D1570970

God's Body

God's Body

Jewish, Christian, and Pagan Images of God

Christoph Markschies

Translated by
Alexander Johannes Edmonds

BAYLOR UNIVERSITY PRESS

Cover design by Savanah N. Landerholm
Cover image: "Jupiter and Thetis," 1811 (oil on canvas), Ingres, Jean Auguste Dominique (1780–1867) / Musee Granet, Aix-en-Provence, France / Bridgeman Images
Book design by Scribe Inc.

Originally published as *Gottes Körper* (München: C.H.Beck, 2016). © Verlag C.H.Beck oHG, München 2016.

The translation of this work was funded by Geisteswissenschaften International – Translation Funding for Humanities and Social Sciences from Germany, a joint initiative of the Fritz Thyssen Foundation, the German Federal Foreign Office, the collecting society VG WORT, and the Börsenverein des Deutschen Buchhandels (German Publishers & Booksellers Association).

The Library of Congress has cataloged this book under ISBN
978-1-4813-1168-7.

Contents

List of Images

Preface

Over the course of their lives, a great many of the present inhabitants of Europe and America have come to conclude that divine images (should there be a reason to believe in God at all) must be more enlightened and "modern" than is traditional, meeting contemporary standards of reason and eschewing a depiction of God patterned after the human person. "Anthropomorphism," the conception of God in human form, is generally held to be archaic, naïve, and primitive. *Sigmund Freud* (1856–1939) deemed such an image "so overtly infantile, so unrealistic, that it would be painful to a humane spirit to think that the vast majority of mortals will never surmount this conception of life." Yet, just as problematic as male-connoted "anthropomorphism" to the founder of psychoanalysis was also the attempt to replace a personal God conceived in the form of a man with an "impersonal, shadowy abstract principle."[1] Even when the philosopher *Ludwig Feuerbach* (1804–1872) justified his theory of projection, first formulated in his 1841 work "The Essence of Christianity," with the *general traits* of the divine image and not a *specific* conception of a divine body,[2] the concept of a perfect divine body (in comparison to the human form) readily lends itself to supporting the thesis that God is nothing but "the personified divinity conceived as a being, or a godhead of man."[3] As will be seen in the following chapter, criticism of anthropomorphic divine images has long been in vogue. In addition, misgivings regarding divine images which depict God in any manner whatsoever corporeally, and insofar ascribe him a certain form of bodiliness, are pervasive.

Thus, from the perspective of personal religious development, is the conception of God's body merely a childish belief, and, in regard to the collective development of religious consciousness, a long surmounted, antiquated evolutionary step? Or might there also be a strong case in the present day for imagining God as corporeal?

Until well into the European Modern era, a consensus existed within Judaism and Christianity at the very least (if not Islam as well) that while, indeed, God possessed no human form, he was nevertheless a *person*; the rejection of anthropomorphism in the three so-called Abrahamic religions did not, in fact, imply the dismissal of his personality.[4] In the past couple of hundred years, at the very least within philosophy, and also somewhat so within Christian theology, less so within Jewish theology, and hardly at all in that of Islam, a *depersonalization* has become one of the guiding principles in discussing God. Goethe had already criticized the idea of contemplating God within the category of a human person, attacking those warring theologians of the time resisting such a depersonalization with the scathing lines: "What is with your scorn / upon the all and one? / the professor is a person / God is none."[5] Nevertheless, both the conventional theologies of Christianity, Judaism, and Islam, and the quotidian practice of piety within these three world religions strongly maintain that God possesses a personality, regardless of scholarly and educated bourgeois reservations. In comparison to all other persons, generally defined since Antiquity as individuated substances with mind albeit always thought of as reason *within a body* or as a *corporeal* reason, God is described as an *incorporeal* (and inasmuch *bodiless*) reason within the collective consciousness.[6] A certain exception to this is provided by those pantheist conceptions wherein the world is understood as the body or form of God, albeit in a metaphorical sense.

Although it usually provokes astonishment within the context of a modern mentality and education to discuss a "divine body" as distinguishable from the world as the person of God, there has, in fact, occasionally also been doubt within early modern Europe as to this widely disseminated image of God: Thus, for example, pointedly reacting to a certain strand of Protestant Enlightenment theology, the Swabian prelate *Friedrich Christoph Oetinger* (1702–1782), a prominent theologian of Pietism, deemed corporeality "the end of God's works" and posited that "if all that is corporeal is to be divorced from God, so is God naught."[7] Indeed, influenced by both diverse Classical and medieval intellectual traditions and contemporaneous radical movements, the Görlitz shoemaker and religious thinker of a decidedly singular ilk *Jakob Böhme* (1575–1624) had already speculated well before Oetinger upon the question of whether God might require nature as his body.[8] Nevertheless, views such as those propounded by Oetinger or Böhme, whether more or less influential, admittedly remain dissenting opinions within the European Modern era.

At any rate, the result just described of a generally prevalent conception of a bodiless, incorporeal personality of God does not apply to Antiquity, and, that is, *for the religions of Antiquity in their entirety*, ranging from pagan religiosity to Judaism, Christianity, and everything between: On the contrary, the notion that God possesses a body and form was thoroughly common sense. Within scholarly circles, this fact has long been known; in 1974, the American philosopher of religion *William J. Wainwright* noted, "The belief that God has a body is by no means uncommon in the history of religious thought, nor is that belief confined to the primitive and unsophisticated. The Manicheans, Tertullian, certain Egyptian anchorites, and the Mormons have all maintained that God has (or is) some particular body."[9] With his reference to the Mormons, Wainwright also drew attention to the phenomenon in the Modern era of God being ascribed a "figure" or "body," as has already been seen in the example of Böhme. Thus, this topic can hardly be approached through a mere juxtaposition of Antiquity and the Modern epoch, but rather by means of the careful tracing of the developments in the process by which once commonly held notions were marginalized, becoming minority beliefs.

Given this remarkable transformation in the image of God between the antique and modern worlds, the idea to reflect upon the *body of God in Antiquity* and to publish the fruits of this contemplation emerged in the course of a research project lasting several years funded by the German Research Council on the conception of the *human* body in Christian Antiquity which I was able to undertake in Heidelberg and Berlin alongside various colleagues; I mention, above all, the philologists Eva Elm, Anna Rack-Teuteberg, and Dorothea Zeppezauer, as well as the archaeologist Tomas Lehmann. During our discussion of the relationship between healing and salvation in Antiquity, I realized that while there is a realm of academic literature on the *human* body in Antiquity, which, at least within the realms of Christianity, follows both chronologically and in content Peter Brown's landmark 1988 book "Body and Society," there was next to no work on the body of *God*.[10] This marked deficit is also applicable to the great and meritorious overviews of the topic, for example, to the comprehensive tome "God in Patristic Thought" by the Oxonian scholar of patristics and Anglican theologian *George Leonard Prestige* (1889–1955).[11]

The book then developed over the course of a total of six years: First, I presented an initial and still highly preliminary sketch at the invitation of Bärbel Friedrich at the Alfried Krupp Academic Lecture in Greifswald in 2008, then, in starkly altered form, in 2009 as the Alexander Böhlig Memorial Lecture at the Protestant Theological Faculty of the Eberhard-Karls-University Tübingen, and then in the German Protestant Institute of Archaeology in Jerusalem at the invitation of Dieter Vieweger, repeated thereafter on the occasion of the emeritation of Theofried Baumeister at the Faculty of Catholic Theology at the Johannes-Gutenberg-University Mainz, and, within the excellence cluster "Cultural of Foundations of

Integration," in Constance at the invitation of Rudolf Schlögl. During the years spent presiding over the Humboldt-University at Berlin, any more thorough an elaboration of this sketch was unthinkable. Thereafter, I thankfully seized upon the opportunity to hold the Deichmann Annual Lecture Series at the Ben-Gurion-University at Beersheba on this topic. To the German study program of the Abbey of the Dormition on Mount Zion in Jerusalem, its director and the incumbent of the Laurentius Klein Chair at the time, the New Testament scholar Margareta Gruber, and the monks of the Benedictine abbey I extend my thanks for the opportunity to prepare a first draft of these lectures there, and, above all, to Roland Deines for the invitation to Beersheba.

This notwithstanding, I am also particularly grateful to my former Heidelberg colleague in Ancient History, Angelos Chaniotis, and to the other fellows of the Institute for Advanced Study at Princeton. During the spring and summer of 2011, this place presented me with the chance to further work upon my manuscript. At Princeton, the resident Judaist, Peter Schäfer, and I had already discussed the relevant Jewish texts with students in the spring of 2010 while I could engage in research as the Stewart Visiting Research Scholar in the Humanities Council, Program of Jewish Studies. Our joint classes in Princeton and Berlin and diverse discussions particularly influenced the five chapters concerning the Jewish texts. During both sojourns at Princeton, I had the opportunity time and time again to discuss at lunch or dinner the problems of divine and human bodies in Antiquity with Peter Brown, Glen Bowerstock, Caroline Walker Bynum, Patricia Crone (†), Christian Habicht, Peter Schäfer, and Heinrich von Staden. I was able to present the results of my stays at the Institute in 2011 in lectures, and at a seminar in Pisa at the Scuola Normale Superiore and discuss them with Glenn Most. In light of these manifold stimuli, I feel as if that which I present here might somewhat be termed my "Princeton book." In Princeton, I also came to realize that the consideration as to whether God possesses a body was closely connected in the philosophical discussions of Antiquity to the question as to how the soul is related to its bodies. Hence, this book is also concerned with these philosophical debates in Antiquity on the body-soul relationship insofar as they are relevant to the essential topic. Conversations with the members of a pertinent workgroup on the soul in the Berlin excellence cluster "Topoi" and, in particular, its leader Christoph Helmig, now active in Cologne, were of central importance to this. I also pleasantly recall the discussions following a presentation of the main theses of this book at the North American Patristic Society in May 2014 in Chicago, to which I had been invited by Susanna Elm. In the final phase, the advice of Candida R. Moss in New York was of great importance to me.

Nevertheless, the book begun in Jerusalem and Princeton could only be completed because Trinity College, Oxford, hosted me for a second time in Hilary Term 2013 as a visiting fellow, permitting me discussions with Oxford colleagues and friends, most prominently Peggy Chadwick, Mark Edwards, Guy and Sarah Stroumsa, and Johannes Zachhuber. Even in the face of the Lower Reading Room of the Bodleian having been thoroughly rearranged prior to my stay for the first time since its creation (much to the dismay of many of its users), I still frequented it gratefully on grounds of this library's wonderful inventory, and I sped back and forth between the rooms for *Patristica* and *Classica* with an industriousness matched only by that marking my journeys between the Bodleian and Sackler Libraries. In Oxford, I also realized that my investigations into the intellectual history of the body of God could be read as comprehensive prolegomena to the writings of the Tübingen Protestant theologian Eberhard Jüngel, wherein he had made the claim to have found a way back to a "well-considered anthropomorphic discourse" of God.[12] Even if it is clear to me that the question as to the validity and applicability of anthropomorphic discourse on God is not only of great significance to a reflective handling of church practice, traditional literature, and lived piety, and I have gladly embraced the connection to the work of a venerated teacher from Tübingen, the study here presented only provides the material for a systematic theological discussion which now must be revisited as much within Judaism and Islam as within Christianity. In the best case, the historical scholarship presents answers from the past to questions which are still apt in the current day; for the most part, the solutions of the past do not lend themselves to unaltered adoption or sheer repristination. In such a sense, the modernity of an antique theme as maintained in this work is hardly the sole product of that understandable tendency within Ancient Studies to depict topics as "modern" in order to convince more individuals to read the books in question, to motivate foundations to finance certain projects, or, indeed, to find meaning in one's own doings.[13]

The manuscript born of Jerusalem, Princeton, and Oxford was not yet publishable. In Berlin, colleagues at my chair took up the text: Mirjam Wulff very reliably translated back into German passages which I had composed in the English language and Juliane Zachhuber had then thoroughly revised. The student assistants, most notably Magdelena Rauner and Saskia Triesscheijn, supplied the distantly sojourning author with what literature he lacked locally despite the exquisite libraries of Oxford and Princeton; Renate Burri, Simon Danner, Marie-Dorothee Schubert, and Katharina Weigel tended to these formalities. I discussed the text extensively with my Berlin colleagues Angelica Dinger and Hannah Schiller; their objections and advice induced me to undertake various changes. The assistants

Marc Bergermann, Jan Bobbe, Emmanouela Grypeou, Sarah-Magdalena Kingreen, and Vera von der Osten-Sacken read the entire manuscript, identifying every oversight and making useful suggestions regarding the organization of the ample material. The German version of this book was published within the Munich press of C.H. Beck; here gratitude must be extended to the publisher Wolfgang Beck, his lector Ulrich Nolte, and the Fritz Thyssen Foundation. That this book could now be translated into the English language in its entirety a mere two years thereafter is due first and foremost to Baylor University Press and its former editor Carey Newman, who spares no effort in the dissemination of the fruits of German research within the Anglophone world. It was a pleasure to continue the well-established collaboration I have enjoyed with this press. Alexander Johannes Edmonds rendered a translation of my sentence structure in German as sensitive as it is precise, for which I also thank him profusely. The printing of this book was made possible by its decoration by the German Publishers and Booksellers Association with its translation prize in 2018. Little was altered from the German edition; Luca Giuliani in Berlin is to be thanked for some critical remarks regarding the third chapter.

With this, the author thankfully concludes his work and hopes that also in its English translation his book will for many who read it be conducive to their own study and reflection upon a matter *quo nihil maius cogitari possit*.

Christoph Markschies

Translator's Note

A few brief remarks are necessary regarding the translation of this work, which proved a very enjoyable, if exacting, undertaking. I should like to thank both the author and Carey Newman of Baylor University Press for their patience and assistance during this process. For her forbearance, I must further thank Chiara Konishi de Toffoli.

Firstly, it must be noted that terminology was the source of much reflection during the translation, and some divergences from the German original were inevitable: the most central of these was in the issue of translating the German words *Körper* and *Leib*, which roughly distinguish between body in a more formal, abstract sense and body in a more immanent, fleshy, bodily sense respectively. I have sought to translate this brace of terms contextually as they occur within the text, as the introduction of any rigid terminology would probably have proven more confusing than illuminating to the Anglophone reader. Another notable terminological point was the key distinction made within the German text between *Verkörperung* and *Einkörperung*, particularly in the second chapter; I elected to translate these as *manifestation* and *embodiment* respectively when they were juxtaposed to each other but was freer with their translation when they occurred alone in other contexts. The keen reader may note a few other less important terminological decisions made in the same vein; none of these impinge upon the book's arguments.

Another crucial issue was the great many quotations from various authors from Antiquity. In selecting English translations, I have generally privileged newer and more accessible translations wherever possible; while the specialist will already have a good handle of the pertinent editions, a decent Loeb or the like is within the grasp of any interested reader. Nevertheless, this work's exploration of intellectual paths recently less trodden means that editions of many key passages are often already a century old. The notes make clear my own relative fidelity to said editions old and new in tailoring these to Christoph Markschies' own German translations and, more broadly, the arguments within any specific passage. Naturally, some quotations in the original were from works which have never been translated into English; in such cases, I followed the German translation with some recourse to the source text, my translations being thereafter reviewed by the author.

It remains to mention that biblical quotations are generally patterned after the King James Version, and that I have sought to render Christoph Markschies' erudite yet accessible text somewhat in the tone of the Oxbridge scholar, trusting that the lively yet precise character of the original prose has thereby remained more or less intact. While I cannot confess to have always held to it, I nevertheless endeavoured to remain mindful of Jerome's words: *non verbosa rusticitas, sed sancta simplicitas*.

Alexander Johannes Edmonds
Heidelberg and Tübingen, November 2018

1

The Body of God after Antiquity

In both the collective consciousness and scholarly texts of the Modern era, God possesses neither a body nor a form in the material sense, save in the beliefs of some particular groups as disparate as the Mormons and Pantheists. This striking deficit has characterized fundamental assumptions regarding God as much in North America as in the British Isles or on the Continent, that is, essentially in regions which have been shaped by Christianity and, more specifically, the Judeo-Christian Bible.

The Natures of Christ

Yet, to this collective consciousness might not regardless belong a precise recollection that, at the very least, the Christian god, according to the confession of the majority of occidental Christianity, is trinitary in composition and that the second divine figure of this trinity, Christ, possesses not merely a corporeal form but, indeed, a body? The antique notion of the corporeality of Christ, who was understood at the very latest from the Councils of Nicaea (325) and Chalcedon (451) onwards as the second figure within a godhead conceived of as a trinity,[1] plays as little of a role as that of the existence of a divine body in of itself in today's general discussion and imagination. According to the classical, conventional form of Christian dogma developed in Antiquity, Christ not only possessed a body as he walked the earth in human form after incarnation, but was also corporeally enthroned at the Father's right in heaven following his death and resurrection, a notion propagated in Christian art and music.[2] With respect to Jesus Christ's divine personage, Christian theology was for centuries hardly averse to ascribing God a body and a corporeal nature. Formulated more precisely, it had accorded *one* of the three modes of God's existence a body and a corporeal nature. Regardless, Western Christianity (in

1

contrast to certain forms of Eastern Christianity) had received that form of late antique Christology wherein, following the confession of faith issued by the Imperial Council of Chalcedon in 451,[3] the terrestrial, corporeal, *human nature* of the Son was strictly distinguished from the incorporeal *divine nature* of Son and Father alike. The so-called two-nature Christology, also termed "dyophysitism" from an originally late antique Greek coinage,[4] understands this specific body of God as merely a special *human* body, and insofar also only as a divine body in a restricted sense after his ascension to God's right. Phrased differently, "two-nature Christology" permits both the ascribing of God a (human) body, and also the maintenance of the fundamental conviction of God's incorporeality. With the Council of Chalcedon, mainstream Christianity had repudiated the notion of a "divine flesh" or an "unincarnate flesh" (σάρξ Χριστοῦ ἐπουράνιος or σάρξ Χριστοῦ ἄκτιστος), and thereby a non-terrestrial body of Jesus Christ in a particular divine corporeality. In the wake of this thereby rejected perspective, Christ possessed, according to influential theologians, a particularly divine body for eternity, and could make use of it after his ascension if he did not use it upon earth (this confession presented by the Council, along with the religious conception described, will be extensively explored in this work).[5] The privileging of the dyophysite position within the Imperial Council of Chalcedon, and the rejection of the view that Christ had possessed a special divine body instead of a human one, reinforced the belief in God's incorporeality, and contributed thereby to the marginalization of belief in God's corporeality. Occasional reworking of antique learning regarding the "heavenly flesh" of Christ, such as by *Kaspar Schwenckfeld* (1490–1561)[6] during the Reformation, would hardly alter the status quo. This unremitting tendency towards marginalization reinforced itself once more in the eighteenth century: The mounting criticism by Protestant theologians in the European Early Modern era of the late antique teaching of Christ's two natures, articulated most pointedly by the Berlin clergyman and professor *Friedrich Daniel Ernst Schleiermacher* (1768–1834),[7] further encouraged a collective amnesia regarding the corporeality or even bodiliness of God—at least in that portion of the Protestant world generally affected by de-Christianization. Today, the classical question as to the corporeality of the human existence of Jesus Christ (on earth as in heaven) plays a role in neither the contemporary theologically unschooled collective consciousness of the "layman" nor academic theorising, let alone the once hotly debated question as to whether God might be accorded a body.

Maimonides and Jewish Conceptions of a Divine Incorporeality

Alongside the tendency to marginalise the notion of a heavenly or terrestrial body of the divinity in *Christian theology* and the *Christian understanding of faith* since the Modern era have come developments within both Judaism and the broader philosophical theory of God. Also in these contexts, the concept of a divine corporeal form or body in a literal, non-metaphorical sense was rejected at times with marked vehemence: The conviction that God did not possess a human voice or form has connected Christian and Jewish thought since the Middle Ages at the very latest; both intellectual traditions have evidently alternately influenced one another. The medieval Jewish doctor, philosopher, and legal scholar *Moses Ben Maimon*, commonly known as Maimonides or by his acronym RaMBaM (1135–1204),[8] was likely the first Jewish thinker to argue both extensively and principally against anthropomorphic conceptions of God. Naturally, in the course of such an argumentation, he was compelled to explain this at length with appropriate passages from his own holy Scripture, the Hebrew Bible. For Maimonides, all of the biblical descriptions of God which accorded God a voice, other anatomical details, or even an entire body were to be interpreted metaphorically. This polymath supposed that these references were for the edification of the unphilosophical, uneducated listening and reading audience of the biblical books; the philosophically inclined, educated male reader (a female readership was still inconceivable to him) would extract meaning with which to sensibly think by means of allegorical interpretation of the metaphorical language of the holy Scripture.

In the first part of his religio-philosophical magnum opus "Guide of the Perplexed" (*Dalālat al-ḥā'irīn* or *More Nevuchim*, מורה נבוכים),[9] according to the dedication intended for a student called Rabbi Joseph and compiled between 1180 and 1190/91 in Fustat (Old Cairo), Maimonides offered explanations for biblical passages and terms which, at least to the uninitiated readership, apparently attested to the corporeality of God. In the eyes of the Jewish medieval thinker, God's incorporeality was "the third of the three most fundamental truths, the preceding ones being the existence of God and His unity."[10] Indeed, God's existence and unity are indisputable in the context of Judaism; the fundamental creed that "the Lord our God is one" (Deuteronomy 6:4) must ultimately prevail.[11] Yet, with respect to God's incorporeality, things become more complicated: Several biblical texts seem, in fact, to prove that God possesses a body and is corporeal. For all intents and purposes, this might follow from the fact, also indubitable for Maimonides, of God's fashioning of humanity in his image. Creation in the likeness of God would seem to imply that God had fashioned humanity in *this* image and according to *the very* form of his own body (Genesis 1:27f.). Maimonides refutes this position (to him misguided) by means of an extensive discussion of the pertinent biblical passages, invoking thereby, for example, Numbers 12:8 wherein it is said of Moses that "he beholds the Lord in his form" (in the Hebrew version; in the Greek text of the Septuagint "He beholds the Lord in his splendor").[12] Indeed, the Hebrew word here employed, usually translated as "form," can, in fact, express corporeality.[13] Nevertheless, Maimonides was deeply convinced that the belief that God possessed a body imperilled confidence in God's unity, and thereby might result in the dispelling of belief in God's existence. A body is an entity composed of combined parts, but God, by definition, an uncompounded unity. Corporeality and unity are opposites: "For a body cannot be one, but is composed of matter and form, which by definition are two."[14] *Unity* is conceptually understood by him as an undifferentiated *individuality*:

> For there is no oneness at all except in believing that there is one simple essence in which there is no complexity or multiplication of notions, but one notion only; so that from whatever angle you regard it and from whatever point of view you consider it, you will find that it is one, not divided in any way and by any cause into two notions; and you will not find therein any multiplicity either in the thing as it is outside of the mind or as it is in the mind, as shall be demonstrated in this Treatise.[15]

This argument against a divine body on grounds of the difference between the principal uncompoundedness of God, on the one hand, and the composite nature of a body, on the other, makes it clear that, besides the Neoplatonic concept of undifferentiated individuality, the One (τὸ ἕν), Maimonides is employing fundamental concepts of Aristotelian ontology (such as, for example, the dual of content and form) in order to reject the notion of a divine body as contrary to reason.[16] In his "Guide of the Perplexed" he had not only demonstrated that the idea of a divine body implied the absurd conception of a composite, and thereby divisible, God, but also that this conception is an application to God of the Aristotelian idea of a substance and its attributes, which would have utterly preposterous consequences for the conception of God:

> Now every such essence is necessity endowed with attributes, for we do not ever find an essence of a body that while existing is divested of everything and is without an attribute. This imagination being pursued, it was thought that He, may He be exalted, is similarly composed of various notions, namely, His essence and the notions that superadded to

His existence. Several groups of people pursued the likening of God to other beings and believed Him to be a body endowed with attributes.[17] Another group raised themselves above this consequence and denied His being a body, but preserved the attributes. All this was rendered necessary by their keeping to the external sense of the revealed books as I shall make clear in later chapters that will deal with these notions.[18]

For Maimonides, the conception of a divine body is so erroneous because firstly it implies composite parts within God, and, moreover, the notion that corporeal accidents impinge upon his substance. An immaterial substance such as God cannot, according to Maimonides, be tied to a particular time or place as it does not command such accidents, qualities

> predicated of a thing that has a relation to something other than itself. For instance, it is related to a time or to a place or to another individual . . . At first thought it seems that it is permissible to predicate of God, may He be exalted, attributes of this kind. However, when one knows true reality and achieves greater exactness in speculation, the fact that this is impossible becomes clear. There is no relation between God, may He be exalted, and time and place; and this is quite clear. . . . Motion, on the other hand, is one of the things attached to bodies, whereas God, may He be exalted, is not a body. Accordingly there is no relation between Him and time, and in the same way there is no relation between Him and place.[19]

In addition to such arguments, generally formulated from the background of Aristotelian metaphysics, the Jewish philosopher also employs lines of argumentation which are rather from a Platonic context: In his "Tractate on the Resurrection of the Dead," Maimonides employs the relationship between body and soul as an argument. As the "body as a whole is only the tool for the soul, by which the soul carries out all its acts,"[20] the notion of a divine body would imply that God would need his body in order to perform actions, which would likewise be inacceptable.

Within his "Guide of the Perplexed," a third line of argumentation is taken from the Targum Onkelos (אונקלוס), the official Babylonian version of the Aramaic translation of the Hebrew Bible, which can be dated to the era of the early Roman Empire but may well have first been compiled in Late Antiquity.[21] According to Maimonides, this Aramaic translation substituted incorporeal terms in the place of the corporeal designations of the Hebrew Bible.[22] The Jewish philosopher could use the Aramaic translation as an argument because his readers evidently accepted it as the authoritative exegesis of the Bible. In actual fact, it had indeed been sought within the translation of the Bible within Targum Onkelos to avoid, or at least reduce, the anthropomorphisms of the source text. In such a manner, the translators of the Targum amended the aforementioned biblical verse Numbers 12:8 with the word "the glory" so that the sense of the passage was strikingly altered "and he (Moses) can behold the image of *the glory* of the Lord" (ובדמות יקרא דייי סתתכל).[23] This approximates the Greek translation of the Septuagint: "and he had seen the splendor of the Lord" (καὶ τὴν δόξαν κυρίου εἶδεν).

To summarize, the notion that God has a body, or is in some manner to be conceived of as corporeal, is, following Maimonides, the consequence of a literal misinterpretation of the biblical text. At the same time, belief in God's corporeality is a grave sin as, in this manner, the believer is behaving idolatrously (or even worse).[24] With such remarks, the medieval Jewish philosopher railed not only against a naïve folk religiosity of the unlettered masses, but also against a very precise Jewish mystic tradition. This had developed, as will be seen, from the foundations of biblical and postbiblical texts during the early Byzantine period, and supplemented the simple discussion of the corporeality of God with elaborate speculations as to the exact dimensions of his body. Within academic literature, these are termed "Shiʿur Qomah" texts (שיעור קומה), literally texts concerning the "measurements of the form [of the divine body]."[25]

Comprehensive in scope and rich in examples and biblical texts, the significance of the here merely tersely summarized arguments of Maimonides for Jewish religious life and thought cannot be emphasized enough. Moreover, his influence upon Christian theology is also not to be underestimated. The medieval philosopher "was not the first Jewish thinker to reject anthropomorphism, but none of his predecessors had denied this so clearly as an article of faith, incumbent on all levels of society" (Sarah Stroumsa).[26] Maimonides did not take the comfortable expedient otherwise resorted to by both Platonic philosophers and Jewish and Christian Platonizing theologians of conceding to the unlearned masses an intellectually wanting anthropomorphism irrespective of its sundry problems, and only surmounting this for the educated elite by means of metaphorical interpretation. Rather, he had definitively stopped in its tracks one practice of handling the anthropomorphic statements within biblical and other religious texts previously self-evident to both Platonizing and anti-Platonic Jewish theology—and thereby also influenced Christian thought, as will now be witnessed.

Anselm of Canterbury and Thomas Aquinas

Naturally, medieval Christian theology was already generally convinced that God could not be conceived of as a corporeal being or as analogous to such before it encountered via Maimonides the strict rejection of anthropomorphic discourse on God's body. The Council of Chalcedon had already seen to this in the year 451 by means of its repudiation of the notion of a "heavenly flesh of Christ." This might be read in the *Proslogion* of the Benedictine monk *Anselm of Canterbury* (1033–1109), who lived roughly a hundred years before Maimonides, wherein the answers may be found as to "how he (God) senses, although he is not body."[27] Anselm argued for his self-evident dismissal of a corporeality of God with the Platonic hierarchy of the good and bad, wherein the body was attributed to the bad without any further discussion: "utmost spirit" is "better than the body."[28] All the same, he granted the highest spiritual being a sentiency which is admittedly not corporeal (*corporeus*), but rather pure cognition.[29] In the entirety of Western and Eastern Christian tradition of the Middle Ages and early modern Era, there is no book comparable to the "Guide of the Perplexed" in its elaborate polemic against anthropomorphic conceptions of God. This is at once apparent in the polemic writings against Jewish philosophers. In a refutation of the "errors" of Maimonides composed in 1270 by *Giles of Rome* (*Aegidius Romanus*), the archbishop of Bourges (ca. 1243–1316), the author left the question of God's body, central to Maimonides' treatise, completely untouched.[30] Quite evidently, there was no controversy regarding this topic between learned Jewish and Christian theologians in this period.[31]

Approximately a century after Maimonides, *Thomas Aquinas* (1225–1274), Giles' teacher, summarized some of the arguments against a corporeal conception of God in his works *Summa contra gentiles* and *Summa theologicae*. Like Maimonides, he employed the basal paradigms of Aristotelian philosophy within his argumentation,[32] despite harshly criticizing the Jewish philosopher:[33]

[2] Every body, being a continuum, is composite and has parts. But, as we have shown, God is not composite,[34] and is, therefore, not a body.[35]

[3] Again, everything possessed of quantity is in a certain manner in potency. For a continuum is potentially divisible to infinity, while numbers can be increased to infinity. But every body has quantity and is therefore in potency. But God is not in potency, being pure act, as has been shown. Therefore, God is not a body.[36]

[4] Furthermore, if God is a body, He must be some natural body, since, as the Philosopher proves,[37] a mathematical body is not something self-existing, since dimensions are accidents. But God is not a natural body, being immobile, as we have shown, whereas every natural body is movable. God is, therefore, not a body.[38]

[5] Again, every body is finite, as is proved in *De caelo* I [I, 5] of a circular body and a rectilinear body.[39] Now, we can transcend any given finite body by means of the intellect and the imagination. If, then, God is a body, our intellect and imagination can think of something greater than God. God is thus not greater than our intellect—which is awkward. God is, therefore, not a body.[40]

[6] Intellectual knowledge, moreover, is more certain than sensitive knowledge. In nature we find an object for the sense and therefore for the intellect as well. But the order and distinction of powers is according to the order of objects. Therefore, above all sensible things there is something intelligible among things. Now, every body having actual existence is sensible. Therefore, we can find something nobler above all bodies. Hence, if God is a body, He will not be the first and greatest being.[41]

[7] A living thing, likewise, is nobler than any non-living body, and the life of a living body is nobler than it, since it is this life that gives to the living body its nobility above other bodies. Therefore, that than which nothing is nobler is not a body. This is God. God is, therefore, not a body.[42]

[8] Then, too, there are the arguments of the philosophers to the same effect,[43] based on the eternity of motion. They are as follows. In every everlasting motion, the first mover cannot be moved either through Himself or by accident, as is clear from the above. Now, the body of the heavens is moved in a circle with an everlasting motion. Therefore, its first mover is not moved either through Himself or by accident. Now, no body moves locally unless it be moved, since the mover and the moved must be together. The moving body must thus be moved in order to be together with the moved body. But no power in a body moves unless it itself be moved by accident, since, when a body is moved, its power is by accident moved. The first mover of the heavens, therefore, is neither a body nor a power in a body. Now, that to which the motion of the heavens is ultimately reduced as to its first unmoved mover is God. God is, therefore, not a body.[44]

Much akin to Maimonides, Aquinas demonstrated by means of dismissing the absurd consequences borne of his premises ("God is a composite entity") that God is not compounded, and that as a pure act (*actus purus*) without unrealized contingencies must hence be understood as infinite and immobile. As a body is by definition a composite entity, it does not possess realized contingencies, is finite, and mobile. Thus, God cannot have a body and the corporeality of God is a contradiction in of itself. Interestingly, like Anselm, Aquinas used a manner of ontological hierarchy of Platonic provenance as an argument: Intellectual entities are "nobler" (*nobilius*) than things capable of sensation. It is clear that, from the basis of such a Platonic hierarchy, any corporeality of God is simply unthinkable.[45] Yet, also working from the basis of the Aristotelian concept of God as the unmoved mover (οὐ κινούμενον κινεῖ),[46] divine corporeality cannot be conceived of without serious contradictions.[47]

Philosophical and Theological Criticism of Anthropomorphism in the Modern Era

On account of such equally obvious and fundamental problems within a conception of the corporeality of God, only a minority within Western philosophical and theological thought concerned itself with this question with any systematic intent. Its contrary seemed all too clearly a fundamental tenet of every rational theory about God. Caspar Schwenckfeld, Jakob Böhme, and Friedrich Christoph Oetinger, all rather marginalized figures within mainstream modern Protestant university theology, have already been named as representatives of this minority. Since Maimonides at the latest, as has been demonstrated, general philosophical and theological discourse on the corporeality of God has been tied to polemic against anthropomorphic images of God, which today are just as invariably the mark of an unenlightened manner of thinking and conceiving of God. At best, anthropomorphic discourse on God is permitted purely as an accommodation to the needs of the recipients of revelation. Regardless, the conception of a personal God composed of a body runs utterly counter to the perspective held by the vast majority of people as to God's nature.

Strident polemic against corporeal conceptions of God may be found, for example, in the treatment of anthropomorphic passages of biblical Scriptures in both the Jewish and Christian biblical criticism of the Early Modern era, which initially developed outside of the respective institutions of church and university or synagogue and house of learning. For *Baruch de Spinoza* (1632–1677), the idea that God had assumed a human nature and hence possessed a body was "just as preposterous as if someone sought to claim that the circle had assumed the nature of the square"[48] — Eberhard Jüngel carefully traced some time ago the argumentations of Spinoza and their significance for the emergence of critical biblical hermeneutics.[49] The notion of a divine body seems to modern philosophers as much as theologians to be so absurd, that often they never experience the need even to formulate it explicitly.

Anthropomorphism is also far more than merely discourse on a divine body. Within his work *Causa Dei Asserta per Justitiam Ejus*, an appendix to his "Theodicy," the Baroque polymath *Gottfried Wilhelm Leibniz* (1646–1716) even labeled *every* attempt to minimize God's size as "anthropomorphism,"[50] and thus not only as a concept of the corporeality of God.[51] The Scottish philosopher, economist, and historian *David Hume* (1711–1776) attempted in his "Dialogues concerning Natural Religion" (1739/40) to demonstrate that every concept of God relating to or based upon experience leads to an absurd anthropomorphism, and that this was, in turn, due to an inherent tendency in humans to anthropomorphic divine images. On the other hand, according to Hume, every concept which attempts to avoid anthropomorphism implies propositions about God which are empirically vacuous.[52] The Konigsberg Enlightenment philosopher *Immanuel Kant* (1724–1804) discussed Hume and argued that, in a certain respect, anthropomorphic divine images are ineluctable. In his "Prolegomena to any future Metaphysics" (1783) he formulated that "for we then do not attribute to the supreme being any of the properties *in themselves* by which we think the objects of experience, and we thereby avoid *dogmatic* anthropomorphism; but we attribute those properties, nonetheless, to the relation of this being to the world, and allow ourselves a *symbolic* anthropomorphism, which in fact concerns only language and not the object itself."[53] Following medieval parlance, Kant termed this "*symbolic* anthropomorphism" a "cognition according to analogy," although, in contrast to the conventional meaning of this term, he understands "analogy" as "a perfect similarity between two relations in wholly dissimilar things."[54] Even when here the possibility of a positivist philosophical or theological assessment of anthropomorphic discourse on God presents itself (following Kant, this discourse can indeed reveal the *essentials* regarding God and his causality for all things, and insofar does not directly run counter to the nature of God), casting votes for a rehabilitation of a "well-considered anthropomorphic discourse" are few and far between within philosophical and theological discussion. The Protestant theologian *Eberhard Jüngel* (*1934) warrants mention,[55] as do, in respect to the christological discussion, his teacher *Karl Barth* (1886–1968) and most recently the American Catholic theologian *Stephen H. Webb* (*1961).[56] Naturally, the aforementioned authors hardly elect to return to a naïve confusion of God and man (should within the history of man's contemplation of God such naïveté have ever existed in so copious a quantity). Rather, they plead for, on the one hand, the limits of language to be taken seriously, and, on the other, to linguistically chart a movement of God to the world—and thereby to corporeality.

It becomes clear from these recent and current works that the question as to God's corporeality is thus already an inevitable consequence of any reflections upon God in either a Jewish or Christian context; this is not only because it has shaped the biblical texts fundamental to this activity, but also because the trusted denigration of this manner of discourse as "anthropomorphism" clearly falls short in its critique. The all-too-evident suspicion in the modern age that such formulations might be the expression of a "premodern worldview" of putatively simple, uneducated people testifies more to prejudice than to fundamental analysis of the pertinent texts. The tradition of a corporeal conception of God is not only more broadly attested than might conventionally be thought, but also was propounded by highly erudite and intellectually ambitious people. Above all, however, it has profoundly shaped the Scriptures collected in both the Jewish and Christian Bibles, and inasmuch also all postbiblical thought and writings within these religions. On this point, Christianity and Judaism are in no manner to be distinguished from the religions of the Near East and Antiquity surrounding them. In many Jewish and Christian biblical texts, discourse on a divine body is definitively not to be understood according to the antique conventions of metaphorical discourse,[57] as if there might exist twixt the body of God and the body of man merely an analogy (of whatever type). Were all similarities always to accompanied by dissimilarities, indeed otherness, these texts could be meant metaphorically. "A metaphor is the application of a word that belongs to another thing" (μεταφορὰ δέ ἐστιν ὀνόματος ἀλλοτρίου ἐπιφορά) said Aristotle after all.[58] Yet, such a relation of dissimilarity or otherness between the divine and human bodies is programmatically denied by many biblical texts in their discourses on God's body. Attention has been most recently been brought to this by the American biblical scholar Benjamin D. Sommer of the Jewish Theological Seminary of America within a book entitled "The Bodies of God and the World of Ancient Israel":

> The God of the Hebrew Bible has a body. This must be stated at the outset, because so many people, including many scholars, assume otherwise.[59]

Sommer deems the conception that God possesses a body to be "the standard notion of ancient Israelite theology"[60] and contrasts within the introduction of his monograph "the formidable authority of childhood teachers and the less robust influence of theologians" who sought to convince him from childhood onwards that, exactly the other way around, the notion of an *incorporeal* God conformed to contemporaneous Jewish (and Christian) thought, and thereby had likewise profoundly influenced nonreligious Western thought.[61]

Guiding Questions and Structure

This brief overview of how the prevalent conception in Antiquity of a
divine body fared in the periods thereafter up until its general marginalization provokes the guiding questions to be answered in the following
chapters: How influential really were biblical concepts of God's body in
later—that is, Hellenistic to late antique—Jewish thought and in the reflections of antique followers of Christ? Are there characteristic distinctions
in the reception of different biblical concepts of God's body (Sommer
has demonstrated in his monograph how truly diverse biblical concepts
of divine corporeality are applied within solely the Hebrew Bible) between
differing currents of Judaism and Christianity in the Early Roman Empire
and in Late Antiquity? Which circumstances in the pagan environment
benefited concepts of God's body? Which circumstances obstructed the
dissemination of this concept and its popularization in various communities? Did the self-evident conception of God's body only exist in Jewish
and Christian thought, or would one also imagine the pagan gods with
bodies? Finally, a rather more systematic question should not be spared at
the conclusion: Is there an intellectual hierarchy between the concept of a
noncorporeal God and the concepts of God's body?

The answers to these questions are approached in six steps, to each
of which a chapter is devoted: The *second chapter* will initially detail the
evidence from the Hebrew Bible and its Greek translation, then the reception of individual biblical conceptions alongside their transformation in
the writings of the so-called intertestamental period up to the beginnings
of a Christian theology in the second and early third centuries after Christ,
including their contexts within philosophical discussion contemporaneous
to them. The *third chapter* will proceed with the reconstruction of concepts of God's body in pagan Greco-Roman culture, and treat, in particular, religious daily practice, insofar as this is still possible with the sources
at hand. With the question of the corporeality of the soul in late antique
discussions, the *fourth chapter* will scrutinize a question seemingly only
peripheral to the question of God's body. In reality, the question is as to
whether the soul belongs to an incorporeally conceived God, or rather
as a part of an *in toto* corporeally conceived creation will be found to be
pertinent to the present topic and not merely as a snapshot of debates in
Late Antiquity. A *fifth chapter* will take into account the relevant antique
Jewish texts. Particular attention will be drawn to an interesting text corpus of late antique and Early Medieval Jewish mysticism termed "Shi'ur
Qomah" (שיעור קומה), texts on the "measurements of the form (of the
divine body)"—an approach to God and his heavenly realm as mythic as it
is mystical. A *sixth chapter* will analyze corporeal conceptions of God in

late antique Christian theology, in particular the concepts of the so-called anthropomorphites. The *seventh and last chapter* will address the difficult question as to whether there are explicit connections or perhaps hidden links between the biblical and postbiblical concepts of God's body and the aforementioned lively discussions of the divine and human natures of Christ including their specific bodilinesses. In regard to this, biblical texts are returned to, also including those which were accepted into the New Testament later. The question will be posed thereby as to whether the concept of the incarnation of God can be understood as in line with the prevalent antique, biblical, and postbiblical concepts of God's body, or if here a definitively new avenue of interpretation had been opened within antique Christianity.

The Body within the "History of Body"

In an introduction to a monograph on God's body in Jewish, Christian, and pagan Antiquity, it does not suffice to depict merely the problems which these conceptions engendered within philosophical and theological deliberation after the end of Antiquity. It is at least as important to locate briefly the topic of the divine body within more general academic discussion on the "history of body" (and in this manner simultaneously to explain as to why such a book was not written until now). As surprising as it may seem to occupy oneself with the conception of divine bodies, it is not particularly original to concern oneself with the general history of the idea of the body. A vast number of publications now exist dedicated to the theme of the "body"; "body history" is presently establishing itself as its own branch of the disciplines of history and cultural studies, especially within the history of the Middle Ages and the Early Modern period, but also within anthropology and ever more within religious studies.[62]

To study the history of the thematization of the body is, as the Zurich historian *Jakob Tanner* (*1950) once put it, a very recent form of approach to the past: Until well into the twentieth century, the human body was no topic for classical history,[63] and the same held for religious history and Christian ecclesiastical history: The human body was not an independent subject of interest, but rather more an implication of the basal concept of human subjectivity and human behavior in history which had not been explicitly thematized. It was only in the years preceding the Great War in Germany and following it in France, when the discipline of history, which had worked until then rather in the history of ideas and events, took up cultural-historical issues that the body became an independent topic, for example, in the analysis of the history of birth, childhood, dying, and death. The Leipzig historian *Karl Lamprecht* (1856–1915) already

described his own present in bodily, or more precisely psychic, categories (i.e., "Reizsamkeit" [sensitivity, excitability] as the mark of the Wil-
helmine epoch),[64] but it was the French *Annales* school, established in the
wake of 1918 at the newly French University of Strasbourg, which well
and truly began to undertake investigations into the history of the body,
and inaugurated thusly in the proper sense this new avenue of research:
In 1924, the Strasbourg historian *Marc Bloch* (1886–1944) published his
study "Les rois thaumaturges," in 1957, the historian and German émigré
to Princeton *Ernst Kantorowicz* (1895–1963) "The King's Two Bodies:
A Study in Medieval Political Theology," to name only two of the monographs most influential in the establishment of this new field of research.[65]

A *second phase of body history*, influenced by social anthropological,
sociological, and philosophical theories, began in the sixties and lasted
into the seventies.[66] *Michel Foucault* (1926–1984), *Norbert Elias* (1897–
1990), and *Mary Douglas* (1921–2007) were the protagonists within this
field during that period,[67] although mention must also be made of the French
ethnologist and sociologist *Marcel Mauss* (1872–1950) and the later translation into English of his lecture on "Techniques of the Body" which he had
originally held in 1934 before the Société de Psychologie but only began to
become influential after his death.[68]

Since the seventies, in a *third phase of body history*, perspectives on
the body clearly shifted once more, sharply influenced by feminist crit-
icisms of academia and the nascent Gender Debate: The unthematized,
ahistorical, and implicit body as found in literature prior to the emergence
of the issue of body history was, on account of perspectives from anthropological and historical research, now less regarded as an object of its
biological evolution (consider thus Lamprecht and his notion of a rising
"Reizsamkeit" in the Wilhemine era), but rather more as a phenomenon of
historical development and conscious construction. In the eighties, in light
of the generally anti-essentialist paradigm of Cultural Studies, *the* body
was substituted by a variety of differing concepts of body. As a result, "the
body" was no longer really viewed as an independent subject, but rather
as the construct which "is no topic or, perhaps, almost all topics" as is
described by the American medievalist *Caroline Walker Bynum* (*1941).[69]
Since the eighties, buffeted by the myriad "turns" and beholden to fashion,
characteristic shifts in the theoretical frameworks of the humanities and
social sciences occurring due to new paradigms such as the "cultural,"
"linguistic," or "performative" turns respectively marked, as Jakob Tanner
describes it, "discursive, semiotic, and performative approaches . . . the
beginning of a new era in the history of the body, which also lead to a
post-structuralist reassessment of key authors of the 1960s, especially of
Foucault."[70] This process of transformation led to a widely disseminated

but not unproblematic *anti-essentialist* foundational character within the field of body-historical research. Hence, as Bynum further notes, almost nobody in the humanities and social sciences presently employs the concept of an *essential bodiliness* anymore, or of a *corporeality* prior to all constructions.[71] Occasional exceptions, wherein the authors of which reckon more strongly with a biological basis to all constructions, serve only to prove the rule.[72]

The same impression is applicable to most of the recent and current body-historical contributions within the field of the study of antique Christianity: For example, the Constance Latinist *Barbara Feichtinger* (*1963) accordingly argued in her introduction to the first of two collections on concepts of the body in antique Christianity[73] that "the body" of antique Christians was constructed through diverse patterns of behavior, techniques, and practices as well as through representations and discourse. For Feichtinger "the body" is also not an epoch-distant reality preceding these constructions.[74] These observations (and others upon the field of Religious Studies which need not be specifically discussed)[75] accord perfectly with the anti-essentialist tendency noted by Caroline Walker Bynum in respect to the treatment of the body in Cultural Studies and some of the most disparate disciplines of the humanities and social sciences.

Such a fundamental anti-essentialist stance facilitates, on the one hand, the depiction of the history of the conceptions of divine corporeality in Antiquity, as the differing antique notions thereof, taken as pure constructs, might be better understood from the perspective of the history of ideas, gender, and culture, but also in terms of their social, political, and religious backgrounds. On the other hand, a programmatically anti-essentialist position—even when it is concerned with a manner of trendiness most strikingly found in the field of Cultural-Historical Studies[76]—engenders problems inasmuch as the focus upon the constructivist character of all apparently "pure" corporeality is certainly plausible, but simultaneously contributes to concealing the fact that the construction does not occur upon a *tabula rasa*, but rather upon the basis of specific natural dispositions. This complicated state of affairs wherein constructions and the biological basis of all constructions, accessible only through constructions, are entangled, already sows confusion from its sheer language. Particularly in quotidian communication, "body" can refer, on the one hand, to "the organs on which a physician operates" but, on the other, "assumptions about race and gender implicit in a medical textbook, to the particular trajectory of one person's desire or to inheritance patterns and family structures."[77] Most likely, the contemporary, all but self-evident anti-essentialist concept of the body is also responsible for the "welter of confusing and contradictory usages" of the designation "body" documented by Caroline Walker Bynum around two decades ago in an article entitled "Why All the Fuss about the Body? A Medievalist's Perspective."[78] Hence, in the analysis of antique texts containing the conception of a divine corporeality, the differing levels of language and content must be considered; the question as to how the biological basis of all constructions also permeates them cannot be dispensed with, even when it can only be answered with the greatest of difficulty.

Caroline Walker Bynum and others have demonstrated that, despite the multitude of contributions to the history of the perception and thematization of the body in the past years and, indeed, decades, blind spots remain within research. One of these blind spots, not mentioned in her foundational article, is the history of the conceptions of divine corporeality in Antiquity. In the monograph "The Corporeal Imagination: Signifying the Holy in Late Ancient Christianity" written by the American scholar of patristics *Patricia Cox Miller* (*1941),[79] to name merely a single example, there is only a short passage wherein the author deals with the heavy criticism which late antique monastic circles leveled against assertions of God's bodilessness.[80] Yet, the real interest of the author is directed towards the question as to which consequences followers of Christ drew from this in respect to their own bodies (a topic which will later be discussed).[81] Miller does, indeed, mention the incarnate body of Christ, but she does not enquire after the concealed or hardly explicit connections between this incarnate body and the debate over God's corporeality.

Five Perspectives

Five perspectives are to be taken away from this exploration: A brief examination of the history of the body history demonstrates *first* that the study of conceptions of God's corporeality in Antiquity are an urgent desideratum.

Second, it already becomes evident in regard to the sheer linguistic complexities of the term "body" that a purely intellectual-historical portrait in the classical sense is hardly meaningful. In the spirit of a "new intellectual history,"[82] backgrounds in terms not only of gender and cultural history, but also of society, politics, and religion, must be taken into account.

Third, the result of a procession through the history of research is that, in respect to the obvious internal proximity of conceptions of human and divine bodies (notwithstanding all of their differences), Jewish, Christian, and pagan concepts of God's body from Antiquity can only be analyzed when they are incessantly compared with parallel concepts of the human body in Antiquity. Nevertheless, a history of divine and human corporeality in the ancient world naturally will not be presented here; it suffices to refer time and again to the excellent works on the history of the body in the Imperial period and Late Antiquity, upon which the central works have already been named: Since *Peter Brown* published the monograph "The Body and Society" in 1988,[83] a slew of pertinent contributions has appeared. The more recent important publications within the long chain of studies stimulated by Brown are, in addition to the aforementioned investigation by Patricia Cox Miller, the American Byzantinist and art historian *Glen Peers'* 2001 work "Subtle Bodies: Representing Angels in Byzantium" alongside the monograph "Corporeal Knowledge: Early Christian Bodies" by the American biblical scholar *Jennifer A. Glancy* from the year 2010.[84]

A *fourth result* of this journey through the history of research is an endeavor to avoid dualistic simplifications in the depiction of the present subject matter. Caroline Walker Bynum demonstrated in her essay that conventional but simplified dualistic concepts such as "body and soul," "matter and spirit," or "human and social body" are not particularly helpful in interpreting sources from Antiquity or the Middle Ages: "Dualities or binaries were frequently not at stake."[85] Antique (and also medieval) thinkers propounded "a technical conception of embodiment that departs (for better or worse) as radically as do the theories of Judith Butler from an understanding of body as stuff or physicality."[86] Likewise, in Christian and Jewish theology, all basal orientations towards foundational paradigms of Platonic philosophy on corporeality were discussed from the background of an Aristotelian scheme of thought: Body was thereby never mere matter but also form, never only act but also potential, and always *bodily*.[87] In such a manner Maimonides' criticism comes into play, according to which the idea of a divine body is a simple anthropomorphic concept wherein naïve uneducated individuals ascribe a fleshy body to God's intellect, also at this juncture hardly historical reality: In Antiquity, for man as much as God, "body" was by no means the sheer material, fleshy substrate of the intellect as, under the spell of a very simplified dual conceptualization loosely borrowed from *René Descartes* (1596–1650), was thought for a long time in at least the Occident.[88]

A *fifth* and final impression from the perspective of history of body history is that "body" is not a fixed stable entity but rather—already in its very basal biological dimension—a single instance in disparate processes of *embodiment*. Here, the term "embodiment" will not be understood as a more or less arbitrary synonym for some manner of implicit knowledge, or as an open metaphor for an unspecified fashion of acquisition or appropriation of knowledge.[89] The term will herein be used very precisely for the internalization of belief and thought in the form of corporeal practices.

When religious belief in this sense is embodied through religious practices (which according to this precise understanding of the term "embodiment" mean *appropriated by means of corporeal practices*),[90] then all of those religious practices tied in Antiquity to conceptions of divine corporeality should be attentively studied.

After such introductory remarks, attention might now be turned to Antiquity. More specifically, it should be demonstrated that concepts of divine bodies and divine corporeality were widespread from biblical times onwards in not only Judaism and Christianity, but also in their pagan surroundings. It will be shown that in antique Christianity there was not only a single, isolated form of "heresy" among the Egyptian monks of the fourth and fifth centuries AD, the so-called *anthropomorphites*, who ascribed God a body, but rather that an entire stream of early Christian reflection upon this topic existed, which had followed this notion since the second century for differing reasons. The same held for antique Judaism: There was not merely an isolated band of a few Jewish mystics, but rather an entire strand of antique Jewish reflection following that idea of God's corporeality. In order to reconstruct the origins and development of these movements, our point of departure will be the Jewish Bible, since the second century the Old Testament to Christendom.

2

The Body of God in the Judeo-Christian Bible and the Early Christian Theologians

Why was God's body a cause for reflection within the Judaism and Christianity of the Imperial period and Late Antiquity? Certainly, above all, because the articulation of this concept was so self-evidently to be found *in the biblical texts themselves*. With the marginalization since Antiquity of the notion of a divine body, the progress of which has been briefly charted in the preceding chapter, the pertinent biblical passages were thus also marginalized, or somewhat "explained away" as purely metaphorical passages. In his aforementioned book "The Bodies of God and the World of Ancient Israel," *Benjamin Sommer* resolutely stands against these interpretative tendencies and blind spots within the field:

> The God of the Hebrew Bible has a body. This must be stated at the outset, because so many people, including many scholars, assume otherwise.[1]

Sommer's thesis appears at first glance to be paradoxical, as a widely held assumption exists within the monotheism central to both the Jewish and Christian Bible that the divine is completely transcendent. The key evidence readily resorted to is the prohibition against graven images from the Ten Commandments:

> Thou shalt not make unto thee any graven image, or any likeness of any thing that is in heaven above, or that is in the earth beneath, or that is in the water under the earth. Thou shalt not bow down thyself to them, nor serve them: for I the LORD thy God am a jealous God, visiting the iniquity of the fathers upon the children unto the third and fourth generation of them that hate me; And shewing mercy unto thousands of them that love me, and keep my commandments. (Exodus 20:4-6)[2]

Yet, this perspective is one sided, if not false. The injunction against graven images proscribes prayer to a depiction of the body of God. The conclusion that God thus *does not possess* a body is, on the contrary, premature: No mention of this topic may be found under the heading of the prohibition of graven images.

The Bible

Anthropomorphism and Rhetoric of the Body

Within the Roman Empire, both Jewish and Christian communities used Greek translations of the Hebrew Bible, a collection of Scriptures wherein, in at least some strata of tradition, God was depicted as corporeal. Andreas Wagner writes even "of the uninhibitedness with which the text of the O(ld) T(estament) discusses conceptions of body, (that is) God's body image."[3] To cite Sommer once more, God was ascribed, in at least some layers of the biblical texts, "a fixed body," that is, one that is spatially and temporally fixed. This denotes a body conceived of as present at a particular place at a particular time, independent of its assumed form or substance, or as to whether God was imagined as visible to human beings or not. God's answer to Moses in Exodus 33:20 ("And he said, Thou canst not see my face: for there shall no man see me, and live."[4]) is obviously based upon the certainty that there is a face of God, albeit this may well only be visible to angels, and in any case not to humans.[5] Sommer might again be cited at this juncture:

> As one moves forward in Genesis, one quickly arrives at additional verses that reflect the physicality of God—and although some of these verses point toward a nonmaterial anthropomorphism, others reflect a more concrete conception of God's body. We can term this conception *material anthropomorphism*, or the belief that God's body, at least at times, has the same shape and the same sort of substance as a human body. In Genesis 2:7 God blows life-giving breath into the first human—an action that might suggest that God has a mouth or some organ with which to exhale. Less ambiguously, in Genesis 3:8, Adam hears the sound of God going for a stroll in the Garden of Eden at the breezy time of the day. A being who takes a walk is a being who has a body—more specifically, a body with something closely resembling legs. . . . *The divine body portrayed in these texts was located in a particular place at a particular time.*[6]

Since the epoch of the Enlightenment, such conceptions have conventionally been termed "anthropomorphism" within classical modern philosophical and theological terminology:[7] With reference to its Greek cognate, the term "anthropomorphism" describes conceptions of God "in human form" or, more inclusively, a certain "humanization of God" which renders any descriptive distinction between God and man whatsoever difficult or utterly impossible.[8] Contrary to what is often reported, the Greek term "anthropomorphic" (ἀνθρωπόμορφος), "human-shaped," was probably neither first employed by *Epicurus* in the fourth and third centuries of the pre-Christian era,[9] nor by his contemporary, the historian and ethnographer *Hecataeus of Abdera*, nor indeed by the Stoic philosopher *Chrysippus* in the third century.[10] Its first attestation is far more likely to hail from the late Hellenistic period, perhaps within the writings of the Stoic philosopher, ethnographer, and geographer *Posidonius of Apamea* in Syria (135–51 BC).[11] Within German-speaking philosophical and theological discourse, it was first introduced by Leibniz and Kant.[12]

It must, however, be acknowledged that the term "anthropomorphism" would not have made the slightest sense to an inhabitant of Antiquity, who after all understood him- or herself as a being created by God in his image and likeness,[13] as is formulated in the Judeo-Christian Bible. He or she would likely have been far more proud of being made (as is recounted in Psalm 8) "a little lower than God"[14] so that man is described in theomorphic language as crowned "with glory and honor." When the biblical passages wherein God's body is mentioned are labeled as "anthropomorphic," this demonstrates that fundamental categories and perspectives in interpreting Scripture have shifted since the period of the genesis of these texts: One does not describe the anthropology of the text as "theomorphic," but rather its theology as "anthropomorphic." The discussion of an "anthropomorphism" presupposes categorical ontological differentiations between God and man, while the conception of the human as the likeness of God is instead interested in the ontological connection between man and God.

Such a *categorical ontological differentiation between God and man* is no discovery of the European Modern era. This can already be substantiated from the later textual strata of the Old Testament, for example, in the postexilic Psalms. It was already explicitly employed in respect to the biblical writings in Antiquity, namely when the corporeal terminology of these texts were understood as *metaphorical language* or interpreted allegorically. Regardless, this interpretation of the pertinent "anthropomorphic" passages became normal by the European Modern era, particularly in academic theological treatment of biblical Scripture.[15] Critical reflection upon this self-evident practice is made all the more difficult when, on the other hand, the categorical *necessity* of such an approach is affirmed with historical tradition. Indeed, the Marburg Old Testament scholar Otto Kaiser (*1924) speaks in such a manner of *necessary metaphors*; without them, it would be impossible to describe God in his complete otherness in respect to the world.[16] Such a concept of interpreting the anthropomorphic parlance in the Hebrew Bible as a network of necessary metaphors might well be a viable approach within the realms of a contemporary understanding of biblical texts within Jewish and Christian theology alike, but it certainly is not new. As has been seen, it is the final consequence of a method of interpreting holy texts introduced in Antiquity which, well before it was adopted by Judaism and Christianity, had already been preserved in the exegesis of Homer's works.[17]

Most recently, doubts have multiplied within exegetical discourse as to the assumption that this hermeneutic treatment of biblical discussion of the divine body was actually originally intended, undermining thereby historically the secureness of its ostensible philosophical or theological necessity. The Munich Old Testament scholar Friedrich Hartenstein (*1960) has already demonstrated in the thesis of his habilitation, "The Countenance of YHWH," that the discussion of God's body in the Hebrew Bible is not usually as heavily allegorized as in, for example, the antique pagan allegorical interpretations of Homer.[18] The Old Testament does indeed know a *body rhetoric*, a very precise handling of the language of God's body, but no *body metaphor* as is characteristic for the Hellenistic and Imperial-era treatment of the canonical texts of the pagan world: As an example, in a pagan writing with allegorical interpretations of Homer attributed to a grammarian called *Pseudo-Heraclitus* which should hail from the first century of the Christian era, the wings of Hermes are explained with the swiftness of the words and the description of this speed in Homer as "winged" (πτερόεντα).[19]

Comparable learned *body metaphor* is lacking within the Hebrew Bible. *Body rhetoric*, by comparison, is in a quite literal sense an integral component of the religious symbolic system of ancient Israel (to follow Hartenstein in employing pertinent terminology coined by the American ethnologist *Clifford Geertz* [1926–2006]).[20] It has already been demonstrated that the mention of a divine body within the biblical texts was definitely not understood according to the antique rules of metaphorical discourse. On this count already, these texts cannot be meant metaphorically, as the programmatic dissimilarity or foreignness of the divine and human body is stated practically nowhere within them. Yet, metaphor is under the conditions of a trope-based theory of metaphors (a word-oriented substitution theory) "the application of a word that belongs to another thing" (μεταφορὰ δέ ἐστιν ὀνόματος ἀλλοτρίου ἐπιφορά).[21] Such a programmatic statement of dissimilarity is only first necessary when otherness can be experienced or perceived through either religious experience or philosophical-theological reflections. Such experiences of otherness or corresponding reflections ultimately lead to theories of categorical onto-logical difference, as, for example, in antique Platonism and its many transformations in Antiquity and indeed thereafter. The same is applicable to the allegorical interpretation of such "anthropomorphic" passages, for antique rhetoricians understand but only a certain combination of meta-phors as allegory: According to the Epicurean active in first-century BC Italy *Philodemus*, "allegory" is a rhetorical trope which is closely adja-cent to metaphor;[22] the contemporary Alexandrian grammarian *Tryphon* defined it as logos which, based upon a relationship of similarity, says something different from what it means;[23] *Cicero* later explains allegory with reference to Philodemus as a form of speech composed of multiple metaphors (*plures translationes*) and is to be understood figuratively.[24] The allegorical interpretations of extracts from the Hebrew Bible discussing a body of God presuppose the experience of otherness and the theoretical conception of ontological difference. Nevertheless, this stance regarding the biblical texts is to be further distinguished from the putative intention of their authors. The French classical philologist *Jean-Pierre Vernant* (1914–2007) additionally warned against exploring the meddlesome question of as to why the inhabitants of Antiquity could speak more uninhibitedly of God's body, and counseled rather concerning oneself with how the symbolic sys-tem functioned and how the relationship between the human and divine was conceived of in connection to the conception of the body of God.[25]

Prior to strict experience or description of a categorical ontologi-cal difference between God and man or body and spirit, the meaning of "body," and naturally also of each individual body part, was clearly distin-guished from those terminological dimensions apparent *after* the introduc-tion of categorical difference. In the aforementioned biblical texts, "body" evidently once did not in the first instance relate to a biological body in the modern sense, confined to its physical, somatic, psychic dimensions, but rather—as Jean-Pierre Vernant emphasized—a "field of force of diverse energies and powers": "'corporeity' still does not acknowledge a distinc-tion between body and soul, nor does it establish a radical break between the natural and the supernatural. Man's corporeality also includes organic realities, vital forces, psychic activities, divine inspirations or influxes."[26] Andreas Wagner states, "Depictions of body are axes of communication": In the case of the discussion of "God's head" "it does not concern the bodily aspect of the head. . . . That God has a head makes clear the follow-ing: God is a real counterpart to me, the head of God serves as an opportu-nity for communication between God and man."[27]

Interesting for an exact description of the images of divine bodies in biblical texts is the question as to which human body parts are not brought into association with God, thus marking a difference between the divine and human body. In a congress paper from 1960,[28] the Scottish scholar of the Old Testament *James Barr* (1924–2006) already warned of the danger of overestimating biblical passages wherein "references to God's hands, feet, ears, nose, his speaking, smelling, walking in gardens, shutting doors, laughing, whistling, treading winepresses, riding early in the morning, rejoicing, being disgusted, changing his mind, being jealous and so on" are discussed.[29] The theophany scenes of the Old Testament showed that God mostly appears in human form, but this is need not strictly be a case; these examples could rather relate to a messenger (מלאך) or even simply his impersonal "splendor" (כבור) in his place.[30] Regardless of how his bodily form might be constituted, it is lethal for humans to see him.[31] That God's body is hardly some arbitrary frail human frame bedecked with aged flesh and wizened skin is stated beyond a doubt more or less explicitly in various passages. Indeed, it might be noted again and again that mention of a "flesh of God" is lacking; in other words, that the item of vocabulary בשׂר is not used with reference to God in the Hebrew Bible, with the exception of an example within the prophetic book of Hosea (9:12) which textual criticism has demonstrated to be questionable.[32] The same applies for bones, blood, and insides, and for the tongue and lips (with the sole exception of Isaiah 30:27-30), stomach, fat, and for the left hand. That God nevertheless possesses a very special body of splendor and that man is only a deficient image thereof is here self-evident. This also should not be understood as a fundamental polemic within the Hebrew Bible against the "anthropomorphic" conceptions of God, as the data on the expressions used to describe God's body demonstrate that there is also a body part ascribed to only God which humans lack: Akin to many Near Eastern gods, he enjoys a winged form (כְּנָפַיִם).[33] It might thus be maintained that the divine body upon which many passages of the Hebrew Bible play was evidently composed of an airy materiality in the eyes of the faithful, and not of bones, flesh, and blood. It is furthermore evident that he displays no deficiencies such as a left, or indeed sinister, hand,[34] but nevertheless acts with consummate emotionality. Regardless, in the opinion of these individuals, God does possess a manner of face, eyes, nose, nostrils, mouth, and teeth. Moreover, these body parts might not only be distinguished from those of mortals in their quality, but also in their size: The fringe of his robe fills the temple (Isaiah 6:1), and his hand conceals an entire human (Exodus 33:22). Behind such descriptions is a body quite evidently envisioned along masculine lines, even if (as with flesh, blood, bones, and innards) any impression of an explicit sex is strictly avoided. In addition, references are lacking regarding those body parts with which individualities might be described: For example, one never reads about the length, thickness, or color of hair. An exception as characteristic as it is rare is supplied by a famous description within the Book of Daniel: "The hair of his head like the pure wool" (7:9).

Corporeality, Materialization, Embodiment

Now, it must not be thought that there was a *single* conception of a spatially and temporally fixed body within the Scriptures of the Hebrew Bible adopted by Christendom as the Old Testament which was then no longer understood literally from the Hellenistic period onwards, but rather interpreted allegorically or taken as metaphorical speech. In actual fact, the traces of a theological discussion on God's corporeality can already be detected within these texts. Benjamin Sommer distinguished from a *first model* of a spatially and temporally circumscribed body of God a second concept of God in the Hebrew Bible and its religious surroundings which he terms "a mysterious fluidity and multiplicity of divine Embodiment and Selfhood." One might speak of a concept of *multiple embodiments or materializations of God*. Sommers' examples for the second concept initially hail from Mesopotamia and Canaan: In the Near Eastern religions there prevalent could be found the tendency to describe gods in disparate local forms of realization. Ishtar accordingly also existed in the form of seven local manifestations. The mighty authority manifest in the form of the highest god, Anu, also realized itself in Marduk, and consequently the word of Anu was Marduk.[35] The emphasis upon God's corporeal presence upon Zion, for example in the Psalms, is explicitly directed against the reception of such a model of a fluid divine body in ancient Israel.[36] The biblical and extrabiblical attestations for such multiple embodiments and materializations of God are known and oft-discussed: Sommer mentions two painted pithoi, clay storage jars, and an inscription on a wall which were found between 1975 and 1976 in the excavations upon the fortification Kuntillet 'Ajrûd in the eastern Sinai and dated to the early to middle eighth century before Christ. On these may be epigraphically attested a "YHWH of Samaria" and a "YHWH of Teman."[37] To this extrabiblical evidence might be added the biblical: The Hebrew Bible mentions a "YHWH in Hebron" (2 Samuel 15:7) and a "YHWH of Zion" (Psalm 99:2).[38] In the Book of Genesis, a votive stele (*massebe*) in Bethel is mentioned, which is discussed as if the seat, in a certain manner, of a God conceived of as material in time and place, and thereby perhaps as a *materialization* thereof (Genesis 31:11-13; cf. ibid. 48:15-16). Whether the Hebrew sentence "I am the God of Bethel" (Genesis 31:13) can also be translated, as Sommer suggests, as "I am the God in Betyl" or "I am the God Bethel"[39] is heavily debated within academia. Indeed, the Phoenician scholar Philo of Byblos precisely distinguishes between "Bethel" (Βαίτυλος) and "bethyls"

(Βαίτυλοι/*baetylia*),[40] which he describes as "ensouled stones" (λίθους ἐμφύχους).[41] Most likely the god *in* Bethel is meant, a much more general embodiment of God as in the case of the god of Hebron, Semaria, Teman, or, indeed, upon Zion. A very concrete, strictly locally confined embodiment of the god as stone would relate back to very archaic, aniconic, nomadic forms of religion as prevalent among Bedouin-influenced peoples such as the Nabateans.[42] Certainly, a cult practice and divine conception of this manner were still present in later times and brought to the very heart of the Roman Empire by Emperor *Marcus Aurelius Antoninus* (AD 204–222), otherwise known as *Elagabalus*: Various sources report that the emperor erected a Heliogabalium on the Palatine Hill, and installed there a betyl from his Syrian home city of Emesa/Homs and priestesses.[43] The temple was consecrated in AD 221 and did not outlive its inaugurator;[44] archaeological remains are most likely to be found in the area of the former "Vigna Barberini," the eastern corner of the Palatine beyond the Colosseum.[45] Otherwise, depictions of the Betyl of Emesa exist from some coins minted in Elagabalus' reign.

Such a biblical reception of the Near Eastern model of simultaneous divine fluidity and multiple embodiments, as the local embodiments of God in Bethel, Hebron, Samaria, Teman, and atop Zion would seem to indicate (and, indeed, the conception of an embodiment of God in Betyl), are vehemently opposed by some layers of redaction within the Hebrew Bible, above all the so called Priestly sources and those from the Deuteronomic-Deuteronomistic school: There is only *one* place of worship and not *many* for a variety of corporeal manifestations of God. The texts from the Priestly schools particularly mention a body: God is

Fig. 2.1   Temple of Elagabalus with betyl from Emesa
BMC Galatia, Cappadocia, and Syria 241 Nr. 24[46]

characterized as the one who "sitteth between the cherubims" (Psalm 99:1; 2 Samuel 6:2; 1 Kings 6:23-25 and 8:6f.[47]), has a footstool for his feet, and lives at the peak of Zion in Jerusalem in his holy temple.[48]

This concludes the recapitulation of Benjamin Sommer's argumentation. A more exhaustive discussion of his theses would be necessary, as all of the further biblical texts pertaining to Sommer's perspective would need to be reexamined, more, indeed, than Sommer himself handled in his publication. For example, the cycle of visions in the Book of the Prophet Amos 7 to 9—the prophet sees how "the LORD stood upon a wall made by a plumbline, with a plumbline in his hand" (Amos 7:7),[49] and he saw "the LORD standing upon the altar" (Amos 9:1)[50]—the famous scene of Isaiah's vocation as a prophet in the sixth capital of the eponymous biblical book where God "sitting upon a throne, high and lifted up, and his train filled the temple" (Isaiah 6:1)[51] is described, but also the Deuteronomistic rejection of a corporeal image of God in the First Book of Kings, where it is said that (a day's journey distant from Beersheba) God was not in the wind, not in the earthquake, not in fire, but rather in "a still small voice" (or, translated more precisely from the Hebrew "in the sound of a sheer still," or indeed, in the words of Martin Buber and Franz Rosenzweig "voice of floating hush" [1 Kings 19:12]).[52] This text cannot here be extensively discussed; this has been partially accomplished by Aaron Schart and Andreas Wagner. For present purposes, it suffices to remember that both the Hebrew Bible and its Greek translation are characterized by a rich usage of corporeal terms for God which were originally not meant allegorically or metaphorically. It has also become clear that there are entirely different concepts of God's body within the biblical books—in part, different materializations and embodiments of God must be reckoned with, and, in part, with his occurrence in individual locations. It must also be made clear that the corporeality of God must again be differentiated from his presence at a particular place; as a rule, the *corporeality* of God is already simply from a logical standpoint the precondition of his *materialization* in a particular place, or his embodiment.

The Jewish-Hellenistic Biblical Exegesis

Although, in recent years, new attention has been steered towards the passages of the Hebrew Bible which describe or presuppose the body of God, an account investigating the lines of transmission of these textual passages into the Judeo-Hellenistic and Imperial-period Jewish and Christian literature and contrasting these traditions with pagan discussion of divine bodies remains a desideratum. Indeed, just as interesting as the question as to whether and to what extent the conception of the divine body in the Hebrew Bible was influenced by notions from Israel's ancient Near Eastern surroundings is that of how the encounter of Judaism with Hellenistic culture affected the treatment of these biblical passages. This meeting, a portrait of which has prominently been painted by the Tübingen New Testament scholar *Martin Hengel* (1926–2009),[53] will now be examined.

Upon first inspection, it would seem that the concept of a divine body with a face, eyes, lashes, ears, nose, nostrils, mouth, and teeth, as informs many texts from the Hebrew Bible, must have proven to be extremely problematic to most people under the conditions of a globalized Hellenistic civilization in the wake of the accession of Alexander the Great (336 BC).[54] This civilization is generally credited with a move towards rationalization (well known under the memorable phrase "from mythos to logos"),[55] progressing from a purely narrative thematization of the divine world found wanting within this burgeoning thought to the rationalized conceptualizing thereof. Aside from the inherent problematic of such a dual conception and of any assessment built upon this (which, much like the definition of mythos, need hardly be broached here), the question is immediately posed as to whether such a development really representatively describes popular and cultural tendencies alike. In fact, intellectual reservations with "anthropomorphic" divine bodies only arose among those who had been shaped by very particular fundamental assumptions from Hellenistic philosophy and were interested additionally in identifying the God of Abraham, Isaac, and Jacob as revealed upon Mount Sinai with divine conceptions within Greek philosophy; these included the Jewish-Hellenistic biblical exegete *Aristobulus* and later *Philo of Alexandria*.

According to a testimonial within the Second Book of the Maccabees (1:10) *Aristobulus* is said to have belonged to a priestly family and to have resided in Egypt as the tutor of a king Ptolemy (probably Ptolemy VI Philometor, 180–145 BC). In later tradition he was called a "peripatetic" and was said to have lived during the middle of the second century BC.[56] The Christian church historian and bishop Eusebius of Caesarea transmits in his *Preparatio evangelica* at the beginning of the fourth century of the Christian era a passage wherein Aristobulus "declared concerning the passages in the Sacred Books which are currently understood to refer to limbs of God's body" (according to Eusebius in his introduction).[57] It appears thereby, when Aristobulus is followed and this is not held to be pure literary fiction, that the Ptolemaic king had presented to his tutor the question as to why (from the perspective of the Jew Aristobulus) "by our law there are intimations given of hands, and arm, and face, and feet, and walking, in the case of the Divine Power."[58] The Jewish interpreter of the Torah answers by first outlining the general hermeneutic preconditions of the treatment of such passages within the Hebrew Bible: the necessity to think of God with a "fitting conception" and to connect those words seemingly bound to "appearance" (ἐπιφάνεια) instead with "major circumstances" (μεγάλα πράγματα) so as to interpret them metaphorically:

> But I would entreat you to take the interpretations in a natural way, and to hold fast the fitting conception of God, and not to fall off into the idea of a fabulous anthropomorphic constitution. For our lawgiver Moses, when he wishes to express his meaning in various ways, announces certain arrangements of nature and preparations for mighty deeds, by adopting phrases applicable to other things, I mean to things outward and visible. Those therefore who have a good understanding admire his wisdom, and the divine inspiration. . . . But to those who are devoid of power and intelligence, and only cling close to the letter, he does not appear to explain any grand idea.[59]

Then, Aristobulus runs through the individual examples (evidently presented to him by the king) one after another and, in addition to the biblical examples, ties in political rhetoric common within the Ptolemaic court: "For when you as a king send out forces, wishing to accomplish some purpose, we say 'The king has a mighty hand,' and the hearers' thoughts are carried to the power which you possess."[60] From this and a few further biblical passages it evidently follows that "the 'hands' are understood of the power of God."[61] "Standing" is explained as the "constitution (. . .) of the world" while the "descent" from Mount Sinai is interpreted as the real epiphany of an actually very much ubiquitous God at a single place.[62] In examining the fragments related by Eusebius it may be realized that from the order which the king was supposed to have submitted for explanation ("hands, and arm, and face, and feet, and walking") that only the upper and lower limbs are explained.[63] Only in a passage noticeably further on within his work does the Christian bishop and scholar relate yet another interpretation from Aristobulus regarding the expression "divine voice" which certainly belongs to the "anthropomorphic" expressions of the Hebrew Bible but is absent from the king's questioning as recounted by the Jewish interpreter of the Torah. The divine voice should be understood "not as words spoken, but as construction of works, just as Moses in the Law has spoken of the whole creation of the world as 'words' of God."[64] As the crowning witness to such an interpretation of biblical texts, Aristobulus then calls upon Pythagoras, Socrates, and Plato, Orpheus, and the Hellenistic didactic poet Aratus (c. 310–245 BC) who is also cited within the Gospel of Luke, although in his quotation from the "Appearances" (Φαινόμενα) by Aratus he replaces the designation for the chief Greek god (Ζεύς and Δίς) with the neutral word "God" (θεός).[65]

Thus, it was already a certainty to this Jewish-Hellenistic interpreter of the Hebrew Bible that "anthropomorphic" discourse regarding a divine body (Aristobulus refers to a "mythological and human condition" of discourse on God: τὸ μυθῶδες καὶ ἀνθρώπινον κατάστημα) did not exemplify within a learned Alexandrian context what might be understood as a "fitting conception" with which to consider God. As a result, one interpreted the biblical formulations describing the divine body "in a loftier meaning" (τὸ μεγαλεῖον in Aristobulus' own words)[66] allegorically as metaphors. As has been seen, it is very much unlikely that such an allegorizing treatment of the "anthropomorphic" passages of the biblical Scriptures had characterized Jewish thought from its very inception—even if exactly this is asserted in the universal history of the historian *Diodorus Siculus* from the first century before Christ. Therein, it is stated that Moses did not produce any cultic statues of the gods "being of the opinion that God is not in human form."[67] The Byzantine patriarch Photius, who excerpted the paragraph from Diodorus in the ninth century of the Christian era, ascribed these lines to *Hecataeus of Miletus*, a historian and geographer of the sixth century BC. He had, however, most likely confused him with *Hecataeus of Abdera*, who had lived two hundred years later during the reigns of Alexander the Great and his Egyptian successor Ptolemy I.[68] It is, indeed, uncertain as to whether the passage in question accords in language or content with others certainly from Hecataeus of Abdera transmitted by Diodorus. It seems rather more likely that the entire text represents another (Jewish?) compilation from the Hasmonean period, or even later, comparable to the Pseudo-Hecataeus texts and presupposing the relevant Jewish-Hellenistic argumentations and pagan ethnographic accounts of Judaism.[69]

Why was it "appropriate" or "in accordance with the rules" in the Ptolemaic era to substitute the literal meaning of biblical passages with a "loftier meaning" in order to preserve divine conceptions deemed "appropriate" or "in accordance with the rules" (τὴν ἁρμόζουσαν ἔννοιαν περὶ θεοῦ κρατεῖν)? One must understand that already in the pre-Socratic tradition of Greek philosophy harsh criticism of "anthropomorphism" occurred, which in its radicalism is only paralleled by the biblical tradition. Whosoever thought along their lines must have seen in the conception of a divine body a more or less absurd notion born of stupid, fatuous individuals.

Ancient Philosophy

Xenophanes

Within a philosophical theology which identified the practical reason for all things with *a* god absolutely transcendental to all that is worldly, but certainly not one *single* god (εἷς θεός), it was above all the pre-Socratic philosopher *Xenophanes* (c. 570 to after 470 BC) who railed against allegedly "naïve," "anthropomorphic" concepts of god: "But mortals think gods are begotten, / and have the clothing, voice, and body of mortals."[70] Xenophanes justifies his argumentation with the neat thought experiment of asking as to how cattle, horses, and lions would conceive of divine bodies (σώματ᾽ ἐποίουν):

> Now if cattle, \<horses\> or lions had hands
> and were able to draw with their hands and perform works like men,
> horses like horses and cattle like cattle would draw the forms of gods,
>   and make their bodies just like the body \<each of them\> had.[71]

In another passage of the didactic poem, Xenophanes presents the ethnological observation that: "Africans \<say their gods are\> snub-nosed and black, Thracians blue-eyed and red-haired!"[72] Quite evidently, this forms the empirical basis for the thought experiment of imagining theriomorphic divine images in analogy to the anthropomorphic examples of humans. Both seemed equally absurd to Xenophanes and inappropriate for the being of his supreme deity. As for the pre-Socratic thinkers the rational cause for all earthly things could not be identified with any of these earthly things, it was incumbent upon them to purge divine images from all anthropomorphic (or theriomorphic) conceptions.[73] God is utterly different from humans and hence inconceivable to them.

    Yet, it should not be thought that Xenophanes considered God to be entirely bodiless (in the sense in which the Christian philosopher Clement of Alexandria integrated the previously cited fragments of this didactic poem into his work "Patchwork" at the end of the second century AD, as will presently be seen). Following earlier speculations upon nature which conceived of the Earth, Oceanus, and the cosmos in the form of a perfect sphere, Xenophanes seems to have adopted for his god a spherical corporeal form (καὶ σφαιροειδὲς αὐτό) which remains "ever in the same place," "moving not at all"; at the very least, such a stance is ascribed to him in later doxological literature, and this attribution cannot be dismissed offhand as a mere contamination from later teachings (e.g., those of Parmenides).[74] Ultimately, the sphere is mathematically an absolutely symmetrical, and hence perfect, body and is immobile (unless it is pushed); it does indeed remain "ever in the same place moving not at all." A major uncertainty admittedly remains in view of the situation of its transmission; it has become somewhat obscure as to what Xenophanes genuinely meant in this passage.[75] It is known from the surviving fragments that Xenophanes said of his upmost god that "all of him sees, all thinks, all hears." Additionally, Xenophanes discusses a motion of his mind.[76] Thus, according to the perspective of this pre-Socratic philosopher, a certain form, materiality, and capacity for sensation is evidently at God's disposal—and thereby properties characteristic of a body.

As has been seen, Xenophanes did not primarily oppose the conception of God having a body. Rather, he merely opposed "anthropomorphic" concepts of God and inasmuch a divine body along human lines analogous to that described within the Hebrew Bible in discussion of God's face, eyes, lashes, ears, nose, nostrils, mouth, and teeth. This pre-Socratic hence formulated exactly the notion of otherness between God and man, and the divine and human body, which is a fundamental requisite for a metaphorical or allegorical interpretation of the pertinent passages of religious or mythological literature such as the biblical texts. It is only in the trajectory of the traditional but deeply problematic model of "from mythos to logos" that one might, in the manner of the Berlin classical philologist *Werner Jaeger* (1888–1961), pronounce that the first sign of an open conflict between the new path of philosophical thought and the traditional path of a mythological worldview may be detected in the words of Xenophanes.[77]

Criticism of Xenophanes in Christian Authors

Already in Antiquity, the exact sense of Xenophanes' words had become unclear and debated alike.[78] The previously quoted sentences have only been transmitted to us because (as has already been alluded to) a Christian author cites them as he wishes to use the pre-Socratic philosopher's opposition to "anthropomorphism" as proof for his own far more fundamental opposition to any conception of a divine corporeality.[79] *Clement of Alexandria*, one of the first truly philosophically cultivated Christian thinkers with a Platonic bent, cited the two passages of Xenophanes in his miscellany *Stromata* ("Patchwork," Στρομ ατεῖς) at the turn of the second to the third century AD. The aim of Clement's argumentation is to "exhibit now with greater clearness the plagiarism of the Greeks from the Barbarian philosophy," that is, to prove that the knowledge of the books of the Hebrew Bible translated into Greek through the great Greek philosophers such as Plato, Aristotle, the Stoics, or Epicurus, and indeed, not only in terms of teachings on God, but also in cognition theory and ethics.[80] A portion of the argumentation would be cited a bit more than three hundred years after its composition by the learned bishop *Eusebius of Caesarea* in his *Praeparatio Evangelica*.[81] Therein, Clement also accentuates the difference between the human body and his divine creator, which he counts as the shared heritage of biblical and philosophical tradition (admittedly on grounds of the "plagiarism of the Hellenes"): "And founding on the formation of man from the dust, the philosophers constantly term the body earthy."[82] Under the auspices of an extensive paralleling of biblical conceptions of creation and pagan creation accounts (up to and including the number of days of creation)[83] Xenophanes is then introduced: "Rightly, then, Xenophanes of Colophon, teaching that God is one and incorporeal. . . ."[84] Both of the fragments just quoted are prefaced by Clement with a programmatic quotation which should evidence the quasi-biblical monotheism of Xenophanes and thereby secure the "Christianness" of the pagan philosopher: "One God there is, midst gods and men supreme / in form, in mind, unlike to mortal men." Both the aforementioned scholarly bishop Eusebius in Palestinian Caesarea and the bishop Theodoret roughly 120 years later in Syrian Cyrrhus (near Apamea) made reference to this passage.[85] Clement comes to discuss Xenophanes once more in a second passage within his "Patchwork." Therein, he elevates the pre-Socratic philosopher above "the Greeks":

> Now, as the Greeks represent the gods as possessing human forms, so also do they as possessing human passions. And as each of them depict their forms similar to themselves, as Xenophanes says, "Africans [say their gods are] snub-nosed and black, Thracians blue-eyed and red-haired!" so also they assimilate their souls to those who form them: the Barbarians, for instance, who make them savage and wild; and the Greeks, who make them more civilized, yet subject to passion.[86]

Plato

In the depiction of antique beliefs in God and in historical outlines of the criticism of "anthropomorphic" divine images alike, a line is eagerly drawn from this pre-Socratic critique in the sixth century BC to the Christian thinkers of the late Imperial era such as Clement or Eusebius. In this trajectory, the Platonic philosophy upon which both Jewish and Christian thinkers drew understandably assumes a central position: Indeed, Plato, "stimulated by Xenophanes, formulates a withering critique of the anthropomorphic polytheism of the myth."[87] Even when controversial debate occurred in Antiquity as to how Plato's solely orally transmitted doctrine of principles was to be interpreted, it was still incontestable that the (supreme) Platonic god is particularly characterized by unity, goodness, immutability, and completeness and, as pure mind (νοῦς) must be conceived of as bodiless.[88] In the Platonic dialogue "The Republic" (*Respublica*) these fundamentals of the "true doctrine of the gods" are elaborated at more length.[89] They might also be found in other passages within the dialogues: in the *Phaedrus*,[90] "the divine is beauty, wisdom, goodness, and all such qualities"; God "always remains simply" in his "own shape" according to the relevant passage in the *Respublica*.[91]

These fundamental premises of a Platonic conception of God apply regardless of whether one identifies this god with the totality of ideas as conceived of as a mind, and (like *Speusippus*, 410/407–339/338 BC, Plato's nephew, student, and successor as scholarch of the Academy) furthermore elevated above that god the One (τὸ ἕν) as highest principle,[92] or identified both in whatsoever form, and then took that all-embracing "One" to be supreme god. Indeed, according to the Platonic dialogue *Parmenides*, the One can only be determined negatively in its absolute unity,[93] and not on grounds of similarity and difference to other things.[94] Along with rest and movement and time and eternity, it lacks all categories of corporeality or bodiliness. As the infinite and the absolute simplest, the One is without a form; thus, it does not partake of the rounded, straight, or circular.[95] With this, Plato distanced himself from theories of a spherical form of the supreme god as most likely already propounded by Xenophanes, and certainly by other pre-Platonic philosophers. The Platonists of the Academy and their founder broke radically with not only all "anthropomorphic" images of a divine corporeality, but also with all earlier assumptions regarding divine "being": as the One "is not being but reaches even farther beyond it in rank and power,"[96] it is "beyond being" (ἐπέκεινα τῆς οὐσίας).

If, in the Imperial era of Antiquity, the formulation "beyond being" (oft-cited even today) was the subject of allusions, it was no longer necessary to emphasize expressly that this negation naturally also implies the negation of *corporeal* being — this implication was self-evident to all those with even the most superficial acquaintance with Plato. This presents itself already in the general evaluation of the body and corporeality within Platonic philosophy. In common with other passages of the dialogues, it is made clear within Plato's *Sophista* that the simple identification of "body" with "being" is philosophically inacceptable. Individuals who "maintain stoutly that that alone exists which can be touched and handled; for they define existence and body, or matter, as identical," and "drag down everything from heaven and the invisible to earth" have no philosophical sense for immaterial existence and are thus somewhat limited.[97] As is articulated in the *Phaedrus*, however, higher being assumes in the form of the soul "an earthy body" (σῶμα γήϊνον), "something solid, when it settles down," "and the whole, compounded in soul and body, is called a living being, and is further designated as mortal."[98] Of all corporeal things, this thusly incorporated soul possesses the most godliness.[99] When, however, such a rarefied, incorporeal, and purely immaterial being as the soul or ideas exists, then by definition the divine cannot be conceived of at the level of lower corporeal being. Even when this "absolute being" (τὸ παντελῶς ὄν) must be ascribed life, as it cannot stand immobile and thereby movement must be claimed for it, it is of course not a corporeal motion which is imagined, but rather an immaterial mobility.[100] Only the corporeal is, as is formulated in the *Phaedrus*, "something solid" which might be encountered, and which must be moved by the higher, spiritual being.[101]

This Platonic concept of a purely spiritual, incorporeal God who— now quite self-evidently identified with the "One" (τὸ ἕν)—might be conceived of as "beyond being" (ἐπέκεινα τῆς οὐσίας) and thus often as consequently transcending a spiritual being, and hence entirely indeterminate (ἐπέκεινα νοῦ καὶ οὐσίας),[102] deeply influenced both Jewish and Christian thought during the period of the Roman Empire. Regardless of the degree to which one gravitated towards the fundamental principle of Platonic philosophy (that is as to whether "almighty God" might be described "as spirit or as beyond spirit and essence") many educated adherents of these two monotheistic religions were convinced that he was "simply invisible and incorporeal"[103]—albeit not all, as will soon be seen. At any rate, the doxographic tradition of the philosophical and philosophical historical teachings and handbooks of Plato pronounced without much ado that he deemed God to be "bodiless" (ἀσώματος), although *expressis verbis* the Athenian philosopher had never done so.[104]

Philo of Alexandria

A good example for the completely self-evident reception of these fundamental elements of Platonic teachings on God (and their intensification in part) through a Jewish-Hellenistic interpreter of the Greek Bible is *Philo of Alexandria*, a contemporary of Paul the Apostle, who inhabited this Mediterranean scholarly metropole during the first half of the first century AD. As an esteemed member of the city's Jewish community he had left an extensive oeuvre of biblical exegetical and philosophical writings which were nevertheless transmitted primarily in Christian contexts after the end of Antiquity. His interpretations of biblical texts later influenced many Christian theologians such as Origen in the east or Ambrose in the west.[105] Although from a modern perspective tensions between a rather Platonically sourced philosophical concept of God and a decidedly biblical divine image are entirely discernible, and Philo, for example, alternates between the more *philosophically* connoted terminology of "the being" (τὸ ὄν) and "absolute being" (τὸ ὄντος ὄν) and the *biblical* sounding "the one who is being" (ὁ ὤν with Exodus 3:14 LXX),[106] the *bodilessness* of God is for him indubitable. It is both a founding axiom of his discussion of God and implicit in his strict adherence to the categorical transcendence of God.[107] As Philo—in comparison to Plato and Aristotle—holds God to be categorically unknowable, he emphasizes the differences between God and man. The categorical difference between the two is that humans have a body and God conversely none. Hence, it might be read within the framework of an argumentation regarding the creation of humans in God's image which Philo should like to see as limited to humans' intellect (νοῦς): "Neither is God in human form, nor is the human body God-like" (οὔτε γὰρ ἀνθρωπόμορφος ὁ θεὸς οὔτε θεοειδὲς τὸ ἀνθρώπειον σῶμα).[108] With such pronouncements, Philo refers to a biblical phrase which is often cited as being fundamental to his teachings: "God *is* not a man" (Numbers 23:19 LXX).[109] As this fundamental statement must stand to rights, and it assists in rising "superior to all the human conceptions of Him," God may not be ascribed a human form. That would not only be a "monstrosity" but also an "impious thought" as it would, in turn, imply human emotions and passions for God. On these conceptual grounds, one equally cannot accord God "hands and feet, incomings and outgoings, enmities, aversions, estrangements, anger, in fact such parts and passions as can never belong to the Cause."[110] God also has no countenance, "transcending as He does the peculiarities that mark all created things." He does not reside in a single part as "He contains all and is not Himself contained by anything."[111] In the tractate "On the Unchangeableness of God" this translates into Philo's conversational style accordingly:

For consider, if He uses our bodily parts or organs He has feet to move from one place to another. But whither will He go or walk since His presence fills everything? To whom will He go, when none is His equal? And for what purpose will He walk? For it cannot be out of care for health as it is with us. Hands He must have to receive and give. Yet He receives nothing from anyone, for, besides that He has no needs, all things are His possessions, and when He gives, He employs as minister of His gifts the Reason wherewith also He made the world. Nor did He need eyes, which have no power of perception without the light which meets our sense. But that light is created, whereas God saw before creation, being Himself His own light. Why need we speak of the organs of nourishment? If He has them, He eats and is filled, rests awhile and after the rest has need again, and the accompaniments of this I will not dwell upon. These are the mythical fictions of the impious, who, professing to represent the deity as of human form, in reality represent Him as having human passions.[112]

As God's essence is without any characteristics (the usual divine predications of, for example, "immeasurability" or "unchangableness" are not tied to his essence but rather qualify his works),[113] there can naturally be no divine body parts—"but the Existent Being is in need of nothing, and so, not needing the benefit that parts bestow, can have no parts at all."[114] Evidently God also does not occupy any delineated space either within the world (as conceived of by the Stoics) or between the worlds (following the Epicureans):[115]

> We must consider the point which naturally comes next, our third point, namely what the place is which he lights upon or meets, for we read "he met a place" (Genesis 28:11). Now "place" has a threefold meaning, firstly that of a space filled by a material form, secondly that of the Divine Word, which God Himself has completely filled throughout with incorporeal potencies; "for they saw," says Moses, "the place where the God of Israel stood" (Exodus 24:10). Only in this place did he permit them to sacrifice, forbidding them to do so elsewhere: for they were expressly bidden to go up "to the place which the Lord God shall choose" (Deuteronomy 7:5), and there to sacrifice "the whole burnt offerings and the peace offerings" (Exodus 20:24) and to offer the other pure sacrifices. There is a third signification, in keeping with which God Himself is called a place, by reason of His containing things, and being contained by nothing whatever, and being a place for all to flee into, and because He is Himself the space which holds Him; for He is that which He Himself has occupied, and naught encloses Him but Himself. I, mark you, am not a place, but in a place; and each thing likewise that exists; for that which is contained is different from that which contains it, and the Deity, being contained by nothing, is of necessity Itself Its own place.[116]

God is eternal, but not in the sense of an eternal duration of a certain time in a certain place, but rather as eternity (αἰών), the *principle* of time. He is he who always is (ἀεὶ ὄν). In this manner, as John Whittaker has demonstrated, Philo identifies the apersonal reality of the ideas of Plato with a personal god, "eternity" (αἰών) bound with "life" (βίος).[117] The soul thus attains a true vision of God only through the liberation from the body, through disembodiment.[118]

It is hence hardly surprising that Philo understands those biblical passages concerning the body of God as metaphorical speech and allegorizes them:[119] Thus, for example, the biblical discussion of the "hand of God" is connected to divine reason (λόγος) or his powers.[120] Moreover, the revelatory voice to be heard upon Sinai bore not the slightest resemblance to a human voice because "whatever God says is not words but deeds, which are judged by the eyes rather than the ears."[121] Hence, they cannot be heard, but rather solely beheld on a purely intellectual level. God does also not rove in a corporeal sense about paradise as (as the unmoved mover) he is unmoved.[122] Direct contact between a human and God in the sense originally envisaged and reported within biblical Scripture can certainly not occur. Nevertheless (in contrast to Plato), Philo delights in the notion within Homer that "the gods . . . put on all manner of shapes, and visit the cities, beholding the violence and the righteousness of men."[123] As, in fact, the "anthropomorphic" discourse here as elsewhere is "to help us, his pupils, to learn our lesson."[124] Such edification is necessary for those "body lovers," the uneducated of the street. These people envisage God in human form and confuse thereby that which may not be confused: God and man.[125] With his strict insistence upon the unknowability of God (from which divine incorporeality follows), and his sound reception by important Christian theologians, Philo of Alexandria doubtless numbers among the founding fathers of the movement which would come over the course of centuries ultimately to deprive God of his body.

Conceptions of Divine Bodies

At first glance, it might well be thought that Werner Jaeger and others are right in claiming that a deeper conflict between a somewhat philosophical worldview and a mythological engagement with the world is revealed by the question as to the existence and constitution of a divine body.[126] This paradigmatic conflict between "mythos" and "logos" would be understood as having implicitly existed prior to the articulation of the aforementioned sentences by Xenophanes in the fifth century BC.

At second glance: naturally for such a stance there is a plethora of evidence, from which only one example might be quoted: Within a fragment of his writing "On Superstition" (*De superstitione*), later preserved by Augustine, the Roman polymath and Stoic philosopher *Seneca*, who committed suicide at the order of the Emperor Nero in the year AD 65, protested "anthropomorphic" and, indeed, "theriomorphic" conceptions of a divine body which formed the divine images found in temples during his age, countering them with teachings on divinity of a Stoically inspired philosophical theology:

To beings who are sacred, immortal and inviolable they consecrate images of the cheapest inert material. They give them the shapes of men or beasts or fishes; some, in fact, make them double creatures of both sexes combined or unlike bodies united. They are called divinities, but if they were successfully brought to life and encountered, they would be regarded as monsters.[127]

Nevertheless, things are hardly as simple as might be inferred from an initial examination. As has already been seen, Xenophanes likely did not seek with his polemic against "anthropomorphism" to deny that his supreme deity had a body—how else might this be all-seeing, all-hearing, and all-understanding?[128] The pre-Socratic philosopher was merely convinced that the divine body was "dissimilar or precisely the same reason that a god's capacity for thought (νόημα)—with which the gods are abundantly endowed—is dissimilar to human thought" as Jean-Pierre Vernant once explained this. Bodies and God's capacity for thought possessed according to Xenophanes, as has been seen, *copiously* (or even *"entirely"*) what bodies and the human mental capacity for thought only *deficiently* display, or, formulated from the perspective of the ancients: Human bodies and capacities for thought possess only *deficiently* what the bodies and capacities of thought of God possess *copiously* (or even *"entirely"*).[129] Furthermore, even with respect to Platonic philosophy, only half the truth is told by that previous sentence stating that the (supreme) Platonic god is characterized in particular by unity, goodness, immutability, and completeness and, as pure intellect (νοῦς), must be understood as bodiless. Plato, indeed, was very much capable of discussing a body of God: In his dialogue the *Timaeus*, it is recounted as to how the world, the cosmos (κόσμος), was fashioned by the demiurge in the form of a sphere as a "complete entirety," and was set rotating. At the center of the cosmos-body and simultaneously spread about it may be found a soul endowed with reason which renders the cosmos itself to a "blissful" god "perceptible to the senses" (εὐδαίμων θεός or θεός αἰσθητός), namely the *world-soul*:[130]

Such, then, was the sum of the reasoning of the ever-existing God concerning the god which was one day to be existent, whereby He made it smooth and even and equal on all sides from the centre, a whole and perfect body compounded of perfect bodies. And in the midst thereof He set Soul, which He stretched throughout the whole of it, and therewith He enveloped also the exterior of its body; and as a Circle revolving in a circle He stablished one sole and solitary Heaven, able of itself because of its excellence to company with itself and needing none other beside,

sufficing unto itself as acquaintance and friend. And because of all this
He generated it to be a blessed God.[131]

And now at length we may say that our discourse concerning the Universe has reached its termination. For this our Cosmos has received the
living creatures both mortal and immortal and been thereby fulfilled;
it being itself a visible Living Creature embracing the visible creatures,
a perceptible God made in the image of the Intelligible, most great and
good and fair and perfect in its generation—even this one Heaven sole
of its kind.[132]

According to Plato, it might hence be said that at least *one* god among
the many supposed by him possesses a spherical body, albeit this refers
to a very special and complete body, as with Xenophanes. The world-soul
is the "the best of things generated";[133] it is related to, similar to, and the
same (ὅμοιος) as the divine, the immortal, the intelligible, the monomor-
phic, the insoluble, the same, and that which is always identical to it.[134]

The Middle Platonic philosopher *Plutarch*, who wrote in the second half of the first century AD, described the cosmos as an "inchoate
deity."[135] In so-called Orphic texts, the (also spherically conceived) world
was explicitly understood as "God's body."[136] Analogous conceptions
are attested by the magical papyri, templates with texts for magical practices, with their predications of the pantokrator who is here termed the
"good daemon" (Ἀγαθὸς Δαίμων). His body also encompasses the entire
cosmos:

Heaven is your head; ether, body; earth, feet; and the water around you,
ocean, [O] Agathos Daimon. You are lord, the begetter and nourisher
and increaser of all.[137]

Regardless, Imperial-era philosophy has not been exhaustively handled
with respect to Platonism. As Mark Edwards most recently emphasized
once more, the received impression of Platonic philosophy's dominance
during the Imperial era and Late Antiquity is potentially due to a later
preference for this thought within Christian theology, and should not necessarily be understood as mirroring reality within the antique "philosophy
market."[138] From the Hellenistic period until Late Antiquity, other schools
of Greek philosophy were far more open to concepts of a divine corporeality, and propounded these in wildly varying forms, as might be demonstrated for the Epicurean, Stoic, and Aristotelian schools.

Epicurus and the Epicurean School

Thus, *Epicurus*, for example, and *Epicurean philosophy* were accorded the belief that the gods possessed a manner of bodies, even if these divine bodies were clearly different from a human body.[139] With respect to the strict materialism which distinguishes this philosophical direction, it is hardly surprising when the gods in Epicureanism are *also* thought of as material existences, despite it already being heavily debated in Antiquity as to which manner of existence and degree of reality should be conceded in this school to those gods. According to an antique scholion on the first proposition of Epicurus, the gods, who inhabit immortal intermediate worlds, "are discernible by reason alone . . . in human form (ἀνθρωποειδεῖς)."[140] The Roman poet and Epicurean philosopher *Lucretius*, who probably lived during the first century BC and may have been a student of Philodemus, considered it an ideal "to approach their shrines with placid heart" and "receive with tranquil peace of spirit the images which are carried to men's minds from their holy bodies, declaring what the divine shapes are."[141] In the dialogue *De natura deorum*, written around 45 BC by *Marcus Tullius Cicero*, the author has a certain Gaius Velleius assert that, according to Epicurus, the Gods might possess "a semblance of body" (*tamquam corpus*) and "a semblance of blood" (*tanquam sanguis*).[142] This formulation most likely means that the bodies of the gods are not composed of flesh and blood, but rather out of something similar (this is Kirk Sanders' understanding of the passage).[143] This body of the gods is described within another record within *De divinatione*, a dialogue of his which appeared shortly prior to *De natura deorum*, as a very fine, transparent (*perlucidus*) material which is also imperishable and inasmuch endless in perpetuity. These two statements from the dialogues of Cicero can be connected together, so that, according to the Epicurean stances here relayed, the gods have human-shaped bodies, but that these are not of flesh and blood, but rather of a very fine transparent matter. Furthermore, as Cicero has Gaius Velleius relate, were the gods to have body parts, they would not use them.[144]

Difficult to explain and, indeed, disputed within the field, is how this conception of an imperishable, intangible body of the gods exactly relates to the epistemological positions attested in Epicurus' own writings, namely that the gods produce these acutely fine images (εἴδολα or *simulacra*) from thin strata of atoms which enter into the soul through those atoms responsible for vision that permit cognition of God. Yet, most likely, it was thought that these images sent from the divine bodies underlying human cognition were conceived of by Epicurus as particles which are lost in the emission of the divine body's fine matter but nevertheless do not result in any damage to the integrity of this body.[145] The reason for this particular quality in the divine body is in the stance of the Epicureans that the atomic conglomeration out of which it is composed evidences, in contrast to terrestrial bodies, no voids between atoms, and losses of matter are abidingly supplemented by the forces conserved from related matter.[146]

While it is not possible to find literal attestations for a turn of phrase analogous to a "certain corporeality" of the gods in authentic texts by Epicurus or Lucretius, such formulations may be found in the work "On the Gods" (Περὶ θεῶν / *De Diis*) by the Epicurean philosopher and poet *Philodemus of Gadara* (in eastern Jordan), who lived in Herculaneum in the second half of the first century BC. These suggest (among other things) that Cicero directly referred to either these writings or their sources in his aforementioned remarks within *De natura deorum*:[147] Possibly, the "semblance of a body" and "semblance of blood" within the fragments of Philodemus transmitted by Cicero correspond to the statement that bodies "appropriate to this (sc. human body)" may be "analogously" discussed in respect to the gods. In other words, the gods have "the semblance of a body and the semblance of blood" because an analogy exists between divine and human bodies: τὸ κατ᾽ ἀναλογίαν.[148] If an only very fragmentarily preserved papyrus from the library of the "Villa of the Papyri" at Herculaneum is ascribed to the Epicurean philosopher of the second and first centuries BC *Demetrius of Lacon* (thus likely from Laconia), and its text (untitled in the papyrus but conventionally captioned "On the Form of the Gods") identified as a theological writing (Pap. Herc. 1055),[149] then Philodemus had readily adopted such views from his own academic teacher: Indeed, on the one hand, the author of "On the Form of the Gods" clearly taught the human form of God (μορφὴν τὴν ἀνθρώπου) and even explicitly formulated that "God is anthropomorphic" (ἀνθρωπόμορφον . . . εἶναι τὸν θεόν), but, on the other, also emphasized the immaterial character of the gods (as οἱ λόγῳ θεωρητοί).[150] For Philodemus "the gods seem to be labeled as λεπτομερεῖς, i.e., they have a fine structure; in the same passage we learn that God is a σύγκριμα νοητὸν ἔχον πυκνότητα νοητήν 'a cognitively discernible entity with cognitively discernible cohesiveness.'"[151] In other words, gods hence possess a body in the form of a particularly fine conglomerate of atoms, so that they cannot be externally touched. They are so fine that they also cannot be destroyed. In another point in the text, the philosopher deems them to be "eternal and immortal living beings."[152] Philodemus can thus be trusted to have drawn attention to the what he would have seen as the contradictory stances of Plato, much in the same manner as Cicero's dialogue partner Gaius Velleius over the course of the argumentation in *De natura deorum*. Moreover, it might also be assumed that Cicero also adopted these ideas from Philodemus: Plato is to have taught, on the one hand, that God is entirely bodiless, but, on the other, an entirely bodiless God would be devoid of the sensory capacity, practical reason (*prudentia*), and many other things essential to the Platonic conception of God.[153] Cicero himself criticized such conceits from Epicureans as reported by him for what he considered to be their wanting logical precision: He could not imagine as to what a "semblance of a body" meant with respect to divine corporeality. Besides this, he rendered the conception of a fine material of divine corporeality laughable by qualifying the transparency of divine bodies with wind permeability (*perlucidus et perfabilis*).[154] In a neutral account, a description of the divine bodies as permeable, shadowy matter would be more appropriate.

In respect to the heavy criticism of Epicurean philosophy in Antiquity, of which Cicero's polemic is merely an example, the influence of these conceptions of a divine corporeality upon more general perceptions and philosophical debate should not be underestimated. On the contrary, should a philosophical orientation in Antiquity which is readily accused in extremely polemic emphasis of "atheism," and a belief in God feigned merely on grounds of convention, argue for a divine body conceived in analogy to the human figure, this can hardly be opportune for the general plausibility of this idea. It might be suspected that God might in the very least also have been deprived of his body during the Imperial era because the Epicurean philosophy maintained such a stance and—as might be seen with Philodemus—knew to defend it verbosely.

The Stoic School

More significant was conversely the weight of *Stoic philosophy*, the positions of which on many points—among these teachings on God—were markedly directed by their proponents against Epicurean philosophy.[155] Naturally, there were myriad similarities between these warring brothers: In the Stoic school, the concept of a "certain" divine corporeality was, in fact, maintained—albeit with a somewhat different rationale from that found within the Epicurean tradition, and in its details strictly to be differentiated from this. Stoic philosophy is also distinguished by a basal materialism: According to this teaching, *every* thing in existence possesses a *material*, indeed, *corporeal* reality. Thus, in contrast to Platonic doctrine, there are no purely immaterial and thereby incorporeal entities such as ideas underpinning material realities which befit a higher, more stable being than reality itself. Put otherwise: Only bodies exist in any real sense. Incorporeal things such as time, place, or syllables merely "subsist" (ὑφεστός); it is first when a body exists in time and space that place and time subsist in relation to exactly this concrete, material, corporeal existence.[156] Materiality and corporeality are also necessary for both principles (ἀρχαί) of all things, namely passive matter (ὕλη), on the one hand, and a forming, active principle animating it, on the other, which is also varyingly termed spirit (πνεῦμα), reason (λόγος), world (κόσμος), or even God[157]—these principles always exist together as material, corporeal reality. Inasmuch, following Stoic teachings, *the* gods (as a natural implication of their existence) should also have a body. In the "Lives of Eminent Philosophers" of Diogenes Laërtius, a likely Imperial-era author, the report may be found that the five most prominent Stoics of the Hellenistic period concurred that both of the eternal principles constituting the ephemeral elements (fire, water, earth, and air) are bodies. This information seemed so strange to modern, evidently Platonically influenced editors that they altered the wording so that the principles might be *incorporeal*.[158] In such a manner, the late antique "victory" of the Platonic opinion that God and the supreme principles are incorporeal is further transposed onto the earlier Hellenistic and Imperial-era texts arguing for the exact opposite.

The corporeality of the active principle understood as God, cosmos, and reason belongs to the central tenets of Stoic philosophy. Accordingly, it is already recounted regarding *Zeno of Citium* in Cyprus, the founder of the Stoa (around 333–264 BC), that he taught the corporeality of the active, divine principle of reason (the logos: λόγος), and hence the corporeality of God.[159] Naturally, an anthropomorphic or similar corporeality was decidedly not imagined thereby: The now repeatedly aforementioned Roman Epicurean Philodemus of Gadara transmitted in his work "On Piety" (Περὶ εὐσεβείας, *De pietate*) a strident polemic from the third head of the Stoa, *Chrysippus of Soli/Cilicia* (281/276–208/204 BC), against the "anthropomorphism" of Epicurus' and the Epicurean school's teachings on deities. While the relevant papyrus (Pap. Herc. 1428) wherein Philodemus quotes from the first book of Chrysippus' work "On the Gods" was dramatically damaged by the eruption of Vesuvius in AD 79 and hence, as with much of the contents of his private library in the "Villa of the Papyri" at Herculaneum, is barely legible at all,[160] it nevertheless becomes evident that Chrysippus deems it "childish" (παιδαριωδῶς) "to represent the gods, in speaking, in painting, or sculpture, in human form, the way we do with cities and rivers and places and ethical states."[161] The same is incidentally already reported by Zeno, who described God as "a living being, immortal, rational, perfect or intelligent in happiness, admitting nothing evil into him, taking providential care of the world and all that therein is, but . . . not of human shape."[162] In the context of the polemic transmitted within Philodemus, analogous central statements of Stoic theology may be found in a putative paraphrase of Chrysippus' "On the Gods":

But indeed Chrysippus too, referring everything to Zeus, says in the first book of his "On the Gods" that Zeus is the principle of reason that rules over everything and is the soul of the universe; and that by virtue of a share in it, all things—humans and beasts and even the stones—are alive, on account of which it is also called Zena and Dia, since it is the cause and ruling element of all things. The world, he says, is a living thing and a god, and so is its ruling element and the soul of the whole; thus one gathers analogously that Zeus, and the universal nature of all things, and Fate and Necessity are God too. Eunomia and Dike and Homonoia and Eirene and Aphrodite and everything of this sort are all the same being. There are no male or female gods, just as cities and virtues are really neither male or female, but are only called masculine or feminine, though their substances are the same, just like Selene and Men. Ares, he says, is about war and Arrangement and Opposition. Hephaestus is fire, Kronos the flowing of the flow. Rhea is earth, Zeus Aether, although some people say he is Apollo, and Demeter is earth or the pneuma in it.[163]

In the course of this, Philodemus refers also to a detail of the teachings of the most important Stoic teacher after Chrysippus, *Diogenes of Babylon* (or *Seleucia*, where the philosopher taught, dying at around 150 BC): This thinker also stated that "anthropomorphic gods" (as was common within Epicurean philosophy) "are a childish and impossible story." In his text "On Athene," Diogenes asserts "that the cosmos is the same as Zeus, or it comprises him as a man does a soul."[164] The Epicurean Philodemus commented in his summary upon the stances of these two important Hellenistic Stoics with wit both dry and wry:

They have not even thought fit to leave us those gods of the form like that in which they are universally worshipped, and with which we are in agreement. For they credit no gods in the shape of humans, but only airs and breezes and aethers.[165]

In the face of such polemics, it comes perhaps as unexpected to learn that there are, in fact, texts of Stoic provenance marked by a deep piety and a personal divine image, most prominently the celebrated Zeus hymn supposedly composed by Zeno's successor as head of the school, *Cleanthes* from Assos/Troas, in the third century BC. Herein, similarity between God and man is explicitly referenced (θεοῶ μίμημα).[166]

The corporeality of the active principle, which can be labeled God, is somewhat less precisely described within Stoic philosophy, being "a creative (or artistic) fire which methodically progresses to begetting."[167] One might hardly err in identifying the materiality of the divine corporeality of the active principle as a simultaneous gathering of power, breath/spirit (πνεῦμα), and fire (πῦρ τεχνικόν) and, in this manner, set categorically apart from a human body. The "creative" or "artistic" fire is already to be categorically distinguished from conventional fire, inasmuch as it does not consume oil or wax but rather, on the contrary, rationally forms matter.[168] Plutarch also bears witness to the Stoic conception of God as "invisible . . . single, a great and continuous fire."[169] The peripatetic philosopher *Alexander of Aphrodisias*, an inhabitant of Asia Minor at the turn of the second to third centuries AD, related as to how the exact relationship of "creative" or "artistic" fire and breath/spirit was described within Stoic philosophy: A mixture of the two dimensions of the active principle was reckoned with akin to that of water and oil: Both entities remain intact within a shared existence (Alexander labeled this particular form of mixing [μίξις] "blending," κρᾶσις, but did not use the expression ἀσύγχυτος ἕνωσις, "mixed union," frequently employed in this context and later adopted by Christian doctrine on the two natures of Christ).[170] The description of the materiality of the active divine principle as "mixing" wherein the character of the mixed entities is retained presupposes once more its corporeality (albeit in a special form which is categorically differentiated from human corporeality): As formulated by the American historian of philosophy Dirk Baltzly, "God" is understood within Stoic theology as "a single, biological individual" conceptualized as a person with a body and mind.[171] The sense cannot be shaken off that the polemic of the Stoics Chrysippus and Diogenes against the "anthropomorphism" of Epicurean philosophy (as extant in the work of the Epicurean Philodemus) hardly leaves all so convincing an impression from a modern perspective—a certain analogy between divine and human bodies characterizes both schools' discourse on the divine body (and possibly also explains thereby the heft of the polemic sent back and forth).

Yet, the overwhelming majority of references to the Stoic conception of a corporeality of the gods hails from the doxographic tradition of antique *Christian* authors, and hence from a tradition predominantly (if not entirely) *critical* of the Stoa.[172] Most often, arguments are made against the backdrop of a Platonically motivated rejection of God's corporeality. It is hardly coincidental, as will be seen further on, that it is above all the first Christian polymath *Origen* (died AD 253/254) who discusses extensively the views of the Stoics on corporeality; he was, indeed, the first Christian theologian to have at his disposal a very thorough knowledge of Platonic philosophy at a professional level and contributed to academic discourses within the Platonic school's contemporaneous debates (for example with his theology of the Trinity).[173] Thus, in his great apologetic work against the Middle Platonist philosopher Celsus (already deceased at the time of writing), Origen reported on *Stoic* theory against the background of *Platonic* premises that corporeal existences (as with all terrestrial bodies) are *ephemeral*, something which Stoic philosophy had just categorically excluded. He forces Stoic theology into an almost untenable position contrary to all classical theology, namely that it teaches the ephemerality of the "supreme God":

> According to the opinion of the Stoics, who maintain that the first principles are corporeal, and who on this account hold that everything is destructible and venture even to make the supreme God Himself destructible (unless this seemed to them to be utterly outrageous), even the Logos of God that comes down to men and to the most insignificant things is nothing other than a material spirit.[174]

Another passage makes it clear that Origen arrived at the view that the "supreme God" of the Stoics is a mortal being on the strength of his interpretation of the Stoic doctrine of world conflagration (ἐκπύρωσις). However, this Christian Alexandrian's interpretation is rather unlikely from a historical perspective; the surviving references to the destruction and identical recreation of the world mention a god as a constantly acting subject within this process.[175] Origen was, nevertheless, correct in his conviction that, in contrast to the single, supreme God, the many gods of the classical Greek pantheon, inasmuch as they are (following the report of Chrysippus as recorded in Philodemus) merely personifications of earth, war, water, and similar, would, in fact, perish with the world within which they exist and then be immediately recreated at the advent of the next world. Furthermore, it must be conceded to Origen that, considering the identification of God with the world in other texts, a not inconsiderable logical problem arises when the continuity of God following the destructions is reckoned with:

> Furthermore, the God of the Stoics, in that He is corporeal, at one time when the conflagration occurs consists entirely of mind, while at another time, when the new world-order comes, He becomes a part *of* it. Not even they have been able to perceive clearly the true conception of God's nature, as being entirely incorruptible, simple, uncompounded, and indivisible.[176]

The belief that Stoic philosophy teaches the corporeality of God, however, belonged to the fundamental knowledge on this school of thought for other Christian theologians who did not scale the dizzying intellectual heights of Origen. Thus might be found, for example, in the Roman urbanite theologian *Hippolytus* at the beginning of the third century AD that "Chrysippus

and Zeno were united in their opinions. For their part, they also supposed
that the first principle of all things is god, who is the purest body, and that his
providence pervades all things,"[177] and later Church Fathers such as *Eusebius of Caesarea* in the fourth century or *Theodoret of Cyrrhus* in the fifth
relate that the gods have a corporeal form (σωματοειδής) composed of a
force of fire.[178] A few years before Hippolytus, *Clement of Alexandria* precisely recounted the position of the Stoics in his "Patchwork" (Στροματεῖς
or *Stromata*) and commented upon it from a Christian perspective:

> Now the Stoics say that God, like the soul, is essentially body and spirit.
> You will find all this explicitly in their writings. . . . Well, they say that
> God pervades all being; while we call Him solely Maker, and Maker by
> the Word.[179]

Markedly better disposed regarding the Stoics is *Quintus Septimus
Florens Tertullianus* (Tertullian for short) who lived at the turn of the second to the third centuries AD in the North African provincial capital of
Carthage. He related the position conceding God a body as one of many
options among the philosophical teachings on God:

> Some are sure He is incorporeal, others that He has a body—the Pla-
> tonists, that is, and the Stoics. Others say He consists of atoms, others of
> numbers, as do Epicurus and the Pythagoreans. Another says, of fire—
> the view of Heraclitus.[180]

The Aristotelian School

After scrutiny of the Platonic, Epicurean, and Stoic schools, this overview
of the philosophical theories relevant to antique conceptions of the body of
God is still not yet complete. A detail from *Aristotelian* philosophy became
of significance to discussion of the divine body, namely the doctrine of a
"first body" (πρῶτον σῶμα), later also frequently described as the "fifth
element" (πέμπτη οὐσία or *quinta essentia*).[181] The question thereby as to
whether the intellectual origins of the teachings of the Stagirites fall under
the heading of Pythagoreanism or Platonism is for the present context is of
little consequence and contested regardless.

In his work "On the Heavens" (*De caelo*), *Aristotle* (384–322 BC)
introduces this "first body" as "one (body)," which is "separate from those
around us here, and of a higher nature in proportion as it is removed from
the sublunary world."[182] He presupposes with this a series of *five* elements,
as found in the pseudo-Platonic work *Epinomis*, which likely is to be
attributed to *Philip of Opus* (in Locris, Central Greece), and are connected

in this work to the so-called five Platonic bodies, polyhedra: "The bodies, then, being five, we must name them as fire, water, and thirdly air, earth fourth, and ether fifth."[183] Each of these elements is also accorded by Philip a living being, fire, for example, receiving the astral deities, and aether certain demons.[184] Aristotle altered this doctrine of five elements likely to be attributed to Philip once more, as, in contrast to the passage from the *Epinomis* just touched upon, he assumed that the stars and astral deities did not have a fiery nature, but rather were composed of the "first body." Yet, Aristotle understands the first body (πρῶτον σῶμα) as orbiting aether. The heavenly bodies are thus eternal and divine.

In the fourth century BC, it was further discussed within the philosophical schools as to whether, in addition to heavenly bodies such as stars and astral deities, the soul was also originally composed of the "first body" or the "fifth element," and it cannot be excluded that the young Aristotle was also a proponent thereof; Cicero certainly ascribed him this.[185] Regardless, this was definitely taught by *Heraclides Ponticus*, like Aristotle a student of Plato, whose lectures he may well have heard as a young man, and an unsuccessful candidate for leadership of the Platonic Academy in 339/338 BC. With Heraclides Ponticus at the very latest the doctrine emerged that, before its earthly incarnation, the soul possesses not only a luminous (φωτοειδής) body, but also an ethereal one. Whether this philosopher used the expression "ethereal body" (αἰθέριον σῶμα) for the soul as is ascribed to him by late antique doxographic tradition remains just as uncertain as the relationship of this teaching to the thought of young Aristotle.[186] It is, however, attested that Heraclides was the first to combine "a form of the Academic theory of five elements (depicted as a heavenly material) with Plato's mythical accounts of the origins of the soul from heaven."[187]

It is first when the views of *Aristotle* on the "first body" (or indeed the "fifth element") are analyzed a little closer that it might be understood as to why after his death his own teachings were so heavily modified, so that ultimately in a few texts of the Imperial era it was even God (and not the heavenly bodies or the soul) who was ascribed a body composed of the fifth element or fifth nature. Aristotle argues in his text "On the Heavens" (*De caelo*) for the existence of a first body which constantly orbits the center, is indestructible, and more exalted and divine (θειοτέρα) than the other four elements.[188] This first body bears the name "aether" (αἰθήρ) because according to Aristotle this word means "runs always."[189] The first body is spherical[190] and is neither heavy nor light, nor does it grow or shrink.[191] Moreover, as a sky element (like water and air), the aether possesses the capacity to become transparent: In the presence of a source of light, it becomes pellucid and insofar mediates between the object viewed and the

sense of sight.[192] In respect to the passages in *De caelo* briefly summarized
here, numerous questions admittedly remain open, which served as food for
thought thereafter and remain key points of contention even today within
academic research: Did the heavenly body possess a soul? How would this
heavenly soul have related to Aristotle's rejection of a world-soul as found
in Plato? How does the eternal proper motion of the element coexist with
the concept of an unmoved mover, and how does the first body relate to
a supreme god?[193] In particular, the *theological* consequences of the cos-
mological, doctrinally motion-oriented argumentation of Aristotle were not
clear enough and were very differently interpreted in the ensuing period.

The Debates over Aristotle

Not least due to the imprecision of Aristotle's views on the first body, his
reported views on the fifth element were clearly altered during the Imperial era and Late Antiquity; the character of the fifth element transformed
into an almost intangible substance, more immaterial than material, and
simultaneously into an incorporeal body. Considering the body-critical
inclinations within the philosophy of Plato and its decisive rejection of the
conception of a corporeality of the supreme principles, it is reasonable to
discuss a "Platonization" of the Aristotelian doctrine of the *quinta essentia*. The Middle Platonic philosopher *Plutarch*, who mostly lived from AD
45 to 125 in his hometown of Chaeronea in Boeotia, but had studied in
Athens and lectured in Rome, wrote an (unfortunately lost) five-volume
work on the fifth element.[194] On occasion, the Middle Platonist philosophers (as with the heavily anti-Aristotelian-inclined *Atticus*, who possibly taught in Athens in the last third of the second century AD) discussed
an *immaterial*, indestructible, and insensible body (σῶμ' ἀπαθές),[195] so
that the Aristotelian discourse on a *body* and the Platonic concept of an
incorporeality of the supreme being were seemingly connected. In reality,
however, the Aristotelian perspective was marginalized to the benefit of
the Platonic option.

    Paradoxically enough, it was precisely this disembodiment of the
Aristotelian first body, combined with the aforementioned identification
(now ascribed to Plato himself) of aether with the air demons, which led
Christian authors in the Imperial era and in Late Antiquity to occasionally
consider whether the angels were composed of such a light or near to
immaterial matter analogous to the *quinta essentia* (these contexts will
be more thoroughly discussed in chapter 6).[196] Regardless, the demate-
rialized first body of Aristotle was not only identified with the soul and
the angels; in his commentary of the Gospel of John, the Christian Alexandrian polymath *Origen* attests to the fact that there were followers of

Christ who accorded God a body composed of the fifth element: "But I make the following remarks as a refutation of those who say there is a fifth nature of bodies in addition to the (four) elements." In the "following remarks" to which the exegete relates in the sentence just quoted, the absurd consequences when God is considered as a body are handled (these passages will be discussed shortly).[197] A trace of this association of God's body with the fifth element may also be found in the *Pseudo-Clementine Recognitions* which also hail from the fourth century but contain earlier material. Therein it is stated: "Aristotle also introduces a fifth element, which he called ἀκατονόμαστον; that is, that which cannot be named; without doubt indicating Him who made the world, by joining the four elements into one."[198] There are also pagan attestations of such a position; for example, the *Corpus Hermeticum*, a series of eighteen philosophical tractates from Egypt complete with relevant texts which must have developed in the early Imperial era, allege that the substance of God's body is identical to the *quinta essentia*: In the Latin treatise *Asclepius* from the *Corpus Hermeticum*, mind is distinguished as the "fifth part" (*quinta pars*) of humans in contrast to their otherwise material components which are constituted of the four elements. This intellect is immaterial and is God's gift to man, justifying his "being-related divinity."[199] This point may well pertain to those to whom Origen refers in his commentary of John, or indeed to others who understood the notoriously obscure passages in Aristotle's work "On the Heavens" by means of a particular doxographic tradition whereby planets and fixed stars were God's ethereal body which as his soul was moved by logos, his reason, a view propounded by, for example, the apologist *Athenagoras*:

> Aristotle, again, and his followers, recognising the existence of one whom they regard as a sort of compound living creature, speak of God as consisting of soul and body, thinking His body to be the ethereal space and the planetary stars and the sphere of the fixed stars, moving in circles; but His soul, the reason which presides over the motion of the body, itself not subject to motion, but becoming the cause of motion to the other.[200]

Additionally, there were also Christian theologians in the Imperial period and Late Antiquity who precisely connected the "fifth body" or πέμπτον σῶμα with the substance of the stars or sky characterized by a steady circular orbit, rather more in the vein in which Aristotle most likely originally intended in *De caelo*, such as Basil of Caesarea in the last third of the fourth century AD:[201]

Others have rejected this system as improbable, and introduced into the
world, to form the heavens, a fifth element after their own fashioning.
There exists, they say, an ethereal body which is neither fire, air, earth,
nor water, nor in one word any simple body. These simple bodies have
their own natural motion in a straight line, light bodies upwards and
heavy bodies downwards; now this motion upwards and downwards is
not the same as circular motion; there is the greatest possible difference
between straight and circular motion.[202]

From the Hellenistic period onwards, *Aristotelian teachings on the first
body* were synthesized with *Stoic notions on the fiery aether* into a single
doctrine on the fifth element or *quinta essentia*, although the ideas of the
two schools not only barely meet at all on some points, but in fact sharply
differ.

In contrast to Aristotle, the Stoics derived the word "aether" (αἰθήρ)
from αἴθειν and αἰθεῖσθαι ("to burn" or "be burned"), denoting thereby
the element fire insofar as it is present in the heavenly sphere.[203] Although
they retained the traditional terminology of Aristotle, they did not count
ether as the fifth element, but rather as a particular occurrence of one of
the conventional four elements (fire, air, water, and earth), namely fire. As
in Aristotle, aether (αἰθήρ) and air (ἀήρ) are strictly distinguished from
one another, and, akin to his "first body," the Stoic "fiery" aether is already
for Zeno and Chrysippus the first or foremost of the four elements and
travels in circular motions. Moreover, according to Cicero, he was already
termed the "supreme god" by Zeno, "who directs all things."[204] However,
Aristotle's assumption that the fifth element is imperishable and categorically distinct from the other four elements does not play a role within this
school's thought; while from a Stoic perspective the ethereal fire indeed
permeates everything, it also takes part as matter within the circulation of
matter and is not categorically removed from this as with the Stagirites.[205]

For example, Aristotelian, Platonic, and Stoic thought is mingled and
altered in a characteristic manner by *Philo of Alexandria*. Yet, no consistent theory might be recognized, but rather a more situational handling of
the problem: The Jewish scholar makes the distinction at one point in his
copious oeuvre between the nature of the firmament and that of the easily identified three terrestrial elements of earth, water, and air. He knows,
however, not to mention as to whether this nature is composed of solid-
ified crystalline material, pure fire, or a fifth body journeying in circular
motions.[206] At another point, he is conversely certain that the heavens are
composed of aether; this fifth, circular element shares in divine nature.[207]
Elsewhere, the domain of the stars is distinguished from the other four elements.[208] Here, then, in contrast to Aristotle, a doctrine of a fifth element

(πέμπτη οὐσία or *quinta essentia*) is also terminologically coined; Philo believes that not only stars and sky are composed of this particular element, but also the human soul.[209] When it is understood that, within the biblical texts which he interprets, Philo considers the soul to be a "breath of God,"[210] then God and the ethereal bodies which the scholar freely imagines to be bodiless and immaterial would be thrust much closer together, but paradoxically so, inasmuch as a body deprived of its corporeality, the "first body" of the "fifth element" or the "fifth nature" would simultaneously function as God's "body." Regardless, it has been seen that, in the interest of strict transcendence of his definition of God, Philo deliberately avoids drawing such conclusions.

For the remainder of the Imperial era and Late Antiquity, the doctrine of a heavenly spiritual body was discussed as extensively as it was critically;[211] this theme will further be returned to in the course of this study, as, under the requirements of a strict transcendence of God, the heavenly spiritual body is something of a haven for traditional conceptions of a divine body—certainly when, as in Christian and Jewish theology, the human soul in its heavenly body is firmly described as the likeness and similitude of God. In comparison, particularly for the periods in which a certain species of Christian Platonism formed in Alexandria spread uniformly across Late Antiquity, traces of the perspective explicitly denied within Platonism that God possesses a (potentially special) body must be sought after far more patiently. However, the evident signs of later, secondary marginalization cannot be understood as indications that these views were only shared by a few or not disseminated at all.

When it is further deduced that in Jewish postbiblical and pagan philosophical texts of the Hellenistic period alike two concepts (as has been seen) stood equally next to one another—those of a *corporeality* of God and, simultaneously, an *incorporeality* of God—then it hardly surprises to learn that these two traditions of thought on God and gods continued into the Imperial era and Late Antiquity in both Judaism and Christianity. Both concepts were championed by influential groups and left traces in the relevant authoritative texts. The proper description of historical reality is poorly served by the simplifications of these complex findings disseminated in secondary literature, such as those claiming that only simple, uneducated people held the conception of a corporeal existence of God or the gods. The Epicurean or Stoic philosophies were definitely not influenced by philosophers any less erudite or more naïve than those of Platonism. Before one of these streams of thought—that of God's body—was marginalized over the course of the Imperial period and Late Antiquity, an extensive debate unfolded within the new Christian religion on the applicability and extent of this notion.

Early Christian Theology

Considering this portrait of two equally privileged traditions of thought up until this point, it is hardly unexpected that examples of this phenomenon might be found among the thinkers who attempted to explain this newly emerged religion of Christianity to the educated of the antique metropoles at the margins of the Roman Empire from the second century onwards. Indeed, the problem of the existence and constitution of the divine body was not only heavily discussed in early Christianity in respect to Jesus Christ, but also God the Father. These perspectives—both that wherein God possessed a body rather more based upon the biblical texts, and that resting rather upon the Alexandrian allegorical interpretations of the Bible wherein passages from the Holy Scripture would be but the expression of metaphorical speech—were current in the religious debates of this new faith from the second century AD onwards. This was the age wherein Christianity reached and began to impact upon not only Antiquity's great metropoles such as Rome, Alexandria, and Antioch, but also midrange provincial capitals such as Ephesus, Carthage, and Lyon.

It might thus be presumed that among those educated Christian popular philosophers termed "theologians" today who wished to explain this new religion to a curious audience within these metropoles in either philosophical schools or public lectures (comparable to those which Maximus of Tyre had held before interested circles in Rome on philosophical topics),[212] there would have been a consensus that God had *no* body, and that literal interpretations of so-called anthropomorphic conceptions were laughable. Yet, this assumption would be false. The question as to whether God should be ascribed a body in the literal sense was, in fact, further heavily debated.

Origen

Such animated discussions are attested by the first Christian "theologian" educated to the level of contemporaneous professional philosophers, *Origen of Alexandria* (died AD 254), who showcased "Christian philosophy" in a privately founded academy in Caesarea, the provincial capital of the province of Palestine, from the late 230s onwards.[213] This highly educated thinker was already a characteristic representative of the concept of an *incorporeality* of God on grounds of his intellectual background in Platonism.[214] Nevertheless, that many educated individuals evidently thought differently from him is evidenced by his elaborate argumentations on this subject within the tomes of his work "On First Principles" (Περὶ ἀρχῶν / *De principiis*), a text which probably draws upon the lectures held by him in Alexandria before he was compelled to leave the city in AD 231 or 232.[215] This work, transmitted in the form of four volumes, begins (according to the rendering of the late antique translator Rufinus of Aquileia from AD 397) with the pointed sentence:

> I know that some will try to say that even according to our Scriptures God is a body, since they find it said in the writings of Moses, "God is a consuming fire," (Deuteronomy 4:24) and in the Gospel according to John, "God is spirit, and those who worship him must worship him in spirit and truth" (John 4:24). Fire and spirit, according to them, will be reckoned to be nothing other than a body.[216]

For the first line of a writing upon the fundamentals of Christian teaching, this opening from Origen comes across, on one hand, as surprising, inasmuch as he begins with a reference to opposing views, and not with his own theses as to the correct Christian, Trinitarian teachings on God, which would be *the* fundamental trinitary "principle" (ἀρχή or *principium*) of Christian theology.[217] Such was already announced, however, in the foreword to the work: It seems, as Origen states, necessary "first of all to lay down a definite line and clear rule regarding each one of these matters,"[218] that is, namely, "concerning God or the Lord Jesus Christ or the Holy Spirit." On the other hand, it is contextually entirely understandable as to what the opposing position claims and here reports: It has already been seen, for example, that "fire" and "spirit" (*ignis vero et spiritus*) counted indeed as *body-constitutive elements* of heavenly material (if categorically distinct and removed from terrestrial matter) for all those who ascribed God a body of ethereal fire in the Stoic tradition and moreover invoked the originally Aristotelian "fifth element" of a "first body" in one manner or another. Individuals who maintained such a perspective on the special materiality of the divine body as being of spirit and fire would have as "first principles" (ἀρχαί or *principia*) not only (as for Origen) the Trinity of Father, Son, and Holy Ghost, but also in Platonic and Stoic tradition perhaps also God *and* matter. Regardless of wildly varying numbers of principles, the contemporaneous doxographic reports on philosophical first principles readily agree in respect to these two particular principles.[219] With his work "On First Principles," Origen thus simultaneously formulates an antithesis on the "principles": Neither "God" and "matter," nor "God," "ideas," and "matter" are attested in the Bible or sought to be understood by the faithful, but rather first and foremost the trinitarily constituted Christian God.

From this, it might be thought that Origen's criticism of a divine body might primarily be meant as an argumentation on the theory of principles.

Yet, it may remarkably be noted from the previously quoted introductory
sentences of "On First Principles" that for those targeted by Origen (certainly according to Origen's account in Rufinus) it was also an argument
of Scripture: These individuals sought "to try to say that even according
to our Scriptures God is a body."[220] This "even" could be understood as
meaning that in strengthening their case they had recourse to both biblical
and philosophical arguments. Origen not only mentions such argumentation in "On First Principles": In one fragment, probably hailing from a
commentary on the first book of the Bible composed in Alexandria, albeit
after "On First Principles," the learned biblical exegete irritably states that
"some, indeed, find the limbs of God named (sc. in the Bible)," understanding these in the literal sense as statements on real body parts of God, and
"bring together thousands of attestations mentioning the limbs of God."[221]

The beginning of "On First Principles" comes across as rather erratic
and abridged, considering that he begins so abruptly with opposing view-
points. Should this impression not be attributed to the spoken nature
of the original lecture or the author's occasionally confusing style of writing, then it may well reflect the well-known inclinations of his translator
Rufinus of Aquileia towards (stylistically impelled) abridgment and (theologically motivated) omission.[222]

If, however, it is conversely to be understood from the first sentence
of "On First Principles" (*De principiis*) that those certain individuals (i.e.,
"some," *quidam*) targeted by Origen sought in addition to their biblical
rationale for the corporeality of God to argue philosophically for this
doctrine, then this would also explain a passage in his foreword. Already
in the *praefatio*, Origen had indicated that usage of the term "bodiless"
(ἀσώματος or *incorporeus*) belonged neither to quotidian Greek language,
nor to biblical attestation. Evidently the philosophical term "bodiless,"
first documented in the writings of Plato and the philosophical literature
following him (albeit not initially in respect to God),[223] played a role in
the argumentations of Origen's opponents, revealing thereby their level
of philosophical education.[224] It is surprising that Origen already mentions
at this early point in his foreword an argument of the group which he
intended first to refute in the text following the foreword, necessarily doubling somewhat thereby the amount of biblical quotations at the beginning
of the main text of "On First Principles." It might be noted in passing how
strangely detached from its context this passage of the foreword is (which
may well again rest on Rufinus' translation). At any rate, already in this
introduction, Origen concerns himself with an alleged dominical saying
used by his opponents in favor of the corporeality of God, namely Jesus'
supposed statement "I am not a bodiless daemon."[225] He refers here to an
"agraphon" (a term within modern research denoting a saying unattested

within the canonized Scriptures of the New Testament) from the "Teachings of Peter" (*Doctrina Petri*, most likely Κήρυγμα Πέτρου in Greek), although it is also attested from the letters of Bishop Ignatius of Antioch at the beginning of the second century, in Eusebius' "Ecclesiastical History," and within Jerome, and is therein attested to Hebrews or another Jewish-Christian gospel.[226] The original sense of this agraphon (most likely a uncanonical parallel transmission of Luke 24:39 "for a spirit hath not flesh and bones") and its erstwhile context are of little consequence for either Origen or present discussion. It is merely important to note that in this Alexandrian scholar's times there were evidently Christians who employed this reference as an authoritative scriptural argument for their stance on divine corporeality.[227] The author of "On First Principles" denies that this agraphon can be employed as an argument as first "this work is not itself included among the ecclesiastical books, and it can be shown that it is not a writing of Peter nor of anyone else who was inspired by the Spirit of God."[228] Moreover, Origen rejects the view that "bodiless" in the agraphon's expression "bodiless daemon" means the same "bodiless" "as that intended by Greek and pagan authors, when philosophers discuss bodiless nature": In the case of the quotation from the now-apocryphal Scripture "bodiless" describes the body of demons "which is naturally fine and thin like air, and because of this is considered or called 'bodiless' by man." Indeed, in the general speech of "the simple or uneducated," "bodiless" means anything which does not have "a solid and palpable body":[229]

> just as one says that the air we breathe is bodiless, because it is not a body that can be grasped and held or resist pressure.[230]

Over the further course of the *praefatio*, Origen announces his intention to demonstrate in comparison that a very precise usage of the term "bodiless" may be evidenced for the Greek philosophers, and that this meaning, connected with another term (admittedly left undisclosed by him in the *praefatio*), is also to be found in the Holy Scripture. Unfortunately, a passage explicitly fulfilling all of these promises is lacking from both the Greek fragments extant today and the Latin translations of his "On First Principles," as will be further explored. Moreover, Origen presents in the aforementioned foreword the prospect of answers to the following questions: "how God Himself is to be understood, whether as bodily and formed according to some shape, or of a different nature than bodies, a point which is not clearly indicated in our preaching. The same is also to be investigated even regarding Christ and the Holy Spirit, and indeed it is to be investigated no less of every soul and every rational nature."[231] Here there is a play once more upon the "principles," which Origen seeks to

investigate in his accordingly entitled work, and to which, in contrast to the
practice of most philosophical schools, matter again will not be counted.

Can a slightly more precise reconstruction of these evidently somewhat philosophically educated individuals arguing for the notion of a
divine corporeality with not only canonized scriptural evidence, but also
apocryphal dominical sayings, be attempted? When both "On First Principles" and Origen's other works are considered in this regard, the sense
is garnered that they do not belong to any single, fixed group (such as
those Christian circles eagerly termed by scholars "Judeo-Christian" or
"gnostic"), but rather a multitude of rather differently inclined figures. It
is certain that such a notion was not only propounded within the Christian
community of *Alexandria*. Indeed, in his homilies on the first book of the
Bible, which, unlike his commentary of Genesis, must certainly have been
held in *Caesarea* within the last period of his life before his death in AD
254,[232] the preacher argues anew against the conception of divine corporeality, now admittedly not in the mode of the conventional philosophical
digression, but rather in the direct style of his sermons,[233] and, moreover,
in this case, in strident polemic:

> We read in many passages of the divine Scripture that God speaks to
> men. For this reason the Jews indeed, but also some of our people, sup-
> posed that God should be understood as a man, that is, adorned with
> human members and human appearance. But the philosophers despise
> these stories as fabulous and formed in the likeness of poetic fictions.
> Because of this it seems to me that I must first discuss these few matters
> and then come to those words which have been read.[234]

The preacher uses the interpretation of the text of the sermon on the circumcision of Abraham (Genesis 17), which must have been directly read
out before his homily, as a pretext to fundamentally clarify the question
as to whether one may somewhat (*quasi*) imagine God like a human with
a body, and outright dispels this notion: In the aforementioned sermon,
Origen rather professes to his community in a characteristic assortment
of epithets of Platonic theory of God as piercingly as possible that God
"is incorporeal and omnipotent and invisible."[235] Such an essential clarifi-
cation would only have been necessary in the context of a parish sermon,
had Jewish and Christian communities existed in the port town of Caesarea, where Origen had lived, taught, and preached since the AD 230s,
which "somewhat" considered God in corporeal form, much as in Alexandria twenty years before. Incidentally, these passages cannot be termed as
anti-Jewish because, likely in the same period, albeit in a different place
in his work, Origen approvingly cited the Middle Platonic philosopher

Numenius, who lived in the second century AD: "In the first book of his work on *The Good* where he (sc. Numenius) speaks of the nations that believe God to be incorporeal, he also included the Jews among them."[236] It was thereby entirely clear to Origen that, in the Jewish and Christian communities alike, *both* views were represented, that both incorporeality and corporeality were opted for on occasion.

In "On First Principles," Origen counts the question as to God's corporeality as one of the central points of his investigation into the first, divine principle of the Trinity. Explicitly or implicitly, this question preoccupies him in all three main sections of this work. The tract closes with the answer to a question provoked by the strict rejection of the notion of a divine corporeality: How, asks Origen, can the trinitary God understood as incorporeal at all be recognized, when, in fact, cognition has a basis primarily in the perception of human senses, but these senses perceive bodies and surfaces?[237] In comparison to the thoroughly stringent argumentation within *De principiis* (irrespective of the slightly chaotic impression left by the surviving Latin translation as has been discussed), Origen unceremoniously dismisses both swiftly and clearly the opposing position as philosophically unsatisfying in his aforementioned sermon "On the Circumcision of Abraham," held before a small community in a port town on the Mediterranean. On first scrutiny, it might be wondered as to why under the heading of "the philosophers" within the Caesarean sermon only the Platonically informed rejection of every conception of a divine corporeality is mentioned but not the opposing stances of the Stoics and the various syntheses of disparate philosophical backgrounds. Yet, at the very latest upon second inspection, it hardly surprises that Origen—deeply influenced by contemporary Platonic philosophers, likely the pupil of the Middle Platonic thinker Ammonius Saccas, who also taught the Neoplatonist Plotinus, and furthermore acquainted with Porphyry, Plotinus' greatest student[238]—drastically reduced the plurality of contemporaneous philosophy to a single position on grounds of homiletic simplification in the interests of a not particularly educated flock. Nevertheless, the energy with which he seeks to disprove notions of God's corporeality at this and various other points should not be traced solely back to his Platonic education and the strident interests of this philosophical orientation in a bodiless, immaterial transcendence of God; as is demonstrated by his previously quoted opening remarks in "On First Principles," Origen always argued on the strength of insights won from reading the biblical texts. First and foremost, he was (like Philo of Alexandria) convinced that merely the "inner man" could be interpreted as the semblance and likeness of God, and (in comparison to Irenaeus of Lyon) not the transitory raiment of his flesh: "We do not understand, however, this man indeed whom Scripture says was made 'according to the image of God' to be corporeal. . . . But it is our inner man, invisible, incorporeal, incorruptible, and immortal which is made 'according to the image of God.'"[239] Were, however, man created in God's image to have been fashioned incorporeally, then this must also apply to his maker, God himself, who must then also be incorporeal:

> But if anyone suppose that this man who is made "according to the image and likeness of God" is made of flesh, he will appear to represent God Himself as made of flesh and in human form. It is most clearly impious to think this about God. In brief, those carnal men who have no understanding of the meaning of divinity suppose, if they read anywhere in the Scriptures of God that "heaven is my throne, and the earth my footstool," (Isaiah 66,1) that God has so large a body that they think he sits in heaven and stretches out his feet to the earth.[240]

If contemplation on God's creation, *protology*, makes it clear that bodiliness is, in fact, not "the end of God's work," but rather bodilessness, then there must also be consequences for Origen's teachings on the end of all things, *eschatology*. It was understood that protology and eschatology should reflect one another, according to an apocryphal dominical saying "See: I do the last things as the first."[241] The resurrection of the dead would hence also imply for Origen (to simplify a complicated body of evidence not altogether without contradiction)[242] no simple restoration of terrestrial corporeality, but rather a recreation in transformed splendor: As is intoned by Origen in another sermon, the righteous will become angels.[243] The systematic weight conceded by the theologian to the incarnation of Jesus Christ as a divine embodiment and corporealization is accordingly light.[244] The systematic fundamental problem of such a Christian doctrine of belief, which both follows biblical insights and also seeks to understand exactly these convictions by contemporaneous standards of rationality, poses, however, the question thereby as to the *incorporeality* of the trinitarily composed God relates to the *corporeality* of his most illustrious creation, humanity. The dynamic development of this creation's corporeality from the birth of an individual as a soul *in a body* to its resurrection in transcendental corporeality, and even a potentially bodiless final state at the end of all things, is hence the central theme of the theological depiction of the history of salvation, albeit also its central problem, as the discussions of his doctrines in the Imperial era and Late Antiquity soon after his death would demonstrate.

It has already been seen that, on reason of principles, Origen is at pains to ground biblically his argumentation on the corporeality of God. On the other hand, it can hardly be overlooked that this author of "On First

Principles" belabors Christian doctrines of faith, seeking to develop the very same with the greatest possible consonance with Middle Platonic thought on God (even in terms of language) and, as previously mentioned, maintaining this even in sermons to a modest community in a Mediterranean port town, if in abbreviated polemic.

The fundamental agreement between the teachings of God advanced by both this Christian thinker and contemporary Middle Platonic philosophy in respect to an incorporeal first principle becomes apparent when the only extant scholastic handbook of so-called Middle Platonic philosophy is consulted as comparison. This work, the *Didascalicus* (Διδασκαλικός) or "Textbook of the Essentials of Plato," from the pen of an otherwise unknown author named *Alcinous*, was likely composed in the second century AD.[245] Alcinous first argues that God cannot have prerequisites, as "nothing is earlier" than him. Hence, he cannot be a part of something, as a part is predicated by a whole, not a body, as the (two dimensional) level precedes the (three dimensional) body, not anything moved, as a mover would have to have preceded him.[246] Alcinous further writes:

> This can be demonstrated also in the following way: if God were a body, he would be composed of form and matter, because every body is a combination of matter and form combined with it, which has a likeness to the forms and participates in them in a manner difficult to express; but it is absurd that God should be composed of matter and form (for he could not then be simple or primordial); so God must be incorporeal.[247]

Alcinous is thus convinced that the simplicity, originality, and complete unity of God necessarily implies his incorporeality.[248] Were God body, then he would be ephemeral, engendered, and mutable.[249]

The Apologists

In his attempt to render Christian teaching intelligible to both the educated of his detractors and his own Christian clientele, Origen was not the first to adopt this philosophical argumentation as the standard for contemporary doctrine on God, but his predecessors limited themselves to only a few remarks on this topic: The philosophical term "incorporeal" (ἀσώματος) is already attested in the writings of the so-called Apologists, that is, the first to explain Christianity at the level of contemporaneous popular philosophers, the "Christian philosophers" of the second century AD such as Justin, Tatian, and Athenagoras. In the context of a sketch of his philosophical education, *Justin the Martyr*, a mid-second-century AD denizen of Rome, elaborates in his "Dialogue with Trypho" that "perception of incorporeal things," the contemplation of purely immaterial existences born of all sensual perception, particularly interested him within Platonic thought.[250] Justin's student *Tatian*, a Syrian, wrote an apology "Against the (sc. pagan) Greeks" sometime before AD 170 in either Rome or Greece. Therein is stated with extreme brevity: "Someone says that the perfect God is body, I that he is bodiless."[251] A scholiast felt compelled to note on the margins of a high medieval Parisian manuscript that the pronouncement of this "someone" reflected Stoic teachings.[252] It also becomes apparent from writings such as Tatian's terse comment that the highly polemic opposition to Stoic materialism (as has been seen in Origen's homily on the Book of Genesis) is not solely due to an individual predilection of this scholar for Platonism, but rather a tradition shared among various apologetically oriented Christian thinkers of the second and third centuries. Indeed, the apologist *Athenagoras*, whose life during the last third of the second century AD remains generally obscure, stresses the primacy of incorporeality over corporeality within a discussion of the resurrection of the dead.[253]

Clement of Alexandria

By contrast, Clement of Alexandria, who inhabited this Mediterranean seat of culture and learning from the AD 280s to the beginning of the third century AD, outlines far more extensively the relationship between God as a purely immaterial reality and his incorporeality in his "Patchwork" (Στρωματεῖς): To be purely immaterial (νοητός) implies being purely incorporeal (ἀσώματος).[254] Previously in the presentation of the pre-Socratic Xenophanes' polemic, transmitted above all by Clement, it has been seen that Clement vigorously emphasizes the difference between the human body and its divine creator, and counts these as the joint heritage of both the biblical and philosophical traditions (if admittedly on grounds of the "plagiarism of the Greeks").[255] Particularly pertinent, provided its authenticity, is a fragment from "On Providence" (Περὶ προνοίας). Therein it is stated that the divine substance is "without beginning or end, incorporeal, and the cause of existing things."[256] Even were this fragment to be a later invention (a corresponding writing by Clement cannot be attested any earlier than this fragment), its contents fully reflect the views of the authentic Clement. As was the case for Origen, questions are already raised for Clement as to the progress of the salvation history considering the incorporeality of God (and the corporeality of Jesus Christ since his incarnation). He asks:

> Without the body, how could dispensation for us, the Church, achieve its end? It was here that he, the Church's head (cf. Ephesians 1:22 and 5:23),

came in the flesh but without beauty of form (cf. Isaiah 53:3), teaching us to fix our gaze on the formless incorporeality of the divine cause.[257]

Hence, in decisively declaring for the incorporeality of God, Origen stands in a Christian apologetic tradition already almost eighty years old, and present in his hometown of Alexandria by means of Clement. Yet, through both his arguments' thoroughness and his interest in grounding them biblically, his voice remains of a very much unique tenor among the chorus of those for God's incorporeality within Imperial-era Christianity.

Origen and the Incorporeality of God

Origen develops the arguments already announced in the aforementioned preface to "On First Principles" (Περὶ ἀρχῶν / *De principiis*) in favor of the conception of an incorporeal God in multiple stages spread over the three main sections of his books, concluding them, as has already been seen, by engaging with the consequences for the question of God's recognizability. Here, he follows Philo of Alexandria in emphasizing the principal unknowableness of God. If God is limitless and immaterial in nature and thus is not confined to a body, surpassing thereby in every sense human thought, then only indirect knowledge of God may be derived from the glory of creation, and no answer as to what God is in and of himself.[258] Perhaps on account of the state of transmission and Rufinus of Aquilea's manner of translation, the argumentation is less clear and stringent than was advertized in the foreword. In the first section on God the Father at the beginning of the work, the incorporeality of God is deduced from biblical light metaphors—that these passages could refer to a bodily light would be inconceivable[259]—and only then is it first demonstrated that a literal, corporeal interpretation of the biblical passages which "some" have cited from Deuteronomy and the Gospel of John must be excluded. While not explicitly mentioned by Origen, the opponents combatted by him in *De principiis* are quite evidently Christian: They are versed in the Scriptures of both testaments well enough to cite them, and an apocryphal dominical saying to wit, and know that according to Stoic thought the body of God is composed of fire and spirit. They were perhaps also aware that various Jewish and Christian texts of the time analogously regarded the bodily nature of the angels as being of fire and spirit. It also cannot entirely be excluded that the supporters of Marcion numbered among the opponents adhering to the stance that their postulated creator god or demiurge apparently evidenced in the Old Testament was a corporeal being.[260] Regardless, Origen's adversaries' lines of argumentation are simple: They likely sought out only those biblical passages which supported a certain Stoic or at least Stoically analogous theory of God. The argument that Origen poses them in response comes across as equally conventional, and corresponds to the usual Platonically grounded polemic against a Stoically inspired materialism in the conception of God:

> And if God is declared to be a body, then, since every body is made of matter, God will also be found to be made of matter; but if he is made of matter, and matter is undoubtedly corruptible, then God, according to them, will be corruptible.[261]

Origen's rebuttal seems not only rather conventional but also hardly to have hit the nail of his opponents' arguments (likely among them those "some" he invokes) upon the head: Ultimately, as has been seen, fire and spirit were generally conceived of as specific divine, transcendent, and eternal matter, and hence to be strictly distinguished from normal, terrestrial, and perishable matter. Nevertheless, as he states in his treatise "On Prayer" (Περὶ εὐχῆς), for Origen "every body is divisible, material, corruptible." Thus, "to prevent anyone from saying that God is in a place after the manner of a body," particularly in the interpretation of the address of the Lord's Prayer ("who art in Heaven": Matthew 6:9), he argues that the supposition that God is a body is

> a tenet which leads to most impious opinions, namely, to suppose that he is divisible, material, corruptible. For every body is divisible, material, corruptible.[262]

A very similar argument on the quality of matter may be found in "On First Principles."[263] When Origen himself does not venture into the underlying notion of a specific divine, transcendental, and eternal material evidently held by his opponents, this should not be understood as rhetorical subterfuge; rather, for Origen every form of corporeality, including the ethereal form of the corporeality of the stars or the pneumatic bodiliness of the resurrection, was a manner of burden upon immaterial existence, and hence fundamentally unbefitting of God. The clearly negative assessment of body is so self-evident to the Christian thinker that he does not even justify this, nor does he sense any contradiction between this stance and the biblical texts interpreted by him which underlie his argumentation as authoritative passages. Even if a form of immaterial bodiliness might exist within the context of eschatological completion (Origen is here uncertain), then this bodiliness must nonetheless be deficient.[264] Thus, Origen explains consistently all those biblical passages mentioning God's body as imagistic or metaphorical speech, as he expounds in an extensive excursus regarding his great commentary on the Gospel of John composed in Caesarea before AD 248:

Many have produced lengthy discussions of God and his essence. Some have even said that he has a bodily nature which is composed of fine particles and is like aether. Others have said that he is incorporeal and is of a different essence which transcends bodies in dignity and power. For this reason it is worthwhile for us to see if we have resources from the divine Scriptures to say something about God's essence.[265]

Origen first tersely reports upon the position of Stoic and Platonic philosophy (incidentally with a charming variant of the Platonic divine predicate of "beyond being" ἐπέκεινα οὐσίας in the shape of ὑπεπέκεινα οὐσίας),[266] in order then to proceed with the exact same three biblical passages which he had employed years earlier in "On First Principles."

In this passage (sc. the Gospel of John 4:24) it is stated as if his essence were spirit, for it says, "God is spirit." But in the law, it is stated as if his essence were fire, for it is written, "Our God is a consuming fire" (Deuteronomy 4:24). In John, however, it is stated as if he were light, for John says, "God is light, and there is no darkness in him" (1 John 1:5). If, then, we should listen to these words literally, making no inquiry beyond the letter, we would have to say that God is a body. Now, most people are incapable of knowing what absurd things we encounter when we say this, for few have had an understanding concerning the nature of bodies, and especially of bodies fitted out by reason and providence.[267]

After remarks regarding a definition of body[268] and the problems logical and philosophical alike in an application of this term, Origen concludes:

In these matters, then, we must either accept so many absurd and blasphemous things about God in preserving the literal meanings, or, as we also do in many other cases, examine and inquire what can be meant when it is said that God is spirit, or fire, or light. First we must say that just as when we find it written that God has eyes, eyelids, ears, hands, arms, feet, and even wings, we change what is written into an allegory, despising those who bestow on God a form resembling men, and we do this with good reason, so also must we act consistently with our practice in the case of the names mentioned above.[269]

The aforementioned and evidently earlier commentary on the first book of the Bible demonstrates that Origen also took a certain pleasure in demonstrating the absurdity of a literal interpretation of biblical texts on the corporeality of God, and could argue not only with basic philosophical axioms on the principles. According to a fragment of this currently incomplete commentary, he penned the following polemic against those who conceived of God with a body and made recourse to biblical texts within his extensive interpretation of the verse describing the creation of man in the image of God (Genesis 1:26f.):

> We will present those who know nothing but the letters with quotations which counter their hasty supposition. Thus from Zechariah: "those seven; they are the eyes of the LORD, which run to and fro through the whole earth": if God has seven eyes, but ourselves only two, then we are not fashioned "in his own image" (Genesis 1:27). Indeed, we are also not created with wings, yet in the ninetieth Psalm it states of God that "under his wings shalt thou trust" (Psalm 90/91:4): If, however he possesses wings but we are unwinged creatures, then man is not created "in the image" of God! How, in turn, might the firmament, which is spherical and ever in motion, be the "throne" of God, as they allege? Moreover, they also wish to inform us that the "earth" should be his "footstool" (Isaiah 66:1). Indeed, should the space between heaven and earth encompass his body from the knees to the sole of his feet, but the earth lies in the centre of the world and comprises its entirety, as may be demonstrated geometrically, are the soles of his feet hereabouts, or in the Antipodes? Do they fill the entire inhabited earth, or only a greater or lesser part of it? Are his feet separated by the seas and rivers, or do they also touch water? How can it be that he, whose "throne" is that large "heaven" and whose "footrest" is the "earth," might be met strolling Paradise (Genesis 3:8–10), or appearing to Moses on the peak of Sinai (Exodus 19:20)? And how might someone who maintains this of God, not be taken for a moron?[270]

In addition to the polemic against an absurd interpretation of biblical body rhetoric in its literal sense, instructions as to interpretation in a higher literary sense might also be found in Origen. Therein, the commentary on John's relevant avenue of interpretation tallies exactly with that of "On First Principles": For example, according to Origen, biblical passages reporting that someone might see God's countenance or his back detailed *intellectual vision* without the participation of the corporeal senses. The God who has no body can only be seen by means of the incorporeal "eyes of the soul" and other incorporeal, immaterial sense organs:

> But if someone lays before us the question why it was said, "Blessed are the pure in heart, for they shall see God" (Matthew 5:8), from that very passage, in my opinion, will our argument be much more firmly established; for what else is seeing God in the heart than . . . to understand and to know him with the intellect? For the names of the organs of sense are frequently applied to the soul, so that it may be said to see with the eyes of the heart (Ephesians 1:18), that is, to infer some intellectual conclusion by means of the faculty of intelligence.[271]

After basic remarks on the unknowableness of God and the problems which such a perspective engenders in the interpretation of biblical texts, Origen concludes accordingly at the end of his introductory section on the bodilessness of God in the first main part of "On First Principles" with overt reference to philosophical argumentation of the like already encountered in Alcinous' "Handbook":

> God, therefore, is not to be thought to be either a body or existing in a body (ἐνσώματος), but to be a simple intellectual being, accepting in Himself no addition whatever; so that he cannot be believed to have in Himself a more or a less, but is, in all things, unity, or, if I may say, oneness, and the intellect and source from which all intellectual being and intellect takes its beginning. Now an intellect, to move and operate, needs no bodily space, nor sensible magnitude, nor bodily shape or colour, nor does it need anything else whatever of things proper to bodies or matter.[272]

As Origen evidently draws upon Platonic handbooks in the dictates of such passages, he could also form very much similar thoughts in other texts, for example in his tract against the long dead but still influential Middle Platonist philosopher Celsus composed before AD 248 in Caesarea. Here, as has been seen, Origen protests far more precisely than in "On First Principles" against the "opinion of the Stoics, who maintain that the first principles are corporeal" and thereby consider logos, the all-pervading reason, a "material spirit."[273] God the Word, the second person of the Trinity, would thereby be a corporeal being prior to the incarnation, a thought insufferable to Origen and already rebuffed in by him in "On First Principles." He notes just as critically in his writings against Celsus:

> But in the view of us Christians, who try to show that the rational soul is superior to any material nature and is an invisible and incorporeal being, the divine Logos is not material. "Through him all things were made" (John 1:3), and in order that all things may be made by the Logos, he extends not to men only but even to the things supposed to be insignificant which are controlled by nature. The Stoics may destroy everything in a conflagration if they like. But we do not recognize that an incorporeal being is subject to a conflagration, or that the soul of man is dissolved into fire, or that this happens to the being of angels, or "thrones, or dominions, or principalities, or powers" (Colossians 1:16).[274]

Origen's fundamental conviction that there is no incorporeal corporeality in the manner of the Platonic interpretation of the "fifth element" also pertained to the question of the resurrected body of Christians, although this debate, both interesting and convoluted alike, cannot be entered into here.[275] In particular, should the scholar genuinely have begun from the premise that the resurrected body of humans would be "spherical" (σφαιροειδές),[276] as is ascribed to him by later (critical) tradition, then this would naturally be an interesting parallel with pagan notions of the corporeality of the gods as spherical in form, this being the most perfect conceivable shape.[277]

In the preface to "On First Principles," Origen announced the intention to demonstrate that a precise use of the term "bodiless" may be observed among the Greek philosophers, and that this meaning may be found in Holy Scripture in association with another term.[278] Yet, did he explicitly name this other term within the work and demonstrate its biblical credentials? Only from very careful reading of the text might it be noted that this term, which should qualify the term "bodiless" in the sense of the Greek philosophers, is, in fact, the term "invisible" (ἀόρατος/*invisibilis*). In contrast to the expression "bodiless" (ἀσώματος), it may actually be found within the Bible, for example in the passage of the Deutero-Pauline Epistle to the Colossians in which Christ is labelled as "the image of the invisible God" (ὅς ἐστιν εἰκὼν τοῦ θεοῦ τοῦ ἀοράτου).[279] The initially somewhat surprising connection of discussion regarding the *corporeality* of God with the question of his visibility, something presupposed by Origen rather than explained, may well originate from contemporary debate with supporters of Marcion.[280] This identification of the terms "invisible" (ἀόρατος/*invisibilis*) and "bodiless" (ἀσώματος) is first made explicit in a recapitulation within the third part of "On First Principles" at the end of the fourth book; moreover, Origen supplies in connection only the one aforementioned quote from the Epistle to the Colossians (should Rufinus of Aquilea's Latin translation be trusted at this point):

> Just as, for example, when it is inquired whether there is any substance in which neither colour nor form nor touch nor magnitude is to be understood to be visible to the mind alone, which anyone names as he pleases; for the Greeks call such "bodiless": while the divine Scriptures name it "invisible"; for Paul declares that God is invisible, for he says that Christ is "the image of the invisible God" (Colossians 1:15).[281]

This reflection as is preserved in the extant text of "On First Principles," heralded already in the foreword, hardly comes across as all that well developed. As has already been seen, it lacks any detailed depiction of the connection between "incorporeality" and "invisibility" within Greek philosophy; this is claimed but not demonstrated. A similar state of affairs is evidenced by the remaining answers—Origen had announced answers to the questions as to whether God is "bodily and formed according to some shape, or of a different nature than bodies, a point which is not clearly indicated in our preaching. The same is also to be investigated even regarding Christ and the Holy Spirit, and indeed it is to be investigated no less of every soul and every rational nature."[282] Did he provide answers over the course of his investigation? Yes and no. The answers appear rather unclearly and in multiple attempts within "On First Principles," but they are preserved extensively in Origen's critique of the Middle Platonist Celsus and in many exegetical commentaries and sermons.

The frequency and thoroughness with which Origen argues against the position of God having a body makes apparent that an evidently not-so-insignificant number of individuals, and not merely faithful but also well-educated Christians thought in such a manner. Origen's polemic demonstrates that not only did a modest so-called anthropomorphism conceive of an enlarged human frame as a divine body, but also that a particular bodiliness of this divine figure was accepted with recourse to philosophical concepts.

Tertullian

The most striking example of a philosophical foundation for the conception of a divine body within mainstream Christianity may be found at the end of the second century in the writings of the Christian rhetorician and theologian *Quintus Septimus Florens Tertullianus* from North Africa. It has already been seen that, in his defense of his own faith, the *Apology* (likely composed in AD 197), Tertullian is finely attuned to the different philosophical schools with respect to the potential for divine corporeality and seeks to orient himself accordingly: "Some are sure He is incorporeal, others that He has a body—the Platonists, that is, and the Stoics."[283] The stance assumed by the author himself is not yet revealed in this passage. It was only a decade later that Tertullian displayed his colors and argued extensively for his *own* position within a polemic work on the theology of the Trinity aimed against *Praxeas*, an inhabitant of Rome likely originally hailing from Asia Minor.[284] Therein, he posed the rhetorical question as to whether anyone would contest that God is body if he is also spirit. In addition to this philosophical justification may further be found a biblical argumentation: Tertullian understood the reference to Christ "being in the form of God" (Philippians 2:6) within the Pauline Epistle to the Philippians as indicating a *corporeal* "form of God" the Father:[285]

> In what form of God? Evidently in some form, not in none: for who will deny that God is body, although God is a spirit? For spirit is body, of its

own kind, in its own form[286] (*spiritus enim corpus sui generis in sua effigie*).

Many decades ago, Adolf von Harnack already observed that Tertullian could only come to this conclusion because for him a *bodiless being*— very much in the scheme of Stoic philosophical tradition, as has been seen—was identical with the nonexistence of an entity:

> Everything that exists is body of some kind or another. Nothing is incorporeal except what does not exist.[287]

For this North African Christian thinker, that God possesses a body is an unshakeable certainty born of principally philosophical reasons never made explicit in themselves. At the same time, however, (according to Harnack) Tertullian emphasizes that "everything anthropopathic and anthropomorphic should be excluded for him (sc. God)."[288] As within Stoic philosophy, hence, the central point is a body of a particular materiality which is categorically distinguished from all terrestrial bodies. This becomes particularly apparent when Tertullian rails against the watering down of these categorical distinctions. Thus, in his great work "Against Marcion" which was composed a few years before his polemic against Praxeas, it becomes indirectly evident that the proponents of this urban Roman teacher assigned the creator god and demiurge a body of terrestrial materiality visible to terrestrial eyes (at least according to the mainstream Christian critics of Tertullian and Origen). As before with the text of Origen quoted, it may be noted that, at least within mainstream ecclesiastical circles, the image prevailed that Marcionistic groups had thus interpreted the relevant texts of the Old Testament in such a literal sense, and hence had elevated an incorporeal, invisible, unknown God and father of Jesus Christ above an accordingly terrestrially corporeally conceived creator God.[289] Whether Marcion truly preached a corporeality composed of terrestrial materiality for the biblical creator God (in particular because he otherwise interpreted the Old Testament literally), and if, indeed, he so strictly distinguished between two gods, as his opponents in the mainstream church claimed of him, must here on grounds of the scarcity of sources remain an open question.[290] Tertullian certainly pronouncedly juxtaposes this to his creed on the unity of God: "It was he also who in the Old Testament had already declared 'there shall no man see me, and live' (Exodus 33:20)."[291]

It might be presumed that the association of the corporeality of God with the heretical name of Marcion (however justified this may or may not be) would have fatal consequences for the broader reception of this idea within mainstream ecclesiastical Christianity: Marcion's name probably marred both profoundly and momentously the widespread view that God possessed figure and body with the suspicion of heresy. This besmirching was probably so successful because within Marcion's teachings (once more according to mainstream church heresiology) the corporeally conceived creator god was clearly inferior and more deficient than the good God and father of Jesus Christ,[292] and Christ in this account only appeared in an impassible spirit body after the fashion of angels, and thus fell under the suspicion of the theories of docetism and modalism.[293]

Melito of Sardis

Admittedly, not only those Christians like Tertullian of decidedly Stoic background or those influenced by the teacher and denizen of Rome Marcion were for the thesis that God might be accorded a body. Origen mentions *Melito of Sardis*, an inhabitant of this city in Asia Minor during the second century AD, as the author of a tract entitled "On the Corporeal God"; both the theologian and his work in question will be extensively treated in chapter 7.[294] Regardless, in contrast to Marcion and also Tertullian, Melito stood at the center of the mainstream church in Asia Minor and was a highly respected representative of his church elsewhere.

"Gnostic" Texts

Finally, certain texts are to be mentioned at this point which are generally ascribed to the so-called gnostic movement. Although, in fact, "Gnosticism" follows (were one to generalize) rather a Platonizing tendency towards the characterization of its diverse divine principles by means of negative epithets such as "imperishable," "unspeakable," or "invisible,"[295] the notion of a heavenly corporeality of God and the conception of an existence of a divine body serve as the backdrop for various individual "gnostic" models. Guy Stroumsa has noted in this context the notion of a polymorphism of Christ which presupposes a material substrate for his shifting forms.[296] The attestations of this conception within those writings attributed to so-called Gnosis need not be elaborated upon in full; a characteristic example here suffices ("Gnostic" conceptions of the body of Jesus Christ will also be extensively revisited in chapter 7): Thus, in the "Second Treatise of the Great Seth," a tract from the gnostic library cache of Nag Hammadi (NHC VII,2) likely composed in the third century AD, the savior says: "For when I came down [from the cross] no one saw me. For I kept changing my forms above, transforming from appearance to appearance."[297] Polymorphism, as is permitted the savior while journeying through hostile territory unrecognized in the "Second Treatise of the Great Seth," does not pertain to any surviving text ascribed to the alleged gnostic

movement the *supreme, absolutely transcendent* god, but rather merely to
secondary forms of the same at various levels of the redemptive event.[298]
The utterly transcendent god evidently possesses neither a corporeal form,
nor a body in the material sense: As the longer recension of the "Secret
Book of John" (also known as the Apocryphon of John, NHC II,1/IV,1)
notes, he is "not corporeal; he is not incorporeal"[299]—hence, as Platonic
philosophy also teaches, he is "beyond being."

Much as in the case of Marcion (at least according to his perception
by the mainstream church), it must hence be stated that individual movements counted among "Gnosis" also brought divine corporeality under
suspicion of heresy by means of associating (as was conventional to them)
this conception with apparently inferior divine forms.

Summary

This journey through the development of Christian theology in the early
Imperial period may be halted at the present juncture; it will be resumed in
the sixth and seventh chapters of this work. It has not only become apparent as to what weight the notion of a divine body bore in the most diverse
of intellectual currents, but also as to how differently these conceptions
were configured in their fine details, not only already in the Hebrew Bible,
the Old Testament of Christians, but also in the various philosophical
schools established since Hellenism influencing Christianity's emerging
theology. It has been seen that within Antiquity there were wildly disparate
groups and movements which proceeded quite naturally from the premise
that God could only be appropriately conceived of in corporeal form and
with a body. This might be found, on the one hand, in the Scriptures of the
Hebrew Bible with their so-called anthropomorphic depictions of God, but
also, on the other hand, in the influential schools of Epicurean and Stoic
philosophy with their conceptions of divine bodies. Nevertheless, as certain as their stance on the particular reality of a godly body on whichever
grounds might have been, this was matched by the convictions of others,
influenced by Platonism both deeply and superficially alike, who repudiated such discourse on a divine body as a more or less absurd teaching.
Here, the first Christian polymath Origen lends himself well as an example.

Even if a *Feuerbachian* perspective (wherein a given anthropology
determines entirely a respective theory of God) is rather a simplification
of complex interrelationships of rationalization and verification, the following correlation most evidently characterizes both of these fundamental
positions witnessed within Antiquity since Hellenism in the most disparate
of milieus:[300] The more that individuals understood themselves as integral,
synthetic entities of body *and* soul, the more clearly that they thought of

body and soul as integral, synthetic entities within their own image of God.[301] The reverse also stands: The more that individuals understood themselves as essentially souls,[302] the surrounding bodies of which were described as deficient and insofar also transitory, the more they came to reject the conception of divine corporeality. Naturally, the plausibility of both schools of thought on the doctrine of God was not exclusively the product of anthropology, but rather always also of concomitant assumptions on the structure and constitution of matter and the soul, and deliberations on the general theory of principles, all thematized philosophically according to contemporaneous standards of rationality in arguments. On account of the diversity of persons and groups which avowed themselves as members of one or the other of the intellectual traditions, and the evident variety of pertinent texts opining for or against divine corporeality, one must already be wary of neat dualities. Thus, the stance that there were, on the one hand, a "Jewish-Old Testament tradition with a strongly holistic appreciation of the person ('I' *am* an animate body)," and, on the other, a tradition of "a Hellenistic-(Neo-)Platonic heritage with its (more or less dualistic) division between soul and body ('I' am a soul which— temporarily—*possesses* a body)"[303] is a striking oversimplification of a clearly complicated situation. This follows the traditional model wherein the development of Christian theology is described as a contest between (and synthesis of) biblical tradition and Platonism respectively; yet, the Oxford ancient historian Mark Edwards has demonstrated with good reason that the generally accepted assumption of a dominance on the part of Platonism in the Imperial era and Late Antiquity may well be the product of a biased preference for this approach within Christian theology, and not reflect the realities of the antique "philosophy market."[304]

Neither Judaism nor Christianity is as monolithic in terms of the notion of a divine body as an Origen in Antiquity would wish, a Maimonides or Thomas in the Middle Ages would normalize, and a Leibniz in the Baroque era would canonize. Here (as elsewhere) the intellectual historical divides run perpendicular to the seemingly abrupt borders of religious orientation and philosophical schools. Exploration of Imperial and late antique history will first be resumed after a visit to the pagan temple and the conceptions therein of both divine corporeality and incorporeality.

3

The Body of God
and Divine Statues in Antiquity

God and Man at Once

Greek philosophers such as Xenophanes or Plato, and Jewish and Christian thinkers who followed them more or less explicitly, were convinced
that the existence of God did not imply corporeal form in the slightest, or
indeed anything at all which might be understood in the simplest sense as a
"form." With this emphasis upon the incorporeality of God, they believed
that they were depicting God as he *is*: "I think you should present god
as he really is," intones the Platonic Socrates in "The Republic."[1] Yet,
what would the visitors to pagan temples in Antiquity who saw the divine
images therein installed and were not influenced by such philosophical
underpinnings have thought? Would they have held these splendid depictions of a stunning corporeality for pure metaphors? Were they convinced
that "anthropomorphic" depictions of the gods' natures are fundamentally
inappropriate?

The presently disseminated definitions of the term "anthropomorphic"
presuppose a *categorical difference* between a divine being in pure immateriality transcendental to all mortals, on the one hand, and a human in a limited, mortal coil, on the other: Derived from the Greek ἀνθρωπόμορφος
"anthropomorphic," the term "anthropomorphism" describes conceptions
of God "in human form" or, put more broadly, the "humanization of God."
Such "humanization," however, practically rules out a categorical differentiation (howsoever it might be described) between God and man,[2]
unless the human features of divine images are understood as *pure metaphors* for the categorically different aspects of divine beings. Yet, a strict
categorical differentiation between god and man hardly numbers among
the suppositions implicit within every antique religion, but rather within
Greco-Roman religion was confined to very specific groups, times, and

periods. In the Imperial era of Antiquity, such a categorical differentiation between divinities and humans belonged by no means to the general piety of most people, and certainly also did not characterize most of the various pagan cults, or at least not in the same strict sense as Judaism and Christianity. The boundaries between human and divine were far more fluid, something made clear from a remark by the Berlin Greek philologist *Ulrich von Wilamowitz-Moellendorff* (1848–1931) from his commentary on the Athenian poet Euripides' tragedy "Heracles." The eponymous figure is God and man at once:

> been man, become god, suffered trials, attained heaven: this is what is essential to Heracles, in whom the Hellenes, all Hellenes, believed. One can lack neither man nor god when one seeks to grasp their initial core, and one who has understood so much is now free of every interpretation merely emphasising one side of this double nature.[3]

Nevertheless, these permeable boundaries may also be somewhat overstated with respect to the Imperial-era incarnation of Greco-Roman religion: "Divinities are immortal humans. Humans are accordingly mortal divinities, which implies that the boundary between the two could be crossed entirely. Divinities were thought of as human even if there were philosophically educated individuals who sought to visualise a godhead without bodily limitations; these remained exceptions."[4] Since god and human were not as strongly differentiated as in many Jewish and some Christian traditions, the gods were frequently not only revered in human form, but also corporeally; their manner of existence could be explained far more readily in analogy to that of humans.[5] These blurred lines permitted statements on the close relationship between the human and divine surprising in their proximity to those of the Judeo-Christian tradition. The early Imperial-era author *Ovid* (43 BC–after AD 17), for example, pronounced in verse that man is "moulded into the form of the all-controlling gods."[6] Many aspects of pagan quotidian lived religious practice are reminiscent of what might be learned from biblical texts of Israelite piety. The ritual praxis in handling divine statues in Greek temples demonstrates that, much like worshippers in Mesopotamia and Canaan, the visitors to these temples from the Hellenistic period until Late Antiquity ascribed the gods a certain fluidity which permitted them to be ostensibly present in multiple places at once. As the classical philologist from Tel Aviv Margalit Finkelberg has reminded,[7] not only was Pheidias' celebrated cult statue in the Temple of Zeus erected in the fifth century BC at the center of the installation, but also an independent altar to the god lying between the Pelopion and the Temple of Hera.[8] Moreover, Olympian Zeus was not only present in

Olympia: The building of the famed Temple of Olympian Zeus in Athens having already been initiated in the sixth century BC, albeit only finally completed by Emperor Hadrian in the second century AD.[9] Moreover, many additional cultic sites revering Olympian Zeus existed.[10] The question as to whether, for example, in entering one of these temples, a humble Greek peasant would have thought that the Olympian Zeus he worshipped possessed a "locally circumscribed body" or not is difficult to answer. Probably, without thematizing this in philosophical terminology, he implicitly supposed a particular corporeality of the god not subject to the constraints of terrestrial bodies and present in multiple places at the same time. It remains uncertain as to how he would have dealt with the existence of diverse local cultic forms of this god and other gods and goddesses—for example, Zeus Panamaros in Stratonicaea, Asia Minor, in addition to Olympian Zeus—and, in turn, with the appearance, in some cases, of these local variants in the same locations, also in iconographically entirely distinct forms. It is only certain that, in the Imperial era, gods and goddesses were present in utter droves: The late antique Christian poet *Aurelius Prudentius Clemens* (AD 348–after 405) lampooned Julian the Apostate, the famed imperial revenant to the pagan religion of his fathers, stating that he became the lover of three hundred thousand gods: Julian "cared . . . not for maintaining true religion, for he loved myriad (lit. three hundred thousand) gods."[11] This is naturally formulated polemically: Hesiod gives the number thirty thousand, while from texts and inscriptions a total of approximately forty thousand gods and goddesses have currently been identified today.[12] Of course, this is dependent upon the point at which a line is drawn between divine and non-divine existence; at the end of the second century AD, in his oration "Plato on God," the rhetorician Maximus of Tyre notes:

> But if you are not strong enough to see the Father and Creator, then it must suffice for the moment to contemplate his works and to worship his offspring, who are many and varied, far more numerous than the Boeotian poet says. God's divine children and relatives are not a mere thirty thousand in number, but countless: the stars and planets in the heavens, and the *daimones* in the ether too.[13]

In the face of such a horde of divine figures, answering the question as to the reflections of pious pilgrims before their cultic images already seems only possible in a rudimentary fashion. It is clear what the experts thought: In a lemma from the Suda, the most voluminous of the Byzantine lexica, a Neoplatonist in Alexandria named *Heraiscus*, student of Proclus and teacher of Isidore in the fifth century AD,[14] is accorded a particular

capacity (the text may be understood as hailing from the life of the philosopher Isidore, compiled as a work of philosophical history by the Neoplatonist Damascius, Isidore's pupil and the last scholarch of the Athenian
Academy):[15] According to this lemma in the Suda, by means of his particular nature, allegedly closer to that of a god than a mortal, Heraiscus was
able to distinguish between *live* and *lifeless* divine statues. In glancing
at a living divine statue "immediately his heart was afflicted by divine
frenzy while both his body and soul leapt up as if possessed by the god."[16]
A "living" divine statue is glossed in the lexical note as "animate."[17]
From this biographical anecdote about Heraiscus, the sense is gained that
for the last antique pagan Neoplatonists the materiality and corporeality of
a divine statue had nothing to do with its potential vitality, as from their perspective the liveliness of the statue was enabled solely by means of divine
ensoulment. The corporeality of divine statues composed of earthly matter is extraneous for Heraiscus, at least according to his student Isidore's
account. Nevertheless, there were attempts within Neoplatonic philosophy
to relate this corporeal materiality to the divine: For example, in the third-
century writings of the Neoplatonist *Iamblichus*, it remained with respect
to divine statues "not derogatory to sacrifice to them bodies subject to the
direction of nature; for all the works of nature serve them and contribute
something to their administration."[18] The material corporeality of a statue
is hence not directly associated with the gods (although, like all Platonists,
Iamblichus naturally knows the corporeal gods as stars[19]), but nevertheless
indirectly: One can also explain as a philosopher by means of rational
arguments why the gods in the temples are consecrated bodies composed
of matter and sacrifices. In both cases, this does not necessarily hinge upon
"dead matter": "And let there be no astonishment if in this connection we
speak of a pure and divine form of matter; for matter also issues from the
father and creator of all,[20] and thus gains its perfection, which is suitable
to the reception of gods."[21] Certain matter may hence serve as a complete
and pure receptacle for a god.[22]

Did such a differentiation between "living," "animate" divine images
and their "lifeless" counterparts reflect the thoughts of pious (or indeed less
than pious) pilgrims before their idols? The evidence necessary for the reconstruction of the piety of the humbler social strata can hardly be gathered.

To some degree, these lacunae may be made up for by examining conceptions of the divine within the *Homeric* epics, as Homer's works were
widely circulated on account of their use within elementary school curricula in the Imperial era, and thereby molded popular opinion.[23] Beyond this,
recourse may be made to descriptions of divine statuary in temples (so-
called ekphraseis), as, for example, found in the Imperial-era author *Pausanias*; moreover, comparable accounts may also be found within *Plutarch*,

Dio Chrysostom, and *Lucian*. Finally, a few characteristic Imperial-era inscriptions permit the drawing of some inferences as to the significance of conceptions of divine bodies within the religiosity commonplace to individuals during this epoch. With some caveats, Imperial-era novels may also be considered. It seems prudent to begin by examining the Archaic- and Classical-period prerequisites of these Imperial-era divine conceptions, so as to depict thereafter the situation within a globalized Roman Antiquity.

The Image of Olympian Zeus by Pheidias

In the middle of the *cella* in the vast majority of pagan temples in Antiquity stood a religious image, at least from the Classical and post-Classical periods onwards (the question as to a potentially aniconic prehistory of Greek and Roman religion need not be considered at this juncture). Certain of these images were widely renowned. Among the Seven Wonders of the World in the general consciousness of Antiquity numbered the statue of Olympian Zeus in the Temple of Zeus at Olympia ("the Alphaic Zeus"), fashioned by the Athenian artist *Pheidias* together with a workshop in the mid-part of the fifth century BC.[24]

In the Classical and Hellenic periods, this image, the exact appearance of which cannot be reconstructed more precisely for want of more significant archaeological remains, was disseminated within the collective consciousness of the ancients by means of the so-called temple coins of Olympia whereupon the image was depicted (albeit in heavily schematized form).[25] Interestingly, a Classical pattern probably schematizing the head of the statue was still minted in the reign of Hadrian, or the design at least emulated. This bronze coinage is, however, only preserved in four examples and depicts on the obverse the head of the emperor, and on its reverse that of the god (Fig. 3.1).[26]

At the end of the pre-Christian era, the geographer *Strabo* described this already celebrated artwork (and the famous raising of the eyebrows as an emblem of Zeus' all-encompassing power) with slightly critical undertones:

> But the greatest of these was the image of Zeus made by Pheidias of Athens, son of Charmides; it was made of ivory, and it was so large that, although the temple was very large, the artist is thought to have missed the proper symmetry, for he showed Zeus seated but almost touching the roof with his head, thus making the impression that if Zeus arose and stood erect he would unroof the temple.

It is related of Pheidias that, when Panaenus (the painter) asked him after what model he was going to make the likeness of Zeus, he replied that he was going to make it after the likeness set forth by Homer in these words:

"Cronion spake, and nodded assent with his dark brows,
and then the ambrosial locks flowed streaming from the lord's immortal
    head,
and he caused great Olympus to quake."

A noble description indeed, as appears not only from the brows but from the other details in the passage, because the poet provokes our imagination to conceive the picture of a mighty personage and a mighty power worthy of a Zeus.[27]

The statue's viewer was compelled to tilt back the head to see it, and thereby to raise the head considerably higher than in any comparable daily communication. The conditioning within this act of viewing already emphasized the distance between the religious image and human viewers, especially as otherwise inferiors were to lower their gaze and bow their heads before their betters. Simultaneously, the corporeal form of the god also conveyed that this distance was not *categorical* in nature, as would be the case between an essentially incorporeal god and the individuals corporeally present before him.

An extremely thorough description of the image's statue and throne (indeed, the most extensive ekphrasis of an ancient artwork extant)

Fig. 3.1   So-called temple coin from Elis, AD 134
Münzkabinett, Staatliche Museen Berlin Preußischer Kulturbesitz[28]

Fig. 3.2   Didrachm, obverse, Zeus enthroned, ca. 450 BC
Kestner Museum, Hannover, inventory number 1999.4.26[29]

appears within the ten volumes of the "Description of Greece" (Ἑλλάδος περιήγησις) compiled for a Roman audience by the geographer and native of Asia Minor *Pausanias* in the last third of the second century AD; the author lists its materials and comments on its dimensions.[30] The visitors cajoled the statue with their rather concrete concerns: It becomes apparent from a discourse composed by the philosopher *Epictetus* in the first century AD that pilgrims to the image expected assistance with the "unpleasant and hard things" which "happen in life," despite the heat, claustrophobia, "tumult and shouting and other annoyances" marking the visit to the evidently completely overrun sanctuary.[31] Nevertheless, it noted in Pausanias that the religious image was cordoned off, and hence one could not pass underneath the statue's throne.[32] He also relates the charming story that, upon completing the statue, Pheidias "prayed the god to show by a sign whether the work was to his liking. Immediately, runs the legend, a thunderbolt fell on that part of the floor where down to the present day the bronze jar (hydria) stood to cover the place."[33] It need not be considered here as to whether, as von Wilamowitz-Moellendorff suggested in a lecture on "Zeus of Olympia"[34] that Pheidias' cult statue should be understood as emblematic of a "religion become spiritual and moral," the enthroned figure superseding in this manner prior depictions consisting of a naked striding figure hurling thunder. Rather, it is clear that all of these depictions of Zeus quite evidently display a body. There is little to support the assertion that artists and pilgrims were convinced that this was "the incorporeal corporeally" depicted (as is the case for von Wilamowitz-Moellendorff) and considered the god to be bodi*less*.[35] Indeed, such a stance on religious images was declaimed in AD 101 or 105 by the popular philosopher *Dio* *of Prusa*, dubbed *Chrysostom*, in his work "The Olympic Discourse on Man's First Conception of God"—insofar as it might be permitted to take the literary fiction of a temple debate for a reflection of reality.[36] Therein, the speaker poses from his Stoically influenced background on the image of god the question as to whether Pheidias realized an appearance "appropriate to a god and . . . its form worthy of the divine nature" when he "not only used a material which gives delight but also presented a human form of extraordinary beauty and size."[37] In his answer, Dio has the artist Pheidias hold forth on the traditional conventions and practices of earlier artists and poets alike before replying as follows:

> For mind and intelligence in and of themselves no statuary or painter will ever be able to represent; for all men are utterly incapable of observing such attributes with their eyes or of learning of them by inquiry. But as for that in which this intelligence manifests itself, men, having no mere inkling thereof but actual knowledge, fly to it for refuge, attributing to God a human body as a vessel to contain intelligence and rationality, in their lack of a better illustration, and in their perplexity seeking to indicate that which is invisible and unportrayable by means of something portrayable and visible, using the function of a symbol and doing so better than certain barbarians, who are said to represent the divine by animals—using as his starting-point symbols which are trivial and absurd. . . . For certainly no one would maintain that it had been better that no statue or picture of gods should have been exhibited among men.[38]

In contrast to the Stoic thinkers presented in the previous chapter, Zeus is for Dio primarily an *immaterial* being who separates the elements of "hard residuary substance."[39] Within the "The Olympic Discourse," the materiality of god, otherwise far more strongly accentuated within Stoic philosophy, is not drawn upon as a justification for his artistic representation of the god in material form. The divine conception of Dio is recognizably influenced by the rudiments of a Platonic concept of a pure immateriality. Nevertheless, his text is not concerned with the question of the corporeality of *god*, but rather that of *human* corporeality: According to Dio, the artist uses a *human* body (ἀνθρώπινον σῶμα) as the "vessel" (ἀγγεῖον) for the representation of the intellectual faculties and reason; it remains unresolved as to whether, in turn, the god possesses a *divine* body as a vessel. From Aristotle onwards, "vessel" is a widespread metaphor for the body; indeed, Emperor Marcus Aurelius describes earthly life as "lackeying the bodily vessel," understanding this as the unavoidable necessity of not only serving lofty ideals on earth with the spirit, but also the body.[40]

In any case, the reflective stance of Dio the Imperial-era rhetorician and philosopher is hardly appropriate to addressing the question as to what many centuries before the Attic sculptor Pheidias and the peregrine throngs might have thought on this topic. *Plutarch*, a contemporary of Dio Chrysostom, indirectly evidences in a polemic passage that "there are some among the Greeks who have not learned nor habituated themselves to speak of the bronze, the painted, and the stone effigies as statues of the gods and dedications in their honour, but they call them gods."[41] Despite all of his interest in philosophically modernizing the divine conceptions conventionally bound up with the statue, even Dio Chrysostom falls under the spell of the Classical literary traditions on this site: As in Strabo roughly a hundred years before, a connection is made between the cult image of Pheidias and Homer. This occurs when Dio has the artist state: "But if you find fault with me for the human figure, you should make haste to be angry with Homer first":[42]

> for he not only represented a form most nearly like this statue of mine by mentioning the flowing locks of the god and the chin too at the very beginning of his poem, when he says that Thetis made supplication for the bestowal of honour upon her son; but in addition to these things he ascribes to the gods meetings and counsellings and harangues, then also journeyings from Ida to the heavens and Olympus, and sleep-scenes and drinking-bouts and love-embraces, clothing everything in very lofty poetical language and yet keeping close to mortal likeness.[43]

Antique religious images were consecrated, and it was believed that the "living gods" (οἱ ἔυψυχοι θεοί) thus "could be more potent" as is said by Plato.[44] The divinities (*numina*) were present in their statues, as is evidenced by the Imperial-era Latin Christian poet *Commodian* in his didactic poem *Instructiones adversus gentium*.[45] In the *Corpus Hermeticum*, a collection of Hermetic tractates from the period between the first century BC and the fourth century AD, this is phrased as follows: "Adore the statues, because they, too, possess forms from the intelligible cosmos."[46]

Religious Statues in Temples

The overarching term "cult image" (ἄγαλμα, ἀπεικόνισμα or εἰκών, more rarely ἀνδριάς)[47] conceals, however, the fact that there were two very different types of cultic statues in temples from the Classical period onwards, as has been demonstrated by Margalit Finkelberg and others: *On the one hand*, the large statues within the interior rooms of the temple were understood as *votive offerings* (ἀναθήματα, "votive images,"

"images offered to the god") in the same manner as the many small votive offerings in the form of figural divine portraits left within the grounds.[48] *On the other hand*, these were understood as the veritable embodiments of a divine person, appearing to act independently and thus able to become objects of cultic reverence ("cult image" or "image of the god").[49] Pausanias, above all, provides a great deal of evidence for this notion:[50] Accordingly, he reports in a digression that at Magnesia on the Maeander in a cave at a place called Aulai/Hylai,[51] is an image of Apollo "very old indeed" which "bestows strength equal to any task. The men sacred to the god leap down from sheer precipices and high rocks, and uprooting trees of exceeding height walk with their burdens down the narrowest of paths."[52] The presence of a religious image was as a guarantor of the presence of the power appertaining to the divinity depicted in the image.[53] From the examples of the Athena Parthenos, a roundly celebrated *oblation* on the part of Athens, and the considerably older Athena Polias in the Erechtheion, a classic *cult statue*, it might be observed that both ritual approaches towards statues could occur in one and the same place, in this case, the Athenian Acropolis.[54]

At the end of the second century AD, in a collective decree on the cult practices of their chief deities, Zeus and Hecate, the popular assembly of the city of Stratonicaea in Caria of Asia Minor (in the vicinity of the modern village of Eskihisar) documented for all those who could read that the statues of Zeus Panamaros and Hecate found at their assembly place, or Bouleuterion, had performed widely seen "feats of strength" and should thus be praised through the singing of hymns.[55] Within the sanctuary of the god Zeus Panamaros, belonging to the municipality of Stratonicaea and connected to the center by means of a sacred street, may be read on the base of a statue of Athene: "Before the unworthy, my hand is without mercy; but when a pious individual venerates me, I will swing above them (protectively) my spear."[56] When the statue of Zeus Panamaros was brought on visits to Stratonicaea from Panamara by the priests by means of horse, this was said to be a "visit of the god" (ἐπιδημία τοῦ θεοῦ).[57] An oracle of the god Apollo preserved in an inscription from Ephesus from the second century AD, probably from the nearby cultic site of Klaros, encourages the inhabitants of a city on the River Hermos, likely Sardis, to erect a golden statue of the goddess Artemis of Ephesus in a temple of Artemis Coloene. The power of the goddess within the statue should aid the city in overcoming a plague. The practices regarding the cult image are described precisely:

> Her form bring in from Ephesus, brilliant with gold. Put her up in a
> temple, full of joy: she will provide deliverance from your affliction and

will dissolve the poison (or: magic) of pestilence, which destroys men,
and will melt down with her flame-bearing torches in nightly fire the
kneaded works of wax, the signs of the evil art of a sorcerer.[58]

The burning of wax models of bodies and body parts in order to request
healing from the worshipped deity, still practiced today in Roman Catholic shrines such as that at Fátima, demonstrates how unencumbered and
directly a power suspected to be within religious images might be called
upon within daily religiosity.[59] Naturally, one might expect particular
potency from a statue finished with particularly precious material. If, by
contrast, a statue was lacking from a temple, the temple was understood
as having been forsaken by that respective divinity. Pausanias recounts
that Sulla fell ill after sacrilegiously looting the ivory-embellished cult
image of Athene from Alalcomenae (Boeotia) in 87/86 BC. The shrine,
"deprived of the goddess, was hereafter neglected."[60] A divine image dis-
playing the god enchained (such as that of Ares Enyalos / Mars Enyalius
in Sparta) hindered the god in forsaking the place in the populace's eyes;
"This image is the same as the Athenians express by their Wingless Victory (in the temple of Nike on the Acropolis); . . . the Athenians think that
victory, having no wings, will always remain where she is."[61]

The seriousness with which the educated in the Imperial period understood the corporeality of religious images is indicated by diverse antique
accounts, wherein signs of the quasi-corporeal animation of these sculp-
tures is portrayed: Changes in expression, nodding of figures to one wor-
shipper or another, sweating, and movements are all recounted. Such is
accordingly related by the satirist *Lucian of Samosata* from Syrian Heirop-
olis/Mabbug, present day Membij:[62]

> In it . . . are images worth of divinity. The gods are especially manifest to
> them. Among them the statues sweat, and move, and deliver oracles, and
> there are often cries in the sanctuary when the temple has been locked
> up, which many have heard.[63]

In the *Acta Hermaisci*, counted as one of the so-called Acts of the
Pagan Martyrs (*Acta Alexandrinorum*), it is reported in a clearly anti-
Roman tenor that the bust of Serapis, the *patronus Alexandrinorum*,
found in the imperial chambers on the Roman Palatine began to sweat
in response to the allegedly less than cordial behavior of Emperor Trajan
towards an Alexandrian delegation, and that the emperor was perplexed by
this.[64] According to *John Lydus* (ca. AD 490–560) the sweating or crying
of divine images prefigures *inner* turmoil to come;[65] thus, this corporeal
sign on the divine image of Serapis might be understood as portending

the military difficulties faced by Trajan during the Parthian War and the Rebellion of the Diaspora between the years AD 115 and 117.[66] In addition to such signs of bodily reaction may also be noted various human ritual behaviors towards the images expressing their corporeality. Thus, many images of gods were dressed in festive robes for particular religious holidays. This not only applied to the wooden statue of Athena Polias, said to have fallen from the sky and housed within the Erechtheion, which annually received a peplos, a newly woven richly embroidered saffron-colored mantle during the summer Panathanaea, but also the wooden cult image of Hera on Samos, among many others.[67]

This Athenian ritual has survived as custom in an altered form, inasmuch as on Greek islands in particular women bestow upon Mary woven textiles such as scarves or gloves on the occasion of her Dormition in August (at roughly the same time of year as the Panathanaea).[68] In *Magnesia on the Maeander*, twelve gods were festively clothed once a year, borne into the marketplace, seated in upholstered couches, and symbolically waited upon on. This is evidenced by a law recorded in an inscription from 196 BC set at the ante of the temple of Zeus Sosipolis "Saviour of the City" legible to all:

> The wreath-bearer leading the procession should have images of all twelve gods garbed in their finest robes carried along, he should have a tholos erected in the agora before the altar of the twelve gods, and set up three most splendid couches. He should further provide a flute player, a piper, and a cithara player for musical accompaniment.[69]

At the altar was thus erected a wooden hut in the form of a tholos and beds for a divine banquet of the twelve Olympian gods (the Δωδεκάθεοι: Zeus and his siblings Demeter, Hera, Hestia, and Poseidon, and his progeny Ares with Hephaistos, Artemis with Apollo, Athene, Aphrodite, and Hermes).

The ritual handling of the corporeality of the gods represented by the religious images was naturally hardly confined to the provisioning of a new robe on certain holidays, but also patterned daily life: in the Isis temples of the Imperial era, the goddess was ceremonially awoken in the morning with the announcement of the time, greeted, washed, dressed, salved, combed, adorned with jewellery, and perfumed by means of various procedures.[70] A similar state of affairs was applicable to cults in Rome, both indigenous and of Greek origin: Seneca noted (if with every symptom of horror at so much superstition) in his only fragmentarily preserved text *De superstitione* that on the Capitol, in the temple of Capitoline Jupiter, "one servant informs Jupiter of the names of his worshippers, another announces the hours." Moreover, he asserts that "there are women who sit in the Capitol, who imagine that Jupiter is their lover."[71] Statues of Aphrodite, in particular, were especially liable to provoke erotic acts, indeed, even to have inspired autoerotic behavior: "There is a story that a man once fell in love with it and hiding by night embraced it, and that a (semen) stain betrays this lustful act."[72] Furthermore, a divine image of Jupiter at the capital of the Imperium Romanum allegedly reacted with jealousy, were it visited too seldom.[73] In part, religious images moved themselves; in part, they were moved: In the late antique Christian novel *De gestis in Perside* (the so-called religious discussion at the Sassanid court) it is stated that the divine effigies had danced the entire night "both the males and females" to demonstrate their joy at the birth of a son (in fact, Jesus Christ) to the mother goddess.[74] Every year on 27 March, at the festival of the *Lavatio*, an image of the goddess Cybele, the *Magna Mater*, left her temple on the Palatinate on a wagon drawn by cows, was driven before the city to the sound of song, and bathed in the river Almo near the Porta Capena along with wagon and cows.[75]

The list of such quotidian signs of a universally held antique piety which reckoned with a corporeal form and found these potently represented in religious images could easily be added to;[76] these examples are sufficient to convey a representative impression of an aspect characteristic to pagan religiosity. Such views were by no means the preserve of the uneducated, but rather were also espoused by erudite individuals: *Apuleius of Madaurus*, a contemporary of Marcus Aurelius in the second century AD, mentions "breathing effigies" in connection to images within his "Metamorphoses" (also known as "The Golden Ass").[77] This might seem surprising at first glance for a Middle Platonist, who precisely recounts in his work "On Plato and his Doctrine" that the Athenian philosopher "thinks of God, however, that he is incorporeal."[78] Yet, such contradictions between an author's philosophical theory and his daily religiosity may also be found in Cicero, to name an example. Naturally, not all of the intelligentsia maintained such a stance: *Plutarch*, by contrast, is at pains to demythologize (put anachronistically) these respective phenomena, presenting thereby enlightened criticism of quotidian religious handling of divine corporeality:

> These words were actually uttered twice, as the story runs, which would have us believe what is difficult of belief and probably never happened. For that statues have appeared to sweat, and shed tears, and exude something like drops of blood, is not impossible; since wood and stone often contract a mould which is productive of moisture, and cover themselves with many colours, and receive tints from the atmosphere; and there is

nothing in the way of believing that the Deity uses these phenomena sometimes as signs and portents. It is possible also that statues may emit a noise like a moan or a groan, by reason of a fracture or a rupture, which is more violent if it takes place in the interior. But that articulate speech, and language so clear and abundant and precise, should proceed from a lifeless thing, is altogether impossible; since not even the soul of man, or the Deity, without a body duly organized and fitted with vocal parts, has ever spoken and conversed.[79]

As to how little such an intellectual protest against quotidian piety affected the public in the period of the Roman Empire is well demonstrated in a question of a priestess of Demeter Thesmophorus named Alexandra addressed at some point in the second or third centuries to the Apollo oracle at Didyma in Asia Minor. She worriedly asked the god what it might portend that the gods were appearing so seldom in corporeal form:[80]

Since from the time when she assumed the office of priestess the gods have not been so frequently manifest (in dreams) through their appearances, partly through maidens and women, partly also through men and children, why is this and is it auspicious?

Unfortunately, only the beginning of the answer supplied in hexameter by the god Apollo is preserved in an inscription found on Büyük Çakmaklık near Miletus; it seeks to console the nervous priestess:

Immortals accompany mortal men . . . and make their will known and the honour which (they should be accorded).[81]

Oracle inquiries and answers evidence how much the population of the High Imperial era were engaged with the corporeal presence of their gods and goddesses, and how implicitly they reckoned with divine corporeality. Energetic championing of the difference between a corporeal image and an incorporeal archetype as is found in Seneca or Plutarch cannot be homogenized within general discourse on pagan religiosity in Antiquity.[82] In most cases, it is philosophers who accentuate this difference: Hence, according to an account of Diogenes Laërtius, the Megarian philosopher *Stilpo* (died after 280 BC) concluded from the statement that Athene is "not by Zeus but by Phidias" that she "then is not a god."[83] Another case is the pagan Neoplatonist *Sallust* in the late fourth century AD, who viewed religious images as inanimate imitations (μίμησις) of life.[84] The lyricist *Diagoras of Melos* (ca. 475–410 BC), also occasionally known by the moniker "the atheist," is supposed to have even thrown a wooden image of Heracles into a fire and to have uttered, "Well, then, dear Heracles, get up, accomplish your thirteenth task for us, and cook breakfast."[85] All of this is hardly daily religiosity, however, but rather learned reflection upon lived religion and, in the last example, also even an act of religious sacrilege punishable in Antiquity.

Epiphanies of Divine Bodies in the Novels of Antiquity

Gods and goddesses were called ἐπήκοος within lived religion, experienced thus as "listeners," described as ἐπιφανής, as "manifesting" beings, and thus regarded as ἐναργής or "visible."[86] In addition to descriptions of temple images in general literature and inscriptions, certain passages from the novels of Antiquity recounting epiphanies of divine bodies within the medium of literary diversion are highly pertinent. An excellent example of this is the romantic novel "Chaereas and Callirhoe" (Τὰ περὶ Χαιρέαν καὶ Καλλιρρόνη), the earliest surviving "historical novel" (it is set around the fifth to fourth centuries BC), and thus in eight books one of the earliest examples of the broader genre, composed by one *Chariton* from Aphrodisias/Caria, probably in the first century AD. Discoveries of papyri demonstrate that the text was widely disseminated as literary entertainment during the Imperial era.[87] In the novel, the protagonist, Callirhoe, is separated from her husband, Chaereas, and sold as a slave into the household of a certain Dionysius, the wealthiest land baron in Miletus. The wife of its steward, a woman named Plagon, suggests to Callirhoe in her desperate state to pray for solace before a statue of Aphrodite:

Fig. 3.3   The new peplos (*left*), Athene (*center*), and Hephaistos
Eastern Frieze of the Parthenon, 438 BC, London, British Museum

"Come to Aphrodite's shrine and offer up a prayer for yourself. The goddess makes her appearance here; and, besides our neighbours, people from the city come here to sacrifice to her. She listens especially to Dionysius, and he has never failed to stop at her shrine." They then told her of the appearances of the goddess, and one of the peasant women said, "Lady, when you see Aphrodite, you will think you are looking at a picture of yourself." When Callirhoe heard this, her eyes filled with tears, and she said to herself, "What a disaster! Even here Aphrodite reigns, the cause of all my woes. But I will go, for I have many complaints to lay before her."[88] Over the course of the narrative, Dionysius attempts to marry Callirhoe, and, as he seeks to bring her by ship from his estates to Miletus, the fishermen claim to see in Callirhoe's form the goddess Aphrodite herself embarking, and thus rush forward and prostrate themselves before her.[89] Her original husband, Chaereas, sadly left behind in his home city of Syracuse, learns of his wife Callirhoe's woeful tale, and sails out to her from Sicily, and enters the temple of Aphrodite on the estate of Dionysius near Miletus during his search. There he faints and, once woken, is spoken to by a priestess:

> "Be not alarmed, my son; the goddess has frightened many besides you, for she appears in person and lets herself be clearly seen.[90] However, this is a sign of good luck."[91]

The appearance of the gods and goddesses in corporeal form analogous to that of humans evidently concealed the real danger of confusion within daily life, as the fishermen's groveling reverence in the novel demonstrates. As the protagonist, pregnant by her first spouse, Chaereas, but believing him dead, finally yields to her master Dionysius' overtures, and is brought to be wed clad in festal Milesian raiment, the multitudes thronging the alleys and even rooftops proclaim: "Aphrodite is the bride!" The scene accordingly mirrors a divine epiphany: "Beneath her feet they spread purple cloth and roses and violets. As she passed they sprayed her with perfume. Not a person, young or old, was left inside the houses or even at the harbors."[92]

For the central figures of "Chaereas and Callirhoe," Aphrodite serves as the "initiatrix" of these various imbroglios, which are only finally happily resolved in the eighth and final book of the novel. The question as to whether the author also considered her responsible for causing fate need not impact upon examining the piety portrayed in the novel.[93] The goddess of love is present again and again within this novel as a divine power believed to act in corporeal form. For *Erwin von Rohde* (1845–1898), Friedrich Nietzsche's occasional friend and partisan, this concept "of the appearance of the gods where and when they wished" recalled "rather certain remnants of a now-unsettling paganism still haunting the Christendom."[94] Yet, this thesis of anachronistic remnants of a vanquished piety is easily challenged: One need only think of the episode in the Acts of the Apostles wherein the inhabitants of Lystra took Paul and Barnabas for Hermes and Zeus.[95]

The same might be suspected for the Imperium's Latin west: In the *Satyricon*, the first Latin novel albeit only preserved in fragments, composed in the first century AD by the Roman senator *Titus Petronius Arbiter*, a priestess of the god Priapus called Quartilla says: "Indeed the gods (*numina*) walk abroad so commonly in our streets that it is easier to meet a god than a man."[96] Even when, appropriately enough for this novel, the utterance falls within an explicitly erotic scene, its sense may scarcely be doubted.

The conception shared by a great many people in Antiquity that gods and goddesses were usually present in corporeal form must, nevertheless, be qualified once more, inasmuch as, according to general perception, they could also adopt *specific* corporeal forms. This religious view expressed in divers myths of gods such as Zeus or Hera was naturally also disputed by philosophers: In his dialogue "The Republic," for example, *Plato* rejects the notion that a god could assume another form than that of his own, inasmuch as a god is "not lacking in beauty or virtue" in respect to his divine nature, and hence warrants being inwardly and outwardly beautiful.[97] "But does that mean that a god would be willing in word or deed to falsify himself by presenting an apparition to us?"[98]

Divine Forms in Mythology

The commonplace ritual contact in temples with the gods' corporeal presences as described in the ekphraseis of religious images, in novels, and in inscriptions was both expanded upon and interpreted by means of a religious rhetoric of divine bodies within mythology, which must certainly have defined not only religious communication, but also everyday speech and sensibilities: The French Classical philologist *Jean-Pierre Vernant* (1914–2007) demonstrated in his essay on the divine body that in Archaic Greece not only was a strict differentiation between body and soul lacking, there was also no categorical separation between natural and supernatural bodies.[99] Vernant referred to a wealth of terms with which Homer described the body in its vitality, and these did not merely comprise body parts (στῆρος, the breast; ἦτορ or καρδία, the heart; φρήν or πραπίδες, the diaphragm; θυρός, the vital spirit; μένος, strength; and νοῦς, mind).[100] According to Vernant, an inspection of Homer also makes clear that here, on the one hand, the gods evidently possess bodies with all essential bodily functions, yet, on the other hand, their bodies markedly differ from those of humans due to their status as gods. While the human body is characterized as bodily deficient, and fleeting to boot, it might rather be said of the gods that they are "they who always are" (οἱ ἀεὶ ὄντες).[101] Nevertheless, there is hardly a sense that a purely literary device or even metaphorical speech is propounded in these texts with their descriptions of corporeality; here, the differences between "Iliad" and "Odyssey" are of little consequence to the question of the strata of historical tradition within the texts.[102] Inasmuch as they possess real bodies in Homer, therein gods have blood, although not of a kind which might be spilled and cause them to lose their lives, but rather "immortal blood" (ἄμβροτον αἷμα).[103] Humans require sustenance to live and must consume food and drink. The gods require nothing (from Plutarch and Philo onwards, this situation is described in philosophical texts with the word ἀπροσδεής, "needing for nothing"[104]), and hence do not need to eat to maintain their bodies. It follows that they excrete no waste products surplus to their bodies' composition. Yet, even if the gods, as Homer intones, "eat not bread nor . . . drink ruddy wine,"[105] they still come together time and time for communal meals. They imbibe a special drink, nectar, and consume a special dish, ambrosia. The divine nymph Calypso receives such nectar and ambrosia; Odysseus, who shares her bed, in contrast, "food and drink, of such sort as mortal men eat."[106] Some gods also partake of earthly fare: Dionysus drinks wine, while Kore, daughter of Demeter, falls under Hades' sway for the love of a pomegranate; the results of both are less godly than they are disastrous. All gods savor the aroma of roast meat offered up to them by humans. In the "Iliad," the notion of the family of the gods holding communal meals without conventional food as with mortals is frequently evoked ("The gods of Homer are an aristocratic society which happens to be immortal"[107]). A comparable ambivalence also characterizes other points of divine notions within Homer; they are immortal and yet still vulnerable. Accordingly, it is described in the "Iliad" during the battle of Troy in which gods fought on both sides with the aid of their divine bodies, the mortal hero Diomedes, guided by Athena, wounds the dainty skin of Aphrodite with a spear, as a result of which her vital fluids (ἰχώρ) leak out:

> And out flowed the immortal blood of the goddess,
> The ichor such as flows in the blessed gods;
> For they eat not bread nor do they drink ruddy wine,
> And so they are bloodless and are called immortals.[108]

Olympian gods have bodies; they beget and give birth—at least some of them according to Homer and Hesiod. Their bodies are admittedly particularly beautiful, as is said in the Homeric Demeter Hymn of the goddess in question:

With these words the goddess changed her form and stature,
Thrusting old age away; beauty wafted all about her,
A lovely fragrance spread from her scented dress
And a radiance shone afar from her immortal body;
Flaxen locks bestrewed her shoulders,
and the sturdy house was filled with a brilliance as of
    lightening
as she went out through the hall . . .[109]

While human bodies exist within strict confines, the divine powers
can somewhat lift these limitations and imbue these bodies with forti-
tude (ἀκλή) or power (κράτος), but naturally also with terror (φόβος)
or romantic longing (ἔρως), so that the usual human limits imposed by
the body might be surpassed.[110] As is demonstrated by the Trojan War,
gods can also make themselves invisible: Athena silently steps behind
Achilles and pulls him by the hair in order to restrain him from an altercation with Agamemnon, "allowing herself to be seen by him alone, and
of the rest no one saw her."[111] Gods can also change their shape:[112] Aphrodite transforms into a geriatric maidservant in order to rescue Helen,
but Helen sees through this on grounds of the flashing eyes and sump-
tuous bosom of the individual before her.[113] The Judgment of Paris and
many other stories in Homer attest that the gods also occasionally present themselves to humans in their true forms—and that these are corporeal, indeed, corporeal enough, that mortals and gods can sleep with one
another to produce offspring. They are depicted with appropriate abandon both on vases and elsewhere within art. A few gods love human men
or women, and mortal children result from these trysts. Nevertheless,
it is always clear in what manner divine and mortal coils differ: Divine
bodies are larger than those of humans, and shapelier, more radiant, and
better smelling.[114]

Vernant vehemently rejects the notion conventionally conveyed by
the term "anthropomorphic" of the divine body as patterned after that
of humans: In the ancients' perception, the relationship is exactly the
reverse; the human body reflects the divine model in its spiritual and
bodily strength.[115] This is already made clear when Hesiod writes in his
"Theogony" that the gods existed prior to humanity as their archetypes. In
Pindar, the commonalities between gods and humans are also emphasized
alongside their closeness (ca. 465 BC):

There is one race of men, the other gods; but from one mother
We both draw our breath. Yet the allotment of a wholly
Different power separates us, for one race is nothing.[116]

These lines were often cited in Antiquity, even by Christian authors.[117] Only the philosophically well educated would have come to the idea of limiting this shared origin to the *soul* or at all to *immaterial* contexts. The Munich classical archaeologist Bert Kaeser recently remarked that "one might polemically say against the god-is-spirit philosophy (which began with Greek philosophy . . .) that the gods of the Greeks are pure bodies, or, better yet, pure persons who exist in an indivisible unity of body, soul, sense, mind, and will (or whatever else humans might be able to separate within themselves)."[118] Admittedly, this hardly pertains to a conventional human body upon which these decriptions might be modeled. For the Greeks, in turn, the corporeal rhetoric in their passages regarding God's body is patterned on a model of a "superbody."[119] Sociological and literary analyses of the figure of the "superhero" demonstrate regardless that, as in Antiquity, the description of such figures within contemporary literature follows certain conventions which seek to structure vast social groups by means of a *special* body which simultaneously always exhibits *general and quotidian* characteristics: In such a manner, particularities in appearance or behavior (in Antiquity certain godly attributes or typical characteristics, for example, of Zeus and Jupiter) are accentuated, so that the place of the "superhero" in question within the collective consciousness is easier assured. In their actions and influence, these figures are intimately socially engaged with those individuals with whom they have contact; for example, Zeus is the "father of gods and men."[120]

Depictions of God in Synagogues

Despite the prohibition of graven images standardized within biblical Scripture and theological texts, neither Jewish nor Christian iconography were ever able to relinquish such conventions of depicting God in corporeal form:[121] A particularly telling example might be evidenced in depictions from Imperial-era Jewish synagogues which an uninitiated visitor might have taken to be representations of God's body. This does not apply to the well-known depictions of the sun at the center of the zodiac as might, for example, be found in the late antique synagogues at Na'aran, Beth-Alpha or Hammat-Tiberias, Isfiya, Khirbet Susiya, Japhia, and En Gedi in the Holy Land.[122] These are related to the conventional antique pagan iconography of the sun;[123] to suggest that this might be a depiction of the Jewish god would run counter to the norms of orthodox conceptions of God within this religion. Far more pertinent, by contrast, is the central register of the wall paintings of the *synagogue* in Syrian *Dura Europos*, on the present-day Syrian-Iraqi border, above a Torah niche embellished with columns.[124] The synagogue was erected in 244/245 BC on top of the remains of a prior construction. Separated from the western wall only by a small alleyway, it lay by the Palmyrene Gate, only two housing blocks away from the famous Christian house church. The frescoes on plaster, discovered in 1932 and now housed in the National Museum at Damascus, were so exemplarily preserved because they became part of a glacis in the mid-third century intended to protect the city wall from undermining by Persian siege troops, and hence were protected by glacis' layers of earth until they were excavated. These defensive precautions were nevertheless in vain; the city fell in 256 AD to its besiegers; it was destroyed and never resettled.

In the center of the rectangular meeting room could be found a Torah shrine and a so-called Moses cathedra on a raised place. The Torah niche projecting out of the wall as an aedicule belongs to the first phase of the painting of the space. Above the niche enclosed by a white mussel shell, stylized in golden paint on a now-faded blue background, the entrance to the Herodian temple in Jerusalem is visible. On the left-hand side of the temple façade appear a menorah, lulav, and etrog and, on the right, a scene of the Sacrifice of Isaac (Genesis 22:12). Within this scene may be found a stone altar, upon which Isaac lies with flung out feet; over this may be seen the hand of God protruding into the scene.[125] In the background stands a tent. "The hand is curved inwards, the fingers hardly open. This gesture of the half-opened, downward-pointing h(and) expresses an aloof pleni-tude of power, as is characteristic for the image of the Rom(an) ruler since Augustus";[126] this recurs within four other scenes within the synagogue of Dura Europos and must have been a representational device already common for some time.[127]

Atop the aedicule is the central field of the western wall. Unfortu-nately, the appearance of the field above the Torah niche (described in academic literature as a "reredos") immediately after it was unearthed can only be understood with difficulty; in securing the discovery before its transportation from Dura Europos to Damascus, a conservator had doubt-less already undertaken some rudimentary reconstruction work upon it.[128] It is at least certain that this middle field had been overpainted twice in ten years, and (at least in its restored state) comes across as rather unprepos-sessing. This frequent and seemingly amateurish overpainting yielded a strange result: Ultimately, visitors could probably hardly have recognized anything, seeing instead a continuous red-painted expanse from which rather more schematic individual depictions emerge. In this sense, the middle field differs from the synagogue's remaining wall paintings, from the clearly contoured illustrations of which it was (and is) easy to divine what the artists had intended to depict. It might be cautiously be deduced from this find that it was evidently more important to those responsible

Fig. 3.4   Dura Europos, Synagogue (AD 244/245)
Central field of the western wall with aedicule, Damascus, National Museum

within the community that certain depictions were swiftly removed and others inserted than that the results were aesthetically pleasing. It also cannot entirely be excluded that the overpainted and now only vaguely recognizable fields above the aedicule were concealed along with the Torah shrine by means of a mechanism for a curtain or similar, and thus may intermittently even no longer have been visible. Perhaps (and, indeed, this interpretation can hardly be ruled out) the depictions in the central register were consciously kept vague and imprecise.

In order to understand this discovery (today in Damascus) the likely genesis of the painting of the central register above the aedicule must be reconstructed.

The large field above the niche probably originally displayed a foliate bush in the manner of a grapevine (without grapes) extending over both registers not yet divided by a decorative band. In the *second phase*, two figures in Persian robes and a lion were painted within this bush.

In a *second phase* within the lower part of the scene, a lyre-playing figure clad in Persian dress following the conventional iconography of Orpheus was painted on the left side.[129] In the upper part (probably at the same time) appeared the enthroned figure of a ruler also apparelled in Persian style, the head of whom had sadly already been lost in 1932. Two further figures were inserted before the throne, and under it the aforementioned lion. It was first in a *third phase* that both parts were separated into two scenes by means of a decorative band, and the bush disappeared as far as was possible, as the enthroned figure was surrounded by eleven further figures also dressed in the Persian manner.

The majority of those who have interpreted this discovery since its excavation construe both the figure seated to the left with a lyre and the enthroned form as depictions of a Davidic Messiah.[130] The question as to why not only a lyre-plucking David as is known from diverse Jewish synagogue mosaics (as, for example, in Jerusalem or Gaza[131]) is depicted, but also a further enthroned figure is, on the contrary, varyingly answered. Kurt Weitzmann and Peter Schäfer have interpreted the second, enthroned figure as an "antithesis of the Christian portrayal of Jesus as king and messiah in the apses of Christian churches."[132] Following Goldstein, they take the two assistants flanking the throne of the elevated messiah-king to be Moses and Elijah.[133] By contrast, the David strumming the lyre is in accordance with conventional messianic iconography within late antique synagogues.

This interpretation of the two figures in Persian garb from the overpainting of the second phase of the image above the Torah shrine as a double portrait of the Davidic messiah-king could, in fact, have once been the intended meaning of its commissioners within the synagogue's community

Fig. 3.5 Dura Europos, Synagogue (AD 244/245)
*Central field of the western wall ("reredos"), draw-
ing of the first two phases*[134]

Fig. 3.6   Dura Europos, Synagogue (AD 244/245)
Central upper field of the western wall, third and final phase[135]

of Dura Europos. Nevertheless, many questions remain open, the most
striking of these being why such a large thorn bush was to be found over
the Torah shrine (ultimately, there are no indications that the burning bush
was once intended thereby), why it was partially overpainted with hardly
completely satisfactory results in such a short space of time,[136] and why
the Davidic messiah needed to be painted twice at all. The question could
also be posed as to how many of those who beheld the western wall of the
synagogue simply interpreted the hand in the Torah niche's superstructure
as a corporeal depiction of the Jewish god. Certainly, it cannot be excluded
that the enthroned figure might occasionally have been understood as a
corporeal depiction of the Jewish god, particularly after it received a privy
council of sorts in a further overpainting.

Early Christianity also depicts God the Father very seldom.[137] Nevertheless, as with the synagogue at Dura Europos, particular corporeal
details such as the hand of God were certainly portrayed.[138] Jewish synagogues and Christian houses of God characteristically differed from pagan
temples inasmuch as sacrifices were not made, and religious images were
not to be found within these spaces. Yet, the example of the synagogue
of Dura Europos demonstrates, much like the apse decorations of many
Christian churches in Antiquity, that a representation of an enthroned person could be realized right at the center of the installation (as in the Temple
of Zeus at Olympia). The question as to whether the fine distinction that
this enthroned figure did not depict the god himself but rather his messiah

or his Christ was really so firmly rooted in the collective consciousness of its visitors, as is usually thought, can quite rightly be doubted. Ultimately, remaining with the example of the Syrian border garrison city of Dura Europos, it might be recalled that only two housing blocks, or roughly a hundred meters, separated the Christian and Jewish houses of God from one another. Moreover, a jaunt from the synagogue to the mithraeum was but a matter of a few meters more; it lay four blocks away.[139] Put in other words: None of these buildings stood isolated; they were all part of a multi-religious environment, and must be interpreted accordingly.

4

The Bodies of Gods and the Bodies of Souls in Late Antiquity

At first glance, it would seem as if, within the *ordinary piety* of Imperial-era Antiquity, divine bodies were just as implicitly venerated as they were present in the majority of temples, while *learned reflection* rather emphasized the difference between the material corporealities of the statues and the gods' form of existence or, indeed, roundly rejected each and any corporeality on the part of the gods.[1] A second round of scrutiny demonstrates that this neat perspective of a quotidian piety of the masses and a reflective religiosity on the part of the intelligentsia modeled upon the classical dual only applies in a restricted sense: *Apuleius of Madaurus*, a contemporary of Marcus Aurelius in the second century AD, described cult images as "breathing likenesses"[2] despite being convinced as a Middle Platonist that God is to be thought of as incorporeal.[3] *Lucian of Samosata*, who lived at the same time, reported that divine images in Syrian Hieropolis/Mabbug changed their form, nodded to one or another devotee, sweated, and moved themselves, all without any contentual or literary act of distancing himself therefrom.[4] In his satire "The Passing of Peregrinus" and his text "Alexander the False Prophet," Lucian delighted in exposing religious charlatans, simultaneously parodying the role of the religious enlightener.[5] Apuleius is (like Cicero) testament to the fact that individuals of strictly Platonic or even moderately Skeptical worldviews[6] could nevertheless comprehend religious acts in tension with their own theoretical assumptions on the corporeality of the gods. Lucian demonstrates, in turn, that such individuals were also prepared to give credence to accounts of dimensions of divine corporeality which, in light of their theoretical principles, they should really have judged as the stuff of fables.

An approach to the realities of Antiquity shaped by neat duals must also be avoided in respect to philosophical reflection. Here, it might seem on first inspection that the Platonist tradition opts to be strictly *against* the supposition of a divine body, while Stoicism is rather *for* this. Yet, it might be recognized in the "Olympian Discourse" of the rhetorician *Dio Chrysostom*, who lived a generation before Apuleius and Lucian at the turn of the first to second centuries AD and whose thought was rather more colored by Stoic philosophy, that thinkers of this orientation did not always thoroughly emphasize the basal materiality of all being where (as with the example of Pheidias' cult image at Olympia) appearance "appropriate to a god and . . . a form worthy of the divine nature" is concerned.[7] Astoundingly, divine bodies might even be discussed within the remits of Platonic philosophy. How a religiously mundane notion of an implicit divine corporeality gained ground within Platonic philosophy (and thus within the Christian theology of Late Antiquity) should be outlined in what follows, initially with regard to certain debates within Platonic, and, in particular, Neoplatonic philosophy, and then concerning an apparently highly specific controversy on the corporeality of the soul within Christian theology in late antique Gaul.

Platonism

Plato thought of his supreme deity as bodiless. Regardless of all manners of controversy in interpretation of details within the Platonic theory of principles and anthropology, nobody in Imperial-era Antiquity questioned that, according to Plato, the supreme god, the "One" (τὸ ἕν), is characterized by unity, goodness, immutability, and completeness, and must be envisioned *incorporeally* as pure spirit (νοῦς). The doxographic tradition of philosophical and historical philosophical textbooks and handbooks ascribed to Plato without further comment the view that he deemed God bodiless (ἀσώματος), although, as has been discussed, the Athenian philosopher never did such a thing *expressis verbis*, but rather his student Aristotle. Regardless, if the Platonic doctrine on God is scrutinized more closely, it becomes apparent that the teaching of a strict incorporeality of God only applies to the *supreme* principle, or the supreme and first god. Following the *Timaeus*, there is a "heavenly kind of gods" formed by the demiurge "for the most part out of fire" (τὴν πλείστην ἰδέαν ἐκ πυρός) in addition to the supreme god.[8] These subaltern gods possess thereby bodies of the same light, fiery matter as is also supposed for the gods within Stoicism. Planets and other celestial bodies also belong to this category of "living" heavenly bodies fashioned by the demiurge, and are hence divine beings equally possessing a certain corporeality.[9] In the *Phaedrus*, Plato notes that God is to be imagined as "an immortal being which has both a soul and a body."[10] It might be summarized (if somewhat simplistically) that the incorporeal god is the exception among the corporeal gods. Dirk Baltzly phases this accordingly: "One striking thing about both the latter gods—i.e., cosmic god and planetary gods—is that they are gods with *bodies*."[11] By means of a rather wayward reading of the *Timaeus*, the pseudo-Platonic *Epinomis* (a protreptic dialogue probably composed by Plato's student Philip of Opus) introduces "demons" (δαίμονες) with bodies composed of air as intermediate beings.[12]

In Imperial-era Platonism—should the "Handbook of Platonism" compiled by one Alcinous be taken to be representative—the bodilessness of the utmost god would appear at first to be markedly more emphasized than the corporeality of the created gods. As previously demonstrated, the section on the first god within the "Handbook" closes with a series of arguments as to why "God must be incorporeal."[13] Yet, the particular fiery corporeality of the seven planets, which are not designated *expressis verbis* as gods, is only very briefly alluded to in connection to the creation of the spheres and planetary orbits: "God fashioned seven visible bodies, mainly composed of fire."[14] Alcinous follows Plato's *Timaeus* at this point; nevertheless, he asserts in later passages that the bodies of the planetary gods are composed of ether. This contradiction may best be explained by inferring that an ethereal fiery matter in the Stoic tradition is here assumed.[15] The demons (here, Alcinous follows the interpretation of the *Timaeus* justified by the pseudo-Platonic *Epinomis*[16]) are also composed of ether and populate the air. According to Alcinous, the supreme "God is in fact Himself the creator of the universe, and of the gods and daemons," which are here understood as (corporeal) intermediate beings between gods and humans.[17]

Within Classical and Imperial-era Platonism, the soul did not yet number among these divine, heavenly beings possessing a body before terrestrial embodiment. As with the qualities and the supreme god, it counts as bodiless. This only changes with the second and third generations of Neoplatonic thinkers in the third and fourth centuries AD. The philosopher *Porphyry*, Plotinus' greatest student (ca. AD 233–305) taught, for example, that the world-soul also has a luminous body of the same fine and simple substance as the remaining celestial bodies.[18] How might this fundamental shift in the image of the soul have come about, with its transmigration of sorts from the realm of an incorporeal god to that of the many corporeal gods?

The Debate over the Body of the Soul in Christian Theology

The decisive change in Platonic teachings on the soul found in the late Neoplatonists is more easily understood when examined as to how it was received by late antique Christian theologians, as the question of whether a heavenly *spiritual body* existed had intensively preoccupied some of these theologians: In the midst of an extremely politically friable and turbulent period at the end of the fifth century AD in the south of Gaul, a spirited debate on the corporeality of the soul took place within the triangle of Clermont-Ferrand, Riez, and Vienne, accompanied by conflict with the Visigoths whose status as *foederati* had hardly placated them. At first glance, this would admittedly seem to have little to do with the question of God's corporeality.

Embroiled in this debate were *Claudianus Mamertus*, who wrote a book against the notion of a corporeal soul, *Faustus of Riez*, who had propounded said views, and *Sidonius Apollinaris*, to whom Claudianus dedicated his book. All three individuals involved in this dispute belonged to the Roman elite of Gaul which struggled in the face of Germanic peoples (most prominently the Visigoths) to maintain Roman order during the political turmoil of the age, ultimately failing.[19] Claudianus Mamertus was a Gallic philosopher and presbyter in Vienne in the last third of the fifth century AD who belonged to the extended circle of friends and acquaintances of Sidonius Apollinaris, who was bishop of Clermont at the time.[20] Clermont was conceded along with the Auvergne to the Visigoths in the peace treaty of AD 475. Bishop Sidonius initially attempted to refrain from entering the debate over the corporeality of the soul, but this was ultimately futile—much spoke for his restraint, not least the close relationship of Sidonius Apollinaris to both combatants: Faustus had baptized him, Claudianus Mamertus theologically educated him.[21]

Of the evidently multitudinous rhetorical, philosophical, theological, and church musical works by Claudianus Mamertus, only one single text is presently preserved, "On the Nature of the Soul" (*De statu animae*),[22] which comprises almost two hundred pages in its 1885 critical edition (urgently in need of revision).[23] In his letters, Sidonius repeatedly praised the work "On the Soul," initially from Clermont, where, formerly a city prefect, he had just become bishop. This fresh incumbent thanked Claudianus Mamertus for the dedication which he had received (*praefectorio patricio doctissimo et optimo uiro Sollio Sidonio*[24]), stating that this was an inestimable gift (*munus potissimum*), priceless in its richness of knowledge and style. In this context, Bishop Sidonius exuberantly praises the author, his epistolary correspondent, Claudianus Mamertus:[25]

> Lastly, no one in my age has shown the ability of my friend to establish points which he wished to prove. . . . He makes judgements like Pythagoras, distinguishes like Socrates, unfolds like Plato, and enfolds like Aristotle; he cajoles like Aeschines and storms like Demosthenes, luxuriates like Hortensius, and seethes like Cethegus; incites like Curio, holds

back like Fabius, simulates like Crassus and dissimulates like Caesar, advises like Cato, dissuades like Appius, and persuades like Cicero. If we now turn to the hallowed Fathers for purposes of comparison, he is instructive like Jerome, destructive like Lactantius, constructive like Augustine; he exalts his tone like Hilary and subdues it like John (Chrysostom); he rebukes like Basil and comforts like Gregory (Nazianzen); he is diffuse like Orosius and compressed like Rufinus; he narrates like Eusebius, urges like Eucherius, challenges like Paulinus (of Nola) and perseveres like Ambrose.[26]

It is something of a point of delicacy, however, that the much-trumpeted Claudianus Mamertus had previously (albeit politely) rebuked Bishop Sidonius for not passing comment on the tome dedicated to him (and, indeed, likely also commissioned by him):[27]

> Another grievance, which I shall likewise ruefully refrain from airing, is that you have never favoured with a word of acknowledgement those little books, to which you graciously lend the lustre of your name. But it may be that you cannot spare a few moments for the claims of a very great friendship.[28]

Sidonius' topically exaggerated reaction can nevertheless hardly be dismissed as being born of sheer courtesy or purely a gesture of apology in light of events, as similar accolades may be found in another, admittedly abbreviated letter from AD 471 to a certain Nymphidius.[29] Jill Harries has explained the delay in the answer of Sidonius Apollinaris as being as a result of a jarring realization that his revered theological teacher Claudianus Mamertus and Faustus of Riez, the bishop who had baptized him, were at odds. He would hence have initially elected to demure.[30] It is certainly conspicuous that Sidonius does not adopt a theological position within his letters but rather extols primarily the literary style of his teacher's work. This may well not only be the result of the genre of such letters, but potentially also, as Harries proposes, of a reluctance on his part to involve himself, or to declare for, Claudianus' position. Regardless, there was scarce little time for the protagonists to argue in depth; Claudianus Mamertus died relatively soon after the completion of his tractate and the correspondence with his student. Only a little later, in AD 473, Sidonius was compelled to write a letter of condolence to a certain Petreius and lauds once more Claudianus Mamertus, Petreius' uncle:

> He was a man both provident and prudent, learned, eloquent, ardent, the most talented among men of his time, his country, and of his people, and

one who ceaselessly devoted himself to philosophy without detriment to religion—indeed, although he did not let his hair and beard grow long, and although he sometimes ridiculed, sometimes even execrated the philosopher's cloak and cudgel, it was only in is dress and in his religion that he parted company with the Platonic brotherhood.[31]

Indeed, Sidonius appended moreover a *carmen* to his letter, wherein he characterizes the deceased as follows:

Under his teaching three literatures were illumined,
Latin, Greek, and Christian:
All of them as a monk in his prime
He absorbed in his unobtrusive studies.
He was prose-writer, philosopher, poet, preacher, geometer,
    and musician.[32]

It might be learned from the letter that Claudianus was a monk in his earlier years and had worked for the church administered by his brother in Vienne as a pastor and preacher, but also belonged to a club of Platonic philosophers.[33] Additional information on Claudianus may be found in the catalog of writers *De uiris illustribus*, by his contemporary Gennadius of Marseille: *uir ad loquendum artifex et ad disputandum subtilis* is how Gennadius terms the presbyter Claudianus, further describing precisely the points of his argumentation in *De statu animae*: In the text, it is considered as to what extent anything other than God is incorporeal.[34] Put otherwise: It handles whether incorporeality is solely a divine predicate or may also be applied to other things.

Claudianus Mamertus was motivated to compose the text of "On the Nature of the Soul" (*De statu animae*) by a lengthy, anonymously circulated letter generally dated to AD 468.[35] This letter may only be found completely intact within a St. Gallen codex from the ninth century AD along with the letters of Bishop Faustus of Riez (captioned *incipit epistula s[an]c[t]i Fausti*), but may also be encountered in a mutilated state in transmitted manuscripts of Claudianus Mamertus, and, finally, in citations from Claudianus' aforementioned text.[36] Claudianus presented this *opusculum* without naming the author;[37] on grounds of the transmission it may likely be ascribed to Faustus. His probable authorship is further evidenced by Gennadius, who catalogs this letter among the works of Faustus as a "little tome" (*paruum libellum*), and quite rightly interprets it as an anti-Arian text.[38] This text is less of a real letter and more of an extended tractate, and begins with the words *Quaeris a me, reuerentissime*[39] *sacerdotum*, meaning that it had been addressed to an individual

priest.[40] The tractate treats three questions posed by Arians—the supporters of Homoean imperial theology in southern Gaul were described with
this term, which, in comparison to mainstream Christian Nicaean and
Neo-Nicaean Trinitary theology of the imperial councils at Nicaea (325)
and Constantinople (381), subordinated the Christ to God the Father;[41] in
reality it must have referred to members of Visigothic tribes. The third of
these "Arian" questions which the anonymous priest evidently conveyed
to Faustus the author relates as to how "corporeal and incorporeal things
are to be considered by humans."[42] Faustus intends to answer this question in his tractate by means of recourse to the opinions of the Church
Fathers. The bishop of Riez quite naturally proceeds from the assumption
that all creations are fashioned *corporeally*—and thereby also the entire
individual, body *and* soul. On this basis, he argues in the form of a *reduc-
tio ad absurdam* against Visigothic Homoean theology: If all creations
are corporeal, then the "Arian" Christians must, according to Faustus,
also take Christ, whom they held to be a creation (if, indeed, complete),[43]
to be corporeal in his heavenly existence *before* the incarnation. Such a
heavenly corporeality of Jesus Christ before the adoption of an earthly
body by means of Mary would be a grave logical contradiction; its logical exclusion would hardly have only been self-evident to Faustus. Thus,
working from the premise that all created things were fashioned corporeally, the bishop of Riez disproved the description of Jesus Christ as a
creation according to "the Arians."

   In the ensuing line of argumentation within his tractate, Faustus
admittedly problematizes this premise of his argument, and busies himself with the question as to whether *all* created things were truly fashioned
corporeally, or as to whether rather the invisible created things (such as
angels or souls) are *in*corporeal beings. If, in fact, the latter might apply
(and not the former), then the argument against the "Arians" would also be
refuted: Should *bodiless* divine creations exist, then it would also be possible to imagine that, as an originally bodiless complete creation existing in
heaven, Jesus Christ then assumed a body through Mary in the incarnation.
From this, the bishop of Riez steers his tractate towards the fundamental
question as to how incorporeality relates to invisibility, and, as promised,
employs thereby texts from the Church Fathers: Some of the most learned
Fathers would have affirmed that there is a distinction between incorporeal and invisible things: "Not a few of the most learned Fathers hold that
the invisible things are one, the incorporeal things another."[44] Faustus
nevertheless does not name the Fathers who adhered to exactly this; this
would hardly have been a simple matter. For example, roughly 250 years
before, the Alexandrian Christian scholar Origen explicitly challenged as to
whether such a difference between invisible and incorporeal things might

really exist: In the interpretation of the pair of opposites of *uisibilia* and *inuisibilia* from Colossians, he maintained rather that the Greeks would speak of an "incorporeal" substance (ἀσώματος/*incorporeus*), the biblical Scriptures, in comparison, of an "invisible."[45] "Invisible" and "incorporeal" are for him thus different appellations for the same thing. Those beings invisible and immaterial would irrespectively occasionally employ bodies[46] because no created nature can exist without a material substrate, and insofar from the Trinity alone they must be considered to be entirely incorporeal: *ex toto incorporea est.*[47] Such a differentiation between corporeal existence and the use of a body through incorporeal existences as may, for example, be found in Origen, is rejected by Faustus of Riez on grounds of his strict monotheism: All that is created is matter and hence visible, is corporeal, and is encompassed by the creator. The nature of souls and the angels is thus also corporeal as they would have beginnings and limitations.[48] Faustus substantiates this position of a constant corporeality of creations with a quotation from the Fathers: Jerome terms the stars *corporatos . . . spiritus*, "spirits furnished with bodies," and the angels *caelestia corpora*—two positions which incidentally stand very much in the tradition of Origen.[49] With a further literal citation[50] from the "Conferences with the Fathers" of *John Cassian* (ca. AD 360–435), whom he may well have met during his sojourn on the monastic isle of Lerina/Saint-Honorat (near Cannes), Faustus declares (albeit does not himself prove within the text) that angels, archangels, and other powers, including human souls and fine air (*subtilis aer*), are spiritual natures (*spiritales naturae*) which by no means may be understood as incorporeal:

> They have a body appropriate to themselves by which they subsist, although it is far more refined (*tenuis*) than our own bodies. In the words of the Apostle: "There are heavenly and earthly bodies" (1 Corinthians 15:40). . . . From this it is clear that nothing is incorporeal but God alone, and therefore only to him can every spiritual and intellectual substance be penetrable.[51]

For Faustus of Riez, God *alone* is incorporeal, and not the angels, nor the remaining powers, nor even the soul: "Nothing is incorporeal but God alone."[52] As, according to Faustus, the "Arians" (ultimately, as has been seen, Visigothic Homoeans) dispute that spatiality, quality, and quantity might be pronounced for the soul, the bishop wishes to demonstrate to them the spatiality and quantity of the soul; for him, these two lines of argumentation are sufficient to compel his opponents to recant.[53]

If, however, for Faustus, the quantity of the soul and its spatiality are so closely connected, then he must have been aware that an extensive contemporary philosophical discussion existed as to the relationship between body and place. Traces of this discourse may be found in the commentary on Aristotle's "Physics" by the pagan Neoplatonist philosopher *Simplicius* (ca. AD 490–560). This focuses upon the question as to whether the location of the body always subsides with the body (the Stoic position) or as to whether it possessed an independent ontological status (the Neoplatonic perspective). Simplicius relates the controversy in the Neoplatonist Iamblichus' own words, also referring to a Neopythagorean tractate probably of the first century, which was incorrectly attributed to the Pythagorean Archytas:[54]

> And he says that if, as the Stoics say, place subsists (merely) as an append-age (παυφίσταται) to bodies, then its will also adopt its definition from them, to the extent that it is completed by the bodies (sc. on which it depends). If, on the other hand, place has being (οὐσία) per se, and no body can exist unless it exists in place—as Archytas seems to want to signify—then place itself defines bodies and delimits them in itself.[55]

Faustus evidently follows the Stoic opinion that location is implied by the body, should for him the *locality* of the soul follow from its *quantity*. He asks as to how the soul might not have a specific place when it is incorporated within limbs and "tied to the innards" (*et inligata uisceribus*), and when although it roams about the senses and is diffused within thoughts, it is confined to the body through the "conditions of its substance" (*conditione substantiae*).[56] For example, someone thinking of Peter and Paul does not automatically bodily encroach upon them in paradise, that is, the place which they now inhabit. Whosoever might spiritually permeate Alexandria and Jerusalem in a local sense must be able to render account as to the visages, motions, and behaviors of its inhabitants. Affects of the heart and thoughts of the soul alike can hardly constitute the substance of the soul, as their retention or loss do not impact upon this substance. Even the abandonment of the body by means of the soul at death is conceived by Faustus as local: The body is the residence (*habitaculum*) of the soul.[57] As is demonstrated by his take on the story of Lazarus, resurrection means the return of the soul to a particular space. The spatial form of the soul also presupposes a spatial division between heaven and hell. Yet, spatial form implies quantity, and quantity body.[58] This would apply to not only the soul but also angels and, moreover, the devil,[59] which might be considered to be a mixture of air and fire. God alone is bereft of body and place, as he is wont to permeate all substances (corporeal and incorporeal, immaterial, and intellectual); the soul is local, has quantities, and is thereby corporeal. Were this not to be the case, then it would rather be a part of God than a creation.[60] The application of this argumentation to the Son, Jesus Christ, ensues in a strangely brief manner at the end of the tractate: As the Son, Christ is just as eternal as the Father, and hence insofar incorporeal. A further theological problem of the tractate exists in the fact that while Faustus maintains the corporeality and thereby also the locality of the soul, at no point does he provide a concrete location for the soul.[61]

How did Faustus come to his conviction that the soul must be considered as corporeal? As will be seen, this stance had been held by certain theological and philosophical circles alike.

Tertullian: "On the Soul"

This position had been adopted by quite a number of Christian theologians prior to Faustus: *Tertullian* was the first Latin theologian who advocated for the corporeality of the soul, and probably coined the relevant term "corporeality" (*corporalitas*).[62] In his work "On the Soul" (*De anima*), dated to between AD 210 and 213, the author summarizes more extended remarks on the soul with the following definition:

> The soul, therefore, we declare to be born of the breath of God, immortal, corporeal, possessed of a definite form, simple in substance, conscious of itself, developing in various ways, free in its choices, liable to accidental change, variable in disposition, rational, supreme, gifted with foresight, developed out of the one original soul.[63]

In "On the Soul" Tertullian relates at length various conceptions of the corporeality of the soul, before he declares for the Stoic conception, wherein the soul is to be understood as *pneuma* ($\pi\nu\varepsilon\hat{\upsilon}\mu\alpha$ or *spiritus*)[64] in respect to its materiality. This stance could easily be connected with biblical terminology: In the first book of the Bible according to its early Latin translation, God breathed into man "the spirit of life" (*flatum vitae*), whereupon it "became a living soul" (*et factus est homo in animam viventem*).[65] It is already here apparent that "corporeality" for Tertullian is not any material corporeality of fire, water, blood, atoms, or a fifth element (Aristotle's *quinta essentia*), but rather a pneumatic substance.[66] In other passages, the North African theologian maintained that the soul must then also be corporeal, "possessing that which is invisible: . . . If it does possess something by which it exists, this must be its body. Everything that exists is body of some kind or another."[67] In other words: as with everything, corporeality is fashioned in its own particular, individual manner (*sui generis*), and thus also the soul. While human bodies are distinguished by a corporeality which is visible, the corporeality of the soul is invisible to anyone but God on grounds of its fine materiality. In contrast to classic Stoic philosophy, such a corporeality *sui generis* is also maintained for God; as has been seen, he differentiates between the corporeality of God, the corporeality of souls, and the corporeality of the cosmos.[68]

In his commentary to the Gospel of Matthew, probably composed in the mid-fourth century AD, *Hilary of Poitiers* thought in the same vein as Tertullian, albeit without the same grounding in philosophical discourse: "For all kinds of souls, whether they possess bodies or are departing from them, possess a corporeal substance according to their nature because everything that is created must be within something (sc. corporeal)."[69] God and soul may insofar be compared, as Hilary writes in his commentary to the Psalms:

> Nothing is void of God, nothing without him. He is everywhere like the soul in the body, which is present in all parts. While it has in the whole body its own and royal seat, it permeates even the marrow, fingers, and limbs.[70]

Arnobius the Younger, a monk hailing from North Africa and resident in Rome between AD 428/432 and 455, further emphasized the corporeality of the soul in a debate with a miaphysite named Serapion shortly before the Council of Chalcedon in 451. Arnobius attempts in this text to prove that "soul and spirit and angels are corporeal":[71] "All that possesses dimensions is body . . . God alone is incorporeal and immensurable."[72] Evidence for this stance is proffered by the fact that the soul can be touched and touches, is furthermore contained within a certain space (namely the body), resides therein, and may abandon this once more (in death).[73] Views such as these were evidently widely held within Gallic monasticism; this is phrased accordingly in the *Liber sine diffinitio ecclesiasticorum dogmatum* of (Pseudo-?)Gennadius of Marseille, composed around AD 470, and thereby at approximately the same time as Faustus of Riez's tractate:

> One may not believe in any incorporeal and invisible natures save God alone, meaning the Father, Son, and Holy Spirit, who is held to be incorporeal, as he, wherever he might be, both fills and binds all. Thus, he is for all creations as invisible as he is incorporeal. All of creation is corporeal and all heavenly forces are composed of bodies, naturally not through flesh. Thus, however, we believe that intellectual natures are corporeal as they are spatially circumscribed, as with the human soul which is enclosed in flesh, and the demons who are of the nature of angels on the basis of their substance.[74]

There was hence a tradition within Latin Christian theology wherefrom Faustus may have gained his conviction that the soul is to be thought of as corporeal. *On the other hand*, Faustus may well also have come to this conclusion due to his own passing acquaintance with philosophy, this position also being held by certain philosophical circles.

Within his extensive 1959 study, Ernest L. Fortin, a Boston Assumptionist father, described the text of Faustus as *Stoic* at its core, albeit with an argumentation markedly less subtle in comparison to Tertullian, but, in turn, far more practical, focused upon the Bible and everyday experience.[75] In contrast, Martin Schulze pronounced in 1883 that Faustus' text was devoid of "almost all philosophical content" and was "merely an assortment of citations from the Fathers, scriptural evidence, and original ideas drawn not from philosophical thought, but rather vulgar modes of thought and belief."[76] Yet, the consistency with which the sentence "God alone is incorporeal" is justified within the text does speak for a certain intellectual vigor and philosophical education: Indeed, the sentence with which Faustus concludes his argument reads, "A single incorporeal God," *unus deus incorporeus*.[77] Faustus even held the notion of an incorporeal soul to be diabolical as it removes the categorical distinction between an incorporeal God and a corporeal humanity, leading to fundamentally absurd positions within both Christology and eschatology.[78]

Hence, it is hardly as simple as it would seem to evaluate the argumentation presented by Faustus as less subtle, but far more practical, and focused upon the Bible and everyday experience. Tracing this back unilinearly to Stoic thought is also not the straightforward business envisioned by Fortin. This impression is swiftly garnered when the second- and third-generation Neoplatonists are taken into account.

The "Astral Bodies" of Souls: The Neoplatonists

It was taught by these (Neo)Platonists that, in its descent from the Milky Way through the spheres, the soul gathered particles which clad it in layers with a *body*. This body was not considered to be entirely immaterial, but it was also not accepted that it was composed of terrestrial matter. It was, hence, a special heavenly body of the soul to be distinguished from the terrestrial one which the soul embodied, as it were, at the end of its process of descent.[79] In the opinion of Porphyry, the pneumatic soul (*anima spiritalis*) somewhat darkened during its descent, becoming thereby materialized and visible.[80] These invisible, immaterial celestial bodies were described with metaphors such as "boat,"[81] "vehicle," or "wagon" (ὄχημα), but also "spiritual pneuma" or "pneumatic soul."[82] It is interesting in respect to the present context that Neoplatonists such as

Proclus conventionally discussed a celestial and insofar "eternal body" of the soul (ἀΐδιον σῶμα).[83]

At first glance, this discourse on an eternal heavenly body of the soul astonishes, as Plato never designated the soul as a "body" or accorded it one:[84] For him, the spiritual and corporeal spheres would have been far too removed from one another; indeed, they stand in many respects in mutual opposition. Middle Platonists such as Apuleius also emphasized that the soul is *not* corporeal.[85] Nevertheless, as a passage from Galen demonstrates, notions of a celestial body of the soul must already have existed in the philosophical discourse of the Imperial era: This doctor and philosopher was evidently uncertain as to whether the soul might possess a "lustrous and ethereal body" (αὐγοειδὲς καὶ αἰθερῶδες σῶμα) or an "incorporeal substance" (ἀσώματος οὐσία); Galen ascribed the former position to Aristotle and the Stoics.[86] It was only in later Neoplatonism that mention of a "heavenly body" of the soul was all but implicit, no longer posing any difficulties.

The onset of this may be dated with marked precision: In the third century AD, *Porphyry* still very pointedly defined the soul as bodiless (ἀσώματος οὐσία);[87] following Heinrich Dörrie, the term "bodiless" (ἀσώματος) must be "understood as *the* expression which described the potent transcendent in its fullest."[88] *Iamblichus of Chalkis* (ca. AD 240/245–320/325), also breaking with his erstwhile teacher Porphyry on this point, reported to the contrary quite unreservedly (in an account of positions of earlier Platonists on the descent of the soul into the material world) on the view of the Hellenistic thinker *Eratostrathenes* (of Cyrene?) and the Imperial-era Platonist *Ptolemy* that the soul is "always to be found in a body." Nevertheless, the "fine material" of the celestial body (λεπτότερα)[89] differed from the mortal coil into which the soul would descend. According to Iamblichus, this body was not composed of a mixture, but rather was itself made of aether (παντὸς τοῦ αἰθέρος).[90] Iamblichus can also discuss unreservedly "divine bodies" (meaning *heavenly* bodies such as the sun, moon, and five planets), the influence of which upon the "materialization" of the body of the soul during its descent he irrespectively seeks rigorously to minimize.[91]

This usage is followed by practically all of the presently known late antique Neoplatonists, evidently without regarding the classical Platonic dual of body and soul as a philosophical or (at the very least) terminological problem thereby. *Macrobius*, a contemporary of Augustine of Hippo, ascribes the soul an "astral body" (*sidereum corpus*),[92] and indeed a "luminous body" (*luminosum corpus*).[93] In the fifth century AD, *Proclus* mentions as if it were quite self-evident an "astral body" (ἀστροειδὲς σῶμα) of the soul, the form of which is spherical.[94] According to *Hermias of*

Alexandria, who also lived in the fifth century AD, this spherical body (reflecting thereby the ideal form of the human body) is nevertheless not fashioned in three dimensions (τριχῇ διαστατόν), but rather two (ἐπίπεδον).⁹⁵ For Olympiodorus, active around a generation later, the body of the soul is composed of the fifth element, and is thus eternal and lustrous.⁹⁶

Naturally, despite such shared fundamental views on the corporeality of the celestial soul, various debates existed within philosophical discussions of a Neoplatonic bent, for example, as to the temporality of this body of the soul, and occasionally also on the possible *complete* bodilessness of the soul,⁹⁷ or the question as to whether different types of such heavenly bodies might be reckoned with for different types of souls. These debates as to the specific constitution of the celestial bodies, often drawn out with much vehemence, need not here be further explored. It is rather striking how united the Neoplatonists were besides such controversies as to the *material* constitution of this heavenly body of the soul. *Galen*, as has been seen, entertained the notion of its material being radiance and aether (αὐγή and αἰθέρ). *Macrobius*, who wrote his commentary to Cicero's "Scipio's Dream" (*Somnium Scipionis*) roughly two generations before the compilation of Faustus' text, wrote of an "ethereal wrapping" (*aetheria obuolutio*) and distinguished this from the "shell-like garb" (*indumentum testeum*) of the earthly body.⁹⁸ In the writings of the Neoplatonic philosopher and Christian bishop *Synesius of Cyrene* (ca. AD 370–412) may be found its literal equivalent ("shell-like garb," ὀστρεῶδες περίβλημα),⁹⁹ which, for its own part, hails from the Platonic dialogue *Phaedrus*. Therein, the expression also refers to the earthly body.

Matthias Baltes suspected that the notion of strata which collect around the soul during its descent through the heavenly spheres, forming thus the wagon of the soul, or celestial body, infiltrated Platonism from the "Chaldean Oracles."¹⁰⁰ Whatever its origins, this concept markedly reinforced once more an earlier tendency to emphasize the materiality of the soul, and propagated the notion of discourse on the heavenly body of the soul as a matter of course. In an exegesis of the "Chaldean Oracles," which incidentally contain earlier material, the medieval Byzantine theologian *Psellus* (AD 1017/18–ca. 1078) discusses (much like Galen and Proclus) a clothing of the soul which is "resplendent, light, and without depths" and termed "surface";¹⁰¹ the last scholarch of the Academy, *Damascius*,¹⁰² was of a similar mind, as had previously been the aforementioned *Hermias*.

The Gallic Christian theologian Faustus of Riez did not distinguish between terrestrial and heavenly bodies; no acquaintance with the subtle differentiation and developed metaphors of the Neoplatonists may be detected. Yet, it is clear within his tractate that, in Faustus' own time, reason to speak of a corporeality of the soul was hardly the preserve of the Stoics. On the contrary, the abrupt dichotomy between Platonic and Stoic doctrine on the soul still colouring the argumentations within Tertullian's "On the Soul" had essentially been shattered by the fifth century AD, certainly when one takes into account the novel developments within Neoplatonism at the time. Hence, the assuredness with which the monk and bishop Faustus of Riez began from the premise of the corporeality of the soul does not come across as a sign of his wanting philosophical education but rather as being emblematic of the influence of Greek culture and learning in Gaul, something which Pierre Courcelle had sought already many years ago to prove.[103]

Claudianus Mamertus

Claudianus Mamertus reacted to Faustus, as already described. He began his rebuttal *De statu animae* "On the Nature of the Soul"[104] with a general polemic against "arrogant ignorance and obstinate adherence to erroneous assumptions,"[105] which might be traced back to hatred of God and one's own neighbors.[106] Individuals shore up such fallacious positions by resorting to the reason or authority of church tradition as the need arises. Claudianus considers himself justified in such preliminary remarks on grounds of a certain text which he had discovered just prior to this among certain individuals by whom it was fervently consumed:

> The first impression of the book is that the unknown author ramblingly discusses the unincarnate and incarnate God in a superficial manner, and then seeks with great effort to demonstrate the capacity of God to suffer, and finally explains that the soul of humans seems to be body. Without strength of argumentation, without decree of law, without conviction of reason, the third discussion in this worthless undertaking is concluded. . . . If you argue in good faith, then why do you conceal your own name? . . . It is now apparent from that revealed by this page and concealed by its author that the compiler of it (sc. the page) is one damned (by the church).[107]

In the first book of his text, which comprises three tomes in total, Claudianus argues prominently on the basis of a general rationality and empiricism with very occasional reference to biblical passages. Yet, the point of departure for the work is very much theological, namely, the demonstration that God can fashion incorporeal substances (such as the soul), and thus had indeed done so. The first argument for incorporeal substances presented by Claudianus is the benevolence of the Creator: Were there to be no incorporeal substances, then the abundance of creation would lack that most important. If, on the contrary, God had fashioned the lowly, the corporeal substances, but had not created incorporeal substances, then this would hardly be a sign of his benevolence. Furthermore, the soul is the divine similitude (*similitudo*); the divine likeness cannot exist in a corporeal soul (or in a body at all) (*in corpore autem nulla esse potest similitudo diuina*).[108] "The human soul is, however, fashioned in the likeness of God; thus, the human soul is incorporeal."[109] The fashioning of an incorporeal substance does not, thereby, engender a being equal (*aequalis*) to God, but rather merely one similar (*similis*) to him. This is documented in the wording of the pertinent passage within Genesis cited by Claudianus. He concludes: "Yet the soul is the image of the incorporeal, and is thus incorporeal. Being created, it is not God; being, however, the image of God, it is not a body."[110]

Thereafter, Claudianus criticizes the what is for him all-too-neat identification of "visible" with "corporeal" in Faustus' work by drawing attention to *invisible* corporeal things (such as sounds). All corporeal things would only then be visible when they are understood to be "intelligible to the five senses." As, however, each of the five senses corresponds to an element (vision to fire, hearing to thin air or aether, smell to thick air or aer, taste to water, and touch to the earth),[111] it must be so with the soul: Were it corporeal, then it would have to be composed of one or more of the elements (which, as has been seen, some Neoplatonists taught in respect to the astral body of the soul). Claudianus refutes the view that the soul is an "airy substance": In this case, it would be subordinated to the developed senses of animals and be illuminated or darkened by the sun.[112] The evidence which is produced by Faustus from (Pseudo-)Jerome is not held by Claudianus to be authoritative testimony from a Church Father, but rather an utter misunderstanding of Jerome's texts; in reality, this Church Father had not ascribed celestial bodies (*caelestia corpora*) to the angels, but rather merely to the stars. Angels possess precisely the incorporeal spiritual body (*corpora spiritalia*) to be received by the risen after the resurrection of the dead.[113] The soul supersedes its body after death, and is thereby itself hardly a species of body spiritual or otherwise, but rather pure bodiless spirit within a new spiritual body. The sentence cited by Faustus from the Gallic monastic theologian John Cassian stating that souls "have a body appropriate to themselves by which they subsist, although it is far more refined than our own bodies"[114] is only meaningful when the soul relates to its spiritual body after the resurrection; as a statement in itself as to the soul's own alleged corporeality, it is meaningless. When the soul is conceived of corporeally, it fills a body "like water a hose," when composed of air, it is still divisible, and the loss of a part of the body brings with it the detachment of a part of the soul.[115] God is not subject to any of the categories of Aristotle, soul not to the categories of space and quantity (certainly, however, to quality, having, relation, place, time, action, affection, and substance): qualities of the soul are their affects.[116] The eye of the soul is mind (*mens*),[117] the vision of the soul is an immaterial sight, as in the case of geometrical bodies, which might also be appreciated without sensory perception, or of numbers, which must be counted according to the principle of numbers, and not through the empiricism of the countable alone.[118] At this point, Claudianus is thinking in a rather Platonic vein, as is made apparent from the following sentence: "These forms which we behold with the spirit shape the intelligible, eternal world, the image of which is this visible, transient world."[119] Irrespective of this, he is wont to argue highly empirically: One can be sunk in thoughts and be entirely turned away from sensory experience, as then the soul has turned away from the senses and retreated into itself. Indeed, even when the body sleeps, the soul thinks and does not rest like the body.[120] Thought is hence no accident of the soul, but rather its substance, as it never ceases to think.[121]

The second book of Claudianus Mamertus' work provides arguments from contemporaneous philosophical discussion in support of the position developed in the first book that the soul stands with its incorporeality between humanity as corporeally composed and an equally incorporeal God. Franz Bömer, Einar Hårleman, and Ernest Fortin have already extensively demonstrated the remarkable level of philosophical learning within these passages. The chapters demonstrate once more that the high praise of Claudianus' erudition which might repeatedly be found within Sidonius Apollinaris cannot be interpreted as sheer topical panegyric. Nevertheless, there is also the risk of exaggeration: Pierre Courcelle has shown that many, if not most, of Claudianus' references are drawn from Porphyry's (lost) work *De regressu animae*, also rather excessively employed by the North African bishop Augustine in *De ciuitate Dei*.[122]

Among the quotations from philosophical literature within Claudianus Mamertus may, on the one hand, be found such well-known texts as an extended passage on the doctrine of the soul from Plato's dialogue the *Phaedo*, wherein the categorical difference between body and soul is clarified through classic Platonic dogma: As the soul moves itself and had witnessed truth before all birth, it cannot be corporeal.[123] On the other hand, markedly less famous antique philosophers are repeatedly referenced, for example, the Pythagorean Philolaus, a contemporary of Socrates, twice. Claudianus claims to quote from the third tome of Philolaus' book on "Weight and Measure" dedicated to the soul; in this manner, he refutes his opponent, who evidently was of the opinion that Philolaus taught the "embodiment" of the soul in matter.[124] Quite to the contrary, as Claudianus Mamertus argues in the second book of his work, he propounded the view that the soul was implanted into the body by means of "number" (through its capacity to conceive of numbers and to count with them[125]) and an "immortal and incorporeal harmony" (*conuenientia* or ἁρμονία), but as number and harmony are themselves incorporeal. Moreover, the pure soul leads a bodiless life in the cosmos (*mundus* or κόσμος) after the separation from the body at death. This second account is evidenced by means of a quotation from a (most likely inauthentic) fragment of Philolaus.[126]

Nevertheless, these authors have no independent authority for Claudianus: Thus, he emphasizes the consonance between Holy Scripture and philosophical argumentation through the example of the Pythagorean Philolaus:[127] The "measure and number and weight" by which God ordered all (Wisdom of Solomon 11:20)[128] do not substantiate the materiality of the soul as had been argued by Faustus in his tractate on the strength of this scriptural passage (otherwise a weight of the soul could be rendered in pounds), but rather its principal character: Comparable to Platonic thought, measure, number, and weight are rather more the eternal forms of the world; "all three at once eternal, ever-indivisible, everywhere, and complete throughout: They are the one God Himself."[129] The soul has an incorporeal size, can think in numbers, and its weight is comprised in its love with which it loves others.[130]

In support of this interpretation, three Pythagoreans are introduced with quotations as philosophical authorities, namely the aforementioned Philolaus, a contemporary of Socrates; Archytas of Tarentum, who lived in the time of Plato; and Hippo of Metapontus.[131] Accompanying them is a lengthy enumeration of further Pythagoreans: "Archippus, Epaminondas, Aristeus, Gorgiades, Diadorus, and all later Platonists."[132] As already alluded to, two textual passages considered to be from Plato follow: an initial brief formulation purportedly from a book of his called "On Nature" (Περὶ Φυσικῆς),[133] and a second, longer passage in the form of a translation from the dialogue *Phaedo*.[134] The allegedly Platonic sentence ("the soul of all animate things is not corporeal, it is always in motion in of itself, and also a driving force for others which are immobile by nature") recalls strikingly a formulation from the text "On Plato and His Doctrine" by the North African (Middle) Platonist Apuleius of Madaura composed in the middle of the second century AD.[135] Finally, a further pointed sentence from the Neoplatonist Porphyry stemming from his lost text *De regressu animae*, best attested within Augustine, follows: "If we wish to be happy, we must flee the body entirely."[136] Bömer suspected that Claudianus had not only read Augustine, but also Porphyry himself (and in the Latin translation of Marius Victorinus to wit[137]). Writings from those Neoplatonists who taught the celestial body of the soul

(such as texts from Iamblichus) were evidently unknown to him. This lack
of acquaintance with the doctrine on the soul in late Neoplatonism may be
recognized in the fact that he does not enter into discussion of the Neoplatonic theory of the soul's astral body or, indeed, engage with it at all. He
rather argues on the general strength of the dualism of body and soul against
the concept of an *earthly* body of the soul; most likely, the theory of a *heavenly* astral body of the soul was not familiar to him in any real detail.

These references to pagan philosophers are initially concluded with
a quotation ascribed to *Quintus Sextius*, albeit without differentiating
between father or son.[138] In the Republican era, the father, Quintus Sextius
the Elder, founded the "School of the Sextii," which incorporated both
Stoic and Platonic ideas; his son likely also belonged to this institution.
Nevertheless, much in the original Platonic sense, the quotation maintains quite *contrary* to the Stoic position that the soul exists incorporeally
without specific place, and must be thought of as a virtually impercepti-
ble force.[139] This line of reasoning closes with an array of witnesses as
colorful as it is lofty: Varro, Cicero, Zoroaster, the Brahmins, the fabled
Anacharsides (one of the Seven Sages), Cato, and Crispus.[140]

It becomes once more clear from the continuation of the chapter that
the meaning of these philosophical authorities to Claudianus Mamertus is
merely derivative; they are valid insofar as they bear witness to the biblical
testimony attested by significant Church Fathers. Thus, the philosophical authorities are associated with references to the Church Fathers Gregory of Nazianzen,[141] Ambrose,[142] Augustine,[143] and Eucherius of Lyon[144]
(the latter three often with extensive quotations). At this point it becomes
apparent as to how far all of this is removed from the subtleties of the fifth
century's christological and philosophical debates. While the Council of
Chalcedon rejected "a mixture or blending" (σύγχυτος καὶ κρᾶσις or
confusionem permixitionemque)[145] of the two natures of Christ in AD 451,
it is outright stated in the work of Eucherius of Lyon, who had possibly
already died before the council,[146] that there are two incorporeal things
within Christ, the soul and God, bound and mixed together with a corporeal
thing, namely man.[147] The Stoic and Neoplatonic notion of an "unmixed
union" (ἀσύγχυτος ἕνωσις) between body and soul, which carefully distinguishes this form of unity differentiated within itself from a "blending"
(κρᾶσις)[148] seems unknown to both Eucherius and Claudianus Mamertus. While Eucherius is praised for his careful differentiation between the
incorporeal soul of Christ and his corporeal body, Claudianus Mamertus harshly criticizes Hilary of Poitiers for his aforementioned lines on
the corporeality of all creation: With such assertions he compromises
salvation.[149]

Augustine of Hippo

Within his argumentation, it is startling as to how little Claudianus Mamertus drew upon *Augustine*, within whose own work a plethora of passages against the corporeality of soul might be found. Indeed, in his later years, Augustine left scarce doubt that he held God, the angels, and the soul to be bodiless. In his voluminous literal interpretation of Genesis, compiled before AD 417, the bishop of Hippo wrote:

> Accordingly, we should pay no attention either to the idea some people have entertained, that there is a sort of fifth bodily element from which souls may be made, which is neither earth nor water nor air nor fire, whether this more tempestuous kind on earth, or that pure and bright fire of heaven but heaven knows what different kind of thing, which lacks any familiar name, but is still some kind of body.[150] If those who hold this opinion mean by "body" the same as we do, which is anything which has length, breadth, and height so as to occupy some local space, then this is not soul nor we may suppose that soul is made from it.[151]

Were it to be asked why Augustine so stridently sided against the notion of a corporeality of God, the angels, and souls, despite the fact that, at the very least, he had intensively engaged with Neoplatonist thought during his Milanese years between AD 384–391, then reference must first be made to his Manichean phase starting in AD 373. Prior to this phase, following the conceptions of the mainstream Catholic Church, Augustine was, on his own account, temporarily convinced that spirit, soul, and God must be understood as *corporeal* in some manner. At a somewhat uncertain point in time in Carthage, the rhetorician had embraced the Stoic notion of a fine corporeality of God.[152] This is learned from various passages (certainly not without problems in respect to their historicity) within his "Confessions" (*Confessiones*). This is initially rendered summarily in the characteristic prayer address of the Christian convert Augustine to God as follows:

> Not that I was imagining you, O God, in the shape of a human body: from the time when I began to listen to philosophical teaching I always avoided this and was delighted that I had found the same principle in the faith of our spiritual mother, your Catholic Church. But I had no other idea what kind of entity you might be.[153]

In the same passage, Augustine describes his erstwhile conception of the bodily form of God: "I was still compelled to imagine you, although not in the shape of a human body, as something corporeal existing in space, whether permeating the world or indeed outside the world and diffused through boundless space." Quite evidently, he had formerly shared the Stoic view that only pure nothingness was to be considered bodiless.[154] Nevertheless, the formulation that God is either "infused" (*infusum*) within the world, or "diffused" (*diffusum*) into the infinite evidences a meta-phorical discourse on a godhead's "overflowing" not at all typical for the Stoa, but rather characteristic for Neoplatonism.[155] This detail may well be thanks to the fact that, many years after his radical confrontation with Neoplatonism in Milan,[156] Augustine is looking back to the beginnings of his philosophical contemplation in Carthage: Employing the language of Neoplatonism, he describes the Stoic stance that the divine pneuma per-meates all things of this world. It remains uncertain as to whether Augus-tine ever propounded the notion that God possessed "the form of human flesh" and be confined "within the physical shape of a human body" before his first philosophical readings.[157] Soon after his so-called Milanese con-version, Augustine railed against such a conception, which he found to be childish, and forbidden to believe within "Catholic teaching" (*catholica disciplina*).[158]

It is also unknown when precisely Augustine encountered the Stoically grounded conception of a fine corporeality of God, which, in Stoic tradi-tion, he presumably also applied to the corporeality of the spirit and the soul. In the passage cited from the "Confessions," this realization appears to date to the early seventies of the fourth century, as, under the influ-ence of Cicero's protreptic dialogue *Hortensius*, he began to be enthralled by philosophy, and read a great number of texts ("from the time when I began to listen to philosophical teaching").[159] Regardless, some twenty-seven years later in the "Confessions," he maintained that after AD 373 he was shaken once more in his beliefs by followers of Manichaean groups. Augustine reports that these individuals polemically asked with respect to the mainstream ecclesiastical notion of man's likeness to God questions such as "Is god bounded by a physical form, and does he have hair and nails?"[160] Similar fare might be found around a decade previously within his exegesis of Genesis against the Manicheans which Augustine compiled soon after his return to North Africa.[161] At the same time, the Manicheans left no doubt that the supreme God designated "Father of Greatness" was to be thought of as absolutely transcendent and removed from any form of corporeality, despite the fact that in the Latin version of the "Funda-mental Epistle" of Mani, the founder of Manichaeism, mention is made of this deity's "limbs" and "substance."[162] The accusation of Augustine that, within Manichaeism, the divine substance, the *diuina substantia*, is conceived of as a "somewhat unformed mass" (*uelut informis molis*)[163] may be the product of mere polemic on the part of a Manichaean or a report from a "lay Manichaean," but a certain terminological ambivalence in respect to the discourse on a divine body does seem to have been characteristic of *North African* Manichaeism at the very least: Word and body are pitted against one another within this markedly Christian-influenced variety of Manichaeism,[164] as, indeed, in other forms of this gnostic universal religion, but man as fashioned from darkness has divine substance shackled within his body.[165] Hence, during his Manichean phase, it cannot be excluded that Augustine still retained some residual Stoically inspired notions as to a corporeality of God and the soul in the form of Manichean discourse on a divine "light-substance."

It was only in Milan, under the influence of Neoplatonism and the sermons of Ambrose, that Augustine abandoned such positions; this renunciation has already been accomplished within the dialogues composed by Augustine in the autumn of AD 386 at the country estate of Cassiacum after his so-called conversion:[166]

> For I have noticed frequently in the sermons of our priest (Ambrose), and sometimes in yours (those of his Milanese patron Theodore), that, when speaking of God, no one should think of Him as something corporeal; nor yet of the soul, for of all things the soul is nearest to God.[167]

On the way to North Africa, Augustine even worked upon a text with which he sought to demonstrate that the soul "lacks corporeal quantity and yet is something great," namely, the essay "On the Quantity of the Soul" (*De quantitate animae*).[168] Therein, the thesis that the soul is incorporeal is justified by means of reference to justice, which is equally incorporeal and yet tangible, along with the absent physical dimensions of the soul and its capacity to collect abstract geometric elements within itself. Detailed contentions built upon these arguments follow within the enormous text, alongside objections. Strikingly, Augustine refuses to state anything positive regarding the substance of the soul:

> As for its substance, I really cannot find a name. I certainly do not think that it belongs to those ordinary and familiar things of which we are aware through our senses. I do not think that the soul is composed either of earth or water or air or fire, or of all of these together, or of any combination of them. . . . (For the soul) appears to be simple and with a substance of its own.[169]

Although Augustine no longer propounds the Stoic view that the soul must be thought of as corporeal, he is still convinced that it possesses a substance *sui generis*. Even if he does not know what exactly to pronounce regarding this substance, he can positively maintain that the soul is "not long, or wide, or strong, or any of those things that one usually looks for in measuring bodies."[170] The soul is not "there where God is," yet it must be assumed that "nothing is nearer to God among all the things He has created than the human soul."[171] By contrast, any terminological proximity to talk of a divine or spiritual body was consistently avoided in the later texts from his North African period. In the second half of his life, Augustine no longer entertained any doubt in the slightest that the notion of a corporeality of God and soul was an absurd and, indeed, heretical position. Nevertheless, a modest tribute to his own thought's tortuous route may well be detected in a section of his antiheretical work "On Heresies," which is concerned with a group of "Tertullianists" named after the eponymous thinker, when Augustine admits that God could well in a certain sense be termed body.[172] This text emerged shortly before his death and may depict a last, somewhat reconciliatory pronouncement on the topic.[173]

These differing stances assumed by Augustine reveal in their own manner as to how closely connected the notions of a corporeality of the soul and a corporeality of God are to each other. They also demonstrate that even one of the greatest Christian adepts of Neoplatonism in the fourth and fifth centuries did not perceive that Neoplatonic discourse had thoroughly adopted the Stoic notion of a body of the soul in altered form — that is, in the guise of discourse on a heavenly astral body. Hence, Augustine may well be responsible for the fact that the classic choice between Stoic and Platonic beliefs endured unchanged within the Christian sphere; he may well also have played his part in the further popularization of classical Platonic thought within Christianity.

Claudianus Mamertus: "De statu animae"

Returning to the Gallic debate at the end of the fifth century AD, any reference to Augustine as the chief witness against those opinions in favor of the corporeality of God and the soul also present in Christianity is, as has been mentioned, lacking within Claudianus Mamertus' work.[174] Quite evidently, the author was not concerned with completeness in his citation of pagan philosophers and Christian authorities within his tractate. Accordingly, the second book of his text on the soul closes once more with biblical quotations and lines of argumentation based thereupon. Above all, the Apostle Paul should demonstrate that body and bodiless, immaterial souls are already to be differentiated from one another on grounds of biblical standards.[175] In the penultimate chapter of the second book, it is argued on the strength of the famous passage from the second Pauline epistle to the

Corinthians (2 Corinthians 12:2) and further biblical references that there are multiple heavens:[176] In the third and uppermost resides God, and thus this must reflect an intelligent heaven.[177] As he does not know as to whether he had been within or without the body, the account of the rapture of Paul evidences that something incorporeal dwells in man.[178]

In the third book, the argumentation is also pursued by means of biblical texts; for example, it is reasoned from the appearance of Gabriel before Mary (Luke 1:26–38), also employed by Faustus of Riez in order to prove the corporeal existence of angels,[179] that angels are somewhat composite beings: They must be composed of body and spirit, with one of which they manifest before humans, and with the other of which they perpetually behold God's countenance.[180] Expressions such as "into Abraham's bosom" (Luke 16:22–26) and other spatial descriptions within the biblical texts must naturally also be understood as metaphors.[181]

The book concludes in a rather didactically adroit fashion with a *Summary* in the shape of a brief recapitulation of important themes within the work; in the edition, a *Letter as Epilogue* then follows—albeit only untitled and anonymously transmitted in a Carolingian hand. The *Summary* briskly presents curt mnemonic phrases on the incorporeality of God, the bodiless vitality of the soul, and its further functions; each of the mnemonics ends with a formulation such as "hence the soul is incorporeal" or "thus is the soul not body."[182] Without any indications as to its transmission, the *Letter* addressed to a "venerable lord" provided by the critical edition as the *Epilogue* to Claudianus Mamertus' work on the soul, ends in extreme didactic abbreviation with a diagram.[183] The graphic assembles three sentences about God, the spirit, and the body, respectively. It is notable that the term "spirit" (*spiritus*) occupies the place of "soul" (*anima*) within this diagram; this may imply that the chart already existed and was merely appended to the end of the book as an illustration.

The illustration is to be read accordingly: God is the "supreme good *without* quality," the spirit "the great good *with* quality," but the body "good *with* quality and quantity"; God is moved without time and place, spirit in time without place, and the body spatially and temporally; God judges and is not judged, the spirit judges and is judged, and the body neither judges nor is judged. Despite its recourse to a biblical passage featured both in the argumentation of Faustus and that of Claudianus Mamertus within the tractate on the soul, the "Epilogue" can also be read as a separate text.[184] It demonstrates, moreover, as to how important the dissemination of the correct views regarding God and the soul within late antique Gaul was to the latter and his circle.

In summary, should the argumentations of Claudianus in the three tomes of his work *De statu animae* be examined, then it might be concluded

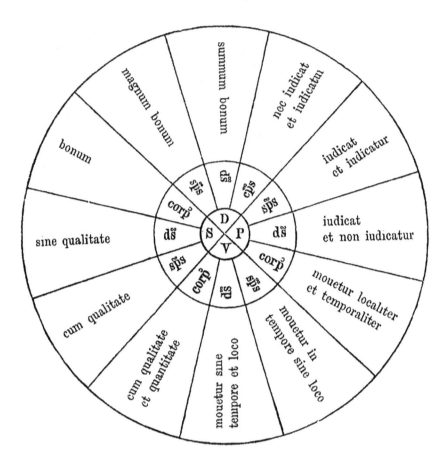

Fig. 4.1 Claudianus Mamertus, illustration from the so-called Epilogue of *De statu animae*
Codex Bibliothecae Universitatis Lipsiensis 286, saec. XI/XII, fol. 77[185]

that the Gallic author had knowledge of an astonishing number of Platonic and Neoplatonic texts, some of these even in their original Greek editions, as has been demonstrated by Franz Bömer and Ernest Fortin. Nevertheless, Claudianus either had not become acquainted with one of the central points in the contemporaneous Neoplatonic discussion on the soul, namely, the question as to how the astral body of the soul might be fashioned, and to what extent it differs from a terrestrial body, or had determined to dismiss it on grounds of the problems it posed to his argumentation. He follows thereby the stance of probably the finest Christian authority on Neoplatonism within the fifth-century Latinate world, Augustine of Hippo. As Claudianus (like Augustine) was uncertain as to how close

Stoic and Neoplatonic theories had become to each other, he could refute (in contrast to Faustus) the Stoic theory of a light, heavenly corporeality of God and soul as energetically as Augustine had. The problem as to how an incorporeal God and the incorporeal soul might precisely be distinguished from one another is resolved by resorting to the Judeo-Christian vision of creation: The soul is fashioned, God its creator. Hence, the criticism (as made by Martin Schulze) that "a sharp division between the aspatiality of God and the aspatiality of the soul" is lacking, "leading to the blurring of the line between God and man"[186] because divine predicates are stated of humans (or more precisely of human souls), is hardly warranted. The graphic at the end of the nominal epilogue evidences that Claudianus had adopted the central Platonic insight that the soul stands between God and man. Nevertheless, exactly the same systematic problem existed for those who propounded the opposing thesis: Were God to display a certain corporeality akin to the soul, then it would equally have to be explained as to where precisely God and soul differ from one another—certainly when a close relation or even shared identity as found in many varieties of Stoic philosophy is not stated, but rather, as in Judeo-Christian tradition, a categorical division.

Conclusion

This glimpse into the contentions of the fourth and fifth centuries AD within Latin-speaking theology demonstrates why the question as to the *corporeality of the soul*, which is systematically and closely tied to the question as to the *corporeality of God*, could be discussed separately from Late Antiquity onwards, and also treated discretely. While, under the influence of Stoic philosophy, both questions were perceived as part of the same debate (as the writings of the North African rhetorician Tertullian demonstrate), later Neoplatonism uncoupled the two questions: In late antique Neoplatonic philosophy, the question as to the specific corporeality of the soul was disputed despite a firm conviction in the bodilessness of the transcendent, primal God. When the grounds for this initially rather surprising development within the Platonic scholastic tradition are sought, then much recommends the supposition that one cause would have been the argumentative plausibility of Stoic materialism: In assuming an ascent of the purely immaterially conceived soul from the body, not only are spatial metaphors which might therein be tied to materiality (such as that of "ascent") necessarily presupposed, but also the question is more significantly posed as to the meaning of spatiality and materiality for this process, as it is philosophically well-nigh (if not utterly) impossible to sustain the conception of a pure immateriality without at least a constitutive connection antitypical to materiality.

Regardless, this debate within pagan Neoplatonist philosophy did not find reception within Christian theology; the most influential Christian writings on the soul continued to follow the classical Platonic and original Neoplatonic paradigms that soul and God are to be thought of as equally bodiless.[187] This was not in the least due to the conspicuousness with which, as *the* Church Father of the Occident, Augustine distanced himself from an earlier Stoically grounded period, making the Stoic conception of a corporeality *sui generis* as a material implication of existence lose its plausibility within Christian theology. The same was the case for the Gallic monastic theologians such as Faustus of Riez, who sought with his Stoically informed notion of an airy corporeality of the soul to argue against "Arianism" (that is, the Homoean imperial theology among the Visigothic groups). This tradition of thought also disintegrated.

In comparison to the debates regarding the so-called *anthropomorphites* in the East the corporeality of *God* was no longer explicitly key to these Western discussions; on the contrary, Faustus and Claudianus Mamertus alike are convinced that God *did not* possess a body, and debated solely the question as to whether the soul might be understood as belonging to the realms of an incorporeal God, or rather *in toto* as a corporeally conceived creation. It might hence be stated that under the influence of Augustine and, indeed, John Cassian, who (as will be seen) railed in strident polemic against the Egyptian anthropomorphites, the question as to God's corporeality was definitively resolved within Christian theology at the end of the fifth century in the West. The answer was resoundingly in the negative.

5

*The Body of God and
Late Antique Jewish Mysticism*

Testaments to Piety

The notion of God possessing a body, even if of a special materiality, was for a great many people in Antiquity entirely self-evident. This was not only implied and, indeed, popularized by means of the statues of gods in pagan temples, but also propounded and taught by individual philosophical schools. It is hence hardly surprising that individuals within antique Christianity were also informed by the notion of the corporeality of God. Ultimately, this may also be found in the canonical Holy Scripture of both the Old and New Testaments, which molded from the very beginning onwards the liturgical life and theological reflections of this religion.[1] Yet, what role might these conceptions have played within late antique Judaism?

It has been seen that, on the one hand, Jewish thinkers such as Aristobulus or Philo of Alexandria were influenced by classical Platonic philosophy, interpreted the relevant biblical passages allegorically, and vehemently rejected the notion of a corporeality of God. On the other hand, however, the influence of the Platonic critique of the notion of a corporeality of the absolutely transcendental God may not be overestimated, as is demonstrated by the painting of the Synagogue of Dura Europos: As indeed applies to Judaism as much as to Christianity and the entire world of Imperial-era Antiquity, quite contrary to that which the research of the nineteenth and twentieth centuries in particular would seek to convince, not everyone implicitly or explicitly adhered to Platonism.

Should one seek to bring further depth to the image of antique Judaism at this juncture, then parallel to both the texts marked by Alexandrian philosophical discussion of an Aristobulus or Philo, or, indeed, the individual testimonials of piety found at a very particular synagogue on the empire's border, rabbinic and non-rabbinic late antique works must be examined. It is important thereby to reckon with the particular, independent coinage of these texts, and not to approach these as mere parallels to Christian or pagan writings—the American Judaist Samuel Sandmel (1911–1968) coined the rather telling usage "parallelomania" for such an abuse of Jewish texts.[2] In addition, it must be made clear that, in contrast to many pagan and Christian sources, these Jewish texts are only dateable to a limited extent, as they were transmitted orally within certain institutional contexts, and shifted thereby in both form and scope. These were only seldom composed by a single, precisely identifiable author and are accordingly difficult to date, and are hardly ever transmitted as a fixed textual corpus (somewhat canonized by means of the author). In order to express appropriately the fluidity of these sources, a term from Literary Studies which is currently enjoying popularity in describing liturgical texts may be employed: "living literature."[3]

Particularly striking discussion of a body of God may be found in the so-called "Shiʿur Qomah" texts (שיעור קומה), literally translated, in texts on the "measurements of the form (of the divine body)." This refers to passages from the corpus of what is termed "Hekhalot literature." To phrase this more precisely, the "Shiʿur Qomah" texts represent a "microform" within the extensive corpus of Hekhalot literature, a collection of "macroforms" of pre-Kabbalistic medieval Jewish mystical literature. This terminological differentiation may be attributed to the Judaist Peter Schäfer, who first critically edited these texts, rendered them accessible by means of translations, and further explored them by means of diverse research contributions.

It has become commonplace to refer to this pre-Kabbalistic form of Jewish mysticism as "Merkavah mysticism" and the corpus of literary texts as "Hekhalot literature"; this modern terminology might be traced back to Gerschom Scholem (1897–1982) and his foundational publications on Jewish mysticism,[4] but this also points to original titles of works from the corpus, which contain the Hebrew terms "hekhal" (היכל), "(heavenly) palace," and "merkavah" (מרכבה), "throne-chariot (of God)." As the Hebrew expression "hekhal" is also used to refer to the Temple in Jerusalem,[5] the plural of the expression "hekhalot" (היכלות) oscillates in meaning between "heavenly palaces" and "heavenly temples."

The Vision of Ezekiel and Its Early Reception

A passage within the book of the Prophet Ezekiel in the Hebrew Bible serves as the chronologically earliest description of the divine throne-chariot;[6] it occurs in the context of the prophet's inaugural vision, and in its essentials may well hail from the fifth century BC. Should the text be read in its final, canonical form, however, without inquiring as to its alleged literary development, then a throne-chariot is not explicitly mentioned in the slightest—rather, *a vision in three stages* is described: Ezekiel, who finds himself at the Kebar Canal, modern Šatt-en-nîl, near the city of Nippur, initially sees a meteorological phenomenon, from the midst of which it shone "as the color of amber" (Ezekiel 1:4).[7] At the center of the phenomenon, albeit only at the end of the vision, proves to be the divine throne with God himself seated thereupon (1:26). A tripartite vision of the enthroned God befalling a prophet in Babylonian exile is hence recounted; the enthroned God being described from the bottom upwards, as is usual. From the light of a white-gold shine becomes concrete "the form" of four winged "living creatures" (חיות) of humanoid appearance (1:5) with the faces of a human, lion, bull, and eagle, respectively. These beings are thus clearly optically differentiated from the cherubim as described elsewhere in the Bible, even though they are readily identified with such, and an according interpretation was presumably originally intended (as is later demonstrated within the tenth chapter).[8] The entities can maneuver in any direction "in perfect harmony and unity, and never turn around, since they always face the direction in which they move."[9] The task of these "living creatures" is evidently to bear the plate the "color of the terrible crystal" (1:22) explicitly mentioned later within the vision's account, and the divine throne with the "appearance of a sapphire stone" (1:26) standing thereupon, even if this is not directly stated anywhere.[10] According to the vision, upon the throne something with "the likeness as the appearance of a man" (1:26) was visible— the vision thus hardly contains a clear and comprehensive anthropomorphic description of God's form, excluding reference twice to "the appearance of his loins" (1:27), but it evokes anthropomorphic notions with the term "man" (אדם). Next to each of the creatures may be found "one wheel upon the earth" (that is, there where the seer Ezekiel stands in the midst of the exiled Jewish community) and the "appearance of the wheels and their work was like unto the color of a beryl" (1:15f.).[11] The entire section "emphasizes the unity and harmony of the creatures and their wheels, which always move in the same direction, both on and above the ground."[12] Regardless, as to how exactly it is to be pictured that wheels may be found next to the beings, and that simultaneously one wheel is situated inside another (1:16) is not thematized within the text; it is difficult to judge whether the image of a wheeled chariot with a throne really already featured in the composition of the original scene. First and foremost, this concerns wheels, and not a throne-chariot: "By each being stands a single wheel" (Zimmerli).[13]

The biblical image from the Book of Ezekiel is difficult to visualize: If, at all, the image of a wheeled chariot genuinely prefigured this scene, then it was promptly repudiated by the text, and insofar transcended: "And when the living creatures went, the wheels went by them: and when the living creatures were lifted up from the earth, the wheels were lifted up . . . for the spirit of the living creature was in the wheels" (1:19, 21).

Consequently, the term *merkavah* (מרכבה), "throne-chariot," also does not yet occur in the Book of Ezekiel's original Hebrew.[14] The chronologically earliest technical use of this term for God's throne in the earthly Temple may be found in the Books of Chronicles; therein, it is stated of David that he presented Solomon with a plan for the Temple, including "gold for the pattern of the chariot of the cherubims, that spread out their wings, and covered the ark of the covenant of the LORD" (1 Chronicles 28:18).[15] It is only in the Book of Jesus Ben Sirach that, in the so-called praise of the worthies, Ezekiel's revelation is described as a "vision of glory" which "he (sc. God) showed him (sc. Ezekiel) above the chariot of the cherubim" (following the Greek recension in Sirach 49:10) and "forms of throne-chariot" (following the Hebrew version in Sirach 49:8). Moreover, attempts at visualization also only first appear in post-antique Christian art; earlier depictions of throne tabernacles[16] are only tangentially related to the account of the vision in this book of prophesy. Yet, even in the depictions of the High Middle Ages, the wheels and the four entities were not always combined into a chariot with wheels and cherubim upon which a throne was mounted. Rather, wheels and creatures occasionally stood next to one another in the same manner in which they stand side-by-side in the biblical text canonical in this period (Fig. 5.1).[17]

Given that, indeed, the word *merkavah* (מרכבה) is only seldom explicitly employed to denote the heavenly throne-chariot, within the Judaism of the Hellenistic period, this vehicle and more generally the throne-vision of Ezekiel nevertheless already play a central role in theological speculation as to the corporeality of God and the design of the heavenly temple (or heavenly palace) wherein God resides.[18] A possible reason for the particular attention lavished is that, within the vision of Ezekiel, the Hebrew expression "man" (אדם) is directly employed in relation to God, somewhat in reference to the notion of humanity's fashioning in God's image within the creation narrative (Genesis 1:26): "Hence, if 'man' is created in the 'likeness' of God, it is only fair to conclude that God looks like 'man' (אדם), and this is precisely what Ezekiel does."[19]

An almost more prominent interest in the physical form of God is betrayed by a vision from the Book of Daniel, presently dated to the second century BC.[20] In a certain sense, the vision within the Book of Ezekiel is already presupposed: a wheeled throne, that is, a throne-chariot, is

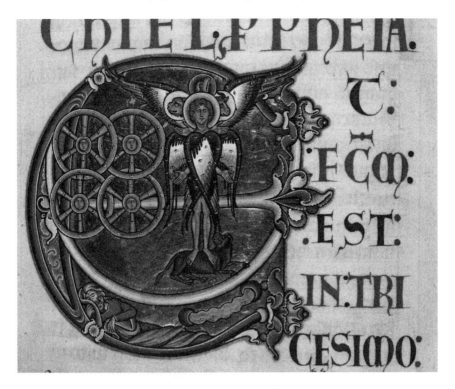

Fig. 5.1   Initial to the Book of Ezekiel from the Winchester Bible (1180)
So-called Morgan Master, Winchester Cathedral Library, fol. 172

evidently represented, albeit without the appearance of the term "throne-chariot" in and of itself. The Prophet Daniel beholds the throne of an "Ancient of days" (עתיק יומין or παλαιὸς ἡμερῶν). Remarkably, further details are rendered as to this figure "whose garment was white as snow, and the hair of his head like the pure wool: his throne was like the fiery flame, and his wheels as burning fire" (Daniel 7:9).[21] The text thus vacillates between the description of a very aged man in woollen white robes and the attempt to express the eternalness of God without employing otherwise commonplace liturgical or philosophical terminology.[22] The "Ancient" is joined by "one like the Son of man" (7:13); yet, no mention is made of a throne shared by the two figures (as in Psalm 109/110:1: "Sit thou at my right hand"), but rather, the one resembling a son of man is brought before the divine throne.[23] In this context, "Son of man" (בר אנש or υἱὸς ἀνθρώπου) genuinely means nothing more than "man" in a generic sense, albeit in somewhat elevated parlance.[24]

This scene from the Book of Daniel was thereafter a keen point of reference; accordingly, in the "parables" of the *first, Ethiopic Book of Enoch* (chapters 37–71), perhaps to be dated to the turn of the Christian era, or, indeed, possibly to the first century AD, the following is said about the enthroned:[25] "There I saw one who had a head of days, and his head was like white wool. And with him was another, whose face was like the appearance of a man; and his face was full of graciousness like one of the holy angels."[26]

Further numbering among the copious mass of Enochian literature is the *second, Slavic Book of Enoch*. Posing substantial difficulties in its dating, it presents a new narrative based upon the Ethiopic book, its Greek original version appearing perhaps in the first century AD in Alexandria.[27] While only extant in a redactional passage from two early modern hand copies of the long recension, a tenth heaven (Aravot, ערבות)[28] is mentioned therein. In this heaven, as of yet undescribed within the Ethiopic Enoch, the titular figure sees a "view of the face of the Lord":

> like iron made burning hot in a fire and brought out, and it emits sparks and is incandescent. Thus even I saw the face of the Lord. But the face of the Lord is not to be talked about, it is so very marvellous and supremely awesome and supremely frightening. (22:1)[29]

Here, a renewed attempt is made to describe the materiality of a body which categorically differs from that of any human. Yet, recourse is not made to any philosophical terminology such as an "ethereal fire" from which this materiality is composed, or a *quinta essentia* beyond all other materiality, but rather to a mundane image from the smithy, admittedly in the mode of a metaphorical distancing from this very scene: "like iron made burning hot in a fire and brought out, and it emits sparks and is incandescent."[30] With this image, it is rendered apparent that the specific materiality of the divine countenance cannot be examined any closer in the slightest, but rather that one must retreat to a safe distance in wonderment and fear. The passage stands thereby in the tradition of depicting meetings between Moses and God on Sinai from the Book of Exodus in the Hebrew Bible, where it is recounted that "the LORD spake unto Moses face to face, as a man speaketh unto his friend" (Exodus 33:11).[31]

Somewhat earlier, namely from the second century BC, may be dated the description of God within a vision of Moses preserved in the fragments of a drama entitled "The Exodus" (Ἐξαγωγή) composed by a Jewish-Hellenistic author named Ezekiel. Moses therein recounts a vision on Mount Sinai:

> I had a vision of a great throne on the top of mount Sinai
> and it reached till the folds of heaven.

A noble man was sitting on it,
with a crown and a large sceptre in his left hand. (lines 68–72)[32]

It is also here apparent how strikingly the conception of a stately man seated upon a throne is influenced by the vision of Ezekiel in the eponymous prophetic book of the Hebrew Bible and, in turn, the conceptions underlying the aforementioned passages of the Book of Daniel. Here, the focus is not upon details of clothing or age, but rather upon good birth and magnanimous disposition; God's body is modeled after the example of a Hellenistic noble.

Evidently focused upon God's corporeality, the description of the form of the Most High within the drama of Ezekiel the Tragedian serves, however, rather as something more of an exception among the apocalyptic texts of the so-called Intertestamental period. A demonstrably far greater sum of texts is at pains to emphasize the inconceivability of God, and has his form somewhat disappear behind his radiance or a fieriness, or at the very least be rendered inaccessible.

In the *Apocalypse of Abraham*, originally probably composed in the Hebrew language in Palestine in the wake of the Temple's destruction in the year AD 70 but only preserved in a medieval Church Slavonic translation, Abraham also sees the four creatures from Ezekiel under the divine throne and "behind the Living Creatures a chariot with fiery Wheels. Each Wheel was full of eyes round about." Yet, nothing is learned of as to who is seated on the throne. The throne is "covered with fire . . . and an indescribable light surrounded the fiery people."[33] Hence, all that may be seen of God is the special materiality of a light which cannot be described as it does not resemble any earthly light. The contours of God's (corporeal) figure are somewhat concealed behind this light's sheer effulgence. Once again, a loose connection is made to the conception of a light, ethereal fire-matter is perceptible, if not rendered terminologically explicit. In the case of visions such as that of Ezekiel, wherein a divine body is characterized by means of detailed descriptions of a human body, a later correction within the tradition may hence be proposed: Following the Apocalypse of Abraham, God is invisible and unnameable.[34] Similar characterizations of God which more or less repudiate his (corporeal) frame may be found in further passages within apocalyptic literature: According to the "Ascension of Isaiah," the titular figure witnesses in the seventh heaven "one whose glory surpassed that of all, and his glory was great and wonderful" (9:27), and, moreover, "another glorious (person) who was like him" (9:33).[35] In this passage, the core of which hails from the early second century AD, a Christian notion of a parity of Father and Son may already underpin the text, although it must remain uncertain as to if and when this was added to the original apocalypse.[36] This passage may well be tentatively traced back to the conception of a second divine figure upon or beside the throne as is present in ancient Judaism; this is to be found within a certain interpretative tradition discussing the Son of man in the biblical Book of Daniel.[37]

Much akin to the Apocalypse of Abraham, a Greek fragment from the *Apocalypse of Sophonias* (or *Zephaniah*) emphasizes that the supreme God is *unnameable*; the prophet merely witnesses in the fifth heaven angels who are named as "lord" (κύριος) and are approximated to the regal figure of God as depicted elsewhere by means of their crowns:

> And the Spirit of the Lord took me, and brought me up to the fifth heaven, and I beheld angels called Lords; and their diadem was set on in the Holy Spirit; and each of them had a throne sevenfold brighter than the light of the rising sun and they dwelt in temples of salvation, and hymned the ineffable, Most High God.[38]

Insofar as might be deduced from this fragment of the apocalypse, the prophet does not see God. Interestingly, Clement compares the restraint in the description of God found in "statements like those of Zephaniah the prophet"[39] with a famous letter of Plato from which he quotes the following decisive sentence:

> Rightly, then, in the great epistle he (Plato) says "For it is not capable of expression, like other branches of study. But as the result of great intimacy with this subject, and living with it, a sudden light, like that kindled by a coruscating fire, arising in the soul, feeds itself."[40]

The point of comparison permitting Clement to muse as to whether the passage from the Apocalypse of Sophonias/Zephaniah might perhaps imply something similar (ὅμοια)[41] to the sentence from Plato's epistle is the Greek term "unnameable" (in Plato: ῥητὸν γὰρ [sc. θεόν] οὐδαμῶς ἐστιν; in the Apocalypse of Sophonias/Zephaniah: (. . .) θεὸν ἄρρητον ὕψιστον). Regardless, this discussion of light in Plato demonstrates that for those who conceived of God's form as luminescence the categorical difference between the Platonic tradition and the biblical-apocalyptic texts which is today professed need not necessarily have applied: Both traditions connected God with light, whether this meant that they associated every material form of transcendent hyperreality with light, or its bright and airy materiality.[42]

This tendency to have God's form vanish somewhat behind impenetrable light results in the conferral of the individual aspects of the description of God's form from the Book of Ezekiel upon the angels. The most striking testimony to this transfer are the so-called "Songs of the Sabbath

Sacrifice" (*Shirot 'Olat Ha-Shabbat,* שירות עולת השבת). These are preserved in manuscripts from Qumran and Masada, having evidently been
sung by the community of Qumran. The keenly debated question as to
whether they originated from this community can here be left open.[43] Borrowing closely from Ezekiel, the service of the cherubim in the heavenly
temple is described in the twelfth hymn: The cherubim prostrate themselves before God

> and they bl[es]s. When they rise, a sound of divine stillness
> [is heard]; and there is a tumult of jubilation at the lifting up of
> their wings, a sound of divine [stillnes]s. The image of the chariot
> (מרכבה)[44]
> do they bless (which is) above the expanse of the Cherubim.
> [And the splend]our of the expanse of light do they sing
> (which is) beneath the seat of his glory. And when the wheels move,
> the holy angels return.
> They go out from between its glorious [h]ubs. Like the appearance of
>   fire
> (are) the spirits of the holy of holies round about,
> the appearance of streams of fire like hashmal.[45]
> And there is a [ra]diant substance
> gloriously multi-coloured, wondrously hued, brightly blended.[46]

As Peter Schäfer has observed, the entire section "reads like an interpretation of Ezekiel, taking up many of his key terms":[47] in the Book of Ezekiel,
above the heads of the "creatures" here interpreted as cherubim may be
found the plate of the firmament from which the throne of God projects.
It is here described as the "image of the chariot," and thus possesses the
moving wheels (האופנים) of the biblical text. This notwithstanding, it is
now the angels who are described like God himself in the hymns from
Qumran; like he who projects from above his loins a gold-silver shine and
from below the loins of whom streams of fire emerge, they are surrounded
by fire. "In other words, what Ezekiel encounters as a vision of God has
been transferred to the angels" in the twelfth of the hymns for the Sabbath
sacrifice: "The angels move to center-stage; God's physical appearance
recedes into the background and is hardly mentioned at all."[48] In place of
a divine message rendered by a godly voice or a particular angel comes
the divine stillness, the great silence. Even if the term "divine stillness"
(קול דממת אלוהים) is reminiscent of the occidental tradition of mysticism,[49]
the text from the twelfth hymn here cited does not concern a "mystical"
experience or "mystical" practice at all. In the interest of preserving God's
divinity and transcendence at all costs, the description of the divine throne

from the biblical Book of Ezekiel is foisted upon the angels. The angels nevertheless perform a service in heaven, and the earthly congregation liturgically encourage them with the hymns in performing these heavenly deeds modeled upon their own actions.[50]

To the history of the reception and transformation of the canonized throne visions of Ezekiel and Daniel further numbers the *Christian Apocalypse of John*, wherein a description of an entirely disembodied God is attempted which nevertheless leaves an impression of materiality: "and, behold, a throne was set in heaven, and one sat on the throne. And he that sat was to look upon like a jasper and a sardine stone: and there was a rainbow round about the throne, in sight like unto an emerald" (Revelation 4:2f.).[51] When it is recognized that the three stones of jasper, sardine stone (i.e., sard/carnelian), and emerald may also be found among the stones upon the high priest's breastplate as described in the Hebrew Bible (Exodus 28:6-21), then it also becomes evident that, according to the author of the revelation, a relationship exists between the tabernacle of the Temple in Jerusalem and the heavenly temple, and the earthly temple yields the model for the heavenly sanctuary. As to whether the Twelve Tribes, and thereby the Nation of Israel, are here concurrently alluded to need not presently be answered.[52]

On the Definition of a Difficult Pair of Terms

Yet, to what extent might one discuss in terms of these traditions, and in particular in Hekhalot literature, "Jewish mysticism," and ascribe this to a "Merkavah mysticism"? Before the not unproblematic implications of the conventional distinction between the literary corpus of Hekhalot literature and a "Merkavah mysticism" might be closer scrutinized, it must first be clarified as to how the ubiquitous but markedly vague term "mysticism" should at all be understood. Right at the beginning of his book "The Origins of Jewish Mysticism," Peter Schäfer already indicated that it would be "hopeless" to seek a definition both acceptable to all and applicable to sundry phenomena and texts tied to "mysticism."[53] The problems begin with the term itself: The substantive "mysticism" first appears in the Early Modern era in French (*la mystique*) before then generally establishing itself.[54] This hence hardly refers to a term from antique source languages. Were one to depart from the Greek verb (μύειν) etymologically underlying the term "mysticism," which means "to close," and, in particular, "to close the eyes,"[55] then a "mystic," as Schäfer posits, is accordingly "someone who shuts his or her eyes in order to shut out the mundane world and experience other realities."[56] Such an etymologically reconstructible terminological dimension to the closure of the senses to the mundane was still very much present in Late Antiquity: The birth of the aforementioned Alexandrian Neoplatonist Heraiscus, a student of Proclus and the teacher of Isidore, is deemed as "mysterious" (μυστικός) within the Suda: Like Horus or Helios, the philosopher-to-be was born of his mother's womb with his index finger fused to his lips as if hushing; this had to be separated surgically, leaving an enduring scar as testament to this miraculous birth.[57] Silence and secrecy indicate that, in the case of Heraiscus, the realm of a *divine* nature may also be perceived within a *human* life: According to the Suda, his own nature as somewhat more divine than human enabled him to distinguish between animate and inanimate divine statues; upon regarding a divine statue imbued with soul, he experienced an inspiration and was as affected body and soul as if he were seized by that very divinity.[58]

Resonating above all within the everyday speech of today, this "secret" and "arcane" dimension to the term "mysticism" and the adjective "mystical" derives from its linguistic proximity to the terminology of antique mystery cults, although no demonstrable etymological connection exists between the aforementioned verb "to close" (μύειν) and the vocabulary characteristic of these cults (that is, μυέειν, "to initiate into the mysteries," or μυεῖσθαι and the substantives μύστης, "initiate," and μυστήριον, "mystery," derived therefrom).[59] In the Neoplatonic philosophy of Late Antiquity, teachings such as those of Parmenides could also receive the label "arcane transmission" (μυστικὴ παράδοσις).[60] This term finds parallels in the philosophical practice of this thinker: In the opinions of Proclus and Parmenides alike, one must convey the secret truths covertly and never reveal ineffable teachings on the gods publicly.[61]

Peter Schäfer has suggested that as a result of ancient mystery cults (such as the cult of Mithras), a hint of secrecy and privacy has accompanied the sematic field of "mysticism" from the very beginning until the present day, even if any link to specific religious practices ended with the decline and death of Greco-Roman mystery cults, this further hastened by the anti-pagan legislation of Christian sovereigns.[62] The Greek expression underlying the modern English term "mystic" (μυστικός, the adjective derived from the verb μύειν) means primarily "belonging to the mystery cults" and then also "dark," "esoteric," or "mysterious" (its linguistic antonym is φανερός, "open").[63]

Admittedly, the abundantly vague and indistinct contemporary English term "mysticism" is not the product of this antique etymology or semantic context, but rather of more or less precisely quoted medieval definitions. Peter Schäfer sought to distinguish between *two* manners of such definitions. In one of these, the definition is characterized by the notion of a "mystical unity" (*unio mystica*) between God and man, wherein a precise differentiation of both instances is diffused or disappears—as in the definition of Dionysus the Carthusian (Dionysius Cartusianus, 1402–1471) also known as Denys van Leeuwen or Denis Ryckel, who explained "mystical theology" (*mystica theologia*) very much in the tradition of Pseudo-Dionysius as the "most ardent intuition of divine darkness" (*ardentissima divinae caliginis intuitio*).[64] The other option is to draw upon the definition of his contemporary Jean Gerson (or John Gerson, 1363–1429), chancellor of the Sorbonne in Paris; standing in the tradition of Thomas Aquinas and Bonaventura, he described this as a "cognition of God by means of experience, born of the unifying love's embrace" (*cognitio experimentalis habita de Deo per amoris unitivi complexum*):[65] "Mysticism is precisely that form of theology which rests upon the inner experiences of the religious subject."[66] As dissimilar as these two types of definition may well be, it is unmistakeable that *both* the *unio mystica*–oriented definition and that privileging experience (*experientia*) have their roots in the Christian theology of the late antique *Corpus Dionysiacum*, the writings of a probably Syrian author from Late Antiquity who portrayed himself as Dionysus the Areopagite, a convert of Paul (Acts 17:34), and hence is dubbed Pseudo-Dionysus: In these writings, discussion of "divine darkness" (ὁ θεῖος γνόφος or σκότος) perennially occurs. Accordingly, the tract "The Mystical Theology" begins with explanations regarding the question as to what "divine darkness" is: The Trinity is invoked, which leads the one praying "up beyond unknowing and light," to "where the mysteries of God's Word lie simple, absolute, and unchangeable in the brilliant darkness of a hidden silence."[67]

As to whether such definitions, evidently influenced by pagan and Christian Greek thought of Late Antiquity, and naturally also medieval Christian Latin philosophy, might be applied to antique and medieval Jewish texts need not here be discussed; Gershom Scholem and Peter Schäfer alike have already done so comprehensively. Indeed, Scholem already doubted that "mystic as such" exists: "There is no mysticism as such, there is only the mysticism of a particular religious system, Christian, Islamic, Jewish mysticism and so on."[68] Naturally, in such a differentiation, the search for commonalities between various "mysticisms of religions" is hardly excluded. Schäfer also suggests differentiation, and that the Jewish mysticism of Late Antiquity and the early Middle Ages not be defined in the sense of the *unio mystica*, which is rather appropriate for certain texts to be assigned to "Christian mysticism." He cites accordingly stipulations from Bernard McGinn (*1937) who published a five-volume "History of Western Christian Mysticism." Schäfer initially adopts three aspects of the theme "mysticism" from McGinn: "mysticism as a part or element of a religion; mysticism as a process or way of life; and mysticism as an attempt to express a direct consciousness of the presence of God."[69]

McGinn himself indicates that a definition of "mysticism" by means of "the experience of some kind of union with God, particularly a union of absorption or identity in which the individual personality is lost," that is, the *unio mystica*, results in the confinement of the designation "mystic" to a comparatively small group. This characteristic applies only to a few texts conventionally ascribed to the corpus of late antique and early medieval Christian mysticism, meaning that "one wonders why Christians ever used the qualifier 'mystical' so often."[70] McGinn eschews the classical, ambiguous term "mystical experience."[71] Rather, in the tradition of Bernard Lonergans, he employs the term "consciousness of the presence of God" and understands mysticism as comprising the following for Christianity: "The mystical element in Christianity is that part of its belief and practices that concerns the preparation for, the consciousness of, and the reaction to what can be described as the immediate or direct presence of God."[72] Regardless, it must be driven home that such a description is first and foremost quiescent as to whether this consciousness of immediate or direct presence of God is only described literarily (i.e., fashioned fictionally), or as to whether descriptions are generated from the experience of this consciousness. The eagerly posed question as to the "nature of the reality" of such experiences must hardly be examined here in any depth, but does, nevertheless, demonstrate that literature, and not experience, takes center stage, although admittedly Scholem was convinced that the corpus of Hekhalot literature was not solely the product of purely fictional, literarily manufactured experience: "They are essentially descriptions of a genuine religious experience for which no sanction is sought in the Bible."[73]

The *Hekhalot texts* which will now be considered are a part of *Merkavah* ("God's throne-chariot") mysticism. Gershom Scholem distinguished three phases of Merkavah mysticism: "the anonymous conventicles of the old apocalyptics; the Merkavah speculation of the Mishnaic teachers who are known to us by name; and the Merkavah mysticism of late and post-Talmudic times, as reflected in the (*Hekhalot*[74]) literature which has come down to us."[75] Such a model, wherein the Hekhalot texts become a subset of the literary form, or, indeed, a subset of Merkavah mysticism, runs the risk, on the one hand, of falsely construing avenues of development and references to traditions, and, on the other, of also failing to recognize sufficiently differences between the aforementioned textual groups. Peter Schäfer has noted that already in Scholem the beginning of the first phase of Merkavah mysticism, the anonymous conventicles of the early apocalyptics, is comparatively imprecise in chronological terms, and the third phase of Hekhalot literature is extended well into the Middle Ages, as, according to Scholem, the Kabbalah follows from this phase. For Scholem, Merkavah mysticism is *pre-Kabbalistic* Jewish mysticism.[76]

The line of development between the apocalyptic texts in emulation of the Prophet Ezekiel's vision and the late Hekhalot texts from the period of Byzantine Judaism in Babylonia as sketched by Scholem and problematized by Schäfer has recently been repeatedly defended, for example, by Rachel Elior and Andrei Orlov.[77]

In her monograph "The Three Temples,"[78] *Rachel Elior* sought to fill the chronological lacunae of Scholem's argument and to present the notion of a heavenly counterpart to the destroyed or desecrated earthly Temple at Jerusalem, initially a throne-chariot (Merkavah) and then a complete heavenly sanctuary (Hekhalot). As the decisive preconditions and prehistory of a Merkavah mysticism understood in such a manner, she reconstructs a strand of biblical thought stretching from the account of the tabernacle (Leviticus 25:18-27) to the concept of the Temple, within the Holy of Holies of which the throne of cherubim stood (1 Kings 6:24-27; 1 Chronicles 28:18), and further from the earthly models of heavenly cherubim in the early shrine (Exodus 25:9, 17-22, 40; 1 Chronicles 28:18-19) to a "mystical transformation" of these heavenly cherubim in the vision of the Prophet Ezekiel (Ezekiel 1:10), and moreover the particular cycles of prayers and hymns of the heavenly sanctuary which were recited in the earthly Temple (Psalm 92:1; 1 Chronicles 6:17 and 2 Chronicles 7:6):[79] The vision of the Prophet Ezekiel figures not only as the endpoint towards which this prehistory is destined, but also simultaneously the *first phase of early Jewish mysticism*. Thereafter, the mystical literature of the "secessionist priests," alleged to have found refuge in the community of Qumran in the Desert of Judah, serves as the *second phase*, thereafter the corpus of Hekhalot literature finally constituting the *third phase*.[80] In particular, the aforementioned "Songs of the Sabbath Sacrifice" (*Shirot 'Olat Ha-Shabbat*, שירות עולת השבת), which Carol Newsom reconstructed from various manuscripts from the discoveries at Qumran and first published in 1985 (three years after the death of Scholem),[81] play a vital role during the second phase of early Jewish mysticism according to Rachel Elior's reconstruction; she understands these as evidence of her thesis that Merkavah mysticism was not only shaped by a mere textually accessible tradition, but also by means of the personal continuity of schools and, moreover, student-teacher relationships during the period of the early Roman Empire and Late Antiquity. For Elior, all three phases of early Jewish mysticism are characterized by the absence of an earthly temple, by means of which the yearning for a notional heavenly sanctuary massively increased. On the strength of this thesis' premise, the concept of a mystical journey to the heavenly shrine could be understood as spiritualization after a fashion of pilgrimages to the terrestrial shrine in Jerusalem, no longer possible after the loss of the cult sanctuary itself. This tradition was formed in all three phases by "secessionist priests," initially by those such as Ezekiel who were compelled to leave the First Temple's site after its destruction in 586 BC, living thereafter in Babylonian exile without a temple, then by means of the Zadokite priests who were expelled from the Temple in the course of a conflict over the office of high priest in the second century BC, and finally by the priests left somewhat unemployed in the wake of the Second Temple's destruction in AD 70.[82] In a book on the Enoch-Metatron tradition, *Andrei Orlov* does not only argue for the continuity of a tradition of mystical speculation over the interpretation of Ezekiel's vision in the form of an unbroken chain of Merkavah mystics from the Second Temple of yore until the medieval era ("the working of the throne-chariot," *Ma'aseh Merkavah*, מעשה מרכבה), but also opts for the existence of contextual and personal connections between the aforementioned texts of early Jewish apocalypticism such as the passages from Enochian literature, the Apocalypse of Abraham, the Sabbath hymns from Qumran, and the later texts of the Hekhalot corpus.[83]

As has been demonstrated by Schäfer and Himmelfarb, the historical lines of tradition for a Jewish Merkavah mysticism extending from the vision of the Prophet Ezekiel to the texts of the Hekhalot corpus proposed by Elior and Orlov combine highly disparate texts which historically do not really share any clear traditional or institutional context.

This becomes apparent when the material employed within this debate (in addition to the account of Ezekiel's vision, most prominently the early Jewish apocalyptic texts) is examined in respect to conceptions of God's corporeality: It has been seen that these texts also markedly differ from one another in this respect: While, according to the *Vision of Ezekiel*, something with "the likeness as the appearance of a man" (1:26) may be witnessed upon the godly throne, but no clear or extensive anthropomorphic description providing even vague intimations, excepting two references to "the appearance of his loins" (1:27), the Prophet Daniel describes much more precisely the form of an "Ancient of days" (עתיק יומין / παλαιὸς ἡμερῶν) on the throne, even further rendering details as to his hair and garb (Daniel 7:9). In the similitudes of the *first, Ethiopic book of Enoch*, the image of a hoary old man with a white mane is also briefly sketched. In contrast, the authorship of the *second, Slavic Book of Enoch*, another entry within the extensive genre of Enochian literature, seeks to describe the "face of the Lord" by means of comparison to glowing, sparking iron (22:1) but implies thereby that, in their own eyes, the materiality of the divine body categorically differs from that of humans. Yet, in the *Drama of Ezekiel the Tragedian*, seated once more upon the throne is a "noble man . . . with a crown and large sceptre in his left hand" (lines 68–72). In addition to a small number of texts with such terse intimations as to a divine corporeality by means of anthropomorphic images may also be found a far greater sum of emphasizing the inconceivability of God, somewhat concealing his form behind his radiance or a fire so as to render God's figure inaccessible regardless. This applies to the *Apocalypse of Abraham*: Here, all that might be seen of God is an ineffable effulgence. Further to these are descriptions which demonstrate through use of superlatives the categorical difference between divine and human form: According to the extant texts of the Ascension of Isaiah, the titular prophet beholds in the seventh heaven "one whose glory surpassed that of all, and his glory was great and wonderful" (9:27), and "another glorious (person) who was like him" (9:33) to wit. Finally, similarly to the Apocalypse of Abraham, the fragment from the *Apocalypse of Sophonias* (or *Zephaniah*) transmitted by Clement of Alexandria maintains that the supreme God is *unnameable*; the prophet merely sees angels in the fifth heaven who are addressed as "lord" (κύριος) and are likened to the regal form of God as elsewhere depicted by means of their crowns. The same applies to the "Songs of the Sabbath Sacrifice" from Qumran, wherein God is not described, but rather the angels as if God himself.[84] Like he who projects from above his loins a gold-silver shine and from below the loins streams of fire, they are surrounded by fire. "In other words, what Ezekiel encounters as a vision of God has been transferred to the angels."[85]

From this corpus it seems neither possible to establish a coherent trajectory resulting in the texts of the "Shi'ur Qomah" passages of Hekhalot literature and their extremely extensive description of God's body, nor to conclude that the texts of early Jewish apocalypticism are in any fashion agreed as to a "canonical" depiction of God's body or form. In comparison to the pagan descriptions of the eroticising effect of statues of female deities upon (male) spectators, it also becomes apparent that comparatively self-evident male attributes and characteristics are employed to depict God's body, if it is at all qualified. Within the texts describing more closely the divine throne and its incumbent, the female sides to God otherwise variously attested within biblical texts, or indeed the philosophical categories of asexuality or oversexuality, do not play the slightest role.

Merkavah Mysticism in the High Imperial Era

At this juncture, the intricate debate as to how exactly these early stages of throne visions might be related to the texts of Hekhalot mysticism might be forsaken, inasmuch as the question as to the corporeality of God within the "Shi'ur Qomah" passages is presently the chief concern, and not the development and intellectual history of a movement within Jewish mysticism, namely that of the "Merkavah." It is nonetheless certain that since the rabbinic period, roughly the era of the high Roman Empire, "many expounded the Merkavah" (הרבה דרשו במרכבה), that is, that many learned in Scripture interpreted publicly in the synagogue the biblical passage from the Book of Ezekiel in which the word "throne-chariot" (Merkavah) appears[86] "and never saw it (the throne-chariot) in their life." At the very least, the Tosefta, a supplement to the Mishnah in a sense, states as much, ascribing the passage to a rabbi from the second century AD.[87] The Mishnah itself differs, ruling that the "passage of the throne-chariot" may not be used as haftarah, as a reading from the prophets, in public synagogue services.[88] How do the Mishnah and the Tosefta relate to one another at this juncture? It need not be answered as to whether a development towards more marked reticence in respect to the biblical passage in question was accomplished between these two difficult to date texts (following David Halperin), or as to whether divergent views on approaching the Ezekiel vision of the throne-chariot of God in synagogue services were simply propounded by different authorities at roughly the same time (following Peter Schäfer).[89] For the latter view might speak a postscript from the Mishnah: "Rabbi Yehuda permitted it" (i.e., to read the biblical passage in the synagogue as haftarah).

It becomes evident from this postscript that also in the opinion of the compilers of the Mishnah, differing views were adopted regarding this topic. This is expressed with similar reticence in another famous passage of the Mishnah, wherein it is forbidden to interpret before gratuitously large classrooms certain biblical passages concerning central theological topoi such as creation or sexuality usually supplied within esoteric classes. After remarks on biblical passages about illicit sexual relationships and the achievement of the divine creation, it is stated: "The Merkavah (may not be expounded) by/to an individual, unless he is wise (a scholar) and understands on his own."[90]

The passages cited from the Mishnah and the Tosefta demonstrate that speculation as to the interpretation of the throne-chariot vision of Ezekiel had become a subject of teaching both meaningful and mysterious alike within Imperial-era rabbinic Judaism, and an either ignorant or curious public needed to be shielded from it. It is remarkable that the Christian polymath Origen, who maintained particularly close contact with Jewish scholars during the second phase of his life in Caesarea, recounts something very similar in the introduction to his commentary to the Song of Songs composed in Caesarea:

> It is said that the custom of the Jews is that no one who has not reached full maturity is permitted to hold this book (sc. Song of Songs) in his hands. And not only this . . . they defer to the last the following four

(texts): the beginning of Genesis, where the creation of the world is described; the beginnings of the prophet Ezekiel, where (the story) of the Cherubim is told; the end (of the same book) which contains (the description of) the building of the (future) Temple; and this book of the Song of Songs.[91]

Peter Schäfer has demonstrated that the motivation of rabbinic texts seeking to limit or entirely prohibit speculation as to the throne and the throne-chariot was, to a certain degree, the protection of God's private sphere:[92] The interest behind quashing speculation as to the form in which God is seated upon his heavenly throne was not prompted first and foremost by philosophical reservations in regard to the conception of a divine corpo-reality, but rather "the rabbis' sense of decency" in respect to speaking appropriately about God.

Tangible within texts such as the Mishnah, Tosefta, and Talmudim, the rabbinic milieu of synagogues wherein scriptural passages were publicly expounded and schools wherein a teacher commented upon texts before his pupils nevertheless has nothing to do with the "immediate consciousness of the presence of God"[93] which McGinn termed "mysticism." Intimations as to such a consciousness may first be found in the Tosefta, transmitted in two medieval manuscripts: Recounted therein is the famed story of four rabbis who enter a garden (Hebrew: *Pardes*, פרדס), incur damage, and are even mortally imperiled.[94] As is stated at the beginning of the story after the Viennese manuscript, however, only "one ascended safely and descended safely." At the narrative's conclusion, this is phrased more precisely and in other word: "Rabbi Aqiva entered safely and went out safely."[95] With the words "ascend" and "descend," the terms with which the ascent of the mystic to the heavenly palace is described probably appear for the first time within the relevant literature; these individuals are paradoxically dubbed "those who descended to the chariot" (*Yorde Merkava*, ירדי מרכבה), although they were in fact "the ascenders to the chariot."[96] In the reading of the story, one garners the impression that, in the garden, Rabbi Aqiba had experienced a mystical ascension to the heavenly sanctuary, and most certainly also found his way back to earthly reality. Most likely, the relevant technical terms "ascend" and "descend" secondarily entered the text, as it is far more probable within the narrative that—as is, after all, recounted at the end of the story within the Tosefta—Rabbi Aqiba safely entered and exited the garden as one of four rabbis, and that originally at the beginning the text it might have been read that he "entered safely and went out safely" (following Peter Schäfer).[97] The narrative's statement, likely originally meant metaphorically, was later understood as an account of a mystical ascent within a garden. In the corpus of Hekhalot literature—cited in what follows according to the individual manuscripts within his edition of the Genizah Fragments and Schäfer's translation of the material[98]—the mystical ascent in the garden is ascribed to one additional rabbi of the four present in the garden, namely, an almost proverbial heretic born in the first century AD: "Elisha Ben Abuyah said: As I ascended in the garden (פרדס), I saw the 'KTRY'L YH, the God of Israel, the lord of the hosts, who sits at the entrance to the garden, and 120 myriad attendant angels surround him."[99] Regardless, the story of the four rabbis in the garden is also quoted twice within the corpus with little in the way of deviations; as in the Tosefta, the ascension in the garden is attributed therein to Rabbi Aqiba, a contemporary and erstwhile friend of Elisha Ben Abuyah, who is depicted in the textual tradition as an orthodox antitype of sorts.[100] Hence, this might be understood as reflecting the literary traces of a gradually growing tradition of reporting on the mystical experiences of individual, famous rabbis over the course of Late Antiquity, which increasingly penetrated these textual traditions originally bereft of even the slightest reference to mystical experience.

The Textual Material of the "Shi'ur Qomah"

Classification

Within the corpus of Hekhalot literature, the so-called "Shi'ur Qomah" passages are of particular interest in respect to the question as to the conception of a body of God, as has been noted. "Shi'ur Qomah" (שיעור קומה) means, translated literally, "measurements of the form (of the divine body)." Within academic discourse, the Hebrew terminology has three different meanings, among which one should distinguish:

First, "Shi'ur Qomah" represents a modern research definition for a *microform* within the five *macroforms* of Hekhalot literature (according to the terminology of Peter Schäfer). "Macroform" describes a superordinate albeit fluid literary unit, and "microform" a part of this superordinate whole. The macroforms of the Hekhalot are: *Hekhalot Rabbati* ("the Greater Palaces"), *Hekhalot Zutarti* ("the Lesser Palaces"), *Ma'aseh Merkavah* ("the Working of the Throne-chariot"), *Merkavah Rabba* ("the Great Throne-chariot"), and the so-called Third or Hebrew Book of Enoch.[101] "Shi'ur Qomah" pieces are attested within most of the manuscripts of the macroform *Merkavah Rabba* (§§ 688–704), in *Hekhalot Rabbati* (§167), and after the contents of one individual manuscript in *Hekhalot Zutarti* (according to MS New York 8128: § 367–376[102] and MS Munich 22: §§480–484).

Second, extended textual contexts also exist which are directly "Shi'ur Qomah" (in Schäfer's synopsis: §§ 939–978). Two microforms of "Shi'ur Qomah" might be found therein (§§ 939 and 947–951). Insofar, Shi'ur Qomah is not only a neat microform of the five macroforms of Hekhalot literature, but also describes a larger unit. Nevertheless, the "Shi'ur Qomah" might hardly be simultaneously termed a *micro- and macroform of Hekhalot literature*: It is doubtful as to whether the "Shi'ur Qomah" was ever understood as a macroform in its own right within the corpus of Hekhalot literature.[103]

Third, "Shi'ur Qomah" in Hekhalot literature itself is employed as a *terminus technicus* for anthropomorphic speculations on the measurements of the body of God seated upon his throne.[104] Accordingly, Rabbi Yishma'el, a real-life friend and contemporary of Rabbi Aqiba, is portrayed as engaging in dialogue with an angel addressed as the guardian of the Law, the Torah, at the beginning of the "Shi'ur Qomah" passage in the macroform *Merkavah Rabba* from the Hekhalot corpus:

> R. Yishma'el said:
> I saw the king of the world
> Seated on a high and lofty throne
> And all of His forces standing
> And the entire heavenly host of the heights
> Bow (and) station themselves by Him
> At His right and His left.
> I spoke to the Prince of the Torah:
> "Rabbi, teach me his dimensions."
> And he told the dimensions of our creator
> And spoke the size of the form
> May they be exhalted and praised.[105]

Rabbi Yishma'el requests from this particular angel statements as to the "dimensions of the form" and receives, in turn, answers.

This request and the detailed description of the divine "dimensions of the form" stand out within the texts of Hekhalot literature, as this is otherwise very much reserved where descriptions of God are concerned.[106] Certainly, in the macroform *Hekhalot Rabbati*, God is described as overwhelmingly attractive, and his winsome and decorated countenance is discussed:

> He who looks at him
> will immediately be torn;
> he who views his beauty
> will immediately be poured out like a jug.[107]

At this juncture, while not explicitly stated, a linguistic convention elsewhere employed for the reaction of a man to female beauty serves to
describe God's body. Beyond the extraordinarily fine features, the godly
"shirtlike robe" (חלוק) is discussed in the macroform *Hekhalot Rabbati*.
This robe is bedecked from top to bottom and both "from the inside and
from the outside" with the unspeakable tetragrammaton YHWH.[108] For this
reason, moreover, even the mystic schooled in ascension cannot regard the
robe itself. In the macroform *Hekhalot Zutarti*, the "beauty of the throne-
chariot" is discussed: The mystic should understand what is within his
heart and remain silent about it so as to be "worthy of the beauty of the
Merkavah."[109] If he is worthy of this beauty, then he can witness God and
is dubbed as one "who is worthy of beholding the king in his beauty."[110]

Certainly, in contrast to the *Hekhalot Rabbati* and *Hekhalot Zutarti*,
the word "beauty" (יופי) is not directly employed with descriptions of God
in biblical texts,[111] but there is at the very least a tendency within biblical
pronouncements on God to characterize him as exceptionally beautiful.
This characterization of God also touches upon a late antique tradition
in discourse on the divine: In the wake of a differentiation by Plotinus,
the absolutely transcendent One in Neoplatonism is not itself identified
with "beauty" (κάλλος), but rather is the "source and origin of beauty."[112]
Similar fare may be found in later Neoplatonists such as Proclus.[113] In
comparison, Plato identified his supreme principle with the beautiful more
directly and without circumlocution.[114] According to Plotinus, the beautiful can also astound upon first being encountered, inducing "wonder and
shock and pleasure mingled with pain."[115] In the Neoplatonizing Christian
mysticism of the Pseudo-Dionysian corpus, the close relationship between
"beauty" and the absolutely transcendent One from the Platonic tradition
was completely adopted: In this corpus, "beauty" (κάλλος) is rather Platonically described as "that which has a share in beauty," that is, in God:

> We call "beautiful" that which has a share in beauty, and we give the
> name of "beauty" to that ingredient which is the cause of beauty in
> everything. But the "beautiful" which is beyond individual being is
> called "beauty" because of that beauty bestowed by it on all things each
> in accordance with what it is.[116]

By contrast, the Hekhalot texts stand firmly in the biblical tradition
when the goal of the mystical ascent within them, the "descent to the
Merkavah" is to look upon this particularly beautiful countenance — and
yet, as is conveyed by statements in the *Hekhalot Zutarti*, it is simultaneously impossible to regard this countenance of God. In the tradition
of biblical storm theophanies, the statement is made, employing terms

from the vision of the Prophet Ezekiel, that God's holy ones look "as the appearance of a flash of lightning."[117] The following description of God is intoned by Rabbi Aqiba:

> He is, so to say, as we are,
> but he is greater than everything
> and his glory consists in this,
> that he is concealed from us.[118]

The essentials of the "Shi'ur Qomah" passages are already present in this statement: God presents himself in human likeness, but he possesses titanic proportions categorically distinct from all human forms.[119] As in all biblical and postbiblical passages, the text naturally leaves no doubt that a human form can only "somewhat" (כביכול) be evidenced for God. The exciting question in and of itself as to whether God "really" is entirely different, as to whether (in the anachronistic terms of Greek philosophy) a distinction must be made between the "appearance" of a gigantic figure and a further distinguished "nature" of God, would be dismissed by "those who descended to the chariot" (*Yorde Merkava*, ירדי מרכבה) as a foolish question of the uninitiated, as it further ponders upon something already shared with single, particular individuals as a special and exclusive revelation, about which nothing greater may be thought or experienced.

Transmission

The manuscript transmission of the microform within Hekhalot literature dubbed "Shi'ur Qomah" within the secondary literature is confusing as the overarching designation "Hekhalot literature" describes various fluid movements of pieces of medieval traditions in early modern manuscripts which might only be systematized with difficulty. With Peter Schäfer's "Synopse zur Hekhalot-Literatur" and a critical edition of the "Shi'ur Qomah" texts by Martin Samuel Cohen, two editions of the material exist which already differ fundamentally in their very inception. The relationship between the manuscripts upon which Schäfer founded his synopsis[120] and those presented in Cohen's edition is no easy task to articulate.[121] Peter Schäfer introduces his attempt to depict the transmission of the material as precisely as possible with the following words:

> The literary development of the various recensions of the texts termed Shi'ur Qomah is among the most complicated and enigmatic phenomena of late antique / early medieval Jewish literary history.[122]

While Schäfer eschews the construing of an *"Urtext"* on grounds of the state of transmission, juxtaposing instead different manuscripts synoptically, Cohen posits in his edition that he had "found a single manuscript copy of what is, perhaps, the Urtext" of all surviving compositions and transmissions in the form of a London manuscript dated by him to the tenth century AD. As is demonstrated by its watermarks, however, this manuscript was actually written in the eighteenth century, and from its content also represents a rather later variant of the transmission.[123] The main part of this text, which Cohen edited under the heading of *Merkavah Rabba* (lines 1–214) on grounds of the later text is a parallel version to the "Shi'ur Qomah" passages (§§ 939–978) edited by Schäfer on the basis of two clearly earlier manuscripts. As to how, furthermore, the recensions termed *Sefer Razi'el* and *Sefer ha-Qomah* ("The Book of the [Divine] Form") by Cohen exactly relate to one another[124] need not be discussed here at length as they are supposedly secondary in nature.[125] In the Middle Ages, many versions circulated which were integrated into divers literary contexts and manuscripts; "any attempt to track down an alleged *Urtext* of Shi'ur Qomah proves futile."[126] Gershom Scholem considered (in Schäfer's terminology) the "Shi'ur Qomah" to originally have been a genuine part of the macroform *Merkavah Rabba* within Hekhalot literature (§§ 688–706), but was later transmitted as a separate unit.[127] In reality, however, it is very much uncertain as to whether the "Shi'ur Qomah" texts were "ever independent units in the sense of 'finalised' compositions": As elsewhere within Hekhalot literature, these must be understood as traditional material in a state of flux (albeit within a specific redactionally circumscribed domain) able to appear in various redactional contexts.[128]

When were, then, these passages on the "dimensions of the form" of the divine body composed? An interesting hint as to the dating of this extremely difficult material might be noted: As will be seen, the "Shi'ur Qomah" texts employ with great frequency the term "parasangs" (פרסות) in describing the dimensions of the divine body. The "parasang" (פרסה) is actually a Persian measure of distance also known in the Greco-Roman world (as παρασάγγης/*parasanga*). In Herodotus, it might be read that an army can advance some five parasangs in a day; therein, the parasang is given as the equivalent as a unit of measurement to thirty *stadia* (roughly 4.8 kilometers), but the antique attempts to provide an equivalent vary.[129] The "parasang" is evidently understood differently within the "Shi'ur Qomah" passages of Hekhalot literature: Therein may be found an interesting pronouncement as to the length of a parasang featuring within a dialogue between Rabbi Yishma'el, the paradigmatic ascender to the throne-chariot, and "Metatron," the "great prince of testimony":[130]

But he (sc. Metatron) said to me: Say, the reckoning of a parasang, what is its distance? Each individual parasang: three miles. And each individual mile: 10,000 ells. And each individual ell: two spans according to His span, and His span fills the (entire) world, as it is said: "Who hath measured the waters in the hollow of His hand, and meted out heaven with the span" (Isaiah 40:12).[131]

A "parasang" hence does not represent a distance of roughly four to six kilometers as was customary in Antiquity, but rather a countable multiple of the diameter of the entire world. At the literary level, this world-encompassing diameter is nevertheless equated with a handspan, roughly a length of twenty centimeters. Two spans did, in fact, equal approximately one ell in antique metrology. Nevertheless, a Roman mile normally encompassed around 3,000 ells and not 10,000. The figures of the classical antique system are better reflected by a reading from another manuscript stating 4,000 ells which, within this passage, could offer a better textual version than the Munich reference manuscript otherwise consulted by Schäfer.[132] Were the relationship between ells and miles correct in Antiquity to be supposed, then the statements as to the relationship between parasangs and miles are also roughly correct. For example, according to Vitruvius, an ell (*cubitus*) was composed of 6 handbreadths (*palmi*) or 24 fingerbreadths (*digiti*); the ideal total length of the body encompasses 6 feet or 8 large handspans or 24 handbreadths or 96 inches.[133] Yet, as Klaus Herrmann (a student of Peter Schäfer[134]) has stated, with the introduction to the quotation from the biblical Book of the Prophet Isaiah, all measurability is neutralized and elevated from terrestrial statistics to the categorically different level of God's realm: "according to His span, and His span fills the (entire) world."[135] The length of the divine body's frame would thus be 450,000 times the extent of the entire world, but naturally the calculation is not meant in this manner. Realistic relationships between distance measurements are taken, and these are transformed on the basis of the calculation of relativity, the handspan, reaching a categorically different plane of heavenly measurements, which by definition may never occur within terrestrial calculations as these are confined to the "span of this world." The formulation of this categorical difference between earthly and heavenly sizes is not described with appropriate Neoplatonic jargon such as "all-transcending" (ὑπερούσιος), as is the case in the Greek philosophical tradition also adopted by the Neoplatonically grounded Christian mysticism in the *Corpus Dionysiacum*;[136] rather, this is voiced by means of the monstrously large numbers found in the biblical tradition. There is also no reference to the originally Orphic concept that the cosmos constitutes God's body.[137] The "neutralization" is stated even more clearly in the macroform *Merkavah Rabba*, wherein (after a slew of measurements as to the limbs of the divine body) it is frankly stated: "We have no measurement in our hands, but the names are revealed to us."[138]

It is thereby evident that, at least for those who transmitted the macroform, it was less about the dimensions of the body parts and more about their mystical names, which are related in consummate detail within this macroform. The fundamental premise that such apparently "foreign language" (divine) names (ὀνόματα βαρβαρικά, *nomina barbara*), actually artificial constructions with theophoric or angelophoric syllabic components, possess potency by means of their untranslatability, and conversely that translation would render them impotent, was widespread within Antiquity. In the "Chaldean Oracles," an Imperial-era didactic poem on cosmology and doctrine of the soul, this is phrased as "do not change the nomina barbara." Moreover, the Byzantine author Psellus commented on the quotation: "You should not translate these into Greek, much like Seraphim, Cherubim, Michael, Gabriel. For, when they are spoken in Hebrew they have an ineffable power in the initiation rites. Yet, when they are spoken in Greek, they lose all power."[139] In much the same vein, Iamblichus stated the following in a passage on the *nomina barabara*: "For the barbarian names possess weightiness and great precision, participating in less ambiguity, variability and multiplicity of expression. For all these reasons, then, they are adapted to the superior beings."[140] Foreign names are, in fact, "wholly suitable for sacred rituals."[141] Such texts proffer philosophical explanations of a phenomenon which is rather to be assigned to the sphere of magic: Whosoever knows the "real" names of the gods, along with being able to speak some words of the "actual" language of the gods, has a share of their power. Within the "Shi'ur Qomah" texts of Hekhalot literature, this magical phenomenon transposed onto the body of God, inasmuch as the *nomina barbara* for the divine body parts are revealed by the angelic prince. This form of magic is naturally categorically distinguished from that which is presented, for example, in the magical papyri of Antiquity wherein many theophoric and Hebrew-sounding are used to ensure the authenticity of the text: The "Shi'ur Qomah" texts hardly concern a neighborhood, an anonymous thief or demons who are compelled by magic to whatever the magician or those who commissioned him wished, or, indeed, erotically connoted affection, destructive magic, return of stolen goods, or protection from malevolent spirits. The listing of dimensions demonstrates to all that the focus is upon something of an entirely different nature, namely, God.

As to whether it might be deduced from this finding that "parasangs" had already fallen out of use as a commonplace measure of distance[142] may here be left open. It is more likely that on account of the prominent employment of a Persian unit of measurement the "Shi'ur Qomah" texts transmitted in the different macroforms of Hekhalot literature were orig-inally composed within the Jewish community resident in Persia, and are thus probably testament to Babylonian Judaism. Yet, to when exactly might they be dated?

Most likely, the recension found in those Early Modern–era manu-scripts reproduced in Schäfer's synopsis may originate from prior recen-sions from the Middle Byzantine era or perhaps even Late Antiquity, albeit here one is still reliant upon hypotheses, whether more or less established. The datings to be found in the secondary literature before the publication of Peter Schäfer's critical text edition vary extremely: *Heinrich Graetz* (1817–1891) declared for the ninth century AD and deemed the texts "through and through un-Jewish and anti-Jewish." *Adolf Jellinek* (1820–1893) and *Moses Gaster* (1856–1939) propounded a very early dating to the second century AD on account of putative parallels to the Christian gnostic Marcus who inhabited that age and was counted among the Val-entinian school; this datation was adopted by Gershom Scholem along with the reference to so-called Christian gnosis, which he built upon by means of further evidence within his respective books.[143] Within his comprehen-sive history of research in the introduction to his edition of the so-called Third Book of Enoch, *Hugo Odeberg* opted for a redaction of the material in the Jewish community of Babylon during the third to fourth centuries AD, an age in which the religion was tolerated by Sassanid rulers; a few of the traditions were further dated by him to the period of the New Tes-tament.[144] Indications of possible parallels (and thereby the phenomenon of a so-called Jewish Gnosis in the period of the early Roman Empire)[145] will further be discussed after the relevant passages from the "Shi'ur Qomah" tradition supposedly closely related to them have been analyzed. It suffices to note at the present juncture that, on the basis of a careful analysis of the purported parallels, Peter Schäfer espouses a dating to the beginning of the Middle Byzantine period of the seventh to ninth centuries AD, that is, to the period of the Babylonian Geonim. Moreover, Schäfer suggests that the extensive description of the "dimensions of the form" of the divine body is a reaction to Christian conceptions of the colossal corporeal form of Jesus Christ.[146]

God's Body in the "Shi'ur Qomah" Texts

Being now in the possession of the necessary information, some of the texts of the "Shi'ur Qomah" microform from the macroforms of Hek-halot literature might be analyzed, and it can be asked which conceptions of God's body underpin the passages. It has already become clear that the distance between God's eyes does not reflect some absurd, "through and through un-Jewish and anti-Jewish" sidetrack of the mystically inclined pious, but rather a neat transformation of those biblical traditions as to a corporeality of God which were to be banished to the intellectual fringes by the medieval mainstream theologies of Judaism and Christianity alike, while never entirely vanishing from the ken of both Jewish and Christian thought.

The analysis will begin with the most extensive complex of "Shi'ur Qomah" traditions from two Early Modern–era manuscripts from Munich which, as has been seen, possess certain attributes of a macroform (§§ 939–978), and will be supplemented by means of three additional passages within the macroforms *Hekhalot Rabbati* (§ 167), *Hekhalot Zutarti* (§ 367–376), and the *Merkavah Rabba* (§§ 688–704). It is difficult to chronologically arrange these four passages; that from the *Hekhalot Rabbati* may be the earliest, and the large passage the latest (§ 939–978). The longer passage begins with the first description of the size of the form, which is attributed to the repeatedly aforementioned Rabbi Yishma'el as a revelatory speech of the supreme lord of the angels, a certain Metatron:[147]

> R. Yishma'el said: Metatron, the great prince of testimony, said to me: I witness through this testimony of the Lord, the God of Israel, . . . from the centre of His seat, His elevation upwards: 118 myriad parasangs. (from the centre of His seat, his elevation downwards: 118 myriads. His height: 236 myriads and a thousand parasangs[148]) From His right arm to His left arm: 77 myriads. From the right eyeball to the left eyeball: 30 myriads. The crown (of His head): (333 and a third). The diadem on His head: 60 myriads for the 60 myriads of Israel. Thus, He is named the great, heroic, and awesome God.[149]

The angelic prince Metatron—whose name, whether understood as Greek borrowing meaning "the one enthroned with (God)" (μετάθϱονος)[150] or a loan from Latin as "he who takes the (divine) measurements" (*metator*),[151] expresses a particular closeness to God—enumerates the decisive measurements of the divinity's form: The mensuration begins in the notional center of the throne, and thus the center of the divine body: Both upwards and downwards, he measures 118 myriad parasangs—that is, 1,180,000 parasangs—the word "parasang" must be placed within quotation marks because, as has been seen, it already depicts an almost unimaginable size.[152] The sum of the total height of God at 2,360,000 "parasangs" demonstrates that God possesses a body with its exact center at the navel (or more precisely, its divine equivalent). In the "Shi'ur Qomah" passage from the macroform *Hekhalot Rabbati* (§ 167), it is preserved in one manuscript that "His arms are twice as long as His shoulders are wide";[153] it is also recounted therein that God's frame measures 2,360,000 parasangs.[154] In the *Hekhalot Zutarti*, only one manuscript relays the correct figure,[155] while, as has been seen, no statement as to total size is provided by the *Merkavah Rabba*. The breadth marked by the arms adjoining the body is approximately a third of the length of the body, the distance between the eyes roughly an eighth. Even though the figures in the corrupted transmission of the Early Modern–era codex do not exactly fit, this body accords with antique notions as to a well-proportioned and thereby beautiful body.

In this context, symmetry (συμμετρία) does not yet denote the modern concept of a mirrored symmetry, but rather the harmoniously proportioned relationship of two or more things to one another in terms of size.[156] The Imperial-era doctor and philosopher Galen reported in the second century AD upon the earlier Stoic theory that beauty lies in the proportions of the limbs of the body: Beauty is not present in the individual limbs,

> but in the proper proportion of the parts, such as for example that of finger to finger and of all these to the hand and wrist, of these to the forearm, of the forearm to the whole arm and of everything to everything else, just as described in the Canon of Polycleitus.[157]

Such a canon of harmonious proportions as the foundation of beauty hailing from Classical Antiquity also underpins the quoted passage of the Hekhalot corpus—thus, remarkably, the passage is *not* influenced by the notion of a categorical and principal beauty of God independent from such a canon's harmonious proportions, as is known of God in other passages in the corpus.[158] As the majority of antique writings on symmetry and proportions are lost, much like the "Canon" of Polycleitus as mentioned by Galen,[159] and the quotation from Galen cannot be converted into precise measurements,[160] one must turn to the description of the proportions of the *homo bene figuratus* in the first century BC by *Vitruvius* in his "Ten Books on Architecture," later tentatively depicted by Leonardo da Vinci, in order to locate detailed statements as to the proportions of a harmoniously built body. Vitruvius writes (possibly on the strength of the measurements found in the "Canon" of Polycleitus):

> Now the navel is naturally the exact centre of the body. For if a man lies on his back with hands and feet outspread, and the centre of a circle is placed on his navel, his figure and toes will be touched by the circumference. Also a square will be found described within the figure, in the same way as a round figure is produced. For if we measure from the sole of the foot to the top of the head, and apply the measure to the

outstretched hands, the breadth will be found equal to the height, just like sites which are squared by rule.[161]

According to Vitruvius, on an ideally proportioned human, the distance between the respective fingertips of the horizontally outstretched arms of an adult male should be exactly equivalent to the height of his body. Chest and forearm come to a quarter of the height of the body, the foot a sixth, the head from chin to crown an eighth, the face a tenth, the exact same for the flat of the hand from the base of the hand to the tip of the middle finger.[162] These Vitruvian proportions inspired Leonardo's celebrated sketch (see Fig. 5.2).[163]

Should it be assumed that it might already have been read in the "Canon" of Polycleitus that a well-proportioned statue was composed of many figures, that is, many proportions ("this achievement comes about through many ratios, wherein the smallest detail might tip the scales"),[164] then the many figures quoted in the "Shi'ur Qomah" passages of Hekhalot literature surprise even less. It is also stated in Plutarch that "beauty is achieved through the congruence of numerous factors, so to speak, brought into union (Kairos) under the rule of a certain due proportion and harmony."[165]

With regard to the "Shi'ur Qomah" passages, one must nevertheless establish two differences in the manner by which, according to the Classical Greek canon of harmonious proportions, the dimensions of a harmoniously built and thereby beautiful body might be determined: *On one hand*, Galen maintains in a paraphrase of the "Canon" of Polycleitus in respect to measurements that they are directed towards "the mean . . . in all things"—that is, not of particular length, breadth, or height, but of mean values.[166] By contrast, the lengths provided in the "Shi'ur Qomah" hardly relate to mean values, but rather to inconceivably huge dimensions. *On the other hand*, quite evidently no interest in copying the figures with absolute precision (a negligence which engenders comparisons between these texts and certain writings from so-called Christian Gnosticism).[167] This may be noted when the introductory passage from the longer section is not only quoted according to the according to the Early Modern–era manuscripts and fragments presented by Peter Schäfer in his synopsis, but also according to the later manuscript employed by Cohen (from the part termed by the editor "Siddur Rabba"):

Said R. Ishmael: Metatron, the Great Beadle, said this testimony to me: I swear by the Lord, the God of Israel, that the height of His body when He sits on His Throne of Glory is 1,189,500 parasangs. The width of his right eye is 33,000 parasangs, and so is his left eye. From His right arm to His left arm is 770,000 parasangs, . . . ". . . the great, mighty, and awesome God."[168]

The difference is, as stated, marginal in terms of the argumentative thrust of the passage and fundamentally an insignificant alteration caused by the both long and complicated process of textual transmission: God's height is somewhat raised by 500, namely from 1,180,000 to 1,180,500 "parasangs"; instead of a distance between the eyes of 300,000 "parasangs," the breadth of the eye itself is measured at 33,000 "parasangs"; finally, the distance between left and right arms remains exactly the same. That this passage might be a secondary transmission is potentially implied by the fact that the text is clearly abbreviated in comparison to the version from the Munich manuscript edited by Schäfer. In the section titled by Cohen, its editor, "Sepher ha-Qomah," the measurements of the passage are also relayed in slightly altered form (and introduced as being related by Rabbi Aqiba rather than by Rabbi Yishma'el):

> His height is 2,300,000,000 parasangs. From the right arm (across) until the left arm is 770,000,000 parasangs. And from the right eyeball until the left eyeball (is a distance of) 300,000,000 parasangs. The skull of His head is 3,000,003 and a third (parasangs). The crown on his head is 600,000 (parasangs).[169]

This assortment from the transmission of the introductory passages of one of the central "Shi'ur Qomah" texts from Hekhalot literature may be summarized accordingly: Evidently there were relatively fixed elements in the tradition such as the figures as to the total height of the frame of the divine body and its two halves above and below the throne, but also many divergences and, most prominently, downright errors and oversights: Nobody measuring 2,300,000 "parasangs" in height can span 770,000,000 "parasangs" from the left to right arm—either the copyist did not realize that (as in the other manuscripts) 770,000 parasangs would be appropriate to the ideal of the harmonious and thereby beautiful proportions of a *homo bene figuratus*, or it was more important to him to emphasize the immensurable size of God than the harmony of the proportions of his form. Regardless, as in certain texts ascribed to the nominal genre of Christian-gnostic literature, there was quite evidently no real interest among those transmitting Hekhalot literature in ultimately presenting a coherent, mathematically precise argumentation as to the size of the form of God's body. Indeed, in the four different visions of the Apocrypha of John from the discoveries at Nag Hammadi and from the Berlin Gnostic Codex, it is not only the case that the figures in the different lines of transmission sharply diverge from one another; indeed,

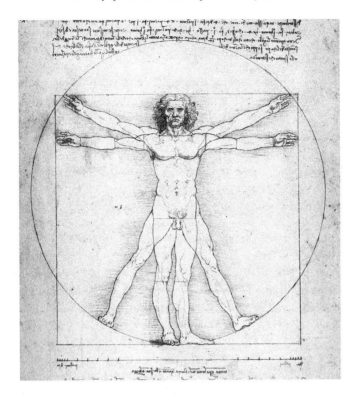

Fig. 5.2   Leonardo da Vinci, sketch of the Vitruvian Man (ca. 1492)
Venice, Galleria dell'Accademia

through certain alterations of figures, entire avenues of argumentation occasionally cease to make sense, or at least sense according to the paradigms of a theology founded in mathematics taught within the Platonic Academy.[170]

Nevertheless, the description of the form of God's body in the long "Shi'ur Qomah" passage within Hekhalot literature is not restricted merely to the fundamental measurements just discussed, but rather preserves further extensive detail. The passages on the size of body parts are repeatedly interrupted by longer quotations on their magical names and doxological sections—in the following, these are left out so as to aid in the understanding of the rather more central elements to the passages. It is one more explicitly noted that this concerns a revelation of Metatron to Rabbi Yishma'el:[171]

> The height of His soles: 3,000 myriad parasangs. . . . From the soles of His feet to His ankles: 1,000 myriads and 500 parasangs high, and the same on the left (side).[172] . . . From His ankles to His knees: 19,000 myrids and 5,200 parasangs in height, and the same on the left (side). . . .

From His knees to His thighs: 12,000 thousand myriad parasangs in height, and the same on the left (side). . . . From His thighs to His neck-throat: 24,000 myriad parasangs. . . . His throat: 13,000 myriads and 800 parasangs in height. . . . The circumference of His head: 300,033 and a third.[173] . . . His beard: A myriad and 1500 parasangs. . . . His tongue (reaches) from one end of the world to the other. . . . The width of His brow: 13,000 myriad parasangs.[174]

(The black) which is in His right eye: A myriad and 1,500 parasangs, and the same on the left (side). . . . The (white) in his right eye: Two myriads and 2000 parasangs, and also the left (side). . . . From His right shoulder to His left shoulder: 16,000 myriad parasangs. . . . From His right arm to His left arm: twelve myriad parasangs. His arms are twice (as long, as his shoulders are wide). . . . The fingers of His (right) hand: 15,000 myriad parasangs. 3,000 myriad parasangs (measured) on each individual finger, and the same on the left (hand). The palm of (His hand): (4,000 myriad) parasangs and also the left. . . . The toes of his feet: (10,000 myriad) parasangs, 2,000 myriad parasangs (measured) on each toe.[175]

The description begins, as is appropriate to a pious individual beholding the godhead with lowered gaze, from the bottom with the feet, and travels then upwards towards the head, which is described with comparatively rich detail. In comparison to biblical texts, the tongue of God is discussed, encompassing a handspan ("from one side of the world to the other"). Then the focus turns from the head to God's fingers and feet, starting with the shoulders. The divine body is characterized in the passage on the strength of its different limbs: Soles of the feet, ankles, knees, thighs, neck, head, beard, brow, eyes, shoulders, arms, fingers, and toes. This is undoubtedly the most detailed depiction of the figure of the divine body within Jewish literature.

The extent to which this comprehensive description in the "Shi'ur Qomah" passage differs from the rather more subtle intimations as to God's body in biblical and postbiblical texts is demonstrated by a passage on the size of God's nose and other body parts:

R. Natan, the student of R. Yochanan,[176] says: "Also he gave me a measurement of the nose, and (indeed) a (correct) measurement, and also (of) the (lips), and also (of) the (cheeks). Although he gave me the size of the brow, he gave me (regardless) the dimensions (of) ells. The width of the forehead is the length of the neck, and such is the shoulders (as) with the length of the nose, the length of the nose is (like the length) (of the) small fingers. The height of the cheeks is as the half of the circumference of the head, and such is the dimensions of every human.[177]

This passage distinguishes itself from others within the "Shi'ur Qomah" as here no absolute numbers are used, but rather quite generally *proportions* in relation to one another. Evidently, the focus is not only upon the nose. It has even been suggested that within the cited passage God's penis and vagina are discussed[178] — but even the most direct of the descriptions of God's body do not venture so far.[179] Ultimately, it is not only on account of the creation of humanity in the likeness of God that a certain analogy exists between the divine and human body, but also that, on grounds of the harmonious proportions of the entire body, his individual limbs find themselves in a harmonious relationship to one another as depicted in proportionate lengths and heights. In the macroform *Hekhalot Zutarti*, these relationships are possibly expressed in the line "his ends are like his form":[180] For the divine body it is also the case that a harmony between the micro- and macroproportions must exist.

In the large "Shi'ur Qomah" passages of Hekhalot literature, *three manners* in which the form of God's corporeality is described may be encountered: *First*, seemingly precise figures are given which nevertheless come across as fantastically high and are also time and time again discounted or neutralized by means of "rulings." *Second*, proportional relationships without figures are introduced. *Finally*, nomina barbara are provided for individual body parts. These three approaches in describing God's corporality are clearly deployed side by side within the texts, and are neither employed in a strict order, nor in a logical hierarchy.[181] The impression is also hardly gained that at the beginning of the development leading to the modern "Shi'ur Qomah" texts originally only one manner existed to describe this form, and that the two others emerged secondarily. Indeed, in the present shape of this material, these texts are concerned with relating the "dimensions of the form" of the divine body, as is demonstrated by the scenic introduction to the passages. At the same time, however, as has been seen, at the very least, this description is also fundamentally directed at revelation of the magical names of the body parts and not only their inconceivable size; hundreds of names are scattered within the relevant passages, partially in veritable clusters of names. The name of God's right thigh, for example, is ŠŠWWST PRNSY, and according to an Oxford fragment from the Cairo Genizah ŠŠNWST WPRNGSYY.[182] The passages which maintain proportionalities without measurements are by comparison rather subordinate; regardless, the notion of microproportionality is ultimately implied by the concept of macroproportionaility.

How might then the revelation of the names of the divine body parts and their sizes relate to one another? First and foremost, *both* acquaintance with the dimensions of the form of God's body and the esoteric name of God (unpronounceable in human language) constitute the cryptic knowledge of the mystic, and signify that he possesses knowledge of the secret revelation related by the angelic prince Metatron to Rabbi Yishma'el (in some traditions Rabbi Aqiba). Yet, the manner of knowledge pertaining to size and name respectively differs. Cognisance of the dimensions is something of a *negative knowledge*, as is also directly expressed in one passage: "We have in our hands no measurement (מידה), but the names are revealed to us."[183] Peter Schäfer concludes that "all attempts to 'measure' and describe" the measurements of the creator are "futile and illustrate the opposite of that which they want most to achieve; namely, that God's dimensions surpass any comprehensible 'measurement.'"[184] Gershom Scholem formulated this similarly:

> What is really meant by these monstrous length measurements is not made clear; the enormous figures have no intelligible meaning or sense-content, and it is impossible really to visualise the "body of the Shekhinah" which they purport to describe; they are better calculated, on the contrary, to reduce every attempt at such a vision to absurdity.[185]

Fundamentally, a factual, if not tradition-historical analogy to so-called *Theologia negativa*[186] is presented here: Within the texts, by means of inconceivably large measurements which are neutralized or utterly discounted by "rulings," the negative knowledge is conveyed that God is greater than anything of which one might even conceive—and precisely this also applies to his corporeal form. In classical *Theologia negativa*, this is expressed by means of characteristic attributes such as "inconceivable"; here, this is accomplished through inconceivable measurements. A sheer paradox might accordingly be articulated: Apparently precise knowledge proves itself to be ignorance upon closer inspection. Yet, in both Greek and Jewish traditions, it is through such "ignorance" that knowledge as to the categorical difference of God to all worldly things is conveyed. In contrast, knowledge of the names revealed by the "Shi'ur Qomah" is an eminently *positive* knowledge. Indeed, should it be taken seriously that the secret names of the divine body parts only accessible to the mystic stand in a general antique magical tradition of such *nomina barbara*, then this is neither a negative nor a static knowledge: The mystic reading Hekhalot literature meditates and pictures himself in the role of "those who descended to the chariot" (*Yorde Merkava*, ירדי מרכבה)[187] *possesses*, according to Peter Schäfer, not only a special knowledge, but also needs his knowledge in order to bring himself into an even closer relationship with God (for example, through incantation with the assistance of the secret names). Through the measurements and names, such a mystic wields (to a certain extent) the magical power to compel God to enter into a closer relationship with himself.[188] This purpose, that of approaching God himself through hallowed turns of phrase from the divine speech accessible to only a few at all, is served by the extensive liturgical passages within the "Shi'ur Qomah" sections, for example, in the introduction to the purportedly earliest section of the macroform *Hekhalot Rabbati*:

> Be lofty, be lofty, ye lofty ones!
> Be exalted, be exalted, ye exalted ones!
> Be mighty, be mighty, ye mighty ones!
> Be majestic, be majestic, majestic ones![189]

Peter Schäfer has termed the form of "mysticism" characterizing these texts "unio liturgica," as a union primarily born of liturgy occurring between the mystic, the angels, and God himself. He thereby differentiated this from the more starkly individualistic (and, in places, even ontologically conceived of as amalgatory) "unio mystica" of some medieval texts from the Christian tradition. The objective is to integrate the mystic into the heavenly liturgy, inasmuch as it is permitted him to hear, know, and pray along to the hymns and doxologies of this liturgy. A simultaneous "unio theurgica" standing next to the "unio mystica" may well be discussed: Both before the heavenly powers and in concert with them, the negative and positive knowledge alike helped the mystic to act appropriately and perform that which was required in relation to God.[190] It must also be supposed that measurements and names were not revealed visually,[191] but rather aurally: Metatron imparts this revelatory wisdom upon a privileged recipient from the rabbinic tradition.

The "Shi'ur Qomah" texts hence hardly paint the portrait of some "makrotheos"[192] in an unreflective or naïve manner by means of enlarging to giganticness the measurements of a well-proportioned human according to antique conceptions; rather, they employ a method which classical Western metaphysics termed *via eminentiae* in order to exclude through exaggeration of figures any comparison between the divine and human bodies. This excess in quantity must be understood as a metaphor for a categorical difference in quality between godly and human frames. In other words, God certainly possesses a body, but his well-proportioned, harmonious corporeality is separated from that of humans by means of a qualitative jump, and not merely a quantitative distance. These abstract, rather philosophical thoughts are expressed by the "Shi'ur Qomah" texts through names and numbers and remain as such in a certain sense within the tradition of biblical and postbiblical thought. Thus, for example, in macroform *Third Enoch*, the "hand of God" is ascribed an emotion, namely a "sorrow of the hand" which indicates that an absolutely superhuman, even

God's Body

categorically different divine corporeality is here being dealt with: "In that hour, the right hand of God wept, and five streams of tears flowed from their five fingers, fell into the great sea, and made the earth quake."[193] Nevertheless, the difference between the logically coherent argumentation of antique philosophical texts and these late antique or Byzantine Jewish mystical texts need also not be exaggerated. At least one passage from the "Shiʻur Qomah" texts might also be read very Platonically:

> The image of His face and the image of His cheeks is as the dimensions of the spirit and as the creation of the soul, such that no one can recognize it. "His body is *tarshish*" (Daniel 10:6).[194]

In this difficult to interpret sentence, Platonic scholars could certainly recover the notion of an immaterial apparition of God, a form of intellectual "vision" which, according to this theory, was as vital in grasping immaterial and spiritual realities and the transcendent reality of God alike. Read accordingly, the sentence cited would mean the following: For "those who descended to the chariot," the spirit and soul exist in the state in which they were originally created by God: These mystics "see" God, but as his body is not composed of conventional earthly materiality, but rather shines like a precious gem, it is also scarcely to be recognized like some terrestrial object, but rather to be beheld solely intellectually.

"Shiʻur Qomah" Traditions in Christian Authors

This observation on the multiple readings of a sentence from Hekhalot literature invites the question as to how the "Shiʻur Qomah" traditions, which appear to be very much particular and unique, relate to other contemporaneous traditions of discourse on God's body. Might the "Shiʻur Qomah" texts merely represent the late product of a development within post-antique, medieval Babylonian Judaism, or is it, in fact, meaningful to search for traditions within the Imperial-era religious koine from which these specific "dimensions of the form" of the divine body might have emerged?

In the Christian literature of Late Antiquity, certain indications exist that there was a complete awareness of certain Jewish groups' speculation as to the body of God, although the evidence is not entirely without problems. Already in the middle of the second century AD, in his "Dialogue with Trypho," the apologist and denizen of Rome *Justin* railed against a literal interpretation of biblical passages in which Christ or angels are discussed, that is, in his opinion, of divine substantialities which a human or humanoid body might assume:

And when he says, "When I consider thy heavens, the work of thy fingers" (Psalm 8:3), unless I comprehend the operation of his Word, I shall not understand the passage. Then I would be like your teachers, who imagine that the Father of the universe, the unbegotten God, has hands and feet and fingers and a soul like a compound creature. As a result of this belief, they claim that the Father Himself appeared to Abraham and Jacob.[195]

It becomes apparent from this passage that, in the opinion of Justin, who hailed from Samaria and was in dialogue with rabbis, there were "Jewish teachers" who accorded God appurtenant limbs as if a composite living creature of both body and soul. As has been seen, the same is attested by Origen for both the cities of Alexandria and Caesarea in the mid-third century AD. This notwithstanding, his remarks allude rather to piety within the communities, and not to Jewish scholars, rabbinical or otherwise, and most certainly not to "those who descended to the chariot." Reference to these groups possibly only first occurs at the onset of the following century: Within a relatively conventional polemic against pagan anthropomorphism, *Arnobius of Sicca*, a North African rhetorician and apologist for Christianity in the face of the Diocletianic Persecution of AD 303–305, accordingly accuses some very particular Jewish circles of possessing anthropomorphic conceptions of God:

Now let us come to the appearance and shapes by which you believe that the gods above have been represented, with which, indeed, you fashion, and set them up in their most splendid abodes, your temples. And let no one here bring up against us Jewish fables and those of the sect of the Sadducees, as though we, too, attribute to the Deity forms (for this is supposed to be taught in their writings and asserted as if with assurance and authority); for these stories either do not concern us, and have nothing at all in common with us, or if they are shared in [by us], as you believe, you must seek out teachers of greater wisdom, through whom you may be able to learn how best to overcome the dark and recondite sayings of those writings.[196]

On first glance, Arnobius' statements come across as strange. Yet, even if the notion that, of all things, the Sadducees argued for an anthropomorphic image of God relates rather poorly with what might otherwise be believed to be known about this group (according to the Acts of the Apostles in the New Testament, they deny the resurrection and the existence of angels and spirits: 23:8[197]), such a tradition may also be found in other, admittedly later sources.[198] In turn, the (somewhat faint) memory seems to have been retained that there are Jewish Scriptures which teach the corporeality of God and, without additional interpretative help, come across as abstruse to a Christian reader. As the Sadducees' biblical basis of argumentation was formed exclusively by the Torah, that is, the five books of Moses, and given that as temple priests they were the guardians of a space considered God's apartment, it might incidentally be presumed that a corporeal image of God prevailed among this group.

Moreover, in an anonymously transmitted late antique homily eagerly attributed nevertheless to *Basil of Caesarea* entitled "On the Creation of Man," it might not only be read that God is "formless and simple," but also that the "dreaming up" of a divine body might be termed "Jewish" (Ἰουδαϊκῶς):

> You should not dream up any form for him. You should not shrink that which is great in the Jewish manner. You should not grasp God in corporeal form, not confine him according to the measure of your mind. . . . Do not picture a form—God must be conceived of on the strength of his power—for the simplicity of his nature, nor a quantity for his size.[199]

Whether this polemic is directed towards the "Shi'ur Qomah" traditions is even less certain than the case of Arnobius' testimony a few decades before. Indeed, the preacher's polemic is directed against "simple, uneducated, unscholarly conceptions of God" within Christian communities;[200] by contrast, the polemic against Judaism is all too schematic.

Hence, it is rather more sensible to search after direct parallels to "dimensions of the form" of the divine body within Christian and pagan texts. Naturally, this does not concern the narrative framework within which an individual who has ascended into heaven holds forth on particular revelations as to a godhead. Richard Reitzenstein has accordingly pointed to Hellenistic astrological fragments of Egyptian or pseudo-Egyptian provenance such as is known from, for example, the introduction to a "Handbook of Astrology" by certain individuals named *Nechepso* and *Petosiris* transmitted in an anthology of the second century AD: "I decided then, (to gaze in prayer) all night long up to the sky, . . . and a shout sounded forth from heaven. Around its flesh a mantle of dark blue colour was wrapped, stretching out darkness before itself."[201] Heavenly journeys were generally in vogue, and also do not render the specifics here sought after.[202] If Platonic philosophy in a general sense is to be eschewed, particularly its theory of principles initially only accessible to initiated members of tight scholastic circles, then it is difficult to find any direct pagan parallel in Antiquity. Certainly, in so-called Middle Platonism (for example, in *Eudorus of Alexandria* in the first century BC), solid mathematical competence is presumed and the absolutely transcendent God in Neopy-thagorean tradition termed "the One" (τὸ ἕν), in Eudorus even within a complicated juxtaposition of two principles, serving to "leave the One as principle of all things, but in another way introduce the highest ele-ments as two. . . . It is clear that the One as principle of all things is quite distinct from the One opposite to the Dyad, which they also call Monad."[203] Naturally, as the "Monad" as a principle of numbers is categor-ically different from all countables, no attempt is made to count or mea-sure the utter unity of the Monad. The same fundamentally holds for the philosophical theory of Neoplatonic ideal numbers as is elaborated upon within an Imperial-era introduction, difficult to date any more precisely, known as the "Arithmetic Theologumena" of Pseudo-Iamblichus.[204] Here, in addition to the "Monad," the "Dyad," "Triad," "Tetrad," and so forth are inserted into the theory of principles (and individual formations of sys-tems attributed to so-called Christian Gnosticism adopt these ideal num-bers or apply them at their divine instances). Nevertheless, it is strictly excluded that the dimensions characterized by ideal numbers might be completed by means of further measurements; on the contrary, such an act of mensuration would hardly be possible for these purely immaterial dimensions: Oneness is the origin of numbers and does not possesses as such spatial extent, or, indeed, any concomitant corporeality.[205]

The "Book of Elchasai"

Parallels to the particular combination of theory of numbers and magic marking out the "Shi'ur Qomah" texts may best be found in writings from groups *on the fringes of the nascent mainstream Christian church*. The most striking parallel hails from reports as to a book today lost with the exception of only a few fragments, the "Book of Elchasai" or "Elxai,"[206] likely written during the reign of Emperor Trajan.[207] This book may possibly have been composed in the same region as later the Jewish mystical texts, namely Persia. As may be supposed from the biography of the Persian gnos-tic *Mani* (AD 216–276),[208] founder of Manicheanism, being, as he was, a member of such a Persian "Elcesaite" baptist community, and having later debated with other members as to the validity of his new teachings,[209] this must still have been used within baptist communities in Persia in the third century AD. Whether, within the confusing religious landscape of Persia, the "Book of Elchasai" or "Elxai" falls under the rubric of "Jewish," "Chris-tian," "Judeo-Christian," or even "syncretistic-gnostic Judeo-Christianity," or (in analogy to the system of teachings of Manichaean Gnosis) enjoyed a multiplicity of religious readerships and applications, need not here be explored.[210] From the critical discussion of this book among theologians of

God's Body

the mainstream Christian church, it is certainly evident that the text was
also used by Christian groups in the era of the Roman Empire. Somewhat
difficult to explain is the name *Elchasai* or *Elxai* and its original function
in the context of the book. The book possibly bore at first the Aramaic title
"The Book of the Hidden Strength" after the figure of the revelatory angel
termed therein a "hidden strength" (חיל כסי).[211] Eusebius quotes one fragment from an (otherwise lost) sermon of Origen in the Palestinian port town
of Caesarea wherein the preacher states that people claim on the authority of
the "Heresy of the Helkesaites" (τῆς Ἐλκεσαιτῶν αἵρεσις) that this book
fell from heaven.[212] The book was already associated with the mythological
figure of a prophet named "Elchasai" (Ἠλχασαΐ) or "Elxai" (Ἠλξαΐ) in
the third century AD, or may well have even been tied to a historical figure
of this name from its very inception who was perhaps its author—this
remains, however, uncertain.[213] It is no longer distinguishable as to whether
Elchasai or *Elxai* might be understood as the byname of a historical personage (as with Simon Magus, the Samaritan followers of whom had taken to
calling "great power" according to the testimony of the Acts of the Apostles,
associating him thereby with the redemptive God[214]) or regarded as a proper
name.[215] It is, by contrast, relatively certain that this was linked from the
very beginning with a movement which offered an immersive bath in order
to forgive sins, and insofar counted among the baptismal movements found
on both sides of the eastern border of the Imperium Romanum, regardless of
whether a Christian origin in the notion of a (second) baptism is to be reckoned with, or rather with an analogy to divers forms of Jewish purification
rituals.[216]

The "Book of Elchasai" or "Elxai" was evidently relayed and employed
by groups within Persia and the eastern Jordan. *Epiphanius of Salamis*
reports that Elchasai's (alleged) progeny still lived in the age of Emperor
Constantine in the shape of two sisters. On one hand, due to his origins,
Epiphanius had at his disposal local knowledge of the region of the eastern Jordan, yet, on the other, he recounts without circumspection the most
absurd of rumors, so that here as well scarce certitude as to this might be
gained. Epiphanius maintains that this brace of sisters, Marthus and Mar-
thana, were worshipped as gods, and their saliva along with other bodily
refuse was used for healing purposes by "deluded sectarians in that country" merely because they were apparently Elxai's kin.[217] The employment
of spittle may be reminiscent of the healing treatments of Jesus, who healed
the man born blind with his saliva (Mark 8:22–26). It may also, however, be
connected with the therapeutic powers actually present within this secretion,
which were highly esteemed in both the Jewish and pagan worlds.[218]

Should the accounts from theologians of the mainstream Christian
church be trusted, then the "Book of Elchasai" or "Elxai" contained, *on the*

one hand, provisions as to the Christian life in the form of a church ordinance (for example, on the second baptism, ritual cleansing, prayer in the direction of Jerusalem, circumcision, and the keeping of the Sabbath) and, *on the other*, speculations as to the gigantic scale of divine bodies. Reports upon this are once more only preserved today in the Christian heresiologies of the third and fourth centuries AD, that is, in authors who pursued their own respective polemic agendas in discussing the book. Pertinent to a comparison with the "Shi'ur Qomah" texts is a passage transmitted, on the one hand, by the Roman heresiologist Hippolytus in his "Refutation of all Heresies" in the early third century AD and, on the other, in three parallel versions independent of this, by Epiphanius of Salamis, metropolitan of Cyprus, at the end of the fourth century AD, in his "Medicine Chest against Heresies." In *Hippolytus*, the following might be read:

> A man by the name of Alcibiades (who was deceitful and stark raving mad) observed this affair while living in Apamea of Syria. He, judging himself more monstrous and more naturally suited for scams than Callixtus, came to Rome bringing a certain book. He claimed that a certain righteous man named Elchasai had received it from the Seres of Parthia. Elchasai handed it on to a man called Sobiai, as if it were an oracle from an angel who was twenty-four schoeni high (or ninety-six miles),[219] four schoeni wide, and six schoeni from shoulder to shoulder. His footprints were three and a half schoeni in length (or fourteen miles), one and a half schoenus wide, and half a schoenus high. There was a female with him too, whose measurements, he says, accorded with the preceding. Now the male is the son of god, whereas the female is called "Holy spirit."[220]

Hippolytus describes the "Book of Elchasai" within his highly critical examination of Callixtus, bishop of Rome between AD 217/218 and AD 222/223 (a theme marking his entire anti-heretical work); Hippolytus defames him as not only an arch-heretic, but also as an irresponsible fraud and an unprincipled coward. According to his account, an Elcesaite called Alcibiades is supposed to have arrived in Rome during this period and to have touted his teachings within Rome's Christian community, which had already been rendered confused by Callixtus; Hippolytus claims also to know that Bishop Callixtus of Rome influenced Alcibiades in respect to his views on baptism and forgiveness of sins. The book had likely already been translated from Aramaic into Greek,[221] as is demonstrated by the conversion of the "schoeni" into Roman miles, which rendered the measurements legible for circles outside of the Aramaic-speaking cultural orbit. In addition, it might be noted that within Hippolytus' account (which, on his own part, may touch upon Alcibiades' own account of the book), the measurements are starkly abbreviated: When the height, the breadth of the shoulders and waist are described, on the one hand, and also the length of the feet, on the other, then most likely statements as to the nose, eyes, arms, and hands might also have been found in the book, exactly as in the "Shi'ur Qomah" texts. Hippolytus not only recounts this, but also identifies the Elchasaites with Pythagoreanism within the remits of his heresiological concept of associating all Christian heresies with pagan philosophical schools[222]—certainly, it has already been seen that such a connection would quite immediately suggest itself to the antique reader, as generally redolent as the connection between God and numbers is of Neopythagoreanism and its arithmetic theology.

The independent parallel transmission of this text more than 150 years later in the "Medicine Chest against Heresies" of Epiphanius, metropolitan of Salamis on Cyrus, demonstrates that, just as is the case between individual relayed versions of the "Shi'ur Qomah" fragments, statements as to measurements could vary wildly. Evidently, here, the exactitude of the transmission was not the most important consideration, but rather a general impression of the largest numbers possible. Epiphanius quotes the passage from a Greek translation of the "Book of Elxai" and does not merely report on it through indirect speech in the manner of his predecessor, with the work of whom he evidently is entirely unfamiliar. The *first transmission* parallel to Hippolytus may be found in Epiphanius within a passage on the "Ossaeans" (a group only attested by him, perhaps another name for the "Essenes"[223]), according to his account, a Jewish group in the eastern Jordan, who had merged into the more Christian group of the "Sampsaeans" by this time.[224] "Elxai," a false prophet, is supposed to have later joined them. The account then concentrates upon questions of ethics and Christology, thereafter continuing:

> Then he describes Christ as a kind of power, and even gives his dimensions—his length of 24 schoeni, or 96 miles, and his width of twenty-four miles, or six schoeni, and similar prodigies about his thickness and feet, and the other stories. And the Holy Spirit—a feminine one at that—is like Christ too, and stands like an image, above a cloud and in between two mountains.[225]

Epiphanius and Hippolytus marginally differ from one another: Hippolytus offers more measurements; Epiphanius abbreviates the account, in particular regarding the difference between waist and shoulder widths, and the very extensive pronouncements upon the feet. Either more figures could be found in the original text consulted by Hippolytus than in that referred to by Epiphanius, or the Cypriot bishop had no interest in enumerating any further figures. Moreover, the Christianization of the book appears to have markedly progressed in the copy employed by Epiphanius in comparison to the version extant in the times of Hippolytus a century and a half prior, as the measurements which concern first and foremost a single revelatory angel (with an attendant second angel) according to Hippolytus, and are only secondarily identified with Christ within the text, describe according to Epiphanius the Christ who appears in a vision along with the Holy Ghost. The more archaic angelic Christology characterizing the first stage of redaction according to Hippolytus has now entirely fallen by the wayside, and angels are no longer mentioned. The notion likely derived from the vision of the Prophet Isaiah in the eponymous biblical book that two angels, seraphs, stand before the divine throne and wait upon it (Isaiah 6:1–3)[226] has here coalesced with the stardardized Christian Trinitarian theology of Late Antiquity.

The account in Hippolytus could provenance from the initial part of the book, inasmuch as its contents originate from a revelatory angel and are legitimated by means of a vision. Interestingly, Epiphanius relates in his account of the "Ebionites" a *second, strikingly parallel version* of its stated contents and, after the measurements, a further literally quoted passage which must be directly related to the reports of the two angels in Hippolytus and Epiphanius:

> Thus they believe that Christ is a manlike figure invisible to human eyes, ninety-six miles—or twenty-four schoeni, if you please!—tall; six schoeni, or twenty-four miles wide; and some other measurement through. Opposite him the Holy Spirit stands invisibly as well, in the form of a female, with the same dimensions. "And how did I (sc. Elchasai/Elxai[227]) find the dimensions?" he says. "I saw from the mountains that the heads were level with them, and from observing the height of the mountain, I learned the dimensions of Christ and the Holy Spirit."[228]

Finally, a *third account* may be found in the section on the Sampsaeans:

> He is called Christ, and the Holy Spirit is his sister, in female form. Each of them, Christ and the Holy Spirit, is ninety-six miles in height and six in width; and they blab out a lot of other nonsense.[229]

The third report is so heavily abbreviated that, without knowledge of both previous examples, one would be compelled to assume that the width consisted of six miles (and not schoini), indicating either drastically narrowed shoulders or a wasp waist.

In his monograph "The Origins of Jewish Mysticism," Peter Schäfer has drawn attention to the differences of this passage from the "Book of Elchasai" to the "Shi'ur Qomah" traditions:[230] In the extant pieces, no measurements are relayed for individual body parts (excluding momentarily the feet), but rather only very general body dimensions provisioned. The gargantuan body in the "Book of Elchasai" does not belong to the "greatest and supreme" God,[231] but rather two angels. However, large angels are also found elsewhere in passages within pagan[232] and Christian literature,[233] for example, in the now-apocryphal Gospel of Peter (as assistants to the risen Christ).[234] The rabbinic tradition preserves the notion that an originally gigantically fashioned Adam was shrunk in punishment for the fall; it was first thereby that he transformed from an angelic being to a mortal human.[235] Probably, these two angels were also first identified with the Son of God and the Holy Ghost at a secondary stage of the textual transmission, as is demonstrated by a strangely unconnected sentence in Hippolytus reminiscent of a scholion: "There was a female with him too, whose measurements, he says, accorded with the preceding. Now the male is the son of god, whereas the female is called 'Holy spirit.'"[236] Certainly, this insertion of a particular, rather Judeo-Christian form of the Christian Trinity, evidencing a linguistic consciousness of the grammatical gender of the Hebrew word "spirit" (*ruakh*, רוח) and its Aramaic and Syriac derivates, is clearly secondary. Indeed, in Hippolytus, the passage concerns a revelatory angel who—much like Metatron in the "Shi'ur Qomah" fragments—confers the revelation, albeit, in the "Shi'ur Qomah" fragments, it is not the revelatory angel, but rather God himself who is described in more detail. Moreover, the dimensions are not all that comparable. Were one to calculate on the basis of the allegedly original "schoina," then the height of the angel is 252 kilometers, the shoulder breadth 63 kilometers, the waist 42 kilometers, and the foot length a little more than 36 kilometers. Quite evidently, the notion of a beautiful body with regular proportions hardly seems to underpin this description: Should these figures reflect the original values, then the angels have markedly longer feet than would be acceptable within the ideal dimensions espoused by Vitruvius (and Polycleitus). Additionally, the angels are clearly too tall to accord with the ideal proportions (by around fifty kilometers), and must be considered to be relatively ill-proportioned beings according to the information rendered by the textual evidence presently extant. It might also be asked as to which mountain was imagined in respect to these exorbitant statements as to height—in the "Book of Elchasai" or "Elxai," this angelic stature is correlated with the mountain height in order to ascertain exact measurements.

So as to understand correctly the "Book of Elchasai" and to be able to relate it appropriately to the "Shi'ur Qomah" fragments, it must further be emphasized that, in terms of genre, it fundamentally differs from later texts within Jewish mysticism. It was F. Stanley Jones who first indicated that this work need not represent, as was keenly thought, an "Apocalypse of Elchasai"—this apparently self-evident genre-historical allocation is the result of, for example, its inclusion in the collection of "New Testament apocrypha" articulated by Edward Hennecke in 1904, and its repeated publication in editions thereafter by Wilhelm Schneemelcher.[237] Jones could demonstrate on the strength of a complete collection of the fragments that, according to the vast majority of the fragments, this tome rather concerns church ordinances which are merely garbed in an apocalypse so as to lend authority to the regulations therein (which in many points starkly diverge from those of the mainstream church).[238] Due to a dearth of pertinent texts, it remains unknown which historical events might well underpin this authorizing passage—Wilhelm Brandt suggested sheer autosuggestion on the part of Elchasai or deceit.[239]

A further fundamental difference between the fragment from the "Book of Elchasai" and the "Shi'ur Qomah" passages becomes thereby evident. As has been seen, the measurements within these fragments of Jewish mystical tradition perform a very precise function: They seek to accent the categorical difference between the use of divine names in the everyday world, and the employment of magical names in the heavenly sphere. The measurements given in the "Book of Elchasai" seek, in contrast, merely to demonstrate that the revelatory angel (or even Christ) commands such an authority that dissenting regulations on matter such as baptismal and supplicatory practice or interaction with astrology and fire within Christian factions in Persia might thereby be justified. Should the implicit connection between the "Book of Elchasai" and the literary genre of apocalypse posited by earlier generations of researchers be done away with (and this must at the very least be considered with great seriousness), then the parallelization between "Shi'ur Qomah" passages and this book proves far more to be sheer "parallelomania," as Peter Schäfer has already maintained in the relevant passages of his book "The Origins of Jewish Mysticism."

So-Called Gnosis

The texts of the "Shi'ur Qomah" are also keenly compared with so-called Christian Gnosticism,[240] primarily with that which is reported about the Christian gnostic *Marcus* in Rome.[241] Marcus is conventionally counted among the school of the Christian teacher Valentinus active in

Rome, but this was most likely actually—as the present author has demonstrated elsewhere—a school of the Christian teacher Ptolemy, who inhabited
Rome in mid-second century AD.[242] As at some point in the AD 160s Val-
entine abandoned Rome in favor of Asia Minor (for reasons presently still
obscure),[243] the urbanite Roman scholastic circle of his student Ptolemy evidently named itself after its revered teacher Valentinus (or was termed so by
its critics) without the far-removed or perhaps even deceased eponym being
able to fend off this usurpation of his authority. According to many critics
from the mainstream church such as the aforementioned Irenaeus, bishop of
Lyon, the teacher Marcus also belonged to the network of the "Valentinian
school"[244] which—as the famous letter of Ptolemy to the Roman matron
Flora demonstrates[245]—possessed a certain cachet in intellectual circles
beyond the Christian community of the imperial capital on account of more
than just this name. Nevertheless, it is unknown in which time and place
exactly this Marcus taught. Irenaeus claims that "some of his disciples" also
"wandered about"[246] the region and that "such things as these they prattled
and practised also in our own regions around the Rhône and deceived many
women."[247] On the strength of this alone, these details already fall under
suspicion of not exactly reflecting the historical situation of Lyon in the AD
180s, as they betray the bishop's conviction that, as especially credible creatures, women could be misled with marked ease by heretics. Moreover, it
is not yet stated thereby that Marcus instructed in the same place where his
students taught and evidently so successfully proselytized (namely in the
region of the Rhône), being as he was also active in Asia Minor.[248]

Should the text of Marcus, preserved above all in the great heresiological work of Bishop Irenaeus of Lyon and in extensive citations in Epiphanius of Salamis, be compared with the "Shi'ur Qomah" tradition, then
no parallels may here be found to the "Dimensions of the Form" of the
body of God. Certainly, Marcus identified the so-called Aeons (αἰῶνες) of
the Valentinian scholastic tradition, a manner of contrafaction to Platonic
notions, with biblical terminology, explicitly referring to the Gospel of
Matthew's angels surrounding the divine throne. Yet, this is all very much
removed from any species of "throne-chariot mysticism": The very specific form of speculation upon letters of the alphabet in Marcus is certainly
an adaptation of traditions from Jewish apocalyptic and, in particular, Jewish gematria,[249] but still remains largely beholden to the fundamental concept of so-called Valentinian Gnosticism, namely the interpretation of the
biblical stories of creation and salvation against the backdrop of a Middle
Platonic philosophy often contradicting their own sense:[250]

> The restoration of all things will take place, he said, whenever all have
> descended upon the one letter, and sound one and the same pronunciation.

He supposes the Amen, which we pray in unison, to be the image of this pronunciation. But the sounds, he claims, are those which formed the Aeon that is immaterial and ingenerate. They are likewise the forms which see the face of Father unceasingly, which the Lord calls angels (Matthew 18:10).[251]

Here, from the background of gematria and speculation on letters, the fundamental conviction common to all systems of so-called Valentinian Gnosticism is explained, namely that, at the end of a story of fall and dispersion, the different Aeons become once more unified and collectively give thanks by way of singing a hymn which naturally is concluded with an "Amen."[252] The end of the story is qualified with terminology from the New Testament's Acts of the Apostles as the "restitution of all things" (3:21). The mythological telling of the end of (salvation) history at the level of Aeons somewhat depicts the paragon of the earthly story of the fall and redemption of humanity, which—in Platonic terms—is the model of terrestrial reality at the level of the idea, which nevertheless (as is often the case in antique Christianity) was not described with the Platonic term "idea" (ἰδέα, "immaterial form").[253] The notion of eschatological unity characterizing so-called Valentinian Gnosis is now explained by Marcus against the backdrop of alphabetic speculation in such a manner that at the end—in a very much Platonic sense—everything becomes thereby once more the Monad, inasmuch as one single letter will stand in place of many characters and pronunciations, one single sound, the perfect harmony of One and Many. The fallen world is represented by means of an endless slew of letters, the redeemed world wherein God will exist "all in all" (1 Corinthians 15:28) through one.

Most viable for comparison with Hekhalot literature are secret names of divine instances, which are not actually named by Irenaeus and the other Christian critics, but rather merely generally characterized: Accordingly, the final letter of a secret divine name known to Marcus through a special revelation, by means of which God speaks and creates, is composed of thirty letters containing within them every further letter; in turn, the Christ-figure is distinguished by a profusion of written characters which represent the "fullness" (τὸ πλήρωμα) of the Aeons in the system of Ptolemy's students, and thereby a contrafacture of the world of ideas:[254]

For Jesus indeed is a symbolical name, having six letters[255] and being known by all who belong to those who are called. The name, however, which is among the Aeons of the Fullness, has many parts, being of another form and another type; it is known by those companions (of Saviour) whose Greatnesses (angels) are always with him.[256]

Should the report hold true, then Marcus differentiated between different names for divine instances (in addition to "Jesus" perhaps "Christ," or the aforementioned secret divine name with thirty characters), knowledge of which was reserved to disparate groups; this point is at once suggestive of the differentiation between followers of the mainstream church communities and those who might be thought of as adhering additionally to relevant gnostic groups generally expressed in the Pauline tradition by means of the designations "psychics" and "pneumatics."[257]

Probably the closest parallel to the "Shi'ur Qomah" passages may be found in the description of an Aeon from the Valentinian fullness of Aeons—the contrafacture of a notion—known as "the Truth." It is explained as follows, possibly through a quotation:

> I wish to show you Truth itself. I have brought her down from the dwellings on high that you might look on her unveiled and learn of her beauty and admire her wisdom. See, then, alpha and omega are her head on high; beta and psi are her neck; gamma and chi are her shoulders with hands; her breast is delta and phi; epsilon and upsilon are her diaphragm; zeta and tau are her stomach; eta and sigma are her private parts; theta and rho are her thighs; iota and psi are her knees; kappa and omicron are her legs; lambda and xi are her ankles; mu and nu are her feet. This, according to the magician, is the body of Truth; this is the shape of her character; this is the impression of her letter. And he calls this character Man.[258]

Certainly, this concerns the description of a figure from head to toe (via the upper and lower body) which is expressly termed a "body," but the body is not composed of flesh, or, indeed, other airy materiality, but rather from characters of the Greek alphabet, wherein the first and last letters ("alpha" and "omega") are combined, and then the next in descending and ascending order, until both sequences meet at "Mu" and "Nu." Comparable orders may be found in antique astrology, for example, when two letters are assigned to each symbol of the Zodiac (as in Teucer/Teukros, who most likely lived in the first century AD in Babylon / Old Cairo).[259] At the same time, this also reflects a process implemented within Jewish texts for encryption and decryption (*Ath-bash*, אתבש), finding use in the antique magical papyri.[260] Much remains unclear in the passage quoted from the writings of Marcus: As to whether here a connection between the heavenly notion of humanity and the astrological determinants of the fate of terrestrial humans should be implied cannot really be determined from the highly abbreviated account within Irenaeus (and Epiphanius). It is not once even clear whether Marcus uses the term "body" (σῶμα) in a metaphorical sense, as he conceived of the "Aeons" in analogy to notions in the strictly Platonic sense as bodiless, immaterial forms, and also only took the letters as metaphors for spiritual reality, or as to whether he described a particular materiality borne by these signs. Whatever might be concluded, both fragments from Marcus extant within Irenaeus and the reports on his writings contain no calculations as to the measurements of God's body, fundamentally ruling out comparison with the "Shi'ur Qomah" traditions. Not only is "Truth" nowhere mentioned as possessing a giant body, but also no particular names are given for any individual limbs as such, and any identification of "Truth" with God himself is lacking. At best, analogies exist *generally* between Hekhalot literature and what is transmitted of Marcus' writings: Both cases are concerned with the revelation of secret names of divine instances, most likely also presented within Marcus in the form of *nomina barbara*, albeit not recapitulated by his mainstream church opponents. Insofar, in respect to potential analogies and parallels to the "Shi'ur Qomah" texts, this branch of so-called Christian Gnosis, Peter Schäfer's pronouncement is apt: "True, the parallel is striking, but so are the differences."[261]

Gershom Scholem himself alluded to a few further, independently transmitted Christian-gnostic texts found most prominently in the tractates of the Codices Askewianus and Brucianus, London and Oxford manuscripts, namely the *Pistis Sophia*, the two *Books of Jeû*, and the so-called *Untitled Text*.[262] The manuscripts hail from the late fourth or early fifth centuries AD; the Coptic texts have been dated for the most part to the third century AD but may well be markedly younger. Conventionally, they are numbered among the writings of so-called Sethian Gnosticism, albeit it is debated as to whether this designation might not constitute a modern construct on the part of academia.[263] This results in the broaching of the difficult question as to whether a "Jewish Gnosis"[264] existed, either as a prerequisite of Christian gnosis, or, indeed, as a roughly contemporary emergence; the answer to this question would only be of interest to the present question were it to yield thereby clear parallels to the "Shi'ur Qomah" texts within Christian gnostic literature. Yet, no such parallels to these catalogs of astoundingly exact measurements of the form of God's body might be found. Certainly, a "garment of light" which Jesus dons is repeatedly discussed in the *Pistis Sophia*,[265] but reference is never made to the form of the supreme deity. Body is only discussed in the context of inferior divine instances: "Now it is that *matter* of the Barbelo which is a *body* to thee today."[266] The two *Books of Jeû* do, in fact, contain all manner of *nomina barbara* for divine instances, but nevertheless, the supreme deity is never the topic of discussion, but rather merely subordinate divine forces; dimensions or bodily descriptions are nowhere to be found.[267]

The systematic reason for this reticence is the same in the two *Books of Jeû* as that rendered by the *Untitled Text*:

> There is again another *place* which is called "deep." There are three fatherhoods within it. The first (father) there is the *covered one* who is the hidden God. In the second father there stand the five trees, and there is a table in their midst. And an only begotten *logos* . . . In the third (father) is the silence and the source . . .[268]

Howsoever, as always, the relationship of this text might be understood as relating to so-called Valentinian Gnosticism, inasmuch as the supreme deity might gladly be termed "deep" (βυθός or βάθος) and "logos," "silence," and "source" are employed as names for the Aeons, functioning hence as divine instances,[269] it is very much certain that the transcendence of the supreme god in the *Untitled Text* is meant to be emphasized through a particularly elaborate description of his otherworldliness employing the aforementioned epithets "deep," "silence," and "source," the communicative element of which is Logos, God's word, as within mainstream Christian theology. This form of Christian Gnosis (irrespective of whether it is to be termed Sethian) comes into contact with the Platonic tradition at this juncture, as has been most prominently demonstrated by John D. Turner.[270]

In a great many texts ascribed to Christian Gnosis, these divine instances are naturally conceived of as bodiless due to this interest in the absolute categorical transcendence of the divine. This is not in the least due to the fact that these texts are more or less in accordance with the fundamental principles of the philosophy of the (Middle) Platonic school. This may, for example, be observed in the *Excerpta ex Theodoto*. This comprises a collection of excerpts from writings by the so-called Valentinian school, and, in particular, from a "Valentinian" perhaps resident in Egypt in the second third of the second century AD, one Theodotus. This was compiled by Clement of Alexandria at the beginning of the third century AD as a manner of notebook for a tractate against the "Valentinian" Gnostics which was never completed.[271] "Bodilessness" is an important keyword within this collection, so much so that even the matter and passions with which the fashioning of the earthly world begin are expressly described as "incorporeal" in two groups of excerpts from "Valentinian" texts,[272] thus rendering it unnecessary even to maintain explicitly the incorporeal and purely immaterial existences of the supreme deity and the subordinate divine instances known as Aeons. Here, the "Valentinian" texts give free rein to the Platonic impetus to stress the absolute transcendence of God as an immaterial being. In spite of this, a passage may also be found in the *Excerpta* which astoundingly emphasizes the materiality of the world of the angels and of the creator of Christ. This passage probably hails from neither Clement nor Theodotus, nor indeed any "Valentinian" gnostic:

> But not even the world of spirit and of intellect, nor the archangels and the First-Created, no, nor even He Himself is shapeless and formless and without figure, and incorporeal; but he also has his own shape and body corresponding to his pre-eminence over all spiritual beings, as also those who were first created have bodies corresponding to their pre-eminence over the beings subordinate to them.[273]

Yet, even within this quotation variously assigned to the lost lectures of Clement's teacher, Pantatenus,[274] or even to the oeuvre of Clement himself (although a stridently Stoic phase would then have to be assumed for this Christian Platonist),[275] the archangels, a particular group of seven primeval higher spirits, and the remaining angelic entities are all accorded a (presumably Stoically gossamer) materiality, and also the creator and Christ, albeit, strikingly enough, not God himself, provided one trusts Clement, who either excerpted this from an unknown source or composed it himself. These may well represent notes for the introduction, with which Clement evidently sought to unseat the radical emphasis upon the corporeality of the divine principles within so-called Valentinian Gnosticism—however, this must admittedly remain uncertain. Valentinian or Jewish groups wherein such a stance might be taught might easily enough be imagined to have existed. By contrast, as a dyed-in-the-wool Platonist, it seems rather unlikely that this passage might be ascribed to Clement.

From these observations, it becomes clear that there is also no uniform conception of divine figures within the texts ascribed to so-called Christian Gnosis. Essentially, that which had applied to postbiblical Jewish literature also held for this form of Christian literature: Many (but not all) texts argue vehemently against the notion of a divine corporeality, and, in the vein of the Platonic school, rail against an ultimately biblical concept of God's body considered to be unphilosophical, absurd, and uneducated. When, however, divine corporeality is discussed, then the manner of direct realism found in the "Shi'ur Qomah" texts with their clear organization of body parts and measurements (albeit also repeated repudiations of realism) is eschewed.

While the identification of clear parallels with the "Shi'ur Qomah" passages from Hekhalot literature within Jewish and Christian antique and late antique literature alike is not forthcoming, it may hardly be believed that such seemingly absurd and linguistically challenging passages of Hekhalot literature pertain to completely isolated texts from particularly pious and marginalized fringe groups. Of course, the mystical groups of "those who descended to the chariot" hardly lived removed from any contact with their intellectual environment; rather, as Peter Schäfer has demonstrated in many publications, there was a fruitful dialogue, and exchange was enjoyed. Naturally, should it be sought to contextualize the attempts hailing from the Byzantine era of these groups to describe the "Dimensions of the Form" of the divine body, one need not elect to employ the writings of so-called Christian Gnosticism, the teachings of the "Valentinian" Marcus, and the texts of the "Book of Elchasai" in comparison. Although such connections were already made very early on between these Christian traditions and the "Shi'ur Qomah" fragments, indeed by protagonists of the new "Wissenschaft des Judentums" such as Moses Gaster, the Sephardic chief rabbi of England and a leading Zionist to wit, and attention has frequently been drawn to them ever since, most recently by Josef M. Baumgarten,[276] the dearth of clear parallels is once more an argument against an early dating to the second century AD for the versions and texts of the "Shi'ur Qomah" traditions presented in the macroforms of Hekhalot literature. This notwithstanding, as has been seen, the localization of the latter traditions and texts within Babylonia, or, indeed, southern Babylonia is rendered possible by means of such comparisons.[277]

Pertinent comparison to the Christologies developed within the mainstream Byzantine Church is also of little further aid in understanding many passages within "Merkavah mysticism,"[278] as practically no attempt was made within Byzantine Christology to render the exact dimensions of the heavenly form of Jesus Christ. While the appearance of Christ was certainly briefly described by means of very generic characteristics on occasion within Christian literature of the Imperial era,[279] the first truly detailed ekphrasis of his form may be found in a Jerusalem synodical letter from the year AD 836 preserved in a tenth- to twelfth-century Middle Byzantine recension, a difficult period for the reverence of images. The complicated relationship of the redactions to one another going back to the original (lost save for a single fragment) was first studied and elucidated in 1994.[280] In the secondary literature, a textual version from the twelfth century is frequently cited which styles itself as a letter of *John of Damascus* to Emperor Theophilus. This is, however, from the outset, a chronological impossibility: Theophilus reigned from AD 829 to 842, while John had already died in AD 754 in the monastery of Mar Saba in the Judean desert near Bethlehem. The text contains so many quotations from the work of this "last Church Father of Antiquity," and from the earlier authors cited, in turn, within his work, that it is nevertheless quite understandable why the compiler had claimed this venerable name in authorship.[281] The work may well have been composed within the Sabaite monastery itself, its monks having been entrusted with John's oeuvre.[282] At the very beginning of the letter, the following is stated:

> A rational being, mortal, with reason and intellect, three ells tall, described in the same manner of appearance and embonpoint in the visible form pertaining to us, displaying the traits of his mother's side and the form of the lineage of Adam. Thus, he is portrayed as the time-honoured historians described his appearance: Shapely, with conjoined eyebrows, with beautiful eyes, with a large nose, waved hair, stooped, of a healthy pallor, with a dark beard, with wheat-coloured skin, taking after his mother in appearance, with long fingers, with a pleasing voice, speaking lovingly, mild-mannered, taciturn, noble, patient, and embued with all gifts in the field of virtue.[283]

Certainly, a measurement is provided for a body (three ells, just under 1.60 meters, was characteristic of the average fully grown adult)[284] but this is hardly an elaborate description of this body; rather, this consists of a compilation of the characteristics important to a painter of the human, rather than divine nature of Jesus Christ. The entire test is strikingly worded on the basis of the two-nature Christology of the Council of Chalcedon, and its discourse on the "unmixed unity" of both natures,[285] "constant and unchanged" in his human nature (even after the resurrection). According to his divine nature, Christ is by comparison "without inception, everlasting, invisible, matter-less, bodiless, indescribable, without quality, without quantity, formless, borderless in size, untouched."[286]

Depictions of this type are preserved, for example, in the sixth- or seventh-century icon of Christ today to be found in the Monastery of Saint Catherine at the foot of Mount Moses on the Sinai Peninsula. Following Kurt Weitzmann, it must have been painted in Constantinople, reproducing a celebrated original of the time which must have influenced Byzantine depictions of Christ in many facets.

The depiction upon the icon roughly accords with that which is stated in the Jerusalem synodical letter of AD 836, albeit the eyebrows are not conjoined, the hair comes across as straighter than waved,[287] and the face displays more of an ivory than a wheat-hued complexion. Regardless, Christ may be seen to possess a large nose, a healthy skin color, a dark beard, and long fingers. It has been stated that here "the aura of a divine image" is combined with "the features of a human portrait ennobled with the bearing of a philosopher."[288]

Regardless, detailed measurements of the earthly, or, indeed, heavenly form of Jesus Christ enthroned with the Father are never found. Quite to

Fig 5.3   Christ Pantocrator (sixth/seventh century)
Sinai, Monastery of Saint Catherine[289]

the contrary, clear alternatives are set in opposition to one another in an alternative edition of the Jerusalem synodical epistle from AD 835, among these number: "with and without matter; . . . without quantities, and three ells in size," wherefrom it becomes apparent that the characteristics of

Jesus' outward appearance as attested from the redaction of the monks of Mar Saba must also have featured in the synodical letter of AD 835.[290]

When, however, as has been seen, no real parallels may be found within Christian literature to the "Shi'ur Qomah" passages, then the likely most plausible explanation for these fragments from Hekhalot literature is that they were probably in more or less conscious competition with the Christology developed in Late Antiquity and the Byzantine era. The brusque debates producing vast reams of literature within Christian theology and the church also signaled a high measure of professional knowledge on "figure on the divine throne next to God" to the unchurched.[291] In response to this evidently professional (and for them quite certainly heretical) knowledge, the Jewish mystical groups of "those who descended to the chariot" established another categorically distinguished knowledge without any real competition within Antiquity. Consciously or unconsciously, they enhanced the attractiveness of their own very specific form of Judaism by now commanding a "unique selling point" (in today's speech) within globalized Antiquity's religious marketplace. Concurrently, in an age in which the Platonic esteem for mathematics belonged to general consciousness of specialist knowledge, they offered a mathematization of sorts of the divine image. This permitted the presentation of this particular species of Jewish mysticism as completely original and autonomous, yet also reminded the educated of what was intellectually familiar to them; moreover, it perhaps even rendered the classical biblical tradition of a divine corporeality more credible to them. It must here be assumed that knowledge of the divine body allowed the adherents of these mystical groups to transform their own bodies, as the magically connoted lore promised to aid in being delivered from "the spirits, demons, and robbers, from all wild animals, (and) from snakes, scorpions, and (from) every sort of imp" (according to the *Merkavah Rabba*).[292] This is, to a certain extent, a clear parallel to the manner of bodily deification which might also be seen within Christian monastic texts, and will be examined more closely within the following, penultimate chapter. Within the final chapter, it will be then considered what consequences might ensue when the conception of a divine corporeality is applied to a figure believed to be the Son of God.

6

The Body of God in
Late Antique Christian Theology

"On the Body and the Soul"

In the previous chapters, it was sought to reconstruct a presently largely neglected line of tradition for various Jewish and Christian conceptions of divine corporeality. This consisted of relevant biblical passages, some philosophical concepts, most prominently from the Hellenistic period, and certain Imperial-era Christian theologians who termed themselves "philosophers" or, more precisely, "Christian philosophers."[1] In this present chapter, the path of Christian thought and, insofar as is possible, Christian piety, is further traced from the High Imperial era to Late Antiquity. Accordingly, two Christian theologians will first be introduced, one of whom was described at some length at the end of the second chapter, the other of whom has at least been mentioned in passing, namely *Melito of Sardis* and *Irenaeus of Lyon*, respectively. Subsequently, the question will be examined as to how the notion of a divine body and of divine bodiliness survived in the cloistered circles of Egyptian monasticism, while being energetically banished to the intellectual fringes within the episcopally driven mainstream theology of Late Antiquity. Above all, it will be critically assessed as to whether the Egyptian monks propounding such views were cognizant of the texts from the second and third centuries, and from which other traditions they might otherwise have been influenced.

As has been seen, the erudite Christian thinker Origen argued most prominently in "On First Principles," which originated from lectures in the ancient cultural metropole of Alexandria in the AD 220s, against individuals who envisioned God with a body and, indeed, knew how to justify these views with not only biblical references, but also recourse to philosophical reflections of a generally Stoic bent. It may be noted from not only this foundational text, but also from Origen's sermons and biblical commentaries from Alexandria and Caesarea of Palestine alike that those propounding such stances evidently knew their Bible well, and were not without philosophical instruction. Certainly, it is premature to dismiss those Origen dubbed "naïfs" (*simplices* or οἱ ἁπλούστεροι) as merely individuals of unsophisticated spiritual training, as is often the case in secondary literature.[2] Even if he had sought in the most diverse of contexts to convince those individuals opting for a divine corporeality to interpret the biblical Scriptures in a deeper, and insofar rather more erudite, sense, his argumentations demonstrate that these opponents (male and, perhaps, female) comprised the *educated*. Nevertheless, it seems as if in the following decades of the third century AD, and most strikingly in the fourth and fifth centuries AD, this particular branch of the intelligentsia suddenly disappeared. The sense is garnered (at least from acquaintance with the pertinent literature) that now it was only very naïve individuals within Christian communities who read the Bible in such an unvarnished manner and understood its purport verbatim, imagining God with a material body regardless of all of the grave difficulties engendered by such a conception. Yet, such a picture may well once more be attributable to mere heresiological motives, namely the wish to combat a stance found to be heretical with all means available, and to defame and disparage its sundry adherents. This suspicion fell particularly upon a group attested from the fourth and fifth centuries AD alike, the members of which were tellingly termed "anthropomorphites" by opponents, as they allegedly conceived of God in human form. Was this, in fact, a movement standing in the tradition of the educated followers of Christ attested in Origen who accorded God a body of some gossamer materiality on the strength of a Stoically founded reading of biblical texts, or in reference to certain Jewish biblical interpretations in the apocalyptic or mystical tradition? Or, conversely, might rather these have been far less intellectually highbrow individuals, who by antique standards, or at least from the perspective of an educated, urbanite theologian, might genuinely have been labeled "naïfs," that is, as *simpliciores* or ἁπλούστεροι in Origen's terminology? In spite of a difficult situation in respect to sources, this question deserves renewed examination on account of recent publications on the so-called anthropomorphites.[3]

Melito of Sardis

In order to answer this question appropriately, a return must be effected to an Imperial-era theologian who, much like the North African Tertullian, proceeded implicitly from the premise that God possesses a body and form, decidedly assuming thereby a standpoint opposing Origen's own; the figure in question is Melito, who inhabited Sardis in Asia Minor in the latter half of the second century AD.[4] It is unlikely that he was bishop of said city, although this might often be read.[5] Interestingly, in turn, there is an intimation that Tertullian had read Melito, albeit critically.[6] That this may have contributed to his own stance on divine corporeality must presently remain the stuff of conjecture. As has been previously discussed, Origen mentions Melito as having been the author of a text entitled "On the Corporeality of God" (Περὶ τοῦ ἐνσώματον εἶναι τὸν Θεόν).[7] Within a list of Melito's works transmitted within his "History of the Church," Eusebius, bishop of Caesarea, the city wherein Origen was active in the second half of his life, who was something of a grandson of his in academic terms, includes a piece with a similar title (Περὶ ἐνσωμάτου θεοῦ):[8] The Middle Greek term ἐνσώματος found in the title means (as the antonym of ἀσώματος "incorporeal") first and foremost "corporeal."[9] Accordingly, this linguistically not unproblematic title should be translated literally as "On the Corporeal God," or, perhaps somewhat more freely in English, as "The Book on God's Corporeality" (as is the case in the antique translations from the Greek original),[10] but not, as might occasionally be encountered, "On the Incarnation of Christ," as it was only markedly later that the aforementioned Greek word was associated with Jesus Christ in this technical sense.[11] The context of the aforementioned passage in Origen speaks for such an interpretation, hailing as it probably does from his sizeable commentary to the first book of the Bible, albeit only transmitted in the form of a Byzantine catena, a chain commentary by divers authors.[12] In this text, Origen busies himself with the exegesis of the famous passage on the creation of humans in God's image (according to Genesis 1:26: ποιήσωμεν ἄνθρωπον κατ᾽ εἰκόνα ἡμετέραν καὶ καθ᾽ ὁμοίωσιν). He notes that some exegetes of the biblical words "in the image" (κατ᾽ εἰκόνα) relate this to the human body, others to the soul, and continues:

> We shall next see as to which arguments they who first pronounced upon this employed; among them numbers Melito, who left writings stating that God has a body.[13]

Regrettably, nothing is extant of this text, or, indeed, respective "texts," should the plural employed by Origen be taken seriously, and no clear traces of an argumentation which might be ascribed to the supposed bishop of Sardis within the short fragment from Origen's commentary on Genesis. It hence remains entirely uncertain whether Origen really had the writings of Melito mentioned by him readily to hand, or whether he knew them only from hearsay. In the extant fragments of his commentary, the different scriptural arguments mentioned are merely ascribed by Origen to an unfortunately anonymous plurality. Accordingly, the following is intoned within another fragment of the commentary:

> How else, they say, might the Lord have "appeared unto Abraham" (Genesis 12:7 and 17:1), and unto Moses and the Saints, were he not to possess a figure? Should he indeed have a frame, then what form should it be in, if not that of humans? And they bring forth thousands of textual references to name God's limbs.[14]

Origen is also unlikely to be referring to Melito in this passage. It is more probable that the argument presented here is from his opponents in Alexandria (the place in which this commentary to the first book of the Bible had been compiled prior to AD 234) than that it might genuinely reflect a paraphrase from Melito's tome "On the Corporeality of God."[15] Finally, Origen employs the plural twice within his argumentation when introducing the opinions of his opponents; evidently, he recalled at this moment that there was a pertinent treatise by Melito on this subject, if not multiple works, but the individuals whom he refuted were rather the previously discussed opponents from "On First Principles," who displayed not only a certain level of philosophical education, but also evidently were well versed in the Bible.

The aforementioned gazetteer of Melito's writings probably quoted by Eusebius unfortunately sheds no further light upon the contents of his "On the Corporeality of God." Remarkable, however, is that, within his catalog of authors called "Illustrious Men" (*De viris illustribus*), Jerome leaves the Greek title of the work untranslated in stark contrast to his handling of the remainder of Melito's oeuvre,[16] perhaps because he found it to be problematic in either language or content.[17]

In the face of such uncertainties, addressing the question as to whether traces of Melito's concept of God's corporeality as mentioned by Origen may be found elsewhere within the former's oeuvre takes on special meaning. *Gregor Wurst* has discussed possible intimations of such a concept within Melito's extant works and fragments alike, particularly with respect to the very complex transmission of his sermons. Noteworthy here is the famous Pascha Homily, almost completely intact in a papyrus codex of the third or fourth centuries AD today conserved in Geneva (Bodmer XIII), fragmentarily preserved in a further, somewhat later papyrus codex (Chester Beatty XII/Michigan Inv. Nr. 5553), and additionally extant in a Latin epitome and in the remnants of a Coptic translation within the Cosby-Schøyen Codex.[18] Also pertinent is an additional homily entitled "On the Soul and the Body" (*De anima et corpore*).[19] One such sermon by Melito, "On the Soul and the Body," is quoted in the aforementioned catalog of Eusebius in an unfortunately highly textually corrupt passage as "The (Discourse) on the Soul and the Body" and directly thereafter as "On the Soul and the Body"—most likely this refers to exactly the same text, the title of which had been excerpted from two different catalogues, or was present in two copies within the library of Caesarea; due to the corrupt textual edition in the case of the first title, the duplication evidently went unnoticed by copyists.[20] Regardless, the latter homily is lost with the exception of two fragments transmitted in Syriac which are additionally suspected either of not originating from Melito at all, or at least of having been heavily altered. Yet, should a longer homily, only well known in Syriac, entitled "On the Soul and the Body and on the Passion of the Lord" (*De anima et corpore deque passione Domini*) and ascribed in its Syriac, Coptic, and Georgian recensions to Athanasius of Alexandria, be associated with Melito's lost homily, then an attempt may be made to reconstruct Melito's text from the different transmissions by Pseudo-Athanasius, at least in terms of its content; in addition to the pseudo-Athanasian homily's three Syriac textual witnesses, exist one Coptic and one Georgian recension respectively,[21] and additionally various smaller Greek texts and fragments in the Christian languages of the Orient attributed to neither Athanasius, nor Melito.[22] The aforementioned brace of Syriac fragments must, nevertheless, serve as the point of departure, as they are explicitly ascribed to Melito's homily in a miaphysite florilegium of the fifth or sixth centuries AD, the *Florilegium Edessenum anonymum*:[23] "Melito, Bishop of Sardis, from his text 'On Soul and Body.'"[24] A synoptic edition of all of this material with a German translation and an extensive commentary was presented some time ago by Gregor Wurst.[25]

It is unnecessary at this juncture to recapitulate the complicated debate as to the history of transmission,[26] which has been superseded by Wurst's new scheme or, indeed, that regarding to which of the antique authors it should be attributed (in addition to Athanasius, his predecessor Alexander of Alexandria has been named).[27] Indeed, in neither the Syriac fragment explicitly ascribed to Melito, nor the variously transmitted pseudo-Athanasian homily, may be found any account of the body of God. This text is far more concerned with the *human body of Jesus Christ* and its function for humanity, and with death, which, in accordance with a conception preponderant in Antiquity, is described as the division of body and soul:

> For the soul and the body were sundered, and death separated them from one another. The soul was bound in the underworld, the flesh dissolved within the earth, and there was a great distance between them both, the flesh and the soul. The flesh disappeared and dissipated within the earth

within which it was buried, yet the soul was powerless in the chains of the underworld.[28]

As similar ideas may be found in the homily on Pascha, which might be ascribed to Melito with likelihood bordering upon certainty, it might be presumed that these passages were, in fact, to be encountered within his lost sermon "On the Soul and the Body," and the pseudo-Athanasian homily preserved its original avenue of thought.[29] The dualistic perspective of humans as fragile compounds of body and soul now characterizes the entire extant text: At no stage within the homily is it particularly emphasized that God fashioned humans from their very inception onwards as integral body-soul units;[30] the body only explicitly appears (in rather biblical terminology) in conjunction with the term "flesh"—"and there was a great distance between them both, the flesh and the soul." In death, the body without the soul is "become as a ship without a helmsman"—destined thereby to sink.[31] What the image expresses is also explicitly stated: The human body perishes and is not thematized as the genuine likeness of the divine body anywhere within the pseudo-Athanasian homily. Not the slightest ring of Stoic materialism might be discerned at any point; the argumentation rather follows a widespread, popular-Platonist paradigm of a dichotomic anthropology, and thereby the Platonic definition then commonplace of death as the "loosing and separation of the soul from the body."[32] Just once, in a soul's lament in Hades stylized as a song, is it mentioned that the soul cries and bewails the loss of its "good body": "Where is this my body, within which I prayed to God?"[33] This initially somewhat outlandish idea, the apostrophizing of the putrid, decomposing body as "beautiful" regardless of its state also finds a parallel in Melito's Pascha homily.[34] The terrestrial body is otherwise painted in such a pessimistic light that it seems rather difficult to conceive that any divine corporeality might genuinely be sighted from such a vantage point. The drabness of corporeal existence begins already in the womb, continues through childhood, and endures into seniority; it is driven home to the sermon's readership or listenership with suggestive questions: "Yet, when he was an infant and crawled about the floor, was he happy?"[35] The intention "to display the propensity of humans to death as urgently as possible" stands markedly in the foreground of the homily's first part.[36] A second part of the sermon is concerned with the incarnation and works of salvation of Jesus Christ. Christ is dispatched to the earth (as is intoned in the fragment ascribed to Melito)

> Without body, that he might, once he had assumed a body through the womb of the virgin and was born as a man, bring man to life, and collect his limbs.[37]

The notion here elaborated belongs to the debate on the bodily resurrection and is formulated with a clear anti-gnostic point directed at those who doubt a resurrection of the body: According to the Coptic and Georgian versions, Christ collects the human limbs scattered by death and reinstates the unity of body and soul for all by means of his own resurrection. In contrast, according to the various Syriac recensions, it is the adoption of a human body, the incarnation, which paradigmatically restores the lost unity of body and soul.[38] This latter version, which in a strict sense may not be divided from the first (as ultimately it is first at the resurrection of the crucified body that it might be proven that the incarnatory unity of body and soul is an inseparable one) should be the earlier from a historical perspective. Probably, it was already to be found in Melito's sermon, who may have adopted this from the Anatolian tradition, as this is also attested in Irenaeus of Lyon, also a probable native of Asia Minor.[39]

Here, in reaction to a gnostic spiritualization of salvation critical of the role of the body, and its concomitant restriction of redemption to the soul, the body of humans is considered just as capable of (and requiring of) salvation. As significant as these beginnings of an anti-gnostic "doctrine of physical salvation" might be,[40] nothing is learned of the specific *reason* why the human body is capable of redemption within the late antique transmissions of Melito's homily "On the Soul and the Body." The argument that, as the "image and likeness of God," the body was and remains intended for salvation could be inferred from Origen's report on Melito in the passage quoted at the outset of this section and inserted into this text, but it cannot be found anywhere in either the editions of the pseudo-Athanasian homilies or in the two Syriac fragments. Unfortunately, nothing is learned either as to any particular materiality of the body obtained by Jesus from the Virgin (or, indeed, received through the resurrection). In turn, there is no mention as to the relationship of this body of Jesus Christ to any divine body; at best, an "indestructible body" is discussed once in one single version of the pseudo-Athanasian homily.[41] In this passage, it was evidently thought that man (supposedly before the fall) possessed an indestructible body which was immortal and hence did not disintegrate into parts in death. Resurrection of the dead by Jesus Christ means in this elsewhere well attested paradigm of antique Christian theology that this incorruptible body is restored once and for all, and granted to humans after death during the general awakening of the dead. Nothing of all of this may be found within the various editions of the homily with the exception of the allusion to a "proper and indestructible body" of man previously quoted. Rather, the argumentation is oriented towards Christ: He was sent from heaven without a body (there is much in favor of following Rucker in assuming that in the original Greek "fleshless," ἄσαϱϰος, appeared at this juncture) and acquires flesh from the Virgin.[42]

The reader of these lines in the *Florilegium Edessenum anonymum* must (and should) have felt reminded of the central formulations of miaphysite theologians, such as may be found in *Apollinaris of Laodicea* (ca. AD 315–392), a manner of spiritual founder of the miaphysite trajectory within Christian theology: "A true God is the fleshless (God) who was visible in the flesh."[43] In other words, in the Syriac fragment from Melito's homily "On the Soul and the Body" from the miaphysite *Florilegium Edessenum anonymum*, Christ is not conceived of as an unmixed unity of divine and human natures as per the Council of Chalcedon, but rather as a hypostatic unity of godhead and human flesh in a typically miaphysite manner. The interface of christological and anthropological doctrine in the fragment is also hardly coincidental: Prominent miaphysite theologians such as *Severus of Antioch* (died AD 538) eagerly explain the relationship between humanity and divinity in Jesus Christ with the analogy of that between body and soul—just as the body is not to be understood as an independently subsisting hypostasis, but rather as only able to exist in combination with the soul, so too Christ must be understood as an independently subsisting compound hypostasis comprising a hypostasis which cannot subsist independently (the human body) and one which can (the godhead).[44] The similarities between the fragment and these ideas from post-Chalcedonian christological debate are striking; nevertheless, they do not strictly suffice as any conclusive argument against the authenticity of the fragment.

Should another fragment from the late antique miaphysite *Florilegium Edessenum anonymum* be ascribed to Melito, then this Anatolian theologian would actually have differentiated very carefully between godhead and human body, as in this fragment it is stated of Christ (following the translation of Gregor Wurst):

Attracting the body, he did not confine the simplicity of his divinity.[45]

Were this fragment genuinely to be authentic, then Melito would first and foremost have been of an opinion completely viable as mainstream within Christian theology and the church, namely, that a human body is not suited to grasping divinity. Admittedly, the authenticity of the fragment prompts considerable thought, as the *Florilegium* displays two passages in the direct vicinity of these words cited which recognizably presuppose knowledge of the heated disputes on the nature of Christ surrounding the Council of Chalcedon. The question as to whether the human body now encompasses the godhead of Jesus Christ or not actually would also seem to assume familiarity with the debates of the fifth century.[46] Hence, considerable uncertainty must be acknowledged in respect to this passage: Should these thoughts expressed in the Syriac fragments of the *Florilegium Edessenum anonymum* at all be traced back to Melito, and thereby the Christian theology of Asia Minor in the late second century AD, then they permit essentially *no* reconstruction of Melito's views on the *divine* body, as they were recognizably transmitted for their christological import and state nothing as to the body of Christ's father. It might only then be recognized that, for this Anatolian theologian, Jesus Christ's path to salvation does not directly begin with a body, but rather "bodilessly" (or, more precisely: "fleshlessly"). Nevertheless, the salient question remains whether—as is maintained by Origen—the second-century Anatolian theologian Melito propounded the stance of a divine corporeality, according to which the "image and likeness" of man were fashioned by God. It is also of interest in the context of this notion as to which traces of theological debates in late antique Syria or Egypt may be identified in the Syriac and Coptic editions of the pseudo-Athanasian homily.[47]

Yet, the findings revealed by analysis of the transmission of the homily "On the Soul and the Body" hardly accord all that well with Origen's report that Melito also held the human body to be a part of the divine likeness, God's ascription of a body becoming thereby a necessity, should this then be considered cogently. A sole, brief reference to an "indestructible body" which humans are granted (once more) by means of Jesus Christ could, but hardly must, point in such a direction. This ambivalent result may well be connected to the loss of the original wording of the sermon, meaning that, at the very best, its foundational premises may be identified as transmitted within texts of the fourth and fifth centuries, which were more or less shaped by the heated disputes at the time on Christology and the theology of the Trinity. As will be seen, the notion of a divine body was far less suited to this antique Christian theological landscape of the fourth and fifth centuries than to that of the second and early third.

The doubts as to the reports that Melito propounded the notion of a divine body are amplified when it is asked how God the Father and Jesus Christ actually related to one another in the Anatolian theologian's mind. Melito is generally counted among the so-called monarchianistic theologians who identified as closely as possible God the Father, Son, and Spirit respectively as one in the interest of creed: "inasmuch as he begets, Father / inasmuch as he is begotten, Son" in the words of the Pascha Homily.[48] The monarchianist identificatory theologians eschewed the strict differentiation of so-called Logos theology which professed the Christ to be Logos and the Son of the Father.[49] Such an identificatory theology leads in the case of Melito to (retrospectively) relatively drastic statements as to the identity of Father and Son in the Passion of Jesus Christ termed "patri-passianistic" within the field of theological history. In addition to these statements are those in which Melito distinguishes between a passible part of Jesus Christ which he terms "man," "flesh," or "body," and another part incapable of suffering; the impassible, godly part suffers along.[50] As evidence for "patripassianistic" pronouncements, the brusque anti-Jewish phrasing in the Pascha homily might, in turn, be referenced, according to which God was killed on the cross and the King of Israel eliminated by Israel's hand.[51] This assertion as well was employed within the miaphysite argumentation against the Chalcedonian Creed in a form both abbreviated and exaggerated alike: The monk *Anastasius of Sinai*, who lived in the seventh century AD, quotes a fragment purported to originate from a work of Melito entitled "On the Passion," quoted approvingly by miaphysite opponents of the Chalcedonians according to Anastasius (the *Florilegium Edessenum anonymum* also hailing, of course, from such miaphysite circles): "God suffered through an Israelite's right hand."[52] Should, however, God, the Father, and Christ, his Son, be identified so closely, then the statement in the *Florilegium Edessenum anonymum* that Christ did *not* possess a body before the incarnation, but rather only once he obtained one from the Virgin Mary would simultaneously apply to the Father: He would then also be incorporeal in Melito's eyes.

In the face of such ambiguities of transmission, examination of the only sermon purportedly transmitted verbatim, the Homily on Pascha, becomes even more vital. Here, the likeness of God is discussed directly following a description of death as the dissolution of the unity of soul and a "good body":[53]

> For man was being divided by death;
> for a strange disaster and captivity were enclosing him,
> and he was dragged off a prisoner under the shadows of death,
> and desolate lay the Father's image.
> This, then, is the reason why the mystery of the Pascha
> has been fulfilled in the body of the Lord.[54]

Despite conflicting interpretations,[55] there can be no doubt that the expression "the Father's image" does not denote the soul as in the case of many other antique Christian theologians. The soul is detained "under the shadows of death" and is the "gift of God" incarcerated in Hades.[56] Thus it might be said of the body that, abandoned by the soul imprisoned in Hades, it languishes alone in the earth which serves as its grave.[57] Therefore, the expression "the Father's image" must refer solely to the body, and hence Origen had correctly relayed Melito's position.

If, however, Melito accorded God a body and genuinely identified Father and Son so closely, as is assumed within scholarly research, then the fragment transmitted within the *Florilegium Edessenum anonymum* must accordingly be interpreted critically, and the miaphysite conception of a "fleshless" or bodiless logos (λόγος ἄσαρκος) should not simply be integrated into Melito's thought. Of course, this does not exclude that individual expressions from this fragment do not originate with Melito, for example, the statement that the "immensurable is measured"[58] as the body which Jesus Christ receives from the Virgin may, in contrast to a divine body, be measured. After all, the philosophical divine predicate of God's "immensurability" was propounded both by those who thought of God as corporeal and those who did not.[59] Rather, remains of Melito's thoughts on the divine body may be found in a fragment from a codex from the Vatican wherein the bath of Jesus during his baptism in the Jordan is likened to the setting of the sun at sea, described as "the sun's swimming pool":[60]

> When the sun has with fiery chariotry fulfilled the day's course, having in the whirling of his course become like fire and flared up like a torch, and when he has blazed through his course's meridian, (then) as though reluctant, if he should appear close by, to burn up the land with ten radiant lightning-shafts, he sinks into the Ocean. Just as a ball of bronze, full of fire within, flashing with much light, is bathed in cold water, making a loud noise, and in the polishing process stops glowing; yet the fire within is not quenched, but flares up again when roused: just so also the sun, inflamed like lightning, wholly undying bathes in cold water, but keeps his fire unsleeping.[61]

Here, the divine body is described in precisely the tradition which has been repeatedly already encountered, namely as ethereal, resplendent fire, and, as is fitting for a theologian who identified Father and Son, albeit in the mode of comparison, the body of Jesus Christ stepping into the Jordan is associated with the fiery body of God. When it is accepted that, according to the testimony of the canonized Gospels, Jesus becomes aware of his status as Son of God by means of the heavenly voice during the baptism scene,[62] then the connection between the divine fiery body and the body of Christ is hardly a cause for astonishment. Just as unsurprising is that this dimension of Melito's theology was pruned from the late antique transmission, especially among the miaphysites.

Thus, despite all uncertainties, this hardly contradicts in any strict sense the further supposition that Melito propounded the notion of a corporeality of God in the now lost work "On the Corporeal God," and that Origen, if not personally acquainted with this text, would nevertheless have been sufficiently well informed of its contents. As, at the very least, the homily "On the Pascha" was translated into Coptic in the late third or early fourth century AD, and the homily edited by Melito "On the Soul and the Body," it might be presumed that the movement of the so-called *anthropomorphites* attested in Egypt were inspired by Melito, or perhaps reacted to him, although explicit references to this second-century theologian from Asia Minor are not extant in what scarce few texts might be attributed to this movement.[63] This notwithstanding, it is conspicuous how prominent within literature translated into Coptic, which was largely intended for rural areas and monks, texts which might be associated with Melito in one manner or another are at all represented. In an overview of Coptic translations of Greek Christian texts, Tito Orlandi has shown that in addition to biblical and by then apocryphal parabiblical texts, and the celebrated gnostic texts, it was most saliently homilies which were translated into Coptic, and among these—should it be assumed that the author was still known to the translators in the second case—two homilies of Melito, namely that of his on the Pascha and "On Soul and Body."[64] Moreover, both famous codices rendering the Greek text of the Pascha homily hail from Egypt: Spread between the Chester Beatty Library in Dublin and the University of Michigan in Ann Arbor, the pages of one should provenance from Aphroditopolis (modern Atfih, eighty kilometers south of Cairo on the right bank of the Nile, and hence opposite the Fayyum Basin), while Codex Bodmer XIII, obtained by Martin Bodmer in 1952 and residing in the library of the same name in Cologny-Genève should originate from a place near Dishna in Middle Egypt.[65] That in Egypt in Late Antiquity there was a particular interest for the long-dead Anatolian theologian Melito is quite indubitable even if all other details (such as the exact provenances of these aforementioned codices from monastic contexts) remain suspect.

Irenaeus of Lyon

Melito and Tertullian are two representative voices within the antique Christian mainstream church of the late second and early third centuries, which evidently propounded the notion of a divine body quite implicitly, even if this doctrine's Stoic underpinnings are only still somewhat perceptible in Tertullian, while for Melito the state of the sources is such that nothing more may be reconstructed. It remains obscure as to what impelled this learned theologian towards his views. Yet, it cannot be claimed that only theologians explicitly influenced by the fundamental principles of Platonic theology vehemently rejected the notion of a divine corporeality, and in contrast to Melito, only associated the biblical passage of the creation of humanity in the "image and likeness" of God with the soul, but not the body.[66] This may be seen in the by now oft-mentioned Irenaeus, bishop of Lyon, who refers to this passage of the Bible repeatedly within his anti-gnostic text *Adversus haereses*, written in the AD 180s and hence some thirty to forty years before Origen's remarks.[67] Precisely as Irenaeus does not repudiate the conception of a divine corporeality on the grounds of a Platonically inspired theoretical framework, his arguments are of a very much unique tenor.

Irenaeus quite evidently does not solely identify the notion of a creation of humanity in the "image and likeness" with the *soul*. In interpreting this Old Testament passage, the bishop rather differentiates between "image" and "likeness," understanding the former as *corporeal existence*, as he writes in his work "Demonstration of the Apostolic Preaching" which supplements his (chronologically earlier) anti-gnostic text, summarizing:

> But man He formed with His own hands, taking from the earth that which was, purest and finest, and mingling in measure His own power with the earth. For He traced His own form on the formation, that that which should be seen should be of divine form: for (as) the image of God was man formed and set on the earth.[68]

It would be very helpful to know as to which divine "forms" are responsible for that which is visible in humans—quite certainly the body—coming across in the manner of a "divine form"; unfortunately, the Armenian word does not permit any unequivocal translation into Greek, and thereby the reconstruction of the original text: It simply means "outline."[69] Yet, is it really meant that God bestowed upon man the outline of his corporeal forms as his image, by means of which humans may be deemed as divine in form? Should a reconstruction of the underlying Greek terminology be attempted, then two terms stand out within the narrow set of options: σχῆμα and εἶδος. The former term distinguishes "the external form or shape of empirically tangible things" (and thereby approximates closely the word μορφή), while the latter vacillates between a pure cognition of external conditions or, precisely to the contrary, the perception of not only the visible outline, but also the internal structure and corporeal capacities.[70] It is, however, clear that, in the Greek original, the "outline of the divine form" was not meant in a modest sense, but rather the *figura*, the concrete form of an individual entity both born of and insoluble from a concrete materiality.[71] Hence, this is a matter not only of a mere outline, but rather of the internal structure and facilities of a divine body which humans received from God, albeit naturally reduced in size so as to conform to a terrestrial materiality and representational structure. In other words, when Irenaeus discusses humanity as the "image of God" (εἰκὼν θεοῦ), this refers to the body imbued with spirit, rather than to merely the body alone.[72] Does, then, Irenaeus genuinely presuppose a *body* for God the Father, or does this actually relate to the earthly body of his Son incarnated as a human? The interpretation of this sentence (and thereby the answer to this question) is disputed. The researcher who deems every reference to a body of God unrelated to the human body of Jesus as "crass anthropomorphism standing in stark contradiction to notions of God found elsewhere"[73] fails to recognize that Irenaeus leaves not the slightest doubt that the subject in the passage quoted is the *Father* and not his word, the Logos: "God the father of all," created the world through his word, his Son, and formed man with his hands.[74] Irenaeus qualifies God in the same text as "not made, invisible," as "spirit,"[75] and yet is simultaneously hardly averse to discussing a corporeality of the Father in a circumspect manner (this can scarcely be said to reflect any "crass anthropomorphism"). Here, "corporeality" quite evidently does not refer to the materiality of divine bodies categorically different from all terrestrial materiality (for example, that of ethereal fire as described in Stoic philosophy), but rather merely the (immaterial) forms of a material body. From such a perspective, according to Irenaeus, God does not possess a material body in any strict sense, but rather a body in the form of immaterial structures of a material corporeality. Admittedly, Irenaeus hardly expressed this position all that clearly within his extant works.

By contrast, there can be no doubt from the Armenian text of Irenaeus' "Demonstration of the Apostolic Preaching" that the bishop genuinely means the human body when referring to the creation of man in the image of God. Indeed, Irenaeus emphasizes at various other points within his surviving work that, in order to restore the "image and likeness" lost in the fall, Christ "took the same dispensation of entry into flesh" as humans:[76] The "likeness of Adam's entry into flesh,"[77] that is, the similarity between the fashioning of Adam's body and the assumption of a human body by Jesus, restores the lost likeness to God,[78] but when he (sc. the preexisting Christ) became incarnate and was made man, he recapitulated in himself the long unfolding of humankind, granting salvation by means of compendium, that in Christ Jesus we might receive what we had lost in Adam, namely to be according to the image and likeness of God.[79]

Through the incarnation of Jesus Christ, it becomes apparent that humans were designed as the visible "image and likeness" of the invisible God,[80] so that there might be no doubt that this representational nature of humans also applies to their visible parts, and not merely the invisible soul. In other passages, it is stated explicitly that, within the biblical pronouncement on the creation of humanity in the likeness of God, "image" refers to the body, and "likeness" rather to the soul.[81] As in Melito, this is again naturally directed against the gnostic thesis that only the spiritual-immaterial portions of humans might be redeemed and partake in this representational relationship.

Irenaeus of Lyon was convinced that it is actually principally impossible for humans to see God, as God is invisible, however, in his words, if God wishes for humans to see him, then "He is seen by men, by whom He wills, and when He wills, and as He wills. For God is powerful in all things." The bishop of Lyon also leaves no doubt that when he discusses "God," the incorporeal Father is here meant:

> Having been seen at that time indeed, prophetically through the Spirit, and seen, too, adoptively through the Son; and He shall also be seen paternally in the kingdom of heaven, the Spirit truly preparing man in the Son of God, and the Son leading him to the Father, while the Father, too, confers (upon him) incorruption for eternal life, which comes to every one from the fact of his seeing God.[82]

This possibility that individuals might see him is created by God with the goal of granting humans life: "And for this reason, He, (although) beyond comprehension, and boundless and invisible, rendered Himself visible, and comprehensible, and within the capacity of those who believe, that He might vivify those who receive and behold Him through faith."[83] Irenaeus propounds the remarkable theory of a somewhat *temporary visibility of God*; God reveals himself occasionally (when is his wont), so that he may be seen and appreciated. Phrased differently, on account of a specific divine act within the history of the salvation of the human race, the "economy of God" (οἰκονομία),[84] God is visible to a chosen few believers. Yet, what manner of "seeing" and "grasping" is here implied? Did Irenaeus have a process of *spiritual* vision in mind, what might be dubbed "intuition" in English, and entails an intellectual conceptualization, or is, in fact, a manner of seeing intended occurring in respect to not only the spiritual, but also the bodily senses? Might, then, a *temporary visibility of God* be inferred? The divine qualities and the human faculties associated with them which are enumerated in mirrored form (incomprehensible, boundless, and invisible, on the one hand, and visible, comprehensible, and within the capacity of those who believe, on the other)[85] by Irenaeus in the passage quoted relate in Latin rather to the performance of intellectual actions and not to the actual of seizing or grasping of matter or a corporeal process of vision. A fragment of the mostly lost original Greek text preserved only in a late antique Latin translation demonstrates, nevertheless, that the Greek expression for "seeing" may also be employed with respect to corporeal instances of vision: "those who see God" (οἱ βλέποντες τὸν

Θεόν).[86] Hence, it cannot be strictly excluded that God the Father possesses not only the immaterial form of material corporeality, but also on occasion a form of material realization of these immaterial forms.

Although Irenaeus accordingly held the human body to be an "image" of God, it remains somewhat uncertain, as has been seen, what exactly this image portrays. A downright material body (in the sense taught by Tertullian or Melito) as the equivalent of human bodies seems unlikely, and is certainly unattested. It is, however, certain that Irenaeus did not battle every corporeal conception of God with the same ardor as Origen would a few decades later. His diction is also hardly in so distant a style as the anonymous author of a text entitled "On the Resurrection" attributed to the Roman urbanite theologian Justin (mid-second century AD) but perhaps composed by his contemporary Athenagoras, wherein it is stated that "flesh is a worthy possession to God" so as to prevent the reader from coming to the conclusion that God himself possesses flesh should the creation in his image extend also to the flesh.[87]

As for Melito, one may pose the question in respect to Irenaeus as to whether the so-called anthropomorphites of the fourth and fifth centuries were influenced by his writings. This issue was raised some time ago by Dmitrij Bumazhnov (and before him already Georges Florovsky).[88] Such an interpretation could be supported by the fact that not only has a passage of the third book of the anti-gnostic work "Against the Heresies" been found on a papyrus of the late second or early third centuries AD from Oxyrhynchus ("this seems to comprise the remains of a bookseller's exemplar, rather than of a functional tome"), but also a fragment of the fifth book in a papyrus of the late third or early fourth centuries AD from Edfu or Akhmîm ("numerous mistakes, above all textual omissions and misreadings of the source text").[89] Irenaeus' chief oeuvre was hence principally known within Egypt's Greek-speaking circles. Moreover, exactly the same Armenian fragments of Irenaeus of Lyon might be found in texts from a theological direction prominently propounded in Egypt and also extant in Syriac fragments of the "On the Body and the Soul" of Melito of Sardis. These hail from the Egyptian miaphysite, anti-Chalcedonian tradition: Among the writings of *Timothy Aelurus* ("the weasel," perhaps on account of his slight frame) who served as patriarch of Alexandria from AD 456 to 477[90] may be found a tractate transmitted in its entirety in Armenian and abbreviated in Syriac (along with fragments of the lost Greek original) called "Against Those Who Speak of Two Natures."[91] Timothy compiled this last and most comprehensive of texts between AD 460 and 475 during his exile to the Chersonese in the Crimea. Three christological fragments are preserved therein which, in marked contrast to the transmitted texts attributed to Melito, contain nothing preserved as to the body of God the

Father (although one of the fragments incidentally displays very close parallels to the Melito tradition) and are interpreted by their editor as (concluding) passages from lost homilies of Irenaeus of Lyon.[92] Moreover, in
his polemic against the presbyter and grammarian John of Caesarea who
wrote an apologia on the Council of Chalcedon,[93] the miaphysite *Severus
of Antioch* quotes the passage wherein the expression "image and likeness"
is associated by Irenaeus with both body *and* soul.[94] Yet, the context of the
controversy is the human bodiliness of the incarnate Jesus, not the divine
body of the heavenly God; both problems are of only indirect relevance to
one another.[95] In contrast to the transmission ascribed to Melito, there are
hence no indications in the otherwise pertinent florilegia and compilations
that Irenaeus' texts played a significant role in the late antique disputes
over the corporeality of God the Father.

The Pseudo-Clementine *Homilies*

A further, highly exciting attestation for antique traditions on God's corporeality may be found in one of the so-called *pseudo-Clementine Homilies*,
more precisely in the seventeenth of these. This title does not indicate a
"sermon" in the manner of late antique ecclesiastical "sermons" but rather
is a play upon the "didactic lectures" (ὁμιλίαι) of Peter, which pattern a
text which might perhaps best be characterized in terms of modern genre
designations as a fictional novel with voluminous dialogues, "fabricated
history," as this was called by Eduard Schwartz.[96] A currently widely
held position is that the homilies likely composed in the first half of the
fourth century (much like the remarkably parallel *Recognitiones*) may be
traced back to a "literary archetype" developed between AD 220 and 250
in Coele-Syria; in other words, passages from the homilies for which no
parallels may be found in the secondary transmission of the *Recognitiones*
cannot have originated in the "literary archetype."[97] According to this perspective, the text of the pseudo-Clementine "literary archetype" belongs
in a manner difficult to explain more precisely to Judeo-Christian traditions, rendering comparison with Jewish textual transmissions meaningful.[98] This notwithstanding, it must not be forgotten that all of the versions
extant ultimately hail from the mainstream Christian church of Late Antiquity (in turn, the *Recognitiones* are only preserved in a Latin translation by
Rufinus of Aquilea[99]) and should not be resorted to in order to reconstruct
the theological positions of marginalized groups from the first three centuries of the history of theology (such as Judeo-Christian movements); these
are first and foremost *late antique* texts.[100] The Syriac transmission of
individual homilies additionally demonstrates that the Greek text of both
medieval manuscripts relaying the homilies represents a clearly redacted

and corrupted late stage of transmission;[101] unfortunately, no Syriac translations are published for the sections here of interest to the present study. Furthermore, the classic systematic model of a "literary archetype" extant in two editions has shown itself ever more strikingly to be an unreliable simplification of a complicated literary and tradition-historical process of growth which cannot be satisfactorily elucidated by means of classic literary criticism.[102] The passage pertinent to the present context concerning the shape (μορφή) of God nevertheless possesses no parallel in the *Recognitiones* and is hence also a separate part of the tradition as the homilist's "personal contribution," that is, according to the established model for the textual history of pseudo-Clementine literature and its transmission. Regardless, it must still be discussed as to whether it was actually developed by the author of the homilies, simply is lacking from the Recognitiones, or represents the product of an entirely independent tradition (in the classic terminology of discerning sources, an "excursus"); Hans Waitz[103] and Jürgen Wehnert[104] consider the passage at hand to be an original component of the literary archetype. The complicated question as to the sources of their already hypothetical literary archetype need not be here explored.

The passage featuring God's form belongs to a debate between Peter and Simon Magus in Laodicea, which serves within the homilies' scheme to refute the doctrines of the Rome-dwelling Christian teacher Marcion of Sinope.[105] The section itself is directed against the notion that the goodly God and Father of Jesus Christ is immaterial, purely spirit, and to be distinguished from a material "just God." The question as to whether such views were really propounded in this form by Marcion, who was compelled to leave the mainstream Roman Church in AD 144 and found his own church,[106] or merely ascribed to him need not here be answered.[107] The dialogue begins with a lively debate on the thesis that God has a form: In the guise of the magus Simon, an adherent of Marcion accuses mainstream ecclesiastical theology in the shape of Peter of falsely describing the Christian God as a "God extremely just"—that is, of not separating the dimension of divine righteousness from the solely benevolent father of Jesus Christ as a distinct divine figure, as Marcion is said to have taught according to the classical heresiology of the mainstream antique Christian church. This false unity of two actually different gods implies, however, the introduction of God in a shape (μορφή),[108] in a "terrible shape" which strikes fear and dismay into the soul. The text has Simon state the following counterarguments built upon one another, which construing a dialectical coup de grâce in interrogative form:

> But has God a shape? If He has, He possesses a figure. And if He has a figure, how is He not limited? And if limited, He is in space. But if He is in

space, He is less than the space which encloses Him. And if less than anything, how is He greater than all, or superior to all, or the highest of all?[109]

The use of the two terms "shape" (μορφή) and "form" (σχῆμα), which at
least colloquially in Greek lie semantically closely to one another, perhaps
can be explained as follows with the assistance of antique philosophical
definitions: Should God possess a perceptible outer form (for example, by
means of angels), an outline (even if of limitless extension, as will be seen),
then this would simultaneously imply an outer form of an empirically tangible object[110] and thereby imply existence within a space (τόπος). This,
however, would be preposterous, as then form and space would impose
boundaries upon the immeasurably immense God, and would encompass
more than God. In contrast to Aristotle, for example, "space" is quite evidently not understood as something identical to the object; rather space is
also understood in a very colloquial sense as that within which an object
may be found.[111]

Peter, representative of the mainstream church and the opponent of
the Marcionite position embodied by Simon, argues, in contrast, enthusiastically for the notion that God has a shape (μορφή). This stance was
already prepared for by means of an argumentation on the function of
humanity's creation in the image of God in correct cognition of God in
the preceding homily. Peter says therein to Simon: "We moulded the form
of Him who truly exists, coming to the knowledge of the true type from
our own shape."[112] Creation in the image of God as the representationality
of forms is here taken radically seriously: The pseudo-Clementines are
convinced that humans can distinguish the true God (with the true form)
from false gods (with false forms) by means of regarding their own human
shape (μορφή). A further passage, in which Peter asserts once more that
the "shape of man has been moulded after the shape of God," that is, in
analogy to the impression of a seal,[113] depicts a symmetrical representation
of the pattern, which becomes invisible when the body is disintegrated by
means of death, or disappears through ethical impropriety.[114]

In the course of the debate within the seventeenth pseudo-Clementine
homily, the mainstream church in the shape of Peter answers the magician
Simon in respect to his chain of arguments against the supposition of a
body of God with the indication that God, in fact, is to be feared according
to Christ's word, recalls as further evidence of this the scenario wherein
the heavenly court of angels is before God's countenance,[115] and then continues as follows:

For He has shape, and He has every limb primarily and solely for beauty's sake, and not for use. For He has not eyes that He may see with them;

for He sees on every side, since He is incomparably more brilliant in His body than the visual spirit which is in us, and He is more splendid than everything, so that in comparison with Him the light of the sun may be reckoned as darkness. Nor has He ears that He may hear; for He hears, perceives, moves, energizes, acts on every side. But He has the most beautiful shape on account of man, that the pure in heart (cf. Matthew 5:8) may be able to see Him, that they may rejoice because they suffered. For He moulded man in His own shape as in the grandest seal, in order that he may be the ruler and lord of all, and that all may be subject to him. Wherefore, judging that He is the universe, and that man is His image (for He is Himself invisible, but His image man is visible),[116] the man who wishes to worship Him honors His visible image, which is man.[117]

Interesting here is the fact that God commands a shape (μορφή) and a body (σῶμα) on grounds of his beauty—evidently the authors of this passage could not conceive of beauty without the materiality it predicates, and thereby not without a certain form of corporeality. At later points within the homily, this is accordingly also explicitly explained.[118] Such a perspective closely associating beauty and corporeality is very much within the remits of the canonized biblical texts' tendencies. While, in these texts (in contrast to later Jewish literature such as the Hekhalot corpus), the word "beauty" (יופי) is not directly employed for descriptions of God,[119] the tendency still remains to characterize God as extraordinarily beautiful. Indeed, a great deal of semantic fields tend to be used in respect to God, among which number the terms "powerful" or "splendid" (אדיר), "splendor" or "majesty" (הדר), "holy adornment" (הדרה), "glory" or "splendor" (הוד), "glory" or "radiance" (כבד), "ornament" or "wondrousness" (צבי), and even "good" in its semantic aspect as "fine" (טוב), all stand in relative terminological propinquity to what might be colloquially termed "beautiful" in English, without needing to explore the exact linguistic relationships between Hebrew semantic fields and the English meaning.[120] Such a view is already supported by the fact that a few of both the aforementioned Hebrew terms (for example, יופי, כבד, and טוב), and some further examples, can be translated with the pertinent Greek term καλός within the Septuagint, even if this term is not explicitly tied to God.[121] The notion that God or the gods may be distinguished on the strength of particular beauty may naturally also be found at various points within *pagan* religiosity, literature, and philosophy. Therein, the respective conceptions of God differ from one another markedly: The gods in *Homer* have especially beautiful bodies, as, for example, is expressed within the Homeric Demeter Hymn in respect to the eponymous goddess: "Beauty wafted all about her."[122] By comparison, *Plato* rejects the concept of a corporeality of the supreme divine principle but maintains that this god is "not lacking in beauty or virtue,"[123] as befits his divine nature. He goes so far as to identify straightforwardly his utmost principle with *the* truly beautiful without circumlocution.[124] Christian texts may be more or less directly ordered according to these different pagan traditions; among the Platonic tradition, for example, numbered *Clement of Alexandria* at the turn of the second to the third centuries AD. For him, all terrestrial, corporeal beauty is only an image of the beauty of the soul as fashioned by God in the manner of an artist. Yet, beholding this bodiless beauty spiritually leads to the equally incorporeal "true beauty":

> For, on the other hand, he who in chaste love looks on beauty, thinks not that the flesh is beautiful, but the spirit, admiring, as I judge, the body as an image, by whose beauty he transports himself to the Artist, and to the true beauty.[125]

The passage within the pseudo-Clementine homilies does not belong to such a Platonic intellectual tradition of divine bodilessness and incorporeal true beauty, but rather combines divine (and thus not only human) beauty with a "shape" (μορφή). As the term "body" (σῶμα) is lacking, "shape" can hardly be meant in the sense of a two-dimensional outline, and must hence imply corporeality. Admittedly, influences from the tradition of Platonic thought may also definitely be found in the passage. This becomes paradoxically apparent in the description of the bodily functions of the divine form: The capacity to see should not be limited to the eyes (which thus do not serve any purpose for vision, but rather belong to the form on grounds of beauty); God sees far better than any human by means of the incomparable radiance of his body. With the discussion of the incomparable resplendence of his body, reference is also evidently made—in an antique sense—to the concept of vision being based upon rays (ῥεῦμα τῆς ὄψεως or *radius oculis profecti*) emitted by the eye which affect things, scanning them much like a modern scanner, and send back an image of the seen thing to the eye.[126] This antique theory of vision, propounded by Plato, among others, and disputed by Aristotle, underpins this passage without direct mention of the classic formulation of this, wherein the "pure fire within us, which is akin to that of day" is caused in humans "to flow through the eyes."[127] Visual rays and bodily radiance are composed of the same matter. Nevertheless, the phrasing "the visual spirit which is in us" demonstrates[128] that Stoic notions of a pneuma-ray "which the hegemonikon of the soul emits through the pupil in the direction of the object to be detected" also underpin this.[129] Such a connection of Platonic and Stoic ideas on visual rays may also, for example, be found in the thought of the doctor Galen in the second century AD.[130]

The tour of the senses and faculties characterized by the body is halted after hearing and vision, as the message is already appreciable: While in human bodies specific senses are functionally bound to certain organs, in God, the senses characterize the entire body beyond any particular functional relationship—in this passage, totality and completeness are the mark of the divine body in comparison to the deficiencies of the human body. This notwithstanding, the radiant divine corporeality is not visible to all, but rather only for those "pure in heart." This is, on one hand, a neat repetition of a biblical line from the Sermon on the Mount drawn from the language of the Psalms,[131] but at the same time it also indicates that the radiant divine bodiliness may only be perceived by means of the "eyes of the soul," that is, with a pertinent organ of inner being.[132] Thereby the particular features are listed, meaning that the human shaped by the divine body "may be the ruler and lord of all, and that all may be subject to him."[133]

In the course of the argumentation, the dialectical conclusion of Simon Magus' introductory series of questions previously invoked, namely, that not only the "form" (σχῆμα) of God follows from his "shape" (μορφή), but also a specific space within which this shape resides (τόπος), is dismissed.[134] After a curt remark that such notions were forbidden by the biblical Scriptures, the author of the homily explains "space" (τόπος) to be the "non-existent" (μὴ ὄν), but God to be "that which exists," stressing thereby that both can hardly be compared with each other: What exists, exists in a container of nothing:

> The space of God is the non-existent, but God is that which exists. But that which is non-existent cannot be compared with that which is existent. For how can space be existent? Unless it be a second space, such as heaven, earth, water, air, and if there is any other body that fills up the vacuity, which is called vacuity on this account, that it is nothing. For "nothing" is its more appropriate name. For what is that which is called vacuity but as it were a vessel which contains nothing, except the vessel itself? But being vacuity, it is not itself space; but space is that in which vacuity itself is, if indeed it is the vessel. For it must be the case that that which exists is in that which does not exist. But by this which is non-existent I mean that which is called by some, space, which is nothing.[135]

That "the vacuity is nothing" was already pronounced by the pre-Socratic Eleatic philosopher Melissus in the mid-fifth century BC;[136] albeit this thesis was contested within the philosophical discussion on space at the time.[137] Discourse on the "non-existent" also originates with the Eleatics.[138] In addition to this philosophically colored argumentation on space, a further argument, less than seamless in its suitability—less than seamless because it suddenly presupposes space to be *filled* substance, and no longer understands this as *vacuity*, as pure nonexistence of substance. In the same manner in which the first argument might be somewhat mis-construed as pantheistic (God fills as being the entire, otherwise empty space), God now suddenly does, in fact, differ from the filled space.[139] The second argument for a shape of God who (irrespective of all of the logical problems which such a notion poses) exists *within* a space runs as follows: That which encompasses something does not exceed that which it encom-passes; the sun fills, after all, the air which it surrounds. Hence, nothing contradicts that God might possess shape and form and beauty, and (as is stated in the text rather Platonically) the participation (μετουσία) of that which is endlessly emanated from him.[140]

Moreover, the homily offers an interesting and very much distinct attempt to liberate the notion of a divine shape (that is, a divine body) from all too anthropomorphic images by means of recourse to arithmetic and geometric coherences:

> (He) (sc. God) is proved to be a substance infinite in height, boundless in depth, immeasurable in breadth, extending the life-giving and wise nature from Him over three infinites. It must be, therefore, that this infinite which proceeds from Him on every side exists, having as its heart Him who is above all, and who thus possesses figure; for wherever He be, He is as it were in the centre of the infinite, being the limit of the universe. And the extensions taking their rise with Him, possess the nature of six infinites; of whom the one taking its rise with Him pene-trates into the height above, another into the depth below, another (the third) to the right hand, another (the fourth) to the left, another (the fifth) in front, and another (the sixth) behind; to whom He Himself, looking as to a number that is equal on every side,[141] completes the world in six temporal intervals, Himself being the rest, and having the infinite age to come as His image, being the beginning, and the end. For in Him the six infinites end, and from Him they receive their extension to infinity. This is the mystery of the hebdomad. For He Himself is the rest of the whole who grants Himself as a rest to those who imitate His greatness within their little measure. For He is alone, sometimes comprehensible, some-times incomprehensible, (sometimes limitable,) sometimes illimitable, having extensions which proceed from Him into infinity. For thus He is comprehensible and incomprehensible, near and far, being here and there, as being the only existent one, and as giving a share of that mind

which is infinite on every hand, in consequence of which souls breathe and possess life.[142]

The notion that God's corporeal form described adequately is an extension of the infinite[143] in three different dimensions (height, breadth, and depth), and, moreover, in six further dimensions, upwards and downwards, right and left, and backwards and forwards, and that God retains a seventh dimension of eschatological sabbath rest (ἀνάπαυσις),[144] is without parallels in contemporaneous literature. Yet, the remark that precisely this sevenfold dimensionality of God's shape is the "mystery of the hebdomad"[145] (and thereby also probably of the seventh day of the week of creation) indicates the Pythagorean theory of numbers as its source, although the concept is also attested within Christian authors, and may well have been thence adopted.[146] In an Imperial-era introduction to this matter which remains difficult to date, the "Arithmetic Theologumena" of Pseudo-Iamblichus, a pertinent quotation from an arithmetic text by the bishop *Anatolius of Laodicea* (second half of the third century AD) may be found. Therein, it is stated that the hebdomad is composed of the three dimensions of height, width, and depth, and the four thresholds of point, line, surface, and body, so that there are hence seven motions: upwards, downwards, forwards, backwards, right, left, and orbiting in a circle.[147] Moreover, the statement that the number six is "a number equal from each side" and implies completion and rest, as has presently been seen, is practically a quotation from the aforementioned text of Pseudo-Iamblichus. In this work, the number six is also associated with the three dimensions of height, width, and depth — each of these three dimensions must be confined on two sides, which would produce from three dimensions six boundaries, these, in turn, forming the six dimensions of a concrete body — forwards, backwards, upwards, downwards, left, and right. According to Neopythagorean numerical theory, the number six also stands for "consolidation" (that is, the terrestrial embodiment) "of the soul."[148]

The passage in the pseudo-Clementine homilies only resembles a didactic piece, "the argumentation of which induces head-shaking,"[149] if one overlooks the creative attempt to present a distinct argumentative justification for the biblical doctrine of divine corporeality with recourse to the Neopythagorean theory of number as developed in Pseudo-Iamblichus or Anatolius of Laodicea — for, indeed, the teachings on the divine form within the pseudo-Clementine homilies is nothing other than precisely this. When a Christian bishop of the third century such as Anatolius of Laodicea already possessed such a command of Neophythagorean numerical theory, then so-called Christian or gnostic groups need hardly further

be invoked in order to understand why this passage may be found in a
Christian text of the fourth century.[150]

Should the standing of numbers and numerical theory within the Platonically based philosophy and science of the era be accounted for, then
the passage in the pseudo-Clementines comes across as far less astonishing. Rather, it contains statements towards which many other forms of
Christian reflection upon biblical texts referring to contemporaneous philosophical standards point, such as those that as God is simultaneously
infinite and yet tangible within his dimensions, he is "comprehensible and
incomprehensible, near and far, being here and there."[151] Subsequently, the
author maintains:

> What affection ought therefore to arise within us if we gaze with our
> mind on His beautiful shape! But otherwise it is absurd (to speak of
> beauty). For beauty cannot exist apart from shape; nor can one be
> attracted to the love of God, nor even deem that he can see Him, if God
> has no form.[152]

This means, on the contrary, that it is devilish, running counter to the truth,
as to how the Marcionite false teaching represented by Simon holds God
to be shapeless and formless, for then he also cannot be seen:

> For the mind, not seeing the form of God, is empty of Him. But how can
> any one pray if he has no one to whom he may flee for refuge, on whom
> he may lean? For if he meets with no resistance, he falls out into vacuity.[153]

Hence, the discussion led by the author as to whether God should be
conceived of as corporeal within Christianity is by no means exclusively
theoretical; indeed, he is rather preoccupied with demonstrating that the
consequences of the false divine conception depriving God of his shape
and corporeality are disastrous for religious practice: There would then no
longer be any reason for prayer or piety.

The author of the pseudo-Clementines touches upon the topic a final
time when the framing debate between Simon Magus and Peter comes
to concern whether visions (as, for example, reported in the Acts of the
Apostles) substantiate Peter's authority—whether these consist of visions
induced by God or purely delusions.[154] Peter does not question that there
are genuine dreams and visions occasioned by God. Yet, there are also
those which the devil must answer for, as he formulates accordingly:

> For I maintain that the eyes of mortals cannot see the incorporeal form
> of the Father or Son, because it is illumined by exceeding great light.

Wherefore it is not because God envies, but because He pities, that He cannot be seen by man who has been turned into flesh. For he who sees (God) cannot live (cf. Exodus 33:20).[155] For the excess of light dissolves the flesh of him who sees; unless by the secret power of God the flesh be changed into the nature of light, so that it can see light, or the substance of light be changed into flesh, so that it can be seen by flesh. For the power to see the Father, without undergoing any change, belongs to the Son alone. But the just shall also in like manner behold God; for in the resurrection of the dead, when they have been changed, as far as their bodies are concerned, into light and become like the angels, they shall be able to see Him. Finally, then, if any angel be sent that he may be seen by a man, he is changed into flesh, that he may be able to be seen by flesh.[156]

The author of the pseudo-Clementine homilies was hence convinced that God has shape (μορφή), form (σχῆμα or ἰδέα), and even a body (σῶμα), that he possesses extensions in particular directions and a location, although he is infinite. He has organs at his disposal such as eyes and ears, although he does not need them to see and hear. On the other hand, he shines so incomparably brightly and intensively that no human eye might see him.[157] Angels are also beings of light, albeit they do not effulge as acutely as the one God; human flesh is transfigured into such light after the resurrection,[158] the light of the angels incarnate when they appear to humans.

The passage on the corporeal form of God preserved in the pseudo-Clementine homilies thus demonstrates that—contrary to what Origen accused his opponents of—not all who propounded a concept of divine corporeality were by any means convinced that God possesses a *human* body like all other individuals. The redactor who inserted these thoughts into the narrative of the original text so as to present the material in the form of homilies was evidently at pains to here make a distinction: God's shape is "incomparably" divorced from that of man.[159] On the strength of this, the traditional biblical notion of a divine body, on the one hand, and the basal standards of divine sovereignty, on the other, are combined in this passage: According to general antique notions, God is naturally presented as requiring nothing (ἀπροσδεής),[160] needing thus neither eyes to see, nor ears to hear, and simultaneously the corporeal dimensions of his intellectual capacities (meaning, for example, his senses) exceed all visible human intellectual faculties. The body's purpose is not any specific utility as this could hardly be the case for God; but rather God has a body solely for the sake of beauty.[161] Additionally, God's body is incomparable in the third dimension to a human body: God has a shape (μορφή) which only the pure heart can see. Those possessing such a heart must accept two dimensions of God's corporeality: They must accept that God has a body, but also accept that this body is completely different from human corporeality, although God employed his own corporeal shape as the form and stamp in order to fashion the human body.

Whence might such notions stem, and how did they enter a collection of texts which the latest compiler of the Greek critical edition deemed the "homilies" of an author who "may be identified as an Arian theologian" and should have composed this "between AD 300 and 320" (although the dating should indicate that a personal student of the presbyter Arius is not meant, but rather most likely an adherent of the subordinated theology of the Trinity inspired by Origen which—like the ecclesiastical historian Eusebius of Caesarea—Arius supported on grounds of some fundamental convictions, although they certainly did not partake of all of his radical stances)?[162] Shlomo Pines, Alon Goshen Gottstein, and David H. Aaron (with critical remarks regarding Gottstein's thesis) already pointed to perceived rabbinical and non-rabbinical parallels to the pseudo-Clementine homilies, concentrating upon parallels to the notion of a particular radiance of the divine form.[163] Regardless, this refers to rabbinic texts which, at the very best, suppose *implicitly* a body of God. These passages, within which the first human, the "image and likeness of God," is described as a body of light, in which the body of Adam (prior to the Fall[164]) shines brighter than the sun ("The balls of the feet of the first man darkened the ball of the sun, how much more the appearance of his countenance"),[165] or Adam and Eve receive "raiment of light" rather than a "garb of skins" after the fall,[166] all may only be seriously entertained as possessing a historical transmission with the pseudo-Clementine homilies with some caveats. Moreover, in terms of their history of transmission, rabbinical texts are not actually required in order to explain the derivation of the pseudo-Clementine homilies' concepts: For example, man's radiant garb is mentioned repeatedly within the "Hymn of the Pearl" from the now-apocryphal Acts of Thomas,[167] and the biblical Book of Exodus had already described the skin of Moses' face as having shone during his descent from Mount Sinai because God had conversed with him.[168] Few other explanations present themselves other than that the radiance of God's countenance has passed to Moses' own face and is now somewhat reflected back. As to whether this radiance was meant by the text's authors metaphorically, or as to whether real rays were implied,[169] hardly alters the fact that a heavenly, special light is regardless described. In the homily of an anonymous Christian author which was later often identified in manuscripts with the Egyptian monastic father Macarius, or, on occasion, with one Symeon of Mesopotamia (hence usually termed pseudo-Macarius or Macarius/ Symeon in secondary literature),[170] which likely originated from late antique

Syria, the radiance on Moses' face and that of Adam are explicitly associated with one another.[171] Naturally the notion that beauty "makes the visage shine" is also known to rabbinical literature, and is stated of Adam.[172] Yet, might this genuinely suffice to establish a particularly close connection between the texts at hand and Judaism, and thereby to uphold the thesis of a Jewish-Christian origin of the traditions which they contain (whatever "Jewish-Christian" might actually mean)? The Dutch scholar of religion *Gilles Quispel* (1916–2006) once suggested naming concepts such as that of that of the pseudo-Clementines "mysticism of form" (*Gestaltmystik*) and to distinguish this from a Greek "mysticism of being" (*Seinsmystik*).[173] Might not, however, such dualistic models which seek to differentiate between Jewish and Greek, and Hebrew and Hellenistic thought be hopelessly oversimplified in nature? Regardless of all "mysticism of form," the author of the pseudo-Clementine homilies evidently adopted certain elements of the Greek "mysticism of being" (under the heading of which a specific philosophical ontology might be understood), for example, God's (or the gods') absolute lack of wanting for anything, the Neopythagorean theory of numbers, and an argumentation combining light and beauty, on the one hand, and shape, form, and body, on the other. Moreover, as Eduard Schwartz already noted, the conceptions of God in the homilies are markedly influenced by the late antique stance that Father and Son are of the same substance[174]—this was famously standardized under the heading of ὁμοούσιος at the Council of Nicaea in AD 325, and permeated the mainstream Christian church over the course of an extended process of discussion during the fourth century. The Father changes corporeal substance into the shape which he wishes, and brings forth the form of his Son, Jesus Christ (from the same substance as him), within one such metamorphosis, who cannot change form by himself without his Father's consent:[175]

> Wherefore much more does the power of God change the substance of the body into whatever He wishes, and whenever He wishes; and by the change that takes place He sends forth what, on the one hand, is of similar substance, but, on the other, is not of equal power. Whatever, then, he who sends forth turns into a different substance, that he can again turn back into his own; but he who is sent forth, arising in consequence of the change which proceeds from him, and being his child, cannot become anything else without the will of him who sent him forth, unless he wills it.[176]

Schwartz deduces that there "must have been Homoousians who understood the incarnation as a transformation of the Logos into the flesh of Christ; Apollinaris and Cyril protest constantly against the assignment of this doctrine to them."[177] This notion of a transformation of divine substance, regardless conceived of as a form, into flesh, and the reverse metamorphosis into a fleshless form influence throughout the passages quoted from the pseudo-Clementine homilies; to derive a tradition which might be assigned to an Early Imperial-era "Judeo-Christian" stream of transmission from these clear terminological and theological shifts in agenda in the fourth century would be a daring hypothesis. Most likely, the compositional context as described by Eduard Schwartz rings truest in this situation, holding forth as he does on the "religion of the educated strata of the Constantinian imperial church" which indulged in neither the Platonically inspired allegorical interpretations of the biblical texts nor in the speculations on Trinitarian theology of the fourth century.[178] This certainly cannot be stated with as much certitude as once did Bernhard Rehm, student of Eduard Schwartz and meritorious editor of the pseudo-Clementine homilies, who doubted "that it might ever be possible to attribute successfully these views, as far removed from orthodoxy as they are, to any particular Christian sect or group. The author is more of a theological adventurer than a serious heretic."[179] Indeed, the views on God's body and the various transformations of God, the angels, and humanity are less a matter of adventurousness and rather more part and parcel of a religiosity and theology prevalent in many sectors of the mainstream church.

It suffices for the present purposes to maintain once more that the impression on the part of Origen that only naïve and uneducated Christians would have propounded the concept of God's corporeality is formulated far too stridently and harshly—Melito of Sardis, Irenaeus of Lyon, Tertullian of Carthage, and the anonymous author of the pseudo-Clementine homilies represent four utterly different argumentative trajectories for the notion of a divine body, hailing from diverse chronological and geographical contexts within antique Christianity. They are also only systematized with great difficulty. The Italian scholar of patristics *Manlio Simonetti* held on the basis of the existence of two categorically divergent positions within the debate on the corporeality of God that these hardly occur in such different contexts by means of sheer happenstance, but rather that they are geographically and culturally *contingent*. Both assumptions seem admittedly problematic: As to whether an *Alexandrian* tradition critical of corporeality and an *Anatolian* theology of the corporeality of God might genuinely be distinguished from one another[180] is questionable: While Melito of Sardis was of good Anatolian Christian stock, the same might hardly be said of Tertullian of Carthage, active as he was in North Africa. Simonetti's assertion must also be doubted that *cultural* particularities within these two broader regions of antique Christendom might be held responsible for this difference in theological conceptions. The particular cultural character of a place or region hardly impinged upon its capacity to bear Stoically derived thinking; this phenomenon might be observed almost everywhere. A comparably dualistic simplification is, as stated, also that there is a "Jewish" or "Hebrew" concept of the corporeality of God and a rather more "Greek" notion of God's corporeality.[181] As has been repeatedly witnessed, concepts of divine corporeality are in equal parts Jewish and non-Jewish.

Christian Debates in the Fourth Century

As Christianity gradually rose in the fourth century AD from a status of mere toleration to that of massive privilege and then of state religion of the Imperium, the debates over God's body did not wane in the slightest despite the growing influence of Platonic Philosophumena upon Christian theology. Already before the outbreak of a heated argument over the veracity and applicability of the notion of God's body at the end of the century, the topic had been discussed by a wide range of Christian thinkers of the East and West. Regarding this history prior and parallel to the clashes over so-called anthropomorphism, Lactantius, active in Nicomedia and Trier, the Syrian bishop Eusebius of Emesa/Homs, and the North African bishop Augustine of Hippo are presently of particular pertinence.

Lactantius on Divine Emotions

L. Caecilius Firmianus, also known as Lactantius, wrote, as was remarked by Jerome in his catalog of "Eminent Men," the "particularly fine text 'On the Wrath of God,' *De ira Dei.*"[182] When it is understood that the African author Tertullian had already occupied himself with the question of God's corporeality, then it is quite striking that, according to Jerome, Lactantius also hailed from Africa, probably being born there around the mid-third century AD. Much like Tertullian, he is a product of Stoic thought, even though he was posted to Nicomedia under Diocletian, and hence to the eastern half of the Imperium. Stoic influences evince themselves already in his first text, which he composed as a Christian at the beginning of the fourth century, in *De opificio* (a work cited by Jerome as *De opificio Dei uel formatione hominis*[183]). Nevertheless, as Antonie Wlosok has demonstrated, the Stoic definition of God already in this work was also invariably reshaped by the Roman conception of God as "Father and Lord" (*pater et dominus*).[184] The connection between benevolent ministration and strict authority expressed in this predication reflects precisely a classic Roman conception of God borrowed from the notion of the paterfamilias. Lactantius summarizes this succinctly as follows: "We should love him as sons and fear him as slaves."[185]

Already in this early writing, a detail of human corporeality is associated with God, namely an upright gait and vision pointed heavenwards ("And so of man alone the right reason, the upright position, and countenance, in close likeness to that of God the Father, bespeak his origin and his Maker"), but no conclusions are drawn from this as to God's corporeality or materiality otherwise. In reality, nevertheless, human corporeal and spiritual connections to God are not immediately meaningful; on the contrary, the relationship of mind and body in respect to humanity is described very much within a Platonic hierarchy:

> His mind, nearly divine, since it has been assigned the domination not only of the living creatures of the earth, but also of his own body, placed in the top of his head as though on a lofty summit, gazes out upon all things and beholds them.[186]

Lactantius hence propounded a Platonically confined Stoic theory of God such as anthropology, and (at least in comparison to Tertullian) a *Stoicism pruned* in regard to materialism.

The tractate "On the Wrath of God" (*De ira Dei*), which is of particular relevance to the present context, evidently hails from the period in which Lactantius was engaged as tutor to the emperor's son Crispus in Trier, probably from the years following AD 314/315. The object of the tractate is *not* wrath as *corporeal* emotion and thus as an affect in the sense of a feeling,[187] but rather the logical necessity of a *term*, namely that of the "wrath of God." This reflects exactly the Stoic understanding of emotion along with sundry concomitant affects (πάθη or *affectus*) not as spiritual phenomena accompanied by inclination and disinclination, as with Aristotle, but rather logically as an incorrect practical judgment.[188] This notwithstanding, Philo of Alexandria, and later Clement of Alexandria and Origen, emphasized God's strict absence of emotions and affects, and hence explained mention of God's wrath as improper language.[189] Yet, it was not only the prominent and learned proponents of Christianity who busied themselves with such a topic: In a rather enigmatic fragmentary Coptic text, the "Berlin Coptic Book" (Papyrus Berolinensis 20915), God's anger is evidently also the central topic, albeit the highly fragmentary state of the manuscript does not permit any entirely unambiguous statements as to the contents.[190] This demonstrates once more that the Alexandrian conception of an emotionless and affectless God during Imperial-era early Christianity was hardly the sole option within Christian theory of God. For example, Tertullian, very much in the vein of his opinions of the divine body, was completely assured of the existence of divine emotions and affects alike, although he also categorically distinguished these from those of humans.[191] Even when he holds anger to be an emotion, that is, to be "suffering" or pathos (πάθος), as within the classical theory, and generally all divine acts upon earth to be such a suffering and thereby a voluntary abasement of God, he prefers rather to discuss *severitas*, "severity," in relation to God. This emotion expresses itself in the affect *ira*, "wrath," albeit in an art and manner specific to God.

> Severity therefore is good because it is just, if indeed the judge is good—that is, is just. So also are the rest of those (activities) good by which the good work of good severity takes its course—whether it be anger or hostility or ferocity. All these are debts owed to severity, as severity is a debt to justice.[192]

Nevertheless, severity does not belong to the original nature of God, but rather is contingent upon the fall of mankind and the consequences thereof.[193] Such are Tertullian's views. Certainly, Lactantius already defamed him as a "Montanist," and as a heretically regarded Christian theologian albeit not by name, meaning that he must have known of his stances on divine emotions and affects.[194]

Lactantius demonstrates in his text "On the Wrath of God" initially with the help of logical inferences and arguments that wrath and mercy are to be ascribed to God in the same manner.[195] Oddly, a definition of wrath as emotion or affect first appears incidentally in the last third of this relatively slender tome. Lactantius formulates his own definition by means of engagement with a Stoic held by him in high regard,[196] namely with the Roman philosopher Seneca. He cites first from the latter's work "On Anger" (only fragmentarily preserved in this crucial passage) the definition which Seneca developed with recourse to a comparable classification in Aristotle. Lactantius writes:

> That the philosophers did not know what was the nature of anger is clear from their definitions which Seneca has enumerated in the books which he wrote *On Anger*. ". . . Aristotle's definition is not much different from our own, for he says that anger is the desire of paying back pain."[197]

Despite his reverence for the Stoic Seneca, Lactantius rejects his definition: Wrath according to Seneca's definition is described by Lactantius as unacceptable "unjust anger"; "just anger," for example, against criminals is not preceded by any affront, and thus punishment is not the consequence of an injury, instead occurring "that discipline be preserved, morals corrected, and license suppressed."[198] This rather comes across as a variation of Tertullian's concept of the good severity from which appropriate wrath stems.

Peculiarly enough, the question as to whether God can be enraged at all is explained in Lactantius' volume by means of logical deduction without any discussion of the presupposed definition of the term "anger." In the course of this initial argumentation, he repudiates the stance attributed to the Epicureans that God is emotionless and affectless in every sense as "He cares for nothing, and He neither has any concern Himself, nor does He show it for another."[199] This Epicurean opinion would lead to the position that God is distinguished by neither wrath nor clemency. Lactantius counters:

> What is so worthy, so befitting to God as providence? But if he cares for
> nothing, provides for nothing, He has lost all divinity. He who takes away
> all force, therefore, all substance from God, what else does he say except
> that there is no God at all?[200]

According to Lactantius, God has emotions, and, having emotions, he also possesses the affect of wrath: "So, he who is not angered, surely is not moved by kindness either, which is contrary to anger. Accordingly then, if there is neither anger nor kindness in him, surely there is neither fear nor joy nor grief nor compassion."[201] Lactantius (incorrectly) ascribes the Stoics the stance that "kindness resides in God but not anger." It is an ugly transformation for humans, and only appropriate to God, when, in anger, as a great storm whips up floods, "the eyes take fire, the mouth quivers, the tongue stammers, the teeth chatter, and now a red flush suffuses and marks the countenance and now a white pallor."[202] This description incidentally possesses an incomparably detailed parallel in Seneca, within which the corporeal symptoms are likened to the "specific symptoms" of "madmen":

> their eyes blaze and flicker, . . . their lips quiver and their teeth grind,
> their hair bristles and stands on end, their breathing is forced and rag-
> ged, their joints crack as they're wrenched, they groan and bellow, their
> speech is inarticulate and halting, they repeatedly clap their hands
> together and stamp the ground.[203]

Lactantius argues against that which he holds for Stoic teaching, namely that, when confronted by opposites, one motions either in both directions or in neither:

> Thus, he who loves the good also hates the evil, and he who does not
> hate the evil does not love the good, because, on one hand, to love the

good comes from hatred of evil, and to hate the evil rises from love of the good.[204]

Hence, Lactantius has proven the applicability of a statement "which has never been taken up nor at any time defended by the philosophers, namely, that God's anger is a consequence of His kindness."[205] Over the course of the entire argumentation, however, (very much in Stoic tradition) the body is not discussed as the seat of the emotions and affects. Indeed, Lactantius argues with a range of nonnegotiable entirety of emotions from which individual emotions and affects cannot be broken off, but the question as to how emotions and all affects are constituted is only addressed indirectly in the description of the body of an enraged human which is altered, or even distorted, at divers points. Only after the conclusion of this argumentation is man considered with a view to God's likeness, and (as already mentioned in *De opificio Dei*) his upright gait and the countenance raised towards heaven introduced as evidence that "there is in man something divine."[206] In no mean tension to this stands, nevertheless, in other passages, that the body of humans is described somewhat by means of a dualistic tendency as representing darkness, fragility, and mortality—in short, as the "depravity of his nature" and the cause of ill thoughts and deeds alike.[207] Towards both portions of man, his wicked striving for evil in body and his pursuit of good in soul, God responds with mercy and wrath.[208] Also in marked tension with the argument outlined at the ouset of "On the Wrath of God" that emotions and affects form a unity, from which nothing may be isolated, stands the reflection at its close that dread, envy, and avarice are emotions lacking in God, but not mercy, wrath, and compassion.[209] When comparison is made to Aristotle's enumeration of the emotions ("I call feelings desire, anger, fear, boldness, spite, joy, love, hatred, longing, envy, pity, in general what is attended by pleasure and distress"[210]), it becomes evident that Lactantius is unable to persevere entirely with his decision for a Stoically grounded concept of emotions and affects. Even his apparently strict dismissal of the conception of a divine corporeality begins to totter; as becomes clear at the end of the tract, the author maintains this to be Stoic because his reception of the Stoa is stunted at materialism:

> I do not mention the figure of God, since the Stoics say that God has not any form, and another mass of material should spring up if I wished to refute them. I speak only of the spirit.[211]

Quite obviously Lactantius would have liked to have disproved the Stoic position that God has no form[212] but employed the pretext of a ream of

connected material to allege that he could not accomplish this in his work
"On the Wrath of God." Stoic philosophy's conception of God's lack of
(human) form (but possession of a body composed of matter) was even
lampooned by Seneca himself in his "Gourdification" of the apotheosed
emperor Claudius: "As for a Stoic God, that sort is, according to Varro,
a perfectly rounded whole—in fact completely globular without either a
head or sexual organs. He (sc. Claudius) can't be that sort. Or can he? If
you ask me, there is something of the Stoic God about him: He has no head
and no heart either."[213] For whatever reason it might be, any passage on
the shape of God (*figura* or *forma*) is lacking within Lactantius' work
"On the Wrath of God." Were it elsewhere to be found within his surviving
work, then it would demonstrate as to whether the author reached once
more the notion of a divine form composed of airy material via the detour
of the reception and interpretation of biblical texts, as Tertullian already
had, and which evidently disappeared from sections of Stoicism in the
following century. Yet, even without such a passage it is still apparent
that the classical Stoic doctrine on God, according to which God certainly
possesses a material, fiery, and spherical body, but may not be conceived
of in human form, had largely stepped back from the limelight, much to
the benefit of the Platonic conception of an absolutely transcendent, and
completely immaterial and bodiless God.

Eusebius of Emesa on God's Corporeality

Nevertheless, there were exceptions. Among these numbered the bishop
Eusebius in Syrian Emesa/Homs. Details of his life are only known from a
lost panegyric on Eusebius (ἐγκώμιον) composed by his contemporary and
friend George, bishop of nearby Laodicea, later excerpted by the church
historians Socrates and Sozomen.[214] Within the heated ecclesiopolitical
and theological altercations, in which both George and Eusebius were
involved, this laudation served as a "partisan" advertisement,[215] meaning
that its information is to be taken with something of a grain of salt. Any
independent opposing transmission admittedly does not exist. According
to this allegedly "partisan" information, Eusebius hailed from a leading
family from Edessa/Urfa, was versed in both Syriac and Greek by birth,
studied with Bishops Eusebius of Caesarea and Patrophilius of Scythopo-
lis/Beth Shean, learned exegetes of the Bible in the Alexandrian tradition,
and went on to briefly study in Antioch, and finally studied philosophy
in Alexandria.[216] In Caesarea, he could probably work in the library of
Origen and make use of not only the biblical teaching aids located there,
but also the interpretation of biblical texts from Origen's own pen. Bas ter
Haar Romeny has characterized Eusebius of Emesa as "a Syrian in Greek

dress," although the Greek influence in Caesarea and shortly thereafter in Antioch and Alexandria alike was of more than superficial impact.[217] In particular, his studies under Eusebius of Caesarea, very prominent already in his time, may well demonstrate that Eusebius belonged to a theologically profiled network which was already dubbed "the Eusebians" in Late Antiquity after the eponymous metropolitans of Caesarea and Nicomedia, and endeavored in close collaboration with Emperor Constantine and his son Constantius to alleviate the heated Trinitarian theological clashes within the Christian church by means of an intercessory course.

Eusebius of Emesa must have been born around AD 300 and his study in Alexandria may be dated to AD 333.[218] These and the following years witnessed severe controversies over the theological and ecclesiopolitical alignment of the Christian church; Eusebius of Emesa was clearly heavily embroiled in these debates, even if only scarce details of this might be known, and moreover from an unbalanced tradition. Indeed, in the years AD 338/339, he was even earmarked by the "Eusebian" network to be the successor of Bishop Athanasius of Alexandria, an influential and energetic opponent of the "Eusebians" who had been forced into exile with political support. Socrates and Sozomen disclose that Eusebius, in fact, refused ordination as bishop of Alexandria as he feared that he would find no support among the metropole's Christian community. After he had refused this outstanding episcopal seat,[219] he instead became bishop in seemingly less embattled Emesa. Yet, there were also conflicts there; Eusebius was compelled to abandon his Syrian see and to resort to his friend George in Laodicea. As to whether the accusation that he devoted himself to astrology had sparked this conflict must remain open; it cannot be ruled out, however, that umbrage was taken within the community at certain professional expertise which he might have gained in Alexandria.[220] It is certain, regardless, that Eusebius belonged to the supporters of the ecclesiastical politics of Emperor Constantine, who collaborated closely with the network of the "Eusebians" and who had likely also won its trust.[221] In the face of the later empire-wide standardization of an agenda directed against the theological and ecclesiopolitical intentions of this group in the years following the death of Eusebius (probably before AD 359),[222] it hardly astounds to learn that, from an originally rich record of his literary works, now only fragments and remnants remain, mostly also only in translations and revisions of the original Greek versions. This also applies to his evidently extensive homiletic oeuvre which must have been wildly popular: Jerome attests in a not uncritical passage within his catalog of authors entitled "On Illustrious Men" to Eusebius' fine rhetorical talent, rendering his works "most eagerly read by those who practice public speaking."[223] Here pertinent are six sermons "On (sc. God's) Incorporeality" (*De incorporali et invisibili Deo* and *De incorporali liber primus, secundus, tertius, quartus et quintus*) which the Jesuit Jacques Sirmond (1559–1651) published in 1643 from a now lost manuscript probably from the twelfth century containing a total of fourteen homilies.[224] Eligius M. Buytaert could demonstrate in various studies that the translation's Latin points to late antique Gaul.[225] On the strength of the close relationship between these texts and a collection of homilies from a manuscript in Troyes' municipal library also dating from the twelfth century ascribed in the manuscript to Eusebius of Emesa, and from the Greek originals of which two other authors are cited under this name,[226] the attribution of the six sermons at hand to Eusebius of Emesa seems justifiable, despite these being assigned to his teacher Eusebius of Caesarea in the manuscript. Irrespective of this, the latter learned bishop may certainly be excluded as their author.

The incorporeality of God is of central significance to Eusebius of Emesa within these six sermons on this theme—as important as it was also to Origen, the scholar and preacher venerated at Eusebius' alma mater in Caesarea. Yet, Eusebius articulates this in a manner markedly different than his predecessor had sought a century before. At the very beginning of the first relayed sermon, "On the Incorporeal and Invisible God," the homilist maintains that he professes loudly and firmly that God is incorporeal, as also souls are.[227] Remarkably, the incorporeality of God is not deduced from the definition of God, but rather inferred from a biblical verse which holds that the body is mortal but the incorporeal soul immortal (Matthew 10:28: "And fear not them which kill the body, but are not able to kill the soul"). This *anthropology* hence forms the foundation for the doctrine on God: God has rendered souls their incorporeal nature and is hence incomparably "more incorporeal" than the soul.[228] Subsequently, Eusebius turns to the question as to whether God is visible and answers this on the basis of the biblical quotation that humanity will see the pure heart of God (Matthew 5:8), with the note that God is beheld by means of the heart, and that one who regards in such a manner does not see with the (corporeal) eye.[229] In a similar manner, a further biblical passage, namely a dialogue from the Book of Isaiah (63:1: "Who is this that cometh from Edom, with dyed garments from Bozrah?"), is interpreted verse by verse as an allegorical discourse on incorporeal issues. In the narrative course of the Old Testament passage cited, God explains himself to be this person questioned: "I that speak in righteousness, mighty to save" (63:1). A question in response ensues: "Wherefore art thou red in thine apparel, and thy garments like him that treadeth in the winefat?" (63:2), this following finally with the answer "I have trodden the winepress alone; and of the people there was none with me" (63:3). The preacher here indicates that this biblical passage does not pertain to an "incorporeal winepress," rejecting thereby a primitive, literally allegorizing interpretation evidently held within the community, but rather the "deliverance through blood," that is, the salvation on the cross.[230] Here, the incorporeality of God no longer seems to be disputed, but rather it should be demonstrated within these biblical passages how this might be evidenced during interpretation of the texts, or, in other words, how an all but contrived allegorization might be avoided within the liturgical readings. This somewhat sober and reserved approach to the allegorical method within the sermon permits the association of it with the educational career of the homilist himself, which featured stints in Alexandria *and* Antioch, namely in one place where biblical exegesis was taught in a *positive* light as regarded allegory, and in another where it was rather received *critically*.[231] In practice, the differences were nevertheless only slight: Origen accordingly interpreted the Old Testament passage in his commentary to the Gospel of John as meaning that Christ ascended to the Father after the crucifixion and had to be purified by the Father.[232] Theodoret of Cyrrhus, who may rather be accorded an "anti-Antiochite" exegesis,[233] interpreted the passage in his commentary to the Book of Isaiah in the fifth century, around a hundred years later than Eusebius, similarly; in the context of the christological debate contemporary to him, the mention of clothing was understood by this Syrian bishop as a statement as to Jesus Christ's humanity.[234]

From the fact that within Eusebius of Emesa's sermon the polemic against the conception of a divine body only plays a dominant role at the beginning and around the conclusion, it may be recognized that, at least at the time of the homily's delivery in the Syrian locality's episcopal church, this notion had become something of a dogmatic specter which, as a homilist, one might impute as sheer absurdity without much ado, and which, in turn, evidently was not accorded serious credence by all that many the congregation's members:

> Pay heed to that which you speak! When you render him (sc. God) a body, you would sequester him a location, you would imagine for him a simple nature, you would render He who is easily propitiated then one who cannot be placated. You would have invented him, who is free from place, at a specific location. You permit thereby eyes, you allow ears in respect to God, and both language and sentiment, and bones and entrails, and muscles and veins; and you know not of what you speak. Be gone the delusion, that you might grasp not how great nature is, but how greatly you might know something.[235]

By means of preposterous queries, the listeners to the bishop of Emesa's sermon should once more consider the ludicrousness of the notion of a divine body: Should God be body, then who may be found beneath him who sits in heaven? Where was God before he fashioned heaven? Is the world his footstool? Where then were his feet before he created the earth?[236] As little earnest engagement with the philosophical theories conducive to models of the corporeality of the Christian God occurs here as honest discussion of relevant images of piety. The final section of the sermon is dedicated to those who still insist that God has a body and flesh. Eusebius emphasizes in response that God is free of emotions, "he fills everything, but not in a corporeal sense," and is pure intellect, *mens pura*.[237] It hence becomes entirely clear that the sermonizer possesses a Platonically founded image of God entirely in Alexandrian tradition (such as, for example, Origen),[238] but merely alludes to this in a few keywords, and never invokes it as the background to this argumentation or at all profiles it in engagement with contributions from the complicated Neoplatonic debates over theories of principles.

Entirely different is the impression gained from scrutiny of the five homilies on "incorporeality" which succeed the sermon "On the Incorporeal and Invisible God" in the collection edited by Sirmond, and the manuscripts are labeled as "five books" of a theological tractate despite their liturgical conclusions. These five sermons treat the topic of "incorporeality" quite fundamentally; only the two final homilies are explicitly concerned with the incorporeality of *God*.[239] Yet, the first homily of the pentalogy of sermons already demonstrates that the questions initiating the topic of the series of homilies were provoked by the biblical reading of a church service (likely Exodus 19:9–20:22), and more likely from those passages which today would be termed anthropomorphic sections. Evidently, this reading prompted the query as to whether God descended to Sinai corporeally, and to what extent God was present in the pillar of clouds on the mountain (Exodus 19:16).[240] Once more the preacher unceremoniously answers such questions initially thetically: "God encompasses nothing, but everything encompasses God, but not in a corporeal manner."[241] The text of the thus evidently incendiary reading is taken up once more at the beginning of the fifth and final sermon, and cited at length, serving as an argument for the five sermons "On the Incorporeality" belonging together from their very inception as a single planned composition.[242] In all five sermons, it is emphasized time and again how markedly already nature demonstrates that God must be conceived of as incorporeal; here, a specific theological interest on the part of the preacher is present. In such a manner, the first three homilies presage the final two in which the incorporeality of God is directly thematized. The penultimate, fourth sermon contains the interesting depiction of an ascension of the mind, in the course of which all corporeal senses are discounted. Yet, the aim of this ascent is not the contemplation of God as, for example, a pure intellect, but rather the inculcation of the hierarchy between body and soul:[243]

> So let us rouse ourselves, let us leap from the sea and the land on which we stand, and let the air be rent by us and let even heaven be split open for us. For rational thought will not be held back. And let us draw closer to an even loftier heaven on the wings of desire, leaving the body with its kind in this place and leaving the feet on earth because they do not run to heaven and the hands here where they are able to touch and the ears here where they can hear voices and smell where it has what it requires and taste among those who eat and let sight remain with the visible things. Let rational thought, stripping away its garment, lay down the weight of this body and move its own wings and let it cut off whatever might lead it downward; such will it be at the crest of (upper) heaven.[244]

Inasmuch as the senses are merely termed the "garment" of thought, they are determined to be merely exterior "instruments" (also claimed by Nemesius of Emesa, possibly an erudite successor of Eusebius at the end of the fourth century: "The organs of imagination are the frontal cavities of the brain, [and] the psychic pneuma within them"[245]), and not as integral parts of the soul. Should the metaphor be followed to its logical conclusions, then this, in turn, leads to the presumably unintended consequence that the individual stands deprived of sense and naked before God.

The lines of argumentation of the homily "On the Incorporeal and Invisible God" and of the five sermons on incorporeality nevertheless run very much parallel to one another despite all of their differences; once more, the incorporeal soul is a striking argument for the incorporeality of its fashioner.[246] While the first three sermons are concerned most saliently with comparative examples from nature so as to demonstrate rather conventionally that the soul is superior to the body and incorporeal, the last two are devoted once more to the incorporeality of God. In long, occationally somewhat longwinded passages, it is attempted to demonstrate again and again that all corporeal contexts are externally constituted, temporally limited, and deficient, and hence cannot be predicated by God. Curt rhetorical questions depicting the absurd consequences of the conception of divine corporeality in any literal sense punctuate once more individual passages of both sermons.[247]

The thoroughness of the argumentation demonstrates in the case of the five sermons "On the Incorporeality" that individuals were present at church services who imagined God in corporeal form. Perhaps the homily "On the Incorporeal and Invisible God," which argues less fervently at this point, was held in another time and place; the six sermons were only ordered consecutively in a secondary stage of transmission. As in the first sermon, theories of a philosophical bent play no role in the five homilies, focusing as they do only upon followers of Christ who read the Bible naïvely: "Do you believe that God is sea? The earth? The air?"[248] The rather scholarly theories of Stoic origin regarding an ethereal or fiery materiality of God were evidently either unknown to the community or seemed less than pertinent to the sermonist. As, in the fourth homily, the "swan-shaped god," the god who transforms himself into a bull to stalk young girls, is attacked, most probably freshly converted Christians or members of the congregation who could not yet rid themselves entirely of pagan cultism also came under fire. Eusebius of Emesa asks these individuals, whom he directly addresses (whether or not they were actually present in the room): Do gods have something akin to wives, like us?[249]

Should the findings from the analysis of the Latin translation of a late antique collection of six Greek homilies from Syria be taken seriously, then the lively discussion among the educated as to the corporeality of God had already waned—probably as much in Emesa as in southern Gaul. Describing those within Christian communities who propounded such views as naïve bumpkins was no longer rhetorical artifice as was still the case with Origen, but rather somewhat an articulation of reality: Naturally it cannot be known precisely whether the learned of Emesa still debated over the eligibility of a concept of God's body grounded in Stoicism, but, from the testimony of the sermons of Eusebius of Emesa, this seems less than likely.

Augustine of Hippo

That the conception of a bodiless God had by no means become implicit within Christian communities and theology may be witnessed in a prominent example, the North African theologian Augustine (13 November 354 to 28 August 430). Scrutiny of his biography and, more precisely, of the story of his manifold conversions to different forms of antique Christianity which may be more or less reconstructed from his arrestingly contrived autobiography entitled *Confessiones* ("Confessions"), demonstrates that Augustine did not propound this stance in all of the phases of his life and thought. It has already been seen that he had quite evidently supposed the corporeality of God during his first intellectual phase in Stoic and Manichean tradition, and even the corporeality of the human spirit and the soul. Nevertheless, no contemporaneous texts are extant from this period, which was marked by the reading of a protreptic dialogue of Cicero entitled *Hortensius*, now lost save for fragments, and his membership of a Manichean group which understood itself to be Christian, but rather only later recollections. It was only after this phase (probably lasting from AD 373 to 382), following his advancement in 384 from a post as teacher of rhetoric in Carthage to the position of resident rhetorician of the imperial seat in Milan, that Augustine became acquainted with certain elements of Neoplatonic philosophy in the summer of AD 386 from pertinent texts (he terms these the "books of the Platonists," *libri Platonicorum*),[250] and turned thereby towards the Platonic conception of a bodiless, absolutely transcendent God as an "incorporeal truth" (*incorporea veritas*).[251] It is disputed which Platonic writings Augustine had read at the time,[252] and how far the contemporary influence of Ambrose, bishop of Milan, who doubtless knew and paraphrased Plotinus,[253] extended (while Willy Theiler enthusiastically argued for Plotinus' student Porphyry, Paul Henry decided for Plotinus himself; Alfred Schindler seems along with Pierre Courcelle to maintain as likely a combination of both authors in the Latin translation of Marius Victorinus[254]). It is nevertheless certain as to what consequences these readings would have for the thought of Augustine: As he himself reports in the "Confessions," the northern Italian imperial seat's resident rhetorician recognized on the strength of these Platonic writings God and his eternal Word to be incorporeal, as being itself, by means of which all of creation—albeit in a graded manner—has its being and is good. This realization of the fundamental incorporeality of God would mark his life thereafter.

Yet, even after this profound reconfiguration of the essential premises of his thought, the question as to the corporeality of God remains present—indeed, in the shape of the question of whether and how God might be seen. The significance of this topic for Augustine in the years following this Milanese revision of his thought is demonstrated by his description of the celebrated "Vision at Ostia" which he experienced with his mother Monica in the Mediterranean port town before departing for North Africa in AD 387.[255] A slew of problems accompanies this text, for example, the question as to the role of mysticism, or as to the exact relationship between "Christianity" and "Neoplatonism" in Augustine; the following study will restrict itself solely to describing the connection between this "vision" (the term does not appear within Augustine) and his discarded Stoic and Manichean notions of a body of God.

What is the story behind the "Vision at Ostia"? In a retrospective some thirteen years later, in the "Confessions," it becomes apparent that the author was recalling a very special conversation between mother and son in which, for a brief moment, the pair completely escaped the earthly hurly burly and, indeed, terrestrial existence itself, and "touched" the divine wisdom itself, "the One" (*id ipsum*).[256] In the address to God characteristic of the "Confessions," Augustine formulates this as follows:

Our conversation concluded that the enjoyment of the physical senses, however great, and however effective in giving earthly enlightenment, is not worthy to be preferred—not even considered—in comparison to the joy of eternal life. We raised ourselves up and with hearts aflame for the One we made our gradual ascent through the physical world and even heaven itself, where sun and moon and stars shine upon the earth. And now we were climbing still further by pondering, discussing and marvelling at your works. We entered into our own minds and transcended them, to reach that place of unfailing abundance, where you feed Israel for ever with the food of truth. There, life is the wisdom by which all other things come to be, both past and future—wisdom which is not created but rather exists just as it always has been and always will be. In fact it does not have the capacity either to have existed or to come to exist. It simply is, because it is eternal. While we spoke, we also gazed upon wisdom with longing; we reached out and touched it as best we could, with every beat of our heart. Then we sighed and left behind us, where they belonged, those firstfruits of the Spirit. We returned to the clamour of our usual kind of speech, in which words have both beginnings and endings. Yet what can compare with your Word, our Lord, who is everlasting, never ageing, yet making all things anew?[257]

The text supposes a tripartite division between a world of the body (*corporalia*), the spiritual world (*in mentes nostras*),[258] and a world beyond the spiritual world wherein God resides as wisdom. For the length of a heartbeat, his bodiless, "animate" being is "touched"—such a beholding of incorporeal being by means of the bodiless "eye of the soul" as categorically distinguished from corporeal vision of corporeal things is also present in Neoplatonic philosophy at the end of a path of ascent in multiple stages. Admittedly, the fact that all of the notions and, in part, terminology used by Augustine might be evidenced within Plotinus and later Neoplatonists,[259] and that he probably obtained the concept of such a graduated ascent from Plotinus' student Porphyry[260] neither excludes the authenticity of such an experience in Ostia, nor does it state anything thereby as to the "Christianness" of the experiences behind such an account. Regarding the authenticity of the experiences recounted many years later, what James O'Donnell so tersely remarked remains, nevertheless, applicable: "What happened at Ostia? We will never know."[261] As Paul Henry has demonstrated, Augustine, who peppered his later account in the "Confessions" with biblical quotations, was at pains to display to the reader the consistency of his erstwhile experience with a Christian religion drawing upon both testaments. Howsoever this later account of a vision in Ostia might be interpreted, it is certain that a God who cannot be conceived of as corporeal can be "touched" (Augustine uses the Latin word *attingere*[262]; nothing is stated as to "seeing" or "beholding"). Naturally, the question immediately poses itself as to whether the "touching" (and, of course, also "seeing" or "beholding") of a noncorporeal being only employs these underlying corporeally grounded terms metaphorically for purely mental motions, or as to whether material implications are contained within these preceedings.

In later years, Augustine remarked upon this at length by letter, and considered whether God might be seen with the senses by means of the corporeal eyes of the earthly or transfigured body, or not, in fact, by means of the "eyes" of the pure hearted or the soul. Yet, the semantic field of "touch" no longer occurs within this context;[263] this may underline that Augustine held the experience at Ostia to be special in some manner. The bishop of Hippo engaged with the aforementioned problem between AD 410 and 413 in a tractate-like didactic letter also entitled "Can We See God?" (*De uidendo Deo*) which is listed as Number 147 within his corpus of letters.[264] The letter was provoked by the question of a woman called Paulina (presumedly living as an ascetic) as to whether God might be simultaneously spirit (as stated in John 4:24) and yet be witnessed in bodily form according to the testimony of so many biblical texts. The woman had evidently been inspired by a rather polemic sentence which had been pronounced in another epistle on the topic: "Let the flesh, drunk with its carnal thoughts, take heed: 'God is a spirit, and therefore they that adore God must adore Him in spirit and in truth.'"[265] This sentence which had so unsettled Paulina stems from a highly spirited and provocative letter of Augustine to a widowed lady of rank named Italica from AD 408/409, in which, at its very beginning, he indicates in unequivocal terms that one might, in turn, also know something when it (for example a face) cannot be seen in a bodily sense: Italica's deceased husband also knew himself when he could not see himself, according to Augustine. Here it would also be the spirit (of the human) doing the detecting.[266] Divine light could then be seen neither now nor after the resurrection by the bodily eye, but rather first in the future by means of the risen human spirit:

> Doubtless, that light is God Himself, since "God is light and in Him there is no darkness" (1 John 1:5), but He is the light of purified minds, not of these bodily eyes. For then the mind will be capable of seeing that light, which now it is not yet able to do.[267]

According to Augustine, such a spiritual vision of God presupposes becoming similar to God, that is, the regaining of the likeness to God damaged by the fall. Whosoever does not, however, associate the likeness to God with inner man, but rather with the body (and thereby the vision of God with live eyes), is "utterly lacking in intelligence."[268] Evidently, as the letter demonstrates, in certain circles not further named, the question was discussed as to whether Christ could see God with his bodily eyes. Augustine currishly dismisses this question: "Many arguments can be adduced to refute that madness," and recommends his correspondent read the letter to such individuals out loud.[269] Unfortunately, it is not known with which figures Augustine is engaging in his letter to Italica. One small intimation is rendered by the concomitant, unfortunately fragmentarily preserved letter to the father of the correspondent Italica, in which Augustine asks the father to deliver the epistle to his daughter personally. Therein it is stated of the letter which the father, a "fellow priest" called Cyprian, should convey to her:

> In it I said something against the opinion of those who can hope nothing of God except what they experience in the body, although they do not dare to say that God is a corporeal being. However, they state this another way when they assert that He can be seen by bodily eyes, which he created for seeing corporeal objects only. Truly, it seems to me that they do not know what a body is, nor how far from a body is a God who is a spirit.[270]

Clearly, Augustine was not so agitated on account of Italica, or at all due to the fact that he had replied to a woman, but rather on account of the opinions of certain persons, unfortunately not further named, which the accompanying letter to the father Cyprian characterizes somewhat closer—it is not even known as to whether this individual moved in circles in Rome, where Italica lived, or in North Africa, where she possessed property. Regardless, the letter conveyed by Cyprian to his daughter must have become known to the aforementioned Paulina;[271] Augustine alludes repeatedly to it in the didactic missive to her, and is at pains to adopt a more reconciliatory tone without altering his fundamental views.[272] Nevertheless, there are differences within the details: In contrast to his exposé within the letter to Italica, Augustine passes over the question as to what the eyes of the resurrected and risen body might achieve within his didactic text to Paulina on grounds of its complexity—on the strength of passages in his text on the City of God, it might be supposed that Augustine assumed that they would be functional after the resurrection, but no longer employed in a neat sense for the corporeal performance of life.[273]

    The previously mentioned didactic missive of Augustine to Paulina begins with a manner of preliminary epistemological clarification (Augustine terms this *praelocutio*, "preamble"[274]), which is nevertheless not consistently applied as such: Here, as in the entire text, there is a dearth of expounded references to philosophical theories and contexts; biblical quotations and general experience serve as the brunt of the argumentation. Using examples for Paulina, the bishop of Hippo initially distinguishes between *corporeal* vision with the eyes (seeing the sun) and an *inner* vision by means of spiritual observation (I know that I live and that I want something); both forms of vision do not enable the sighting of *God*.[275] In contrast to terrestrial and heavenly bodies, he is not visible as both manners of seeing imply blatancy in the sense of a circumscribed and present substantiality (Augustine admittedly only appends this somewhat later). Delineated and present substantiality distinguish both the sun and one's own existence or certain of one's own executions of volition: That which is seen with the corporeal eye commands features such as "colors, noises, odors, tastes, warmth," while that which is beheld by the spirit is (at least in the example chosen by Augustine) characterized by some manner of more active presence such as "will, thought, memory, understanding, knowledge, faith." That which does not belong to these two types which "may be perceived either by bodily or mental senses," concludes Augustine, must be *believed*.[276] Naturally, this differentiation of two manners of sight including the terminology employed may be traced back to Platonic philosophy, and equally the rendering of the procedures of cognition for the spirit or soul by means of metaphors with recourse to corporeal processes; within the classical Platonic terminology adopted and expanded upon by the Christian Platonists such as Origen, "cognition" is described as a "vision" for the inner human.[277] Something which, like a corporeal face, is initially seen corporeally is in memory viewed incorporeally as something absent within the mind; in other words, that seen corporeally is retained only as something witnessed incorporeally.[278] Remarkably enough, however, in this passage, God belongs for Augustine just as historical events (such as the founding of the city of Constantinople by Constantine) to the realm of the *believable* and thereby to the believer, and not to the realm of that which might be seen, in both senses of the word. As followers of Christ believe the Holy Scripture, wherein it might be read, "Blessed are the pure in heart: for they shall see God" (Matthew 5:8), "we do not doubt that it is an act of piety to believe," to believe that God exists and may be beheld.[279] With this, the bishop names the problem which he intends to treat in his didactic epistle to Paulina: Viewing God is impossible due to his absence of corporeality and substantiality, yet it is to be believed according to the testimony of the Scriptures. Stated otherwise, God does not belong to the "evident things" (*res evidentes*) such as objects such as the sun and the fact of one's own cognitive and volatative existence simply are.[280] Such a notion of "evident things" refers to the Skeptical epistemological tradition which was conveyed into the Latin realm by Cicero (from whom the use of the Latin term *evidens* for Greek ἐνάργεια stems),[281] of which Augustine hence was also cognizant from his Skeptical phase. An "evident thing" stands before the senses of the soul or the body and is hence present.[282] It certainly cannot be stated that the North African bishop exhibited a flawless Platonism; at a descisive point, something of an entire block of Stoic epistemology has remained. This was likely permitted to endure because for Augustine it touched upon the Neoplatonic tradition of negative theology.[283] Nevertheless, from a comparison of this threefold epistemological differentiation of corporeal and spiritual vision along with a state of belief without any vision and the tripartite Platonic ontological differentiation between a world of the body (*corporalia*), the spiritual world (*in mentes nostras*), and a world beyond that of the spiritual wherein God dwells as wisdom, which Augustine, as has been seen,[284] presupposes repeatedly in the "Confessions," it may be determined that the two tripartite divisions hardly really align. In contrast to the epistemological threefold distinction, the ontological example recognizes a realm reserved for God alone; "belief" also relates, for example, to historical occurences, and as a term or activity is by no means the preserve of God alone.

The author of the didactic text addressed to Paulina concludes his "preamble" with a renewed affirmation that belief is to be categorically distinguished from vision with the body or the soul, even when that belief occurs within the spirit, and individual elements of belief (such as the hope of one's own resurrection) should somehow be illustrated by the senses.[285]

Augustine answers Paulina's question as to how it might coincide that God cannot be seen and yet simultaneously might be believed by means of biblical texts that he makes himself visible by means of an extended quotation from the Milanese bishop Ambrose's commentary on the Gospel of Luke.[286] This citation is explicitly introduced as such but probably may be traced back in many parts to Origen's sermons on this gospel. Evidently, it was imperative to the bishop of Hippo Regius to have recourse to a further, unquestioned authority, proven in combatting the positions on the theology of the Trinity rejected by Augustine, in addition to his own when approaching such a controversial question.[287] Regardless, it was also apparent to him that biblical passages might be resorted to to justify either position, be it that of the visibility of God or the principle invisibility of God; Augustine does as much in his didactic letter.[288] The nub of the argumentation from Ambrose cited ejects the problem of the visibility of God from theological epistemological theory, migrating it thereby from anthropology to doctrine of God: When God might wish, writes Ambrose, he might appear in a very precise form as he did to Abraham, or Isaiah, or Stephen; when he might not be so desiring, he does not appear and is also not to be seen. The "fulness of the Godhead" (Colossians 2:9) can as a human be neither seen with corporeal eyes nor grasped with the spirit:[289]

> Certainly it is not possible to refute the argument that the Father or the Son, or at least the Holy Spirit (if, however, the Holy Spirit can be seen) are seen under the appearance which their will has chosen, but their nature has not originated. . . . Therefore, "no one hath seen God at any time," because no one has beheld that fullness of the divinity which dwells in God; no one has experienced it with mind or eyes, for the word "seen" is to be referred to both.[290]

Augustine refers repeatedly to this text from Ambrose over the further course of the letter and proffers relatively little in the way of his own ideas additional to this. Among these is most salient the opinion that humans will first witness God upon eternal life. In order to explain this, Augustine makes reference to a passage in the First Epistle of John (3:2 "Beloved, now are we the sons of God, and it doth not yet appear what we shall be: but we know that, when he shall appear, we shall be like him; for we shall see him as he is."):

> Not as men saw Him when He willed under the appearance that He willed; not in His nature under which He lies hidden within Himself even when He is seen, but as He is. This is what was asked of Him by the one who spoke to Him face to face, when he said to Him: "Show me thyself," but no one can at any time experience the fullness of God through the eyes of the body any more than by the mind itself.[291]

According to Augustine, Moses certainly requested to see God "as he is," but could not see him;[292] to see God is first granted those "pure in heart," that is those cleansed of earthly sin, after the general resurrection in their risen bodies. In the interim, he will only seen (as the bishop of Hippo formulates astoundingly circumspectly) "perhaps, by some of the angels."[293]

Within his didactive missive to Paulina, Augustine takes advantage of a debate over the question as to whether God might be seen with bodily eyes in order to further radicalize his rejection of the stance he once held himself that God possesses a body: Bolstered by the authority of Ambrose of Milan, he maintains that not one of the forms in which God lets himself be seen by the corporeal eyes of humans is formed from God's nature and substance.[294] Inferences as to God's substance on grounds of his appearances are hence entirely excluded. In place of any speculation as to the body of God, Augustine turns to Jesus Christ: In the final judgment, it will prove that, in realty, the hungered and tormented Jesus Christ in the sense of the famous formulation from the Epistle to the Philippians of the Apostle Paul is the form of God (*forma Dei*; Philippians 2:6).[295] On earth, Christ is already afforded access to the Father, albeit only within the limitations imposed upon this process by terrestrial vision in its corporeal and immaterial forms.

When, according to the testimony of the Gospel of John, Christ brings tidings (*narratio*), no word for corporeal ears is meant, but rather that he is "an image giving knowledge to our minds, that it may shine there with an inner, indescribable light. This is what was said to Philip in the words, 'He that seeth me, seeth the Father also.'"[296] Moreover, whosoever "is transported beyond the bounds of his mind to understand this sees God even when He is thought absent; whoever cannot do this should ask and strive to deserve to be able to do it." As God cannot be seen corporeally or spiritually within this world, readings and debates on this topic are scarcely of help, but rather only prayer on the redeeming, merciful intervention of God who can grant humans sight when he wills.[297] Through such divine grace, it was accorded individual, selected figures such as Moses and Paul from the salvation history reported in both testaments of the Bible that they might see the substance of God.[298] This substance is described with a phrase from the New Testament as dwelling "in the light which no man can approach unto" (1 Timothy 6:16).[299] For others who do not warrant this grace remains only prayer and the path of faith. Within such a prayer-oriented pedagogy of correct cognition of God, Christ naturally plays a central role, particularly the example of his earthly life as the pathway to belief, and thereby to the Trinitary God himself.[300] Insofar as Augustine maintains in an impressive exegesis of a passage from the Epistle to the Ephesians already cited and interpreted by Ambrose, the one who follows Jesus Christ's path, aligns his or her life to his cross, and seeks to love it similarly approaches best this future vision of God in Christ after death. For Augustine, naturally, it is a gift of grace should one discover this way of the cross, accordingly described by him as the "mystery of the cross."

Then, explaining by what sort of men God is seen as he is in that contemplation, he (sc. Bishop Ambrose of Milan) says: "He who knew 'what is the breadth and length and height and depth, and the charity of Christ which surpasseth all knowledge,' saw both Christ and the Father" (Ephesians 3:18f.). I generally understand these words of the Apostle Paul thus: by the "breadth," all the good works of charity; by the "length," perseverance to the end; by the "height," hope of heavenly rewards; by the "depth," the unsearchable judgments of God, from whom that grace has come to men. This interpretation I also adapt to the mystery of the cross: for the breadth I take the transverse beam on which the hands are stretched, because it signifies works; for the length, that part of the upright which extends from the transverse beam down into the earth, where the whole crucified Body was seen erect, which signifies to persevere, that is, to be steadfast and long-suffering; by the height, that part which extends upward from the transverse beam, where the Head is conspicuously seen, because of the expectation of heavenly things. This is to prevent us from believing that good works ought to be done and persevered in for the sake of the earthly and temporal favors of God, rather than for that heavenly and eternal good which "faith that worketh by charity" hopes for. By the depth I understand that part of the cross which is plunged into the hidden part of the earth and is not seen, but from which rises the whole part above, which is visible, just as man is called from the secret will of God to a share in such great grace, "one after this manner, and another after that" (Galatians 5:6); but that charity of Christ which surpasseth all knowledge is undoubtedly found where "that peace is, which surpasseth all understanding" (Philippians 4:7).[301]

Considering the sober, in parts downright negative, perspective of fallen humanity characteristic to Augustine, it hardly surprises when he accords no particular intellectual faculty for a vision of God adequate to his being — Paul van Geest has discussed that the negative anthropology in the didactic letter to Paulina is closely related to a negative theology.[302] Nevertheless, it must be recognized that the negative theology here serves to steer contemplation on God's figure into a program of life informed by the Pauline theology of the cross, as Basil Studer has demonstrated in his interpretation of the didactic missive to Paulina.[303] The energetic reference to the maltreated, needy, hungry, and thirsty body of Christ on the cross is probably actually the most potent cure for any speculation as to a divine body born of a particular materiality. With such an allusion to the battered body of Christ, Augustine sought to render Paulina and other Christians who read his didactive epistle immune to musings on God's body. The fervent energy which he brought to bear is better understood[304] when it is explored as to which clashes on the theme of the body of God shook neighboring Egypt in his lifetime.

The Anthropomorphite Controversy

We now turn to this dispute, a marked climax (and simultaneously a chronological endpoint) to the divers debates in antique Christianity over the question as to whether God is to be conceived of with a body in whatsoever manner. Seemingly, this controversy concerned merely a more or less minor group of monks who have already been mentioned repeatedly in passing and now recur a final time as propounding the conception of a divine body with fervor and zeal. In reality, however, this encompassed a bitter conflict within the Christian churches of Egypt and the Holy Land at the end of the fourth and beginning of the fifth centuries hardly confined to some small factions of monks, the core of which formed the *anthropomorphites* (a coinage of their adversaries) within later, primarily heresiologically motivated ecclesiastical historiography, that is, those who allegedly pictured God in "human form." While it appears on first glance that, merely through this group and those it provoked, a heated debate as to the corporeality of God broke out anew (indeed, research until recently described this as such[305]), it must rather be stated that an orientation of piety and theology ever present within ancient Christianity which implicitly thought of God as having a body became suddenly once more a bone of strident contention. Put differently, the "anthropomorphites" did not constitute a more or less large group within monasticism with specific views, but rather a still-widespread manner of orientation within religiosity and theology which was marginalized by its opponents as a small group of the uneducated on heresiological grounds. It is scarcely coincidence that within these bitter debates as to the legitimacy of this manner of theology and religiosity, the validity and applicability of the theology of Origen was also at stake, being the opinions of a Christian theologian who had already stridently attacked the theological position and practice of piety of followers of Christ who imagined and revered God with a body. The outbreak anew of heated clashes in the fouth century is hence closely bound to the so-called *first Origenite controversy*, a dispute over the orthodoxy of Origen in not only Egypt, but also in the three provinces of Palestine, in Rome, and in Constantinople between the years of AD 393 and 404.[306] Naturally, these contexts cannot be presented here in all of their intricacies.

Even should the heresiological perspective already established in Antiquity (and still pervasive today) of particular groups of simple rustic ascetics with their especially naïve anthropomorphic image of God becoming the object of contention within the controversy not be adopted, but rather, more precisely, the specific reasons for such a serious renewed conflict between two long-opposed differing lines of tradition within Christian theology and piety, the problem of the peculiar term "anthropomorphites" first attested in the fifth century, which lent its name to the dispute termed within academia the "anthropomorphite controversy," remains to be explained. This must first be addressed before the controversies categorized under this heading might be depicted discretely according to the transmission of individual sources.

The Term "Anthropomorphites"

The word "anthropomorphite" (in English something akin to "one who imagines God in human form") stems from the Greek term (of abuse) ἀνθρωπομορφιανοί or ἀνθρωπομορφῆται, evidently first employed by the ecclesiastical historians Socrates and Sozomen in the fifth century, and Timonthy of Constantinople in the sixth.[307] It has already been seen that the underlying Greek expression "anthropomorphic," "human-shaped" (ἀνθρωπόμορφος), is first attested in late Hellenism, perhaps first in the Stoic philosopher, ethnographer, and geographer *Posidonius of Apamea* in Syria (135–51 BC); it was initially employed neutrally in Imperial-era and late antique philosophical historiography. In contrast to this original, rather descriptive designation, the polemic undertone of "anthropomorphite" is already tangible; ultimately, the conception of a body of God as propounded by Christian theologians such as Tertullian of Carthage and Melito of Sardis never concerned a divine body analogous or even identical to the human body, but rather, as has been noted, a body of special, gossamer materiality, being composed, for example, of ether and fire. The polemical context of the designation "anthropomorphites" becomes even more apparent once it is deduced as to which individual presumably coined it: *Socrates* is party to the conflict; he reveres Origen, that critic of all conceptions of a divine body par excellence exceedingly highly: "The Alexandrian master suffers not the slightest negative word, or, indeed, reservations of any kind. In dogmatic issues to be debated, Socrates proceeds very much in the vein of the dictum *Origenes locutus, causa finita.*"[308] Yet, *Sozomen* can also hardly serve as an unbased source, as he merely expands upon the pertinent passage within Socrates. As to whether the brief report from Timothy of Constantinople which states that the "anthropomorphites" say that "God is human-shaped" stems from earlier sources and possesses any grain of truth need not here be answered.[309] The aforementioned brace of terms ἀνθρωπομορφιανοί and ἀνθρωπομορφῆται were not previously employed in pagan Greek parlance; they are part of a "specific Christian language" (or *Sondersprache*, to employ a term coined by Christine Mohrmann) particular to adherents of the Christian religion and solely influenced by them. This terminology already signals to followers of Christ antique and modern that those subsumed by the designation are to be characterized as naïve individuals with absurd notions — it may certainly quite rightly be doubted whether such a neat duality of an allegedly simple "folk piety" and a reflective religion of intellectuals applies to the late fourth century.[310]

Socrates, who along with Sozomen is responsible for the appellation for this group still used today, begins the account in his "Ecclesiastical

History" with the introductory remark that the question as to "whether God
is a corporeal existence, and has the form of man; or whether he is incorporeal, and without human or, generally speaking, any other bodily shape"
brought the church into vehement disputes and turmoil.[311] In Socrates may
already be found the explanation of the debate (still often employed today)
as being due to the apparently very low standard of education among the
anthropomophites: He maintains that "very many of the more simple
ascetics asserted that God is corporeal, and has a human figure."[312] Conspicuous in this account is the juxtaposition of the adjectives "corporeal"
and "has a human figure" (σωματικὸν καὶ ἀνθρωπόμορφον), that is,
of the placement next to one another of a rather more neutrally described
and a heresiologically disqualified term. In this manner, it is already made
clear by means of the choice of terminology that, heresiologically seen,
less than stellar minds are meant. Sozomen, who lived almost contempo-
raneously to Socrates and also wrote an "Ecclesiastical History," albeit
one heavily indebted to his predecessor, characterizes the anthropomorphites with equal disdain as simple and unschooled monks but nevertheless
concedes that this relates not to a small group, but rather the "mainstream
theology" of Egyptian monasticism:

> A question was at this period agitated in Egypt, which had been pro-
> pounded a short time previously, namely, whether it is right to believe
> that God is anthropomorphic. Because they laid hold of the sacred words
> with simplicity and without any questioning, most of the monks of that
> part of the world were of this opinion; and supposed that God possessed
> eyes, a face, and hands, and other members of the bodily organization.[313]

Directly at the beginning of his account of the controversy, Sozomen
also mentions that these "anthropomorphite" teachings were disputed by
"others." He does not state whether this pertained to monks—evidently,
persons are meant who were theologically oriented towards Origen and
interpreted the biblical texts allegorically:

> But those who searched into the hidden meaning of the terms of Scrip-
> ture held the opposite; and they maintained that those who denied the
> incorporeality of God were guilty of blasphemy.[314]

On the strength of the testimony of both ecclesiastical historians, a key
figure in the outbreak of heated clashes between the majority of Egyptian
monks and an evidently statistically smaller group of "Origenistically"
minded monks appears to have been the Alexandrian patriarch *Theophilus III*
(AD 385–412),[315] the fortunes of whose image "mired by the parties in

goodwill and hate" fluctuate throughout history. Should it be sought to understand the progress of the altercations, then a more detailed study of his theological decisions and (ecclesiastical) political deeds is necessary.

Patriarch Theophilus II of Alexandria
and the Beginning of the Controversy

A famous depiction from a late antique Alexandrian world chronicle displays the patriarch Theophilus standing upon the roof of the Serapeum (beneath him a cult statue of the god visible), the largest temple in Alexandria, founded in the Ptolemaic period and splendidly enlarged in the Imperial era. Probably at some point between June 391 and April 392,[316] this temple was plundered in the wake of violent metropolitan clashes and partially destroyed, serving as a beacon conspicuous throughout the entire Imperium.[317] The miniature on the margin of the text of the chronicle depicts the patriarch, clearly identified by means of an accompanying ([ὁ] ἅγιος Θ[ε]όφι[λος]), with a manner of disc in one hand and a book in the left as the vanquisher of heathendom (according to Josef Strzygowski[318]). With this prominent example of the "Christianization" of the Serapeum, it illustrates a widespread contemporary image of Bishop Theophilus as might be found at the end of another version of this chronicle text likely originating from the age of Emperor Justinian (AD 527–565): "And he chased away those who sinned against the true religion."[319]

It may remain open at this point as to whether the statement "and he chased away those who sinned" pertains to devotees of the pagan cults, or to those who tended towards dissenting Christian groups, or to any manner of deviation from the form of Christianity with which the patriarch identified himself. Indeed, the metropole's pertinent intraurban conflicts, within each of which Patriarch Theophilus was considerably embroiled, were closely connected:[320] In the corpus of the letters of Jerome, who lived as an ascete in Bethlehem at the time, a Latin translation of the letter of Theophilus to the bishops of the ecclesiastical provinces of Palestine and Cyrus on a synod convened in Alexandria in the autumn of AD 400 may be found.[321] The Alexandrian patriarch here reports on a visitation of monasteries in the Nitrian Desert, and maintains that the so-called Origenist monks which he there encountered, "forming a party," "tried to put pressure on me at my see in Alexandria." To this belonged a spell of rabble-rousing with the aid of a mother and her son in an animated quarter of the city, "inciting the pagan populace against us with the kind of things that unbelievers will readily give ear to."[322]

Page 236 — God's Body

Fig. 6.1 Theophilus of Alexandria on the roof of the Serapeum in Alexandria (?)
Papyrus Golenishev Inv. Nr. 310/8 fol. 6^{verso} B (sixth century)
Pushkin Museum, Moscow (in its 1905 condition)[323]

Among the things they shouted, even reminding them in passing, so to speak, of the destruction of Serapis and other idols, was the cry: "(Outrages) against the rights of temples have not been (committed) in the Nitrian monasteries!"[324]

In other words, the heated clashes between groups which vehemently propounded the validity of a notion of a divine body and those who just as fervently acted against against it in the tradition of Origen can hardly be separated from the general, simmering state of religious and political conflict within the city. Should what Theophilus here claims hold true, then the opponents of the nominal anthropomorphites sought also to secure the support of the pagan population.[325] From other sources, it is known that, in particular, the aforementioned woman and her son may well have possessed a reason to proceed with all available means against the Alexandrian bishop (as Theophilus is supposed to have encouraged the youth to provide false testimony against a rival within the church by means of bribery[326]); it need not be presently answered as to what exactly occurred here in Alexandria. It must equally be left open whether Theophilus actually was a "weathervane" "possessed of a truly pharaonic craze for building," as the sources allege of him.[327]

Yet, why was Theophilus responsible for such a radical escalation of the long-latent conflict between the majority of Egyptian monks with their theology denounced as "anthropomorphic" and a minority of "Origenistically" informed monks? As the writings of this energetic church leader have only survived in fragments, translated in part into every language of Christian Antiquity,[328] his actions within the clashes around the anthropomorphites must today be reconstructed by means of texts authored by critics of Theophilus. The two aforementioned ecclesiastical historians Socrates and Sozomen number among these critics; they hold that, at the beginning of the controversy, Theophilus principally agreed with the party attacking the "anthropomorphites," and thus taught that "God is incorporeal."[329] Were this information to be accurate, then it would mean that Theophilus more or less sympathized with the Origenists from after his inauguration as bishop in AD 385 well into the 390s, and found himself in agreement with the fundamental principles of the doctrine of God of this previously discussed Alexandrian polymath. Nevertheless, this congruence in thought between Patriarch Theophilus and Origen is not claimed by either of the pertinent church historians but rather only somewhat implicitly stated.

As somewhat authentic sources on the strength of which such an orientation could be verified, the fragments extant from his dated festal letters before the outbreak of the controversy are available (preserved are fragments from the years 386, 388, 390, 391, 395, and 401). By comparison, the later and mostly extremely partisan reports on his actions in the conflicts over the theology of Origen are naturally less relevant. Moreover, the short fragments of the homilies of Theophilus are also of little use, as they can scarcely be dated to precise years of his episcopate.[330] Unfortunately, evaluation of the festal letters hardly aids in precisely establishing the relative proximity or distance of the bishop's theology to that of Origen: A very brief fragment of the first festal letter of the patriarch transmitted by an anonymous globetrotter of the sixth century dubbed "Cosmas who sailed to India" (Κοσμᾶς Ἰνδικοπλεύστης) demonstrates, for example, merely that the Metropolitan of Alexandria knew to interpret the story of the passion allegorically in respect to the salvific meaning of Easter.[331] Two pieces from festal letters of the 90s are known among other things because the still-powerful successor and nephew of Theophilus, Cyril of Alexandria, incorporated them at the Council of Ephesus in 431 into a florilegium with representative Church Fathers so as to support his own christological position (both fragments are also transmitted variously elsewhere in other florilegia in respect to the christological debate):[332] The fifth festal letter from AD 390 contains a brusque statement on the human body, which is composed of "pleasure and sleep" (stemming, in fact, from the Old Testament's Wisdom of Solomon 7:2);[333] the sixth festal letter from the following year of 391 rejects that Christ assumed "a heavenly body made, as it were, from some precious material," and ripostes that instead he "accepted the weakness of *our* nature."[334] Despite the fact that, considering the small quantity of texts, judgments must be made with the utmost care, the cited passages relatively critical of the human body fit well with what might be reconstructed of the views of the Origenistically informed factions in the context of the great controversies following AD 399. Stated somewhat more cautiously, the few surviving fragments from Patriarch Theophilus' incumbency *before* the great clashes do not contradict the view of the two ecclesiastical historians Socrates and Sozomen that he began his career as bishop influenced by the theology of Origen, and that this orientation would first become troublesome for him later. It is somewhat more difficult to combine this image from the historians of the church with what is known of his actions during the considerable controversies over Origen before 399: Indeed, in these turmoils engulfing Palestine in the 390s, featuring Bishop Epiphanius of Salamis and Jerome on the one side and Bishop John of Jerusalem and Rufinus of Aquileia on the other, the Alexandrian bishop seems to have assumed something of a mediating or even neutral position, at least for a time. Certainly, he did not declare openly for Origen and the party of his radical supporters. As these events belong very much to a specific context (that of the so-called First Origenist Crisis) and, in reality, a strikingly broad network of persons in both the west and the east of the Imperium were involved in addition to the previously mentioned actors,[335] the various imbroglios can only be presented in brief with a focus upon Theophilus.

The first reports as to Theophilus' engagement as mediator interestingly do not pertain to the latent debates on the theology of Origen already

emerging in *Egypt*, but rather his intervention within the respective conflicts in the neighboring ecclesiastical provinces of *Palestine*. The bishop
of Alexandria was evidently entreated to arbitrate by his counterpart in
Jerusalem, John, roughly two years before the outbreak of the conflict
in the neighboring region, that is, at some point before Pentecost 396.
Theophilus had previously mediated with success in ecclesiastical feuds
within the parishes of Antioch and Bostra. In terms of ecclesiastical law,
the Alexandrian bishop was in no way responsible for these two Syrian
localities; quite evidently he had been requested by John as a prominent
prince of the church from a significant episcopal seat and a prolific umpire
of disputes within the church.[336] In response to this petition, Theophilus
sent an Alexandrian presbyter called Isidore to Jerusalem with letters to
Bishop John and his most prominent opponent Jerome.[337] Admittedly, this
attempt at mediation is alleged to have failed initially in a particularly dramatic fashion, and to have only heightened tensions, very much counter
to the wishes of the bishops of Alexandria and Jerusalem alike. The mission failed, on the one hand, because Isidore, from all that which might
be gathered, nevertheless sided behind the scenes markedly for John, and
Jerome, upon uncovering this partisanship, quite understandably reacted
rather ill-humoredly and irreconcilably. On the other, it may quite justifi-
ably be asked whether Theophilus could really act as an impartial arbiter in
such a dispute considering his own theological preferences, and whether his
emissary Isidore truly chose sides on his own authority. In order to judge in
regard to this context, it must first be established why and how this crisis in
which Theophilus was to mediate had come about.

The Outbreak of the So-Called First Origenist Crisis

From what is presently known, the conflict was first ignited in Palestine
due to the metropolitan of Cyprus at the time, *Epiphanius of Salamis*, who
originally hailed from the environs of Jerusalem and had there lived for
a stint as a monk.[338] Unfortunately, information as to these beginnings
comes only from the polemic accusations directed by Jerome in his text
"Against John of Jerusalem" from either AD 396 or 397 at the Holy City's
incumbent as bishop.[339] These allegations, which on grounds of their own
partisanship submit unfortunately less than reputable testimony as to an
adversary within the church, nevertheless cautiously permit the reconstruction of an extremely dramatic scene, in which Bishops Epiphanius of
Salamis and John of Jerusalem first engaged in dispute over the theology of
Origen before a broad public:[340] Probably during a visit to Jerusalem in AD
393 or 394 (either for the chuch consecration festival in September 393 or
for Easter 394[341]), Epiphanius had heard a sermon of the local bishop John

in the Church of the Sepulchre, in which the teachings of Origen on "the Trinity, the assumption of our Lord's body, the cross, hell, the nature of angels, the condition of souls, the Savior's resurrection and our own" were evidently treated favorably.[342] Likely directly thereafter Epiphanius began himself to preach, attacking sharply the incumbent bishop in his own episcopal church during the festive liturgy due to the reference to Origen. A graver affront to general decorum and convention would likely have been unimaginable in this period. John hence instructed an archdeacon to interrupt Epiphanius in his sermon, and thus himself seriously infringed upon convention. Furthermore, the Hierosolymitan ordinary held a (presumably improvised) afternoon sermon the very same day against the "anthropomorphites" in order to defend himself against the accusation of heresy. Regrettably, practically nothing is learned of this homily from the report of Jerome, being chronologically secondary in nature and polemic in content. After having explained the term "anthropomorphites" to his readers in his text "Against John of Jerusalem" (namely in the manner that anthropomorphites believe in rustic credulousness that God actually possesses those body parts ascribed to him in the Bible), he proceeds to note that Bishop John spoke in an infuriated and unbecoming manner during his improvised counter-sermon to that of Epiphanius. Furthermore, Jerome maintains that John had gestured at Epiphanius with his eyes, hands, and entire body so as to foster the suspicion that he might adhere to this heresy.[343] According to Jerome's polemic portrayal of events, the markedly older Epiphanius is supposed to have answered to the sermon of John, "All that has been said by one who is my brother in the episcopate, but my son in point of years, against the heresy of the anthropomorphites, has been well and faithfully spoken, . . . But it is fair that, as we condemn this heresy so we should also condemn the perverse doctrines of Origen." This shrewd statement prompted laughter and applause according to Jerome,[344] although it cannot be excluded that John of Jerusalem understood this laughter as derision. Epiphanius then evidently exited the Church of the Sepulchre after another exchange of words and, after a brief halt among the monks in Bethelehem (home also to Jerome), fled the Holy Land that very night in the direction of Cyprus.[345] Much attests to the view that the bishop of Salamis considered the church community to be aghast at John of Jerusalem; in particular, monks in Bethlehem, influenced by their former confrère Epiphanius, began to turn away from John, their ordinary.[346] This much might be deduced of the likely events at the beginning of the altercation from the polemic testimony of Jerome. These demonstate that, from the very beginning, certain circles held "anthropomorphism" and "Origenism" alike to be two connected, equally overdrawn and thereby heretical positions.

The crisis which broke out in AD 393 or 394 escalated to openly declared war as, some time later but no more than three years hence, in his erstwhile monastery at Eleuthropolis near Jerusalem, Epiphanius ordained a Latin monk as priest for a monastery in Bethlehem. John complained about this ordination, disputed within ecclesiastical law, and appealed to the unity of the church against this alleged Cypriot troublemaker. The monk in question ordained by Epiphanius was none other than Jerome's brother, Paulianus.[347] Quite evidently, it was contested between the parties as to whether monks of Western origin who had settled in the Holy Land and inhabited Judean monasteries fell under the jurisdiction and right of ordination of the bishop of Jerusalem, or of the bishop of Eleuthropolis.[348] In response to John's protest, Epiphanius now sent from his quarter a brusque letter of accusation to his Hierosolymitan colleague,[349] preserved in Latin translation among the letters of Jerome, which culminates in the sentence, "Withdraw, dearly beloved, from the heresy of Origen and from all heresies."[350] The topic of anthropomorphism so vital to the duel of sermons in the Church of the Sepulchre, nevertheless plays no role in this letter of denouncement, which is likely to be dated to AD 393/394; Origen is rather described as the "the spiritual father of Arius, and the root and parent of all heresies" and hence clearly viewed instead against the backdrop of the debates on Christology and the theology of the Trinity of the third century AD.[351] Nevertheless, a great deal of information has also been lost, and those indications extant remain difficult to understand: Thus, it is known that *Rufinus of Aquileia*, who lived in a monastery on the Mount of Olives and was a central protagonist in the disputes on the side of John of Jerusalem, had promised one of the female ascetics living there the translation of the pseudo-Clementine *Recognitiones*.[352] This woman was named Silvia and arrived in Jerusalem in AD 394 (or perhaps even as late as 400) and may also have been the sister-in-law of the earlier *Praefectus pro praetorio* in the East, Flavius Rufinus.[353] It becomes evident in this small note that within the monastic environs of the city of Jerusalem, that is, at the heart of the fervent debates, a corpus of texts was discussed within which, as has been seen, the question as to the figure of God was central. Nevertheless, nothing more than this may be evinced from this mention. As to whether Rufinus as a former student of Didymus of Alexandria, who expounded biblical texts in the Origenist tradition,[354] was pursuing something more of a critical agenda and sought to unmask the pertinent passages in the pseudo-Clementine corpus cannot be stated as he only realized his intent to translate this markedly later, and the Greek original he employed is lost. It comes across as natural to suppose on grounds of this scattered information that the question as to whether God possesses a body and how this body might be fashioned was discussed at length within the monastic circles of Jerusalem and Bethlehem, and that John of Jerusalem had long been an annoyance in such debates on grounds of his "Origenist leanings." The thematic reference to the "Anthropomorphism" in the second sermon of John could also be explained by positing that the bishop of Jerusalem, deeply disgusted by the unbecoming behavior of Epiphanius, could attack him best with this keyword and accuse him thereby of absurd teachings.[355]

In this early stage of the controversy, Theophilus seems not to have engaged with the debate; certainly, nothing is heard of him either taking sides with his opposite number John, bishop of Jerusalem, or proclaiming in favor of Epiphanius and the monks supported by him, most prominently Jerome in Bethlehem.[356] About two and a half years after the homiletic contest in the Church of the Sepulchre between John and Epiphanius which provoked the crisis, in June 396,[357] the Alexandrian presbyter Isidore embarked upon his mission to Jerusalem as a mediator at Theophilus' bequest. In addition to Bishop John and his theological counselor Rufinus of Aquilea, Jerome was of particular import to the mission, being at once Epiphanius' representative among the monks in the vicinity of Jerusalem and his most avid propagator by means of his translations. Nevertheless, it had already become clear to Jerome from letters of Isidore actually intended for Bishop John and Rufinus which had, nevertheless, come into his possession, that the Alexandrian emissary could hardly be considered a neutral arbitrator.[358] Subsequently, the mediatory deputation followed its aforementioned disastrous course: Jerome refused to speak with Isidore and felt maligned by Theophilus by means of Rufinus. According to the reconstruction of Pierre Nautin, it was no longer possible for the Alexandrian bishop's envoy to deliver two identically worded letters of apology to *both* addressees.[359] John gave Isidore an apologia against the aforementioned epistolary accusations of Epiphanius destined for Alexandria and answered simultaneously a letter of his episcopal colleague Theophilus.[360] As an incensed Jerome relates in his thoroughly polemic work against John of Jerusalem, the latter must have been very much satisfied with proceedings.[361] Were such information from Jerome not to be merely interpreted as sheer polemic against the master of Isidore the mediator, whom he saw as biased, that is, against Theophilus, then it might indicate that Isidore did not act independently of the fundamental ecclesiastical-political and theological intentions of his commissioner Theophilus in clearly siding with the "Origenistically" minded Bishop John of Jerusalem and Rufinus of Aquileia, on the one hand, and against the "anti-Origenistically" oriented Bishop Epiphanius of Salamis, on the other hand. Quite evidently, the Alexandrian metropolitan was very much in agreement with his Hierosolymitan colleague, and, just as obviously, Theophilus could not shed the emphatic defense of Origen by John from his politics.

In the apologia of John, nevertheless, the question as to the corporeality of God played only a subordinate role; ultimately, merely a single sentence in this text belonging to a "private creed"[362] of John concerns this: "We anathematise those who state something large or small or unequal or visible in respect to the godhead of the Trinity; rather, as we call the Father incorporeal and invisible and eternal, so do we also deem incorporeal and invisible <and eternal> the Son and the Holy Ghost."[363] As the observations following the "private creed" in the apologia of John of Jerusalem for Theophilus of Alexandria also demonstrate, the bodiliness of Jesus and the resurrected body of humans formed a topic in addition to the canonical question as to whether Epiphanius was entitled to ordain as priest a monk hailing from the West. Yet, as connected as these questions were to implicit concepts on the body of God, a few years later, these would be debated with markedly greater intensity in Egypt than in Palestine and Jerusalem (should the surviving sources be correct on this point).

Considering the prior history and the failure of Isidore's mission, the swift and peaceful outcome of such an escalated conflict is astounding; this was the product of the initiative of the Theophilus the bishop of Alexandria, who proved himself once more to be a seasoned mediator of ecclesiastical conflicts: After Jerome had concluded his aforementioned polemic text against John of Jerusalem (presumably in 396 or 397), a conversation resulted between him and Bishop Theophilus (according to Nautin immediately thereafter, in the winter of AD 396/397, in 399 at the very latest)[364] which concerned less theological questions than it did church discipline, and ended with Jerome relenting. As to whether Theophilus in actuality came to Jerusalem and Bethlehem to intercede personally, as he promised to Jerome, remains unclear.[365] Regardless, Theophilus' written request to Jerome to soften his tone towards his local bishop prevailed,[366] and hence he could conclude successfully the mission asked of him by his colleague John of Jerusalem despite Isidore's failure.

Should the reconciliation between John and Jerome, into which Rufinus and Epiphanius were included, be dated first to the end of the fourth century, then events in early AD 398 in Constantinople could also be seen as the catalyst for these developments: At the time, Theophilus of Alexandria was compelled, contrary to his original intentions, to consent to the election of John Chrysostom as bishop of Constantinople, considered an "Origenist,"[367] and to ordain the new appointee, as, with the publication of information relevant to criminal proceedings, he was threatened with prosecution and conviction.[368] In the face of such a threat, a tranquil situation in Alexandria must very much have been in his interest, and this reality could also explain his actions during the first phase of the Origenist controversy. Regardless, this may well have been a motive for his deeds in the years AD 339/400, as the conflict spread to Egypt.

The Motives of the Patriarch

Howsoever one thinks in regard to the difficult questions as to the chronology of the heated clashes in Palestine and the various efforts at intervention in the 390s, it is entirely possible that the perspectives of the ecclesiastical historians Socrates and Sozomen regarding the altered stance of the bishop, who declaimed vehemently the personage and thology of Origen, provide a valid account of actual circumstances: Much supports the premise that Alexandria's metropolitan Theophilus was initially mildly "Origenistically" minded, much in the vein of his immediate predecessors (and, in particular, Athanasius[369]) and, at the least, did not oppose fundamentally Origen's theology. Far more gladly a mediator in disputes, he may well have had bad experiences with the potential for conflict of theology in the Origenian vein during the first phase of the Origenist Crisis in Palestine, and have been confronted by energetic "anti-Origenist" monks in his own diocese with presumably shocking details as to the teachings of Origen, have discarded increasingly his prior views, and have finally sought to combat them. The chronology of this alienation may be reconstructed with some accuracy: As Theophilus learned by means of the conflict in Jerusalem of the details of the doctrine of a theologian who viewed many of his predecessors highly critically, he must have become suspicious. Then he came to appreciate the extent to which conflict over Origen escalated and was further informed by "anthropomorphites," monks from his own ecclesiastical province, as to the alleged heresies of Origen. Individual fragments of his texts and letters illustrate how he read almost hatefully "On First Principles" and the exegetical and homiletical works of Origen under these auspices. Naturally, he also found therein the heresies which he sought.[370] What today would carefully be distinguished from one another as political and theological motives went here hand in hand; certainly, as has been stated, the theological and ecclesiastical-political development of Bishop Theophilus may be understood in such a manner. Nevertheless, for want of insight into his inner workings it can also hardly be categorically excluded that his altered stance on the theology of Origen was merely the purely tactical, actually theologically unfounded masquerade of an individual behaving much in the manner of the proverbial "weathervane."

Why might Theophilus of Alexandria have seen such bitter scrimmages within his own diocese and in the entirety of Egypt shortly after having surprisingly enough settled amicably the heated conflict in

Palestine? The closely related question as to why the monks in Palestine and Egypt alike suddenly developed such a profound suspicion of Origen and those they held to be his adherents is frequently answered within the field with a reference to the previously quoted opinion of Bishop Epiphanius of Salamis that over the course of the controversy as to the theology of the Trinity it was increasingly agreed upon that Origen was the spiritual "father of Arius."[371] This would then mean that these groupings were first hostile to the Alexandrian presbyter Arius and later extended the focus of their enmity to Origen as they already understood him as the spiritual father of the heresy of Arius on grounds of their shared Alexandrian origin.[372] Yet, should the reconstructions of Elizabeth Clark and Antoine Guillaumont be followed,[373] then, at the very least in Egypt, the personage of *Evagrius Ponticus* and his theology evidently played a vital role in the escalation of a clearly long-simmering conflict—more precisely, the doctrine of Evagrius that, for pure prayer, the monk should transcend "the contemplation of corporeal nature" and correspond, indeed, to the incorporeal God thereby.[374] This teaching popularized an already significantly older form of the theology arguing against the conception of a body of God by means of instructions as to a concrete practice of religiosity which accompanied and structured the daily routine of a monk, namely prayer.

Evagrius Ponticus and His Polemic

Evagrius was educated in the milieu of the two Cappadocian theologians Basil of Caesarea and Gregory of Nazianzus, both of whom were heavily influenced by Origen.[375] Gregory bequeathed to him in his will "as a small gesture of friendship . . . a shirt . . . , a tunic, two cloaks, and thirty gold pieces."[376] Since AD 383, Evagrius lived first with monks in the Nitrian Deserts, and then in Kellia further to the west, an expansive monastic settlement with large, homestead-like hermitages ("cells," τὸ κέλλιον) for the monks. He died there in AD 399 and thus escaped the measures instituted by Patriarch Theophilus.[377]

As Evagrius journeyed by way of Jerusalem to Egypt, he encountered an ascetism influenced by Origen's theology to which "the most eminent" numbered and "appear to have adopted the monastic life" according to Epiphanius of Salamis.[378] The centers of this were the *Deserts of Nitria and Scetis*, the former lying on the edge of cultivated land near a canal between Lake Mareotis and the western, Rosetta arm of the Nile at a natron lake (near the modern village of Al Barnuji), the second in the present-day Wadi an-Natrun (Natron Valley) some hundred kilometers southeast of Alexandria, halfway to Giza. Kellia developed after the founder of Nitria, *Amun* (ca. AD 288–356), a student of

Anthony, retreated in AD 338, after roughly a decade, fifteen kilometers farther south into the desert, founding a new settlement with some brethren in order to find more peace. In the period of its greatest extent, it encompassed a hilly area of over a hundred square kilometers along the Al Nubanya Canal, which connects the western arm of the Nile with Lake Mareotis at Alexandria, well beyond the pale of the sown in this period.[379]

When it is recognized that a brisk exchange of ideas prevailed between Alexandria and Nitria, as is demonstrated, for example, by the influential teacher and exegete *Didymus the Blind* (AD 311–398), and thereby that a flourishing ascetic tourism led ever more prominent visitors such as Jerome or Rufinus,[380] but also Evagrius Ponticus, to the three aforementioned settlements, then it hardly surprises to learn that Origen's theology originally developed in Alexandria had adherents among monks sixty to one hundred kilometers afield to the east and southeast. Perhaps "the most eminent" who "appear to have adopted the monastic life" referred in particular to Didymus the Blind, the orientation of whom towards Origen can hardly be doubted in respect to either his method of biblical exegesis or his theology.[381] Additional to this prominent "Origenist" was a whole tonsure of monks informed by Origen, who need not here be discussed in detail, incidentally, not only in Lower but also in Upper Egypt.[382] The doctrine of Evagrius can be termed (following Jon F. Dechow) a synthesis of the approaches propounded by these individuals, wherein, born of these individual references, a remarkable transformation of the fundamental thought of Origen occured within a monastic context.[383]

In the writings of Evagrius, the aspect within the theology of Origen directed against the body is strikingly honed, truly creating thereby the content fundamental to a heated battle against the "anthropomorphites" for the first time. As it is hardly possible to expound the distinct and complex theology of this thinker in a merely rudimentary manner, one of his various texts will be concentrated upon, namely his short tractate "On Prayer" (Περὶ προσευχῆς), certainly translated into many ancient Christian languages and hence presumably much prized both within and without the Imperium. In the Greek manuscripts, it is mostly ascribed to the ascetic Nilus but can be attributed to Evagrius with a high probability by means of the Syriac tradition.[384] Only a very crude dating to the years AD 383–399 is at all possible;[385] it consists of a collection of apophthegms, that is, aphorisms captioned as "chapters" (κεφάλαια). These could, indeed, be termed "meditative sayings" which (much as in the Neoplatonic tradition) should enable a literate community to memorize the contents therewith expressed.[386] Evagrius outlines a sort of practical rule for correct prayer, namely, to distance oneself from all possible conceptions of corporeality.

Fig. 6.2 Present-day preservation of the ruins of the partially excavated hermitages of Kellia
Subregion of Qouçoûr / Qusur el-ʿIzeila (probably sixth to eighth centuries AD)[387]

In other words, he demands a "prayer of the spirit" and accordingly draws radical conclusions from the traditional definition of prayer as the "communion of the mind with God":[388]

> When you pray do not form images of the divine within yourself, nor allow your mind to be impressed with any form, but approach the Immaterial immaterially and you will come to understanding.[389]

The notion of a corporeal form is inappropriate as the godhead is without quantity and form.[390] This fundamental conviction is characteristic to the author and may already be found in a long theological letter which Evagrius composed at some point between AD 379 and 381, as he sojourned with Gregory of Nazianzus: There already he pointedly excludes that God is "one in number," as only that which might be counted is corporeal, but God possesses "no material and circumscribed nature":

> Number is a property of quantity; and quantity is linked to bodily nature; therefore, number is a property of bodily nature. We have affirmed our faith that our Lord is the fashioner of bodies. So every number designates

those things that have been allotted a material and circumscribed nature; but "One and Only" is the designation of the simple and uncircumscribed essence.[391]

In the *Kephalaia Gnostica*, a further work of Evagrius, it is also tersely maintained that number represents a quantitative size, and quantity is tied to a corporeal dimension.[392] With the terms "One and Only," Evagrius takes up a double expression within Origen's theory of God borrowed from Platonic philosophy, which he then further develops: In the work on principles of his teacher, never mentioned by name, this double expression is already applied to themes of the body, as has been seen:

> God, therefore, is not to be thought to be either a body or existing in a body, but to be a simple intellectual being, accepting in Himself no addition whatever; so that he cannot be believed to have in Himself a more or a less, but is, in all things, *Monad* (unity).[393]

Evagrius also adopts Origen's doctrine of a first creation of rational and incorporeal beings (λογικά or *rationabiles creaturae*).[394] Accordingly, he is also convinced that God's first creations were bodiless, intelligent, immaterial beings, λογικοί, as also God is incorporeal as a simple and unfathomable substance.[395] Indeed, in Evagrius, this cosmologically and protologically oriented teaching is concretely associated with the prayer of the monk, as this yields the opportunity to recognize this utterly transcendent, incorporeal God—or at least where "pure prayer" is concerned. In one such prayer, man observes his "own light" (τὸ οἰκεῖον φέγγος),[396] considering himself to be "luminescent" (φωτοειδής) and "formless" (ἀνείδεος), that is, bare of any sensory clarity.[397] In such a manner, one's creation in the likeness of God also becomes apparent, who himself is intrinsically light.[398] Ultimately, then, the individual's immaterial, bodiless body becomes the space of the merciful presence of God,[399] a "place of God."[400] In his biography of Evagrius, Palladius of Helenopolis claims that the monastic father was able after fifteen years of hard asceticism (that is, in approximately AD 396) by means of incessant prayer to free himself from all of the passions, vices, and other corporeal hindrances of such intellectual show, meaning that he could actually see such a pure, holy light.[401] At the end of his tractate "On Thoughts," closely related to "On Prayer,"[402] Evagrius gives very concrete suggestions from monastic practice as to how this particular state may be approached so that the mind shines as brightly as a star, namely, by means of controlling the emotions, particularly rage, and the cravings of the body, especially the stomach: One should not fill the stomach with bread, drink water moderately, avoid strife, and spend the night in prayer: "Knock on the door of Scripture with the hands of Virtues."[403] By contrast, in "On Prayer," less is stated as to light or as to the "place of God" and far more as to God himself. Rather than focusing upon "mental representations," one should persevere in prayer in deep quietude.[404] An empirically appreciable image is demonic:

> When the mind finally achieves the practice of pure prayer free from the passions, then the demons no longer attack it on the left, but on the right. They suggest to it a notion of God along with some form associated with the senses so that it thinks that it has perfectly attained the goal of prayer.[405]

Thus, for Evagrius, corporeal conceptions of God are not only impossible and preposterous notions to the reasonable individual which should be restricted from one's thoughts merely on grounds of rationality, as Origen held; rather, they are demonic attempts to lead a follower of Christ astray from the righteous path of his belief, from the way to God, and indeed from the route to heaven, and to cast this individual into hell by means of unreason, passion, and turmoil. In other words, Evagrius loaded the brusque polemic of Origen against the notion of a body of God with a great deal of theology, combining the entire discourse on demons, sins, judgment, and hell with a classical Christian conception of God believed by many adherents of Christianity. Quite certainly, he saw in the prevalent notion of a body of God all that which a monk should combat in thought, word, and works. Evagrius presumably also, as has been seen, undertook this heavy embellishment with theology of the rather philosophically argumented work of Origen in order somewhat to ground Origen's intellect-associated thesis within monastic life. The controversy around Origen might hence also never be described as merely a dispute over different forms of theology, but rather a debate between forms of religiosity.[406]

As is clearly demonstrated by the passages from his work "On Prayer" and other of his tracts, Evagrius' intensification of Origen's theology simultaneously renewed the Alexandrian theologian's erstwhile thrust against individuals who imagined God with a body within his book on first principles. That which Origen had formulated around 160 years previously in his "On First Principles" as a polemic for the educated was revitalized by Evagrius and disseminated within Egypt and Alexandria by means of the daily practice of prayer in a burgeoning monastic colony. In place of a prayer to God, which might be marred by the bodily imagination of a corporeally conceived God, the so called Jesus Prayer was introduced, the uninterrupted invocation of Jesus by means of the exclamation of the words "Lord Jesus" (Κύριε Ἰησοῦ) or "Lord Jesus Christ, have mercy

upon us" (Κύριε Ἰησοῦ Χριστέ, ἐλέησον ἡμᾶς). According to Antoine
Guillaumont, contemporary evidence of such a practice may already be
found in the fifth century (on the contrary, Irénée Hausherr remained skeptical of such an early dating).[407] The Jesus Prayer was nevertheless less than
evident to monks of the Origenite tradition—one well-known albeit later
and now-destroyed inscription upon the wall of an oratorium in a kellion
reflects late antique debates on the theology of Origen.[408] In the inscription, a demon is depicted as objecting to the Jesus Prayer: "When you
constantly exclaim 'Lord Jesus!' Then you are not praying to the Father
or the Holy Ghost."[409] According to the inscription, the monk replies to
this objection by stating that inasmuch as he prays to Jesus, he is also
praying "to the Father with him, and to the Holy Ghost of his Father with
him." This demonic dissent sounds like a crude recapitulation of Origen's
criticism of the monastic practice of calling upon Jesus in prayer. Origen
famously writes the following in his work on prayer:

> If we understand what prayer is, perhaps we ought not to pray to anyone
> born [of woman], nor even to Christ himself, but only to the God and
> Father of all, to whom also our Saviour prayed . . . and teaches us to
> pray.[410]

Precisely this remark from Origen was repeatedly attacked by Bishop
Theophilus as heretical during the first Origenite controversy within,
among other places, an aforementioned synodical missive from AD 400,
in his Easter festal letter from 401, and in a further text.[411] The fact that
within a later inscription Origen's criticism was intoned by a demon
demonstrates that the theological charging of the Alexandrian's polemic,
as might be observed in Evagrius Ponticus, was not without consequence,
resultantly leading to a marked increase in criticism also of Origen. There
is hence much to recommend the view that the radicalization of Origen's
positions via Evagrius Ponticus had ultimately provoked the heated disputes over Origen in Egypt which will now be considered.

The "Anthropomorphites'" Criticism of Radical Origenism

The fact that a radicalized Origenism entails an equally pointed anti-
Origenism does not yet elucidate why at all there were still monks in
Egypt who might be denounced as "anthropomorphites." An examination
of the personage and work of Evagrius Ponticus can somewhat explain the
resurgence of the furor with which Origen had fought those who assumed
or even conceived of a body of God for the late fourth century; this notwithstanding, it remains difficult to understand why there were so many

individuals, and in particular ascetics, who adhered to such conceptions despite the striking decline in the influence of Stoic materialism within Christian theology already witnessed. This prompts the question as to why not only ascetics informed by the theology of Origen existed within the Egyptian desert but also these very "anthropomorphites." This question has been answered in very different manners: It was already held in Antiquity that this consisted of the remnants of pagan religiosity, in particular of an Egyptian bent, within Christian piety deemed to be *survivals*.[412] Yet, on the other hand, the lively dissemination of translated texts of those Imperial-era theologians who propounded notions of the divine body demonstrates that this explanation hardly suffices and, indeed, could well be entirely false. Naturally, it should not be excluded that "survivals" of pagan religiosity aided, for example, the reception of certain forms of piety and theology among monks, but the influence of the *Christian* theological traditions outlined is rather underestimated. Moreover, a glance at the texts of Evagrius already demonstrates that within "anthropomorphite theology" the focus was not only on theological doctrine, but also the practice of prayer.

Whence did these monks hail, who presumably sojourned in the Sketis, modern-day Wadi Natrun, when, as has been deduced, Nitria and Kellia were prominently influenced by Origenists?[413] The question is certainly presented should the "anthropomorphites" not be taken for a sheer invention of their opponents (as does, for example, Rubenson).[414] A convincing answer might only be attained for these questions when the sources depicting the outbreak of the Origenist clashes in Egypt are critically analyzed. Here, the two previously discussed ecclesiastical historians must be revisited.

Socrates and, following him, Sozomen recount the story that Patriarch Theophilus withdrew his originally "Origenist" position and taught for a space of time in the manner of the "anthropomorphites." He is supposed to have been coerced to do so by means of naked force: Both ecclesiastical historians report that Theophilus was assailed by some "anthropomorphites" who sought to kill him, that he (understandably) feared for his life, and attempted to placate the aggressive monks by stating, "In seeing you, I behold (in your face) the face of God."[415] Therewith, according to the narrative of both church historians, Theophilus conceded that an "image and likeness" of the divine countenance might be seen in the *corporeal* face of a human, and that thereby a certain manner of corporeality is to be conferred upon God. After a demand presented as an ultimatum by the monks, the patriarch was also supposed to have uttered critical remarks on the writings of Origen (according to Socrates),[416] or generally critical statements regarding the admirers of Origen (following Sozomen).[417] Both historians hold the words exclaimed by Theophilus while facing death to be a dishonest change in stance, perhaps also because as Origenistically minded theologians they could not imagine in the slightest that a bishop could at all propound "anthropomorphite" positions: "By these means he deluded the brethren, and broke up the sedition."[418]

At this juncture, it must first be understood that the intervention of monks in the interest of certain networks within state, church, and theological politics at the end of the fourth century was something of a fixture within Alexandria's workings: As has been seen, Theophilus is supposed to have been compelled to revise his opinions on Origen publicly in the spring of AD 399 by a group of "anthropomorphically" influenced monks. Conversely, in the aforementioned letter from an Alexandrian synod from AD 400, Theophilus himself may be witnessed stating that his life was threatened by some "Origenistically" informed monks from the Nitrian Desert.[419] Furthermore, it is known from a saying transmitted in the context of a monastic collection of sentences that (in the case of the Serapeum) Theophilus also was hardly adverse to employing groups of monks in accomplishing a certain aim: "Summoned by Patriarch Theophilus, came once fathers to Alexandria to convene a prayer and destroy the heathen temple."[420] Quite evidently, Theophilus was not only a political virtuoso in mobilizing support from large demographic groups (in this case, monks), much like his great predecessor Athanasius, but also attempted, under the circumstances of the Christian state religion once more massively privileged by Emperor Theodosius, a new form of politically potent "authoritative spiritual leadership" (Edward J. Watts) in order to conclude the Christianization of the metropolis.[421] Already with Athanasius, the close connection between the ascetics (such as Anthony) belonged to the brief of "spiritual leadership"; Theophilus hardly associated with this tradition by chance.[422] Violence, also in bloodily form, had marked conflicts in the city for a long time; it clearly belonged to the political methods deemed appropriate within the Christian community.[423]

This perspective from the two church historians Socrates and Sozomen that the formerly "Origenistically" sympathetic patriarch Theophilus switched his position in AD 399 to one critically opposed to Origen may be well attested within the scattered remains of his own oeuvre's transmission (and certainly, as has been seen, markedly better than his "mild Origenism" *prior* to the change of stances). Supporting this is, for example, a first, highly critical synodical text from an Alexandrian synod probably composed by him which can be dated to autumn/winter of AD 399 or the first months of 400.[424] This consists of a vehement assault upon the person and position of Origen, in particular upon his views on the pre-existence and terrestrial embodiment of the soul. Origen is described as a "maniac and enemy of God."[425] A second text, likely also written by Theophilus, from this synod or a further example in AD 400, addressed to the bishops of the church provinces of Syria and Palestine, is transmitted in a probably highly accurate Latin translation by Jerome[426] and contains, as has been seen, not only renewed and ever more extensive recriminations against Origen, but also complaints about monks from the Nitrian desert, within which the "heresy of Origen" had allegedly spread. Not only may the accusation that these monks poison the hearts of simple followers of Christ here be found,[427] but also the allegation quoted that these monks attempt to bury the reputation of the Patriarch Theophilus in Alexandria even among the pagan urban population. Questions as to the corporeality of God are not directly engaged within the text, but rather the bishop accused his opponents (the Origenists) of so great an obsession against their own bodies that they (in the words of Theophilus) "turned their hands against themselves and cut off their own members with a knife":

> They foolishly thought on this account that if they went about with mutilated face and severed ears they were proving themselves to be religious and humble. One of them has even amputated his tongue by biting it off.[428]

One might initially hold such accusations to be pure polemic, as such charges had famously already been leveled at Origen in the context of disputes in the third century AD, claiming that he had severed a member (namely, his penis) with a knife.[429] On the other hand, for example, the so-called *Sentences of Sextus* demonstrate that there were not only "people cutting off and throwing away their own limbs in order to keep the rest of the body strong (or healthy)," but also that the recommendation circulated among adherents of Christianity to practice this "in order to observe moderation."[430] In the sentences, it is even directly exhorted to sever those limbs of the body which hinder restrained and abstemious life: "For it is better to live moderately without the part than to live ruinously with it."[431] Other contemporaneous sources confirm that Christians living as ascetics would cut off body parts, attempting in this manner to demonstrate their complete apathy towards the body.[432] In the hagiography of the Palestinian monastic father Sabas, who died in AD 532 and was an energetic supporter of Origen's theology, it is recounted that a hermit named Jacobus castrated himself: "Heavily embattled from the demons of unchastity . . . , be it from ignorance of the canons of the church, or from the forgetting of the same, he took hold of a knife and cut off his testicles." As, according to the report of the hagiography, the castrated monk could not endure the blood loss and pain, he had to be cared for by a doctor from

Sabas' lavra.[433] Self-amputation of the tongue is attested by the famous example from Antiquity of the pre-Socratic philosopher Zeno of Elea (ca. 490–430 BC), who wished to unseat a tyrant and bit off his own tongue and spat it out in the tyrant's face in order to impress the masses and incite them to participate.[434] A similar anecdote is told of the Hellenistic philosopher Anaxarchos from the school of Democritus in Abdera/Thrace (ca. 360–320 BC), who during his extremely brutal torture at the hands of the tyrant Nicocreon of Cyprus bit off his own tongue to preempt its planned extraction.[435] These and other stories were widespread in Antiquity; even Tertullian refers (if now anonymously) to an "Attic prostitute" who spits her own tongue in the face of the tyrant who seeks to torture her, so as to avoid betraying her fellow conspirators.[436] Ultimately, it is no longer possible to tell whether the Alexandrian synod and Patriarch Theophilus sought to cast the most gruesome of aspersions upon their adversaries, or whether these monks were genuinely riven by a particularly obsessive hatred of the body and all corporeality. It is, by contrast, certain that the second synodical letter of AD 400 establishes a connection between such behavior towards one's own body and the teachings of Origen. The screed further contains a manner of catalog of Origen's heresies which outlines and expands upon relevant comparisons to Epiphanius of Salamis.[437] Within this catalog may be found the assertion that Origen stated:

> that after the passage of many centuries our bodies will gradually be reduced to nothing and will dissolve into thin air, and, in case we should think this a small matter, adding that "the resurrected body will not only be corruptible but also mortal"?[438]

Naturally, this sentence cannot be found within the surviving works of Origen and must be interpreted as sheer malevolent polemic against this Alexandrian theologian of yesteryear. Regardless of such questions of authenticity, the quotation of this sentence in the Alexandrian synodical letter may well indicate why Theophilus turned from the Origenistically informed networks to the "anthropomorphites": Considering that raving monks presented him with such sentences as "quotations" from the text on first principles (something which, in fact, cannot be excluded), then perhaps he saw at work in the adherents of Origen a stance extremely hostile towards the body which impinged upon or even threatened to eliminate both the physical existence of the terrestrial body and the future existence of the heavenly resurrected body. It can, nevertheless, also scarcely be excluded that it might have been imperative for Theophilus to cite the most scandalous sentences once allegedly written by Origen and now also propounded by the latter's followers: Within a florilegium directed against

Origen first compiled in Palestine (the manuscript of which hails from the twelfth century),[439] a fragment from a letter of Theophilus from AD 403 is preserved[440] wherein the Alexandrian metropolitan not only repeats the allegation just quoted; rather, he also contests the apparent teaching of Origen that "the risen bodies do not have apposite forms, but rather a spherical shape."[441] Additionally, he recapitulates the supposed argument of the Origenists that a spherical form is "the best shape." Although it cannot be excluded that monks influenced by Origen and Evagrius within the diocese of Theophilus adhered to such conceptions (for example, the notion of an original spherical body of humanity may also be found in the Platonic dialogue *Timaeus* during a description of the spherical form of the world),[442] such a sentence is ideally suited to defaming Origen and his supporters. God and his body are hardly discussed in either the entire fragment of the letter of Theophilus from AD 403 or the second synodical letter of AD 400; rather, without reference to the creation in the likeness of God, it is maintained that the present human body is the best possible form for humans.

For Bishop Theophilus, the question as to the nature and consistency of the resurrected body of humans was not closely bound to the question as to the actuality of the human nature of Jesus Christ (and thereby to the reality of the incarnation). Within the second synodical letter of AD 400, it may be read that Origen sought in his tome on first principles to convince individuals "that the living Word of God did not assume a human body."[443] This assertion also owes itself to a heavily exaggerated and thereby false reading of his work on first principles.[444] Nevertheless, for those who read Origen in such a manner, this must have led to the conclusion that, according to him, the soul of Jesus Christ *alone* reproduces the form and likeness of the divine majesty: This position was naturally contested by the synodical letter.[445] Despite only fragments of the synodical declarations and episcopal letters from the years between AD 399 and 403 surviving, not only ecclesiastical-political, but also thoroughly theological motives might be presumed from these: Perhaps, influenced by such assertions and alleged quotations from Origen, Theophilus had genuinely become convinced that the root of the theological ill was in the false conception of an incorporeal God and the notion constructed thereupon of a likeness to God confined purely to the human soul. Such a line of argumentation can certainly be imagined as having been expressed by the "anthropomorphically" minded circles of monks ranged against Origen which had harassed the patriarch since AD 399.

The Beginning of the Conflict

The apparently only colorfully recounted, but in fact clearly contrived scenes in Socrates and Sozomen are merely *part* of the whole story—this applies also to the beginning of the conflict which must be reconstructed from other sources, being omitted by the two ecclesiastical historians. The initial events occuring prior to the aforementioned synodical text of AD 399/400 and the letter of AD 403, evidently presaging all of the clashes and plunging the patriarch into considerable difficulties, are nowhere to be found within Socrates (and Sozomen). These opening deeds are related by the ascetic *John Cassian*, who sojourned during precisely this period within Egypt's monastic landscapes and recorded his impressions many years later (probably shortly after AD 419) in his *Collationes Patrum* ("Conversations with the Fathers").[446] As he belonged to a group of monks who were favorably inclined towards the theology of Origen and their transformation in Evagrius Ponticus, he was (akin to all other witnesses to the controversy) a partisan. It was presumably on account of this theological orientation that John Cassian, along with many other Origenistically informed monks, abandoned the monastic settlement of Sketis in AD 399/400 as Bishop Theophilus of Alexandria turned on the "Origenists," and settled (by way of Constantinople and Rome) in Marseille;[447] here, the *Collationes* were also composed (probably for the brethren of the newly founded monastic settlements on the Île Saint-Honorat of the Îles de Lérins, a manner of monastic retreat for the northern Gallic aristocracy).[448] As is already denoted by the title, in the *Collationes Patrum* this work presents these Egyptian experiences in the form of fictive discussions with monks living there.[449] At the same time, this constitutes a manner of "initiatiory text" which should introduce Gallic monks to the theology and practice of Egyptian monasticism, and also as an advertisement for certain theological positions. The text most certainly may not be understood as something of an inadvertent historical depiction of the past.[450]

The outbreak of the controversy is reported by Cassian in the second conversation with a sketic monk named Isaac on perpetual prayer. Most likely, this ascetic is identical with an Origenistically minded monk of Sketis by the name of Isaac, who like John Cassian sought refuge in Constantinople after AD 399. It is possible that he even belonged to the immediate circle of Evagrius Ponticus in Kellia.[451] In this text, it is stated:

> In the region of Egypt, the following custom is observed according to an ancient tradition: When the day of Epiphany has been celebrated—which the priests of that province understand to be both the day of the lord's baptism and that of his birth according to the flesh, meaning that they

celebrate the solemnity as in the Western provinces—a letter from the bishop of Alexandria is sent to all the churches of Egypt. It is both the beginning of the Lenten season and the day of Easter are designated not only for each town but also for all the monasteries. In accordance with this custom, then, a very few days after the previously mentioned conference with Abba Isaac had taken place, there arrived the solemn letter of Theophilus, bishop of the aforesaid city. Along with the Easter announcement he also argued extensively against the foolish heresy of the anthropomophites and demolished it at great length. Because of their errant naïveté, however, this was received with great bitterness by nearly all the various sorts of monks who were living throughout the province of Egypt that the vast majority of the elders decided that the aforementioned bishop should be abominated by the entire body of the brothers as a person who had been tainted by a very serious heresy. For this seemed to go contrary to the words of Holy Scripture by denying that Almighty God had a human form, although Scripture very clearly testified to the fact that Adam had been created in his image. To such an extent was this letter repudiated by those who dwelt in the desert of Scetis and who, in perfection and knowledge, surpassed all who lived in the monasteries of Egypt that, apart from Abba Paphnutius, the priest of our community, none of the other priests who presided over the other three churches in that desert would allow it to be read at all, either privately or publicly, in their communities.[452]

Opposing this overwhelming majority of both simple and educated, accomplished monks alike accusing as one Theophilus of teaching unbiblically, was according to John Cassian, "Abba Paphnutius, the priest of our community" alone. An ascetic of this name recurs frequently within the *Collationes Patrum*; therein, he is a hermit, and priest for one of the groups in Scetis, also leading the minority of Origenistically minded monks there. Cassian already regards him highly on grounds of their shared theological orientation.[453]

Should Cassian's portrayal be followed, which admittedly is just as laden with heresiological motives as those of the ecclesiastical historians, and hardly paints Theophilus or the "anthropomorphite" monks in a good light, then the conflicts centered initially upon an Easter festal letter which Theophilus wrote in the spring of AD 399[454] (as the patriarch of Alexandria endeavored to do so as to announce the exact date of the feast of Easter and to discuss some theological themes of general interest).[455] In this, presumably his fourteenth, letter in the series of Easter festal epistles, Theophilus evidently harshly criticizes the position of the "anthropomorphites"—although the missive is lost, a brief summary of his deeds is most likely to be found in the aforementioned nevertheless fragmentarily preserved letter of the patriarch from Constantinople from some four years later in AD 403:[456]

> We have not only anathematized Origen's heresies, but also another heresy that attempted to cause serious disturbance to the monasteries. Since certain people of the more rustic and uncultivated sort claimed that it was necessary to conceive of God in human form, we did not remain silent but also refuted this heresy, Christ having lent us vigilance, with written proofs in official ecclesiastical letters.[457]

Theophilus mentions his actions against the anthropomorphites, who, as a theologian active in an urban context, he alleges to be artless individuals from the countryside; nevertheless, he mentions letter*s* in the plural, and not one single festal text. As to what his interventions constituted, practically nothing is learned from the passage cited from his own letter; Cassian merely describes in the previously cited passage that the patriarch "denied that Almighty God had a human form." Regardless, the sentence presents two problems: *On the one hand*, the Latin terminology used to depict the relationship of similarity between human form and God is conceivably imprecise: *compositio* can describe both a neat connection of limbs in the sense of the Greek term for combination (σύνθεσις) and a comparison on grounds of a relationship of similarity in the sense of the Greek term "analogy" (ἀναλογία).[458] It is probably meant in the sense that the "anthropomorphites" maintained a certain analogy (admittedly not qualified any further here) between God and human corporeal form, and that Theophilus contested this similarity. *On the other hand*, it is unusual that the description of the relationship of similitude in Cassian's text takes *God* as its starting point rather than man. This reveals the polemic undertone of the description: Theophilus quite evidently accused the anthropomorphites of the cardinal error of approaching God by way of humanity rather than humanity by way of God. Yet, that any recollection in the slightest of the genuine teachings of those monks condemned as "anthropomorphites" might be intact within such heady polemic may quite rightly be doubted.

Different once more are the circumstances relayed by *Gennadius of Masillia* in his catalog of authors from the second half of the fifth century: Gennadius, who like John Cassian hailed from Marseille, mentions in his section on Theophilus of Alexandria an "extensive book" wherein the patriarch opposed not only Origen, but also the "anthropomorphite heretics who say that the Lord comprises a human form and limbs." Against this heresy, Theophilus is supposed to have demonstrated by means of detailed argumentation that God is bodiless, in no way confined by corporeal members, and of an indestructible, immutable, and incorporeal nature.[459] Whether a further tract by Theophilus or, at the least, additional epistles from him against the "anthropomorphites" might genuinely be expected, or whether Gennadius here is merely describing the aforementioned festal letter (most likely of AD 399), and thereby somewhat exaggerates remains, unfortunately, presently unclear.[460] As the festal letter itself is lost, it is difficult to obtain a precise image of the arguments and counterarguments. Graham Gould made recourse to that information within Gennadius relating to this allegedly comprehensive book in reconstructing the original position of Theophilus. According to this, Theophilus taught that but God alone is incorporeal, immutable, and indestructible, that is, he "who only hath immortality" (1 Timothy 6:16), while "all intellectual natures are corporeal, all corruptible, all mutable, that He alone should not be subject to corruptibility of changeableness, who alone has immortality and life."[461] Whether Theophilus here referred to the intangible element of humans such as the soul or intellect (the opinion of Gould[462]), or actually rather angels and other spiritual beings is fundamentally immaterial to the argument: His position was more radically formulated than that of Origen, as he accorded all spiritual existences save God himself a corporeal nature both mutable and destructible alike.

Whatever might be thought regarding the question as to in which forms Patriarch Theophilus adopted a stance against the anthropomorphites, the harsh criticism which the patriarch expressed in his festal letter (probably of AD 399) was the reason why he was so fervently and vehemently attacked by certain monks and accused (as Socrates relates) of being "an impious person and an enemy of God."[463]

The Conflicts within the Life of Aphou of Oxyrhynchus/Pemdjé

Fortunately, a further, albeit highly literarily reworked, depiction of a scene from the early days of the heated conflict is preserved in the *Coptic life of an Upper Egyptian monk named Aphou* who initially lived in the vicinity of the famous city of Oxyrhynchus/Pemdjé in a monastic community as a hermit and thereafter became bishop of said city. The biography composed in the Sahidic dialect of Coptic is preserved in a single manuscript, a papyrus with fragments of a Coptic menology first edited in 1883.[464] This papyrus is kept in Turin and was dated by its first editors to the second half of the fifth century AD. By contrast, Tito Orlandi opts for the seventh century; when exactly the hagiography itself was composed must remain open.[465] Considering the text's possible significance in reconstructing the theology and religiosity of the anthropomorphites, there are sundry recent translations into different languages and a few studies.[466]

Aphou, the monastic father and later bishop, is known not only from his Coptic hagiography, but also from two further late antique Christian sources which relay apophthegmata and brief scenes from his life respectively. Admittedly, the account of his life was not carried over to the Arabic menologies still employed until today within the Coptic Church.[467] It is rather unlikely that Aphou possessed ties to a monastic group probably resident in Asia Minor termed "Audians" in Epiphanius[468] and further accused by the Metropolitan of Cyprus of "anthropomorphism."[469] Such a group cannot be attested for Upper Egypt but rather—should Epiphanius of Salamis be followed—must originally have been resident within the Taurus, Palestine, Arabia, and on Cyprus, and later also in a few of the monasteries of Chalcidice, in the environs of Damascus, and in portions of Mesopotamia, the territory from which its eponymous heresiarch Audius proportedly hailed.[470]

In the hagiography of Aphou, it is now reported that the hermit Aphou once a year left his hermitage and came to Oxyrhynchus for the Easter sermon "in the church of Pemdjé."[471] This introductory statement already demonstrates the text's level of hagiographic stylization, as, according to tradition, the late antique city of Oxyrhynchus, the third-largest city in Egypt at the time, possessed more than thirty churches, and not the solitary example of the narrative.[472] Typical of its genre, the hagiography concentrates on those events salient to the understanding of the hero, underlines a few central theological notions,[473] and presents only those details most vital for this purpose. One of these central ideas is the care with which Aphou approaches Holy Scripture and seeks to protect it from every species of dereliction, derision, and denial.[474] Indeed, the aforementioned narrative belongs within such a context: The *Vita* recounts that Aphou once heard in one such Easter sermon "an expression (λέξις) which was not in accord with the knowledge of the Holy Spirit, so that he was much troubled by that discourse."[475] The statement found to be so deeply unsettling is quoted verbatim: "It is not the image of God which we men bear."[476] Much recommends the view that this consists of a literal quotation from the bishop of Alexandria's already repeatedly mentioned albeit unfortunately lost Easter festal letter for AD 399, which would have been read forth in Oxyrhynchus as elsewhere, and which Aphou would have heard. This letter is here termed a "sermon," as the announcement of the date of the Feast of Easter was conventionally accompanied in the festal letters with extended theological remarks on a current theme, and hence could scarcely be distinguished from a sermon. According to the Coptic *Vita*, the reading aloud of the sermon (and the festal letter) provoked considerable unrest: After the reading of the incriminating passage, not only was Aphou "much troubled by that discourse," but "indeed, all those who heard it were afflicted and troubled."[477] The narrative proceeds thereafter in a heavily reworked legendary fashion typical of the genre: An angel instructs Aphou to explain the incriminating expression and dispatches him to the bishop in Alexandria, some two hundred kilometers away, the Coptic name of which is naturally reproduced within the Coptic text: "Thou art ordered by the Lord to go to Rakote to set this word aright."[478] There, "wearing a wornout tunic," Aphou initially waits "at the bishop's gate for three days, and no one let him in (sc. to see Bishop Theophilus), for they took him for a common man (ἰδιώτης)."[479] According to the hagiography's narrative, Aphou nevertheless finally succeeds in gaining admittance thanks to the intercession of a cleric. A debate then ensues at this point in the text between the bishop and Aphou wherein the boundaries of the politeness due to a prince of the church are increasingly abandoned by Aphou. After a few introductory pleasantries, Aphou cuts to the heart of the matter and his concerns:

> Aphou answered him (sc. Bishop Theophilus): "Let my Lord command that the original of the sermon be read to me, wherein I heard the sentence that was not in agreement with the Scriptures inspired by God. Personally, I did not believe that it had come from you, but I thought that the clerk had committed a scribal error, regarding which a goodly number of pious people blunder to the point of being greatly troubled."

> Then Apa Theophilus, the archbishop, gave an order. The original of the sermon was brought to him. When the reading had begun, that phrase was reached.

> Then Apa Aphou bowed down, saying: "This sentence like that is not correct; I, on the other hand, will maintain that it is in the image of God that all men have been created."

> The Archbishop replied: "How is it that you alone have spoken against this reading, and that there has not been anyone in agreement with you?"

> Apa Aphou said: "But indeed I am sure that you will be in agreement with me and will not argue with me."

> The Archbishop said: "How could you say of an Ethiopian that he is the image of God, or of a leper, or of a cripple, or of a blind man?"

Blessed Aphou replied: "If you proclaim that in such fashion, you will be denying that which He said, namely, 'Let us make man in our likeness and in our image' (Gen. 1:26)."

The Archbishop replied: "Far be it! But I believe that Adam alone was created in His likeness and image, but that his children whom he begot after him do not resemble him. . . . I hesitate to say of an ailing man or one passible that he bears the image of God, who is impassible and self-sufficient, while (the former) squats outside and performs his necessities. How could you think of him (as being one) with God, the true light whom nothing can surpass?" (cf. 1 Timothy 6:16).[480]

The debate between Apa Aphou and Theophilus, his bishop, reveals a great deal as to how the author of the hagiography wished to understand the theology of the two protagonists: Theophilus is stylized as an "Origenist." While Origen's name does not occur in this passage (or, indeed, at all in the "Life" of Aphou), the position proportedly held by Theophilus in his conversation with Aphou that Adam was the sole human to possess the likeness of God and to have lost it as a consequence of the fall is clearly ascribed by contemporaries such as Epiphanius of Salamis to Origen.[481] Thus, for a learned reader of the "Life" of Aphou, Theophilus was evidently characterized as being a follower of Origen. Apa Aphou reacts to the extremely pointed objections of Theophilus according to the hagiography in a manner by which he concedes to the bishop of Alexandria that the splendor of God "can be seen by no-one due to its ineffable light and also in respect to the fragility of humans and insignificance according to the frailty of nature."[482] He plays literally thereby upon the sentences from Theophilus with which the latter concludes his previously cited observations at the beginning of the debate. After this conciliatory recourse to a basis common to both discussants, Aphou refutes very soberly the opinion of Theophilus that only Adam before the fall might be described as having been fashioned in the likeness of God with a traditional argumentation: He observes that images of emperors are hardly fashioned of the same material as the individuals they should depict, but rather of markedly more modest and indeed more fragile matter: "All will proclaim that it is the image of the king, but at the same time all know that it is wood and colours."[483] When Aphou imagined God corporeally, it was naturally clear to him that the body of the divine likeness could not have been composed of the same material as the divine body. A categorical distinction exists between a living person and a piece of wood—as exists also between a divine and a human body. After this explanation, it is stated literally:

> When he heard these words, the blessed Archbishop arose and bent his head, saying: "This is fitting that instruction come from those who search in solitude, for, as for us, the reasonings of our hearts are mixed in us, to the point that we err completely in ignorance." And immediately he wrote within all the country, retracting that phrase, saying: "It is erroneous and proceeds from my lack of intelligence in this respect."[484]

A simple monk (as noted, characterized by means of the Greek word ἰδιώτης) living before the gates of a medium-sized city thus converts the metropolitan of Alexandria and the entirety of Egypt. Naturally, it is difficult to determine what grain of historical truth might lie within this thoroughly and carefully constructed and animatedly recounted scene.[485] Questions remain at the very least: Might it really be imagined that it was Apa Aphou who converted the bishop with his arguments, and even rendered the demons responsible for his error? Is it plausible that Theophilus might so neatly have confined the creation in the divine likeness to Adam, the protoplast, without the differentiation made by Origen? Would the Alexandrian bishop have denied that the divine similitude might be predicated from the human body on grounds of the necessity for precisely this body to leave abodes to relieve itself in open latrines or the great outdoors? As has been seen, already in the second century, the Roman urbanite theologian Valentinus had indicated that a divine body which needs nothing for its sustenance, also digests nothing, excretes nothing, and hence experiences no need to "squat outside" to heed nature's call. Much recommends the stance that, so as to extol Apa Aphou, bishop of Oxyrhynchus, here a story was constructed or, at the very least, heavily embellished according to the generally prevalent rules of hagiographic discourse, assigning this renowned ascetic an absolutely central role within a conspicuous shift in stance on the part of Bishop Theophilus.[486] In the interests of exciting dialogue, the positions of the historical figures are markedly accentuated: According to the image conveyed of him by the *Vita*, Theophilus reduces the creation in God's image no longer to the soul, but to merely the protoplast Adam prior to the fall. Aphou does not unequivocally betray at any point within the text of the *Vita* that he is an "anthropomorphite"—accordingly, his theology is interpreted despite the lack of clear indications within the text very much contrastingly either as "anthropomophite" (prominently Drioton, Florovsky, and Golitzin[487]) or as decidedly *not* "anthropomophite" (thus, recently, Bumazhnov[488]). Certainly, it must be accepted that for the authors of the hagiography of an Egyptian bishop in the fifth century it would hardly seem opportune to render explicit the conversion of the Alexandrian bishop to the stances of the anthropomorphites, and also to accord his foil in the debate, the

main protagonist, precisely this heresy. Finally, the context of the manuscript of the Life of Aphou (a monologue with readings for 18 September)
evinces that the *Vita* was read for a time within the Coptic church service
on the bishop and ascetic's death day. Thus, for the reconstruction of the
clashes elsewhere attested, it must be maintained that Theophilus turned to
"anthopomorphite" positions and was more or less energetically pressured
into this by similarly minded monks to wit. In the dialogue relayed within
the "Life" of Aphou, a literarily highly inflated and theologically censored
memory of such embattled conversations may be glimpsed: No more, but,
indeed, also no less.

Nevertheless, it still warrants consideration as to whether the *Vita*
demonstrates that in the clashes over "anthropomorphism" within theology and religiosity alike at the end of the fourth century, that this pertained, in fact, rather more to the divine likeness, the *imago Dei*, and in
particular, to the countenance of God.[489] Two decisive sentences may be
advanced in justification of this stance: According to the "Life" of Aphou,
the Alexandrian bishop had written in the incriminating festal letter of
AD 399 to the chagrin of many monks: "It is not the image of God which
we men bear."[490] As he was assailed by these very same infuriated monks
and revoked this in the very same year, he is supposed, according to the
testimony of the ecclesiastical historians Socrates and Sozomen, to have
said to them: "In seeing you, I behold (in your face) the face of God."[491]
Naturally, it is unlikely that the bishop stated exactly this sentence, albeit
this cannot be excluded; Antiquity remembered significant turns of phrase.
It is clear, however, that the bishop according to the "Life" of Aphou lays
the focus upon the *countenance* in the revocation of the position pronounced in the festal letter. The reason for this may have been quite unsophisticated: The face is at once the most important part of the body and
frequently the most decisive for the human body in initial contact. The
question as to how this material might be understood must be returned to
once more. Moreover, the opinion of Dmitrij Bumazhnov that the "Life"
rather betrays an intermediate position between radical "Origenists" and
radical "anthropomorphites," the adherents of which considered the closer
details of the relationship of the likeness to the archetype to be inscrutable,
may well apply to those who once composed this text; this "intermediate
position" will be revisited once more in the clash between "Origenism"
and "anthropomorphism."

The Conflicts within the *Collationes Patrum* of John Cassian

A further scene, perhaps even more vital for the reconstruction of the theology of the "anthropomorphites," is recounted within the aforementioned

Collationes Patrum ("Conversations with the Fathers") by John Cassian: A hoary Egyptian monk named Serapion was moved by a monk visiting him from Cappadocia called Photinus to interpret the central biblical attestation for the creation in the likeness of God (Genesis 1:26)[492] "not according to the lowly sound of the letter, but in a spiritual way" (*non secundum humilem litterae sonum, sed spiritualiter*). Photinus, who had been summoned by Paphnutius, the spiritual father and priest of the Origenistically minded monks, in order to avail himself of aid in the evidently taxing debate with Serapion, explains to his brother monk

> that nothing of this sort could be the case with that immeasurable and incomprehensible and invisible majesty—that it could be circumscribed in a human form and likeness, that indeed a nature which was incorporeal and uncomposed and simple could be apprehended by the eye or seized by the mind.[493]

Interestingly, this argumentation from Photinus, kept very much along the lines of a classical Origenistic and Evagrian theory, found acceptance among most monks, but not among the venerable Serapion, although it was aimed at him. From the report in John Cassian, Serapion found it extremely difficult to combine the new theoretical perspective with his prior practice of personal piety:

> But the old man got so confused in his mind during the prayers, when he realized that the anthropomorphic image of the Godhead which he had always pictured to himself while praying had been banished from his heart, that he suddenly broke into the bitterest tears and heavy sobbing and, throwing himself to the ground with a loud groan, cried out: "Woe is me, wretch that I am! They have taken my God from me (cf. John 20:2, 13), and I have no one to lay hold of, nor do I know whom I should adore or address."[494]

The aged monk's utterances are somewhat reminiscent of a critical commentary to those views formulated by Evagrius Ponticus in respect to correct prayer which has already been discussed (the name of Evagrius nevertheless appears as infrequently as that of Origen within the *Collationes Patrum*).[495] Regardless, the account comes across as decidedly contrived, as Columba Stewart has noted with reference to the personal names: While the proponent of the correct doctrine (in Cassian's eyes) from Cappadocia, homeland of the deeply Origenistically influenced theologians Basil of Caesarea, Gregory Nazianzen, and Gregory of Nyssa, bears the name Photinus (Φωτεινός) "the emitter of light," his opponent is redolent of the pagan demon from which the Christian community had just freed itself: Serapion.[496] Deeply influenced by Evagrius Ponticus, John Cassian rather discusses in regard to the divine image of the Serapeum a "serious error," which almost spells perpetual death, that is, eternal consignment to hell.[497]

The reaction of Serapion the monk to the argumentation of Photinus does not incidentally indicate that he was "very much a simple man"[498] (as Cassian intends) who "had hardly been educated as to the substance and nature of the Godhead," and hence frankly imagined God as some manner of modern human. Indeed, it is hardly probable that Serapion, "as is the way of that error, according to which they used to worship demons in human form," also holds "that the incomprehensible and ineffable majesty of the true Deity should be adored under the limitations of some image," that is, still languishes in paganism's residue.[499] All of this could be put down to polemicism from John Cassian, a theologian influenced by Origen and Evagrius. In the vein of Tertullian or Melito, Serapion would rather have pictured God with a corporeality categorically distinguished from that of humans—and, by means of the Origenistically informed monks of Scetis, would have been compelled to envision something immaterial and completely inconcrete, were the story to contain a kernel of historical truth, and hence (from his perspective) nothing.[500]

The Theological Profile of the "Anthropomorphites"

In respect to the problems of the pertinent sources, it is a difficult task to clearly reconstruct the theological profile of "anthropomorphism." It was certainly not as the ecclesiastical historians and monastic theologians more or less influenced by Origen would have gladly had it on heresiological grounds: A conception of simple monks who believed literally that which stood written in the Bible and were too foolish to interpret appropriately metaphorically biblical mention of a hand, voice, or eye of God. It is moreover not known whether many individuals at the end of fourth century actually still propounded the classical anthropomorphite positions which may be unambiguously attested within the initial centuries of Christian theological history. Skepticism in the face of all-too-grandiose statements within the sources is very much the order of the day: "The bulk of illiterate, anti-Origenist monks with anthropomorphite views are simply not visible before they appear as the foes in the descriptions by John Cassian and Socrates."[501] The statement in John Cassian that anthropomorphism was caused by "delusion of the demons . . . the ignorance which characterized the earliest pagans,"[502] demonstrates that, in the circles influenced by Origen (and Evagrius), every register of antique heresiology was drawn upon so as to diabolize the notion of a divine corporeal form as naïve, uneducated, and, indeed, demonic. The idea that only simple, aged rustics, tied in some manner or other to very traditional pagan divine images, lapsed into the heresy of anthropomorphism has been widespread since Antiquity, albeit misleading. Indeed, by means of such a classification, the heresiologically motivated images of the movement have prevailed (and, indeed, still do so today), rather than the actual theology of an Egyptian monastic group.

This also applies for later polemics against the so-called anthropomorphites such as, for example, those composed by the nephew and successor of Theophilus in the office of the patriarch of Alexandria, Cyril. This consists of a group of three writings which belong together which were collected into a single text at an unknown point in the Middle Ages. This tractate, transmitted under the title "Against the Anthropomorphites" and reproduced in the *Patrologica Graeca* by Jacques Paul Migne in 1859, being composed of an introductory letter and twenty-eight *capitula*, compiles three independent essays by Cyril, namely the "Doctrinal Questions and Answers," the "Answers to Tiberius and His Companions," and the "Letter to Colosirius" together with some fragments from a sermon of Gregory of Nyssa. The "Answers to Tiberius and His Companions" are only completely extant in a Syriac translation, the others also separately in Greek manuscripts.[503] As Cyril had lived in Egypt as a monk for a stint, he was presumably optimally informed about the theological conflicts, and not only as a result of his uncle. Nevertheless, the legend that Cyril was instructed in Christian belief by John of Jerusalem, and insofar would have been informed firsthand as to the conflicts within this city in AD 399, is without any grounding in historical reality.[504] This notwithstanding, Cyril might be expected to be well oriented in regard to the Palestinian prologue to the controversies. In the three texts composed by him, "anthropomorphites" are understood, very much in the acquainted manner, as a group of deranged and simple souls who had not comprehended that God must be thought of and envisioned as incorporeal. Irrespective of this, a closer reading of the texts offers some insights in describing more precisely the theological profile of the monks dubbed by their opponents "anthropomorphites." The three texts suppose a concrete historical situation: A certain Tiberius, deacon of a Palestinian monastery,[505] had posed questions prompted by certain individuals who (at least in the case of the second text) hailed in part from Egypt and are probably to be identified with exactly those anthropomorphites who had induced Bishop Theophilus to alter his stance in AD 399. These queries are answered by Cyril in the first two texts, which might be dated from AD 431 to 434 (following Lionel R. Wickham) and thus exist within the context of the heated debates between Bishops Cyril and Nestorius on the form of the unity between God and man in Christ. Nevertheless, cloistered circles from the northwestern environs of Damascus, the Abilene, might also be factored into this perspective.[506] The Greek term "anthropomorphites" does not occur in these texts; already in the first text, the targets are rather those whose beliefs are such "that they somehow suppose and think the all-transcending divine nature to be human in appearance or form."[507]

As the arguments repeat themselves, the second text with answers to Tiberius will here be concentrated upon, namely the "Doctrinal Answers." In this composition, Cyril initially maintains, in regard to the introductory question as to the meaning of discussion of God's "eyes or ears, or indeed hands, feet, and wings" in the biblical texts[508] (akin to Aphou in the dispute with Theophilus), that God dwells "in the light which no man can approach unto" (1 Timothy 6:16) and, as such an inaccessible entity, must be considered "completely incorporeal" (ἀσώματον παντελῶς).[509] A body would imply form, quantity, place, parts, and limbs.[510] This would be entirely excluded in respect to God, even if "one elects to conceive of such things not as they exist in palpable, gross bodies but as existing in fine-drawn immateriality and in correspondence with God's nature."[511] With this addendum to his argumentation, Cyril indicates clearly that, irrespective of the polemic typical of his time and institution against intellectually impoverished monastic circles which envisioned God with a finite human body in their cognitive simplicity, he actually understood very well the real theological context: the notion of a particular divine materiality of the divine body categorically separated from human corporeality as found within Stoic tradition.[512]

Nevertheless, the theological point of departure for the anthropomorphites of the fourth century cannot, in contrast to the heresiological constructions of their teachings in John of Jerusalem, Theophilus, and Cyril, have been Stoic materialism and the question as to how this might be combined with Christian doctrine of God. The surviving texts prompt the suspicion that the starting point would rather have been the well-considered idea that humans were fashioned with body *and* soul according to the divine archetype. In contrast to earlier Christian notions of the body of God from the second and third centuries, the point of departure for "anthropomorphism" would hence have shifted somewhat from *theory of God* into *anthropology*. For a theology propounded above all by Christian ascetics (perhaps of both sexes), this hardly astonishes: The close relationship between the body of the monk and the body of God supposed by the theology of the anthropomorphites was likely received by such circles as a principle fundament (or, indeed, perhaps as *the* principle fundament) of Christian life which enabled at all the monk's treading of the path to perfection: The monk knew himself as the image and likeness of God's body to be principally already complete, and was at once also still on the path to perfection, in order to bring his own body closer to that original model in the similitude of which he had been fashioned. The "anthropomorphites" were convinced that Adam had never lost entirely the image of God, while the Origenists maintained the loss of a considerable part of the likeness to God.[513] "Anthropomorphites" and their adversaries were hence also distinguished from one another in how they appraised the consequences of the primeval fall of man in paradise.[514] Thus, the requirement for these monks to express such thoughts humbly and to think modestly, as marks, for example, Aphou's hagiography, should not be misconstrued: Monastic humility is not to be confused with intellectual simplicity (the pertinent Greek word in the biography of Aphou is ἁπλοῦς, which might better be translated as "sincere" than "simple"):[515] In the *Vita* of Aphou, Bishop Theophilus, who abandoned Origenism at the instigation of the monk Aphou, becomes a prominent example of an individual who spurns pride and encounters "the purity and sincerity of childhood."[516] As might also be seen in the narrative in John Cassian of the monk Serapion, who was deprived of his God in the most elementary sense, anthropomorphism served as a path by which God might be imagined somewhat akin to a living person within a concretely experienced monastic religiosity, thereby not thinking of him and believing in him as a mere transcendent principle far removed from the world and the individual daily routine.

Should "anthropomorphism" be interpreted foremostly as a form of piety by which God might be envisioned as close to human needs and problems, then the textual witnesses preserved might perhaps be best accounted for accordingly. "Anthropomorphism" in the late fourth and early fifth centuries may be described as a monastic transformation of the classical Christian stances on the body of God for the purposes of ascetic communities and stands, nevertheless, (as is demonstrated, for example, by Cyril of Alexandria) in the tradition of the Christian doctrines of the second and third centuries. This applies, even if such a continuity has keenly been contested within the field over the past decades.

It is harder to address the question as to whether "anthropomorphism" might at the least have occasionally been associated with the experience of a corporeal vision of God's countenance, meaning, in a certain sense, mystical experience, in the center of which, some form of corporeal impression of the divine visage existed in the anthropomorphic figure of Jesus Christ.[517] Recently, Alexander Golitzin has most prominently suggested to interpret the surviving texts and reports in such a manner.[518] Inasmuch, he holds the "anthropomorphism" understood accordingly to be an appendage of the "mystical visions" discussed in Jewish texts such as

Hekhalot literature,[519] and justifies his opinion most strikingly with apophthegmata of Egyptian monks reporting heavenly journeys and visions;
nevertheless, a body of God is never directly mentioned in these texts,
but rather invariably divine luminescence or the body of Jesus Christ.[520]
An exception is presented by an apophthegma ascribed to Apa Arsenius,
although it remains nevertheless uncertain as to whether the sentence
is not, in fact, meant metaphorically: "He also said, 'If we seek God,
He will show Himself to us, and if we keep Him, He will remain close
to us.'"[521]

An argument for such an interpretation of the sources emphasizing a
"vision" of a more or less corporeally conceived divine visage not mentioned by Golizin might be won from an extended tractate anonymously
transmitted in two manuscripts of the eleventh and twelth centuries
between works from Origen and Jerome within the abbey library of Monte
Cassino; it is conventionally cited under the title "Tractate against Origen
on the Vision of Isaiah" and mostly ascribed to Patriarch Theophilus of
Alexandria.[522] Quite evidently, the text was composed *after* the bishop's
abandonment of his earlier, rather more Origenistically inclined or at least
more neutral stance, as, while he certainly betrays "a remarkable measure
of autonomy and . . . speculative flair and solid literary ability," nevertheless, as an "anti-Origenist polemic, by contrast, the work is of a low
standard; indeed, the criticism of the exegesis of Origen eschews every
hallmark of objectivity."[523] Yet, this corresponds exactly to the tenor of the
already repeatedly mentioned two Alexandrian synodical letters from
the years AD 399/400, the authorship of which might also be attributed
to Theophilus. Like the second synodical letter, this tractate was probably
translated into Latin by Jerome.[524] The author of the text is preoccupied
with questions as to the interpretation of the vision related in the Book of
the Prophet Isaiah of an appearance of God in the Temple at Jerusalem
(Isaiah 6:1–13), and states:

> For it was not God's face—that which enables God to be seen—that the
> Seraphim covered with their two wings, as he (sc. Origen) imagined, but
> their own, since the prophets showed that God's face—that which God
> is—cannot be seen by mortal eyes. Hence when Moses said to the Lord:
> "Reveal thyself to me clearly that I may see thee" (Exodus 33:18), he
> heard from him: "No one shall see my face and live" (Exodus 33:30). By
> these words he is taught to place a limit on his desire, and to understand
> the extent of his own weakness. John, too, cries: "No one has ever seen
> God; the only Son, who is in the bosom of the Father, he had made him
> known" (John 1:18). The explanation of this saying teaches that not only
> human beings but rational creatures as a whole and whatever is outside

God cannot see God as he really is, but only as He has deigned to reveal Himself to his creatures.[525]

Such a polemic only makes sense were there to have genuinely been individuals within Christian communities who reckoned that the seraphim concealed a somehow corporeally composed and thereby visible countenance of God. Even though Origen, in fact, did not propound this, he is accused of such by the author of the tractate, presumably Theophilus of Alexandria: "Although Origen does not state it explicitly, (it) is a consequence of what he says."[526] It is thus polemically omitted that Origen sought initially only to resolve a *philological* point of debate. In the biblical passage from Isaiah, it remains unanswered as to whether the seraphim cover their own faces and feet, or rather God's visage and feet:[527] In the Hebrew original, the referant of the pertinent possessive pronouns is unclear, as, indeed, is illustrated by Origen (and, following him, Jerome) in interpretations of the passage.[528] Origen decidedly declared for grammatically relating the passage to God, and Jerome followed him in doing so. Theophilus now argues that such an interpretative statement detailing something being concealed by something else implicitly presupposes at the very least spatiality, and thereby corporeality: "But if the Seraphim cover his face and his feet, they would be greater than God, in that, so to speak, they cover him from head to toe."[529]

Circles which propounded such spatially and bodily accentuated opinions as to the sight of God were not confined to Egypt or the East, as might be seen when it is noted that Augustine was at considerable pains to refute this position (incidentally with presumably very much a similar approach to his colleague in the East in his tractate against Origen: God permits himself to be seen in corporeal form when he wishes; he is not, however, in and of himself corporeal). Learned exegetes of biblical texts such as Jerome propounded for a time such views at the very least implicitly, if not, indeed, voicing them openly.[530] Like Augustine in the West, the author of the Eastern tractate translated into Latin pleads for a negative theology so as to stave off what for him are misleading notions:

For we know that God exists, and we know what he is not; but what he is, and of what nature, we cannot know. Because it belongs to his goodness and mercy descending upon us that we may be capable of determining something about him, we perceive him to exist through benefits he confers. But what his nature is, on account of the gulf separating us from him, no creature can comprehend; and, to put it succinctly, we know what God is not, but we cannot know what he is. Not by reason of his having something which afterwards he ceased to have, but by reason of that which is joined to us through the weakness of our nature which he does not have; for example, that he should have a mutable body, or that he should be in need of anything, or that he should be accessible to human vision or subject to anything else that pertains to the creature.[531]

It remains peculiar within the "Tractate against Origen on the Vision of Isaiah" that here Origen is accused of a position which, absurdly enough, is very close to that which (as far as might be known) the "anthropomorphites" thought — and it remains furthermore strange, provided that the text was the work of Patriarch Theophilus, that this text distances itself from the aforementioned position in the interests of a negative theology although, according to the testimony of the ecclesiastical historians Sozomen and Socrates, he had apparently elected, in fact, at least in that present moment in AD 399, for the position of the "anthropomorphites."[532] Might the accusation from both ecclesiastical historians that the metropolitan never actually shifted in the direction of the "anthropomorphites" ring true? Had he only altered his rather friendly or at the very least neutral stance towards Origen under duress from the accordingly minded monks? Then for Theophilus the theological principle behind a new coalition with the "anthropomorphites" is not their "anthropomorphitism" but rather his own newly critical stance towards the closest foe of the "anthropomorphites" and of "anthropomorphism," that is, against the "arch-heretic" Origen, who had been dead for 150 years; this had all very much occurred after the timeworn adage "the enemy of my enemy . . ." In the context of the heated debates engaged in already regarding Origen in Egypt and Palestine, the decision to position oneself against these theologians would hardly have proven difficult for a bishop of Alexandria to reach; the first synodical letter from AD 399/400 preserved in Justinian makes reference to the confrontations between Origen and the Alexandrian bishop Heraclas in the AD 230s and 240s.[533]

Howsoever the intellectual development of Bishop Theophilus of Alexandria and his political actions might be evaluated, it is certain, as has been seen, that he supported for a time the monks termed by their opponents "anthropomorphites" but probably himself never propounded on the strength of his own convictions any positions within which a body of God played a prominent role. Much recommends the notion that the association between the Alexandrian metropolitan and the monks was more or less a marriage of convenience from which the bishop decidedly profited (inasmuch as peace reigned within his notoriously turbulent church province), but not the "anthropomorphite" bretheren. Certainly, this unequal situation served as yet another reason for the decline in the influence of the conception of a divine body within Christian theology. Nevertheless, the "anthropomophites" hardly disappeared from the scene without a trace.

The Aftermath

Evidently, only a single group survived from among the erstwhile "anthropomorphites" for an extended time; this has been highlighted most prominently by Dimitrij Bumazhnov in past years, and he has also counted (as has been seen) that the compilers of the hagiography of Aphou numbered among its ranks. Bumazhnov indicated that, in addition to an "anthropomorphite" group of monks who vehemently supported the idea of a corporeality of God and their Origenistically informed opponents, there was also a further third intermediary group. Beyond the "Life," traces of this group may, on the one hand, be found in a passage from Epiphanius of Salamis and, on the other, also from further monastic texts.[534] In this passage, Epiphanius reckons with the notion that it was possible for the prophets of the old covenant to see the Son of God prior to his incarnation with corporeal eyes: "So he saw, and he did not see. But as he was able, in truth he saw, but he did not see, as one who has an infinite inability to comprehend."[535] Yet, the bishop of Salamis admonished against the notion which might be drawn therefrom that every follower of Christ might actually see God with corporeal eyes, and thereby conceive of God as corporeal. A sentence of a monk from the Egyptian desert attests to such an intermediate position which nevertheless still supposed the possibility that God's true, inaccessible being has corporeal dimensions:

> Someone asked Abba Sopatrus, "Give me a commandment, abba, and I will keep it." He said to him, "Do not allow a woman to come into your cell and do not read apocryphal literature. Do not get involved in discussions about the image. Although this is not heresy, there is too much ignorance and liking for dispute between the two parties in this matter. It is impossible for a creature to understand the truth of it."[536]

Beyond such residual beliefs, a gradual decline in the conception of a corporeality of God seems to have set in after the heated debates at the end of the fourth century, this, in turn, heralding the one-sided medieval and Early Modern–era context from which this present work initially departed. The traces of a Stoically founded materialism in the Christian doctrine of God as could still be observed in Tertullian at the beginning of the third century evidently vanished completely from discourse after they already ceased to play a central role among the anthropomorphites.

Accordingly, in a *debate between an unknown philosopher named Phaedo and bishops* compiled by an anonymous author long after the end of the Imperial Council in Nicaea and preserved in an anonymously transmitted ecclesiastical history from the middle of the fifth century[537] as an alleged citation from the (in fact, at that time, lost) Acts of the Council, not the slightest trace of any Stoically colored argument at all might be found within the debate on the anthropomorphic passages of the biblical texts. Naturally, it is highly unlikely that such a debate had taken place at the first imperial council, but the anonymously transmitted text of a disputation could retain memories of genuine disputes between pagan philosophers and Christian bishops. According to the anonymous text, the philosopher remonstrates with the bishops about the biblical verse, "Let us make man in our image, after our likeness" (Genesis 1:26), remarking that one might be misled by this biblical passage into "explaining God to be anthropomorphic":

> "And yet we know that God is simple and without form. Tell me what this designation seeks to relate. Is the godhead thus somewhat human in form?" Answer of the Holy Fathers through the Bishop Eustathius of Antioch: "Not so, my dear philosopher, but rather when God states 'let them have dominion . . . over all the earth, and over every creeping thing that creepeth upon the earth' (Genesis 1:26.28), then this is hence the actual meaning of the creation of humans in God's image and his dominion of the entire earth."[538]

The philosopher with a name hardly coincidentally reminiscent of Plato's dialogue *Phaedo* returns once more in the course of the fictitious dialogue with the council to the fact that this biblical quotation poses "considerable difficulties" to him and must be discussed. The anonymous author has Hosius of Cordoba, the emperor's court bishop, answer the philosopher. He states:

> This "in the image," my dear philosopher, may not be understood in the sense of corporeal composition, but rather is a consequence of the doctrine of the truth that the image is formed in the spiritual realm. Listen and know: God, who is good by nature, planted in the spiritual substance of humans which is in his "image" and "likeness," for example, the goodness, the simplicity, the holiness, the purity, the selflessness, the warmth of heart, the rapture, and the similitude of that which is his nature, can also be possessed by humans created by him by means of God's grace, that is, his spiritual realm.[539]

Indeed, in two other texts of the fifth and sixth centuries devoted to debates featuring philosophical objections to Christian theology, Stoic arguments for the supposition that God possesses a body of fine matter also play as little of a role as their corresponding notions within Christian religiosity. In his dialogue *Theophrastus*, probably composed between AD 485 and 490, *Aeneas of Gaza* considers the creation of the world and the fate of the human soul, and thereby also the question as to the resurrection and corporeality. With little in the way of ado, it is maintained that the creator is incorporeal and limitless.[540] The only interesting question is whether any at all of the "upper bodies," that is the moon and the stars, are uncreated.[541] The same holds for *Zacharias Rhetor*, who was ordained as bishop of Mytilene on Lesbos after AD 527. In his dialogue *Ammonius*,[542] likely composed already in his student days in Berytus/Beirout and featuring a pagan Neoplatonist philosopher of the same name and a doctor called Gessius, he confines the extent of creation in the divine likeness merely to the human soul in the interpretation of Genesis 1:26f., so that the question as to divine corporeality need not be treated in the slightest.[543] These dissenting participants of the dialogue are united in their view that God is bodiless.[544] As Zacharias had also studied in Alexandria,[545] his quiescence might be taken as representative for the issues taught in the curricula of the scholarly metropole.[546] The notion of a corporeality of God evidently no longer numbered among these.

The Body of the Monk

At the end of this section, the interesting albeit difficult to answer question may be posed as to whether the differing stances on the question as to the existence of God's body in whatever manner would have consequences for the approach of antique Christians to their own bodies. On grounds of a dearth of sources, this question may only be answered in respect to monasticism, as, at least in part, those circles which adhered to the notion of a divine body (the anthropomorphites) and those which vehemently rejected such an idea can here be distinguished from one another. The question, then, is more precisely as follows: Are there different attitudes towards one's own body present in a monk informed by "anthropomorphic" conceptions of God and another who is strictly against such an "anthropomorphic" image of God, being, for example, influenced by the hostile stance towards the "anthropomorphites" in the tradition of Origen?

A conclusive answer to this question is, as noted, difficult. Nevertheless, there is much to commend the notion that monks critical of any manner of corporeal conception of God tended towards the destruction of their own bodies, the body accordingly constituting the difference between the monk and his God. This has already been witnessed in the debate over whether monks in the theological tradition of Origen and Evagrius laid hands on themselves and, for example, castrated themselves. Moreover, the converse is also applicable: A monk who thought that God possessed a specific heavenly body likely attempted to transform his own earthly body into this specific manner of a divine heavenly body. In any case, both approaches to the monastic body existed in Late Antiquity; both avenues will be sought to be identified with their respective specific position on the conception of a divine body.[547]

This will begin with the notion of destroying the body as visible evidence of a stark difference between God and man: In addition to those previously mentioned, all manner of further interesting examples from the period of Late Antiquity exist for such a radical destruction of the body. The repeatedly mentioned ascetic and theologian Jerome, who lived in Bethlehem as a monk, described the life of the earlier *grammaticus* and hermit *Hilarion of Gaza* soon after Hilarion's death around AD 371 in his *Vita Hilarionis*.[548] The beginnings of the hagiography are usually dated to AD 386;[549] soon afterwards, it was translated from the Latin into Greek. Naturally, this text is less concened with a historiographically correct portrayal of the biography of an ascetic than it is with advertising a particular lifestyle.[550] According to the description of Jerome, the hermit wore nothing more than sackcloth and only a pelt or a coat in the peasant style only in the event of extreme cold.[551] He copied thereby (certainly not by chance) the dress of Anthony the "Father of the Monks"; Jerome is here, as elsewhere in his biography, concerned with the stylization of Hilarion, the foundational figure of Palestinian monasticism, as a second Anthony.[552] Thus, Jerome, himself a *grammaticus*,[553] states literally:

> He clipped his hair once a year, at Easter, and until his death slept on rushes strewn on the bare ground. He never washed a sackcloth he once donned, saying that it was superfluous to seek cleanliness in Cilician goat skins, nor did he change to another tunic until the old was was worn to shreds.[554]

The manner here described of approaching one's own body had nothing to do with the path generally prevalent among Christians, that of associating with Greek popular-philosophical attitudes to human bodies. Hilarion did not groom his beard and hair in something of a modest manner (as, for example, Clement of Alexandria advised at the beginning of the third century:[555] "Since cropping is to be adopted not for the sake of elegance, but on account of the necessity of the case [. . .]"[556]), rather he ceased to care for them. Jerome's depiction of the hermit Hilarion resembles the art and manner in which the apocryphal Acts of Peter describe the female, black, Ethiopian devil:

a very ugly woman, according to her appearance an Ethiopian, no Egyptian, but very black, clad in filthy rags, but with an iron chain about the neck and a chain on her hands and feet; she danced.[557]

The clothes of this she-devil are, like those of Hilarion, dirty and torn to shreds. Hence, the body of Hilarion while not entirely destroyed, is neglected in a manner which approaches this ruin. This closeness to voluntary destruction will become obvious when the description of Hilarion is followed more closely.

Jerome recounts a few additional details as to his hero Hilarion, which render even clearer the destructive potential of his disposition towards his body: Hilarion's cell, which could still be visited and inspected in the time of Jerome, was smaller than Hilarion himself (four feet wide and five feet high[558]). Moreover, Jerome relays further detailed information as to Hilarion's astoundingly simple diet:

> For the first half of the time between his twenty-first to his twenty-sixth year, he lived on a half a pint of lentils a day, soaked in cold water; for the last half, on dry bread with salt and water. Then, from his twenty-seventh to his thirtieth year, he kept himself alive on wild herbs and the raw roots of some shrubs. From thirty-one to thirty-five, he had for his daily food six ounces of barley bread and a slightly cooked green vegetable without oil. Perceiving after a while that his eyes were weakening and that his whole body was shrinking from a scabby eruption of the skin and a kind of mange, he added olive oil to his slender diet and maintained this rigid degree of abstinence until his sixty-third year, tasting nothing beyond that, either of fruit, or legumes, or anything else. Then, when he realized that he was exhausted and felt that he was very close to death, from sixty-four to eighty, he abstained from bread with unbelievable fervor (*fervor mentis*)[559] and was serving God as a novice at an age when others are inclined to live a little less strenuously. A small mess of meal and crushed vegetables was made for him; his food and drink together weighed scarcely five ounces. We may note, finally, that he never broke his fast before sunset, not even on feast days or because of serious illness.[560]

What Jerome describes in these passages from the *Vita Hilarionis* may well be heavily exaggerated or, indeed, not (the quotient of truth is admittedly difficult to gauge), but it illustrates very well as to how a large group of antique Christians leading an ascetic or monastic life approached their own bodies. These individuals sought more or less to destroy their own bodies — as this body was imagined to be *the* enemy of the ascetic purposes of the monk, and seen as *the* hindrance to a life according to God's instructions. A great many further examples for such a life might be cited from the relevant monastic literature, most prominently from Egypt: Modest or consciously neglected dress and grooming, extremely restricted and ever-dwindling nutrition, and finally the attempt to force an upright gait into a humble posture by means of inhabiting a cell far too small in size.[561]

There are additionally far more radical examples than the ascetic behavior of Hilarion according to Jerome's portrayal. An extreme example appeared some years ago in modern Israel: In the excavation of a hermit's tower on the Hebron Road between Jerusalem and Bethlehem near the Monastery of Mar Elias (Khirbet Tabaliya), a skeleton was found from the sixth century AD. The skeleton belongs to an ascetic who was shackled by a thick iron chain wrapped multiple times around the lower abdomen and crossing on the back.[562] At the time of his death, the man was between twenty-four and twenty-six years of age; the manner of his self-enchainment is particuly well attested in Syria.[563]

Even should this fettered ascetic be dated to markedly later than the texts discussed from the end of the fourth and the beginning of the fifth centuries, he represents an extreme attempt within a region which openly opposed the thought of Origen to destroy one's own body, and somewhat to bind in chains corporeal needs, thoughts "of the flesh," and all that which might hinder the body of the ascetic in the ascent to heaven.

Conversely, however, probably not only was the body of the ascetic somewhat destroyed, but the attractiveness of Christianity was also enhanced to some degree by means of the results of such a manner of public competition, as this demonstrated very openly the new religion's sway.[564] Some pagan contemporaries such as, for example, the Platonic philosopher Eunapius not only took notice of these extremely radical and destructive stances towards the body, but also commented upon them highly critically: "monks, as they called them, who were men in appearance but led the lives of swine."[565]

Yet, in the ascetic behavior of antique followers of Christ, not only the attempt to destroy the body through ascesis which might be bound to the critical stance of many monks against corporeal conceptions of God might be attested. Quite evidently, the guiding notion of perfecting one's own body and transforming its attributes with reference to those of the heavenly body or the divine body itself also existed. It was not only motives from biblical writings or inspirations from contemporaneous philosophy which were responsible for this friendlier conduct towards one's own body, but also widespread practices of caring for one's own body in antique societies: Reinhold Merkelbach already attested years ago[566] that, for Christians and non-Christian contemporaries alike, within the relevant

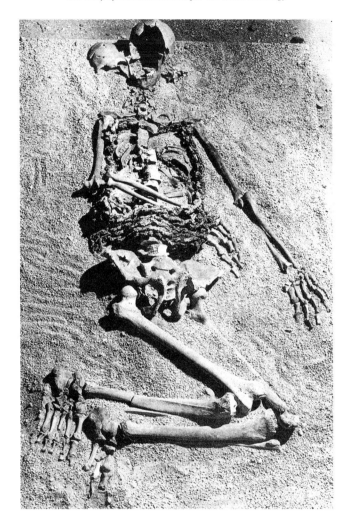

Fig. 6.3 Monk in chains
*Find from a grave from Horvat Tabalia near Jerusalem
(sixth century)
Collection of the Greek Orthodox Patriarchate in Jerusalem*[567]

terms of "ascetic" (ἀσκητής) and "athlete" (ἀγωνιστής) could connote a
"Christian sportsman," a well-trained athlete who (incidentally, the pagan
athletes alike) prosecuted a "relentless battle against one's own body,"[568]
albeit not so much with the aim to destroy the body, but rather to bring it
to perfection.

While certainly attempts to perfect in such a manner one's own body,
and thereby to deify it, cannot be observed in the "anthropomorphites" of

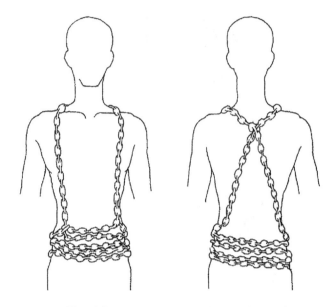

Fig. 6.4 Reconstruction of a monk's chain
Find from a grave from Horvat Tabalia near Jerusalem (sixth century)[569]

the late fourth century, they may be found in other many other texts from antique Egyptian and Syrian monasticism. These sources demonstrate that the attempt to transform a mortal coil into a divine body was a widespread attitude in Christian asceticism of Late Antiquity. In the present context, a few characteristic examples suffice:

The body of the great Egyptian abbot *Shenoute*, who died at over one hundred years in age in his "White Monastery" near the Middle Egyptian city of Sohag in AD 466, should through constant fasting have been transformed "into little more than bones, sinews, and leather, and thereby became almost indestructible."[570] Incorruptibility is naturally a divine attribute; the body of Shenoute becomes in his own monastery a model for the community of the monks, from which concrete instructions for the ascetic behavior within the community are drawn.[571] Nevertheless, it should not be surmised from such sentences and their ritualization in the monastery that the body was at all abhorred there: In Shenoute's tractate *Contra Origenistas*, views on the body explicitly at loggerheads to one another may be found: "Pray tell, did they not say that this body is a chastisement of the soul and its prison? I for one say that the body of the truly righteous is the joy and the relief of the soul."[572]

A particularly spectacular manner of placing one's own body in analogy to the body of God may be found in the famous Syrian stylites. Bishop

Theodoret of Cyrrhus in Syria commented in his biography of the celebrated Syrian pillar-saint Simeon Stylites (ca. AD 390–459), written while Simeon was still alive in approximately AD 444, on the constant raising of the pillar whereupon Simeon stood[573] with the following words: "He wished to fly to heaven and to free himself from earthly commotion."[574] Although the incessant raising of the pillar actually had an entirely trivial reason (Simeon raised it due to mounting irritation from pilgrims who wished to touch him and cut off pieces of the hide he wore), contemporaries found his program of deification of the body through constant standing and incessant bowing down of the head to be a "new and marvellous spectacle" (θέαμα καινὸν καὶ παράδοξον).[575] The mixture of bowing and standing makes it at least clear that Simeon led his entire life as if he stood immediately before the divine throne, directly before God's countenance. Incidentally, in Jewish-Hellenistic and Samaritan tradition alike God is also termed "the standing one."[576] When, according to the account of the hagiography, a man from Rabaena[577] once asked the ascetic as to whether he might be a man or an angel (in Greek: "an incorporeal nature," ἀσώματος φύσις),[578] Simon displayed a horrific wound on his foot which he had acquired from the constant standing and which discharged a great deal of pus unceasingly.

Naturally, a corporeally understood similitude with God which might be conceived of as a consequence of the creation in the likeness of God is not discussed within these texts. Yet, in the texts, the angels are introduced as intercessory figures: This is accordingly stated, within a text ascribed to Shenoute within which the monks are exhorted to lead an angelic life: "You transform into the form (βίος) of the angels and imitate the prophets and the apostles and all saints, not only by means of your garb and the contentless names . . . but also by means of your burdens which you take upon yourselves through the name of the Lord, of Jesus Christ."[579] "Angelic life" (ἀγγελικὸς βίος) was expected.[580] The one who remodeled, transformed, or willed his body to be angelic, was naturally bound to occasional misunderstandings. The widespread Platonic idea of an "assimilation with God as far as possible" (ὁμοίωσις τῷ θεῷ κατὰ τὸ δύνατον) and, moreover, the idea of "deification" (θεοποίησις) already provoked confusion and discussion during Antiquity.[581] The notion of an angelic life could have helped to avoid these misunderstandings, even if those who employed this conception actually refered to the bodies of God.

Summary and Prospect

It has been seen that the biblical concept of a divine body was, in fact, propounded by a few prominent Christian authors of the second and early third centuries such as Melito of Sardis or Tertullian, and evidently adopted once more by a group of Christian monks in Egypt in the fourth century, although a great number of educated theologians such as Origen in the third and fourth centuries sharply contested such images of God. It could be entirely possible that the entire controversy as to the validity and applicability of Origen's theology in the fourth and fifth centuries in Egypt and the Holy Land alike was not provoked by the "anthropomorphites" but rather, on the contrary, by means of the stringent measures taken by the Alexandrian patriarch Theophilus against "anthropomorphism." Might not the question as to the *human body* of Jesus of Nazareth have played a role in the debates, being soon thereafter professed to be a divine person, or even a divinity, throughout antique Christendom? What might be learned as to antique conceptions of divine bodies from the debates on the human body of Jesus Christ? The final chapter will be devoted to this question.

7

The Body of God and Antique Christology

When notions of the divine body in Antiquity are more closely examined, it swiftly becomes evident how close ancient Judaism and Christianity stand to one another: At this seemingly very specific point of Christian doctrine it becomes apparent that Judaism and Christianity did not occur during the High Imperial-era and Late Antiquity as, for example, they are modeled in the widespread research heuristic of the "parting of the ways"[1]: This concept imagines a divergence of antique Judaism into two separate religions, that is, Judaism and Christianity, *respectively*, and dates such a process primarily to the second century AD. Although the narrative of parted ways which originates with Philip Alexander is already a revision of the markedly more problematic model built upon familial analogies (according to which Christianity is understood as playing daughter to Judaism's mother, and thereby implied to be more modern and contemporary than Judaism), it has become clearer in recent years how little the correlating dynamics of shared development come into view when such a metaphor of bifurcation underlies a model. Daniel Boyarin has additionally indicated[2] that strict distinctions between two or more entities in the model of a family tree or a forking of ways can regardless hardly be justified for the multiple phenomena of mixture and hybridization factually present. This becomes exemplary in its clarity, should the development of the festal calendars and liturgical texts in antique Judaism and Christianity respectively be compared (as has been done by Israel Yuval[3] or Clemens Leonhard[4]); here, it is demonstrable as to how strongly communities keenly modeled as dual entities remained somewhat connected to one another as if in a network.

While attractive in postmodern times, such disillusions of boundaries and fluidities of ostensibly stable entities seem rather to hit something of a wall when the various antique Christian concepts of reflecting upon Jesus of Nazareth as the Christ of God are considered: The Christian confession of the crucified Messiah Jesus of Nazareth as the form of realization of the one unitary God seems to have served as a perennial dividing line, separating unequivocally creeds and communities within the Roman Imperium from one another.

The Incarnation as a Specificum?

Certainly, a few elements of the Christian account of Jesus of Nazareth are also to be found in rabbinical and non-rabbinical Jewish texts; Daniel Boyarin has thus demonstrated that the notion of a divine person adjacent to God who is hypostatized as the "Word of God" is not a preserve of Christian teaching in the High Imperial period.[5] This present work's inspection of late antique and early Byzantine Jewish Hekhalot literature has additionally concluded that cases of such convergences of Jewish and Christian teaching on the (to abbreviate) plural dimensions of the one and only God do not comprise early phenomena of a spiritual neighborliness, these being increasingly excluded considering the later differentiation of the two religions from one another. It has rather been seen that still within Late Antique and early Byzantine periods in Judaism it was still thought that certain analogies to Christianity are conspicuous. Nevertheless, nothing approaching an *incarnation*, a "rendering in flesh" of such privileged *divine* intermediary figures within a concrete earthly body (as indeed in that of the Nazarene Jesus), may be found within any of these Jewish texts of highly varied provenance.[6] Corporeal manifestations remain limited to angels. The notion of an incarnation of eternal God in the person of Jesus of Nazareth seems to associate Christianity more with the pagan than the Jewish manner of belief, although *incarnation* in the *confined sense* (becoming flesh in a concrete person from birth to death) must be distinguished from this in the *extended sense* (temporary manifestations of gods) as a matter of course: Proper, if temporary, appearances of divine figures in human form were at least according to the mythology of pagan Antiquity entirely possible, and insofar did not spring entirely from only the realms of the interpretations of reality at the time.[7] This is documented by a vivid scene from Luke's Acts of the Apostles wherein a crowd of Lyconian Lystra's population is portrayed as proclaiming, originally allegedly in Lyconian Lystra's popular cant, the following acclamatory sentence: "The gods are come down to us in the likeness (or equivalence) of men" (Acts 14:11).[8] The scene reported in the Acts of the Apostles (namely that, in Lystra, the Christian missionaries Barnabas and Paul were held within such an epiphany-related religiosity to be Zeus and Hermes on grounds of their healing of an invalid) is reminiscent of another famous story: According to the Imperial-era poet Ovid, Jupiter appears together with Hermes before Philemon and Baucis *specie mortali*, "in the form of a mortal."[9] Something quite comparable is also stated in the Acts by means of the thronged masses: "The gods are come down to us in the likeness of men." Hence, it is already stated in Homer that

> the gods do in the guise of strangers from afar put on all manner of shapes, and visit the cities, beholding the violence and the righteousness of men.[10]

As to whether, according to Luke's conception, this divine form is, in turn, the *equivalent* or only the *likeness* of man, cannot be precisely determined from the Greek wording.[11] This somewhat fine linguistic differentiation does not initially seem to have been found to be a problem; rather, it came to become one later, in the course of reflection upon this and other passages of the Christian Bible during Antiquity.

Even should the Lucan text very subtly intimate a difference between the human (that is, corporeal) form of gods, and the body of humans, such reports on the temporary or more extended manifestations of a god or gods, as has been demonstrated by Hans Ulrich Gumbrecht, on grounds of the strict transcendentalization of the definition of God in late antique and medieval mainstream Judaism not only came to be perceived ever more as something of a stumbling block, but rather served and still serves in the Modern era among an intelligentsia more or less influenced by Christianity as a vanquished mythological conception of the world. This hardly surprises: The notion of a temporary or lifelong incarnation of transcendent divine immateriality is, as Gumbrecht notes, something of the counter-model to the concept originating in René Descartes which reduces the human body as far as possible to its function as a mere source of energy for human spirituality.[12] It is only in the last decades that, following a post-Cartesian tendency, the voices for a markedly higher appraisal of the body and corporeality have multiplied; in this context, the long-neglected notion of the "incarnation" has received attention anew, Gumbrecht himself being an interesting example of such a recent tendency. Already on these grounds, the end of this present study on the conceptions of a divine corporeality in Antiquity must once more—if briefly—explore the specific Christian notion that, in the case of Jesus, the divine body does not consist of a particular materiality becoming of the divinity of God, but rather is more or less identical to a human body—at least for a certain period of time. Does this idea of a complete identity perhaps serve as the truly Christian contribution to the debate over the divine body in Antiquity? Or might it rather be merely a radicalized form of classical Jewish thought on the likeness of God, which, without consideration of contemporary philosophical standards of discussion, once more was considered by means of the example of an individual human? Or might, in fact, the notion of an identity of divine and human bodies be ill suited to delineating Christianity from the other monotheistic and pagan religions of Antiquity?

Debates over the Divinity of the Body of Jesus Christ

Naturally, in answering this question, a complete history of the development of the Christian doctrine of the incarnation in some fashion, possibly simultaneously taking into account convergent Jewish, Muslim, and pagan conceptions, can hardly now be presented. In the present context, a few characteristic examples must suffice, and general reference be made to the comprehensive depiction of the development of Christian thought on Jesus of Nazareth as a divine personage and the concomitant religiosity from the pen of *Alois, Kardinal Grillmeier* (1910–1998). This unfinished portrait encompasses a total of five volumes and proceeds well into the debates branching off in the wake of the Council of Chalcedon (AD 451).[13] The present point of departure is, in contrast to that of Grillmeier's portrayal, the impression that, already in the texts which later (that is, from the second century onwards) would be incorporated into the canonical New Testament of Christendom, the specific constitution of the human body of Jesus of Nazareth was of great import to the mostly unknown authors of these texts, as they were concurrently convinced that here (formulated in consciously vague terms) more was in play than a merely human body. The meaning of this central dimension of the corporeality of the (once more phrased unspecifically) divine human Jesus for the formation of a doctrine of the Christ of God referring to Jesus of Nazareth—classically termed "Christology"—is barely touched by Grillmeier. This question would enjoy an important role most prominently within inter-Christian debates from the second century onwards, albeit with entirely different accentuations, as Walter Bauer already brought to the fore more than a century ago in an overview of the pertinent texts from the apocryphal literature of antique Christianity.[14] A salient statement within the New Testament which might be named without analogy in regard to its contents serves to mark the problem well: In the epistle to the community in Anatolian Colossae, to which tradition ascribes incorrectly Paul's authorship, originating nevertheless certainly from the first century, it is stated that in Christ "dwelleth all the fullness of the Godhead bodily" (Colossians 2:9).[15] With this opinion that the entire "fullness of the Godhead"[16] alighted in a body (σωματικῶς),[17] the task of describing the consequences of this statement for the understanding of the body about which this was stated presented itself somewhat directly within antique Christianity. In the present context, it is thus unimportant whether this verse was originally meant against the backdrop of those pertinent Stoic philosophical concepts[18] wherein the entire plenitude of the godhead was present in the *world* (ὁ κόσμος) as the body of the divinity, and thus that Christ should here be accorded a *cosmic body*, or whether the sentence was read as a statement as to the *earthly* and *human* body of Jesus Christ (certainly the Letter to the Colossians knows of an earthly body of Jesus Christ composed of flesh and concedes it a salvific significance):[19] The business of also clarifying the relationship between divinity and humanity in the body of Jesus Christ proved itself to be inevitable, and the solutions to this task permit interesting insights as to the concepts of God's body propounded thereby.[20] Here, roughly *two* fundamental directions within which this relationship was explicated may be discerned: The demotion of the body to the status of an illusory frame and the promotion of the body to the status of a completely human body.

The extent to which all of these questions were contingent upon the fundamental problem of the corporeality of God the Father is demonstrated by a passage from a report of an alleged disputation between a Christian named Acacius and an official of the Roman emperor Decius called Marcianus in the *Acta Acacii*. Therein, testimony as to events such as the generation of Christ is debated, Marcianus asking according to the text's own testimony, stylized as the protocol of a conversation: "Is God thus corporeal?" to which Acacius, accused of being a Christian, replies: "That is known by Him alone; in truth, we do not recognize his invisible form, rather we worship his strength and power."[21] The text's composition may be located in fourth century Anatolia, and it documents that, in late antique catechistic contexts, the question as to whether God possesses a body was openly answered in certain Christian circles and a close connection to the question as to the corporeal existence of Jesus Christ was perceived.[22]

The Promotion of the Human Body of Jesus Christ

A few authors and schools emphasize the human corporeality of Jesus Christ particularly strongly. Thus, for example, the North African Christian teacher *Tertullian* discusses in relation to Christ a *sermo in carne*, "God, the word, in flesh," within his polemic against a theology which identified Father and Son.[23] In the course of this, Tertullian critically engages with a statement of his adversaries which equates God and flesh with one another without any differentiation: "And so it was flesh that was born, and so the flesh will be the Son of God" (*Caro itaque nata est, caro itaque erit filius dei*).[24] The North African theologian insists that God was not *transformed* into flesh, as "the Word abides in his form." Only insofar is it "made flesh" (John 1:14), which means, according to Tertullian, that it "comes to be in flesh, and is manifested and seen and handled by means of the flesh": Jesus is "one substance composed of two, flesh and spirit, a kind of mixture."[25] This is precisely to be understood in the sense of the Stoic "unmixed unity" (ἀσύγχυτος ἕνωσις) that within this "certain mixture" the identity of both elements, "word" and "flesh," remains intact—in contrast to a complete mixture leading to a new body or a new fluid with new characteristics ("blending," σύγχυσις), or to a sheer juxtaposition of two elements such as might occur in a pile of pebbles (παράθεσις).[26] Nevertheless, what is missing in this early study of the reflection (Tertullian being the first Latinate author to concern himself with fundamental questions of Christology in such detail) is any extended contemplation of those features of Jesus characteristic to human corporeality and to these specific individuals, and, in turn, problematic for a god. Conceivable would be human wants such as thirst, hunger, or sleep, which a deity by definition cannot possess, inasmuch as he wants for nothing (ἀπροσδεής).[27] The degree to which such questions were discussed is evinced by the fact that Tertullian composed an original work entitled "On the Flesh of Christ," wherein he sought to argue that it is already entirely visible from biblical texts that Jesus Christ possesses a "human and derived from man," "not composed of spirit, any more than it is composed of soul or of the stars, or is a *phantasm*."[28] At the same time, however, as has already been seen, for the Stoic Tertullian, it was already on philosophical grounds that Jesus Christ existed as a body, namely because he existed on earth: "Nothing is incorporeal except what does not exist."[29]

The Demotion of the Human Body of Jesus Christ to an "Illusory Body"

In turn, there are intimations that this human corporeality was demoted to the status of a merely apparent corporeality in the interest of preserving an intact divinity, although little in the way of direct sources exist for such notions, generally termed "docetism," and the position must rather be reconstructed from the polemic accounts of so-called antique Christian heresiologies, that is, its nominal opponents.[30] The problems with the historical reconstruction of such doctrines begin already with the terminology employed and its definition: While the term "docetism" (despite possessing roots in Late Antiquity) is a modern coinage of rather unclear or indeed hazy meaning and supplies wildly varying definitions,[31] already at the end of the second century attestations of the hitherto-unevidenced Greek word "illusionists" (Δοκηταί) occur. Accordingly, it is suggested to differentiate between these historically attested "illusionists" ("docetes") and their doctrine ("illusion" or, indeed, "docetic doctrine"), on the one hand, and a collective term formed on the basis of content for various groups, on the other hand, associated with a unified contextual rejection of a concrete human corporeality for the terrestrial Christ ("docetists," "docetic," and "docetism").[32]

In the present context, these "docetic" positions are of less interest— for example, the alleged opinion of the teacher *Cerdo* active in Rome in the mid-second century,[33] according to which Christ was "not in flesh" but rather "merely present as an image."[34] *Phantasma* (φάντασμα), the Latinized Greek word employed within the account, has a broad spectrum of meaning, signifying "image," "illusion," "ghost," or simply "apparition." Most likely, with such statements cited as those of *Cerdo*, considered to be the teacher of the "arch-heretic" Marcion, positions were foisted upon him which were assumed at the end of the second and the beginning of the third centuries AD to have been propounded by *Marcion*.[35] Nevertheless, it remains highly uncertain as to whether Marcion himself had deemed the human body of Christ a *phantasma*: Tertullian accuses Marcion of having taught that Jesus Christ was not that which he appeared to be: Flesh and yet not flesh, human and yet not human. Nevertheless, he announces that, from his own knowledge, Marcion did not *expressis verbis* discuss a phantasma, but rather this notion is merely the logical consequence of the stances of Marcion in Tertullian's eyes.[36] As figures are repeatedly mentioned as maintaining that the body of Christ is to be thought of analogously to the angels taking form upon their appearances on earth (such as before Abraham in Genesis 21:1–5[37]), much recommends the notion that Marcion also assumed that Jesus Christ possessed the body of an angel,[38] and thereby an "image of human substance."[39] Harnack had already correctly noted that, according to the general contemporary understanding, angels "which came to Abraham were not spirits, but rather acted and ate like living and real humans; hence, Christ was also no spirit, but rather God appearing in human form."[40] Should he have thought thus, Marcion would scarcely be the only Christian of the second century to comprehend Christ in analogy to an angel.[41] Unfortunately, it remains completely unclear as to whether the following sentences cited, offered by Tertullian as a literal quotation from Marcion, were actually meant by the latter as a polemic against the now canonical story of Jesus' birth, or as to whether these are not rather a rhetorical exaggeration on the part of Tertullian many years after the death of his literary adversary:

> "Away," he says, "with Caesar's enrolments, always a nuisance, and with inns with no room; away with dirty rags and hard mangers; let the angel host take the responsibility when it gives honour to its own God, and that

> by night; the shepherds had better watch over their flocks; no need for the
> wise men to be fetched along from afar; for all I care, they may keep
> their gold; also let Herod be a better man, lest Jeremiah have something
> to boast of; and let not the Child be circumcised, lest he feel pain, nor
> brought to the temple, lest he burden his parents with the expense of
> an offering, nor put into the hands of Simeon, lest he make the old man
> sorry because he is soon to die; also let that old woman hold her tongue,
> lest she put the evil eye upon the boy."[42]

It is regardless certain that mainstream church circles from the second century onwards already leveled at the "arch-heretic" Marcion
the accusation that he did not accord Jesus a human body. From such interpretations aimed at particular teachings, rumors must then evidently have
swiftly emerged, and thereafter, on the basis of reports taken as truth, certain "heretics" would have been purported to have described the human
body of Jesus Christ as a *phantasma*.

Potentially also supporting such a critical appraisal of Imperial-era accusations of heresy is the fact that, in the classical heresiological doxographies,
these or comparable positions are already thrust upon very diverse range of
individuals and serve somewhat as the salient feature by which "Gnostic"
teaching might be recognized. Thus, it is recounted of the Syrian teacher
Satornilus, conventionally held to be an "early Gnostic," that he taught that
the redeemer was "unborn, incorporeal, and without form, only seemingly
of human appearance."[43] Even if here the term "seemingly" is expressed
with Latin putative, and thus was certainly translated in Late Antiquity with
Greek δοκήσει, the context does not concern a divine body, but rather
the *incorporeality* of God (*incorporalis*/ἀσώματος). The accusations
found in the corpus of letters ascribed to the Antiochian bishop *Ignatius*,
supposedly dating from beginning of the second century, remain equally
schematic.[44] These are addressed to followers of Christ from communities
in different cities in Asia Minor. In letters to the communities in Smyrna,
modern İzmir, and Tralles (near modern Aydın), "unbelievers" are attacked
who say that "he suffered only in appearance."[45] This position must have
been received particularly explosively considering that Ignatius himself
also suffered and died—this notion of the suffering and dying martyr's
mimetic conformity to the suffering and dying Christ in the theology of
Christian martyrdom will also be further explored elsewhere herein.[46]
Moreover, in these texts addressed to the parishes of Smyrna and Tralles,
"suffering" (πάθος) is understood not only as the designation of a certain
portion of Jesus' life, but also *pars pro toto* as an expression for the "entire
Christ event with all of its individual occurrences."[47] Hence, the author of
this letter is convinced that it must be professed that Jesus Christ bore a

body of flesh and blood, as he would otherwise have worn something life-less such as a corpse, and, in such a manner, the salvation performed on the cross would have been an illusion.[48] The letters to the parishes of Smyrna and Tralles exist in various manuscript versions of differing length; much warrants the stance that, in Late Antiquity, the terse thetic statements of an earlier version were expanded into a so-called long recension of the letters ascribed to Ignatius. In this long version, one can find an extensive affir-mation of the truth and reality of the incarnation of Jesus Christ at birth, which recognizably terminologically presupposes the heated confronta-tions of the fourth and fifth centuries, and demonstrates as to how implicit the avowal of the human body of Jesus Christ on the part of antique Chris-tianity had become in the wake of these different controversies:

> Mary then did truly conceive a body which had God inhabiting it. And God the Word was truly born of the Virgin, having clothed Himself with a body of like passions with our own. He who forms all men in the womb, was Himself really in the womb, and made for Himself a body of the seed of the Virgin, but without any intercourse of man. He was carried in the womb, even as we are, for the usual period of time; and was really born, as we also are; and was in reality nourished with milk, and partook of common meat and drink, even as we do. And when He had lived among men for thirty years, He was baptised by John, really and not in appearance; and when He had preached the gospel three years, and done signs and wonders, He who was Himself the Judge was judged by the Jews, falsely so called, and by Pilate the governor; was scourged, was smitten on the cheek, was spit upon; He wore a crown of thorns and a purple robe; He was condemned: He was crucified in real-ity, and not in appearance, not in imagination, not in deceit. He really died, and was buried, and rose from the dead, even as He prayed in a certain place, saying, "But do Thou, O Lord, raise me up again, and I shall recompense them."[49]

What exactly the Christian groups attacked in purportedly the earliest version of the letter attributed to Ignatius actually taught in the second century remains obscure, along with many other details. It also remains unknown how large these groups were or whether they were widespread within Ignatius' hometown, Syrian Antioch, or in the Anatolian cities of Smyrna and Tralles, or even in all three locations. It is also possible to reconstruct the motivations behind this position with some difficulty — the notion of many that a shameful death on the cross did not hold so well with the affirmation of his divinity may well be one reason for this, albeit noth-ing precise may be discerned through such a tangle of vehement polemic.

This means, however, that the different assignments of position treated underneath the heading of "docetism," over the authenticity of which much ink might be spilled, need not be outlined and critically studied at length in their entirety. Soon thereafter, the discourse on an earthly body of Jesus Christ as a *phantasma* would become the distinguishing mark of the doctrine of "many heretics" without any attempt at differentiation, as might be read, for example, in the Spanish author *Gregor of Elvira* in the fourth century;[50] yet, such stereotypes can hardly be effectively evaluated, and hence the movements of which they were born can no longer be depicted appropriately.

Interesting as a starting point for the present study are rather the individuals who were already explicitly labeled "illusionists" in the High Imperial period, and their positions, as they propounded a sophisticated "illusory doctrine," and, in this context, opinions as to the body of Jesus Christ. For such individuals, *two* pertinent sources exist among their Christian adversaries from the late second and early third centuries.[51]

The Opinions of Julius Cassianus

Clement of Alexandria mentions at the end of the second century the term "illusionist" for individuals named after their independent doctrines but does not expound as to wherein the independence of the teachings lies: "But of the heresies, some are called after the name of the founder . . . other heresies are called from the place where they arose . . . others from their practice . . . others from peculiar opinions, as the Illusionists."[52] Moreover, Clement acknowledges elsewhere a "doctrine of illusion," for the popularization of which he blames in particular a Christian teacher called *Julius Cassianus*.[53] This prompts the association of both terms: "Illusionists" propound an "illusory teaching." Initially, it is not explicitly learned from the second passage in Clement what exactly this teacher taught on the human body of Jesus Christ (that is, wherein the "illusory doctrine" precisely lay), nor, indeed, anything as to whether and how he justified his own ethics hostile to the body and sexuality with pertinent theological stances. Regardless, Clement wishes to suggest to those reading the passage that Julius Cassianus explained his stand for complete sexual abstinence inasmuch as he considered sexuality to have been adopted by humans from the bestial practices of the animal world following the fall. Moreover, Clement intimates that Julius Cassianus accorded Jesus Christ an "illusory" or "apparent" fleshy body. This was certainly how Jerome understood Julius Cassianus some two centuries after Clement.[54] Considering his beginnings within the circles of so-called Valentinian Gnosis, yet another explanation may suggest itself:

Potentially he assumed, as was the case with certain teachers which might be numbered among the Valentinian school,[55] that Jesus Christ possessed a "spiritual body" (τὸ σῶμα τὸ ψυχικόν). It was meant thereby (according to a particularly thorough report upon the Valentinians in Irenaeus of Lyon) that he was "so prepared with such ineffable artifice that he was visible, tangible, and passible."[56] Yet, according to Irenaeus' account, Christ possesses these qualities not because he is composed of matter (ὕλη),[57] but rather because the actually invisible, intangible, and impassible substance of the soul miraculously assumes such characteristics from free particles. It is entirely possible that Julius Cassianus followed Valentinian teachings at this juncture. Should it be asked, following this premise, how such a "purely immaterial" or only "apparently fleshy body" should be envisioned concretely, then inferences might be drawn from a quotation in Clement of Alexandria verbatim from a text by Julius Cassianus entitled "Concerning Continence and Celibacy":

> And let no one say that because we have these parts, that the female body is shaped this way and the male that way, the one to receive, the other to give seed, sexual intercourse is allowed by God.[58]

Quite evidently, for Julius Cassianus, the male penis along with the testes and the female vagina were not integral to the human being first created by God, but rather they arrived (likely with surrounding flesh) as a consequence of the fall and it was only from thereafter that humans engaged in sexual dealings with one another and were able to receive progeny. Julius Cassianus clearly culled this notion from the moment within the narrative of the creation wherein "dressing in skins" is discussed.[59] Were this, however, to be the case, and Clement to have ascribed a docetic doctrine to Julius Cassianus, then this ascetic would presumably have taught that Jesus of Nazereth only apparently (δοκήσει) possessed a male penis and testicles, but in reality, as the true "likeness of God," was free from this member, the purpose of which, after all, was only to be found in the bilious emulation of animal practices of procreation and lust. Admittedly, this specific teaching of Julius Cassianus could not have attained any mainstream status within Imperial-era Christianity, as the conception was commonly maintained that the child Jesus of Nazareth, like any Jewish youngster, had undergone the circumcision of precisely this penis.[60] In certain regions, the late antique festal calendar accordingly also contained a "Feast of the Circumcision of the Lord" (*Circumcisio Domini*) celebrated eight days after his birth on 1 January; nevertheless, pertinent relics were only first exhibited from the early Middle Ages onwards.[61]

Valentinus of Rome

It is not only the "Gnostic" school originating with the teacher and inhabitant of Rome *Valentinus* which is key to the present context due to its
notion of a "spiritual body." The teacher after whom the school named
itself had evidently also devoted thought to this fundamental problem. A
fragment from Valentinus demonstrates that in the second century AD the
consequences of the abstinence (ἐγκράτεια) of Jesus for his body could
be described very differently from how this had been approached by Julius
Cassianus—incidentally, this solution as to the question of how the godliness of Jesus might be rendered visible in his body also reveals that the
second century served as something of a laboratory within Christian theological history, as here highly individual and unusual (at least from the
perspective of later centuries) "solutions" were conceived of and developed. Within the context of his account of positions which sought to live
by and justify a code of abstinence (ἐγκράτεια), Clement of Alexandria
reports the following on Valentinus:

> And Valentine says in the letter to Agathopus: "Jesus endured all
> things and was continent; it was his endeavour to earn a divine nature;
> he ate and drank in a manner peculiar to himself, and the food did not
> pass out of his body. Such was the power of his continence that food
> was not corrupted within him; for he himself was not subject to the
> process of corruption."[62]

Here once more, the exceptionality of the human body of Jesus who
patently possessed the usual organ for receiving food and drink in
the human manner (namely, a mouth) is emphasized not by means of the
absence of a penis with testicles, but rather through a dearth of digestion
and excretion; this warrants much musing as to whether in Valentinus' eyes
Jesus did, in fact, possess stomach, intestines, and *anus*, only apparently
possessed these, or, indeed, possessed these organs but elected not to use
them. Unfortunately, no answer is forthcoming in the extant fragment. It
might only be stated with certainty that other Christian authors of the time
(such as Irenaeus and Clement of Alexandria) were convinced that Jesus
of Nazareth would have eaten and drunk quite normally, that is, in the
manner imagined within antique academia, namely by absorbing into the
body certain necessary substances by means of the digestion, and excret-
ing the indigestible remainder.[63] Quite evidently, there were time and again
voices according to which Jesus did eat and drink, but did not existentially
require these daily aspects of life like other individuals—in a late antique
Latin version of the apocryphal Acts of Peter, it is accordingly stated:

Whereas "he is in the Father and the Father in him" (cf. John 17:21); in him also is the fullness of all majesty (cf. Colossians 2:9), who has shown us all his benefits. He ate and drank on our account, though he was neither hungry nor thirsty; he suffered and bore revilings for us, he died and rose for us.[64]

Interestingly, the sentence "He ate and drank in a peculiar way, not delivering up His food again" from Valentinus' letter is cited as an "orthodox" teaching on Christ in an epistle ascribed to the Cappadocian bishop and theologian *Basil of Caesarea* in the last third of the fourth century without reference to the author himself Valentinus, already notorious at the time as a "gnostic."[65] This quotation, most likely taken from Clement, clearly indicates that, especially in Encratic and monastic circles, also in the fourth century, a markedly strong interest still existed in expressing the singularity of the human body of Jesus Christ in such a manner that sexuality and digestion might be kept well away from him wherever possible. On the other hand, there were also clearly earlier voices which rejected any differentiation at this juncture. Accordingly, it might be read in a fragment of the Roman urbanite apologist Justin that the discourse on an "immaterial body" of Jesus Christ is essentially tantamount to the "fantasy of a body."[66]

On the Teachings of the "Illusionists"

A tradition on the "illusionists" (Δοκηταί) completely divergent from that of Clement of Alexandria and his remarks on Julius Cassianus might be found somewhat later in an anti-heretical work ascribed to the presbyter and Roman urbanite *Hippolytus*; the manner by which such a doubling of traditions came to pass now eludes any real elucidation. As in all comparable passages which might be counted among the so-called gnostic material unique to Hippolytus, any parallel transmission in Irenaeus, Clement, or any other anti-gnostic author is lacking.[67] Quite evidently, at the onset of the third century, there was a consensus within Christian circles that there was a more or less stable group of individuals with a particular set of teachings departing from those of the mainstream church, namely these "illusionists" or Δοκηταί, but, as the differences between Clement and Hippolytus demonstrate, there was no quorum as to what this group exactly believed.[68] In *Hippolytus*, a detailed mythological system of a development of divine principles is articulated. Within the mythological (or, indeed, one might even say gnostic) remits expounded, it is recounted that the Savior and only born Son received through bathing in the Jordan "in the water the form and seal of the body that had been born by the virgin."[69] This adoption of an image is elucidated by means of two comparisons which cannot be entirely aligned with the subject level. He concentrated

himself like a bright flash of lightning in the tiniest body. To use a better
analogy: he contracted himself like the light beam of the eyes withdrawn
under the eyelids.[70]

That stated here on lightning and light corresponds to antique conceptions.
Thus, the "Optics" of the Greek mathematician Euclid begin with the opening postulate "Let it be assumed that lines (of sight) drawn directly from
the eye pass through a space of great extent."[71] In the lost first book of his
"Optics" from the second century AD, Claudius Ptolemy, likely another
inhabitant of Egypt, associated visual rays and light with each other as two
types (*species*) of one and the same category and was of the opinion that
both (as visual πνεῦμα) consist of aether, the finest element.[72] While the
comparison explains how an absolutely transcendent force may be enclosed
within a spatially restricted body, it is evidently presupposed that, by means
of bathing in a silhouette of a body on the surface of the water, this particular force might clothe itself in precisely this silhouette.[73] The notion that
only first during the baptism the particular combination of divine and human
parts was constituted in Jesus Christ must hardly astonish (or at all prompt
the alteration of the Greek text in the original report); this is also attested
elsewhere. Its unique feature is that, in comparison to other passages on the
baptism of Jesus, the emphasis is on the *corporeal* dimension; otherwise,
in these interpretations of the narrative of the baptism of Jesus, the focus
is upon the imbuement of the baptized Christ with the Holy Spirit, or his
establishment as the Son of God.[74] As might be reconstructed with no mean
circumspection, the connection of the baptismal event and light metaphors
is reminiscent of notions of light phenomena during the baptism in the Syrian cultural sphere, as found in the apocryphal Gospels of the Ebionites and
of the Hebrews respectively,[75] and also in the widespread, and for a time
canonical Diatessaron compiled by Tatian.[76] Unfortunately, it is not learned
within the extract quoted from Hippolytus which particular characteristics
distinguished the shadow-body assumed from the Jordan and how it existed
with him on a daily basis. Only in the summary of the section, with which
Hippolytus closes his anti-heretical work two books later,[77] may yet another
reference be found as to how the shadow loaded with the luminous force
differs from a normal body:

> Jesus clothed himself with that only-born power. Accordingly, he could
> not be seen by anyone, because he changed the magnitude of his glory.
> Everything happened to him, they say, as is written in the gospels.[78]

Christ was also invisible, as has been seen, according to the description
excerpted by Bishop Epiphanius of Salamis on Cyprus from the "Book of

Elchasai" (or "Elxai") and ascribed to one of the Judeo-Christian groups termed by him the "Ebionites." In this source, nevertheless, the invisibility is expressed in relation to a Christ of gargantuan dimensions whose exorbitant size now certainly articulates a remarkable difference to all other humans:

> Thus they believe that Christ is a manlike figure invisible to human eyes, ninety-six miles—or twenty-four schoeni, if you please!—tall; six schoeni, or twenty-four miles wide; and some other measurement through.[79]

The connection between the divine body and the body of Jesus Christ is made more apparent within the discourse on Christ taking his flesh from the stars and ether in his descent to the earth, and accordingly possessing—akin to God—an "astral and ethereal body" (as Novatian polemically states).[80] Origen famously testifies that there were Christians who ascribed God such a stellar body composed of ether or who understood the stars to be God's body, perhaps on the strength of the pertinent passages in Aristotle or other authors, as has been seen. The position that Jesus Christ also had such a body was foisted upon a student of Marcion named Apelles in a later heresiological text. Nevertheless, there is also a competing tradition that Apelles accorded Christ a body combined from the four elements,[81] which corresponded to the appreciation of the natural sciences prevalent at the time, as might be found, for example, in Justin.[82] Tertullian mentions the doctrine of astrally formed bodies in his systematization of erroneous teachings, wherein the reality of a normal human body of Jesus is gainsaid as an independent teaching, without according it any certain originator.[83]

The apocryphal Acts of John attempts in yet another manner to grasp the singularity of the body of Jesus. In one passage, which is incidentally only relayed in one high medieval manuscript in a poor textual condition and does not belong to the prevalent late antique version of these acts, this particularity is made clear in the detail that the body of Christ can be periodically touched. According to this text, at times, in turn, he does not leave footprints and thus also does not possess a material body. He transforms from human corporeality to divine bodilessness. John recounts this radical mutability of the body of Jesus as follows:

> I will tell you another glory, brethren; sometimes when I meant to touch him I encountered a material, solid body; but at other times again when I felt him, his substance was immaterial and incorporeal, and as if it did not exist at all. . . . And I often wished to see if his footprint appeared on the ground—for I saw him raising himself from the earth—and I never saw it.[84]

Hence, in this passage, this does not relate to a docetic concept in the strict sense, but rather first and foremost to the notion of the so-called polymorphism of Christ. According to this conception, Jesus Christ possesses such a special human body that it can assume various different states of aggregation (to employ scientific terminology), from the solid form of aggregation, the entire material body in another state of aggregation.[85] The one, solid state of aggregation, represents the conventional human body composed of matter (ὕλη), the other corresponds to the usual divine body, and is without terrestrial matter and thereby is no longer tangible to hands. Jesus Christ thus appears, on the one hand, in human, and, on the other hand, in divine form, with a visible form and without visible corporeality. *Incorporeality* in the strict sense is, nevertheless, not claimed, along with various states of aggregation of an object which presuppose his lingering substantiality. Naturally, there are also texts within canonical Scripture which belong to the prior history of such images of a mutable body of Jesus, such as, for example, the narrative of his transfiguration (Matthew 17:1–8 and parallels), the journey after Easter to Emmaus (Luke 24:13-35), or other post-Easter appearances.[86] This notwithstanding, the radical transformation of corporeality to incorporeality is not yet expressed therein. In the aforementioned section of the text of the Acts of John which was not incorporated into the more prevalent version, the mutability of the body of Jesus is, however, not only described as a radical metamorphosis from corporeality to bodiliness, but also as the transformation of a solid state of aggregation of corporeality to a less firm example thereof, somewhat serving as the beginning of the path to a disintegration of the body and as an intimation as to his potential incorporeality. This is demonstrated by various details within the section,[87] such as by his eyes, the size of his body, and the consistency of his chest.

> But then there appeared to me a yet more amazing sight; I tried to see him as he was, and I never saw his eyes closing, but always open. But he sometimes appeared to me as a small man with no good looks, and also as wholly looking up to heaven. And he had another strange (property); when I reclined at table he would take me to his breast, and I held (him) to me; and sometimes his breast felt to me smooth and soft, but sometimes hard like rock; so that I was perplexed in my (mind) and said: "What does (*) this mean?"[88]

It hardly surprises that this rather experimental attempt to ascribe Jesus Christ simultaneously a human body (albeit a special example) and a divine incorporeality was not satisfactorily received in a period of sophisticated christological reflection within Late Antiquity and — as is demonstrated by the extremely thin testimony from manuscripts—was hardly copied with the remainder of the text of the Acts of John all that often. It comes across almost unhelpfully as to how, in this section, it is attempted by means of various, less than consistent avenues to ascribe Jesus Christ simultaneously a special human body which is inherently mutable and, at the same time, to portray him as possessing unchangeable divine attributes, such as the constant surveillance of all things, corresponding to religious tradition in the ancient world: "Not sleeping is the eye of Zeus, but rather near, although it is far."[89] The descriptions in the passage from the Acts of John oscillate between gradations of material fixity and the neat dual of corporeality and bodilessness; this ambivalence need not be a consequence of the presumably complex literary development of the passage, but rather may be the narrational attempt to bring that to expression which, for example, was described on the basis of Stoic philosophumena with philosophical terminology as the special corporeality of the gods, which concurrently stands in categorical opposition to all human corporeality.

Quite evidently, such passages focus upon making it apparent through the notion of the polymorphy of Jesus Christ that the Son of God possessed at once both a human and a divine body (or, indeed, like a God, *no* body). Erik Peterson has correctly drawn attention to the fact that the impression of mutability only emerges because that which is always contiguous in the absolute timelessness of God is separated within the human perception into the temporal stages of past, present and future: What humans perceive to be changeable forms is thus rather simultaneous and to be conceived of together as the hallmark of the divine human.[90] This is most evident in those scenes in which Jesus appears sequentially as a child, adult, and geriatric.[91]

At this juncture, as mentioned, it is impossible to compile a complete inventory of the notions of the human body of Jesus Christ in vogue within antique Christianity, or propounded by learned Christians. Nevertheless, despite something of a dearth of complete elaborations, the corpus permits the recognition of something very much fundamental: Until the outbreak of the heated clashes over the relationship between God and man in the person of Jesus Christ from the fourth century onwards, the majority of the positions championed in the High Imperial era and Late Antiquity could be categorized in terms of whether they (as in the case of Tertullian) emphasized the complete identification of the corporeality of Jesus with generally human corporeality or rather laid stock upon differences.

The Resurrected Body of Jesus Christ

Increasingly, this controversy no longer merely concerned the question as to the terrestrial bodiliness of Jesus Christ, but rather also the constitution of his *resurrected body*. This extensive debate over the composition of the human body after the resurrection need not and, indeed, cannot be reviewed here in detail;[92] it rather represents an outlier of the contestations over the human body of Jesus on earth, which has already been documented to some extent. Once more, only a few characteristic examples are to be excerpted from an expansive and complex transmission: When they seek to argue for the reality of the human body of Jesus Christ after the resurrection, various texts within antique Christian literature refer to an apocryphal dominical saying which was not incorporated into the canonical Gospels: "I am not a bodiless daemon" (οὐκ εἰμὶ δαιμόνιον ἀσώματον).[93] The dominical saying emphasizes that which the resurrected Christ says in Emmaus according to the Gospel of Luke: "For a spirit hath not flesh and bones, as ye see me have" (Luke 24:39). The canonized text and the apocryphal pronouncement alike document a prevalent belief within ancient Christendom:[94] The resurrected Jesus also possesses a body; he is not a bodiless demon.

There were innumerable debates from the second to fifth centuries AD on the question as to whether and in which manner this body of the revenant differed from the earthly body of Jesus, and as to whether, for example, he was a transformed spiritual body.[95] Even the Alexandrian theologian Origen, who has been encountered as a staunch critic of any notion of God's body, made this differentiation and explains accordingly within an exposition of this apocryphal dominical saying:

> Rather what he said must be understood according to the intention of the author of the pamphlet,[96] that is, that he did not have such a body as the daemons have (which is naturally fine and thin like air, and because of this is considered or called "bodiless"[97] by many), but that he had a solid and palpable body.[98]

Evidently, Origen was also of the opinion that Christ had a solid, material, and tangible body after his resurrection, and even took his flesh with him (at least initially) to heaven.[99]

Most of the Christian theologians (with the exception of individual gnostics who argued in a more differentiated manner) professed the corporeality of the resurrection of Jesus Christ. As has been seen from the debates which occurred in the third and fourth centuries, Origen was compelled to defend his position against all kinds of misunderstandings and, indeed, his students and their students more so.[100] The quasi-materialistic tack taken by these controversies within the late antique mainstream Christian church is documented by a pronouncement of the North African bishop *Augustine* regarding a Spanish episcopal colleague from the Balearic Isles named Consentius[101] from AD 419 or 420. Accordingly, Augustine writes in this late phase of his life, in which he had reconciled far more his thought with that of the mainstream ecclesiastical consensus:

> You ask whether the body of the Lord now has flesh and blood or the other features of the flesh. . . . I believe that the body of the Lord is in heaven as it was on earth when he ascended into heaven. But he said unto his disciples, as we read in the gospel, when they were doubtful about his resurrection and thought that what they were seeing was not a body but a spirit, "Behold my hands and my feet, that it is I myself: handle me, and see; for a spirit hath not flesh and bones, as ye see me have."[102]

Augustine assumes—very much in agreement with the pertinent passages in the letters of Paul—with a transformation of the terrestrial body by means of the resurrection, but also, in turn, with a resurrection of the *flesh*, which preserves this flesh with blood and bones for eternity. It is transformed to an "immaterial flesh" (for example, through a new moral quality of its actions), but it remains corporeal flesh with blood and bone.[103] According to Augustine, the identity of the sexes as man and woman is also preserved, but he presumes the eschatological perfection of the body, as he explains roughly eight years after the aforementioned letter to Consentius in his great work on the "City of God" (*De civitate Dei*): Certain deficiencies of age or infirmity, or disfigurations are corrected by means of the spontaneous perfection of the body so that the state of an ideal age of roughly thirty is restored, or created for those who experienced an early death. Naturally, not all of the nails and hair are regained which were shed over the course of an earthly life.[104] The eschatological completion also implies the immortality, weightlessness, and impassibility of the resurrected body. Those risen can use their limbs and organs, such as the stomach; they participate in heavenly banquets, although they actually no longer need anything more to eat. To a certain degree, admittedly never specified precisely by Augustine, the eschatological perfection is oriented towards the ideal of an antique beauty constituted on the grounds of proportionality and symmetry.[105] The model and benchmark of the resurrected body of humans is fundamentally the body of Jesus Christ as "image and likeness of God." Nevertheless, the resurrected body of Christ in the flesh is effectively only commensurate in regard to his ideal age of thirty years and the fundamental quality of having been born and having died, and not in any literal sense of a yardstick for height, weight, or other bodily details, which would have to lead to identical copies:

> But in any case Christ rose with the same bodily size as that with which he died, and it is wrong to say that when the time of the general resurrection comes his bodily size will increase, so that he will be equal to the tallest, though he had no such size in the body when he appeared to his disciples with the size in which he was known to them. But if we say that all larger bodies must be reduced to the size of the Lord's body, much will have to be taken from the bodies of many, though he promised that not a hair would perish (cf. Matthew 10:30). Hence it follows that each one is to receive his own measure, either the size that he had in youth, if he died an old man, or if he died in childhood, the size that he would have reached.[106]

Evidently, Augustine was well acquainted with the tradition that the body of Jesus was of average height (this is, as has been seen, nevertheless, first textually attested in a post-antique Byzantine source ascribed to John Damascene), as it is only so that the problem could first have been posed for him and other Christians as to how the bodies of particularly large individuals might relate to the medium-sized resurrected body of Jesus Christ.

A very similar argumentation using the corporeal reality of the manifestations of the revenant may already be found in the text *De resurrectione*, the ascription of which to the Roman urbanite apologist Justin Martyr is disputed, but almost certainly hails from the second century AD.[107] Here, the communal meal of fish and honey attended, according to the account of the Gospel of Luke, by Jesus and his disciples,[108] is also employed as an argument that the risen Christ possessed his complete human body after the resurrection, and that this will also remain for all those who will be resurrected:

> Why did He rise in the flesh in which He suffered, unless to show the resurrection of the flesh? And wishing to confirm this, when His disciples did not know whether to believe He had truly risen in the body, and were looking upon Him and doubting, He said to them, "Ye have not yet faith (Mark 4:40/Luke 24:39), see that it is I!" (cf. Luke 24:39f.) and He let them handle Him, and showed them the prints of the nails in His hands. And when they were by every kind of proof persuaded that it was Himself, and in the body, they asked Him to eat with them, that they might thus still more accurately ascertain that He had in verity risen bodily; and He did eat honey-comb and fish (cf. Luke 24:42f.). And thereby He had thus shown them that there is truly a resurrection of the flesh.[109]

Such a resurrection-derived affirmation of the reality of the human body of the person Jesus Christ represents (in particular within Late Antiquity) a broad mainstream ecclesiastical consensus[110] but, as has been seen, not nearly the only position propounded in antique Christianity. The aforementioned differing accentuations concerning the human body of Jesus Christ may well have been arrived at because the sparse transmission of sources as may be found within the canonical or apocryphal writings on Jesus of Nazareth was interpreted in differing manners within antique Christianity. Already long before the "christological controversies" proper, since the fourth century, all of the passages within the canonized Gospels which depicted Jesus of Nazareth as someone who was—to formulate this as generally as possible—in a certain sense influenced by his body or, indeed, even directly dependent upon his corporeality, were controversially debated (for example, between the so-called gnostic and mainstream church circles). The later clashes between theologians from the so-called Antiochian school of a certain Diodorus of Tarsus and Theodore of Mopsuestia[111] and their opponents such as Cyril of Alexandria are also merely part of an extended history of controversial debates over whether the Jesus professed to be God might be accorded all of the senses and sentiments characteristic to such a human body—that is, also the feeling of hunger, thirst, or despondency. The aforementioned creed of the Council of Chalcedon in AD 451 discusses that "one and the same" Lord Jesus Christ was "complete in the divinity and . . . complete in the humanity . . . truly God and truly human from reason-gifted body and soul," "of the substance of one" alike to humans in all things apart from sin.[112]

The Disputes over the "Incorruptibility" of the Body of Jesus Christ

Notoriously, this conciliatory statement of compromise did not prevail in soothing the flared tempers of the disputants. The question as to how exactly the human body of Jesus of Nazareth, whose complete reality was hardly disputed by anyone by this point, related to the godhead of Jesus Christ was further debated and, indeed, with great controversy. A certain endpoint is nevertheless presented by the mainstream rejection of the notion that the terrestrial body of Jesus Christ is "incorruptible" (ἄφθαρτος) prior to the resurrection. After the Council of Chalcedon, such views of the imperishability of the body of Jesus were not only propounded by theologians who endorsed the results of the council, but also by those who rejected them. The discourse on an incorruptible body initially corresponded precisely to those notions which had previously been entertained by Christians (albeit also, naturally, adherents of other religions and spiritual movements) regarding God's body: Among those thoroughly topical features of God (and thereby also to the classical characteristics of a divine body) numbered simply that, in contrast to humans, he was incorruptible; this terminology was hardly informed alone by all of the philosophical doctrines of God of the various schools (Epicurus writes of a generally widespread conception of God: ἡ κοινὴ τοῦ θεοῦ νόησις),[113] but rather may also be found in the canonized Scripture of the New Testament.[114] "Incorruptible" implies thereby not only the impossibility of the physical destruction of a body, but also the moral annihilation of the same; the Word consequently possesses ontological and ethical dimensions alike. Insofar, it readily suggested itself also to employ the term "incorruptible" (ἄφθαρτος) in respect to the earthly body of Jesus of Nazareth, the term having already been implicit for the resurrected body since Paul,[115] as this body had been very closely associated with his godhead. Yet, by contrast, it is surprising how late it was that a debate as to the divine features of the body of Jesus actually broke out in relation to this term: First at the beginning of the sixth century may groups be attested which employed the designation "incorruptible" in respect to the human body of Jesus of Nazareth; it is also in this period that the polemical moniker "Aparthatodocetics," derived from the Greek term for "incorruptible," may first be found (nevertheless, only in the title of a writing of the grammatician John of Caesarea as of yet evading precise dating[116]), which is also still used today within the field for this orientation. The play upon the earlier designation "docetics" (individuals who only accorded Christ an "apparent" incarnation) was obviously intended in this term's coinage: Such individuals who ascribed Christ a particular, incorruptible body, denied as much as the "docetics" (at the least in the eyes of their opponents) the truth of the assumption of flesh in a human body. A comprehensive portrayal of the contexts of this theological avenue of thought and those who propounded or contested it in the sixth century can hardly be recounted here.[117] A terse overview of the positions in the context of the clashes of the time over the relationship between divinity and humanity in Jesus Christ will serve for the present purposes: *On the one hand*, there were theologians who believed on the basis of the decisions in doctrine of the Council of Chalcedon that they were to distinguish the body of Jesus as "incorruptible." These become tangible in a polemic against this ruling which was composed by *Leontius of Byzantium*, who originally hailed from so-called Origenistic monastic circles in the Holy Land, in roughly AD 535/536.[118] Leontius claims that the pertinent theologians were of the opinion that while Christ assumed a "somewhat corruptible" (φθαρτόν) example from Mary during the incarnation, it was immediately metamorphosed into a state of "incorruptibility" (ἀφθαρσία).[119] In other words, the divine Logos assumed a corruptible body and transformed it at the very moment of assumption into one incorruptible—and, indeed, through the act of assumption within a unity of divinity and humanity. Evidently this group did not thereby deny that Jesus of Nazareth truly suffered bodily on the cross, but rather merely supposed that the divine Logos would first have to permit explicitly such a torment upon the, in fact, incorruptible body: "It is not on grounds of nature . . . that we say that the body is free of suffering and incorruptible, but rather because of the unification with the God-Logos."[120] In other words, when the Logos was unwilling, then the body would not partake of any of the physical alterations, corruption, or destruction which might befall it. As to how many individuals propounded such a theology as here described is, nevertheless, indiscernible from the remarks of Leontius. A more defined profile may, *on the other hand*, be won of a second group of individuals who maintained stances comparable in content, but rather positioned themselves critically against the theology of the Council of Chalcedon. They were represented most prominently by Bishop *Julian of Halicarnassus* in Asia Minor, who lived during the first quarter of the sixth century, and to whom individuals had recourse as late as the eighth century.[121] As his writings are lost, his views can only be reconstructed from fragments preserved in the corpus of the former patriarch *Severus of Antioch*—this strident polemicist against the theology of the Council of Chalcedon initially lived as a monk in Gaza before he was named in AD 512 as the first miaphysite patriarch in the aforementioned Syrian metropole, leaving for Egyptian exile some six years later, where he died two decades later.[122] Controversy between Julian and Severus already presented itself in AD 510 as they encountered one another in Constantinople, but first truly broke in AD 520, in Egypt, to which they had both fled. While both were avowed opponents of the theology of the Council of Chalcedon, they elected not to unite on the question of the incorruptibility of the human body of Jesus prior to the resurrection, and their spat split the miaphysitically oriented anti-Chalcedonian movement. The clashes, which embraced multiple levels and writings, need not here be described in any detail; that the position may have been presaged in the writings of Cyril of Alexandria and Severus himself (to whom Julian has recourse) is also hardly of pertinence to the present context.[123] From the testimony of the fragments, Julian's stance corresponds in content to a great extent to the view of those opponents battled by Leontius; Christ is certainly, following humanity, "consubstantial" (ὁμοούσιος) with the remainder of humans but, this notwithstanding, he is incapable of suffering on grounds of the hypostatic union of divinity and humanity. He must first willingly render his consent in order for his body to suffer, so that the inherently incorruptible body might be corrupted in death on the cross (physically, but not morally). In a second edition of a didactic missal, he formulates these connections accordingly:

> We do not require the expression "consubstantial with us" on grounds of the fact that he (Christ) was fashioned like a conventional, necessarily passible substance, but rather on account of the fact that he is from the same substance (as us), so that, even if he is impassible, even if he is incorporeal, he is consubstantial with us due to the fact that he is of the same nature as us: Not, namely, because he himself suffered freely, we suffering without conscious assent, is he thus of a different nature (to us).[124]

Following Julian, evidence for the incorruptibility of the human body of Christ is the reality that "he suffered for others of his own free will."[125] As he specified the "corruptibility" of the body (that is, every form of physical alteration of the body), so that a body is subject to the rule of sin and hence morally corrupted, he notes accordingly of his opponents, "They assume that he was mortal before the resurrection; then they should also posit that he was in sin."[126] "Incorruptibility" hence also means that the necessity born of sin of experiencing detrimental physical or psychic states, and of morally decaying, is not applicable to Christ in the same manner. In the emphasis of the categorical impeccability of Jesus, Julian was in agreement with all critics; in the identification of impeccancy and incorruptibility, he markedly differed from many contemporaries. The energetic criticism of Severus of Antioch regarding these remarks from Julian of Halicarnassus, which he held to be a mere recapitulation of the position of the Constantinopolitan monk Eutyches[127] prior to the Council of Chalcedon,[128] would nevertheless hardly prove to spell the end of the attractiveness of this position, which, as has been noted, was championed not only by the Council of Chalcedon's proponents, but also by its critics, within the notoriously quarrelling Christianity of the eastern half of the Imperium. The degree to which, in fact, this position remained appealing may be witnessed in the account (disputed in respect to its historicity) of Emperor Justinian (AD 527–565) turning to this idea near the end of his life: Accordingly, the information may be found in the ecclesiastical history of Evagrius the Scholiast, the last ecclesiastical historian of Late Antiquity to write in Greek, born in the reign of the aforementioned suzerain, that Justinian was in his final year a convert to "Aphthartodocetism," and supported this in an edict. Friedrich Loofs has labeled this alleged conversion of the emperor in quotation marks as "heresy" ("Ketzerei") and viewed this as being in "the vein of Cyrillic-Chalcedonian orthodoxy as he understood it" ("Bahnen cyrillisch-chalcedonensischer Orthodoxie, wie er sie verstand"); Karl Heinz Utheman characterized the edict as an "unsolved puzzle."[129] Evagrius writes of the emperor:

> Justinian issued what is called by the Romans an edict, in which he described the body of Christ as incorruptible and not susceptible to the natural and blameless passions, thus stating that the Lord ate before the Passion just as He ate after the resurrection, and that from the time of its formation in the womb His all-holy body did not experience any change or variation in respect to the voluntary and natural passions, not even after its resurrection.[130]

Although this edict is mentioned in additional sources, its original wording is lost.[131] The pursuit of an answer to the highly contested question of what exactly the emperor really thought, and likely sought thereby to reorganize through this edict to the bishops of the realm, need not be undertaken in the present context as, irrespective of a possible imperial intervention, the controversy described on "incorruptibility" during the sixth century developed into a consensus that the earthly body of Jesus of Nazareth was just as ephemeral as any other terrestrial body prior to his resurrection. Should the information preserved be correct, Justinian himself evidently wished to integrate into his ecclesiastical politics, otherwise at pains to reflect the consensus, those theologians who wished to assert the particularity of this earthly body in contrast to those other human bodies characterized by sin.[132] Yet, even resolute opponents of the Council of Chalcedon saw in such a doctrine the unrelinquishable avowal of the true humanity of Jesus of Nazareth as no longer being preserved. Therewith also vanished the notion (already generally discarded from the theory of God) of an incorruptible, divine body of a special materiality from christological teaching, and thereby essentially from Christian theology as a whole.

At this present juncture, the chronological survey via selected debates over the character of the corporeality of Jesus might be brought to a close, inasmuch as in the theology informed by the Council of Chalcedon and the anti-Chalcedonian theology alike, it was henceforth clearly maintained that "incarnation" is, in fact, not the assumption of a somehow "divine" body, but rather the assumption of humanity of an inherently bodiless God in another example of himself, that is, in a whole and entirely human body.

Yet, how might it be that it came to such a protracted debate over the reality of the body of a human who had doubtless existed in a particular time and place like any other human being? In order to answer this question, the canonized Scriptures of the Christian Bible must be examined, in particular the Gospels.

The Corporeality of Jesus Christ in the Canonized Gospels

In the present context, it does not suffice in the reconstruction of the history of this problem to offer merely an Imperial-era history of the tradition of the so-called "christological sovereign titles" and "formulae and hymns"[133] bestowed upon or associated with Jesus of Nazareth such as "Son of David," "Servant of God," "Jesus, the Prophet," "Son of Man," and "Messiah" (or, in the Greek language, "Christ"), as Grillmeier did in his comprehensive standard work on antique Christian teaching under the heading of "The Biblical Points of Departure of Patristic Christology." Rather, one must inspect those stories within the canonized Gospels within which the human body of Jesus is relevant in a certain sense to the narrative of the particular account in question.[134] Accordingly, two manners of relevance may already be distinguished between within the canonical texts:

There are, *on the one hand*, accounts in which the body of Jesus is capable of "more" than the bodies of his disciples—and this difference between two human bodilinesses is for the most part not recounted somewhat in and of itself within the Christian Bible, but rather employed to signal to readers that Jesus himself is "more" than his disciples. In the Gospel of Mark, probably the oldest surviving Gospel, the story of a boat journey on the "Sea of Galilee," the Lake of Gennesaret, a classic miracle of salvation is related:[135]

> And there arose a great storm of wind, and the waves beat into the ship, so that it was now full. And he was in the hinder part of the ship, asleep on a pillow: and they awake him, and say unto him, "Master, carest thou not that we perish?" And he arose, and rebuked the wind, and said unto the sea, Peace, be still. And the wind ceased, and there was a great calm. And he said unto them, "Why are ye so fearful? how is it that ye have no faith?" And they feared exceedingly, and said one to another, "What manner of man is this, that even the wind and the sea obey him?" (Mark 4:37–41)[136]

In this narrative, the description of the slumbering body of Jesus is undertaken for a particular reason; it serves to illustrate a biblical verse hailing from the Psalms: "It is vain for you to rise up early, to sit up late, to eat the bread of sorrows: for so he giveth his beloved sleep" (Psalm 127/126:2). Jesus is this beloved who is granted sleep in situations of extreme peril which others who arose early and awoke are unable to receive. He is thus "more than Jonah" (Matthew 12:41//Luke 11:32), as Jonah also slept deeply and securely in a ship (Jonah 1:5). In contrast to him, however,

Jesus is able himself to soothe the storm. In the moment, in which the disciples are full of fear and definitively unable to sleep, Jesus demonstrates power and sovereignty, inasmuch as he slumbers, should the scene be read from its conclusion according to the report of the oldest canonized gospel. Phrased otherwise, as a sleeper, he does not form part of the anxious and powerless group of disciples in their boat, but rather part of the group of those chosen and beloved by God of whom the Psalms spoke. The focus of the author thus essentially did not lie initially in the body of Jesus, but this is rather a stylistic element in order to state something as to the entire person (and not only regarding his body).[137] At the same time, however, it becomes evident that the particularity of Jesus is depicted in the corporeal performances—he is so serene that he can also find peace in the most turbulent situations and sleep.

Naturally, there are many further examples within the canonized Gospels for the exceptionality of the human body of Jesus which here might be discussed—reports of wonders wherein not only are demons expelled by the fingers of Jesus but also God's sovereignty becomes reality,[138] or the so-called words of institution of the Last Supper, according to which Jesus of Nazareth expressly assigns a salvific meaning to his own blood and body. The difference between the human body of Jesus of Nazareth and the bodies of other individuals is perhaps most tangible in the account of the "transformation" of Jesus on a mountain in Galilee localized since Late Antiquity at Mount Tabor, and conventionally termed in the Anglophone sphere as "transfiguration." Here, in contrast to the aforementioned story, the focus is genuinely upon the human body of Jesus Christ and its categorical singularity. Here, the key sentence relevant to understanding this may be found directly at the outset of the narrative as recounted in the Gospel of Mark:

> And (sc. Jesus) was transfigured before them (i.e., Peter, James, and John): and his face did shine as the sun, and his raiment was white as the light. (Matthew 17:2)[139]

While in the parallel synoptic version in the Gospel of Luke, the transformation of the face as the most important part of the human body is mentioned, albeit not discussed in any more depth ("And as he prayed, the fashion of his countenance was altered, and his raiment was white and glistering," Luke 9:29),[140] the Gospel of Matthew illustrates the process of the metamorphosis with the six words "like the sun" and "like the light" (ὡς ὁ ἥλιος [. . .] ὡς τὸ φῶς). The visage of Jesus thereby assumes a form associated with divine corporeality during Antiquity, as has already been witnessed within a passage from the Pseudo-Clementines. Therein,

310   *God's Body*

it is stated that "He is incomparably more brilliant in His body than the visual spirit which is in us, and He is more splendid than everything, so that in comparison with Him the light of the sun may be reckoned as darkness."[141] Yet, in the Judaism of the time of the Second Temple and the High Imperial era, there were also traditions according to which Adam's face before the fall or after his eschatological restoration shined like the sun: David H. Aaron has collected many Jewish texts which document as to how widespread this conception was (in addition to the apocalyptic literature, particularly in the Midrashim Leviticus Rabba, Qohelet Rabba, and Mishle).[142]

In light of this, the conceptions from the Epistle to the Colossians mentioned at the beginning of this chapter come across as a theological reflection upon the transfiguration: The changes of the face into a form which refers simultaneously both to the first human as he was originally intended and to God himself renders it apparent that Christ as the Word of God was the image after which humanity was fashioned in the first human: In transfigured form, he, Jesus Christ, is even more recognizable than otherwise as "the image of the invisible God" (Colossians 1:15a).[143] As also formulated by Philo of Alexandria, the remaining individuals in the scene are only an "image of the image" (εἰκὼν εἰκόνος). The actual image is the Word of God, the Logos (ὁ λόγος); humans were fashioned as the image and likeness of this image, as the "image of the image":

> Now if even the part is image of an image, it is plain that this is also the case for the whole. But if this entire sense-perceptible cosmos, which is greater than the human image, is a representation of the divine image, it is plain that the archetypal seal, which we affirm to be the intelligible cosmos, would itself be the model and archetypal idea of the ideas, the Logos of God.[144]

It is often rendered that in the Christian form of the so-called Logos theology, the history of which in Christianity begins with the prologue of the fourth gospel, the identification of the originally apersonal Stoic world-intellect with the spirit of the God of the Greek Bible within Hellenistic Judaism is taken a step further, inasmuch as a carpenter's son from Galilee becomes a part of this identificatory chain. Decisive in this, however, is that this always concerns the concrete earthly bodiliness of a human: "And the Word was made flesh, and dwelt among us, (and we beheld his glory, the glory as of the only begotten of the Father,) full of grace and truth" (John 1:14).[145] The sentence from the Epistle to the Colossians should be understood in light of this context, according to which Christ is the "image of the invisible God, the firstborn of every creature," as Helmut

Merklein has demonstrated:[146] According to the author of the Letter to the Colossians, the invisible God becomes apparent in a concrete, historical person, who lived as a human with a human body, was crucified, and was resurrected from the dead. The narrative of the transfiguration of Jesus from the canonized Gospels even goes a step further: In the transformed (or, indeed, transfigured) face of the savior, the metamorphosed visage of the invisible God might be sighted. Simultaneously, in the transfiguration, it becomes evident how the marred likeness of the first human can and should be restituted.

On the other hand, there are also accounts in the Gospels in which the body of Jesus is definitively not "more" than the bodies of his disciples. In these texts, the body then appears rather as a mere ornamental or inconsequential detail within statements as to the relevance of Jesus for the divine salvation history. Particularly notable as examples of the so-called "passion narrative" of the canonized Gospels, for instance, is the story of the sojourn of Jesus in a garden "which was named Gethsemane" (Mark 14:32).[147] Here might be read a sentence formulated by the author of the Gospel expressing his despair and fear in a moving manner, who does not find the sympathy in the companionship of his followers for which he had hoped: "And (sc. Christ) saith unto them (sc. his disciples), 'My soul is exceeding sorrowful unto death: tarry ye here, and watch.'" (Mark 14:34). In turmoil, the conflicted Jesus prays to his father: "And he said, 'Abba, Father, all things are possible unto thee; take away this cup from me: nevertheless not what I will, but what thou wilt.'" (Mark 14:36). Clearly, in the composition of this passage, the body of Jesus himself was of no particular interest to the author: Corporeal intimations of fear and dismay are scarcely expressed, with the exception of the phrase in which he "began to be sore amazed, and to be very heavy" (Mark 14:33)[148]—a description relativized once more by means of the sentence: "The spirit truly is ready, but the flesh is weak" (Mark 14:38). This tendency is continued in the portrayal of the crucifixion—the fourfold depiction of a crucifixion in the Gospels is the most detailed description of this mode of execution known from Antiquity, but this is quite evidently told without any interest in the bloody details of this extremely gruesome and degrading form of executing one sentenced to death.[149] This becomes apparent from a comparison: The Jewish historian Flavius Josephus reports upon a Jewish prophet named Jesus, son of Ananias.[150] Shortly before the outbreak of the Jewish War, the latter announced again and again the looming destruction of the Temple in Jerusalem. Due to these threats against the Temple, the cultic center of the Jewish religion, he was incarcerated (exactly as his namesake Jesus bar Joseph of Nazareth) by the High Council, the Sanhedrin, interrogated, and delivered to the Roman procurator Albinus. The latter sentenced

Jesus the prophet to flogging and let him free after the scourging. Josephus described the scourging far more brutally and in greater detail than the authors of the Gospels: Jesus bar Ananias was brought before the Roman procurator, and

> there, although flayed to the bone with scourges, he (sc. Jesus bar Ananias) neither sued for mercy nor shed a tear, but, merely introducing the most mournful of variations into his ejaculation, responded to each stroke with "Woe to Jerusalem!"[151]

Moreover, from both the only demonstrable archaeological remains of a crucifixion from Antiquity, a calcaneal bone of a crucified man pierced by a long formidable nail excavated by Vasilis Tsaferis in the Jesusalem quarter of Giv'at ha-Mivtar in 1968,[152] and an anatomical reconstruction of the conditions of death on a cross, it might be surmised that the canonical Gospels were in fact somewhat reserved in describing the ceaseless agony of the gradual death by asphyxiation of the human through whose joints nails were driven. Indirect at best is the authors' attempt to render recognizable the sovereignty and power of Jesus and to downplay the indications of despair ("My God, my God, why hast thou forsaken me?" Mark 15:34 with Psalm 22:2).

Yet, it is precisely because the human body of Jesus in the last days and hours of his life can be so little distinguished from other suffering human bodies that it becomes such an indispensable instrument within salvation history and also becomes at this point an image of real, true humanity. This is demonstrated by a hymn from the First Epistle of Peter:

> For even hereunto were ye called: because Christ also suffered for us, leaving us an example, that ye should follow his steps: Who did no sin, neither was guile found in his mouth: Who, when he was reviled, reviled not again; when he suffered, he threatened not; but committed himself to him that judgeth righteously: Who his own self bore our sins in his own body on the tree, that we, being dead to sins, should live unto righteousness: by whose stripes ye were healed. For ye were as sheep going astray; but are now returned unto the Shepherd and Bishop of your souls. (1 Peter 2:21-25)[153]

The body of Jesus is, as is here evidenced by means of a quotation verbatim from the so-called Servant Song of the Prophet Isaiah ("Surely he hath borne our griefs, and carried our sorrows: . . . and with his stripes we are healed"),[154] certainly no insignificant detail within God's salvation history. Formulated otherwise, the incarnated body is most saliently in its form as a *sacrificed* body *the* inalienable instrument of God's salvation for humanity.

Hence, a *corporeal* salvific concept in some of the texts of the canonized New Testament may be readily discussed, which (regarded from the vantage point of Imperial-era and late antique theological reflection) is one of the grounds for antique Christians to profess Jesus of Nazareth to be simultaneously a divine and a human entity. One example of such a corporeal salvific concept is that well into Late Antiquity, in complete continuation of Jewish theologumena, repeated mention was made of the redemptive function of the blood of Jesus Christ—Karlmann Beyschlag had already drawn attention to this now frequently overlooked line of tradition within Christian theological history some time ago.[155] Even if the idea of an incarnation of God in a preferred human body evidently served as an impetus for many individuals, the acceptance of this identification with the person of Jesus of Nazareth would aid in the interpretation of the suffering and death of Jesus according to the model of the voluntary vicarious death for society, as may be observed for Judaism not only in the example of the Servant Song of Isaiah, but also in the interpretation of the so-called Maccabean martyrs;[156] admittedly, it is unnecessary to discuss these comparatively oft-studied contexts here in any real detail, as they are only rather tangentially connected to the present question regarding the divine body.

The Creed of Agathonius of Tarsus

At the outset, it was asked as to whether the Christian idea according to which, in the case of Jesus, the divine body is not composed of a particular materiality appropriate to the divinity of God, but rather is more or less *completely* identical to a human body, was perhaps actually the Christian contribution to the debate over the divine body in Antiquity. At the end of the present paradigmatic survey of various antique Christian texts within which the body of Jesus of Nazareth was an object of reflection, a curt and unambiguous answer to this question is something of a galling prospect. Indeed, on the one hand, it has been seen that by no means all Christians in Antiquity assumed Christ to possess such a real human body. Those who did, in turn, tended to imagine it in wildly varying manners, marking at divergent points differences of this special human body of Jesus Christ to conventional human bodies. Inferences on the body of God from the body of Jesus Christ were not undertaken in Christian Antiquity, although the notion of the likeness to God certainly played a marked role. In the controversy over the so-called anthropomorphites, treated thoroughly in the previous chapter, Christian theologians even even explicitly warned against associating the human body of Jesus Christ and his divine nature.

An impressive example for this is an alleged avowal made by an otherwise unknown bishop named *Agathonicus of Tarsus* at a synod in Ancyra/Ankara at some point at the beginning of the fifth century against the so-called anthropomorphites; this is preserved with other alleged writings of the bishop in a Sahidic Coptic dossier. Moreover, texts exist in the Fayumic dialect and a further Sahidic transmission from the White Monastery at Sohag.[157] This dossier with the writings of the alleged Agathonicus may be found in a papyrus-codex probably hailing from the monastic library at Thebes which once belonged to the collection of Thomas Philipps (Philipps 18833) and is now preserved in the Bodmer Papyrus Collection in Geneva.[158] Admittedly, much recommends the notion that these writings consist of pseudepigraphic fragments from the quill of an Egyptian monk, as, according to all that is known, no bishop called Agathonicus of Tarsus ever exited in Late Antiquity—his invention would have served to legitimate a certain position within a conflict within Egypt by means of the authority of an Anatolian bishop.[159] In the synodical affirmation purportedly professed (*Fides Agathonici*), it is stated:

> We believe in God, that He was the Creator of all things beneath heaven and those above heaven of which Solomon spoke,[160] that he consists of a complete, unrecognisable, and ineffable substance (οὐσία), that (sc. the substance) does not consist of the matter from which He created all things. And whosoever compares the substance of the godhead in his heart and erects in his heart a form, saying thereby: "God is in this form," and (thereby) maligns the godhead—it is the ruler of darkness who sketches these squalid substances in the hearts of the unknowing by lying to them that the godhead is in this form, and they serve unbeknownst idols. It is right to think of the body which Christ bore with integrity. Yet, the godhead which united itself with the flesh, it is ineffable. The body is called Christ, for the meaning of "Christ" is "the anointed one." You (also may) not think of it (sc. the godhead) in any manner of shape, so that you might avoid error. For, we believe in the Son, that He is the Word of the Father, and the Holy Ghost, that it is His breath, and we believe in the Trinity of equal beings, that it is bodiless, without beginning and without end.[161]

Despite the absence of the key christological term "one single nature" (μία φύσις), the avowal is nevertheless bound to the Alexandrian model of not imagining Christ as an inherently differentiated unity of two entirely divine and entirely human entities respectively, but rather, very much in the tradition of Apollonaris of Laodicea, as being a tight unity of a human body and a divine soul. Nevertheless, a differentiation is made between the two in the text:

> And the word of the Father manifested itself in the Virgin as impassible. Yet, He became passible of His own will, not by means of powerlessness. He died of His own will, and He rose from the dead on the third day. He took the flesh with Him into heaven; it comes also with him to bring order, and will order everything. This (flesh) is that which combines on the table with the bread, when it is blessed, as Paul stated. And it is also His blood which combines with the (wine) chalice, after this becomes blood when the priest announces aloud: "Body and blood of Christ."[162]

Although, like the official Alexandrian theology prior to the Council of Chalcedon (AD 451), the text is at pains to emphasize the personal *unity* of Jesus Christ, certain elements are simultaneously adopted which belong rather within a tradition of a distinction between human and divine portions within Jesus Christ; Alois Grillmeier would be correct in tracing these elements back to the tradition of Origen and to seek the one or more individuals who forged this text in the circles of Origenistically inclined monks who turned against their "anthropomorphite" brothers in faith.[163] Indeed, such a polemic avowal of the division between the human body, on the one hand, and the divinity of Jesus Christ, on the other, as might be found in the alleged creed of Bishop Agathonicus of Tarsus, might only be explained by inferring monks from the groups of so-called anthropomorphites who identified the transfigured body of Jesus Christ with the body of the godhead, or understood this specific body of Jesus Christ as being a part of the body of the Trinitary divinity.[164] In contrast, the anonymous author emphasizes that God in his creative almightiness can assume different forms at whim:

> God assumes the likeness of a human; He also accords his likes (to humans) to any form He wills; that is: Every form He wishes to assume, He assumes. For humans, who are fashioned in certain forms, are incapable of exchanging these; they have their nature within which they are fashioned, namely form. God, by contrast, possessing no creator, assumes thus whatever figure is His fancy. He manifested Himself before Abraham in the form of a human, for it is written "And he lift up his eyes and looked, and, lo, three men stood by him." He manifested Himself to Moses in that he was a flame. He manifested Himself to Paul, in that he was a light more luminous than the rays of the sun. . . . These examples should suffice to compel prudent listeners not to confine the divinity

within a small, weak substance, in the manner of humans, (a substance)
which from its miserableness changes nothing.[165]

At this point, the present journey through the various manners by which
the body of Jesus Christ might be reflected upon may come to a close;
naturally it would be rewarding to dwell further upon the different traditions which associate particularly closely the human body of Jesus Christ
with his godhead and, in addition to theological teachings, to take also
into account, for example, the pictoral depictions of the vera icon, the
authentic image of Christ, and antique debates over how this image was
to be revered.[166] Yet, this notwithstanding, it has become apparent how
markedly the forms of Christian reflection on a human body of God may
be distinguished from the Jewish and pagan discourse of the time, and how
much uncertainty these attempts to describe this body betray.

The Divine Body of Jesus Christ and the Human Body

As something of an appendix to the investigations as to various conceptions of divine bodies in Antiquity, a glance might once more be made at
the close of this present chapter as to how much such notions also influenced the daily lives of followers of Christ who believed in a human incarnation of God. Accompanying the particular meaning of the human body
of Jesus would be a process by which the general model of an "emulation"
recalling Jesus of Nazareth in the testimony of the canonized Gospels
would become a model of mimetic conformity, a model of the "imitation
of Christ" (*imitatio Christi*) concretized and thereby, at once, radicalized.
Such a radical alignment of the Christian body and the body of Christ
formed the core motif of Christian life for individual groups and particular texts—and demonstrates once more the marked significance of the
different notions of the body of the divine human Jesus Christ in antique
Christendom.

The radicality with which Christians lived according to the maxim
of transforming their bodies after the model of the human body of Jesus
Christ or, indeed, having them transformed, could already be illustrated by
means of the example of the canonized letters of the Apostle Paul. Yet, far
more exciting is the analysis of the transformation of pertinent statements
from these apostolic epistles in the correspondence ascribed in its first version to the Antiochian bishop *Ignatius* and conventionally dated to AD 115
(admittedly, as has been seen, later editions exist: The dating of this foundational version is equally controversial).[167] The author dubs his readership "imitators" or "mimics" of God (μιμηταὶ ὄντες θεοῦ).[168] Indeed, he
claims further that mimetic conformity with the suffering Christ can only

be attained by means of one's own martyrdom; only so may the presence as a disciple of Christ be fulfilled.[169] In other words, the author argues that only the martyr, whose body is abused just as much as that of Christ, and who is brought to death precisely as Christ, can be the consummate imitator and perfect player of Christ.[170] The content of the text reflects the historical situation he seeks to describe: Ignatius, who as a Roman citizen is on the way from Antiochia to Rome for his trial, wishes from Asia Minor to have sent in advance of him a notice to the Christian communities in Rome in which he has frantically pled to be left to suffer until the bitter end, as only then may the congruence with Christ be attained on earth. The author manifestly conceives of this with recourse to the Pauline idea that one can only become part of the heavenly glory of Christ by means of the path of vicarious suffering: "Allow me to be an imitator of the suffering of my God."[171]

Intended accordingly is the letter to the parish of the city of Rome sent ahead by Ignatius to the community, it being his final destination; it is simultaneously a warning not to undertake anything which might hinder the protagonist's martyrdom. Such admonitions riddle the entire letter:

> For I will have no other such opportunity to attain to God, nor can you be enlisted for a better work—if, that is, you keep silent. For if you keep silent about me, I will be a word of God; but if you desire my flesh, I will once again be a mere noise. . . . I urge you, do not become an untimely kindness to me. Allow me to be bread for the wild beasts; through them I am able to attain to God. I am the wheat of God and am ground by the teeth of the wild beasts, that I may be found to be the pure bread of Christ. . . . Fire and cross and packs of wild beasts, cuttings and being torn apart, the scattering of bones, the mangling of limbs, the grinding of the whole body, the evil torments of the devil—let them come upon me, only that I may attain to Jesus Christ.[172]

The author desires no longer to "live like a human" (κατὰ ἀνθρώπους ζῆν),[173] but rather wishes to learn to "live according to Christianity" (κατὰ Χριστιανισμὸν ζῆν)[174]—the term "Christianity" (Χριστιανισμός) famously appears for the first time in antique writings.[175] For the author of the letters, living "according to Christianity" means the complete abolition of the earthly body and the desire for all possible manners of destroying his body in the arena.

A discussion both extensive and erudite exists regarding the question as to whether the passionate longing of Ignatius after martyrdom is the individual quest for meaning of a Christian on the way towards his own execution and anticipating his own death, or as to whether such a Christian form of yearning for martyrdom is a specific form of suicide.[176] Yet, this discourse on the so-called voluntary (or voluntarily provoked)[177] martyrdom is not of any particular relevance to the present context, especially considering that it first appears at all in the third century.[178] Ignatius did not exhort the Christian parishes in Asia Minor with which he communicated by letter to emulate him in commiting collective suicide. First, late antique Christian authors criticized the explicit longing for martyrdom as something of a concealed form of mere suicide, which was prohibited to followers of Christ according to the doctrine of the mainstream antique church.

Besides the example of Ignatius, under whose name a mimetically construed identification of his own mortal body with the mortal body of Jesus Christ was propagated, there were also other ways by means of which a conformity might be accentuated between Christ and a suffering martyr, the defeat of whom was celebrated by the Christian community with great rhetorical and theological effort so as to reinterpret it as a victory. Here of particular interest is the account from the Christian parish of Smyrna/İzmir of the martyrdom of the Bishop Polycarp. Polycarp of Smyrna also appears as a correspondent in the corpus of the letters of Ignatius, according to which the report of his martyrdom, probably to be dated to AD 155/156,[179] is readily taken to be authentic, although the most-employed version hails from liturgical sources of the seventh and eighth centuries AD and was probably reworked for the purposes of liturgical reading.[180] Yet, the earliest accessible version of the report is a terse and abbreviated quotation in the "Ecclesiastical History" of Bishop Eusebius of Caesarea at the beginning of the fourth century: As Eusebius had also edited his sources before he inserted them into his work of history, the foundational text of the Martyrdom of Polycarp must be considered lost. Quite obviously, the description of the execution of the geriatric Polycarp already belonged to the original text: According to the narrative, the body of the bishop, who had reached eighty-six years of age and was hence on grounds of both age and personality effectively the leader of the Christian communities in Asia Minor, was not devoured by the fire which should burn him to death as he was bound to a stake. As if a miracle, a wind kept the flames distant from the condemned bishop. This narrative from Polycarp's martyrdom naturally need not be taken as a report of historical events, being rather highly artificially construed in nature and referencing the account of the martyrdom of three young men in the furnace of the Greek version of the Book of Daniel:[181]

> For the fire, taking on the appearance of a vaulted room, like a boat's sail filled with the wind, formed a wall around the martyr's body. And he was in the center, not like burning flesh but like baking bread or like gold and

silver being refined in a furnace. And we perceived a particularly sweet aroma, like wafting incense or some other precious perfume.[182]

Ernst Lohmeyer and others have demonstrated that fine fragrances (εὐωδία and ὀσμή) are symbols of divine presence,[183] precisely as the indestructibility (ἀφθαρσία) of the body is a divine attribute. The terrestrial body of the martyr thus becomes part of a divine, immortal, special corporeality, that which humans once possessed as the likeness to God but lost in paradise and now may redeem. The concept of a divine body and divine corporeality also had manifold consequences in daily life among antique Christians. For the author of the letters of Ignatius, martyrdom alters in the most terrible manner—the form of the deeply harrowing story of the passion of Christ—a human body into a divine body in imitation of Christ, the image of God. The report of the martyrdom of Polycarp questions this position of a strict proximity between the body of the martyr and the divine body of Christ, as here the human body is not horrifically destroyed in the sequence of Christ's torments, but rather preserved in the midst of all suffering and attributed divine features.

Conclusion

The significance of these conceptions as to the human body of the divine human Jesus Christ is usually neglected because, as has been seen, from Antiquity onwards, there were considerable difficulties bound with every anthropomorphic conception of God, in pagan philosophical traditions, but also in Jewish and Christian literature from the postbiblical period onwards. The notion of a human body of God is perhaps the most potent form by means of which the antique imagination of a divine body survived the strident religious and philosophical criticism of this divine image, and, moreover, perhaps the most radical manner in which the originally Jewish idea that humanity was fashioned in the likeness of God continued to be entertained: The divine body is exactly the human body—and vice versa.

Conclusion

Settled Conceptions of God?

In studying the various notions of a divine body, a detail settled today of the divine image of unenlightened forebears is not the subject of scrutiny, but rather a broad stream of Judeo-Christian and pagan tradition: Statements as to the corporeality of God inform practically every page of the Judeo-Christian Bible and accordingly are the shared heritage of Judaism and Christianity until the present day, albeit these traditions have been ever more marginalized and dismissed as naïve.[1] It has been seen that these cannot all be interpreted as simple anthropomorphic concepts; according to these biblical traditions, bodiliness—as is already demonstrated for the notion characteristic to Christianity that God became man in the person of Jesus of Nazareth—is, in a very conscious sense, the end of the works of God.[2] The insight that bodiliness does not only stand at the end of God's works, but also reveals something fundamental about the God discussed in the Jewish and Christian traditions is then inevitable, should these biblical pronouncements be taken seriously. Phrased otherwise, the God witnessed within the biblical Scripture cannot be reduced without substantial loss to a bodiless, absolutely transcendental being in the tradition of a biblical interpretation informed by Platonic philosophy and conventional since Antiquity.

Following Marco Frenschkowski, three forms of discourse on the corporeality of God may be discerned within the Judeo-Christian and pagan-religious traditions alike: *First*, an "'epiphanial' discourse (How can the gods appear? To this belongs also the traditions as to the meals of the gods, etc.)"; *second*, a "cosmic (the cosmos as body of the divinity), which is not necessarily to be understood as pantheistic"; and, *third*, a "monarchic throne room metaphor, as the escalation of which the famed 'Shi'ur Qomah' texts are to be understood, and which is naturally not only attested within Judaism, and additionally 'inherently' is accompanied by a range of other visualizations of the gods."[3] Most prominently, the first and third forms have been treated in detail in this work; the second has only been alluded to in this study. Nevertheless, the image is insofar complete as it has become clear that such notions were completely self-evident and to be encountered in intellectuals and the unlettered alike within pagan, Jewish, and Christian Antiquity—very much in contrast to the Middle Ages and Early Modern era.

Nevertheless, it might also hardly be contested that the notion of the corporeality of God within the biblical texts (and, indeed, not only in these) forms a part of a *mythical worldview*.[4] Regardless of how the irksome academic term "myth" might be defined, it is characteristic of it that all (naturally also the world of the gods and also this present world) is understood to be a unity of the material and spiritual.[5] Moreover, myth is insofar fundamentally transgressive as, much like the dimensions in the "Shiʻur Qomah" texts,[6] it crosses all conceivable borders of time and space. When, by means of such principles of construction, traditional meaningful divine narratives are recounted which seek as stories of origins and central events and transformations alike to explain the present, then, in all attempts to demarcate a boundary between gods and humans, such lines swiftly become blurred: Gods act like humans and they act with a body, as humans act with a body.

In the past few decades, it has become ever more apparent that such a mythological worldview may, regardless, hardly be described by means of a neat dual as the clearly defined alternative to rational thought (for example, with terms such as "jejune" or "prerational"), should, in fact, the results of rational evaluations of God, world, and humans be presented, alongside, incidentally, scarce-considered common-sense and immanent daily experiences.[7] At this juncture, it must only be recognized that such a "rationality" of myth reflected *contemporaneous* standards of reason, merely accepted in part in later epochs. The recent insight that the remains of a mythological divine image are concurrently preserved in the biblical conception of a divine corporeality has admittedly heightened once more the problematic of the hiatus between the historical record and contemporary notions of God for religious thought: The scholar of the New Testament *Rudolf Bultmann* (1884–1976) not only maintained in a famous lecture under particular historical circumstances in April 1941 that the "worldview of the New Testament . . . is a mythic one" (incidentally without recourse to the notion of divine corporeality),[8] but also indicated that it would be impossible to "repristinate the mythic worldview," even if therein "truths are discovered once more which were lost in the Enlightenment."[9] Pointed sentences which let fly a heated debate: "No adult imagines God as a being present above in heaven; indeed, 'heaven' in the old sense no longer exists for us."[10] In the manner of a cantus firmus, the word "settled" (*erledigt*) recurs throughout the first half of Bultmann's lecture.[11] For this Marburg scholar, among those conceptions which have been settled also numbers the Platonically rooted notion of a God to be conceived of as purely immaterial who acts within a world both shaped and contingent upon "natural bodiliness": "Humans who understand themselves purely biologically do not appreciate that a supernatural something, πνεῦμα, might permeate and be active within the dense fabric of the natural forces at all."[12] From this position (as from the very being of myth itself) follows for Bultmann the task of "demythologizing" theological discourse.[13] Already in a 1925 portrayal of the thought of Luther and Kierkegaard interpreted as existential, he had formulated the central statement of this: "Should one wish to speak of God, one must evidently *speak of oneself.*"[14] Against such a backdrop, statements on divine corporeality do, indeed, come off as "settled," as they do not respect modern consensus on logically necessary limits of statements. It might additionally be argued that conceptions of the corporeality of God, in terms of corporeal details, came to a standstill in the pre-Modern era, as *Robert Musil* (1880–1942) stated in his novel "The Man without Qualities" (*Der Mann ohne Eigenschaften*) from 1930/1932:

> God is most deeply unmodern: We are not able to imagine him in a frock, clean-shaven, sporting a parting, but rather do as the patriarchs were wont.[15]

Regardless, in fact, the problem that within religious discourse statements are formulated as to God which only partially correspond to *contemporary* standards of rationality, scarcely affects only the conception of a divine corporeality: This is demonstrated by the heated disputes concerning the polemic of the philosopher *Johann Gottlieb Fichte* (1762–1814) against the notion of a personality and substantiality of God which accompanied the publication of a treatise in 1798, termed the so-called "Atheism Dispute" (*Atheismusstreit*), which the Jena professor brought upon his chair.[16] In this controversy, it became apparent that the arguments against a conception of God's corporeality could also be submitted in opposition to discourse on his *substance* as being a particular substance categorically distinct from all others: Fichte already argued in his initial work which sparked the debate that the term "substance" implies the connection of time, place, and extent, meaning that the conception of God as an independent substance should be dismissed as untenable.[17] God is a manner of liminal term for a moral world order which consequently cannot be appropriately predicated by means of "substance" or, indeed, other related predicates. Fostered by means of such objections, the conception of a God "who cannot state '*I am*,' a God without personality, without existence, who creates nothing and grants nothing" (as the Zurich reformed pastor *Johann Casper Lavater* [1741–1801] noted in a private letter)[18] was not modified by Fichte in his reactions to the controversy, but rather further honed.[19]

The statement that the notion of a divine corporeality is untimely and may be deemed "settled" in view of the present-day rationalist culture serves as a more or less well-grounded philosophical judgment, but, in terms of religious studies, hardly as a description of contemporary religiosity. Conceptions of this manner, in fact, continue into the present day.[20] Thus, the concept of God's corporeality in *Mormonism* represents a key theological theme. Mormons hold for a sin of the traditional Christian churches that, within their conventional beliefs and doctrinal systems, the biblical notion of a corporeality of God was at least watered down, if not, indeed, dismissed in its entirely.[21] *Joseph Smith* (1805–1844) who received, according to Mormon beliefs, the "Book of Mormon" in 1820 by means of an angel, explained in an explicit stand against an allegorical interpretation of the relevant biblical passages that the "Father has a body of flesh and bones as tangible as man's; the Son also; but the Holy Ghost has not a body of flesh and bones, but is a personage of Spirit."[22] This notwithstanding, certain aspects of the body rhetoric of the Hebrew Bible, such as those passages within which God is ascribed wings, are interpreted by Smith as metaphorical discourse. Moreover, his perspective differs from the classical mainstream theology of the Trinity of both Eastern and Western ilk, inasmuch as the Son is clearly subordinate to the Father.[23] Recently, such positions have also come to receive attention within the large mainstream Christian creeds. Accordingly, the American Roman Catholic theologian *Stephen H. Webb* recently suggested entering into a dialogue with individuals propounding this stance, even declaring such a dialogue to be "necessary."[24] Webb reaches this appraisal as he considers the antique Christian attempts to accord God a body to still be a viable form of Christian theology today—he accordingly poses the question as to what might have occurred, were the "anthropomorphites" of Late Antiquity to have triumphed in their struggle.[25] Such an "anthropomorphic" theory of God in the biblical tradition as championed by Mormonism is possible for Webb because, in this manner, recourse might be made once more to certain entirely self-evidently propounded positions of the mainstream church during the epoch prior to the Council of Nicaea at the beginning of the fourth century and the Origenistic clashes marking that century's end. According to Webb's perspective, this not only applies to the marked subordination of the Son beneath the Father, which as a manner of pre-Nicaean form of Christian theology is opposed to the equal standing normalized by the council in Nicaea, but also belongs to the theological tradition (if rejected in Late Antiquity) of the present-day mainstream church.[26]

In brief, Webb terms the theology of the Mormons as a "counterfactual history of post-Nicene developments of pre-Nicene theology"[27] as a realization of a counter-development to the trajectory of mainstream ecclesiastical theological doctrine. Such a process of the pluralization of Roman Catholic theology by means of recourse to marginalized traditions corresponds to the process enacted within the French "Nouvelle Théologie" in the wake of 1945, arraying certain pre-Nicene "Church Fathers" such as Origen against the hegemony of a Neo-Scholastic theology informed by a certain modern reading of the medieval Dominican Thomas Aquinas.[28] Against the backdrop of Roman Catholic dogma's characteristic principle of always formulating in harmony with tradition, no other process by which to pluralize theological concepts is even possible.

Yet, in the course of a prevalent contemporary criticism of Platonic thought (including its transformations) born of reflection upon the Jewish and Christian religions, is it easier said than done to ignore the multifaceted misgivings and heavy censure voiced regarding the notion of the body of God since Antiquity? May, in fact, those who feel compelled to enact such a project of "de-Platonization" within Jewish and Christian theology, completely ignore the insights ultimately produced by the "Platonization" of the theologies of both of these world religions? The Platonic interest (put in simplistic terms) in a categorical difference between earthly corporeality and transcendent immateriality is, indeed, also ultimately to be interpreted as the adoption of biblical notions as to the categorical distinction between God and man, as is, for example, expressed in the First Commandment. An anthropomorphic discourse of divine corporeality is perennially in danger of blurring this distinction and accordingly is deemed by modern Christian theologians such as Bultmann as a "sin."[29] It almost seems as if a corresponding criticism of the Platonization of Christianity in Antiquity, having already been propounded in the late nineteenth and early twentieth centuries by Protestants such as the Berlin historian of dogma *Adolf von Harnack* (1851–1930),[30] is now also in vogue within Roman Catholic theology, as the opinions of Stephen H. Webb demonstrate. Yet, even if the classical Platonic notion of a divine "being," termed moreover "beyond being" or even the "all-transcending" in Neoplatonism,[31] is presently held to be problematic, if not entirely impossible, in the course of general criticism of classical metaphysics, the question still remains as to whether the classical conception of the corporeality of God can at all serve to assert the otherworldliness of God which now categorically belongs to every definition of God.[32]

The monograph here presented does not comprise a systematic contribution to the Christian (or, indeed, Jewish) theory of God,[33] but rather a historical study. Hence, it hardly renders at its close any conclusive answer to the question as to whether the classical conception of the corporeality of God might at all be asserted for the otherworldliness of God which belongs to his definition. In many cases within this work's analysis of text and image alike, it was recognizable that in Judaism and Christianity, but also in pagan philosophical concepts and religious notions, clear traces were visible of attempts to assert also (in Platonic terms) the otherworldliness of this body, for example in the Stoic supposition of a particularly light materiality, or in the Jewish notion of exorbitant and thereby inconceivably large dimensions. Occasionally, a simple, terse statement such as "akin to" is sufficient to express verbally the difference between the terrestrial and transcendent bodies. At no point is to be found within the Judeo-Christian texts dialogue meant genuinely naïvely, for example, regarding the deity's favorite dishes, and nowhere (with the exception of the "Shi'ur Qomah" literature) are any details of clothing, or, indeed, of skin hue or hair color related (with the exception of a later description of the human nature of Christ). Discourse on the body of God is always a discussion of details of the corporeality, a discourse which in its reservations in depiction disclaims to a certain extent the foundational thesis of complete corporeality. This also applies when the question is posed as to which sex actually underpins mention of divine corporeality: When conventionally the image of an enthroned monarch is painted, a male figure is evidently envisioned. Yet, with the striking exception of a passage of the "Shi'ur Qomah" (transmitted in only a single manuscript to wit) which describes the divine genitals,[34] the description of specific male attributes and corporeal details hardly stands at the forefront or is overemphasized. Nevertheless, among the texts examined, nothing may be found seeking to problematize or deny the constriction of these descriptions to the mental image of a man. It must at least be stated that the divine image possesses something of a bias in this respect.[35]

Moreover, one result of this study may be witnessed in the observation that concepts of pure immateriality *without* any materiality have the tendency of being supplemented by the notion of a materiality: It is not only that from the Neoplatonic conception of a celestial body of the soul for the purely immaterial soul, it becomes apparent that those who assume an ascent of a purely immaterially conceived soul from the body presume by necessity spatial and thereby also materially related metaphors (for example, "ascent"), but also that, in a prominent topos of Platonic philosophy, it becomes recognizable that the notion of a pure immateriality cannot be philosophically tolerated without an at least constitutive antitypical reference to materiality.

Thus, both are applicable: Inspection of conceptions of God's corporeality demonstrates "the truth of myth *and* the necessity of demythologization."[36] *The truth of myth* becomes evident insofar as the conception can prevent the transposition of neat dualisms between body and spirit or matter and spirit, between nature and supernature, onto God, and the appreciation of him as a purely immaterial being without consideration of the rational costs of this notion. The rational toll of this transposition consists *first* of the fact that it becomes ineluctable to authorize within God's pure immateriality in an unparalleled manner the hierarchization (in and of itself already problematic) within this dualism (that is, that the immaterial should be of greater worth than the corporeal) by means of the overemphasis of such a pyramid of being. All known negative consequences of such a hierarchization thereby (beginning with aspects of hostility towards the body, scorn of the body, and destruction of the body) may, in actuality, still be kept at bay, but are nevertheless already sanctioned, and potentially authorized. Should, for example, it be sought to think of God as an "all-determining reality"[37] or as "the reason for the possibility of all possibilities," then, within such attempts to express absoluteness and totality categorically distinct from all terrestrial relativity, no particularity may actually be permitted to remain intact, even that in which corporeality is excluded *per definitionem* from the definition of God expressed in such terms. If God is to be understood as the reason for the plethora of all conceivable possibilities, and insofar actually as is formulated by Platonic tradition, exists "beyond being"[38] as that which provides all possibility as the reason for possibility, then the discourse (naturally anachronistic in its literal sense) of his body is an indication that neither the reasons for possibility nor the possibilities exist as purely immaterial structures without material substrate. Indeed, a logical possibility is, moreover, to be distinguished once more inasmuch as it is conceived of as a possibility by an individual, and is realized thereby both as a thought and as the material substrate bound to this thought. Naturally, this capacity for realization of possibility is, in turn, to be distinguished from the actual reality of possibility, but also from the logical possibility of fundamental dismissal.[39] In pure, logical possibility, spirit and matter also form a unit (indeed, as possibility) just as in possibility conceived of as possibility, and then in realized possibility. Different between these two levels of the realization of possibility are only the forms of the materiality; in one case, this comprises the materiality with which every thought is laden, in the other case, of the one specific possibility, for example, for a ham sandwich, the adequate materiality of bread, butter, and ham.

The *necessity of demythologization* is evident in the concept of God's body insofar as the notion of a corporeality of God cannot (as is evidently the case in Mormonism) be identified with discourse of a sheer human corporeality. At the latest since the objections of Feuerbach and Freud,[40] a divine body can no longer be imagined in the manner of a human body; the confusion between man and God coming to expression in such notions had already been defined by the Judeo-Christian Bible as humanity's most classical aberrant stance, as sin. Naturally, considering the peril of misunderstandings and the hardly refutable necessity among adults to consider and to formulate that lent credence in childhood in the form of an age-appropriate adult belief, it may scarcely be doubted that the notion of a body of God in its literal sense is demonstrably anachronistic — were it ever to have been championed in so straightforward a literalness.

This double insight of the truth of myth and the necessity of demythologization inherent to myth is, in a certain sense, also expressed in the classical theology of the Trinity, inasmuch as it is distinguished between the person of Jesus Christ, who following his ascension forms with his deified body one of three persons of the Trinity, and the persons of the Father and the Holy Ghost, for the latter of which bodilessness is usually principally claimed. The quite implicit and usually never explicit emphasis of these differences admittedly poses a daunting theological problem, as it very conspicuously brings to the fore the differences between two of the three persons of the Trinity. The monotheistic intention, a feature characteristic, indeed, essential to Jewish and Christian tradition alike, would probably be better accommodated were such a tension between corporeality and incorporeality to be assumed for all three persons of the Trinity, so as to prevent the differences from growing so great that the fundamental creed of the unity of the three persons might no longer convince.

Once more, the monograph here presented does not represent a systematic contribution to the Christian (or, indeed, Jewish) theory of God; rather, it is intended as a historical investigation. At the same time, it closes with the suggestion as to whether it might not, in fact, also be sensible in the interests of the human body to engage with the topic with which this work has been concerned, in turn, with markedly greater awareness: "God's Body: Jewish, Christian, and Pagan Images of God." A circumspect anthropomorphism of the divine image[41] prevents religious discourse from losing sight of the humanity of God. Inasmuch, however, as God is God in that he grants humans humanity, Jewish and Christian thought is in agreement despite of all their respective differences; God remains God in such humanity already merely in that, unlike humans, he does not permit the repeated appearance of inhumanity at the juncture of such human turns, and delivers humans to true humanity which is visible once more in the person of Jesus of Nazareth.[42] In such a sense, it might be stated, following Immanuel Kant, that one may "permit without reproach or shyness . . . certain anthropomorphisms" in the discussion of God.[43] Indeed, a critical and self-ironic objection Lichtenberg wrote in probably his last letter, send to his brother Ludwig Christian six days before his death, also holds true:

> We finer Christians abhor idolatry, that is, our dear God comprises wood and gold foam, but he remains only an image, which is only another entry in precisely the same series, finer, but an image. When the spirit wishes to tear away from this idolatry, then it ultimately encounters the Kantian idea. Yet, it is presumptuousness to believe that so mixed a being as man would ever recognize everything so *purely*.[44]

Above all, it might thoroughly be asked as to whether such attention to the corporeality of God might not aid in avoiding certain imbalances within philosophical anthropology which emerge within classical concepts by means of the devaluation of corporeality: Body is, as Johannes Schelhas states, actually not only a frame, but also the medium fashioned by God after his own similitude by means of which humans are realized as social beings and their humanity is achieved.[45] With a position which takes seriously the bodiliness of humanity in such a sense, certain cul-de-sacs might be avoided in contestations with the natural sciences over the material basis of certain intellectual processes and contexts.

The rich field presenting itself when conceptions of the body of God in Antiquity are studied, and thereby Judaism, Christianity, and also the pagan cults taken into account, has hardly been explored in its entirety. When it is accepted that the Qur'an, and thereby the genesis of Islam, may also be assigned with good reason to Late Antiquity,[46] then at least some reference to this third religion must be made at the close of this book. While certainly the Qur'an does not know the notion of the creation in the divine likeness and every manner of anthropomorphism is rejected within Islamic theology, naturally mention of the eyes and hands of God occurs.[47] Yet, the comparison of the Christian notion of a manifestation of God in the human Jesus of Nazareth with God's taking shape in the orally recited Qur'an is justifiable; Navid Kermani terms this the "inverbation" of God within the Qur'an recitation and parallels this with the incarnation of God in Jesus Christ: "Theological discussion in Christianity, for example, has focused on the question of Jesus' human-divine nature, while Islamic scholars have devoted themselves with similar ardour to the question of the 'creation of the Quran' . . .—that is, whether the Quran is part of God's eternal Being, or whether God created it at a point in time."[48] The

earlier concept of an "inlibration" of God in the Qur'an (the term of Henry
A. Wolfson) is thereby modified: "It is not a book which serves as the
manifestation of the Word of God in place of the incarnation, . . . but rather
an empirically perceived acoustic-verbal manifestation . . . appears at this
juncture."[49] Angelika Neuwirth wishes even to observe (admittedly contextually heavily modified) traces of the Judeo-Christian theology of the
Word (λόγος) of God in the Qur'an.[50] When it is said of the Qur'an that
"the Quran possesses a unique style that was different from everything
known and held a rank in beauty that exceeded all forms of oratory, and
even verse, which is the best form of discourse,"[51] then the poetic pulchri-
tude of the recited Qur'an embodies the beauty of God. "We can understand this only as a kind of aesthetic proof of the existence of God."[52]
Even if no speculation is made within such Islamic texts on the body of an
absolutely transcendent God, the conception of a corporeality of God, as
in particular configurations of Judaism and Christianity, is migrated into a
certain manner of incarnation.

This migration in the notion of a divine body from the classical doctrine of God still continues, incidentally, in the present day, and, indeed,
in the form of a process which (following Carl Schmitt) may be labeled
the secularization of theological terms.[53] At the present juncture, a prominent example suffices: As demonstrated by Ernst Kantorowicz, English
jurists of the Early Modern era transposed the medieval notion of the "two
bodies of the king," one *natural*, the other *political*, onto the state. The
political body is (as expressed by the Elizabethan jurist Edmund Plowden
[1518–1585] in respect to a legal case of 1562) "a Body that cannot be
seen or handled, . . . this Body is utterly void of Infancy, and old Age, and
other natural Defects and Imbecilities, which the Body natural is subject
to, and for this Cause, what the King does in his Body politic, cannot be
invalidated or frustrated by any Disability in his natural Body."[54] It
becomes far more apparent that the pedigree of such conceptions lies in
the antique notion of a divine body when claims are made that this body
"never dies," that is, lives forever and does not experience any passions
or might at all be injured.[55] While in Kantorowicz it is not entirely proven
as to which avenues within intellectual history precisely lead from the
Middle Ages to the conception of an eternal and indestructible "political
body" of the king composed of a particular matter.[56] Nevertheless, it is
also quite evident without such attestations that an important intellectual-
historical supposition of the modern conception of the sovereignty of
the state and the inalienable dignity of each and every person alike was
here taken into account. Naturally, the field has hardly been exhausted by
means of Kantorowicz's monograph; for example, a great number of lines
may be traced with intellectual history leading towards the notion of an

unalienable dignity: Hans Joas very recently maintained the "sacralization of the person" since the nineteenth century to be a root of the notion of universal human rights; he distinguishes thereby the conception that also under the precepts of a programmatic atheism "the human person would itself become a holy object."[57] The notion completely divorced from the divine or human body alike that the spirit or the soul depicts the likeness of God in man is, as Joas demonstrates, one among many preconditions of this development towards the sacredness of the person. Yet, the concept of the human person's sacredness may naturally also be derived without any recourse to a transcendent archetype of the human likeness: In other words, the European Modern era features concepts justifying the inalienable dignity of humans which not only eschew the notion of a divine body, but also any fundamental justification by means of a divinity at all. Seen accordingly, the gradual disappearance of the concept of a divine body appears for the idea of God as the first great motion in the direction of secularization within intellectual history.

As has been witnessed repeatedly, the notion of a divine body abides in altered form. These various medieval and early modern transformations of the idea of a divine body cannot be examined here at any further length. Inasmuch, this monograph may be read as something of a prospectus for future research, and not as the evaluation of the results of an extended intellectual project now more or less concluded.

Notes

Preface

1 Sigmund Freud, *Das Unbehagen in der Kultur* (1930), Studienausgabe Bd. 9 (Frankfurt am Main: S. Fischer, 1974), 206: "Diese Vorsehung kann der gemeine Mann sich nicht anders als in der Person eines großartig erhöhten Vaters vorstellen. Nur ein solcher kann die Bedürfnisse des Menschenkindes kennen, durch seine Bitten erweicht, durch die Zeichen seiner Reue beschwichtigt werden. Das Ganze ist so offenkundig infantil, so wirklichkeitsfremd, daß es einer menschenfreundlichen Gesinnung schmerzlich wird zu denken, die große Mehrheit der Sterblichen werde sich niemals über diese Auffassung des Lebens erheben können. Noch beschämender wirkt es zu erfahren, ein wie großer Anteil der heute Lebenden, die es einsehen müssen, daß diese Religion nicht zu halten ist, doch Stück für Stück von ihr in kläglichen Rückzugsgefechten zu verteidigen sucht. Man möchte sich in die Reihen der Gläubigen mengen, um den Philosophen, die den Gott der Religion zu retten glauben, indem sie ihn durch ein unpersönliches, schattenhaft abstraktes Prinzip ersetzen, die Mahnung vorzuhalten: 'Du sollst den Namen des Herrn nicht zum Eitlen anrufen!' Wenn einige der größten Geister vergangener Zeiten das gleiche getan haben, so darf man sich hierin nicht auf sie berufen."

2 Feuerbach cites in his work's appendix Thomas Aquinas who argues *against* the notion of a divine body: Thomas de Aquino, *Summa contra gentiles* I 20.7 (Thomas von Aquin, *Summa contra gentiles*, Bd. 1, *Buch I*, hg. und übers. von Karl Albert und Paulus Engelhardt unter Mitarbeit von Leo Dümpelmann [Darmstadt: Wissenschaftliche Buchgesellschaft, 1974 = ibid., 2001], 74 [Latin text], 75 [German translation]): "Si igitur Deus est corpus, intellectus et imaginatio nostra aliquid maius Deo cogitare possunt. Et sic Deus non est maior intellectu nostro. Quod est inconveniens. Non est igitur corpus." From this argumentation presented by the famous Aquinian, Feuerbach concludes: "In dem unendlichen Wesen ist mir nur als Subjekt, *als Wesen* Gegenstand, was ein *Prädikat*, eine *Eigenschaft von mir selbst ist. Das unendliche Wesen ist nichts als die personifizierte Unendlichkeit des Menschen, Gott nichts als die personifizierte, als ein Wesen vorgestellte Gottheit oder Göttlichkeit des Menschen*" (Ludwig Feuerbach, *Das Wesen des Christentums*, bearbeitet von Wolfgang Harich und Werner Schuffenhauer, *Gesammelte Werke*, Bd. 5 [Berlin: Akademie-Verlag, 1984], 461).

3 See the reference in the previous note.

4 Hartmut Rosenau, "Gott höchst persönlich: Zur Rehabilitierung der Rede von der Personalität Gottes im Durchgang durch den Pantheismus- und Atheismusstreit," in *Marburger Jahrbuch Theologie XIX: Personalität Gottes*, hg. Wilfried Härle und Reiner Preul (Leipzig: Evangelische Verlagsanstalt, 2007), 47–76; and idem, *Mit Gott reden—von Gott reden: Das Personsein des dreieinigen Gottes; Votum des Theologischen Ausschusses*

der Union Evangelischer Kirchen (UEK) in der EKD, hg. Michael Beintker und Martin Heimbucher, Evangelische Impulse 3 (Neukirchen-Vluyn: Neukirchener, 2011), 28–31, 40–49.

5 "Was soll mir euer Hohn / Über das All und Eine? / Der Professor ist eine Person, / Gott ist keine" (Johann Wolfgang VON GOETHE, Zahme Xenien, siebente Abteilung [here cited according to GOETHE, *Berliner Ausgabe: Poetische Werke; Gedichte und Singspiele*, Bd. 2, *Gedichte: Nachlese und Nachlaß* (Berlin: Aufbau-Verlag, ³1979)], 357; in the commentary, p. 789, it is stated: "Vermutlich 1829 entstanden. Der Titel 'Der Pantheist,' den die Weimarer Ausgabe aus der Ausgabe letzter Hand übernahm, ist ein Zusatz der Nachlaßherausgeber."

6 I quote the classic definitions of Boethius, later adopted, for example, by Thomas Aquinas: "naturae rationabilis individua substantia"; and "Persona est rationalis naturae individua substantia" (Boethius, *Opuscula sacra V Contra Eutychen et Nestorium 3* [PhB 397, 74 ELSÄSSER = BiTeu 170–172 MORESCHINI]; and De personis et duabus naturis 3 [PL 64, 1343 C]; cf. Thomas de Aquino, *Quaestio unica, "De unione verbi incarnati"* art. 1 ad arg. 17 [28 OBENAUER]). See Corinna SCHLAPKOHL, *Persona Est Naturae Rationabilis Individua Substantia: Boethius und die Debatte über den Personbegriff*, MTS 56 (Marburg an der Lahn: N. G. Elwert, 1999), 56–71 and 199–201.

7 Friedrich Christoph OETINGER, Art. "Leib, Soma," in idem, *Biblisches und emblematisches Wörterbuch*, hg. Gerhard Schäfer in Verbindung mit Otto Betz, Reinhard Breymayer, Eberhard Gutekunst, Ursula Hardmeier, Roland Pietsch und Guntram Spindler, 2 Bde., Bd. 1: *Text*, und Bd. 2: *Anmerkungen*, Texte zur Geschichte des Pietismus 7/3 (Berlin/ New York: De Gruyter, 1999), 223.5f. = (o. O. [Heilbronn/Neckar]: o. V., 1776), 407: "Leiblichkeit ist das Ende der Werke Gottes, wie aus der Stadt Gottes klar erhellet . . ." See also idem, Art. "Offenbaren, Phaneroo," in idem, *Biblisches und emblematisches Wörterbuch*, 246.30–248.4 = 456–458. On the topic of the "bodiliness of God," see also the remarks in the introduction to ibid., xvii; and Oswald BAYER, "Gottes Leiblichkeit: Zum Leben und Werk Friedrich Christoph Oetingers," in idem, *Leibliches Wort: Reformation und Neuzeit im Konflikt* (Tübingen: Mohr Siebeck, 1992), 94–104.

8 Pierre DEGHAYE, "Die Natur als Leib Gottes in Jacob Böhmes Theosophie," in *Gott, Natur und Mensch in der Sicht Jacob Böhmes und seiner Rezeption*, hg. Jan Garewicz und Alois Maria Haas, Wolfenbütteler Arbeiten zur Barockforschung 24 (Wiesbaden: Harrassowitz, 1994), 71–111. See also, more generally, Eberhard H. PÄLTZ, s.v. "Böhme, Jacob (1575–1624)," *TRE* 6: 748–754; and now, in particular, Christian BENDRATH, *Leibhaftigkeit: Jakob Böhmes Inkarnationsmorphologie*, Theologische Bibliothek Töpelmann 97 (Berlin/ New York: De Gruyter, 1999), esp. 48 and 107–110.

9 William J. WAINWRIGHT, "God's Body," *JAAR* 42 (1974): 470–481, esp. 470.

10 Peter BROWN, *The Body and Society: Men, Women and Sexual Renunciation in Early Christianity*, Lectures on the History of Religions 13 (New York: Columbia University Press, 1988). Appeared 2008: idem, *The Body and Society*, twentieth anniversary ed. with a new introduction, Columbia Classics in Religion (New York: Columbia University Press, 2008). See also Peter BROWN, *A Life of Learning*, Charles Homer Haskins Lecture for 2003, ACLS Occasional Paper 55, 12–15 (available online at http://www.acls.org/ Publications/OP/Haskins/2003_PeterBrown.pdf [last accessed May 2019]).

11 George L. PRESTIGE, *God in Patristic Thought* (London: Heinemann, 1936 = Eugene, Ore.: Wipf & Stock, 2008). See also Andrew Brian McGOWAN, Brian E. DALEY, and Timothy J. GADEN, eds., *God in Early Christian Thought: Essays in Memory of Lloyd G. Patterson*, Supplements to Vigiliae Christianae 94 (Leiden: Brill, 2009); Franz COURTH, *Trinität: In der Schrift und Patristik*, Handbuch der Dogmengeschichte, Bd. 2, *Der trinitarische Gott—die Schöpfung—die Sünde*, Fasc. 1a (Freiburg im Breisgau: Herder, 1988); Robert M. GRANT, *The Early Christian Doctrine of God* (Charlottesville: University Press of Virginia, 1966); Clemens THOMA, s.v. "Gott III. Judentum," *TRE* 6: 626–654; and George Christopher STEAD, "Gott V. Alte Kirche," *TRE* 6: 652–657.

12 Eberhard Jüngel, "Anthropomorphismus als Grundproblem neuzeitlicher Hermeneutik," in idem, *Wertlose Wahrheit: Zur Identität und Relevanz des christlichen Glaubens*, Theologische Erörterungen 3, 2. um ein Register erweiterte Auflage (Tübingen: Mohr Siebeck, 2003), 110–131, esp. 123–131.

13 Aloys Winterling, "Wie modern war die Antike? Was soll die Frage?" in *Geschichte denken: Perspektiven auf die Geschichtsschreibung heute*, hg. Michael Wildt (Göttingen: Vandenhoeck & Ruprecht, 2014), 12–34.

1   The Body of God after Antiquity

1 Alois Kardinal Grillmeier†, *Jesus der Christus im Glauben der Kirche*, Bd. 1, *Von der Apostolischen Zeit bis zum Konzil von Chalcedon (451)*, 3. verbesserte und ergänzte Aufl. (Freiburg/Basel/Vienna: Herder, 1990).

2 Ferdinand Kattenbusch, *Das apostolische Symbol: Seine Entstehung, sein geschichtlicher Sinn, seine ursprüngliche Stellung im Kultus und in der Theologie der Kirche*, Bd. 2, *Verbreitung und Bedeutung des Taufsymbols* (Leipzig: Hinrichs, 1900), 651–655; John Norman Davidson Kelly, *Early Christian Creeds* (London: Longman, 1972), 152f.; and also Christoph Markschies, "'Sessio ad Dexteram.' Bemerkungen zu einem altchristlichen Bekenntnismotiv in der christologischen Diskussion der altkirchlichen Theologen," in *Le trône de Dieu*, éd. Marc Philonenko, WUNT 69 (Tübingen: Mohr Siebeck, 1993), 252–317, esp. 278–283 = idem, *Alta Trinità Beata: Gesammelte Studien zur altkirchlichen Trinitätstheologie* (Tübingen: Mohr Siebeck, 2000), 1–69, esp. 32–37.

3 From the definition (Acta Conciliorum Oecumenicorum 2/I/II, 129.30f., Schwartz): ἕνα καὶ τὸν αὐτὸν Χριστὸν υἱὸν κύριον μονογενῆ ἐν δύο φύσεσιν ἀσυγχύτως, ἀτρέπτως, ἀδιαιρέτως, ἀχωρίστως. See on the text André de Halleux, "La définition christologique à Chalcédoine," *Revue théologique de Louvain* 7 (1976): 3–23, 155–170, esp. 9 = idem, *Patrologie et Oecuménisme: Recueil d'Études*, Bibliotheca ETL 93 (Leuven: Peeters, 1990), 445–480, esp. 451; German translation in Grillmeier, *Jesus der Christus im Glauben der Kirche*, 1: 54f.

4 In Late Antiquity, only the word μονοφυής ("of *one* nature") is attested: Geoffrey William Hugo Lampe, *Patristic Greek Lexicon* (Oxford: Clarendon, 1987 = 1961), s.v. (p. 884); also from the seventh century onwards the term μονοφυσίτης: Evangelinus Apostolides Sophocles, *Greek Lexicon of the Roman and Byzantine periods (from B.C. 146 to A.D. 1100)* (Hildesheim: Olms 1992 = Cambridge, Mass./London: Harvard University Press; London: Oxford University Press 1914), s.v. (p. 769).

5 See generally Hans Joachim Schoeps, *Vom himmlischen Fleisch Christi: Eine dogmengeschichtliche Untersuchung*, Sammlung gemeinverständlicher Vorträge und Schriften aus dem Gebiet der Theologie und Religionsgeschichte 195/196 (Tübingen: Mohr Siebeck, 1951); Stephen H. Webb, *Jesus Christ, Eternal God: Heavenly Flesh and the Metaphysics of Matter* (Oxford: Oxford University Press, 2012).

6 Horst Weigelt, s.v. "Kaspar Schwenckfeld," *TRE* 30: 712–719, esp. 715f. See also Schoeps, *Vom himmlischen Fleisch Christi*, 25–36; Paul L. Maier, *Caspar Schwenckfeld on the Person and Work of Christ: A Study of Schwenckfeldian Theology at Its Core*, Van Gorcum's theologische bibliotheek 33 (Assen: van Gorcum, 1959 = Eugene, Ore.: Wipf and Stock, 2004); and Webb, *Jesus Christ, Eternal God*, 153–157. On Schwenckfeld's relationship to Paracelsus, from whom Schwenckfeld evidently received inspiration, see Ute Gause, *Paracelsus (1493–1541): Genese und Entfaltung seiner frühen Theologie*, Spätmittelalter und Reformation. Neue Reihe 4 (Tübingen: Mohr Siebeck, 1993) 40–47.

7 Admittedly, Schleiermacher attempted a critical reformulation of this theologoumenon: Friedrich Daniel Ernst Schleiermacher, *Der christliche Glaube nach den Grundsätzen der evangelischen Kirche im Zusammenhange dargestellt*, 2. Aufl., Berlin 1830/1831, hg. Rolf Schäfer, Kritische Gesamtausgabe 1/13, Tlbd. 1 (Berlin/New York: De Gruyter 2003), 173f. See also Kurt Nowak, *Schleiermacher: Leben, Werk und Wirkung*

(Göttingen: Vandenhoeck & Ruprecht, 2002), 279–281; Martin Oнsт, *Schleiermacher und die Bekenntnisschriften: Eine Untersuchung zu seiner Reformations- und Protestant-ismusdeutung*, BHT 77 (Tübingen: Mohr Siebeck, 1989), 121–129; and Franz Christ, *Menschlich von Gott reden: Das Problem des Anthropomorphismus bei Schleiermacher*, Ökumenische Theologie 10 (Einsiedeln/Zürich/Köln: Benziger & Gütersloh: Gütersloher Verlagshaus Mohn, 1982), esp. 220–231.

8   Most recently: Sarah Stroumsa, *Maimonides in His World: Portrait of a Mediterranean Thinker* (Princeton, N.J.: Princeton University Press, 2011).

9   The page numbers of the Arabic text are cited according to the following critical edition: *Le guide des égarés: Traité de théologie et de philosophie par Moïse Ben Maimoun dit Maï-monide*, publié pour la première fois dans l'original arabe et accompagné d'une traduction Française et des notes critiques littéraires et explicatives par Salomon Munk, tome 1 (Paris: Franck, 1856 = Osnabrück: Zeller, 1964). ET from *The Guide of the Perplexed by Moses Maimonides*, trans. with an introduction and notes by Shlomo Pines, with an introductory essay by Leo Strauss (Chicago: Chicago University Press, 1963). Cf. Adolf Weiß's 1923 German translation: *Mose Ben Maimon, Führer der Unschlüssigen*, Übersetzung und Kom-mentar von Adolf Weiß, mit einer Einleitung von Johann Meier, Philosophische Bibliothek 184a-c (Hamburg: Meiner, ²1995).

10 Leo Strauss, "How to Begin to Study the *Guide of the Perplexed*," in *The Guide of the Perplexed by Moses Maimonides*, trans. Shlomo Pines, xi–lvii, esp. xxi. On the work, see the introduction in Moses Maimonides, *Wegweiser für die Verwirrten: Eine Textauswahl zur Schöpfungsfrage*, Arabisch/Hebräisch, Deutsch, übers. von Wolfgang von Abel, Ilya Levkovich, Frederek Musall, eingel. von Frederek Musall und Yossef Schwartz, Herders Bibliothek der Philosophie des Mittelalters 19 (Freiburg/Basel/Vienna: Herder, 2009), 21–27 (on the title: p. 23 n. 25). On the Latin reception in the Middle Ages, see Görge K. Hasselhoff, *Dicit Rabbi Moyses: Studien zum Bild von Moses Maimonides im lateinischen Westen vom 13. bis 15. Jahrhundert*, 2. Aufl. mit ein Nachwort (Würzburg: Königshausen & Neumann, 2005), 88–220.

11 The Hebrew is not understood in the sense of "one God" (as it is translated in the Septua-gint: Κύριος ὁ Θεὸς ἡμῶν Κύριος εἷς ἐστι·), but rather in the sense of "one, oneness." This interpretation is naturally also pointedly aimed at the Christian teaching of the Trin-ity of God.

12 Maimonides, *Führer der Unschlüssigen* I 5 (16ᵇ–17ᵃ Munk = *Führer der Unschlüssigen*, 40 Weiss = *The Guide of the Perplexed*, 29 Pines).

13 The Hebrew word can be translated into English with "appearance," "image," "form," or "shape." See on this in detail Christoph Dohmen, *Das Bilderverbot: Seine Entstehung und seine Entwicklung im Alten Testament*, BBB 62, 2., durchges. und um ein Nachwort erweit-erte Aufl. (Frankfurt am Main: Athenäum, 1987), 216–223 ("Exkurs 4: תמונה *im AT*"); and Ernst-Joachim Waschke, s.v. "תמונה," in *Theologisches Wörterbuch zum Alten Testa-ment* (Stuttgart: Kohlhammer, 1995), 8: 677–680. This does not entirely correspond to the semantic range of the term δόξα, which is employed in the Greek translation of Num 12:8 in contrast to the otherwise conventional ὁμοίωμα: καὶ τὴν δόξαν κυρίου εἶδεν. Δόξα emphasizes much more stridently the apparitional character of a thing and is not used as the equivalent for terms which describe the body in the Septuagint (above all σῶμα and σάρξ). See for this Otfried Hofius, "'Der in des Vaters Schoß ist' Joh 1.18," in idem und Hans-Christian Kammler, *Johannesstudien: Untersuchungen zur Theologie des vier-ten Evangeliums*, WUNT 88 (Tübingen: Mohr Siebeck, 1996), 24–32, esp. 31 nn. 52–54 for the references from rabbinic literature.

14 Maimonides, *Führer der Unschlüssigen* I 35 (42ᵇ Munk = *Führer der Unschlüssigen*, 111 Weiss = *The Guide of the Perplexed*, 81 Pines).

15 Maimonides, *Führer der Unschlüssigen* I 51 (58ᵇ Munk = *Führer der Unschlüssigen*, 158 Weiss = *The Guide of the Perplexed*, 113 Pines). Maimonides refers to I 53.

16 On the philosophical sources of the "Guide of the Perplexed," see Pines, *The Guide of the Perplexed*, lvii–lxiii; and also Harry Austryn Wolfson, "The Aristotelian Predicables

and Maimonides' Division of Attributes," in idem, *Studies in the History of Philosophy and Religion*, ed. Isadore Twersky and George H. Williams (Cambridge, Mass.: Harvard University Press, 1977), 2: 161–194, originally published in *Essays and Studies in Memory of Linda R. Miller*, ed. Israel Davidson (New York: Jewish Theological Seminary of America, 1938), 201–234.

17 Weiss notes in the footnotes of his translation the critical glosses (*hassagot*) of Rabbi Abraham ben David from Posquières (RABaD III) on Maimonides, *Mishne Torah*, Hilkhot Teshuva (Regeln der Umkehr) 3.7 (*Führer der Unschlüssigen*, 160 n. 32); cited according to Gershom Scholem, *Origins of the Kabbalah*, ed. R. J. Zwi Werblowsky, trans. Allan Arkush (Princeton, N.J.: Princeton University Press, 1987), 210.

18 Maimonides, *Führer der Unschlüssigen* I 51 (59ᵃ Munk = Führer der Unschlüssigen, 160 Weiss = The Guide of the Perplexed, 114 Pines).

19 Maimonides, *Führer der Unschlüssigen* I 52 (60ᵃ/60ᵇ Munk = Führer der Unschlüssigen, 165f. Weiss = *The Guide of the Perplexed*, 116f. Pines).

20 Maimonides, *Maamar Teḥyyat ha-Metim* (Tractate on the Resurrection of the Dead), here cited according to Joshua Finkel, *Maḳ'āla fi teḥiyat ha-metim: Maimonides' Treatise on Resurrection*, Proceedings of the American Academy for Jewish Research 9 (New York: ha-Aḳademyah ha-ameriḳanit le-mada'e ha-yahadut, 1939), 7: "[The] body as a whole is only the tool for the soul, by which the soul carries out all its acts"; cf. also ibid., 16: "The body is only the combination of tools for the acts of the soul." For an ET and commentary, see Sarah Stroumsa, "Twelfth Century Concepts of Soul and Body: The Maimonidean Controversy in Baghdad," in *Self, Soul, and Body in Religious Experience*, ed. Albert I. Baumgarten, Jan Assmann, and Guy G. Stroumsa, SHR 78 (Leiden/Boston/Köln: Brill, 1998), 313–334, esp. 324f.

21 Uwe Glessmer, *Einleitung in die Targume zum Pentateuch*, TSAJ 48 (Tübingen: Mohr Siebeck, 1995), 84–94; Peter Schäfer, s.v. "Bibelübersetzungen II. Targumim," *TRE* 6: 216–228, esp. 220f.; Israel Drazin, "Dating Targum Onkelos by Means of the Tannaitic Midrashim," *JJS* 50 (1999): 246–258.

22 Maimonides, *The Guide of the Perplexed* I 21, 27, 28, 36 (26ᵃ, 30ᵃ, 31ᵇ, 44ᵇ Munk = *Führer der Unschlüssigen*, 66f., 76f., 80f., 114f. = *The Guide of the Perplexed*, 49, 57f., 59f., 85 Pines. See Siegmund Maybaum, *Die Anthropomorphien und Anthropopathien bei Onkelos und den späteren Targumin mit besonderer Berücksichtigung der Ausdrücke Memra, Jekara und Schechintha* (Breslau: Schletter'sche Buchhandlung, 1870), 3–6 and 48–51.

23 *The Bible in Aramaic Based on Old Manuscripts and Printed Texts*, ed. Alexander Sperber, with a foreword by Robert P. Gordon, vol. 1, *The Pentateuch according to Targum Onkelos* (Leiden/New York/Cologne: Brill, 1992), 242; *The Aramaic Bible*, vol. 8, *The Targum Onqelos to Leviticus and The Targum Onqelos to Numbers*, trans. with apparatus and notes by Bernard Grossfeld (Collegeville, Minn.: The Liturgical Press, 1988), 105.

24 Maimonides, *Führer der Unschlüssigen* I 36 (42ᵇ–45ᵃ, 51ᵇ, 54ᵇ Munk = *Führer der Unschlüssigen*, 112–117 = *The Guide of the Perplexed*, 49, 57f. 59f. 85 Pines).

25 Details in Stroumsa, *Maimonides in His World*, 71f.

26 Stroumsa, *Maimonides in His World*, 70.

27 Anselmus Cantuariensis, *Proslogion* 6 (*S. Anselmi Cantuariensis Archepiscopi Opera Omnia*, vol. 1, *Continens opera quae prior et Abbas Beccensis composuit*, ad fidem codicum recensuit Franciscus Salesius Schmitt [Edinburgh: Thomas Nelson, 1946], 104.19).

28 Anselmus Cantuariensis, *Proslogion* 6 (I, 104.23–26 Schmitt).

29 Anselmus Cantuariensis, *Proslogion* 6 (I, 105.4–6 Schmitt).

30 Giles of Rome [= Aegidius Romanus], *Errores Philosophorum: Critical Text with Notes and Introduction*, ed. Josef Koch, trans. John O. Riedl (Milwaukee, Wis.: Marquette University Press, 1944), 56–67. In § XII,5 Aegidius defends against the notion that the heavens are spiritually imbued, super-heavenly bodies ("supercaelestia corpora . . . animate": 60.17 Koch). See Hasselhoff, *Dicit Rabbi Moyses*, 370, 399; and, particularly, Silvia Donati, "Ägidius von Roms Kritik an Thomas von Aquins Lehre der hylomorphen

Zusammensetzung der Himmelskörper," in *Thomas von Aquin: Werk und Wirkung im Licht neuer Forschungen*, hg. Albert Zimmermann, Miscellanea mediaevalia 19 (Berlin/ New York: De Gruyter, 1988), 377–396.

31 Hence also HASSELHOFF, *Dicit Rabbi Moyses*, 122–220.

32 Thomas de Aquino, *Summa contra gentiles* I 20.2–7. On the argumentative sequence and the various problems associated therewith, see WAINWRIGHT, "God's Body," 471; and also John F. WIPPEL, "Quidditative Knowledge of God according to Thomas Aquinas," in *Graceful Reason: Essays in Ancient and Medieval Philosophy Presented to Joseph Owens on the Occasion of His Seventy-Fifth Birthday and the Fiftieth Anniversary of His Ordination*, ed. Lloyd Philip Gerson, Papers in Mediaeval Studies 4 (Toronto: Pontifical Institute of Mediaeval Studies, 1983), 273–299.

33 Jennifer HART WEED, "Maimonides and Aquinas: A Medieval Misunderstanding?" *Revista Portuguesa de Filosofia* 64 (2008): 379–396; cf. on reception also Maimonides, *Wegweiser für die Verwirrten*, 35f.

34 Thomas de Aquino, *Summa contra gentiles* I 18.

35 Thomas de Aquino, *Summa contra gentiles* I 20.2. ET from *Saint Thomas Aquinas: On the Truth of the Catholic Faith: Summa contra Gentiles*, book 1, trans. Anton C. PEGIS (Garden City, N.Y.: Image Books, 1955), 106. Cf. Thomas von Aquin, *Summa contra gentiles*, 72 (Latin text), 73 (German translation). On the historical-philosophical background to the passage, see Klaus KREMER, *Die neuplatonische Seinsphilosophie und ihre Wirkung auf Thomas von Aquin*, Studien zur Problemgeschichte der antiken und mittelalterlichen Philosophie 1 (Leiden: Brill, 1966), 424–437.

36 Thomas de Aquino, *Summa contra gentiles* I 20.3. ET from PEGIS, *Saint Thomas Aquinas: On the Truth of the Catholic Faith*, 106.

37 Aristoteles, *Metaphysica* XIII 1, 1076 a 32–37; and also XIII 2, 1077 b 12–16.

38 Thomas de Aquino, *Summa contra gentiles* I 20.4. ET from PEGIS, *Saint Thomas Aquinas: On the Truth of the Catholic Faith*, 106.

39 Aristoteles, *De caelo* I 5 271 b–273 a. See Edward GRANT, *Planets, Stars, and Orbs: the medieval Cosmos, 1200–1687* (Cambridge: Cambridge University Press, 1994), 23–33.

40 Thomas de Aquino, *Summa contra gentiles* I 20.5. ET from PEGIS, *Saint Thomas Aquinas: On the Truth of the Catholic Faith*, 106.

41 Thomas de Aquino, *Summa contra gentiles* I 20.6. ET from PEGIS, *Saint Thomas Aquinas: On the Truth of the Catholic Faith*, 107.

42 Thomas de Aquino, *Summa contra gentiles* I 20.7. ET from PEGIS, *Saint Thomas Aquinas: On the Truth of the Catholic Faith*, 107.

43 Naturally, Aristotle is primarily meant.

44 Thomas de Aquino, *Summa contra gentiles* I 20.8. ET from PEGIS, *Saint Thomas Aquinas: On the Truth of the Catholic Faith*, 107.

45 Wainwright is entirely correct in noting that the reasons for this ontological hierarchies are entirely lacking within the argument. As the arguments "are only sound if materialism is false, they cannot be successfully employed against theists like Tertullian and Pratt" (idem, "God's Body," 473). The same holds true for the premise that all bodies are incomplete. Inasmuch, "the argument remains incomplete" (idem, "God's Body," 471).

46 See Aristoteles, *Metaphysica* XII 7, esp. 1072 a 25f. (οὐ κινούμενον κινεῖ, ἀΐδιον καὶ οὐσία καὶ ἐνέργεια οὖσα); and, on the reception of this within Thomas, John F. WIPPEL, *The Metaphysical Thought of Thomas Aquinas: From Finite Being to Uncreated Being*, Monographs of the Society for Medieval and Renaissance Philosophy 1 (Washington, D.C.: Catholic University of America Press, 2000), 412–441.

47 Some of the arguments are also employed by him in the theological summae, cf. Thomas de Aquino, *Summa Theologiae* I quaest. 3, art. 1. Here, five arguments may also be found for the assumption of a divine corporeality, namely: (1) three-dimensionality, (2) humanity's creation in the likeness of God as an indication of a divine *figura*, (3) body parts mentioned in Scripture, (4) movements such as sitting within Scripture, and (5) *a quo*

and *ad quem* as mentioned in Scripture. In *respondeo decendum*, Thomas argues thereby that it was demonstrated that "Deus est primum movens immobile" and "id quod est nobilissimum in entibus" (*S. Thomae Aquinatis Summa Theologica*, diligenter emendata de Rubeis, Billuart et aliorum, notis selectis ornata, Pars 1ᵃ [Turin: Marietti, 1927], 16f).

48 Baruch de Spinoza, *Epistula* 73 from December 1673 (Baruch de Spinoza, *Epistolae, Stelkonstige Reeckening van den Regenboog, Reeckening van Kanssen—(Nachbericht)*, Spinoza Opera, im Auftrag der Heidelberger Akademie der Wissenschaften Carl Gebhardt ed. [Heidelberg: Winter 1972 = 1925], 4: 309).

49 Eberhard JÜNGEL, "Anthropomorphismus als Grundproblem neuzeitlicher Hermeneutik," in idem, *Wertlose Wahrheit: Zur Identität und Relevanz des christlichen Glaubens*, Theologische Erörterungen 3, 2. um ein Register erweiterte Aufl. (Tübingen: Mohr Siebeck, 2003), 110–131, esp. 123–131; idem, *Gott als Geheimnis der Welt: Zur Begründung der Theologie des Gekreuzigten im Streit zwischen Theismus und Atheismus*, 8. erneut durchgesehene Aufl. (Tübingen: Mohr Siebeck, 2010), 352–357; and also Hans-Walter SCHÜTTE und Rainer FABIAN, s.v. "Anthropomorphismus II.," in *Historisches Wörterbuch der Philosophie* (Basel/Stuttgart: Schwabe, 1971), 1: 377f.

50 Within Leibniz, as is correctly noted by Jüngel, the term may be discerned as being a still-contemporary neologism: JÜNGEL, "Anthropomorphismus als Grundproblem neuzeitlicher Hermeneutik," 126 n. 75.

51 Leibniz, *Causa Dei Asserta per Justitiam Ejus* 2: "Error Magnitudinem Dei infrigentium Anthropomorphismus, Bonitatem tollentium Despotismus appellari potest"; here cited after Gottfried Wilhelm Leibniz, "Causa Dei Asserta per Justitiam Ejus cum Caeteris Ejus Perfectionibus Cunctis Actionibus Conciliatam," in idem, *Opera Philosophica Quae Exstant Latina Gallica Germanica Omnia*, instruxit Johann Eduard Erdmann, Faksimiledruck der Ausgabe 1840 durch weitere Textstücke ergänzt und mit einem Vorwort versehen v. Renate Vollbrecht (Aalen: Scientia, 1959), 653–665, esp. 653 = *Die philosophischen Schriften von Gottfried Wilhelm Leibniz*, Bd. 6, hg. Carl Immanuel Gerhardt (Hildesheim: Olms, 1961), 439–462, esp. 439.

52 David Hume, *Dialogues concerning Natural Religion*, pt. 4, *A Treatise of Human Nature Being an Attempt to Introduce the Experimental Method of Reasoning into Moral Subjects and Dialogues concerning Natural Religion by D. Hume*, ed. with preliminary dissertations and notes by Thomas Hill Green and Thomas Hodge Grose, vol. 2 (Aalen: Scientia, 1964 [= London, 1886]), 406–409. See Elisabeth HEINRICH, "Religionskritik im Spannungsfeld von logischer und genealogischer Argumentation," in *Kritik der Religion: Zur Aktualität einer unerledigten philosophischen und theologischen Aufgabe*, hg. Ingolf U. Dalferth und Hans-Peter Großhans, Religion in Philosophy and Theology 23 (Tübingen: Mohr Siebeck, 2006), 95–116, esp. 98–102; and Hans GRAUBNER, "Zum Problem des Anthropomorphismus in der Theologie (Hume, Kant, Hamann)," in *Johann Georg Hamann und England: Hamann und die englischsprachige Aufklärung; Acta des siebten Internationalen Hamann-Kolloquiums zu Marburg/Lahn 1996*, hg. Bernhard Gajek, Regensburger Beiträge zur deutschen Sprach- und Literaturwissenschaft B/69 (Frankfurt am Main/Berlin/Bern: Lang, 1999), 381–395.

53 Immanuel Kant, *Prolegomena zu einer jeden künftigen Metaphysik, die als Wissenschaft wird auftreten können*, Kants Gesammelte Schriften, hg. von der Königlich Preußischen Akademie der Wissenschaften, Bd. 4 (Berlin: De Gruyter, 1903–1911), 357 (Tl. 3 § 57). ET from Gary Carl HATFIELD, *Immanuel Kant: Prolegomena to Any Future Metaphysics That Will Be Able to Come Forward as Science: With Selections from the "Critique of Pure Reason,"* rev. ed., Cambridge Texts in the History of Philosophy (Cambridge: Cambridge University Press, 2004), 108. The original German reads: "Alsdann eignen wir dem höchsten Wesen keine von den Eigenschaften *an sich selbst* zu, durch die wir uns Gegenstände der Erfahrung denken, und vermeiden dadurch den *dogmatischen* Anthropomorphismus; wir legen sie aber dennoch dem Verhältnisse desselben zur Welt bei und

erlauben uns einen *symbolischen* Anthropomorphism, der in der That nur die Sprache und nicht das Object selbst angeht."

54 Kant, *Prolegomena zu einer jeden künftigen Metaphysik*, 357 (§ 58): "Eine solche Erkenntniß ist die nach der Analogie, welche nicht etwa, wie man das Wort gemeiniglich nimmt, eine unvollkommene Ähnlichkeit zweier Dinge, sondern eine vollkommne Ähnlichkeit zweier Verhältnisse zwischen ganz unähnlichen Dingen bedeutet." See also JÜNGEL, "Anthropomorphismus als Grundproblem neuzeitlicher Hermeneutik," 127f.; and idem, *Gott als Geheimnis der Welt*, 360–363.

55 JÜNGEL, "Anthropomorphismus als Grundproblem neuzeitlicher Hermeneutik," 110–131; and idem, *Gott als Geheimnis der Welt*, 352–363.

56 WEBB, *Jesus Christ, Eternal God*. Webb engages with not only Barth (57–59, 209–242, and 287–292), but also somewhat more briskly Jüngel (94–96). A prior proponent of taking biblical "anthropomorphism" seriously may be found in Edmond La Beaume CHERBONNIER, "The Logic of Biblical Anthropomorphism," *HTR* 55 (1962): 187–206.

57 Aristotle, *Poetica* 21, 1457 b 7–9, states: "A metaphor is the application of a word that belongs to another thing: either from genus to species, species to genus, species to species, or by analogy." ET from *Aristotle: Poetics. Longinus: On the Sublime. Demetrius: On Style*, trans. Stephen HALLIWELL, W. Hamilton FYFE, Doreen C. INNES, and W. Rhys ROBERTS, rev. Donald A. Russell, LCL 199 (Cambridge, Mass.: Harvard University Press, 1995), 105. Cf. the German translation from Manfred FUHRMANN: *Aristoteles: Poetik: Griechisch/Deutsch*, hg. und übers. von Manfred Fuhrmann, Reclams Universal-Bibliothek 7828, bibliographisch ergänzte Ausgabe (Stuttgart: Reclam, 1994 = 2012), 66f.: "Eine Metapher ist die Übertragung eines Wortes (das somit in uneigentlicher Bedeutung verwendet wird), und zwar entweder von der Gattung auf die Art oder von der Art auf die Gattung oder von einer Art auf eine andere, oder nach den Regeln der Analogie."

58 Cf. the references in the previous footnote; on the historical contextualization of the definition of metaphors according to Aristotle in discourse ancient and modern, cf. for example, Harald WEINRICH, s.v. "Metapher," in *Historisches Wörterbuch der Philosophie* (Basel: Schwabe, 1971), 5: 1179–1186.

59 Benjamin D. SOMMER, *The Bodies of God and the World of Ancient Israel* (Cambridge: Cambridge University Press, 2009), 1.

60 SOMMER, *The Bodies of God and the World of Ancient Israel*, 1.

61 SOMMER, *The Bodies of God and the World of Ancient Israel*, 1.

62 See Susan BORDO and Monica UDVARDY, s.v. "Body, the," in *New Dictionary of the History of Ideas*, ed. Maryanne Cline Horowitz (Detroit: Thomson Gale, 2005), 1: 230–238; Seymour FISHER, s.v. "Body Image," in *International Encyclopedia of the Social Sciences*, ed. David L. Sills (New York: Macmillan, 1968), 2: 113–116; Jakob TANNER, s.v. "Body, History of," in *International Encyclopedia of the Social & Behavioral Sciences*, ed. Neil J. Smelser and Paul B. Baltes (Amsterdam: Elsevier, 2001), 2: 1277–1282; and also Maren LORENZ, *Leibhaftige Vergangenheit: Einführung in die Körpergeschichte*, Historische Einführungen 4 (Tübingen: edition discord, 2000).

63 Hence, there is only a brief article entitled "Körper" within the "Grosse vollständige Universal-Lexicon aller Wissenschaften und Künste" published by Johann Heinrich ZEDLER: s.v. "Leib, lat. *Corpus*, franz. *Corps*," in *Grosses vollständiges Universal-Lexicon* (Graz: Akademische Verlagsanstalt, 1961 = Halle/Leipzig: Johann Heinrich Zedler, 1737), 16: 1504f.

64 Karl LAMPRECHT, *Deutsche Geschichte: Ergänzungs-Band; Zur jüngsten deutschen Vergangenheit*, Bd. 2/2, *Innere Politik, äußere Politik*, 4. Aufl. (Berlin: Gaertner, 1921), 26: "Die Reizsamkeit ist ein besonderer seelischer Zustand, in dem große Massen von Reizen oder Eindrücken, die in früheren Entwicklungszeitaltern der Völker der europäischen Staatengemeinschaft unter der Schwelle des Bewusstseins blieben, bewusst zu werden beginnen: sie bedeutet also eine Intensivierung der Leistungen des Nervensystems." More

generally on the author, see Luise SCHORN-SCHÜTTE, *Karl Lamprecht: Kulturgeschichtss-chreibung zwischen Wissenschaft und Politik*, Schriftenreihe der Historischen Kommission bei der Bayerischen Akademie der Wissenschaften 22 (Göttingen: Vandenhoeck & Ruprecht, 1984), esp. 110–137; Roger CHICKERING, *Karl Lamprecht: A German Academic Life (1856–1915)* (Atlantic Highlands, N.J.: Humanities Press, 1993); Matthias MIDDELL, *Weltgeschichtsschreibung im Zeitalter der Verfachlichung und Professionalisierung: Das Leipziger Institut für Kultur- und Universalgeschichte 1890–1990*, 3 Bde. (Leipzig: Akademische Verlagsanstalt, 2004).

65 Marc BLOCH, *Les rois thaumaturges: Étude sur le caractère surnaturel attribué à la puissance royale, particulièrement en France et en Angleterre* (Strasbourg: Istra, 1924); Ernst H. KANTOROWICZ, *The King's Two Bodies: A Study in Medieval Political Theology* (Princeton, N.J.: Princeton University Press, 1957).

66 TANNER, s.v. "Body, History of," 1279.

67 Norbert ELIAS, *Über den Prozess der Zivilisation: Soziogenetische und psychogenetische Untersuchungen*, Bd. 1, *Wandlungen des Verhaltens in den weltlichen Oberschichten des Abendlandes*, Bd. 2, *Wandlungen der Gesellschaft: Entwurf zu einer Theorie der Zivilisation* (Basel: Verlag Haus zum Falken, 1939); ET: *The Civilizing Process*, trans. Edmund Jephcott (New York: Urizen Books, 1978); Mary DOUGLAS, *Purity and Danger: An Analysis of Concepts of Pollution and Taboo*, with a new preface by the author (New York/London: Routledge 2002 = New York: Praeger, 1966); idem, *Natural Symbols: Explorations in Cosmology* (New York: Pantheon Books, 1970), esp. chapter 5, "The Two Bodies," 69–87.

68 Marcel MAUSS, "Techniques of the Body," *Economy and Society* 2 (1973): 70–88; originally in *Journal de psychologie normale et pathologique* 32 (1935): 271–293.

69 Caroline Walker BYNUM, "Why All the Fuss about the Body? A Medievalist's Perspective," *Critical Inquiry* 22 (1995): 1–33: "In a sense, of course, 'the body' is the wrong topic. It is no topic or, perhaps almost all topics" (2). This might be an allusion to Mary Douglas: "Just as it is true that everything symbolizes the body, so it is equally true that the body symbolizes everything else" (idem, *Purity and Danger*, 122).

70 TANNER, s.v. "Body, History of," 1279.

71 BYNUM, "Why All the Fuss about the Body?" 2. Cf. also the history of research in Bryan S. TURNER, *The Body and Society: Explorations in Social Theory*, 3rd ed. (London/Los Angeles: SAGE, 2008), 33–61.

72 Cf., for example, Barbara DUDEN, *Geschichte unter der Haut: Ein Eisenacher Arzt und seine Patientinnen um 1730* (Stuttgart: Klett-Cotta, 1987), 18–21.

73 Barbara FEICHTINGER, "Einleitung," in *Die Christen und der Körper: Aspekte der Körperlichkeit in der christlichen Literatur der Spätantike*, hg. Barbara Feichtinger und Helmut Seng, Beiträge zur Altertumskunde 184 (Leipzig/München: Saur, 2004), 9–26. See some other objections from Peter DINZELBACHER in his discussion of the collection of papers in *Plekos* 8 (2006): 73–76; and also the subsequent volume: Barbara Feichtinger, Stephen Lake und Helmut Seng, hg., *Körper und Seele: Aspekte spätantiker Anthropologie*, Beiträge zur Altertumskunde 215 (Leipzig/München: Saur, 2006).

74 FEICHTINGER, "Einleitung," 11: "Es mag die–mit den Tieren geteilte–'Unentrinnbarkeit' des biologischen Körpers als unabdingbare Voraussetzung des menschlichen Lebens sein, die Körperlichkeit zu einem zentralen Phänomen des menschlichen Seins macht, doch es ist der reflektierte 'Körper,' der diskursiv repräsentierte 'Körper,' der gleichsam als 'Text' zu definieren und zu lesen ist, der Körperlichkeit zu einem zentralen Phänomen des Menschseins, zu einem Element menschlicher Kultur, werden lässt." BYNUM similarly pronounces: "the body dissolves into language" (idem, "Why All the Fuss about the Body?" 2).

75 Maurice BLOCH, "From Cognition to Ideology," in *Ritual, History and Power: Selected Papers in Anthropology*, London School of Economics Monographs on Social Anthropology 58 (London/Atlantic Highlands, N.J.: Athlone Press, 1989), 106–136; Sarah

COAKLEY, "Introduction: Religion and the Body," in *Religion and the Body*, ed. Sarah Coakley, Cambridge Studies in Religious Traditions 8 (Cambridge/New York: Cambridge University Press, 1997), 1–12, esp. 6f.; Bryan S. TURNER, "Recent Developments in the Theory of the Body," in *The Body: Social Process and Cultural Theory,* ed. Mike Featherstone, Mike Hepworth, and Bryan S. Turner (London/Newbury Park, Calif.: SAGE, 1991), 1–35; and Richard C. POULSEN, *The Body as Text: In a Perpetual Age of Nonreason* (New York: Lang, 1996).

76 See Christoph MARKSCHIES, "Der genaue Blick: Welche Moden haben uns wo die Qualität verdorben?" in *What the Hell Is Quality? Qualitätsstandards in den Geisteswissenschaften*, hg. Elisabeth Lack und Christoph Markschies (Frankfurt am Main/New York: Campus, 2008), 134–144.

77 BYNUM, "Why All the Fuss about the Body?" 5.

78 BYNUM, "Why All the Fuss about the Body?" 2.

79 Patricia Cox MILLER, *The Corporeal Imagination: Signifying the Holy in Late Ancient Christianity* (Philadelphia: University of Pennsylvania Press, 2009).

80 MILLER, *The Corporeal Imagination*, 36–38.

81 MILLER, *The Corporeal Imagination*, 122–130.

82 See Christoph MARKSCHIES, "Vergangenheit, Gegenwart und Zukunft der Ideengeschichte: Zum Werk Hans von Campenhausens," in *Hans Freiherr von Campenhausen: Weg, Werk und Wirkung*, hg. Christoph Markschies, Schriften der Philosophisch-historischen Klasse der Heidelberger Akademie der Wissenschaften 43/2007 (Heidelberg: Winter, 2008), 9–27, esp. 21–24; and Quentin SKINNER, "Bedeutung und Verstehen in der Ideengeschichte," in *Die Cambridge School der politischen Ideengeschichte*, hg. Martin Mulsow und Andreas Mahler, suhrkamp taschenbuch wissenschaft 1925 (Berlin: Suhrkamp, 2010), 21–87, esp. 69–80.

83 BROWN, *The Body and Society*. See also idem, "Report," in *Symbolae Osloenses Debate: The World of Late Antiquity Revisited = Symbolae Osloenses* 72 (1997): 5–30, esp. 21f. (on the influence of Mary Douglas upon Peter Brown); and Lawrence E. SULLIVAN, "Knowledge of the Body in the Study of Religion," *History of Religions* 30 (1990): 86–99.

84 Glenn PEERS, *Subtle Bodies: Representing Angels in Byzantium*, The Transformation of the Classical Heritage 32 (Berkeley/Los Angeles/London: University of California Press, 2001); and Jennifer A. GLANCY, *Corporal Knowledge: Early Christian Bodies* (New York/Oxford: Oxford University Press, 2010), esp. "What She Knew in Her Body: An Introduction," 3–23. See also Aline ROUSSELLE, *Porneia: On Desire and the Body in Antiquity* (Oxford: Blackwell, 1988); ET from the French: *Porneia. De la maîtrise du corps à la privation sensorielle; IIᵉ–IVᵉ siècles de l'ère chrétienne*, Les chemins de l'histoire (Paris: Presses Universitaires de France, 1983); Susan Ashbrook HARVEY, "Locating the Sensing Body: Perception and Religious Identity in Late Antiquity," in *Religion and the Self in Antiquity*, ed. David Brakke, Michael L. Satlow, and Steven Weitzman (Bloomington: Indiana University Press, 2005), 140–162; Kallistos WARE, "'My Helper and My Enemy': The Body in Greek Christianity," in *Religion and the Body*, ed. Sarah Coakley, Cambridge Studies in Religious Traditions 8 (Cambridge/New York: Cambridge University Press, 1997), 90–110; and Andrew LOUTH, "The Body in Western Catholic Christianity," in ibid., 111–130.

85 BYNUM, "Why All the Fuss about the Body?" 13. See idem, "The Female Body and Religious Practice in the Later Middle Ages," in idem, *Fragmentation and Redemption: Essays on Gender and the Human Body in medieval Religion* (New York: Zone Books, 1992), 181–238, esp. 226f.

86 BYNUM, "Why All the Fuss about the Body?" 18. See also Judith BUTLER, *Bodies That Matter: On the Discursive Limits of "Sex"* (New York/London: Routledge, 1993); and Thomas LAQUEUR, *Making Sex: Body and Gender from the Greeks to Freud* (Cambridge, Mass./London: Harvard University Press, 1990).

87 Philip VAN DER EIJK, "The Matter of Mind: Aristotle on the Biology of 'Psychic' Processes and the Bodily Aspects of Thinking," in *Aristotelische Biologie: Intentionen, Methoden, Ergebnisse*, hg. Wolfgang Kullmann and Sabine Föllinger, Philosophie der Antike 6 (Stuttgart: Steiner, 1997), 221–258.

88 Rom HARRÉ, s.v. "Mind-Body Dualism," in *International Encyclopedia of the Social & Behavioral Sciences*, ed. Neil J. Smelser and Paul B. Baltes (Amsterdam: Elsevier, 2001), 14: 9885–9889; Alice SOWAAL, "Cartesian Bodies," *Canadian Journal of Philosophy* 34 (2004): 217–240.

89 Margaret LOCK, "Cultivating the Body: Anthropology and Epistemologies of Bodily Practise and Knowledge," *Annual Review of Anthropology* 22 (1993): 133–155, esp. 137f.; Honi Fern HABER and Gail WEISS, eds., *Perspectives on Embodiment: The Intersections of Nature and Culture* (New York: Routledge, 1999); Almut-Barbara RENGER and Alexandra STELLMACHER, "Der Asketen- als Wissenskörper: Zum verkörperlichten Wissen des Simeon Stylites in ausgewählten Texten der Spätantike," *ZRGG* 62 (2010): 313–338, esp. 315–317.

90 COAKLEY, "Introduction: Religion and the Body," 8.

2 The Body of God in the Judeo-Christian Bible and the Early Christian Theologians

1 SOMMER, *The Bodies of God and the World of Ancient Israel*, 1. Published the following year without knowledge of Sommer's manuscript: Andreas WAGNER, *Gottes Körper: Zur alttestamentlichen Vorstellung der Menschengestaltigkeit Gottes* (Gütersloh: Gütersloher Verlagshaus, 2010); previously: Aaron SCHART, "Die 'Gestalt' YHWHs: Ein Beitrag zur Körpermetaphorik alttestamentlicher Rede von Gott," *Theologische Zeitschrift* 55 (1999): 26–43.

2 Cf. Deut 5:7-10 and, on its interpretation, see DOHMEN, *Das Bilderverbot*, 211–216; WAGNER, *Gottes Körper*, 25–31; and also Sven PETRY, *Die Entgrenzung JHWHs: Monolatrie, Bilderverbot und Monotheismus im Deuteronomium, in Deuterojesaja und im Ezechielbuch*, FAT 2/27 (Tübingen: Mohr Siebeck, 2007), 40–43.

3 WAGNER, *Gottes Körper*, 32 (with attestations on pp. 32–36).

4 See Friedhelm HARTENSTEIN, "Vom Sehen und Schauen Gottes: Überlegungen zu einer theologischen Ästhetik aus der Sicht des Alten Testaments," *Marburger Jahrbuch Theologie* XXII = *MTS* 110 (Leipzig: Evangelische Verlagsanstalt, 2010), 15–37, esp. 18–22.

5 SOMMER, *The Bodies of God and the World of Ancient Israel*, 1.

6 SOMMER, *The Bodies of God and the World of Ancient Israel*, 2.

7 For the history of this term, see Franz CHRIST, *Menschlich von Gott reden: Das Problem des Anthropomorphismus bei Schleiermacher*, Ökumenische Theologie 10 (Einsiedeln/ Zürich/Köln: Benziger; Gütersloh: Gütersloher Verlagshaus Mohn, 1982), 15–31. On the history of the subject, see Wolfhart PANNENBERG, *Systematische Theologie*, Bd. 1 (Göttingen: Vandenhoeck & Ruprecht, 1988), 401–416.

8 Following the definition in CHRIST, *Menschlich von Gott reden*, 13f.

9 Epicurus is said to have described "anthropomorphic gods" (θεοὺς ἀνθρωπομόρφους) as the result of fantastic human dreams about the gods, and thus employed the word ἀνθρωπόμορφος with the sense here relevant: Sextus Empiricus, *Adversus Mathematicos* IX 25 (BiTeu II, 218.9–15 MUTSCHMANN) = *Epicurea*, hg. Hermann Usener (Leipzig: Teubner, 1887), frag. 353, 238.12–16 (missing from *Epicuro: Opere*, introduzione, testo critico, traduzione e note di Graziano ARRIGHETTI, Classici della Filosofia 4 [Turin: Einaudi, 1960]). The employment of this term with regard to Epicurus is regardless more commonplace, as Pseudo-Galenus, *De historia philosophica* 16 (*Doxographi Graeci* 608.16–609.1 DIELS).

10 Thus accordingly, the account in the Imperial-era historian of philosophy Diogenes Laertius on Chrysippus in his *Vitae Philosophorum* VII 147 (SCBO II, 360.11 Long = SVF II, 1021 [II, 305.17 von Arnim]): μὴ εἶναι (sc. Gott) μέντοι ἀνθρωπόμορφον; on this passage, see below. Considering the attetations preserved and its phrasing, it can only contain a paraphrase, and not a quotation from Chrysippus.

11 Strabo, *Geographica* XVI 2.35 (BiTeu III, 1061.15f. Meineke = IV, 340.33f. Radt): οἱ Ἕλληνες (sc. τὸ θεῖον) ἀνθρωπομόρφους τυποῦντες·. The passage is possibly to be ascribed to the philosopher Posidonius, frag. 133, S. 113.3f. Theiler = *Greek and Latin Authors on Jews and Judaism*, ed. with introduction, translations, and commentary by Menahem Stern, vol. 1, *From Herodotus to Plutarch*, Publications of the Israel Academy of Sciences and Humanities (Jerusalem: Academy of Sciences and Humanities, 1974), frag. 115, 294. In favor of the ascription to Posidonius, see Karl Reinhardt, *Poseidonios über Ursprung und Entartung: Interpretation zweier kulturgeschichtlicher Fragmente*, Orient und Antike 6 (Heidelberg: Winter, 1928), 6–34, esp. 9–14; and Martin Hengel, *Judentum und Hellenismus: Studien zu ihrer Begegnung unter besonderer Berücksichtigung Palästinas bis zur Mitte des 2. Jahrhunderts vor Christus*, 3. durchg. Aufl., WUNT 10 (Tübingen: Mohr Siebeck, 1988), 469–472; seen differently in Eduard Norden, "Jahve und Moses in hellenistischer Theologie," in *Festgabe von Fachgenossen und Freunden A. von Harnack zum siebzigsten Geburtstag dargebracht*, hg. Karl Holl (Tübingen: Mohr Siebeck, 1921), 292–301, esp. 294–297; and Jörg-Dieter Gauger, "Eine missverstandene Strabonstelle (zum Judenbericht XVI 2.37)," *Historia* 28 (1979): 211–224. Cf. Strabo, *Geographica* XVII 1.28 (1123.26). See also, most recently, René S. Bloch, *Antike Vorstellungen vom Judentum: Der Judenexkurs des Tacitus im Rahmen der griechischrömischen Ethnographie*, Historia 160 (Stuttgart: Steiner, 2002), 42–53.

12 Details in Christ, *Menschlich von Gott reden*, 16–23.

13 Thus Gen 1:27. On the interpretation of this passage, see Walter Gross, "Die Gottesebenbildlichkeit des Menschen nach Gen 1.26.27 in der Diskussion des letzten Jahrzehnts," *Biblische Notizen* 68 (1993): 35–48; and, in detail, below. For friendly advice on the following section, I thank my Berlin colleague Bernd U. Schipper.

14 Ps 8:6; characteristically modified within the Septuagint, inasmuch as only man's "parity with angels" is considered.

15 A brief history of research into this within German scholarship of the Old Testament may be found in Wagner, *Gottes Körper*, 45–51. Schart, "Die 'Gestalt' YHWHs," 34, differentiates between a "naïve anthropomorphic conception of God" and "metaphorical statements." See now also Howard Schwartz, "Does God Have a Body? The Problem of Metaphor and Literal Language in Biblical Interpretation," in *Bodies, Embodiment, and Theology in the Hebrew Bible*, ed. S. Tamar Kamionkowski and Wonil Kim, Library of Hebrew Bible 465 (New York/London: T&T Clark, 2010), 201–237.

16 Otto Kaiser, *Der Gott des Alten Testaments: Theologie des Alten Testaments*, Tl. 2, *Jahwe, der Gott Israels, Schöpfer der Welt und des Menschen*, Uni-Taschenbücher, Wissenschaft 2024 (Göttingen: Vandenhoeck & Ruprecht, 1998), 315f.

17 Ilaria Ramelli, s.v. "Allegory: II. Judaism," in *Encyclopedia of the Bible and Its Reception* (Berlin/New York: De Gruyter, 2009), 1: 785–793; Margaret M. Mitchell, "Allegory: IV. Christianity; A. Greek Patristics and Orthodox Churches; B. Latin Patristics and Early Medieval Times," in ibid., 1: 796–800.

18 Hans-Josef Klauck, *Allegorie und Allegorese in synoptischen Gleichnistexten*, Neutestamentliche Abhandlungen, Neue Folge 13 (Münster: Aschendorff, 1978), 35–66; Ilaria Ramelli e Giulio Lucchetta, *Allegoria*, vol. 1, *L'età classica*, introduzione e cura di Roberto Radice, Temi metafisici e problemi del pensiero antico, Studi e testi 98 (Mailand: Vita e Pensiero, 2004), 147–204.

19 Ps.-Heraclitus, *Allegoriae* 67.6f. (CUFr 72 Buffière). Cf. the English edition with commentary: *Heraclitus: Homeric Problems*, ed. and trans. Donald Andrew Russell and David Konstan, Society of Biblical Literature Writings from the Greco-Roman World 14

(Atlanta: Society of Biblical Literature, 2005), 208f. Cf. Cornutus, *Theologiae Graecae* 16 (BiTeu 22.3–5 Lang = SAPERE 14, 52.362–368 Berdozzo) and the commentary on this passage within the Italian edition: *Anneo Cornuto: Compendio di teologia greca*, saggio introduttivo e integrativo, traduzione e apparati di Ilaria Ramelli (Mailand: Bompiani, 2003), 336 fn. 92; and now also Mark Sheridan, *Language for God in Patristic Tradition: Wrestling with Biblical Anthropomorphism* (Downers Grove, Ill.: IVP Academic, 2015), 50–55.

20 Friedhelm Hartenstein, *Das Angesicht JHWHs: Studien zu seinem höfischen und kultischen Bedeutungshintergrund in den Psalmen und in Exodus 32–34*, FAT 55 (Tübingen: Mohr Siebeck, 2008), 10–14, esp. 12 with n. 36; also idem, "JHWHs Wesen im Wandel: Vorüberlegungen zu einer Theologie des Alten Testaments," *Theologische Literaturzeitung* 137 (2012): 3–20, esp. 12–15.

21 Aristotle, *Poetica* 21, 1457 b 7–9, states: "A metaphor is the application of a word that belongs to another thing: either from genus to species, species to genus, species to species, or by analogy." ET is that of Stephen Halliwell. On this passage, see *Aristoteles: Poetik*, übers. und erl. von Arbogast Schmitt, 2. durchges. und erg. Aufl., Aristoteles Werke in deutscher Übersetzung 5 (Berlin: Akademie, 2011), 623f.; and on the theory of metaphors, see the remarks in Hartenstein, *Das Angesicht JHWHs*, 11f.

22 Philodem, *Rhetorica* III col. 4 (BiTeu I, 164.20–23 Sudhaus); also ibid., IV col. 14 (174.20–23 Sudhaus). Furthermore, see Klauck, *Allegorie und Allegorese in synoptischen Gleichnistexten*, 40f.; and, on the practice of allegorical interpretation in Philodemus, Ramelli, *Allegoria*, 1: 260–264.

23 Tryphon, *De tropis* 1 (BiTeu III, 193.9–11 Spengel = Martin L. West, "Tryphon *De tropis*," *Classical Quarterly* 15 [1965]: 230–248, text 236–248, here 236).

24 Cicero, *Orator* 27.94 (SCBO Z. 8–11 Wilkins). Cf. idem, *Epistulae ad Atticum* II 20[=40].3 (Cambridge Classical Text and Commentaries 1, 252 Shackleton Bailey with commentary, 393): "Si erunt mihi plura ad te scribenda, ἀλληγορίαις obscurabo." In Klauck, *Allegorie und Allegorese in synoptischen Gleichnistexten*, 41–62, may be found further attestations from the Imperial-era theory and practice of allegorical interpretation.

25 Jean-Pierre Vernant, "Mortals and Immortals: The Body of the Divine," in idem, *Mortals and Immortals: Collected Essays*, ed. Froma I. Zeitlin (Princeton, N.J.: Princeton University Press, 1992), 27–49, esp. 31. Hartenstein suggests employing the term "sociomorphism" over "anthropomorphism" (Hartenstein, *Das Angesicht JHWHs*, 22).

26 Vernant, "Mortals and Immortals," 29f. See on this also Hartenstein, *Das Angesicht JHWHs*, 19f.; Wagner, *Gottes Körper*, 14–17 (with further literature, pp. 16f. with n. 6); Dörte Bester, *Körperbilder in den Psalmen: Studien zu Psalm 22 und verwandten Texten*, FAT 2/24 (Tübingen: Mohr Siebeck, 2007), 38–40; and the collected papers *Corps de Dieux*, sous la direction de Charles Malamoud et Jean-Pierre Vernant, Collection Folio: Histoire 120 (Paris: Gallimard, 2003 = Le temps de la reflexion 7 [Paris: Gallimard, 1986]).

27 Wagner, *Gottes Körper*, 18, 145f. See also idem, "Das synthetische Bedeutungsspektrum hebräischer Körperbezeichnungen," *Biblische Zeitschrift* 51 (2007): 257–265.

28 James Barr, "Theophany and Anthropomorphism in the Old Testament," in *Congress Volume Oxford 1959*, Supplements to Vetus Testamentum 7 (Leiden: Brill, 1960), 31–38.

29 Barr, "Theophany and Anthropomorphism in the Old Testament," 31. On the other hand, the author states on p. 38: "The God whom Israel worships appears, if he wills to appear at all, in living human likeness."

30 Barr, "Theophany and Anthropomorphism in the Old Testament," 33f.

31 See in addition to Exod 33:20 also Judg 13:22; or literally in LXX: Θανάτῳ ἀποθανούμεθα, ὅτι θεὸν ἑωράκαμεν. See now Hartenstein, "Vom Sehen und Schauen Gottes," 31–36.

32 Evangelia G. Dafni, "ΣΑΡΞ ΜΟΥ ΕΞ ΑΥΤΩΝ (LXX-Hosea IX 2): Zur Theologie der Sprache in der Septuaginta," *VT* 51 (2001): 336–353, esp. 336f. The author infers a

translation influenced by the Stoic conception of divine bodies (pp. 352f.). On the absence of the bodily expressions "flesh" (בשר), "blood" (דם), and "bones" (עצם), see also Schart, "Die 'Gestalt' YHWHs," 32–34; and Wagner, *Gottes Körper*, 135–137.

33 Schart, "Die 'Gestalt' YHWHs," 28–35 and 42, provides such an overview as to the body parts of humans and God. See also Wagner, *Gottes Körper*, 105–109 and 137f. On God's wings, cf. Pss 17:8; 36:8; 57:2; 61:5; 63:8; 91:4; and also Ruth 2:12. See also Bernd Janowski, "Keruben und Zion: Thesen zur Entstehung der Zionstradition," in idem, *Gottes Gegenwart in Israel*, Beiträge zur Theologie des Alten Testaments 1 (Neukirchen-Vluyn: Neukirchener, 1993), 247–280, esp. 264–269 (wings on throne of cherubs); and Klaus Koenen, "'Süßes geht vom Starken aus' (Ri 14.14): Vergleiche zwischen Gott und Tier im Alten Testament," *Evangelische Theologie* 55 (1995): 174–197, esp. 184f.

34 Schart, "Die 'Gestalt' YHWHs," 30.

35 Sommer, *The Bodies of God and the World of Ancient Israel*, 36. See also Tzvi Abusch, s.v. "Ishtar," in *Dictionary of Deities and Demons in the Bible (DDD)*, ed. Karel van der Toorn, Bob Becking, and Pieter W. van der Horst (Leiden/New York/Köln: Brill, 1995), 847–855, esp. 851; and idem, s.v. "Marduk," in ibid., 1014–1026, esp. 1017–1020. On the relationship between god and the divine image, see Manfried Dietrich, "Das Kultbild in Mesopotamien," in *"Jahwe und seine Aschera": Anthropomorphes Kultbild in Mesopotamien, Ugarit und Israel; Das biblische Bilderverbot*, hg. Manfried Dietrich und Oswald Loretz, Ugaritisch-Biblische Literatur 9 (Münster: UGARIT-Verlag, 1992), 7–38.

36 On the rise and development of the Zion tradition, see Janowski, "Keruben und Zion," 257–269; and Corinna Körting, *Zion in den Psalmen*, FAT 48 (Tübingen: Mohr Siebeck, 2006), 163–219.

37 Pithos A (inscription 3.1): "lyhwh šmrn wl'šrth"; a "YHWH of Teman" is also twice attested on Pithos B (inscriptions 3.6; 3.9), also in the wall inscription 4.1 (in Phoenician script): "l[y]hwh[]tymn.wl[]'šrt[h]." See now the long-awaited excavation report of Ze'ev Meshel, *Kuntillet 'Ajrud (Horvat Teman): An Iron Age II Religious Site on the Judah-Sinai Border* (Jerusalem: Israel Exploration Society, 2012), 87–90, 95–98, and 105, and commentary on pp. 130f.; Jeremy M. Hutton, "Southern, Northern and Transjordanian Perspectives," in *Religious Diversity in Israel and Juda*, ed. Francesca Stavrakopoulou and John Barton (London/New York: T&T Clark, 2010), 149–174, esp. 152–156; and Wagner, *Gottes Körper*, 38–40. A divergent interpretation is found in Erhard Blum, "Die Wandinschriften 4.2 und 4.6 also die Pithos-Inschrift 3.9 aus *Kuntillet 'Ağrūd*," *Zeitschrift des Deutschen Palästina-Vereins* 129 (2013): 21–54, here 44–50.

38 2 Sam 15:7; also Ps 99:2. See Sommer, *The Bodies of God and the World of Ancient Israel*, 38f.; and now critically Henrik Pfeiffer, "Die Herkunft Jahwes und ihre Zeugen," *Berliner Theologische Zeitschrift* 30 (2013): 11–43, here 36–40.

39 Cf. for this text from Gen 31:13; the Septuagint translated the verse without recourse to "Bethel": ἐγώ εἰμι ὁ θεὸς ὁ ὀφθείς σοι ἐν τόπῳ θεοῦ. Possibly the *massebah* also marked the place wherein a particular closeness to God is possible (epistolary communication from Bernd U. Schipper, 5 February 2013).

40 Herennius Philo, *Phoenicica* apud Eusebium, *Praeparatio Evangelica* I 10.16 (GCS Eusebius VIII/1, 47.1 Mras/Des Places) = FGrH, Tl. 3, Geschichte von Städten und Völkern (Horographie und Ethnographie) C Autoren über einzelne Länder nr. 608a–856 (Zweiter Bd.: Illyrien-Thrakien nr. 709–856) (Leiden: Brill, 1958), nr. 790 (809.23) = Albert I. Baumgarten, *The Phoenician History of Philo of Byblos: A Commentary*, Études préliminaires aux religions orientales dans l'Empire romain 89 (Leiden: Brill, 1981), 15.23; see the commentary in ibid., 202f. See also Otto Eissfeldt, "Der Gott Bethel," *Archiv für Religionswissenschaft* 28 (1930): 1–30 = idem, *Kleine Schriften*, Bd. 1, hg. Rudolf Sellheim und Fritz Maas (Tübingen: Mohr Siebeck, 1962), 206–233; J. Philip Hyatt, "The Deity Bethel and the Old Testament," *Journal of the American Oriental Society* 59 (1939): 81–89; Klaus Koenen, *Bethel: Geschichte, Kult und Theologie*, Orbis Biblicus et Orientalis (Fribourg, Schweiz/Göttingen: Universitätsverlag /

Vandenhoeck & Ruprecht, 2003), 81–95, 133f.; and Edward R. DALGISH, S.V. "Bethel (Deity)," in *The Anchor Bible Dictionary* (New York: Doubleday, 1992), 1: 706–710; with the objections of Günther ZUNTZ, "Baitylos und Bethel," *Classica et Mediaevalia* 8 (1945): 169–219, esp. 178f.

41 Herennius Philo, *Phoenicica* apud Eusebium, *Praeparatio Evangelica* I 10.23 (GCS Eusehius VIII/1, 48.10 MRAS/DES PLACES = FGrH nr. 790, 810.29 JACOBY). On the βαίτυλοι at length, see ZUNTZ, "Baitylos und Bethel," 180–185.

42 Robert WENNING, "The Betyls of Petra," *Bulletin of the American School of Oriental Research* 234 (2001): 79–95; generally: Tryggve N. D. METTINGER, *No Graven Image? Israelite Aniconism in Its Ancient Near Eastern Context*, Coniectanea biblica Old Testament Series 42 (Stockholm: Almqvist & Wiksell International, 1995).

43 *Scriptores Historiae Augustae* XVII, *Aeli Lampridii Antoninus Heliogabalus* 3.4 (BiTeu I, 225.5–11 HOHL); See the detailed commentary in *Histoire Auguste*, tome 3/1, *Vies de Macrin, Diaduménien, Héliogabale*, texte établi, traduit et commenté par Robert Turcan, Collection des Universités de France, (Paris 1993), 162f.; and Theo OPTENDRENK, *Die Religionspolitik des Kaisers Elagabal im Spiegel der Historia Augusta*, Habelts Dissertationsdrucke, Reihe Alte Geschichte, Heft 6 (Bonn: Habelt, 1969), 84–106; Timothy D. BARNES, "Ultimus Antoninorum," in *Bonner Historia-Augusta-Colloquium 1970*, unter Mitwirkung von Johannes Straub, hg. Andreas Alföldi, Antiquitas, Reihe 4, Beiträge zur Historia-Augusta-Forschung, Bd. 10 (Bonn: Habelt, 1972), 53–74, esp. 60–62; Martin FREY, *Untersuchungen zur Religion und Religionspolitik des Kaisers Elagabal*, Historia, Einzelschriften 62 (Stuttgart: Steiner, 1989), 74 with n. 4; and Stephan BERRENS, *Sonnenkult und Kaisertum von den Severern bis zu Constantin I. (193–337 n. Chr.)*, Historia, Einzelschriften 185 (Stuttgart: Steiner, 2004), 51–57; further antique reports in Herodianus, *Regnum post Marcum* V 5.8–10 (BiTeu 115.28–116.16 LUCARINI); and (Ps.-)Aurelius Victor, *De Caesaribus* 23.1 [1–3] (BiTeu 102.20–25 PICHLMAYR = CUFr 31 FESTY).

44 *Passio S. Philippi ep. Heracleae et sociorum* (BHL 6834), in *Acta Sanctorum Octobris IX*, 545–548, esp. 546f.; and also Joseph FÜHRER, "Zur Geschichte des Elagabaliums und der Athena Parthenos des Pheidias," *Römische Mitteilungen* 7 (1892): 158–165, esp. 158.

45 On the temple and its excavation, see Henri BROISE and Yvon THÉBERT, "Élagabal et le complexe religieux de la Vigna Barberini: Heliogabalium in Palatino monte iuxta aedes imperatorias consecravit eique templum fecit (HA, Ant. Heliog., III, 4)," *Mélanges de l'École française de Rome: Antiquité* 111 (1999): 729–747; Martijn ICKS, *The Crimes of Elagabalus: The Life and Legacy of Rome's Decadent Boy Emperor* (London: I. B. Tauris, 2011), 27f. (with tables 11/12); and Filippo COARELLI, S.V. "Heliogabalus, templum; Heliogabalium," in *Lexicon Topographicum Urbis Romae*, a cura di Eva Margareta Steinby (Rome: Edizioni Quasar, 1996), 3: 10f.

46 Coin from Emesa, in the British Museum since 1846, London: Warwick WROTH, *Catalogue of the Greek Coins of Galatia, Cappadocia and Syria*, A Catalogue of the Greek Coins in the British Museum 20 (London: Printed by the Order of the Trustees of the British Museum, 1899), 241 nr. 24 (plate XXVIII/2), with the legend ΑΥΤΟΚ ΣΟΥΛΠ ΑΝΩΝΕΙΝΟΣ ΣΕ ΕΜΙΣΩ[N] ΚΟΛΩΝ from year 565 of the Seleucid era (= AD 253/254). See also Richard DELBRÜCK, "Uranius of Emesa," *Numismatic Chronicle and Journal of the Royal Numismatic Society* 8 (1948): 11–29; further references at http://www.wildwinds.com/coins/ric/elagabalus/i.html s.v. "sacred stone" (last accessed on 1 May 2019).

47 On the underpinnings of this conception, see Friedhelm HARTENSTEIN, "Wolkendunkel und Himmelsfeste: Zur Genese und Kosmologie der Vorstellung des himmlischen Heiligtums JHWHs," in *Das biblische Weltbild und seine altorientalischen Kontexte*, ed. Bernd Janowski and Beate Ego with the collaboration of Annette Krüger, FAT 32 (Tübingen: Mohr Siebeck, 2001), 125–179.

48 SOMMER, *The Bodies of God and the World of Ancient Israel*, 58–79.

49 Amos 7:7in the LXX, God becomes a simple "man," evidently to object to the passage καὶ ἰδοὺ ἀνὴρ ἑστηκὼς ἐπὶ τείχους ἀδαμαντίνου, καὶ ἐν τῇ χειρὶ αὐτοῦ ἀδάμας. See generally Charles Theodore Fritsch, *The Anti-anthropomorphisms of the Greek Pentateuch*, Princeton Oriental Texts 10 (Princeton, N.J.: Princeton University Press, 1943); and, most recently, Staffan Olofsson, *God Is My Rock: A Study of Translation Technique and Theological Exegesis in the Septuagint* (Stockholm: Almqvist & Wiksell International, 1990), 17–19 ("The Avoidance of Attributing Physical Form to God."

50 Amos 9:1.

51 Isa 6:1. The LXX reduces once more the body terminology, as instead of the hem of the robe which fills the temple, it mentions only very neutrally his "glory" which fills the house of the temple.

52 1 Kgs 19:12.

53 Hengel, *Judentum und Hellenismus*. See also idem, *Juden, Griechen und Barbaren: Aspekte der Hellenisierung des Judentums in vorchristlicher Zeit*, Stuttgarter Bibelstudien 76 (Stuttgart: Verlag Katholisches Bibelwerk, 1976); and idem (in collaboration with Christoph Markschies), *The "Hellenization" of Judaea in the First Century after Christ* (London: SCM Press, 1989). I have published a terminological and research history on the topic, treating thereby Hengel's work: Christoph Markschies, *Hellenisierung des Christentums: Sinn und Unsinn einer historischen Deutungskategorie*, Forum Theologische Literaturzeitung 25 (Leipzig: Evangelische Verlags-Anstalt, 2012), 5f. and 33–36.

54 See for this dating Hans-Joachim Gehrke, *Geschichte des Hellenismus*, Oldenbourg Grundriss der Geschichte 1B, 4. Aufl. (München: Oldenbourg, 2008), 1–4; and Markschies, *Hellenisierung des Christentums*, 114–116.

55 Thus Wilhelm Nestle, *Vom Mythos zum Logos: Die Selbstentfaltung des griechischen Denkens von Homer bis auf die Sophistik und Sokrates*, 2. Aufl. (Stuttgart: Kröner, 1975), passim. For a critical position: Glenn W. Most, "From Logos to Mythos," in *From Myth to Reason? Studies in the Development of Greek Thought*, ed. Richard Buxton (Oxford: Oxford University Press, 1999), 25–47, esp. 28.

56 On his biography, see, most prominently, Nikolaus Walter, *Der Thoraausleger Aristobulos: Untersuchungen zu seinen Fragmenten und zu pseudepigraphischen Resten der jüdisch-hellenistischen Literatur*, TU 86 (Berlin: Akademie-Verlag, 1964), 10–26. Walter attempts to show that the statements as to the philosophical orientation and the identification of the king are rather more learned work of the Christian copyists of the fragments without precise knowledge of the actual living conditions. Somewhat more optimistic is Hengel, *Judentum und Hellenismus*, 295–298, regarding the authenticity of the information. Lester L. Grabbe, s.v. "Aristobulus of Alexandria (the Philosopher)," in *Encyclopedia of the Bible and Its Reception* (Berlin/New York: De Gruyter, 2009), 2: 724–726, describes Hengel's opinion as "widely accepted" (p. 724).

57 Eusebius, *Praeparatio Evangelica* VIII 9.38 (GCS Eusebius VIII/1, 451.7f. Mras/Des Places). German translation and commentary in Nikolaus Walter, "Fragmente jüdisch-hellenistischer Exegeten: Aristobulos, Demetrios, Aristeas," in *Jüdische Schriften aus hellenistisch-römischer Zeit*, Bd. 3, Lfg. 2, *Unterweisungen in lehrhafter Form* (Gütersloh: Gütersloher Verlagshaus Mohn, 1975), 270. On the text, see Walter, *Der Thoraausleger Aristobulos*, 36f.; and, recently, Sheridan, *Language for God in Patristic Tradition*, 63–65.

58 Aristobulus, frag. 2 = Eusebius, *Praeparatio Evangelica* VIII 10.1 (GCS Eusebius VIII/1, 451.13–17 Mras/Des Places). German translation and commentary in Walter, "Fragmente jüdisch-hellenistischer Exegeten," 271. ET from *Eusebius of Caesarea: Praeparatio Evangelica (Preparation for the Gospel)*, vol. 3, pt. 1, trans. E. H. Gifford (1903), 375.

59 Aristobulus, frag. 2 = Eusebius, *Praeparatio Evangelica* VIII 10.2–5 (GCS Eusebius VIII/1, 451.17–452.7 Mras/Des Places). German translation and commentary in Walter, "Fragmente jüdisch-hellenistischer Exegeten," 270f. ET from Gifford, *Eusebius of Caesarea: Praeparatio Evangelica*, 376.

60 Aristobulus, frag. 2 = Eusebius, *Praeparatio Evangelica* VIII 10.7 (GCS Eusebius VIII/1, 452.10–14 Mras/Des Places). German translation and commentary in Walter, "Fragmente jüdisch-hellenistischer Exegeten," 271. ET from Gifford, *Eusebius of Caesarea: Praeparatio Evangelica*, 376.

61 Aristobulus, frag. 2 = Eusebius, *Praeparatio Evangelica* VIII 10.8 (GCS Eusebius VIII/1, 452.18f. Mras/Des Places). German translation and commentary in Walter, "Fragmente jüdisch-hellenistischer Exegeten," 271. ET from Gifford, *Eusebius of Caesarea: Praeparatio Evangelica*, 376.

62 Aristobulus, frag. 2 = Eusebius, *Praeparatio Evangelica* VIII 10.9–17 (GCS Eusebius VIII/1, 452.21–454.8 Mras/Des Places). German translation and commentary in Walter, "Fragmente jüdisch-hellenistischer Exegeten," 271–273. ET from Gifford, *Eusebius of Caesarea: Praeparatio Evangelica*, 377.

63 Walter, *Der Thoraausleger Aristobulos*, 62: στάσις and κατάβασις could "perhaps correspond to πόδες and περίπατος" ("vielleicht als Entsprechungen für πόδες und περίπατος gelten").

64 Aristobulus, frag. 4 = Eusebius, *Praeparatio Evangelica* XIII 12.3–8 (GCS Eusebius VIII/2, 191.9–195.11 Mras/Des Places). German translation and commentary in Walter, "Fragmente jüdisch-hellenistischer Exegeten," 664. ET from Gifford, *Eusebius of Caesarea: Praeparatio Evangelica*, 274–276. See also Peter Kuhn, *Offenbarungsstimmen im Antiken Judentum: Untersuchungen zur Bat Qol und verwandten Phänomenen*, TSAJ 20 (Tübingen: Mohr Siebeck, 1989), 144–149.

65 Aristobul, frag. 4 = Eusebius, *Praeparatio Evangelica* XIII 12.7 (GCS Eusebius VIII/2, 195.4–7 Mras/Des Places). German translation and commentary in Walter, "Fragmente jüdisch-hellenistischer Exegeten," 275. See on this point also Ps.-Aristeas, *Epistula ad Philocratem* 16 (SC 89, 110 Pelletier = BiTeu 6.3–10 Mendelsohn/Wendland); and Hengel, *Judentum und Hellenismus*, 298f.

66 Aristobulus, frag. 2 = Eusebius, *Praeparatio Evangelica* VIII 10, 5 and 9 (GCS Eusebius VIII/1, 452.6f. 21f.). See also Walter, *Der Thoraausleger Aristobulos*, 129–141; and already Edmund Stein, *Die allegorische Exegese des Philo aus Alexandria*, BZAW 51 (Gießen: Alfred Töpelmann, 1929), 6–12.

67 Diodorus Siculus, *Bibliotheca historica* XL 3.4 (BiTeu IV, 180.32–181.3 Dindorf) = Photius, *Bibliothecae codex* 244 (CUFr VI, 135.37–40 Henry = FGrH 264 F 6 [III A, 14.23–25 Jacoby; new edition online, accessible at http://referenceworks.brillonline.com/entries/brills-new-jacoby/hekataios-264-a264#BNJTEXT264_F_6 (last accessed on 1 May 2019)]) = *Greek and Latin Authors on Jews and Judaism* I, frag. 11, 26.20–23 Stern. ET follows Stern, p. 28. On the text, see Felix Jacoby, s.v. "Hekataios 4) Hekataios aus Abdera," PW 7/2: 2750–2769, esp. 2765f.; Werner Jaeger, "Greeks and Jews: The First Greek Records of Jewish Religion and Civilization," *Journal of Religion* 18 (1938): 127–143, esp. 139–141 (Jaeger supposes a literal quotation from Hecataeus in Diodorus: 139 n. 37); and Hengel, *Judentum und Hellenismus*, 465f. See also now Bloch, *Antike Vorstellungen vom Judentum*, 29–41.

68 Photius, *Bibliothecae codex* 244 (CUFr VI, 137.7f. Henry). According to René Henry this is a "conclusion de Photius" (137 n. 2).

69 Thus Daniel R. Schwartz, "Diodorus Siculus 40.3 — Hecataeus or Pseudo Hecataeus?" in *Jews and Gentiles in the Holy Land in the Days of the Second Temple, the Mishnah, and the Talmud: A Collection of Articles*, ed. Menachem Mor, Aharon Oppenheimer, Jack Pastor, and Daniel R. Schwartz (Jerusalem: Yad Ben-Zvi Press, 2003), 181–198; dated even later by Russell E. Gmirkin: *Berossus and Genesis, Manetho and Exodus: Hellenistic Histories and the Date of the Pentateuch*, Library of Hebrew Bible/Old Testament Studies 433 (New York/London: T&T Clark, 2006), 38–62; most prominently critical of Gmirkin: Bezalel Bar-Kochva, *The Image of the Jews in Greek Literature: The Hellenistic Period*, Hellenistic Culture and Society 51 (Berkeley/Los Angeles/London: University of California Press, 2010), 106f. with n. 48; also Lester L. Grabbe, *A History of the Jews*

and Judaism in the Second Temple Period, vol. 2, *The Early Hellenistic Period (335–175 BCE)*, Library of Second Temple Studies 68 (London/New York: T&T Clark, 2008), 113–119.

70 Clemens Alexandrinus, *Stromata* V 109.2f. (GCS Clemens Alexandrinus II, 399.19f. Stählin/Früchtel/Treu = Hermann Diels/Walther Kranz, *Die Fragmente der Vorsokratiker: Griechisch und Deutsch*, unveränderter Nachdruck der 6. Aufl. 1951 [Zürich: Weidmann, 2004], 132.16f. [DK 21 B 14]); Greek text modified according to *Poetarum elegiacorum testimonia et fragmenta*, ediderunt Bruno Gentili et Carolus Prato, Bibliotheca scriptorum Graecorum et Romanorum Teubneriana, 2. verbesserte Aufl. (Leipzig: Teubner, 1988), 175. ET is from the edition and brief commentary in *The Texts of Early Greek Philosophy: The Complete and Selected Testimonies of the Major Presocratics*, pt. 1, ed. and trans. Daniel W. Graham (Cambridge: Cambridge University Press, 2010), 109 (31 [F19]). See also the extensive commentary in James H. Lesher, *Xenophanes of Colophon: Fragments; A Text and Translation with a Commentary*, Phoenix Supplementary vol. 30 = Phoenix Pre-Socratics 4 (Toronto/London: University of Toronto Press, 1992), 24f., 85–89, and 114–119; and Ernst Heitsch, "Das Wissen des Xenokrates," *Rheinisches Museum* 109 (1966): 193–235, esp. 216–219.

71 Clemens Alexandrinus, *Stromata* V 109.2f. (GCS Clemens Alexandrinus II, 400.1–5 Stählin/Früchtel/Treu); cf. DK 11 B 15 (I, 60.17–61.2 Diels/Kranz = 32 [F20], 108–111 Graham). Differently, 176 Gentili/Prato with conjecture of Diels; also differently, 24 Lesher. See the extensive commentary in Lesher, *Xenophanes of Colophon: Fragments*, 89–94 and 114–119; also, most recently, Wolfgang Drechsler and Rainer Kattel, "Mensch und Gott bei Xenophanes," in *Gott und Mensch im Dialog: Festschrift für Otto Kaiser zum 80. Geburtstag*, Bd. 1, hg. Markus Witte, BZAW 345 (Berlin/New York: De Gruyter, 2004), 111–129.

72 Thus also Clemens Alexandrinus, *Stromata* VII 22.1 (GCS Clemens Alexandrinus III, 16.6 Stählin/Früchtel/Treu = DK 21 B 16 [I, 133.6f. Diels/Kranz] = 33 [F21], 110 Graham). Accordingly the text in Clement, seen differently in Diels/Kranz and following him 175 Gentili/Prato.

73 See Otto Kaiser, "Der eine Gott und die Götter der Welt," in idem, *Zwischen Athen und Jerusalem: Studien zur griechischen und biblischen Theologie, ihrer Eigenart und ihrem Verhältnis*, BZAW 320 (Berlin/New York: De Gruyter, 2003), 135–152, esp. 147–150; and, in particular, Aryeh Finkelberg, "Studies in Xenophanes," *Harvard Studies in Classical Philology* 93 (1990): 103–167.

74 Admittedly otherwise in Pseudo-Aristoteles, *De melisso* 7 977 b 19f. (Barbara Cassin, *Si Parménide: Le traité anonyme De Melisso Xenophane Gorgia*, édition critique et commentaire, Cahiers de Philologie 4 [Lille: Presses Universi-taires de Lille 1980], 344.1–4 = DK 21 A 28 [I, 118 Diels/Kranz]); also Jaap Mansfeld, "De Melisso Xenophane Gorgia: Pyrrhonizing Aristotelianism," *Rheinisches Museum für Philologie* 131 (1988): 239–276, esp. 254.

75 Thus DK 21 A 31.3–9 (I, 121.28–122.14 Diels/Kranz) = Simplicius, *In Aristotelis physicorum libros commentaria* I 2 ad p. 184 b 15 (CAG IX, 22.30–23.20 Diels). See on this Bruno Snell, *Die Entdeckung des Geistes: Studien zur Entstehung des europäischen Denkens bei den Griechen*, 9. Aufl. (Göttingen: Vandenhoeck & Ruprecht, 2009), 131f.; with markedly different emphasis: Finkelberg, "Studies in Xenophanes," 109–114, 118–127, and 163–165. An ET is given in Lesher, *Xenophanes of Colophon: Fragments*, 212f.; on the question of the spherical body, see ibid., 100–102.

76 So DK 21 B 24 (I, 135.7 Diels/Kranz) = Sextus Empiricus, *Adversus mathematicos* IX 144 (BiTeu II, 246.23–25 Mutschmann); cf. Diogenes Laertius IX 19 (SCBO II, 446.12–16 Long = DK 21 A 1 [I, 113, 26]): οὖλος ὁρᾶι, οὖλος δὲ νοεῖ, οὖλος δέ τ' ἀκούει; also DK 21 B 25 (I, 135.9) = Simplicius, *In Aristotelis physicorum libros commentaria* I 2 ad p. 184 b 15 (23.19 Diels, as above): ἀλλ' ἀπάνευθε πόνοιο νόου φρενὶ πάντα

κραδαίνει. An extensive commentary is given in Lesher, *Xenophanes of Colophon: Fragments*, 30 (Text), 102–106, and 114–119.

77 Werner Jaeger, *Die Theologie der frühen griechischen Denker* (Stuttgart: Kohlhammer, 2009 [= 1953]), 54.

78 Attestations in Drechsler/Kattel, "Mensch und Gott bei Xenophanes," 112f. and 119–121.

79 On this *in extenso*: Mark J. Edwards, "Xenophanes Christianus?" *Greek, Roman and Byzantine Studies* 32 (1991): 219–228, esp. 223–228.

80 Clemens Alexandrinus, *Stromata* V 89.1 (GCS Clemens Alexandrinus II, 384.15–17 Stählin/Früchtel/Treu). ET from *The Writings of Clement of Alexandria*, vol. 2, trans. William Wilson, Ante-Nicean Christian Library 4 (Edinburgh: T&T Clark, 1867), 274

81 Cf., for further parts of the section, Clemens Alexandrinus, *Stromata* V 98.1–134.1 (GCS Clemens Alexandrinus II, 390.19–417.14 Stählin/Früchtel/Treu); and Eusebius, *Praeparatio Evangelica* XIII 13.1–65 (GCS Eusebius VIII/2, 198.4–228.8 Mras/Des Places).

82 Clemens Alexandrinus, *Stromata* V 99.4 (GCS Clemens Alexandrinus II, 392.7 Stählin/Früchtel/Treu). Cf. Gen 2:7 and *Stromata* V 94.3 (GCS Clemens Alexandrinus II, 388.9–11 Stählin/Früchtel/Treu) with Ps.-Plato, *Axiochus* 365 E–366 A. ET from Wilson, *The Writings of Clement of Alexandria* 2: 280.

83 Clemens Alexandrinus, *Stromata* V 106–108 (GCS Clemens Alexandrinus II, 397.6–399.13 Stählin/Früchtel/Treu).

84 Clemens Alexandrinus, *Stromata* V 109.1 (GCS Clemens Alexandrinus II, 399.14–17 Stählin/Früchtel/Treu). ET from Wilson, *The Writings of Clement of Alexandria* 2: 285. Cf. also the editions of the collections of fragments: DK 21 B 23 (I, 135.4f. Diels/Kranz = 35 [F23], 108–110 Graham = 178 Gentili/Prato and in Lesher, *Xenophanes of Colophon: Fragments*, 30, with commentary: pp. 96–102 and 114–119). Should the authentic meter of verse in Xenophanes be held to have remained the same (seen otherwise by Wilamowitz and Heitsch: Lesher, *Xenophanes of Colophon: Fragments*, 85), then it must be maintained that Eusebius of Caesarea here attempts (unsuccessfully) to rework the iambic trimeter of the original in *Praeparatio Evangelica* XIII 13.36 (GCS Eusebius VIII/2, 212.8f. Mras/Des Places) into a hexameter, thus, for example, Mark Edwards: idem, "Xenophanes Christianus?" 221: εἷς θεός ἔν τε θεοῖσι καὶ ἀνθρώποισι μέγιστος, | οὔ τι δέμας θνητοῖσιν ὁμοίιος, οὐδὲ νόημα. | ἀλλ' οἱ βροτοὶ δοκοῦσι γεννᾶσθαι θεούς, | τὴν σφετέρην δ' ἐσθῆτα ἔχειν φωνήν τε δέμας τε·.

85 Eusebius, *Praeparatio Evangelica* XIII 13.36 (GCS Eusebius VIII/2, 212.8f. Mras/Des Places); also Theodoretus Cyrrhensis, *Graecarum Affectionum Curatio* III 72 (BiTeu 88.19–89.1 Raeder).

86 Clemens Alexandrinus, Stromata VII 22.1 (III, 16.3–9 Stählin/Früchtel/Treu). ET from Wilson, *The Writings of Clement of Alexandria* 2: 241.

87 Jens Halfwassen, s.v. "Platonismus II. Religionsphilosophisch," in *Religion in Geschichte und Gegenwart: Handwörterbuch für Theologie und Religionswissenschaft*, 4. Aufl. (Tübingen: Mohr Siebeck, 2003), 6: 1387–1389, quotation on 1387; see also Friedrich Solmsen, "The Background of Plato's Theology," *Transactions and Proceedings of the American Philological Association* 67 (1936): 208–218.

88 See now in particular Stephen Menn, *Plato on God as Nous*, Journal of the History of Philosophy Monograph Series (South Bend, Ind.: St. Augustine's Press, 2002 = Carbondale: Southern Illinois University Press, 1995), 7–15 (contra Harold Cherniss); also idem, "Aristotle and Plato on God as Nous and as the Good," *Review of Metaphysics* 45 (1992): 543–573, esp. 555–558.

89 Plato, *Respublica* II 18, 379 B. On the gods of the Greek pantheon in Plato, see Gustav E. Mueller, "Plato and the Gods," *Philosophical Review* 45 (1936): 457–472, esp. 463–466.

90 Plato, *Phaedrus* 246 D. ET from *Plato: Euthyphro. Apology. Crito. Phaedo. Phaedrus*, trans. Harold North Fowler, LCL 36 (Cambridge, Mass.: Harvard University Press, 1914), 473.

91 Plato, *Respublica* II 19, 381 C. ET from *Plato: Republic, Books 1–5*, ed. and trans. Chris EMLYN-JONES and William PREDDY, LCL 237 (Cambridge, Mass.: Harvard University Press, 2013), 211.

92 Thus, most prominently, the doxographically transmitted fragment (fr. 38 LANG = 89 ISNARDI PARENTE), in the reconstruction of the Φυσικαὶ δόξαι of Aëtius (after Ioannes Stobaeus, *Anthologium* I 1 [I, 35.3f. WACHSMUTH]) in Hermann DIELS, *Doxographi Graeci collegit, recensuit prolegominis indicibusque instruxit*, 4th ed. (Berlin: De Gruyter, 1965), 303.20–22. Also see Hans KRÄMER, "Die ältere Akademie," in *Die Philosophie der Antike*, Bd. 3, *Ältere Akademie—Aristoteles—Peripatos*, hg. Hellmut Flashar, Grundriss der Geschichte der Philosophie, begründet von Friedrich Ueberweg, völlig neu bearb. Ausg. (Basel/Stuttgart: Schwabe, 1983), 1–174, esp. 22–43 (§ 2. Speusippus); on the fragment itself, see ibid., 37.

93 Plato, *Parmenides* 137 B: τὸ ἓν αὐτό. I follow in my interpretation Jens HALFWASSEN, *Der Aufstieg zum Einen: Untersuchungen zu Platon und Plotin*, Beiträge zur Altertumskunde 9 (Stuttgart: Teubner, 1992), 298–307, though he himself does not justify the fundamental choice made for the Plato interpretation here propounded.

94 Cf. Plato, *Parmenides* 139 E–140 A. On its interpretation, see HALFWASSEN, *Der Aufstieg zum Einen*, 336–363.

95 Plato, *Parmenides* 137 D–138 A. On its interpretation, see HALFWASSEN, *Der Aufstieg zum Einen*, 312–316.

96 Plato, *Respublica* VI 19, 509 B. ET from *Plato: Republic, Books 6–10*, ed. and trans. Chris EMLYN-JONES and William PREDDY, LCL 237 (Cambridge, Mass.: Harvard University Press, 2013), 95. See also John WHITTAKER, "Ἐπέκεινα νοῦ καὶ οὐσίας," *VC* 23 (1969), 91–104 = idem, *Studies in Platonism and Patristic Thought*, Collected Studies Series CS 201 (London: Variorum Reprints, 1984), nr. XIII.

97 Plato, *Sophista* 246 A/B. ET from *Plato: Theaetetus. Sophist*, trans. Harold North FOWLER, LCL 123 (Cambridge, Mass.: Harvard University Press, 1921), 378.

98 Plato, *Phaedrus* 246 C/D. ET from FOWLER, *Plato: Euthyphro. Apology. Crito. Phaedo. Phaedrus*, 437. Cf. here, as elsewhere, the German translation of Friedrich Schleiermacher: Platon, *Sämtliche Werke*, Nach der Übersetzung von Friedrich Schleiermacher und Hieronymus Müller mit der Stephanus-Numerierung hg. Walter F. Otto†, Ernesto Grassi und Gert Plamböck, Bd. 4, *Phaidros, Parmenides, Theaitetos, Sophistes*, Rowohlts Klassiker der Literatur und der Wissenschaft 39, Griechische Philosophie Bd. 5 (Hamburg: Rowohlt, 1958), 28.

99 Plato, *Phaedrus* 246 D.

100 Plato, *Sophista* 248 E/249 A (Fremder).

101 Plato, *Phaedrus* 246 C/D.

102 Attestations for this formula in WHITTAKER, "Ἐπέκεινα νοῦ καὶ οὐσίας," 92–103.

103 Thus Origenes, *Contra Celsum* VII 38 (GCS Origenes II, 188.11f. KOETSCHAU).

104 *Doxographi Graeci*, collegit, recensuit, prolegomenis indicibusque instruxit Hermann DIELS, editio iterata (Berlin/Leipzig: De Gruyter, 1929), 537 (apparatus for Cicero, *De natura deorum* I 12.30). Diels names the following passages: Alcinous, *Didascalicus* 10.7 καὶ τὸ ἀσώματον αὐτὸν εἶναι (CUFr 25[166],1 WHITTAKER/LOUIS); Apuleius, *De Platone* I 192 (BiTeu 93.8–14 MORESCHINI); Aristocles apud Eusebium, *Praeparatio evangelica* XV 14.1: ἀλλ' οὗτος ἄμφω σώματά φησιν εἶναι, καὶ τὸ ποιοῦν καὶ τὸ πάσχον (sc. the active and passive principles for Zeno bodies), ἐκείνου τὸ πρῶτον ποιοῦν αἴτιον ἀσώματον εἶναι λέγοντος (according to Plato, the first, active principle is bodiless: GCS Eusebius VIII/2, 378.20–379.2 MRAS/DES PLACES = *Aristocles of Messene: Testimonia and Fragments*, ed. with translation and commentary by Maria Lorenza Chiesara, Oxford Classical Monographs [Oxford: Oxford University Press, 2001], frag. 3, 18f. with commentary on p. 81); Diogenes Laertius, *Vitae philosophorum* III 77: δοκεῖ δ' αὐτῷ τὸν θεὸν ὡς καὶ τὴν ψυχὴν ἀσώματον εἶναι; also V 32 (SCBO I, 152.10f., 213.5f. LONG); Pseudo-Galenus, *Historia philosophorum* 16 (*Doxograpi Graeci* 608.16–18

Diels); Hippolytus, *Refutatio omnium haeresium* I 19.3 (GCS Hippolyt III, 19.12f. Wendland = PTS 25, 76.9f. Marcovich); and Seneca apud Augustinum, *De civitate Dei* VI 10 (BiTeu I, 267.22–24 Dombart/Kalb); cf. on this also Ps.-Plato, *Epinomis* 981 B.

105   Michael Mach, s.v. "Philo von Alexandrien," *TRE* 26: 523–531.

106   Mach, s.v. "Philo von Alexandrien," 526: "Zwischen dem persönlichen Gott der Bibel und dem wirkenden Prinzip des sog. philosophischen Monotheismus klafft eine Lücke, die so nie wirklich in Philos Blick kommt. Je geistiger der philonische Gott gedacht wird, desto mehr muß Philo die irdische Stofflichkeit abwerten (worin er weit über die Ansätze Platos hinausgeht)." See also on the topic also David T. Runia, *Philo of Alexandria and the Timaeus of Plato*, Philosophia Antiqua 44 (Leiden: Brill, 1986), 258–266 and 431–438; and Dieter Zeller, "Gott bei Philo von Alexandrien," in *Der Gott Israels im Zeugnis des Neuen Testaments*, hg. Ulrich Busse, Quaestiones Disputatae 201 (Freiburg/Basel/Vienna: Herder, 2003), 32–57 = idem, *Studien zu Philo und Paulus*, BBB 165 (Göttingen: Vandenhoeck & Ruprecht Unipress / Bonn University Press, 2011), 13–36.

107   See John M. Dillon and Wilhelm H. Wuellner, eds., *The Transcendence of God in Philo: Some Possible Sources*, The Center for Hermeneutical Studies in Hellenistic and Modern Culture, Protocol of the Sixteenth Colloquy, 20 April 1975, Series Colloquy 16 (Berkeley: Graduate Theological Union and University of California, 1975); John M. Dillon, "The Nature of God in the '*Quod Deus*,'" in David Winston and John Dillon, *Two Treatises of Philo of Alexandria: A Commentary on De Gigantibus and Quod Deus Sit Immutabilis*, Brown Judaic Studies 25 (Chico, Calif.: Scholars Press, 1983), 217–227; and Gerhard Sellin, "Gotteserkenntnis und Gotteserfahrung bei Philo von Alexandrien," in *Monotheismus und Christologie: Zur Gottesfrage im hellenistischen Judentum und im Urchristentum*, hg. Hans-Josef Klauck, Quaestiones Disputatae 138 (Freiburg/Basel/Vienna: Herder, 1992), 17–40.

108   Philo, *De opificio mundi* 69 (Philonis Alexandrini Opera quae supersunt I, 23.2–7 Cohn). ET from *Philo: On the Creation: Allegorical Interpretation of Genesis 2 and 3*, trans. F. H. Colson and G. H. Whitaker, LCL 226 (Cambridge, Mass.: Harvard University Press, 1929), 55. Cf. the German translation in *Philo von Alexandria: Die Werke in deutscher Übersetzung*, hg. Leopold Cohn, Isaak Heinemann und Willy Theiler, 2. Aufl., Bd. 1 (Berlin: De Gruyter, 1962). 50. See also *Philo of Alexandria: On the Creation of the Cosmos according to Moses*, trans. with an introduction and commentary by David T. Runia, Philo of Alexandria Commentary Series 1 (Leiden/Boston/Köln: Brill, 2001), 225.

109   Num 23:19 LXX. In Philo cf., among others, *Quod Deus sit immutabilis* 53, 62, 69 (Opera II, 68.16, 70.15, 72.7 Wendland); *De confusione linguarum* 98 (Opera II, 247.25–248.1 Wendland); *De somniis* I 237 (Opera III, 255.13 Wendland); and also *De decalogo* 32 (Opera IV, 276.1–3 Wendland).

110   Philo, *De sacrificiis Abelis et Caini* 94–97 (Opera I, 241.7–242.1 Cohn). ET from *Philo: On the Cherubim. The Sacrifices of Abel and Cain. The Worse Attacks the Better. On the Posterity and Exile of Cain. On the Giants,* trans. F. H. Colson and G. H. Whitaker, LCL 227 (Cambridge, Mass.: Harvard University Press, 1929), 165–167. Cf. the German translation in Cohn/Heinemann/Theiler, *Die Werke in deutscher Übersetzung*, 3: 251.

111   Philo, *De posteritate Caini* 7 (Opera II, 2.11–13 Wendland). ET from Colson and Whitaker, *Philo: On the Cherubim. The Sacrifices of Abel and Cain. The Worse Attacks the Better. On the Posterity and Exile of Cain. On the Giants*, 331. Cf. also Aristoteles, *Physica* IV 4 212 a 5 and Philo, *De somniis* I 234f. (Opera III, 254.19–22 Wendland).

112   *Quod Deus sit immutabilis* 57–59 (Opera II, 69.12–70.2 Wendland). ET from *Philo: On the Unchangeableness of God. On Husbandry. Concerning Noah's Work As a Planter. On Drunkenness. On Sobriety,* trans. F. H. Colson and G. H. Whitaker, LCL 247 (Cambridge, Mass.: Harvard University Press, 1930), 39–41. Cf. the German translation in Cohn/Heinemann/Theiler, *Die Werke in deutscher Übersetzung*, 4: 85f.

113   Cf. Philo, *Legum allegoriae* I 36 (Opera I, 70.10f. Cohn); and ibid., III 36 (120.30–121.7). See also Anna Passoni Dell'Acqua, "Innovazioni lessicali e attributi divini:

Una caratteristica del giudaismo alessandrino?" in *La parola di Dio cresceva (At 12.24): Scritti in onore di Carlo Maria Martini nel suo 70. compleanno*, a cura di Rinaldo Favris, supplementi alla Rivista Biblica 33 (Bologna: EDB, 1998), 87–108, esp. 87–90.

114 Philo, *De posteritate Caini* 4 (Opera II, 1.15f. WENDLAND). ET from COLSON/WHITAKER, *Philo: On the Cherubim. The Sacrifices of Abel and Cain. The Worse Attacks the Better. On the Posterity and Exile of Cain. On the Giants*, 331.

115 Philo, *De somniis* I 184 (Opera III, 244.15–18 WENDLAND). On its interpretation against the backdrop of contemporary philosophical doxography, see David T. RUNIA, "The Beginning of the End: Philo of Alexandria and Hellenistic Theology," in *Traditions of Theology: Studies in Hellenistic Theology, Its Background and Aftermath*, ed. Dorothea Frede and André Laks, Philosophia Antiqua 89 (Leiden/Boston/Cologne: Brill, 2002), 281–316, esp. 284–286.

116 Philo, *De somniis* I 61–64 (Opera III, 218.9–24 WENDLAND). ET from *Philo: On Flight and Finding. On the Change of Names. On Dreams*, trans. F. H. COLSON and G. H. WHITAKER, LCL 275 (Cambridge, Mass.: Harvard University Press, 1934), 329. Cf. the German translation in COHN/HEINEMANN/THEILER, *Die Werke in deutscher Übersetzung*, 6: 185f.

117 John WHITTAKER, "God and Time in Philo of Alexandria," in idem, *God—Time—Being: Two Studies in the Transcendental Tradition in Greek Philosophy*, Symbolae Osloenses, Fasc. Suppl. 23 (Oslo: Universitetsforlaget, 1971), 33–57, esp. 37 with n. 16 on p. 51.

118 MACH, s.v. "Philo von Alexandrien," 526: "Zwar gilt ihm der menschliche Körper als Gefängnis der Seele, aber eben nicht unbedingt als Gefängnis des jeweiligen menschlichen Logos. Entsprechend ist die Befreiung der Seele keine Rückführung des partiellen Logos in den allgemeinen, sondern im Idealfall eine Entkörperlichung, womit die Möglichkeit gegeben wird, daß die Seele in den rein geistigen Bereich gelangt, hier Gott selbst wirklich wahrnehmen kann und so ihr Ziel erreicht."

119 STEIN, *Die allegorische Exegese des Philo aus Alexandria*, 26–31. See also Jean PEPIN, "Remarques sur la théorie de l'exégèse allégorique chez Philon," in *Philon d'Alexandrie: Lyon, 11–15 Septembre 1966*, Colloques nationaux du Centre National de la Recherche Scientifique (Paris: Éditions du Centre National de la Recherche Scientifique, 1967), 131–167, esp. 161–167.

120 Philo, *Quod deus sit immutabilis* 57 (n. 118). See also Anna Maria SCHWEMER, "Gottes Hand und die Propheten: Zum Wandel der Metapher 'Hand Gottes' in frühjüdischer Zeit," in *La main de Dieu. Die Hand Gottes*, éd. René Kieffer et Jan Bergman, WUNT 94 (Tübingen: Mohr Siebeck, 1997), 65–85, esp. 70f.

121 Philo, *De decalogo* 47 (Opera IV, 279.14–16 WENDLAND). ET from *Philo: On the Decalogue. On the Special Laws, Books 1–3*, trans. F. H. COLSON, LCL 320 (Cambridge, Mass.: Harvard University Press, 1937), 31. See SCHWEMER, "Gottes Hand und die Propheten," 71; and KUHN, *Offenbarungsstimmen im Antiken Judentum*, 153–175.

122 Philo, *Quaestiones in Genesim* I 42 (Les Œuvres de Philon d'Alexandrie 34A, 108 MERCIER = LCL 380, 24 MARCUS).

123 Homer, *Odyssea* XVII 485–487. ET from *Homer: Odyssey, Books 1–12*, trans. A. T. MURRAY, rev. George E. Dimock, LCL 104 (Cambridge, Mass.: Harvard University Press, 1998), 191. Cf. Philo, *In somniis* I 232f. (III, 254.11–18 WENDLAND); and Plato, *Respublica* II 380 D–381 D. See Howard JACOBSON, "A Philonic Rejection of Plato," *Mnemosyne* 57 (2004): 488f.

124 Philo, *De confusione linguarum* 135 (Opera II, 254.19–21 WENDLAND). ET from *Philo: On the Confusion of Tongues. On the Migration of Abraham. Who Is the Heir of Divine Things? On Mating with the Preliminary Studies*, trans. F. H. COLSON and G. H. WHITAKER, LCL 261 (Cambridge, Mass.: Harvard University Press, 1932), 83.

125 Philo, *Quod Deus sit immutabilis* 55 (Opera II, 68.21f. WENDLAND). ET from COLSON/WHITAKER, *Philo: On the Unchangeableness of God. On Husbandry. Concerning Noah's Work As a Planter. On Drunkenness. On Sobriety*, 37. See also DILLON, "The Nature of God in the 'Quod Deus,'" 221.

126 JAEGER, *Die Theologie der frühen griechischen Denker*, 54.
127 Augustinus, *De civitate Dei* VI 10 (BiTeu I, 267.13–18 DOMBART/KALB) = Lucio Anneo
Seneca, *I frammenti*, a cura di Dionigi Vottero (Bologna: Pàtron Editore, 1998), frag.
65 (= 31 HAASE), 180f. with commentary on p. 303f.; and, previously, Marion LAUS-
BERG, *Untersuchungen zu Senecas Fragmenten*, Untersuchungen zur antiken Literatur
und Geschichte 7 (Berlin: De Gruyter, 1970), 201–206. ET from *Augustine: City of God,
Books 4–7*, trans. William M. GREEN, LCL 412 (Cambridge, Mass.: Harvard University
Press, 1963), 353.
128 Thus, DK 21 B 24 (I, 135.7 DIELS/KRANZ) = Sextus Empiricus, *Adversus mathematicos* IX
144 (BiTeu II, 246.23–25 MUTSCHMANN).
129 VERNANT, "Mortals and Immortals," 29: "dissimilar or precisely the same reason that a
god's capacity for thought (νόημα)—with which the gods are abundantly endowed—is
dissimilar to human thought."
130 On this, see Wolfram BRINKER, s.v. "Seele," in *Platon-Lexikon: Begriffswörterbuch zu
Platon und der platonischen Tradition* (Darmstadt: Wissenschaftliche Buchgesellschaft,
2007), 253–258; Christoph MARKSCHIES, "Die Seele als Bild der Welt—gestern, heute,
morgen," *Berichte und Abhandlungen der Berlin-Brandenburgischen Akademie der
Wissenschaften* 14 (2009): 9–24; and Gyburg RADKE, *Die Theorie der Zahl im Platonismus: Ein systematisches Lehrbuch* (Tübingen/Basel: Francke, 2003), 488–496. See also
Johannes ZACHHUBER, s.v. "Weltseele," in *Historisches Wörterbuch der Philosophie*
(Darmstadt: Wissenschaftliche Buchgesellschaft, 2004), 12: 516–521.
131 Plato, *Timaeus* 34 A/B. ET from *Plato: Timaeus. Critias. Cleitophon. Menexenus. Epistles*, trans. R. G. BURY, LCL 234 (Cambridge, Mass.: Harvard University Press, 1929),
35. Cf. Platon, *Sämtliche Werke*, Bd. 5, *Politikos, Philebos, Timaios, Kritias*, Rowohlts
Klassiker der Literatur und der Wissenschaft 47, Griechische Philosophie Bd. 6 (Hamburg: Rowohlt, 1959), 158; and Plato, *Leges* 821 A.
132 Plato, *Timaeus* 92 C. ET from BURY, *Plato: Timaeus. Critias. Cleitophon. Menexenus.
Epistles*, 253.
133 Plato, *Timaeus* 36 E–37 A: "And whereas the body of the Heaven is visible, the Soul is
herself invisible but partakes in reasoning and in harmony, having come into existence by
the agency of the best of things intelligible and ever-existing as the best of things generated." ET from BURY, *Plato: Timaeus. Critias. Cleitophon. Menexenus. Epistles*, 73.
134 Plato, *Phaedo* 78 B–80 B; also *Timaeus* 47 B–C.
135 Plutarchus, *Moralia* 67. *Platonicae Quaestiones* 8.4, 1007 C/D (BiTeu VI/1, 132.14–
16 HUBERT/DREXLER). On its interpretation, see Charlotte KÖCKERT, *Christliche Kosmologie und kaiserzeitliche Philosophie: Die Auslegung des Schöpfungsberichtes bei
Origenes, Basilius und Gregor von Nyssa vor dem Hintergrund kaiserzeitlicher Timaeus-
Interpretationen*, Studien und Texte zu Antike und Christentum 56 (Tübingen: Mohr Siebeck, 2009), 47–49.
136 As verified in *Corpus Hermeticum*, tome 1, *Traités I–XII*, texte établi par Arthur Darby
Nock et traduit par André-Jean Festugière, CUFr, 2. éd. du 7. tirage revu et corrigé (Paris:
Société d'Édition "Les Belles Lettres," 1999), 137f. (Appendice A; cf. *Corpus Hermeti-
cum* X 11); but in particular Macrobius, *Saturnalia* I 20.16f. (SCBO 116.14–17 KASTER
= PEG II/2 [Orphicorum et Orphicis similium testimonia et fragmenta], frag. 861, 381
BERNABE = *Orphicorum fragmenta*, 265 KERN): "Learn, that the nature of my divinity is
one that I wish to tell you: The firmament of heaven is my head, my stomach is the sea, the
earth my feet, my eyes are in the air, and the radiant light of the sun is my far-shining eye."
See also Roelof VAN DEN BROEK, "The Sarapis Oracle in Macrobius, *Sat.* I, 20, 16f.," in
*Hommages à Maarten J. Vermaseren: Recueil d'études offert par les auteurs de la Série
Études préliminaires aux religions orientales dans l'Empire romain à Maarten J. Vermaseren à l'occasion de son soixantième anniversaire le 7 avril 1978*, vol. 1, éd. Margreet
B. de Boer et T. A. Edridge, Études préliminaires aux religions orientales dans l'Empire
romain 68 (Leiden: Brill, 1978), 123–141, esp. 138–141.

137 *Papyri Graecae Magicae* XII 242–244 (PGM II, 74.32–34 PREISENDANZ). Cf. on this XIII 766–772 (PGM II, 122.19–25); XXI 3–7 (PGM II, 146.1–10). See Jan ASSMANN, "Primat und Transzendenz: Struktur und Genese der ägyptischen Vorstellung eines höchsten Wesens," in *Aspekte der ägyptischen Religion*, hg. Wolfhart Westendorf, Göttinger Orientforschungen, Reihe 4 Ägypten 9 (Wiesbaden: Harrassowitz, 1979), 7–42, esp. 7–13. See also Wolfgang FAUTH, *Helios Megistos: Zur synkretistischen Theologie der Spätantike*, Religions in the Graeco-Roman World 125 (Leiden: Brill, 1995), 105. ET from *The Greek Magical Papyri in Translation: Including the Demotic Texts*, ed. Hans Dieter BETZ (Chicago/London: University of Chicago Press, 1986), 162.

138 Mark EDWARDS, "Further Reflections on the Platonism of Origen," *Adamantius* 18 (2012): 317–324, esp. 323.

139 Pseudo-Galenus, *Historia philosophorum* 16 (*Doxographi Graeci* 608.16–609.1 DIELS).

140 Scholion on Epicurus, *Ratae sententiae* 1, transmitted by Diogenes Laertius, *Vitae philosophorum* X 139 (SCBO II, 559.5 LONG = frag. [5] 139.3–7 p. 121 ARRIGHETTI): "Elsewhere he says that the gods are discernible by reason alone, some being numerically distinct, while others result uniformly from the continuous influx of similar images directed to the same spot and in human form." ET from *Diogenes Laertius: Lives of Eminent Philosophers, Books 6–10*, trans. R. D. HICKS, LCL 185 (Cambridge, Mass.: Harvard University Press, 1925), 663–665. On the difficult passage's interpretation, and, indeed, history of interpretations, Jaap MANSFELD, "Aspects of Epicurean Theology," *Mnemosyne* 46 (1993): 172–210, esp. 201–208.

141 Lucretius, *De rerum natura* VI 75–78 (SQAW 32, 376 MARTIN). ET from *Lucretius: On the Nature of Things*, trans. W. H. D. ROUSE, rev. Martin F. Smith, LCL 181 (Cambridge, Mass.: Harvard University Press, 1992), 499. See T. Lucretius Carus, *De rerum natura: Lateinisch und Deutsch*, von Hermann Diels, Bd. 2, Lukrez, *Von der Natur*, übers. von Hermann Diels (Berlin: Weidmann, 1924), 261). For the "holy bodies of the gods," cf. also I 1015 (88 MARTIN).

142 Cicero, *De natura deorum* I 25f.,71 (BiTeu 45, 27.26–28.5 AX). On the interpretation of this passage, cf. the extensive commentary in M. Tulli Ciceronis, *De natura deorum liber primus*, ed. Arthur Stanley Pease (Cambridge, Mass.: Harvard University Press, 1955), 311–323; and, most prominently, Robert PHILIPPSON, "Die Quelle der Epikureischen Götterlehre in Ciceros erstem Buche De natura deorum," *Symbolae Osloenses* 19 (1939): 15–40; Joseph MOREAU, "Épicure et la physique des dieux," *Revue des Études Anciennes* 70 (1968): 286–294; and Kirk R. SANDERS, "Cicero *De natura deorum* 1.48f.: Quasi Corpus?" *Mnemosyne* 4 (2004): 215–218.

143 SANDERS, "Cicero *De natura deorum* 1.48f.: Quasi Corpus?" 216.

144 Cicero, *De divinatione* II 27.40 (BiTeu 46, 95.20–24 GIOMINI).

145 See on this Lucretius, *De rerum natura* VI 75–78; and furthermore Daniel BABUT, "Sur les dieux d'Epicure," *Elenchos* 26 (2005): 79–110; Adam DROZDEK, "Epicurean Gods," *Classica et Mediaevalia* 56 (2005): 155–166, esp. 156f.; Dirk OBBINK, "'All Gods Are True' in Epicurus," in *Traditions of Theology: Studies in Hellenistic Theology, Its Background and Aftermath*, ed. Dorothea Frede and André Laks, Philosophia Antiqua 89 (Leiden: Brill, 2002), 183–222. See also Jaap MANSFELD, "Aspects of Epicurean Theology," *Mnemosyne* 46 (1993): 172–210; and Marianne WIFSTRAND SCHIEBE, "Sind die epikureischen Götter 'thought-constructs'?" *Mnemosyne* 56 (2003): 703–727. Cf. Cicero, *De natura deorum* I 19.49 (BiTeu 45, 20.14–24 AX); and Diogenes Laertius, *Vitae philosophorum* X 31 (SCBO II, 509.17–20 LONG = 23.8 ARRIGHETTI).

146 Aëtius, *Placita philosophorum* I 3.18 (*Doxographi Graeci* 285.1–7 DIELS corrected in the apparatus). On this, see Robert PHILIPPSON, "Zur epikureischen Götterlehre," *Hermes* 51 (1916): 568–608, esp. 590f.

147 Philodemus, *De Diis* (Περί θεῶν) III frag. 8.6 (p. 45 DIELS): ... μήτε σάρκι]νον εἶναι[ι κα]τ' ἀναλογίαν [ἔχ]ον τι σῶμ' ὅπερ] ἡγεῖται [ἄ]ναλογ[. .... I cite Philodemus' work according to Hermann DIELS, *Philodemos über die Götter, erstes und drittes Buch*,

griechischer Text und Erläuterung I–III, Abhandlungen der Königlich Preussischen Akademie der Wissenschaften, Philosophisch-historische Klasse 7/1915, 4/1916 und 6/1916 (Leipzig: Zentralantiquariat der Deutschen Demokratischen Republik, 1970 = Berlin: Verlag der Königlichen Akademie der Wissenschaften, in Kommission bei Georg Reimer, 1916/1917). See also, in detail, PHILIPPSON, "Zur epikureischen Götterlehre," 568–608, esp. 577–592; and now OBBINK, "'All Gods Are True' in Epicurus," 189, which pleads for a direct depenedence.

148   Philodemus, *De Diis* III frag. 9.3 (p. 45 DIELS). Regardless, in this case, this concerns "flesh in its actual sense" ("das Fleisch im eigentlichen Sinne"): σαρκὶ τῇ κυρίως (frag. 9.1 ibid.).

149   For this, see Michael ERLER, "§ 18. Demetrios Lakon," in *Die hellenistische Philosophie*, hg. Hellmut Flashar, Grundriss der Philosophie, begründet von Friedrich Ueberweg, völlig neu bearb, Ausgabe, Die Philosophie der Antike, Bd. 4 (Basel: Schwabe, 1994), 256–267, esp. 264; and Tiziano DORANDI, s.v. "Démétrios Lacon," in *Dictionnaire des philosophes antiques*, publié sous la direction de Richard Goulet (Paris: Éditions du Centre national de la Recherche scientifique, 1994), 2: 637–641.

150   Demetrius Lacon, *De forma dei* (Περὶ τῆς θεοῦ μορφῆς) 3 and 5; cited after Demetrio Lacone, *La Forma del Dio (PHerc. 1055)*, edizione, traduzione e commento a cura di Mariacarolina Santoro, La scuola di Epicuro (Neapel: Bibliopolis, 2000), 91–101, here col. 14.9–17.1 (96f.).

151   Philodemus, *De Diis* III col. 11.13 and 19f. (p. 32 DIELS); WIFSTRAND SCHIEBE, "Sind die epikureischen Götter 'thought-constructs'?" 706.

152   Philodemus, *De Diis* I col. 2.7–11 (p. 10 DIELS; fol. 51): . . . τὸν θεὸν ζῷιον ἀΐδιον καὶ ἄφθαρτον; after DIELS, *Philodemos über die Götter*, 50, certainly a paraphrase of the introductory sentence beginning the letter of Epicurus to Menoeceus (fr. [4] 123.2–5 [107 ARRIGHETTI]).

153   Cicero, *De natura deorum* I 12.30 (BiTeu 45, 13.17–22 AX). An attempt to explain these contradictions by means of the example of the "ambigua materiae . . . qualitas" which only appear corporeally "according to their disposition and capacity" ("vi et ratione [. . .] corpoream"), may be found in Apuleius, *De Platone* I 5.192 (BiTeu III, 93.5–18 MORESCHINI; quotes 93.12f, 17f.).

154   Cf. the texts from *De natura deorum* I 26.71 and *De divinatione* II 27.40.

155   Max POHLENZ, *Die Stoa: Geschichte einer geistigen Bewegung*, 7. Aufl. (Göttingen: Vandenhoeck & Ruprecht, 1992), 93f.; most recently: David SEDLEY, "The Origins of Stoic God," in *Traditions of Theology: Studies in Hellenistic Theology, Its Background and Aftermath*, ed. Dorothea Frede and André Laks, Philosophia Antiqua 89 (Leiden: Brill, 2002), 41–84.

156   Plutarchus, *Moralia 72. De communibus notitiis adversus Stoicos* 30, 1073 E (BiTeu VI/2, 95.1–3 POH-LENZ/WESTMAN; also CUFr Plutarque, Œuvres morales XV/2, 89 CASEVITZ/BABUT, with extensive commentary on pp. 257f. = SVF II, 525 [II, 167.24–26 VON ARNIM]). Cf. Ioannes Stobaeus, *Anthologium* I 8.42 (I, 106.18–23 WACHSMUTH = SVF II, 509 [II, 164.26–30 VON ARNIM]); also Galenus, *De methodo medendi* II 7 (*Claudii Galeni opera omnia* X, 155 KÜHN = SVF II 322 [II, 115.32f.]). See also Victor GOLDSCHMIDT, "ὑπάρχειν et ὑφεστάναι dans la philosophie stoïcienne," *Revue des Études Grecques* 85 (1972): 331–444; and Marcelo D. BOERI, "The Stoics on Bodies and Incorporeals," *Review of Metaphysics* 54 (2001): 723–752, esp. 729–735 (with a critical turn against Panayiotis TZAMALIKOS, "Origen and the Stoic View of Time," *Journal of the History of Ideas* 52 [1991]: 531–561, esp. 540).

157   Dirk BALTZLY, "Stoic Pantheism," *Sophia* 34 (2003): 3–33, has insightfully traced this identification back to the pre-Hellenistic *medical* traditions (p. 24; with recourse to Heinrich von STADEN, "Body, Soul, and Nerves: Epicurus, Herophilus, Erasistratus, the Stoics, and Galen," in *Psyche and Soma: Physicians and Metaphysicians on the Mind-Body*

Problem from Antiquity to Enlightenment, ed. John P. Wright and Paul Potter [Oxford: Clarendon, 2000], 79–116, esp. 80–86).

158 Diogenes Laertius, *Vitae philosophorum* VII 134 (SCBO II, 354.8–18 LONG = SVF I, 85 [I, 24.5–9 VON ARNIM]; also SVF II, 299 [II, 111.4–7 VON ARNIM]). For the justicifation of this reading and on its interpretation, cf. BOERI, "The Stoics on Bodies and Incorporeals," 725 with n. 5. The edition by Miroslav MARCOVICH (*Diogenis Laertii Vitae Philosophorum*, BiTeu [Stuttgart/Leipzig: Teubner, 1999], 523.19) also reads σώματα.

159 Aristocles apud Eusebium, *Praeparatio evangelica* XV 14.1: ἀλλ᾽ οὗτος ἄμφω σώματά φησιν εἶναι, καὶ τὸ ποιοῦν καὶ τὸ πάσχον (sc. the active and passive principles are bodies according to Zeno: GCS Eusebius VIII/2, 378.20–379.1 MRAS/DES PLACES = *Aristocles of Messene: Testimonia and Fragments*, ed. with translation and commentary by Maria Lorenza Chiesara, Oxford Classical Monographs [Oxford: Oxford University Press, 2001], frag. 3, 18f.). Cf. Diogenes Laertius, *Vitae philosophorum* VII 134 (SCBO II, 354.8–11 LONG = SVF I, 85 [I, 24.5–8 VON ARNIM] = SVF I, 493 [I, 110.25–29]).

160 The text in DIELS (*Doxographi Graeci*) and VON ARNIM (*Stoicorum Veterum Fragmenta*) follows *Philodem über Frömmigkeit*, bearb. und erläutert von Theodor Gomperz, Der Text und photo-lithographische Beilagen, acht und zwanzig Tafeln, Herkulanische Studien 2 (Leipzig: Teubner, 1866), 5–151, esp. 77–79. As of yet, only the first part of the work exists in a new critical text edition: *Philodemus, On Piety*, pt. 1, *Critical Text with Commentary*, ed. Dirk OBBINK (Oxford: Clarendon, 1996); cf. the text and translation by Albert HENRICHS, "Die Kritik der stoischen Theologie im P. Herc. 1428," *Cronache Ercolanesi* 4 (1974): 5–32, here 12–25 (without information on all papyrological details). Surprisingly, the fragment is lacking from Chrysippe, *Œuvre philosophique*, textes traduits et commentés par Richard Dufour, 2 Bde. (Paris: Les Belles Lettres, 2004). An introduction to this topic may be found in vol. 1, L–LII, a selection of the fragments in vol. 2, 485–531.

161 Philodemus, *De pietate* 11 (Pap. Herc. 1428, Col. V,28–VI,1; *Doxographi Graeci* 546b,28–36 DIELS = SVF II, 1076 [II, 315.17–19 VON ARNIM]). Interestingly, no parallel to this sentence exists within Cicero.

162 Diogenes Laertius, *Vitae philosophorum* VII 147 (SCBO II, 360.9–11 LONG = SVF II, 1021 [II, 305.15–17 VON ARNIM]). ET from HICKS, *Diogenes Laertius: Lives of Eminent Philosophers, Books 6–10*, 251.

163 Philodemus, *De pietate* 11 (Pap. Herc. 1428, Col. IV,12–V,28; *Doxographi Graeci* 545b,13–546b,28 DIELS = SVF II, 1076 [II, 315.2–17 VON ARNIM]). In DIELS, op. cit., synoptically with the paraphrase of Philodemus or a source of Philodemus from Cicero, *De natura Deorum* I 15.39 (BiTeu 45, 16.23–17.8 AX); a preliminary version of the critical edition also appears in OBBINK, "'All Gods Are True' in Epicurus," 199–201, from which the ET is adapted.

164 Philodemus, *De pietate* 15 (Pap. Herc. 1428, Col. VIII,14–28 [*Doxographi Graeci* 548b,14–549b,28 DIELS = SVF III, 33 [II, 217.9–14 VON ARNIM]; text after HENRICHS, "Die Kritik der stoischen Theologie im P. Herc. 1428," 19). Cicero only adopted the passage from Philodemus in very abbreviated form: *De natura Deorum* I 15.41 (BiTeu 45, 17.22–25 AX), synopsis in DIELS, op. cit.; and also in OBBINK, "'All Gods Are True' in Epicurus," 206f., from which the ET is adapted.

165 Philodemus, *De pietate* 16 (Pap. Herc. 1428, Col. X,29–XI,5; text after HENRICHS, "Die Kritik der stoischen Theologie im P. Herc. 1428," 21). ET from OBBINK, "'All Gods are true' in Epicurus," 210.

166 Cleanthes, *Hymnus* (apud Ioannes Stobaeus, *Anthologium* I 1.12 [I, 25.3–27.4 WACHSMUTH] = SVF I, 537 [I, 121.34–123.5 VON ARNIM]). See the extensive commentary and the enumeration of suggestions for the restoration of the notoriously corrupt †ἤχου along with a detailed justification for the reconstruction θεοῦ μίμημα in Johan C. THOM, *Cleanthes' Hymn to Zeus: Text, Translation, and Commentary*, Studien und Texte zu Antike und Christentum 33 (Tübingen: Mohr Siebeck, 2005), 54–66.

167 Aëtius, *Placita philosophorum* I 7.33 (*Doxographi Graeci* 305.15–306.11 DIELS = SVF II, 1027 [II, 306.19–25 VON ARNIM]).

168 BALTZLY, "Stoic Pantheism," 6–9.

169 Plutarchus, *Moralia* 60, *De facie in orbe lunae* 12, 926 C/D (BiTeu V/3, 45.20–22 and 27–46.1 HUBERT/POHLENZ/ DREXLER = SVF II, 1045 [II, 308.19–28 VON ARNIM]). ET from *Plutarch: Moralia, concerning the Face Which Appears in the Orb of the Moon. On the Principle of Cold. Whether Fire or Water Is More Useful. Whether Land or Sea Animals Are Cleverer. Beasts Are Rational. On the Eating of Flesh*, trans. Harold CHERNISS and W. C. HELMBOLD, LCL 406 (Cambridge, Mass.: Harvard University Press, 1957), 81. In SVF, the unlikely reconstruction ἡμῖν from Pohlenz is used, which is offered by BiTeu only in the apparatus.

170 Alexander von Aphrodisias, *De mixtione* 3 (CAG. suppl. II/2, 216.25–217.2 BRUNS; here cited after *Alexander of Aphrodisias on Stoic Physics: A Study of the De mixtione*, with preliminary essays, text, translation and commentary by Robert B. TODD, Philosophia Antiqua 29 [Leiden: Brill, 1976], 116). See also BALTZLY, "Stoic Pantheism," 7f.; and for the expression ἀσύγχυτος ἕνωσις, cf. Luise ABRAMOWSKI, "συνάφεια und ἀσύγχυτος ἕνωσις als Bezeichnungen für trinitarische und christologische Einheit," in idem, *Drei christologische Untersuchungen*, BZNW 45 (Berlin/New York: De Gruyter, 1981), 63–109, esp. 66–70.

171 BALTZLY, "Stoic Pantheism," 8, 11. On the connections of this theology to the debate in the Platonic Academy, see SEDLEY, "The Origins of Stoic God," 60–82.

172 Naturally, there are exceptions—the aforementioned tractate *De mixtione* of Alexander of Aphrodisias or the (admittedly much later) commentator of Aristotle, Sophonias (a monk). Cf. Sophonias, *In libros Aristotelis De anima paraphrasis* ad *De anima* 5, 411 a 7 (CAG XXIII, 36.11–13 HAYDUCK = SVF II, 1046 [II, 308.32–34 VON ARNIM]).

173 Christoph MARKSCHIES, *Christian Theology and Its Institutions in the Early Roman Empire: Prolegomena to a History of Early Christian Theology*, trans. Wayne Coppins, Baylor-Mohr Siebeck Studies in Early Christianity (Waco, Tex.: Baylor University Press; Tübingen: Mohr Siebeck, 2015), 59–91. See also Henning ZIEBRITZKI, *Heiliger Geist und Weltseele: Das Problem der dritten Hypostase bei Origenes, Plotin und ihren Vorläufern*, BHT 84 (Tübingen: Mohr Siebeck, 1994), 260–266.

174 Origenes, *Contra Celsum* VI 71 (GCS Origenes II, 141.15–20 KOETSCHAU = SVF II, 1051 [II, 310.21–25 VON ARNIM] = frag. 1061 [524–527 DUFOUR]). ET from *Origen: Contra Celsum*, trans. with an introduction and notes by Henry CHADWICK (Cambridge: Cambridge University Press, 1953), 385. See on this Josiah B. GOULD, *The Philosophy of Chrysippus*, Philosophia Antiqua 17 (Leiden: Brill, 1970), 155.

175 See on the theory of ἐκπύρωσις in the early Stoa, Ricardo SALLES, "Ἐκπύρωσις and the Goodness of God in Cleanthes," *Phronesis* 50 (2005): 56–78. On the background of the debate between Origen and Celsus, see still Carl ANDRESEN, *Logos und Nomos: Die Polemik des Kelsos wider das Christentum*, Arbeiten zur Kirchengeschichte 30 (Berlin: De Gruyter, 1955), 73–77.

176 Origenes, *Contra Celsum* IV 14 (GCS Origenes I, 284.23–28 KOETSCHAU = SVF II, 1052 [II, 310.30–34 VON ARNIM] = frag. 1063 [526 DUFOUR]). Cf. on this also *Contra Celsum* I 21 (72.15). And in *Dialogus cum Heraclide* § 12 (SC 67, 80 SCHERER = Textes et Documents IX, 146.19 SCHERER).

177 Hippolytus, *Refutatio omnium haeresium* I 21.1 (GCS Hippolyt III, 25.12–16 WENDLAND/ PTS 25, 83.1–4 MARCOVICH = SVF II, 1029 [II, 306.35–39 VON ARNIM = Doxographi Graeci 571.7–10 DIELS]). ET from *Hippolytus: Refutation of All Heresies*, trans. with an introduction and notes by M. David LITWA, Writings from the Greco-Roman World 40 (Atlanta: SBL Press, 2016), 67–69.

178 Theodoretus Cyrrhensis, *Graecarum affectionum curatio* II 113 (BiTeu 66.12–16 RAEDER = SVF II, 1028 [II, 306.33f. VON ARNIM]). See also Eusebius Caesariensis, *Praeparatio Evangelica* III 9.9 (GCS Eusebius VIII/1, 129.6–9 MRAS/DES PLACES = SVF II, 1032 [II,

307.5–7 VON ARNIM]): ἐν οἷς (sc. the verses 14–19 of the Orphic hymn Ζεὺς πρῶτος γένετο, . . . κτλ.; cf. III 9.2 [126.14–19 = 129.2–5 MRAS/DES PLACES = *Poetae Epici Graeci* II/1, 208.8–209.13 BERNABÉ; cf. VAN DEN BROEK, "The Sarapis Oracle in Macrobius, Sat. I, 20, 16f.," 125–129]).

179   Clemens Alexandrinus, *Stromata* V 89.2–4 (GCS Clemens Alexandrinus II, 384.18–385.2 STÄHLIN/FRÜCHTEL/TREU = SVF II, 1035 [II, 307.15–17 VON ARNIM]). Cf. also ibid., I 51.1 (33.12–14) = SVF II, 1040 (II, 307.30f.): "The Stoics too, of whom he also speaks, say wrongly that God is corporeal and moves through matter of the most disreputable kind." ET from *Clement of Alexandria: Stromateis, Books 1–3*, trans. John FERGUSON, Fathers of the Church 85 (Washington, D.C.: Catholic University of America Press, 1991), 60.

180   Tertullianus, Apologeticum 47.6 (CChr.SL 1, 163.21–23 DEKKERS) = SVF II, 1034 (II, 307.10f. VON ARNIM). ET from *Tertullian: Apology. De Spectaculis. Minucius Felix: Octavius*, trans. T. R. GLOVER and Gerald H. RENDALL, LCL 250 (Cambridge, Mass.: Harvard University Press, 1931), 207. Cf. also Lactantius, *Divinae institutiones* VII 3.1–4 (BiTeu IV, 648.19–13 HECK/WLOSOK = SVF II, 1041 [II, 307.33–44 VON ARNIM]). On Tertullian's own position, see below in more detail.

181   Paul MORAUX, s.v. "Quinta Essentia," PW 24: 1171–1263. See also Henry John EASTERLING, "Quinta natura," *Museum Helveticum* 21 (1964), 73–85; and Mary L. GILL, "The Theory of the Elements in *De Caelo* 3 and 4," in *New Perspectives on Aristotle's "De Caelo,"* ed. Alan C. Bowen and Christian Wildberg, Philosophia Antiqua 177 (Leiden: Brill, 2009), 139–162. See also the excursus of Alberto JORI, "Geschichte der Lehre vom ersten Körper (Äther)," in *Aristoteles: Über den Himmel*, übers. und erläutert von Alberto Jori, Aristoteles Werke in deutscher Übersetzung 12/3 (Berlin: Akademie, 2009), 193–259. For the Christian reception, see Jean PEPIN, *Théologie cosmique et théologie chrétienne (Ambroise, Exam. I 1, 1–4)*, Bibliothèque de philosophie contemporaine, Histoire de la philosophie et philosophie générale (Paris: Presses universitaires de France, 1964), 486–492; with reference to Ps.-Clemens Romanus, *Recognitiones* VIII 15.4f. (GCS Pseudoklementinen II, 226.1–9 REHM/STRECKER).

182   Aristoteles, *De caelo* I 2, 269 b 13–17.

183   Ps.-Plato, *Epinomis* 981 C. Cf. MORAUX, s.v. "Quinta essentia," 1187–1192.

184   Ps.-Plato, *Epinomis* 984 D–985 B. On the teaching of demons, see Friedrich ANDRES, s.v. "Daimon," PW Suppl. 3: 267–322, esp. 296; also Franz CUMONT, *Die orientalischen Religionen im römischen Heidentum*, bearb. von August Burckhardt-Brandenberg, 9. unveränd. Aufl., reprogr. Nachdr. der 3. dt. Aufl. (Stuttgart: Teubner, 1989 = 1931), 309.

185   Cicero, *Tusculanae disputationes* I 10.22 (BiTeu 44, 228.19–229.2 POHLENZ); discussion at length in MORAUX, s.v. "Quinta essentia," 1213–1231. The discussion concerns, above all, the lost early dialogue De philosophia of Aristotle: Aristotele, *Della filosofia*, introduzione, testo, traduzione e commento esegetico di Mario UNTERSTEINER, Temi e testi 10 (Rome: Edizioni i storia e letteratura, 1963). Cf. also (very much shorter) *Aristotelis Opera*, vol. 3, *Librorum deperditorum fragmenta*, collegit et annotationibus instruxit Olof GIGON (Berlin/New York: De Gruyter, 1987), 267–270. The pertinent Cicero passages are in UNTERSTEINER as frag. 27 = 30 (op. cit., 54–57 and commentary 265–280).

186   Ioannes Philoponos, *In Aristotelem De anima* I prooemium (CAG XV, 9.4–9 HAYDUCK; cf. frag. 99 in *Die Schule des Aristoteles: Texte und Kommentar*, hg. Fritz Wehrli, 2. ergänzte und verbesserte Aufl. [Basel/Stuttgart: Schwabe, 1969], 34.20–23 and commentary p. 93 = *Heraclides of Pontus: Texts and Translation*, ed. Eckart Schütrumpf, Rutgers University Studies in Classical Humanities 14 [New Brunswick, N.J.: Transaction, 2008], frag. 47, 120f.). On this see DIELS, *Doxographi Graeci*, 214; MORAUX, s.v. "Quinta Essentia," 1193–1196; and Hans B. GOTTSCHALK, *Heraclides of Pontus* (Oxford: Clarendon, 1980), 102–127.

187   JORI, "Geschichte der Lehre vom ersten Körper (Äther)," 217 (almost literally taken from MORAUX, s.v. "Quinta Essentia," 1196).

188 Aristoteles, *De caelo* I 2, 269 a 30–34. See the commentary to the passage in JORI, *Über den Himmel*, 384f.; and also Christian WILDBERG, *John Philoponus' Criticism of Aristotle's Theory of Aether*, Peripatoi 16 (Berlin/New York: De Gruyter, 1988), 64–68.

189 Aristoteles, *De caelo* I 3 270 b 20–24. ET from *Aristotle: On the Heavens*, trans. W. K. C. GUTHRIE, LCL 338 (Cambridge, Mass.. Harvard University Press, 1939), 25.

190 Aristoteles, *De caelo* II 4, 286 b 10–287 b 21. Cf. ibid., 286 b 10. See the commentary ad. loc. in JORI, *Über den Himmel*, 436–439. The circular body is nevertheless restricted: *De caelo* I 5, 271 b 25–273 a 6.

191 Aristoteles, *De caelo* I 3, 269 b 18–23. Cf. ibid., 269 b 29–35. Also 270 a 12–14. See on this also the attempt to make visible the traditional underpinnings of such conceptions in Richard BODÉÜS, *Aristotle and the Theology of the Living Immortals* (Albany: State University of New York Press, 2000), 40–45.

192 Aristoteles, *De anima* II 7, 418 b 7–9. Cf. JORI, "Geschichte der Lehre vom ersten Körper (Äther)," 235.

193 See on this JORI, "Geschichte der Lehre vom ersten Körper (Äther)," 220, 223–225; most prominently, however, MORAUX, s.v. "Quinta Essentia," 1198–1204. In MORAUX also is given a depiction of comparable teachings, in particular, in *De generatione animalium* (vital pneuma), which are here ignored (op. cit., 1204–1209).

194 Cf. nr. 44 in the late antique list of works known as the "Lamprias Catalogue," the titles of which are conveyed in Konrat ZIEGLER, *Plutarchos von Chaironeia*, 2. durch Nachtr. erg. Aufl. (Stuttgart: Druckenmüller, 1964), 61–64 (revised version of idem, s.v. "Plutarchos [2] von Chaironeia," PW 21/1: 636–962, esp. 696–702, here 698); and briefly JORI, *Über den Himmel*, 247: Περὶ τῆς πεμπτῆς οὐσίας βιβλία ε'.

195 Atticus apud Eusebium, *Praeparatio Evangelica* XV 7 (GCS Eusebius VIII/2, 363.8–365.21 MRAS/DES PLACES = frag. 5 [CUFr 55–57 DES PLACES], cf. esp. 7.6). See MORAUX, s.v. "Quinta essentia," 1173.

196 See, above all, MORAUX, s.v. "Quinta essentia," 1256–1259; and now Glenn PEERS, *Subtle Bodies: Representing Angels in Byzantium*, The Transformation of the Classical Heritage 32 (Berkeley/Los Angeles/London: University of California Press, 2001), 67–80.

197 Origenes, *Commentarii in Euangelium Ioannis* XIII 21.125f. (GCS Origenes IV, 245.1–5 PREUSCHEN). ET from *Origen: Commentary on the Gospel of John, Books 13–32*, trans. Ronald Heine (Washington, D.C.: Catholic University of America Press, 1993), 93. Cf. on the translation of καθ' ὑπεξαίρεσιν in Origène, *Commentaire sur Saint Jean: Tome III (Livre XIII)*, texte grec, avant propos, traduction et notes par Cécile Blanc, SC 222 (Paris: Les éditions du Cerf, 1975), 98f. with n. 2; also Origenes, *De principiis* III 6.6 (GCS Origenes V, 288.21–26 KOETSCHAU = TzF 24, 660 GÖRGEMANNS/KARPP) and *Contra Celsum* IV 56 (GCS Origenes I, 329.11–16 KOETSCHAU).

198 Pseudo-Clemens, *Recognitiones* VIII 15.4 (GCS Pseudoklementinen II, 226.1–5 REHM/STRECKER). On its interpretation and on its history of tradition, see MORAUX, s.v. "Quinta essentia," 1228. Remarkably, the first sentence, Ἀριστοτέλης καὶ πέμπτον ἀκατονόμαστον, may also be found in the scholia on Basilius, *Homiliae in Hexaëmeron* I 2 (226.1f. REHM/STRECKER). Cf. also Giorgio PASQUALI, "Doxographica aus Basilius-scholien," Nachrichten der Königlichen Gesellschaft der Wissenschaften zu Göttingen, philosophisch-historische Klasse (Berlin: Weidmann, 1910), 194–228, esp. 195f.

199 *Corpus Hermeticum Asclepius* 6 (CUFr II, 303.5–8 NOCK/FESTUGIÈRE). Cf. ibid., 302.6. See the commentary in Walter SCOTT, *Hermetica: The Ancient Greek and Latin Writings which Contain Religious or Philosophic Teachings Ascribed to Hermes Trismegistus*, vol. 3, *Commentary: Latin Asclepius and Stobaei Hermetica* (Oxford: Clarendon, 1936), 39–42.

200 Athenagoras, *Supplicatio pro Christianis* 6.4 (PTS 31, 33.25–30 MARCOVICH). See on this MORAUX, s.v. "Quinta Essentia," 1128; and, for the notion that Jesus Christ had possessed a body, below.

201 Cf. on this Basilius Caesariensis, *Homiliae in Hexaëmeron* I 11 (GCS.NF 2, 18.17–24 AMAND DE MENDIETA/RUDBERG); Ambrosius Mediolanensis, *Homiliae in Hexaëmeron* I 6.23 (CSEL 32, 21.1–22.4 SCHENKL; see also PÉPIN, *Théologie cosmique et théologie chrétienne [Ambroise, Exam. I 1, 1–4]*, 226–247); and Nemesius Emesanus, *De natura hominis* 5.165f. (BiTeu 52.20–53.6 MORANI). Clearly further removed from Aristotle is what Hermias (*Irrisio gentilium philosophorum* 11 [SC 388, 108.6–12 HANSON/JOUSSOT = *Doxographi Graeci*, 654.1–3 DIELS).

202 Cf., for this, Basilius Caesariensis, *Homiliae in Hexaëmeron* I 11 (GCS.NF 2, 18.17–24 AMAND DE MENDIETA/RUDBERG). Pagan doxographic accounts are found in MORAUX, s.v. "Quinta Essentia," 1227; on the Christian accounts, cf. André-Jean FESTUGIERE, *L'idéal religieux des Grecs et l'Évangile*, Études bibliques, 2ᵉ éd. (Paris: Librairie Lecoffre / J. Gabalda, 1981), 221–263.

203 Philo, *De confusione linguarum* 156 (II, 259.2f. WENDLAND = SVF II, 664 [II, 197.31–33 VON ARNIM]). Cf. Cornutus, *Theologiae Graecae compendium* 1 (BiTeu 2.12–14 LANG = SAPERE 14, 30.14–16 BERDOZZO); and Diogenes Laertius, *Vitae philosophorum* VII 135–137 (SCBO II, 355.3–20 LONG = SVF II, 580 [II, 179.35–180.13 VON ARNIM], ascribed in 136 [II, 355.10–12 L. = 180.14–16 v.A.]). Cf., in particular, § 137 (II, 355.17–20 L. = 180.10–13 v.A.). Cf. also Cicero, *De natura deorum* II 24.64 (of Chrysippus; BiTeu 45, 73.27–74.2 AX). See the commentary in *M. Tulli Ciceronis De natura Deorum: Libri secundus et tertius*, ed. Arthur Stanley PEASE (Cambridge, Mass.: Harvard University Press, 1958), 708f.; JORI, "Geschichte der Lehre vom ersten Körper (Äther)," 242; and MORAUX, s.v. "Quinta Essentia," 1232–1235 with attestations on 1233.

204 Cicero, *Academica priora* (Lucullus) II 126 (BiTeu 42, 91.9–11 PLASBERG = SVF I, 154 [I, 41.32–34 VON ARNIM]).

205 Cf. on this Ioannes Stobaeus, *Anthologium* I 10.16c (I, 129.1–11 WACHSMUTH = SVF II, 413 [II, 136.6–14 VON ARNIM]). Moreover, cf. also SVF II, 642 (II, 194.4–8) = Arius Didymus, *Physica frag.* 29.8 (*Doxographi Graeci* 465.8–10 DIELS); and SVF II, 1014 (II, 303.10–14) = Sextus Empiricus, *Adversus Mathematicos* IX 123–126 (BiTeu II, 242 [418.10–419.3]). On circular motion, cf. for Zeno SVF I, 101 (I, 28.11–13) = Aëtius, *Placita* I 14.6 (*Doxographi Graeci* 313b,1f. DIELS); and for Chrysippus SVF II, 527 (II, 168.28–31) = Ioannes Stobaeus, *Anthologium* I 21.5 (I, 185.1–8 WACHSMUTH). Cf. also SVF II, 579 (II, 179.32–34) = Plutarchus, *Moralia* 70, *De Stoicorum repugnantiis* 41, 1053 A (BiTeu VI/2, 48.17f. POHLENZ/WESTMAN).

206 Cf. Philo, *De somniis* I 21 (III, 209.8–14 WENDLAND). See Paul WENDLAND, "Eine doxographische Quelle Philo's," *Sitzungsberichte der königlich preussischen Akademie der Wissenschaften zu Berlin* 23 (1897): 1074–1079; and, in detail, MORAUX, s.v. "Quinta Essentia," 1235–1237. See also Wilhelm BOUSSET, *Jüdisch-christlicher Schulbetrieb in Alexandria und Rome: Literarische Untersuchungen zu Philo und Clemens von Alexandrien, Justin und Irenäus*, FRLANT 23 (Göttingen: Vandenhoeck & Ruprecht, 1915), 40–43.

207 Philo, *De plantatione* 3 (II, 133.15–134.2 WENDLAND). Cf. also *Quaestiones in Genesim* III 6 also IV 8 (LCL 380, 190 also 280f. MARCUS); and *Quaestiones in Exodum* II 73 (LCL 401, 122 MARCUS). See André-Jean FESTUGIERE, *La révélation d'Hermès Trismégiste*, tome 2, *Le dieu cosmique* (Paris: Les Belles Lettres, 1986 = Paris: Gabalda, 1949), 531.

208 The stars themselves are also souls, and thereby spiritual beings for which circular motion is the most appropriate movement, as is explained by Philo in *De gigantibus* 8 (II, 43.14–17 WENDLAND). Striking here is the synthesis of an etherial doctrine of the Aristotelian model with the views of Plato on circular motion.

209 Philo, *Quis rerum divinarum heres sit* 283 (III, 64.18–22 WENDLAND). See MORAUX, s.v. "Quinta Essentia," 1249–1251.

210 Philo, *De plantatione* 18f. (II, 137.8–13 WENDLAND). Cf. *De opificio mundi* 135 (I, 47.4–11 COHN); and *Legum allegoriarum* III 161 (I, 148.6–4 COHN).

211 On the critical discussion of the notion that the soul is composed of the fifth substance, in Hellenism, see now, most prominently, Andrea FALCON, *Aristotelianism in the First Century BCE: Xenarchus of Seleucia* (Cambridge: Cambridge University Press, 2011), 25–32 (with the following presentation of the pertinent texts, translation, and commentary from Simplicius, *In Aristotelis De caelo* [T2] CAG VII, 13.22–28, 14.13–21 HEIBERG; [T3] 21.33–22.17, 20.10–36; [T4] 23.11–31; [T5] 23.31–24.7; [T6] 24.20–27; [T7] 25.11–28; [T8] 42.6–16; [T9] 50.21–24; [T10] 55.25–31, 56.12–17; also [T11] 70.20–29, op. cit., on pp. 63–113); and Christian WILDBERG, *John Philoponus' Criticism of Aristotle's Theory of Aether*, Peripatoi 16 (Berlin/New York: De Gruyter, 1988), 103–233. The question as to *God's* body does not play any role in the argumentation.

212 Javier CAMPOS DAROCA and Juan Luis LOPEZ CRUCES, s.v. "Maxime de Tyr," in *Dictionnaire des philosophes antiques*, publié sous la direction de Richard Goulet (Paris: Éditions du Centre national de la Recherche scientifique, 2005), 4: 324–348.

213 Gilles DORIVAL, s.v. "Origène d'Alexandrie," in *Dictionnaire des philosophes antiques*, 4: 807–842, esp. 810–813; and Rowan WILLIAMS, s.v. "Origenes/Origenismus," *TRE* 25: 397–420. On the topic of "bodiliness," see also, in particular, Eugène DE FAYE, *Origène: Sa vie, son oeuvre, sa pensée*, tome 3, *La doctrine* (Paris: Leroux, 1928), 27–30; Hal KOCH, *Pronoia und Paideusis: Studien über Origenes und sein Verhältnis zum Platonismus*, Arbeiten zur Kirchengeschichte 22 (Berlin: De Gruyter, 1932), 21 n. 1; Monique ALEXANDRE, "Le statut des questions concernant la matière dans le *Peri Archôn*," in *Origeniana: Premier colloque international des études origéniennes (Montserrat, 18–21 septembre 1973)*, dirigé par Henri Crouzel, Gennaro Lomiento, et Josep Rius-Camps, Quaderni di "Vetera Christianorum" 12 (Bari: Istituto di letteratura cristiana antica, Università di Bari, 1975), 63–81; David L. PAULSEN, "Early Christian Belief in a Corporeal Deity: Origen and Augustine as Reluctant Witnesses," *HTR* 83 (1990): 105–116, esp. 107–114; Lawrence R. HENNESSEY, "A Philosophical Issue in Origen's Eschatology: The Three Senses of Incorporeality," in *Origeniana Quinta: Historica—Text and Method—Biblica—Philosophica—Theologica—Origenism and Later Developments; Papers of the 5th International Origen Congress Boston College, 14–18 August 1989*, ed. Robert J. Daly, BETL 105 (Leuven: Peeters, 1992), 373–380; and SHERIDAN, *Language for God in Patristic Tradition*, 27–38 and 110–114.

214 Admittedly, Mark EDWARDS has drawn attention to the fact that this influence should also not be overestimated in respect to Origen's theology: idem, *Origen against Plato*, Ashgate Studies in Philosophy & Theology in Late Antiquity (Aldershot: Ashgate, 2002); and now idem, "Further Reflections on the Platonism of Origen," *Adamantius* 18 (2012): 317–324.

215 Basilius STEIDLE, "Neue Untersuchungen zu Origenes' Περὶ ἀρχῶν," *ZNW und die Kunde der älteren Kirche* 40 (1941): 236–243; Manlio SIMONETTI, "Osservazioni sulla struttura del *De principiis* di Origene," *Rivista di filologia e di istruzione classica* 90 (1962): 273–290, 372–393; Paul KÜBEL, "Zum Aufbau von Origenes' DE PRINCIPIIS," *VC* 25 (1971): 31–39; Gilles DORIVAL, "Remarques sur la forme du Peri Archôn," in Crouzel, Lomiento, et Rius-Camps, *Origeniana*, 33–45; idem, "Nouvelles remarques sur la forme du *Traité des Principes* d'Origène," *Recherches Augustiniennes* 22 (1987): 67–108. Critical of Dorival: Charles KANNENGIESSER, "Origen, Systematician in *De Principiis*," in Daly, *Origeniana Quinta*, 395–405.

216 Origenes, *De principiis* I 1.1 (TzF 24, 98–100 GÖRGEMANNS/KARPP = GCS Origenes V, 16.19–17.4 KOETSCHAU). ET from *Origen: On First Principles*, vol. 1, ed. and trans. John BEHR (Oxford: Oxford University Press, 2017), 25. Cf. the translations in GÖRGEMANNS/KARPP. On the work, see Lothar LIES, *Origenes' "Peri Archon": Eine undogmatische Dogmatik; Einführung und Erläuterung*, Werkinterpretationen (Darmstadt: Wissenschaftliche Buchgesellschaft, 1992), esp. 46.

217 Hence also ALEXANDRE, "Le statut des questions concernant la matière dans le *Peri Archôn*," 64: "Ces passages, abruptement situés en des positions-clés du traité . . ."

218 Origenes, *De principiis* I 1.1 (TzF 24, 84 GÖRGEMANNS/KARPP = GCS Origenes V, 8.14–20 KOETSCHAU). ET from BEHR, *Origen: On First Principles*, 1: 13.

219 Cf. only the third chapter of the Φυσικαὶ δόξαι (*Placita philosophorum*) of Aëtius, insofar as it can be reconstructed from the two epitomies in Pseudo-Plutarch and Joannes Stobaeus (a new edition of the material is being prepared by Oliver Primavesi, Munich; I cite the text here according to the synoptic edition by Hermann Diels [*Doxographi Graeci* 276.3 DIELS]): γ´. Περὶ ἀρχῶν τί εἰσιν. Here, three fundamental principles are provided for *Plato* (287.17–288.1): Σωκράτης Σωφρονίσκου Ἀθηναῖος καὶ Πλάτων Ἀρίστωνος Ἀθηναῖος . . . τρεῖς ἀρχάς, τὸν θεὸν τὴν ὕλην τὴν ἰδέαν; and two for *Aristotle* and the five "elements" including an "ethereal body" (288.7–11): Ἀριστοτέλης δὲ Νικομάχου Σταγειρίτης ἀρχὰς μὲν ἐντελέχειαν ἤτοι εἶδος ὕλην στέρησιν· στοιχεῖα δὲ τέτταρα, πέμπτον δέ τι σῶμα αἰθέριον, ἀμετάβλητον. The account closes with the two principles of the Stoic *Zeno*: Ζήνων Μνασέου Κιτιεὺς ἀρχὰς μὲν τὸν θεὸν καὶ τὴν ὕλην, ὧν ὁ μέν ἐστι τοῦ ποιεῖν αἴτιος ἡ δὲ τοῦ πάσχειν, στοιχεῖα δὲ τέτταρα. Further accounts in Heinrich DÖRRIE†/Matthias BALTES, *Die philosophische Lehre des Platonismus: Einige grundlegende Axiome/Platonische Physik (im antiken Verständnis) I; Bausteine 101–124; Text, Übersetzung, Kommentar*, Der Platonismus in der Antike, Grundlagen—System—Entfaltung 4 (Stuttgart-Bad Cannstatt: Frommann-Holzboog, 1996), 118–201.

220 Origenes, *De principiis* I 1.1 (TzF 24, 98 GÖRGEMANNS/KARPP = GCS Origenes V, 16.19f. KOETSCHAU). ET from BEHR, *Origen*, 13.

221 Origenes, *Commentarii in Genesim* D 11 = *Collectio Coisliniana*, frag. 73 PETIT (OWD 1/1, 158.21–28 METZLER = CChr.SG 15, 73.5–15 PETIT).

222 Friedhelm WINKELMANN, "Einige Bemerkungen zu den Aussagen des Rufinus von Aquileia und des Hieronymus über ihre Übersetzungstheorie und -methode," in *Kyriakon: Festschrift Johannes Quasten*, vol. 2, ed. Patrick Granfield and Josef A. Jungmann (Münster: Aschendorff, 1970), 532–547, esp. 535–537.

223 Plato, *Phaedo* 85 E (from the ἁρμονία of a lyre); and Aristoteles, *Physica* IV 1 209 a 16 (στοιχεῖα νοητά as geometrical bodies are ἀσώματα) do not employ this in respect to God. Aristoteles, *De anima* I 2 404 b 31, characterizes with the term (first?) the Platonic theory of principles. On the term ἀσώματος in Imperial-era accounts of the Platonic theory of principles. For additional references, see LSJ s.v., 267.

224 Thus Guy STROUMSA, "The Incorporeality of God: Context and Implications of Origen's Position," *Religion* 13 (1983): 345–358, esp. 346, "chrétiens stoïcisants"; referring to André BECKAERT, "L'évolution de l'intellectualisme grec vers la pensée religieuse et la relève de la philosophie par la pensée chrétienne," *Revue des études byzantines* 19 (1961): 44–62, esp. 59.

225 Origenes, *De principiis* I *praef.* 8 (TzF 24, 94 GÖRGEMANNS/KARPP = GCS Origenes V, 14.16–15.5 KOETSCHAU). ET from BEHR, *Origen: On First Principles*, 1: 19.

226 Agraphon 72 in *Agrapha: Aussercanonische Schriftfragmente, mit fünf Registern gesammelt und untersucht und in zweiter, völlig neu bearb., durch alttestamentliche Agrapha vermehrter Aufl. . . .* hg. Alfred RESCH, TU 30/3f. (Leipzig: Hinrichs, 1906), 96–98; following the version of Ignatius, *Epistula ad Smyrneos* 3.2 (SUC I, 206.5 FISCHER). Cf. Eusebius, *Historia ecclesiastica* III 36.11 (GCS Eusebius II/1, 278.13–16 SCHWARTZ). RESCH argues (op. cit., 97f.) for an Aramaic precursor text. Now otherwise with references to further secondary literature see Jörg FREY, "B.V.1.1. Fragmente judenchristlicher Evangelien," in *Antike christliche Apokryphen in deutscher Übersetzung*, hg. Christoph Markschies und Jens Schröter, Bd. 1, *Evangelien und Verwandtes* (Tübingen: Mohr Siebeck, 2012), 560–592, esp. 585; *Le parole dimenticate di Gesù*, a cura di Mauro Pesce, Scritti Greci e Latini (Rome: Fondazione Lorenzo Valla, 2004), 322, 711; and already Ernst VON DOBSCHÜTZ, *Das Kerygma Petri kritisch untersucht*,

Texte und Untersuchungen zur altchristlichen Literatur XI/1 (Leipzig: Hinrichs, 1893), 82–84. Cf. also Agraphon 29 (op. cit., 246f.) in Origenes, loc. cit.; also Hieronymus, *Commentarii in Isaiam* XVIII *prol.* (CChr.SL 73A, 741.48f. ADRIAEN): ". . . iuxta euangelium, quod Hebraeorum lectitant Nazaraei, incorporale daemonium . . ."; and idem, *De viris illustribus* 16.4 (BiPatr 12, 106 CERESA-GASTALDO = 180 BARTHOLD; on Ignatius of Antioch).

227 Markus VINZENT, "'Ich bin kein körperloses Geistwesen': Zum Verhältnis von κήρυγμα Πέτρου, 'Doctrina Petri' und IgnSm 3," in Reinhard M. Hübner, *Der paradox Eine: Antignostischer Monarchianismus im zweiten Jahrhundert*, mit einem Beitrag von Markus Vinzent, Supplements to Vigiliae Christianae 50 (Leiden/Boston/Köln: Brill, 1999), 241–286.

228 See the Latin text of *De principiis* I *praef.* 8 (TzF 24, 94 GÖRGEMANNS/KARPP = GCS Origenes V, 15.2–5 KOETSCHAU). ET from BEHR, *Origen: On First Principles*, 1: 19.

229 Origenes, *De principiis* I *praef.* 8 (TzF 24, 94–96 GÖRGEMANNS/KARPP = GCS Origenes V, 15.5–16 KOETSCHAU). On this subject, see Mark EDWARDS, "Origen No Gnostic; Or, on the Corporeality of Man," *JTS* 43 (1992): 23–37, esp. 24f.

230 Origenes, *De principiis* I *praef.* 8 (TzF 24.96 GÖRGEMANNS/KARPP = GCS Origenes V, 15.17–19 KOETSCHAU). ET from BEHR, *Origen: On First Principles*, 1: 19.

231 Origenes, *De principiis* I *praef.* 9 (TzF 24.96 GÖRGEMANNS/KARPP = GCS Origenes V, 15.20–27 KOETSCHAU). ET from BEHR, *Origen: On First Principles*, 1: 21.

232 Antonio GRAPPONE, "Annotazioni sulla cronologia delle omelie di Origene," *Augustinianum* 41 (2001): 27–58, esp. 51–58.

233 Christoph MARKSCHIES, "'. . . für die Gemeinde im Grossen und Ganzen nicht geeignet . . .'? Erwägungen zu Absicht und Wirkung der Predigten des Origenes," in idem, *Origenes und sein Erbe: Gesammelte Studien*, TU 160 (Berlin/New York: De Gruyter, 2007), 35–62, esp. 41–56. See also Éric JUNOD, "Wodurch unterscheiden sich die Homilien des Origenes von seinen Kommentaren?" in *Predigt in der Alten Kirche*, hg. Ekkehard Mühlenberg und Johannes van Oort, Studien der Patristischen Arbeitsgemeinschaft 3 (Kampen: Kok Pharos, 1994), 50–81.

234 Origenes, *Homiliae in Genesim* 3.1 (GCS Origenes VI, 58.3–8 HABERMEHL). ET from *Origen: Homilies on Genesis and Exodus*, trans. Ronald HEINE (Washington, D.C.: Catholic University of America, 1982), 89. Cf. the German translation in Origenes, *Die Homilien zum Buch Genesis*, eingel. und übers. von Peter HABERMEHL, Origenes Werke mit deutscher Übersetzung 1/2 (Berlin/Boston und Freiburg/Basel/Vienna: De Gruyter und Herder, 2011), 90.

235 Origenes, *Homiliae in Genesim* 3.2 (GCS Origenes VI, 59.3–8 HABERMEHL). ET from HEINE, *Origen: Homilies on Genesis and Exodus*, 89. Generally on the views of Origen regarding circumcision, see Andrew S. JACOBS, *Christ Circumcised: A Study in Early Christian History and Difference* (Philadelphia: University of Pennsylvania Press, 2012), 122–125.

236 Origenes, *Contra Celsum* I 15 (GCS Origenes I, 67.21–25 KOETSCHAU) = Numenius, Περὶ τἀγαθοῦ frag. 1b (CUFr 42 DES PLACES). ET from CHADWICK, *Origen: Contra Celsum*, 17. On this passage, see Henri CROUZEL, *Origène et la philosophie*, Théologie 52 (Paris: Aubier, 1962), 45f.

237 Thus the appropriate observation in Marguerite HARL, "Structure et cohérence du Peri Archôn," in Crouzel, Lomiento, et Rius-Camps, *Origeniana*, 11–45, esp. 19. Harl refers to *De principiis* IV 4.9f. (TzF 24, 812–820 GÖRGEMANNS/KARPP = GCS Origenes V, 361.14–364.16 KOETSCHAU).

238 See Thomas BÖHM, "Origenes—Theologe und (Neu-)Platoniker? Oder: Wem soll man mißtrauen—Eusebius oder Porphyrius?" *Adamantius* 8 (2002): 7–23; Christoph MARKSCHIES, *Kaiserzeitliche christliche Theologie und ihre Institutionen: Prolegomena zu einer Geschichte der antiken christlichen Theologie* (Tübingen: Mohr Siebeck, 2007), 73–107; and ZIEBRITZKI, *Heiliger Geist und Weltseele*, 30–43, 260–266.

239 Origenes, *Homiliae in Genesim* I 13 (GCS Origenes VI, 24.1–6 HABERMEHL). ET from HEINE, *Origen: Homilies on Genesis and Exodus*, 69. Cf. also on this the aforementioned fragment from the commentary on the pertinent passage: Origenes, *Commentarii in Genesim* D 11 = *Collectio Coisliniana* frag. 73 PETIT (OWD 1/1, 160.22–28 METZLER = CChr. SG 15, 74.43–51 PETIT); and, above all, Henri CROUZEL, *Théologie de l'image de dieu chez Origène*, Théologie 34 (Paris: Aubier, 1956), 148–153. See Christoph MARKSCHIES, s.v. "Innerer Mensch," in *Reallexikon für Antike und Christentum* (Stuttgart: Hiersemann, 1998), 18: 266–312 (on Origen: 289–293); EDWARDS, *Origen against Plato*, 102–107; and idem, "Further Reflections on the Platonism of Origen," 320.

240 Origenes, *Homiliae in Genesim* I 13 (GCS Origenes VI, 24.8–25.3 HABERMEHL). ET from HEINE, *Origen: Homilies on Genesis and Exodus*, 63f.

241 *Epistula Barnabae* 6.13 (SAC 2, 154 WENGST = TU 30/3f., Agraphon 123, S. 167 RESCH = PESCHE, *Le parole dimenticate di Gesù*, 152f. 633f.).

242 See Gerald BOSTOCK, "Quality and Corporeity in Origen," in *Origeniana Secunda: Second colloque international des études origéniennes (Bari, 20–23 septembre 1977)*, textes rassemblés par Henri Crouzel et Antonio Quacquarelli, Quaderni di "Vetera Christianorum" 15 (Rome: Edizioni dell'Ateneo, 1980), 323–337; Henry CHADWICK, "Origen, Celsus, and the Resurrection of the Body," *HTR* 41 (1948): 83–102; Gilles DORIVAL, "Origène et la résurrection de la chair," in *Origeniana Quarta: Die Referate des 4. Internationalen Origeneskongresses (Innsbruck, 2.–6. September 1985)*, hg. Lothar Lies, Innsbrucker Theologische Studien 19 (Innsbruck/Vienna: Tyrolia, 1987), 291–321 (with additional literature on p. 319 in n. 1); EDWARDS, "Origen No Gnostic," 28–31; HENNESSEY, "A Philosophical Issue in Origen's Eschatology," 374–376; and most recently Panagiōtēs TZAMALIKOS, *Origen: Philosophy of History & Eschatology*, Supplements to Vigiliae Christianae 85 (Leiden/Boston: Brill, 2007), 343.

243 Origenes, *Homiliae in Leviticum* IX 11 (GCS Origenes VI, 439.1–10 BAEHRENS). In Methodius, *De resurrectione* III 10.2 (G. Nathanael BONWETSCH, *Methodius von Olympus*, Bd. 1, *Schriften* [Erlangen/Leipzig: Deichert, 1891], 266.4–6 = GCS Methodius 409.14–405.2 BONWETSCH), a description may be found preserved only in Church Slavonic of immaterial bodiliness with reference to 1 Cor 15:35–49 as "not heavy nor hard as of this earth, of flesh and limb, rather soft and as of air, such is the spirit," which Methodius presents as a quotation from Origen's *De resurrectione*. See Pamphilus von Caesarea, *Apologia pro Origene: Apologie für Origenes*, übers. und eingel. von Georg RÖWEKAMP, Fontes Christiani 80 (Turnhout: Brepols, 2005), 165; BOSTOCK, "Quality and Corporeity in Origen," 334f.; Henri CROUZEL, "Les critiques adressées par Méthode et ses contemporains à la doctrine origénienne du corps ressuscité," *Gregorianum* 53 (1972): 679–716; idem, "La doctrine origénienne du corps ressuscité," *Bulletin de littérature ecclésiastique* 81 (1980): 175–200, 241–266 (= idem, *Les fins dernières selon Origène*, Collected Studies Series CS 320 [Aldershot: Variorum, 1990], nr. VI and VII); and Holger STRUTWOLF, "Gnosis als System: Zur Rezeption der valentinianischen Gnosis bei Origenes," Forschungen zur Kirchen- und Dogmengeschichte 56 (Göttingen: Vandenhoeck & Ruprecht, 1993), 339–356. On the possible spherical form of the resurrected body, see below; on the positions in the Origenistic Crisis of the fourth century, most prominently for Theophilus of Alexandria, see below.

244 Thus KOCH, *Pronoia und Paideusis*, 62–65; with a somewhat different accentation: Rolf GÖGLER, *Zur Theologie des biblischen Wortes bei Origenes* (Düsseldorf: Patmos, 1963), 307–319; Marguerite HARL, *Origène et la fonction révélatrice du verbe incarné* (Paris: Éditions du Seuil, 1958), 113–115, 238f.; ALEXANDRE, "Le statut des questions concernant la matière dans le *Peri Archôn*," 71–74; GRILLMEIER, *Jesus der Christus im Glauben der Kirche*, 1: 266–280, esp. 274–27; and Basil STUDER, s.v. "Incarnazione," in *Origene: Dizionario; La cultura, il pensiero, le opere*, a cura di Adele Monaci Castagno (Rome: Città Nuova Editrice, 2000), 225–229.

245 Tryggve Göransson: *Albinus, Alcinous, Arius Didymus*, Studia Graeca et Latina Gothoburgensia 61 (Göteborg: Acta Universitatis Gothoburgensis, 1995), 105–136. See also Matthias Baltes, "Muß die 'Landkarte des Mittelplatonismus' neu gezeichnet werden?" in idem, *ΔΙΑΝΟΗΜΑΤΑ: Kleine Schriften zu Platon und zum Platonismus*, hg. Annette Hüffmeier, Marie-Luise Lakmann und Matthias Vorwerk, Beiträge zur Altertumskunde 123 (Stuttgart/Leipzig: Teubner, 1999), 327–350; and the introduction in the critical edition: Alcinoos, *Enseignement des doctrines de Platon*, introduction, texte établi et commenté par John Whittaker et traduit par Pierre Louis, Collection des Universités de France (CUFr) (Paris: Les Belles Lettres, 1990), VI–XXXI.

246 Alcinous, *Epitome doctrinae Platonicae sive Διδασκαλικός* 10.7 (CUFr 25 Whittaker/ Louis = 165.34–42 Hermann). A comparable philosophical derivation of the subordination of the body (in this case in respect to ὕλη, "matter") in Calcidius, *Commentarius in Platonis Timaeum* 319 (Corpus Platonicum Medii Aevi. Plato Latinus IV, 314.17–315.2 Waszink).

247 Alcinous, *Epitome doctrinae Platonicae sive Διδασκαλικός* 10.7 (CUFr 25 Whittaker/ Louis = 165.42–166.6 Hermann). ET from *Alcinous: The Handbook of Platonism*, trans. with an introduction and commentary by John Dillon (Oxford: Clarendon, 1993), 19. Cf. Alkinoos, *Didaskalikos: Lehrbuch der Grundsätze Platons*, von Orrin F. Summerell und Thomas Zimmer, Sammlung wissenschaftlicher Commentare (Berlin/New York: De Gruyter, 2007), 29.

248 Alcinous demonstrates "that the simplicity, the perfect unity of God, implies his incorporeality"—thus Stroumsa, "The Incorporeality of God," 345. See also on this Koch, *Pronoia und Paideusis*, 256–258; and André-Jean Festugiere, *La révélation d'Hermès Trismégiste*, tome 4, *Le dieu inconnu et la gnose*, Études Bibliques (Paris: Gabalda, 1954), 95–102.

249 Alcinous, *Epitome doctrinae Platonicae sive Διδασκαλικός* 10.8 (CUFr 25f. Whittaker/ Louis = 166.12–14 Hermann).

250 Iustinus Martyr, *Dialogus cum Tryphone* 2.6 (93 Goodspeed = PTS 47.73.36–43 Marcovich). ET from *St. Justin Martyr: Dialogue with Trypho*, trans. Thomas B. Falls, rev. with a new introduction by Thomas P. Halton, ed. Michael Slusser, Selections from the Fathers of the Church 3 (Washington, D.C.: Catholic University of America Press, 2003), 6. Cf. the quotation of the contemporary Platonist Atticus in Eusebius, *Praeparatio evangelica* XV 13.5 (GCS Eusebius VIII/2, 377.14 Mras/Des Places = frag. 9 [CUFr 69 Des Places]). And in Iustinus himself: *Apologia* 63.10 (72 Goodspeed = PTS 38, 122.22 Marcovich = SC 507.296.24 Munier): ποτὲ δὲ καὶ ἐν εἰκόνι ἀσωμάτῳ (or with the MSS, ἀσωμάτων of the appearances of Jesus before the incarnation). Cf. ibid., 63.17 (73 Goodspeed = 123.41f. Marcovich = 298.46f. Munier).

251 Tatianus, *Oratio ad Graecos* 25.3 (TU 4/1, 27.5f. Schwartz = 291 Goodspeed = PTS 43, 49.17f. Marcovich = BHTh 165, 150.17f. Trelenberg). ET from *Tatian: Oratio ad Graecos and Fragments*, ed. and trans. Molly Whitaker, Oxford Early Christian Texts (Oxford: Clarendon, 1982), 49.

252 Accordingly, the Codex Arethae after Parisinus Graecus 174 (TU 4/1, 47 Schwartz): τῶν Στωϊκῶν αὕτη ἡ δόξα.

253 Athenagoras, *Supplicatio pro Christianis* 36 (357 Goodspeed = TU 4/2, 46.23f. Schwartz = PTS 31, 112.20f. Marcovich).

254 See on this Robert P. Casey, "Clement of Alexandria and the Beginnings of Christian Platonism," *HTR* 18 (1925): 39–101, esp. 78–80; and Harold W. Attridge, "The Philosophical Critique of Religion under the Early Empire," *ANRW* II/16.2: 45–78.

255 Clemens Alexandrinus, *Stromata* V 99.4 (GCS Clemens Alexandrinus II, 392.7 Stählin/ Früchtel/Treu). Cf. *Stromata* V 94.3 (GCS Clemens Alexandrinus II, 388.9–11 Stählin/Früchtel/Treu). See Dietmar Wyrwa, *Die christliche Platonaneignung in den Stromateis des Clemens von Alexandrien*, Arbeiten zur Kirchengeschichte 53 (Berlin/ New York: De Gruyter, 1983), 268–282.

256	Clemens Alexandrinus, *De providentia frag.* 37 (GCS Clemens Alexandrinus III, 219.17–22 Stählin/Früchtel/Treu) = Maximus Confessor, *Capita de substantia* (PG 91, 264). See on the authenticity of the remarks *Clavis Patrum Graecorum*, vol. 1, *Patres Antenicaeni*, cura et studio Maurice Geerard (Turnhout: Brepols, 1983), nr. 1390, 138f.

257	Clemens Alexandrinus, *Stromata* III 103.3 (GCS Clemens Alexandrinus II, 243.32–244.3 Stählin/Früchtel/Treu). ET from *Clement of Alexandria: Stromateis, Books 1–3*, trans. John Ferguson, Fathers of the Church 85 (Washington, D.C.: Catholic University of America Press, 1991), 321f.

258	Thomas Böhm, "Unbegreiflichkeit Gottes bei Origenes und Unsagbarkeit des Einen bei Plotin—ein Strukturvergleich," in *Origeniana Octava: Origen and the Alexandrian Tradition; Papers of the 8th International Origen Congress Pisa, 27–31 August 2001*, ed. Lorenzo Perrone in collaboration with Paolo Bernardini and Diego Marchini, BETL 164 (Leuven: Peeters, 2003), 1: 451–463, esp. 452–455. See also Basil Studer, "Zur Frage der dogmatischen Terminologie in der lateinischen Übersetzung von Origenes' *De Principiis*," in idem, *Dominus Salvator: Studien zur Christologie und Exegese der Kirchenväter*, Studia Anselmiana 107 (Rome: Pontificio Ateneo S. Anselmo, 1992), 67–89, esp. 76–78.

259	Origenes, *De principiis* I 1.2 (TzF 24, 100–102 Görgemanns/Karpp = GCS Origenes V, 17.18–21 Koetschau).

260	Stroumsa, "The Incorporeality of God," 348f., indicates that Origen identifies his adversaries with *Gnostics in the Marcionite mould* in his text on the "first principles." In *De principiis* II 4.3 it is argued against the adherents of Marcion, in particular against their alleged dualistic sundering of the one God in twain, and maintained that they held the creator God witnessed in the Old Testament to be *visible* (*visibilis*) and corporeal (*corporeus*: TzF 24, 336 Görgemanns/Karpp = GCS Origenes V, 130.12–20 Koetschau). Naturally, there are gnostic groups which championed notions of divine corporeality, and, indeed, possibly Origen even polemically labeled the followers of Marcion as "Stoics": *Commentarii in epistulam ad Romanos* II 9 [13] (AGLB 16, 169.467f. Hammond Bammel after the particular reading of the Copenhagen MS 1338 4°, saec. IX, which might be found in *Opera Omnia* VI, 137 Lommatzsch and also in FChr 2/1, 288.15 Heither): *Stoici aiunt. . .* ; thus accordingly also Adolf von Harnack, *Der kirchengeschichtliche Ertrag der exegetischen Arbeiten des Origenes*, Tl. 2, *Die beiden Testamente mit Ausschluss des Hexateuchs und des Richterbuchs*, TU 42/4 (Leipzig: Hinrichs, 1919), 68; and, following him, Crouzel, *Origène et la philosophie*, 43.

261	Origenes, *De principiis* II 4.3 (TzF 24, 336 Görgemanns/Karpp = GCS Origenes V, 130.17–20 Koetschau). ET from Behr, *Origen: On First Principles*, 1: 187.

262	Origenes, *De oratione* 23.3 (GCS Origenes II, 351.1–7 Koetschau). ET from Henry Chadwick and J. E. L. Oulton, *Alexandrian Christianity: Selected Translations of Clement and Origen* (Philadelphia: Westminster Press, 1954), 284.

263	Origenes, *De principiis* IV 4.6 (TzF 24, 802 Görgemanns/Karpp = GCS Origenes V, 357, 16–28 Koetschau). See on the passage Alexandre, "Le statut des questions concernant la matière dans le Peri Archôn," 67f.

264	Origenes, *De principiis* I 7.5 (TzF 24, 242 Görgemanns/Karpp = GCS Origenes V, 92.9–12 Koetschau).

265	Origenes, *Commentarii in Euangelium Ioannis* XIII 21.123 (GCS Origenes IV, 244.19–24 Preuschen). *Origen: Commentary on the Gospel of John, Books 13–32*, trans. Ronald Heine, Fathers of the Church 89 (Washington, D.C.: Catholic University of America, 1993), 93.

266	Plato, *Respublica* VI 19, 509 B. See on the anti-Stoic orientation of Origen also the passages from *Contra Celsum* cited above, p. 47 with n. 174; ibid. with n. 176; Crouzel, *Origène et la philosophie*, 41–45; Bostock, "Quality and Corporeity in Origen," 324–326; Henry Chadwick, "Origen, Celsus, and the Stoa," *JTS* 48 (1947): 34–49; and Eleuterio

ELORDUY, "El influjo estoíco en Orígenes," in Crouzel, Lomiento, et Rius-Camps, *Origeniana*, 277–288, esp. 279–281.

267 Origenes, *Commentarii in Euangelium Ioannis* XIII 21.124f. (GCS Origenes IV, 244.24–32 PREUSCHEN). ET from HEINE, *Origen: Commentary on the Gospel of John. Books 13–32*, 93f.

268 Origenes, *Commentarii in Euangelium Ioannis* XIII 21.125 (GCS Origenes IV, 244.32–245.1 PREUSCHEN). ET from HEINE, *Origen: Commentary on the Gospel of John. Books 13–32*, 94.

269 Origenes, *Commentarii in Euangelium Ioannis* XIII 21.130–22.131 (GCS Origenes IV, 244.24–32 PREUSCHEN). ET from HEINE, *Origen: Commentary on the Gospel of John. Books 13–32*, 95.

270 Origenes, *Commentarii in Genesim* D 11 = *Collectio Coisliniana*, frag. 73 PETIT (OWD 1/1, 160.1–20 METZLER = CChr.SG 15, 73.16–74.40 PETIT).

271 Origenes, *De principiis* I 1.9 (TzF 24, 120 GÖRGEMANNS/KARPP = GCS Origenes V, 26.15–27.2 KOETSCHAU). ET from BEHR, *Origen: On First Principles*, 1: 39. See also on this topic Origenes, *Contra Celsum* VII 43 (GCS Origenes II, 194.7–24 KOETSCHAU); and STROUMSA, "The Incorporeality of God," 351.

272 Origenes, *De principiis* I 1.6 (TzF 24, 110 GÖRGEMANNS/KARPP = GCS Origenes V, 21.10–17 KOETSCHAU). ET from BEHR, *Origen: On First Principles*, 1: 31–33

273 Origenes, *Contra Celsum* VI 71 (GCS Origenes II, 141.15–20 KOETSCHAU). ET from BEHR, *Origen: On First Principles*, 1: 385. An exact parallel to the expression πνεῦμα σωματικόν may be found in the Stoic texts collected by Hans VON ARNIM, certainly not (the present passage of Origen is freely numbered as SVF II, 1051 [II, 310.16–25]), the comparable discussion of a πνεῦμα φυσικόν: Pseudo-Galenus, *Introductio seu medicus* 9 (*Claudii Galeni opera omnia* XIV, 697.6–8 KÜHN = SVF II, 716 [II, 16–18 VON ARNIM]). See on the Stoic parallels and Platonic underpinnings also BOSTOCK, "Quality and Corporeity in Origen," 325–327.

274 Origenes, *Contra Celsum* VI 71 (GCS Origenes II, 141.20–28 KOETSCHAU). ET from CHADWICK, *Origen: Contra Celsum*, 385f.

275 See alongside the literature enumerated above, p. 364 nn. 242 and 243, also in summary Caroline Walker BYNUM, *The Resurrection of the Body in Western Christianity, 200–1336*, Lectures on the History of Religions, New Series 15 (New York: Columbia University Press, 1995), 59–71.

276 For Origen, cf. most prominently the statement of the anathematisms in the edict of Emperor Justinian against Origen from AD 543: Iustinianus Imperator, *Edictum contra Origenem = Epistula ad Menam* (ACO III, 204.10f. SCHWARTZ = Legum Iustiniani Imperatoris Vocabularium, Subsidia III, 98.10f. AMELOTTI/ZINGALE). Cf. also ibid., Anathematismus 5 (213.25f. = 116.25f. = TzF 24, 822 GÖRGEMANNS/KARPP). Also from the anathematisms of AD 553, nr. 10 (ACO IV/1, 249.23 STRAUB = TzF 24, 828 GÖRGEMANNS/KARPP). Origen was evidently convinced that angels have spherical bodies: *De oratione* 31.3 (on the angels: GCS Origenes II, 397.5f. KOETSCHAU). The Stoic Chrysippus already taught the sphericalness of souls according to a transmission in the scholia on Homer: Scholion on *Ilias* Ψ 66 (*Scholia Graeca in Homeri Iliadem* V, 377.42–44 ERBSE = SVF II, 815 [II, 224.39 VON ARNIM]): Χρύσιππος δὲ μετὰ τὸν χωρισμὸν τοῦ σώματός φησιν αὐτὰς σφαιροειδεῖς γενέσθαι.

277 The ideal form is already in Plato the ideal form which the Demiurge grants the cosmos as a living entity: *Timaeus* 33 B. Cf. also the doxographic accounts on the divine spherical form in Xenophanes and Parmenides.

278 See pp. 43–48.

279 Origenes, *De principiis* I 1.28 (TzF 24, 118 GÖRGEMANNS/KARPP = GCS Origenes V, 26.2f. KOETSCHAU). For the biblical passage, cf. op. cit. (116 = 25.3f.). See KANNENGIESSER, "Origen, Systematician in De Principiis," 400f.

280 Origenes, *De principiis* II 4.3 (TzF 24, 336 Görgemanns/Karpp = GCS Origenes V, 130.12–20 Koetschau).
281 Origenes, *De principiis* IV 3.15 (TzF 24, 778 Görgemanns/Karpp = GCS Origenes V, 347.9–14 Koetschau). Cf. already ibid., IV 4.5 (800 = 356.9f.). ET from Behr, *Origen: On First Principles*, 1: 559.
282 Origenes, *De principiis* I *praef.* 9 (TzF 24, 96 Görgemanns/Karpp = GCS Origenes V, 15.20–27 Koetschau). ET from Behr, *Origen: On First Principles*, 1: 21.
283 Tertullianus, *Apologeticum* 47.6 (CChr.SL 1, 163.21f. Dekkers = SVF II, 1034 [II, 307.10f. von Arnim]). ET from Glover/Rendall, *Tertullian: Apology. De Spectaculis. Minucius Felix: Octavius*, 207. Richard Heinze, *Tertullians Apologeticum, Berichte über die Verhandlungen der Königlich Sächsischen Gesellschaft der Wissenschaften*, Philologisch-historische Klasse 62, Bd. 10, Heft (Leipzig: Teubner, 1910), 474, refers to an excerpt of a collection of δόξαι περὶ θεοῦ in Theophilus of Antioch and Joannes Stobaeus, the original author of which is no longer identifiable, as possible parallels to the passage. Cf. Hermann Diels, "Eine Quelle des Stobäus," *Rheinisches Museum für Philologie* 30 (1875): 172–181. Regardless, this comprises a florilegium with citations from poets, also Nicole Zeegers-Vander Vorst, *Les citations des poètes grecs chez les apologistes chrétiens du IIe siècle*, Université de Louvain, Recueil de travaux d'histoire et de philologie sér. 4, 47 (Louvain: Bureau du Recueil, Bibliothèque de l'Université, 1972), 115–123, 123–132, 132–137.
284 Joseph Moingt, *Théologie trinitaire de Tertullien*, tome 1, *Histoire, Doctrine, Méthodes*, Théologie 68 (Paris: Aubier, 1966), 183–224. Moingt demonstrated that Praxeas cannot be labeled as a "modalistic Monarchian," as prior German-speaking academia had assumed: "Le monarchianisme n'est pas un modalisme" (p. 190). The views of Praxeas might better be described (employing a term from my academic teacher Luise Abramowski) as "identificatory theology" (*Identifikationstheologie*). See on this also Christoph Markschies, "'. . . et tamen non tres Dii, sed unus Deus . . .' Zum Stand der Erforschung der altkirchlichen Trinitätstheologie," in idem, *Alta Trinità Beata: Gesammelte Studien zur altkirchlichen Trinitätstheologie* (Tübingen: Mohr Siebeck, 2000), 286–309, esp. 294.
285 The Latin term *effigies* is here translated as μορφή: "qui cum in effigie (in the Vulgate: *forma*) Dei constitutus (Vulgata: *esset*) non rapinam existimavit (Vulgate: *arbitratus est*) . . ."; Greek: ὃς ἐν μορφῇ θεοῦ ὑπάρχων οὐχ ἁρπαγμὸν ἡγήσατο τὸ εἶναι ἴσα θεῷ. For the corpus in Tertullian, see VL 24/2 109; Frede and Blaise, *Dictionnaire Latin-Français des auteurs chrétiens*, s.v. 300.
286 Tertullianus, *Adversus Praxean* 7.8 (FC 34, 128.11f. Scarpat/Sieben). ET from *Tertullian: Adversus Praxean*, trans. Ernest Evans (London: SPCK, 1948), 138. See the extensive commentary of the passage in Q. S. F. Tertulliano, *Contro Prassea*, edizione critica con introduzione, traduzione italiana, note e indici a cura di Giuseppe Scarpat, Corona Patrum 12 (Turin: Società Editrice Internazionale, 1985), 281–283; and, for context, Sheridan, *Language for God in Patristic Tradition*, 118–122.
287 Tertullianus, *De carne Christi* 11.4 (CChr.SL 2, 895.23f. Kroymann = SC 216, 258.23f. Mahe). On the subject itself, see Gerhard Esser, *Die Seelenlehre Tertullians* (Paderborn: Schöningh, 1893), 48–52; Eric Weil, "Remarques sur le matérialisme des Stoïciens," in *Mélanges Alexandre Koyré*, publiés à l'occasion de son soixante-dixième anniversaire, tome 2, *L'aventure de l'esprit*, Histoire de la pensée 13 (Paris: Hermann, 1964), 556–572; and Marcia L. Colish, *The Stoic Tradition from Antiquity to the Early Middle Ages*, vol. 2, *Stoicism in Christian Latin Thought through the Sixth Century*, second impression with addenda et corrigenda (Leiden: Brill, 1990), 9–29, esp. 15.
288 Adolf von Harnack, *Lehrbuch der Dogmengeschichte*, Bd. 1, *Die Entstehung des kirchlichen Dogmas*, 4. neu durchgearbeitete und vermehrte Aufl. (Tübingen: Mohr Siebeck, 1909), 574 n. 6. Cf., however, Joseph Moingt, *Théologie trinitaire de Tertullien*, tome 2, *Substantialité et individualité*, Théologie 68 (Paris: Aubier, 1966), 333–338; and Michel Spanneut, *Le Stoïcisme des pères de l'Église: De Clément de Rome à Clément*

d'Alexandrie, Patristica Sorbonensia 1, nouv. éd., revue et augmentée (Paris: Éditions du Seuil, 1969), 164–167.

289   See Origenes, *De principiis* II 4.3 (TzF 24, 336 Görgemanns/Karpp = GCS Origenes V, 130.12–20 Koetschau). On the Marcionite theory of God, see Winrich Löhr, "Did Marcion Distinguish between a Just God and a Good God?" in *Marcion und seine kirchengeschichtliche Wirkung. Marcion and His Impact on Church History: Vorträge der internationalen Fachkonferenz zu Marcion, gehalten vom 15.–18. August 2001 in Mainz*, hg. Gerhard May und Katharina Greschat in Gemeinschaft mit Martin Meiser, TU 150 (Berlin/New York: De Gruyter, 2002), 131–146.

290   Barbara Aland, "Sünde und Erlösung bei Marcion und die Konsequenz für die sog. beiden Götter Marcions," in *Marcion und seine kirchengeschichtliche Wirkung*, 147–157, esp. 155.

291   Tertullianus, *Aduersus Marcionem* II 27.5 (CChr.SL 1, 506.22–25 Kroymann). ET from *Tertullian: Adversus Marcionem, Books 1–3*, trans. Edward Evans, Oxford Early Christian Texts (Oxford: Clarendon, 1972), 163.

292   See additionally the pertinent accounts of mainstream church heresiology in Adolf von Harnack, *Marcion: Das Evangelium vom fremden Gott; Eine Monographie zur Geschichte der Grundlegung der katholischen Kirche*, Neue Studien zu Marcion, TU 45 und 44/4, 2. verb. und verm. Aufl. (Leipzig: Hinrichs, 1924 und 1923 = Darmstadt: Wissenschaftliche Buchgesellschaft, 1960), 274*–276* and 286* (therein ascribed to the "antitheses" of Marcion); and (critical of this tendency from Harnack) Gerhard May, "Markions Genesisauslegung und die 'Antithesen,'" in idem, *Markion: Gesammelte Aufsätze*, hg. Katharina Greschat und Martin Meiser, Veröffentlichungen des Instituts für Europäische Geschichte Mainz, Abteilung für abendländische Religionsgeschichte, Beiheft 68 (Mainz: Zabern, 2005), 43–50.

293   Tertullianus, *Aduersus Marcionem* III 9.1 (CChr.SL 1, 519.16–24 Kroymann).

294   Origenes, *Commentarii in Genesim* D 11 = *Collectio Coisliniana*, frag. 73 Petit (OWD 1/1, 158.19–21 Metzler = CChr.SG 15, 73.3–5 Petit).

295   See on this, at length and with references, Christoph Markschies, "Der religiöse Pluralismus und das antike Christentum—eine neue Deutung der Gnosis," in idem, *Gnosis und Christentum* (Berlin: Berlin University Press, 2009), 53–82.

296   Guy G. Stroumsa, "Polymorphie divine et transformations d'un mythologème: L' 'Apocryphon de Jean' et ses sources," *VC* 35 (1981): 412–434. See also Carola Barth, *Die Interpretation des Neuen Testaments in der valentinianischen Gnosis*, TU 37/3 (Leipzig: Hinrichs, 1911), 52.

297   Second Logos of the Great Seth (NHC VII,2 p. 56.20–25 [NHMS 30, 166 Riley]). ET from *The Coptic Gnostic Library: A Complete Edition of the Nag Hammadi Codices*, ed. James M. Robinson (Leiden: Brill, 2000), 4: 167. The original Greek text still shines through in the Coptic translation: μορφή and ἰδέα. Cf. Irenaeus, *Aduersus haereses* I 30.12 (FChr 8/1, 346.1–18 Rousseau/Doutreleau/Brox). Further attestations in Stroumsa, "Polymorphie divine et transformations d'un mythologème," 415–419.

298   On the image here presupposed of the gnostic theory of God from the example of so-called Valentianism, see Christoph Markschies, "Individuality in Some Gnostic Authors: With a Few Remarks on the Interpretation of Ptolemaeus, *Epistula ad Floram*," *ZAC* 15 (2011): 411–430.

299   Apocryphon of John (NHC II,1 p. 3.22f. [NHMS 33.25 Waldstein/Wisse]). ET from Robinson, *The Coptic Gnostic Library*, 2: 24f., 184f. Further attestations on the topic in Stroumsa, "The Incorporeality of God," 348f.

300   Thus Manlio Simonetti, "Modelli culturali nella cristianità orientale del II–III secolo," in *De Tertullien aux Mozarabes: Mélanges offerts à Jacques Fontaine, membre de l'institut, à l'occasion de son 70ᵉ anniversaire, par ses élèves, amis et collègues*, Institute de Recherche et d'Histoire des Textes, comité, éd. Louis Holtz, tome 1, *Antiquité tardive et christianisme ancien (IIIᵉ–VIᵉ siècles)*, Collection des études augustiniennes 132 (Paris:

Institute d'Études Augustiniennes, 1992), 381–392 = idem, *Orthodossia ed eresia tra I e II secolo*, Armarium 5 (Soveria Manelli/Messina: Rubbettino, 1994), 315–331, esp. 327f.; with reference to Irenaeus, *Adversus haereses* V 6.1 (FChr 8/5, 56.3–10 ROUSSEAU/BROX); and Jean PEPIN, *Idées grecques sur l'homme et sur Dieu*, Collection d'Études anciennes (Paris: Les Belles-Lettres, 1971), 167f.

301 Irenaeus, *Adversus haereses* V 6.1 (FChr 8/5, 56.8f. ROUSSEAU/BROX).

302 (Ps.-?) Plato, *Alcibiades* I 130 C: "But since neither the body nor the combination of the two is man, we are reduced, I suppose, to this: either man is nothing at all, or if something, he turns out to be nothing else than soul." ET from *Plato: Charmides. Alcibiades I and II. Hipparchus. The Lovers. Theages. Minos. Epinomis*, trans. W. R. M. LAMB, LCL 201 (Cambridge, Mass.: Harvard University Press, 1927), 201. Cf. Origenes, *De principiis* IV 2.7 (ἀνθρώπους δὲ νῦν λέγω τὰς χρωμένας ψυχὰς σώμασιν: TzF 24, 722 GÖRGEMANNS/KARPP = GCS Origenes V, 318.12–319.1 KOETSCHAU); very similarly *Contra Celsum* VII 38 (GCS Origenes II, 188.24 KOETSCHAU). See on the topic STROUMSA, "The Incorporeality of God," 351.

303 Thus FEICHTINGER, "Einleitung," 9–26, here 12.

304 EDWARDS, "Further Reflections on the Platonism of Origen," 323.

3 The Body of God and Divine Statues in Antiquity

1 Plato, *Respublica* 379 A. ET from EMLYN-JONES/PREDDY, *Plato: Republic, Books 1–5*, 201.

2 Thus the definition of Franz CHRIST, *Menschlich von Gott reden: Das Problem des Anthropomorphismus bei Schleiermacher*, Ökumenische Theologie 10 (Einsiedeln/Zürich/Köln: Benziger; Gütersloh: Gütersloher Verlagshaus Mohn, 1982), 13f.

3 Ulrich VON WILAMOWITZ-MOELLENDORFF, *Euripides Herakles erklärt*, Bd. 1, zweite Bearb. (Berlin: Weidmann, 1895), 38.

4 Manfred CLAUSS, *Kaiser und Gott: Herrscherkult im römischen Reich* (Stuttgart/Leipzig: Teubner, 1999), 30f. The author refers to the explanation of his thesis in idem, *Mithras: Kult und Mysterien* (München: Beck, 1990), 19–23.

5 Aristoteles, *Politica* 1.2, 1253 a 24–27.

6 Publius Ovidius Naso, *Metamorphoses* I 83 (BiTeu 4 ANDERSON; cf. *Publius Ovidius Naso, Metamorphosen*, in deutsche Hexamter übertragen von Erich Rösch, mit einer Einführung von Niklas Holzberg, Tusc-Bü, 11. überarb. Aufl. [Darmstadt: Wissenschaftliche Buchgesellschaft, 1988], 10). ET from *Ovid: Metamorphoses, Books 1–8*, trans. Frank Justus MILLER, rev. G. P. Goold, 3rd ed., LCL 42 (Cambridge, Mass.: Harvard University Press, 1984), 9. See on the passage Wolfgang SPEYER, "Spuren der 'Genesis' in Ovids Metamorphosen," in *Kontinuität und Wandel: Lateinische Poesie von Naevius; Franco Munari zum 65. Geburtstag*, hg. Ulrich Justus Stache (Hildesheim: Weidmann, 1986), 90–99.

7 Margalit FINKELBERG, "Two Kinds of Representations in Greek Religious Art," in *Representations in Religion: Studies in Honor of Moshe Barash*, ed. Jan Assmann and Albert I. Baumgarten, SHR 89 (Leiden: Brill, 2001), 27–41.

8 Pausanias, *Graeciae descriptio* V 13.8 (BiTeu II, 33.1–3 ROCHA-PEREIRA).

9 Renate TÖLLE-KASTENBEIN, *Das Olympieion in Athen*, Arbeiten zur Archäologie (Köln/Weimar/Vienna: Böhlau, 1994), 136–162. Cf. also Stavros VLIZOS, "Das Vorbild des Zeus aus Olympia," in *Römische Götterbilder der mittleren und späten Kaiserzeit*, hg. Dietrich Boschung und Alfred Schäfer, Morphomata 22 (Paderborn: Wilhelm Fink, 2015), 41–69.

10 Cf. s.v. Ὀλύμπιος in Hans SCHWABL, s.v. "Zeus Tl. II," PW Suppl. 15: 994–1411, esp. 1071f., 1466–1468 (supplements).

11 Prudentius, *Apotheosis* 453 (CUFr II, 19 LAVARENNE). ET from *Prudentius*, trans. H. J. THOMSON, vol. 1, LCL 387 (Cambridge, Mass./London: Harvard University Press, 1949),

154. See Elias J. BICKERMAN, "Diva Augusta Marciana," *American Journal of Philology* 95 (1974): 362–376, esp. 369 n. 31. Bickerman references Hesiod, *Opera et dies* 251–253.

12 Hesiodus, *Opera et dies* 251–253. See, moreover, CLAUSS, *Kaiser und Gott*, 22.

13 Maximus Tyrius, *Dissertationes* XI 12 (BiTeu 99.274–280 TRAPP = 141.237–242 KONIARIS). ET from *Maximus of Tyre: The Philosophical Orations*, trans. with an introduction and notes by M. B. TRAPP (Oxford: Clarendon, 1979), 105f. With the invocation of πατὴϱ καὶ δημιουϱγός, Maximus alludes to his philosophy's Platonic frame of reference and, in turn, to one of the most celebrated passages from the *Timaeus* during his era: Plato, *Timaeus* 28 C; and verbatim from *Timaeus* 41 A.

14 Michel TARDIEU, s.v. "Heraiskos," in *Der neue Pauly: Enzyklopädie der Antike* (Stuttgart/ Weimar: Metzler, 1998), 363; and, on the urban context, Christopher HAAS, *Alexandria in Late Antiquity: Topography and Social Conflict* (Baltimore: Johns Hopkins University Press, 1997), 129–131.

15 Cf. now Polymnia ATHANASSIADI, *Damascius, The Philosophical History: Text with Translation and Notes* (Athen: Apamea, 1999). Rather than calling it by its conventional title, the *Vita Isidori*, Athanassiadi suggests to follow the Suda (*Suda* Δ 39 [II, 3.28–4.2 ADLER] = Testimonia I, 334 ATHANASSIADI) in terming it the Φιλόσοφος Ἱστοϱία or *Historia philosophica* on account of its extant contents (p. 58). According to Athanassiadi, this title may also be traced back to Damascius. This notwithstanding, its traditional title is employed in the references which follow. On the redaction of the texts of Damascius in the Suda, cf. Rudolf ASMUS, "Zur Rekonstruktion von Damascius' Leben des Isidorus," *Byzantinische Zeitschrift* 18 (1909): 424–480, here 438–440; on its title: 443–445.

16 Suda H 450 (II, 579.7–10 ADLER) = Damascius, *Vita Isidori frag.* 174 (Bibliotheca Graeca et Latina Suppletoria I, 147.2–5 ZINTZEN = frag. 76 E [194 ATHANASSIADI]). ET from ATHANASSIADI, *Damascius, The Philosophical History*, 195.

17 Suda H 450 (II, 579.10–14 ADLER) = Damascius, *Vita Isidori frag.* 174 (Bibliotheca Graeca et Latina Suppletoria I, 147.5–8 ZINTZEN = frag. 76 E [194 ATHANASSIADI]).

18 Iamblichus, *De mysteriis* V 19 (CUFr 168.15–21 SAFFREY/SEGONDS/LECERF). ET from *Iamblichus: De mysteriis*, trans. with an introduction and notes by Emma C. CLARKE, John M. DILLON, and Jackson P. HERSHBELL (Atlanta: Society of Biblical Literature, 2003), 259.

19 On this, cf., for example, Iamblichus, *De mysteriis* I 19 (CUFr 45.14–20 SAFFREY/ SEGONDS/LECERF).

20 Plato, *Timaeus* 41 A. See the commentary in *Jamblique, Réponse à Porphyre (De Mysteriis)*, texte établi, traduit et annoté par Henri Dominique Saffrey et Alain-Philippe Segonds† avec la collaboration de Adrien Lecerf, CUFr (Paris: Les Belles Lettres, 2013), 264.

21 Iamblichus, *De mysteriis* V 23 (CUFr 173.12–16 SAFFREY/SEGONDS/LECERF). ET from CLARKE/DILLON/HERSHBELL, *Iamblichus: De mysteriis*, 267.

22 Iamblichus, *De mysteriis* V 23 (CUFr 173.19–21 SAFFREY/SEGONDS/LECERF). In *Über die Geheimlehren von Jamblichus*, aus dem Griechischen übers., eingel. und erklärt v. Thedor Hopfner, Quellenschriften der griechischen Mystik 1 (Leipzig: Theosophisches Verlagshaus, 1922), 151, this is translated as "ein vollkomenes und lauteres Immanenzmittel."

23 Robert LAMBERTON, "Homer in Antiquity," in *A New Companion to Homer*, ed. Ian Morris and Barry Powell (Leiden: Brill, 1996), 33–54, esp. 41–43 and 44–48; and MARKSCHIES, *Kaiserzeitliche christliche Theologie und ihre Institutionen*, 48f., 68 (references).

24 *Anthologia Graeca* IX 58 (Antipater of Sidon, second/first century BC: TuscBü III, 42 BECKBY): καὶ τὸν ἐπ᾿ Ἀλφειῷ Ζᾶνα κατηυγασάμην. Hyginus, *Fabulae* 223.4 (BiTeu II, 173.6f. MARSHALL): "signum Iouis Olympii, quod fecit Phidias ex ebore et auro sedens, pedes LX." See Kai BRODERSEN, *Die sieben Weltwunder: Legendäre Kunst- und Bauwerke der Antike*, 7. Aufl., C. H. Beck Wissen in der Beck'schen Reihe 2029 (München: Beck, 2007), 10f. Concerning the problem of the traditional wording "cult image," see Alice A. DONOHUE, "The Greek Images of the Gods: Considerations on Terminology and Methodology," *Hephaistos* 15 (1997): 31–45; and now Fernande HÖLSCHER, *Die Macht*

der Gottheit im Bild: Archäologische Studien zur griechischen Götterstatue (Heidelberg: Verlag Antike, 2017), 13–42. Many thanks to Luca Giuliani for valuable suggestions on this topic.

25 Charles T. SELTMAN, *The Temple Coins of Olympia*, repr. from "Nomisma" VIII, IX, XI, with a foreword by William Ridgeway (Cambridge: Bowes & Bowes, 1921). It is admittedly completely uncertain as to whether the coins were genuinely struck on the sanctuary's grounds, as is thought by Seltman, and thereby warranting the designation "temple coins": Johannes NOLLÉ, "Die Münzen von Elis *(Kat.-Nr. 1–50)*," in *Olympia: Geld und Sport in der Antike*, hg. Manfred Gutgesell und Anne Viola Siebert, Museum Kestnerianum 7 (Hannover: Kestner-Museum, 2004), 17–30, esp. 18.

26 Julius FRIEDLÄNDER, "Die unter Hadrian in Elis geprägte Münze mit der Darstellung der Bildsäule des olympischen Zeus von Phidias," *Berliner Blätter für Münz-, Siegel- und Wappenkunde* 3 (1866): 21–26; Josef LIEGLE, *Der Zeus des Phidias* (Berlin: Weidmann, 1932), esp. 9, 114–167 with tables 1 and 6; and Christopher P. JONES, "The Olympieion and the Hadrianeion at Ephesos," *JHS* 113 (1993): 149–152, who demonstrates that, for example, coins with the image of Olympian Zeus were also struck in Ephesus.

27 Strabo, *Geographica* VIII 3.30 (II, 444.29–446.12 RADT). ET from *Strabo: Geography, Books 8–9*, trans. Horace Leonard JONES, LCL 196 (Cambridge, Mass.: Harvard University Press, 1927), 89. See the commentary in *Strabons Geographika*, Bd. 6, *Buch V–VIII: Kommentar*, mit Übersetzung und Kommentar, hg. Stefan RADT (Göttingen, Vandenhoeck & Ruprecht, 2007), 420f. The passage is paraphrased, or a similar source excerpted, in Valerius Maximus, *Factorum et dictorum memorabilium libri novem* III 7 (*De fiducia sui*) *Externi* 4 (295.14–296.6 KEMPF). Cf. also Macrobius, V 13.23 (BiTeu I, 296.12–23 WILLIS); Quintilianus, *Institutio oratoria* XII 10.9 (BiTeu II, 403.8–13 RADERMACHER); Plinius, *Naturalis historiae* XXXIV 8.19 (TuscBü XXXIV, 24 KÖNIG/BAYER); and Seneca Maior, *Controversiae* VIII 2 also X 5.8 (BiTeu 229.8–31. 318.11–13 HÅKANSON). Cf. also *Anthologia Graeca* XVI 81 (TuscBü IV, 346 BECKBY).

28 *Accessions number*: 1936/184; *object number*: 18200646; *obverse*: [ΑΥΤ]ΟΚΡΑΤΩΡ- [ΑΔΡ]ΙΑΝΟΣ. Draped bust of Hadrian, chest view, right-facing, *reverse*: ΗΛΙ[ΕΩΝ]. Head of Zeus after the statue of Phidias with a laurel wreath, right-facing, *material*: bronze; *mass*: 25.64 g; *diameter*: 33 mm. See also the notes on the page in the "interactive catalogue" of the Münzkabinett (last accessed 15 May 2019): http://www.smb.museum/ikmk/object.php?id=18200646.

29 NOLLÉ, "Die Münzen von Elis *(Kat.-Nr. 1–50)*," Katalog Nr. 3, S. 23. *Material*: bronze; *mass*: 12.05 g; *diameter*: 11 mm. On the type, cf. also SELTMAN, *The Temple Coins of Olympia*, AZ βϱ, p. 26; and Stefan RITTER, "Münzbilder im Kontext: Zeus und Olympia auf elischen Stateren des 4. Jahrhunderts v.Chr.," in *Konstruktionen von Wirklichkeit. Bilder im Griechenland des 5. und 4. Jahrhunderts v.Chr.*, hg. Ralf von den Hoff und Stefan Schmidt (Stuttgart: Steiner, 2001), 89–105.

30 Pausanias, *Graeciae descriptio* V 11.1–12.2 (BiTeu II, 25.6–29.6 ROCHA-PEREIRA). On the cult image, see LIEGLE, *Der Zeus des Phidias*, 245–288 ("Der Zeus des Phidias als Kultbild"); Alfred MALLWITZ, *Olympia und seine Bauten* (München: Prestel, 1972), 228–234; Ulrich SINN, "Olympia—Zeustempel und Wettkampfstätte," in *Erinnerungsorte der Antike: Die griechische Welt*, hg. Elke Stein-Hölkeskamp und Karl-Joachim Hölkeskamp (München: Beck, 2010) 79–97; Wolfgang SCHIERING, *Die Werkstatt des Pheidias in Olympia*, Tl. 2, *Werkstattfunde*, Olympische Forschungen 18 (Berlin/New York: De Gruyter, 1991); Stavros VLIZOS, *Der thronende Zeus: Eine Untersuchung zur statuarischen Ikonographie des Gottes in der spätklassischen und hellenistischen Kunst*, Internationale Archäologie 62 (Rahden, Westfalen: Leidorf, 1999), 5–21; Balbina BÄBLER, "Der Zeus von Olympia," in Dio Chrysostomus, *Oratio* XII, *De dei cognitione*, Dion von Prusa, *Olympische Rede oder über die erste Erkenntnis Gottes*, eingel., übers. und interpretiert von Hans-Josef KLAUCK, mit einem archäologischen Beitrag von Balbina Bäbler, Scripta Antiquitatis Posterioris ad Ethicam REligionemque pertinentia (SAPERE) 2 (Darmstadt:

Wissenschaftliche Buchgesellschaft, 2000), 216–238; and Tanja Susanne SCHEER, *Die Gottheit und ihr Bild. Untersuchungen zur Funktion griechischer Kultbilder in Religion und Politik*, Zetemata 105 (München: Beck, 2000), 55–61. Texts in *Die antiken Schriftquellen zur Geschichte der bildenden Künste bei den Griechen*, gesammelt von Johannes Overbeck (Leipzig: Engelmann, 1868 = Hildesheim: Olms 1959), nr. 692–743, pp. 125–135. See also now Verity PLATT, *Facing the Gods: Epiphany and Representation in the Graeco-Roman Art, Literature and Religion*, Greek Culture in the Roman World (Cambridge: Cambridge University Press, 2011), 224–235.

31 Epictetus, *Dissertationes ab Arriano digestae* I 6.23 (BiTeu 27.13–17 SCHENKL). ET from *Epictetus: Discourses, Books 1–2*, trans. W. A. OLDFATHER, LCL 131 (Cambridge, Mass.: Harvard University Press, 1925), 45–47.

32 Pausanias, *Graeciae descriptio* V 11.4–6 (BiTeu II, 26.12–27.2 ROCHA-PEREIRA).

33 Pausanias, *Graeciae descriptio* V 11.9 (BiTeu II, 27.29–28.2 ROCHA-PEREIRA). ET from *Pausanias: Description of Greece*, trans. W. H. S. JONES and H. A. ORMEROD, vol. 2, LCL 188 (Cambridge, Mass./London: Harvard University Press, 1926), 443.

34 Ulrich VON WILAMOWITZ-MOELLENDORFF, "Der Zeus von Olympia," in idem, *Reden und Vorträge*, 3. verm. Auflage (Berlin: Weidmann, 1913), 199–221, here 209.

35 VON WILAMOWITZ-MOELLENDORFF, "Der Zeus von Olympia," 218.

36 Dio Chrysostomus, *Oratio* XII, *De dei cognitione*. Also discussed at length in Hermann FUNKE, s.v. "Götterbild," in *Reallexikon für Antike und Christentum*, 11: 752–755.

37 Dio Chrysostomus, *Oratio* XII 52 (BiTeu I, 216.12–16 DE BUDÉ = SAPERE 2, 84 KLAUCK). ET from *Dio Chrysostom*, trans. J. W. COHOON, vol. 2, LCL 339 (Cambridge, Mass.: Harvard University Press, 1939), 57.

38 Dio Chrysostomus, *Oratio* XII 59f. (BiTeu I, 216.12–16 DE BUDÉ = SAPERE 2, 88–91 KLAUCK). ET from COHOON, *Dio Chrysostom*, 2: 63–65. See the commentary in KLAUCK, Dion von Prusa, *Olympische Rede*, 142–145 and 205–213; and now PLATT, *Facing the Gods*, 227–235.

39 Dio Chrysostomus, *Oratio* XII 81 (BiTeu I, 226.18 DE BUDÉ = SAPERE 2, 104f. KLAUCK). ET from COHOON, *Dio Chrysostom*, 2: 83.

40 Aristoteles, *Historia Animalium* 511b17 and 521 b 6; Marcus Aurelius, *Ad se ipsum* III 3 (BiTeu 17.1f. DALFEN): καὶ λατρεύων τοσούτῳ χείρονι τῷ ἀγγείῳ, <ὅσῳ κρεῖττον τὸ κυριεῦον> ἤπερ ἐστὶ τὸ ὑπηρετοῦν. Cf. on this Secundus, *Sententiae* 8 (quoted after B. E. PERRY, *Secundus the Silent Philosopher*, American Philological Association Philological Monographs 22 [Ithaca, N.Y.: American Philological Association, 1964], 78–90, here 82.8–12 = *Fragmenta Philosophorum Graecorum*, collegit, recensuit, vertit, annotationibus et prolegomenis instruxit Friedrich Wilhelm August MULLACH [Paris: Editore Ambrosio Firmin Didot, 1860], 513). ET from *Marcus Aurelius*, ed. and trans. C. R. HAINES, LCL 58 (Cambridge, Mass.: Harvard University Press, 1916), 49.

41 Thus Plutarchus, *Moralia* 23, *De Iside et Osiride* 71, 379 C (BiTeu II, 68.24–69.2 NACHSTÄDT/SIEVEKING/TITCHENER), from *Plutarch: Moralia, Isis and Osiris. The E at Delphi. The Oracles at Delphi No Longer Given in Verse. The Obsolescence of Oracles*, trans. Frank Cole BABBITT, LCL 306 (Cambridge, Mass.: Harvard University Press, 1936), 165. Cf. also Fritz GRAF, "Plutarch und die Götterbilder," in *Gott und die Götter bei Plutarch: Götterbilder—Gottesbilder—Weltbilder*, hg. Rainer Hirsch-Luipold, Religionsgeschichtliche Versuche und Vorarbeiten 54 (Berlin/New York: De Gruyter, 2005), 251–266.

42 Dio Chrysostomus, *Oratio* XII 62 (BiTeu I, 219.20f. DE BUDÉ = SAPERE 2, 90 KLAUCK). ET from COHOON, *Dio Chrysostom*, 2: 65. On this topic, see also LIEGLE, *Der Zeus des Phidias*, 250–259.

43 Dio Chrysostomus, *Oratio* XII 62 (BiTeu I, 219.21–220.3 DE BUDÉ = SAPERE 2, 90 KLAUCK). ET from COHOON, *Dio Chrysostom*, 2: 65–67.

44 Plato, *Leges* XI 931 A. ET from *Plato: Laws*, trans. R. G. BURY, vol. 2, LCL 192 (Cambridge, Mass./London: Harvard University Press, 1926), 449.

45   Commodianus, *Instructiones adversus gentium* I 18.5 (CChr.SL 128, 16 Martin): "Mittebant capita sub numine quasi praesenti." Cf. also 16f. (17 Martin): "Monstra deo ista fincta sunt per uiniuoraces, / Audacia quorum damnabilis numina fingit." See on the text Franz Joseph Dölger, *Sol salutis: Gebet und Gesang im christlichen Altertum, mit besonderer Rücksicht auf die Ostung in Gebet und Liturgie*, 3. um Hinweise verm. Aufl., Liturgiewissenschaftliche Quellen und Forschungen 16/17 (Münster: Aschendorff, 1971), 9 n. 2.

46   *Corpus Hermeticum* XVII (CUFr II, 243.11f. Nock/Festugière). ET from *Hermetica: The Greek Corpus Hermeticum and the Latin Asclepius in a New English Translation, with Notes and Introduction*, trans. Brian P. Copenhaver (Cambridge: Cambridge University Press, 1992), 62.

47   Funke, s.v. "Götterbild," 11: 659–828; on the terminology: 663–666; Pascale Linant de Bellefonds et al., s.v. "Rites et activités relatifs aux images de culte," in *Purification, Initiation, Heroization, Apotheosis, Banquet, Dance, Music, Cult, Images*, Thesaurus cultus et rituum antiquorum, vol. 2, ed. Jean-Charles Balty (Los Angeles: Getty, 2004), 418–507; Dietrich Boschung, "Kultbilder als Vermittler religiöser Vorstellungen," in *Kult und Kommunikation: Medien in Heiligtümern der Antike*, hg. Christian Frevel und Henner von Hesberg, Schriften des Lehr- und Forschungszentrums für die antiken Kulturen des Mittelmeerraumes 4 (Wiesbaden: Reichert, 2007), 63–87; Burkhard Gladigow, "Epiphanie, Statuette, Kultbild: Griechische Gottesvorstellungen im Wechsel von Kontext und Medium," *Visible Religion* 7 (1990): 98–121; and idem, "Zur Ikonographie und Pragmatik römischer Kultbilder," in *Iconologia sacra: Mythos, Bildkunst und Dichtung in der Religions- und Sozialgeschichte Alteuropas; Festschrift Karl Hauck zum 75. Geburtstag*, hg. Hagen Keller und Nikolaus Staubach, Arbeiten zur Frühmittelalterforschung 23 (Berlin/New York: De Gruyter, 1994), 9–24; Richard L. Gordon, "The Real and the Imaginary: Production and Religion in the Graeco-Roman World," *Art History* 2 (1979): 5–34; and Platt, *Facing the Gods*, 86–91.

48   Strabo, *Geographica* VIII 3.30 (II, 444.27–29 Radt). See Finkelberg, "Two Kinds of Representations in Greek Religious Art," 30; and the commentary in Radt, *Strabons Geographika*, 6: 420.

49   Finkelberg, "Two Kinds of Representations in Greek Religious Art," 27–41; and Sylvia Estienne, "*Simulacra Deorum* versus *Ornamenta Aedium*: The Status of Divine Images in the Temples of Rome," in *Divine Images and Human Imaginations in Ancient Greece and Rome*, ed. Joannis Mylonopoulos, Religions in the Graeco-Roman World 170 (Leiden: Brill, 2010), 257–271.

50   Thus already (albeit strongly influenced by Christian premises) Karl Friedrich Nägelsbach, *Die nachhomerische Theologie des griechischen Volksglaubens bis auf Alexander* (Nürnberg: Geiger, 1857 = Hildesheim: Olms, 2004), 5f.

51   In the manuscript, Ὕλαι is reconstructed by Ulrich von Wilamowitz-Moellendorff as Αὐλαί in his review of Otto Kern, hg., *Die Inschriften von Magnesia am Maeander* (Berlin: Spemann, 1900): idem, *Kleine Schriften*, Bd. 5/1, *Geschichte, Epigraphik, Archäologie* (Berlin: Akademie-Verlag, 1971), 343–368, here 359 n. 3.

52   Pausanias, *Graeciae descriptio* X 32.6 (BiTeu III, 167.7–14 Rocha-Pereira). ET from *Pausanias: Description of Greece*, trans. W. H. S. Jones, vol. 4, LCL 297 (Cambridge, Mass.: Harvard University Press, 1935), 557. On this passage see *Steinepigramme aus dem griechischen Osten*, hg. Reinhold Merkelbach und Josef Stauber, Bd. 1, *Die Westküste Kleinasiens von Knidos bis Ilion* (Stuttgart/Leipzig: Teubner, 1998), 190f., with depictions of such dendrophoroi on coins.

53   Further references to benevolent and malevolent divine images in Funke, s.v. "Götterbild," 720–727.

54   Pausanias, *Graeciae descriptio* I 24.3–5 (BiTeu I, 53.16–54.5 Rocha-Pereira); and Finkelberg, "Two Kinds of Representations in Greek Religious Art," 33. See on the sculpture

also Walter-Herwig SCHUCHHARDT, "Athena Parthenos," in *Antike Plastik: Forschungen zur griechischen und römischen Skulptur* 2 (1963): 31–53.

55 Inscription on the wall of the Bouleterion: *Corpus Inscriptionum Graecorum* II, nr. 2715, p. 481–484 BOECKH = Franciszek SOKOLOWSKI, *Lois sacrées de l'Asie Mineure*, École française d'Athenes, Trauvaux et mémoires 9 (Paris: De Boccard, 1955), nr. 69, p. 162–165 = Mehmet Çetin ŞAHIN, *Die Inschriften von Stratonikeia*, Tl. 2/1, *Lagina, Stratonikeia und Umgebung*, Inschriften griechischer Städte aus Kleinasien 22/1 (Bonn: Habelt, 1982), nr. 1101, p. 155, line 5f. On the inscription, see Robin Lane FOX, *Pagans and Christians in the Mediterranean World from the Second Century AD to the Conversion of Constantine* (London: Penguin Books, 1986), 135; and Angelos CHANIOTIS, "Das Bankett des Damas und der Hymnos des Sosandros: Öffentlicher Diskurs über Rituale in den griechischen Städten der Kaiserzeit," in *Ritualdynamik: Kulturübergreifende Studien zur Theorie und Geschichte rituellen Handelns*, hg. Dietrich Harth und Gerrit Jasper Schenk (Heidelberg: Synchron, 2004), 291–304, esp. 296–300 (with additional bibliography).

56 Mehmet Çetin ŞAHIN, *Die Inschriften von Stratonikeia*, Tl. 1, *Panamara*, Inschriften griechischer Städte aus Kleinasien 21 (Bonn: Habelt, 1981), nr. 41a, p. 31 = MERKELBACH/ STAUBER, *Steinepigramme aus dem griechischen Osten*, 1: nr. 02/06/01, p. 212.

57 ŞAHIN, *Die Inschriften von Stratonikeia*, Tl. 2/1, *Panamara*, nr. 242, p. 120, lines 15–18. Cf. on this also Hans OPPERMANN, *Zeus Panamaros*, Religionsgeschichtliche Versuche und Vorarbeiten 19/3 (Gießen: Töpelmann, 1924), 60f.

58 MERKELBACH/STAUBER, *Steinepigramme aus dem griechischen Osten*, 1: nr. 03/02/01, p. 296. On the inscription, cf. Fritz GRAF, "An Oracle against Pestilence from a Western Anatolian Town," *Zeitschrift für Papyrologie und Epigraphik* 92 (1992): 267–279, from which (268–269) the present ET is taken; and Irene HUBER, *Rituale der Seuchen- und Schadensabwehr im Vorderen Orient und Griechenland: Formen kollektiver Krisenbewältigung in der Antike*, Oriens et Occidens 10 (Stuttgart: Steiner, 2005), 136–139.

59 Albeit models of the afflicted body parts are burnt in Fátima, while, in contrast, wax dolls which would have been used on site for black magical purposes (μάγματα; curse dolls) were probably burnt before the Ephesian statue of Artemis, with the oracle ascribing responsibility for the plague to their use (thus GRAF, "An Oracle against Pestilence from a Western Anatolian Town," 277f.).

60 Pausanias, *Graeciae descriptio* IX 33.6 (BiTeu III, 65.13–22 ROCHA-PEREIRA). ET from JONES/ORMEROD, *Pausanias: Description of Greece*, 4: 321.

61 Pausanias, *Graeciae descriptio* III 15.7 (BiTeu I, 238.14–19 ROCHA-PEREIRA). ET from JONES/ORMEROD, *Pausanias: Description of Greece*, 2: 93. On the rivalry between the cities of Athens and Sparta, see Christa FRATEANTONIO, *Religion und Städtekonkurrenz: Zum politischen und kulturellen Kontext von Pausanias' Periegese*, Millennium-Studien 23 (Berlin/New York: De Gruyter, 2009), 253. For additional references, see s.v. "Götterbild," 716f.; Christian August LOBECK, *Aglaophamus Sive de Theologiae Mysticae Graecorum Causis, Idemque Poetarum Orphicorum Dispersas Reliquias Collegit, Libri Tres Scripsit* (Königsberg: Borntraeger, 1829 = Darmstadt: Wissenschaftliche Buchgesellschaft, 1961), 1: 275f.; and the fragment reconstructed by way of Reinhold Merkelbach from Karl MEULI, "Die gefesselten Götter," in idem, *Gesammelte Schriften*, mit Benutzung des Nachlasses hg. Thomas Gelzer (Basel: Schwabe, 1975), 2: 1035–1081. See in summary also Reinhold MERKELBACH, "Gefesselte Götter," in idem, *Hestia und Erigone: Gesammelte Aufsätze*, hg. Wolfgang Blümel u.a. (Stuttgart/Leipzig: Teubner, 1996), 17–30.

62 These statues are born of "the influence of Asia Minor"; thus Carl CLEMEN, "Tempel und Kult in Hierapolis," in *Pisciculi: Studien zur Religion und Kultur des Altertums; Franz Josef Dölger zum sechzigsten Geburtstage dargeboten von Freunden, Verehrern und Schülern*, hg. Theodor Klauser und Adolf Rücker (Münster: Aschendorff, 1939), 66–69, here 69; and

now Jane L. Lᴉɢʜᴛғᴏᴏᴛ, *Lucian: On the Syrian Goddess*, ed. with introduction, translation, and commentary (Oxford: Oxford University Press, 2003), 72–83.

63   Lucianus, *De Syria dea* 10 (252.10–12 Lᴉɢʜᴛғᴏᴏᴛ). ET from Lᴉɢʜᴛғᴏᴏᴛ, *Lucian: On the Syrian Goddess*, 253. As Jane Lightfoot demonstrates in her commentary, this presages § 36 (op. cit., 332f.). Lucian recounts that the oracle of Apollo/Nebo is said to "move, and deliver oracles," sweating when unobserved by priests (252.7–14 Lᴉɢʜᴛғᴏᴏᴛ).

64   *Acta Alexandrinorum 8. Acta Hermaisci* (= Pap. Oxy. 1242, col. III, 50–53 [BiTeu 34 Mᴜsᴜʀɪʟʟᴏ]). On the text, see Andrew Hᴀʀᴋᴇʀ, *Loyalty and Dissidence in Roman Egypt: The Case of the Acta Alexandrinorum* (Cambridge: Cambridge University Press, 2008), 84–95; and Andreas Hᴀʀᴛᴍᴀɴɴ, "Judenhass und Martyrium: Zum kulturgeschichtlichen Kontext der *Acta Alexandrinorum*," in *Zwischen Antike und Moderne: Festschrift für Jürgen Malitz zum 65. Geburtstag*, dargebracht von Kollegen, Freunden, Schülern und Weggefährten, hg. Andreas Hartmann und Gregor Weber (Speyer: Brodersen, 2012), 119–209, esp. 157f.

65   Ioannes Lydus, *De ostentis prooemium* 8 (BiTeu, 3–5 Wᴀᴄʜsᴍᴜᴛʜ).

66   Hᴀʀᴛᴍᴀɴɴ, "Judenhass und Martyrium," 157 n. 192.

67   Pausanias, *Graeciae descriptio* I 26.6 (BiTeu I, 59.21–24 Rᴏᴄʜᴀ-Pᴇʀᴇɪʀᴀ). On the clothing custom in Athens and on Samos, see Ludwig Dᴇᴜʙɴᴇʀ, *Attische Feste* (Berlin: Keller, 1932 = Berlin: Akademie-Verlag, 1956), 22–35, esp. 29–33; Herbert W. Pᴀʀᴋᴇ, *Festivals of the Athenians*, Aspects of Greek and Roman Life (London: Thames and Hudson, 1986), 33–50; Evy Johanne Håʟᴀɴᴅ, "Athena's Peplos: Weaving as a Core Female Activity in Ancient and Modern Greece," *Cosmos* 20 (2004): 155–182; and Hans Wᴀʟᴛᴇʀ, *Das griechische Heiligtum, dargestellt am Heraion von Samos* (Stuttgart: Urachhaus, 1990), 88f.

68   Håʟᴀɴᴅ, "Athena's Peplos," 172f.

69   *Die Inschriften von Magnesia am Maeander*, hg. Otto Kern (Berlin: Spemann, 1900), nr. 98, pp. 82–84 = Wilhelm Dɪᴛᴛᴇɴʙᴇʀɢᴇʀ, *Sylloge Inscriptionum Graecarum, Volumen alterum*, 3. Aufl. (Leipzig: Hirzel, 1917 = Hildesheim u.a.: Olms, 1982), nr. 589, pp. 111–116 = Sᴏᴋᴏʟᴏᴡsᴋɪ, *Lois sacrées de l'Asie Mineure*, nr. 32, pp. 88–92, esp. lines 41–46. See Orhan Bɪɴɢöʟ, *Magnesia am Mäander. Magnesia ad Maeandrum*, Homer Reihe: Antike Städte 6 (Istanbul: Homer Kitabevi, 2007), 113–115; and Martin P. Nɪʟssᴏɴ, *Griechische Feste von religiöser Bedeutung mit Ausschluss der attischen* (Leipzig: Teubner, 1906), 23–27.

70   Jaime Aʟᴠᴀʀ Eᴢǫᴜᴇʀʀᴀ, *Romanising Oriental Gods: Myth, Salvation, and Ethics in the Cults of Cybele, Isis, and Mithras*, trans. and ed. Richard Gordon, Religions in the Graeco-Roman World 165 (Leiden: Brill, 2008), 305–309 (with literary and epigraphic references; most prominently: Porphyrius, *De abstinentia* IV 9 [BiTeu 242.3–10 Nᴀᴜᴄᴋ] = Reinhold Mᴇʀᴋᴇʟʙᴀᴄʜ, *Isis Regina—Zeus Sarapis: Die griechisch-ägyptische Religion nach Quellen dargestellt*, 2. Aufl. [München/Leipzig: Teubner, 2001], 151; Apuleius, *Metamorphoses* XI 9.3 [SQAW 1, 332.2–6 Hᴇʟᴍ]). On the clothing, see Gʟᴀᴅɪɢᴏᴡ, "Epiphanie, Statuette, Kultbild," 104f. with additional references.

71   Seneca, *De superstitione frag.* 36 Hᴀᴀsᴇ = frag. 69 Vᴏᴛᴛᴇʀᴏ = Augustinus, *De civitate Dei* VI 10 (BiTeu I, 268.24–28, 269.7–10 Dᴏᴍʙᴀʀᴛ/Kᴀʟʙ). On the passage, see now Jörg Rüᴘᴋᴇ, *Aberglauben oder Individualität? Religiöse Abweichung im römischen Reich* (Tübingen: Mohr Siebeck, 2011), 50–54.

72   Plinius Maior, *Naturalis historiae* XXXVI 4.21 (TuscBü XXXVI, 26 Köɴɪɢ/Hᴏᴘᴘ). ET from *Pliny: Natural History, Books 36–37*, trans. D. E. Eɪᴄʜʜᴏʟᴢ, LCL 419 (Cambridge, Mass.: Harvard University Press, 1962), 17. In more depth, with source attestations, cf. Clemens Alexandrinus, *Protrepticus* 57.3 (GCS Clemens Alexandrinus I², 45.1–5 Sᴛäʜʟɪɴ/Fʀüᴄʜᴛᴇʟ/Tʀᴇᴜ); and cf., very abbreviatedly, contra, Lucianus, *Imagines* 4 (SCBO II, 362.15–18 Mᴀᴄʟᴇᴏᴅ). See Fᴜɴᴋᴇ, s.v. "Götterbild," 735f.; and Pʟᴀᴛᴛ, *Facing the Gods*, 183–188.

73   Augustus dreams that the Capitoline Jupiter takes affront at his visits to *Iupiter Tonans* and complains "that his followers were stripped from him" from such imperial behavior: Suetonius, *De vita caesarum* 2, *Divus Augustus* 91 (BiTeu 99.25–30 Iʜᴍ).

74 Quoted after Eduard Bratke, *Das sogenannte Religionsgespräch am Hof der Sasani-den*, TU 19/3 (Leipzig: Hinrichs, 1899), 12.2–4. The ET follows *Religious Discussion at the Court of the Sassanids*, trans. Andrew Eastbourne (2010), 8, accessible at https:// ia800207.us.archive.org/10/items/ReligiousDiscussionAtTheCourtOfTheSassanids .religionsgesprchAmHof/Religionsgesprach_am_Hof_der_Sasaniden.pdf. Cf. the Ger-man translation in Hermann Usener, *Das Weihnachtsfest: Kapitel I–III*, Religions-geschichtliche Untersuchungen, Tl. 1, 2. Aufl. (Bonn: Cohen, 1911), 33 (with parallels in n. 17a). See the introduction to the text in Katharina Heyden, *Die "Erzählung des Aph-roditian": Thema und Variation einer Legende im Spannungsfeld von Christentum und Heidentum*, Studien und Texte zu Antike und Christentum 53 (Tübingen: Mohr Siebeck, 2009), 118–170.

75 Ovidus, *Fasti* IV 337–348 (TuscBü 166 Gerlach/Holzberg). Further references in Georg Wissowa, *Religion und Kultus der Römer*, Handbuch der Altertumswissenschaften IV 5, 2. Aufl., (München: Beck, 1912 = 1971), 319 with n. 7.

76 Many further references in Funke, s.v. "Götterbild," 716–720; most prominently for the Roman temple in Gerhard Bauchhenss, "Wie die Römer die Götter gebildet—Gottesbild und Götterbilder," in *Götterbilder—Menschenbilder: Religion und Kulte in Carnuntum*, hg. Franz Humer und Gabrielle Kremer (Wien: AV + Astoria Druckzentrum, 2011), 30–43, esp. 38–41. Unfortunately less than intelligible is the highly fragmentary Pap. Vindob. Gr. Inv. 25 942, possibly a protocol, inasmuch as it perhaps concerns the completion of a cult image of Isis: Robert Paul Salomons, *Einige Wiener Papyri*, Studia Amstelodamensia ad Epigraphicam, Ius Antiquum et Papyrologicam Pertinentia 4 (Amsterdam: Hakkert, 1976), 23–35 (edition and detailed commentary).

77 Apuleius, *Metamorphoses* XI 17.1 (SQAW 1, 338.25 Helm): *simulacra spirantia*. On its interpretation, see *Apuleius of Madauros: The Isis-Book (Metamorphoses, Book XI)*, ed. with translation and commentary by John Gwyn Griffiths, Études preliminaires aux religions orientales dans L'empire romain 39 (Leiden: Brill, 1975), 264f., who interprets the expression as indicating the real vitality of the religious images: "If Apuleius . . . is following a traditional manner of expression, yet his meaning is not simply that these images had been with such artistic skill that the gods were present in their images. . . . It follows that *spirantia* here is most apposite."

78 Apuleius, *De Platone et eius dogmate* 5.190 (BiTeu III, 92.8 Moreschini = CUFr 64 Beaujeu). Attestations of sources and parallels within the doxographic tradition in the commentary of Beaujeu ad. loc., op. cit., 256.

79 Plutarchus, *Vitae parallelae: Coriolanus* 38.1–3 (BiTeu I/2, 223.21–224.9 Ziegler). ET from *Plutarch's Lives*, trans. Bernadotte Perrin, vol. 4, LCL 80 (Cambridge, Mass.: Harvard University Press, 1916), 211–213. A very similar, albeit markedly shorter argu-mentation regarding the purported perspiration of divine images is found in Cicero, *De Divinatione* II 58 (TuscBü 186.26–30 Schäublin): "nec enim sanguis nec sudor nisi e corpore" (186.30).

80 On the religious-historical background of the extract, see "Mantik und Orakelwesen: das Erlöschen der Orakel," in Marco Frenschkowski, *Offenbarung und Epiphanie*, Bd. 1, *Grundlagen des spätantiken und frühchristlichen Offenbarungsglaubens*, WUNT 2/79 (Tübingen: Mohr Siebeck, 1995), 41–64.

81 *Didyma*, Tl. 2, *Die Inschriften*, hg. Albert Rehm und Richard Harder (Mainz: Zabern/ Berlin: Mann, 1958), nr. 496 A, p. 299 = Joseph Fontenrose, *Didyma: Apollo's Oracle, Cult, and Companions* (Berkeley/Los Angeles/London: University of California Press, 1988), nr. 22, pp. 196f. ET also after Fontenrose. See on the text also Louis Robert, *Hel-lenica: Recueil d'épigraphie, de numismatique et antiquités grecques*, tome 11 (Limoges/ Paris: Adrien-Maisonneuve, 1960), 543–546; Merkelbach/Stauber, *Steinepigramme aus dem griechischen Osten*, 1: nr. 01/19/05, p. 82; and Donald F. McCabe, *Inscriptions of Ionia* (Princeton, N.J.: Institute for Advanced Study, 1984), Milet, nr. 481.

82 FUNKE, s.v. "Götterbild," 714–716; and PLATT, *Facing the Gods*, 78f. with further litera-
ture. Alternately: Christoph AUFFARTH, "Götterbilder im römischen Griechenland: Vom
Tempel zum Museum," in *Ritual Dynamics and Religious Change in the Roman Empire:
Proceedings of the Eighth Workshop of the International Network Impact of the Empire
(Heidelberg, July 5–7, 2007)*, ed. Olivier Hekster, Sebastian Schmidt-Hofner, and Christian
Witschel, Impact of Empire 9 (Leiden/Boston: Brill, 2009), 306–325: "Dass den Griechen
die Differenz zwischen der Gottheit und ihrem Abbild bewusst war, ist in den Quellen klar
zu sehen. Jedenfalls kam es nicht zu der Anbetung eines materiellen Bildes, wie es die
intellektuelle (auch christliche) Polemik später darstellte" (p. 313f.). See also idem, "Das
angemessene Bild Gottes: Der Olympische Zeus, antike Bildkonvention und die Christologie," in *Tekmeria: Archäologische Zeugnisse in ihrer kulturhistorischen und politischen
Dimension: Beiträge für Werner Gauer*, hg. Natascha Kreutz und Beat Schweizer (Münster:
Scriptorium, 2006), 1–23; and, similarly but more abbreviatedly, BOSCHUNG, "Kultbilder als
Vermittler religiöser Vorstellungen," 86.
83 Diogenes Laertius, *Vitae philosophorum* II 116 (SCBO I, 106.10–14 LONG). ET from
Diogenes Laertius: Lives of Eminent Philosophers, Books 1–5, trans. R. D. HICKS, LCL
184 (Cambridge, Mass.: Harvard University Press, 1925), 245. Cf. Klaus DÖRING, *Die
Megariker: Kommentierte Sammlung der Testimonien*, Studien zur antiken Philosophie 2
(Amsterdam: Grüner, 1971), nr. 183, pp. 55f.
84 Sallustius, *De deis et mundo* 15 (28.11–17 NOCK). Further passages in FUNKE, s.v. "Götterbild," 714–716.
85 Scholia in Aristophanem, *Nubes* 830 g (here cited according to: Douwe HOLWERDA, *Prolegomena de Comoedia: Scholia in Acharnenses, Equites, Nubes*, Scholia in Aristophanem I 3/1 [Groningen: Bouma, 1977], 168.1–4). Cf. also the pertinent *testimonia* of the
story in slightly differing redactions in *Diagorae Melii et Theodori Cyrenaei Religiae*,
ed. Marcus WINIARCZYK, BiTeu (Leipzig: Teubner, 1981), testimonia 27–33, pp. 10–12
(in particular: Athenagoras, *Legatio* 4.1–2 [318f. GOODSPEED]; Clemens Alexandrinus,
Protrepticus 24.4 [GCS Clemens Alexandrinus I, 18.17–21 STÄHLIN/FRÜCHTEL/TREU];
and Epiphanius, *Ancoratus* 103.8 [GCS Epiphanius I², 124.12–17 HOLL/BERGERMANN/
COLLATZ; also Ulrich VON WILAMOWITZ-MOELLENDORFF, "Ein Stück aus dem Ancoratus
des Epiphanios," in *Sitzungsberichte der preußischen Akademie der Wissenschaften,
philologisch-historische Klasse* (Berlin: Verlag der Königlichen Akademie der Wissenschaften, 1911), 759–772]); *Theosophia Graeca Tubingensis* 70 (BiTeu 48.590–597
ERBSE); and Bruno KEIL, "Ein neues Bruchstück des Diagoras von Melos," *Hermes* 55
(1920): 63–67. See also Felix JACOBY, *Diagoras ὁ ἄθεος*, Abhandlungen der Deutschen
Akademie der Wissenschaften zu Berlin, Klasse für Sprachen, Literatur und Kunst
3/1959 (Berlin: Akademie, 1959), 14.
86 Elpidius PAX, s.v. "Epiphanie," in *Reallexikon für Antike und Christentum* (Stuttgart:
Hiersemann, 1962), 5: 832–909, esp. 838–860; and FRENSCHKOWSKI, *Offenbarung und
Epiphanie*, 1: 278f. A great number of pertinent pagan epiphany texts are collected
together in Alfred WIKENHAUSER, "Die Traumgesichte des Neuen Testaments in religionsgeschichtlicher Sicht," in Klauser und Rücker, *Pisciculi*, 320–333, esp. 329–332.
87 Cf. the entries in both relevant digitally accessible catalogues of literary papyri: on the
one hand, in the Mertens-Pack 3 online database (as of June 2006) under nr. 241–244
(accessible online at http://promethee.philo.ulg.ac.be/cedopal/getPackAuteuranglais.asp
[last accessed 13 May 2019]); and, on the other, in the Leuven Database of Ancient Books
(http://www.trismegistos.org/ldab/) with a total of four entries. On the novel more generally: Consuelo RUIZ MONTERO, "Chariton von Aphrodisias: Ein Überblick," *ANRW* II/34.2:
1006–1054. An ethusiastic argument from an earlier dating is to be found in Carl Werner
MÜLLER, "Chariton von Aphrodisias und die Theorie des Romans in der Antike," in *Antike
und Abendland* 22 (1976): 115–136 = idem, *Legende—Novelle—Roman: Dreizehn Kapitel zur erzählenden Prosaliteratur der Antike* (Göttingen: Vandenhoeck & Ruprecht,
2006), 445–475. For the idea of employing this novel as an example, I am indebted to

Ulrich VICTOR, "Die Religionen und religiösen Vorstellungen im Römischen Reich im 1. und 2. Jahrhundert n.chr.," in *Antike Kultur und Neues Testament: Die wichtigsten Hintergründe und Hilfsmittel zum Verständnis der neutestamentlichen Schriften*, hg. Ulrich Victor, Carsten Peter Thiede und Urs Stingelin (Basel/Gießen: Brunnen, 2003), 87–170, esp. 93f.; and Fox, *Pagans and Christians in the Mediterranean World from the Second Century AD to the Conversion of Constantine*, 138–140.

88 Chariton, *De Callirhoe narrationes amatoriae* II 2.5f. (BiTeu 26.74–84 REARDON). ET from *Chariton: Callirhoe*, ed. and trans. G. P. GOOLD, LCL 481 (Cambridge, Mass.: Harvard University Press, 1995), 91–93.

89 Chariton, *De Callirhoe narrationes amatoriae* III 2.14 (BiTeu 45.116–46.119 REARDON).

90 On this translation of ἐναργής, see Henry George LIDDELL and Robert SCOTT, *A Greek-English Lexicon*, rev. and augmented by Henry Stuart Jones (Oxford: Oxford University Press, 1983), s.v. (p. 556). In *Chariton von Aphrodisias, Kallirhoe*, eingel., übers. und erläutert von Karl PLEPELITS, Bibliothek der Griechischen Literatur 6 (Stuttgart: Hiersemann, 1976), 80, this is translated: "Weißt du, hin und wieder erscheint sie hier leibhaftig."

91 Chariton, *De Callirhoe narrationes amatoriae* III 6.4 (BiTeu 55.398–400 REARDON). ET GOOLD, *Chariton: Callirhoe*, 169.

92 Chariton, *De Callirhoe narrationes amatoriae* III 2.16f. (BiTeu 46.131–136 REARDON). ET from GOOLD, *Chariton: Callirhoe*, 145.

93 Chariton, *De Callirhoe narrationes amatoriae* VII 5.3 (BiTeu 121.232f. REARDON). See on this topic Erwin ROHDE, *Der griechische Roman und seine Vorläufer*, 3. durch einen zweiten Anhang verm. Aufl. (Leipzig: Breitkopf und Härtel, 1914), 520–531. Rohde takes the author to be a Christian (p. 525), but this is rather unlikely: Isolde STARK, "Religiöse Elemente im antiken Roman," in *Der antike Roman: Untersuchungen zur literarischen Kommunikation und Gattungsgeschichte*, von einem Autorenkollektiv unter Leitung von Heinrich Kuch (Berlin: Akademie-Verlag 1989), 135–149, esp. 144f.

94 ROHDE, *Der griechische Roman und seine Vorläufer*, 525.

95 Acts 14:11f. On the passage's historical basis in a particular manner of worship of Zeus found in the region of Lystra, see Cilliers BREYTENBACH, *Paulus und Barnabas in der Provinz Galatien: Studien zu Apostelgeschichte 13f.; 16.6; 18.23 und den Adressaten des Galaterbriefes*, AGAJU 38 (Leiden: Brill, 1996), 68–73.

96 Petronius, *Satyrica* 17.5 (BiTeu 13.3f. MÜLLER). ET from *Petronius: Satyricon. Seneca: Apocolocyntosis*, trans. Michael HESELTINE and W. H. D. ROUSE, rev. E. H. Warmington, LCL 15 (Cambridge, Mass.: Harvard University Press, 1913), 23. On the text more generally, see the introduction in Peter HABERMEHL, *Petronius, Satyrica 79–141: Ein philologisch-literarischer Kommentar*, Bd. 1, *Sat. 79–110*, Texte und Kommentare 27/1 (Berlin/New York: De Gruyter, 2006), xi–xxx. On its religious-historical context, see Hubert PETERSMANN, "Religion, Superstition and Parody in Petronius' Cena Trimalchionis," in *Groningen Colloquia on the Novel*, Bd. 6, hg. Heinz Hofmann (Groningen: Forsten, 1996), 75–85.

97 Plato, *Respublica* II 381 C. ET from EMLYN-JONES/PREDDY, *Plato: Republic, Books 1–5*, 211.

98 Plato, *Respublica* II 382 A. ET from EMLYN-JONES/PREDDY, *Plato: Republic, Books 1–5*, 213.

99 VERNANT, "Mortals and Immortals," 27–49, esp. 29.

100 VERNANT, "Mortals and Immortals," 30f.

101 Hesiodus, *Theogonia* 33 and 105: γένος αἰὲν ἐόντων. See Ernst HEITSCH, "Hesiod," in idem, *Gesammelte Schriften*, Bd. 2, *Zur griechischen Philosophie*, Beiträge zur Altertumskunde 153 (Berlin/New York: De Gruyter, 2002), 17–37, esp. 25–27. Cf. Plato, *Timaeus* 27 D: τὸ ὂν ἀεί, γένεσιν δὲ οὐκ ἔχον.

102 On conceptions of the gods in Homer, see particularly Karl Friedrich VON NÄGELSBACH, *Carl Friedrich von Nägelsbach's Homerische Theologie*, 2. Aufl., nach dem Auftrag des

verewigten Verfassers bearbeitet von Georg Autenrieth (Nürnberg: Geiger, 1861), 13–23; Jasper GRIFFIN, *Homer on Life and Death* (Oxford: Oxford University Press, 1980), 144–204; Wolfgang KULLMANN, "Gods and Men in the *Iliad* and *Odyssey*," in idem, *Homerische Motive: Beiträge zur Entstehung, Eigenart und Wirkung von "Ilias" und "Odyssee,"* hg. Roland J. Müller (Stuttgart: Steiner, 1992), 243–263 = *Harvard Studies in Classical Philology* 89 (1985): 1–23; Hartmut ERBSE, *Untersuchungen zur Funktion der Götter im homerischen Epos*, Untersuchungen zur antiken Literatur und Geschichte 24 (Berlin/New York: De Gruyter, 1986), 121, 269–273, 286; and Emily KEARNS, "The Gods in the Homeric Epics," in *The Cambridge Companion to Homer*, ed. Robert Fowler (Cambridge: Cambridge University Press, 2004), 59–73.

103　Homerus, *Ilias* V 339, 870; XVI 381, 670, 680, 867; XVII 194, 202; XX 358; XXII 9; XXIV 460; and *Odyssea* V 347; VII 260, 265; VIII 365; X 222; XI 330; XVIII 191; and XXIV 59, 445.

104　Plutarchus, *Vitae Parallelae: Comparatio Aristidis et Catonis* 31[4],2, 354 F (BiTeu I/1, 328.25–27 ZIEGLER); and Philo Alexandrinus, *Quod deus sit immutabilis* 56 (Opera II, 69.6 WENDLAND); *De agricultura* 54 (Opera II, 106.16 WENDLAND); *De Abrahamo* 30 (Opera IV, 8.2 COHN). Cf. 2 Macc 14:35. See Wolfgang HOFFMANN, Ὁ θεὸς ἀπροσδεής: *Gottes Bedürfnislosigkeit in den Schriften der frühen Väterzeit*, Tl. druck einer maschinenschriftlichen Dissertation an der Gregoriana Rom 1965 (Bonn: n.n., 1966); and Katharina BRACHT, "God and Methodius: Use of, and Background to, the Term ἀπροσδεής as a Description of God in the Works of Methodius of Olympus," in McGowan, Daley, and Gaden, *God in Early Christian Thought*, 105–122, esp. 110. Comparable to Sallustius, *De deis et mundo* 15 (28.8–10 NOCK).

105　Homerus, *Ilias* V 341. ET from *Homer: Iliad, Books 1–12*, trans. A. T. MURRAY, rev. William F. Wyatt, LCL 170 (Cambridge, Mass.: Harvard University Press, 1999), 237.

106　Homerus, *Odyssea* V 197–200. ET from *Homer: Odyssey, Books 1–12*, trans. A. T. MURRAY, rev. George E. Dimock, LCL 104 (Cambridge, Mass.: Harvard University Press, 1998), 197.

107　Werner JAEGER, *Paideia: Die Formung des griechischen Menschen* (Berlin/Leipzig: De Gruyter, 1934), 1: 32. See also GRIFFIN, *Homer on Life and Death* (Oxford: Oxford University Press, 1980), 146f.

108　Homerus, *Ilias* V 339–342. ET from MURRAY, *Homer: Iliad, Books 1–12*, 237. See on ἰχώρ VON NÄGELSBACH, *Carl Friedrich von Nägelsbach's Homerische Theologie*, 17. Plutarch recounts repeatedly of Alexander the Great that he contested that ἰχώρ flowed in his veins: Plutarchus, *Vitae Parallelae, Alexanderus* 28, 681 B (BiTeu II/2, 190.9–11 ZIEGLER); *Regum et imperatorum apophthegmata = Moralia* 15; *Regum et imperatorum apophthegmata Alex.* 16, 80 E (BiTeu II/1, 28.1–4 NACHSTÄDT/SIEVEKING/TITCHENER) and *Moralia* 21b; *De Alexandri Magni fortuna et virtute oratio* II 9, 341 B (BiTeu II/2, 111.19–25 NACHSTÄDT/SIEVEKING/TITCHENER).

109　*Hymni Homerici in Cererem* 275–281. ET from *Homeric Hymns, Homeric Apocrypha, Lives of Homer*, ed. and trans. Martin L. WEST, LCL 496 (Cambridge, Mass.: Harvard University Press, 2003), 55. See *The Homeric "Hymn to Demeter": Translation, Commentary, and Interpretative Essays*, ed. and trans. Helene P. FOLEY (Princeton, N.J.: Princeton University Press, 1993), 52 and 84–97; and PLATT, *Facing the Gods*, 60–72.

110　VERNANT, "Mortals and Immortals," 37f.

111　Homerus, *Ilias* I 194–198. ET from MURRAY, *Homer: Iliad, Books 1–12*, 27.

112　VERNANT, "Mortals and Immortals," 30f.

113　Homerus, *Ilias* III 396–398.

114　GLADIGOW, "Epiphanie, Statuette, Kultbild," 98f. with references.

115　VERNANT, "Mortals and Immortals," 35: "It is rather the reverse: in all its active aspects, in all the components of its physical and psychological dynamism, the human body reflects the divine model as the inexhaustible source of a vital energy when, for instance, the brilliance of divinity happens to fall on a mortal creature, illuminating him, as in a fleeting glow, with a little of that splendor that always clothes the body of a god."

116 Pindarus, *Nemeische Ode* VI 1–3 (BiTeu 141.1–3 SNELL/MAEHLER). ET from *Pindar: Nemean Odes. Isthmian Odes. Fragments*, ed. and trans. William H. RACE, LCL 485 (Cambridge, Mass.: Harvard University Press, 1997), 61. See Peter VON KLOCH-KORNITZ, "Zum Anfang von Pindars Nemea VI," *Hermes* 89 (1961): 370f. (his interpretation follows this translation: "Eines ist der Menschen Geschlecht, ein anderes das der Götter, doch von einer Mutter her atmen wir beide, getrennt durch ganz und gar verschiedene Macht; denn auf der einen Seite ist ein Nichts"); Douglas E. GERBER, "Pindar, Nemean Six: A Commentary," *Harvard Studies in Classical Philology* 99 (1999), 33–91, esp. 43–45; Michael THEUNISSEN, *Pindar: Menschenlos und Wende der Zeit*, 2. durchges. Aufl. (München: Beck, 2002), 227–234; and Frederico LOURENÇO, "A 'Cloud of Metaphysics' in Pindar: The Opening of Nemean 6," *Humanitas* 63 (2011): 61–73. Eduard NORDEN, *Agnostos Theos: Untersuchungen zur Formengeschichte religiöser Rede* (Leipzig: Teubner, 1912 = Darmstadt: Wissenschaftliche Buchgesellschaft, 1956), 353, interprets the verses as a "lyrical paraphrase" of Hesiod, *Opera et dies* 108: ὡς ὁμόθεν γεγάασι θεοὶ θνητοί τ' ἄνθρωποι.

117 Clemens Alexandrinus, *Stromata* V 102.2 (GCS Clemens Alexandrinus II, 395.1 STÄHLIN/FRÜCHTEL/TREU); Eusebius, *Praeparatio Evangelica* XIII 13.27 (GCS Eusebius VIII/2, 207.6f. MRAS/DES PLACES); Ioannes Stobaeus, *Anthologium* II 7.13 (II, 121.19f. WACHSMUTH); and Themistius, *Orationes* VI 78a (BiTeu I, 115.13f. DOWNEY/NORMAN). Cf. also PEPIN, *Idées grecques sur l'homme et sur Dieu*, 36–38.

118 Bert KAESER, "Die Körper der Götter und die Wahrheit der Bilder," in *Die Unsterblichen: Götter Griechenlands*, hg. von den Staatlichen Antikensammlungen und Glyptothek München (Lindenberg im Allgäu: Fink, 2012), 52–79.

119 VERNANT, "Mortals and Immortals," 41.

120 James CARNEY, Robin DUNBAR, Anna MACHIN, Tamás DÁVID-BARRETT, and Mauro SILVA JÚNIOR, "Social Psychology and the Comic-Book Superhero: A Darwinian Approach," *Philosophy and Literature* 38 (2014): A195–A215.

121 FUNKE, s.v. "Götterbild," 768–771. See principally Pierre PRIGENT, *Le judaïsme et l'image*, TSAJ 24 (Tübingen: Mohr Siebeck, 1990), passim.

122 Rachel HACHLILI, "The Zodiac in Ancient Jewish Art," *Bulletin of the American Schools of Oriental Research* 228 (1977): 61–77; Günter STEMBERGER, "Die Bedeutung des Tierkreises auf Mosaikfußböden spätantiker Synagogen," *Kairos* 17 (1975): 23–56; and PRIGENT, *Le judaïsme et l'image*, 159–173 (overview of fidings from the respective areas and their various interpretations). For background, see also Ludwig WÄCHTER, "Astrologie und Schicksalglaube im rabbinischen Judentum," *Kairos* 11 (1969): 181–200, esp. 194–200.

123 Karl LEHMANN, "The Dome of Heaven," *Art Bulletin* 22 (1945): 1–17; and Wilhelm ROSCHER, s.v. "Helios," in *Ausführliches Lexikon der griechischen und römischen Mythologie* (Leipzig: Teubner, 1890), 1/2: 1993–2026.

124 Carl H. KRAELING, *The Synagogue*, repr. with new foreword and indices, The Excavations at Dura-Europos Conducted by Yale University and the French Academy of Inscriptions and Letters, Final Report 8/1 (New York: KTAV, 1979 = New Haven, Conn.: Yale University Press, 1956); Lee L. LEVINE, "The Synagogue of Dura-Europos," in *Ancient Synagogues Revealed* (Jerusalem: Israel Exploration Society, 1981), 172–177; Hans-Peter STÄHLI, *Antike Synagogenkunst* (Stuttgart: Calwer, 1988), 69–99; PRIGENT, *Le judaïsme et l'image*, 179–263; Jonathan GOLDSTEIN, "The Central Composition of the West Wall of the Synagogue in Dura-Europos," *Journal of the Ancient Near Eastern Society* 16, no. 17 (1984/1985): 99–142, esp. 118–131; most recently, Peter SCHÄFER, *Die Geburt des Judentums aus dem Geist des Christentums*, Tria Corda, Jenaer Vorlesungen zu Judentum, Antike und Christentum 6 (Tübingen: Mohr Siebeck, 2010), 126–128; and Lee I. LEVINE, *Visual Judaism in Late Antiquity: Historical Contexts of Jewish Art* (New Haven, Conn./London: Yale University Press, 2012), 97–118.

125   Lieselotte Kötzsche, s.v. "Hand II (ikonographisch)," in *Reallexikon für Antike und Christentum* (Stuttgart: Hiersemann, 1986), 13: 402–482, esp. 418–420; Prigent, *Le judaïsme et l'image*, 230f. 240f.; and Schwemer, "Gottes Hand und die Propheten," 65–86, esp. 74f. On the temple, see Pamela Berger, "The Temples/Tabernacles in the Dura-Europos Synagogue Paintings," in *Dura Europos: Crossroads of Antiquity*, ed. Lisa R. Brody and Gail L. Hoffman (Chestnut Hill, Mass.: McMullen Museum of Art, Boston College, 2011), 123–140.

126   Kötzsche, s.v. "Hand II (ikonographisch)," 418.

127   Kraeling, *The Synagogue*, 57; cited in agreement in Kötzsche, s.v. "Hand II (ikonographisch)," 418.

128   Kraeling, *The Synagogue*, 217; Clark Hopkins, "The Excavation of the Dura Synagogue Paintings," in *The Dura-Europos Synagogue: A Re-evaluation (1932–1972)*, ed. Joseph Gutmann (Chamberburg, Pa.: American Academy of Religion, 1973), 15f.; Goldstein, "The Central Composition of the West Wall of the Synagogue in Dura-Europos," 100–102; and now Margaret Olin, "'Early Christian Synagogues' and 'Jewish Art Historians': The Discovery of the Synagogue of Dura-Europos," *Marburger Jahrbuch für Kunstwissenschaft* 27 (2000): 7–28.

129   A good schematization in Prigent, *Le judaïsme et l'image*, 189 (as fig. 44).

130   Divergent interpretations (Joshua, Elias, Moses) in Prigent, *Le judaïsme et l'image*, 190–193. Opting for Jacob is Jacob Milgrom, "The Dura Synagogue and Visual Midrash," in *Scriptures for the Modern World*, ed. Paul R. Cheesman and C. Wilfred Griggs (Provo, Utah: Religious Studies Center, Brigham Young University, 1984), 29–60.

131   Goldstein, "The Central Composition of the West Wall of the Synagogue in Dura-Europos," 114 with fig. 7.

132   Kurt Weitzmann and Herbert L. Kessler, *The Frescoes of the Dura Synagogue and Christian Art*, Dumbarton Oaks Studies 28 (Washington, D.C.: Dumbarton Oaks Research Library and Collection, 1990), 91–94; and Goldstein, "The Central Composition of the West Wall of the Synagogue in Dura-Europos," 120–128. See also Schäfer, *Die Geburt des Judentums aus dem Geist des Christentums*, 127. In this direction tended already Georg Kretschmar, "Jüdische und christliche Kunst," in *Abraham unser Vater: Juden und Christen im Gespräch über die Bibel; Festschrift für Otto Michel zum 60. Geburtstag*, hg. Otto Betz, Martin Hengel und Peter Schmidt, Arbeiten zur Geschichte des Spätjudentums und Urchristentums 5 (Leiden/Köln: Brill, 1963), 295–319, esp. 307–313.

133   Goldstein, "The Central Composition of the West Wall of the Synagogue in Dura-Europos," 118–131; and Schäfer, *Die Geburt des Judentums aus dem Geist des Christentums*, 127f.

134   Drawings from Henry F. Pearson from 1934/1935 reproduced in Erwin R. Goodenough, *Symbolism in the Dura Synagogue,* vol. 3, *Illustrations*, Jewish Symbols in the Greco-Roman Period 11 = Bollingen Series 37/11 (New York: Pantheon, 1964), fig. 73–77 = Schäfer, *Die Geburt des Judentums aus dem Geist des Christentums*, 181, Abb. 2/3. See also Pearson's reconstruction of the space in Michael Rostovtzeff, *Dura Europos and Its Art* (Oxford: Clarendon, 1938), plate XX after sp. 108; and the reproductions of the drawings of Pearson and Herbert J. Gute in Prigent, *Le judaïsme et l'image*, 183.

135   Goldstein, "The Central Composition of the West Wall of the Synagogue in Dura-Europos," 105 (with further literature). On the Christian aftermath, see Christoph Markschies, "Odysseus und Orpheus—christlich gelesen," in *Griechische Mythologie und frühes Christentum*, hg. Raban von Haehling (Darmstadt: Wissenschaftliche Buchgesellschaft, 2005), 227–253 (with further literature).

136   Parts of the bush must also have still remained visible during the third phase: Goldstein, "The Central Composition of the West Wall of the Synagogue in Dura-Europos," 111 (as in Kraeling and Goodenough, op. cit., for the references). Prigent, *Le judaïsme et l'image*, 182, explains the bush with Targum Neofiti on Gen 3:24 (Torah as the Tree of Life).

137 A small few and, moreover, rather difficult examples are named by Henri LECLERCQ, s.v. "Dieu," in *Dictionnaire d'archéologie chrétienne et de liturgie* (Paris: Letouzey et Ané, 1920), 4/1: 821–824, esp. 822f.: (1) *Cotton-Genesis zum dritten Schöpfungstag (Genesis 1.11)* in a reproduction of a now-lost illustration, Paris, Bibliothèque Nationale, ms. français 9530. See also Herbert L. KESSLER, "409 Two Copies of Minatures from the Cotton Genesis," in *Age of Spirituality: Late Antique and Christian Art, Third to Seventh Century: Catalogue of the Exhibition at the Metropolitan Museum of Art, November 19, 1977, through February 12, 1978*, ed. Kurt Weitzmann (Princeton, N.J.: Princeton University Press, 1977), 458 (surely a depiction of Christ); and (2) a depiction of a head in the scene in which Moses receives the law, on a narrow side of the reliquary of Brescia, in *Dictionnaire d'archéologie chrétienne et de liturgie* 2/1: 1152f., Abb. 1627. On possible depictions of God the Father on late antique Christian sarcophagi, see MARKSCHIES, "'Sessio ad dexteram,'" in idem, *Alta Trinità Beata*, 1–69, esp. 62; (3) *Sarkophag aus Trinquetaille* (Arles, Musée lapidaire d'art chrétien; see KAISER-MINN, *Die Erschaffung des Menschen auf den spätantiken Monumenten des 3. und 4. Jahrhunderts*, JAC, Ergänzungsbände 6 [Münster: Aschendorff, 1981], 19–28 with table 9); and (4) the so-called dogmatic sarcophagus in the Museum of the Vatican (Ex-Lateran. 104; see Helga KAISER-MINN, *Die Erschaffung des Menschen auf den spätantiken Monumenten des 3. und 4. Jahrhunderts*, Abb. nr. 140/141; and Josef ENGEMANN, "Zu den Dreifaltigkeitsdarstellungen der frühchristlichen Kunst: Gab es im 4. Jahrhundert anthropomorphe Trinitätsbilder?" *JAC* 19 [1976]: 157–172).

138 Pierre PRIGENT, "La main de Dieu dans l'iconographie du paléo-christianisme," in Kieffer et Bergman, *La Main de Dieu*, 141–156; and Klaus WESSEL, s.v. "Hand Gottes," in *Reallexikon zur byzantinischen Kunst* (Stuttgart: Hiersemann, 1971), 2: 950–962.

139 Patricia DELEEUW, "A Peaceful Pluralism: The Durene Mithraeum, Synagogue, and Christian Building," in *Dura Europos: Crossroads of Antiquity*, ed. Lisa R. Brody and Gail L. Hoffman (Chestnut Hill, Mass.: McMullen Museum of Art, Boston College, 2011), 189–199.

4 The Bodies of Gods and the Bodies of Souls in Late Antiquity

1 The scholarly Antique polemic against cult images is reconstructed in detail within FUNKE, s.v. "Götterbild," 11: 659–828, esp. 745–752.

2 Apuleius, *Metamorphoses* XI 17.1 (SQAW 1, 338.25 HELM): *simulacra spirantia*.

3 Apuleius, *De Platone et eius dogmate* 5.190 (BiTeu III, 92.8 MORESCHINI = CUFr 64 BEAUJEU).

4 Lucianus, *De Syria dea* 10 (252.10–12 LIGHTFOOT). As Jane Lightfoot demonstrates in her commentary, this presages § 36 (op. cit., 332f.). Lucian recounts that the oracle of Apollo/ Nebo is said to "move, and deliver oracles," sweating when unobserved by priests (252.7–14 LIGHTFOOT).

5 Jens GERLACH, "Die Figur des Scharlatans bei Lukian," in *Lukian, Der Tod des Peregrinos: Ein Scharlatan auf dem Scheiterhaufen*, hg., übers. und mit Beiträgen versehen von Peter Pilhofer, Manuel Baumbach, Jens Gerlach und Dirk Uwe Hansen, SAPERE 9 (Darmstadt: Wissenschaftliche Buchgesellschaft, 2005), 150–152. On the difference between the two texts, see Ulrich VICTOR, hg., *Lukian von Samosata: Alexandros oder der Lügenprophet*, Religions in the Graeco-Roman World 132 (Leiden: Brill, 1997), 17–26, albeit Victor stylizes the text on the "lying prophet" a touch too strongly as a "factual report." See Angelos CHANIOTIS, "Old Wine in a New Skin: Tradition and Innovation in the Cult Foundation of Alexander of Abonouteichos," *Electrum* 6 (2002): 67–85, esp. 68 with n. 5; and Wolfgang SPICKERMANN, "Lukian und die (Götter)bilder," in *Römische Götterbilder der mittleren und späten Kaiserzeit*, hg. Dietrich Boschung und Alfred Schäfer, Morphomata 22 (Paderborn: Wilhelm Fink, 2015), 87–108.

6 The question as to whether Lucian possessed a philosophical credo is answered accordingly by Heinz-Günther NESSELRATH, "Lukian und die antike Philosophie," in *Lukian,*
   ΦΙΛΟΨΕΥΔΕΙΣ Η ΑΠΙΣΤΩΝ: Die Lügenfreunde oder; Der Ungläubige, eingel., übers.
   und mit interpretierenden Essays versehen von Martin Ebner, Holger Gzella, Heinz-
   Günther Nesselrath und Ernst Ribbat, SAPERE 3, 2. Aufl. (Darmstadt: Wissenschaftliche Buchgesellschaft, 2002), 135–152, esp. 150–152. The answer to the question comes
   across even more skeptically should (as is done by Peter VON MÖLLENDORFF in his review
   of the volume, *Plekos* 4 [2002]: 1–10) the literary character of all of these pertinent statements by Lucian be further emphasized, believing less of the conclusions which might be
   drawn about his personal views than Nesselrath.
7 Dio Chrysostomus, *Oratio* XII 52 (BiTeu I, 216.12–16 DE BUDÉ = SAPERE 2, 84
   KLAUCK). ET from COHOON, *Dio Chrysostom*, 2: 57.
8 Plato, *Timaeus* 40 A. ET from BURY, *Plato: Timaeus. Critias. Cleitophon. Menexenus*,
   83–85. See Gerd VAN RIEL, *Plato's Gods*, Ashgate Studies in the History of Philosophical
   Theology (Surrey/Burlington, Vt.: Ashgate, 2013), 34–59; and John F. FINAMORE, *Iamblichus and the Theory of the Vehicle of the Soul*, American Classical Studies 14 (Chico,
   Calif.: Scholars Press, 1985), 66.
9 Cf. Plato, *Timaeus* 30 C 9–31 A 1.
10 Plato, *Phaedrus* 246 D 1. ET from FOWLER, *Plato: Euthythro. Apology. Crito. Phaedo.
   Phaedrus*, 473.
11 Dirk BALTZLY, "Is Plato's Timaeus Panentheistic?" *Sophia* 49 (2010): 193–215, esp. 206f.;
   and now VAN RIEL, *Plato's Gods*, 45f.
12 Ps.-Plato, *Epinomis* 984 D 3–E 1; 985 A 3–7. See Frederick E. BRENK, "In the Light of
   the Moon: Demonology in the Early Imperial Period," *ANRW* II/16.3: 2068–2145, esp.
   2085–2091.
13 Alcinous, *Epitome doctrinae Platonicae sive Διδασκαλικός* 10.7 (CUFr 25 WHITTAKER/
   LOUIS = 165.42–166.6 HERMANN). ET from Alcinous, *The Handbook of Platonism*, trans.
   with an introduction and commentary by John DILLON (Oxford: Clarendon, 1993), 19.
14 Alcinous, *Epitome doctrinae Platonicae sive Διδασκαλικός* 14.7 (CUFr 34 WHITTAKER/
   LOUIS = 170.42–171.3 HERMANN). ET from DILLON, *The Handbook of Platonism*, 25. For
   the term πυρώδης (Plato, *Critias* 226 C), cf. the parallel passages within Imperial-era
   Platonism in WHITTAKER, CUFr, 118 n. 293; and Eusebius Caesariensis, *Praeparatio
   Evangelica* III 9.9 (GCS Eusebius VIII/1, 129.7 MRAS/DES PLACES = SVF II, 1032 [II,
   307.4f. VON ARNIM]).
15 Alcinous, *Epitome doctrinae Platonicae sive Διδασκαλικός* 15.4 (CUFr 36 WHITTAKER/
   LOUIS = 171.34f. HER-MANN). ET from DILLON, *The Handbook of Platonism*, 25.
16 DILLON, *The Handbook of Platonism*, 132f. For demonology in Middle Platonism in
   detail, see, in addition to the literature named in n. 12, also Jean BEAUJEU, *Apulée, Opuscules Philosophiques (Du dieu de Socrate, Platon et sa doctrine, du monde) et fragments*,
   texte établi, traduit et commenté, CUFr (Paris: Les belles lettres, 1973), 183–201.
17 Alcinous, *Epitome doctrinae Platonicae sive Διδασκαλικός* 15.2 (CUFr 35 WHITTAKER/
   LOUIS = 171.20–23 HERMANN).
18 Proclus, *In Platonis Rem Publicam commentarii* II 196.24–30, 197.12–16. See Werner
   DEUSE, *Untersuchungen zur mittelplatonischen und neuplatonischen Seelenlehre*, Akademie der Wissenschaften und der Literatur, Abhandlungen der Geistes- und Sozialwissenschaftlichen Klasse, Einzelveröffentlichung 3 (Wiesbaden: Steiner, 1983), 222.
19 Jill HARRIES, *Sidonius Apollinaris and the Fall of Rome AD 407–485* (Oxford: Oxford
   University Press, 1994), 169–242; Oliver OVERWIEN, "Kampf um Gallien: Die Briefe
   des Sidonius Apollinaris zwischen Literatur und Politik," *Hermes* 137 (2009): 93–117;
   Raymond VAN DAM, *Leadership and Community in Late Antique Gaul*, The Transformation of the Classical Heritage 8 (Berkeley/Los Angeles/London: University of California
   Press, 1985), 157–178; Karl Friedrich STROHEKER, *Der senatorische Adel im spätantiken
   Gallien* (Darmstadt: Wissenschaftliche Buchgesellschaft, 1970; Tübingen: Alma Mater,

1948), 217–219; and naturally Pierre Courcelle, *Les lettres grecques en Occident: De Macrobe à Cassiodore*, Bibliothèque des écoles françaises 159 (Paris: Boccard, 1948), 221–246. More recently considered in brief in Peter Brown, *The Ransom of the Soul: Afterlife and Wealth in Early Western Christianity* (Cambridge, Mass./London: Harvard University Press, 2015), 124–147.

20 Wolfgang Schmid, s.v. "Claudianus Mamertus," in *Reallexikon für Antike und Christentum* (Stuttgart: Hiersemann, 1957), 3: 169–179; Martin Schulze, *Die Schrift des Claudianus Mamertus, Presbyters zu Vienne, über das Wesen der Seele (De statu animae)*, diss. phil. Leipzig 1883 (Dresden: Rammingsche Buchdruckerei, 1883); René de la Broise, *Mamerti Claudiani Vita Ejusque Doctrina de Anima Hominis: Thesim Facultati Litterarum Parisiensi Proponebat* (Paris: Retaux-Bray, 1890); Franz Zimmermann, "Des Claudianus Mamertus Schrift: 'De statu animae libri tres,'" *Divus Thomas* 1 (1914): 238–256, 332–368, and 440–495; Ernest L. Fortin, *Christianisme et culture philosophique au cinquième siècle: la querelle de l'âme humaine en Occident*, Études Augustiniennes (Paris: Études Augustiniennes, 1959), 15–21; and Michele Di Marco, *La polemica sull'anima tra "Fausto di Riez" e Claudiano Mamerto*, Studia Ephemeridis Augustinianum 51 (Roma: Institutum patristicum Augustinianum, 1995), 7–9.

21 Harries, *Sidonius Apollinaris and the Fall of Rome*, 18, 105. On the baptism see Sidonius, *Carmen* XVI 84 (CUFr I, 123 Loyen); and André Loyen, "La mère de Fauste de Riez (Sidoine Apollinaire C. XVI v. 84)," *Bulletin de la littérature ecclésiastique* 73 (1972): 167–169.

22 CPL 983: *Claudiani Mamerti Opera*, recensuit et commentario critico instruxit Augustus Engelbrecht, CSEL 11 (Vienna: Gerold, 1885); Eligius Dekkers and Emil Gaar enumerate manuscripts not taken into account by Engelbrecht: idem, *Clavis Patrum Latinorum*, 3rd ed. (Steenbrugge: In Abbatia Sancti Petri/Brepols, 1995), 317.

23 CPL 984: *Epistula ad Sapaudum* (in CSEL 11, 203–206 Engelbrecht) and a letter to Sidonius transmitted within his corpus of letters and probably hailing from roughly AD 470/471 (Claudianus Mamertus, *Epistula* apud Sid., *Epistulae* IV 2 [CUFr II, 114f. Loyen]). The authenticity of CPL 1960 (*Epistula Ps. Hieronymi ad Constantium*, PL 30, 487) is discussed by Germain Morin, "Notes liturgiques," *Revue Bénédictine* 30 (1913): 226–234, esp. 228–231. The fourth book of Sidonius' letters have received extensive commentary: David Amherdt, *Sidoine Apollinaire, le quatrième livre de la correspondance: Introduction et commentaire* (Bern: Lang, 2001).

24 Claudianus Mamertus, *De statu animae praef.* (CSEL 11, 18.2f. Engelbrecht).

25 Sidonius, *Epistulae* IV 3.2 (CUFr II, 116f. Loyen).

26 Sidonius, *Epistulae* IV 3.6f. (CUFr II, 118 Loyen). ET from *Sidonius: Poems and Letters*, trans. W. B. Anderson, vol. 2, LCL (Cambridge, Mass.: Harvard University Press 1965), 73–75. See Courcelle, *Les lettres grecques en Occident*, 240–244.

27 Claudianus Mamertus, *De statu animae praef.* (CSEL 11, 18.4f. Engelbrecht).

28 Claudianus Mamertus, *Epistula apud Sidonium*, *Epistulae* IV 2.2 (CUFr II, 114 Loyen). ET from Anderson, *Sidonius: Poems and Letters*, 67.

29 Sidonius, *Epistulae* V 2 (CUFr II, 175f. Loyen).

30 Harries, *Sidonius Apollinaris and the Fall of Rome*, 110.

31 Sidonius, *Epistulae* IV 11.1 (CUFr II, 135 Loyen). ET from Anderson, *Sidonius: Poems and Letters*, 103. Commentary in Harries, *Sidonius Apollinaris and the Fall of Rome*, 110f.

32 Sidonius, *Epistulae* IV 11.6 (CUFr II, 137 Loyen). ET from Anderson, *Sidonius: Poems and Letters*, 109. Commentary in Harries, *Sidonius Apollinaris and the Fall of Rome*, 110f.; and in Fortin, *Christianisme et culture philosophique*, 17f.

33 Sidonius, *Epistulae* IV 11.6 (CUFr II, 137 Loyen: in the *carmen*, line 6): *Quam totam monachus uirente in aeuo*. For his assistance to the bishop, see ibid., *Epistula* IV 11.5 (136f.).

34 Gennadius, *De viris illustribus* 84 (TU 14, 90.11–14 Richardson).

35   Edition and philological commentary (on CPL 963[iii]): Arvid G. ELG, *Epistula Fausti Reiensis tertia* (Uppsala: Almquist & Wiksell, 1946); idem, *In epistulam Fausti Reiensis tertiam adnotationes* (Lund: Ohlsson, 1945). Elg takes up observations from Bernhard REHLING, *De Fausti Reiensis epistula tertia: Commentatio historica*, diss. phil. Münster 1898 (Münster: Aschendorff, 1898), and presents a photomechanical reproduction of Engelbrecht's edition with a new critical apparatus for variants.

36   Sangallensis 190 membr. saec. IX pp. 92–110 = CSEL 21, 168.5–181.7 ENGELBRECHT; also in CSEL 11, 3–17 ENGELBRECHT; Neuedition des Apparates bei ELG, *Epistula Fausti Reiensis tertia*, 8–21. See on the topic Marino NERI, *Dio, l'anima e l'uomo: L'epistolario di Fausto di Riez* (Rome: Aracne, 2011), 53–81; COLISH, *Stoic Tradition from Antiquity to the Early Middle Ages*, vol. 2, *Stoicism in Christian Latin Thought through the Sixth Century*, 128f.; and José MADOZ, "Un caso de materialismo en España en el siglo IV," *Revista española de teología* 8 (1948): 203–230, esp. 206–210.

37   Claudianus Mamertus, *De statu animae* I praef. (CSEL 11, 19.6f. ENGELBRECHT). Cf. ibid., I 1 (CSEL 11, 24.3–7 ENGELBRECHT). See NERI, *Dio, l'anima e l'uomo*, 53f.; and DI MARCO, *La polemica sull'anima tra "Fausto di Riez" e Claudiano Mamerto*, 7f.

38   Gennadius Massiliensis, *De viris illustribus* 86 (TU 14, 91.12–16 RICHARDSON). See on this Manlio SIMONETTI, "Fausto di Riez e i Macedoniani," *Augustinianum* 17 (1977): 333–354.

39   Accordingly (with the Hss.) in CSEL 21 and p. 8.5 ELG, in CSEL 11: *reuerendissime*.

40   Faustus Rhegiensis, *Epistula* 3 (CSEL 21, 168.5 ENGELBRECHT = 8.5 ELG). See REHLING, *De Fausti Reiensis epistula tertia*, 6–11; FORTIN, *Christianisme et culture philosophique*, 43–74. On Faustus, see Roger John Howard COLLINS, s.v. "Faustus von Reji," *TRE* 11: 63–67.

41   DI MARCO, *La polemica sull'anima tra "Fausto di Riez" e Claudiano Mamerto*, 8–11; and NERI, *Dio, l'anima e l'uomo*, 56f.

42   Faustus Rhegiensis, *Epistula* 3 (CSEL 21, 173.10f. ENGELBRECHT = 13.10f. ELG).

43   Thus Arius and fellow presbyters in their letter to Alexander of Alexandria (ca. AD 320; Urkunden zum arianischen Streit 6.2 = Dokumente zum arianischen Streit 1.2 = Athanasius Werke III/1, 12.9 OPITZ).

44   Faustus Rhegiensis, *Epistula* 3 (CSEL 21, 173.17–19 ENGELBRECHT = 13.17–19 ELG). On this passage, in detail, see FORTIN, *Christianisme et culture philosophique*, 48–53.

45   Origenes, *De principiis* IV 3.15 (347.11 KOETSCHAU). Cf. ibid., I 7 (86.18); and *prol.* (14.1); also Augustinus, *Epistula* 238.15 (CSEL 57, 544.4 GOLDBACHER). See FORTIN, *Christianisme et culture philosophique*, 49.

46   Origenes, *De principiis* IV 3.15 (GCS Origenes V, 347.18 KOETSCHAU = TzF 24, 778 GÖRGEMANNS/KARPP).

47   Origenes, *De principiis* IV 3.15 (GCS Origenes V, 347.21f. KOETSCHAU = TzF 24, 780 GÖRGEMANNS/KARPP). Cf. ibid., II 2.1 (112.4f. = 296).

48   Faustus Rhegiensis, *Epistula* 3 (CSEL 21, 173.19–22 ENGELBRECHT = 13.19–22 ELG). See also REHLING, *De Fausti Reiensis epistula tertia*, 45–48.

49   See on this Alan B. SCOTT, *Origen and the Life of the Stars: A History of an Idea*, OECS (Oxford: Clarendon; New York: Oxford University Press, 1991), 113–149, esp. 128–131 and 133–143. Jerome discusses a *caeleste corpus* with regard to the sun, moon, and stars in his work *Contra Iohannem* 27 (CChr.SL 79A, 49.19 FEIERTAG).

50   This may well indicate that Faustus' original text is, in fact, no longer extant. Ultimately, the argumentation was heralded by texts from the Fathers, and only a scarce few readers would have been able to attribute the anonymous quotation to Cassian.

51   Faustus Rhegiensis, *Epistula* 3 (CSEL 21, 174.16–23 ENGELBRECHT = 14.16–23 ELG) = Ioannes Cassianus, *Collationes* VII 13.2 (CSEL 132, 192.26–193.7 PETSCHENIG/KREUZ = SC 42[bis], 446 PICHERY) with minor abbreviations. ET from *John Cassian: The Conferences*,

trans. and annotated by Boniface RAMSEY, Ancient Christian Writers 57 (New York, N.Y./ Mahwah, N.J.: Newman Press, 1997), 256–257. On the impermeability of the matter for the substance, cf. also Faustus Rhegiensis, *De spiritu sancto* II 1 (CSEL 21, 131.15–24 ENGELBRECHT).

52 Faustus Rhegiensis, *Epistula* 3 (CSEL 21, 174.21 ENGELBRECHT = 14.21 ELG) = Ioannes Cassianus, *Collationes* VII 13.2 (CSEL 132, 193.5f. PETSCHENIG/KREUZ = SC 42bis, 446 PICHERY): *nihil esse incorporeum nisi solum deum.* ET from RAMSEY, *John Cassian: The Conferences*, 257.

53 Faustus Rhegiensis, *Epistula* 3 (CSEL 21, 175.3–5 ENGELBRECHT = 15.3–5 ELG).

54 Thomas Alexander SZLEZÁK, *Pseudo-Archytas über die Kategorien: Texte zur griechischen Aristoteles-Exegese*, Peripatoi 4 (Berlin/New York: De Gruyter, 1972), 13–19.

55 Simplicius, *Commentarium IX ad Aristotelis Categorias* 11 b 11 (CAG VIII, 361.10–15 KALBFLEISCH). ET from *Simplicius: On Aristotle's "Categories 9–15*," trans. Richard GASKIN (Ithaca, N.Y.: Cornell University Press, 2000), 95. See Max JAMMER, *Concepts of Space: The History of Theories of Space in Physics* (Cambridge, Mass.: Harvard University Press, 1954), 8; Richard SORABJI, *Matter, Space and Motion: Theories in Antiquity and Their Sequel* (Ithaca, N.Y.: Cornell University Press, 1988), 3–22 and 202–215; and Carl A. HUFFMAN, *Archytas of Tarentum: Pythagorean, Philosopher and Mathematician King* (Cambridge: Cambridge University Press, 2005), 595–599.

56 Faustus Rhegiensis, *Epistula* 3 (CSEL 21, 175.7–13 ENGELBRECHT = 15.7–13 ELG).

57 Faustus Rhegiensis, *Epistula* 3 (CSEL 21, 177.8–12 ENGELBRECHT = 17.8–12 ELG). This statement can naturally also be employed metaphorically: Prudentius, *Cathemerinon* X 39f. (CUFr I, 56 LAVARENNE); and Ps.-Augustinus, *Sermo* 368.1 = Caesarius Arelatensis, *Sermo* 173.1 (CChr.SL 104, 705.8 MORIN). The parallel Greek expression is κατοικητήριον.

58 Faustus Rhegiensis, *Epistula* 3 (CSEL 21, 178.2–12 ENGELBRECHT = 18.2–12 ELG).

59 Faustus Rhegiensis, *Epistula* 3 (CSEL 21, 178.7–179.16 ENGELBRECHT = 18.7–19.16 ELG).

60 Faustus Rhegiensis, *Epistula* 3 (CSEL 21, 179.21–180.1 ENGELBRECHT = 19.21–20.1 ELG).

61 See COLLINS, s.v. "Faustus von Reji," *TRE* 11: 65.

62 On *corporalitas*: Thesaurus Linguae Latinae IV, 995 s.v.

63 Tertullianus, *De anima* 22.2 (CChr.SL 2, 814.8–13 WASZINK). ET from *Tertullian: Apologetical Works; Minucius Felix: Octavius*, trans. Rudolf ARBESMANN, Emily Joseph DALY, and Edwin A. QUAIN, Fathers of the Church 10 (Washington, D.C.: Catholic University of America Press, 1950), 230. A more extensive commentary is in Jan Hendrik WASZINK, *Quinti Septimi Florentis Tertulliani De Anima*, Supplements to Vigiliae Christianae 100 (Leiden/Boston: Brill, 2010), 297. See also more generally Claudio MORESCHINI, "Tertulliano tra Stoicismo e Platonismo," in *Kerygma und Logos: Beiträge zu den geistesgeschichtlichen Beziehungen zwischen Antike und Christentum; Festschrift für Carl Andresen zum 70. Geburtstag*, hg. Adolf Martin Ritter (Göttingen: Vandenhoeck & Ruprecht, 1979), 367–379; in particular Petr KITZLER, "*Nihil enim anima si non corpus*: Tertullian und die Körperlichkeit der Seele," *Wiener Studien* 122 (2009): 145–169, esp. 147; and Heinrich HOPPE, *Beiträge zur Sprache und Kritik Tertullians*, Publications of the New Society of Letters at Lund 14 (Lund: Gleerup, 1932), 134.

64 Jean-Baptiste GOURINAT, *Les stoïciens et l'âme*, Philosophies (Paris: Presses Universitaires de France, 1996), 17–21.

65 Tertullian accordingly translates Gen 2:7. See the attestations in *Genesis*, hg. Bonifatius FISCHER, Vetus Latina 2 (Freiburg: Herder, 1951–1954), 40f.

66 Tertullianus, *De anima* 5.2 (CChr.SL 2, 786.5–13 WASZINK). Evidence for Hippaeus, Hippo, Thales, Empedocles, Critias, Epicurus, and Critolaus in WASZINK, *Quinti Septimi Florentis Tertulliani De Anima*, 127f. See on this line of argument KITZLER, "*Nihil enim anima si non corpus*," 147–165.

67 Tertullianus, *De carne Christi* 11.3–4 (CChr.SL 2, 895.17–24 Kroymann). ET from *Tertullian's Treatise on the Incarnation: The Text*, ed. with an introduction, translation, and commentary by Ernest Evans (London: SPCK, 1956), 43.

68 See also Kitzler, "*Nihil enim anima si non corpus*," 149; and Neri, *Dio, l'anima e l'uomo*, 73–79.

69 Hilarius Pictaviensis, *In Matthaeum* V 8 (SC 254, 158.17–20 Doignon). Cf. *De Psalmo* 118.19.8 (CSEL 22, 527.8 Zingerle). ET from *St. Hilary of Poitiers: Commentary on Matthew*, trans. D. H. Williams, Fathers of the Church 125 (Washington, D.C.: Catholic University of America Press, 2012), 78.

70 Hilarius, *De Psalmo* 118 Koph 8 (CSEL 22, 183.11–15 Zingerle).

71 Arnobius Iunior, *Conflictus Arnobii et Serapionis* II 2.5.14 (PL 53, 276 D = Corona Patrum 14, 142.4f. Gori): *Ergo animae et spiritus et angeli corporei sunt.* The notion of a corporeality of angels and demons is argued against in detail by Augustine in *De civitate Dei* XXI 10 (BiTeu II, 510.16–512.4 Dombart/Kalb); and *Enchiridion* 59 (CChr.SL 46, 81.66–85 Evans; 81.77): *angeli contrectabilia corpora non habere.*

72 Arnobius Iunior, *Conflictus Arnobii et Serapionis* II 2.5.15f. (PL 53, 276 D = Corona Patrum 14, 142.6–10 Gori).

73 Arnobius Iunior, *Conflictus Arnobii et Serapionis* II 2.5.19f. (PL 53, 277 A = Corona Patrum 14, 142.15–17 Gori).

74 Gennadius Massiliensis, *Liber sive diffinitio ecclesiasticorum dogmatum* 11f. (JThS 7, 1905, 91f. Turner). On the text, see José Madoz, "Un caso de materialismo en España en el siglo VI," *Revista Española de Teología* 8 (1948): 203–230, here 206f.

75 Fortin, *Christianisme et culture philosophique*, 47. See also, already, Schulze, *Die Schrift des Claudianus Mamertus*, 10.

76 Schulze, *Die Schrift des Claudianus Mamertus*, 56f.

77 Faustus Rhegiensis, *Epistula* 3 (CSEL 21, 180.23 Engelbrecht = 20.23 Elg). Cf. *Epistula* 5 (188.20f.).

78 Faustus Rhegiensis, *Epistula* 3 (CSEL 21, 180.18–22 Engelbrecht = 20.18–22 Elg).

79 *Proclus: The Elements of Theology; A Revised Text with Translation, Introduction, and Commentary*, ed. and trans. Eric R. Dodds (Oxford: Oxford University Press, 1963), 304–311 and 313–321; Finamore, *Iamblichus and the Theory*, 11–32; and Otto Geudtner, *Die Seelenlehre der chaldäischen Orakel*, Beiträge zur klassischen Philologie 35 (Meisenheim am Glan: Hain, 1971), 18–24, with bibliography 18 n. 83.

80 Porphyrius, *Fragmenta* 382 Smith (BiTeu 462.1–466.71 Smith) = Ioannes Stobaeus, *Anthologiae* I 60 (I, 445.14–448.3 Wachsmuth). Cf. Porphyrius, *De Antro Nympharum* 11 (BiTeu 64.10–25 Nauck).

81 Synesius, *De insomniis* 7 (CUFr II, 157.10 Terzaghi): ὥσπερ σκάφους ἐπιβᾶσα. However, Synesius employs Porphyry, in turn, as his source in *De insomniis* (Deuse, *Untersuchungen zur mittelplatonischen und neuplatonischen Seelenlehre*, 222f.).

82 Synesius, *De insomniis* 7 (CUFr II, 156.8f. Terzaghi). See Helmut Seng, "Seele und Kosmos bei Macrobius," in *Körper und Seele: Aspekte spätantiker Anthropologie*, hg. Barbara Feichtinger, Stephen Lake und Helmut Seng, Beiträge zur Altertumskunde 215 (München/Leipzig: Saur, 2006), 115–141, esp. 126f.; and Robert Christian Kissling, "The OXHMA—ΠΝΕΥΜΑ of the Neo-Platonists and the *De insomniis* of Synesius of Cyrene," *American Journal of Philology* 43 (1922): 318–330.

83 Proclus Atheniensis, *Institutio theologica* 207 (180.35–182.3 Dodds). According to Proclus, *Theologia Platonica* III 5 (CUFr III, 19.3–9 Saffrey/Westerink), he is immaterial. According to Proclus, *Commentarii in Platonis Timaeum* III, *ad Platonis Timaeum* 32 D/33 A (BiTeu II, 60.2–6 Diehl), he is impassible. See in detail "Appendix II: The Astral Body in Neoplatonism," in Dodds, *Proclus: The Elements of Theology*, 313–321.

84 Franz Bömer, *Der lateinische Neuplatonismus und Neupythagoreismus und Claudianus Mamertus in Sprache und Philosophie*, Klassisch-philologische Studien 7 (Leipzig: Harrassowitz, 1936), 34.

85 Apuleius, *De Platone et eius dogmate* I 9.199 (BiTeu III, 97, 16–18 MORESCHINI = CUFr 68 BEAUJEU). See DEUSE, *Untersuchungen zur mittelplatonischen und neuplatonischen Seelenlehre*, 100.

86 Galenus, *De placitis Hippocratis et Platonis* VII 7.25 (CMG V 4/1/2, 474.23–26 DE LACY).

87 Heinrich DÖRRIE, *Porphyrios' "Symmikta zetemata": Ihre Stellung in System und Geschichte des Neuplatonismus nebst einem Kommentar zu den Fragmenten*, Zetemata 20 (München: Beck, 1959), 9, 43f. (reconstructed from Nemesius, *De natura hominis* 3 [BiTeu 38.18 MORANI] = Porphyrius, Σύμμικτα ζητήματα frag. 259F [BiTeu 280.19–21 SMITH]), also 166 and 185f.; and idem, "Platons Begriff der Seele und dessen weitere Ausgestaltung im Neuplatonismus," in *Seele: Ihre Wirklichkeit, ihr Verhältnis zum Leib und zur menschlichen Person*, hg. Klaus Kremer, Studien zur Problemgeschichte der antiken und mittelalterlichen Philosophie 10 (Leiden/Köln: Brill, 1984), 18–45, here 38.

88 DÖRRIE, *Porphyrios' "Symmikta zetemata*," 186.

89 Iamblichus Chalcidensis, *De anima* 26 (*Iamblichus' De Anima: Text, Translation, and Commentary*, ed. and trans. John F. FINAMORE and John M. DILLON, Philosophia Antiqua 92 [Leiden/Boston/Köln: Brill, 2002], 54.4–7 [with literature on the Platonists enumerated in the commentary: op. cit., 152f.] = Stobaeus, *Anthologiae* I 49.39 [I, 378.6–9 WACHSMUTH] = Heinrich DÖRRIE, *Die geschichtlichen Wurzeln des Platonismus: Bausteine 1–35: Text, Übersetzung, Kommentar*, aus dem Nachlass hg. Annemarie Dörrie, Der Platonismus in der Antike: Grundlagen—System—Entwicklung (Stuttgart-Bad Cannstatt: Frommann-Holzboog, 1987), 1: Baustein 9, 132f. [commentary on p. 378f.] = Heraclides Ponticus, frag. 50, text and translation: *Heraclides of Pontus: Texts and Translation*, ed. Eckart SCHÜTRUMPF, Rutgers University Studies in Classical Humanities 14 [New Brunswick, N.J./London: Transaction, 2008], 122–125 with further literature on the Platonists mentioned within the commentary, op. cit.).

90 Iamblichus, *Fragmentum in Platonis Timaeum* 84 (*Iamblichi Chalcidensis in Platonis dialogos commentariorum fragmenta*, ed. with translation and commentary by John DILLON, Philosophia Antiqua 23 [Leiden: Brill, 1973], 196.4f., with commentary on p. 380). See FINAMORE, *Iamblichus and the Theory*, 11–14; and text, translation, and commentary in Heinrich DÖRRIE und Matthias BALTES, *Die philosophische Lehre des Platonismus: Von der "Seele" als der Ursache aller sinnvollen Abläufe, Bausteine 151–168; Text, Übersetzung, Kommentar*, Der Platonismus in der Antike: Grundlagen—System—Entwicklung (Stuttgart-Bad Cannstatt: Frommann-Holzboog, 2002), 6/1: Baustein 165, 122–125. Baltes is of the opinion that the fine immaterial body is only there to "permit the soul's transitory sojourn in the fine, heavenly realm" and should not be associated with the topic of the "vehicle of the soul" (p. 382).

91 Iamblichus, *Fragmentum in Platonis Timaeum* 81 (DILLON, *Iamblichi Chalcidensis in Platonis dialogos commentariorum fragmenta*, 194.7), directly criticizing Porphry (op. cit., 373; and FINAMORE, *Iamblichus and the Theory*, 11f.). On Porphry's doctrine, see DEUSE, *Untersuchungen zur mittelplatonischen und neuplatonischen Seelenlehre*, 218–230; and, previously, Heinrich DÖRRIE, "Porphyrius' Lehre von der Seele," in *Porphyre: Huit exposés suivis de discussions: Vandoeuvres-Genève, 30 août–5 sept. 1965*, éd. Heinrich Dörrie, Entretiens sur l'antiquité classique 12 (Genève: Fondation Hardt, 1966), 165–192 = idem, *Platonica Minora*, Studia et testimonia antiqua 8 (München: Fink, 1976), 441–453.

92 Macrobius, *Somnium Scipionis* I 11.12 (BiTeu II, 47.21–29 WILLIS).

93 Macrobius, *Somnium Scipionis* I 12.13f. (BiTeu II, 50.11–24 WILLIS).

94 Proclus, *Commentarii in Platonis Timaeum* I, *ad Platonis Timaeum* 23 F (BiTeu I, 138.26–139.3 DIEHL); III, *ad Timaeum* 36 B (II, 236.28–337.1); IV, *ad Timaeum* 40 B/C (III, 135.16–23); IV, *ad Timaeum* 40 B/C (III, 136.6–11); V, *prol.* (III, 167.13–20); V, *ad Timaeum* 41 A (III, 194.30f.): ἡλιοειδῆ γὰϱ αὐτῶν ἐστι τὰ ὀχήματα καὶ μιμούμενα τὴν νοεϱὰν αἴγλην; V, *ad Timaeum* 41 A (III, 204.8–10: Position des Syrianus); V, *ad*

Timaeum 41 D/E (III, 268.26–32); and *In Platonis Cratylum commentaria* 73, *ad Platonis Cratylum* 391 D/E (BiTeu 35.20–26 Pasquali). Cf. Hierocles, *In aureum Pythagoreorum carmen commentarius* 26.1f. (BiTeu 111.3–16 Köhler; see Hermann S. Schibli, "Hierocles of Alexandria and the Vehicle of the Soul," *Hermes* 121 [1993]: 109–117); Herm., *in Plat. Phdr.* I 64 (69.14–18 Couvreur); and Augustinus, *Epistula* 158.8 (CSEL 44, 494.1–23 Goldbacher). See Dörrie/Baltes, *Die philosophische Lehre des Platonismus*, 400f.

95 Hermias, *In Platonis Phaedrum scholia* II 15 (130.25–28 Couvreur). See on the relationship to Syrianus, *In Aristotelis metaphysica commentaria ad Aristotelis Metaphysicam* 2 1076 a 38 (CAG VI/1, 85.23–25 and 86.2–7 Kroll), Karl Praechter, s.v. "Syrianos," in *Realencyclopädie der classischen Altertumswissenschaften* (Stuttgart: Druckenmüller, 1932), IV A 2: 1728–1775, esp. 1759.

96 Olympiodorus, *In Platonis Alcibiadem commentarii* 17, *ad Platonis Alcibiadem* 1 103 A / B (14.1–4 Westerink). See D. Baltzly, "What Goes Up: Proclus against Aristotle on the Fifth Element," *Australasian Journal of Philosophy* 80 (2002): 261–287.

97 Thus Damascius, *In Phaedonem* I 551, *ad Platonis Phaedonem* 115 A/118 A (VKNAW, Afd. Letterkunde, Nieuwe Reeks 93, 283.1–5 Westerink); and previously already Porphyrius, *Fragmentum De regressu animae* 301 a.f. Smith = Augustinus, *De civitate Dei* XIII 19.49 (BiTeu 346.8f. Smith = BiTeu I, 583.5f. Dombart/Kalb).

98 Macrobius, *Somnium Scipionis* I 11.12 (BiTeu II, 47.27 Willis); from *testa*, "musselshell."

99 Synesius, *De insomniis* 6 (II, 155.1 Terzaghi). See Seng, "Seele und Kosmos bei Macrobius," 128f.

100 Dörrie/Baltes, *Die philosophische Lehre des Platonismus*, 388–402.

101 Michael Psellus, *Opuscula philosophica* 38.

102 Damascius, *In Phaedonem* I 168.5–8, *ad Platonis Phaedonem* (I, 47.5–7 Westerink/Combès).

103 Courcelle, *Les lettres grecques en Occident*, 210–253.

104 As Schulze, *Die Schrift des Claudianus Mamertus*, 15, correctly noted, *status* stands in place of *natura* or *essentia*: evidence on p. 15 n. 1.

105 Claudianus Mamertus, *De statu animae* I 1 (CSEL 11, 21.5–7 Engelbrecht).

106 Claudianus Mamertus, *De statu animae* I 1 (CSEL 11, 22.11f. Engelbrecht): *Oderunt igitur proximum, oderunt et deum.*

107 Claudianus Mamertus, *De statu animae* I 2 (CSEL 11, 24.10–26.6 Engelbrecht).

108 Claudianus Mamertus, *De statu animae* I 4 (CSEL 11, 38.9–14 Engelbrecht).

109 Claudianus Mamertus, *De statu animae* I 4 (CSEL 11, 38.14–16 Engelbrecht).

110 Claudianus Mamertus, *De statu animae* I 5 (CSEL 11, 41.1–3 Engelbrecht).

111 Claudianus Mamertus, *De statu animae* I 7 (CSEL 11, 45.8–46.6 Engelbrecht).

112 Claudianus Mamertus, *De statu animae* I 12 (CSEL 11, 52.23–53.12 Engelbrecht).

113 Claudianus Mamertus, *De statu animae* I 12 (CSEL 11, 53.16–54.1 Engelbrecht): The quotes' provenance is from the *Commentarius in Iob* of Philip Presbyter (CPL 643: PL 26, 727), and they were evidently transmitted under the name of his teacher, Jerome.

114 Claudianus Mamertus, *De statu animae* I 16 (CSEL 11, 61.10–12 Engelbrecht); and Faustus Rhegiensis, *Epistula* 3 (CSEL 21, 174.16–18 Engelbrecht). The quote hails from Ioannes Cassianus, *Conlationes* VII 13 (CSEL 13², 192.26–193.4 Petschenig/Kreuz). ET from Ramsey, *John Cassian: The Conferences*, 256.

115 Claudianus Mamertus, *De statu animae* I 17 (CSEL 11, 63.1–11 Engelbrecht).

116 Claudianus Mamertus, *De statu animae* I 19–21. Cf., in particular, I 20 (CSEL 11, 70.14–17 Engelbrecht). On this reference to Aristotle's categories, see Bömer, *Der lateinische Neuplatonismus*, 87–96 (Marius Victorinus as a source Claudianus shares with Augustine). A Latin reading text and a German translation of the paragraphs may be found in Jörg-Jochen Berns, *Gedächtnislehren und Gedächtniskünste in Antike und Frühmittelalter (5. Jahrhundert v.Chr. bis 9. Jahrhundert n.Chr.): Dokumentensammlung mit Übersetzung, Kommentar und Nachwort*, Documenta Mnemonica I/1 (Tübingen: Niemeyer, 2003), 419–425.

117 Claudianus Mamertus, *De statu animae* I 23 (CSEL 11, 82.22–83.13 ENGELBRECHT).
     German translation in BERNS, *Gedächtnislehren und Gedächtniskünste in Antike
     und Frühmittelalter*, 437/439. On the semantic field of *inlocalitas* or *inlocalis*, only
     found in Claudianus Mamertus (Thesaurus Linguae Latinae VII/1, 386 s.v.), see
     BÖMER, *Der lateinische Neuplatonismus*, 111–128; and FORTIN, *Christianisme et cul-
     ture philosophique*, 87: This translates ἀδιάστατος rather than ἄτοπος. Ernst BICKEL,
     "Inlocalitas: Zur neupythagoreischen Metaphysik," in *Immanuel Kant: Festschrift zur
     zweiten Jahrhundertfeier seines Geburtstages*, hg. Albertus-Universität in Königsberg
     in Preußen (Leipzig: Dietrich'sche Verlagsbuchhandlung, 1924), 17–26, here 22f.,
     interprets this differently.
118 Claudianus Mamertus, *De statu animae* I 25 (CSEL 11, 92.25–93.4 ENGELBRECHT).
119 Claudianus Mamertus, *De statu animae* I 25 (CSEL 11, 91.25–92.1 ENGELBRECHT). Ger-
     man translation in BERNS, *Gedächtnislehren und Gedächtniskünste in Antike und Früh-
     mittelalter*, 437/439.
120 Claudianus Mamertus, *De statu animae* I 24 (CSEL 11, 85.22–86.5 ENGELBRECHT).
121 Claudianus Mamertus, *De statu animae* I 24 (CSEL 11, 86.7f. ENGELBRECHT). German trans-
     lation in BERNS, *Gedächtnislehren und Gedächtniskünste in Antike und Frühmittelalter*, 439.
122 COURCELLE, *Les lettres grecques en Occident*, 226–235. Courcelle refers critically to
     BÖMER, *Der lateinische Neuplatonismus*, 2–30. See also Terenzio ALIMONTI, "Apuleio e
     l'arcaismo in Claudiano Mamerto," in *Forma futuri: Studi in onore del Cardinale Michele
     Pellegrino*, a cura di Terenzio Alimonti, Francesco Bolgiani, et al. (Turin: Bottega
     d'Erasmo, 1975), 191f. Bömer opted for a source which is "pre-Neoplatonic, and, in
     fact, Neopythagorean" (op. cit., 163). Einar HÅRLEMAN, *De Claudiano Mamerto Gallicae
     Latinitatis Scriptore Quaestiones* (Uppsala: Lundequistska Bokhandeln, 1938), 57–80,
     contrary to Bömer, views Claudianus as having himself translated Plato, *Phaedon* 66
     B-67 A in *De statu animae* II 7 (CSEL 11, 125.14–127.2 ENGELBRECHT).
123 Cf. Plato, *Phaedon* 67 A (on the period after death): τότε γὰρ αὐτὴ καθ' αὑτὴν ἡ ψυχὴ
     ἔσται χωρὶς τοῦ σώματος, πρότερον δ' οὔ, with *De statu animae* II 7 (CSEL 11,
     125.14–127.2 ENGELBRECHT): "Defunctorum enim animus liber est et solutus a corpore."
124 Claudianus Mamertus, *De statu animae* II 3 (CSEL 11, 105.5–15 ENGELBRECHT). On the
     passage, see primarily August BOECKH, *Philolaos des Pythagoreers Lehren nebst den
     Bruchstücken seines Werkes* (Berlin: Vossische Buchhandlung, 1819), 28–32; and then
     BÖMER, *Der lateinische Neuplatonismus*, 143–154 (for the term *incorporatio*, ibid., 171–
     172, translates Greek ἐνσωμάτωσις); and COURCELLE, *Les lettres grecques en Occident*,
     232–234.
125 Claudianus Mamertus, *De statu animae* II 5 (CSEL 11, 116.17–117.17 ENGELBRECHT).
126 Claudianus Mamertus, *De statu animae* II 7 (CSEL 11, 120.12–20 ENGELBRECHT). The
     fragment is incorporated into the edition of the fragments of Philolaus: *Philolaus of Cro-
     ton: Pythagorean and Presocratic: A Commentary on the Fragments and Testimonia with
     Interpretive Essays*, ed. and trans. Carl A. HUFFMAN (Cambridge: Cambridge University
     Press, 1993), 412.
127 Claudianus Mamertus, *De statu animae* II 3 (CSEL 11, 105.12–14 ENGELBRECHT).
128 Claudianus Mamertus, *De statu animae* II 3 (CSEL 11, 105.13f. ENGELBRECHT); Faustus
     Rhegiensis, Epistula 3 (CSEL 21, 179.19–22 Engelbrecht).
129 Claudianus Mamertus, *De statu animae* II 4 (CSEL 11, 112.6–13 ENGELBRECHT).
130 Claudianus Mamertus, *De statu animae* II 5 (CSEL 11, 118.5–14 ENGELBRECHT).
131 Claudianus Mamertus, *De statu animae* II 7 (CSEL 11, 120.15–20, 121.7–9, 121.14–
     18 ENGELBRECHT). For Philolaus, see the reference above, n. 126. For the fragment of
     Archytas see also above BÖMER, *Der lateinische Neuplatonismus*, 137–143; and *Archytas
     of Tarentum: Pythagorean, Philosopher and Mathematician King*, ed. Carl A. HUFFMAN
     (Cambridge: Cambridge University Press, 2005), 607. For *Hippo*, see Hermann DIELS and
     Walther KRANZ, *Die Fragmente der Vorsokratiker: Griechisch und Deutsch*, unveränder-
     ter Nachdruck der 6. Aufl. 1951 (Zürich: Weidmann, 2004), 389.10–14 (DK 38 B 4).

132 Claudianus Mamertus, *De statu animae* II 7 (CSEL 11, 122.2f. ENGELBRECHT). See COURCELLE, *Les lettres grecques en Occident*, 232; and prominently BÖMER, *Der lateinische Neuplatonismus*, 128–131.

133 Claudianus Mamertus, *De statu animae* II 7 (CSEL 11, 124.17–20 ENGELBRECHT). On this passage, see BÖMER, *Der lateinische Neuplatonismus*, 34–42.

134 For Claudianus Mamertus, *De statu animae* II 7 (CSEL 11, 125.14–126.4 ENGELBRECHT) = *Phaedon* 66 b–c, see FORTIN, *Christianisme et culture philosophique*, 150–154; and previously already BÖMER, *Der lateinische Neuplatonismus*, 1–30 (synopsis of the Greek text and its Latin translation: pp. 3f.).

135 Apuleius, *De Platone* I 192 (BiTeu 97.16–14 MORESCHINI = 60 BEAUJEU).

136 Claudianus Mamertus, *De statu animae* II 7 (CSEL 11, 128.13–17 ENGELBRECHT). Cf. Augustinus, *De civitate Dei* X 29 (BiTeu I, 449.25–28 DOMBART/KALB). See Joseph BIDEZ, *Vie de Porphyre: Le philosophe néo-platonicien*, receuil de travaux publiés par la Faculté de philosophie et lettres, Université de Gand 43 (Gand: van Goethem, 1913 = Hildesheim: Olms, 1964/1980), 38* with n. 4 for further attestations; and BÖMER, *Der lateinische Neuplatonismus*, 76. A synopsis of the passages is also to be found in COURCELLE, *Les lettres grecques en Occident*, 229.

137 BÖMER, *Der lateinische Neuplatonismus*, 84; also COURCELLE, *Les lettres grecques en Occident*, 228f.

138 See in detail on the quote BÖMER, *Der lateinische Neuplatonismus*, 132–137. Bömer takes the *inquiunt* from Claudianus Mamertus, *De statu animae* II 8 (CSEL 11, 129.13 ENGELBRECHT), as evidence of a pre-Neoplatonic doxographic source, into which the quotation was inserted as the view of both Sextii; according to Bömer, Claudianus Mamertus would have excerpted from this source.

139 Claudianus Mamertus, *De statu animae* II 8 (CSEL 11, 129.6–15 ENGELBRECHT). On this passage, see ALIMONTI, "Apuleio e l'arcaismo in Claudiano Mamerto," in Alimonti, Bolgiani, et al., *Forma futuri*, 189–228, esp. 224; and COURCELLE, *Les lettres grecques en Occident*, 232–234.

140 Claudianus Mamertus, *De statu animae* II 8 (CSEL 11, 130.2–16 ENGELBRECHT). On the passage, see BÖMER, *Der lateinische Neuplatonismus*, 154–160.

141 COURCELLE, *Les lettres Grecques en Occident*, 225 n. 2, refers in respect to this passage to the first *Oratio* of Gregory as translated by Rufinus: I 7 (CSEL 46, 11.9 ENGELBRECHT).

142 Claudianus Mamertus, *De statu animae* II 9 (CSEL 11, 131.7–15 ENGELBRECHT). The fragment of Ambrose cited possibly stems, as with a further example in II 9 (CSEL 11, 132.11–133.8 ENGELBRECHT), from his lost text *De sacramento regenerationis siue de philosophia* (CPL 161): Goulven MADEC, *Saint Ambroise et la philosophie* (Paris: Études Augustiniennes, 1974), 260–262.

143 Claudianus Mamertus, *De statu animae* II 9 (CSEL 11, 133.10–19 ENGELBRECHT), citing Augustinus, *Epistula* 166.4, *De origine animae hominis* (CSEL 44, 550.10–551.4 GOLDBACHER), probably from AD 415. On this, see Gerard J. P. O'DALY, s.v. "Anima, animus," in *Augustinus-Lexikon* (Basel: Schwabe, 1986–1994), 1: 315–340, here 321f.; Robert J. O'CONNELL, "Augustine's Rejection of the Fall of the Soul," Augustinian Studies 4 (1973): 1–32, here 17–29; and DI MARCO, *La polemica sull'anima tra "Fausto di Riez" e Claudiano Mamerto*, 138–142.

144 Claudianus Mamertus, *De statu animae* II 9 (CSEL 11, 135.20–136.10 ENGELBRECHT). The quotation originates from a lost homily (CPL 494); Claudianus and Eucherius may well have known one another (as is considered by FORTIN, *Christianisme et culture philosophique*, 15f.).

145 Prologue to the council's definition from *Actio* V: *Concilium Universale Chalcedonense*, ed. Eduard SCHWARTZ, vol. 1, pars 2, Actio Secunda. Epistularum Collectio B, Actiones III–VII, ACO II/1/2 (Berlin/Leipzig: De Gruyter, 1933), 128.21 (App.: κρᾶσιν ἢ σύγχυσιν). Cf. ACO II/3/2, 136.22 (according to the original MS: *confusionem permixtionemque*).

146 Lionel R. Wickham, s.v. "Eucherius von Lyon," *TRE* 10: 522–525, here 523.

147 Claudianus Mamertus, *De statu animae* II 9 (CSEL 11, 136.2–10 Engelbrecht).

148 See on this Luise Abramowski, "συνάφεια und ἀσύγχυτις ἕνωσις als Bezeichnungen für trinitarische und christologische Einheit," in idem, *Drei christologische Untersuchungen*, BZNW 45 (Berlin/New York: De Gruyter 1981), 63–109; Dörrie, *Porphyrios' "Symmikta zetemata,"* 36–90; Ernest Fortin, "Saint Augustin et la doctrine néoplatonicienne de l'âme (Ep. 137.11)," in *Augustinus Magister: Congrès international Augustinien, Paris, 21–23 Septembre 1954, Actes* (Paris: Études Augustiniennes, 1954), 3: 371–380; idem, *Christianisme et culture philosophique au cinquième siècle*, 111–128; and Jean Pepin, "Une nouvelle source de saint Augustin: Le ζητήματα de Porphyre; Sur l'union de l'âme et du corps," in *Revue des études anciennes* 66 (1964): 53–107.

149 Claudianus Mamertus, *De statu animae* II 9 (CSEL 11, 134.16–135.7 Engelbrecht).

150 Cf. the heavily reworked (at the very least) passages of an account from Aristotle in Cicero, *Tusculanae disputationes* I 22; 41; 65f. (= Aristoteles, *De philosophia frag.* 27 b–d [SCBO 94–96 Ross]). Cf. also the polemic in Augustinus, *De civitate Dei* XXII 11 (BiTeu II, 585.25–586.7 Dombart/Kalb); and his remarks from AD 388 in *De quantitate animae* 14.23 (CSEL 89, 158.9–15 Hörmann).

151 Augustinus, *De Genesi ad litteram libri duodecim* VII 21 (CSEL 28/1, 217.13–21 Zycha). ET from *Augustine: On Genesis*, trans. with notes by Edmund Hill, ed. John E. Rotelle (Hyde Park, New York: New City Press, 2002), 337. On this passage and futher examples from Augustine, see Di Marco, *La polemica sull'anima tra "Fausto di Riez" e Claudiano Mamerto*, 138f.; and O'Daly, s.v. "Anima, animus," in *Augustinus Lexikon*, 1: 325.

152 On this topic, see prominently Paulsen, "Early Christian Belief in a Corporeal Deity," esp. 107–114; and the ensuing debate: Kim Paffenroth, "Notes and Observations: Paulsen on Augustine; An Incorporeal or Nonanthropomorphic God," *HTR* 86 (1993): 233–235; David L. Paulsen, "Reply to Kim Paffenroth's Comment," *HTR* 86 (1993): 235–239; Kitzler, "*Nihil enim anima si non corpus,*" 166f.; and Carl W. Griffin/David L. Paulsen, "Augustine and the Corporeality of God," *HTR* 95 (2002): 97–118.

153 Augustinus, *Confessiones* VII 1 (BiTeu 124.6–10 Skutella). ET from *Augustine: Confessions, Books 1–8*, trans. Carolyn J.-B. Hammond, LCL 26 (Cambridge, Mass./London: Harvard University Press, 2014), 293. Phrased very similarly in VI 4 (103.28–104.3): Augustine learns that those who are made in spirit anew by "our mother the Catholic Church" do not believe that "te creatorem omnium in spatium loci quamvis summum et amplum, tamen undique terminatum membrorum humanorum figura contruderet." See on the discussion of this passage Griffin and Paulsen, "Augustine and the Corporeality of God," 108; and Johannes van Oort, "The Young Augustine's Knowledge of Manichaeism: An Analysis of the Confessions and Some Other Relevant Texts," *VC* 62 (2008): 441–466.

154 Augustinus, *Confessiones* VII 1 (BiTeu 124.24–125.7 Skutella). ET from Hammond, *Augustine: Confessions, Books 1–8*, 293. On the passage in depth, see Charles Baguette, "Une période stoïcienne dans l'évolution de la pensée de saint Augustin," *Revue des études augustiniennes* 16 (1970): 47–77; and James J. O'Donnell, *Augustine Confessions*, vol. 2, *Commentary on Books 1–7* (Oxford: Clarendon, 1992), 392–396.

155 Thus Colish, *The Stoic Tradition from Antiquity to the Early Middle Ages*, vol. 2, *Stoicism in Christian Latin Thought through the Sixth Century*, 148. She also argues for an inconsistent reception of the Stoa in Augustine. Interpreted differently by Baguette, "Une période stoïcienne dans l'évolution de la pensée de saint Augustin," 55–57, who points to the influence of Plotinus; also Robert J. O'Connell, "Ennead VI,4 and 5 in the Works of Saint Augustine," *Revue des études augustiniennes* 9 (1963): 1–39, here 10 n. 36.

156 Pepin, "Une nouvelle source de saint Augustin," 59–70.

157 Augustinus, *Confessiones* V 19 (BiTeu 92.21–28 Skutella). ET from Hammond, *Augustine: Confessions, Books 1–8*, 221.

158 Augustinus, *De moribus ecclesiae catholicae et de moribus Manichaeorum* I 17 (Augustinus Opera XXV, 66.10–16 RUTZENHÖFER).

159 Augustinus, *Confessiones* VII 1 (BiTeu 124.7 SKUTELLA): . . . *ex quo audire aliquid de sapientia coepi* . . . ET from HAMMOND, *Augustine: Confessions, Books 1–8*, 293. For the interpretation of this statement, see BAGUETTE, "Une période stoïcienne dans l'évolution de la pensée de saint Augustin," 48–51.

160 Augustinus, *Confessiones* III 12 (BiTeu 45.18–24 SKUTELLA). ET from HAMMOND, *Augustine: Confessions, Books 1–8*, 111. Cf. on this also Erich FELDMANN, *Der Einfluss des Hortensius und des Manichäismus auf das Denken des jungen Augustinus*, Diss. theol. (Münster, 1975), 617–631.

161 Augustinus, *De Genesi contra Manichaeos* 27 (CSEL 91, 94.5–13 WEBER). Conjecture by Weber for *interiora*: idem, "Textprobleme in Augustinus, De Genesi contra Manichaeos," *Wiener Studien* 111 [1998]: 211–230, here 217f.; On this passage, see Dorothea WEBER, "Augustinus, *De Genesi contra Manichaeos*. Zu Augustins Darstellung und Widerlegung der manichäischen Kritik am biblischen Schöpfungsbericht," in *Augustine and Manichaeism in the Latin West: Proceedings of the Fribourg-Utrecht Symposium of the International Association of Manichaean Studies (IAMS)*, ed. Johannes van Oort, Otto Wermelinger, and Gregor Wurst, Nag Hammadi and Manichaean Studies 49 (Leiden/Boston/Köln: Brill, 2001), 298–306, here 304–306. Cf. also Augustinus, *De moribus ecclesiae catholicae et de moribus Manichaeorum* II 43 (Augustinus Opera XXV, 200.10–13 RUTZENHÖFER). Equally, *Contra Secundianum liber* 20 (CSEL 25/2, 938.7–11 ZYCHA).

162 *Manichaei epistula fundamenti* frag. 2 (Papyrologica Coloniensia XXVII/2, 22.12–18 STEIN) = Augustinus, *Contra epistulam fundamenti* 13 (CSEL 25/1, 209.11–20 ZYCHA).

163 Augustinus, *Contra epistulam fundamenti* 43 (CSEL 25/1, 248.11–21 ZYCHA). Characterized as a polemic by Volker Henning DRECOLL/Mirjam KUDELLA, *Augustin und der Manichäismus* (Tübingen: Mohr Siebeck, 2011), 147; cf. also, however, François DECRET, *L'Afrique Manichéenne (IVᵉ–Vᵉ siècles): Étude historique et doctrinale* (Paris: Études Augustiniennes, 1978), 1: 306–322 ("a Vulgärmanichäismus": p. 306).

164 *Manichaei epistula fundamenti* frag. 2 (Papyrologica Coloniensia XXVII/2, 20.1–3 STEIN) = Augustinus, *Contra epistulam fundamenti* 12 (CSEL 25/1, 207.25–208.4 ZYCHA). Commentary in Erich FELDMANN, *Die "Epistula Fundamenti" der nordafrikanischen Manichäer: Versuch einer Rekonstruktion* (Altenberge: CIS, 1987), 35f.; and in Markus STEIN, *Manichaica Latina*, Bd. 2, *Manichaei epistula fundamenti: Text, Übersetzung, Erläuterungen*, Abhandlungen der Nordrhein-Westfälischen Akademie der Wissenschaften, Sonderreihe Papyrologica Coloniensia XXVII/2 (Paderborn/München/Vienna/Zürich: Schöningh, 2002), 76f. (on the various possibilities in identifying Patticus). Generally: DRECOLL/KUDELLA, *Augustin und der Manichäismus*, 21–30; and Therese FUHRER, "Augustins Modellierung des manichäischen Gottesbildes in den Confessiones," in *Monotheistische Denkfiguren in der Spätantike*, hg. Alfons Fürst, Luise Ahmend, Christian Gers-Uphaus und Stefan Klug, Studien zu Antike und Christentum 81 (Tübingen: Mohr Siebeck, 2013), 179–195.

165 On the continual confinement of the divine substance though each act of begetting, see Augustinus, *De haeresibus ad Quoduultdeum* 46.13 (CChr.SL 46, 317.39–41 VANDER PLAETSE/BEUKERS).

166 Augustinus, *Soliloquia* II 17.31 (CSEL 89, 88.11–17 HÖRMANN).

167 Augustinus, *De beata uita* 4 (CChr.SL 29, 67.91–94 GREEN). ET from *Saint Augustine: The Happy Life. Answer to Skeptics. Divine Providence and the Problem of Evil. Soliloquies*, trans. Ludwig SCHOPP, Dennis J. KAVANAGH, Robert P. RUSSELL, and Thomas F. GILLIGAN, Fathers of the Church 5 (New York: Cima, 1948), 47–48.

168 Hence the characterization of the content in *Retractationes* I 8.1 (CChr.SL 57, 21.1–22.9 MUTZENBECHER). ET from *Saint Augustine: The Retractions*, trans. Mary Inez BOGAN, Fathers of the Church 60 (Washington, D.C.: Catholic University of America Press, 1968), 28. See on the work Karl-Heinrich LÜTCKE, s.v. "Animae quantitate (De-)," in

Augustinus-Lexikon (Basel: Schwabe, 1986–1994), 1: 350–356; and Concetta Giuffre Scibona, "The Doctrine of Soul in Manichaeism and Augustine," in *"In Search of Truth": Augustine, Manichaeism and Other Gnosticism; Studies for Johannes van Oort at Sixty*, ed. Jacob A. van den Berg, Nag Hammadi and Manichaean Studies 74 (Leiden: Brill, 2011), 377–418, here 383–385.

169 Augustinus, *De quantitate animae* 2 (CSEL 89, 132.11–17, 25–133.27 Hörmann). ET from *Saint Augustine: The Immortality of the Soul. The Magnitude of the Soul. On Music. The Advantage of Believing. On Faith in Things Unseen*, trans. Ludwig Schopp, John J. McMahon, Robert Catesby Taliaferro, Luanne Meagher, Roy Joseph Deferrari, and Mary Francis McDonald, Fathers of the Church 4 (New York: Cima, 1947), 60. Cf. the German translation in Karl-Heinrich Lütcke, *Augustinus, philosophische Spätdialoge: Die Größe der Seele. Der Lehrer*, Bibliothek der Alten Welt, Antike und Christentum (Zürich/München: Artemis, 1973), 44–245, here 47.

170 Augustinus, *De quantitate animae* 4 (CSEL 89, 135.13–16 Hörmann). ET from Schopp/McMahon/Taliaferro/Meagher/Deferrari/McDonald, *Saint Augustine: The Immortality of the Soul. The Magnitude of the Soul. On Music. The Advantage of Believing. On Faith in Things Unseen*, 63.

171 Augustinus, *De quantitate animae* 77 (CSEL 89, 225.19–22 Hörmann). ET from Schopp/McMahon/Taliaferro/Meagher/Deferrari/McDonald, *Saint Augustine: The Immortality of the Soul. The Magnitude of the Soul. On Music. The Advantage of Believing. On Faith in Things Unseen*, 144.

172 Augustinus, *De haeresibus ad Quoduultdeum* 86 (CChr.SL 46, 338.8–339.16 Vander Plaetse/Beukers).

173 Madeleine Scopello, s.v. "Haeresibus ad Quoduultdeum (De-)," in *Augustinus-Lexikon* (Basel: Schwabe, 2004), 3: 278–290, here 280f.

174 Although it is to be completely expected that Claudianus knew texts by Augustine: Fortin, *Christianisme et culture philosophique*, 90–93, 101–105, and 148f. See also Terenzio Alimonti, "Apuleio e l'arcaismo in Claudiano Mamerto," in *Forma futuri: Studi in onore del Cardinale Michel Pellegrino*, a cura di Terenzio Alimonti, Francesco Bolgiani et al. (Turin: Bottega d'Erasmo, 1975), 216–219.

175 Claudianus Mamertus, *De statu animae* II 11 (CSEL 11, 142.12–19 Engelbrecht).

176 Claudianus Mamertus, *De statu animae* II 12 (CSEL 11, 148.2–8 Engelbrecht).

177 Claudianus Mamertus, *De statu animae* II 12 (CSEL 11, 150.4–11 Engelbrecht).

178 Claudianus Mamertus, *De statu animae* II 12 (CSEL 11, 152.9–17 Engelbrecht).

179 Faustus Rhegiensis, *Epistula* 3 (CSEL 21, 178.12–24 Engelbrecht = 18.12–24 Elg).

180 Claudianus Mamertus, *De statu animae* III 5 (CSEL 11, 164.15–23 Engelbrecht).

181 Claudianus Mamertus, *De statu animae* III 9 (CSEL 11, 170.4–21 Engelbrecht).

182 Claudianus Mamertus, *De statu animae* III 16.3 and 5 (CSEL 11, 186.4. 14f. Engelbrecht): *Igitur incorporalis est anima* or *Non igitur corpus est animus*. A German summary may be found in Zimmermann, "Des Claudianus Mamertus Schrift," 470–490.

183 On academic illustrations and diagrams in Antique Christian literature generally see Christoph Markschies, "Gnostische und andere Bilderbücher in der Antike," *ZAC* 9 (2005): 100–121 = idem, *Gnosis und Christentum* (Berlin: Berlin University Press, 2009), 113–160.

184 Faustus Rhegiensis, *Epistula* 3 (CSEL 21, 179.20f. Engelbrecht = 19.20f. Elg); Claudianus Mamertus, *De statu animae epilogus* (CSEL 11, 193.28–194.1 Engelbrecht). Cf. *De statu animae* II 3 (105.13f.) and II 4 (111.5f.).

185 CSEL 11, 197 Engelbrecht. See also op. cit., p. III; Rudolf Helssig, *Die lateinischen und deutschen Handschriften der Universitätsbibliothek Leipzig*, Bd. 1, *Die theologischen Handschriften*, Tl. 1 (Ms 1–500) (Wiesbaden: Harrassowitz, 1995), 417f.

186 Schulze, *Die Schrift des Claudianus Mamertus*, 73.

187 On Claudianus Mamertus' later influence during the Middle Ages, see Fortin, *Christianisme et culture philosophique*, 23.

5   The Body of God and Late Antique Jewish Mysticism

1   MARKSCHIES, *Christian Theology and Its Institutions in the Early Roman Empire*, 191–299.

2   Samuel SANDMEL, "Parallelomania," *JBL* 81 (1962): 1–13 = "'Parallelomania': The Presidential Address Given before the Society of Biblical Literature, December 27, 1961," in *Presidential Voices: The Society of Biblical Literature in the Twentieth Century*, ed. Harold W. Attridge and James C. VanderKam, Biblical Scholarship in North America 22 (Leiden/Boston: Brill, 2006), 107–118.

3   This might be understood as "material which circulates within a community and forms part of its heritage and tradition but which is constantly subject to revision and rewriting to reflect changing historical and cultural circumstances": Paul BRADSHAW, *The Search for the Origins of Christian Worship: Sources and Methods for the Study of Early Liturgy*, 2nd ed. (London: SPCK; New York: Oxford University Press, 2002), 5. See also idem, "Liturgy and 'Living Literature,'" in *Liturgy in Dialogue: Essays in Memory of Ronald Jasper*, ed. Paul Bradshaw and Bryan Spinks (London: SPCK, 1994), 138–153.

4   Gershom SCHOLEM, *Major Trends in Jewish Mysticism*, 3rd ed. (London: Thames and Hudson, 1955). On the placement of the work within the history of research, see Peter SCHÄFER, *The Origins of Jewish Mysticism* (Princeton, N.J.: Princeton University Press, 2009), 9–13; and also Gershom SCHOLEM's *Major Trends in Jewish Mysticism: 50 Years After; Proceedings of the Sixth International Conference on the History of Jewish Mysticism*, ed. Peter Schäfer and Joseph Dan (Tübingen: Mohr Siebeck, 1993). This terminology may not yet be found in Philipp BLOCH, "Die Yorede Merkavah, die Mystiker der Gaonenzeit und ihr Einfluss auf die Liturgie," *Monatsschrift für Geschichte und Wissenschaft des Judentums* 37 (1893): 18–25, 69–74, 257–266, 305–311.

5   Cf., e.g., 1 Sam 3:3; 1 Kgs 6:33; 7:50; Ezra 5:14; 6:5; Isa 6:1; Jer 7:4; Ezek 41:1, 21; and Dan 5:2-3. See also Magnus OTTOSSON, s.v. "היכל," in *Theologisches Wörterbuch zum Alten Testament* (Stuttgart: Kohlhammer, 1977), 2: 408–415.

6   On the introduction, see Frank-Lothar HOSSFELD, "Das Buch Ezechiel," in *Einleitung in das Alte Testament*, hg. Christian Frevel, 8. vollständig überarb. Aufl., Kohlhammer Studienbücher Theologie 1/1 (Stuttgart: Kohlhammer, 2012), 592–621.

7   Cf. throughout the translation of Walther ZIMMERLI, *Ezechiel*, Tlbd. 1, *Ezechiel 1–24*, 2. verb., durch ein neues Vorwort und einen Literaturnachtrag erweiterte Aufl., Biblischer Kommentar Altes Testament XIII/1 (Neukirchen-Vluyn: Neukirchener, 1979), 1–85. On this passage, see also SCHÄFER, *The Origins of Jewish Mysticism*, 34–50; and Moshe GREENBERG, *Ezekiel 1–20: A New Translation with Introduction and Commentary*, The Anchor Bible 22 (Garden City, N.Y.: Doubleday, 1983), 37–59.

8   David J. HALPERIN, *The Faces of the Chariot: Early Jewish Responses to Ezekiel's Vision*, TSAJ 16 (Tübingen: Mohr Siebeck, 1988), 41: "Ezekiel's Ḥayyot do not look very much like cherubim."

9   SCHÄFER, *The Origins of Jewish Mysticism*, 39.

10   ZIMMERLI, *Ezechiel*, 1: 52.

11   Cf. Ezek 1:16. On the differences between the Hebrew text and the Septuagint, see HALPERIN, *The Faces of the Chariot*, 55–60.

12   SCHÄFER, *The Origins of Jewish Mysticism*, 40f.

13   ZIMMERLI, *Ezechiel*, 1: 66. See also SCHÄFER, *The Origins of Jewish Mysticism*, 41: "For, strictly speaking, his creatures and wheels do not constitute a chariot. The wheels and the creatures are not joined together." On this topic, see also GREENBERG, *Ezekiel 1–20*, 47.

14   Albeit certainly in the Greek translation of Ezek 43:3. Here the throne-chariot is compared to a war chariot: "Die Verse 15–21 vermeiden die ausdrückliche Rede vom 'Wagen,' offenbar ist die Terminologie erst im Werden begriffen" (ZIMMERLI, *Ezechiel*, 1: 66).

15   See Peter WELTEN, "Lade—Tempel—Jerusalem: Zur Theologie der Chronikbücher," in *Textgemäß: Aufsätze und Beiträge zur Hermeneutik des Alten Testaments; Festschrift für Ernst Würthwein zum 70. Geburtstag*, hg. Antonius H. J. Gunneweg und Otto Kaiser (Göttingen: Vandenhoeck & Ruprecht, 1979), 169–183.

16 Andreas ALFÖLDI, "Die Geschichte des Throntabernakels," *La nouvelle Clio* 1/2 (1949/1950): 537–566. The association of the passage in the Hebrew Book of Ezekiel with the Persian baldachin cart as attempted by Alföldi is contested by ZIMMERLI, *Ezechiel*, 1: 65.

17 See Larry M. AYRES, "The Work of the Morgan Master at Winchester and English Painting of the Early Gothic Period," *Art Bulletin* 56 (1974): 201–223 (identification of the illustrator of the initials as the "Morgan Master" and dating); see also http://freechristimages.org/biblebooks/Book_of_Ezekiel.htm (last accessed 16 May 2019).

18 HALPERIN, *The Faces of the Chariot*, 49–193; Christopher ROWLAND, "The Visions of God in Apocalyptic Literature," *JSJ* 10 (1979): 137–154; and also SCHÄFER, *The Origins of Jewish Mysticism*, 53–154.

19 SCHÄFER, *The Origins of Jewish Mysticism*, 44f.

20 Herbert NIEHR, "Das Buch Daniel," in *Einleitung in das Alte Testament*, 8. vollst. überarb. Aufl., hg. Christian Frevel, Kohlhammer Studienbücher Theologie 1/1 (Stuttgart: Kohlhammer, 2012), 610–621, here 616.

21 See the commentary in Otto PLÖGER, *Das Buch Daniel*, Kommentar zum Alten Testament 18 (Gütersloh: Gütersloher Verlagshaus Mohn, 1965), 110–115.

22 Hans SCHMOLDT, s.v. "עתק," in *Theologisches Wörterbuch zum Alten Testament* (Stuttgart: Kohlhammer, 1989), 6: 487–489, here 488. See also HALPERIN, *The Faces of the Chariot*, 74–78.

23 See on this also Martin HENGEL, "'Setze dich zu meiner Rechten!' Die Inthronisation Christi zur Rechten Gottes und Psalm 110.1," in idem, *Studien zur Christologie: Kleine Schriften IV*, hg. Claus-Jürgen Thornton (Tübingen: Mohr Siebeck, 2006), 281–367, here 311–334 = Philonenko, *Le trône de Dieu*, 108–194, here 158–161. Hengel points to the Syro-hexaplar version of Dan 7:22 (*Codex Syro-Hexaplaris Ambrosianus*, photolitographice ed., curante, et adnotante Antonio Maria Ceriani, Monumenta Sacra et Profana ex Codicibus praesertim Bibliothecae Ambrosianae 7 [Milan: Bibliotheca Ambrosiana, 1874], 148ʳ); and the pertinent Greek editions (Septuaginta XVI/2, 342f. ZIEGLER/MUNNICH/FRAENKEL).

24 The development into a title (disputed in its details) is not here of immediate concern. See, e.g., Carsten COLPE, s.v. "υἱὸς τοῦ ἀνθρώπου," in *Theologisches Wörterbuch zum Neuen Testament* (Stuttgart: Kohlhammer, 1969), 8: 407–481, esp. 422–425; John J. COLLINS, "The Son of Man in First-Century Judaism," *NTS* 38 (1992): 448–466, here 450f.; Gerd THEISSEN und Annette MERZ, *Der historische Jesus: Ein Lehrbuch*, 2. durchges. Aufl. (Göttingen: Vandenhoeck & Ruprecht, 1997), 470–492, here 472.

25 John J. COLLINS, *The Apocalyptic Imagination: An Introduction to Jewish Apocalyptic Literature*, 2nd ed., The Bible Resource Series (Grand Rapids/Cambridge: Eerdmans, 1998), 178. See also SCHÄFER, *The Origins of Jewish Mysticism*, 48–77.

26 Ethiopic Enoch 46:1 (Ethiopic text in Michael E. KNIBB, *The Ethiopic Book of Enoch: A New Edition in Light of the Aramaic Dead Sea Fragments* [Oxford: Oxford University Press, 1978], 28; German translation in Siegbert UHLIG, *Das äthiopische Henochbuch*, Jüdische Schriften aus hellenistisch-römischer Zeit V/6 [Gütersloh: Gütersloher Verlagshaus Mohn, 1984], 461–780). ET from George W. E. NICKELSBURG and James C. VANDERKAM, *1 Enoch*, Hermeneia (Minneapolis: Fortress Press, 2012), 59. See also James MUILENBURG, "The Son of Man in Daniel and the Ethiopic Apocalypse of Enoch," *JBL* 79 (1960): 197–209; Christfried BÖTTRICH, "Konturen des 'Menschensohnes' in äthHen 37–71," in *Gottessohn und Menschensohn: Exegetische Studien zu zwei Paradigmen biblischer Intertextualität*, hg. Dieter Sänger, Biblisch-theologische Studien 67 (Neukirchen-Vluyn: Neukirchener, 2004), 53–90; COLLINS, "The Son of Man in First-Century Judaism," 451–459; COLPE, s.v. "υἱὸς τοῦ ἀνθρώπου," 425–429; HALPERIN, *The Faces of the Chariot*, 85f.; HENGEL, "'Setze dich zu meiner Rechten!'" 334–337; and SCHÄFER, *The Origins of Jewish Mysticism*, 60–67 and 72–77.

27 Thus Christfried Böttrich, "Das slavische Henochbuch," in *Apokalypsen*, Jüdische
    Schriften aus hellenistisch-römischer Zeit 5/7 (Gütersloh: Mohn, 1995), 783–1040, here
    807–813.
28 Certainly meaning a particular form of "cloud." See on this Schäfer, *The Origins of Jew-
    ish Mysticism*, 79 n. 101.
29 Grant Macaskill, *The Slavonic Text of 2 Enoch*, Studia Judaeoslavica 6 (Leiden/Boston:
    Brill, 2013), 101. Cf. Böttrich, "Das slavische Henochbuch," 890. ET from F. I. Ander-
    sen, "2 (Slavonic Apocalypse of) Enoch," *The Old Testament Pseudepigrapha*, vol. 1,
    ed. J. H. Charlesworth (Garden City, N.Y.: Doubleday, 1985) 91–221, here 136. Böt-
    trich refers to Georg Nathanael Bonwetsch, *Die apokryphe "Leiter Jakobs,"* Nachrichten
    der königlichen Gesellschaft der Wissenschaften zu Göttingen, Philologisch-historische
    Klasse 7 (Göttingen: Vandenhoeck & Ruprecht, 1900), 76–87, here 77f.: "Und die Spitze
    der Leiter war ein Angesicht wie eines Menschen, aus Feuer gehauen." See also A. Orlov,
    "'Without Measure and without Analogy': The Tradition of the Divine Body in *2 (Sla-
    vonic) Enoch*," in idem, *From Apocalypticism to Merkabah Mysticism: Studies in the
    Slavonic Pseudepigrapha*, Journal for the Study of Judaism Supplements 114 (Leiden:
    Brill, 2007), 149–174; idem, "God's Face in the Enochic Tradition," in *Paradise Now:
    Essays on Early Jewish and Christian Mysticism*, ed. April D. DeConick, Symposium
    Series 11 (Atlanta: Society of Biblical Literature; Leiden: Brill, 2006), 179–193; also
    idem, "The Face as the Heavenly Counterpart of the Visionary in the Slavonic Ladder of
    Jacob," in *Of Scribes and Sages: Early Jewish Interpretation and Transmission of Scrip-
    ture*, ed. Craig A. Evans, Studies in Scripture in Early Judaism and Christianity 9 (Lon-
    don: T&T Clark, 2004), 2: 59–76 = idem, *From Apocalypticism to Merkabah Mysticism*,
    399–422. In contrast to Orlov, Böttrich admits that within "Jacob's Ladder" probably the
    "countenance of God is not meant, but rather the face/representation of the last usurper
    king" (nicht das Gesicht Gottes, sondern . . . nur das Gesicht/die Repräsentation des letz-
    ten Usurpatorkönigs) and that "the text is regardless rather unclear" (der Text ist jedoch
    nicht ganz eindeutig) (communicated by letter, March 19, 2014).
30 Schäfer, *The Origins of Jewish Mysticism*, 80, deems this metaphor both at once "quite
    a prosaic image for the brightness of God's face," and yet also "not particularly imagina-
    tive" by means of contrast, and concludes that this is "not the most flattering image for
    God's face." Cf. 2 En. 39:3: "And now, my children, it is not from my own lips that I am
    reporting to you today, but from the lips of the LORD who has sent me to you. As for
    you, you hear my words, out of my lips, a human being created equal to yourselves; but
    I, I have heard the words from the fiery lips of the LORD. For the lips of the LORD are a
    furnace of fire." ET from Andersen, "2 (Slavonic Apocalypse of) Enoch," 163.
31 On this passage, see also Andrei Orlov, "Ex 33 on God's Face: A Lesson from the Enochic
    Tradition," in *Seminar Papers 39: Society of Biblical Literature Annual Meeting 2000*
    (Atlanta: Society of Biblical Literature, 2000), 130–147 = idem, *From Apocalypticism
    to Merkabah Mysticism*, 311–326. On the biblical discourse, see Friedhelm Hartenstein,
    *Das Angesicht JHWHs: Studien zu seinem höfischen und kultischen Bedeutungshintergr-
    und in den Psalmen und in Exodus 32–34*, FAT 55 (Tübingen: Mohr Siebeck, 2008), 265–
    268; and Joseph Reindl, *Das Angesicht Gottes im Sprachgebralso des Alten Testaments*,
    Erfurter Theologische Studien 25 (Leipzig: St. Benno, 1970), 72f.
32 Ezechiel Tragicus, *Fragmenta* 68–71 = Eusebius, *Praeparatio Evangelica* IX 29.5 (from
    Alexander Polyhistor, Περὶ Ἰουδαίων: GCS Eusebius VIII/1, 529.5–9 Mras/Des Places
    = Tragicorum Graecorum Fragmenta I, frag. 128, p. 292.68–72 Snell). ET from Howard
    Jacobson, *The Exagoge of Ezekiel* (Cambridge: Cambridge University Press, 1983), 55.
    On this passage, see Hengel, "'Setze dich zu meiner Rechten!'" 338f. = 165f.; Andrei
    Orlov, "In the Mirror of the Divine Face: The Enochic Features of the Exagoge of Eze-
    kiel the Tragedian," in *The Significance of Sinai: Traditions about Sinai and Divine Rev-
    elation in Judaism and Christianity*, ed. George J. Brooke, Hindy Najman, and Loren
    Stuckenbruck, Themes in Biblical Narrative 12 (Leiden: Brill, 2008), 183–199; Pieter

VAN DER HORST, "Moses' Throne Vision in Ezekiel the Dramatist," *JJS* 34 (1983): 21–29 = idem, *Essays on the Jewish World of Early Christianity*, NTOA 14 (Göttingen: Vandenhoeck & Ruprecht; Fribourg: Universitäts-Verlag, 1986), 63–71; and idem, "Some Notes on the 'Exagoge' of Ezekiel," *Mnemosyne* 37 (1984): 354–375, esp. 364–368 = idem, *Essays on the Jewish World of Early Christianity*, 72–93, esp. 82–86.

33 Apocalypse of Abraham 18 (Studien zur Geschichte der Theologie und Kirche I/1, 29.5–30.3 BONWETSCH). ET from Alexander KULIK, *Retroverting Slavonic Pseudepigrapha: Toward the Original of the Apocalypse of Abraham* (Leiden/Boston: Brill, 2005), 24. German translation in Belkis PHILONENKO-SAYAR und Marc PHILONENKO, "Die Apokalypse Abrahams," in *Apokalypsen*, JSHRZ V/5 (Gütersloh: Gütersloher Verlagshaus Mohn, 1982). On the passage in more length see Ithamar GRUENWALD, *Apocalyptic and Merkavah Mysticism*, AGAJU 14 (Leiden: Brill, 1980), 55–57; HALPERIN, *The Faces of the Chariot*, 103–114; Martha HIMMELFARB, *Ascent to Heaven in Jewish and Christian Apocalypses* (New York/Oxford: Oxford University Press, 1993, 61–66); Christopher ROWLAND, *The Open Heaven: A Study of Apocalyptic in Judaism and Early Christianity* (Eugene, Ore.: Wipf and Stock, 2002 = London: SPCK, 1982), 86–88; SCHÄFER, *The Origins of Jewish Mysticism*, 86–93.

34 Andrei A. ORLOV, *Heavenly Priesthood in the Apocalypse of Abraham* (Cambridge: Cambridge University Press, 2013), 154–189; ROWLAND, *The Open Heaven*, 86–88; and Phillip B. MUNOA, *Four Powers in Heaven: The Interpretation of Daniel 7 in the Testament of Abraham*, Journal for the Study of the Pseudepigrapha, Supplement 28 (Sheffield: Sheffield Academic Press, 1998), 141–148. At length on the polemic against depictions of God in the Apocalypse, see Alexander KULIK, "The Gods of Nahor: A Note on the Pantheon of the Apocalypse of Abraham," *JJS* 54 (2003): 228–232; and Andrei ORLOV, "'The Gods of My Father Terah': Abraham the Iconoclast and the Polemics with the Divine Body Traditions in the Apocalypse of Abraham," *Journal for the Study of the Pseudepigrapha* 18 (2008): 33–53 = idem, *Divine Manifestations in the Slavonic Pseudepigrapha*, Orientalia Judaica Christiana 2 (Piscataway, N.Y.: Gorgias, 2009), 217–235.

35 CChr.SA 7, 105 PERRONE/NORELLI. ET from M. A. KNIBB, "Martyrdom and Ascension of Isaiah," *The Old Testament Pseudepigrapha*, vol. 2, ed. J. H. Charlesworth (Garden City, N.Y.: Doubleday, 1985 [1983]) 143–176, here 171f. On the text, see SCHÄFER, *The Origins of Jewish Mysticism*, 93–99.

36 Enrico NORELLI, *Ascensio Isaiae: Commentarius*, CChr.SA 8 (Turnhout: Brepols, 1995), 487–489. On the question as to the identification of the religious-historical milieu wherein the text was composed, see HIMMELFARB, *Ascent to Heaven in Jewish and Christian Apocalypses*, 55–58; Robert G. HALL, "Isaiah's Ascent to See the Beloved: An Ancient Jewish Source for the Ascension of Isaiah," *JBL* 113 (1994), 463–484; and SCHÄFER, *The Origins of Jewish Mysticism*, 94 with n. 31 (with an energetic argument against neatly distinguishing between Judaism and Christianity; similarly, HALL, "Isaiah's Ascent to See the Beloved," 466: "the terms 'Jewish,' 'Christian,' and 'Gnostic' are notoriously slippery when applied to texts from early in the second century").

37 HALL, "Isaiah's Ascent to See the Beloved," 468–470.

38 Clemens Alexandrinus, *Stromata* V 77.2 (GCS Clemens Alexandrinus II, 377.20–24 STÄHLIN/FRÜCHTEL/TREU). ET from WILSON, *The Writings of Clement of Alexandria*, 2: 267. On this apocalypse, in the alleged Coptic fragments of which nevertheless no parallels to the fragment transmitted in Greek may be found, see, in summary, Bernd Jörg DIEBNER, *Zephanjas Apokalypse*, Jüdische Schriften aus hellenistisch-römischer Zeit V/9 (Gütersloh: Gütersloher Verlagshaus Mohn, 2003), 1141–1246, here 1200–1230; HIMMELFARB, *Ascent to Heaven in Jewish and Christian Apocalypses*, 51–55; and SCHÄFER, *The Origins of Jewish Mysticism*, 99–102.

39 Clemens Alexandrinus, *Stromata* V 77.1 (GCS Clemens Alexandrinus II, 377.19f. STÄHLIN/FRÜCHTEL/TREU). ET from WILSON, *The Writings of Clement of Alexandria*, 2: 267.

40 Clemens Alexandrinus, *Stromata* V 77.1 (GCS Clemens Alexandrinus II, 377.15–19 STÄHLIN/FRÜCHTEL/TREU) = Plato, *Epistula* VII 341 C/D (BiTeu 33.22–25 MOORE-BLUNT). ET from WILSON, *The Writings of Clement of Alexandria*, 2: 266f.

41 Clemens Alexandrinus, *Stromata* V 77.2 (GCS Clemens Alexandrinus II, 377.19f. STÄHLIN/FRÜCHTEL/TREU).

42 On the notion that the "solar eye" of the soul can perceive the (divine) light (Plato, *Timaeus* 45 B), see Albrecht DIHLE, "Vom sonnenhaften Auge," in *Platonismus und Christentum: Festschrift für Heinrich Dörrie*, hg. Horst-Dieter Blume und Friedhelm Mann, JAC, Ergänzungsband 10 (Münster: Aschendorff, 1983), 84–91.

43 The *editio princeps* opts for an origin in Qumran: Carol NEWSOM, *Songs of the Sabbath Sacrifice: A Critical Edition*, Harvard Semitic Studies 27 (Atlanta: Scholars Press, 1985), 4. For an introduction to prior academic discourse thereon see SCHÄFER, *The Origins of Jewish Mysticism*, 130f. Critical text edition: Carol NEWSOM, "Shirot 'Olat Hashabbat," in *Qumran Cave 4*, vol. 6/1, *Poetical and Liturgical Texts*, ed. Esther Eshel et al. (Oxford: Clarendon, 1998), 173–401. Cf. the German translation: Johann MAIER, *Die Qumran-Essener: Die Texte vom Toten Meer*, Bd. 2, *Die Texte der Höhle 4*, Uni-Taschenbücher 1863 (München: Reinhardt, 1995), 377–417.

44 Literally: "of a throne chariot's throne."

45 The term חשמל is taken from Ezek 1:27; its meaning remains uncertain: Wilhelm GESENIUS, *Hebräisches und Aramäisches Handwörterbuch über das Alte Testament*, begonnen v. Rudolf Meyer, unter zeitweiliger, verantwortlicher Mitarbeit von Udo Rüterswörden und Johannes Renz bearb. und hg. Herbert Donner, 18. Aufl. (Heidelberg: Springer, 2013), s.v. (p. 408f.), renders the meanings: "Bernstein," "Elektron," or "hellgelbe Goldlegierung."

46 4QShirShab after 4Q405 frag. 20 col. ii and frag. 21, lines 7–11. ET follows SCHÄFER, *The Origins of Jewish Mysticism*, 137. Cf. MAIER, *Die Qumran-Essener*, 2: 406f. An interpretation of all twelve songs may be found in Anna Maria SCHWEMER, "Gott als König und seine Königsherrschaft in den Sabbatliedern aus Qumran," in *Königsherrschaft Gottes und himmlischer Kult im Judentum, Urchristentum und in der hellenistischen Welt*, hg. Martin Hengel und Anna Maria Schwemer, WUNT 55 (Tübingen: Mohr Siebeck, 1991), 45–119, here 107–112.

47 SCHÄFER, *The Origins of Jewish Mysticism*, 137. Individual references also in NEWSOM, *Songs of the Sabbath Sacrifice*, 313 (lines 7f. and Ezek 1; also 10:16–17a), 314 (lines 8f. and Ezek 1:26), 315 (lines 9f. and Ezek 1:12–14), 315 (line 10 and Ezek 1:4, 27), and 316 (lines 10–11 and Ezek 1:28).

48 SCHÄFER, *The Origins of Jewish Mysticism*, 138.

49 Cf. 1 Kgs 19:12 and Job 4:16. Diverse parallels from Hekhalot literature in Laurence H. SCHIFFMAN, "Merkavah Speculation at Qumran: The 4Q Serekh Shirot Olat ha-Shabbat," in *Mystics, Philosophers, and Politicians: Essays in Jewish Intellectual History in Honor of Alexander Altmann*, ed. Jehuda Reinharz and Daniel Swetschinski with the collaboration of Kalman P. Bland, Duke Monographs in Medieval and Renaissance Studies 5 (Durham, N.C.: Duke University Press, 1982), 15–47, here 36f.; and Dale C. ALLISON, "The Silence of the Angels: Reflections on the Songs of the Sabbath Sacrifice," *Revue de Qumrân* 13 (1988): 189–197.

50 Thus also the emphatic interpretation of SCHÄFER, *The Origins of Jewish Mysticism*, 142–144.

51 See GRUENWALD, *Apocalyptic and Merkavah Mysticism*, 62–69; ROWLAND, *The Open Heaven*, 403–441; and also SCHÄFER, *The Origins of Jewish Mysticism*, 103–111. The text is located in the tradition of a merkava myticism by Christopher ROWLAND, "Things to Which Angels Long to Look: Approaching Mysticism from the Perspective of the New Testament and the Jewish Apocalypses," in Christopher ROWLAND and Christopher R. A. MORRAY-JONES, *The Mystery of God: Early Jewish Mysticism and the New Testament*, Compendia Rerum Iudaicarum ad Novum Testamentum 3/12 (Leiden/Boston, 2009), 3–215, here 72–90.

52 Thus Schäfer, *The Origins of Jewish Mysticism*, 105. The account of the biblical passage in Epiphanius, *De XII gemmis* 2.7 (here cited after *Epiphanius von Salamis: Über die zwölf Steine im hohepriesterlichen Brustschild (De duodecim gemmis rationalis)*, nach dem Codex Vaticanus Borgianus Armenus 31, hg. und übers. v. Felix Albrecht und Arthur Manukyan [Piscataway, N.J.: Gorgias, 2014], 46f.) demonstrates that the three stones mentioned in the revelation were chosen more or less at random from the ensemble of twelve (own translation, following ibid.): "Earlier were they thus set in four rows, for the breastplate was divided into four parts, and was itself quadrilateral: one handspan in length, and as broad as the length. At the beginning is sardion, the first stone, then topazion, then emerald; and in the second row the first stone is ruby, then saphire, and then jasper; and in the third row is lyngurium, then agate, and then amethyst; and in the fourth row, which is the last, the first stone is chrysolith, then beryl, then onyx. And these are the twelve stones, which were placed upon the breastplate hanging from the shoulders; this is their selection and order." Epiphanius identifies the emerald with Levi (12), jasper with Naphtali (28), and ruby with Ruben (8).

53 Schäfer, *The Origins of Jewish Mysticism*, 1. Kurt Ruh, *Geschichte der abendländischen Mystik*, Bd. 1, *Die Grundlegung durch die Kirchenväter und die Mönchstheologie des 12. Jahrhunderts* (München: Beck, 1990), 26: "Ich weiß also mit Flasch, dass 'Mystik' in geschichtlicher Darstellung wie alle epochalen Benennungen nur ein—freilich notwendiges—historiographisches Schema ist. Was 'Mystik' ist, erweist sich immer erst am konkreten Text." Ruh thus employs texts with recourse to "mysticism" within a corpus, and not a definition. For a justification, see idem, "Vorbemerkungen zu einer neuen Geschichte der abendländischen Mystik im Mittelalter," in idem, *Kleine Schriften*, Bd. 2, *Scholastik und Mystik im Mittelalter*, hg. Volker Mertens (Berlin/New York: De Gruyter, 1984), 337–363: "Es verhält sich also nicht so, daß es zuerst einer Begriffsbestimmung bedürfte, um die Schriften zusammenzustellen, die Gegenstand einer Geschichte der Mystik sein sollen. Da gibt es schon längst so etwas wie einen Kanon" (342f.).

54 Volker Leppin, *Die christliche Mystik*, C. H. Beck Wissen in der Beck'schen Reihe 2415 (München: Beck, 2007), 7. See also on this Louis Bouyer, "Mysticism: An Essay on the History of the Word," in *Understanding Mysticism*, ed. Richard Woods (London: Athlone Press, 1980), 42–55; and Michel de Certeau, "'Mystique' au XVIIᵉ siecle: Le probleme du langage 'mystique,'" in *L'Homme devant Dieu: Mélanges Henri de Lubac* (Paris: Aubier, 1964) 2: 267–291.

55 Pierre Chantraine, *Interférences de vocabulaire entre le grec et les langues européennes*, Studii clasice 2 (Bucarest: Ed. academiei republicii populare romîne, 1960), 69f.; Peter Heidrich, s.v. "Mystik, mystisch," in *Historisches Wörterbuch der Philosophie* (Darmstadt: Wissenschaftliche Buchgesellschaft, 1984), 6: 268–273, here 268f.; also the entry s.v. μύειν in Henry George Liddell and Robert Scott, *A Greek-English Lexicon*, rev. and augmented by Henry Stuart Jones with the assistance of Roderick McKenzie (Oxford: Clardendon Press, 1983), 1157.

56 Schäfer, *The Origins of Jewish Mysticism*, 1.

57 Suda H 450 (II, 579.24–29 Adler) = Damascius, *Vita Isidori* frag. 174 (Bibliotheca Graeca et Latina Suppletoria I, 148.1–6 Zintzen) = frag. 76 E (196 Athanassiadi). Parallels to the hushing index finger on the lips in Zintzen are found within the apparatus of the section. See also Clemens Zintzen, "Mystik und Magie in der neuplatonischen Philosophie," *Rheinisches Museum* 108 (1965): 71–100 = idem, *Athen—Rom—Florenz: Ausgewählte Kleine Schriften*, hg. Dorothee Gall und Peter Riemer (Hildesheim: Olms, 2000), 53–96.

58 Suda H 450 (II, 579.7–10 Adler) = Damascius, *Vita Isidori frag.* 174 (Bibliotheca Graeca et Latina Suppletoria I, 147.2–5 Zintzen) = frag. 76 E (194 Athanassiadi). Cf. the German translation in *Das Leben des Philosophen Isidoros von Damaskios aus Damaskos*, wiederhergestellt, übers. und erklärt v. Rudolf Asmus, Philosophische Bibliothek 125 (Leipzig: Meiner, 1911), 64.

59 On terminology, see also Christoph RIEDWEG, *Mysterienterminologie bei Platon, Philon und Klemens von Alexandrien*, Untersuchungen zur antiken Literatur und ihrer Geschichte 26 (Berlin/New York: De Gruyter, 1987), 158–161.

60 Proclus, *In Platonis Timaeum Commentaria* IV, *ad Platonis Timaeum* 37 D (BiTeu III, 12.27–30 DIEHL). Cf. ibid., *ad Platonis Timaeum* 39 E (BiTeu III, 99.9–11 DIEHL). See HEIDRICH, s.v. "Mystik, mystisch," 268.

61 Proclus, *In Platonis Parmenidem Commentaria* IV, *ad Platonis Parmenidem* 133 B (928.8f. COUSIN).

62 Reinhold MERKELBACH, *Mithras* (Königstein/Taunus: Hain, 1984), 245–250; Karl Leo NOETHLICHS, "Kaisertum und Heidentum im 5. Jahrhundert," in *Heiden und Christen im 5. Jahrhundert*, hg. Johannes van Oort und Dietmar Wyrwa, Studien der Patristischen Arbeitsgemeinschaft 5 (Leuven: Peeters, 1998), 1–31; and idem, s.v. "Heidenverfolgung," in *Reallexikon für Antike und Christentum* (Stuttgart: Hiersemann, 1986) 13: 1149–1190.

63 HEIDRICH, s.v. "Mystik, mystisch," 268. On the meaning of the word among antique Christian authors, see BOUYER, "Mysticism," 46–53.

64 Dionysius Cartusianus, *Sermo Septimus in Festo Johannis Apostolae et Evangelistae*, here cited according to *Sermones de Sanctis*, Pars Prima, Dionysii Cartusiani Opera omnia 31 (Tournai: Typis Cartusiae S.M. de Pratis, 1906), 206ᵇ A. On the author, see Peter DINZELBACHER, *Christliche Mystik im Abendland: Ihre Geschichte von den Anfängen bis zum Ende des Mittelalters* (Paderborn: Schöningh, 1994), 386f.

65 Jean Gerson, *De theologia mystica lectiones sex* IV 28 and VI 43 (Œuvres Complètes III, 273f. 289 GLORIEUX). On the parallels in Thomas and Bonaventura, see DINZELBACHER, *Christliche Mystik im Abendland*, 9f. n. 3; on the interpretation, see Walter DRESS, *Die Theologie Gersons* (Gütersloh: Bertelsmann, 1931), 51f., 91–107; Ulrich KÖPF, s.v. "Erfahrung III. Theologiegeschichtlich 1. Mittelalter und Reformation," *TRE* 10: 109–116, esp. 113; DINZELBACHER, *Christliche Mystik im Abendland*, 380–384; and Christoph BURGER, *Aedificatio, fructus, utilitas: Johannes Gerson als Professor der Theologie und Kanzler der Universität Paris*, BHT 70 (Tübingen: Mohr Siebeck, 1986), 125–143.

66 KÖPF, s.v. "Erfahrung III. Theologiegeschichtlich 1. Mittelalter und Reformation," 113, with reference to Jean Gerson, *De theologia mystica lectiones sex* IV 28 (Œuvres Complètes III, 273f. GLORIEUX).

67 Ps.-Dionysius Areopagita, *De mystica theologia* 1.1 (PTS 67², 141.3–142.4 RITTER). ET from *Pseudo-Dionysus: The Complete Works*, trans. Colm LUIBHEID (Mahwah, N.J.: Paulist Press, 1987), 135. On the history and usage of these expressions, see the evidence of Adolf Martin Ritter in the apparatus (expanded in the second edition) in *Pseudo-Dionysius Areopagita, Über die Mystische Theologie und Briefe*, eingel., übers. und erklärt von Adolf Martin RITTER, Bibliothek der Griechischen Literatur 40 (Stuttgart: Hiersemann, 1994), 74 (translation) and 81f. (commentary); Christoph MARKSCHIES, *Gibt es eine "Theologie der gotischen Kathedrale"? Nochmals: Suger von Saint-Denis und Sankt Dionys vom Areopag*, Abhandlungen der Heidelberger Akademie der Wissenschaften, Philosophisch-historische Klasse 1/1995 (Heidelberg: Winter, 1995), 61 n. 224; and RUH, *Geschichte der abendländischen Mystik*, 1: 59–71.

68 SCHOLEM, *Major Trends in Jewish Mysticism*, 5, cited in SCHÄFER, *The Origins of Jewish Mysticism*, 6.

69 Bernhard McGINN, *The Foundations of Mysticism*, vol. 1, *The Presence of God: A History of Western Christian Mysticism* (London: SCM Press, 1991), xif.; cited in SCHÄFER, *The Origins of Jewish Mysticism*, 7f.

70 McGINN, *The Presence of God*, 1: xvf.; cited approvingly by SCHÄFER, *The Origins of Jewish Mysticism*, 7f.

71 McGINN, *The Presence of God*, 1: xviif.: "The term mystical experience, consciously or unconsciously, also tends to place emphasis on special altered states—visions, locutions, rapture, and the like—which admittedly have played a large part in mysticism but which

many mystics have insisted do not constitute the essence of the encounter with God"; cited approvingly in Schäfer, *The Origins of Jewish Mysticism*, 8.

72 McGinn, *The Presence of God*, 1: xvii. For the shift from "experience" to "consciousness," see p. xx n. 17; McGinn refers to the Canadian theologian and philosopher of religion Bernard Lonergan (1904–1984); attestations on p. 345.

73 Scholem, *Major Trends in Jewish Mysticism*, 46–47

74 Scholem, *Major Trends in Jewish Mysticism*, 43; and Schäfer, *The Origins of Jewish Mysticism*, 11.

75 Scholem, *Major Trends in Jewish Mysticism*, 42–43.

76 Scholem, *Major Trends in Jewish Mysticism*, 40: "The first phase in the development of Jewish mysticism before its crystallization in the medieval Kabbalah is also its longest. Its literary remains are traceable over a period of almost a thousand years, from the first century B.C. to the tenth A.D." On criticism, see Schäfer, *The Origins of Jewish Mysticism*, 9–12.

77 Objections in Schäfer, *The Origins of Jewish Mysticism*, 12–20. See also Martha Himmelfarb, "Merkavah Mysticism since Scholem: Rachel Elior's *The Three Temples*," in *Wege mystischer Gotteserfahrung: Judentum, Christentum und Islam. Mystical Approaches to God: Judaism, Christianity, and Islam*, hg. Peter Schäfer unter Mitarbeit von Elisabeth Müller-Luckner, Schriften des Historischen Kollegs. Kolloquien 65 (München: Oldenbourg Verlag, 2006), 19–36; and idem, "Heavenly Ascent and the Relationship of the Apocalypses and the Hekhalot Literature," *Hebrew Union College Annual* 59 (1988): 73–100.

78 Rachel Elior, "From Earthly Temple to Heavenly Shrines: Prayer and Sacred Song in the Hekhalot Literature and its Relation to Temple Traditions," *Jewish Studies Quarterly* 4 (1997): 217–267; idem, *The Three Temples: On the Emergence of Jewish Mysticism*, The Littman Library of Jewish Civilization (Oxford/Portland, Ore.: Littman Library of Jewish Civilization, 2004).

79 Rachel Elior, "The Foundations of Early Jewish Mysticism: The Lost Calendar and the Transformed Heavenly Chariot," in Schäfer, *Wege mystischer Gotteserfahrung*, 1–18, here 11: "and to the cycles of divine worship and sacred song that were performed in the Temple." See also idem, *The Three Temples*, 63–81.

80 Elior, *The Three Temples*, 165–265. See also Himmelfarb, "Merkavah Mysticism since Scholem," 29–34; and Schäfer, *The Origins of Jewish Mysticism*, 14f. Not considered in the present context are not only the argumentation for the parallelism between earthly and heavenly sanctuary on the strength of calendars, but also the criticism of this interpretation of contemporary calendars, for example, from Qumran; see on this Sacha Stern, "Rachel Elior on Ancient Jewish Calendars: A Critique," *Aleph* 5 (2005): 287–292.

81 Newsom, *Songs of the Sabbath Sacrifice*; James H. Charlesworth and Carol A. Newsom, eds., *Angelic Liturgy: Songs of the Sabbath Sacrifice*, The Dead Sea Scrolls 4B (Tübingen: Mohr Siebeck, 1999); Joseph M. Baumgarten, "The Qumran Sabbath Shirot and Rabbinic Merkabah Traditions," *Révue de Qumrân* 13 (1988): 199–213; and Elisabeth Hamacher, "Die Sabbatopferlieder im Streit um Ursprung und Anfänge der jüdischen Mystik," *JSJ* 27 (1996): 119–154.

82 Elior, *The Three Temples*, 31–33. Summary and criticism in Himmelfarb, "Merkavah Mysticism since Scholem," 23.

83 Andrei A. Orlov, *The Enoch-Metatron Tradition*, TSAJ 107 (Tübingen: Mohr Siebeck, 2005), 3–6. On this, see also Schäfer, *The Origins of Jewish Mysticism*, 12–14.

84 This is common within angelology: Johann Michl, s.v. "Engel II (jüdisch)," in *Reallexikon für Antike und Christentum* (Stuttgart: Hiersemann, 1962), 5: 60–97, here 69–72.

85 Schäfer, *The Origins of Jewish Mysticism*, 138.

86 Schäfer, *The Origins of Jewish Mysticism*, 177.

87 Tosefta Megilla 4.6 (228.1 Zuckermandel after MS Erfurt). Cf. *Die Tosefta*, Bd. 2/4, *Seder Moëd: Taanijjot—Megilla*, übers. und erklärt von Günter Mayer und Carola Krieg, Rabbinische Texte, Reihe 1: Die Tosefta (Stuttgart: Kohlhammer, 2002), 135. Detailed

commentary on the passage in SCHÄFER, *The Origins of Jewish Mysticism*, 177–179; and HALPERIN, *The Faces of the Chariot*, 12f.

88 Mishnah Megilla 4.10. Here quoted according to *Megilla: Rolle*, bearbeitet von Michael Krupp, Die Mischna, Textkritische Ausgabe mit deutscher Übersetzung und Kommentar (Jerusalem: Lee Achim Sefarim, 2002), 25. On the passage, in depth, see HALPERIN, *The Faces of the Chariot*, 20–23.

89 David J. HALPERIN, *The Merkabah in Rabbinic Literature*, American Oriental Studies 62 (New Haven, Conn.: American Oriental Society, 1980), 39–63. On this, critically, see SCHÄFER, *The Origins of Jewish Mysticism*, 179f.

90 Mishnah Chagiga 2.1. On the interpretation, see most recently SCHÄFER, *The Origins of Jewish Mysticism*, 180–185 (translation from 181); and, earlier already, HALPERIN, *The Merkabah in Rabbinic Literature*, 19–27; also idem, *The Faces of the Chariot*, 23–25. In the following section, I have drawn in part upon the observations made during an advanced seminar in Tübingen in the winter semester of 1987/1988 convened under the direction of Martin Hengel (1926–2009) and developed in the previously mentioned advanced seminars with Peter Schäfer in Berlin and Princeton.

91 Origenes/Rufinus, *Commentarium in Cantica Canticorum Prologus* 1.7 (GCS Origenes VIII, 62.22–30 BAEHRENS = SC 375, 84–86 BRÉSARD/CROUZEL/BORRET). ET after SCHÄFER, *The Origins of Jewish Mysticism*, 183. On the passage, see Nicholas R. M. DE LANGE, *Origen and the Jews: Studies in Jewish-Christian Relations in Third-Century Palestine*, University of Cambridge Oriental Publications 25 (Cambridge: Cambridge University Press, 1976), 34f. (on δευτερώσεις) and 60f. (on the passage more generally).

92 SCHÄFER, *The Origins of Jewish Mysticism*, 184f.

93 MCGINN, *The Foundations of Mysticism*, 1: xix.

94 Tosefta Chagiga 2.3 (234.7f. ZUCKERMANDEL). On the interpretation of this story transmitted in multiple variants (Talmud Yerushalmi Chagiga 2.1 [fol. 77b 8–12]; Talmud Bavli Chagiga 14–15b), see SCHOLEM, *Major Trends in Jewish Mysticism*, 52f; Peter SCHÄFER, "New Testament and Hekhalot Literature: The Journey into Heaven in Paul and Merkavah Mysticism," in idem, *Hekhalot-Studien*, TSAJ 19 (Tübingen: Mohr Siebeck, 1988), 234–249, esp. 238–246; idem, *The Origins of Jewish Mysticism*, 196–203; HALPERIN, *The Merkabah in Rabbinic Literature*, 86–92, 107–109; and idem, *The Faces of the Chariot*, 31–37. The "other" (אחר) of the four rabbis is the usually only anonymously described Rabbi Elisha Ben Abuyah, a tannaite of the second generation discredited as a heretic.

95 Tosefta Chagiga 2.3 (234.8f. ZUCKERMANDEL). The sentence is only transmitted within the Viennese MS; cf. ibid., 2.4 (234.11)

96 On this paradoxical terminology and its obscure history, see Peter SCHÄFER, *The Hidden and Manifest God: Some Major Themes in Early Jewish Mysticism*, trans. Aubrey Pomerance (Albany: State University of New York Press, 1992), 2–3 n. 4 (= idem, *Der verborgene und der offenbare Gott: Hauptthemen der frühen jüdischen Mystik* [Tübingen: Mohr Siebeck, 1991]); and already SCHOLEM, *Major Trends in Jewish Mysticism*, 47.

97 SCHÄFER, *The Origins of Jewish Mysticism*, 197f. Cf. on this Talmud Yerushalmi Chagiga 2.1 (fol. 77b 8–12): "one entered in peace and exited in peace." Cf. *Hagiga: Festopfer*, übers. von Gerd A. Wewers, Übersetzung des Talmud Yerushalmi II/1 (Tübingen: Mohr Siebeck, 1983), 37.

98 *Synopse zur Hekhalot-Literatur*, hg. Peter SCHÄFER, Margarete Schlüter und Hans Georg von Mutius, TSAJ 2 (Tübingen: Mohr Siebeck, 1981); and Peter SCHÄFER, *Geniza-Fragmente zur Hekhalot-Literatur*, TSAJ 6 (Tübingen: Mohr Siebeck, 1984). Additionally drawn upon is Martin S. COHEN, *The Shi'ur Qomah: Texts and Recensions*, TSAJ 9 (Tübingen: Mohr Siebeck, 1985). See the overview and history of research in Ra'Anan S. BOUSTAN, "The Study of Heikhalot Literature: Between Mystical Experience and Textual Artifact," *Currents in Biblical Research* 6 (2007): 130–160. Central is a sentence from the introduction to the *Synopse*: "Vorgelegt werden nicht bestimmte Texte der *Hekhalot*-Literatur, d.h.

festumrissene und endredigierte *Schriften*, die zur 'Gattung' *Hekhalot*-Literatur zählen, sondern *Handschriften*" (op. cit., v).

99 *Synopse zur Hekhalot-Literatur* § 597 after N8128 (230.47–49 SCHÄFER). ET from the German of *Übersetzung der Hekhalot-Literatur*, vol. 5, §§ 335–597, in Zusammenarbeit mit Klaus Herrmann, Lucie Renner, Claudia Rohrbacker-Sticker und Stefan Siebers, hg. Peter Schäfer, TSAJ 22 (Tübingen: Mohr Siebeck, 1989), 338. N8128 denotes MS 8128 of the Kabbalah of the Jewish Theological Seminary.

100 *Synopse zur Hekhalot-Literatur* § 338 (Hekhalot Zutarti, N8128; 144.12 SCHÄFER; only quoted with introductory formula). Full wording in § 344 as a statement of Rabbi Aqiba in the first person (146.6–9 SCHÄFER). Also transmitted more literally in the macroform *Merkava Rabba* in § 672 (246.57f. SCHÄFER).

101 As an introduction, see SCHÄFER, *The Origins of Jewish Mysticism*, 243f.; and idem, *The Hidden and Manifest God*, 5–8. The Third Book of Enoch was generally cited from a ubiquitous albeit not unproblematic edition prior to the publication of the *Synopse*: *3 Henoch or the Hebrew Book of Henoch*, ed. and trans. for the first time with introduction, commentary, and critical notes by Hugo Odeberg (Cambridge: Cambridge University Press, 1928).

102 On this, see Klaus HERRMANN, "Text und Fiktionen: Zur Textüberlieferung des Shi'ur Qoma," *Frankfurter Judaistische Beiträge* 16 (1988): 89–142.

103 SCHÄFER, *The Origins of Jewish Mysticism*, 307 with n. 279, where Schäfer indicates that, in the introduction to the *Synopse* and in *Übersetzung der Hekhalot-Literatur*, vol. 4, §§ 598–985, in Zusammenarbeit mit Klaus Herrmann, Lucie Renner, Claudia Rohrbacker-Sticker und Stefan Siebers, hg. Peter SCHÄFER, TSAJ 29 (Tübingen: Mohr Siebeck, 1991), xxxif., he handled these sections as "a macroform 'Shi'ur Qomah' of its own."

104 *Synopse zur Hekhalot-Literatur* §§ 688, 692, and 948 (253.33f., 252.60 [only in N8128], and 294.17). See also SCHÄFER, *Übersetzung der Hekhalot-Literatur*, xxxii.

105 *Synopse zur Hekhalot-Literatur* § 688 after O1531 (252.30–33 SCHÄFER). O1531 refers to MS Oxford, Bodleian Library Michael 9 = Neubauer 1531, saec. XIV.

106 SCHÄFER, *The Hidden and Manifest God*, 15f.

107 *Synopse zur Hekhalot-Literatur* § 159 after O1531 (70.8–10 SCHÄFER).

108 *Synopse zur Hekhalot-Literatur* § 102 after O1531 (48.39f. SCHÄFER). Quoted from *Übersetzung der Hekhalot-Literatur*, vol. 2, §§ 81–334, in Zusammenarbeit mit Hans-Jürgen Becker, Klaus Herrmann, Claudia Rohrbacker-Sticker und Stefan Siebers, hg. Peter SCHÄFER, TSAJ 17 (Tübingen: Mohr Siebeck, 1987), 22. On this topic, see also Raphael LOEWE, "The Divine Garment and Shi'ur Qomah," *HTR* 58 (1965): 153–160.

109 *Synopse zur Hekhalot-Literatur* § 335 after O1531 (142.41–43 SCHÄFER). Quoted from *Übersetzung der Hekhalot-Literatur*, vol. 3, §§ 335–597, in Zusammenarbeit mit Klaus Herrmann, Lucie Renner, Claudia Rohrbacher-Sticker und Stefan Siebers, hg. Peter SCHÄFER, TSAJ 22 (Tübingen: Mohr Siebeck, 1989), 1.

110 *Synopse zur Hekhalot-Literatur* § 407 after O1531 (172.2–5 SCHÄFER). The expression לראות מלך ביופיו, "to behold the king in his beauty," stems from Isa 33:17, and recurs repeatedly in the *Hekhalot Zutarti* (§ 407, 408, 409, 411 etc); also in § 248 (110.21 SCHÄFER) and Genizah Fragment G 8, fol. 2b, 18f. 23 (*Geniza-Fragmente zur Hekhalot-Literatur*, 105). On its interpretation, see SCHÄFER, *The Hidden and Manifest God*, 57–60.

111 Helmer RINGGREN, s.v. "יפה," in *Theologisches Wörterbuch zum Alten Testament* (Stuttgart: Kohlhammer, 1982), 3: 787–790, here 789. See also Alexandra GRUND, "'Aus der Schönheit Vollendung strahlt Gott auf' (Ps 50:2): Bemerkungen zur Wahrnehmung des Schönen in den Psalmen," in *"Wie schön sind deine Zelte, Jakob!" Beiträge zur Ästhetik des Alten Testaments*, hg. Alexandra Grund u.a., Biblisch-Theologische Studien 60 (Neukirchen-Vluyn: Neukirchener, 2003), 100–129; and Silvia SCHROER und Thomas STAUBLI, *Die Körpersymbolik der Bibel* (Darmstadt: Wissenschaftliche Buchgesellschaft, 1998), 24–29.

112 Plotinus, *Enneades* I 6 (Περὶ τοῦ καλοῦ) 9.44 (PhB 211a, 24.40–45 HARDER). Cf. *Enneades* VI 2 18.134f. (PhB 214a, 218.1–8 HARDER); VI 2 18.134f. (PhB 214a, 218.1–8

HARDER); and VI 7 33.255 (PhB 213a, 332.21f. HARDER). See A. Hilary ARMSTRONG, "Beauty and the Discovery of Divinity in the Thought of Plotinus," in *Kephalaion: Studies in Greek Philosophy and Its Continuation Offered to Cornelia Johanna de Vogel*, ed. Jaap Mansfeld and Lambertus Marie de Rijk, Philosophical Texts and Studies 23 (Assen: Van Gorcum, 1975), 155–163 = idem, *Plotinian and Christian Studies*, Variorum Collected Studies Series 102 (Farnham: Ashgate, 1979), nr. XIX; Glenn W. MOST, s.v. "Schöne (das)," in *Historisches Wörterbuch der Philosophie* (Darmstadt: Wissenschaftliche Buchgesellschaft, 1992), 8: 1343–1351; and Mark J. EDWARDS, "Middle Platonism on the Beautiful and the Good," *Mnemosyne* 44 (1991): 161–167.

113 Proclus, *Theologia Platonis* I 24 (CUFr I, 106.6–10 SAFFREY/WESTERINK). Cf. ibid., III 11 (CUFr III, 44.14–17 SAFFREY/WESTERINK) (referring to Plato, *Epistula* 2, 312 E). See on this Christos TEREZIS and Kalomoira POLYCHRONOPOULOU, "The Sense of Beauty (κάλλος) in Proclus the Neoplatonist," in *Neoplatonism and Western Aesthetics*, ed. Aphrodite Alexandrakis and Nicholas J. Moutafakis, Studies in Neoplatonism, Ancient and Modern 12 (Albany: State University of New York Press, 2002), 53–60; and Sergei MARIEV, "Proklos and Plethon on Beauty," in *Aesthetics and Theurgy in Byzantium*, ed. Sergei Mariev and Wiebke-Marie Stock, Byzantinisches Archiv 25 (Berlin/Boston: De Gruyter, 2013), 57–74, here 62–65.

114 (Ps.-?) Plato, *Hippias maior* 296 E.

115 Plotinus, *Enneades* V 5 12.81 (PhB 213a, 98.34–37 HARDER). ET from *Plotinus*, vol. 5, trans. A. H. ARMSTRONG, LCL 444 (Cambridge, Mass./London: Harvard University Press, 1984), 193.

116 Ps.-Dionysius Areopagita, *De divinis nominibus* 4.7 (PTS 33, 151.2–7 SUCHLA). ET from LUIBHEID *Pseudo-Dionysius: The Complete Works*, 76. See also Dimitrios N. KOUTRAS, "The Beautiful according to Dionysius," in Alexandrakis and Moutafakis, *Neoplatonism and Western Aesthetics*, 31–40; and Jens HALFWASSEN, "Schönheit und Bild im Neuplatonismus," in *Neuplatonismus und Ästhetik: Zur Transformationsgeschichte des Schönen*, hg. Verena Olejniczak Lobsien und Claudia Olk, Transformationen der Antike 2 (Berlin/New York: De Gruyter, 2007), 43–57, here 45–47.

117 *Synopse zur Hekhalot-Literatur* § 352 after O1531 (148.19 SCHÄFER). Cf. Ezek 1:14.

118 *Synopse zur Hekhalot-Literatur* § 352 after O1531 (148.22f. SCHÄFER). ET from SCHÄFER, *The Hidden and Manifest God*, 58; and idem, *The Origins of Jewish Mysticism*, 290–292.

119 *Synopse zur Hekhalot-Literatur* § 356 after O1531 (150.24f. SCHÄFER).

120 Cf. SCHÄFER, *Übersetzung der Hekhalot-Literatur*, 4: xxxii: München, Bayerische Staatsbibliothek Cod. Hebr. 40, saec. XV; München, Bayerische Staatsbibliothek Cod. Hebr. 22, saec. XVI; MS Cambridge Taylor-Schechter Cairo Genizah Collection K. 21.95.C (= G8), saec. XI; MS Oxford Hebr. C. 65.6 (= G9), saec. XI; MS Cambridge Taylor-Schechter K. 21.95.I (G4), saec. XII; MS Cambridge Taylor-Schechter K. 21.95.H (G10), saec. XI; MS Cambridge Taylor-Schechter K. 21.95.J (G11), late.

121 COHEN, *The Shi'ur Qomah*. Cohen also published his doctoral dissertation completed at the Jewish Theological Seminary in New York in 1983: idem, *The Shi'ur Qomah: Liturgy and Theurgy in Pre-Kabbalistic Jewish Mysticism* (Lanham, Md./London: University Press of America, 1983).

122 "Die literarische Entwicklung der verschiedenen Fassungen des *Shi'ur Qoma* genannten Textes gehört zu den kompliziertesten und rätselhaftesten Phänomenen der spätantiken/frühmittelalterlichen jüdischen Literaturgeschichte." Peter SCHÄFER, "*Shi'ur Qoma*: Rezensionen und Urtext," in idem, *Hekhalot-Studien*, TSAJ 19 (Tübingen: Mohr Siebeck, 1988), 75–83, here 75.

123 COHEN, *The Shi'ur Qomah*, 1–5 (quotation p. 5): London British Library Or. 10675 = Gaster MS 187. On criticism, see SCHÄFER, "*Shi'ur Qoma*," 75f. Schäfer's edition is based upon MS 40 = München, Bayerische Staatsbibliothek, Cod. Hebr. 40, saec. XV.

124 COHEN, *The Shi'ur Qomah*, 77–124 and 125–128.

125 See the brief summary of the criticism in the introduction of SCHÄFER, *Übersetzung der Hekhalot-Literatur*, 4: xxxiii; in more depth, SCHÄFER, "*Shi'ur Qoma*," 81–83; and *Massekhet Hekhalot: Traktat von den himmlischen Palästen; Edition, Übersetzung und Kommentar*, hg. Klaus HERRMANN, TSAJ 39 (Tübingen: Mohr Siebeck, 1994), 76–91.

126 SCHÄFER, *The Origins of Jewish Mysticism*, 307.

127 Gershom SCHOLEM, *Jewish Gnosticism, Merkabah Mysticism, and Talmudic Tradition: Based on the Israel Goldstein Lectures, Delivered at the Jewish Theological Seminary of America, New York* (New York: Jewish Theological Seminary of America, 1965), 6f.

128 *Synopse zur Hekhalot-Literatur*, vii: "jemals selbständige Einheiten im Sinne von 'fertig redigierten' Schriften gewesen sind."

129 Herodotus, *Historiae* II 6.3 (BiTeu I, 142.11–13 ROSÉN). Cf. *Suda* Π 427 (IV, 40.25 ADLER); Hesychius Π 659 (Sammlung griechischer und lateinischer Grammatiker 11/3, 32 HANSEN); and Xenophon, *Expeditio Cyri* II 2.6 (BiTeu 53.13f. HUDE/PETERS). Nevertheless, breaking with Herodotus and Xenophon, the sixth-century AD Byzantine historian Agathias notes in *Historiae* II 21 (Corpus Fontium Historiae Byzantinae II, 68.22–24 KEYDELL) that in his own time the Persians only counted twenty-one *stadia* to a parasang. Strabo (XI 11.5 [BiTeu II, 728.9–11 MEINEKE]) reports that some equate the parasang with sixty, and others with forty or thirty *stadia*.

130 *Synopse zur Hekhalot-Literatur* § 939 after M40 (293.30 SCHÄFER). Rabbi Yisma'el is the chief protagonist of the *Hekhalot Rabbati* and *Merkava Rabba*; in *Hekhalot Zutarti* it is Rabbi Aqiba.

131 *Synopse zur Hekhalot-Literatur* § 950 after M40 (294.50–53 SCHÄFER). ET after the German of SCHÄFER, *Übersetzung der Hekhalot-Literatur*, 4: 164f.

132 M22: four thousand, albeit M22 has "eight" for the number of miles in a parasang (295.53–55 SCHÄFER). Manuscript M22 hence does not fundamentally provide the better figures, but is rather a sign that, in the process of transmission, the numbers in M22 and M40 lost their order.

133 Vitruvius, *De architectura* III 1.7 (CUFr III, 10 GROS). Cf. ibid., III 1.3 (CUFr III, 7 GROS).

134 HERRMANN, *Massekhet Hekhalot*, 222–225. Herrmann quotes and compares four parallel versions of this sentence; that from *Synopse zur Hekhalot-Literatur* § 950 is held by him to be "possibly the oldest form of this . . . tradition."

135 *Synopse zur Hekhalot-Literatur* § 950 (294.52 SCHÄFER).

136 Johannes ZACHHUBER, s.v. "Überseiend; überwesentlich," in *Historisches Wörterbuch der Philosophie* (Darmstadt: Wissenschaftliche Buchgesellschaft, 2001), 11: 58–63.

137 Cf. on this Macrobius, *Saturnalia* I 20.16f. (SCBO 116.14–17 KASTER = PEG II/2 [Orphicorum et Orphicis similium testimonia et fragmenta], frag. 861, 381 BERNABÉ = *Orphicorum fragmenta*, 265 KERN).

138 *Synopse zur Hekhalot-Literatur* § 699 after O1531 (256.32f. SCHÄFER).

139 *Oracula Chaldaica frag.* 150 (CUFr 103 DES PLACES) = Psellus, Ἐξήγησις τῶν Χαλδαϊκῶν ῥητῶν (PG 122, 1132 c 1): ὀνόματα βάρβαρα μήποτ᾽ ἀλλάξῃς. On the topic, see Fritz GRAF, *Gottesnähe und Schadenzauber: Die Magie in der griechisch-römischen Antike* (München: Beck, 1996), 195–198; and, for the Jewish literature, Peter SCHÄFER, "Jewish Liturgy and Magic," in *Geschichte—Tradition—Reflexion: Festschrift für Martin Hengel zum 70. Geburtstag*, vol. 1, *Judentum*, hg. Peter Schäfer u.a. (Tübingen: Mohr Siebeck, 1996), 541–555; and Hans-Jürgen BECKER, "The Magic of the Name and Palestinian Rabbinic Literature," in *The Talmud Yerushalmi and Graeco-Roman Culture*, ed. Peter Schäfer, TSAJ 93 (Tübingen: Mohr Siebeck, 2002), 391–407. See also Naomi JANOWITZ, "God's Body: Theological and Ritual Roles of *Shi'ur Komah*," in *People of the Body: Jews and Judaism from an Embodied Perspective*, ed. Howard Eilberg-Schwartz (Albany: State University of New York Press, 1992), 183–201.

140 Iamblichus, *De mysteriis* VII 5 (CUFr 168.15–21 SAFFREY/SEGONDS/LECERF). ET from *Iamblichus: De mysteriis*, translated with an introduction and notes by Emma C. CLARKE,

John M. DILLON, and Jackson P. HERSHBELL, Writings from the Greco-Roman World 4 (Atlanta: Society of Biblical Literature, 2003), 299.

141 Iamblichus, *De mysteriis* VII 5 (CUFr 193.5–7 SAFFREY/SEGONDS/LECERF). ET from CLARKE/DILLON/HERSHBELL, *Iamblichus: De mysteriis*, 303.

142 HERMANN, *Massekhet Hekhalot*, 223f.

143 Heinrich GRAETZ, "Die mystische Literatur in der gaonäischen Epoche," *Monatsschrift für Geschichte und Wissenschaft des Judentums* 8 (1859): 67–78, 103–118, and 140–153 (citation from p. 115); Adolf JELLINEK, hg., *Beth ha-Midrasch: Sammlung kleiner Midraschim und vermischter Abhandlungen aus der ältern jüdischen Literatur*, nach Handschriften und Druckwerken gesammelt und nebst Einleitungen hg., Tl. 6 (Jerusalem: Bamberger & Wahrmann, 1938 [= Leipzig/Vienna: Wahrmann, 1877]), xxxxiif.; Moses GASTER, "Das Schiur Komah," *Monatsschrift für Geschichte und Wissenschaft des Judentums* 37 (1893): 179–185, 213–230 = idem, *Studies and Texts*, vol. 2 (New York: KTAV, 1971), 1330–1353; Gershom SCHOLEM, *Origins of the Kabbalah*, ed. R. J. Zwi Werblowsky, trans. Allan Arkush (Princeton, N.J.: Princeton University Press, 1987) 19; idem, *Jewish Gnosticism, Merkabah Mysticism, and Talmudic Tradition*, 36–42; and idem, *The Origins of Jewish Mysticism*, 6–23. On prior research, see also SCHÄFER, *Übersetzung der Hekhalot-Literatur*, 4: xxxvii.

144 Hugo ODEBERG, ed., *3 Enoch, or The Hebrew Book of Enoch*, trans. for the first time with introduction, commentary, and critical notes by Hugo Odeberg (Cambridge: Cambridge University Press, 1928), 38: "This points to a place and time of composition (*i.e., redaction*) such as the Jewish colonies in Babylonia during the third and fourth centuries." SCHOLEM was less than amenable in regard to this edition, as is demonstrated by his remarkably pointed rezension: *Orientalische Literaturzeitung* 33 (1930): 193–197; SCHÄFER's judgment is more reconciliatory: *Übersetzung der Hekhalot-Literatur*, 1: xliv–xlix.

145 The inaugurator of this avenue of research was Moritz FRIEDLÄNDER (1842–1919, Secretary of the "Israelitischen Allianz zu Wien" from 1874 onwards): *Der vorchristliche jüdische Gnosticismus* (Göttingen: Vandenhoeck & Ruprecht, 1898). On this topic, see also Joseph DAN, "Jewish Gnosticism?" in *Jewish Studies Quarterly* 2 (1995): 309–328; and Klaus HERRMANN, "Jüdische Gnosis? Dualismus und 'gnostische' Motive in der frühen jüdischen Mystik," in *Zugänge zur Gnosis: Akten zur Tagung der Patristischen Arbeitsgemeinschaft vom 02.–05.01.2011 in Berlin-Spandau*, hg. Christoph Markschies und Johannes van Oort, Studien der Patristischen Arbeitsgemeinschaft 12 (Leuven/Walpole, Mass.: Peeters, 2013), 43–90 (on Scholem, pp. 44–48).

146 SCHÄFER, *The Origins of Jewish Mysticism*, 313–315.

147 On Metatron and various explanations of his name, see Friedrich AVEMARIE, "Rivalität zwischen Gott und seinen Paladinen. Beobachtungen zum Monotheismus in der rabbinischen Literatur," in *Gott–Götter–Götzen: XIV. Europäischer Kongress für Theologie (11.–15. September 2011 in Zürich)*, hg. Christoph Schwöbel, Veröffentlichungen der wissenschaftlichen Gesellschaft für Theologie 38 (Leipzig: Evangelische Verlagsanstalt, 2013), 353–366, esp. 357–363; and previously already ODEBERG, *3 Enoch, or The Hebrew Book of Enoch*, 79–146; and ORLOV, *The Enoch-Metatron Tradition*, 92–96.

148 Remark in brackets according to the Geniza Fragment T.-S. K 21.95.C (= G8): SCHÄFER, *Geniza-Fragmente zur Hekhalot-Literatur*, 106 (text relayed in the following note).

149 *Synopse zur Hekhalot-Literatur* § 939 after M40 (293.30–36 SCHÄFER). ET after the German of SCHÄFER, *Übersetzung der Hekhalot-Literatur*, 4: 136f. The point marked by (+) is inserted into the ET from the Genizah Fragment G8.

150 The angelic name מטטרון or מיטטרון was explained by ODEBERG as ὁ μετὰ θρόνον, the angel "who sits by the godly throne" (*3 Enoch, or The Hebrew Book of Enoch*, 136–142). SCHOLEM, *Major Trends in Jewish Mysticism*, 69f., objected that a Greek equivalent such as *μετάθρονος is lacking, and θρόνος is not attested as an exonym in Hebrew: "It is quite possible that the word Metatron was chosen on strictly symbolical grounds and represents one of the innumerable secret names which abound in the Hekhalot texts no less

than in the gnostical writings or in the magical papyri." ORLOV, *The Enoch-Metatron Tra-dition*, 93–96, mentions as a further explanation the Koine variant of Greek σύνθρονος, "throne companion" (Saul LIEBERMAN in GRUENWALD, *Apocalyptic and Merkavah Mysti-cism*, 235–241; see also SCHÄFER, *The Hidden and Manifest God*, 29f. n. 70).

151   Such a derivation is first to be found in Samuel KRAUSS, *Griechische und lateinische Lehnwörter im Talmud, Midrasch und Targum*, mit Bemerkungen von Immanuel LÖW (Berlin: Calvary, 1899 = Hildesheim: Olms, 1987), 1: 250–252; and then in Adolph JEL-LINEK, *Beiträge zur Geschichte der Kabbala* (Leipzig: Fritzsche, 1852), 2: 4f., who also refers to the term μέτρον. Of a similar mind is Guy G. STROUMSA, "Form(s) of God: Some Notes on Metatron and Christ," *HTR* 76 (1983): 269–288, here 287. Latin *meta-tor*, "measurer," explains מטטרון or מיטטרון; see also AVEMARIE, "Rivalität zwischen Gott und seinen Paladinen," 357 n. 17 with reference to Midrash Bereshit Rabba 5.5 (34.6 THEODOR/ALBECK). On this, in detail, see Peter SCHÄFER, *Die Geburt des Judentums aus dem Geist des Christentums*, Tria Corda, Jenaer Vorlesungen zu Judentum, Antike und Christentum 6 (Tübingen: Mohr Siebeck, 2010), 107–132.

152   In Hebrew, רבבות reflects Greek μυριάς, that is, ten thousand.

153   *Synopse zur Hekhalot-Literatur* § 167 after B238 (Budapest, Rabbinerseminar, Kaufmann 238, saec. XV; here cited after 75.39f. SCHÄFER).

154   *Synopse zur Hekhalot-Literatur* § 167 after N8128 and V228 (New York, Jewish Theo-logical Seminary 8128 saec. XV/XVI and Biblioteca Apostolica Vaticana, Vat. Ebr. 228; here cited after 75.22–24/74.24–26 SCHÄFER).

155   *Synopse zur Hekhalot-Literatur* § 376: 2,360,000 with M40 (§ 728); by contrast, in N8128 (158.21f. SCHÄFER): "230 myriad parasangs." Cf. SCHÄFER, *Übersetzung der Hekhalot-Literatur*, 3: 73 n. 21.

156   Hildebrecht HOMMEL, *Symmetrie im Spiegel der Antike*, Sitzungsberichte der Heidelberger Akademie der Wissenschaften, Philosophisch-historische Klasse 5/1986 (Heidelberg: Winter, 1987), 21–23 (with attestations).

157   Galenus, *De placitis Hippocratis et Platonis* V 3.15 (CMG V 4/1/2, 308.17–21 DE LACY). ET from Andrew STEWART, "The Canon of Polykleitos: A Question of Evidence," *JHS* 98 (1978): p. 125 n. 23. The first part of the quotation was ascribed by Hans VON ARNIM to Chrysippus, from the first book of whose work *De affectionibus* Galen quotes according to his own statements: op. cit., V 3.12 (308.4): SVF III, 472 (III, 122.23f. VON ARNIM). See also Arbogast SCHMITT, "Symmetrie und Schönheit: Plotins Kritik an hellenistischen Proportionslehren und ihre unterschiedliche Wirkungsgeschichte in Mittelalter und früher Neuzeit," in *Neuplatonismus und Ästhetik: Zur Transformationsgeschichte des Schönen*, hg. Verena Olejniczak Lobsien und Claudia Olk, Transformationen der Antike 2 (Berlin/New York: De Gruyter, 2007), 59–84, here 60f.; and also Hans Jürgen HORN, "Stoische Symmetrie und Theorie des Schönen in der Kaiserzeit," *ANRW* II/36.3: 1454–1472, esp. 1458–1462.

158   Naturally, this does not concern the harmonious motions of a harmoniously proportioned body as evidently in Polycleitus.

159   Hanna PHILIPP, "Zu Polyklets Schrift 'Kanon,'" in *Polyklet: Der Bildhauer der griech-ischen Klassik; Ausstellung im Liebieghaus Museum alter Plastik Frankfurt am Main*, hg. Herbert Beck, Peter C. Bol und Maraike Bückling (Mainz: Zabern, 1990), 135–155.

160   PHILIPP, "Zu Polyklets Schrift 'Kanon,'" 139.

161   Vitruvius, *De architectura* III 1.3 (138 FENSTERBUSCH). ET from *Vitruvius: On Architec-ture, Books 1–5*, trans. Frank GRANGER, LCL 251 (Cambridge, Mass.: Harvard University Press; London: William Heinemann, 1931), 161. On the passage, see Frank ZÖLLNER, *Vitruvs Proportionsfigur: Quellenkritische Studien zur Kunstliteratur im 15. und 16. Jahrhundert*, Manuskripte für Kunstwissenschaft in der Wernerschen Verlagsgesellschaft (Worms: Werner, 1987), 1–10.

162   Vitruvius, *De architectura* III 1.2 (136 FENSTERBUSCH). On the passage, see Nikolaus SPE-ICH, *Die Proportionslehre des menschlichen Körpers: Antike, Mittelalter, Renaissance*

(Andelfingen: Akeret, 1957), 57–70; and generally on ancient metrology, see Friedrich HULTSCH, *Griechische und römische Metrologie*, 2. Aufl. (Berlin: Weidmann, 1882), 30–74.

163   See ZÖLLNER, *Vitruvs Proportionsfigur*, 77–82.

164   Accordingly PHILIPP, "Zu Polyklets Schrift 'Kanon,'" 137, with reference to a quotation from Philo Mechanicus, *Mechanicae Syntaxis* IV 1 p. 50.7–9 = DK 40 B 2 (I, 393.5 DIELS/ KRANZ).

165   Plutarchus, *Moralia 3, De audiendo* 13, 45 C/D (BiTeu I, 91.4–6 PATON/WEGEHAUPT/ POHLENZ). ET from BABBITT, *Plutarch: Moralia*, 243. This is likely an allusion to the principles of the Canon of Polycleitus or even a literal citation, certainly according to Dietrich SCHULZ, "Zum Kanon Polyklets," *Hermes* 83 (1955): 200–220, esp. 201f.

166   Galenus, *De temperamentis* I 9 (BiTeu 42, HELMREICH = DK 40 A 3 [I, 391.22 DIELS/ KRANZ]). ET from STEWART, "The Canon of Polykleitos," 125 n. 2. On the passage, see PHILIPP, "Zu Polyklets Schrift 'Kanon,'" 139.

167   Already GASTER, "Das Schiur Komah," 183 = 1334, discusses in regard to the texts "Willkürlichkeit, mit der sie von den Abschreibern und Compilatoren behandelt werden."

168   Siddur Rabba lines 1–6 after COHEN, *The Shi'ur Qomah*, 38.

169   Sefer ha-Qoma lines 12–21 after COHEN, *The Shi'ur Qomah*, 127f.

170   Cf. only Alcinous, *Didascalicus* 7.4 (CUFr 18,[162],2f. WHITTAKER/LOUIS).

171   *Synopse zur Hekhalot-Literatur* § 948f. after M40 (294.19 SCHÄFER).

172   G11 (= TAYLOR-SCHECHTER K 21.95.J): "Von seiner Fußsohle bis zu seinen Fußgelenken: sechs Myriaden und 2.000 Parasangen." Cf. *Geniza-Fragmente zur Hekhalot-Literatur*, 132, 1b.3–5 SCHÄFER; *Übersetzung der Hekhalot-Literatur*, 4: 149.

173   This probably means: "The head is equivalent to a third of the size of the entire body."

174   *Synopse zur Hekhalot-Literatur* § 948f. after M40 (294.2–34 SCHÄFER). ET after the German of SCHÄFER, *Übersetzung der Hekhalot-Literatur*, 4: 148–158.

175   *Synopse zur Hekhalot-Literatur* § 950 after M40 (294.37–53 SCHÄFER); ET after the German of SCHÄFER, *Übersetzung der Hekhalot-Literatur*, 4: 158–163.

176   Accordingly, only M40; the remaining textual sources have R. Yishma'el.

177   *Synopse zur Hekhalot-Literatur* § 951 after M40 (294.58–61 SCHÄFER). ET after the German of SCHÄFER, *Übersetzung der Hekhalot-Literatur*, 4: 165.

178   In his dissertation, COHEN does not translate אמה "arm," but rather "penis" ("genitals": Marcus JASTROW, *A Dictionary of the Targumim, the Talmud Babli and Yerushalmi, and the Midrashic Literature* [Peabody, Mass.: Hendrickson, 2005 = London: Luzac, 1903/1905], 1117 sub. 360). The ET "amah of the pudendum" admittedly shamefully conceals the following paradox: "penis of the vagina." Should this reconstruction prove accurate, then this would be a rather daring attempt to state a male-femaleness in the sense of a Platonic spherical human.

179   COHEN, *The Shi'ur Qomah*, 217 n. 6 refers to ibid., 210 n. 47 and 225f. nn. 1–3; however, not the slightest reference might there be found to divine sexual organs. Examination of Howard EILBERG-SCHWARTZ, *God's Phallus and Other Problems for Men and Monotheism* (Boston: Beacon Press, 1994), yields similar fruits. Here, the "Shi'ur Qomah" traditions are admittedly only explored in means of a single sentence (p. 180).

180   *Synopse zur Hekhalot-Literatur* § 367 after N8128 (154.46 SCHÄFER). ET after the German of SCHÄFER, *Übersetzung der Hekhalot-Literatur*, 3: 61. Schäfer nevertheless suggests, with the parallels in § 953 (296.34 SCHÄFER), to read "his locks" (ibid., 61 n. 11). A new analogy of proportion would thus be created: "His locks are like his form" (beautiful, for example).

181   Seen differently GRUENWALD, *Apocalyptic and Merkavah Mysticism*, 213–217. Critical remarks regarding this in COHEN, *The Shi'ur Qomah*, 29f.

182   *Synopse zur Hekhalot-Literatur* § 948 after M40 (294.11f. SCHÄFER). ET after SCHÄFER, *Übersetzung der Hekhalot-Literatur*, 4: 15. Alternately after G9 (= Hebr. C.65.6): *Geniza-Fragmente zur Hekhalot-Literatur*, 115, 6a.9 SCHÄFER.

183   *Synopse zur Hekhalot-Literatur* § 699 after O1531 (256.32f. SCHÄFER). ET after SCHÄFER, *Übersetzung der Hekhalot-Literatur*, 4: 114

184 Schäfer, *The Hidden and Manifest God*, 102.

185 Scholem, *Major Trends in Jewish Mysticism*, 64.

186 Thomas Rentsch, s.v. "Theologie, negative," in *Historisches Wörterbuch der Philosophie* (Darmstadt: Wissenschaftliche Buchgesellschaft, 1998), 10: 1102–1105.

187 It unfortunately cannot be presently deduced as to whether female mystics employed the liturgical formulae of the "Shi'ur Qoma" passages; considering the restrictions of rabbinical teaching and the absence of evidence, such an assumption seems scarcely all that likely.

188 For the names and appellation, see Schäfer, *The Hidden and Manifest God*, 107–121; Halperin, *The Faces of the Chariot*, 405–407; and Cohen, *The Shi'ur Qomah*, 99–109.

189 *Synopse zur Hekhalot-Literatur* § 167 after O1531 (74.14–17 Schäfer). ET after the German of Schäfer, *Übersetzung der Hekhalot-Literatur*, 2: 101.

190 Schäfer, *The Hidden and Manifest God*, 165; and idem, *The Origins of Jewish Mysticism*, 339–343.

191 According to Schäfer this concerns "in a way, the phenomenon of the 'empty vision'" (*The Origins of Jewish Mysticism*, 341).

192 Albeit this word was unknown to Classical Antiquity.

193 *Synopse zur Hekhalot-Literatur* § 68 after V228 (35.14–16 Schäfer). ET after the German of Schäfer, *Übersetzung der Hekhalot-Literatur*, 1: 151f. On the passage, see Beate Ego, "Trauer und Erlösung: Zum Motiv der Hand Gottes in 3Hen §§ 68–70," in Kieffer et Bergman, *La Main de Dieu*, 171–188, esp. 176–182.

194 *Synopse zur Hekhalot-Literatur* § 949 after M40 (294.25f. Schäfer). ET from Cohen, *The Shi'ur Qomah*, 47. For a parallel cf. § 699 after O1531 (256.30f. Schäfer). See Scholem, *Major Trends in Jewish Mysticism*, 64.

195 Iustinus, *Dialogus cum Tryphone* 114.3 (231 Goodspeed/PTS 47, 14–19 Marcovich). ET from *St. Justin Martyr: Dialogue with Trypho*, trans. Thomas B. Falls, rev. and with a new introduction by Thomas P. Halton, ed. Michael Slusser, Selections from the Fathers of the Church 3 (Washington, D.C.: Catholic University of America Press, 2003), 170.

196 Arnobius Maior, *Adversus nationes* III 12 (Corpus Scriptorum Latinorum Paravianum 170.1–13 Marchesi). ET from *The Seven Books of Arnobius Adversus Gentes*, trans. Archibald Hamilton Bryce and Hugh Campbell, Ante-Nicene Christian Library 19 (Edinburgh: T&T Clark, 1871), 158. See also Guy Stroumsa, "Le couple de l'Ange et de l'Esprit: Traditions juives et chretiennes," *Révue Biblique* 88 (1981): 42–61, here 51f.

197 The latter two views are not attested elsewhere: [Hermann L. Strack and] Paul Billerbeck, *Kommentar zum Neuen Testament aus Talmud und Midrasch*, Bd. 4, *Exkurse zu einzelnen Stellen des Neuen Testaments: Abhandlungen zur neutestamentlichen Theologie und Archäologie* (München: Beck, 1928), 1: 344.

198 Stroumsa, "Le couple de l'Ange et de l'Esprit," 49, references the Karaite Jewish theologian *Jacob Qirqisani* (Hebrew: *Ya'akov ben Ephraim ha-Tzerqesi*; Arabic: *Ya'qūb al-Qirqisānī*) from the first half of the tenth century. In his *Kitab al-Anwar* I 7 (p. 42.5–7 Nemoy) *Ya'akov/Ya'qūb* maintains in the course of an account of a group known as the "Maġārīya," that "Da'ūd ibn Marwān (a Jewish author of the ninth century) says in one of his books that the Sadūkīya (Sadducees) said that the glorious creator has a body and interpret literally those scriptural passages which affirm that He has." ET in Bruno Chiesa and Wilfrid Lockwood, *Ya'qūb al-Qirqisānī on Jewish Sects and Christianity: A Translation of "Kitāb al-anwār"; Book I with Two Introductory Essays*, Judentum und Umwelt 10 (Frankfurt am Main: Lang, 1984), 134). On the account and its context, see also Norman Golb, "Who Were the Maġārīya?" *Journal of the American Oriental Society* 80 (1960): 347–359, here 348 with n. 348.

199 Pseudo-(?)Basilius Caesariensis, *Homilia de creatione hominis* I 5 (SC 160, 176.11–178.19 Smets/van Esbroeck = GNO. Supplementum 9.5–10.1 Hörner). In the final half-sentence, I follow the MSS and do not adopt the conjecture of Hadwiga Hörner: ἁπλότητι φύσεως μέγεθος πόσον; Hörner holds the homily to be redacted excerpts from Basil (op. cit., viiif.).

200 Pseudo-(?)Basilius Caesariensis, *Homilia de creatione hominis* I 5 (SC 160, 176.4–10 SMETS/VAN ESBROECK = GNO. Supplementum 8.12–9.4 HÖRNER).

201 Fragment 1 in *Nechepsonis et Petosiridis fragmenta*, ed. Ernst RIESS, Philologus, Supplement-Bd. VI/1 (Göttingen: Dieterich, 1891); digitalized version online at http://www .hellenisticastrology.com/editions/Riess-Nechepso-Petosiris.pdf (accessed 10 May 2019), 333 = Vettius Valens, *Anthologiae* VI *prooemium* 9 (BiTeu 231.8–15 PINGREE). ET from Stephan HEILEN, "Some Metrical Fragments from Nechepsos and Petosiris," in *La poésie astrologique dans l'antiquité*, textes réunis par Isabelle Boehm et Wolfgang Hübner, actes du colloque organisé les 7 et 8 décembre 2007 par J.-H. Abry avec la collaboration de I. Boehm Collection du Centre d'Études et de Recherches sur l'Occident Romain CEROR, 38 (Paris: de Boccard, 2011), 23–93, here 39. On this passage, see Richard REITZENSTEIN, *Poimandres: Studien zur griechisch-ägyptischen und frühchristlichen Literatur* (Leipzig: Teubner, 1904), 5: "Die Lücke nach dem ersten Verse ist dem Sinne nach zu ergänzen: die ganze Nacht hat Nechepso betend zum Himmel emporgeblickt, da fühlt er sich dem Körper entrückt, und eine Stimme tönt zu ihm aus dem Himmel, deren Leib ein dunkles Gewand umhüllt." See also idem, *Die hellenistischen Mysterienreligionen nach ihren Grundgedanken und Wirkungen*, 3. Aufl. (Leipzig: Teubner, 1927), 189–191.

202 A gamut of material and literature in HENGEL, *Judentum und Hellenismus*, 381–394; and in Alan F. SEGAL, "Heavenly Ascent in Hellenistic Judaism, Early Christianity and Their Environment," *ANRW* II/23.2: 1333–1394.

203 Eudorus Alexandrinus apud Simplicium, *In Aristotelis physicorum libros commentaria* I 5 ad p. 188ᵃ 19 (CAG IX, 181.27–30 DIELS). ET from *Simplicius: On Aristotle Physics 1.5–9*, trans. Han BALTUSSEN, Michael John SHARE, Michael ATKINSON, and Ian MUELLER, Ancient Commentators on Aristotle (London: Bloomsbury, 2014), 19. On the passage, see Heinrich DÖRRIE† and Matthias BALTES, *Die philosophische Lehre des Platonismus: Einige grundlegende Axiome/Platonische Physik (im antiken Verständnis) I; Bausteine 101–124; Text, Übersetzung, Kommentar*, Der Platonismus in der Antike. Grundlagen— System—Entfaltung 4 (Stuttgart-Bad Cannstatt: Frommann-Holzboog, 1996), 176f. (text) and 473–477 (commentary); Mauro BONAZZI, "Eudorus of Alexandria and the 'Pythagorean' Pseudepigrapha," in *On Pythagoreanism*, ed. Gabriele Cornelli, Richard McKirahan, and Constantinos Macris, Studia Praesocratica 5 (Berlin: De Gruyter 2013), 385–404; and Heinrich DÖRRIE, "Der Platoniker Eudoros von Alexandreia," *Hermes* 79 (1944): 25–38 = idem, *Platonica minora*, Studia et testimonia antiqua VIII (München: Fink, 1976), 297–309.

204 The best introduction to the text may be found in the rezension of the critical edition (*[Iamblichi] Theologoumena arithmeticae*, ed. Victorius DE FALCO, BiTeu [Leipzig: Teubner, 1922]) by Hans OPPERMANN, *Gnomon* 5 (1929): 545–558.

205 Ps.-Iamblichus, *Theologumena arithmeticae* 1 (BiTeu 1.4f. DE FALCO): Μονάς ἐστιν ἀρχὴ ἀριθμοῦ, θέσιν μὴ ἔχουσα.

206 Wilhelm BRANDT, *Elchasai, ein Religionsstifter und sein Werk: Beiträge zur jüdischen, christlichen und allgemeinen Religionsgeschichte in späthellenistischer Zeit, mit Berücksichtigung der Sekten der syrischen Sampsäer und der arabischen Mughtasila* (Leipzig: Hinrichs, 1912 = Amsterdam, Philo Press, 1971); with the review of Adolf von HARNACK, *Theologische Literaturzeitung* 37 (1912): 683f.; Georg STRECKER, s.v. "Elkesai," in *Reallexikon für Antike und Christentum* (Stuttgart: Hiersemann, 1959), 4: 1171–1186; Kurt RUDOLPH, *Antike Baptisten: Zu den Überlieferungen über frühjüdische und -christliche Taufsekten*, Sitzungsberichte der Sächsischen Akademie der Wissenschaften zu Leipzig, Philologisch-historische Klasse 4/121 (Berlin: Akademie, 1981), 13–17 = idem, *Gnosis und spätantike Religionsgeschichte: Gesammelte Aufsätze*, Nag Hammadi and Manichaean Studies 42 (Leiden: Brill, 1996), 569–603; Luigi CIRILLO, *Elchasai e gli elchasaiti: Un contributo alla storia delle comunità giudeo-cristiane* (Cosenza: Marra, 1984); Gerard P. LUTTIKHUIZEN, *The Revelation of Elchasai: Investigations into the Evidence for a Mesopotamian Jewish Apocalypse of the Second Century and Its Reception*

by *Judeo-Christian Propagandists*, TSAJ 8 (Tübingen: Mohr Siebeck, 1985); with the detailed review of F. Stanley JONES, *JAC* 30 (1987): 200–209 = idem, *Pseudoclementina Elchasaiticaque inter Judaeochristian: Collected Studies*, OLA 203 (Leuven/Paris/Walpole, Mass.: Peeters, 2012), 417–431; idem, "The *Book of Elchasai* in Its Relevance for Manichean Instruction with a Supplement: *Book of Elchasai* Reconstructed and Translated," in idem, *Pseudoclementina*, 359–397; and Simon Claude MIMOUNI, *Early Judeo-Christianity: Historical Essays*, trans. Robyn Fréchet, Interdisciplinary Studies in Ancient Culture and Religion 13 (Leuven/Walpole, Mass.: Peeters, 2012), 248–276.

207   Accordingly also Epiphanius, *Panarion haereses* 19.1.4 (GCS Epiphanius I², 218.2f. HOLL/BERGERMANN/COLLATZ). Cf. Hippolytus, *Refutatio omnium haeresium* IX 16.4 (GCS Hippolyt IV, 255.1–5 WENDLAND/PTS 25, 362.16–20 MARCOVICH). See STRECKER, s.v. "Elkesai," 1172f.; and Johannes VAN OORT, s.v. "Elkesaiten," in *RGG*, 4. Aufl. (Tübingen: Mohr Siebeck, 2000), 2: 1227f. The analysis of the "Book of Elchasai" here offered was first presented by myself as part of a keynote paper at the close of the conference "Judaism in Transition: Crossing Boundaries in Time and Space; From the Hellenistic-Roman World to Babylonia, from the Orient to Medieval Europe," on the occasion of the 70th birthday of Peter Schäfer on July 3, 2013, in the Berlin-Brandenburgische Akademie der Wissenschaften.

208   *Codex Manichaicus Coloniensis* p. 94.9f. (Papyrologica Coloniensia XIV, 66 KOENEN/RÖMER), four anecdotes and aphorisms of Elchasai follow, transmitted in part by Mani. "Elchasaios" is also attested in the Berlin Turfan fragment M 1344, albeit practically without context: Werner SUNDERMANN, *Mitteliranische manichäische Texte kirchengeschichtlichen Inhalts*, mit einem Appendix von Nicholas Sims-Williams, Schriften zur Geschichte und Kultur des Alten Orients, Berliner Turfantexte XI (Berlin: Akademie-Verlag, 1981), nr. 2.1 Z. 26 S. 19.

209   Further commentary in the *editio princeps*: Albert HENRICHS and Ludwig KOENEN, "Der Kölner Mani-Kodex (P. Colon. inv. nr. 4780) ΠΕΡΙ ΤΗΣ ΓΕΝΝΗΣ ΤΟΥ ΣΩΜΑΤΟΣ ΑΥΤΟΥ: Edition der Seiten 72.8–99.9," *Zeitschrift für Papyrologie und Epigraphik* 32 (1978): 87–199, here 179–195; critically: LUTTIKHUIZEN, *The Revelation of Elchasai*, 25–30, 156–164 (text, translation, and commentary); contra JONES, "The *Book of Elchasai* in Its Relevance for Manichean Instruction," 360f.

210   Most recently on this debate: Annette Yoshiko REED, F. Stanley JONES, and Claude MIMOUNI, "Two Books on Jewish-Christianity," *Annali di Storia dell'Esegesi* 30 (2013): 93–101. The characterization cited of "syncretistic-gnostic Judeo-Christianity" is propounded by STRECKER, s.v. "Elkesai," 1186.

211   Thus Epiphanius, *Panarion haereses* 19.2.1 (GCS Epiphanius I², 219.8–10 HOLL/BERGERMANN/COLLATZ). For an explanation of the name, see BRANDT, *Elchasai, ein Religionsstifter und sein Werk*, 5–8; and LUTTIKHUIZEN, *The Revelation of Elchasai*, 182–188. It is not improbable considering the strict monotheism of the group that one of its number was dubbed אל כסי, "Hidden God."

212   Origenes, frag. ex *Homilia in Psalmum* 82 apud Eusebium, *Historia ecclesiastica* VI 38 (GCS Eusebius II/2, 592.24–594.2 SCHWARTZ). On this passage, see LUTTIKHUIZEN, *The Revelation of Elchasai*, 89–91.

213   Hippolytus, *Refutatio omnium haeresium* IX 13.1 (GCS Hippolyt IV, 251.12f. WENDLAND/PTS 25, 357.5f. MARCOVICH). Cf. Epiphanius, *Panarion haereses* 19.1.4 (GCS Epiphanius I², 221.6–13 HOLL/BERGERMANN/COLLATZ).

214   Acts 8:10: Οὗτός ἐστιν ἡ δύναμις τοῦ θεοῦ ἡ καλουμένη μεγάλη. On the possible Samaritan background to this title (חילה רבה), see Hans G. KIPPENBERG, *Garizim und Synagoge: Traditionsgeschichtliche Untersuchungen zur samaritanischen Religion der aramäischen Periode*, Religionsgeschichtliche Versuche und Vorarbeiten 30 (Berlin: De Gruyter, 1971), 328–349, esp. 345 on the meaning of the expression ἡ δύναμις τοῦ θεοῦ.

215   Thus, already, Hans WAITZ, "Das Buch des Elchasai, das heilige Buch der judenchristlichen Sekte der Sobiai," in *Harnack-Ehrung: Beiträge zur Kirchengeschichte, ihrem Lehrer Adolf von Harnack zu seinem siebzigsten Geburtstage (7. Mai 1921) dargebracht von einer Reihe seiner Schüler* (Leipzig: Hinrichs, 1921), 87–104, here 88f.

216   Overview of research in LUTTIKHUIZEN, *The Revelation of Elchasai*, 4–25.

217   Epiphanius, *Panarion haereses* 19.2.3f. (GCS Epiphanius I², 219.13–22 HOLL/BERGERMANN/COLLATZ). Cf. also ibid., 53.1.2 (GCS Epiphanius II², 315.4–7 HOLL/DUMMER). ET adapted from *The Panarion of Epiphanius of Salamis Book I (Sects 1–46)*, trans. Frank Williams SECOND, rev. ed., Nag Hammadi and Manichean Studies 63 (Leiden/Boston: Brill, 2008), 49.

218   [Hermann L. STRACK and] Paul BILLERBECK, *Das Evangelium nach Markus, Lukas und Johannes und die Apostelgeschichte, erklärt aus Talmud und Midrasch*, Kommentar zum Neuen Testament aus Talmud und Midrasch 2, 9. Aufl. (München: Beck, 1989), 15–17; Rudolf HERZOG, *Die Wunderheilungen von Epidauros. Ein Beitrag zur Geschichte der Medizin und der Religion*, Philologus, Supplement 22/3 (Leipzig: Dieterich, 1931), 15–17; and also Ludwig DEUBNER, s.v. "Speichel," in *Handwörterbuch des deutschen Aberglaubens* (Augsburg: Weltbild, 2000 = Berlin: De Gruyter, 1937), 149–155.

219   A *schoinos* (σχοῖνος) is, according to Herodotus, *Historiae* II 6.3 (BiTeu 142.12f. ROSÉN), an Egyptian measurement of distance equaling sixty *stadia*, or roughly ten to twelve kilometers. The "Seren" are a mythological people who cannot be fixed exactly geographically (BRANDT, *Elchasai, ein Religionsstifter und sein Werk*, 11; STRECKER, s.v. "Elkesai," 1173; and, above all, Gerrit Jan REININK, "'Das Land Seiris' [Sir] und das Volk der Serer in jüdischen und christlichen Traditionen," *JSJ* 6 [1975]: 72–85). LUTTIKHUIZEN, *The Revelation of Elchasai*, 60, suggests a textual corruption (Σηρ . . .) and the name of a Persian region without specifying a precise name. Simon Claude MIMOUNI, *Early Judeo-Christianity: Historical Essays*, trans. Robyn Fréchet, Interdisciplinary Studies in Ancient Culture and Religion 13 (Leuven/Walpole, Mass.: Peeters, 2012), 256 n. 32, derives this from צבע, "to plunge in water, wash," and explains this as a misreading of the otherwise attested baptist group of the Μασβώθεοι.

220   Hippolytus, *Refutatio omnium haeresium* IX 13.1–3 (GCS Hippolyt IV, 251.8–20 WENDLAND/PTS 25, 357.1–358.14 MARCOVICH). ET from *Hippolytus: Refutation of All Heresies*, trans. with an introduction and notes by M. David LITWA, Writings from the Greco-Roman World 40 (Atlanta: SBL Press, 2016), 659–661.

221   The inference of an Aramaic original version is held to be excessive by STRECKER, s.v. "Elkesai," 1183.

222   Hippolytus, *Refutatio omnium haeresium* IX 14.1 (GCS Hippolyt IV, 252.24f. WENDLAND/PTS 25, 359.8 MARCOVICH).

223   Alfred SCHMIDTKE, *Neue Fragmente und Untersuchungen zu den judenchristlichen Evangelien: Ein Beitrag zur Literatur und Geschichte der Judenchristen*, TU 37/1 (Leipzig: Hinrichs, 1911), 191 and 228–230; Sakari HÄKKINEN, s.v. "Ebionites," in *A Companion to Second-Century Christian "Heretics*," ed. Antti Marjanen and Petri Luomanen, Supplements to Vigiliae Christianae 76 (Leiden: Brill, 2005), 247–278, here 261–265; and, in further detail, LUTTIKHUIZEN, *The Revelation of Elchasai*, 114–116.

224   Epiphanius, *Panarion haereses* 19.1.1, also 2.1 (GCS Epiphanius I², 217.18f., 219.5–8 HOLL/BERGERMANN/COLLATZ). See BRANDT, *Elchasai, ein Religionsstifter und sein Werk*, 100–133. RUDOLPH, *Antike Baptisten*, 16 = 590, considers "Sampseans," Σαμψαῖοι, to be a "Verballhornung für Σαβαῖοι" (p. 34 n. 55 = 590 n. 55). STRECKER demonstrates that Epiphanius "bestrebt war, den Bereich der elkesaitischen Wirkungen auszuweiten" (s.v. "Elkesai," 1175).

225   Epiphanius, *Panarion haereses* 19.4.1–2 (GCS Epiphanius I², 221.6–13 HOLL/BERGERMANN/COLLATZ). ET adapted from SECOND, *The Panarion of Epiphanius of Salamis Book I (Sects 1–46)*, 50f.

226 On this topic, see Georg KRETSCHMAR, *Studien zur frühchristlichen Trinitätstheologie*, BHT 21 (Tübingen: Mohr Siebeck, 1956), 62–124; on the "Book of Elchasai," ibid., 98f.; and the review of Joseph BARBEL, "Zur 'Engels-Trinitätslehre' im Urchristentum," *Theologische Revue* 54 (1958): 50–58; idem, *Christos Angelos: Die Anschauung von Christus als Bote und Engel in der gelehrten und volkstümlichen Literatur des christlichen Altertums, zugleich ein Beitrag zur Geschichte des Ursprungs und der Fortdauer des Arianismus*, Theophaneia 3 (Bonn: Hanstein, 1941), 277f.; Carl ANDRESEN, "Zur Dogmengeschichte der Alten Kirche," *Theologische Literaturzeitung* 84 (1959): 81–88 = idem, *Theologie und Kirche im Horizont der Antike: Gesammelte Aufsätze zur Geschichte der Alten Kirche*, hg. Peter Gemeinhardt, Arbeiten zur Kirchengeschichte 112 (Berlin/New York: De Gruyter, 2009), 37–45; and STROUMSA, "Le couple de l'Ange et de l'Esprit," 44–47. A more recent critical overview on the discussion is offered by Samuel VOLLENWEIDER, "Zwischen Monotheismus und Engelchristologie. Überlegungen zur Frühgeschichte des Christusglaubens," *ZTK* 99 (2002): 21–44, 28–31, and 34–38.

227 According to the grammatical and contextual logic of the passage in Epiphanius, this must, however, refer to Ebion, the (fabricated) founding father of the "Ebionites."

228 Epiphanius, *Panarion haereses* 30.17.6f. (GCS Epiphanius I², 356.18–357.7 HOLL/ BERGERMANN/COLLATZ). ET adapted from SECOND, *The Panarion of Epiphanius of Salamis Book I (Sects 1–46)*, 145.

229 Epiphanius, *Panarion haereses* 53.1.9 (GCS Epiphanius II², 316.3–7 HOLL/DUMMER). ET adapted from *The Panarion of Epiphanius of Salamis Books II and III: De Fide*, trans. Frank Williams SECOND, rev. ed., Nag Hammadi and Manichean Studies 79 (Leiden/ Boston: Brill, 2013), 72.

230 SCHÄFER, *The Origins of Jewish Mysticism*, 313f.; alternately STROUMSA, "Le couple de l'Ange et de l'Esprit," 42–61; and Joseph M. BAUMGARTEN, "The Book of Elkesai and Merkabah Mysticism," *JSJ* 17 (1986): 212–223, 257–259, here esp. 220–222.

231 Hippolytus, *Refutatio omnium haeresium* IX 15.1.3 (GCS Hippolyt IV, 253.13–16.26 WENDLAND/PTS 25, 360.5–7, 360.17–361.19 MARCOVICH). In depth, see BRANDT, *Elchasai, ein Religionsstifter und sein Werk*, 33–37.

232 *Corpus Hermeticum* I 1 (CUFr I, 7.5–7 NOCK/FESTUGIÈRE).

233 *Pastor Hermae* 83.1 = *Similitudines* IX 6.1 (GCS Apostolische Väter I, 80.30–81.1 WHITTAKER). Cf. *Acta Ioannis* 90.3 (Acta Apostolorum Apocrypha II/1, 195.9–11 BONNET = CChr.SA 1, 195.10–15 JUNOD/KAESTLI); and 5 Ezra 2:43. See Michael WOLTER, "5. Esra-Buch. 6. Esra-Buch," in *Unterweisungen in lehrhafter Form*, Jüdische Studien hellenistisch-römischer Zeit III/7 [Gütersloh: Gütersloher Verlagshaus Mohn, 2001], 818); and *Passio SS. Perpetuae et Felicitatis* 10.8 (SC 417, 138.18f. 21f. AMAT): *uir quidam mirae magnitudinis* or τις ἀνὴρ θαυμαστοῦ μεγέθους. See also GRILLMEIER, *Jesus der Christus im Glauben der Kirche*, 1: 150–157; and DÖLGER, *ΙΧΘΥΣ: Der heilige Fisch in den antiken Religionen und im Christentum* (Rome: Spithöver / Münster: Aschendorff, 1922), 2: 559 n. 4.

234 *Evangelium Petri* 10.39f. (GCS Neutestamentliche Apokryphen I, 42.8–14 KRAUS/ NICKLAS = SC 201, 58.4–9 MARA).

235 Cf., for example, in the Midrash Bereshit Rabba 8.1 (55.6f. THEODOR/ALBECK) ". . . als Gott den ersten Menschen erschuf, war derselbe ein bloßer Kloß und er reichte von einem Ende der Welt bis zum anderen" (cf. Ps 139:16). Further passages in SCHÄFER, *The Origins of Jewish Mysticism*, 314 n. 324; and Alan F. SEGAL, *Two Powers in Heaven: Early Rabbinic Reports about Christianity and Gnosticism*, Studies in Judaism in Late Antiquity 25 (Leiden: Brill, 1977), 110–115. On the context within the Midrash, see ibid., 112–120.

236 Hippolytus, *Refutatio omnium haeresium* IX 13.1–3 (GCS Hippolyt IV, 251.18–20 WENDLAND/PTS 25, 358.12–14 MARCOVICH). ET from LITWA, *Hippolytus: Refutation of All Heresies*, 659–661.

237 Hans WAITZ, "Das Buch des Elchasai, das heilige Buch der judenchristlichen Sekte der Sobiai," in *Harnack-Ehrung: Beiträge zur Kirchengeschichte, ihrem Lehrer Adolf*

von Harnack zu seinem siebzigsten Geburtstage (7. Mai 1921) dargebracht von einer Reihe seiner Schüler, 87–104 (Leipzig: Hinrichs, 1921); Johannes IRMSCHER, "Das Buch des Elchasai," in *Neutestamentliche Apokryphen in deutscher Übersetzung*, Bd. 2, *Apostolisches, Apokalypsen und Verwandtes*, hg. Wilhelm Schneemelcher, 5. Aufl. der von Edgar Hennecke begründeten Sammlung, (Tübingen: Mohr Siebeck, 1989), 619–623.

238   JONES, "The *Book of Elchasai* in Its Relevance for Manichean Instruction," 362–364, 391–395; and idem, "The Genre of the *Book of Elchasai*: A Primitive Church Order, Not an Apocalypse," in idem, *Pseudoclementina*, 398–416. Critically: MIMOUNI, *Early Judeo-Christianity*, 265f.

239   BRANDT, *Elchasai, ein Religionsstifter und sein Werk*, 60: "Vielleicht–es soll wenigstens nicht glatt unmöglich heißen–läßt sich der Inhalt dieses Blattes des Elchasai also so erklären, daß die Hauptsache darin als Erzeugnis einer Autosuggestion in Schutz genommen werden darf. Wie aber dann die Sache zurechtgelegt und mit dem Schein einer nachmeßbaren Realität ausgestattet ist, kann das Ganze doch nur als ein Schwindel bezeichnet werden."

240   See already GASTER, "Das Schiur Komah," 1343: "Am vollkommsten entspricht nun *Valentin's* Gnosis allen diesen Voraussetzungen. Der Stifter derselben wird sogar als Judenchrist bezeichnet. 'Nach seiner hellenistischen Ausdrucksweise und den aramäischen Namen, welche in seinem jüdischen Systeme vorkommen, zu schliessen, stammte er von *jüdischer* Abkunft her,' sagt Neander von ihm. Noch näher läge vielleicht das System des Jüngers des Valentin, Markus, des Hauptes der Markusier." In the footnotes, Gaster references August NEANDER, *Allgemeine Geschichte der christlichen Religion und Kirche*, Bd. 2, (Gotha: Perthes: 1864), 105, which contains the history of Christian doctrine in its first three centuries.

241   Niclas FÖRSTER, *Marcus Magus: Kult, Lehre und Gemeindeleben einer valentinianischen Gnostikergruppe; Sammlung der Quellen und Kommentar*, WUNT 114 (Tübingen: Mohr Siebeck, 1999), 1–5 (brief history of research and overview of literature).

242   Christoph MARKSCHIES, "Valentinian Gnosticism: Toward the Anatomy of a School," in *The Nag Hammadi Library after Fifty Years: Proceedings of the 1995 Society of Biblical Literature Commemoration*, ed. John D. Turner and Anne Marie McGuire, Nag Hammadi Studies 44 (Leiden: Brill, 1997), 401–438; idem, "New Research on Ptolemaeus Gnosticus," *ZAC* 4 (2000): 225–254; and idem, "Nochmals: Valentinus und die Gnostikoi; Beobachtungen zu Irenaeus, haer. I 30.15 und Tertullian, Val. 4.2," *VC* 51 (1997): 179–187.

243   Epiphanius, *Panarion haereses* 31.7.2 (GCS Epiphanius I², 396.1–6 HOLL/BERGERMANN/COLLATZ). Text, translation, and commentary in Christoph MARKSCHIES, *Valentinus Gnosticus? Untersuchungen zur valentinianischen Gnosis mit einem Kommentar zu den Fragmenten Valentins*, WUNT 65 (Tübingen: Mohr Siebeck, 1992), 331–334.

244   Irenaeus, *Aduersus haereses* I 13.1 (SC 264, 188.1–4 ROUSSEAU/DOUTRELEAU). Here cited is the late antique Latin translation of the Greek work; should Hippolytus or Epiphanius cite (or purport to cite) the Greek original, then it is supplementarily provided. Hippolytus identifies the anonymous teacher who wanted to better Marcus with Valentinus himself: *Refutatio omnium haeresium* VI 42.2 (GCS Hippolytus III, 173.19–21 WENDLAND/PTS 25, 259.10–12 MARCOVICH). See on this FÖRSTER, *Marcus Magus*, 56f.

245   Epiphanius, *Panarion haereses* 33.3.1–7.10 (GCS Epiphanius I², 450.16–457.22 HOLL/BERGERMANN/COLLATZ). See also the edition with commentary in *Ptolémée, Lettre à Flora, analyse, texte critique, traduction, commentaire et index grec de Gilles* QUISPEL, Sources Chrétiennes 24bis (Paris: Cerf, 1966).

246   Irenaeus, *Aduersus haereses* I 13.6 (SC 264, 201.102–202.105 ROUSSEAU/DOUTRELEAU). Cf. Epiphanius, *Panarion haereses* 34.3.4 (GCS Epiphanius II², 9.4–6 HOLL/DUMMER). See FÖRSTER, *Marcus Magus*, 389f.

247 Irenaeus, *Aduersus haereses* I 13.7 (SC 264, 204.127–129 ROUSSEAU/DOUTRELEAU). ET
     from *St Irenaeus of Lyon: Against the Heresies, Book 1*, trans. and annotated by Dominic
     J. UNGER with futher revisions by John J. Dillon, Ancient Christian Writers 55 (Mahwah,
     N.J.: Paulist Press, 1992), 51. Cf. Epiphanius, *Panarion haereses* 34.3.4 (GCS Epiphanius
     II², 9.24–26 HOLL/DUMMER). Jerome first maintains that Marcus himself passed through
     "the regions through which the Rhône and Garonne flow, besmirched it with the teaching"
     (*Epistula* 75.3 [CSEL 55², 32.17f. HILBERG]), but this report is better explained as superfi-
     cial readings of Irenaeus by Jerome than as any authentic memory from the region. Thus
     also FÖRSTER, *Marcus Magus*, 41f.
248 Irenaeus, *Aduersus haereses* I 13.5 (SC 264, 200.94 ROUSSEAU/DOUTRELEAU): *in Asia nos-
     tri*. An overview of the debate as to the appropriateness of the image of a "gnostic Casa-
     nova" (Giovanni Filoramo) with history of research in FÖRSTER, *Marcus Magus*, 123–126,
     On the places within which Marcus was active, see ibid., 159f.
249 Shmuel SAMBURSKY, "On the Origin and Significance of the Term Gemaṭria," *JJS* 29
     (1978): 35–38. On the Jewish and pagan underpinnings of the "name speculation" see
     FÖRSTER, *Marcus Magus*, 192–206.
250 Barbara ALAND, "Die frühe Gnosis zwischen platonischem und christlichem Glauben:
     Kosmosfrömmigkeit versus Erlösungstheologie," in *Die Weltlichkeit des Glaubens in
     der Alten Kirche: Festschrift für Ulrich Wickert zum siebzigsten Geburtstag*, hg. Diet-
     mar Wyrwa, BZNW und die Kunde der älteren Kirche 85 (Berlin/New York: De Gruyter,
     1997), 1–24 = idem, *Was ist Gnosis? Studien zu frühem Christentum, zu Marcion und
     zur kaiserzeitlichen Philosophie*, WUNT 239 (Tübingen: Mohr Siebeck, 2009), 103–
     124; Christoph MARKSCHIES, "Welche Funktion hat der Mythos in gnostischen Systemen?
     Oder: Ein gescheiterter Denkversuch zum Thema 'Heil und Geschichte,'" in *Heil und
     Geschichte: Die Geschichtsbezogenheit des Heils und das Problem der Heilsgeschichte
     in der biblischen Tradition und in der theologischen Deutung*, hg. Jörg Frey, Stefan Kra-
     uter und Hermann Lichtenberger, WUNT 248 (Tübingen: Mohr Siebeck, 2009), 513–534
     = idem, *Gnosis und Christentum* (Berlin: Berlin University Press, 2009), 83–112.
251 Irenaeus, *Aduersus haereses* I 14, 1 (SC 264, 210.34–41 ROUSSEAU/DOUTRELEAU). ET from
     UNGER, *St Irenaeus of Lyon: Against the Heresies, Book 1*, 60. Cf. Epiphanius, *Panarion
     haereses* 34.4.7 (GCS Epiphanius II², 11.9–14 HOLL/DUMMER). See the commentary in
     FÖRSTER, *Marcus Magus*, 389f.
252 Cf. from the so-called great notice, the systematic report on the teachings of the "students of
     Ptolemy" in Irenaeus, *Aduersus haereses* I 2.6 (SC 264, 46.86–88 ROUSSEAU/DOUTRELEAU).
     Cf. also Epiphanius, *Panarion haereses* 31.13.4 (GCS Epiphanius I², 405.12–14 HOLL/
     BERGERMANN/COLLATZ).
253 Matthias BALTES, s.v. "Idee (Ideenlehre)," in *Reallexikon für Antike und Christentum*
     (Stuttgart: Hiersemann, 1996), 17: 213–246, here 245.
254 Irenaeus, *Aduersus haereses* I 14.2 (SC 264, 212.54–214.63 ROUSSEAU/DOUTRELEAU).
     Cf. Epiphanius, *Panarion haereses* 34.4.11 and 5.1 (GCS Epiphanius II², 12.2–5. 9–11
     HOLL/DUMMER). See Franz DORNSEIFF, *Das Alphabet in Mystik und Magie*, 2. Aufl., Stoi-
     cheia: Studien zur Geschichte des antiken Weltbildes und der griechischen Wissenschaft
     7 (Leipzig: Reprint-Verlag, 1994 = Leipzig: Teubner, 1925), 126–133.
255 In contrast to the Latin spelling, the Greek Ἰησοῦς does, indeed, consist of six letters.
256 Irenaeus, *Aduersus haereses* I 14.4 (SC 264, 218.99–105 ROUSSEAU/DOUTRELEAU). ET
     from UNGER, *St Irenaeus of Lyon: Against the Heresies, Book 1*, 61. Cf. Epiphanius,
     Panarion haereses 34.6.4 (GCS Epiphanius II², 13.18–14.2 HOLL/DUMMER). Cf. also the
     translation of FChr 8/1, 232.21–24 BROX.
257 Such are the suspicions of FÖRSTER, *Marcus Magus*, 231–233 (with attestations). Com-
     parison with "Shiʿur Qoma" traditions in STROUMSA, "Form(s) of God," 281; criticism in
     Christopher R. A. MORRAY-JONES, "The Body of the Glory: Approaching the New Tes-
     tament from the Perspective of Shiur Koma Traditions," in *The Mystery of God: Early
     Jewish Mysticism and the New Testament*, ed. Christopher Rowland and Christopher R. A.

Morray-Jones, Compendia Rerum Iudaicarum ad Novum Testamentum III/12 (Leiden/ Boston, 2009), 501–610, here 570 n. 142.

258 Irenaeus, *Aduersus haereses* I 14.3 (SC 264, 214.73–216.84 ROUSSEAU/DOUTRELEAU). ET from UNGER, *St Irenaeus of Lyon: Against the Heresies, Book 1*, 61. Cf. Epiphanius, *Panarion haereses* 34.5.5–7 (GCS Epiphanius II², 12.20–13.6 HOLL/DUMMER). See on this the commentary in FÖRSTER, *Marcus Magus*, 221–228.

259 Cf. on the Ram (*Aries* or Κριός) Teucer, *De duodecim signis* (after an excerpt from Rhetorius, Catalogus Codicum Astrologorum Graecorum VII, 194.15 and 195.19–24 BOLL). On the passage, see Franz BOLL, *Sphaera: Neue griechische Texte und Untersuchungen zur Geschichte der Sternbilder* (Leipzig: Teubner, 1903 = Hildesheim: Olms, 1967), 5–21; REITZENSTEIN, *Poimandres*, 286f.; DORNSEIFF, *Das Alphabet in Mystik und Magie*, 132f., 286f.; Wilhelm GUNDEL, *Dekane und Dekansternbilder: Ein Beitrag zur Geschichte der Sternbilder der Kulturvölker*, mit einer Untersuchung über die ägyptischen Sternbilder und Gottheiten der Dekanae von Siegfried Schott, Studien der Bibliothek Warburg 19 (Glückstadt/Hamburg: Augustin, 1936), 115–119; and FÖRSTER, *Marcus Magus*, 221–228. On Teucer/Teukros, see Wilhelm GUNDEL, s.v. "Teukros 5)," PW V A 1: 1132–1134.

260 DORNSEIFF, *Das Alphabet in Mystik und Magie*, 26, cites an attestation from the Babylonian Talmud: Shabbath 104b. On the magical papyri, see ibid., 42f.

261 SCHÄFER, *The Origins of Jewish Mysticism*, 312. For critical remarks as to Scholem's idea of comparing Marcus and the "Shi'ur Qoma" texts, see already, COHEN, *The Shi'ur Qomah*, 24–26.

262 SCHOLEM, *Jewish Gnosticism*, 36f. On datation, see the remarks by Hans-Martin SCHENKE, "Vorwort," in *Koptisch-Gnostische Schriften*, Bd. 1, *Die Pistis Sophia, die beiden Bücher des Jeû, unbekanntes altgnostisches Werk*, hg. Carl Schmidt, 4. um das Vorwort erw. Aufl., hg. Hans-Martin Schenke (mit den Nachträgen der 2. Aufl. von Walter C. Till, 1954), GCS (Berlin: Akademie-Verlag, 1984), xvi–xxxiv; and Carsten COLPE, *Einleitung in die Schriften aus Nag Hammadi*, Jerusalemer Theologisches Forum 16 (Münster: Aschendorff, 2011), 60–64, 277–311, 318–323.

263 Cf. Hans-Martin SCHENKE, "The Phenomenon and Significance of Gnostic Sethianism," in *The Rediscovery of Gnosticism: Proceedings of the International Conference on Gnosticism at Yale, New Haven, Connecticut, March 28–31, 1978*, ed. Bentley Layton, vol. 2, *Sethian Gnosticism*, SHR 41/2 (Leiden: Brill, 1981), 588–616; and, critically opposed to this, Frederik WISSE, "Stalking Those Elusive Sethians," in Layton, *The Rediscovery of Gnosticism* 2: 563–576. Oriented towards present debates are, e.g., Johanna BRANKAER, *Die Gnosis: Texte und Kommentar* (Wiesbaden: Marix, 2010), 78–84; or John D. TURNER, *Sethian Gnosticism and the Platonic Tradition*, Bibliothèque Copte de Nag Hammadi, Section "Études" 6 (Québec: Les Presses de l'Université Laval; Louvain/Paris: Peeters, 2001), 57–92 and 747–759.

264 FRIEDLÄNDER, *Der vorchristliche jüdische Gnosticismus*, does not discuss the Codices Askewianus and Brucianus; the same for DAN, "Jewish Gnosticism?" 309–328. It is handled at some length in HERRMANN, "Jüdische Gnosis?" 62–73, the discussion of a "Little YHWH" (הקטן יוי) in the Third Book of Enoch and of a "Little Jao" in the *Pistis Sophia* (cf. *Synopse zur Hekhalot-Literatur* § 15 after V228 [9.52 SCHÄFER] and *Pistis Sophia* 7 [NHS 9, 12.22 SCHMIDT]).

265 *Pistis Sophia* I 6 (NHC 9, 8.14 SCHMIDT). ET from *Pistis Sophia*, text ed. Carl Schmidt, trans. and annotated by Violet MACDERMOT, Nag Hammadi Studies 9 (Leiden: Brill, 1978), 19. Cf. the German translation in GCS Koptisch-gnostische Schriften I, 5.24 SCHMIDT/SCHENKE, therein also further attestations in the register s.v. "Lichtkleid" (op. cit., 409).

266 *Pistis Sophia* II 63 (NHC 9, 8.14 SCHMIDT). ET from MACDERMOT, *Pistis Sophia*, 257. Cf. the German translation in GCS Koptisch-gnostische Schriften I, 82.22–26 SCHMIDT/SCHENKE, therein also further attestations in the register s.v. "Lichtkleid" (op. cit., 409).

267 The complete name of Jeû, a product of the supreme God (NHS 13, 260.23f. Schmidt), is, for example, repeatedly (260.28, 261.3.5, and 262.13 Schmidt) given as a *nomen barbarum* with sixteen letters (details in Colpe, *Einleitung in die Schriften aus Nag Hammadi*, 280f.). On the manuscript's illustrations, see Markschies, "Gnostische und andere Bilderbücher in der Antike" = idem, *Gnosis und Christentum*, 113–159, here 146–154.

268 *Anonymum Brucianum* 4 (NHS 13, 231.24–232.1. 7f. Schmidt). ET from MacDermot, *Pistis Sophia*, 320f.

269 The sequence of Sethianism historically succeeding Valentianism, long canonical within research, is contested, for example, by Simone Pétrement, *A Separate God: The Christian Origins of Gnosticism* (= *Le Dieu séparé: Les origines du Gnosticisme* [Paris: Les éditions du Cerf, 1984]), trans. Carol Harrison (London: Darton, Longman and Todd, 1991), 17, 135.

270 Turner, *Sethian Gnosticism and the Platonic Tradition*, 502–512, 707–709.

271 See the introduction in François Sagnard, *Clément d'Alexandrie, Extraits de Théodote, Texte Grec, Introduction, Traduction et Notes*, Sources Chrétiennes 23 (Paris: Les éditions du Cerf, 1970), 5–8.

272 Clemens Alexandrinus, *Excerpta ex Theodoto* 45.3–46.2 (GCS Clemens Alexandrinus III, 121.13–16 Stählin/Früchtel/Treu). Closely related is Irenaeus, *Aduersus haereses* I 4.5 (SC 264, 74.103–105 Rousseau/Doutreleau); cf. also Epiphanius, *Panarion haereses* 31.17.12 (GCS Epiphanius I², 412.13f. Holl/Bergermann/Collatz). On the incorporeality of the matter, see also Clemens Alexandrinus, op. cit., 47.4 (122.5–8); and ibid., 50.3 (123.14); also 55.1 (125.8).

273 Clemens Alexandrinus, *Excerpta ex Theodoto* 10.1 (GCS Clemens Alexandrinus III, 109.16–20 Stählin/Früchtel/Treu). ET from *The Excerpta ex Theodoto of Clement of Alexandria*, ed. with translation, introduction, and notes by Robert Pierce Casey, Studies and Documents 1 (London: Christophers, 1934), 47–49.

274 Originally Wilhelm Bousset, *Jüdisch-christlicher Schulbetrieb in Alexandria und Rom: Literarische Untersuchungen zu Philo und Clemens von Alexandria, Justin und Irenäus*, FRLANT 23 (Göttingen: Vandenhoeck & Ruprecht, 1915), 191–195. Accoridng to Eusebius, *Historia ecclesiastica* V 10.1 (GCS Eusebius II/1, 450.18f. Schwartz), Pantaenus was an exponent of the Stoic school; this is problematized by Alain Le Boulluec, "Die 'Schule' von Alexandrien," in *Die Zeit des Anfangs (bis 250)*, hg. Luce Pietri, Die Geschichte des Christentums: Religion—Politik—Kultur 1 (Freiburg: Herder, 2003), 576–621, here 576–579.

275 Sagnard, *Clément d'Alexandrie, Extraits de Théodote*, 12–15; and Casey, *The Excerpta ex Theodoto of Clement of Alexandria*, 105f. and 8–16 from the introduction.

276 Gaster, "Das Schiur Komah," 218–223 = 1341–1346; Scholem, *Jewish Gnosticism, Merkabah Mysticism, and Talmudic Tradition*, 37f.; and Baumgarten, "The Book of Elkesai and Merkabah Mysticism," 212–223, 257–259, esp. 220–222.

277 So Cohen, *The Shi'ur Qomah*, 13–31 and footnotes, 31–41; Schäfer, *Übersetzung der Hekhalot-Literatur*, 4: 38f.

278 Schäfer, *The Origins of Jewish Mysticism*, 327–330: Schäfer is "inclined to locate 3 Enoch's (as well as the rabbis') Metatron in the cultural context of (late) Babylonian Judaism and to regard it as a response to the New Testament message of Jesus Christ." See also Herrmann, "Jüdische Gnosis?" 79–90.

279 These early characterizations are tersely summarized in Nikolaus Müller, s.v. "Christusbilder," in *Realenzyklopädie für protestantische Theologie und Kirche*, 3. Aufl. (Leipzig: Hinrichs, 1898), 4: 63–82, here 63–65; at greater length by Ernst von Dobschütz, *Christusbilder: Untersuchungen zur christlichen Legende, Beilagen*, TU 18/3–4 (Leipzig: Hinrichs, 1899), 294**–297**.

280 Heinz Gauer, *Texte zum byzantinischen Bilderstreit: Der Synodalbrief der drei Patriarchen des Ostens von 836 und seine Verwandlung in sieben Jahrhunderten*, Studien und Texte zur Byzantinistik 1 (Frankfurt am Main: Lang, 1994), l–lx; prior to this already von Dobschütz,

Christusbilder, 207**–211**. On p. 297** Dobschütz enumerates a few texts parallel to Ps.-John Damascene; he provides a synopsis of the ekphrases of these texts (pp. 300f.).

281 GAUER, *Texte zum byzantinischen Bilderstreit*, lvi–lviii with attestations on p. lvii in n. 1. On the historical background to the synodical letter see Alexander Alexandrovic VASILIEV, "The Life of Saint Theodore of Edessa," *Byzantion* 16 (1942/1943), 165–225.

282 GAUER, *Texte zum byzantinischen Bilderstreit*, lxii.

283 *Epistula ad Theophilum imperatorem de sanctis et venerandis* (PG 95, 349.26–42 = 80.12–81.9 GAUER). Cf. GAUER, *Texte zum byzantinischen Bilderstreit*, 74–128.

284 VON DOBSCHÜTZ, *Christusbilder*, 297** n. 1 (Excursus: "Zur Prosopographie Christi"). Cf., however, Epiphanius Monachus, *Vita Mariae* (302**.5 DOBSCHÜTZ): ἐξ ποδῶν τῶν τελείων . . .

285 *Epistula ad Theophilum imperatorem de sanctis et venerandis* (PG 95, 349.23–26 = 80.9–11 GAUER).

286 *Epistula ad Theophilum imperatorem de sanctis et venerandis* (PG 95, 349.17–22 = 78.28–80.2 GAUER).

287 A parallel ekphrasis in Epiphanius Monachus, *Vita Mariae*, mentions (blond) hair, not all too thick and alightly waved (302**.5–8 DOBSCHÜTZ). For frilly hair, see VON DOBSCHÜTZ, *Christusbilder*, 167 n., who points to the coinage of Justinian II, illustration in Manolis CHATZIDAKIS and Gerry WALTERS, "An Encaustic Icon of Christ at Sinai," *Art Bulletin* 49 (1967): 197–208, fig. 10 after p. 200. On the topic, see also Klaus WESSEL, s.v. "Christusbild," in *Reallexikon zur byzantinischen Kunst* (Stuttgart: Hiersemann, 1966), 1: 966–1047, here 970–978.

288 BELTING, *Bild und Kult*, 153. Belting depicts (p. 155 Abb. 79) a votive image from the Pontian Catacombs of Rome which evidences that the type represented by the Sinai Icon was already widesrpread throughout the empire in the sixth century (see also p. 153).

289 See on this CHATZIDAKIS and WALTERS, "An Encaustic Icon of Christ at Sinai"; KURT WEITZMANN, *The Monastery of Saint Catherine at Mount Sinai: The Icons*, vol. 1, *From the Sixth to the Tenth Century* (Princeton, N.J.: Princeton University Press, 1976), 13–15 (nr. B 1 with tables I–II, XXXIX–XLI); and Hans BELTING, *Bild und Kult: Eine Geschichte des Bildes vor dem Zeitalter der Kunst*, 2. Aufl. (München: Beck, 1993 = 1991), 152f.

290 *Epistula synodica patriarchatum orientalium ad Theophilum Imperatorem* (28.1–5 GAUER). Vocally critical of the attempt to reconstruct an earlier text from the traditions is Paul SPECK, *Ich bin's nicht, Kaiser Konstantin ist es gewesen*, ΠΟΙΚΙΛΑ ΒΥΖΑΝΤΙΝΑ 10 (Bonn: Habelt, 1990), 449–534.

291 MARKSCHIES, "'Sessio ad dexteram,'" in Philonenko, *Le trône de Dieu*, 252–317 = idem, *Alta Trinità Beata*, 1–69.

292 *Synopse zur Hekhalot-Literatur* § 705 after O1531 (258.41f. SCHÄFER). Cf. SCHÄFER, *Übersetzung der Hekhalot-Literatur*, 4: 125; and Merkabah Rabba 182f. after COHEN, *The Shi'ur Qomah*, 73 (ET). See ibid., 53; and JANOWITZ, "God's Body."

6   The Body of God in Late Antique Christian Theology

1 Winrich A. LÖHR, "Christianity as Philosophy: Problems and Perspectives of an Ancient Intellectual Project," *VC* 64 (2010): 160–188.

2 Thus already Adele MONACI CASTAGNO, "Origene ed 'i molti': Due religiosità a contrasto," *Augustinianum* 21 (1981): 99–117; differently: Gunnar af HÄLLSTRÖM, *Fides simpliciorum according to Origen of Alexandria*, Societas Scientiarum Fennica, Commentationes Humanarum Litterarum 76 (Helsinki: Finnish Society of Science and Letters, 1984), 64–69. See also Martin HIRSCHBERG, *Studien zur Geschichte der "simplices" in der Alten Kirche: Ein*

Beitrag zum Problem der Schichtungen in der menschlichen Erkenntnis (Berlin: maschinen-schriftlich vervielfältig, 1944), 89–91. On this problem, see in greater detail Norbert BROX, "Der einfache Glaube und die Theologie: Zur altkirchlichen Geschichte eines Dauerprob-lems," *Kairos* 14 (1972): 161–187 = idem, *Das Frühchristentum: Schriften zur Historischen Theologie*, hg. Franz Dünzl, Alfons Fürst und Ferdinand R. Prostmeier (Freiburg: Herder, 2000), 305–336. The prior state of research is weighed up in Heinrich BACHT, s.v. "Einfalt," in *Reallexikon für Antike und Christentum* (Stuttgart: Hiersemann, 1959), 4: 821–840.

3 Cf. Dmitrij BUMAZHNOV, *Der Mensch als Gottes Bild im christlichen Ägypten: Studien zu Gen 1.26 in zwei koptischen Quellen des 4.–5. Jahrhunderts*, Studien und Texte zu Antike und Christentum 34 (Tübingen: Mohr Siebeck, 2006), 1–24.

4 Adolf von HARNACK, *Die Überlieferung der griechischen Apologeten des 2. Jahrhun-derts in der alten Kirche und im Mittelalter*, TU I/1–2 (Leipzig: Hinrichs, 1882 = Ber-lin: Akademie-Verlag, 1991), 243, 248; Hubertus R. DROBNER, "15 Jahre Forschung zu Melito von Sardes (1965–1980): Eine kritische Bibliographie," *VC* 36 (1982): 313–333; and BUMAZHNOV, *Der Mensch als Gottes Bild im christlichen Ägypten*, 16f.

5 Thus, with reference to Eusebius, *Historia ecclesiastica* V 24.5 (GCS Eusebius II/1, 492.3–6 SCHWARTZ). See Gregor WURST, *Die Homilie "De anima et corpore," ein Werk des Meliton von Sardes? Einleitung, synoptische Edition, Übersetzung und Kommentar*, Bd. 2, *Einleitung, Kommentar (Habil. Masch.)* (Freiburg, Schweiz: Verlag, 2000), 10: "Meliton war definitiv kein ἐπίσκοπος." Seen differently in *Méliton de Sardes, Sur la pâque et fragments*, introduc-tion, texte critique, traduction et notes, SC 123 (Paris: Les éditions du Cerf, 1966), 8–10. Eusebius was convinced that Melito was bishop of Sardis: IV 13.8 (330.20f.) and 26.1 (380.21); thus also quite implicitly HARNACK, *Die Überlieferung der griechischen Apologeten des 2. Jahrhunderts in der alten Kirche und im Mittelalter*, 240f.; HALL leaves the question open within his edition (op. cit., xi–xiii). Overview of further discussion in WURST, op. cit., 7–11.

6 Thus Hieronymus, *De viris illustribus* 24.3 (BiPatr 12, 120 CERESA-GASTALDO = 190 BARTHOLD). See also HARNACK, *Die Überlieferung der griechischen Apologeten des 2. Jahrhunderts in der alten Kirche und im Mittelalter*, 241, 250–252. Cf. Gennadius, *Liber ecclesiasticorum dogmatum* 4 (PL 58, 982 B = Cuthbert Hamilton TURNER, "The Liber Ecclesiasticorum Dogmatum attributed to Gennadius," *JTS* 7 [1906]: 89–99, here 90): "Nihil corporeum (sc. in trinitate credamus), ut Melito et Tertullianus."

7 Origenes, *Commentarii in Genesim* D 11 = *Collectio Coisliniana*, frag. 73 PETIT (OWD 1/1, 158.19–21 METZLER = CChr.SG 15, 73.3–5 PETIT).

8 Eusebius, *Historia ecclesiastica* IV 26.2 (GCS Eusebius II/1, 382.7 SCHWARTZ). On the interpretation and the sources of the list, see most recently WURST, *Die Homilie De anima et corpore, ein Werk des Meliton von Sardes?* 2: 14–24.

9 Thus also G. W. H. LAMPE, *A Patristic Greek Lexicon* (Oxford: Clarendon, 1987 = 1961), s.v. (p. 482).

10 On the question of translation in depth, see HARNACK, *Die Überlieferung der griechischen Apologeten des 2. Jahrhunderts in der alten Kirche und im Mittelalter*, 248 n. 351. Har-nack first relates the Latin translation of Rufinus (*De deo corpore induto*: GCS Eusebius II/1, 383.5f. MOMMSEN), to which the Syriac version conforms (*The Ecclesiastical History of Eusebius*, ed. from the manuscripts by the late William Wright and Norman McLean, with a collation of the Ancient Armenian version by Adalbert Merx [Cambridge: Univer-sity Press, 1898], 237.13f.; cf. Eberhard NESTLE, *Die Kirchengeschichte des Eusebius aus dem Syrischen übersetzt*, TU 21/2 [Leipzig: Hinrichs, 1901], 159).

11 See the translation "die Körperlichkeit Gottes" in the German translation from Philipp HAEUSER and Hans Armin GÄRTNER: *Eusebius von Caesarea: Kirchengeschichte*, hg. Heinrich Kraft (Darmstadt: Wissenschaftliche Buchgesellschaft, 3. Aufl. 1989), 225 n. 100; alternately: *Eusebius: The Ecclesiastical History in Two Volumes*, trans. John E.

OULTON and Kirsopp LAKE, vol. 1, LCL 265 (Cambridge, Mass./London: Harvard University Press, 1925), 387: "On God incarnate."

12 The text also tends to be ascribed to Theodoret of Cyrrhus, although his *Quaestiones* is only a source from the collection in Codex Coislin 113 edited by Françoise Petit. Cf. the stemma in *Catenae Graecae in Genesim et in Exodum*, vol. 2, *Collectio Coisliniana in Genesim*, CChr.SG 15 (Turnhout: Brepols; Leuven: University Press, 1986), xix.

13 Origenes, *Commentarii in Genesim* D 11 = *Collectio Coisliniana*, frag. 73 PETIT (OWD 1/1, 158.19–21 METZLER = CChr.SG 15, 73.3–5 PETIT).

14 Origenes, *Commentarii in Genesim* D 11 = *Collectio Coisliniana*, frag. 73 PETIT (OWD 1/1, 158.26–28 METZLER = CChr.SG 15, 73.3–5 PETIT).

15 Also: *Melito of Sardes: On Pascha and Fragments*, ed. and trans. Stuart George HALL, OECT (Oxford: Oxford University Press, 1979), xiii; and WURST, *Die Homilie De anima et corpore, ein Werk des Meliton von Sardes?* 2: 16. According to Pierre NAUTIN, *Origène: Sa vie et son oeuvre*, Christianisme antique 1 (Paris: Beauchesne, 1977), 226f., the list may represent an independent quotation as the third book of the lost *Vita Pamphili* of Eusebius contains *numera indices* of books from the property of the protagonist, also Hieronymus (*Apologia contra Rufinum* II 22 [SC 303.32–35 LARDET]; commentary transmitted in Pierre LARDET, *L'apologie de Jérôme contre Rufin. Un commentaire*, Supplements to Vigiliae Christianae 15 [Leiden: Brill, 1993], 208f.).

16 Jerome cites the title from Eusebius in Greek: *De viris illustribus* 24.2 (BiPatr 12, 120 CERESA-GASTALDO = *Hieronymus, De viris illustribus: Berühmte Männer*, mit umfassender Werkstudie hg., übers. und kommentiert von Claudia Barthold [Mülheim, Mosel: Carthusianus, 2010], 190, 310).

17 See on this Stanislaus VON SYCHOWSKI, *Hieronymus als Litterarhistoriker: Eine quellenkritische Untersuchung der Schrift des Heiligen Hieronymus "De viris illustribus,"* Kirchengeschichtliche Studien 2/2 (Münster: Schöningh, 1894), 116 n. 11; and Carl Albrecht BERNOULLI, *Der Schriftstellerkatalog des Hieronymus: Ein Beitrag zur Geschichte der altchristlichen Litteratur* (Freiburg im Breisgau: Mohr, 1895), 230 d and 84–86.

18 Henry CHADWICK, "The Latin Epitome of Melito's Homily on the Pascha," *JTS* 11 (1960): 76–82; and *The Crosby Schøyen Codex MS 193 in the Schøyen Collection*, ed. James E. GOEHRING, CSCO, Subsidia 85 (Leuven: Peeters, 1990). Gregor Wurst suggested improvements to the reading of the fragmentary manuscript, but the pertinent treatment has not yet been published.

19 WURST, *Die Homilie De anima et corpore, ein Werk des Meliton von Sardes?* 2: 30–44 (*De Pascha*), 18, 57–66 (*De anima et corpore*). On the description of the papyri, see *Repertorium der griechischen christlichen Papyri*, Bd. 2, *Kirchenväter-Papyri*, Tl. 1, *Beschreibungen*, im Namen der Patristischen Arbeitsstelle Münster, hg. Kurt ALAND† und Hans-Udo ROSENBAUM, Patristische Texte und Studien 42 (Berlin/New York: De Gruyter, 1995), KV 54, pp. 359–365 and KV 55, pp. 366–382.

20 Eusebius, *Historia ecclesiastica* IV 26.2 (GCS Eusebius II/1, 382.3.5 SCHWARTZ). In his translaton of the *Ecclesiastical History* of Eusebius, Rufinus translates *de anima et corpore et mente* and *item de anima et corpore* (383.2.4 MOMMSEN); *De viris illustribus* 24.2 (BiPatr 12, 120 CERESA-GASTALDO = 190 BARTHOLD): *De anima et corpore librum unum.* Rufinus had evidently read Περὶ ψυχῆς καὶ σώματος ἢ νοός, which is provided by a few manuscripts, and ἢν ἐν οἶς. Yet others, such as that of the Syriac translation (237.9.11 WRIGHT/McLEAN), do not attest to the crux. The textual version of his edition is explined by Schwartz in the apparatus to this passage accordingly: "ηνενοις scheint aus ἢ ἑνὸς, das in ἢ νοὸς corrigirt werden sollte, entstanden zu sein." WURST, *Die Homilie De anima et corpore, ein Werk des Meliton von Sardes?* 2: 18 n. 109, refers to a conjecture within *Hermiae Philosophi Irrisio Gentilium Philosophorum, Apologetarum Quadrati, Aristidis, Aristonis, Miltiadis, Melitonis, Apollinaris Reliquiae*, illam ad optimos libros MSS. nunc primum aut denuo collatos recensuit prolegomenis, adnotatione versione instruxit has undique collegit praemissis dissertationibus edidit commentariis illustravit Joannes Carl

Theodor Eques de Otto, Corpus apologetarum christianorum saeculi secundi IX (Jena: Mauke [Dufft], 1872), 376 n. 8. Otto had suspected that this might be a gloss in the margin ἤ, ἐν ἐνίοις (in nonnullis codicibus legitur) καί, which had infiltrated the text. HARNACK, *Die Überlieferung der griechischen Apologeten des 2. Jahrhunderts in der alten Kirche und im Mittelalter*, 247 n. 346, would then have expected ἤ ἐν ἐνίοις καὶ νοός; the νοός could then hardly be shed. Like BERNOULLI, *Der Schriftstellerkatalog des Hieronymus*, 196 D, he considers ἤ νοός to be an addition of the fourth century. WURST, op. cit., assumes a slip of the pen originally which was then integrated into the following title: ὁ Περὶ ψυχῆς καὶ σώματος ἤ περὶ λουτροῦ; the gloss ἐν ἐνίοις καὶ ὁ would then slip into the text: ὁ Περὶ ψυχῆς καὶ σώματος ἤ ἐν ἐνίοις καὶ ὁ περὶ λουτροῦ. This (and here Wurst is in agreement with Bernoulli and Harnack) was then corrected to Περὶ ψυχῆς καὶ σώματος ἤ νοός καὶ ὁ περὶ λουτροῦ in the fourth century under the influence of trichotomic anthropology.

21 Michel VAN ESBROECK, "Les Œuvres de Méliton de Sardes en Géorgien," *Bedi Kartlisa: Revue de kartvélologie* 31 (1973): 48–63, here 50; idem, "Nouveaux fragments de Méliton de Sardes dans une homélie grégorienne sur la croix," *Analecta Bollandiana* 90 (1972): 63–99.

22 Overview of the MSS and editions in WURST, *Die Homilie De anima et corpore, ein Werk des Meliton von Sardes?* 2: 57–66. In addition to the Syriac, Coptic, and Georgian versions, a homily of a Ps.-Epiphanius, *De resurrectione*, first edited by Pierre NAUTIN, *Le dossier d'Hippolyte et de Méliton dans les florilèges dogmatiques et chez historiens modernes*, Patristica 1 (Paris: Les éditions du Cerf, 1953), 154–159, occurs, along with other textual witnesses and fragments.

23 On this collection, see the introduction to the edition: Ignaz RUCKER, *Florilegium Edessenum anonymum (syriace ante 562)*, Sitzungsberichte der Bayerischen Akademie der Wissenschaften, Philosophisch-historische Abteilung 5/1933 (München: Beck, 1933), iii–xxi; and Gregor WURST, *Die Homilie De anima et corpore, ein Werk des Meliton von Sardes?* 2: 63f.

24 Melito, frag. XIII (Otto), transmitted in Syriac in British Library Syr. 729 Additional 12156, edited in *Florilegium Edessenum anonymum (syriace ante 562)*, nr. 7$^{1-2}$ frag. 16/17, pp. 12–14 RUCKER. Latin translation in OTTO, op. cit., IX. 419; Greek retroversions in RUCKER, op. cit.; ET in HALL, op. cit., 80f.; French in PERLER, op. cit., 236–239. Detailed introduction in WURST, *Die Homilie De anima et corpore, ein Werk des Meliton von Sardes?* 2: 63f.

25 Gregor WURST, *Die Homilie De anima et corpore, ein Werk des Meliton von Sardes? Einleitung; Synoptische Edition; Übersetzung. Kommentar*, Bd. 1, *Synoptische Edition. Übersetzung (Habil. masch.)* (Freiburg, Schweiz: 2000). German translation of the Coptic text also in BUMAZHNOV, *Der Mensch als Gottes Bild im christlichen Ägypten*, 110–124.

26 Most prominently: NAUTIN, *Le dossier d'Hippolyte et de Méliton dans les florilèges dogmatiques et chez historiens modernes*, 43–73; Wilhelm SCHNEEMELCHER, "Der Sermo 'De anima et corpore': Ein Werk Alexander von Alexandriens?" in *Festschrift für Günther Dehn, zum 75. Geburtstag am 18. April 1957 dargebracht von der Evangelisch-Theologischen Fakultät der Rheinischen Friedrich-Wilhelms-Universität zu Bonn*, hg. Wilhelm Schneemelcher (Neukirchen-Vluyn: Erziehungsverein, 1957), 119–143; and Othmar PERLER, "Recherches sur le Peri Pascha de Méliton," *Recherches de science religieuse* 51 (1963): 407–421 = idem, *Sapientia et caritas: Gesammelte Aufsätze zum 90. Geburtstag*, hg. Dirk van Damme and Otto Wermelinger, Paradosis 29 (Freiburg, Schweiz: Universitätsverlag, 1990), 315–329.

27 According to WURST, *Die Homilie De anima et corpore, ein Werk des Meliton von Sardes?* 2: 78–92, at the beginning is the only slightly reworked frag. XIII, ascribed explicitly to Melito, subsequently the Syriac and Coptic versions of the Pseudo-Athanasian homily as text recension α; the corpus is also described by BUMAZHNOV, *Der Mensch als Gottes Bild im christlichen Ägypten*, 25–34.

28 Ps.-Athanasius, *De anima et corpore* 64–70 (1: 5 Wurst). The transmission of the Syriac version is dispensed with.

29 Wurst not only evidences in his commentary ad. loc. that this concerns "frequently transmitted commonplace philosophy" (um einen häufig rezipierten philosophischen Allgemeinplatz), but also demonstrates that a notion appertaining to this might be found in the Pascha Homily (*De Pascha* 55.390–56.392 [SC 123, 90.405–407 Perler/ OECT 30.390–392 Hall]). Wurst, *Die Homilie De anima et corpore, ein Werk des Meliton von Sardes?* 2: 126.

30 Differently Bumazhnov, *Der Mensch als Gottes Bild im christlichen Ägypten*, 51 on the "Kompositionsrahmen" lines 47–52 (1: 4 Wurst).

31 Ps.-Athanasius, *De anima et corpore* 83 (1: 6 Wurst; no parallels in Syriac). See the commentary in Wurst, *Die Homilie De anima et corpore, ein Werk des Meliton von Sardes?* 2: 132.

32 Plato, *Phaedo* 67 D. Contemporary Jewish and Christian references to this formula in Wurst, *Die Homilie De anima et corpore, ein Werk des Meliton von Sardes?* 2: 126.

33 Ps.-Athanasius, *De anima et corpore* 135 (1: 10 Wurst; no parallels in Syriac). The Coptic nanou corresponds to Greek καλός in both of its fundamental senses as "good" and "beautiful." See Walter Ewing Crum, *A Coptic Dictionary*, compiled with the help of many scholars (Oxford: Clarendon, 1979 = 1939), s.v. (p. 227). Parallels from the monastic literature of late antique Egypt in Bumazhnov, *Der Mensch als Gottes Bild im christlichen Ägypten*, 81–99.

34 *De Pascha* 55.391 (SC 123, 90.406 Perler/30.391 Hall). Further parallels from contemporary literature in Wurst, *Die Homilie De anima et corpore, ein Werk des Meliton von Sardes?* 2: 132.

35 Ps.-Athanasius, *De anima et corpore* 270 (1: 16 Wurst; no parallels in Syriac). The text is also attested in a hagiographic parallel transmission (1: 17 Wurst).

36 Schneemelcher, "Der Sermo 'De anima et corpore,'" 128. The formulation is also employed by Wurst in his commentary: Wurst, *Die Homilie De anima et corpore, ein Werk des Meliton von Sardes?* 2: 146–155.

37 Melito, frag. XIII A lines 334–343 (12 Rucker = 1: 25 Wurst; lines 336 and 341f. are absent within this edition). On the relationship of the versions to one another, see Wurst in his commentary: Wurst, *Die Homilie De anima et corpore, ein Werk des Meliton von Sardes?* 2: 157–169.

38 Ps.-Athanasius, *De anima et corpore* 334–347 (1: 24f. Wurst). For the Georgian text lacking within Wurst, see van Esbroeck, "Nouveaux fragments de Méliton de Sardes," here 74f. Even if the theological concepts of the reassembly of the body-soul unity in the Coptic, Georgian, and Syriac fragments are probably to be placed in a chronological sequence, the linguistic versions of the homily are not: In the largely secondary (from the perspective of theological history) Coptic version l. 336, it is stated of Christ: "as He was Holy Ghost." This predication is characteristic of the theology of identification of Melito and comes across as archaic in the face of the fourth century's differentiations regarding the theology of the Trinity: Wurst, *Die Homilie De anima et corpore, ein Werk des Meliton von Sardes?* 2: 158. On the conception of resurrection within the Coptic version, see, in detail, Bumazhnov, *Der Mensch als Gottes Bild im christlichen Ägypten*, 42–48.

39 Reinhard M. Hübner, *Die Einheit des Leibes bei Gregor von Nyssa: Untersuchungen zum Ursprung der "physischen" Erlösungslehre*, Philosophia Patrum 2 (Leiden: Brill, 1974), 302–305.

40 Hübner has demonstrated that this conception, which plays upon the Parable of the Lost Sheep (Matt 18:12-14 and Luke 15:4-7), takes into account the spiritual-historical roots of the so-called physical doctrine of salvation of the Christian theologians of the fourth century, and he traces this anti-gnostic argument back to Irenaeus, attempting to evidence this in Hippolytus, Pseudo-Hippolytus, Marcellus of Ancyra, and, indeed, Melito: idem, *Die Einheit des Leibes bei Gregor von Nyssa*, 305f.: "Denn physisch ist

die Erlösungsauffassung der Gnostiker, weil hier Identisches (die geistigen Spermen) zu Identischem (Gott) zurückgeführt wird. Und in der Identität ist auch die Universalität begründet: alles Identische, nämlich Geistige, wird geeint. 'Physisch' muß aber auch eine Gegeninterpretation dieser Soteriologie ausfallen, wenn die Identität zwischen Erlöser und Erlöstem vom Geistigen ins Körperliche verlegt wird, denn auch hier bleibt die Identität Grund der Universalität: alle sind *ein* Leib, und da der Leib des Herrn erlöst ist, sind alle Leiber in dem einen Leib erlöst." A discussion of the critical objections which have since arisen may be found in WURST, *Die Homilie De anima et corpore, ein Werk des Meliton von Sardes?* 2: 160–162.

41   Ps.-Athanasius, *De anima et corpore* 360 (1: 26 WURST; no parallels in Syriac). WURST, *Die Homilie De anima et corpore, ein Werk des Meliton von Sardes?* 2: 168, interprets the passage in respect to the body of resurrection: "psalliere deinem Gott, weil du (nun) deinen eigenen und unzerstörbaren Körper hast."

42   RUCKER, *Florilegium Edessenum anonymum*, 12, suggests a retroversion.

43   *Fides secundum partem* 31 (in Hans LIETZMANN, *Apollinaris von Laodicea und seine Schule: Texte und Untersuchungen* [Hildesheim/New York: Olms, 1970 = Tübingen: Mohr Siebeck, 1904], 178.17–179.3). Accordingly, the *Florilegium Edessenum anonymum* already signals in its title that it presents references that Jesus Christ is θεὸς ἀληθινός, in the edition of RUCKER, 1 with commentary on pp. xf.

44   Thus, for example, in Severus Antiochenus, *Epistula* 2 ad Oecumenium (PO XII/2, 189f. BROOKS). See also Roberta C. CHESNUT, *Three Monophysite Christologies: Severus of Antioch, Philoxenus of Mabbug, and Jacob of Sarug*, Oxford Theological Monographs (Oxford: Oxford University Press, 1976), 9–11.

45   Melito, frag. XIV (14 RUCKER = OECT 81 HALL = SC 123, 240 PERLER). Also in the Greek reverse-translation of RUCKER, op. cit. More detailed commentary in WURST, *Die Homilie De anima et corpore, ein Werk des Meliton von Sardes?* 2: 29f.

46   Accordingly, NAUTIN, *Le dossier d'Hippolyte et de Méliton dans les florilèges dogmatiques et chez historiens modernes*, 73, does not hold the fragment to be authentic.

47   On this, in detail, see BUMAZHNOV, *Der Mensch als Gottes Bild im christlichen Ägypten*, 35f. Bumazhnov employs Wurst's synoptic edition but renders his own translations.

48   *De Pascha* 9.58f. (SC 123, 64.63f. PERLER/7.58f. HALL). Translation from HALL, *Melito of Sardis. On Pascha and other Fragments*, 7.

49   Reinhard M. HÜBNER, "Melito von Sardes und Noët von Smyrna," in *Oecumenica et Patristica. Festschrift für Wilhelm Schneemelcher zum 75. Geburtstag*, hg. Damaskinos Papandreou, Wolfgang A. Bienert und Knut Schäferdiek (Stuttgart/Berlin/Köln: Kohlhammer, 1989), 219–240 = idem, *Der paradox Eine. Antignostischer Monarchianismus im zweiten Jahrhundert*, mit einem Beitrag von Markus Vinzent, Supplements to Vigiliae Christianae 50 (Leiden: Brill, 1999), 1–37 (with additional remarks and supplements to the original publication); and GRILLMEIER, *Jesus der Christus im Glauben der Kirche*, 1: 207–212.

50   Thus HÜBNER, "Melito von Sardes und Noët von Smyrna," 26f., in his interpretation of Melito, *De Pascha* 46f., 306–310 (SC 123, 84.328–331 PERLER/OECT 22.306–24.310 HALL).

51   Melito, *De Pascha* 96.715f. (SC 123, 116–118.735–737 PERLER/OECT 54.715f. HALL). HÜBNER, "Melito von Sardes und Noët von Smyrna," 228 = 23, demonstrates that discourse is only so cutting in respect to Judaism (traditionally strong in Anatolia). See also Ingeborg ANGERSTORFER, *Melito und das Judentum* (Diss. theol., masch., Regensburg, 1985), 116–136, 221–227.

52   Anastasius Sinaita, *Viae Dux* XII 2.18 (CChr.SG 8, 203.197f. UTHEMANN).

53   Melito, *De Pascha* 55.390–56.392 (SC 123, 90.405–407 PERLER/OECT 30.390–392 HALL).

54   Melito, *De Pascha* 56.392–397 (SC 123, 90.407–412 PERLER/OECT 30.392–397 HALL). ET from HALL, *Melito of Sardis: On Pascha and Other Fragments*, 31.

55 Othmar Perler, "Méliton 'Peri Pascha' 56 et la traduction géorgienne," in *Forma futuri: Studi in onore del Cardinale Michele Pellegrino*, a cura di Terenzio Alimonti, Francesco Bolgiani, et al. (Turin: Bottega d'Erasmo, 1975), 334–349 = Perler, "Recherches sur le Peri Pascha de Méliton," 407–421 = idem, *Sapientia et caritas: Gesammelte Aufsätze zum 90. Geburtstag*, hg. Dirk van Damme, Otto Wermelinger, u.a., Paradosis 29 (Freiburg, Schweiz: Universitätsverlag, 1990), 349–364. Perler interprets 56.395 (ἡ τοῦ πατρὸς εἰκών) as referring to the soul. Also, in turn, Bumazhnov, *Der Mensch als Gottes Bild im christlichen Ägypten*, 68f.; with Georges Florovsky, "The Anthropomorphites in the Egyptian Desert: Part I," in *Akten des XI. Internationalen Byzantinistenkongresses München 1958*, hg. Franz Dölger und Hans-Georg Beck (München: Beck, 1960), 154–159 = idem, *Collected Works*, vol. 4, *Aspects of Church History*, ed. Richard S. Haugh (Belmont, Mass.: Nordland, 1975), 89–96, here 94.

56 Melito, *De Pascha* 55.389–391 (SC 123, 90.404–406 Perler/OECT 30.392–397 Hall).

57 Wurst, *Die Homilie De anima et corpore, ein Werk des Meliton von Sardes?* 2: 127–129, interprets the passage accordingly, and the ἔκειτο from 55.395 directly, op. cit., 129 as a euphemism for "to bury." Bumazhnov, *Der Mensch als Gottes Bild im christlichen Ägypten*, 66f. concurs with his interpretation.

58 Melito, frag. XIII B line 578 (13 Rucker = 1: 59 Wurst): the fragment was reverse-translated by Rucker, op. cit. Marcel Richard, "Témoins Grecs des fragments XIII et XV de Méliton de Sardes," *Le Muséon* 85 (1972): 309–336 = idem, *Opera minora*, tome 1, (Turnhout: Brepols/Leuven: Peeters, 1976), nr. 7, has pointed to a parallel section within a homily ascribed to Epiphanius entitled *De resurrectione* (Nautin, *Le dossier d'Hippolyte et de Méliton dans les florilèges dogmatiques et chez historiens modernes*, 154–159), which states: Ὁ ἀμέτρητος μετρεῖται καὶ οὐκ ἀντιτάσσεται (157.14f. Nautin = 316.10 Richard = 1: 58.578 Wurst).

59 Parallels from Christian literature are noted by Hübner, "Melito von Sardes und Noët von Smyrna," 226f. = 17f.; in his addenda he relates an interpretation from Hermann Josef Vogt as to the nailing on the cross (op. cit., 35). A somewhat different, anti-gnostic interpretation in Wurst, *Die Homilie De anima et corpore, ein Werk des Meliton von Sardes?* 2: 196–208.

60 Melito, frag. VIIIb (Harnack, *Marcion: Das Evangelium vom fremden Gott*, 422*f. = SC 123.17f. Perler = OECT 72.16f, Hall). Hall, op. cit., xxxii, follows Grant in holding the fragment to be "doubtfully authentic." The fragment stems from a manuscript of the twelfth/thirteenth centuries with predominantly hagiographic texts (Albert Ehrhard, *Überlieferung und Bestand der hagiographischen und homiletischen Literatur der griechischen Kirche von den Anfängen bis zum Ende des 16. Jahrhunderts*, TU 52/2 [Berlin: Akademie-Verlag, 1952], 923): Cod. Vat. Graec. 2022, fol. 238 s.

61 Melito, frag. VIIIb (Harnack, *Marcion: Das Evangelium vom fremden Gott* 423* = SC 123, 228.1–232.4521–30 Perler = OECT 72.20–30 Hall). ET from Hall, *Melito of Sardis: On Pascha and Other Fragments*, 73. On the background to the fragment, probably aimed at Marcion, see Franz Joseph Dölger, *Sol salutis: Gebet und Gesang im christlichen Altertum, mit besonderer Rücksicht auf die Ostung in Gebet und Liturgie*, 3. um Hinweise verm. Aufl., Liturgiewissenschaftliche Quellen und Forschungen 16/17 (Münster: Aschendorff, 1971), 264–271 (cf. the translation of Dölger, op. cit., 265); and Markus Vinzent, *Christ's Resurrection in Early Christianity and the Making of the New Testament* (Farnham, Surrey: Ashgate, 2011), 17f.

62 Matt 3:17 par.

63 This also Bumazhnov, *Der Mensch als Gottes Bild im christlichen Ägypten*, 69, who rejects such an interpretation of Melito. Nevertheless, he closes his pertinent section as follows: "Treffen die hier vorgelegten Überlegungen zur Gottebenbildlichkeit des Menschen bei Ps.-Ath. und in der Pascha-Homilie zu, dann spricht dies eher gegen eine Identifizierung des asiatischen Theologen mit den Anthropomorphiten. Gleichzeitig kann man kaum bestreiten, dass die Ausdrucksweise des hl. Melito einen Anlass für

entsprechende Beschuldigungen gegeben haben könnte, was auch die erwähnte Text-passage bei Origenes indirekt bezeugt."

64 Tito ORLANDI, "Coptic Literature," in *The Roots of Egyptian Christianity*, ed. Birger A. Pearson and James E. Goehring, Studies in Antiquity and Christianity (Philadelphia: Fortress Press, 1992 = 1986), 51–81, here 58f.; and idem, "La tradizione di Melitone in Egitto e l'omelia *De anima et corpore*," *Augustinianum* 37 (1997): 37–50; extensively expounded in BUMAZHNOV, *Der Mensch als Gottes Bild im christlichen Ägypten*, 31f.

65 On the description of Papyri KV 54/55 (P. Chester Beatty XII and P. Michigan Inv. 5553a-d; also P. Bodmer XIII), see ALAND/ROSENBAUM, *Repertorium der griechischen christlichen Papyri*, 2/1: KV 54, pp. 359–365, and KV 55, pp. 366–382. Recently, Nicola Denzey LEWIS and Justine Ariel BLOUNT have pointed to the problems of the respective histories of the finds and demonstrated that the disparate statements as to origin possibly may be traced back to attempts by antiquities dealers and discoverers to conceal or reimagine the real find spots: idem, "Rethinking the Origins of the Nag Hammadi Codices," *JBL* 133 (2014): 399–419, here 407–410, with critical remarks regarding James M. ROBINSON, *The Pachomian Monastic Library at the Chester Beatty Library and the Bibliothèque Bodmer*, Occasional Papers of the Institute for Antiquity and Christianity 19 (Claremont: Institute for Antiquity and Christianity, 1990); see also now idem, *The Story of the Bodmer Papyri: From the First Monastery's Library in Upper Egypt to Geneva and Dublin* (Eugene, Ore.: Cascade, 2011), 88–93.

66 For the prehistory of the interpretation of Gen 1:26 in the Hellenistic Judaism of Alexandria and in Philo, see Stefanie LORENZEN, *Das paulinische Eikon-Konzept*, WUNT 2/250 (Tübingen: Mohr Siebeck, 2008), 69–138; and Robert R. McL. WILSON, "The Early History of the Exegesis of Gen. 1:26," in *Papers Presented to the Second International Conference on Patristic Studies Held at Christ Church Oxford*, ed. Kurt Aland and Frank L. Cross, Studia Patristica 1 = TU 63 (Berlin: Akademie-Verlag, 1957), 420–437.

67 See Gustaf WINGREN, *Man and the Incarnation: A Study in the Biblical Theology of Irenaeus*, trans. Ross Mackenzie (Edinburgh/London: Oliver and Boyd, 1959), 90–100; Peter SCHWANZ, *Imago Dei als christologisch-anthropologisches Problem in der Geschichte der Alten Kirche von Paulus bis Clemens von Alexandrien*, Arbeiten zur Kirchengeschichte und Religionswissenschaft 2 (Halle: Niemeyer, 1969), 117–143; Antonio ORBE, *Antropología de San Ireneo*, Biblioteca de Autores Cristianos 286 (Madrid: La Editorial Católica, 1969), 96–100; Jacques FANTINO, *L'homme, image de Dieu, chez saint Irénée de Lyon* (Paris: Les éditions du Cerf, 1985), 45–181; Anders-Christian JACOBSEN, "The Constitution of Man according to Irenaeus and Origen," in *Körper und Seele: Aspekte spätantiker Anthropologie*, hg. Barbara Feichtinger, Stephen Lake und Helmut Seng, Beiträge zur Altertumskunde 215 (München/Leipzig: Saur, 2006), 67–94, esp. 67–78; and idem, "The Importance of Genesis 1–3 in the Theology of Irenaeus," *ZAC* 8 (2005): 299–316.

68 Irenaeus, *Demonstratio* 11 (PO XII/5, 667.13–16 TER MĒKĒRTTSCHIAN). English translation from *St. Irenaeus: The Demonstration of the Apostolic Preaching*, trans. with introduction and notes by J. Armitage ROBINSON (London: SPCK, 1920), 80. On this see JACOBSEN, "The Importance of Genesis 1–3 in the Theology of Irenaeus," 304f. Cf. the German translation of *Des Heiligen Irenäus Schrift zum Erweise der apostolischen Verkündigung ΕΙΣ ΕΠΙΔΕΙΞΙΝ ΤΟΥ ΑΠΟΣΤΟΛΙΚΟΥ ΚΗΡΥΓΜΑΤΟΣ*, in armenischer Version entdeckt und ins Deutsche übersetzt v. Karapet TER-MĒKĒRTTSCHIAN und Erwand TER-MINASSIANTZ, mit einem Nachwort und Anmerkungen v. Adolf Harnack, TU 31/1 (Leipzig: Hinrichs, 1907), 7. Further passages from *Aduersus haereses* in SCHWANZ, *Imago Dei als christologisch-anthropologisches Problem in der Geschichte der Alten Kirche von Paulus bis Clemens von Alexandrien*, 119f.

69 See Bruno REYNDERS, *Vocabulaire de la "Demonstration" et des fragments de Saint Irénée* (Louvain: Éditions de Chevetogne, 1958), 47; and Matthias BEDROSIAN, *New Dictionary Armenian-English* (Venice: S. Lazarus Armenian Academy, 1875–1879), 606.

70 Bruno REYNDERS, *Lexique comparé du texte grec et des versions latine, arménienne et syriaque de l' "Adversus haereses" de saint Irénée*, tome 2, *Index des mots Latins*,

Notes to Pages 194–195

CSCO 142 Subsidia 6 (Louvain: Durbecq, 1954), 128. See also Ulrich NORTMANN, s.v. "schêma/Figur, Form," in *Aristoteles-Lexikon*, hg. Otfried Höffe, Kröners Taschenausgabe 459 (Stuttgart: Kröner, 2005), 520f., here 520; and Christof RAPP and Tim WAGNER, s.v. "eidos/Gestalt, Art, Form," in *Aristoteles-Lexikon*, 147–158, here 151 and 157.

71 Criticism of a possible derivaton from Platonic philosophy as is assumed by Gerhard MAY, *Schöpfung aus dem Nichts: Die Entstehung der Lehre von der creatio ex nihilo*, Arbeiten zur Kirchengeschichte 48 (Berlin/New York: De Gruyter, 1978), 174 with n. 128, is expressed in Dietmar WYRWA, "Kosmos und Heilsgeschichte bei Irenäus von Lyon," in *Die Weltlichkeit des Glaubens in der Alten Kirche: Festschrift für Ulrich Wickert zum siebzigsten Geburtstag*, in Verbindung mit Barbara Aland und Christoph Schäublin, hg. Dietmar Wyrwa, BZNW 85 (Berlin/New York: De Gruyter, 1997), 443–480, here 459.

72 Irenaeus, *Adversus haereses* V 6.1 (FChr 8/5, 58.5–10 BROX = SC 153, 72.5–9 ROUSSEAU/DOUTRELEAU/MERCIER). On the passage, see SCHWANZ, *Imago Dei als christologisch-anthropologisches Problem in der Geschichte der Alten Kirche von Paulus bis Clemens von Alexandrien*, 120.

73 SCHWANZ, *Imago Dei als christologisch-anthropologisches Problem in der Geschichte der Alten Kirche von Paulus bis Clemens von Alexandrien*, 140; previously already Arnold STRUKER, *Die Gottebenbildlichkeit des Menschen in der christlichen Literatur der ersten zwei Jahrhunderte. Ein Beitrag zur Geschichte der Exegese von Genesis 1,26* (Münster: Aschendorff, 1913), 76–128, in particular 98.

74 Irenaeus, *Demonstratio* 10 (PO XII/5, 667.5–12 TER MĔKĔRTTSCHIAN). ET from ROBINSON, *St. Irenaeus: The Demonstration of the Apostolic Preaching*, 80.

75 Irenaeus, *Demonstratio* 5 (PO XII/5, 663.3–6 TER MĔKĔRTTSCHIAN). ET from ROBINSON, *St. Irenaeus: The Demonstration of the Apostolic Preaching*, 73f. On Irenaeus' divine image, see Eric OSBORN, *Irenaeus of Lyon* (Cambridge: Cambridge University Press, 2001), 36–41.

76 Irenaeus, *Demonstratio* 32 (PO XII/5, 684.8–11 TER MĔKĔRTTSCHIAN).

77 Irenaeus, *Demonstratio* 32 (PO XII/5, 684.8–11 TER MĔKĔRTTSCHIAN). Cf. the German translation of *Des Heiligen Irenäus Schrift zum Erweise der apostolischen Verkündigung*, 19. On the passage, see FANTINO, *L'homme, image de Dieu, chez saint Irénée de Lyon*, 156–160.

78 On this, in greater depth, see Barbara ALAND, "Fides und Subiectio: Zur Anthropologie des Irenäus," in *Kerygma und Logos: Beiträge zu den geistesgeschichtlichen Beziehungen zwischen Antike und Christentum; Festschrift für Carl Andresen zum 70. Geburtstag*, hg. Adolf Martin Ritter (Göttingen: Vandenhoeck & Ruprecht, 1979), 9–28, here 19f.

79 Irenaeus, *Adversus haereses* III 18.1 (FChr 8/3, 220.2–7 BROX = SC 211, 342.7–344.13 ROUSSEAU/DOUTRELEAU). ET from *St. Irenaeus of Lyons: Against the Heresies, Book 3*, trans. and annotated by Dominic J. UNGER OFM Cap with an introduction and further rev. by Ireanaeus M. C. Steenberg, Ancient Christian Writers 64 (New Yoerk/Mahwah, N.J.: Newman Press, 2012), 87–88. On the passage, see Alfred BENGSCH, *Heilsgeschichte und Heilswissen: Eine Untersuchung zur Struktur und Entfaltung des theologischen Denkens im Werk "Adversus haereses" des hl. Irenäus von Lyon*, Erfurter Theologische Studien 3 (Leipzig: St. Benno, 1957), 120–136; FANTINO, *L'homme, image de Dieu, chez saint Irénée de Lyon*, 162f.; and SCHWANZ, *Imago Dei als christologisch-anthropologisches Problem in der Geschichte der Alten Kirche von Paulus bis Clemens von Alexandrien*, 122–130.

80 Irenaeus, *Adversus haereses* V 16.2 (FChr 8/5, 136.1–5 BROX = SC 153, 216.29–32 ROUSSEAU/DOUTRELEAU/MERCIER). or Johannes Damascenus, *Sacra parallela* nr. 167 (TU 20/2, 77.4–9 HOLL).

81 Irenaeus, *Adversus haereses* V 6.1 (FChr 8/5, 56.6–10 BROX = SC 153, 72.5–9 ROUSSEAU/DOUTRELEAU/MERCIER). On the passage, see McL. WILSON, "The Early History of the Exegesis of Gen. 1:26," 432 (with references to parallels in n. 5); FANTINO, *L'homme, image de Dieu, chez saint Irénée de Lyon*, 120f.; and JACOBSEN, "The Importance of Genesis 1–3 in the Theology of Irenaeus," 305f.

82 Irenaeus, *Adversus haereses* IV 20.5 (FChr 8/4, 162.5–13 Brox = SC 100, 638.108–640.117 Rousseau/Hemmerdinger/Doutreleau/Mercier). ET from *The Writings of Irenaeus*, vol. 1, trans. Alexander Roberts and W. H. Rambaut, Ante-Nicene Christian Library 5 (Edinburgh: T&T Clark, 1868), 442. On the passage, see also Bumazhnov, *Der Mensch als Gottes Bild im christlichen Ägypten*, 18.

83 Irenaeus, *Adversus haereses* IV 20.5 (FChr 8/4, 162.17–20 Brox = SC 100, 640.122–125 Rousseau/Hemmerdinger/Doutreleau/Mercier). ET from Roberts/Rambaut, *The Writings of Irenaeus*, 1: 442f.

84 Gerhard Richter, *Oikonomia: Der Gebrauch des Wortes Oikonomia im Neuen Testament, bei den Kirchenvätern und in der theologischen Literatur bis ins 20. Jahrhundert*, Arbeiten zur Kirchengeschichte 90 (Berlin/New York: De Gruyter, 2005), 116–141; and now Katharina Greschat, "Selbstentfaltung Gottes in der Geschichte bei Irenäus von Lyon? Zur Kritik an einer weitverbreiteten Auffassung," in *Gott in der Geschichte: Zum Ringen um das Verständnis von Heil und Unheil in der Geschichte des Christentums*, hg. Mariano Delgado und Volker Leppin, Studien zur christlichen Religions- und Kulturgeschichte 18 (Fribourg: Academic Press/Stuttgart: Kohlhammer, 2013), 71–84, here 79–81.

85 On the attributes ascribed to God, see Osborn, *Irenaeus of Lyon*, 28–32.

86 Irenaeus, *Adversus haereses* IV 20.5 after Johannes Damascenus, *Sacra parallela* nr. 148 (TU 20/2, 62.1–4 Holl = SC 100, 640.122–125 Rousseau/Hemmerdinger/Doutreleau/Mercier).

87 Pseudo-Iustinus Martyr, *De resurrectione* 7 = frag. 107 from Johannes Damascenus (TU 20/2, 44.246–249 Holl; better edition: PTS 54, 118.11–13 Heimgartner). See the commentary in Martin Heimgartner, *Pseudojustin – Über die Auferstehung: Text und Studie*, Patristische Texte und Studien 54 (Berlin/New York: De Gruyter, 2001), 171f.; and in Alberto D'Anna, *Pseudo-Giustino, Sulla Resurrezione: Discorso cristiano del II secolo*, Letteratura Cristiana Antica (Brescia: Morcelliana, 2001), 68–85.

88 Bumazhnov, *Der Mensch als Gottes Bild im christlichen Ägypten*, 17f.; and previously already Florovsky, "The Anthropomorphites in the Egyptian Desert: Part I," 93–95.

89 P. Oxy. III 405: Aland/Rosenbaum, *Repertorium der griechischen christlichen Papyri* 2/1: KV 46, pp. 317–320; and P. Jenensis Irenaeus: Aland/Rosenbaum, *Repertorium der griechischen christlichen Papyri*, 2/1: KV 47, pp. 321–327.

90 On Timotheus Aelurus, see Alois Kardinal Grillmeier, *Jesus der Christus im Glauben der Kirche*, Bd. 2/4, *Die Kirche von Alexandrien mit Nubien und Äthiopien nach 451*, unter Mitarbeit von Theresia Hainthaler (Freiburg: Herder, 1990), 7–35.

91 *Timotheus Älurus' des Patriarchen von Alexandrien Widerlegung der auf der Synode zu Chalcedon festgesetzten Lehre*, Armenischer Text mit deutschem und armenischem Vorwort, zwei Tafeln und dreifachem Register, hg. Karapet Ter-Mĕkĕrttschian und Erwand Ter-Minassiantz (Leipzig: Hinrichs, 1908), 256.25–257.31 (frag. 2 Jordan), 257.33–258.25 (frag. 3 Jordan), and also 258.26–259.23 (frag. 4 Jordan). On this work, see Grillmeier, *Jesus der Christus im Glauben der Kirche*, 2/4: 12f.; Eduard Schwartz, *Codex Vaticanus Gr. 1431: Eine antichalkedonische Sammlung aus der Zeit Kaiser Zenos*, Abhandlungen der Bayerischen Akademie der Wissenschaften, philosophisch-historische Abteilung 32/6 (München: Oldenbourg, 1927), 98–117 (quotation in the Armenian transmission); and (for the Syriac transmission) R. Y. Ebied and Lionel R. Wickham, "Timothy Aelurus: Against the Definition of the Council of Chalcedon," in *After Chalcedon: Studies in Theology and Church History, Offered to Albert van Roey for His Seventieth Birthday*, ed. Carl Laga, OLA 18 (Leuven: Peeters, 1985), 115–166.

92 Edited in Hermann Jordan, *Armenische Irenaeusfragmente*, mit deutscher Übersetzung nach Dr. W[illy] Lüdtke, zum Tl. erstmalig herausgegeben und untersucht, TU 36/3 (Leipzig: Hinrichs, 1913), 3–5.56–60 (Fr. 2; text and translation; on the problem as to whether the fragment originates from Melito, see pp. 84–99), 5–7, 60–62 (Fr. 3), 7f. 62–64 (Fr. 4), and study 64–99.

93 On this, see Alois Kardinal Grillmeier, *Jesus der Christus im Glauben der Kirche*, Bd. 2/2, *Die Kirche von Konstantinopel im 6. Jahrhundert*, unter Mitarbeit von Theresia

Hainthaler (Freiburg/Basel/Vienna: Herder, 1989), 54–74. Evidently a textual tradition on the (earthly) body of Christ attributed to Irenaeus was already a part of John's argumentation: Cf. Iohannis Caesariensis, *Apologia Concilii Chalcedonensis (Excerpta syriaca latine versa)* 118 (CChr.SG 1, 46.1152–1161 RICHARD/AUBINEAU). On the passage, see G. JOUSSARD, "Une citation et un ouvrage de saint Hippolyte sous le nom de saint Irénée?" *Revue des sciences religieuses* 17 (1937): 290–305.

94   Irenaeus, *Adversus haereses* III 18.1 (FChr 8/3, 220.2–7 BROX = SC 211, 342.7–344.13 ROUSSEAU/DOUTRELEAU).

95   Transmitted is Irenaeus, *Adversus haereses* III 18.1 = frag. 11 (II, 440f. HARVEY) = Severus Antiochenus, *Contra impium Grammaticum* III 17 (CSCO 101, 285, 1–15 LEBON).

96   Eduard SCHWARTZ, "Unzeitgemäße Beobachtungen zu den Clementinen," *ZNW* 31 (1932): 151–198, here 185. On the question of genre, most recently in detail with a history of research on the genre-theoretical suppositions, see Meinolf VIELBERG, *Klemens in den pseudoklementinischen Recognitionen: Studien zur literarischen Form des spätantiken Romans*, TU 145 (Berlin: Akademie-Verlag, 2000), 111–169; and previously Mark J. EDWARDS, "The *Clementina*: A Christian Response to the Pagan Novel," *Classical Quarterly* 42 (1992): 459–474.

97   In selection: Adolf HILGENFELD, *Die clementinischen Recognitionen und Homilien, nach ihrem Ursprung und Inhalt* (Jena: Schreiber, 1848), 19–25, 245–280; Hans WAITZ, *Die Pseudoklementinen: Homilien und Rekognitionen:Eine quellenkritische Untersuchung*, TU 25/4 (Leipzig: Hinrichs, 1904), 16–77; Georg STRECKER, Das Judenchristentum in den Pseudoklementinen, TU 70², 2. bearb. und erw. Aufl. (Berlin: Akademie-Verlag, 1981), 35–96; Jürgen WEHNERT, "Literarkritik und Sprachanalyse: Kritische Anmerkungen zum gegenwärtigen Stand der Pseudoklementinen-Forschung," *ZNW* 74 (1983): 268–301; idem, "Abriss der Entstehungsgeschichte des pseudoklementinischen Romans," *Apocrypha* 3 (1992): 211–236; and now his introduction in idem, *Pseudoklementinische Homilien: Einführung und Übersetzung*, Kommentare zur apokryphen Literatur 1/1 (Göttingen: Vandenhoeck & Ruprecht, 2010), 29–46. A history of research may also be found in VIELBERG, *Klemens in den pseudoklementinischen Recognitionen*, 11–23; STRECKER, *Das Judenchristentum in den Pseudoklementinen*, 1–34; F. Stanley JONES, "The Pseudo-Clementines: A History of Research," in idem, *Pseudoclementina*, 50–113; and now in Frédéric AMSLER, "État de la recherche récente sur le roman Pseudo-Clémentin," in *Nouvelles intrigues pseudo-Clémentines. Plots in the Pseudo-Clementine Romance: Actes du deuxième colloque international sur la littérature apocryphe chrétienne, Lausanne– Genève, 30 août–2 septembre 2006*, éd. Frédéric Amsler, Albert Frey, Charlotte Touati, et Renée Girardet, Publications de l'Institut Romand des Sciences Bibliques 6 (Prahins: Éditions du Zèbre, 2008), 25–45.

98   Shlomo PINES, "Points of Similarity between the Exposition of the Doctrine of the Sefirot in the Sefer Yezira and a Text of the Pseudo-Clementine Homilies: The Implications of This Resemblance," *Proceedings of the Israel Academy of Sciences and Humanities* 7 (1989): 63–141, here 64.

99   SCHWARTZ ("Unzeitgemäße Beobachtungen zu den Clementinen," 152) has indicated that it is entirely uncertain as to "wieweit die lateinische Übertragung als ein zuverlässiger, einigermaßen ausreichender Ersatz für das verlorene griechische Original angesehen werden kann. Die Proben von mangelhafter Kenntnis des Griechischen und gewissenloser Flüchtigkeit, die Rufin bei der Übersetzung der Kirchengeschichte des Eusebius in reichlicher Fülle liefert, sind geeignet, ein Mißtrauen zu erwecken." In another passage, Schwartz comments on the translation: "Sie ist ein liederliches, unzuverlässiges Machwerk" (ibid., 154). VIELBERG characterizes the qualities of the translator Rufinus entirely differently: idem, *Klemens in den pseudoklementinischen Recognitionen*, 184–187.

100 Thus, entirely in agreement, Nicole KELLEY, *Knowledge and Religious Authority in the Pseudo-Clementines: Situating the Recognitions in Fourth Century Syria*, WUNT 2/213 (Tübingen: Mohr Siebeck, 2006), 27–35. Already SCHWARTZ, "Unzeitgemäße Beobachtungen zu den Clementinen," 162–164, indicated that Origen and Eusebius evidently

knew of different "Clementines" and not one and the same "foundational text," which according to his opinion preceeds both versions, and thus maintains the supposition of a foundational text and sources incorporated into it to be superfluous. Hans WAITZ defends himself against these perspectives most prominently with two papers: "Neues zur Text- und Literarkritik der Pseudoklementinen?" *Zeitschrift für Kirchengeschichte 52 (1933):* 305–318; and idem, "Die Lösung des pseudoclementinischen Problems," *Zeitschrift für Kirchengeschichte* 59 (1940): 304–341.

101 Wilhelm FRANKENBERG, *Die syrischen Clementinen mit griechischem Paralleltext: Eine Vorarbeit zu dem literargeschichtlichen Problem der Sammlung,* TU 48/3 (Leipzig: Hinrichs, 1937), ix–xxi. Bernhard REHM does not employ the Syriac transmission, by contrast, in the textual reconstruction of the parallel fragments *Homiliae* I–XIV: GCS Pseudoklementinen I, xvi–xx.

102 VIELBERG, *Klemens in den pseudoklementinischen Recognitionen,* 18–20.

103 WAITZ, *Die Pseudoklementinen: Homilien und Rekognitionen,* 27, considers nevertheless whether *Homiliae* XVII 12–20 belongs to the foundational text, as they quote "in the same manner" ("in gleicher Weise") as a passage from the *Recognitiones* Exodus 33:20 (!): Cf. *Homiliae* XVII 16.4 (GCS Pseudoklementinen I, 238.12 REHM/STRECKER) and *Recognitiones* III 29.5 (GCS Pseudoklementinen II, 118.3f. REHM/STRECKER). Nevertheless, comparison with the passage from the *Recognitiones* demonstrates that clear disparities in the interpretation of the passage exist. In the *Recognitiones,* it is stated in III 30.1–3 (118.4–8). The crux of the homilies, that angels will be rendered in flesh so as to be visible for humans, and humans rendered angels, is entirely lacking. It might at the most be stated that the justifiability of visions is disputed by Peter and Simon within the foundational text. WAITZ, op. cit., 99f., justifies at greater length his ascription to the "foundational text" and a source of this foundational text.

104 Jürgen WEHNERT, "'Das Geheimnis der Siebenzahl': Spekulationen über die unendliche Gestalt Gottes in den pseudoklementinischen Homilien, Buch 16 und 17," in *Nouvelles intrigues pseudo-Clémentines. Plots in the Pseudo-Clementine Romance: Actes du deuxième colloque international sur la littérature apocryphe chrétienne, Lausanne– Genève, 30 août–2 septembre 2006,* éd. Frédéric Amsler, Albert Frey, Charlotte Touati, et Renée Girardet, Publications de l'Institut Romand des Sciences Bibliques 6 (Prahins: Éditions du Zèbre, 2008), 461–467, here 461, refers to allegedly literal parallels between *Homiliae* XVII 7.3, 8.8 (GCS Pseudoklementinen I, 232.17–22, 233.23–29 REHM/STRECKER) and *Recognitiones* II 61.6 (GCS Pseudoklementinen II, 88.22–25). The fact that in all three textual extracts God is discussed as light and the light of the sun is described as darkness in contrast to this light (232.18–20 [88.24f.]) does not bear out as an argument the very general thesis "that this doctrine (sc. the teaching on the form of God) was already preserved in the earliest literary stratum" (dass diese Lehre schon in der ältesten Literarschicht enthalten war) and that it constituted "a product of the Judeo-Christian theology of the second century AD" (um ein Produkt judenchristlicher Theologie des 2. Jh.s. n.Chr.).

105 F. Stanley JONES, "Marcionism in the *Pseudo-Clementines,*" in idem, *Pseudoclementina,* 152–171, here 163f. On the literary coherence of the narrative on the speech, SCHWARTZ, "Unzeitgemäße Beobachtungen zu den Clementinen," 167–169.

106 Tertullian, *De praescriptione haereticorum* 30.1–2 (I Talenti 10, 204.1–11 REFOULÉ/ CARPIN); and idem, *Aduersus Marcionem* IV 4.3 (SC 456, 78.20–24 MORESCHINI). See also HARNACK, *Marcion: Das Evangelium vom fremden Gott,* 16*–23* (on the year AD 144).

107 This question is posed most prominently by Barbara ALAND, s.v. "Marcion und die Marcioniten," *TRE* 22: 89–101, here 94–96 = idem, *Was ist Gnosis?* 318–340, here 327–330.

108 Ps.-Clemens Romanus, *Homiliae* XVII 3.3 (GCS Pseudoklementinen I, 230.6f. REHM/ STRECKER).

109   Ps.-Clemens Romanus, *Homiliae* XVII 3.5–7 (GCS Pseudoklementinen I, 230.12–16 REHM/STRECKER). ET from *The Clementine Homilies*, trans. Thomas SMITH, Peter PETERSON, and Dr. DONALDSON, Ante-Nicene Christian Library 17 (Edinburgh: T&T Clark, 1870), 258f. Cf. throughout the following the German translation: Jürgen WEHNERT, *Pseudoklementinische Homilien: Einführung und Übersetzung*, passim, here p. 223.

110   Aristoteles, *Metaphysica* VII 3, 1029 a 2–7. On its interpretation, see NORTMANN, s.v. "schêma/Figur, Form," 520f.

111   Aristoteles, *Physica* IV 4: ὥστε τὸ τοῦ περιέχοντος πέρας ἀκίνητον πρῶτον, τοῦτ' ἔστιν ὁ τόπος, "So that is what place is: the first unchangeable limit of that which surrounds" (212 a 20f.). ET from *Aristotle: Physics, Books III and IV*, trans. with introduction and notes by Edward HUSSEY, new impression with corrections and additions (Oxford: Clarendon, 1993), 28. See on this also Anton Friedrich KOCH, s.v. "topos (1)/Raum," in *Aristoteles-Lexikon*, 603–605.

112   Ps.-Clemens Romanus, *Homiliae* XVI 10.4 (GCS Pseudoklementinen I, 223.8–11 REHM/STRECKER). ET from SMITH/PETERSON/DONALDSON, *The Clementine Homilies*, 249.

113   Naturally a Near Eastern cylinder seal is not meant (thus WEHNERT, "'Das Geheimnis der Siebenzahl,'" 462), but rather a classic metaphorical explication of the likeness to God, as is attested repeatedly in the ancient Christian authors. Cf. Gregorius Nazianzenus, *Orationes theologicae* XXIX, *De filio* 17 (SC 250, 11–14 GALLAY/JOURJON).

114   Ps.-Clemens Romanus, *Homiliae* XVI 19.1–3 (GCS Pseudoklementinen I, 226.22–227.1 REHM/STRECKER).

115   Ps.-Clemens Romanus, *Homiliae* XVII 7.2 (GCS Pseudoklementinen I, 232.13–15 REHM/STRECKER).

116   PINES, "Points of Similarity between the Exposition of the Doctrine of the Sefirot in the Sefer Yezira and a Text of the Pseudo-Clementine Homilies," 103, considers this sentence to be a later gloss.

117   Ps.-Clemens Romanus, *Homiliae* XVII 7.2–6 (GCS Pseudoklementinen I, 232.16–233.1 REHM/STRECKER). Also quoted in Johannes Damascenus, *Sacra parallela* nr. 21 (TU 20/2, 11.5–9 HOLL). ET from SMITH/PETERSON/DONALDSON, *The Clementine Homilies*, 261f. XVII 7.4f. (232.23–25).

118   Ps.-Clemens Romanus, *Homiliae* XVII 10.5 (GCS Pseudoklementinen I, 235.7–9 REHM/STRECKER).

119   Cf. Zech 9:17. See Helmer RINGGREN, s.v. "יפה," s.v. "תמונה," in *Theologisches Wörterbuch zum Alten Testament* (Stuttgart: Kohlhammer, 1982), 3: 787–790, here 789. On this, see also Reinhold GESTRICH, *Schönheit Gottes: Anstösse zu einer neuen Wahrnehmung*, Ästhetik — Theologie — Liturgik 47 (Berlin: LIT, 2007), 92–104.

120   An overview of relevant prior research attempts within German exegetical literature since 1950 is provided by Alexandra GRUND, "'Aus der Schönheit Vollendung strahlt Gott auf' (Ps 50.2): Bemerkungen zur Wahrnehmung des Schönen in den Psalmen," in *"Wie schön sind deine Zelte, Jakob!" Beiträge zur Ästhetik des Alten Testaments*, hg. Alexandra Grund u.a., Biblisch-Theologische Studien 60 (Neukirchen-Vluyn: Neukirchener, 2003), 100–129, here 101–106.

121   Edwin HATCH and Henry A. REDPATH, *A Concordance to the Septuagint and Other Greek versions of the Old Testament (including the Apocryphal Books)* (Graz: Akademische Druck- und Verlagsanstalt, 1954 = Oxford: Clarendon, 1897), s.v. (p. 715f.); and Walter GRUNDMANN, s.v. "καλός," in *Theologisches Wörterbuch zum Neuen Testament* (Stuttgart: Kohlhammer, 1938), 3: 539–553, here 546.

122   *Hymni Homerici in Cererem* 275f. ET from *Homeric Hymns: Homeric Apocrypha; Lives of Homer*, ed. and trans. Martin L. WEST, LCL 496 (Cambridge, Mass.: Harvard University Press, 2003), 55.

123   Plato, *Respublica* II 381 C.

124   (Ps.-?) Plato, *Hippias maior* 296 E.

125 Clemens Alexandrinus, *Stromata* IV 116.2 (GCS Clemens Alexandrinus II, 299.14–17 STÄHLIN/FRÜCHTEL/TREU). ET from WILSON, *The Writings of Clement of Alexandria*, 2: 192.

126 A brief somewhat contemporary account of the theory of vision through emenation is to be found in Apuleius, *Apologia pro se de magia* 15.6 (SQAW 36, 40.5–7 HELM = SAPERE 5, 84 HAMMERSTAEDT = DK 47 A 25 [I, 431.14–16 DIELS/KRANZ]). See also Gérard SIMON, *Der Blick, das Sein und die Erscheinung in der antiken Optik: Anhang; Die Wissenschaft vom Sehen und die Darstellung des Sichtbaren*, aus dem Französischen von Heinz Jatho (München: Fink, 1992), 30–66; and DIHLE, "Vom sonnenhaften Auge," in Blume und Mann, *Platonismus und Christentum*, 84–91, here 84–88.

127 Plato, *Timaeus* 45 B/C. ET from BURY, *Plato: Timaeus. Critias. Cleitophon. Menexenus*, 101. On the philosophical-historical background, see SIMON, *Der Blick, das Sein und die Erscheinung in der antiken Optik*, 38–41; also Wolfgang KULLMANN, *Aristoteles und die moderne Wissenschaft*, Philosophie der Antike 5 (Stuttgart: Steiner, 1998), 246–248.

128 Ps.-Clemens Romanus, *Homiliae* XVII 7.3 (GCS Pseudoklementinen I, 232.16–233.1 REHM/STRECKER).

129 So DIHLE, "Vom sonnenhaften Auge," 85, with reference to a doxographical account of Chrysippus in Aëtius, *Placita philosophorum* IV 15.3 (*Doxographi Graeci* 406.4–14 DIELS), therein regardless, op. cit., 406.6f. Aëtius, *Placita philosophorum* I 3.18 (*Doxographi Graeci* 285.1–7 DIELS): . . . ὑπὸ τοῦ ὁρατικοῦ πνεύματος . . . as a designation.

130 Galenus, *De placitis Hippocratis et Platonis* VII 5.31–41 (CMG V 4/1/2, 460.1–33 DE LACY). See on this the partial translation and commentary in SIMON, *Der Blick, das Sein und die Erscheinung in der antiken Optik*, 44f.

131 Matt 5:8: μακάριοι οἱ καθαροὶ τῇ καρδίᾳ, ὅτι αὐτοὶ τὸν θεὸν ὄψονται. On the background in the language of the Psalms, see Ulrich LUZ, *Das Evangelium nach Matthäus*, Tlbd. 1, *Mt 1–7*, 2. durchges. Aufl., EKKNT I/1 (Zürich: Benziger/Neukirchen-Vluyn: Neukirchener, 1989), 211.

132 Origenes, *Contra Celsum* VII 33 (GCS Origenes II, 184.2–9 KOETSCHAU = SVigChr 54, 487.2–9 MARCOVICH). See Karlmann BEYSCHLAG, "Zur Geschichte der Bergpredigt in der Alten Kirche," *Zeitschrift für Theologie und Kirche* 74 (1977): 291–322, 302f.

133 Ps.-Clemens Romanus, *Homiliae* XVII 7.4 (GCS Pseudoklementinen I, 232.24f. REHM/STRECKER).

134 Ps.-Clemens Romanus, *Homiliae* XVII 8.1 (GCS Pseudoklementinen I, 233.4–7 REHM/STRECKER).

135 Ps.-Clemens Romanus, *Homiliae* XVII 8.3–5 (GCS Pseudoklementinen I, 233.4–19 REHM/STRECKER). ET from SMITH/PETERSON/DONALDSON, *The Clementine Homilies*, 262f.

136 Melissus in Simplicius, *In Aristotelis physicorum libros commentaria* I 2 ad p. 185 a 20 b 5 (CAG IX, 40.12f. DIELS = DK 30 B 7 [I, 80.17f. DIELS/KRANZ]). On this, see Hans-Joachim NEWIGER, *Untersuchungen zu Gorgias' Schrift über das Nichtseiende* (Berlin: De Gruyter, 1973), 94–97.

137 Hans Günter ZEKL, s.v. "Raum I. Griechische Antike," in *Historisches Wörterbuch der Philosophie* (Darmstadt: Wissenschaftliche Buchgesellschaft, 1992), 8: 67–82, here 70f.

138 Theo KOBUSCH, "Nichts, Nichtseiendes," in *Historisches Wörterbuch der Philosophie* (Darmstadt: Wissenschaftliche Buchgesellschaft, 1984), 6: 805–836, here 806f.

139 Thus, accordingly, in his recapitulation of the contents of the argumentation, WEHNERT, "'Das Geheimnis der Siebenzahl,'" 463.

140 Ps.-Clemens Romanus, *Homiliae* XVII 8.9 (GCS Pseudoklementinen I, 233.29–234.3 REHM/STRECKER).

141 Accordingly, in an account of Pythagorean-Orphean theory of number, also Ps.-Iamblichus, *Theologumena arithmeticae* 6 (BiTeu 48.6–10 DE FALCO). The mathematical relationship referred to by Pseudo-Clement and Pseudo-Iambichus alike is the following:

"Six" is a number equal from every side, a so-called triangular number which comes into existence when the first three natural numbers one, two, and three are added together. The units may be ordered in the form of an "equally sided" triangle (and hence these are termed figured numbers). The mathematical relationship described in the Greek sentence quoted ("Accordingly the Pythagoreans named Six ὁλομέλεια . . . either inasmuch as it alone is in sum equal to its parts or limbs and less than 10 . . .") may be explained as follows: "Six" is both the sum of its actual parts one, two, and three, as $1 + 2 + 3 = 6$: Such a number is termed by mathematicians since Antiquity "complete," the next complete number being twenty-eight. From the antique perspective, these numbers reflect the world's harmony, as also becomes clear from the text: ἐμμελές. Hence, it is hardly necessary, as WEHNERT, "'Das Geheimnis der Siebenzahl,'" 465 does, to refer to the equilateral triangle in which the numbers one to six "are thus spread about the end points and midpoints of the sides of the triangle" (auf den End- und Mittelpunkten der Dreiecksseiten so verteilen) so "that the sums of sides are identical" (dass die Seitensummen identisch sind). I thank at this juncture heartily my Berlin colleague Eberhard Knobloch for his insights.

142   Ps.-Clemens Romanus, *Homiliae* XVII 9.1–10.3 (GCS Pseudoklementinen I, 234.7–235.2 REHM/STRECKER). ET from SMITH/PETERSON/DONALDSON, *The Clementine Homilies*, 263f.

143   On the historical-philosophical background in the early Stoa, see PINES, "Points of Similarity between the Exposition of the Doctrine of the Sefirot in the Sefer Yezira and a Text of the Pseudo-Clementine Homilies," 74–76; for the positions in Plato and Aristotle, see Ekkehard MÜHLENBERG, *Die Unendlichkeit Gottes bei Gregor von Nyssa: Gregors Kritik am Gottesbegriff der klassischen Metaphysik*, Forschungen zur Kirchen- und Dogmengeschichte 16 (Göttingen: Vandenhoeck & Ruprecht, 1966), 29–58.

144   On this context, see Jan HELDERMAN, *Die Anapausis im Evangelium Veritatis: Eine vergleichende Untersuchung des valentinianisch-gnostischen Heilsgutes der Ruhe im Evangelium Veritatis und in anderen Schriften der Nag-Hammadi-Bibliothek*, Nag Hammadi Studies 18 (Leiden: Brill, 1984), 47–84.

145   Ps.-Clemens Romanus, *Homiliae* XVII 10.1 (GCS Pseudoklementinen I, 235.5–9 REHM/STRECKER).

146   Clemens Alexandrinus, *Stromata* IV 109.2 (GCS Clemens Alexandrinus II, 296.12f. STÄHLIN/FRÜCHTEL/TREU). Cf. Pseudo-(?)Basilius Caesariensis, *Homilia de creatione hominis* II 5 (SC 160, 250.17 SMETS/VAN ESBROECK = GNO Supplementum 55.13 HÖRNER).

147   Ps.-Iamblichus, *Theologumena arithmeticae* 7 (BiTeu 55.1–4. 10f. DE FALCO). On the author Anatolius, who was likely Iamblichus' teacher, see John DILLON, "Iamblichus of Chalcis (c. 240–325 A.D.)," *ANRW* II/36.2: 862–909, here 866–870.

148   Ps.-Iamblichus, *Theologumena arithmeticae* 6 (BiTeu 43.17–44.1 DE FALCO),

149   "Dessen Argumentation Kopfschütteln verursachen mag": WEHNERT, "'Das Geheimnis der Siebenzahl,'" 464. Wehnert substantiates as to how strongly the section is influenced by biblical and philosophical terminology.

150   Thus, for the talk of the pairs of opposites which God created, one can refer to the pairs of opposites in the principles theory of the so-called Valencian gnosis; the parallels, however, are actually confined to the Greek term συζυγία, which, moreover, is not so central to the doctrine of the pairs of opposites in the pseudo-Clementines: Ps.-Clemens Romanus, *Homiliae* II 15.1f. (GCS Pseudoklementinen I, 40.25–41.6 REHM/STRECKER). For συζυγία, see the attestations s.v. in *Die Pseudoklementinen III Konkordanz zu den Pseudoklementinen*, Tl. 2, *Griechisches Wortregister, Syrisches Wortregister, Index nominum, Stellenregister*, von Georg STRECKER, Die Griechischen Christlichen Schriftsteller (Berlin: Akademie-Verlag, 1989), 347.

151   Ps.-Clemens Romanus, *Homiliae* XVII 10.2 (GCS Pseudoklementinen I, 234.21–235.2 REHM/STRECKER). ET from SMITH/PETERSON/DONALDSON, *The Clementine Homilies*, 264.

152   Ps.-Clemens Romanus, *Homiliae* XVII 10.5 (GCS Pseudoklementinen I, 235.5–9 REHM/STRECKER). ET from SMITH/PETERSON/DONALDSON, *The Clementine Homilies*, 265.

153 Ps.-Clemens Romanus, *Homiliae* XVII 11.2 (GCS Pseudoklementinen I, 235.11–14 REHM/STRECKER). ET from SMITH/PETERSON/DONALDSON, *The Clementine Homilies*, 265.

154 On this passage in detail, see Jürgen WEHNERT, "Petrus *versus* Paulus in den pseudoklementinischen Homilien 17," in *Christians as a Religious Minority in a Multicultural City: Modes of Interaction and Identity Formation in Early Imperial Rome; Studies on the Basis of a Seminar at the Second Conference of the European Association for Biblical Studies (EABS) from July 8–12, 2001, in Rome*, ed. Jürgen Zangenberg and Michael Labahn, Journal for the Study of the New Testament Supplement Series 243 (London/ New York: T&T Clark, 1980), 175–185; Wehnert interprets the passage as a stunted anti-Pauline polemic (pp. 179f.). HILGENFELD, *Die clementinischen Recognitionen und Homilien, nach ihrem Ursprung und Inhalt dargestellt*, 265f., 269, also noted here antiMarcionite polemic, Paul being ultimately the apostle venerated by Marcion.

155 Cf. the use of the biblical passage in question in *Recognitiones* III 29.5 (GCS Pseudoklementinen II, 118.3f. REHM/STRECKER).

156 Ps.-Clemens Romanus, *Homiliae* XVII 16.2–6 (GCS Pseudoklementinen I, 238.9–16 REHM/STRECKER). ET from SMITH/PETERSON/DONALDSON, *The Clementine Homilies*, 269f. On the passage, see STRECKER, *Das Judenchristentum in den Pseudoklementinen*, 191–194 (according to Strcker originally directed at Paul and not Simon).

157 A distant parallel is the discussion between Peter and Simon on the quasi-Marcionite thesis that in addition to God a further immesurable light force exists: *Recognitiones* II 49.3–50.1 (GCS Pseudo-klementinen II, 80.27–81.7 REHM/STRECKER).

158 Cf. also *Recognitiones* III 30.5 (GCS Pseudoklementinen II, 118.11–13 REHM/STRECKER): "futurum enim tempus ostendit, in quo ex hominibus angeli fient, quit in spiritu mentis deum videbunt." See also STRECKER, *Das Judenchristentum in den Pseudoklementinen*, 216.

159 Ps.-Clemens Romanus, *Homiliae* XVII 7.3 (GCS Pseudoklementinen I, 232.18 REHM/ STRECKER).

160 Ps.-Clemens Romanus, *Homiliae* II 44.2 (GCS Pseudoklementinen I, 53.12f. REHM/ STRECKER).

161 Ladislaus MADYDA, *De pulchritudine imaginum deorum quid auctores Graeci saec. 2 p. Chr. n. iudicaverint*, Polska Akademia umiejętności, Archiwum filologiczne 16 (Warschau/Krakau: Gebethner et Wolff, 1939); 34–56.

162 Bernhard REHM, *Die Pseudoklementinen*, Bd. 1, *Homilien*, hg. Bernhard Rehm†, 3. verbesserte Aufl. v. Georg Strecker, GCS Pseudoklementinen I (Berlin: AkademieVerlag, 1992), vii. Seen otherwise in idem, "Zur Entstehung der pseudoclementinischen Schriften," *ZNW* 37 (1938): 77–184, here 158–160; Rehm reckons with a date of composition between the Nicaenum of AD 325 and the Constantinopolitanum of AD 381.

163 PINES, "Points of Similarity between the Exposition of the Doctrine of the Sefirot in the Sefer Yezira and a Text of the Pseudo-Clementine Homilies," 80–114 (criticism: Annette Yoshiko REED, "Rethinking [Jewish-]Christian Evidence for Jewish Mysticism," in *Hekhalot Literature in Context: Between Byzantium and Babylonia*, ed. Ra'anan Boustan, Martha Himmelfarb, and Peter Schäfer, TSAJ 153 [Tübingen: Mohr Siebeck, 2013], 349–377, here 359–376); and Alon G. GOTTSTEIN, "The Body as Image of God in Rabbinic Literature," *HTR* 87 (1994): 171–195, here 173; but cf. David H. AARON, "Shedding Light on God's Body in Rabbinic Midrashim: Reflections on the Theory of a Luminous Adam," *HTR* 90 (1997): 299–314.

164 According to the Midrash Bereshit Rabba 12.6 on Gen 2:4 (102.2f. THEODOR/ALBECK), Adam is stripped of his exorbitant size and his luminescence after the fall. On this passage, see AARON, "Shedding Light on God's Body in Rabbinic Midrashim," 308.

165 Midrash Wajiqra Rabbah 20.1 on Lev 16:1 (131 WÜNSCHE/KRUPP; cf. the digitally accessible collation of the most important manuscripts: http://www.biu.ac.il/JS/midrash/VR/ editionData.htm, last accessed on 18 May 2019). See on this GOTTSTEIN, "The Body as Image of God in Rabbinic Literature," 179; and the criticism of the translation and

employment of the passage in A<small>ARON</small>, "Shedding Light on God's Body in Rabbinic Midrashim," 303–305. On the translation see op. cit., 305; equally on the parallel transmission within the rabbinical literature, op. cit., 305 n. 19.

166 Midrash Bereshit Rabba 20.12 on Gen 5:21 (196.4f. T<small>HEODOR</small>/A<small>LBECK</small>): "In der Pentateuchrolle des Rabbi Meir (eines Tannaiten der dritten Generation im zweiten Jahrhundert) stand geschrieben: 'Lichtgewänder'" (in the place of "Hautgewändern"). See also Nissan R<small>UBIN</small> and Admiel K<small>OSMAN</small>, "The Clothing of the Primordial Adam as a Symbol of Apocalyptic Time in the Midrashic Sources," *HTR* 90 (1997): 155–174; G<small>OTTSTEIN</small>, "The Body as Image of God in Rabbinic Literature," 179f.; and O<small>RLOV</small>, *Heavenly Priesthood in the Apocalypse of Abraham*, 121–124. The contexts for the history of Christian theology are briefly expounded in Erik P<small>ETERSON</small>, "Theologie des Kleides," *Benediktinische Monatsschrift* 16 (1934): 347–356 = idem, *Marginalien zur Theologie und andere Schriften*, hg. mit einer Einführung von Barbara Nichtweiß, Erik Peterson: Ausgewählte Schriften 2 (Würzburg: Echter, 1995), 10–19; see also idem, "Theologie der Kleidung," *Wort und Wahrheit* 2 (1947): 193–199 = idem, *Marginalien zur Theologie und andere Schriften*, 20–27; and Sebastian B<small>ROCK</small>, "Clothing Metaphors as a Means of Theological Expression in Syriac Tradition," in *Typus, Symbol, Allegorie bei den östlichen Vätern und ihre Parallelen im Mittelalter*, hg. Margot Schmidt in Zusammenarbeit mit Carl Friedrich Geyer, Eichstätter Beiträge 4 (Regensburg: Pustet, 1982), 11–40; and idem, "Jewish Traditions in Syriac Sources," *JJS* 30 (1979): 212–232, here 216f.

167 So-called Hymn of the Pearl (*Acta Thomae* 108–113), here lines 9, 14, 72, 76, 82 (Erwin P<small>REUSCHEN</small>, *Zwei gnostische Hymnen* [Gießen: Töpelmann, 1904], 19, 24f. = Paul-Hubert P<small>OIRIER</small>, *L'Hymne de la Perle des Actes de Thomas: Introduction, texte—traduction, commentaire*, Homo religiosus 8 [Louvain-La-Neuve: Université Catholique de Louvain, 1981], 329f. and 334). On the different Greek and Syrian vocabulary, see ibid., 414f.

168 Exod 34:29f.

169 Arguing enthusiastically for a purely metaphorical meaning is A<small>ARON</small>, "Shedding Light on God's Body in Rabbinic Midrashim," 307–309, contra G<small>OTTSTEIN</small>, "The Body as Image of God in Rabbinic Literature," 179.

170 Most recent introduction to the corpus and the question as to its authorship: Klaus F<small>ITSCHEN</small>, *Pseudo-Makarios: Reden und Briefe*, eingel., übers. und mit Anmerkungen versehen, Bibliothek der griechischen Literatur 52 (Stuttgart: Hiersemann, 2000), 1–21.

171 Ps.-Macarius/Symeon, *Homiliae* (after Typ III or C) XX 1 (TU 72, 103.5–12 K<small>LOSTERMANN</small>/ B<small>ERTHOLD</small> = SC 275, 236.31–238.40 D<small>ESPREZ</small>).

172 See on this the parallels in Kohelet Rabbah 8.2. G<small>OTTSTEIN</small>, "The Body as Image of God in Rabbinic Literature," 181; A<small>ARON</small>, "Shedding Light on God's Body in Rabbinic Midrashim," 310 (with ET of the parallel passage); and Hector M. P<small>ATMORE</small>, *Adam, Satan, and the King of Tyre: The Interpretation of Ezekiel 28:11–19 in Late Antiquity,* Jewish and Christian Perspectives 20 (Leiden: Brill, 2012), 18–21.

173 Gilles Q<small>UISPEL</small>, "Sein und Gestalt," in idem, *Gnostic Studies,* vol. 2, Uitgaven van het Nederlands Historisch-Archeologisch Instituut te Istanbul 34/2 (İstanbul: Nederlands Historisch-Archaeologisch Institut in het Nabije Oosten, 1975), 142–145: "Wir stellen dann fest, dass die christliche Mystik verschiedene Wurzeln hat und sich deshalb auch in einer fortwährenden Spannung bewegt. Es gibt, kurz gesagt, eine Seinsmystik und eine Gestaltmystik; die erste ist hellenischen, die andere jüdischen Ursprungs." See also, in more detail, idem, *Makarius, das Thomasevangelium und das Lied von der Perle*, NovT-Sup 15 (Leiden: Brill, 1967), passim, esp. 116–118; and idem, "Ezekiel 1:26 in Jewish Mysticism and Gnosis," *VC* 34 (1980): 1–13, here 12f.; critically Dmitrij B<small>UMAZHNOV</small>, *Visio mystica im Spannungsfeld frühchristlicher Überlieferungen: Die Lehre der sogenannten Antoniusbriefe von der Gottes- und Engelschau und das Problem unterschiedlicher spiritueller Traditionen im frühen ägyptischen Mönchtum*, Studien und Texte zu Antike und Christentum 52 (Tübingen: Mohr Siebeck, 2009), 251f. with n. 338; in agreement, S<small>TROUMSA</small>, "The Incorporeality of God," here 353 with n. 68.

174 S<small>CHWARTZ</small>, "Unzeitgemäße Beobachtungen zu den Clementinen," 172.

175 Christoph MARKSCHIES, "Theologische Diskussionen zur Zeit Konstantins: Arius, der 'arianische' Streit und das Konzil von Nicaea, die nachnizänischen Auseinandersetzungen bis 337," in *Das Entstehen der einen Christenheit (250–430)*, hg. Charles (†) und Luce Piétri, Die Geschichte des Christentums: Religion—Politik—Kultur 2 (Freiburg: Herder, 1996), 271–344; edited and updated in idem, *Alta Trinità Beata: Gesammelte Studien zur altkirchlichen Trinitätstheologie* (Tübingen: Mohr Siebeck, 2000), 99–195.

176 Ps.-Clemens Romanus, *Homiliae* XX 7.6f. (GCS Pseudoklementinen I, 272.21–26 REHM/ STRECKER). ET from SMITH/PETERSON/DONALDSON, *The Clementine Homilies*, 318f. I would not hazard an interpretation wherein ὁμοούσιος is "neutered" ("stark entwertet") and then, thereafter, discussed "in the sense of a decisive Arianism" ("im Sinn eines entschiedenen Arianismus") (notwithstanding REHM, "Zur Entstehung der pseudoclementinischen Schriften," 160). Logical subordination (for example, in the theological salvation-historical or liturgical-practical-pious interests in prayer) is also naturally known from an "orthodox" Nicean theology.

177 SCHWARTZ, "Unzeitgemäße Beobachtungen zu den Clementinen," 173 with extensive references.

178 SCHWARTZ, "Unzeitgemäße Beobachtungen zu den Clementinen," 197. Carl SCHMIDT, *Studien zu den Pseudo-Clementinen, nebst einem Anhange: Die älteste römische Bischofsliste und die Pseudo-Clementinen*, TU 46/1 (Leipzig: Hinrichs, 1929), 240, associates the milieu of the "foundational text" with the *Didascalia* (preserved in its entirety in Syriac), a comprehensive church ordinance which, following BRUNO STEIMER, *Vertex Traditionis: Die Gattung der altchristlichen Kirchenordnungen*, BZNW 63 (Berlin/New York, 1992), 49–52, may be localized in Syria and dated to the third century AD.

179 REHM, "Zur Entstehung der pseudoclementinischen Schriften," 159.

180 Thus Manlio SIMONETTI, "Modelli culturali nella Cristianità orientale del II–III secolo," initially in *De Tertullien aux Mozarabes: Mélanges offerts à Jacques Fontaine . . . à l'occasion de son 70. anniversaire*, vol. 1, *Antiquité tardive et christianisme ancien (IIIᵉ—VIᵉ siècles)*, éd. Louis Holtz, Collection des études augustiniennes, Série Antiquités (Paris: Institut d'Études Augustiniennes, 1992), 381–392; now in idem, *Ortodossia ed eresia tra I e II secolo*, Armarium 5 (Messina: Soveria Manelli, 1994), 315–331, here 327f.; further references to literature and discussion in BUMAZHNOV, *Der Mensch als Gottes Bild im christlichen Ägypten*, 11–15.

181 Carl W. GRIFFIN and David L. PAULSEN, "Augustine and the Corporeality of God," *HTR* 95 (2002): 97–118, here 98: ". . . One would expect that Jewish conceptions of God would be perpetuated within Christianity."

182 Hieronymus, *De viris illustribus* 80.1–3 (BiPatr 12, 186f. CERESA-GASTALDO = 232 BARTHOLD). The section may be found in translation with commentary in *L. Caecilii Firmiani Lactantii De ira Dei liber*, quem ediderunt, transtulerunt, praefatione atque notis instruxit Henricus KRAFT et Antonia WLOSOK, *Laktanz: Vom Zorne Gottes*, eingel., hg., übertragen und erläutert v. Heinrich KRAFT und Antonie WLOSOK, TzF 4 (Darmstadt: Wissenschaftliche Buchgesellschaft, 1983), viif.; further attestations that Jerome highly valued the work in the commentary ad loc in *Hieronymus: De viris illustribus*, Berühmte Männer, mit umfassender Werkstudie hg., übers. und kommentiert von Claudia BARTHOLD (Mülheim, Mosel: Carthusianus, 2010), 361.

183 For Jerome, see the preceding note; on the dating of the text, see Antonie WLOSOK, "§ 570: L. Caecilius Firmianus Lactantius," in *Restauration und Erneuerung: Die lateinische Literatur von 284 bis 374 n.Chr.*, hg. Reinhart Herzog, Handbuch der lateinischen Literatur der Antike, Bd. 5 = Handbuch der Altertumswissenschaft 8/5 (München: Beck, 1989), 383–385.

184 Attestations for the formula, Antonie WLOSOK, *Laktanz und die philosophische Gnosis: Untersuchungen zu Geschichte und Terminologie der gnostischen Erlösungsvorstellung*, Abhandlungen der Heidelberger Akademie der Wissenschaften, Philosophisch-historische Klasse 2/1960 (Heidelberg: Winter, 1960), 232–246, here 231 n. 1: "Die

Gottesprädikation *Pater et Dominus* bei Laktanz in Analogie zum römischen *Pater Familias*"; also see pp. 241–246.

185   Lactantius, *Divinae institutiones* IV 4.2 (BiTeu II, 320.10 HECK/WLOSOK). ET from *Lactantius: Divine Institutes*, trans. with an introduction and notes by Anthony BOWEN and Peter GARNSEY, Translated Texts for Historians 40 (Liverpool: Liverpool University Press, 2004), 230. See on this also WLOSOK, *Laktanz und die philosophische Gnosis*, 242–246; idem, "Römischer Religions- und Gottesbegriff in heidnischer und christlicher Zeit," *Antike und Abendland* 16 (1970): 39–53 = *Res Humanae–Res Divinae: Kleine Schriften*, hg. Eberhard Heck und Ernst August Schmidt, Bibliothek der klassischen Altertumswissenschaften 2/84 (Heidelberg: Winter, 1990), 15–34; and idem, "Vater und Vatervorstellungen in der römischen Kultur," in *Das Vaterbild im Abendland*, Bd. 1, *Rom, frühes Christentum, Mittelalter, Neuzeit, Gegenwart*, hg. Hubertus Tellenbach (Stuttgart u.a.: Kohlhammer, 1978), 18–54 = idem, *Res Humanae–Res Divinae: Kleine Schriften*, 35–83.

186   Lactantius, *De opificio Dei* 8.3 (CSEL 27/1, 27.18–28.4 BRANDT = SC 213, 150.10–16 PERRIN). ET from *Lactantius: The Minor Works*, trans. Sister Mary Francis MACDONALD, Fathers of the Church, New Translation 54 (Washington, D.C.: Catholic University of America Press, 1965), 25. Further evidence of this notion in Lactantius is noted by WLOSOK, *Laktanz und die philosophische Gnosis*, 221f.; on the history, in depth, see ibid., 8–47; and Lactance, *L'ouvrage du Dieu créateur*, tome 2, commentaire et index, par Michel PERRIN, SC 214 (Paris: Les éditions du Cerf, 1974), 305–307.

187   See the attempt at definition by Kurt SOKOLOWSKI, "Emotion," in *Allgemeine Psychologie*, hg. Jochen Müsseler und Wolfgang Prinz, Spektrum Lehrbuch (Heidelberg: Spektrum, 2002), 337–384, here 342: "Im englischen Sprachraum wird nicht so deutlich zwischen affect, emotion und mood unterschieden wie im deutschen Sprachraum zwischen Affekt, Emotion und Stimmung. So werden affect, emotion und mood häufig synonym verwandt, wobei affect zudem häufig als Obergriff eingesetzt wird, während im Deutschen Affekte kurze und intensive Emotionszustände bezeichnen, die starke Verhaltenstendenzen besitzen. Emotionen sind bewertende Stellungnahmen zu Umweltereignissen, die verschiedene physische und psychische Teilsysteme [Komponenten] zum Zwecke einer möglichst optimalen Reaktion koordinieren. Stimmungen unterscheiden sich von Emotionen durch geringere Intensität und längere Dauer–häufig wird Stimmungen auch eine fehlende Objektbezogenheit im Gegensatz zu Emotionen, die immer auf etwas gerichtet sind, zugesprochen." Additional to the definition here related, the classical Greek and Latin terminology is also translated, mostly not distinguishing between "emotion" and "affect" in the sense of a modern differentiation.

188   SVF III, 459 (III, 111.32–38 VON ARNIM, ascribed by the editor to Chrysippus' writing on the affects) = Plutarchus, *Moralia* 28, *De virtute morali* 7, 447 A (BiTeu III, 143.13–20 POHLENZ/SIEVEKING). See on this topic Maximilian FORSCHNER, "Die pervertierte Vernunft: Zur stoischen Theorie der Affekte," *Philosophisches Jahrbuch* 87 (1983): 258–280; and peviously already Jürgen HENGELBROCK, s.v. "Affekt," in *Historisches Wörterbuch der Philosophie* (Darmstadt: Wissenschaftliche Buchgesellschaft, 1971), 1: 89–93, here 90f.

189   This material is summarily relayed in Herbert FROHNHOFEN, *ΑΠΑΘΕΙΑ ΤΟΥ ΘΕΟΥ: Über die Affektlosigkeit Gottes in der griechischen Antike und bei den griechischsprachigen Kirchenvätern bis zu Gregorios Thaumaturgos*, Europäische Hochschulschriften, Reihe 23, Theologie 318 (Frankfurt am Main: Lang, 1987), 108–115 (Philo), 179–212 (Clement and Origen); and previously, more generally, Christiane INGREMEAU, *La colère de dieu*, Introduction, texte critique, traduction, commentaire et notes, Sources Chrétiennes 289 (Paris: Les éditions du Cerf, 1982), 13–24 ("Le theme de la colère divine"). For Clement, see already Theodor RÜTHER, *Die sittliche Forderung der Apatheia in den ersten beiden christlichen Jahrhunderten und bei Klemens von Alexandrien: Ein Beitrag zur Geschichte des christlichen Vollkommenheitsbegriffes*, Freiburger Theologische Studien 63 (Freiburg: Herder, 1949). For Origen, see Adolf PRIMMER, *Απάθεια und Έλεος im Gottesbegriff des Origenes* (Vienna: Diss. phil. masch., 1956); Michel SPANNEUT, "Apatheia ancienne, Apatheia chrétienne: 1ère partie; L'*apatheia* ancienne," in *ANRW* II/36.7:

4641–4717 (on Philo, pp. 4701–4704); and idem, "L' 'apatheia' chrétienne aux quatre premiers siècles," *Proche-Orient chrétien* 52 (2002): 165–302.

190 Cf., for example, nr. 27.5, torgē (ὀργή), here cited after *Das Berliner "koptische Buch" (P 20915): Eine wiederhergestellte frühchristlich-theologische Abhandlung*, bearbeitet von Gesine SCHENKE ROBINSON unter Mitarbeit von Hans-Martin Schenke† und Uwe-Karsten Plisch, CSCO 610, SC 49 (Leuven: Peeters, 2004), 55. On the topic, see also Annewies VAN DEN HOEK, "*Papyrus Berolinensis 20915* in the Context of other Early Christian Writings from Egypt," in Perrone, Bernardini, and Marchini, *Origeniana Octava*, 75–92, here 83f.

191 Tertullianus, *Adversus Marcionem* II 27.1 (CChr.SL 1, 505.23–28 KROYMANN). See, among others, FROHNHOFEN, *ΑΠΑΘΕΙΑ ΤΟΥ ΘΕΟΥ*, 221–231.

192 Tertullianus, *Adversus Marcionem* II 16.1 (CChr.SL 1, 492.1–5 KROYMANN). ET from *Tertullian Adversus Marcionem, Books 1 to 3*, ed. and trans. Ernest EVANS (Oxford: Clarendon, 1972), 129.

193 Tertullianus, *Adversus Marcionem* II 11.2 (CChr.SL 1, 488.22–26 KROYMANN).

194 Hence, KRAFT/WLOSOK in *Laktanz: Vom Zorne Gottes*, xxiii.

195 Lactantius, *De ira Dei* 2.9f. (TzF 4, 6 KRAFT/WLOSOK = SC 289, 96.45–52 INGREMEAU).

196 Lactantius, *Diuinae institutiones* I 5.26 (BiTeu I, 20.13–15 HECK/WLOSOK). See on this Jochen WALTER, *Pagane Texte und Wertvorstellungen bei Lactanz*, Hypomnemata 165 (Göttingen: Vandenhoeck & Ruprecht, 2006), 144–148 (on Seneca, p. 146, It would seem unlikely that Lactantius "independently glimpsed normativising factors in the texts of Seneca" [in den Texten Senecas eigenständig normsetzende Faktoren erblickte]).

197 Lactantius, *De ira Dei* 17.13 (TzF 4, 58 KRAFT/WLOSOK = SC 289, 178.69–77 INGREMEAU). ET from MACDONALD, *Lactantius: The Minor Works*, 101. For this definition, cf. Seneca, *Dialogi* III 3.3 = *De ira* I 3.3 (*L. Annaeus Seneca: De ira. Über die Wut*, Lateinisch/ Deutsch, übers. und hg. Jula WILDBERGER, Reclams Universal-Bibliothek 18456, [Stuttgart: Reclam, 2007] 12; the first part probably stood in a lacuna of the textual transmission of roughly a third of the entire volume appearing after I 2.3): "Aristotelis finitio non multum a nostra abest; ait enim iram esse cupiditatem doloris reponendi"; Aristoteles, *De anima* I 1 403 a 30 (here, admittedly, only one of many definitions repoted by Aristotle): οἷον ὀργὴ τί ἐστιν· ὁ μὲν γὰρ ὄρεξιν ἀντιλυπήσεως ἤ τι τοιοῦτον, ὁ δὲ ζέσιν τοῦ περὶ καρδίαν αἵματος καὶ θερμοῦ; and idem, *Rhetorica* II 2 1378 a 30–32: Ἔστω δὴ ὀργὴ ὄρεξις μετὰ λύπης τιμωρίας [φαινομένης] διὰ φαινομένην ὀλιγωρίαν εἰς αὐτὸν ἤ τι τῶν αὐτοῦ, τοῦ ὀλιγωρεῖν μὴ προσήκοντος. Stated in brief: (Ps.-) Andronicus Rhodius, *De passionibus* 4 (cited after: *Pseudo-Andronicus de Rhodes: Περὶ παθῶν*, édition critique du texte grec et de la traduction latine medievale par Anne GLIBERT-THIRRY, Corpus Latinum commentariorum in Aristotelem Graecorum, Supplementum 2 [Leiden: Brill, 1977], 231.81): Ὀργὴ μὲν οὖν ἐστιν ἐπιθυμία τιμωρίας τοῦ ἠδικηκέναι δοκοῦντος·. In detail, see also Janine FILLION-LAHILLE, *Le De ira de Sénèque et la philosophie stoïcienne des passions*, Études et commentaires (Paris: Klincksieck, 1984), 170–179.

198 Lactantius, *De ira Dei* 17.17 (TzF 4, 58 KRAFT/WLOSOK = SC 289, 180.93–97 INGREMEAU). ET from MACDONALD, *Lactantius: The Minor Works*, 101.

199 Lactantius, *De ira Dei* 4.2 (TzF 4, 8 KRAFT/WLOSOK = SC 289, 98.6–9 INGREMEAU). ET from MACDONALD, *Lactantius: The Minor Works*, 65f. Cf. on this *Epicurea*, hg. Hermann Usener (Leipzig: Teubner, 1887), frag. 365, 244.4–6 (absent in Epicuro, *Opere*, introduzione, testo critico, traduzione e note di Graziano Arrighetti, Classici della Filosofia 4 [Turin: Einaudi, 1960]); further attestations in the commentary in INGREMEAU on the passage (SC 289, 232f.).

200 Lactantius, *De ira Dei* 4.6 (TzF 4, 8 KRAFT/WLOSOK = SC 190.21–24 INGREMEAU). ET from MACDONALD, *Lactantius: The Minor Works*, 66.

201 Lactantius, *De ira Dei* 4.11 (TzF 4, 10 KRAFT/WLOSOK = SC 289, 102.43–45 INGREMEAU). ET from MACDONALD, *Lactantius: The Minor Works*, 67.

202 Lactantius, *De ira Dei* 5.1–3 (TzF 4, 10–12 KRAFT/WLOSOK = SC 289, 104.1–16 INGREMEAU). ET from MACDONALD, *Lactantius: The Minor Works*, 67f.

203 Seneca, *De ira* I 1.3f. (6–8 WILDBERGER). ET from *Seneca: Anger, Mercy, Revenge*, trans. Robert A. KASTER and Martha C. NUSSBAUM, *The Complete Works of Lucius Annaeus Seneca* (Chicago/London: University of Chicago Press, 2010), 14.

204 Lactantius, *De ira Dei* 5.9f. (TzF 4, 12 KRAFT/WLOSOK = SC 289, 106.41–48 INGREMEAU). ET from MACDONALD, *Lactantius: The Minor Works*, 69.

205 Lactantius, *De ira Dei* 6.1 (TzF 4, 14 KRAFT/WLOSOK = SC 289, 119.2–7 INGREMEAU). ET from MACDONALD, *Lactantius: The Minor Works*, 70.

206 Lactantius, *De ira Dei* 7.3–5 (TzF 4, 16 KRAFT/WLOSOK = SC 289, 110.14–112.23 INGREMEAU). ET from MACDONALD, *Lactantius: The Minor Works*, 71. See on this Michel PERRIN, *L'homme antique et chrétien: L'anthropologie de Lactance 250–325*, Théologie historique 59 (Paris: Beauchesne, 1981), 68–85. In the most recent edition, Lactance, *La colère de dieu*, 41–44, a reworking is assumed; against this, in his review of the publication: Eberhard HECK, *Gnomon* 57 (1985): 145–148, here 147.

207 Lactantius, *De ira Dei* 15.3f. (TzF 4, 50 KRAFT/WLOSOK = SC 289, 164.15–166.23 INGREMEAU). ET from MACDONALD, *Lactantius: The Minor Works*, 95. Cf. on this *De ira Dei* 19.1 (TzF 4, 64 KRAFT/WLOSOK = SC 289, 186.1–6 INGREMEAU). See also PERRIN, *L'homme antique et chrétien*, 250–325, 277–280.

208 Lactantius, *De ira Dei* 15.5 (TzF 4, 50 KRAFT/WLOSOK = SC 289, 166.23–27 INGREMEAU).

209 Lactantius, *De ira Dei* 15.10–12 (TzF 4, 52 KRAFT/WLOSOK = SC 289, 168.48–57 INGREMEAU).

210 Aristoteles, *Ethica Nicomachea* II 4, 1105 b 21–23. ET from *Aristotle: Nicomachean Ethics, Books II–IV*, trans. with a commentary by C. C. W. TAYLOR, Clarendon Aristotle Series (Oxford: Clarendon, 2006), 7. On its interpretation, see Christoph RAPP, *Aristoteles Rhetorik, übers. und erläutert*, 2. Halbbd., Aristoteles Werke in deutscher Übersetzung 4/2 (Berlin: Akademie-Verlag, 2002), 545–552; and idem, s.v. "pathos/Widerfahrnis, Affekt," in Höffe, *Aristoteles-Lexikon*, 427–436.

211 Lactantius, *De ira Dei* 18.13f. (TzF 4, 62 KRAFT/WLOSOK = SC 289, 186.66–72 INGREMEAU = SVF II, 1057 [II, 311.34f. VON ARNIM]). ET from MACDONALD, *Lactantius: The Minor Works*, 104.

212 Cf. Aëtius, *Placita philosophorum* I 6.1 (*Doxographi Graeci* 292.22f. DIELS); and SVF II, 1060 (II, 312.9–13 VON ARNIM) = [Metrodorus]/Philodemus, περὶ αἰσθήσεως, Pap. Herc. 19/698, col. XVI and XVIII 484 (compared with Annick MONET, "[Philodème, *Sur les sensations*], PHerc. 19/698," *Cronache Ercolanesi* 26 [1996]: 27–126, here 104f.). See Heinrich KARPP, *Probleme altchristlicher Anthropologie: Biblische Anthropologie und philosophische Psychologie bei den Kirchenvätern des dritten Jahrhunderts*, Beiträge zur Förderung christlicher Theologie 44/3 (Gütersloh: Bertelsmann, 1950), 149 n. 2.

213 L. Annaeus Seneca, *Diui Claudii apocolocyntosis* 8.1 (TuscBü 24 BINDER = SVF II, 1059 [II, 312.3–7 VON ARNIM]). ET from Robert GRAVES, *Claudius the God and His Wife Messalina* (London: Penguin, 1984 [1934]), 432.

214 Socrates, *Historia ecclesiastica* II 9.1–3 (GCS.NF 1, 98.9–16 HANSEN). While Sozomen does not directly state that he employs George of Laodicea as a source, his turns of phrase are strikingly parallel in the pertinent section. Cf. *Historia ecclesiastica* III 6.1f. (FChr 73/2, 348.1–8 HANSEN). A brief recapitulation of the biography is found in Robert E. WINN, *Eusebius of Emesa: Church and Theology in the Mid-fourth Century* (Washington, D.C.: Catholic University of America Press, 2011), 1–5; more detailed in Eligius Maria BUYTAERT, *L'héritage littéraire d'Eusèbe d'Émèse: Étude critique et historique, textes*, Bibliothèque du Muséon 24 (Louvain: Bureaux du Muséon, 1949), 61–96; and in Henning J. LEHMANN, *Per Piscatores: Orsardaukh; Studies in the Armenian Version of a Collection of Homilies by Eusebius of Emesa and Severian of Gabala* (Aarhus: Eget, 1975), 23–36.

215 The word "partisan" is here set in quotation marks because the network-based ecclesio-political activist coalitions in the fourth century were frequently formed ad hoc (for

example, at synods) and are thus scarcely to be compared to modern political parties, as the expression "Kirchenparteien," popular within German-speaking research, would suggest.

216 Socrates, *Historia ecclesiastica* II 9.41f. (GCS.NF 1, 98.16–21 HANSEN). This encompasses, according to BUYTAERT, *L'héritage littéraire d'Eusèbe d'Émèse*, 72f., the conventional sciences and also astrology.

217 Robert Barend ter HAAR ROMENY, *A Syrian in Greek Dress: The Use of Greek, Hebrew and Syriac Biblical Texts in Eusebius of Emesa's Commentary on Genesis*, Traditio Exegetica Graeca 6 (Leuven: Peeters, 1997), 7–12, 140–146.

218 BUYTAERT, *L'héritage littéraire d'Eusèbe d'Émèse*, 70f.

219 BUYTAERT, *L'héritage littéraire d'Eusèbe d'Émèse*, 74–79, dated with Socrates and Sozomen to AD 341; this is incorrect, as had already been concluded by Eduard SCHWARTZ, "Von Konstantins Tod bis Sardika 342," *Nachrichten von der Königlichen Gesellschaft der Wissenschaften zu Göttingen: Philosophisch-historische Klasse* (Göttingen: Vandenhoeck & Ruprecht, 1911), 469–522, here 486–488 = idem, *Zur Geschichte des Athanasius*, Gesammelte Schriften 3. Bd. (Berlin: De Gruyter, 1959), 265–334, here 286–289. Since then, he has been followed by, to name a few, Wilhelm SCHNEEMELCHER, "Die Kirchweihsynode von Antiochien 341," in *Bonner Festgabe Johannes Straub zum 65. Geburtstag am 18. Oktober 1977*, dargebracht von Kollegen und Schülern, hg. Adolf Lippold, Bonner Jahrbücher, Beihefte 39 (Bonn: Habelt, 1977), 319–346, here 334–337 = idem, *Reden und Aufsätze: Beiträge zur Kirchengeschichte und zum ökumenischen Gespräch* (Tübingen: Mohr Siebeck, 1991), 94–125, here 111–114; Timothy BARNES, *Athanasius and Constantius: Theology and Politics in the Constantinian Empire* (Cambridge, Mass./London: Harvard University Press, 1993), 45f. and 205; and Annick MARTIN, *Athanase d'Alexandrie et l'église d'Égypte au IVe siècle (328–373)*, Collection de l'École Française de Rome 216 (Rome: École Française, 1996), 403–420.

220 Socrates, *Historia ecclesiastica* II 9.1f. (GCS.NF 1, 98.21–99.5 HANSEN).

221 Here, Socrates, *Historia ecclesiastica* II 9.1f. (GCS.NF 1, 98.21–99.5 HANSEN), is somewhat terser. On the subject at hand, see BUYTAERT, *L'héritage littéraire d'Eusèbe d'Émèse*, 92–94. An identification with a brutally tortured and executed rhetorician Eusebius with the sobriquet Pittacus from Emesa named by Ammianus Marcellinus, *Rerum gestarum libri* XIV 7.18 and 9.4–6 (SQAW21/1, 82.13–18. 90.25–92.8 SEYFARTH) is unlikely; alternatively David WOODS, "Ammianus Marcellinus and Bishop Eusebius of Emesa," *JTS* 54 (2003): 585–591. Nevertheless, traditions also exist on a martyr called Eusebius from Emesa (attestations in BUYTAERT, *L'héritage littéraire d'Eusèbe d'Émèses*, 94f. with nn. 236 and 237); the question neither need nor must be further explored here.

222 BUYTAERT, *L'héritage littéraire d'Eusèbe d'Émèse*, 94f.

223 Hieronymus, *De viris illustribus* 91.1–3 (BiPatr 12, 196f. CERESA-GASTALDO = 238 BARTHOLD). ET from *Saint Jerome: On Illustrious Men*, trans. Thomas P. HALTON, Fathers of the Church, A New Translation 100 (Washington, D.C.: Catholic University of America Press, 1999), 124.

224 Accessible in a critical edition in Eligius M. BUYTAERT, *Eusèbe d'Émèse: Discours conservés en Latin; Textes en partie inédits*, tome 2, La collection de Sirmond (Discours XVIII à XXIX), Spicilegium Sacrum Lovaniense, Études et Documents 27 (Louvain: Spicilegium Sacrum Lovaniense, 1957); on the history of editions, in addition to BUYTAERT, *L'héritage littéraire d'Eusèbe d'Émèse*, 103–116, see also the terse comments from WINN, *Eusebius of Emesa*, 5–10. Extremely critical words on the tendency of BUYTAERT to normalize the manuscript text according to grammatical and orthographic rules may be found from Vinzenz BULHART in his review in *Gnomon* 30 (1958): 537–540; the review concludes with the sentence: "Aber eigentlich müßte die Ausgabe, kaum daß sie erschienen ist, schon neu gemacht warden" (p. 540).

225 Eligius M. BUYTAERT, "L'authenticité des dix-sept opuscules contenus dans le MS T. 523 sous le nom d'Eusèbe d'Emèse," *Revue d'histoire ecclésiastique* 43 (1948): 5–89, here 25–28.

226 Buytaert, *L'héritage littéraire d'Eusèbe d'Émèse*, 103–115.
227 Eusebius Emesenus, *Sermo* 20.1 (79.2–9 Buytaert).
228 Eusebius Emesenus, *Sermo* 20.2 (79.10–20 Buytaert).
229 Eusebius Emesenus, *Sermo* 20.4 (80.20–27 Buytaert). The heavily abbreviated biblical passage is also quoted in *Sermo* 25.5 (160.11 Buytaert).
230 Eusebius Emesenus, *Sermo* 20.8 (83.15–27 Buytaert).
231 See the classical state of research in, for example, Heinrich Kihn, *Theodor von Mopsuestia und Junilius Africanus als Exegeten, nebst einer kritischen Textausgabe von des letzteren Instituta regularia divinae legis* (Freiburg: Herder, 1880), 9–18; or in Christoph Schäublin, *Untersuchungen zur Methode und Herkunft der antiochenischen Exegese*, Theophaneia 23 (Köln/Bonn: Hanstein, 1974), 11–42.
232 Origenes, *Commentarii in Euangelium Ioannis* VI 55.287 (GCS Origenes IV, 245.1–5 Preuschen).
233 Silke-Petra Bergjan, "Die dogmatische Funktionalisierung der Exegese nach Theodoret von Cyrus," in *Christliche Exegese zwischen Nicaea und Chalcedon*, hg. Johannes van Oort und Ulrich Wickert (Kampen: Kok Pharos, 1992), 32–48. See also Jean-Noël Guinot, *L'exégèse de Théodoret de Cyr*, Théologie historique 100 (Paris: Beauchesne, 1995), 222–230.
234 Theodoretus Cyrrhensis, *Commentaria in Isaiam* XIX 63.2 (SC 315.586–288.594 Guinot).
235 Eusebius Emesenus, *Sermo* 20.24 (94.18–25 Buytaert).
236 Eusebius Emesenus, *Sermo* 20.25 (94.26–95.2 Buytaert).
237 Eusebius Emesenus, *Sermo* 20.39f. (102.3–16 Buytaert).
238 Origenes, *De principiis* I 1.6 (GCS Origenes V, 21.10–14 Koetschau = TzF 24, 110 Görgemanns/Karpp). On its Neoplatonic background, see, for example, Henning Ziebritzki, *Heiliger Geist und Weltseele: Das Problem der dritten Hypostase bei Origenes, Plotin und ihren Vorläufern*, BHT 84 (Tübingen: Mohr Siebeck, 1994), 137f.; on its transformation in Evagrius Ponticus in the fourth century, see below.
239 Eusebius Emesenus, *Sermo* 21, *De incorporali liber primus*; *Sermo* 22, *De incorporali liber secundus* (*De incorporali anima*); *Sermo* 23, *De incorporali tertius*; *Sermo* 24, *De incorporali liber quartus* (*De eo quod Deus incorporalis est*); *Sermo* 25, *De incorporali liber quintus* (*Item de eo quod Deus pater incorporalis est*); cf. 103.1, 115.1, 132.1, 136.1, and 158.1 Buytaert. The fifth and last sermon is preserved fragmentarily and breaks off before the liturgical conclusion (174.5–7).
240 Eusebius Emesenus, *Sermo* 21.1 (102.2–15 Buytaert).
241 Eusebius Emesenus, *Sermo* 21.2 (102.16f. Buytaert).
242 Eusebius Emesenus, *Sermo* 25.6 (161.17–29 Buytaert).
243 Robert Winn, "The Natural World in the Sermons of Eusebius of Emesa," *VC* 59 (2005): 31–53 and idem, *Eusebius of Emesa*, 126–133.
244 Eusebius Emesenus, *Sermo* 24.19 (145.7–21 Buytaert). For this passage, see Robert Winn, *Eusebius of Emesa*, 127f., from which the overwhelming majority of this passage's ET has been taken.
245 Nemesius Emesenus, *De natura hominis* 6.173f. (BiTeu 56.2–6 Morani). ET after *Nemesius: On the Nature of Man*, trans. with an introduction and notes by R. W. Sharples and P. J. van der Eijk, Translated Texts for Historians 49 (Liverpool: Liverpool University Press, 2008), 101. See Eckart Scherer, s.v. "Sinne, die," in *Historisches Wörterbuch der Philosophie* (Darmstadt: Wissenschaftliche Buchgesellschaft, 1995), 9: 824–869, here 831–834.
246 Eusebius Emesenus, *Sermo* 21.2 (104.3–12 Buytaert).
247 Cf., for example, Eusebius Emesenus, *Sermo* 24.28 (150.4–7 Buytaert).
248 Eusebius Emesenus, *Sermo* 24.25 (147.25–148.11 Buytaert).
249 Eusebius Emesenus, *Sermo* 24.25 (152.4–12 Buytaert). Without directly stating names, Eusebius alludes to Jupiter, Leda, and Europa and, indeed, Hera or Juno.

250 Augustinus, *Confessiones* VII 9.13 (BiTeu 137.7–18 Skutella). On the various attempts to identify the person behind *per quendam hominem*, see James J. O'Donnell, *Augustine: Confessions*, vol. 2, *Commentary on Books 1–7* (Oxford: Clarendon, 1992), 419f.

251 Augustinus, *Confessiones* VII 20.26 (BiTeu 149.1–11 Skutella).

252 Cf., in addition to the passages from the "Confessions" cited in the previous notes, also *Confessiones* VIII 2.3 (BiTeu 154.16–23 Skutella). For the question as to whether Marius Victorinus compiled such translations and Augustine in fact read these, see James J. O'Donnell, *Augustine: Confessions*, vol. 3, *Commentary on Books 8–13, Indexes* (Oxford: Clarendon, 1992), 13–15; and Pierre Hadot, *Marius Victorinus: Recherches sur sa vie et ses oeuvres* (Paris: Institut des Études Augustiniennes, 1971), 179–190.

253 Ambrosius, *De Isaac uel anima* 78f. (FChr 48, 148.15–154.15 Dassmann) paraphrases Plotinus; so Pierre Courcelle, *Recherches sur les Confessions de Saint Augustin*, nouvelle édition augmentée et illustrée (Paris: De Boccard, 1968), 106–117; see also pp. 93–106 and 117–138. The entire relevant passage from Courcelle, *Recherches sur les Confessions de Saint Augustin*, 93–138, is translated and reprinted in *Zum Augustin-Gespräch der Gegenwart, mit Bibliographie*, hg. Carl Andresen, Wege der Forschung 5 (Darmstadt: Wissenschaftliche Buchgesellschaft, 1962), 125–181. Important supplements and critical remarks may be found in Willy Theiler, "Rezension Courcelle," *Gnomon* 25 (1953): 113–122, here 114f.

254 Alfred Schindler, s.v. "Augustin, Augustinismus I," *TRE* 4: 646–698, here 649, and 559–661; Paul Henry, *Plotin et l'Occident: Firmicus Maternus, Marius Victorinus, Saint Augustin et Macrobe*, Spicilegium Sacrum Lovaniense 15 (Louvain: Spicilegium Sacrum Lovaniense, 1934), 82–89; and additionally Courcelle, *Recherches sur les Confessions de Saint Augustin*, 153–174 (esp. 160–164 for a synopsis of further relevant passages from the *Confessiones*), 281–284, and 601f.; and the rezension of Theiler, 117f. Most recently, this question has been addressed by (among others) Pier Franco Beatrice, "Quosdam Platonicorum Libros: The Platonic Readings of Augustine in Milan," *VC* 43 (1989): 248–281; O'Donnell, *Augustine: Confessions*, 2: 421–424 (with further literature); Wilhelm Geerlings, "*Libri Platonicorum*: Die philosophische Bildung Augustins," in *Platon in der abendländischen Geistesgeschichte: Neue Forschungen zum Platonismus*, hg. Theo Kobusch und Burkhard Mojsisch (Darmstadt: Wissenschaftliche Buchgesellschaft, 1997), 60–70; and Thomas O'Loughlin, "The 'Libri Platonicorum' and Augustine's Conversions," in *The Relationship between Neoplatonism and Christianity: Proceedings of the First Patristic Conference at Maynooth*, ed. Thomas Finan and Vincent Twomey (Dublin: Four Courts Press, 1992), 101–125.

255 Augustinus, *Confessiones* IX 10.23–25 (BiTeu 199.3–201.21 Skutella).

256 The early Latin translation of ++Ps 4:9 had introduced this Neoplatonically sounding title into Christian discourse: *in pace, in idipsum obdormiam et somnum capiam*. See O'Donnell, *Augustine: Confessions*, 3: 99f.; and also Paul Henry, *La vision d'Ostie: Sa place dans la vie et l'œuvre de saint Augustin* (Paris: Vrin, 1938), 15–103 = "Die Vision zu Ostia," in *Zum Augustin-Gespräch der Gegenwart*, hg. Carl Andresen, Wege der Forschung 5 (Darmstadt: Wissenschaftliche Buchgesellschaft, 1962), 201–270, here 220f.

257 Augustinus, *Confessiones* IX 10.24 (BiTeu 199.20–200.13 Skutella). ET from *Augustine: Confessions, Books 9–13*, ed. and trans. Carolyn J.-B. Hammond, LCL 27 (Cambridge, Mass./London: Harvard University Press, 2016), 47–49.

258 O'Donnell, *Augustine: Confessions*, 3: 129. Already Courcelle, *Recherches sur les Confessions de Saint Augustin*, 129f., demonstrates that the plural *mentes* draws more on Augustine than on Plotinus or Porphyry.

259 Extensive attestations in Henry, *La Vision d'Ostie*, 15–103 = "Die Vision zu Ostia," 201–270. Critical remarks as to the disqualified connection of the text with Plontinus in Theiler, "Rezension Courcelle," 117f. Cf., however, Pierre Courcelle, "La première expérience augustinienne de l'extase"; and also André Mandouze, "'L'extase d'Ostie': Possibilités et limites de la méthode des parallèles textuels," in *Augustinus Magister:*

Congrès International Augustinien, Paris, 21–24 Septembre 1954, Actes, tome 1, *Communications* (Paris: Études Augustiniennes, 1954), 53–57 and 67–84; John A. MOURANT, "Ostia Reexamined: A Study in the Concept of Mystical Experience," *Philosophy of Religion* 1 (1970): 34–45; and O'DONNELL, *Augustine: Confessions*, 3: 122–137.

260 THEILER, "Rez. Courcelle," 117f., refers to Proclus, *Theologia Platonica* II 11 (CUFr II, 64.10–65.26 SAFFREY/WESTERINK). On Porphyry's *De regressu animae*, lost save a few fragments in Augustine, see Ilsetraut HADOT, "Erziehung und Bildung bei Augustin," in *Internationales Symposion über den Stand der Augustinus-Forschung, vom 12. bis 16. April 1987 im Schloss Rauischholzhausen der Justus-Liebig-Universität Gießen*, hg. Cornelius Mayer und Karl Heinz Chelius, Cassiciacum 39/1 = Res et Signa 1 (Würzburg: Augustinus-Verlag, 1989), 99–130, here 127–130. These fragments of *De regressu animae* are part of the text of *De philosophia ex oraculis haurienda*, according to John J. O'MEARA, *Porphyry's Philosophy from Oracles in Augustine* (Paris: Études Augustiniennes, 1959); and idem, "Porphyry's Philosophy from Oracles in Eusebius' *Praeparatio Evangelica* and Augustine's Dialogues of Cassiciacum," *Recherches Augustiniennes* 6 (1969): 103–138. Cf., however, Richard GOULET, "Augustin et le *De regressu animae* de Porphyre," in *Augustin philosophe et prédicateur: Hommage à Goulven Madec*, éd. Isabelle Bochet, Collection des Études Augustiniennes, Série Antiquité 195 (Paris: Institut des Études Augustiniennes, 2012), 67–110.

261 O'DONNELL, *Augustine: Confessions*, 3: 127.

262 Augustinus, *Confessiones* IX 10.24 (BiTeu 200.7f. SKUTELLA).

263 An exception is presented by Augustinus, *Epistula* 147.26 (CSEL 44, 300.15 GOLDBACHER = 150 NAAB): *nec tactu tenetur* (cf. Gen 32:24–30).

264 The relevant texts with translation and commentary: *Augustinus: Über Schau und Gegenwart des unsichtbaren Gottes*, Texte mit Einführung und Übersetzung von Erich NAAB, Mystik in Geschichte und Gegenwart, TU I/14 (Stuttgart-Bad Cannstatt: Frommann-Holzboog, 1998), 118–191 (*Epistula* 147 after CSEL 44, 274.10–331.11 GOLDBACHER without critical apparatus with a German translation), 192–213 (*Epistula* 148 after CSEL 44, 332.1–347.23 GOLDBACHER the same), 214–259 (*Epistula* 187 after CSEL 57, 81.1–119.5 GOLDBACHER the same; *Epistula* 92 and 92A after CSEL 34/2, 436.1–444.3 and 444.4–445.3 GOLDBACHER the same). ETs taken from *Augustine: Letters*, trans. Wilfrid PARSONS, 3 vols., Fathers of the Church 9, 18, and 20 (Washington, D.C.: Catholic University of America Press, 1953).

265 Augustinus, *Epistula* 92.5 (CSEL 34/2, 441.10–12 GOLDBACHER = 260 NAAB). ET from PARSONS, *Augustine: Letters*, 2: 53. On the historical context of the letter and Augustine's correspondent, see NAAB, *Augustinus, Über Schau und Gegenwart des unsichtbaren Gottes*, 2–6.

266 Augustinus, *Epistula* 92.2 (CSEL 34/2, 437.7–12 GOLDBACHER).

267 Augustinus, *Epistula* 92.2 (CSEL 34/2, 437.19–438.2 GOLDBACHER). ET from PARSONS, *Augustine: Letters*, 2: 51

268 Augustinus, *Epistula* 92.3 (CSEL 34/2, 439.1–5 GOLDBACHER = 262 NAAB). ET from PARSONS, *Augustine: Letters*, 2: 52. For the notion of the "inner human" in Augustine, cf. Christoph MARKSCHIES, s.v. "Innerer Mensch," in *Reallexikon für Antike und Christentum* (Stuttgart: Hiersemann, 1997), 18: 266–312, here 305–308.

269 Augustinus, *Epistula* 92.6 (CSEL 34/2, 443.8–10 GOLDBACHER = 268 NAAB). ET from PARSONS, *Augustine: Letters*, 2: 54.

270 Augustinus, *Epistula* 92A (CSEL 34/2, 444.7–14 GOLDBACHER = 268 NAAB). ET from PARSONS, *Augustine: Letters*, 2: 55. On Cyprian, see André MANDOUZE, *Prosopographie de l'Afrique Chrétienne (303–533)*, d'après la documentation élaborée par Anne-Marie La Bonnardière, Prosopographie chrétienne du Bas-Empire 1 (Paris: Éditions du Centre National de la Recherche Scientifique, 1982), 258 (s.v. Cyprianus 5). On his daughter Italica, see NAAB, *Augustinus, Über Schau und Gegenwart des unsichtbaren Gottes*, 6; and Charles PIETRI† et Luce PIETRI, *Prosopographie de l'Italie chrétienne (313–604)*, tome 1,

A–K, Prosopographie chrétienne du Bas-Empire 2/1 (Rome: École Française de Rome, 1999), 1162.

271   MANDOUZE, *Prosopographie de l'Afrique Chrétienne (303–533)*, 837 (s.v. Paulina).

272   NAAB, *Augustinus, Über Schau und Gegenwart des unsichtbaren Gottes*, 4–9 and 14–25.

273   Augustinus, *Epistula* 147.51 (CSEL 44, 326.20–327.4 GOLDBACHER = 184 NAAB).

274   Augustinus, *Epistula* 147.5 (CSEL 44, 279.14 GOLDBACHER = 122 NAAB).

275   Augustinus, *Epistula* 147.3 (CSEL 44, 276.12–18 GOLDBACHER = 120 NAAB). God himself does not require a body to see: 147.50 (325.15–19 = 182).

276   Augustinus, *Epistula* 147.4 (CSEL 44, 278.1–14 GOLDBACHER = 122 NAAB). ET from PARSONS, *Augustine: Letters*, 3: 173. On the implicit terminology of *credere*, see Eugene TESELLE, s.v. "Credere," in *Augustinus-Lexikon* (Basel: Schwabe, 1986–1994), 1: (119–131) 123f.

277   MARKSCHIES, s.v. "Innerer Mensch," 18: 267–275 and 289–293.

278   Augustinus, *Epistula* 147.38 (CSEL 44, 313.4–9 GOLDBACHER = 166 NAAB). On the topic, see Johann KREUZER, "Der Abgrund des Bewusstseins: Erinnerung und Selbsterkenntnis im zehnten Buch," in *Die Confessiones des Augustinus von Hippo: Einführung und Interpretation zu den dreizehn Büchern*, hg. Norbert Fischer und Cornelius Mayer, Forschungen zur europäischen Geistesgeschichte 1 (Freiburg: Herder, 1998), 445–487; James J. O'DONNELL, s.v. "Memoria," in *Augustinus-Lexikon* (Basel: Schwabe, 2004–2010), 3: 1249–1257; Christopher G. STEAD, "Augustine, the Meno and the Subconscious Mind," in *Die Weltlichkeit des Glaubens in der Alten Kirche: Festschrift für Ulrich Wickert zum siebzigsten Geburtstag*, hg. Dietmar Wyrwa in Verbindung mit Barbara Aland und Christoph Schäublin, BZNW 85 (Berlin/New York: De Gruyter, 1997), 339–345; and also Willy THEILER, s.v. "Erinnerung," in *Reallexikon für Antike und Christentum* (Stuttgart: Hiersemann, 1966), 6: 43–54.

279   Augustinus, *Epistula* 147.3 (CSEL 44, 277.14–23 GOLDBACHER = 120 NAAB). ET from PARSONS, *Augustine: Letters*, 3: 172. On the concept of divine authority here presupposed, see also ibid., 147.40 (314.12–315.9 = 168/170); and Karl-Heinrich LÜTCKE, *"Auctoritas" bei Augustin: Mit einer Einleitung zur römischen Vorgeschichte des Begriffs*, Tübinger Beiträge zur Altertumswissenschaft 44 (Stuttgart: Kohlhammer, 1968), 119–148.

280   Augustinus, *Epistula* 147.6 (CSEL 44, 280.7 GOLDBACHER = 122 NAAB).

281   Cicero, *Academica priora (Lucullus)* II 17 (BiTeu 42, 35.20–26 PLASBERG). See for the Greek background of the quotation of Epicurus in Sextus Empiricus, *Adversus Mathematicos* VII 203 (BiTeu II, 48 [235.13–27] MUTSCHMANN = frag. 247 USENER [p. 179.18–180.1] = Epicuro, *Opere*, introduzione, testo critico, traduzione e note di Graziano Arrighetti, Classici della Filosofia 4 [Turin: Einaudi, 1960], 457f.); and *Adversus Mathematicos* VIII 63–65 (BiTeu II, 116 [300.20–301.4] MUTSCHMANN = frag. 253 USENER [p. 187.5–17], not in Arrighetti). See also Wilhelm HALBFASS, s.v. "Evidenz," in *Historisches Wörterbuch der Philosophie* (Basel: Schwabe, 1972), 2: 829–832, here 829f.

282   Augustinus, *Epistula* 147.7 (CSEL 44, 280.23–281.2 GOLDBACHER = 120 NAAB).

283   Implicitly also Paul VAN GEEST, *The Incomprehensibility of God: Augustine as a Negative Theologian*, Late Antique History and Religion 4 = The Mystagogy of the Church Fathers 1 (Leuven: Peeters, 2011), 109–127, here 113; on its philosophical underpinnings, see pp. 24–41.

284   O'DONNELL, *Augustine: Confessions*, 3: 129; and already COURCELLE, *Recherches sur les Confessions de Saint Augustin*, 129f., indicate that the plural form *mentes* is more likely the doing of Augustine than of Plotinus or Porphyry.

285   Augustinus, *Epistula* 147.9f. (CSEL 44, 283.9–15 GOLDBACHER = 128 NAAB). On the expression *praelocutio* see above, with reference to Augustinus, *Epistula* 147.5 (279.14 = 122).

286   Also see Basil STUDER, *Zur Theophanie-Exegese Augustins: Untersuchung zu einem Ambrosius-Zitat in der Schrift "De videndo Deo" (ep. 147)*, Studia Anselmiana 59 (Rome: Herder/Rome: Editrice Anselmiana, 1971), 5–52; and idem, *Gratia Christi—Gratia Dei bei Augustinus von Hippo: Christozentrismus oder Theozentrismus?* Studia Ephemeridis "Augustinianum" 40 (Rome: Institutum Patristicum "Augustinianum," 1993), 227–235.

Inaccessible to me was Michel ALDARIC, *Les sources bibliques du De videndo deo de Saint Augustin* (Paris: Le Saulchoir, 1970).

287 Ambrosius, *Expositio evangelii secundum Lucam* I 24–27 (CChr.SL 14, 18.370–20.430 ADRIAEN) = Augustinus, *Epistula* 147.18 (CSEL 44, 289.7–292.5 GOLDBACHER = 136–140 NAAB). The statement of Ambrose is "not even already ensured by his authority, but on grounds of the truth" (nicht schon aufgrund seiner Autorität, sondern aufgrund der Wahrheit gesichert): 147.52 (328.11–13 = 186). On the relationship between Augustine and Ambrose, see Ernst DASSMANN, s.v. "Ambrosius," in *Augustinus-Lexikon* (Basel: Schwabe, 1986–1994), 1: 270–285, here 277–281. On the references to Origen, see the evidence in NAAB, *Augustinus, Über Schau und Gegenwart des unsichtbaren Gottes*, 39–41. On Ambrose in the clashes over the theology of the Trinity in the fourth century, see Christoph MARKSCHIES, *Ambrosius von Mailand und die Trinitätstheologie. Kirchen- und theologiegeschichtliche Studien zu Antiarianismus und Neunizänismus bei Ambrosius und im lateinischen Westen (364–381)*, BHT 90 (Tübingen: Mohr Siebeck, 1995), 84–216.

288 Augustinus, *Epistula* 147.12–17 (CSEL 44, 285.4–289.6 GOLDBACHER = 130–136 NAAB): Gen 32:30; Exod 33:11; Isa 6:11; John 14:9; Matt 5:8; 18:10; Heb 12:14; 1 John 3:2; Bar 3:38 (for *scimus posse Deum uideri*); John 1:18; 1 John 4:12; 1 Tim 6:16 (for *Deum nemo uidit umquam*).

289 Ambrosius, *Expositio evangelii secundum Lucam* I 24 (CChr.SL 14, 18.377–19.385 ADRIAEN) = Augustinus, *Epistula* 147.18 (CSEL 44, 289.15–290.3 GOLDBACHER = 136 NAAB). Augustine also argues similarly in the letter's summary, 147.47 (322.18–323.7 = 178/180).

290 Ambrosius, *Expositio evangelii secundum Lucam* I 25 (CChr.SL 14, 19.93–99 ADRIAEN) = Augustinus, *Epistula* 147.18 (CSEL 44, 290.8–18 GOLDBACHER = 138 NAAB). ET from PARSONS, *Augustine: Letters*, 3: 185

291 Augustinus, *Epistula* 147.20 (CSEL 44, 294.11–22 GOLDBACHER = 142 NAAB). ET from PARSONS, *Augustine: Letters*, 3: 188f. For further references to this biblical passage in Augustine's oeuvre, see Walter THIELE, VL 26/1 (Freiburg: Herder, 1956–1969), 298–300.

292 Here, Augustine changed his stance over the course of his life: Kari KLOOS, "Seeing the Invisible God: Augustine's Reconfiguration of Theophany Narrative Exegesis," *Augustinian Studies* 36 (2005): 397–420; and VAN GEEST, *The Incomprehensibility of God*, 115f.

293 Augustinus, *Epistula* 147.22 (CSEL 44, 296.24–297.2 GOLDBACHER = 146 NAAB). ET from PARSONS, *Augustine: Letters*, 3: 191. On this topic, see now Ellen MUEHLBERGER, *Angels in Late Ancient Christianity* (Oxford: Oxford University Press, 2013), 43–57.

294 Augustinus, *Epistula* 147.19 (CSEL 44, 292.6–13 GOLDBACHER = 140 NAAB). See also VAN GEEST, *The Incomprehensibility of God*, 116f.

295 Augustinus, *Epistula* 147.28 (CSEL 44, 302.10–21 GOLDBACHER = 152–154 NAAB).

296 Augustinus, *Epistula* 147.29 (CSEL 44, 303.10–19 GOLDBACHER = 154 NAAB). ET from PARSONS, *Augustine: Letters*, 3: 197. On this passage, see STUDER, *Gratia Christi—Gratia Dei bei Augustinus von Hippo*, 229f.

297 Augustinus, *Epistula* 147.29 (CSEL 44, 303.22–304.7 GOLDBACHER = 154/156 NAAB).

298 Augustinus, *Epistula* 147.31 (CSEL 44, 305.3–8 GOLDBACHER = 156 NAAB). Moses is admittedly granted only a limited manner of vision: 32 (306.3–307.4 = 158).

299 Augustinus, *Epistula* 147.44 (CSEL 44, 318.22–319.10 GOLDBACHER = 174 NAAB).

300 STUDER, *Gratia Christi—Gratia Dei bei Augustinus von Hippo*, 17–119, esp. 84–96; and also Goulven MADEC, s.v. "Christus," in *Augustinus-Lexikon* (Basel: Schwabe, 1986–1994), 1: 845–908, here 869f. and 879–882.

301 Augustinus, *Epistula* 147.33f. (CSEL 44, 307.10–308.13 GOLDBACHER = 160 NAAB), quoting Ambrose, *Expositio evangelii secundum Lucam* I 27 (CChr.SL 14, 20.424–427 ADRIAEN) = Augustinus, *Epistula* 147.18 (291.20–292.1 GOLDBACHER = 140 NAAB). ET from PARSONS, *Augustine: Letters*, 3: 201f.

302 VAN GEEST, *The Incomprehensibility of God*, 125–127.

303 STUDER, *Gratia Christi—Gratia Dei bei Augustinus von Hippo*, 227f.

304 These passionate efforts are evident, for example, in the fact that Augustine seeks once more in a recapitulation after a fashion to ensure that Paulina has understood what he sought to outline: Augustinus, *Epistula* 147.37 (CSEL 44, 310.4–312.2 GOLDBACHER = 162–166 NAAB).

305 Recently, numerous contributions have appeared on the so-called anthropomorphite controversy: BUMAZHNOV, *Der Mensch als Gottes Bild im christlichen Ägypten*, 2–24; idem, *Visio mystica im Spannungsfeld frühchristlicher Überlieferungen*, 1–18; Alexander GOLITZIN, "The Form of God and Vision of the Glory: Some Thoughts on the Anthropomorphite Controversy of 399 AD," http://www.marquette.edu/maqom/morphe.html (last accessed 4 June 2019); Romanian translation in *Mistagogia—Experiența lui Dumnezeu în Ortodoxie: Studii de teologie mistică*, Colecția Mistica (Sibiu: Deisis, 1998), 184–267; Graham GOULD, "The Image of God and the Anthropomorphite Controversy in Fourth Century Monasticism," in Daly, *Origeniana Quinta*, 549–557; and Paul A. PATTERSON, *Visions of Christ: The Anthropomorphite Controversy of 399 CE*, Studien zu Antike und Christentum 68 (Tübingen: Mohr Siebeck, 2012), 2–25 (history of research).

306 As an introduction to the present state of research: Elizabeth A. CLARK, *The Origenist Controversy: The Cultural Construction of an Early Christian Debate* (Princeton, N.J.: Princeton University Press, 1992); Jon F. DECHOW, *Dogma and Mysticism in Early Christianity: Epiphanius of Cyprus and the Legacy of Origen*, North American Patristic Society, Patristic Monograph Series 13 (Macon, Ga.: Scholar's Press, 1988). Cf., however, Fred LEDEGANG, "Anthropomorphites and Origenists in Egypt at the End of the Fourth Century," in *Origeniana Septima: Origenes in den Auseinandersetzungen des vierten Jahrhunderts* [7. Internationales Origeneskolloquium, vom 25. bis zum 29. August 1997, Hofgeismar], hg. Wolfgang A. Bienert, BETL 137 (Leuven: University Press / Uitgeverij Peeters, 1999), 375–781; as well as (classically) Karl HOLL, "Die Zeitfolge des ersten origenistischen Streits," in idem, *Gesammelte Aufsätze zur Kirchengeschichte*, Bd. 2, *Der Osten* (Tübingen: Mohr Siebeck, 1928), 310–335; and Adolf JÜLICHER, "Bemerkungen zu der Abh. des Hrn. Holl 'Die Zeitfolge des ersten origenistischen Streits,'" in *Gesammelte Aufsätze zur Kirchengeschichte*, 2: 335–350.

307 For Ἀνθρωπομορφιανοί, see Socrates, *Historia ecclesiastica* VI 7.27 (GCS Sokrates, 324.19 HANSEN); and also Sozomenus, *Historia ecclesiastica* VIII 12.12 (GCS Sozomenus, 366.12 BIDEZ/HANSEN). For Ἀνθρωπομορφῆται, see Timotheus Presbyter Constantinopolitanus, *De receptione haereticorum* (PG 86, 45 A = *Syntagma XIV Titulorum sine scholiis secundum versionem palaeo-slovenicam adjecto textu graeco e vetustissimis codicibus ma-nuscriptis exarato*, vol. 1, Vorwort von Jürgen Dummer, Subsidia Byzantina lucis ope iterata IIb [Saint Petersburg: Kaiserliche Akademie der Wissenschaften, 1906 = Leipzig: Zentralantiquariat, 1974], 732.2f. BENEŠEVIČ).

308 "Es fällt kein negatives oder auch nur zurückhaltendes Wort über den alexandrinischen Meister. Bei dogmatischen Streitfragen verfährt Sokrates ganz nach dem Grundsatz. *Origenes locutus, causa finite*" (Martin WALLRAFF, *Der Kirchenhistoriker Sokrates: Untersuchungen zu Geschichtsdarstellung, Methode und Person*, Forschungen zur Kirchen- und Dogmengeschichte 68 [Göttingen: Vandenhoeck & Ruprecht, 1997], 227–230, quotation on p. 227). See also Glenn F. CHESNUT, *The First Christian Histories: Eusebius, Socrates, Sozomen, Theodoret, and Evagrius*, 2nd. ed., rev. and enlarged (Macon, Ga.: Mercer University Press; Leuven: Peeters, 1986), 177–179.

309 CHESNUT, *The First Christian Histories*, 210.

310 On this highly problematic paradigm, see most recently Peter GEMEINHARDT, "Volksfrömmigkeit in der spätantiken Hagiographie: Potential und Grenzen eines umstrittenen Konzepts," *Zeitschrift für Theologie und Kirche* 110 (2013): 410–438; or also Christoph MARKSCHIES, "Hohe Theologie und schlichte Frömmigkeit? Einige Beobachtungen zum Verhältnis von Theologie und Frömmigkeit in der Antike," in *Volksglaube im antiken*

Christentum, hg. Heike Grieser und Andreas Merkt (Darmstadt: Wissenschaftliche Buch-gesellschaft, 2009), 456–471.

311 Socrates, *Historia ecclesiastica* VI 7.1 (GCS Sokrates 322.7–9 HANSEN). ET from *Socra-tes Scholasticus: Ecclesiastical History*, trans. A. C. ZENOS, in *NPNF²* (New York: Chris-tian Literature, 1890), 142.

312 Socrates, *Historia ecclesiastica* VI 7.3 (GCS Sokrates 322.11–15 HANSEN). ET from ZENOS, *Socrates Scholasticus: Ecclesiastical History*, 142.

313 Sozomenus, *Historia ecclesiastica* VIII 11.1 (GCS Sozomenus, 363.26–364.3 BIDEZ/ HANSEN). ET from ZENOS, *Socrates Scholasticus: Ecclesiastical History*, 405–406.

314 Sozomenus, *Historia ecclesiastica* VIII 11.2 (GCS Sozomemus, 364.3–5 BIDEZ/HANSEN). ET from ZENOS, *Socrates Scholasticus: Ecclesiastical History*, 406.

315 Winrich A. LÖHR, s.v. "Theophilus von Alexandrien," *TRE* 33: 364–368. See also Norman RUSSELL, *Theophilus of Alexandria*, The Early Church Fathers (London/New York: Rout-ledge, 2007), 3–41; earlier already Hans-Georg OPITZ, s.v. "Theophilus von Alexandrien," PW 5A/2: 2149–2165; Massey Hamilton SHEPHERD Jr., "The Anthropomorphic Contro-versy in the Time of Theophilus of Alexandria," *Church History* 7 (1938): 263–273; Agostino FAVALE, *Teofilo d'Alessandria (345 c.–412): Scritti, vita e dottrina*, Biblioteca del Salesianum 41 (Torino: Società Editrice Internazionale, 1958), 43–178; Christopher HAAS, *Alexandria in Late Antiquity: Topography and Social Conflict* (Baltimore: Johns Hopkins University Press, 1997), 180–295; Tito ORLANDI, "Theophilus of Alexandria in Coptic Literature," in *Monastica et ascetica, orientalia, e Saeculo Secundo, Origen, Athanasius, Cappadocian Fathers, Chrysostom, Augustine: Papers Presented to the Sev-enth International Conference on Patristic Studies Held in Oxford 1975*, ed. Elizabeth A. Livingstone, Studia Patristica 16/2 = TU 129 (Berlin: Akademie-Verlag, 1985), 100–104; Claudia RAPP, *Holy Bishops in Late Antiquity: The Nature of Christian Leadership in a Time of Transition*, The Transformation of the Classical Heritage 37 (Berkeley: Califor-nia University Press, 2005), 128f. and 147f.; Norman RUSSELL, "Theophilus and Cyril of Alexandria on the Divine Image," in *Origeniana Octava: Origen and the Alexandrian Tradition; Papers of the 8th International Origen Congress Pisa, 27–31 August 2001*, ed. Lorenzo Perrone in collaboration with Paolo Bernardini and Diego Marchini, BETL 164 (Leuven: Peeters, 2003), 2: 939–946; Duncan H. RYNOR, "The Faith of the Simpliciores: A Patriarch's Dilemma," in *Cappadocian Fathers, Chrysostom and His Greek Contem-poraries, Augustine, Donatism and Pelagianism*, ed. Elizabeth A. Livingstone, Studia Patristica 22 (Leuven: Peeters, 1989), 165–169; and Edward J. WATTS, *Riot in Alexan-dria: Tradition and Group Dynamics in Late Antique Pagan and Christian Communities*, Transformation of the Classical Heritage 46 (Berkeley: University of California Press, 2010), 190–207.

316 Johannes HAHN, "'*Vetustus error extinctus est*'—Wann wurde das Sarapeion von Alexan-dria zerstört?" *Historia* 55 (2006): 368–383. The events and chronology are reconstructed markedly differently from Hahn in LÖHR, s.v. "Theophilus von Alexandrien," 364f.

317 Cf., most prominently, Rufinus, *Historia ecclesiastica* XI 22f. 29–30 (GCS Eusebius II/2, 1025.7–1030.15, 1035.27–1036.2 MOMMSEN); and Eunapius, *Vitae sophistarum* VI 11 (38.10–39.14 GIANGRANDE = 472 BOISSONADE). See Johannes HAHN, "The Conversion of the Cult Statues: The Destruction of the Serapeion 392 A.D. and the Transformation of Alexandria into the 'Christ-Loving City,'" in *From Temple to Church: Destruction and Renewal of Local Cultic Topography in Late Antiquity*, ed. Johannes Hahn, Stephen Emmel, and Ulrich Gotter, Religions in the Graeco-Roman World 163 (Leiden: Brill, 2008), 335–366; idem, *Gewalt und religiöser Konflikt: Studien zu den Auseinandersetzu-ngen zwischen Christen, Heiden und Juden im Osten des Römischen Reiches (von Kon-stantin bis Theodosius II.)*, Klio. Beihefte, Neue Folge 8 (Berlin: Akademie-Verlag, 2004), 78–101; Ramsay MACMULLEN, *Christianizing the Roman Empire A.D. 100–400* (New Haven/London: Yale University Press, 1984), 90–101; Richard W. BURGESS and Jitse H. F. DIJKSTRA, "The 'Alexandrian World Chronicle,' Its *Consularia* and the Date

of the Destruction of the Serapeum (with an Appendix on the *Praefecti Augustales*)," *Millennium* 10 (2013): 39–113, here 96; and generally, on the temple district, Judith S. MᴄKᴇɴᴢɪᴇ, Sheila Gɪʙsoɴ, and Andres T. Rᴇʏᴇs (with an appendix by Günter Gʀɪᴍᴍ and Judith S. MᴄKᴇɴᴢɪᴇ), "Reconstructing the Serapeum in Alexandria from the Archaeological Evidence," *Journal of Roman Studies* 94 (2004): 73–121, here 107–110.

318   See also Joseph Wɪʟᴘᴇʀᴛ, "Beiträge zur christlichen Archäologie XIII: Das Bild des Patriarchen Theophilos in einer alexandrinischen Weltchronik," *Römische Quartalschrift* 24 (1910): 3–29 (pp. 15–17 for criticism regarding the idea that Theophilus is adorned with a nimbus); Josef Sᴛʀᴢʏɢowsᴋɪ, "Wilperts Kritik meiner alexandrinischen Weltchronik," *Römische Quartalschrift* 24 (1910): 172–175 (p. 173: the "doubtlessly present nimbus"); and Bᴜʀɢᴇss/Dɪᴊᴋsᴛʀᴀ, "The 'Alexandrian World Chronicle,' Its *Consularia* and the Date of the Destruction of the Serapeum," 88f.

319   Here quoted after *Excerpta latina barberi* ad annum 384 (Chronica minora I, 370.3–5 Fʀɪᴄᴋ = 310 Gᴀʀsᴛᴀᴅ). The passage has no parallel in the chronicle fragment of Papyrus Golenischev: Bᴜʀɢᴇss/Dɪᴊᴋsᴛʀᴀ, "The 'Alexandrian World Chronicle,' Its Consularia and the Date of the Destruction of the Serapeum," 50.

320   This context is emphasized perennially by Cʟᴀʀᴋ, *The Origenist Controversy*, 8: "A second historical dimension of the Origenist controversy I have highlighted (sc. in addition to the central role of women in the debate) is the role that pagan-Christian conflict played in it."

321   Hieronymus, *Epistula* 92 (CSEL 55², 147.1–155.2 Hɪʟʙᴇʀɢ = CPG II, 2596). On the context of the synod, see Cʟᴀʀᴋ, *The Origenist Controversy*, 105–111; and Rᴜssᴇʟʟ, *Theophilus of Alexandria*, 14–24, 89–91.

322   Hieronymus, *Epistula* 92.3 (CSEL 55², 150.11–20 Hɪʟʙᴇʀɢ). ET from Rᴜssᴇʟʟ, *Theophilus of Alexandria*, 95–96. On the Alexandrian presbyter Isidore and his embroilment within the clashes, see below. See also Rᴜssᴇʟʟ, *Theophilus of Alexandria*, 14–24; and Dᴇᴄʜow, *Dogma and Mysticism in Early Christianity*, 161–164.

323   The so-called Alexandrinische Weltchronik, Papyrus Golenischev inv. nr. 310, fol. 6ᵛ: *Repertorium der griechischen christlichen Papyri*, Bd. 2, *Kirchenväter-Papyri*, Tl. 1, *Beschreibungen*, im Namen der Patristischen Arbeitsstelle Münster hg. Kurt Aland† und Hans-Udo Rosenbaum, Patristische Texte und Studien 42 (Berlin/New York: De Gruyter, 1995), KV 1, pp. 1–10. See also Adolf Bᴀᴜᴇʀ and Josef Sᴛʀᴢʏɢowsᴋɪ, *Eine alexandrinische Weltchronik, Text und Miniaturen eines griechischen Papyrus der Sammlung W. Goleniščev herausgegeben und erklärt*, Denkschriften der Kaiserlichen Akademie der Wissenschaften in Wien, Philosophisch-historische Klasse 51/2 (Vienna: Gerold, 1905), 152f.; and Henri Lᴇᴄʟᴇʀᴄǫ, s.v. "Chronique alexandrine," in *Dictionnaire d'archéologie chrétienne et de liturgie* (Paris: Letouzey et Ané, 1911), 3/1: 1546–1553. The text is now to be found in *Apocalypse of Pseudo-Methodius: An Alexandrian World Chronicle*, ed. and trans. Benjamin Gᴀʀsᴛᴀᴅ, Dumbarton Oaks Medieval Library (Cambridge, Mass. / London: Harvard University Press, 2012), xviii–xxxvi, xxxviii–xxxix (introduction), 141–311 (text), and 347–387 (notes). On its dating, see Otto Kᴜʀᴢ, "The Date of the Alexandrian World Chronicle," in *Kunsthistorische Forschungen, Otto Pächt zu seinem 70. Geburtstag*, hg. Artur Rosenauer (Salzburg: Residenz, 1972), 17–22.

324   Hieronymus, *Epistula* 92.3 (CSEL 55², 150.22–151.4 Hɪʟʙᴇʀɢ). ET from Rᴜssᴇʟʟ, *Theophilus of Alexandria*, 96. The sentence attested in the manuscript, *non sunt in iura tepulorum in nitriae monasteriis*, does not seem to me, as Isidor Hilberg thought, to be a crux interpretum (p. 150.28f. with apparatus), but rather the abbreviated verbal discourse; admittedly (as in the earlier editions) the meaningless word *tepulorum* must be corrected to *templorum*.

325   Hᴀʜɴ, *Gewalt und religiöser Konflikt*, 91.

326   Palladius Helenopolitanus, *Dialogus de vita Sancti Chrysostomi* 6 (SC 341, 130.46–140.139 Mᴀʟɪɴɢʀᴇʏ). On the affair, see, e.g., Cʟᴀʀᴋ, *The Origenist Controversy*, 47–51; and Fᴀᴠᴀʟᴇ, *Teofilo d'Alessandria (345 c.–412)*, 96f.

327 Palladius Helenopolitanus, *Dialogus de vita Sancti Chrysostomi* 6 (SC 341, 128.23f. MALINGREY). For the translation, see Anne-Marie MALINGREY, op. cit., 128f. n. 2 and 6 (132.62f.).

328 *Clavis Patrum Graecorum*, vol. 2, *Ab Athanasio ad Chrysostomum*, cura et studio Maurice Geerard (Turnhout: Brepols, 1974), nr. 2580–2623, pp. 112–123, with *Clavis Patrum Graecorum: Supplementum*, cura et studio Maurice Geerard et Jacques Noret, adjuvantibus François Glorie et J. Desmet (Turnhout: Brepols, 1998), nr. 2585–2681, pp. 90–95. See also RUSSELL, *Theophilus of Alexandria*, 45–49.

329 Socrates, *Historia ecclesiastica* VI 7.4 (GCS Sokrates, 322.15–17 HANSEN).

330 An exception is formed by the only completely preserved sermon, *De mystica cena* (CPG II, 2617 = PG 77, 1016 C–1029 B; ET in RUSSELL, *Theophilus of Alexandria*, 52–60). Although it is attributed to Cyril of Alexandria in the manuscripts, Marcel RICHARD was able to demonstrate that Theophilus had held it at some point during the controversies of the years between AD 399 and 401 in Alexandria, perhaps on Maundy Thursday, 29 March 400 (idem, "Une homélie de Théophile d'Alexandrie sur l'institution de l'Eucharistie," *Revue d'histoire ecclésiastique* 33 [1937]: 46–54 = idem, *Opera minora*, tome 2 [Turnhout: Brepols/Leuven: Peeters, 1977], nr. 37; idem, "Les écrits de Théophile d'Alexandrie." *Muséon* 52 [1939]: 33–50).

331 Theophilus Alexandrinus, *Epistula festalis prima (ad annum 386)* in Cosmas Indicopleustes, *Topographia Christiana* X 17 (SC 197, 257.1–4 WOLSKA-CONUS = CPG II, 2580).

332 Attestations for pro- and anti-Chalcedonian traditions in *Clavis Patrum Graecorum*, 2: 112f.

333 Theophilus Alexandrinus, *Epistula festalis quinta (ad annum 390)* in *Gesta Ephesina* 54 [VIIII] (Collectio Vaticana: ACO I/1/2, 41.18f. SCHWARTZ = CPG II, 2582): . . . ἵνα μὴ ἐξ ἡδονῆς καὶ ὕπνου, καθάπερ ἐπὶ τῶν ἄλλων ἀνθρώπων ἔχει, δέξηται σῶμα. The biblical passage states somewhat divergently ἐκ σπέρματος ἀνδρὸς καὶ ἡδονῆς ὕπνῳ συνελθούσης.

334 Theophilus Alexandrinus, *Epistula festalis sexta (ad annum 391)* in *Gesta Ephesina* 54 [VIIII] (Collectio Vaticana: ACO I/1/2, 41.28, 42.4f. SCHWARTZ = CPG II, 2583). ET from RUSSELL, *Theophilus of Alexandria*, 48

335 The significance of the different networks and their different concentrations is particularly evoked by CLARK, *The Origenist Controversy*, 11–42; see esp. 17–19 on the theory supposed, and pp. 38–40 on the mathematical calculation of the concentration of elite networks.

336 On these intercessory missions, see, in depth, RUSSELL, *Theophilus of Alexandria*, 13–15. For the conflicts in Antiochia, the so-called Melitian schism, see classically Ferdinand CAVALLERA, *Le schisme d'Antioche (IVᵉ–Vᵉ siècle)* (Paris: Picard, 1905), 71–298; and FAVALE, *Teofilo d'Alessandria (345c.–412)*, 72–77; for Bostra, see ibid., 79.

337 Quote from Ioannes Hierosolymitanus, *Apologia ad Theophilum*, in Hieronymus, *Contra Ioannem Hierosolymitanum* 37 (CChr.SL 79A, 73.32–35 FEIERTAG). For the ensuing clashes, cf. the differing chronologies of HOLL, "Die Zeitfolge des ersten origenistischen Streits," 311–323; JÜLICHER (in HOLL, op. cit., 335–350); and Pierre NAUTIN, "La lettre de Théophile d'Alexandrie à l'Église de Jérusalem et la réponse de Jean de Jérusalem (Juin–Juillet 396)," *Revue d'Histoire Ecclésiastique* 69 (1974): 365–394. See also idem, "Études de chronologie hiéronymienne (393–397)," *Revue des Études Augustiniennes* 18 (1972): 209–218; also *Revue des Études Augustiniennes* 19 (1973): 69–86, 213–239; and *Revue des Études Augustiniennes* 20 (1974): 251–284. OPITZ, s.v. "Theophilos 18)," 2135, follows HOLL. Rowan WILLIAMS, s.v. "Origenes/Origenismus," *TRE* 25: 397–420, here 415–417; LÖHR, s.v. "Theophilus von Alexandrien," 365; and RUSSELL, *Theophilus of Alexandria*, 15–17, follow the chronology of Nautin. The differences between Holl and Jülicher (and Nautin) are, for the most part, hardly discussed at any length; also not in CLARK, *The Origenist Controversy*, who appears rather to follow Holl (p. 11 n. 1).

338 Christoph MARKSCHIES, s.v. "Epiphanios von Salamis," in *Der Neue Pauly: Enzyklopädie der Antike* (Stuttgart/Weimar: Metzler, 1997), 3: 1152f. On his early monastic biography, see now, in detail, Oliver KÖSTERS, *Die Trinitätslehre des Epiphanius von Salamis: Ein Kommentar zum "Ancoratus,"* Forschungen zur Kirchen- und Dogmengeschichte 86 (Göttingen: Vandenhoeck & Ruprecht, 2003), 17–76; and previously already CLARK, *The Origenist Controvery*, 85–95; and DECHOW, *Dogma and Mysticism in Early Christianity*, 31–43. Light is shed upon the ecclesiastical-political background in Federico FATTI, "*Pontifex Tantus*: Giovanni, Epifanio e le origini della prima controversia origenista," *Adamantius* 19 (2013): 30–49; and upon the rhetorical dimension in Krastu BANEV, *Theophilus of Alexandria and the First Origenist Controversy: Rhetoric and Power*, OECS (Oxford: Oxford University Press, 2015), 107–149.

339 The various approaches to the dating are protrayed summarily within CLARK, *The Origenist Controversy*, 132 n. 362. Clark opts sensibly (in my own opinion), due to the critical stance regarding the Alexandrian presbyter Isidore in chapter 37 (CChr.SL 79A, 73.37–50 FEIERTAG), rather for AD 397 than for within the two years prior to this. HOLL and JÜLICHER ("Die Zeitfolge des ersten origenistischen Streits," 319) refer to chapter 42, "ante paucos menses, circa dies Pentecostes, cum obscurato sole omnis mundus iamiamque uenturum iudicem formidaret" (79.5–7), and decide for the solar eclipse of 6 April 395. NAUTIN, "Études de chronologie hiéronymienne (393–397)," *Revue des Études Augustiniennes* 18 (1972): 210–215, opts, on the contrary, for AD 397. On the argumentation in the text, see Ilona OPELT, *Hieronymus' Streitschriften* (Heidelberg: Winter, 1973), 64–82.

340 Hieronymus, *Contra Ioannem Hierosolymitanum* 10f. (CChr.SL 79A, 18.13–20.33 FEIERTAG). A colorful of rendition of this scene may also be found in John Norman Davidson KELLY, *Jerome: His Life, Writings, and Controversies* (London: Duckworth, 1975), 195–209.

341 The setting of this date depends upon fundamental alterations in the dating of the first Origenist crisis: HOLL decides ("Die Zeitfolge des ersten origenistischen Streits," 323), due to the statement *post triennium* in Hieronymus, *Contra Ioannem Hierosolymitanum* 1 (CChr. SL 79A, 5.11–6.15 FEIERTAG: "Nosti, Pammachi, nosti me ad hoc opus non inimicitiis, non gloriae cupiditate descendere, sed prouocatum litteris tuis ex ardore fidei, ac uelle, si fieri posset, omnes id ipsum sapere, nec impatientiae ac temeritatis posse reprehendi, qui post triennium loquor"), for Easter AD 390 as the date of the sermon and summer AD 393 as the date of the letter of Epiphanius against John; JÜLICHER (in HOLL, op. cit., 336f.) associates the triennium (in my own opinion, correctly) with the time from the outbreak of the crisis to the composition of the text *Contra Ioannem Hierosolymitanum* and dates the duel of sermons to the church consecration festival of AD 392. Contrary to this, NAUTIN dates the letter of Epiphanius to AD 394 ("La lettre de Théophile d'Alexandrie à l'Église de Jérusalem et la réponse de Jean de Jérusalem [Juin-Juillet 396]," 24f.) and the duel of sermons at the church consecration festival to AD 393 ("Études de chronologie hiéronymienne [393–397]," *Revue des Études Augustiniennes* 19 [1973]: 69–73), as Epiphanius could not have torn himself away from his duties at Easter in Salamis and in Cyprus.

342 Hieronymus, *Contra Ioannem Hierosolymitanum* 10 (CChr.SL 79A, 18.13–22 FEIERTAG). Translation from *The Principal Works of St. Jerome*, trans. W. H. FREEMANTLE with G. LEWIS and W. G. MARTLEY, *NPNF²* 6 (Oxford: James Parker & Co., 1893), 429.

343 Hieronymus, *Contra Ioannem Hierosolymitanum* 11 (CChr.SL 79A, 20.14–22 FEIERTAG).

344 Hieronymus, *Contra Ioannem Hierosolymitanum* 11 (CChr.SL 79A, 20.22–33 FEIERTAG). ET from FREEMANTLE/LEWIS/MARTLEY, *The Principal Works of St. Jerome*, 430.

345 Hieronymus, *Contra Ioannem Hierosolymitanum* 14 (CChr.SL 79A, 24.19–32 FEIERTAG).

346 HOLL, "Die Zeitfolge des ersten origenistischen Streits," 312f., refers in both contexts to *Contra Ioannem Hierosolymitanum* 14 (CChr.SL 79A, 24.26 FEIERTAG); and *Epistula* 51.1 (CSEL 54², 396.5–7 HILBERG). This is seen differently by JÜLICHER (in HOLL, "Die Zeitfolge des ersten origenistischen Streits," 336), who refers to a joint journey of Epiphanius

and John of Jerusalem to Bethel, which is reported upon in the letter of complaint from Epiphanius translated by Jerome (Hieronymus, *Epistula* 51.9 [411.3–11]; on this text, see the note after next). Accordingly, Jülicher supposes that the dramatic scenes in the Church of the Sepulchre in Jerusalem initially had no consequences, and the conflict first truly broke out on account of the ordination; similarly, KELLY, *Jerome*, 199. I consider it to be unlikely that the public duel of sermons could have been without consequences (assuming, of course, that Jerome did not completely exaggerate his description of the scene). Should the journey really have fallen between the homiletic duel and the ordination (which is uncertain), then they should be understood as having served as an attempt at reconciliation.

347   Cf. Epiphanius in Hieronymus, *Epistula* 51.1 (CSEL 54², 396.18–397.24 HILBERG); idem, *Epistula* 82.4, 8 (CSEL 55², 111.15–18, 114.14–115.2 HILBERG); and *Contra Ioannem Hierosolymitanum* 40f. (CChr.SL 79A, 77.1–79.36 FEIERTAG). On the events, see HOLL, "Die Zeitfolge des ersten origenistischen Streits," 313f.; JÜLICHER in HOLL, op. cit., 337f.; NAUTIN, "Études de chronologie hiéronymienne (393–397)," *Revue des Études Augustiniennes* 19 (1973): 76–78 (April/May AD 394); and KELLY, *Jerome*, 200f. See also Young Richard KIM, "Epiphanius of Cyprus vs. John of Jerusalem: An Improper Ordination and the Escalation of the Origenist Controversy," in *Episcopal Elections in Late Antiquity*, ed. John Leemans, Peter van Nuffelen, Shawn W. J. Keough, and Carla Nicoloaye, Arbeiten zur Kirchengeschichte 119 (Berlin/Boston: De Gruyter, 2011), 411–422, here 416–421.

348   Thus, Hieronymus, *Epistula* 82.8 (CSEL 55², 114.21–115.2 HILBERG).

349   The letter (CPG II, 3754) is again only completely preserved in a translation of Jerome: Hieronymus, *Epistula* 51 (CSEL 54², 395.5–412.5 HILBERG). Greek fragments in Paul MAAS, "Die ikonoklastische Episode in dem Brief des Epiphanios an Johannes," *Byzantinische Zeitschrift* 30 (1929/1930): 279–286 = idem, *Kleine Schriften*, hg. Wolfgang Buchwald (München: Beck, 1973), 437–445; and in Wolfgang LACKNER, "Zum Zusatz zu Epiphanios' von Salamis Panarion, Kap. 64," *VC* 27 (1973): 56–58.

350   Hieronymus, *Epistula* 51.3 (CSEL 54², 400.4–7 HILBERG). ET from FREEMANTLE/LEWIS/MARTLEY, *The Principal Works of St. Jerome*, 85.

351   Hieronymus, *Epistula* 51.3 (CSEL 54², 400.7–10 HILBERG). Cf. Epiphanius, *Panarion haereses* 64.42 (GCS Epiphanius II, 410.5–7 HOLL/DUMMER [with attestations to other passages in the appendix]). On the genesis of anti-Origenism in Epiphanius, see now KÖSTERS, *Die Trinitätslehre des Epiphanius von Salamis*, 22f.

352   Rufinus, *Prologus in Clementis Recognitionis* 2 (CChr.SL 20, 281.5–13 SIMONETTI = GCS Pseudoklementinen II, 3.5–12 REHM/STRECKER).

353   Palladius Helenopolitanus, *Historia Lausiaca* 55 (Texts and Studies VI/2, 148.15f. BUTLER). For Silvia/Silviana (according to Palladius) and her familial ties, see Arnold Hugh Martin JONES, John Robert MARTINDALE, and John MORRIS, *The Prosopography of the Later Roman Empire*, vol. 1, *A.D. 260–395* (Cambridge: Cambridge University Press, 1971), s.v. "Silvia" (p. 842); and Martin HEINZELMANN, "Gallische Prosopographie 260–527," *Francia* 10 (1982): 531–718, here s.v. "Silvia 1" (p. 695). Critically regarding this: Charles PIETRI† et Luce PIETRI, *Prosopographie de l'Italie chrétienne (313–604)*, tome 2, *L–Z*, Prosopographie chrétienne du Bas-Empire 2/2 (Rome: École Française de Rome, 2000), 2072. On this topic, see also Stefan REBENICH, *Hieronymus und sein Kreis: Prosopographische und sozialgeschichtliche Untersuchungen*, Historia, Einzelschriften 72 (Stuttgart: Steiner, 1992), 258f.; Edward D. HUNT, "St. Silvia of Aquitaine: The Role of a Theodosian Pilgrim in the Society of East and West," *JTS* 23 (1972): 351–373; with idem, *Holy Land Pilgrimage in the Later Roman Empire AD 312–460* (Oxford: Clarendon, 1998), 159f., 190 n. 55, and 199; Paul DEVOS, "Silvie la sainte pèlerine," *Analecta Bollandiana* (1973): 105–121; and idem, "Silvie la sainte pèlerine: II. En Occident," *Analecta Bollandiana* 92 (1974): 321–343.

354   Rufinus, *Apologia contra Hieronymum* II 15 (CChr.SL 20, 94.14–95.25 SIMONETTI).

355 This seems to be the explanation for the context in CLARK, *The Origenist Controversy*, 45 n. 7, referencing Hieronymus, *Contra Ioannem Hierosolymitanum* 5 (CChr.SL 79A, 11.1–18 FEIERTAG) and the views of Rufinus reported by Jerome: *Apologia contra Rufinum* II 21 (SC 303, 160.1–29 LARDET).

356 Also according to HOLL, "Die Zeitfolge des ersten origenistischen Streits," 314.

357 NAUTIN, "Études de chronologie hiéronymienne (393–397)," *Revue des Études Augustiniennes* 19 (1973): 79–81.

358 Hieronymus, *Contra Ioannem Hierosolymitanum* 37 (CChr.SL 79A, 73.42–73.54 FEIERTAG).

359 NAUTIN, "La lettre de Théophile d'Alexandrie à l'Église de Jérusalem et la réponse de Jean de Jérusalem (Juin-Juillet 396)," 368f. Generally on the events, see FAVALE, *Teofilo d'Alessandria (345 c.–412)*, 88–93, 96–102; and KELLY, *Jerome*, 204–207.

360 The reconstruction of this missive may be found in NAUTIN, "La lettre de Théophile d'Alexandrie à l'Église de Jérusalem et la réponse de Jean de Jérusalem (Juin-Juillet 396)," 370–380 (critical edition of the Latin text, French translation, and commentary). This task had previously been attempted by Carl Paul CASPARI, "Ein Glaubensbekenntniss des Bischofs Johannes von Jerusalem (386–417) in syrischer Übersetzung aus einer nitrischen Handschrift, sammt Allem, was uns sonst von Johannes übrig geblieben," in idem, *Ungedruckte, unbeachtete und wenig beachtete Quellen zur Geschichte des Taufsymbols und des Glaubenssymbols*, Tl. 1 (Christiania: Malling, 1866 = Brüssel: Culture et Civilisation, 1964), 161–212, here 166–172.

361 Hieronymus, *Contra Ioannem Hierosolymitanum* 5 (CChr.SL 79A, 11.1–7 FEIERTAG).

362 On the history and problematics of this terminology, see Christoph MARKSCHIES, "On Classifying Creeds the Classical German Way: 'Privat-Bekenntnisse' ('Private Creeds')," in *Biblica, Philosophica, Theologica, Ethica: Papers Presented at the Sixteenth International Conference on Patristic Studies Held in Oxford 2011*, vol. 11, ed. Markus Vinzent, Studia Patristica 63 (Leuven/Paris/Walpole, Mass.: Peeters, 2013), 259–271.

363 Johannes Hierosolymitanus, *Epistula ad Theophilum* (after NAUTIN, "La lettre de Théophile d'Alexandrie à l'Église de Jérusalem et la réponse de Jean de Jérusalem [Juin-Juillet 396]," 375.6–11; reconstructed from Hieronymus, *Contra Ioannem Hierosolymitanum* 8 [CChr.SL 79A, 15.16–22 FEIERTAG]). The Latin *unius substantiae* translates ὁμοούσιος. See OPELT, *Hieronymus' Streitschriften*, 68; and previously already Pierre NAUTIN, "Ὁμοούσιος *unius esse* (Jérôme, ep. XCIII)," *VC* 15 (1961): 40–45.

364 NAUTIN, "La lettre de Théophile d'Alexandrie à l'Église de Jérusalem et la réponse de Jean de Jérusalem (Juin-Juillet 396)," 384f.; and idem, "Études de chronologie hiéronymienne (393–397)," *Revue des Études Augustiniennes* 20 (1974): 273–275. See for the later dating Ferdinand CAVALLERA, *Saint Jérôme, sa vie et son œuvre*, Spicilegium Sacrum Lovaniense 1 et 2 (Louvain: Spicilegium Sacrum Lovaniense, 1922), 1/1: 270–280 and 1/2: 38–43. Like Nautin, HOLL also assumes only a very brief period to have elapsed: idem, "Die Zeitfolge des ersten origenistischen Streits," 318–322. JÜLICHER (in HOLL, op. cit., 341f.) also situates all of the events and texts in close succession after one another within the year AD 395.

365 Hieronymus, *Epistula* 82.5 (CSEL 55², 112.8–10 HILBERG); following the interpretation of OPITZ, s.v. "Theophilos 18)," 2153.

366 Hieronymus, *Epistula* 82.1 (CSEL 55², 107.19–108.10 HILBERG). The letter from Theophilus to which Jerome answers is not extant.

367 On this, in brief, see CLARK, *The Origenist Controversy*, 22f. 46–49; in depth, Jean-Marie LERAUX, "Jean Chrysostome et la querelle origéniste," in *Epektasis: Mélanges patristiques offerts au Cardinal Jean Daniélou*, éd. Jacques Fontaine and Charles Kannengiesser (Paris: Beauchesne, 1972), 335–341; and Matthieu-Georges DE DURAND, "Evagre le Pontique et le 'Dialogue sur la vie de saint Jean Chrysostome,'" *Bulletin de littérature ecclésiastique* 3 (1976): 191–206. Generally on the bibliographic context, see Rudolf BRÄNDLE, *Johannes Chrysostomus: Bischof–Reformer–Märtyrer* (Stuttgart: Kohlhammer, 1999), 54–69;

and John Norman Davidson KELLY, *Golden Mouth: The Story of John Chrysostom—Ascetic, Preacher, Bishop* (London: Duckworth, 1995), 104–111.

368 Socrates, *Historia ecclesiastica* VI 2.1–12 (GCS Sokrates, 312.4–313.20 HANSEN). Cf. Sozomenus, *Historia ecclesiastica* VIII 2.1–19 (FChr 73/4, 954.1–960.22 HANSEN); and Theodoretus, *Historia ecclesiastica* V 27.1–4 (GCS Theodoret, 328.11–329.7 PARMENTIER/HANSEN). On its interpretation, see Susanna ELM, "The Dog That Did Not Bark: Doctrine and Patriarchal Authority in the Conflict between Theophilus of Alexandria and John Chrysostom of Constantinople," in *Christian Origins: Theology, Rhetoric and Community*, ed. Lewis Ayres and Gareth Jones (London/New York: Routledge, 1998), 68–93, here 69f., and 78–81; RUSSELL, *Theophilus of Alexandria*, 17f.; and now (critically) Wendy MAYER, "John Chrysostom As Bishop: The View from Antioch," *Journal of Ecclesiastical History* 55 (2004): 455–466.

369 Wolfgang A. BIENERT, "Athanasius von Alexandrien und Origenes," in *Liturgica, Second Century, Alexandria before Nicaea, Athanasius and the Arian Controversy: Papers Presented at the Eleventh International Conference on Patristic Studies Held in Oxford 1991*, ed. Elizabeth A. Livingstone, Studia Patristica 26 (Leuven: Peeters, 1993), 360–364; and Charles KANNENGIESSER, "Das Vermächtnis des 'fleißigen' Origenes: Zur Theologie des Athanasius," in Bienert, *Origeniana septima*, 173–186 (in his discussion of Christ as the "image of God," Athanasius refers to Origen: *De decretis Nicaenae synodis* 27.1–3 [Athanasius Werke II/1, 23.17–24.3 OPITZ]).

370 See, in turn, Alfons FÜRST, "Hieronymus gegen Origenes: Die Vision Jesajas im ersten Origenismusstreit," *Revue d'Études Augustiniennes* 53 (2007): 199–233 = idem, *Von Origenes und Hieronymus zu Augustinus: Studien zur antiken Theologiegeschichte*, 239–274, Arbeiten zur Kirchengeschichte 115 (Berlin/New York: De Gruyter, 2011), here 211–224 = 252–266.

371 Hieronymus, *Epistula* 51.3 (CSEL 54², 400.7–10 HILBERG).

372 BUMAZHNOV, *Der Mensch als Gottes Bild im christlichen Ägypten*, 3; and DECHOW, *Dogma and Mysticism in Early Christianity*, 93–107.

373 Antoine GUILLAUMONT, *Les "Kephalaia nostica" d'Évagre le Pontique et l'histoire de l'Origénisme chez les Grecs et les Syriens*, Patristica Sorbonensia 5 (Paris: Éditions du Seuil, 1962), 59–61; and, in more depth, CLARK, *The Origenist Controversy*, 60–84.

374 Evagrius Ponticus, *De oratione* 57 (PG 79, 1180 A). ET in *Evagrius of Pontus, The Greek Ascetic Corpus*, trans. with introduction and commentary by Robert E. SINKEWICZ, OECS (Oxford: Oxford University Press, 2003), 198. See also Doris SPERBER-HARTMANN, *Das Gebet als Aufstieg zu Gott: Untersuchungen zur Schrift De oratione des Evagrius Ponticus*, Early Christianity in the Context of Antiquity 10 (Frankfurt am Main: Lang, 2011), 17–24; and Antoine GUILLAUMONT, *Un philosophe au désert: Évagre le Pontique*, Textes et Traditions 8 (Paris: Vrin, 2004), 298–306.

375 GUILLAUMONT, *Un philosophe au désert*, 31–39. Cf., however, now Ilaria L. E. RAMELLI, "Evagrius and Gregory: Nazianzen or Nyssen? Cappadocian (and Origenian) Influence on Evagrius," *Greek, Roman, and Byzantine Studies* 53 (2013): 117–137, on his relationship to Gregory of Nyssa.

376 Cf. on this Gregorius Nazianzenus, *Testamentum* (158.4–7 PITRA = PG 37, 393 B). Further attestations and bibliography in CLARK, *The Origenist Controversy*, 61 with n. 100.

377 Antoine GUILLAUMONT, s.v. "Evagrius Ponticus," *TRE* 10: 565–570; idem, "Histoire des moines aux Kellia," *Orientalia Lovaniensia Periodica* 8 (1977): 187–203; idem, *Un philosophe au désert*, 13–95. Additional literature can be found in bibliographic form on a relevant platform called "Guide to Evagrius Ponticus, ed. Joel Kalvesmaki" at the following address: http://evagriusponticus.net (last accessed 2 September 2014).

378 Epiphanius, *Panarion haereses* 64.4.1 (GCS Epiphanius II, 409.19–410.1 HOLL/DUMMER). ET from SECOND, *The Panarion of Epiphanius of Salamis, Books II and III. De Fide*, 137. On this pronouncement and the group behind it, see DECHOW, *Dogma and Mysticism in Early Christianity*, 145f.

379 Hugh G. Evelyn White, *The Monasteries of the Wâdi 'n Natrûn*, pt. 2, *The History of the Monasteries of Nitria and of Scetis*, ed. Walter Hauser, Publications of the Metropolitan Museum of Art Egyptian Expedition (New York: Arno Press, 1973 [= New York: Metropolitan Museum, 1932]), 17–144; Joachim Willeitner, *Die ägyptischen Oasen: Städte, Tempel und Gräber in der libyschen Wüste*, Zaberns Bildbände zur Archäologie (Mainz: Zabern, 2003), 104–113; and Rodolphe Kasser, "Sortir du monde: Réflexions sur la situation et le développement des établissements monastiques aux Kellia," *Revue de théologie et de philosophie* 109 (1976): 111–124.

380 Bärbel Kramer, s.v. "Didymus von Alexandrien (311–398)," *TRE* 8: 741–746; Dechow, *Dogma and Mysticism in Early Christianity*, 146–150; and the classic Derwas J. Chitty, *The Desert a City: An Introduction to the Study of Egyptian and Palestinian Monasticism under the Christian Empire* (Crestwood, N.Y.: St Vladimir's Seminary Press, 1995 [= Oxford: Blackwell, 1966]), 20–45 and 46–64. For Evagrius, see Guillaumont, *Un philosophe au désert*, 53–64.

381 Wolfgang A. Bienert, *"Allegoria" und "Anagoge" bei Didymos dem Blinden von Alexandria*, Patristische Texte und Studien 13 (Berlin/New York: De Gruyter, 1972), 3f., 43–49, and 69–153. See also Dechow, *Dogma and Mysticism in Early Christianity*, 159–161.

382 Detailed analysis in Dechow, *Dogma and Mysticism in Early Christianity*, 164–177 (Lower Egypt: Nitria and Kellis) and 183–218.

383 Dechow, *Dogma and Mysticism in Early Christianity*, 177–181 ("Evagrius as Synthesizer"). See also Guillaumont, *Les "Kephalaia nostica" d'Évagre le Pontique et l'histoire de l'Origènisme chez les recs et les Syriens* (Paris: Éditions du Seuil, 1962), 40–43 ("Le problem de l'origénisme d'Évagre"); Gabriel Bunge, "Origenismus-Gnostizismus: Zum geistesgeschichtlichen Standort des Evagrios Pontikos," *VC* 40 (1986): 24–54 = idem, *"Die Lehren der heiligen Väter" (RB 73, 2): Aufsätze zu Evagrios Pontikos aus drei Jahrzehnten*, hg. Jakobus Kaffanke, Weisungen der Väter 11 (Beuron: Beuroner Kunstverlag, 2011), 121–154; and Samuel Rubenson, "Evagrios Pontikos und die Theologie der Wüste," in *Logos: Festschrift für Luise Abramowski zum 8. Juli 1993*, hg. Hanns Christof Brennecke, Ernst Ludwig Grasmück und Christoph Markschies, BZNW 67 (Berlin/New York: De Gruyter, 1993), 384–401.

384 CPG II, 2452. The (by modern standards) rather mediocrely edited Greek text in PG originates from AD 1673 and was compared to Φιλοκαλία τῶν νηπτικῶν συνερανισθεῖσα παρὰ τῶν ἁγίων καὶ θεοφόρων πατέρων ἡμῶν ἐν ᾗ διὰ τῆς κατὰ τὴν Πρᾶξιν καὶ Θεωρίαν Ἠθικῆς Φιλοσοφίας ὁ νοῦς καθαίρεται, φωτίζεται, καὶ τελετοῦται (Athens: Ἀστήρ, 1957), 176–189. See on its authorship Irénée Hausherr, "Le *Traité de l'oraison* d'Évagre le Pontique (Pseudo-Nil)," *Revue d'Ascétique et de Mystique* 15 (1934): 34–93 and 113–70. For the *Syrian* tradition see idem, "Le *De oratione* d'Évagre le Pontique en Syriaque et en Arabe," *Orientalia Christiana Periodica* 5 (1939): 7–71; and Joseph Muyldermans, *Evagriana syriaca: Textes inédits du British Museum et de la Vaticane*, édités et traduits, Bibliothèque du Muséon 31 (Louvain: Publications universitaires, 1952), 39–46 (41f.: critical edition of the Greek prologue text). For the *Greek* text see Karl Heussi, *Untersuchungen zu Nilus dem Asketen*, TU 42/2 (Leipzig: Hinrichs, 1917), 119f. (with important references to textual differences in the manuscript tradition in n. 6); and also Michael Kohlbacher, "Unpublizierte Fragmente des Markianos von Bethlehem (nunc CPG 3898 a-d)," in *Horizonte der Christenheit: Festschrift für Friedrich Heyer zu seinem 85. Geburtstag*, hg. Michael Kohlbacher und Markus Lesinski, Oikonomia 34 (Erlangen: Lehrstuhl für Geschichte und Theologie des christlichen Ostens, 1994), 137–167, here 155 §§ 6b, 7, 9, 20, 28, 31, 42, 49, 59, 105, and 107; and generally Sperber-Hartmann, *Das Gebet als Aufstieg zu Gott*, 3–15; and also Gabriel Bunge, *"In Geist und Wahrheit": Studien zu den 153 Kapiteln "Über das Gebet" des Evagrios Pontikos*, übers. v. Hagia Witzenrath, Hereditas 27 (Bonn: Borengässer, 2010), 48–76.

385 Guillaumont, *Un philosophe au désert*, 165–170; Sperber-Hartmann, *Das Gebet als Aufstieg zu Gott*, 13–15 (critical of *Evagrius Ponticus: The Praktikos; Chapters on*

Prayer, trans. with an introduction and notes by John Eudes Bamberger, Cistercian Studies Series 4 [Kalamazoo, Mich.: Cistercian, 1981], 51: "between 390 and 395").

386 Wilhelm Bousset, *Apophthegmata: Studien zur Geschichte des ältesten Mönchtums* (Tübingen: Mohr Siebeck, 1923), 75: "Euagrius hat fast seiner ganzen Hinterlassenschaft . . . die Form der Apophthegmen-Literatur aufgeprägt." Equally characteristic of his oeuvre are the short sentences called "centuries": Endre von Ivanka, "ΚΕΦΑΛΑΙΑ: Eine byzantinische Literaturform und ihre antiken Wurzeln," *Byzantinische Zeitschrift* 47 (1954): 285–291.

387 Rodolphe Kasser, "Le monachisme copte," in *Les Kellia, ermitages coptes en Basse-Egypte: Musée d'art et d'histoire Genève, 12 octobre 1989–7 janvier 1990* (Genève: Éditions du Tricorne, 1989), 9–20, here p. 17 fig. 1.

388 Evagrius Ponticus, *De oratione* 3 (PG 79, 1168 C). ET from Sinkewicz, *Evagrius of Pontus: The Greek Ascetic Corpus*, 199. Cf. on this Clemens Alexandrinus, *Stromata* VII 39.6 (GCS Clemens Alexandrinus III, 30.15f. Stählin/Früchtel/Treu). See also Lorenzo Perrone, *La preghiera secondo Origene: L'impossibilità donata*, Letteratura Cristiana Antica 24 (Brescia: Morcelliana, 2011), 539–543; Guillaumont, *Un philosophe au désert*, 298–301; and Sperber-Hartmann, *Das Gebet als Aufstieg zu Gott*, 83–102.

389 Evagrius Ponticus, *De oratione* 57 (PG 79, 1181 A). ET from Sinkewicz, *Evagrius of Pontus: The Greek Ascetic Corpus*, 199. On the term "prayer of the spirit," see Gabriel Bunge, *Das Geistgebet: Studien zum Traktat De oratione des Evagrios Pontikos*, Schriftenreihe des Zentrums patristischer Spiritualität Koinonia im Erzbistum Köln 25 (Köln: Luthe, 1987), 62–73 and 78–80.

390 Evagrius Ponticus, *De oratione* 67 (PG 79, 1181 C).

391 Ps.-Basilius, *Epistula* 8.2 = Evagrius Ponticus, *Epistula fidei* 2.7 (CUFr I, 24.36–25.42 Courtonne = Corona Patrum I, 88.34–38 Forlin Patrucco). ET from *Evagrius Ponticus*, trans. A. M. Casiday, The Early Church Fathers (London/New York: Routledge, 2006), 48. As an introduction to the *Epistula fidei*, transmitted in the corpus of the letters of Basil, but attributed in manuscripts also to Nilus, see Bousset, *Apophthegmata*, 335–341; Robert Melcher, *Der 8. Brief des hl. Basilius, ein Werk des Evagrius Pontikus*, Münsterische Beiträge zur Theologie 1 (Münster: Aschendorff, 1923), 72–102; and *Evagrios Pontikos: Briefe aus der Wüste*, eingel., übers. und kommentiert v. Gabriel Bunge, Sophia 24 (Trier: Paulinus, 1986), 190–193. On the key terms μονὰς καὶ ἑνάς, see Gabriel Bunge, "Hénade ou Monade? Au sujet de deux notions centrales de la terminologie évagrienne," *Le Muséon* 102 (1989): 69–91.

392 *Capita Gnostica* IV 19 (here cited according to the Greek retroversion of the so-called first, abbreviated Syriac version in Wilhelm Frankenberg, *Euagrius Ponticus*, Abhandlungen der Gesellschaft der Wissenschaften zu Göttingen, philologisch-historische Klasse Neue Folge 13/2 [Berlin: Weidmann, 1912], 273; cf. the abbreviated and unabbreviated Syriac translation in *Les six centuries des "Kephalaia gnostica" d'Évagre le Pontique*, édition critique de la version syriaque commune et édition d'une nouvelle version syriaque, intégrale, avec une double traduction française par Antoine Guillaumont, Patrologia Orientalis 28/1 [Paris: Firmin-Didot, 1958], 142/143): ἐν τῷ ἀριθμῷ τὸ πόσον κατηγορεῖ ἁρμόζει δὲ πρὸς τὴν σωματικὴν φύσιν· ὁ ἀριθμὸς ἄρα τῆς φυσικῆς θεωρίας τῆς δευτέρας ἐστίν. See on this Clark, *The Origenist Controversy*, 62f.

393 Origenes, *De principiis* I 1.6 (GCS Origenes V, 21.10–14 Koetschau = TzF 24, 110 Görgemanns/Karpp). ET from Behr, *Origen: On First Principles*, 1: 31.

394 Hieronymus, *Epistula* 124.9 (CSEL 56/1², 110.4–12 Hilberg): "'omnis creatura liberabitur a seruitute corruptionis in libertatem gloriae filiorum Dei' (Rom 8:21), sic intellegimus, ut primam creaturam rationabilium et incorporalium esse dicamus, quae nunc seruiat corruptioni, eo quod sit uestita corporibus et, ubicumque corpora fuerint, statim corruptio subsequatur; postea autem 'liberabitur de seruitute corruptionis,' quando receperit gloriam filii dei et 'deus fuerit omnia in omnibus' (1 Cor 15:28)." The passage is probably a translation from *De principiis* III 6.1 (GCS Origenes V, 281.1–6 Koetschau = TzF 24,

646 GÖRGEMANNS/KARPP). See on this, for example, Holger STRUTWOLF, *Gnosis als System: Zur Rezeption der valentinianischen Gnosis bei Origenes*, Forschungen zur Kirchen- und Dogmengeschichte 56 (Göttingen: Vandenhoeck & Ruprecht, 1993), 237–241.

395 *Epistula ad (Ps.-) Melaniam* 29 (British Library Add. 17.192, fol. 62b = Add. 14.578, fol. 191aαβ [619.20–30 FRANKENBERG]). See GUILLAUMONT, *Un philosophe au désert*, 343–345; Gabriel BUNGE, "Mysterium Unitatis: Der Gedanke der Einheit von Schöpfer und Geschöpf in der evagrianischen Mystik," *Freiburger Zeitschrift für Philosophie und Theologie* 36 (1989): 449–469 = idem, *"Die Lehren der heiligen Väter" (RB 73, 2)*, 98–120; and idem, *Evagrios Pontikos: Briefe aus der Wüste*, 396 n. 50. Bunge opts for the term σύμμιξις in the Greek original; it might be considered as to whether (as with the Cappadocians with whom Evagrius had studied) the notion of an ἀσύγχυτος ἕνωσις underpinned this and not an indivisible single unity of, on the one hand, μονὰς καὶ ἑνάς, and, on the other, λογικοί. This question warrants investigation in depth (also considering the letter's difficult state of textual transmission).

396 Evagrius Ponticus, *Practicus* 64 (SC 171, 648.1–3 GUILLAUMONT/GUILLAUMONT). See the commentary in *Evagrios Pontikos: Der Praktikos (der Mönch); Hundert Kapitel über das geistliche Leben*, eingel. und kommentiert von Gabriel BUNGE, 2. verb. und verm. Aufl., Weisungen der Väter 6 (Beuron: Beuroner Kunstverlag, 2008), 226. Cf. Evagrius Ponticus, *Gnosticus* 45 (SC 356, 178.5–8 GUILLAUMONT) = Socrates, *Historia ecclesiastica* IV 23.67 (GCS Sokrates, 255.17–19 HANSEN): τῆς δὲ δευτέρας (sc. γνώσεως): one of the realizations comes from humans, the other from God; cf. ibid., 20 [121 G./G.]). See also Antoine GUILLAUMONT, "La vision de l'intellect par lui-même dans la mystique Évagrienne," *Mélanges de l'Université Saint-Joseph* 50 (1984): 255–262 = idem, *Études sur la spiritualité de l'Orient chrétien*, Spiritualité orientale, Série Monachisme primitif 66 (Bégrolles en Mauges: Abbaye de Bellefontaine, 1996), 143–150.

397 Evagrius Ponticus, *De malignis cogitationibus* 43 (SC 438, 298.1–7 GÉHIN/GUILLAUMONT/GUILLAUMONT). Cf. *Fragmenta Graeca* on the *Capita Gnostica* 28 (Joseph MUYLDERMANS, "Euagriana," *Le Muséon* 44 [1931]: 37–68, here 52 nr. 12).

398 *Capita Gnostica* I 35 (79 FRANKENBERG; cf. PO 28/1, 33/34 GUILLAUMONT). See Hans-Veit BEYER, "Die Lichtlehre der Mönche des vierzehnten und des vierten Jahrhunderts, erörtert am Beispiel des Gregorios Sinaïtes, des Euagrios Pontikos und des Ps.-Makarios/Symeon," *Jahrbuch der Österreichischen Byzantinistik* 31 (1981): 473–512, here 475–491.

399 *Capita Gnostica* III 25 (205 FRANKENBERG = PO 28/1, 106 GUILLAUMONT), in the corrected version of the first Syriac version which is at pains to unburden Evagrius of the anti-Origenistic accusations: Τὸ πνευματικὸν σῶμα, ὃ ἐνδύσουσιν οἱ μέσοι λογικοὶ ἐν τῇ ἐσχάτῃ ἡμέραι οὐκ ἄλλό ἐστι παρὰ τοῦτο ὃ ἐκδοῦσιν ἄφθαρτον ὄρθιον καὶ εὐλογοῦν (cf. 1 Sam 28:14). Counter to this: ibid. (PO 28/1, 107 GUILLAUMONT) in the unabridged, second version: "the immaterial body and its opposite are not formed from our limbs or parts, rather from a body." See also GUILLAUMONT, *Les "Kephalaia Gnostica" d'Évagre le Pontique et l'histoire de l'Origènisme chez les recs et les Syriens*, 240 with n. 140. A new identification of the relationship between both versions of the *Kephalaia Gnostica* is attempted by Augustine CASIDAY, *Reconstructing the Theology of Evagrius Ponticus: Beyond Heresy* (Cambridge: Cambridge University Press, 2013), 46–71. This question is hardly central to the present context.

400 For the notion of a "place of God," see Evagrius Ponticus, *Capita cognoscitiua* 20 (quoted after MUYLDERMANS, "Euagriana," 60). ET in SINKEWICZ, *Evagrius of Pontus: The Greek Ascetic Corpus*, 213.

401 Palladius Helenopolitanus, *Historia Lausiaca* 38 (Texts and Studies VI/2, 122.15f. BUTLER).

402 Columba STEWART, "Imageless Prayer and the Theological Vision of Evagrius Ponticus," *JECS* 9 (2001): 173–204, here 182–184. Rather critical of this thesis is SPERBER-HARTMANN, *Das Gebet als Aufstieg zu Gott*, 62 n. 297.

403   Evagrius Ponticus, *De malignis cogitationibus* 43 (298.1–7 Géhin/Guillaumont/Guil-
      laumont). ET from Casiday, *Evagrius Ponticus*, 116. On the introduction to the text
      falsely entitled *De malignis cogitationibus* and ascribed to Nilus of Ancyra, see, for exam-
      ple, Guillaumont, *Un philosophe au désert*, 115–118; and *Évagre le Pontique. Sur les
      pensées*, Édition du texte grec, introduction, traduction, notes et index par Paul Géhin,
      Antoine Guillaumont, and Claire Guillaumont, Sources chrétiennes 438 (Paris: Les édi-
      tions du Cerf, 1998), 28–33.

404   Evagrius Ponticus, *De oratione* 69 (PG 79, 1181 D). See Stewart, "Imageless Prayer and
      the Theological Vision of Evagrius Ponticus," here 194; also Gabriel Bunge, "Aktive und
      kontemplative Weise des Betens im Traktat *De oratione* des Evagrios Pontikos," *Studia
      Monastica* 41 (1999): 211–227 = idem, *"Die Lehren der heiligen Väter" (RB 73, 2)*,
      23–40.

405   Evagrius Ponticus, *De oratione* 72 (PG 79, 1181 D). ET in *Evagrius of Pontus, The Greek
      Ascetic Corpus*, translated with introduction and commentary by Robert E. Sinkewicz,
      OECS (Oxford: Oxford University Press, 2003), 200. For the conception of "demons" in
      Evagrius, see David Brakke, *Demons and the Making of the Monk: Spiritual Combat in
      Early Christianity* (Cambridge, Mass./London: Harvard University Press, 2006), 48–77;
      see also the introduction to his translation of *Antirrheticus: Evagrius of Pontus, Talking
      Back; A Monastic Handbook Combating Demons*, trans. with an introduction by David
      Brakke, Cistercian Studies Series 229 (Collegeville, Minn.: Liturgical Press, 2009), (1–
      40) 30–35; For the conception of demons in *De oration*, see Sperber-Hartmann, *Das
      Gebet als Aufstieg zu Gott*, 24–28, 70–78, and 102–125.

406   Irénée Hausherr, "Les grands courants de la spiritualité orientale," *Orientalia Christiana
      Periodica* 1 (1935): 114–138, here 130; cited in agreement in Dechow, *Dogma and Mys-
      ticism in Early Christianity*, 105.

407   Antoine Guillaumont, "Das Jesusgebet bei den Mönchen Ägyptens," in idem, *An den
      Wurzeln des christlichen Mönchtums: Aufsätze*, ins Deutsche übertragen v. Hagia
      Witzenrath, Weisungen der Väter 4 (Beuron: Beuroner Kunstverlag, 2007), 120–129;
      contra Irénée Hausherr, *Noms du Christ et voies d'oraison*, Orientalia Christiana
      Analecta 157 (Rome: Pontificium Institutum orientalium studiorum, 1960), 202–
      210. Guillaumont's view is supported by Alois Kardinal Grillmeier, "Das 'Gebet zu
      Jesus' und das 'Jesus-Gebet': Eine neue Quelle zum 'Jesus-Gebet' aus dem Weißen
      Kloster," in Laga, *After Chalcedon*, 187–202; and idem, *Jesus der Christus im Glau-
      ben der Kirche*, 2/4: 191f.

408   For inscription nr. 1 from Qusur al-Rubaiyat/Qouçoûr er-Roubâ'yât, House 219 (Room
      12; roughly between AD 650 and 750), see *Kellia I, Kom 219, fouilles, exécutées en
      1964 et 1965*, sous la dírection de François Daumas et Antoine Guillaumont (Le Caire:
      Institut français d'archéologie orientale, 1969), 99 (Coptic text and translation). Cf., how-
      ever, Antoine Guillaumont, "Une inscription copte sur la 'prière de Jésus,'" *Orientalia
      Christiana Periodica* 34 (1968): 310–325 = idem, *Aux origines du monachisme chré-
      tien: Pour une phénoménologie du monachisme*, Spiritualité orientale 30 (Bégrolles en
      Mauges: Abbaye de Bellefontaine, 1979), 168–183 (text and translation of the inscrip-
      tion: 174f.); and Rodolphe Kasser, "La 'prière de Jésus' Kelliote réexaminée en quelques
      points," *Orientalia Christiana Periodica* 62 (1996): 407–410. For the context of the find,
      see Pierre Corboud, "L'oratoire et les niches-oratoires: Les lieux de la prière," in *Le
      site monastique copte des Kellia: Sources historiques et explorations archéologiques*,
      Actes du Colloque de Genève 13 au 15 août 1984, éd. Philippe Bridel (Carouge: Mis-
      sion Suisse d'Archéologie Copte de l'Université de Genève, 1986), 85–92. Generally, see
      also Clark, *The Origenist Controvery*, 69f. with n. 162; and also Emmanuel Lanne, "La
      'Prière de Jésus' dans la tradition égyptienne: Témoignage des psalies et des inscriptions,"
      Irénikon 50 (1977): 163–203.

409   Lines 2–8; also lines 16–19.

410 Origenes, *De oratione* 15.1 (GCS Origenes II, 333.26–334.1 KOETSCHAU). ET from Henry CHADWICK and J. E. L. OULTON, *Alexandrian Christianity: Selected Translations of Clement and Origen* (Philadelphia: Westminster, 1954), 269. On the passage, see PERRONE, *La preghiera secondo Origene*, 260f.; and, in detail, GRILLMEIER, *Jesus der Christus im Glauben der Kirche*, 2/4: 188–190.

411 Hieronymus, *Epistula* 92.2 = Theophilus Alexandrinus, *Synodica Epistula ad Palestinos et ad Cyprios episcopos missa* 2 (CSEL 55, 149.6–9 HILBERG). See on the topic Thomas GRAUMANN, "Reading *De oratione*: Aspects of Religious Practice in the Condemnation of Origen," in *Origeniana Nona: Origen and the Religious Practice of His Time; Papers of the 9th International Origen Congress, Pécs, Hungary, 29 August–2 September 2005*, ed. György Heidl and Robert Somos, BETL 228 (Leuven: Peeters, 2009), 159–177; DECHOW, *Dogma and Mysticism in Early Christianity*, 440f.; and now Roberto ALCIATI, "Origene, gli antropomorfiti e Cassiano: Le ragioni di una relazione istituita," *Adamantius* 19 (2013): 96–110, here 101f., on the question as to whether a tractate from the bishop against Origen and also the anthropomorphites existed.

412 Already Johannes Cassianus, *Collationes* X 5.1 (CSEL 13, 289.9–12 PETSCHENIG = SC 54bis, 146 PICHERY). CLARK, *The Origenist Controversy*, 52 n. 55, relates with reference to the notion that the phrase *consuetudo erroris antiqui* is evidently associated with paganism the view of her colleague within Art History, Annabel Wharton, that there was a conflict between pagan and Christian believers over "whose image should be revered." An overview of the attestations of surviving pagan religiosity, also in the vicinity of monasteries, is collected in Markus VINZENT, "Das 'heidnische' Ägypten im 5. Jahrhundert," in *Heiden und Christen im 5. Jahrhundert*, hg. Johannes van Oort und Dietmar Wyrwa, Studien der Patristischen Arbeitsgemeinschaft 5 (Leuven: Peeters, 1998), 32–65, here 56–63.

413 EVELYN WHITE, *The Monasteries of the Wâdi 'n Natrûn*, 2: 133f.

414 RUBENSON, "Evagrios Pontikos und die Theologie der Wüste," 388f.; and, in more detail, idem, "Origen in the Egyptian Monastic Tradition of the Fourth Century," in Bienert, *Origeniana septima*, 319–337, here 329–336.

415 The quotation from Theophilus is the same within both church historians. ET after CLARK, *The Origenist Controversy*, 45–47.

416 Socrates, *Historia ecclesiastica* VI 7.7f. (322.22–28 HANSEN).

417 Sozomenus, *Historia ecclesiastica* VIII 11.3–4 (364.9–16 BIDEZ/HANSEN).

418 Sozomenus, *Historia ecclesiastica* VIII 11.5 (364.9–16 BIDEZ/HANSEN).

419 Hieronymus, *Epistula* 92.6 (CSEL 55², 154.3–12 HILBERG).

420 *Apophthegmata Patrum* 306 (Theophilus 3; PG 65, 200 A). See on this WATTS, *Riot in Alexandria*, 198f. On the image of Theophilus within this source, see BANEV, *Theophilus of Alexandria and the First Origenist Controversy*, 182–191.

421 WATTS, *Riot in Alexandria*, 190f.; HAHN, *Gewalt und religiöser Konflikt*, 97–101.

422 David BRAKKE, *Athanasius and the Politics of Asceticism*, OECS (Oxford: Clarendon/ New York: Oxford University Press, 1995), 83–110, 266–272. On the references from Theophilus to Athanasius, see also WATTS, *Riot in Alexandria*, 200–203.

423 Carlos R. GALVAO-SOBRINHO, "Embodied Theologies: Christian Identity and Violence in Alexandria in the Early Arian Controversy," in *Violence in Late Antiquity: Perceptions and Practices*, ed. Harold Allen Drake (Aldershot/Burlington, Vt.: Ashgate, 2006), 321–331; HAHN, *Gewalt und religiöser Konflikt*, 51–120; and Thomas SIZGORICH, *Violence and Belief in Late Antiquity: Militant Devotion in Christianity and Islam*, Divinations: Rereading Late Ancient Religion (Philadelphia: University of Pennsylvania Press, 2009), 81–107 and 108–143.

424 Iustinianus Imperator, *Tractatus aduersus impium Origenem* (ACO III, 202.18–203.10 SCHWARTZ = *Scritti teologici ed ecclesiastici di Giustiniano*, a cura di Mario Amelotti e Livia Migliardi Zingale, Legum Iustiniani Imperatoris Vocabularium, Subsidia III [Milan: Giuffrè, 1977], 94.18–96.10 = CPG II, 2595). See now José DECLERCK, "Théophile

d'Alexandrie contre Origène: Nouveaux Fragments de l'Epistula Synodalis Prima (CPG 2595)," *Byzantion* 54 (1984): 495–507. On its dating, see HOLL, "Die Zeitfolge des ersten origenistischen Streites," 254; DECHOW, *Dogma and Mysticism in Early Christianity*, 405f.; and also CLARK, *The Origenist Controversy*, 105f. with n. 158. A rhetorical analysis is given in BANEV, *Theophilus of Alexandria and the First Origenist Controversy*, 125–130.

425   Verbatim from the quotation from the synodical letter in Iustinianus Imperator, *Tractatus aduersus impium Origenem* (ACO III, 203.4 SCHWARTZ = 96.4 AMELOTTI/ZINGALE).

426   Hieronymus, *Epistula* 92 (CSEL 55², 147.1–155.2 HILBERG = CPG II, 2596). Naturally, it might once more be asked whether Jerome really understood the theological underpinnings of the debate as have been reconstructed by Elizabeth Clark, and whether Theophilus at all wanted to make these accessible to him. The response in the negative to these questions (in CLARK, *The Origenist Controvery*, 7) hardly surprises. On the interpretation of the letter itself, see also ibid., 106–111. Jerome himself wrote regarding the translation of the Alexandrian bishop's [seventeenth] Easter festal letter for AD 402 that the translation had been very exacting of him (Hieronymus, *Epistula ad Theophilum* 99.1 [CSEL 55², 212.8f. HILBERG]): "ut omnes sententias pari uenustate transferrem et graecae eloquentiae latinum aliqua ex parte responderet eloquium" (should I have wished to render all thoughts in the same beauty, and to do any justice to the Greek eloquences in Latin). This seems more likely than the topical modesty of a Greek-translating Latin scholar, who additionally stood markedly lower in the ecclesiastical hierarchy than the author being translated (see also idem, *Epistula ad Theophilum* 114.3 [395.14–23 HILBERG]). For the chonology of the letters, see CAVALLERA, *Saint Jérôme, sa vie et son œuvre*, 1/1: 270–280 and 1/2: 38–43.

427   Hieronymus, *Epistula* 92.1 (CSEL 55², 147.18–24 HILBERG).

428   Hieronymus, *Epistula* 92.1 (CSEL 55², 147.25–148.9 HILBERG). ET from RUSSELL, *Theophilus of Alexandria*, 93–94.

429   Eusebius, *Historia ecclesiastica* VI 8.1–3 (GCS Eusebius II/2, 534.15–336.6 SCHWARTZ). Cf. also Epiphanius, *Panarion* 64.3.13 (GCS Epiphanius II, 409.16–18 HOLL/DUMMER). See Christoph MARKSCHIES, "Kastration und Magenprobleme? Einige neue Blicke auf das asketische Leben des Origenes," in Heidl, Somos, and Németh, *Origeniana Nona*, 255–271 = idem, *Origenes und sein Erbe*, 15–34.

430   *Sententii Sexti* 273 (42 CHADWICK). ET from Walter T. WILSON, *The Sentences of Sextus*, Society of Biblical Literature Wisdom Literature from the Ancient World 1 (Atlanta: Society of Biblical Literature, 2012), 276; see also the commentary on pp. 51–54.

431   *Sententii Sexti* 13 (12 CHADWICK). ET from WILSON, *The Sentences of Sextus*, 46. The aphorism clearly refers to Matt 5:29f. and 19:12 and is, according to Henry CHADWICK, *The Sentences of Sextus: A Contribution to the History of Early Christian Ethics*, Texts and Studies, n.s., 5 (Cambridge: Cambridge University Press, 1959), 109–112, an attestation that Christians living the ascetic life took this biblical passage literally. Incidentally, Origen also polemicizes against such a verbatim interpretation in his commentary on this passage: Origenes, *Commentaria in Evangelium Matthaei* XV 3 (GCS Origenes X, 354.1–357.10 KLOSTERMANN/BENZ). The commentary culminates in this sentence (355.7–9): Ἀλλ' οὐ πιστευτέον αὐτοῖς μὴ τὸ βούλημα τῶν ἱερῶν γραμμάτων περὶ τούτων ἐξειληφόσιν (Yet, they cannot be believed, for they have not understood the sense of the Holy Scripture regarding this question.).

432   Epiphanius, *De fide* 13.5 (GCS Epiphanius III, 513.20f. HOLL/DUMMER). See Richard REITZENSTEIN, *"Historia Monachorum" und "Historia Lausiaca": Eine Studie zur Geschichte des Mönchtums und der frühchristlichen Begriffe Gnostiker und Pneumatiker*, FRLANT 24 (Göttingen: Vandenhoeck & Ruprecht, 1916), 189–209.

433   Cyrillus Scythopolitanus, *Vita S. Sabae* 41 (TU 49/2, 131.19–27 SCHWARTZ).

434   Diogenes Laertius, *Vitae philosophorum* IX 27 (SCBO II, 451.9f. LONG = DK 29 A 1 [I, 247.27–29 DIELS/KRANZ]). The story was perennially invoked in Antiquity, for example,

by Plutarch in a tract against garrulity: Plutarchus, *Moralia* 35, *De garrulitate* 8, 505 D (BiTeu III, 288.4–7 POHLENZ/SIEVEKING); or by Valerius Maximus, *Facta et dicta memorabilia* III 3.3, *Externi* 2–4 (BiTeu I, 182.59–184.105 BRISCOE).

435   Diogenes Laertius, *Vitae philosophorum* IX 59 (SCBO II, 468.14–21 LONG = DK 72 A 1 [II, 235.14–20 DIELS/KRANZ]).

436   Tertullianus, *Apologeticum* 50.7f. (CUFr 107 WALTZING/SEVERYNS = CChr.SL 1, 170.31–36 DEKKERS). On the broader tradition regarding this Athenian woman named Leaena (from Λέαινα, "lioness"), see Plinius, *Naturalis historiae* VII 23.87 and XXXIV 19.72 (TuscBü VII, 66–68 KÖNIG/WINKLER and XXXIV, 56 KÖNIG/WINKLER); or Plutarchus, *Moralia* 35, *De garrulitate* 8, 505 E (BiTeu III, 288.7–19 POHLENZ/SIEVEKING).

437   DECHOW, *Dogma and Mysticism in Early Christianity*, 436–448 (with extensive attestations from sources).

438   Hieronymus, *Epistula* 92.2 (CSEL 55², 149.11–19 HILBERG). ET from RUSSELL, *Theophilus of Alexandria*, 94–95. Cf. for the quotation (unattested within Origen's oeuvre) *De principiis* II 10.1–3 (TzF 24, 418–426 GÖRGEMANNS/KARPP = GCS Origenes V, 172.28–176.20 KOETSCHAU). Theophilus also paraphrases the sentence in his letter from Constantinople (AD 403; CPG II, 2612; here frag. 5, 62.3f. RICHARD). For possible sources for this allegation in Origen, see DECHOW, *Dogma and Mysticism in Early Christianity*, 447; see also pp. 349–390.

439   Marcel RICHARD, "Nouveaux fragments de Théophile d'Alexandrie," *Nachrichten der Akademie der Wissenschaften zu Göttingen* 2/1975 (Göttingen: Vandenhoeck & Ruprecht, 1975), 57–65, here 57f. = idem, *Opera minora*, tome 2 (Turnhout/Leuven: Peeters, 1977), nr. 39, 57f.

440   Fragment nr. 8 of a letter from Constantinople AD 403 (CPG II, 2612) after Codex Athous Vatopedi 236, fol. 123ʳ–125ʳ: RICHARD, "Nouveaux fragments de Théophile d'Alexandrie," 63 = idem, *Opera minora*, tome 2, nr. 39, 63. ET in RUSSELL, *Theophilus of Alexandria*, 142.

441   Theophilus Alexandrinus, *Epistulae* frag. 8 (63.34f. RICHARD). See most prominently Gilles DORIVAL, "Origène et la résurrection de la chair," in *Origeniana Quarta: Die Referate des 4. Internationalen Origeneskongresses (Innsbruck, 2.–6. September 1985)*, hg. Lothar Lies, Innsbrucker Theologische Studien 19 (Innsbruck/Vienna: Tyrolia, 1987), 291–321, here 315–317; and also Emanuela PRINZIVALLI, "Aspetti esegetico-dottrinali del dibattito nel IV secolo sulle tesi origeniane in materia escatologica," *Annali di storia dell'esegesi* 11 (1994): 433–460.

442   Theophilus Alexandrinus, *Epistulae* frag. 8 (64.1–3 RICHARD). Cf. also Plato, *Timaeus* 32 D-34 A; and Proclus Atheniensis, *Institutio theologica* 210 (184.1–10 DODDS).

443   Hieronymus, *Epistula* 92.4 (CSEL 55², 152.15–20 HILBERG). ET from RUSSELL, *Theophilus of Alexandria*, 97.

444   On Origen's Christology, see GRILLMEIER, *Jesus der Christus im Glauben der Kirche*, 1: 266–280.

445   Hieronymus, *Epistula* 92.4 (CSEL 552, 152.20–23 HILBERG).

446   On the biography of Cassian, see generally Owen CHADWICK, *John Cassian: A Study in Primitive Monasticism* (Cambridge: Cambridge University Press, 1950 = 2008), 1–36. 49f.; Adalbert de VOGÜÉ, *Histoire littéraire du mouvement monastique dans l'antiquité*, tome 6, *Les derniers ècrits de Jérôme et l'oeuvre de Jean Cassien*, Patrimoines christianisme (Paris: Les éditions du Cerf, 2002), 173–273; Columba STEWART, *Cassian the Monk*, Oxford Studies in Historical Theology (New York/Oxford: Oxford University Press, 1998), esp. 7–12 (on its dating, p. 16 with n. 134 on p. 151); Christopher J. KELLY, *Cassian's Conferences: Scriptural Interpretation and the Monastic Ideal*, Ashgate New Critical Thinking in Religion, Theology and Biblical Studies Series (Farnham/Burlington, Vt.: Ashgate, 2012), 1–16; and also Richard J. GOODRICH, *Contextualizing Cassian: Aristocrats, Asceticism, and Reformation in Fifth-Century Gaul*, OECS (Oxford: Oxford University Press, 2007), 8–31 and 211f.

447 Palladius Helenopolitanus, *Dialogus de vita Sancti Chrysostomi* 3 (SC 341, 76.83f. MALINGREY). See CLARK, *The Origenist Controversy*, 22f. and 50–58; Salvatore MARSILI, *Giovanni Cassiano ed Evagrio Pontico: Dottrina sulla carità e contemplazione*, Studia Anselmiana 5 (Rome: Herder, 1936), 77–86; and also STEWART, *Cassian the Monk*, 12.

448 Friedrich PRINZ, *Frühes Mönchtum im Frankenreich: Kultur und Gesellschaft in Gallien, den Rheinlanden und Bayern am Beispiel der monastischen Entwicklung (4. bis 8. Jahrhundert)* (München: Oldenbourg, 1965), 47–59; and Mireille LABROUSSE, "Les origines du monastère (Vᵉ–VIIIᵉ siècle)," in *Histoire de l'abbaye de Lérins* (Bégrolles-en-Mauges: Abbaye de Bellefontaine, 2005), 23–124; and also Martine DULAEY, "Les relations entre Lérins et Marseille: Eucher et Cassien," in *Lérins, une île sainte de l'antiquité au moyen âge*, éd. Yann Codou et Michel Lauwers, Collection d'études médiévales de Nice 9 (Turnhout: Brepols, 2009), 63–82. See also recently *Hilarius von Arles: Leben des heiligen Honoratus; Eine Textstudie zum Mönchtum und Bischofswesen im spätantiken Gallien*, hg. Franz Jung (Fohren-Linden: Carthusianus, 2013), 98f.

449 Karl Suso FRANK, "Fiktive Mündlichkeit als Grundstruktur der monastischen Literatur," in *Biblica et apocrypha, orientalia, ascetica: Papers Presented at the Eleventh International Conference on Patristic Studies Held in Oxford 1991*, vol. 2, ed. Elizabeth A. Livingstone, Studia Patristica 25 (Leuven: Peeters, 1993), 356–375; STEWART, *Cassian the Monk*, 28f.; and also Adalbert de VOGÜÉ, "Pour comprendre Cassien: Un survol des Conférences," *Collectanea Cisterciensia* 39 (1979): 250–272, here 252–254 = idem, *De Saint Pachôme à Jean Cassien: Études littéraires et doctrinales sur le monachisme égyptien à ses débuts*, Studia Anselmiana 120 (Rome: Pontificio ateneo S. Anselmo, 1996), 303–330, here 305–307.

450 Generally, see also Marie-Anne VANNIER, "Jean Cassien, historiographe du monachisme égyptien?" in *L'historiographie de l'église des premiers siècles*, éd. Bernard Pouderon et Yves-Marie Duval, Théologie historique 114 (Paris: Beauchesne, 2001), 149–158; and GOODRICH, *Contextualizing Cassian*, 8–31 and 211f.

451 STEWART, *Cassian the Monk*, 136f., in making these interpretations draws upon Palladius Helenopolitanus, *Dialogus de vita Sancti Chrysostomi* 17 (SC 341, 340.101–107 MALINGREY), and also *Apophthegmata Patrum* 372*–383* (Isaak 1–12: Περὶ τοῦ ἀββᾶ Ἰσαὰκ τοῦ πρεσβυτέρου τῶν Κελλίων) PG 65, 224 B–228 A. On this topic, see also VOGÜÉ, *Histoire littéraire du mouvement monastique dans l'antiquité*, 6: 245–273.

452 Johannes Cassianus, *Collationes* X 2.1–3 (CSEL 13, 287.3–24 PETSCHENIG = SC 54ᵇⁱˢ, 140/142 PICHERY). ET from RAMSEY, *John Cassian: The Conferences*, 371f. Cf. also *Johannes Cassianus: Unterredungen mit den Vätern; Collationes Patrum*, Tl. 1, *Collationes 1 bis 10*, übers. und erläutert v. Gabriele Ziegler, mit einer Einleitung und farbigen Abbildungen v. Georges Descoeudres, Quellen der Spiritualität 5 (Münsterschwarzach: Vier-Türme, 2011), 301f. On the background to the translation in the "Cassian-Projekt Münsterschwarzach" see its homepage: www.cassian-projekt.de (last accessed 18 May 2019).

453 STEWART, *Cassian the Monk*, 10f. references *Apophthegmata Patrum* 786–790 (Paphnutius 1–5: Περὶ τοῦ ἀββᾶ Παφνουτίου) PG 65, 377 C–380 D. Cf. also *Collectio systematica* IX 14 (SC 387, 448.1–10 GUY) and XVII 15 (SC 498, 19.1–20.15 GUY). Perhaps this Paphnutius Βούβαλος, "the desert antelope," may be identical with the figure of the same name, Paphnutius Kephalas, in Palladius Helenopolitanus, *Historia Lausiaca* 47 (Texts and Studies 6, 137.2–142.10 BUTLER); also followed by Edward Cuthbert BUTLER, *The Lausiac History of Palladius*, vol. 2, *The Greek Text Edited with Introduction and Notes*, Texts and Studies 6 (Cambridge: Cambridge University Press, 1904), 224f.; and EVELYN WHITE, *The Monasteries of the Wâdi 'n Natrûn*, 2: 120–122. See also KELLY, *Cassian's Conferences*, 63–65; and DECHOW, *Dogma and Mysticism in Early Christianity*, 172–176.

454 This festal letter is lost, but is generally dated to the year AD 399 (CLARK, *The Origenist Controversy*, 45–57). Only GRILLMEIER, *Jesus der Christus im Glauben der Kirche*, 2/4, prefers the years "around 395" ("um 395").

455 Andreas Külzer, "Die Festbriefe (ΕΠΙΣΤΟΛΑΙ ΕΟΡΤΑΣΤΙΚΑΙ): Eine wenig beachtete Untergattung der byzantinischen Briefliteratur," *Byzantinische Zeitschrift* 91 (1998): 379–390, here 386.

456 Fragment nr. 7 of the letter from Constantinople 403 n.chr. (CPG II, 2612): Richard, "Nouveaux fragments de Théophile d'Alexandrie," 63 = idem, *Opera minora*, tome 2, nr. 39, 63. ET in Russell, *Theophilus of Alexandria*, 142.

457 Theophilus Alexandrinus, *Epistula Constantinopoli scripta* (= CPG II, 2612) frag. 7 (63.29–33 Richard). ET from Russell, *Theophilus of Alexandria*, 141–142.

458 *Der neue Georges: Ausführliches Latein-Deutsches Handwörterbuch*, aus den Quellen zusammengetragen und mit besonderer Bezugnahme auf Synonymik und Antiquitäten unter Berücksichtigung der besten Hilfsmittel ausgearbeitet v. Karl-Ernst Georges, hg. Thomas Baier, bearb. v. Tobias Dänzer (Darmstadt: Wissenschaftliche Buchgesellschaft, 2013), 1: 1032. See also *Mittellateinisches Wörterbuch* (München: Beck, 1999), 2: 1099–1103.

459 Gennadius Massiliensis, *De viris illustribus* 34 (TU 14/1, 73.23–74.12 Richardson).

460 Bruno Czapla, *Gennadius als Litterarhistoriker: Eine quellenkritische Untersuchung der Schrift des Gennadius von Marseille "De viris illustribus,"* Kirchengeschichtliche Studien IV/1 (Münster: Schöningh, 1898), 74, opines that the passage is copied completely from Cassian and that no independent knowledge of the text might be evidenced for the author. On this topic, see also Hans Joachim Cristea, *Schenute von Atripe, Contra Origenistas: Edition des koptischen Textes mit annotierter Übersetzung und Indizes einschließlich einer Übersetzung des 16. Osterfestbriefs des Theophilus in der Fassung des Hieronymus (ep. 96)*, Studien zu Antike und Christentum 60 (Tübingen: Mohr Siebeck, 2012), 99f.

461 Gennadius Massiliensis, *De viris illustribus* 34 (TU 14/1, 74.9–12 Richardson). ET from *Gennadius: Lives of Illustrious Men*, trans. with introduction and notes by Ernest Cushing Robinson, in *NPNF²*, 3 (New York: Christian Literature, 1906), 385–404, here 392.

462 Gould, "The Image of God and the Anthropomorphite Controversy in Fourth Century Monasticism," 553.

463 Socrates, *Historia ecclesiastica* VI 7.8 (322.27f. Hansen).

464 CPG II, 2684, first edited (with many mistakes) in Eugène Revillout, "La vie du bienheureux Aphou, évêque de Pemdjé (Oxyrinque)," *Revue Égyptologique* 3 (1883): 27–33; and then (much better) in Francesco Rossi, *Trascrizione di tre manoscritti copti del Museo egizio di Torino*, con tradizione Italiana, Memorie del Reale Accademia delle Scienze di Torino, serie II 37 (Turin: Accademia delle Scienze di Torino, 1886), 5–22 = 67–84; then with important corrections in Oscar von Lemm, "Koptische Miscellen: XLIV Zur Vita des h. Aphu," *Bulletin de l'Académie impériale des sciences de Saint-Pétersbourg* 6/2 (1908): 596–598 = idem, *Koptische Miscellen I–CXLVIII: Unveränderter Nachdruck der 1907–1915 im "Bulletin de l'Académie impériale des sciences de St.-Pétersbourg" erschienenen Stücke*, hg. Peter Nagel unter Mitarbeit von Kurt Kümmel, Subsidia Byzantina 11 (Leipzig: Zentralantiquariat der DDR, 1972), 72–74.

465 Tito Orlandi, "Egyptian Monasticism and the Beginnings of the Coptic Literature," in *Carl-Schmidt-Kolloquium an der Martin-Luther-Universität 1988*, hg. Peter Nagel, Martin-Luther-Universität Halle-Wittenberg, Wissenschaftliche Beiträge 23/1990 (K 9) (Halle: Martin-Luther-Universität Halle-Wittenberg, 1990), 129–142, here 137; and Bumazhnov, *Der Mensch als Gottes Bild im christlichen Ägypten*, 138f. See also Anders Georges Florovsky, "Theophilus of Alexandria and Apa Aphu of Pemdje: The Anthropomorphites in the Egyptian Desert: Part II," in *Harry Austryn Wolfson Jubilee Volume on the Occasion of His Seventy-Fifth Birthday. Sefer hayovel likhevod Tsevi Volfson*, vol. 1, English Section (Jerusalem: American Academy for Jewish Research, 1965), 275–310, here 279 = idem, *Collected Works*, vol. 4, *Aspects of Church History*, ed. Richard S. Haugh (Belmont, Mass.: Nordland, 1975), 97–129 and 290–296, here 101: "The 'Life' seems to have been written in a day when the turbulent events of the times of Theophilus had been forgotten in monastic circles. Some time must have elapsed

before the 'Life' could be included in a *Menologion*. Thus, it seems most probable that the whole collection was completed in the later part of the fifth century."

466 Étienne Drioton, "La discussion d'un moine anthropomorphite Audien avec le patriarche Théophile d'Alexandrie en l'année 399," *Revue de l'orient chrétien* 20 (= 2. sér. 10) (1915–1917): 92–100 and 113–128, here 94–115 (text from Rossi and von Lemm with French translation). An Italian translation is offered by Tito Orlandi, "La Cristologia nei testi catechetici Copti," in *Cristologia e catechesi patristica*, tome 1, *Convegno di studio e aggiornamento Pontificium Institutum Altioris Latinitatis (Facoltà di Lettere cristiane e classiche) Roma, 17–19 febbraio 1979*, a cura di Sergio Felici, Biblioteca di scienze religiose 31 (Rome: LAS, 1980), 213–229, here 219–221 ("Estratto dalla 'Vita di Aphu'"). The text is discussed in detail most prominently in Bumazhnov, *Der Mensch als Gottes Bild im christlichen Ägypten*, 138–218 (with a German translation on pp. 219–228 and a history of research on pp. 144–150); but also in Florovsky, "Theophilus of Alexandria and Apa Aphu of Pemdje," 275–310 = 97–129 and 290–296; Clark, *The Origenist Controversy*, 51f., 59f., 64f., and 74f.; and also Gould, "The Image of God and the Anthropomorphite Controversy in Fourth Century Monasticism," 550–554.

467 Texts, translation, and interpretation in Bumazhnov, *Der Mensch als Gottes Bild im christlichen Ägypten*, 140–142. On the Arabic menologues, see Florovsky, "Theophilus of Alexandria and Apa Aphu of Pemdje," 278 = 100 with attestations in n. 14.

468 However, cf. Drioton, "La discussion d'un moine anthropomorphite Audien avec le patriarche Théophile d'Alexandrie en l'année 399," 116f.; critically opposed to this: Florovsky, "Theophilus of Alexandria and Apa Aphu of Pemdje," 289f. = 111f.; Guillaumont, *Les "Kephalaia Gnostica" d'Évagre le Pontique et l'histoire de l'Origènisme chez les Grecs et les Syriens*, 61 n. 62; and, most recently, Bumazhnov, *Der Mensch als Gottes Bild im christlichen Ägypten*, 145f. On "anthropomorphism" among the Audians, see Epiphanius, *Panarion haereses* 70.2.4f. (GCS Epiphanius III, 234.8–15 Holl/Dummer); Jacques Yarry, "Une semi hérésie syro-egyptienne: L'audianisme," *Bulletin de l'Institut Français d'Archéologie Orientale* 63 (1965): 169–195, here 173–175; and Guy G. Stroumsa, "Jewish and Gnostic Traditions among the Audians," in *Sharing the Sacred: Religious Contacts and Conflicts in the Holy Land, First–Fifteenth Centuries CE*, ed. Arieh Kofsky and Guy G. Stroumsa (Jerusalem: Yad Izhak Ben-Zvi, 1998), 97–108, here 101f. = idem, *Barbarian Philosophy: The Religious Revolution of Early Christianity*, WUNT 112 (Tübingen: Mohr Siebeck, 1999), 258–267, here 261f.

469 Epiphanius, *Panarion haereses* 70.2.4f. (GCS Epiphanius III, 234.8–15 Holl/Dummer). Cf. also ibid., 70.6.1f. (GCS Epiphanius III, 237.27–238.4 Holl/Dummer).

470 Epiphanius, *Panarion haereses* 70.15.5 (GCS Epiphanius III, 248.31–249.2 Holl/Dummer).

471 *Vita Aphunis* 2.7 (ed. Rossi 6a/68a.17–27). See Bumazhnov, *Der Mensch als Gottes Bild im christlichen Ägypten*, 219–228, here 219.

472 Eldon Jay Epp, "The New Testament Papyri at Oxyrhynchus in Their Social and Intellectual Context," in *Sayings of Jesus: Canonical and Non-canonical; Essays in Honour of Tjitze Baarda*, ed. William L. Petersen, Johan S. Vos, and Henk J. de Jonge, NovTSup 89 (Leiden: Brill, 1997), 47–68, here 54 = idem, *Perspectives on New Testament Textual Criticism: Collected Essays, 1962–2004*, NovTSup 116 (Leiden: Brill, 2005), 497–520, here 504; Julian Krüger, *Oxyrhynchos in der Kaiserzeit: Studien zur Topographie und Literaturrezeption*, Europäische Hochschulschriften 3. Reihe Geschichte und ihre Hilfswissenschaften 441 (Frankfurt am Main/New York: Lang, 1990), 69–109; and AnneMarie Luijendijk, *Greetings in the Lord: Early Christians and the Oxyrhynchus Papyri*, Harvard Theological Studies 60 (Cambridge, Mass.: Harvard University Press, 2008), 19–21 and 189–231.

473 Bumazhnov, *Der Mensch als Gottes Bild im christlichen Ägypten*, 152–191.

474 Attestations in Bumazhnov, *Der Mensch als Gottes Bild im christlichen Ägypten*, 155–161.

475 *Vita Aphunis* 5.1f. (ed. Rossi 7c/69c.5–28). ET from Florovsky, "Theophilus of Alexandria and Apa Aphu of Pemdje," 113.

476 *Vita Aphunis* 5.4 (ed. Rossi 8a/70a.26–31). ET from Florovsky, "Theophilus of Alexandria and Apa Aphu of Pemdje," 113. See Bumazhnov, *Der Mensch als Gottes Bild im christlichen Ägypten*, 212–218; and Clark, *The Origenist Controversy*, 74f.

477 See on this *Vita Aphunis* 5.2 (ed. Rossi 7c/69c.22–28).

478 *Vita Aphunis* 5.3 (ed. Rossi 7c/69c.28–8a/70a.12). ET from Florovsky, "Theophilus of Alexandria and Apa Aphu of Pemdje," 113.

479 *Vita Aphunis* 6.1f. (ed. Rossi 8b/70b.8–27). See on this Bumazhnov, *Der Mensch als Gottes Bild im christlichen Ägypten*, 187f.

480 *Vita Aphunis* 7.8–8.11 (ed. Rossi 9b/71b.21–11a/73.24). ET from Florovsky, "Theophilus of Alexandria and Apa Aphu of Pemdje," 114f.

481 Epiphanius, *Epistula ad Iohannem Hierosolymitanum* apud Hieronymum, *Epistula* 51.6f. (CSEL 54[2], 406.24–407.3, 407.9–19 Hilberg). On this passage and the references to Origen, see Dechow, *Dogma and Mysticism in Early Christianity*, 302–315; on its connection to Vita Aphunis, see most prominently Florovsky, "Theophilus of Alexandria and Apa Aphu of Pemdje," 299f. = 121f.

482 *Vita Aphunis* 10.1 (ed. Rossi 12a/74a.22–12b/74b.1). ET from Florovsky, "Theophilus of Alexandria and Apa Aphu of Pemdje," 115f. See on this Bumazhnov, *Der Mensch als Gottes Bild im christlichen Ägypten*, 201–203.

483 *Vita Aphunis* 10.2–9 (ed. Rossi 12b/74b.16–13b/75b.12). See, in particular, 10.2f. (12b/74b.17–25). On this, in depth, see Bumazhnov, *Der Mensch als Gottes Bild im christlichen Ägypten*, 202–210. ET from Florovsky, "Theophilus of Alexandria and Apa Aphu of Pemdje," 116.

484 *Vita Aphunis* 11.1–3 (ed. Rossi 13b/75b,12–13c/75c,19). ET from Florovsky," Theophilus of Alexandria and Apa Aphu of Pemdje," 116f.

485 Florovsky, "Theophilus of Alexandria and Apa Aphu of Pemdje," 279 = 101, argues that "the writer was unaware of that complex and controversial situation in which the dispute had taken place and therefore had no incentive to be tendentious: he had a 'blind accuracy'—*une exactitude aveugle*, as Drioton puts it" (see for this Drioton, "La discussion d'un moine anthropomorphite Audien avec le patriarche Théophile d'Alexandrie en l'année 399," 93f.). Bumazhnov, *Der Mensch als Gottes Bild im christlichen Ägypten*, 192, states on the contrary: "Die Vita scheint eine historisch relativ lang zurückliegende Begebenheit für ihre eigene, durch die aktuellen Zwecke bedingte Situation zu bearbeiten."

486 Seen otherwise by Bumazhnov, *Der Mensch als Bild Gottes im christlichen Ägypten*, 213–215. See esp. p. 214: "Im Zentrum des Interesses des Verfassers liegt somit weder die Diskussion der Gottebenbildlichkeit des Menschen an und für sich noch ihre historischen Begleitumstände, sondern das Problem der Rolle des Mönchtums in der Kirche."

487 Florovsky, "Theophilus of Alexandria and Apa Aphu of Pemdje," 290 and 301–305 = 112 and 123–127; further attestations in Bumazhnov, *Der Mensch als Bild Gottes im christlichen Ägypten*, 210f.

488 Bumazhnov, *Der Mensch als Bild Gottes im christlichen Ägypten*, 192–218.

489 On this position within the field, see below. See also on this, Frances M. Young, "God's Image: The 'Elephant in the Room' in the Fourth Century?" in *Studia Patristica: Including Papers Presented at the National Conference on Patristic Studies Held at Cambridge in the Faculty of Divinity under Allen Brent, Thomas Graumann and Judith Lieu in 2009*, ed. Allen Brent and Markus Vinzent, Studia Patristica 50 (Leuven/Paris/Walpole, Mass.: Peeters, 2011), 57–72.

490 *Vita Aphunis* 5.4 (ed. Rossi 8a/70a.26–31). ET from Florovsky, "Theophilus of Alexandria and Apa Aphu of Pemdje," 113.

491 Theophilus' quotation appears in the same wording in the writings of both ecclesiastical historians: οὕτως ὑμᾶς εἶδον ὡς θεοῦ πρόσωπον. See on this Clark, *The Origenist Controversy*, 45–47.

492 Johannes Cassianus, *Collationes* X 3.1f. (CSEL 13, 288.22–25 Petschenig = SC 54bis, 142 Pichery). See, moreover, the extensive analyses in Stewart, *Cassian the Monk*, 86–99; Bunge, *"In Geist und Wahrheit,"* 63–65; and Bumazhnov, *Der Mensch als Gottes Bild im christlichen Ägypten*, 176–179.

493 Johannes Cassianus, *Collationes* X 3.3 (CSEL 13, 288.22–25 Petschenig = SC 54bis, 142/144 Pichery). ET from Ramsey, *John Cassian: The Conferences*, 372.

494 Johannes Cassianus, *Collationes* X 3.4 (CSEL 13, 289.7–14 Petschenig = SC 54bis, 144 Pichery). ET from Ramsey, *John Cassian: The Conferences*, 373. Stewart, *Cassian the Monk*, 192 n. 10 (viz p. 87), draws attention to the fact that Cassian does not otherwise cite John 20:2, 13. In his view, it is also apparent from this detail that, in fact, the divinity of Jesus Christ stands in the foreground of the argumentation (p. 88).

495 See above for the indirect reference to Origen and Evagrius in Johannes Cassianus. See Stewart, *Cassian the Monk*, 11f., 87, 124; and idem, "John Cassian's Schema of Eight Principal Faults and His Debt to Origen and Evagrius," in *Jean Cassien entre l'orient et l'occident: Actes du colloque international organisé par le New Europe College en collaboration avec la Ludwig Boltzmann Gesellschaft, Bucarest, 27–28 septembre 2001*, éd. Cristian Bădiliţă et Attila Jakab (Paris: Beauchesne/Iaşi: Polirom, 2003), 205–220.

496 See Stewart, *Cassian the Monk*, 87; emphatically concurring: Patterson, *Visions of Christ*, 17–19. On a monk influenced by Origen called "Serapion" see Dechow, *Dogma and Mysticism in Early Christianity*, 155f. Bunge, *"In Geist und Wahrheit,"* 65–69, suggests (as did already Adalbert de Vogüé, *Histoire littéraire du mouvement monastique dans l'antiquité*, tome 3, *Jérôme, Augustin et Rufin au tournant du siècle (391–405)* [Paris: Les éditions du Cerf, 1996], 88 n. 468) identifying this Photinus with Evagrius Ponticus, evidencing parallels to the sentences of Cassian in Evagrius.

497 Johannes Cassianus, *Collationes* X 4.1 (CSEL 13, 289.7–14 Petschenig = SC 54bis, 144/146 Pichery). ET from Ramsey, *John Cassian: The Conferences*, 373.

498 Bumazhnov, *Der Mensch als Gottes Bild im christlichen Ägypten*, 177–179, locates this polemic characterization in the context of a frequently attested (naturally also in Egypt) monastic ideal of being or becoming "simple" so as to avoid arrogance and pride (pp. 161–172).

499 Johannes Cassianus, *Collationes* X 5.1 (CSEL 13, 289.7–14 Petschenig = SC 54bis, 146 Pichery). For Stewart, *Cassian the Monk*, 88, the connection between Serapion's position and paganism is "marginal."

500 On the conception of John Cassian that in prayer to God one might see within the glorified Christ, see *De incarnatione Domini contra Nestorium* III 6.3 (CSEL 17, 267.23–29 Petschenig). See Stewart, *Cassian the Monk*, 95–99.

501 Rubenson, "Origen in the Egyptian Monastic Tradition of the Fourth Century," 333; seen otherwise by Ledegang, "Anthropomorphites and Origenists in Egypt," 379: "Summarizing, it can be said that the conflict at the end of the fourth century in Egypt was originally a sociological controversy between simple and learned monks and a theological one with regard to the biblical anthropomorphisms and to prayer. Finally, however, it became a merely political conflict. Origen's theological views only played a minor part in this."

502 Johannes Cassianus, *Collationes* X 5.1 (CSEL 13, 290.9–11 Petschenig = SC 54bis, 146 Pichery).

503 For the three texts, the edition in Migne (Cyrillus Alexandrinus, *Adversus Anthropomorphitas*, PG 76, 1065–1132) is now superseded by *Cyril of Alexandria: Select Letters*, trans. Lionel R. Wickham, Oxford Early Christian Texts (Oxford: Clarendon, 2007 = 1983). On the MSS and the history of prior editions, see pp. xxviii–xxxi and xlvii–xlix. For the Syriac text, see Rifaat Y. Ebied and Lionel R. Wickham, "The Letter of Cyril of Alexandria to Tiberius the Deacon," *Le Muséon* 83 (1970): 433–482. On the texts, see also Eginhard P. Meijering, "Some Reflections on Cyril of Alexandria's Rejection of Anthropomorphism," *Nieuw Theologisch Tijdschrift* 28 (1974): 295–301; Alexander

GOLITZIN, "The Form of God and Vision of the Glory," 22–24; and PATTERSON, *Visions of Christ*, 61–77.

504 Following the breviary of the Carmelites, thus *Acta Sanctorum . . . , Januarius,* tomus II, *die 28* (Paris: Victor Palmé, 1863), p. 844 = PG 68, 11f.: "Cyrillus Episcopus Alexandrinus claris parentibus ortus, [Alexandrinusne fuerit,] Theophili item Episcopi Alexandrini ex fratre nepos, a quo adolescens Athenas studiorum caussa missus, cum plurimum profecisset, ad Ioannem Episcopum Hierosolymitanum, vt Christianæ vitae perfectione imbueretur, se contulit." Critical of this legend: Félix Marie ABEL, "Saint Cyrille d'Alexandrie dans ses rapports avec la Palestine," in *Kyrilliana: Spicilegia Sancti Cyrilli Alexandrini XV recurrente saeculo; Études variées à l'occasion du XVᵉ centenaire de Saint Cyrille d'Alexandrie (444–1944),* éd. Seminarium Franciscale Orientale Ghizae (Le Caire: Editions du Scribe Egyptien, 1947), 205–230, here 207–213.

505 WICKHAM, *Selected Letters*, xxviiif.; PATTERSON, *Visions of Christ*, 62f. On Cyril's relationship to the church of the three provinces of Palaestina, see ABEL, "Saint Cyrille d'Alexandrie dans sa rapports avec la Palestine," 221–226.

506 PATTERSON, *Visions of Christ*, 63 (with reference to Cyrillus Alexandrinus, *De dogmatum solutione* [547.19–28 PUSEY = 180.19–28 WICKHAM]). On the countryside, see PATTERSON, *Visions of Christ*, 72f.

507 Cyrillus Alexandrinus, *Solutiones ad Tiberium* 1 (137 WICKHAM = 448 EBIED/WICKHAM).

508 Cyrillus Alexandrinus, *De dogmatum solutione quaestio* 1 (549.3–8 PUSEY = 184.3–7 WICKHAM).

509 Cyrillus Alexandrinus, *De dogmatum solutione responsio* 1 (549.9–17 PUSEY = 184.9–18 WICKHAM).

510 Cyrillus Alexandrinus, *De dogmatum solutione responsio* 1 (550.1–6 PUSEY = 184.18–23 WICKHAM).

511 Cyrillus Alexandrinus, *De dogmatum solutione responsio* 1 (550.6–10 PUSEY = 184.23–186.3 WICKHAM). ET from WICKHAM, *Cyril of Alexandria: Select Letters*, 187

512 Naturally, it remains to be discussed as to whether the monastic circles which posed to Cyril the respective questions by means of Tiberius actually propounded these positions; this remains uncertain. PATTERSON, *Visions of Christ*, 73, certainly does not once suggest it.

513 DECHOW, *Dogma and Mysticism in Early Christianity*, 308–311, refers to texts from Ps.-Macarius and Evagrius.

514 GOULD, "The Image of God and the Anthropomorphite Controversy in Fourth Century Monasticism," 550f.

515 BUMAZHNOV, *Der Mensch als Gottes Bild im christlichen Ägypten*, 157–159.

516 *Vita Aphunis* 12.11 (ed. ROSSI 14c/76c.21–29).

517 STROUMSA, "Jewish and Gnostic Traditions among the Audians," 101 = 261, distinguishes between "concrete mysticism," wherein God becomes visible to corporeal eyes, and "metaphorical mysticism," wherein God becomes visible only to the (Platonically meant) eye of the mind. See also PATTERSON, *Visions of Christ*, 19f.

518 Alexander GOLITZIN, "The Form of God and Vision of the Glory," passim; and idem, "'The Demons Suggest an Illusion of God's Glory in a Form': Controversy over the Divine Body and Vision of Glory in Some Late Fourth, Early Fifth Monastic Literature," *Studia Monastica* 44 (2002): 13–43. Critical remarks in BUMAZHNOV, *Der Mensch als Gottes Bild im christlichen Ägypten*, 148–150; largely in agreement: PATTERSON, *Visions of Christ*, 20–24, more critically 70.

519 GOLITZIN, "The Form of God and Vision of the Glory," 29–36.

520 GOLITZIN, "The Form of God and Vision of the Glory," 1–29. A portion of the references treated by Golitzin is discussed in depth within BUMAZHNOV, *Visio mystica im Spannungsfeld frühchristlicher Erfahrungen*, 170–252.

521 *Apophthegmata patrum* 48 (Arsenius 10; PG 65, 89 C). ET from *The Sayings of the Desert Fathers: The Alphabetical Collection*, trans. Benedicta WARD, rev. ed. (Kalamazoo,

Mich.: Cistercian, 1984), 10. On this saying, cf. Dmitrij Bumazhnov, "Kann man Gott festhalten? Eine frühchristliche Diskussion und deren Hintergründe," in *Christianity in Egypt: Literary Production and Intellectual Trends: Studies in Honor of Tito Orlandi*, ed. Paola Buzi and Alberto Camplani, Studia Ephemeridis Augustinianum 125 (Rome: Institutum Patristicum Augustinianum, 2011), 165–176, here 166f.

522 For an introduction to the text (CPG 2, 2683), see *Origenes: Die Homilien zum Buch Jesaja; Im Anhang; Fragmente und Zeugnisse des Jesajakommentars und; Theophilus von Alexandria, Traktat gegen Origenes über die Vision Jesajas*, eingel. und übers. v. Alfons Fürst und Christian Hengstermann, OWD 10 (Berlin/New York: De Gruyter; Freiburg: Herder, 2009), 180f.; and previously already Berthold Altaner, "Wer ist der Verfasser des *Tractatus in Isaiam* VI 1–7 (ed. G. Morin, Anecdota Maredsolana III 3, Maredsous 1903, 103–122)? Ein Forschungsbericht," *Theologische Revue* 42 (1943): 147–151 = idem, *Kleine patristische Schriften*, hg. Günter Glockmann, TU 83 (Berlin: Akademie, 1967), 483–488.

523 Altaner, "Wer ist der Verfasser des *Tractatus in Isaiam* VI 1–7," 147f. = 483f.: "einen beachtlichen Grad von Selbständigkeit und . . . spekulative Begabung und gute Schriftkenntnisse . . . antiorigenistische Kampfschrift dagegen steht die Arbeit auf einem sehr tiefen Niveau; denn die Kritik der Exegese des Origenes lässt jede Sachlichkeit vermissen."

524 So Fürst/Hengstermann in *Origenes: Die Homilien zum Buch Jesaja*, OWD 10, 180–182.

525 Theophilus Alexandrinus, *Tractatus contra Originem de visione Esaie* 2 (OWD 10, 338.1–11 Fürst/Hengstermann). ET from Russell, *Theophilus of Alexandria*, 162f.

526 Theophilus Alexandrinus, *Tractatus contra Originem de visione Esaie* 2 (OWD 10, 338.22–24 Fürst/Hengstermann). ET from Russell, *Theophilus of Alexandria*, 163.

527 Hieronymus, *Commentaria in Esaiam* III 4, in Esaiam 6:2 (AGLB 23, 312.10–15 Gryson). See on this topic Cristea, *Schenute von Atripe*, 62–65.

528 Origenes, *Homilia in Esaiam* 1.2 (GCS Origenes VIII, 244.15–18 Baehrens/OWD 10, 198.9–11 Fürst/Hengstermann).

529 Theophilus Alexandrinus, *Tractatus contra Originem de visione Esaie* 2 (OWD 10, 338.21f. Fürst/Hengstermann). ET from Russell, *Theophilus of Alexandria*, 163.

530 Cf. Hieronymus, *Epistula* 18A, 7 (CSEL 54², 82.17–85.2 Hilberg) with *Commentaria in Esaiam* III 4, in Esaiam 6:2 (AGLB 23, 312.1–315.73 Gryson) and *Commentaria in Abacuc* 113.2 (CChr.SL 76A, 620.60–621.114 Adriaen). The development of the exegesis of the passage in Jerome and the internal incoherences are analyzed by Alfons Fürst, "Hieronymus gegen Origenes: Die Vision Jesajas im ersten Origenismusstreit," *Revue d'Études Augustiniennes* 53 (2007): 199–233 = idem, *Von Origenes und Hieronymus zu Augustinus: Studien zur antiken Theologiegeschichte*, Arbeiten zur Kirchengeschichte 115 (Berlin/New York: De Gruyter, 2011), 239–274, here 244–252.

531 Theophilus Alexandrinus, *Tractatus contra Originem de visione Esaie* 2 (OWD 10, 342.15–23 Fürst/Hengstermann). ET from Russell, *Theophilus of Alexandria*, 164–165.

532 In the Egyptian monastic father Shenoute's tractate *Contra Origenistas* 7 (§§ 331/332 [p. 147 Cristea]), the Trinitary reading of the cherubim in Isa 6 is also protested: Cristea, *Schenute von Atripe*, 59–65.

533 Iustinianus Imperator, *Tractatus aduersus impium Origenem* (ACO III, 202.23–23 Schwartz = 94.23–26 Amelotti/Zingale). On the events leading to the departure of Origen from Caesarea, see Williams, s.v. "Origenes/Origenismus," 397–420. Remarkably, the Alexandrian (!) synodical letter confuses the Alexandrian bishops: Origen left Alexandria during the office of Heraclas' predecessor, Demetrius, although his successor Heraclas also scarcely undertook measures to recall his erstwhile colleague. At the most, Demetrius had "thrown out" (put metaphorically: "examined," ἐξέτιλεν) Origen. See op. cit., 202.27–30 = 94.27–30.

534 Bumazhnov, *Der Mensch als Gottes Bild im christlichen Ägypten*, 217: "Die Übereinstimmung zwischen den Zeugnissen . . . läßt die Frage aufstellen, ob die Ansichten des hl.

Epiphanius, der bekanntlich in seinen jüngeren Jahren 'engen Kontakt zu monastischen Zirkeln' in Ägypten hatte, eine 'dritte' ägyptische Tradition widerspiegeln können, die die Unbegreiflichkeit der Gottebenbildlichkeit des Menschen herausstellte und zwischen den 'Origenisten' und den 'Anthropomorphiten' in gewisser Weise vermittelte." See also idem, "Einige Aspekte der Nachwirkung des Ankoratus und des Panarion des hl. Epiphanius von Salamis in der früheren monastischen Tradition," *Adamantius* 11 (2005): 158–178.

535 Epiphanius, *Ancoratus* 54.1 (GCS Epiphanius I², 63.7–10 HOLL/BERGERMANN/COLLATZ). ET from *St. Epiphanius of Cyprus: Ancoratus*, trans. Young Richard KIM, Fathers of the Church 128 (Washington, D.C.: Catholic University of America Press, 2014), 137. Cf. also Epiphanius, *Panarion haereses* 70.2.7 (GCS Epiphanius III, 234.22–25 HOLL/ DUMMER). Synoptic presentation of these passages with German translation in BUMAZH-NOV, *Der Mensch als Gottes Bild im christlichen Ägypten*, 216f.

536 *Apophthegmata Patrum* 870 (Sopater 1; PG 65, 413 A = *Collectio systematica* XIV 16, SC 474, 264.1–7 GUY). Cf. on this also *Apophthegmata Patrum* 189 (Daniel 7; PG 65, 157 B = *Collectio systematica* XVIII 4, SC 498, 42.17–21 GUY). ET from WARD, *The Sayings of the Desert Fathers*, 225.

537 On the so-called *Anonymus Cyzicenus* (as the anonymous compiler hailed from the city of Cyzicus), earlier also generally known as "Gelasius of Cyzicus," see *Anonymus von Cyzicus: Historia Ecclesiastica; Kirchengeschichte*, übers. und eingel. v. Günther Christian Hansen, FChr 49/1 (Turnhout: Brepols, 2008), 7–49. Hansen suggested that Philip of Side, a Christian universal historian of the period (pp. 27–29), invented the entire dialogue somewhat in the vein of a rhetorical exercise ("what would x have said in this situation?" pp. 40–44).

538 Anonymus Cyzicenus, *Historia ecclesiastica* II 14.1–2 (GCS.NF 9, 50.6–19 HANSEN = FChr 49/1, 194.7–24 HANSEN).

539 Anonymus Cyzicenus, *Historia ecclesiastica* II 15.6–8 (GCS.NF 9, 52.12–24 HANSEN = FChr 49/1, 200.1–19 HANSEN).

540 Aeneas, *Theophrastus sive De animarum immortalitate et corporum resurrectione dialogus* (46.5f. MINNITI COLONNA). On Aeneas' definition of God, see Manfred WACHT, *Aeneas von Gaza als Apologet: Seine Kosmologie im Verhältnis zum Platonismus*, Theophaneia 21 (Bonn: Hanstein, 1969), 38–50.

541 This is not believed by the Neoplatonic collocutor (38.12f. COLONNA). In the Neoplatonic manner, two different types of body are accordingly distinguished, as is stated by Theophrastus, an Athenian (52.5f. COLONNA).

542 On its dating, cf. the critical edition: *Zacaria Scholastico: Ammonio*, introduzione, testo critico, traduzione, commento a cura di Maria MINNITI COLONNA (Neapel: Antrice, 1973), 38. Minniti Colonna opts for ca. AD 486/487, referring thereby to the introductory ὑπόθεσις of the dialogue (Zacharias Rhetor Mitylenaeus, *Ammonius sive De mundi opificio disputatio* 1–8 [93 MINNITI COLONNA]).

543 Zacharias Rhetor Mitylenaeus, *Ammonius sive De mundi opificio disputatio* 1233–1241 (134f. MINNITI COLONNA).

544 Zacharias Rhetor Mitylenaeus, *Ammonius sive De mundi opificio disputatio* 248–260 (103 MINNITI COLONNA).

545 Particularly pertinent to this is *The Life of Severus by Zachariah of Mytilene*, trans. with introduction by Lena AMBJÖRN, Texts from Christian Late Antiquity 9 (Piscataway, N.J.: Gorgias Press, 2008).

546 Geoffrey GREATREX, introduction to *The Chronicle of Pseudo-Zachariah Rhetor: Church and War in Late Antiquity*, ed. Geoffrey Greatrex, trans. Robert R. Phenix and Cornelia B. Horn, with contributions by Sebastian P. Brock and Witold Witakowski, Translated Texts for Historians 55 (Liverpool: Liverpool University Press, 2011), 3–31, esp. 14f.

547 In the following sections, I have drawn in part upon a lecture which I gave on 9 November 2001 at a conference of the project "Imitatio Christi als Körperkonzept: Der leidende

Körper als kulturelles Symbol und Kommunikationsmedium bei der Integration des Christentums in die spätantike Gesellschaft" under the aegis of the Collaborative Research Centre (Sonderforschungsbereich) 485, "Norm und Symbol: Die kulturelle Dimension sozialer und politischer Integration"; the lecture appeared in a collection of papers from the conference: Christoph MARKSCHIES, "Körper und Körperlichkeit im antiken Mönchtum," in *Die Christen und der Körper: Aspekte der Körperlichkeit in der christlichen Literatur der Spätantike*, hg. Barbara Feichtinger und Helmut Seng, Beiträge zur Altertumskunde 170 (München: Saur, 2004), 189–212.

548 Georg GRÜTZMACHER, s.v. "Hilarion," in *Realencyclopädie für protestantische Theologie und Kirche* (Leipzig: Hinrichs, 1900), 8: 54–56, here 54. Other datings in CHITTY, *The Desert a City*, 13f.: born in AD 293. On the hagiography, see also W. ISRAEL, "Die Vita S. Hilarionis des Hieronymus als Quelle für die Anfänge des Mönchtums kritisch untersucht," *ZTK* 23 (1880): 129–165; and Theodor ZÖCKLER, "Hilarion von Gaza: Eine Rettung," *Neue Jahrbücher für deutsche Theologie* 3 (1894): 146–178. See also on the *Vita* in more detail Stephan SCHIWIETZ, *Das morgenländische Mönchtum*, Bd. 2, *Das Mönchtum auf Sinai und in Palästina im vierten Jahrhundert* (Mainz: Kirchheim 1913), 103–119.

549 Ilona OPELT, "Des Hieronymus' Heiligenbiographien," *Römische Quartalschrift* 74 (1979): 145–177, decides for AD 389–392.

550 Philip ROUSSEAU, *Ascetics, Authority, and the Church in the Age of Jerome and Cassian*, 2nd ed. (Notre Dame, Ind.: University of Notre Dame Press, 2010), 134–139; Adalbert de VOGÜÉ, *Histoire littéraire du mouvement monastique dans l'antiquité, Premier Partie: Le monachisme latin*, tome 2, *De l'itinéraire d'Égerie à l'éloge funèbre de Népotien (384–396)*, Patrimoines christianisme (Paris: Les éditions du Cerf, 1993), 163–236. See also Manfred FUHRMANN, "Die Mönchsgeschichten des Hieronymus: Formexperimente in erzählender Literatur," in *Christianisme et formes littéraires de l'antiquité tardive en Occident: Huit exposés suivis de discussions*, avec la participation de Helena Junod-Ammerbauer et Françcois Paschoud, entretiens prepares et presides par Manfred Fuhrmann, Vandoeuvres-Genève, 23–28 août 1976, Entretiens sur l'antiquité classique 23 (Genève: Fondation Hardt, 1977), 41–89.

551 Hieronymus, *Vita Hilarionis* 3.1 (SC 508, 218.1–220.6 MORALES).

552 Cf. the Latin translation of the *Vita* by a friend of Jerome: Evagrius Antiochenus, *Vita Antonii* (cited after Pascal BERTRAND, *Die Evagriusübersetzung der Vita Antonii: Rezeption—Überlieferung—Edition, unter besonderer Berücksichtigung der Vitas Patrum-Tradition* [Diss. phil. masch., Utrecht 2006], accessible at http://dspace.library .uu.nl/bitstream/handle/1874/7821/full.pdf?sequence=16 [last accessed 29 May 2019]). On the translation, see Peter GEMEINHARDT, *Antonius: Der erste Mönch; Leben—Lehre—Legende* (München: Beck, 2013), 143f.; VOGÜÉ, *Histoire littéraire du mouvement monastique dans l'antiquité*, 2: 179 with attestations in nn. 68–70; previously already Julius PLESCH, *Die Originalität und literarische Form der Mönchsbiographien des hl. Hieronymus*, Beilage zum Programm des Wittelsbacher-Gymnasiums München (München: Wolf, 1910), 40–55; FUHRMANN, "Die Mönchsgeschichten des Hieronymus," 41–58; and Przemyslaw NEHRING, "Jerome's Vita Hilarionis: A Rhetorical Analysis of Its Structure," *Augustinianum* 43 (2003): 417–434, here 420.

553 John BINNS, *Ascetics and Ambassadors of Christ: The Monasteries of Palestine 314–631*, OECS (Oxford: Oxford University Press, 1994), 75, draws attention to this point.

554 Hieronymus, *Vita Hilarionis* 4.2 (SC 508, 226.8–13 MORALES). ET from "Life of Hilarion by Saint Jerome," trans. Sister Marie Ligori EWALD, in *Early Christian Biography*, ed. Roy J. Deferrari, Fathers of the Church 15 (Catholic University of America Press, 1952), 250–251. Cf. moreover Evagrius Antiochenus, *Vita Antonii* 47 (176.688–690 BERTRAND). See on the topic Philippus OPPENHEIM, *Das Mönchskleid im christlichen Altertum*, Römische Quartalschrift, 28. Supplementheft (Freiburg: Herder, 1931), 21–56.

555 Clemens Alexandrinus, *Paedagogus* III 60.2f. (GCS Clemens Alexandrinus I, 270.17–23 STÄHLIN/FRÜCHTEL/TREU). For this, see Martin PUJIULA, *Körper und christliche Lebensweise: Clemens von Alexandreia und sein Paidagogos*, Millennium-Studien zur Kultur

und Geschichte des ersten Jahrtausends n. Chr. 9 (Berlin/New York: De Gruyter, 2006), 244–257.

556 Clemens Alexandrinus, *Paedagogus* III 61.1 (GCS Clemens Alexandrinus I, 270.27–31 Stählin/Früchtel/Treu). ET from *The Writings of Clement of Alexandria*, vol. 1, trans. William Wilson, Ante-Nicene Christian Library 4 (Edinburgh: T&T Clark, 1867), 317.

557 *Actus Petri cum Simone* 22 (I, 70.8–10 Lipsius). See Franz Josef Dölger, *Die Sonne der Gerechtigkeit und der Schwarze: Eine religionsgeschichtliche Studie zum Taufgelöbnis*, 2. um hinterlassene Nachträge des Verfassers verm. Aufl., Liturgiewissenschaftliche Quellen und Forschungen 14 (Münster: Aschendorff, 1971), 49–64; and Peter Habermehl, *Perpetua und der Ägypter oder die Bilder des Bösen im frühen afrikanischen Christentum: Ein Versuch zur Passio sanctarum Perpetua[e] et Felicitatis*, TU 140 (Berlin/New York: De Gruyter, 2004), 161–177 ("Exkurs 4: Der Schwarze"). ET from *The Apocryphal Acts of Paul, Peter, John, Andrew and Thomas*, trans. Bernhard Pick (Chicago: Open Court, 1909), 93.

558 Hieronymus, *Vita Hilarionis* 4.1 (SC 508, 224.1–226.8 Morales). See Vogüé, *Histoire littéraire du mouvement monastique dans l'antiquité*, 2: 185–188.

559 As the lexica demonstrate, this is a rather more negatively connotated word, which might be rendered as "zeal" or similar: *Der neue Georges: Ausführliches Lateinisch-Deutsches Handwörterbuch*, aus den Quellen zusammengetragen und mit besonderer Bezugnahme auf Synonymik und Antiquitäten unter Berücksichtigung der besten Hilfsmittel ausgearbeitet v. Karl-Ernst Georges, hg. Thomas Baier, bearb. v. Tobias Dänzer (Darmstadt: Wissenschaftliche Buchgesellschaft, 2013), 2: 2110; and *Mittellateinisches Wörterbuch* (München: Beck, 2009), 4: 178f.

560 Hieronymus, *Vita Hilarionis* 5.1–7 (SC 508, 226.1–228.23 Morales). ET from Ewald, "Life of Hilarion by Saint Jerome," 251–252. For other contemporary reports as to the dietary habits of Christians living as ascetics, see Fuhrmann, "Die Mönchsgeschichten des Hieronymus," 49 with nn. 4–6.

561 Attestations in Markschies, "Körper und Körperlichkeit im antiken Mönchtum," 193–200. See Hannah Hunt, *Clothed in the Body: Asceticism, the Body and the Spiritual in the Late Antique Era*, Ashgate Studies in Philosophy & Theology in Late Antiquity (Farnham, Surrey/Burlington, Vt., Ashgate 2012), 47–61.

562 Elena Kogan-Zehavi, "The Tomb and Memorial of a Chain-Wearing Anachorite at Khirbet Tabaliya, Near Jerusalem," *Atiqot* 35 (1998): 135–148. A depiction may also be found in *Cradle of Christianity*, exhibition at the Israel Museum Jerusalem, Weisbord Exhibition Pavillon, Spring 2000–Winter 2001, ed. Ya'el Israeli and David Mevorah (Jerusalem: Israel Museum, 2000), 184f.

563 Kogan-Zehavi, "The Tomb and Memorial of a Chain-Wearing Anachorite," 146f.; and Ignacio Peña, Pascal Castellana, and Romuald Fernández, *Les reclus syriens: Recherches sur les anciennes formes de vie solitaire en Syrie*, Publications of the Studium biblicum franciscanum, Collectio minor 23 (Milan: Centro Propaganda e Stampa, 1980), 103f.

564 Brown, *The Body and Society*, 241–284 and 366–386; and Christoph Markschies, *Das antike Christentum: Frömmigkeit, Lebensformen, Institutionen*, 2. durchges. und erw. Aufl., Beck'sche Reihe 1692 (München: Beck, 2012), 242–250.

565 Eunapius, *Vitae Sophistarum* VI 11.6 (39.6f. Giangrande = 472 Boissonade). ET from *Philostratus and Eunapius: The Lives of the Sophists*, trans. Wilmer Cave Wright, LCL 134 (London: Heinemann, 1922), 423. See Reinhold Merkelbach, *Isis Regina–Zeus Sarapis: Die griechisch-ägyptische Religion nach den Quellen dargestellt*, 2. Aufl. (München/Leipzig: Teubner, 2001), 329.

566 Reinhold Merkelbach, "Der griechische Wortschatz und die Christen," *Zeitschrift für Papyrologie und Epigraphik* 18 (1995): 101–148.

567 *Cradle of Christianity*, 184f.

568 MERKELBACH, "Der griechische Wortschatz und die Christen," 108. Nevertheless, Merkelbach is above all concerned with martyrs and less so with monastic ascetics. Insofar, the contribution could be supplemented.

569 *Cradle of Christianity*, 184f.

570 Besa, *Vita Sinuthii* (Bohairic, based upon V-VA Copt. 66 ff. 19ʳ-82ʳ) § 10 (CSCO.Co. II/2, 12.24–27 LEIPOLDT/CRUM). On the protagonist's hagiography and conduct, see Nina LUBOMIERSKI, *Die Vita Sinuthii: Form- und Überlieferungsgeschichte der hagiographischen Texte über Schenute den Archimandriten*, Studien und Texte zu Antike und Christentum 45 (Tübingen: Mohr Siebeck, 2007), 22–27 and 171–173; previously already Johannes LEIPOLDT, *Schenute von Atripe und die Entstehung des national ägyptischen Christentums*, TU 25/1 (Leipzig: Hinrichs, 1903), 62–69; and now Caroline T. SCHROEDER, *Monastic Bodies: Discipline and Salvation in Shenoute of Atripe*, Divinations: Rereading Late Ancient Religion (Philadelphia: University of Pennsylvania Press, 2007), 54–157.

571 SCHROEDER, *Monastic Bodies*, 54–59.

572 Sinuthi, *Contra Origenistas* 19 (§§ 409 [p. 172 CRISTEA]). ET from *Selected Discourses of Shenoute the Great: Community, Theology, and Social Conflict in Late Antique Egypt*, trans. with introductions by David BRAKKE and Andrew CRISLIP (Cambridge: Cambridge University Press, 2015), 68. Cf. GRILLMEIER, *Jesus der Christus im Glauben der Kirche*, 2/4: 205.

573 This measured initially six, then twelve, twenty-two, and finally thirty-six or forty ells in height (evidence from various hagiographies: Stephan SCHIWIETZ, *Das morgenländische Mönchtum*, Bd. 3, *Das Mönchtum in Syrien und Mesopotamien und das Aszetentum in Persien* [Mödling bei Wien: Missionsdruckerei St. Gabriel, 1938], 329f.). See on this Hanns Christof BRENNECKE, "Die Styliten als Römer," in *Leitbilder aus Kunst und Literatur*, hg. Jürgen Dummer und Meinolf Vielberg, Altertumswissenschaftliches Kolloquium 5 (Stuttgart: Steiner, 2002), 9–30; idem, "Wie man einen Heiligen politisch instrumentalisiert: Der Heilige Simeon Stylites und die Synode von Chalkedon," in *Theologie und Kultur: Geschichten einer Wechselbeziehung; Festschrift zum einhundertfünfzigjährigen Bestehen des Lehrstuhls für Christliche Archäologie und Kirchliche Kunst an der Humboldt-Universität zu Berlin*, hg. Gerlinde Strohmaier-Wiederanders (Halle: Gursky, 1999), 237–260; SCHIWIETZ, *Das morgenländische Mönchtum*, 3: 315–347.

574 Theodoretus, *Historia monachorum* 26.12 (SC 257, 184.1–9 CANIVET/LEROY-MOLINGHEN).

575 Theodoretus, *Historia monachorum* 26.22 (SC 257, 204.3–7 CANIVET/LEROY-MOLINGHEN).

576 Ἑστώς or קעים: Jarl FOSSUM, "Sects and Movements," in *The Samaritans*, ed. Alan D. Crown (Tübingen: Mohr Siebeck, 1989), 293–396, here 379–389; and Hans G. KIPPENBERG, *Garizim und Synagoge: Traditionsgeschichtliche Untersuchungen zur samaritanischen Religion der aramäischen Periode*, Religionsgeschichtliche Versuche und Vorarbeiten 30 (Berlin: De Gruyter, 1971), 347–349 with n. 136.

577 Ravenna: thus Bernhard KÖTTING, *Peregrinatio Religiosa: Wallfahrten in der Antike und das Pilgerwesen in der alten Kirche*, 2. Aufl., Forschungen zur Volkskunde 33–35 (Münster: Stenderhoff, 1980 = Münster: Regensberg 1950), 122. An alternate identification is found in *Théodoret de Cyr: Histoire des moines de Syrie: "Histoire Philothée" XIV–XXX. Traité sur la charité (XXXI)*, texte critique, traduction, notes et index par Pierre CANIVET et Alice LEROY-MOLINGHEN, SC 257 (Paris: Les éditions du Cerf, 1979), 207 n. 2.

578 Theodoretus, *Historia monachorum* 26.23 (SC 257, 206.8–208.26 CANIVET/LEROY-MOLINGHEN).

579 Sinuti, *opus sine titulo* A22 from *Canon* III (in LEIPOLDT: *De vita monachorum*) after FR-BN copte 130² f. 50 = MONB.YB (transcribed and collated by Stephen Emmel, Paris, October 2014). Translation according to LEIPOLDT, *Schenute von Atripe*, 62. On the fragment itself, see Stephen EMMEL, *Shenoute's Literary Corpus*, vol. 2, Corpus scriptorum Christianorum orientalium, Subsidia 112 (Leuven: Peeters, 2004), 572f. On this topic, see MUEHLBERGER, *Angels in Late Ancient Christianity*, 157–159.

580 Karl S. Frank, *ΑΓΓΕΛΙΚΟΣ ΒΙΟΣ: Begriffsanalytische und begriffsgeschichtliche Untersuchung zum "engelgleichen Leben" im frühen Mönchtum*, Beiträge zur Geschichte des alten Mönchtums und des Benediktinerordens 26 (Münster: Aschendorff, 1964). See therein also on the history of the term, which was initially associated with martyrdom and the abstemious life of virgins (pp. 177–201). For attestation of this notion within monastic literature, see also Muehlberger, *Angels in Late Ancient Christianity*, 148–175; Emmanouela Grypeou, "Höllenreisen und engelgleiches Leben: Die Rezeption von apokalyptischen Traditionen in der koptisch-monastischen Literatur," im *Christliches Ägypten in der spätantiken Zeit: Akten der zweiten Tübinger Tagung zum Christlichen Orient (7.–8. Dezember 2007)*, hg. Dmitrij Bumazhnov, Studien und Texte zu Antike und Christentum 79 (Tübingen: Mohr Siebeck, 2013), 43–54; and Dimitrios Moschos, *Eschatologie im ägyptischen Mönchtum: Die Rolle christlicher eschatologischer Denkvarianten in der Geschichte des frühen ägyptischen Mönchtums und seiner sozialen Funktion*, Studien zu Antike und Christentum 59 (Tübingen: Mohr Siebeck, 2010), 153–158.

581 Hubert Merki, ὁμοίωσις θεῷ. *Von der platonischen Angleichung an Gott zur Gottähnlichkeit bei Gregor von Nyssa*, Paradosis 7 (Freiburg, Schweiz: Paulusdruckerei, 1952), passim.

7 The Body of God and Antique Christology

1 James D. G. Dunn, *The Parting of the Ways between Christianity and Judaism and Their Significance for the Character of Christianity* (London: SCM Press, 1991); Judith Lieu, "'The Parting of the Ways': Theological Construct or Historical Reality?" *JSNT* 17 (1995): 101–119; and Annette Yoshiko Reed and Adam H. Becker, "Traditional Models and New Directions," in *The Ways That Never Parted: Jews and Christians in Late Antiquity and the Early Middle Ages*, ed. Adam H. Becker and Annette Yoshiko Reed, Texts and Studies in Ancient Judaism 95 (Tübingen: Mohr Siebeck 2003), 1–34.

2 Daniel Boyarin, *Dying for God: Martyrdom and the Making of Christianity and Judaism* (Stanford: Stanford University Press, 1999), 1–21.

3 Israel J. Yuval, "Passover in the Middle Ages," in *Passover and Easter: Origin and History to Modern Times*, ed. Paul F. Bradshaw and Lawrence A. Hoffman, Two Liturgical Traditions 5 (Notre Dame, Ind.: University of Notre Dame Press, 1999), 127–160; and idem, "Christianity in the Talmud: Parallelomania or Parallelophobia?" in *Transforming Relations: Essays on Jews and Christians Throughout History in Honor of Michael A. Signer* (Notre Dame, Ind.: University of Notre Dame Press, 2010), 50–74.

4 Clemens Leonhard, *The Jewish Pesach and the Origins of the Christian Easter: Open Questions in Current Research*, Studia Judaica 35 (Berlin/New York: De Gruyter, 2006). See also Albert Gerhards and Clemens Leonhard, eds., *Jewish and Christian Liturgy and Worship: New Insights into Its History and Interaction*, Jewish and Christian Perspectives Series 15 (Leiden/Boston: Brill, 2007).

5 Daniel Boyarin, *Border Lines: The Partition of Judeo-Christianity* (Philadelphia: University of Pennsylvania Press, 2004), 89–150.

6 Jacob Neusner, "Is the God of Judaism Incarnate?" *Religious Studies* 24 (1988): 213–238.

7 Additionally (with many attestations): Dieter Zeller, "Die Menschwerdung des Sohnes Gottes im Neuen Testament und die antike Religionsgeschichte," in *Menschwerdung Gottes—Vergöttlichung von Menschen*, hg. Dieter Zeller, NTOA 7 (Fribourg: Universitätsverlag; Göttingen: Vandenhoeck & Ruprecht, 1988), 141–176.

8 Οἱ θεοὶ ὁμοιωθέντες ἀνθρώποις κατέβησαν πρὸς ἡμᾶς. See on the sentence Colin J. Hemer, *The Book of Acts in the Settings of Hellenistic History*, ed. Conrad H. Gempf, WUNT 49 (Tübingen: Mohr Siebeck, 1989), 110, 178; Zeller, "Die Menschwerdung des Sohnes Gottes im Neuen Testament und die antike Religionsgeschichte," 160–162, also, in depth, Marco Frenschkowski, *Offenbarung und Epiphanie*, Bd. 2, *Die verborgene Epiphanie in Spätantike und frühem Christentum*, WUNT 2/80 (Tübingen: Mohr

Siebeck, 1997), 125–140; and Cilliers BREYTENBACH, *Paulus und Barnabas in der Provinz Galatien: Studien zu Apostelgeschichte 13f.; 16.6; 18.23 und den Adressaten des Gala-terbriefes*, AGAJU 38 (Leiden: Brill, 1996), 31–38 (on the religious-historical local atmosphere).

9   P. Ovidius Naso, *Metamorphoses* VIII 626f. (BiTeu 195 ANDERSON = TuscBü 306 RÖSCH): "Iuppiter huc specie mortali cumque parente/ venit Atlantiades positis caducifer alis." See on the passage FRENSCHKOWSKI, *Offenbarung und Epiphanie*, 2: 11–14, 138f. On the gen-eral context, see Friedrich PFISTER, s.v. "Epiphanie," PW Suppl. 4: 277–323, esp. 286f.; Bernard C. DIETRICH, "Divine Epiphanies in Homer," *Numen* 30 (1983): 53–79; and Hen-drik Simon VERSNEL, "What Did Ancient Man See When He *Saw a God*? Some Reflec-tions on Greco-Roman Epiphany," in *Effigies Dei: Essays on the History of Religions*, ed. Dirk van der Plas, SHR 51 (Leiden: Brill, 1987), 42–55.

10   Homerus, *Odyssea* XVII 485–487. See ZELLER, "Die Menschwerdung des Sohnes Gottes im Neuen Testament und die antike Religionsgeschichte," 160f. ET from MURRAY, *Homer: Odyssey, Books 1–12*, 191.

11   Walter BAUER, *Griechisch-deutsches Wörterbuch zu den Schriften des Neuen Testaments und der frühchristlichen Literatur*, 6., völlig neu bearb. Aufl. im Institut für neutestament-liche Textforschung Münster, unter besonderer Mitwirkung von Viktor Reichmann, hg. Kurt und Barbara Aland (Berlin/New York: De Gruyter, 1988), s.v. "ὁμοίω" (p. 1150).

12   Hans U. GUMBRECHT, "Incarnation, Now: Five Brief Thoughts and a Non-conclusive End-ing," *Communication and Critical/Cultural Studies* 8 (2011): 207–213: Gumbrecht dis-cusses a reduction "to a mere energy base for our minds, struggling to find pleasures and a dignity of their own" (p. 210). I thank Hans Ulrich Gumbrecht for pointing to this article and the extensive discussions on these coherencies in autumn 2010 in Berlin.

13   For the state of publication of the work and its recensions, see the detailed statements at https://www.sankt-georgen.de/institute/alois-kardinal-grillmeier-institut/ (last accessed 29 May 2019).

14   Walter BAUER, *Das Leben Jesu im Zeitalter der neutestamentlichen Apokryphen* (Darm-stadt: Wissenschaftliche Buchgesellschaft, 1967 = Tübingen: Mohr Siebeck, 1909), 29–58.

15   On the understanding of the passage, see most prominently George H. VAN KOOTEN, *Cos-mic Christology in Paul and the Pauline School: Colossians and Ephesians in the Context of Graeco-Roman Cosmology, with a New Synopsis of the Greek Texts*, WUNT 2/171 (Tübingen: Mohr Siebeck, 2003), 11–16.

16   θεότης is a hapax legomenon in the Greek Bible, and was not employed often in Jewish texts; cf., however, for example, *Apocalypsis Sedrach* 2.4; 7.8; 14.8; 15.1 (PVTG 4, 39; 41; 45 WAHL). The rare word means "godhead" and not the more conventional θειότης, "godliness" (also attested in inscriptions). Cf. *Aristeae ad Philocratem epistula* 7.95 (SC 89, 150 PELLETIER) and the extensive references for both terms in the commentary in MARKSCHIES, *Valentinus Gnosticus?* 94–96 (with attestations and literature).

17   On the adverb σωματικῶς, see Ceslas SPICQ, *Lexique théologique du Nouveau Testament*, 2ᵉ éd. (Fribourg: Universitätsverlag, 1991), s.v. (p. 1496). Particularly interesting among the attestations offered by Spicq is a request pronounced by Abraham in the presence of the Archangel Michael according to a manuscript version of the *Testamentum Abrahae* 7:19 (brief recension after the hagiographic compilatory MS Paris, Bibliothèque Natio-nale, Fonds grec 1613, saec. XV; cited after Francis SCHMIDT, *Le testament grec d'Abra-ham: Introduction, édition critique des deux recensions grecques, traduit par F.S.*, Texts and Studies in Ancient Judaism 11 [Tübingen: Mohr Siebeck, 1986], 62).

18   On this, see VAN KOOTEN, *Cosmic Christology in Paul and the Pauline School*, 17–21. See therein also a brief overview on the critical discussion of this thesis (pp. 24–27 and, in particular, 53–57).

19   Cf. Col 1:22.

20 Quite evidently, the σωματικῶς of the biblical passage Col 2:9 first became important in the christological debates of the third and fourth centuries: In Clemens Alexandrinus, *Excerpta ex Theodoto* 31.1 (GCS Clemens Alexandrinus III, 117.4 Stählin/Früchtel/ Treu), an interesting abbreviated version is attested which (were Clement not to have constructed it himself) may perhaps have been current in circles subscribing to so-called Valentinian Gnosticism: ἐν αὐτῷ γὰρ πᾶν τὸ πλήρωμα ἦν. Theognostus, a student of Origen in Alexandria, quotes the biblical passage in his "Outlines" (frag. 4 after Adolf von Harnack, *Die Hypotyposen des Theognost*, TU 24/3 [Leipzig: Hinrichs, 1903], 77.11–78.2) without the σωματικῶς, thus: Καὶ ἐν αὐτῷ οἰκεῖν φασι τὸ πλήρωμα τῆς θεότητος πάσης, οὐχ ὡς ἑτέρου μὲν ὄντος αὐτοῦ, ἑτέρας δὲ ἐπεισιούσης ἐν αὐτῷ τῆς θεότητος, ἀλλ᾽ †αὐτῷ δὴ τούτῳ† τῆς οὐσίας αὐτοῦ συμπεπληρωμένης τῆς θεότητος. On this passage, see Grillmeier, *Jesus der Christus im Glauben der Kirche*, 1: 290–294. Cf., in contrast, the alleged letter of Hymenaeus of Jerusalem and his six colleagues to Paul of Samosata in Gustave Bardy, *Paul de Samosate: Étude historique*, nouvelle éd. entièrement refondue, Spicilegium sacrum Lovaniense 4 (Louvain: Spicilegium Sacrum Lovaniense, 1929), 13–19, here 18 = Eduard Schwartz, *Eine fingierte Korrespondenz mit Paulus dem Samosatener*, Sitzungsberichte der Bayerischen Akademie der Wissenschaften, philosophisch-philologische und historische Klasse 3/1927 (München: Bayerische Akademie der Wissenschaften, 1927), 329.1–3: διόπερ καί τὸ ἐκ τῆς παρθένου σῶμα χωρῆσαν πᾶν τὸ πλήρωμα τῆς θεότητος σωματικῶς τῇ θεότητι ἀτρέπτως ἥνωται καὶ τεθεοποίηται. The pointed emphasis of σωματικῶς also hardly speaks for its authenticity: Henri de Riedmatten, *Les actes du procès de Paul de Samosate: Étude sur la Christologie du IIIᵉ au IVᵉ siècle*, Paradosis 6 (Fribourg: Éditions St-Paul, 1952), 121–134; thus, incidentally, already Schwartz, *Eine fingierte Korrespondenz mit Paulus dem Samosatener*, 49: "eine unverkennbare Spur der Debatten stehen geblieben, die durch die apollinaristische Christologie hervorgerufen waren."

21 *Acta Acacii* 4.6 (SQS.NF 3, 59.25–28 Knopf/Krüger/Ruhbach).

22 On the dating and genre of the *Acta Acacii*, see the introduction in the edition, translation, and commentary of martyr literature by Hans Reinhard Seeliger and Wolfgang Wischmeyer, *Märtyrerliteratur*, hg., übers., kommentiert und eingel., Texte und Untersuchungen zur Geschichte der altchristlichen Literatur 172 (Berlin/Boston: De Gruyter, 2015).

23 Tertullianus, *Adversus Praxean* 27.6 (FChr 34, 234.24–236.4 Sieben). On this passage, see Joseph Moingt, *Théologie Trinitaire de Tertullien*, tome 2, *Substantialité et individualité*, Théologie 68 (Paris: Aubier, 1966), 524f. On the description of the opponents of Tertullian as "identificatory theologians," see idem, *Théologie Trinitaire de Tertullien*, tome 1, *Histoire, Doctrine, Méthodes*, Théologie 68 (Paris: Aubier, 1966), 190; and Christoph Markschies, "'. . . et tamen non tres Dii, sed unus Deus . . .' Zum Stand der Erforschung der altkirchlichen Trinitätstheologie," in idem, *Alta Trinità Beata: Gesammelte Studien zur altkirchlichen Trinitätstheologie* (Tübingen: Mohr Siebeck, 2000), 286–309, here 293–295: "Le monarchianisme n'est pas un modalisme."

24 Tertullianus, *Adversus Praxean* 27.4 (FChr 34, 234.13f. Sieben). ET from *Tertullian: Adversus Praxean*, trans. Ernest Evans (London: SPCK, 1948), 172. See on the entire context Grillmeier, *Jesus der Christus im Glauben der Kirche*, 1: 245–249; and also Moingt, *Théologie Trinitaire de Tertullien*, 2: 326–331.

25 Tertullianus, *Adversus Praxean* 27.7f. (FChr 34, 236.10–19 Sieben). ET from Evans, *Tertullian: Adversus Praxean*, 173. See also Moingt, *Théologie Trinitaire de Tertullien*, 2: 351f.; and René Braun, *Deus Christianorum. Recherches sur le vocabulaire doctrinal de Tertullien*, 2ᵉ éd. revue et augmentée, Études Augustiniennes (Paris: Études Augustiniennes, 1977), 298–317.

26 See also Heinrich Dörrie, *Porphyrios' "Symmikta zetemata": Ihre Stellung in System und Geschichte des Neuplatonismus nebst einem Kommentar zu den Fragmenten*, Zetemata 20 (München: Beck, 1959), 26f.; and Luise Abramowski, "συνάφεια und ἀσύγχυτος

ἕνωσις als Bezeichnungen für trinitarische und christologische Einheit," in idem, *Drei christologische Untersuchungen*, BZNW 45 (Berlin/New York 1981), 63–109.

27　For ἀπροσδεής, see above, p. 380 with n. 104.

28　Tertullianus, *De carne Christi* 15.2 (SC 216, 272.14–274.18 MAHÉ). On the text, see Willamien OTTEN, "Christ's Birth of a Virgin Who Became a Wife: Flesh and Speech in Tertullian's *De carne Christi*," *VC* 51 (1997): 247–260; and Geoffrey D. DUNN, "Mary's Virginity *in partu* and Tertullian's Anti-docetism in *De carne Christi* reconsidered," *JTS* 58 (2007): 467–484. BAUER, *Das Leben Jesu im Zeitalter der neutestamentlichen Apokryphen*, 40–47, takes the passage within Tertullian as a basis from which to reconstruct pertinent stances, most prominently from heresiological literature.

29　Tertullianus, *De carne Christi* 11.4 (SC 216, 258.23f. MAHE).

30　Nobert BROX, "'Doketismus'—eine Problemanzeige," *Zeitschrift für Kirchengeschichte* 95 (1984): 301–314. Winrich A. LÖHR, s.v. "Doketismus," *RGG* 2: 925–927, here 925, proposed the following clear definition: "Doketismus . . . kann man als jegliche Art von Christologie bestimmen, die a) die wahre Menschheit des Gottessohnes Jesus Christus durch die Annahme eines Leibes von bes(onderer) Qualität beschränkt, oder die b) Leiden und Tod Jesu Christi als bloß scheinbar lehrt, oder die c) die Menschheit Christi als nicht zum transzendenten Personenkern gehöriges Akzidenz charakterisiert und somit Erdenwandel, Leiden und Tod so bestimmt, dass sie den Erlöser nicht wirklich betreffen." See also in depth idem, "Deutungen der Passion bei Heiden und Christen im zweiten und dritten Jahrhundert," in *Deutungen des Todes Jesu im Neuen Testament*, hg. Jörg Frey und Jens Schröter, 2., durchges. und mit einer neuen Einleitung versehene Aufl., Universitätstaschenbücher 2953 (Tübingen: Mohr Siebeck, 2012), 545–574, here 552–574.

31　Theodoretus Cyrrhensis, *Epistula* 82 post collectionem Sirmondianam (PG 83, 1264 = IV/2, 1142 SCHULZE).

32　BROX, "'Doketismus'—eine Problemanzeige," 305; and Karl Wolfgang TRÖGER, "Doketistische Christologie in Nag-Hammadi-Texten: Ein Beitrag zum Doketismus in frühchristlicher Zeit," *Kairos* 19 (1977): 45–52, here 46. A careful terminological differentiation, if also as of yet without explicit mention, is also sought by Gustav KRÜGER, s.v. "Doketen," in *Realencyklopädie für protestantische Theologie und Kirche*, 3. Aufl. (Leipzig: Hinrichs, 1898), 4: 764f; and Peter WEIGANDT, *Der Doketismus im Urchristentum und in der theologischen Entwicklung des zweiten Jahrhunderts* (Diss. theol. masch., Heidelberg, 1961), 1–6. The texts were collected by Adolf HILGENFELD, *Ketzergeschichte des Urchristenthums urkundlich dargestellt* (Darmstadt: Wissenschaftliche Buchgesellschaft, 1963 = Leipzig: Fues, 1884), 546–550.

33　For Cerdo, see HARNACK, *Marcion: Das Evangelium vom fremden Gott*, 31*–39*; Gerhard MAY, "Markion und der Gnostiker Kerdon," in idem, *Markion: Gesammelte Aufsätze*, hg. Katharina Greschat und Martin Meiser, Veröffentlichungen des Instituts für Europäische Geschichte Mainz, Abteilung für abendländische Religionsgeschichte, Beiheft 68 (Mainz: Philipp von Zabern, 2005), 63–73; and David W. DEAKLE, "Harnack & Cerdo: A Reexamination of the Patristic Evidence for Marcion's Mentor," in *Marcion und seine kirchengeschichtliche Wirkung: Marcion and His Impact on Church History; Vorträge der Internationalen Fachkonferenz zu Marcion, gehalten vom 15.–18. August 2001 in Mainz*, hg. Gerhard May und Katharina Greschat in Gemeinschaft mit Martin Meiser, TU 150 (Berlin/New York: De Gruyter, 2002), 177–191.

34　Pseudo-Tertullianus, *Adversus omnes haereses* 6.1 (CChr.SL 2, 1408.18–25 KROYMANN).

35　Thus also MAY, "Markion und der Gnostiker Kerdon," 69f. (he assumes a Roman urbanite oral tradition); and DEAKLE, "Harnack & Cerdo," 182.

36　Tertullianus, *Adversus Marcionem* III 8.2f. (CChr.SL 1, 518.3–8 KROYMANN = SC 399, 94.14–96.20 BRAUN). The accusation that Marcion's doctrine led to a *phantasma* or *phantasma carnis* also appears in *Adversus Marcionem* IV 8.2 (CChr.SL 1, 557.10 KROYMANN = SC 456, 106.19 MORESCHINI/BRAUN); 9.5 (559.16 = 118.39); 18.9 (591.16 = 236.87f.); 20.13 (597.21 = 262.109); 40.3 (656.27 = 498.29); 42.7 (660.5 = 516.64); 43.6 (662.11 =

524.47); V 7.5 (683.23 = SC 483, 166.41 MORESCHINI/BRAUN); 8.3 (686.23 = 182.25); and V 20.3 (724.23 = SC 483, 364.27f. MORESCHINI/BRAUN). Cf. also ibid., IV 9.5 (118.38f.): "qui corpus non habebat"; and V 5.9 (677.5 = SC 483, 142.80 MORESCHINI/BRAUN).

37 On antique Jewish and Christian answers to the question as to whether angels might actually have eaten, see MARKSCHIES, *Valentinus Gnosticus?*, 100–104.

38 Tertullianus, *Adversus Marcionem* III 9.1 (CChr.SL 1, 519.17–21 KROYMANN = SC 399, 100.1–6 BRAUN). Further attestations of this conception of the angelic body in HARNACK, *Marcion: Das Evangelium vom fremden Gott*, 286*f.; extensive discussion in VINZENT, "'Ich bin kein körperloses Geistwesen,'" 260–264.

39 As a quotation from Marcion in Tertullianus, *Adversus Marcionem* III 10.2 (CChr.SL 1, 521.16f. KROYMANN = SC 399, 108.8f. BRAUN).

40 "[Die Engel] die zu Abraham kamen, nicht Gespenster waren, sondern als leibhaftige und wirkliche Menschen handelten und aßen; so war auch Christus kein Gespenst, sondern der Gott trat in menschlicher Erscheinung auf" (HARNACK, *Marcion: Das Evangelium vom fremden Gott*, 125).

41 For another example of a so-called angelic Christology, see above, p. 415 with n. 226. The question, incidentally, has also been discussed in respect to Tertullian: Edgar G. FOSTER, *Angelomorphic Christology and the Exegesis of Psalm 8:5 in Tertullian's Adversus Praxean: An Examination of Tertullian's Reluctance to Attribute Angelic Properties to the Son of God* (Lanham, Md.: University Press of America, 2005), 1–18.

42 Tertullianus, *De carne Christi* 2.1f. (SC 216, 212.4–214.14 MAHE). For the conceptions of the body of Christ in Marcion, see also HARNACK, *Marcion: Das Evangelium vom fremden Gott*, 124–126; and Jean-Pierre MAHE, *Tertullien, La chair du Christ*, tome 1, introduction, texte critique, traduction et notes, Sources Chrétiennes 216 (Paris: Les éditions du Cerf, 2008), 74–78. ET from EVANS, *Tertullian's Treatise on the Incarnation: The Text*, 7.

43 Irenaeus, *Adversus haereses* I 24.2 (SC 264, 322.21–23 ROUSSEAU/DOUTRELEAU = FChr 8/1, 296.14f. BROX). Cf. Hippolytus, *Refutatio omnium haeresium* VII 28.4 (GCS Hippolyt III, 209.4f. WENDLAND = PTS 25, 303.16f. MARCOVICH). For Satornilus, see HILGEN-FELD, *Ketzergeschichte des Urchristenthums urkundlich dargestellt*, 190–195.

44 The extensive discussion as to the dating of the different letters ascribed to Ignatius within the Corpus Ignatianum can neither here be documented, nor can an individual position with a justification be outlined; see, however, Reinhard M. HÜBNER, "Thesen zur Echtheit und Datierung der sieben Briefe des Ignatius von Antiochien," *ZAC* 1 (1997): 44–72; Mark J. EDWARDS, "Ignatius and the Second Century: An Answer to R. Hübner," *ZAC* 2 (1998): 214–226; Andreas LINDEMANN, "Antwort auf die 'Thesen zur Echtheit und Datierung der sieben Briefe des Ignatius von Antiochien,'" *ZAC* 1 (1997): 185–194; Georg SCHÖLLGEN, "Die Ignatianen als pseudepigraphisches Briefcorpus: Anmerkungen zu den Thesen von Reinhard M. Hübner," *ZAC* 2 (1998): 16–25; and Hermann Josef VOGT, "Bemerkungen zur Echtheit der Ignatiusbriefe," *ZAC* 3 (1999): 50–63. The earlier debate is already summarized by, for example, Lothar WEHR, *Arznei der Unsterblichkeit: Die Eucharistie bei Ignatius von Antiochien und im Johannesevangelium*, Neutestamentliche Abhandlungen 18 (Münster: Aschendorff, 1987), 24–30; and Thomas LECHNER, *Ignatius adversus Valentinianos? Chronologische und theologiegeschichtliche Studien zu den Briefen des Ignatius von Antiochien*, Supplements to Vigiliae Christianae 47 (Leiden: Brill, 1999), xv–xxvi. The later debate is summarized, for example, in Wolfram UEBELE, *"Viele Verführer sind in die Welt hinausgegangen": Die Gegner in den Briefen des Ignatius von Antiochien und in den Johannesbriefen*, Beiträge zur Wissenschaft vom Alten und Neuen Testament 151 (Stuttgart: Kohlhammer, 2001), 20–27.

45 Ignatius Antiochenus, *Epistula ad Smyrnaeos* 2 (SAC I, 204.19–206.1 FISCHER). Similar accusations also in ibid., 4.1–2. Cf. the almost verbatim parallel against this in *Epistula ad Trallianos* 10.2.

46 See also Candida R. Moss, *The Other Christs: Imitating Jesus in Ancient Christian Ideologies of Martyrdom* (Oxford: Oxford University Press, 2010), 41–44 and 83f.

47 The "gesamte Christusgeschehen mit all seinen Einzelereignissen." Karin Bommes, *Weizen Gottes: Untersuchungen zur Theologie des Martyriums bei Ignatius von Antiochien*, Theophaneia 27 (Köln/Bonn: Hanstein, 1976), 54. See also, in turn, Uebele, *"Viele Verführer sind in die Welt hinausgegangen,"* 71.

48 Ignatius Antiochenus, *Epistula ad Smyrnaeos* 5.2 (SAC I, 208.2–5 Fischer). For the insistence on the reality of the flesh and blood of Jesus, see William R. Schoedel, *Die Briefe des Ignatius von Antiochien. Ein Kommentar*, aus dem Amerikanischen übers. v. Gisela Koester, Hermeneia-Kommentare (München: Kaiser, 1990), 247–249 and 255–259. On the adversaries of the author, see Jerry L. Sumney, "Those Who 'Ignorantly Deny Him': The Opponents of Ignatius of Antioch," *JECS* 1 (1993): 345–365; Michael D. Goulder, "Ignatius' 'Docetists,'" *VC* 53 (1999): 16–30; and Uebele, *"Viele Verführer sind in die Welt hinausgegangen,"* 70–73 and 84–92. Uebele connects this rivalry with that which was reported of Satornilus (p. 161f.)

49 Ps.-Ignatius Antiochenus, *Epistula ad Trallianos* 10.4–6 (II, 106.14–108.6 Diekamp). ET from *The Writings of the Apostolic Fathers*, trans. Alexander Roberts, James Donaldson, and F. Crombie, Ante-Nicene Christian Library 1 (Edinburgh: T&T Clark, 1867), 202f. See the brief commentary in Joseph B. Lightfoot, *The Apostolic Fathers*, pt. 2, *S. Ignatius. S. Polycarp*, rev. texts with introductions, notes, dissertations, and translations, vol. 3, 2nd ed. (London/New York: Macmillan, 1889), 159f.

50 Gregorius Iliberritanus, *Tractatus Origenis* XIV 8 (CChr.SL 69, 108.57–59 Bulhart = 154 Battifol/Wilmart).

51 Bishop Serapion of Antioch claimed that the "Gospel of Peter" was composed by Δοκηταί: *Epistula* apud Eusebium Caesariensem, *Historia Ecclesiastica* VI 12.6 (GCS Eusebius II/2, 546.2–7 Schwartz). On the extensive debates over the relationship of this apocryphal gospel to so-called docetism (which here cannot be further examined), see most recently Matti Myllykoski, "Die Kraft des Herrn: Erwägungen zur Christologie des Petrusevangeliums," in *Das Evangelium des Petrus: Texte, Kontexte, Intertexte*, hg. Thomas J. Kraus und Tobias Nicklas, TU 158 (Berlin/New York: De Gruyter, 2007), 301–326, here 307–311 and 313–325.

52 Clemens Alexandrinus, *Stromata* VII 108.1f. (GCS Clemens Alexandrinus III, 76.20–26 Stählin/Früchtel/Treu). ET from Chadwick and Oulton, *Alexandrian Christianity: Selected Translations of Clement and Origen*, 163.

53 Clemens Alexandrinus, *Stromata* III 91.1 (GCS Clemens Alexandrinus II, 238.9 Stählin/Früchtel/Treu): ὁ τῆς δοκήσεως ἐξάρχων Ἰούλιος Κασσιανός. Cf. ibid., III 102.3 (243.11–14). For Julius Cassianus, see Alain Le Boulluec, *La notion d'hérésie dans la littérature grecque IIe–IIIe siècles*, tome 2, *Clément d'Alexandrie et Origène*, Études Augustiniennes (Paris: Études Augustiniennes, 1985), 348–350. Le Boulluec demonstrates that ἐξάρχων cannot be translated as if Julius Cassianus had *substantiated* this doctrine: p. 349 n. 221. See also Giulia Sfameni Gasparo, "Protologia ed encratismo: Esempi di esegesi encratita di Gen 1–3," *Augustinianum* 22 (1982): 75–89.

54 Hieronymus, *Commentarii in epistulam Pauli apostoli ad Galatas* III ad 6.8 (CChr.SL 77A, 214, Raspanti). Nevertheless, it must be accepted that the accusation of introducing *putatiuam Christi carnem* is also leveled by Jerome at many other heresies and heresiarchs: Ebion, Mani, Marcion, and Photinus in ibid., I ad 1.1 (12.75–13.82); Marcion and other heresies in ibid., II ad 4.4f. (108.5f.). See skeptically Krüger, s.v. "Doketen," 764.

55 According to Clement of Alexandria, Julius Cassianus (or Tatian? The sentence is grammatically ambiguous) hailed from the so-called Valentinian school, that is, the school named after the Roman urbanite teacher Valentinus; thus *Stromata* III 92.1 (GCS Clemens Alexandrinus II, 238.22 Stählin/Früchtel/Treu). On the Egyptian teachers of the Valentinian school, see Christoph Markschies, "Valentinianische Gnosis in Alexandrien und Ägypten," in *Origeniana Octava: Origen and the Alexandrian Tradition. Origene e*

la tradizione Alessandrina; Papers of the 8th International Origen Congress Pisa, 27–31 August 2001, ed. Lorenzo Perrone, BETL 164 (Leuven: Peeters, 2004), 331–346.

56 Irenaeus, *Adversus haereses* I 6.1 (SC 264, 92.602–605 Rousseau/Doutreleau = FChr 8/1, 162.22–24 Brox) = Epiphanius, *Panarion haereses* 31.20.4 (GCS Epiphanius I², 416.24–26 Holl/Bergermann/Collatz). A comprehensive collection and interpretation of so-called Valentinian texts on the "psychic Christ" may be found in Einar Thomassen, *The Spiritual Seed: The Church of the "Valentinians,"* Nag Hammadi and Manichaean Studies 60 (Leiden/Boston: Brill, 2006), 30 and 40–45.

57 Irenaeus, *Adversus haereses* I 6.1 (SC 264, 92.605f. Rousseau/Doutreleau = FChr 8/1, 162.24f. Brox) = Epiphanius, *Panarion haereses* 31.20.4 (GCS Epiphanius I, 416.26–417.2 Holl/Bergermann/Collatz).

58 Clemens Alexandrinus, *Stromata* III 91.1 (GCS Clemens Alexandrinus II, 238.9–14 Stählin/Früchtel/Treu). ET from Chadwick and Oulton, *Alexandrian Christianity: Selected Translations of Clement and Origen*, 83.

59 Clemens Alexandrinus, *Stromata* III 95.2 (GCS Clemens Alexandrinus II, 239.26 Stählin/Früchtel/Treu).

60 Iustinus Martyr, *Dialogus cum Tryphone* 67.5f. (PTS 47, 185.24–26 Marcovich). On the background to the passage, see now in depth, Andrew S. Jacobs, *Christ Circumcised: A Study in Early Christian History and Difference* (Philadelphia: University of Pennsylvania Press, 2012), 46–50.

61 See, e.g., *Missale Gothicum (Vat. Reg. lat. 317)*, hg. Leo Cunibert Mohlberg, Rerum Ecclesiasticarum Documenta, Series Maior, Fontes 5 (Rome: Herder, 1961), 16–23; Theodor Klauser, "Der Festkalender der Alten Kirche im Spannungsfeld jüdischer Traditionen, christlicher Glaubensvorstellungen und missionarischen Anpassungswillens," in *Kirchengeschichte als Missionsgeschichte*, Bd. 1, *Die alte Kirche*, hg. Heinzgünther Frohnes und Uwe W. Knorr (München: Kaiser, 1974), 377–388, here 384; Karl Adam Heinrich Kellner, *Heortologie oder die geschichtliche Entwicklung des Kirchenjahres und der Heiligenfeste: von den ältesten Zeiten bis zur Gegenwart*, 3. Aufl. (Freiburg: Herder, 1911), 109; Jacobs, *Christ Circumcised*, 146–177; and Otto Clemen, "Eine seltsame Christusreliquie," *Archiv für Kulturgeschichte* 7 (1909): 137–144 = idem, *Kleine Schriften zur Reformationsgeschichte (1897–1944)*, Bd. 3, 1907–1911, hg. Ernst Koch (Leipzig: Zentralantiquariat, 1983), 193–200.

62 Valentinus, frag. 3 (Markschies) = Clemens Alexandrinus, *Stromata* III 59.3 (GCS Clemens Alexandrinus II, 223.12–16 Stählin/Früchtel/Treu). ET from Chadwick and Oulton, *Alexandrian Christianity: Selected Translations of Clement and Origen*, 67. Extensive commentary in Markschies, *Valentinus Gnosticus?*, 83–117; on the translation of θεότητα Ἰησοῦς εἰργάζετο, see pp. 92–96.

63 Irenaeus, *Adversus haereses* III 22.2 (435.30–437.34 Rousseau/Doutreleau); and Clemens Alexandrinus, *Stromata* VI 71.2 (GCS Clemens Alexandrinus II, 467.9–13 Stählin/Früchtel/Treu). On this and further passages, see in depth Markschies, *Valentinus Gnosticus?*, 98f.

64 *Acta Petri / Actus Vercellenses* 20 (I, 67.24–28 Lipsius = 344.1–7 Vouaux). ET from Pick, *The Apocryphal Acts of Paul, Peter, John, Andrew and Thomas*, 90. Cf. the translation by Marietheres Döhler, *Acta Petri: Text, Übersetzung und Kommentar zu den Actus Vercellenses* (Diss. theol. masch., Berlin, 2015), 142. On the text's contents, see Matthew C. Baldwin, *Whose Acts of Peter? Text and Historical Context of the Actus Vercellensis*, WUNT 2/196 (Tübingen: Mohr Siebeck, 2005), 216f.

65 Basilius Caesariensis, *Epistula* 366 (Basil to the monk Urbicus, on abstinence; CUFr III, 229.31–35 Courtonne). ET from *St. Basil: The Letters*, vol. 4, trans. Roy J. Deferrari, LCL 270 (Cambridge, Mass.: Harvard University Press, 1934), 353. For the parallels, see Markschies, *Valentinus Gnosticus?*, 84–86; and previously already Walter Völker, "Basilius, Ep. 366 und Clemens Alexandrinus," *VC* 7 (1953): 23–26.

66 Pseudo-Iustinus Martyr, *De resurrectione* 2 apud Johannem Damascenum, *Sacra parallela* nr. 107 (TU 20/2, 38.60–63 Holl = PTS 54, 106.17–19 Heimgartner).

67 See the attempt at tackling this theme in Luise ABRAMOWSKI, "Ein gnostischer Logostheologe: Umfang und Redaktor des gnostischen Sonderguts in Hippolyts 'Widerlegung aller Häresien,'" in idem, *Drei christologische Untersuchungen*, BZNW 45 (Berlin/New York: De Gruyter, 1981), 18–62 (with an enumeration of the appurtenant fragments: p. 18 n. 1).

68 This may lie in the fact that in the lost text of the Roman urbanite author Justin "Syntagma against all Heresies" there is evidently not yet an independent section devoted to the "illusionists" (Δοκηταί). See HILGENFELD, *Ketzergeschichte des Urchristenthums urkundlich dargestellt*, 21–30; and now Geoffrey SMITH, *Guilt by Association: Heresy Catalogues in Early Christianity*, OECS (Oxford: Oxford University Press, 2014), 55–86. On the passage in Hippolytus, see Hans STAEHELIN, *Die gnostischen Quellen Hippolyts in seiner Hauptschrift "Gegen die Häretiker,"* TU 6/3 (Leipzig: Hinrichs, 1890), 32–37 (on the general relation of the account to the others in the corpus; the views as to the body of Jesus are incidently the possession of solely the report on the "docetes"), also 68f. with 71f. and 94f.

69 Hippolytus, *Refutatio omnium haeresium* VIII 10.7 (GCS Hippolyt III, 229.25–230.2 WENDLAND = PTS 25, 328.39–329.43 MARCOVICH). ET from LITWA, *Hippolytus: Refutation of All Heresies*, 593.

70 Hippolytus, *Refutatio omnium haeresium* VIII 10.3 (GCS Hippolyt III, 229.25–230.2 WENDLAND = PTS 25, 327.20–328.25 MARCOVICH). In REITZENSTEIN, *Poimandres*, 145, Egyptian formulae are pointed to within which Amon is predicated as "der sich verborgen hält in seinem Auge." The sense of this present passage is nevertheless more trivial; imagined is an explanation of the inconceivable reality of the incarnation by means of an evocative image from everyday experience. ET from LITWA, *Hippolytus: Refutation of All Heresies*, 591.

71 Euclides, *Optica definitiones* 1 (BiTeu VII, 2.2f. HEIBERG). ET from Harry Edwin BURTON, "The Optics of Euclid," *Journal of the Optical Society of America* 35 (1945): 357–372, here 357.

72 Claudius Ptolemaeus, *Optica* II 1 (here cited after Albert LEJEUNE, *L'optique de Claude Ptolémée dans la version latine d'après l'arabe de l'émir Eugène de Sicile: Édition critique et exégétique*, augmentée d'une traduction française et de compléments, Collection des travaux de l'Académie Internationale d'Histoire des Sciences 31 [Leiden: Brill, 1989], 11.6–11). See also on this, idem, *Euclide et Ptolémée: Deux stades de l'optique géométrique grecque*, recueil de travaux d'histoire et de philologie 3. sér. 31 (Louvain: Bibliothèque de l'Université, 1948), 65f.; and SIMON, *Der Blick, das Sein und die Erscheinung in der antiken Optik*, 93–141.

73 Thus also the interpretation in BAUER, *Das Leben Jesu im Zeitalter der neutestamentlichen Apokryphen*, 130f.

74 BAUER, *Das Leben Jesu im Zeitalter der neutestamentlichen Apokryphen*, 114–141.

75 On this, most recently, see Jörg FREY, "B. V.1.3: Die Fragmente des Ebionäerevangeliums," in *Antike christliche Apokryphen in deutscher Übersetzung*, hg. Christoph Markschies und Jens Schröter in Verbindung mit Andreas Heiser, Bd. 1, *Evangelien und Verwandtes*, Tlbd. 1, 7. Aufl. der v. Edgar Hennecke begründeten und v. Wilhelm Schneemelcher fortgeführten Sammlung (Tübingen: Mohr Siebeck, 2012), 607–622.

76 Gospel of the Ebionites frag. 4 FREY = Epiphanius, *Panarion haereses* 30.14.3 (GCS Epiphanius I², 350.17–351.1 HOLL/BERGERMANN/COLLATZ): εὐθὺς περιέλαμψε τὸν τόπον φῶς μέγα. Further attestations in BAUER, *Das Leben Jesu im Zeitalter der neutestamentlichen Apokryphen*, 135f.; and, most prominently, in Gabriele WINKLER, "Die Licht-Erscheinung bei der Taufe Jesu und der Ursprung des Epiphaniefestes: Eine Untersuchung griechischer, syrischer, armenischer und lateinischer Quellen," *Oriens christianus* 78 (1994): 177–229, here 190–202 (with the evidence for the reconstruction of the Diatessaron).

77 As other passages in the closing tenth book also contain additional or different informations, it must at the least be assumed that Hippolytus inspected his sources once more;

thus also Josef FRICKEL, *Das Dunkel um Hippolyt von Rom: Ein Lösungsversuch; Die Schriften Elenchos und Contra Noëtum*, Grazer Theologische Studien 13 (Graz: Institut für ökumenische Theologie und Patrologie, 1988), 132–134; and idem, *Die "Apophasis Megale" in Hippolyt's Refutatio (VI 9–18): Eine Paraphrase zur Apophasis Simons*, Orientalia Christiana Analecta 182 (Rome: Pontificium Institutum Orientalium Studiorum, 1968), 56–74.

78 Hippolytus, *Refutatio omnium haeresium* X 16.6 (GCS Hippolyt III, 278.12–15 WENDLAND = PTS 25, 396.28–32 MARCOVICH).

79 Epiphanius, *Panarion haereses* 30.17.6 (GCS Epiphanius I², 356.18–357.3 HOLL/ BERGERMANN/COLLATZ). On the passage, see JACOBS, *Christ Circumcised*, 103–118. ET adapted from SECOND, *The Panarion of Epiphanius of Salamis Book I (Sects 1–46)*, 145.

80 Pseudo-Tertullianus, *Adversus omnes haereses* 6.5 (CChr.SL 2, 1409.20–27 KROYMANN). A weak reflection of either the precise information on Apelles or the general information as in Tertullian, may be found in Novatianus, *De trinitate* 10.53 (CChr.SL 4, 27.32–42 DIERCKS). Very similar also in Origenes/Hieronymus, *Homiliae in Lucam* XIV 4 (GCS Origenes IX², 86.13–17 RAUER = FChr 4/1, 168.4–7 SIEBEN).

81 Hippolytus in *Refutatio omnium haeresium* VII 38.3 (GCS Hippolyt III, 224.10–15 WENDLAND/PTS 25, 321.10–16 MARCOVICH) and Epiphanius in *Panarion haereses* 42.3–5 (GCS Epiphanius II, 192.3–6 and 10–14 HOLL/DUMMER) offer a divergent teaching, in which the body is composed of the four elements and no celestial substance. Hippolytus emphatically enumerates the characteristics of the elements (224.12–15/321.13–15).

82 For the notion that the body is composed of the four στοιχεῖα, cf. the respective Stoic attestation in SVF II, 412–438 (II, 136–144 VON ARNIM), esp. frag. 414 from the context of Pseudo-Iustinus Martyr, *De resurrectione* 6 (TU 20/2, 43.201–206 HOLL).

83 Tertullianus, *De carne Christi* 15.2 (SC 216, 272.14–274.18 MAHE). For the christological doctrine of Apelles see, for example, in depth, HARNACK, *Marcion: Das Evangelium vom fremden Gott*, 177–196, 404*–420* (Harnack harmonizes both traditions: p. 189); and more briefly BAUER, *Das Leben Jesu im Zeitalter der neutestamentlichen Apokryphen*, 44f.; also, most recently, Katharina GRESCHAT, *Apelles und Hermogenes: Zwei theologische Lehrer des zweiten Jahrhunderts*, Supplements to Vigiliae Christianae 48 (Leiden: Brill, 2000), 99–109.

84 *Acta Iohannis* 93 (CChr.SA 1, 197.1–4; 10–13 JUNOD/KAESTLI). ET from Knut SCHÄFERDIEK, "Acts of John," in *New Testament Apocrypha*, vol. 2, *Writings Related to the Apostles, Apocalypses, and Related Subjects*, rev. ed. of the collection initiated by Edgar Hennecke, ed. Wilhelm Schneemelcher, ET ed. R. McL. Wilson (Westminster: J. Clark & Co., 2003), 181.

85 WEIGANDT, *Der Doketismus im Urchristentum und in der theologischen Entwicklung des zweiten Jahrhunderts*, 40–56; BROX, "'Doketismus'–eine Problemanzeige," 311; Eric JUNOD, "Polymorphie du Dieu Saveur," in *Gnosticisme et Monde Hellénistique: Actes du Colloque de Louvain-la-Neuve (11–14 mars 1980)*, éd. Julien Ries (Louvain-la-Neuve: Université catholique de Louvain, Institute orientaliste, 1982), 38–46; idem and Jean-Daniel KAESTLI, *Acta Iohannis: Textus alii — Commentarius, Indices*, CChr.SA 2 (Turnhout: Brepols, 1983), 466–493; Pieter J. LALLEMAN, "Polymorphy of Christ," in *The Apocryphal Acts of John*, ed. Jan N. Bremmer, Studies on the Apocryphal Acts of the Apostles 1 (Kampen: Kok Pharos, 1995), 97–118; LÖHR, "Deutungen der Passion bei Heiden und Christen im zweiten und dritten Jahrhundert," 567–572; and Paul FOSTER, "Polymorphic Christology: Its Origins and Development in Early Christianity," *JTS* 58 (2007): 66–99.

86 FOSTER, "Polymorphic Christology," 67–77. Incidentally, similarly already, Adolf HILGENFELD, "Der gnostische und der kanonische Johannes über das Leben Jesu," *ZTK* 43 (1900): 1–61, here 41–43.

87 Eric JUNOD and Jean-Daniel KAESTLI count within their commentary a total of twelve details wherein polymorphy becomes explicit (CChr.SA 2, 474f.). English in FOSTER,

"Polymorphic Christology," 86. Critical remarks in LALLEMAN, "Polymorphy of Christ," 170–172.

88 *Acta Iohannis* 89 (CChr.SA 1, 193.7–15 JUNOD/KAESTLI). ET from SCHÄFERDIEK, "Acts of John," 180.

89 Ioannes Stobaeus, *Anthologium* I 3.9 (I, 53.21f. WACHSMUTH) = Tragicorum Graecorum Fragmenta Adespota 485 (II, 140 KANNICHT/SNELL).

90 Erik PETERSON, "Einige Bemerkungen zum Hamburger Papyrusfragment der Acta Pauli," *VC* 3 (1949): 142–162, here 157 = idem, *Frühkirche, Judentum und Gnosis: Studien und Untersuchungen* (Darmstadt, Wissenschaftliche Buchgesellschaft, 1982 = Freiburg: Herder, 1959), 183–208, here 202f. WEIGANDT, *Der Doketismus im Urchristentum und in der theologischen Entwicklung des zweiten Jahrhunderts*, 48, rejects this interpretation, as this is "far too sophisticated" (überhaupt zu anspruchsvoll) for the readers of these texts who he assumes "hailed from the lower classes and certainly overwhelmingly from vulgar Christian circles" (aus den unteren Klassen und wohl überwiegend aus vulgärchristlichen Kreisen stammten).

91 Cf. only Valentinus frag. 7 (MARKSCHIES) in Hippolytus, *Refutatio omnium haeresium* VI 42.2 (GCS Hippolytus III, 173.22–25 WENDLAND/PTS 25, 259.11–15 MARCOVICH). For further attestations, see MARKSCHIES, *Valentinus Gnosticus?*, 208–211; and WEIGANDT, *Der Doketismus im Urchristentum und in der theologischen Entwicklung des zweiten Jahrhunderts*, 42–45.

92 On the question as to the bodiliness of Christ, who, according to the mainstream classical late antique ecclesiastical notion, is enthroned with the Father in heaven after the resurrection, see Christoph MARKSCHIES, "'Sessio ad Dexteram,'" in Philonenko, *Le trône de Dieu*, 252–317, esp. 278–283 = idem, *Alta Trinità Beata*, 1–69, here 32–37.

93 For the agraphon, see the attestations above and moreover, in particular, Alfred RESCH, *Agrapha: Aussercanonische Schriftfragmente, gesammelt und untersucht*, in zweiter, völlig neu bearb., durch alttestamentliche Agrapha vermehrter Aufl. hg., TU 30/3–4 (Leipzig: Hinrichs, 1906), Agraphon 72 (pp. 96–98); Ernst VON DOBSCHÜTZ, *Das Kerygma Petri kritisch untersucht*, TU 11 (Leipzig: Hinrichs, 1893), 82–84; and, most prominently, VINZENT, "'Ich bin kein körperloses Geistwesen,'" 245–260.

94 A critical perspective is given in Markus VINZENT, *Christ's Resurrection in Early Christianity and the Making of the New Testament* (Surrey/Burlington, Vt.: Ashgate, 2011), 10–25 and 120f. On the book, see the rezension by Peter LAMPE and Adolf Martin RITTER, *ZAC* 17 (2013): 580–588.

95 For Paul, see Peter LAMPE, "Paul's Concept of a Spiritual Body," in *Resurrection: Theological and Scientific Assessments*, ed. Ted Peters, Robert John Russell, and Michael Welker (Grand Rapids/Cambridge: Eerdmans 2002), 103–114; Dag Øistein ENDSJØ, "Immortal Bodies, before Christ: Bodily Continuity in Ancient Greece and 1 Corinthians," *JSNT* 30 (2008): 417–436; and Candida R. MOSS, "Heavenly Healing: Eschatological Cleansing and the Resurrection of the Dead in Early Church," *JAAR* 79 (2011): 991–1017, here 1000–1004.

96 Sc. the "Teaching of Peter," from which, according to Origen, the dominical saying hails. See Origenes, *De principiis* I *praef.* 8 (TzF 24, 95 GÖRGEMANNS/KARPP = GCS Origenes V, 14.18–15.5 KOETSCHAU).

97 For the keyword "incorporeal," see above.

98 Origenes, *De principiis* I *praef.* 8 (TzF 24, 96 GÖRGEMANNS/KARPP = GCS Origenes V, 15.8–15 KOETSCHAU). ET from BEHR, *Origen: On First Principles*, 1: 19.

99 Thus certainly in a fragment from the text *De resurrectione*, which Pamphilus quotes in his apologia for Origen: Pamphilus Caesariensis, *Apologia pro Origene* 130 (SC 464, 212.22–24 AMACKER/JUNOD = FChr 80, 350.14–17 RÖWEKAMP).

100 Pamphilus von Caesarea, *Apologia pro Origene* (Röwekamp), 165.
101 On the Spanish bishop, see Jules Wankenne, s.v. "Consentius," in *Augustinus-Lexikon* (Basel: Schwabe, 1986–1994), 1: 1236–1239. On the question of the resurrection of the flesh in Augustine, see Paula Fredriksen, "Vile Bodies: Paul and Augustine on the Resurrection of the Flesh," in *Biblical Hermeneutics in Historical Perspective: Studies in Honor of Karlfried Froehlich on His Sixtieth Birthday*, ed. Mark S. Burrows and Paul Rorem (Grand Rapids: Eerdmans, 1991), 75–87.
102 Augustinus, *Epistula* 205.1.2 (CSEL 57, 324.11–325.5 Goldbacher). ET from *St. Augustine: Letters*, vol. 2, trans. Boniface Ramsey (New York: New City Press, 2004), 378.
103 So Fredriksen, "Vile Bodies," 86. For the background, see Caroline Walker Bynum, *The Resurrection of the Body in Western Christianity, 200–1336*, Lectures on the History of Religions 15 (New York: Columbia University Press, 1995), 94–104.
104 On this, in depth, albeit not entirely without accentuation, see Augustinus, *De civitate Dei* XXII 19 (BiTeu II, 597.13–600.5 Dombart/Kalb); and *Enchiridion ad Laurentium de fide et spe et caritate* 23.89–91 (CChr.SL 46, 97.58–98.114 Evans).
105 See also Moss, "Heavenly Healing," 1009.
106 Augustinus, *De civitate Dei* XXII 15 (BiTeu II, 592.6–17 Dombart/Kalb). ET after *Augustine: City of God, Books 21–22*, trans. William M. Green, LCL 417 (Cambridge, Mass./London: Harvard University Press, 1972), 277. On the text, in detail, see Virginia Burrus, "Carnal Excess: Flesh at the Limits of Imagination," *JECS* 17 (2009): 247–265, here 250–260; Bynum, *The Resurrection of the Body in Western Christianity, 200–1336*, 95–99; David Dawson, "Transcendence As Embodiment: Augustine's Domestication of Gnosis," *Modern Theology* 10 (1994): 1–26; and Moss, "Heavenly Healing," 1008–1011.
107 Also, most recently, at length, see Martin Heimgartner, *Pseudojustin—Über die Auferstehung: Text und Studie*, Patristische Texte und Studien 54 (Berlin/New York: De Gruyter, 2001), 203–221 (Heimgartner decides for Athenagoras); and Alberto D'Anna, *Pseudo-Giustino, Sulla Resurrezione: Discorso cristiano del II secolo*, Letteratura Cristiana Antica (Brescia: Morcelliana, 2001), 286 ("Deutero-Giustino," an adherent of Justin's school). Previously, for example, see Oskar Skarsaune, s.v. "Justin Märtyrer," *TRE* 17: 471–478, here 472. For the text's authenticity, see, among others, Pierre Prigent, *Justin et l'Ancien Testament: L'argumentation scripturaire du traité de Justin contre toutes les hérésies comme source principale du Dialogue avec Tryphon et de la Première Apologie*, Études bibliques (Paris: Gabalda, 1964), 36–60.
108 This comprises a frequently attested reading from Luke 24:42f.: οἱ δὲ ἐπέδωκαν αὐτῷ ἰχθύος ὀπτοῦ μέρος [καὶ ἀπὸ μελίσσου κηρίου]· καὶ λαβὼν ἐνώπιον αὐτῶν ἔφαγεν. For the attestation of this reading, see Nestle-Aland²⁸ apparatus ad. loc. (p. 290); and Prigent, *Justin et l'Ancien Testament*, 56f.
109 Pseudo-Justinus Martyr, *De resurrectione* 9 = frag. 108 from Johannes Damascenus (TU 20/2, 47.9–48.24 Holl = PTS 54, 124.7–126.19 Heimgartner). On the concept of corporeal resurrection in Pseudo-Justin, see now Moss, "Heavenly Healing," 1004–1006. On the concept within the authentic works, see Gilles Dorival, "Justin et la resurrection des morts," in *La resurrection chez les Pères*, Cahiers de Biblia Patristica 7 (Strasbourg: Université Marc Bloch, 2003), 101–118; and Horacio E. Lona, *Über die Auferstehung des Fleisches: Studien zur frühchristlichen Eschatologie*, BZNW 66 (Berlin/New York: De Gruyter, 1993), 91–110 (Justin) and 135–154 (Ps.-Justin). ET from *The Writings of Justin Martyr and Athenagoras*, trans. Marcus Dodds, George Reith, and B. P. Pratten, Ante-Nicene Christian Library 2 (Edinburgh: T&T Clark, 1909), 351f.
110 Additional passages in Bauer, *Das Leben Jesu im Zeitalter der neutestamentlichen Apokryphen*, 45f. On the early history of the notion, see Angelo P. O'Hagan, *Material Re-creation in the Apostolic Fathers*, TU 100 (Berlin: Akademie-Verlag, 1968); and, in detail, Bynum, *The Resurrection of the Body in Western Christianity, 200–1336*, 34–51.

See also, divergently, Vinzent, *Christ's Resurrection in Early Christianity and the Making of the New Testament*, 111–125.

111 Grillmeier, *Jesus der Christus im Glauben der Kirche*, Bd. 2/3, *Die Kirchen von Jerusalem und Antiochien nach 451 und bis 600*, mit Beiträgen von Alois Grillmeier, Theresia Hainthaler, Tanios Bou Mansour und Luise Abramowski, hg. Theresia Hainthaler (Freiburg/Basel/Vienna: Herder, 2002), 227–261; and idem, *Jesus der Christus im Glauben der Kirche*, 1: 673–686.

112 From the council's definition of faith (Acta Conciliorum Oecumenicorum 2/I/II, 129.23–27 Schwartz). On the text, see the literature cited above, p. 333 with n. 3.

113 Aristotle may first have employed the term in this context; cf. *De caelo* I 10 270 a 18–21. Cf. also idem, *Metaphysica* I 10 1059 a 5–12. According to Diogenes Laertius, *Vitae philosophorum* VII 137 (SCBO II, 355.21–356.1 Long = SVF II, 526 [II, 168.5–7 von Arnim]), the early Stoics are already supposed to have used this term in their theory of God. Epicurus certainly also used it: *Epistula ad Menoeceum* apud *Diogenem Laertium*, ibid., X 123 (II, 552.6–9 = 59.16–60.2 Usener = 107.2–5 Arrighetti). Clearly terminologically influenced by Aristotle is the Middle Platonic handbook literature: Alcinous, *Epitome doctrinae Platonicae sive Διδασκαλικός* 5.5 (CUFr 10 Whittaker/Louis = 157.31–36 Hermann). Cf. also ibid., 12.1 (CUFr 27 Whittaker/Louis = 167.2–4 Hermann).

114 See for this Rom 1:23: . . . καὶ ἤλλαξαν τὴν δόξαν τοῦ ἀφθάρτου θεοῦ ἐν ὁμοιώματι εἰκόνος φθαρτοῦ ἀνθρώπου καὶ πετεινῶν καὶ τετραπόδων καὶ ἑρπετῶν; and 1 Tim 1:17: . . . τῷ δὲ βασιλεῖ τῶν αἰώνων, ἀφθάρτῳ ἀοράτῳ μόνῳ θεῷ, τιμὴ καὶ δόξα εἰς τοὺς αἰῶνας τῶν αἰώνων, ἀμήν. Further pagan, Jewish, and Christian attestations in Günther Harder, s.v. "φθείρω κτλ.," in *Theologisches Wörterbuch zum Neuen Testament* (Stuttgart: Kohlhammer, 1973), 94–106, 96f., 102f., and 105f.

115 1 Cor 15:51f.: ἰδοὺ μυστήριον ὑμῖν λέγω· πάντες οὐ κοιμηθησόμεθα, πάντες δὲ ἀλλαγησόμεθα, ἐν ἀτόμῳ, ἐν ῥιπῇ ὀφθαλμοῦ, ἐν τῇ ἐσχάτῃ σάλπιγγι· σαλπίσει γὰρ καὶ οἱ νεκροὶ ἐγερθήσονται ἄφθαρτοι καὶ ἡμεῖς ἀλλαγησόμεθα.

116 Iohannes Grammaticus, *Aduersus Monophysitas* tit. (CChr.SG 1, 69.1–3 Richard): ἸΩΑΝΝΟΥ ΠΡΕΣΒΥΤΕΡΟΥ ἈΠΟ ΓΡΑΜΜΑΤΙΚΩΝ ΠΡΟΣ ἈΦΘΑΡΤΟ-ΔΟΚΗΤΑΣ. The work, a florilegium, collects the passages from the Fathers for the notion that the body of Christ is perishable prior to the resurrection (2.1 [71.86–88 Richard]); it begins in 1.1 with a sentence which defines the problem and thereby also, even though no definition of the titular term is presented, paraphrases what "aphthardocetes" propound, and which counterpositions are championed by the Neo-Chalcedonian John (69.4–7).

117 For the so-called aphthartodocetes, see most prominently Alois Kardinal Grillmeier, *Jesus der Christus im Glauben der Kirche*, Bd. 2/2, *Die Kirche von Konstantinopel im 6. Jahrhundert*, unter Mitarbeit von Theresia Hainthaler (Freiburg/Basel/Vienna: Herder, 1989), 82–116 and 224–241.

118 On Leontius, see Friedrich Loofs, *Leontius von Byzanz und die gleichnamigen Schriftsteller der griechischen Kirche*, TU 3/1–2 (Leipzig: Hinrichs, 1887), 22–34, in particular 24f.; contra Marcel Richard, "Léonce de Jérusalem et Léonce de Byzance," *Mélanges de Science Religieuse* 1 (1944): 35–88 = idem, *Opera minora*, tome 3 (Turnhout: Brepols/Leuven: Peeters, 1977), nr. 59; and Brian E. Daley, *Leontius of Byzantium: A Critical Edition of His Works with Prolegomena* (microfiche of a dissertation, Oxford: University of Oxford, 1979), lviii–lvix; Grillmeier, *Jesus der Christus im Glauben der Kirche*, 2/2: 190–195.

119 Leontius Byzantinus, *Contra Aphthartodocetas* (PG 86, 1329 B). On the text, see Lorenzo Perrone, "Il 'Dialogo contro gli aftartodoceti' di Leonzio di Bisanzio e Severo di Antiochia," *Cristianesimo nella storia* 1 (1980): 411–442.

120 Leontius Byzantinus, *Contra Aphthartodocetas* (PG 86, 1325 B).

121 René Draguet, *Julien d'Halicarnasse et sa controverse avec Sévère d'Antioche sur l'incorruptibilité du corps du Christ: Étude d'histoire littéraire et doctrinale suivie des fragments dogmatiques de Julien (texte syriacque et traduction grecque)* (Louvain: Smeesters,

1924), 1*–78* (fragments); Grillmeier, *Jesus der Christus im Glauben der Kirche*, 2/2: 82–116; and lastly Cyril Hovorun, *Will, Action and Freedom: Christological Controversies in the Seventh Century*, The Medieval Mediterranean 77 (Leiden: Brill, 2008), 28–30. For the ensuing effects, see Martin Jugie, s.v. "Gaianité," in *Dictionnaire de théologie catholique* (Paris: Letouzey et Ané, 1920), 6: 1002–1022.

122 Iain R. Torrance, s.v. "Severus von Antiochien," *TRE* 31: 184–186; Grillmeier, *Jesus der Christus im Glauben der Kirche*, 2/2: 135–185; and Mischa Meier, *Anastasios I: Die Entstehung des Byzantinischen Reiches* (Stuttgart: Klett-Cotta, 2009), 258–269 and 289–319. A hitherto-unknown source from Harvard Syr. 22 in which Julian is also discussed has recently been edited and translated with a commentary by Sebastian P. Brock: "A Report from a Supporter of Severos on Trouble in Alexandria," in *Synaxis katholike. Beiträge zu Gottesdienst und Geschichte der fünf altkirchlichen Patriarchate für Heinzgerd Brakmann zum 70. Geburtstag*, hg. Diliana Atanassova und Tinatin Chronz, orientalia—patristica—oecumenica 6/1 (Vienna/Berlin: Lit-Verlag, 2014), 47–64.

123 Draguet, *Julien d'Halicarnasse et sa controverse avec Sévère d'Antioche sur l'incorruptibilité du corps du Christ*, 1*–3* (fragments); William H. C. Frend, *The Rise of the Monophysite Movement* (Cambridge: Cambridge University Press, 1972), 253–255; and Grillmeier, *Jesus der Christus im Glauben der Kirche*, 2/2: 25f., 83–85 (on the chronology of the clashes), and 87–93 (on Severus).

124 Iulianus Halicarnassensis, *Additiones Iuliani ad Tomum frag.* 52 (57*/58* Draguet). I follow the retrotranslation of the Syriac text cited by Severus into Greek by Draguet (for the Syriac, see op. cit., 19*/20*).

125 Iulianus Halicarnassensis, Tomus frag. 16 (49* Draguet).

126 Iulianus Halicarnassensis, Tomus frag. 17 (49* Draguet). Grillmeier, *Jesus der Christus im Glauben der Kirche*, 2/2: 104 n. 249, refers to Cyrillus Alexandrinus, *Epistula ad Successum* I 9 (PG 77, 236 B = ACO I/1/6, 155.17f. Schwartz).

127 Eutyches was accused of having championed the view that the human body of Christ descended from heaven, which was contested: See his pertinent statement at a synod in November AD 448, surviving in the minutes from AD 451 1 [nr. 359] (ACO 2/1/1, 124.27–29 Schwartz); and the solemn revocation at the same synod: ibid. [nr. 522] (ACO 2/1/1, 142.26–32 Schwartz).

128 See also Draguet, *Julien d'Halicarnasse et sa controverse avec Sévère d'Antioche sur l'incorruptibilité du corps du Christ*, 12, 96–99, and 172–180. For Eutyches himself, see Adolf Jülicher, s.v. "Eutyches 5," PW 6/1: 1527–1529; Eduard Schwartz, "Der Prozess des Eutyches," *Sitzungsberichte der Bayerischen Akademie der Wissenschaften: Philosophisch-historische Klasse* 5 (1929): 1–52; Grillmeier, *Jesus der Christus im Glauben der Kirche*, 1: 731–733; George A. Bevan and Patrick T. R. Gray, "The Trial of Eutyches: A New Interpretation," *Byzantinische Zeitschrift* 101 (2008): 617–657; and most recently Christian Lange, *Mia energeia: Untersuchungen zur Einigungspolitik des Kaisers Heraclius und des Patriarchen Sergius von Constantinopel*, Studien und Texte zu Antike und Christentum 66 (Tübingen: Mohr Siebeck, 2012), 95–102.

129 Friedrich Loofs, "Die 'Ketzerei' Justinians," in *Harnack-Ehrung: Beiträge zur Kirchengeschichte, ihrem Lehrer Adolf von Harnack zu seinem siebzigsten Geburtstage (7. Mai 1921) dargebracht von einer Reihe seiner Schüler* (Leipzig: Hinrichs, 1921), 232–248, here 247 = idem, *Patristica: Ausgewählte Aufsätze zur Alten Kirche*, hg. Hanns Christof Brennecke und Jörg Ulrich, Arbeiten zur Kirchengeschichte 71 (Berlin/New York: De Gruyter, 1999), 369–385, here 384f.; and Karl-Heinz Uthemann, "Kaiser Justinian als Kirchenpolitiker und Theologe," in idem, *Christus, Kosmos, Diatribe: Themen der frühen Kirche als Beiträge zu einer historischen Theologie*, Arbeiten zur Kirchengeschichte 93 (Berlin/New York: De Gruyter, 2005), 257–331, here 327.

130 Evagrius Scholasticus, *Historia ecclesiastica* IV 39 (FChr 57/2, 540.2–17 Bidez/Parmentier/Hübner). ET from *The Ecclesiastical History of Evagrius Scholasticus*, trans. with an introduction by Michael Whitby (Liverpool: Liverpool University Press, 2000), 250.

131 Eustratius, *Vita Eutychii* IV 33 (PG 86, 2313 B = CChr.SG 25, 32.939–943 Laga). Cf. Theophanes, *Chronica ad annum* 6057 (I, 241.6–10 de Boor); and Michael Syrus, *Chronica* IX 34 (II, 272 Chabot). On the elsewhere-mentioned edict of the emperor, lost in its wording, see most prominently Grillmeier, *Jesus der Christus im Glauben der Kirche*, 2/2: 489–495 (with additional literature on p. 489 n. 583).

132 So Grillmeier, *Jesus der Christus im Glauben der Kirche*, 2/2: 493–495.

133 Grillmeier, *Jesus der Christus im Glauben der Kirche*, 1: 14–132.

134 I should like to thank my colleague, New Testament scholar Margareta Gruber: She was Dean of Studies of the Ecumenical Study Year of the Abbey of the Dormition on Mount Zion in Jerusalem as the first drafts of the following passages were composed in February and March 2011; a brief, albeit provocative treatment by her provided the initial catalyst for further reflections, and additional discussions deepened this initial stimulus. See Margareta Gruber, "Zwischen Bilderverbot und 'Vera Icon' oder: Wie viel Bild ist von Christus erlaubt?," *Lebendiges Zeugnis* 60 (2005): 100–115.

135 Gerd Theissen, *Urchristliche Wundergeschichten: Ein Beitrag zur formgeschichtlichen Erforschung der synoptischen Tradition*, 6. Aufl., Studien zum Neuen Testament 8 (Gütersloh: Gütersloher Verlagshaus Mohn, 1990), 107–111. See also Robert A. Guelich, *Mark 1–8:26*, World Biblical Commentary 34A (Dallas: Word Books, 1989), 261–263; and Albert Fuchs, "Die 'Seesturmperikope' Mk 4.35–41 parr. im Wandel der urkirchlichen Verkündigung," in *Weihbischof Dr. Alois Stöger: Exeget zwischen Bibelkommission und Offenbarungskonstitution*, hg. Ferdinand Staudinger und Heinrich Wurz, Studien zum neuen Testament und seiner Umwelt 15 (St. Pölten: Philosophisch-Theologische Hochschule der Diözese, 1990), 101–133.

136 For the similarities and differences regarding the referenced passages (Pss 65:8; 89:10; 107:28f.; also Jonah 1), see Otto Eissfeldt, "Gott und das Meer in der Bibel," in *Studia Orientalia, Joanni Pedersen septuagenario A.D. VII id. nov. anno MCMLIII a collegis, discipulis, amicis dictata* (Kopenhagen: Munksgaard, 1953), 76–84 = idem, *Kleine Schriften*, Bd. 3 (Tübingen: Mohr Siebeck, 1966), 256–264; Gottfried Schille, "Die Seesturmerzählung Markus 4:35–41 als Beispiel neutestamentlicher Aktualisierung," *ZNW* 56 (1965): 30–40; and Rudolf Pesch, *Das Markusevangelium*, Tl. 1, *Einleitung und Kommentar zu Kap. 1.1–8.26*, 4. Aufl., Herders Theologischer Kommentar zum Neuen Testament II (Freiburg/Basel/Vienna: Herder, 1984), 268–277 with excursus, pp. 277–281.

137 On the intent of this statement, see Pesch, *Das Markusevangelium*, 1: 272–274 and 278f. See also Earle Hilgert, "Symbolismus und Heilsgeschichte in den Evangelien: Ein Beitrag zu den Seesturm- und Gerasenererzählungen," in *Oikonomia: Heilsgeschichte als Thema der Theologie; Oscar Cullmann zum 65. Geburtstag gewidmet*, hg. Felix Christ (Hamburg-Bergstedt: Reich, 1967), 51–56; similarly, Walter Schmithals, *Wunder und Glaube: Eine Auslegung von Markus 4.35–6.6a*, Biblische Studien 59 (Neukirchen-Vluyn: Neukirchener, 1970), 56–68.

138 Luke 11:20. See Michael Wolter, *Das Lukasevangelium*, Handbuch zum Neuen Testament 5 (Tübingen: Mohr Siebeck, 2008), 418f.; and Pieter W. van der Horst, "'The Finger of God': Miscellaneous Notes on Luke 11:20 and Its *Umwelt*," in Petersen, Vos, and de Jonge, *Sayings of Jesus*, 89–103. For religious-historical parallels from the text's surroundings, cf. also Martin Hengel, "Der Finger und die Herrschaft Gottes in Lk 11.20," in Kieffer et Bergman, *La Main de Dieu*, 87–106 = idem, *Jesus und die Evangelien: Kleine Schriften V*, hg. Claus-Jürgen Thornton, WUNT 211 (Tübingen: Mohr Siebeck, 2007), 644–663.

139 Matt 17:2. On the text, see Theissen, *Urchristliche Wundergeschichten*, 102–105 and 121–125; Johannes M. Nützel, *Die Verklärungserzählung im Markusevangelium: Eine redaktionsgeschichtliche Untersuchung*, Forschung zur Bibel 6 (Würzburg: Echter, 1971), 168f., 241f., and 281–287; Markus Öhler, "Die Verklärung (Mk 9:1–8): Die Ankunft der Herrschaft Gottes auf Erden," *Novum Testamentum* 38 (1996): 197–217; idem, *Elia im Neuen Testament: Untersuchungen zur Bedeutung des alttestamentlichen Propheten im frühen Christentum*, BZNW 88 (Berlin/New York: De Gruyter, 1997), 118–135; John

Paul HEIL, *The Transfiguration of Jesus: Narrative Meaning and Function of Mark 9:2–8, Matt 17:1–8 and Luke 9:28–36*, Analecta biblica 144 (Rome: Edizione Pontificio Istituto Biblico, 2000), 26f. and 76–93 (parallels from intertestamental literature on pp. 79–84); Dieter ZELLER, "La metamorphose de Jésus comme épiphanie (Mc 9.2–8)," in *L'Evangile exploré: Mélanges offerts à Simon Légasse à l'occasion de ses soixante-dix ans*, publié sous la direction de Alain Marchadour, Lectio Divina 166 (Paris: Les éditions du Cerf, 1996), 167–186; and idem, "Bedeutung und religionsgeschichtlicher Hintergrund der Verwandlung Jesu," in *Authenticating the Activities of Jesus*, ed. Bruce Chilton, New Testament Tools and Studies 28/2 (Leiden: Brill, 1999), 303–321. Select bibliography in Thomas F. BEST, "The Transfiguration: A Select Bibliography," *Journal of the Evangelical Theological Society* 24 (1981): 157–161.

140   On the interpretation of this passage, see François BOVON, *Das Evangelium nach Lukas*, Tlbd. 1, *Lk 1.1–9.50*, Evangelisch-Katholischer Kommentar zum Neuen Testament III/1 (Zürich: Benziger/Neukirchen-Vluyn: Neukirchener, 1989), 495f.; and, in more detail, FRENSCHKOWSKI, *Offenbarung und Epiphanie*, 2: 184–187.

141   Ps.-Clemens Romanus, *Homiliae* XVII 7.3 (GCS Pseudoklementinen I, 232.17–20 REHM/ STRECKER). ET from SMITH/PETERSON/DONALDSON, *The Clementine Homilies*, 261. For an extensive treatment of the passage, see above.

142   AARON, "Shedding Light on God's Body in Rabbinic Midrashim," 303–307.

143   Eduard LOHSE, *Die Briefe an die Kolosser und an Philemon*, Kritisch-exegetischer Kommentar IX/2 (Göttingen: Vandenhoeck & Ruprecht, 1968), 85–88.

144   Philo Alexandrinus, *De opificio mundi* 25 (I, 7.17–18.4 COHN). Textual reconstruction and ET from RUNIA, *Philo of Alexandria: On the Creation of the Cosmos according to Moses*, 52, 150. Cf. the German translation in COHN/HEINEMANN/THEILER, *Philo von Alexandria: Die Werke in deutscher Übersetzung*, 35.

145   John 1:14. See Udo SCHNELLE, *Antidoketische Christologie im Johannesevangelium: Eine Untersuchung zur Stellung des 4. Evangeliums in der johanneischen Schule*, FRLANT 144 (Göttingen: Vandenhoeck & Ruprecht, 1987), 231–247; and, for an overview of the interpretive possibilities, Hartwig THYEN, *Das Johannesevangelium*, Handbuch zum Neuen Testament 6 (Tübingen: Mohr Siebeck, 2005), 88–100.

146   Helmut MERKLEIN, "Christus als Bild Gottes im Neuen Testament," *Jahrbuch für biblische Theologie* 13 (1998): 53–75 and 64f.

147   For the context, see Detlev DORMEYER, *Die Passion Jesu als Verhaltensmodell: Literarische und theologische Analyse der Traditions- und Redaktionsgeschichte der Markuspassion*, Neutestamentliche Abhandlungen Neue Folge 11 (Münster: Aschendorff, 1974), 124–137; Johannes SCHREIBER, *Die Markuspassion: Eine redaktionsgeschichtliche Untersuchung*, 2. Aufl., BZNW 68 (Berlin/New York: De Gruyter, 1993), 58–74 and 104f.; Wolfgang REINBOLD, *Der älteste Bericht über den Tod Jesu: Literarische Analyse und historische Kritik der Passionsdarstellungen der Evangelien*, BZNW 69 (Berlin/New York: De Gruyter, 1994), 138–145 and 234–240; and Florian HERRMANN, *Strategien der Todesdarstellung in der Markuspassion: Ein literaturgeschichtlicher Vergleich*, NTOA = Studien zur Umwelt des Neuen Testaments 86 (Göttingen: Vandenhoeck & Ruprecht, 2010), 338–356.

148   Cf., however, from Luke 22:44 the mention that "his sweat was as it were great drops of blood falling to the ground," καὶ ἐγένετο ὁ ἱδρὼς αὐτοῦ ὡσεὶ θρόμβοι αἵματος καταβαίνοντος ἐπὶ τὴν γῆν. On the medical background, see François BOVON, *Das Evangelium nach Lukas*, Tlbd. 4, *Lk 19.28–24.53*, Evangelisch-Katholischer Kommentar zum Neuen Testament III/4 (Neukirchen-Vluyn: Neukirchener; Düsseldorf: Patmos Verlag, 2009), 309f., as well as the following comment: "To my own knowledge, the artists of Christian Antiquity did not venture to depict this scene," "Meines Wissens haben die Künstler der christlichen Antike nicht gewagt, diese Szene darzustellen" (p. 310).

149   Martin HENGEL, "Mors turpissima Crucis: Die Kreuzigung in der antiken Welt und die 'Torheit' des 'Wortes vom Kreuz,'" in *Rechtfertigung: FS Ernst Käsemann zum 70. Geburtstag*, hg. Johannes Friedrich, Wolfgang Pöhlmann und Peter Stuhlmacher (Tübingen:

Mohr Siebeck; Göttingen: Vandenhoeck & Ruprecht, 1976), 123–184, here 145–164 = idem, *Studien zum Urchristentum: Kleine Schriften VI*, hg. Claus-Jürgen Thornton, WUNT 234 (Tübingen: Mohr Siebeck, 2008), 594–652, here 614–631.

150 Michael Theobald, "Jesus, Sohn des Ananias, und Jesus, Sohn des Josef," *Welt und Umwelt der Bibel* 56 (2010): 36–39; Paul Winter, *On the Trial of Jesus*, 2nd ed., rev. Tom Alec Burkill and Geza Vermes, Studia Judaica 1 (Berlin/New York: De Gruyter, 1974), 97–109; and Martin Hengel and Anna Maria Schwemer, *Geschichte des frühen Christentums*, Bd. 1, *Jesus und das Judentum* (Tübingen: Mohr Siebeck, 2007), 119f. and 595f. For additional context, see Catherine Hezser, *Lohnmetaphorik und Arbeitswelt in Mt 20.1–16: Das Gleichnis von den Arbeitern im Weinberg im Rahmen rabbinischer Lohngleichnisse*, NTOA 15 (Fribourg: Universitäts-Verlag; Göttingen: Vandenhoeck & Ruprecht, 1990), 267–275.

151 Flavius Josephus, *Bellum Judaicum* VI 304f. (II/2, 52 Michel/Bauernfeind). ET from *Josephus: The Jewish War, Books 5–7*, trans. H. St. J. Thackeray, LCL 210 (Cambridge, Mass./London: Harvard University Press, 1928), 465.

152 Joseph Zias and Eliezer Sekeles, "The Crucified Man from Giv'at ha-Mivtar: A Reappraisal," *Israel Exploration Journal* 35 (1985): 22–27; and now Christoph Markschies, "Kreuz," in *Erinnerungsorte des Christentums*, hg. Christoph Markschies und Hubert Wolf unter Mitarbeit von Barbara Schüler (München: Beck, 2010), 574–591.

153 On its interpretation, see Hugolin Langkammer, "Jes 53 und 1 Petr 2, 21–25: Zur christologischen Interpretation der Leidenstheologie von Jes 53," *Bibel und Liturgie* 60 (1987): 90–98; and Reinhard Feldmeier, *Der erste Brief des Petrus*, Theologischer Handkommentar zum Neuen Testament 15/I (Leipzig: Evangelische Verlagsanstalt: 2005), 111–118.

154 Cf. 1 Pet 2:24f. with Isa 53:4–6 LXX.

155 Karlmann Beyschlag, *Grundriss der Dogmengeschichte*, Bd. 2, *Gott und Mensch*, Tl. 1, *Das christologische Dogma*, Grundrisse 3/1 (Darmstadt: Wissenschaftliche Buchgesellschaft: 1991), 104–114; critical remarks on this passage in Basil Studer, "Kritische Fragen zu einer Geschichte des christologischen Dogmas," *Augustinianum* 34 (1994): 489–500, here 496–499.

156 Christoph Markschies, "Der Mensch Jesus Christus im Angesicht Gottes—Zwei Modelle des Verständnisses von Jesaja 52.13–53.12 in der patristischen Literatur und deren Entwicklung," in *Der leidende Gottesknecht: Jesaja 53 und seine Wirkungsgeschichte*, hg. Bernd Janowski und Peter Stuhlmacher, FAT 14 (Tübingen: Mohr Siebeck, 1996), 197–247.

157 Albert Ehrhard, "Zur literarhistorischen und theologischen Würdigung der Texte," in Walter E. Crum, *Der Papyruscodex saec. VI–VII der Philippsbibliothek in Cheltenham: Koptische theologische Schriften*, mit einem Beitrag von Albert Ehrhard, Schriften der Wissenschaftlichen Gesellschaft in Straßburg 18 (Straßburg: Trübner, 1915), 129–171, here 154–168; Tito Orlandi, "Il *dossier* copto di Agatonico di Tarso: Studia letterario e storico," in *Studies Presented to Hans Jacob Polotsky*, ed. Dwight W. Young (East Gloucester, Mass.: Pirtle & Polson, 1981), 269–299; and idem, s.v. "Agathonicus of Tarsus," in *Coptic Encyclopedia* (New York: Macmillan, 1991), 1: 69f. See also *Faijumische Fragmente der Reden des Agathonicus Bischofs von Tarsus*, hg. und erklärt von Wolja Erichsen, Det Kongelige Danske videnskabernes selskab, Historisk-filologiske meddelelser 19/1 (Copenhagen: Høst & Søn, 1932).

158 Crum, *Der Papyruscodex saec. VI–VII der Philippsbibliothek in Cheltenham*, ix–xiii. On the MS, see also Johannes Irmscher, "Die Anfänge der koptischen Papyrologie," in *Graeco-Coptica: Griechen und Kopten im byzantinischen Ägypten* [Referate der V. Koptologischen Arbeitskonferenz, 25.–27. Mai 1983], hg. Peter Nagel, Wissenschaftliche Beiträge der Martin-Luther-Universität Halle-Wittenberg 48/1984 (Halle, Saale: Universität Halle-Wittenberg, 1984), 121–136, here 126.

159 Wolfgang Speyer, *Die literarische Fälschung im heidnischen und christlichen Altertum: Ein Versuch ihrer Deutung*, Handbuch der Altertumswissenschaft I/2 (München: Beck, 1971), 50; on the contemporary context, see also 193 and 265–277.

160 CRUM refers in his apparatus to the passage in his German translation to 1 Kgs 8:27 (idem, *Der Papyruscodex saec. VI–VII der Philippsbibliothek in Cheltenham*, 77).

161 CRUM, *Der Papyruscodex saec. VI–VII der Philippsbibliothek in Cheltenham*, 22.4–20. Cf. the German translation of op. cit., 76f.; parallel transmission in ORLANDI, "Il *dossier* copto di Agatonico di Tarso," 282f.

162 CRUM, *Der Papyruscodex saec. VI–VII der Philippsbibliothek in Cheltenham*, 25.9–16. Cf. the German translation, op. cit., 80f.

163 Alois Kardinal GRILLMEIER, *Jesus der Christus im Glauben der Kirche*, 2/4: 232. See also ORLANDI, "Il *dossier* copto di Agatonico di Tarso," 277 and 281 (on the presumably secondary title transmitted by means of manuscript).

164 GRILLMEIER, *Jesus der Christus im Glauben der Kirche*, 2/4: 231–234.

165 CRUM, *Der Papyruscodex saec. VI–VII der Philippsbibliothek in Cheltenham*, 23.18–27 and 24.8–10. Cf. the German translation, op. cit., 79.

166 See *Doctrina Addai: De Imagine Edessena/Die Abgarlegende; Das Christusbild von Edessa*, übers. und eingel. von Martin Illert, FChr 45 (Turnhout: Brepols, 2007), 9–18; VON DOBSCHÜTZ, *Christusbilder*; and *Mandylion: Intorno al Sacro Volto, da Bisanzio a Genova* [Genova, Museo Diocesano, 18 aprile–18 luglio 2004], a cura di Gerhard Wolf, Colette Dufour Bozzo, Anna Rosa Calderoni Masetti (Mailand: Skira, 2004).

167 On the difference between (Pauline) "emulation" and (Ignatian) "imitation": Hans FREIHERR VON CAMPENHAUSEN, *Die Idee des Martyriums in der alten Kirche*, 2. durchges. und erg. Aufl. (Göttingen: Vandenhoeck & Ruprecht, 1964), 56–78; and SCHOEDEL, *Die Briefe des Ignatius von Antiochien*, 72–74. Now, in detail, see MOSS, *The Other Christs*, 45–74.

168 Ignatius Antiochenus, *Epistula ad Ephesios* 1.1 (SUC I, 142.8–11 FISCHER).

169 Ignatius Antiochenus, *Epistula ad Ephesios* 1.2 (SUC I, 142.11–14 FISCHER).

170 Most recently, Majella FRANZMANN, "Imitatio Christi: Copying the Death of the Founder and Gaining Paradise," in *A Wandering Galilean: Essays in Honour of Seán Freyne*, ed. Zuleika Rodgers, SuppJSJ 132 (Leiden: Brill, 2009), 367–383.

171 Ignatius Antiochenus, *Epistula ad Romanos* 6.3 (SUC I, 188.16–18 FISCHER). Karin BOMMES, *Weizen Gottes*, 40f., has admittedly demonstrated that μιμητής is not a term restricted to martyrdom.

172 Ignatius Antiochenus, *Epistula ad Romanos* 2.1 (SUC I, 184.3–7 FISCHER). ET from *The Apostolic Fathers*, vol. 1, *I Clement. II Clement. Ignatius. Polycarp. Didache*, ed. and trans. Bart D. EHRMAN, LCL 24 (Cambridge, Mass./London: Harvard University Press, 2003), 271–277.

173 Ignatius Antiochenus, *Epistula ad Romanos* 8.1 (SUC I, 190.10f. FISCHER). ET from EHRMAN, *The Apostolic Fathers*, 1: 281.

174 Ignatius Antiochenus, *Epistula ad Magnesios* 10.1 (SUC I, 168.4–6 FISCHER). ET from EHRMAN, *The Apostolic Fathers*, 1: 251.

175 SCHOEDEL, *Die Briefe des Ignatius von Antiochien*, 215.

176 Glen W. BOWERSOCK, *Martyrdom and Rome*, The Wiles Lectures given at the Queen's University of Belfast (Cambridge: Cambridge University Press, 1995), 59–74 ("Martyrdom and Suicide"); see also the review of Ekkehard MÜHLENBERG, *JTS* 47 (1996): 275–279, here 277; and Christel BUTTERWECK, *"Martyriumssehnsucht" in der Alten Kirche?* BHT 87 (Tübingen: Mohr Siebeck, 1995), 23–35.

177 Daniel BOYARIN, *Dying for God: Martyrdom and the Making of Christianity and Judaism* (Stanford, Calif.: Stanford University Press, 1999), 121.

178 Thus, most recently, Candida R. MOSS, "The Discourse of Voluntary Martyrdom: Ancient and Modern," *Church History* 81 (2012): 531–551, who indicated that there is no antique term for that which has been termed "voluntary martyrdom" since the Early Modern era (p. 533).

179 An overview of the three central dating suggestions (ca. AD 155/156, 167, and 177) in Gerd BUSCHMANN, *Das Martyrium des Polykarp*, übers. und erklärt, Kommentar zu den

apostolischen Vätern 6 (Göttingen: Vandenhoeck & Ruprecht, 1998), 39f. (with bibliographical references).

180   For their Greek text, the editions are, on the one hand, based upon six Greek MSS of the menology for the month of February and, on the other, on the passage in the *Ecclesiastical History* of Eusebius soon to be mentioned. For details, see most recently BUSCHMANN, *Das Martyrium des Polykarp*, 13–16; prior to this, most prominently Boudewijn DEHANDSCHUTTER, *Martyrium Polycarpi: Een literairkritische studie*, BETL 52 (Leuven: University Press, 1979), 27–48 (with a synopsis, pp. 112–129 = BUSCHMANN, op. cit., 17–36); previously already Hans Freiherr von CAMPENHAUSEN, *Bearbeitungen und Interpolationen des Polykarpmartyriums*, Sitzungsberichte der Heidelberger Akademie der Wissenschaften, Philosophisch-historische Klasse 3/1957 (Heidelberg: Winter, 1957), 5–48, here 40–48 = idem, *Aus der Frühzeit des Christentums: Studien zur Kirchengeschichte des ersten und zweiten Jahrhunderts* (Tübingen: Mohr Siebeck, 1963), 253–301, here 293–301; and most recently, Candida R. MOSS, "On the Dating of Polycarp: Rethinking the Place of the *Martyrdom of Polycarp* in the History of Christianity," *Early Christianity* 1 (2010): 539–574, here 541–544.

181   Dan 3:46–50 LXX. On the references to the biblical text, see Candida R. MOSS, "Nailing Down and Tying Up: Lessons in Intertextual Impossibility from the Martyrdom of Polycarp," *VC* 67 (2013): 117–136; idem, "On the Dating of Polycarp," 544–547; and Boudewijn DEHANDSCHUTTER, "The New Testament and the Martyrdom of Polycarp," in *Trajectories through the New Testament and the Apostolic Fathers*, ed. Andrew F. Gregory and Christopher Tuckett (Oxford: Oxford University Press, 2005), 395–406.

182   *Martyrium Polycarpi* 15.2 after the version from the menologies (30 BUSCHMANN/DEHANDSCHUTTER). ET from EHRMAN, *The Apostolic Fathers*, 1: 389.

183   Ernst LOHMEYER, *Vom göttlichen Wohlgeruch*, Sitzungsberichte der Heidelberger Akademie der Wissenschaften, Philosophisch-historische Klasse 9 (Heidelberg: Winter, 1919), esp. 28–31. See also Bernhard KÖTTING, "Wohlgeruch der Heiligkeit," in *Jenseitsvorstellungen in Antike und Christentum: Gedenkschrift für Alfred Stuiber*, hg. Theodor Klauser, JAC, Ergänzungsband 9 (Münster: Aschendorff, 1982), 168–175, esp. 173f. Gerd BUSCHMANN relates the vocabulary in his commentary on the passage instead to the sacrificial context (*Das Martyrium des Polykarp*, 304–309).

Conclusion: Settled Conceptions of God?

1   At the very best, "naïveté" may be a reasonable descriptor for certain contemporary forms of "biblicistic" interpretations: Mark SHERIDAN, *Language for God in Patristic Tradition: Wrestling with Biblical Anthropomorphism* (Downers Grove, Ill.: IVP Academic, 2015), 213–215.

2   "Leiblichkeit ist das Ende der Werke Gottes, wie aus der Stadt Gottes klar erhellet . . .": OETINGER, "Art. Leib, Soma," 223.5f. = (o. O. [Heilbronn/Neckar]: o. V., 1776), 407.

3   "'Epiphaniale' (Wie können die Götter erscheinen? Dazu gehören auch die Traditionen über die Speise der Götter u.ä.) . . . Kosmische (der Kosmos als Leib der Gottheit), die ja nicht etwa notwendig pantheistisch zu verstehen ist" . . . "Monarchische Thronsaalmetaphorik, als deren Steigerung die bekannten 'Shi'ur Qoma'-Texte zu verstehen sind und die natürlich nicht nur jüdisch bezeugt ist, und die zudem ein Umfeld von anderen Verbildlichungen der Götter 'an sich' hat." Epistolary communication from Marco FRENSCHKOWSKI (15 May 2009). On the topic of "epiphany," see idem, *Offenbarung und Epiphanie*, Bd. 1, *Grundlagen des spätantiken und frühchristlichen Offenbarungsglaubens*, WUNT 2/79 (Tübingen: Mohr Siebeck, 1995). On the topic of the "cosmos as the body of the godhead," see Grace JANTZEN, *God's World, God's Body* (Philadelphia: Westminster Press, 1984).

4   Useful attempts at the systematization of ethnological, literary, religious-historical, and philosophical definitions of myth in Werner H. SCHMIDT, s.v. "Mythos III: Alttestamentlich,"

TRE 23: 625–644, here 626–628. See also Axel HORSTMANN, s.v. "Mythos, Mythologie VI: 20. Jahrhundert," in *Historisches Wörterbuch der Philosophie* (Darmstadt: Wissenschaftliche Buchgesellschaft, 1984), 6: 300–318.

5 See Kurt HÜBNER, *Die Wahrheit des Mythos* (München: Beck, 1985), 95–108; and idem, s.v. "Mythos: Philosophisch," *TRE* 23: 597–608, here 599f.

6 On the dimension of transgressing boundaries, see HORSTMANN, s.v. "Mythos, Mythologie VI," 303f.

7 Bernd JANOWSKI, "Das biblische Weltbild: Eine methodologische Skizze," in *Das biblische Weltbild und seine altorientalischen Kontexte*, hg. Beate Ego und Bernd Janowski, FAT 32 (Tübingen: Mohr Siebeck, 2001), 229–260. On the term "worldview" ("Weltbild"), see Horst THOMÉ, s.v. "Weltbild," in *Historisches Wörterbuch der Philosophie* (Darmstadt: Wissenschaftliche Buchgesellschaft, 2004), 12: 460–463; and Johannes ZACHHUBER, "Weltbild, Weltanschauung, Religion: Ein Paradigma intellektueller Diskurse im 19. Jahrhundert," in *Die Welt als Bild: Interdisziplinäre Beiträge zur Visualität von Weltbildern*, hg. Christoph Markschies und Johannes Zachhuber, Arbeiten zur Kirchengeschichte 107 (Berlin/New York: De Gruyter, 2008), 211–82.

8 "Weltbild des Neuen Testamentes . . . ein mythisches." Rudolf BULTMANN, *Neues Testament und Mythologie: Das Problem der Entmythologisierung der neutestamentlichen Verkündigung*, Nachdruck der 1941 erschienenen Fassung, hg. Eberhard Jüngel, Beiträge zur Evangelischen Theologie 96 (München: Kaiser, 1985), 12. In the footnotes, Bultmann defined the term "myth" which he implied in the 1942 lecture: "Mythologisch ist die Vorstellungsweise, in der das Unweltliche, Göttliche als Weltliches, Menschliches, das Jenseitige als Diesseitiges erscheint, in der z.B. Gottes Jenseitigkeit als räumliche Ferne gedacht wird . . ." (p. 23 n. 2).

9 "Wahrheiten wieder neu entdeckt werden, die in einer Zeit der Aufklärung verloren gegangen sind" (BULTMANN, *Neues Testament und Mythologie*, 14).

10 "Kein erwachsener Mensch stellt sich Gott als ein oben im Himmel vorhandenes Wesen vor; ja, den 'Himmel' im alten Sinne gibt es für uns gar nicht mehr" (BULTMANN, *Neues Testament und Mythologie*, 15). The heated discussion is documented in part in the volumes of *Kerygma und Mythos: Ein theologisches Gespräch*, hg. Hans-Werner Bartsch, Theologische Forschung 1, 5. erw. Aufl. (Hamburg-Bergstedt: Reich, 1967); *Kerygma und Mythos: Diskussionen und Stimmen des In- und Auslandes*, Bd. 2, hg. Hans-Werner Bartsch, Theologische Forschung 2 (Hamburg-Bergstedt: Reich, 1965); *Kerygma und Mythos III: Das Gespräch mit der Philosophie*, hg. Hans-Werner Bartsch, Theologische Forschung 5 (Hamburg-Bergstedt: Reich, 1966); and *Kerygma und Mythos IV: Das Gespräch mit der Philosophie*, hg. Hans-Werner Bartsch, Theologische Forschung 8 (Hamburg-Bergstedt: Reich, 1966). Rudolf BULTMANN outlined this stance once more in detail in the second volume of the series in the face of critical objections: "Zum Problem der Entmythologisierung," in *Kerygma und Mythos*, Bd. 2, *Diskussionen und Stimmen des In-und Auslandes*, hg. Hans-Werner Bartsch, Theologische Forschung 2 (Hamburg-Bergstedt: Reich, 1965) 179–208, esp. 180–190 on the definition of myth.

11 BULTMANN, *Neues Testament und Mythologie*, 15: "Erledigt ist . . . der Geister- und Dämonenglaube"; 16: "Die Wunder des Neuen Testaments sind damit als Wunder erledigt"; and 17: "Die mythische Eschatologie ist im Grunde . . . erledigt."

12 "Der rein biologisch sich verstehende Mensch sieht nicht ein, daß überhaupt in das geschlossene Gefüge der natürlichen Kräfte ein übernatürliches Etwas, das πνεῦμα, eindringen und in ihm wirksam sein könne" (BULTMANN, *Neues Testament und Mythologie*, 17f).

13 BULTMANN, *Neues Testament und Mythologie*, 22f.

14 "Will man von Gott reden, so muß man offenbar *von sich selbst reden*" (Rudolf BULTMANN, "Welchen Sinn hat es, von Gott zu reden?" *Theologische Blätter* 4 [1925]: 129–135, here 131 = idem, *Glauben und Verstehen: Gesammelte Aufsätze*, Bd. 1 [Tübingen: Mohr Siebeck, 1933], 26–37, here 28). On the work, see Gerhard EBELING, "Zum Verständnis von R. Bultmanns Aufsatz: 'Welchen Sinn hat es, von Gott zu reden?'" in idem,

Wort und Glaube, Bd. 2, *Beiträge zur Fundamentaltheologie und zur Lehre von Gott* (Tübingen: Mohr Siebeck, 1969), 343–371, esp. 350–361.

15 "Gott ist im tiefsten unmodern: Wir vermögen nicht, ihn uns im Frack, glattrasiert und mit einem Scheitel vorzustellen, sondern tun es nach Patriarchenart" (Robert Musil, *Der Mann ohne Eigenschaften: Roman*, hg. Adolf Frisé, neu durchges. und verb. Ausg. 1978, Rowohlt Jahrhundert 1 = rororo 4001 [Reinbek: Rowohlt, 1990], 197 [49. Kapitel]). See on this also Claus-Dieter Osthövener, "Literarische und religiöse Deutungskultur im Werk Robert Musils," in *Protestantismus zwischen Aufklärung und Moderne: Festschrift für Ulrich Barth*, hg. Roderich Barth, Claus-Dieter Osthövener und Arnulf von Scheliha, Beiträge zur rationalen Theologie 16 (Frankfurt am Main: Lang, 2005), 286–300.

16 For the background, see Rosenau, "Gott höchst persönlich," in Härle und Preul, *Marburger Jahrbuch Theologie XIX*, 47–76, esp. 52–60 and 60–66; and Christian Danz, "Der Atheismusstreit um Fichte," in *Philosophisch-theologische Streitsachen: Pantheismusstreit— Atheismusstreit—Theismusstreit*, hg. Georg Essen und Christian Danz (Darmstadt: Wissenschaftliche Buchgesellschaft, 2012), 135–213.

17 Thus, summarily, Johann Gottlieb Fichte, "Ueber den Grund unseres Glaubens an eine göttliche Weltregierung," *Philosophisches Journal* 8 (1798): 1–20, here 17 = *Fichtes Werke*, hg. Immanuel Hermann Fichte, Bd. 5, *Zur Religionsphilosophie* (Berlin: Veit, 1846 = Berlin: De Gruyter, 1971), 175–189, here 188: "Es kann ebensowenig von der anderen Seite dem, der nur einen Augenblick nachdenken, und das Resultat dieses Nachdenkens sich redlich gestehen will, zweifelhaft bleiben, dass der Begriff von Gott, als einer besonderen Substanz, unmöglich und widersprechend ist: und es erlaubt, dies aufrichtig zu sagen, und das Schulgeschwätz niederzuschlagen, damit die wahre Religion des freudigen Rechtthuns sich erhebe."

18 "Der nicht sagen kann: *Ich bin*, ein Gott ohne Persönlichkeit—ohne Existenz, der nichts schafft und nichts gibt" (letter of Lavater to Reinhold, Zürich, 16 February 1799, quoted after *Appellation an das Publikum . . . Dokumente zum Atheismusstreit um Fichte, Forberg, Niethammer: Jena 1798/99*, hg. Werner Röhr, Reclams Universal-Bibliothek 1179 [Leipzig: Reclam, 1987], 145 [Document IV.21]). On Lavater, see Gerhard Ebeling, "Genie des Herzens unter dem Genius saeculi—J. C. Lavater als Theologe," in *Das Antlitz Gottes im Antlitz des Menschen: Zugänge zu Johann Kaspar Lavater*, hg. Karl Pestalozzi und Horst Weigelt, Arbeiten zur Geschichte des Pietismus 31 (Göttingen: Vandenhoeck & Ruprecht, 1994), 23–60.

19 Fichte, *J. G. Fichte's . . . Appellation an das Publicum über die durch ein Churf. Sächs: Confiscationsrescript ihm beigemessenen atheistischen Aeusserungen* (Jena/Leipzig: Gabler; Tübingen: Cotta, 1799), 55 = *Fichtes Werke*, hg. Immanuel Hermann Fichte, Bd. 5, *Zur Religionsphilosophie* (191–238) 215: They (sc. the opponents) "subsume the Infinite in a finite definition, and wonder at God's wisdom in having arranged everything precisely as they themselves would have" ("fassen den Unendlichen in einen endlichen Begriff; und bewundern die Weisheit Gottes, dass er alles gerade so eingerichtet hat, wie sie selbst es auch gemacht hätten").

20 The Leipzig scholar of the New Testament *Marco Frenschkowski* relayed to me (by letter on 15 May 2009) that the notion of a corporeality of God "astoundingly has once more been adopted at the fringes of the established Churches in recent religious history" ("am Rande der etablierten Kirchen in der jüngeren Religionsgeschichte doch erstaunlicherweise wieder aufgenommen") and helpfully made me aware of the case in respect to the Mormons.

21 Stephen E. Robinson et al., s.v. "God the Father," in *Encylopedia of Mormonism*, ed. Daniel H. Ludlow (New York: Macmillan, 1992), 2: 548–552.

22 *Doctrine and Covenants* Section 130:22 (items of instruction given by Joseph Smith the Prophet, at Ramus, Illinois, 2 April 1843); here quoted after the internet version of the "Church of Jesus Christ of Latter Day Saints," at http://www.lds.org/Scriptures/dc -testament/dc/130.22?lang=eng#21 (last accessed 19 May 2019).

23 On a pertinent web page of the "Church of Jesus Christ of Latter Day Saints" it is stated: "However, just because some statements about God are metaphorical doesn't mean that every statement is. When the Psalmist speaks of God covering us with His feathers, and giving refuge under His wings, the metaphor is completely clear" (https://www .fairmormon.org/answers/Mormonism_and_the_nature_of_God/Corporeality_of_God; last accessed 25 May 2019).

24 WEBB, *Jesus Christ, Eternal God*, 243–270, esp. 243; a detailed interpretation of texts penned by Joseph Smith may be found on pp. 253–257. Previously already: Edmond La Beaume CHERBONNIER, "In Defense of Anthropomorphism," in *Reflections on Mormonism: Judeo-Christian Parallels; Papers Delivered at the Religious Studies Center Symposium, Brigham Young University, March 10–11, 1978*, ed. Truman G. Madsen, Religious Studies Series 4 (Provo, Utah: Religious Studies Center, Brigham Young University and Bookcraft, 1978), 155–174, esp. 162.

25 WEBB, *Jesus Christ, Eternal God*, 244: "What if the monks of Egypt had won their battle in defence of anthropomorphism?"

26 MARKSCHIES, "Theologische Diskussionen zur Zeit Konstantins."

27 WEBB, *Jesus Christ, Eternal God*, 244.

28 Raymond WINLING, s.v. "Nouvelle Théologie," *TRE* 24: 668–675.

29 BULTMANN, "Welchen Sinn hat es, von Gott zu reden?" 26–28.

30 Adolf von HARNACK, *Das Wesen des Christentums* (= Leipzig: Hinrichs, 1929), 33 = hg. und kommentiert v. Trutz Rendtorff (Gütersloh: Kaiser, 1999), 87 = hg. Claus-Dieter Osthövener, 2. durchges. Aufl. (Tübingen: Mohr Siebeck, 2007), 37; idem, *Lehrbuch der Dogmengeschichte*, Bd. 1, *Die Entstehung des kirchlichen Dogmas*, Sammlung Theologischer Lehrbücher 2/1 (Freiburg: Mohr, 1886), 11–23, 121–132; Eginhard P. MEIJERING, *Die Hellenisierung des Christentums im Urteil Adolf von Harnacks*, Verhandelingen der Koninklijke Nederlandse Akademie van Wetenschappen, Afd. Letterkunde, Nieuwe Reeks, deel 128 (Amsterdam: North-Holland, 1985); and MARKSCHIES, *Hellenisierung des Christentums*, 49–58.

31 Cf. Plato, *Respublica* 508 B; and Porphyrius, *Sententiae ad intelligibilia ducentes* 10 (BiTeu 4.7–10 LAMBERZ). See also Johannes ZACHHUBER, s.v. "Überseiend; überwesentlich," in *Historisches Wörterbuch der Philosophie* (Darmstadt: Wissenschaftliche Buchgesellschaft, 2001), 11: 58–63.

32 See the cautious defense of the classical doctrine of God in Eginhard P. MEIJERING, "Some Reflections on Cyril of Alexandria's Rejection of Anthropomorphism," *Nieuw Theologisch Tijdschrift* 28 (1974): 295–301.

33 In such a sense, Franz CHRIST, *Menschlich von Gott reden: Das Problem des Anthropomorphismus bei Schleiermacher*, Ökumenische Theologie 10 (Einsiedeln/Zürich/Köln: Benziger; Gütersloh: Gütersloher Verlagshaus Mohn, 1982), 29–31 and 226–231, seeks in the spirit of his teacher Jüngel to contribute to the revival of a legitimate anthropomorphism within theories of God.

34 In a few ancient Jewish and Christian texts, the sexuality of angels is also discussed: Kevin SULLIVAN, "Sexuality and Gender of Angels," in *Paradise Now: Essays on Early Jewish and Christian Mysticism*, ed. April D. DeConick, Society of Biblical Literature Symposium Series 11 (Leiden: Brill, 2004), 27–35.

35 Cf., however, Christl M. MAIER, "Körperliche und emotionale Aspekte JHWHs aus der Genderperspektive," in *Göttliche Körper—Göttliche Gefühle: Was leisten anthropomorphe und anthropopathische Götterkonzepte im Alten Orient und im Alten Testament*, hg. Andreas Wagner, Orbis Biblicus et Orientalis 270 (Fribourg: Academic Press; Göttingen: Vandenhoeck & Ruprecht, 2014), 171–189.

36 "Die Wahrheit des Mythos *und* die Notwendigkeit der Entmythologisierung" (Eberhard JÜNGEL, "Die Wahrheit des Mythos und die Notwendigkeit der Entmythologisierung," in idem, *Indikative der Gnade–Imperative der Freiheit: Theologische Erörterungen IV* [Tübingen: Mohr Siebeck, 2000], 40–57).

37 Thus, for example, in connection to Bultmann, EBELING, "Zum Verständnis von R. Bult-
    manns Aufsatz," 353.
38 On the Platonic phrase ἐπέκεινα τῆς οὐσίας, see above, pp. 33–35.
39 An account of the classical differentiations in the definitions of the term "possibility" is
    rendered by Horst SEIDL, s.v. "Möglichkeit," in *Historisches Wörterbuch der Philosophie*
    (Darmstadt: Wissenschaftliche Buchgesellschaft, 1984), 6: 72–92. See on this now Mau-
    rizio FERRARIS, *Manifesto of New Realism*, trans. Sarah De Sanctis, foreword by Graham
    Harman (New York: State University of New York Press, 2014), 15–28.
40 See above and now Joachim NEGEL, *Feuerbach weiterdenken: Studien zum religions-
    kritischen Projektionsargument*, Religion—Geschichte—Gesellschaft 51 (Berlin: LIT,
    2014), 35–110.
41 Thus also Eberhard JÜNGEL, "Anthropomorphismus als Grundproblem neuzeitlicher
    Hermeneutik," in idem, *Wertlose Wahrheit: Zur Identität und Relevanz des christlichen
    Glaubens*, Theologische Erörterungen 3, 2., um ein Register erweiterte Aufl. (Tübingen:
    Mohr Siebeck, 2003), 110–131, esp. 127–131; with reference to Immanuel KANT, *Prole-
    gomena zu einer jeden künftigen Metaphysik*, 357 (§ 57). Also arguing for the "right to
    anthropomorphic statements" ("Recht auf anthropomorphe Aussagen") is Klaus BERGER,
    Ist Gott Person? Ein Weg zum Verstehen des christlichen Gottesbildes (Gütersloh: Güters-
    loher Verlagshaus, 2004), 35–38, 59f.
42 JÜNGEL, "Anthropomorphismus als Grundproblem neuzeitlicher Hermeneutik," 131.
43 "Gewisse Anthropomorphismen . . . ungescheut und ungetadelt erlauben" (Imma-
    nuel KANT, *Kritik der reinen Vernunft*, Kants Gesammelte Schriften Bd. 3, hg. von der
    Königlich Preußischen Akademie der Wissenschaften [Berlin: De Gruyter, 1911], B 724f.
    = 457f.).
44 "Wir feineren Christen verachten den Bilderdienst, das ist, unser lieber Gott besteht aus
    Holz und Goldschaum, aber er bleibt immer ein Bild, das nur ein anderes Glied in eben
    derselben Reihe ist, feiner, aber immer ein Bild. Will sich der Geist von diesem Bilder-
    dienst losreißen, so gerät er endlich auf die Kantische Idee. Aber es ist Vermessenheit
    zu glauben, daß ein so gemischtes Wesen als der Mensch das alles je so *rein* anerken-
    nen werde" (letter of G. C. Lichtenberg to Ludwig Christian Lichtenberg, Göttingen, 18
    February 1799, quoted after *Appellation an das Publikum* [Dokument IV.22] = Georg
    Christoph LICHTENBERG, *Briefwechsel*, Bd. 4, *1793–1799*, in *Auftrag der Akademie der
    Wissenschaften zu Göttingen*, hg. Ulrich Joost und Albrecht Schöne (München: Beck,
    1992), 1019 [Brief nr. 2969]; see also Albrecht BEUTEL, *Lichtenberg und die Religion:
    Aspekte einer vielschichtigen Konstellation*, BHT 93 [Tübingen: Mohr Siebeck, 1996],
    237f.).
45 Johannes SCHELHAS, "Der Leib als Schöpfung," *Neue Zeitschrift für Systematische Theol-
    ogie und Religionsphilosophie* 55 (2013): 33–53, here 39; and Volker GERHARDT, *Individ-
    ualität: Das Element der Welt*, Beck'sche Reihe 1381 (München: Beck, 2000), 50–59. I
    thank my Berlin colleague Horst Bredekamp for all manner of discussions regarding this
    context.
46 Angelika NEUWIRTH, *Der Koran als Text der Spätantike: Ein europäischer Zugang* (Ber-
    lin: Verlag der Weltreligionen, 2010), 20–24.
47 Gudrun KRÄMER, "Ja, er kann: Islam als *empowerment*," in *Was ist der Mensch?* hg. Detlev
    Ganten, Volker Gerhardt, Jan-Christoph Heilinger und Julian Nida-Rümelin, Humanpro-
    jekt, Interdisziplinäre Anthropologie 3 (Berlin/New York: De Gruyter, 2008), 159–161.
48 Navid KERMANI, *God Is Beautiful: The Aesthetic Experience of the Quran*, trans. Tony
    Crawford (Cambridge: Polity Press, 2014), 171.
49 NEUWIRTH, *Der Koran als Text der Spätantike*, 167. The expression "inlibration" may
    be traced back to Harry Austryn WOLFSON, *The Philosophy of the Kalam*, Structure and
    Growth of Philosophic Systems from Plato to Spinoza 4 (Cambridge, Mass./London:
    Harvard University Press, 1976), 244f.
50 NEUWIRTH, *Der Koran als Text der Spätantike*, 158–168 (in reference to Sura 55:1–4).

51 Thus ʿAlī ibn ʿĪsā ar-Rummānī, died AD 996, *Talat rasaʿil fi iʿgaz al-qurʿan* [An nukat fi iʿgaz al-qurʿan], ed. Muḥammad Aḥmad Ḥalafallāh, Ḏaḫāʾir al-ʿarab 16 (Miṣr: Dār al-Maʿārif, [circa 1955]), 111; here quoted after KERMANI, *God Is Beautiful*, 192.

52 KERMANI, *God Is Beautiful*, 192.

53 Carl SCHMITT, *Politische Theologie: Vier Kapitel zur Lehre von der Souveränität*, 8. Aufl. (Berlin: Duncker & Humblot, 2004 = 1922), 43: "Alle prägnanten Begriffe der modernen Staatslehre sind säkularisierte theologische Begriffe."

54 Edmund PLOWDEN, *The Commentaries, or Reports of Edmund Plowden: . . . Containing Divers Cases upon Matters of Law, Argued and Adjudged in the Several Reigns of King Edward VI., Queen Mary, King and Queen Philip and Mary, and Queen Elizabeth [1548–1579]. To Which Are Added, the Quæries of Mr. Plowden. In Two Parts* (London: Brooke, 1816), 212a–213: "For the King has in him two Bodies, viz. a Body natural, and a Body politic. His Body natural (if it be considered in itself) is a Body mortal, subject to all Infirmities that come by Nature or Accident, to the Imbecility of Infancy or old Age, and to the like Defects that happen to the natural Bodies of other People. But his Body politic is a Body that cannot be seen or handled, consisting of Policy and Government, and constituted for the Direction of the People, and the Management of the public weal, and this Body is utterly void of Infancy, and old Age, and other natural Defects and Imbecilities, which the Body natural is subject to, and for this Cause, what the King does in his Body politic, cannot be invalidated or frustrated by any Disability in his natural Body." See also KANTORO-WICZ, *The King's Two Bodies*, 7–23; Arnold D. HARVEY, *Body Politic: Political Metaphor and Political Violence* (Cambridge: Cambridge Scholars, 2007), 117–118; and Jonathan Gil HARRIS, *Foreign Bodies and the Body Politic: Discourses of Social Pathology in Early Modern England* (Cambridge: Cambridge University Press 1998), 141–146.

55 PLOWDEN, *The Commentaries, or Reports*, 283: "[T]he King has two Capacities, for he has two Bodies, the one whereof is a Body natural, consisting of natural Members as every other Man has, and in this he is subject to Passions and to Death as other Men are: the other is a Body politic, and the Members thereof are his Subjects, and he and his Subjects together compose the corporation, as Southcote said, and he is incorporated with them, and they with him, and he is the Head, and they are the Members, and he has sole Government of them: and this Body is not subject to Passions as the other is, nor to Death, for as to this Body the King never dies, and his natural Death is not called in our Law (as Harper said) the Death of the King, but the Demise of the King, not signifying by the Word (Demise) that the Body politic of the King is dead, but that there is a Separation of the two Bodies, and that the Body politic is transferred and conveyed over from the Body natural now dead, or now removed from the Dignity royal, to another Body natural."

56 Ulrich KÖPF, "Politische Theologie im Mittelalter," *Theologische Rundschau* 58 (1993): 437–444, here 439. Köpf provides a medieval attestation for the notion that the "political body" of the king is imperishable and thereby eternal (pp. 441–444).

57 Hans JOAS, *Die Sakralität der Person: Eine neue Genealogie der Menschenrechte* (Berlin: Suhrkamp, 2011), 81f.

Bibliography of Secondary Literature

Only titles from the secondary literature are included in this bibliography; the source texts employed may be found directly within the references pertaining to the cited passages.

AARON, David H. "Shedding Light on God's Body in Rabbinic Midrashim: Reflections on the Theory of a Luminous Adam." *HTR* 90 (1997): 299–314.

ABEL, Félix M. "Saint Cyrille d'Alexandrie dans ses rapports avec la Palestine." In *Kyrilliana: Spicilegia Sancti Cyrilli Alexandrini XV recurrente saeculo; Études variées à l'occasion du XVe centenaire de Saint Cyrille d'Alexandrie (444–1944)*, édité par Seminarium Franciscale Orientale Ghizae, 205–230. Le Caire: Editions du Scribe Egyptien, 1947.

ABRAMOWSKI, Luise. "Ein gnostischer Logostheologe: Umfang und Redaktor des gnostischen Sonderguts in Hippolyts 'Widerlegung aller Häresien.'" In idem, *Drei christologische Untersuchungen*, 18–62. BZNW 45. Berlin/New York: De Gruyter, 1981.

————. "συνάφεια und ἀσύγχυτος ἕνωσις als Bezeichnungen für trinitarische und christologische Einheit." In idem, *Drei christologische Untersuchungen*, 63–109. BZNW 45. Berlin/New York: De Gruyter, 1981.

ABUSCH, Tzvi. "Ishtar." In *Dictionary of Deities and Demons in the Bible (DDD)*, edited by Karel van der Toorn, Bob Becking, and Pieter W. van der Horst, 847–855. Leiden/New York/Cologne: Brill, 1995.

————. "Marduk." In *Dictionary of Deities and Demons in the Bible (DDD)*, edited by Karel van de Toorn, Bob Becking, and Pieter W. van der Horst, 1014–1026. Leiden/New York/Cologne: Brill, 1995.

ALAND, Barbara. "Die frühe Gnosis zwischen platonischem und christlichem Glauben: Kosmosfrömmigkeit versus Erlösungstheologie." In *Die Weltlichkeit des Glaubens in der Alten Kirche: Festschrift für Ulrich Wickert zum siebzigsten Geburtstag*, herausgegeben von Dietmar Wyrwa, 1–24. Beihefte zur Zeitschrift für die neutestamentliche Wissenschaft und Kunde der älteren Kirche 85. Berlin/New York: De Gruyter, 1997. (= idem, *Was ist Gnosis? Studien zu frühem Christentum, zu Marcion und zur kaiserzeitlichen Philosophie*, 103–124. WUNT 239. Tübingen: Mohr Siebeck, 2009.)

———. "Fides und Subiectio: Zur Anthropologie des Irenäus." In *Kerygma und Logos: Beiträge zu den geistesgeschichtlichen Beziehungen zwischen Antike und Christentum; Festschrift für Carl Andresen zum 70. Geburtstag*, herausgegeben von Adolf M. Ritter, 9–28. Göttingen: Vandenhoeck & Ruprecht, 1979.

———. "Marcion und die Marcioniten." In *Theologische Realenzyklopädie*, 22: 89–101. Berlin/New York, De Gruyter, 1992. (= idem, *Was ist Gnosis? Studien zum frühen Christentum, zu Marcion und zur kaiserzeitlichen Philosophie*, 318–340. WUNT 239. Tübingen: Mohr Siebeck, 2009).

———. "Sünde und Erlösung bei Marcion und die Konsequenz für die sog. beiden Götter Marcions." In *Marcion und seine kirchengeschichtliche Wirkung: Marcion and His Impact on Church History*, herausgegeben von Katharina Greschat und Gerhard May, 147–157. TU 150. Berlin/New York: De Gruyter, 2002.

ALAND, Kurt, und Hans-Udo ROSENBAUM, Hg. *Repertorium der griechischen christlichen Papyri*. Bd. 2, *Kirchenväter-Papyri*. Tl. 1, *Beschreibungen*. Im Namen der Patristischen Arbeitsstelle Münster. PTS 42. Berlin/New York: De Gruyter, 1995.

ALBARIC, Michel. *Les sources bibliques du De videndo deo de Saint Augustin*. Paris: Le Saulchoir, 1970.

ALCIATI, Roberto. "Origene, gli antropomorfiti e Cassiano: Le ragioni di una relazione istituta." *Adamantius* 19 (2013): 96–110.

ALEXANDRE, Monique. "Le statut des questions concernant la matière dans le *Peri Archôn*." In *Origeniana: Premier colloque international des études origéniennes (Montserrat, 18–21 septembre 1973)*, dirigé par Henri Crouzel, Gennaro Lomiento, et Josep Rius-Camps, 63–81. Quaderni di "Vetera Christianorum" 12. Bari: Istituto di letteratura cristiana antica, Università di Bari, 1975.

ALFÖLDI, Andreas. "Die Geschichte des Throntabernakels." *La nouvelle clio* 1/2 (1949/1950): 537–566.

ALIMONTI, Terenzio. "Apuleio e l'arcaismo in Claudiano Mamerto." In *Forma futuri: Studi in onore del Cardinale Michele Pellegrino*, a cura di Terenzio Alimonti, Francesco Bolgiani, et al., 189–228. Turin: Bottega d'Erasmo, 1975.

ALLISON, Dale C. "The Silence of the Angels: Reflections on the Songs of the Sabbath Sacrifice." *Revue de Qumrân* 13 (1988): 189–197.

ALTANER, Berthold. "Wer ist der Verfasser des *Tractatus in Isaiam* VI 1–7 (ed. G. Morin, Anecdota Maredsolana III 3, Maredsous 1903, 103–122): Ein Forschungsbericht." *Theologische Revue* 42 (1943): 147–151. (= idem, *Kleine patristische Schriften*, herausgegeben von Günter Glockmann, 483–488. TU 83. Berlin: Akademie-Verlag, 1967.)

ALVAR, Jaime Ezquerra. *Romanising Oriental Gods: Myth, Salvation, and Ethics in the Cults of Cybele, Isis, and Mithras*. Translated and edited by Richard Gordon. Religions in the Graeco-Roman World 165. Leiden: Brill, 2008.

AMSLER, Frédéric. "État de la recherche récente sur le roman Pseudo-Clémentin." In *Nouvelles intrigues pseudo-Clémentines. Plots in the Pseudo-Clementine Romance: Actes du deuxième colloque international sur la littérature apocryphe chrétienne, Lausanne—Genève, 30 août–2 septembre 2006*, édités par Frédéric Amsler, Albert Frey, Charlotte Touati, et Renée Girardet, 25–45. Publications de l'Institut Romand des Sciences Bibliques 6. Prahins: Éditions du Zèbre, 2008.

ANDRES, Friedrich. "Daimon." In *Paulys Realencyclopädie der classischen Altertumswissenschaft*. Supplementband 3: 267–322. Stuttgart: Metzler, 1918.

ANDRESEN, Carl. *Logos und Nomos: Die Polemik des Kelsos wider das Christentum*. Arbeiten zur Kirchengeschichte 30. Berlin: De Gruyter, 1955.

———. "Zur Dogmengeschichte der Alten Kirche." *Theologische Literaturzeitung* 84 (1959): 81–88. (= idem, *Theologie und Kirche im Horizont der Antike: Gesammelte Aufsätze zur Geschichte der Alten Kirche*, herausgegeben von Peter Gemeinhardt, 37–45. Arbeiten zur Kirchengeschichte 112. Berlin/New York: De Gruyter, 2009.)

ANGERSTORFER, Ingeborg. *Melito und das Judentum*. Diss. theol. masch., Regensburg, 1985.

ARMSTRONG, Arthur H. "Beauty and the Discovery of Divinity in the Thought of Plotinus." In *Kephalaion: Studies in Greek Philosophy and Its Continuation Offered to Cornelia Johanna de Vogel*, edited by Jaap Mansfeld and Lambertus M. de Rijk, 155–163. Philosophical Texts and Studies 23. Assen: Van Gorcum, 1975. (= idem, *Plotinian and Christian Studies*, nr. XIX. Variorum Collected Studies Series 102. Farnham: Ashgate, 1979.)

ASMUS, Rudolf. *Das Leben des Philosophen Isidoros von Damaskios aus Damaskos*. Philosophische Bibliothek 125. Leipzig: Meiner, 1911.

———. "Zur Rekonstruktion von Damascius' Leben des Isidorus." *Byzantinische Zeitschrift* 18 (1909): 424–480.

ASSMANN, Jan. "Primat und Transzendenz: Struktur und Genese der ägyptischen Vorstellung eines höchsten Wesens." In *Aspekte der ägyptischen Religion*, herausgegeben von Wolfhart Westendorf, 7–42. Göttinger Orientforschungen. Reihe 4 Ägypten 9. Wiesbaden: Harrassowitz, 1979.

ATTRIDGE, Harold W. "The Philosophical Critique of Religion under the Early Empire." In *ANRW* II, *Prinzipat*, 16.2, *Religion (Heidentum: Römische Religion, Allgemeines [Forts.])*, herausgegeben von Wolfgang Haase, 45–78. Berlin/New York: De Gruyter, 1978.

AUFFARTH, Christoph. "Das angemessene Bild Gottes: Der Olympische Zeus, antike Bildkonvention und die Christologie." In *Tekmeria: Archäologische Zeugnisse in ihrer kulturhistorischen und politischen Dimension; Beiträge für Werner Gauer*, herausgegeben von Natascha Kreutz und Beat Schweizer, 1–23. Münster: Scriptorium, 2006.

———. "Götterbilder im römischen Griechenland: Vom Tempel zum Museum." In *Ritual Dynamics and Religious Change in the Roman Empire: Proceedings of the Eighth Workshop of the International Network Impact of the Empire (Heidelberg, July 5–7, 2007)*, edited by Olivier

Hekster, Sebastian Schmidt-Hofner, and Christian Witschel, 306–325. Impact of Empire 9. Leiden/Boston: Brill, 2009.

AVEMARIE, Friedrich. "Rivalität zwischen Gott und seinen Paladinen: Beobachtungen zum Monotheismus in der rabbinischen Literatur." In *Gott— Götter—Götzen: XIV. Europäischer Kongress für Theologie (11.–15. September 2011 in Zürich)*, herausgegeben von Christoph Schwöbel, 353– 366. Veröffentlichungen der wissenschaftlichen Gesellschaft für Theologie 38. Leipzig: Evangelische Verlagsanstalt, 2013.

AYRES, Larry M. "The Work of the Morgan Master at Winchester and English Painting of the Early Gothic Period." *Art Bulletin* 56 (1974): 201–223.

BABUT, Daniel. "Sur les dieux d'Epicure." *Elenchos* 26 (2005): 79–110.

BACHT, Heinrich. "Einfalt." In *Reallexikon für Antike und Christentum*, 4: 821–840. Stuttgart: Hiersemann, 1959.

BÄBLER, Balbina. "Der Zeus von Olympia." In Dio Chrysostomus, *Oratio XII, De dei cognitione*. Dion von Prusa. *Olympische Rede oder über die erste Erkenntnis Gottes*. Eingeleitet, übersetzt und interpretiert von Hans-Josef Klauck, mit einem archäologischen Beitrag von Balbina Bäbler, 216–238. SAPERE 2. Darmstadt: Wissenschaftliche Buchgesellschaft, 2000.

BAGUETTE, Charles. "Une période stoïcienne dans l'évolution de la pensée de saint Augustin." *Revue des études augustiniennes* 16 (1970): 47–77.

BALDWIN, Matthew C. *Whose Acts of Peter? Text and Historical Context of the Actus Vercellensis*. WUNT 2/196. Tübingen: Mohr Siebeck, 2005.

BALTES, Matthias. "Idee (Ideenlehre)." In *Reallexikon für Antike und Christentum* 17: 213–246. Stuttgart: Hiersemann, 1996.

———. "Muß die 'Landkarte des Mittelplatonismus' neu gezeichnet werden?" In idem, *ΔΙΑΝΟΗΜΑΤΑ: Kleine Schriften zu Platon und zum Platonismus*, herausgegeben von Annette Hüffmeier, Marie-Luise Lakmann und Matthias Vorwerk, 327–350. Beiträge zur Altertumskunde 123. Stuttgart/ Leipzig: Teubner, 1999.

BALTZLY, Dirk. "Is Plato's Timaeus Panentheistic?" *Sophia* 49 (2010): 193–215.

———. "Stoic Pantheism." *Sophia* 34 (2003): 3–33.

———. "What Goes Up: Proclus against Aristotle on the Fifth Element." *Australasian Journal of Philosophy* 80 (2002): 261–287.

BANEV, Krastu. *Theophilus of Alexandria and the First Origenist Controversy. Rhetorik and Power*. OECS. Oxford: Oxford University Press, 2015.

BARBEL, Joseph. *Christos Angelos: Die Anschauung von Christus als Bote und Engel in der gelehrten und volkstümlichen Literatur des christlichen Altertums, zugleich ein Beitrag zur Geschichte des Ursprungs und der Fortdauer des Arianismus*. Theophaneia 3. Bonn: Hanstein, 1941.

———. "Zur 'Engels-Trinitätslehre' im Urchristentum." *Theologische Revue* 54 (1958): 50–58.

BAR-KOCHVA, Bezalel. *The Image of the Jews in Greek Literature: The Hellenistic Period*. Hellenistic Culture and Society 51. Berkeley/Los Angeles/ London: University of California Press, 2010.

BARNES, Timothy D. *Athanasius and Constantius: Theology and Politics in the Constantinian Empire.* Cambridge, Mass./London: Harvard University Press, 1993.

———. "Ultimus Antoninorum." In *Bonner Historia-Augusta-Colloquium 1970,* herausgegeben von Andreas Alföldi unter Mitwirkung von Johannes Straub, 53–74. Antiquitas. Reihe 4. Beiträge zur Historia-Augusta-Forschung 10. Bonn: Habelt, 1972.

BARR, James. "Theophany and Anthropomorphism in the Old Testament." In *Congress Volume Oxford 1959,* 31–38. VTSup 7. Leiden: Brill, 1960.

BARTH, Carola. *Die Interpretation des Neuen Testaments in der valentinianischen Gnosis.* TU 37/3. Leipzig: Hinrichs, 1911.

BAUCHHENSS, Gerhard. "Wie die Römer die Götter gebildet—Gottesbild und Götterbilder." In *Götterbilder—Menschenbilder: Religion und Kulte in Carnuntum,* herausgegeben von Franz Humer und Gabrielle Kremer, 30–43. Wien: AV + Astoria Druckzentrum, 2011.

BAUER, Adolf, und Josef STRZYGOWSKI. *Eine alexandrinische Weltchronik, Text und Miniaturen eines griechischen Papyrus der Sammlung W. Goleniščev herausgegeben und erklärt.* Denkschriften der Kaiserlichen Akademie der Wissenschaften in Wien. Philosophisch-historische Klasse 51/2. Wien: Gerold, 1905.

BAUER, Karl-Adolf. *Leiblichkeit, das Ende aller Werke Gottes: Die Bedeutung der Leiblichkeit des Menschen bei Paulus.* Studien zum Neuen Testament 4. Gütersloh: Mohn, 1971.

BAUER, Walter. *Das Leben Jesu im Zeitalter der neutestamentlichen Apokryphen.* Darmstadt: Wissenschaftliche Buchgesellschaft, 1967. (= Tübingen: Mohr Siebeck, 1909.)

BAUMGARTEN, Joseph M. "The Book of Elkesai and Merkabah Mysticism." *JSJ* 17 (1986): 212–223, 257–259.

———. "The Qumran Sabbath Shirot and Rabbinic Merkabah Traditions." *Révue de Qumrân* 13 (1988): 199–213.

BAYER, Oswald. "Gottes Leiblichkeit: Zum Leben und Werk Friedrich Christoph Oetingers." In idem, *Leibliches Wort: Reformation und Neuzeit im Konflikt.* Tübingen: Mohr Siebeck, 1992.

BEATRICE, Pier F. "Quosdam Platonicorum Libros: The Platonic Readings of Augustine in Milan." *VC* 43 (1989): 248–281.

BECKAERT, André. "L'évolution de l'intellectualisme grec vers la pensée religieuse et la relève de la philosophie par la pensée chrétienne." *Revue des études byzantines* 19 (1961): 44–62.

BECKER, Hans-Jürgen. "The Magic of the Name and Palestinian Rabbinic Literature." In *The Talmud Yerushalmi and Graeco-Roman Culture,* edited by Peter Schäfer, 391–407. TSAJ 93. Tübingen: Mohr Siebeck, 2002.

BEDROSIAN, Matthias. *New Dictionary Armenian-English.* Venedig: S. Lazarus Armenian Academy, 1875–1879.

BELLEFONDS, Pascale Linant de, u.a. "Rites et activités relatifs aux images de culte." In *Purification, Initiation, Heroization, Apotheosis, Banquet, Dance, Music, Cult, Images.* Thesaurus cultus et rituum antiquorum, vol. 2, edited by Jean-Charles Balty, 418–507. Los Angeles: Getty, 2004.

BELTING, Hans. *Bild und Kult: Eine Geschichte des Bildes vor dem Zeitalter der Kunst.* 2. Aufl. München: Beck, 1993. (= 1991.)

BENDRATH, Christian. *Leibhaftigkeit: Jakob Böhmes Inkarnationsmorphologie.* Theologische Bibliothek Töpelmann 97. Berlin/New York: De Gruyter, 1999.

BENGSCH, Alfred. *Heilsgeschichte und Heilswissen: Eine Untersuchung zur Struktur und Entfaltung des theologischen Denkens im Werk "Adversus haereses" des hl. Irenäus von Lyon.* Erfurter Theologische Studien 3. Leipzig: St. Benno, 1957.

BERGER, Klaus. *Ist Gott Person? Ein Weg zum Verstehen des christlichen Gottesbildes.* Gütersloh: Gütersloher Verlagshaus, 2004.

BERGER, Pamela. "The Temples/Tabernacles in the Dura-Europos Synagogue Paintings." In *Dura Europos: Crossroads of Antiquity*, edited by Lisa R. Brody and Gail L. Hoffman, 123–140. Chestnut Hill, Mass.: McMullen Museum of Art, Boston College, 2011.

BERGJAN, Silke-Petra. "Die dogmatische Funktionalisierung der Exegese nach Theodoret von Cyrus." In *Christliche Exegese zwischen Nicaea und Chalcedon*, herausgegeben von Johannes van Oort und Ulrich Wickert, 32–48. Kampen: Kok Pharos, 1992.

BERNOULLI, Carl A. *Der Schriftstellerkatalog des Hieronymus: Ein Beitrag zur Geschichte der altchristlichen Litteratur.* Freiburg im Breisgau: Mohr, 1895.

BERRENS, Stephan. *Sonnenkult und Kaisertum von den Severern bis zu Constantin I. (193–337 n. Chr.).* Historia. Einzelschriften 185. Stuttgart: Steiner, 2004.

BEST, Thomas F. "The Transfiguration: A Select Bibliography." *JETS* 24 (1981): 157–161.

BESTER, Dörte. *Körperbilder in den Psalmen: Studien zu Psalm 22 und verwandten Texten.* FAT 2/24. Tübingen: Mohr Siebeck, 2007.

BEUTEL, Albrecht. *Lichtenberg und die Religion: Aspekte einer vielschichtigen Konstellation.* BHT 93. Tübingen: Mohr Siebeck, 1996.

BEVAN, George A., and Patrick T. R. GRAY. "The Trial of Eutyches: A New Interpretation." *Byzantinische Zeitschrift* 101 (2008): 617–657.

BEYER, Hans-Veit. "Die Lichtlehre der Mönche des vierzehnten und des vierten Jahrhunderts, erörtert am Beispiel des Gregorios Sinaïtes, des Euagrios Pontikos und des Ps.-Makarios/Symeon." *Jahrbuch der Österreichischen Byzantinistik* 31 (1981): 473–512.

BEYSCHLAG, Karlmann. *Grundriss der Dogmengeschichte.* Bd. 2, *Gott und Mensch.* Tl. 1, *Das christologische Dogma.* Grundrisse 3/1. Darmstadt: Wissenschaftliche Buchgesellschaft, 1991.

———. "Zur Geschichte der Bergpredigt in der Alten Kirche." *ZTK* 74 (1977): 291–322.

BICKEL, Ernst. "Inlocalitas: Zur neupythagoreischen Metaphysik." In *Immanuel Kant: Festschrift zur zweiten Jahrhundertfeier seines Geburtstages*, herausgegeben von der Albertus-Universität in Königsberg in Preußen, 17–26. Leipzig: Dietrich'sche Verlagsbuchhandlung, 1924.

BICKERMAN, Elias J. "Diva Augusta Marciana." *American Journal of Philology* 95 (1974): 362–376.

BIDEZ, Joseph. *Vie de Porphyre: Le philosophe néoplatonicien.* Receuil de travaux publiés par la Faculté de philosophie et lettres. Université de Gand 43. Gand: van Goethem, 1913. (= Hildesheim: Olms, 1964/1980.)

BIENERT, Wolfgang A. *"Allegoria" und "Anagoge" bei Didymos dem Blinden von Alexandria.* PTS 13. Berlin/New York: De Gruyter, 1972.

———. "Athanasius von Alexandrien und Origenes." In *Liturgica, Second Century, Alexandria before Nicaea, Athanasius and the Arian Controversy.* Papers presented at the Eleventh International Conference on Patristic Studies held in Oxford 1991, edited by Elizabeth A. Livingstone, 360–364. StPatr 26. Leuven: Peeters, 1993.

BINGÖL, Orhan. *Magnesia am Mäander. Magnesia ad Maeandrum.* Homer Reihe: Antike Städte 6. Istanbul: Homer Kitabevi, 2007.

BINNS, John. *Ascetics and Ambassadors of Christ: The Monasteries of Palestine 314–631.* OECS. Oxford: Oxford University Press, 1994.

BLOCH, Marc. *The Royal Touch: Sacred Monarchy and Scrofula in England and France.* Translated from the French by J. E. Anderson. Abingdon, Oxon.: Routledge, 1973. (= idem, *Les rois thaumaturges: Étude sur le caractère surnaturel attribué à la puissance royale, particulièrement en France et en Angleterre.* Strasbourg: Istra, 1924.)

BLOCH, Maurice. "From Cognition to Ideology." In *Ritual, History and Power: Selected Papers in Anthropology.* London School of Economics Monographs on Social Anthropology 58. London/Atlantic Highlands, N.J.: Athlone Press, 1989.

BLOCH, Philipp. "Die Yorede Merkavah, die Mystiker der Gaonenzeit und ihr Einfluss auf die Liturgie." *Monatsschrift für Geschichte und Wissenschaft des Judentums* 37 (1893): 18–25, 69–74, 257–266, 305–311.

BLOCH, René S. *Antike Vorstellungen vom Judentum: Der Judenexkurs des Tacitus im Rahmen der griechisch-römischen Ethnographie.* Historia. Einzelschriften 160. Stuttgart: Steiner, 2002.

BLUM, Erhard. "Die Wandinschriften 4.2 und 4.6 sowie die Pithos-Inschrift 3.9 aus *Kuntillet 'Aǧrūd." Zeitschrift des Deutschen Palästina-Vereins* 129 (2013): 21–54.

BODÉÜS, Richard. *Aristotle and the Theology of the Living Immortals.* Albany: State University of New York Press, 2000.

BOECKH, August. *Philolaos des Pythagoreers Lehren nebst den Bruchstücken seines Werkes.* Berlin: Vossische Buchhandlung, 1819.

BÖHM, Thomas. "Origenes—Theologe und (Neu-)Platoniker? Oder: Wem soll man mißtrauen—Eusebius oder Porphyrius?" *Adamantius* 8 (2002): 7–23.

———. "Unbegreiflichkeit Gottes bei Origenes und Unsagbarkeit des Einen bei Plotin—ein Strukturvergleich." In *Origeniana Octava: Origen and the Alexandrian Tradition; Papers of the 8th International Origen Congress Pisa, 27–31 August 2001,* edited by Lorenzo Perrone in collaboration with Paolo Bernardini and Diego Marchini, 1: 451–463. BETL 164. Leuven: Peeters, 2003.

BOERI, Marcelo D. "The Stoics on Bodies and Incorporeals." *Review of Metaphysics* 54 (2001): 723–752.

BOLL, Franz. *Sphaera: Neue griechische Texte und Untersuchungen zur Geschichte der Sternbilder.* Leipzig: Teubner, 1903. (= Hildesheim: Olms, 1967.)

BÖMER, Franz. *Der lateinische Neuplatonismus und Neupythagoreismus und Claudianus Mamertus in Sprache und Philosophie.* Klassisch-philologische Studien 7. Leipzig: Harrassowitz, 1936.

BOMMES, Karin. *Weizen Gottes: Untersuchungen zur Theologie des Martyriums bei Ignatius von Antiochien.* Theophaneia 27. Köln/Bonn: Hanstein, 1976.

BONAZZI, Mauro. "Eudorus of Alexandria and the 'Pythagorean' pseudepigrapha." In *On Pythagoreanism*, edited by Gabriele Cornelli, Richard McKirahan, and Constantinos Macris, 385–404. Studia Praesocratica 5. Berlin: De Gruyter, 2013.

BONWETSCH, Georg N. *Die apokryphe "Leiter Jakobs."* Nachrichten der königlichen Gesellschaft der Wissenschaften zu Göttingen. Philologisch-historische Klasse 7. Göttingen: Vandenhoeck & Ruprecht, 1900.

BORDO, Susan, and Monica UDVARDY. "Body, the." In *New Dictionary of the History of Ideas*, edited by Maryanne Cline Horowitz, 1: 230–238. Detroit: Thomson Gale, 2005.

BORSCHE, Tilman. "Leib, Körper." In *Historisches Wörterbuch der Philosophie*, 5: 173–178. Darmstadt: Wissenschaftliche Buchgesellschaft, 1980.

BOSCHUNG, Dietrich. "Kultbilder als Vermittler religiöser Vorstellungen." In *Kult und Kommunikation: Medien in Heiligtümern der Antike*, herausgegeben von Christian Frevel und Henner von Hesberg, 63–87. Schriften des Lehr- und Forschungszentrums für die antiken Kulturen des Mittelmeerraumes 4. Wiesbaden: Reichert, 2007.

BOSTOCK, Gerald. "Quality and Corporeity in Origen." In *Origeniana Secunda: Second colloque international des études origéniennes (Bari, 20–23 septembre 1977)*, textes rassemblés par Henri Crouzel et Antonio Quacquarelli, 323–337. Quaderni di "Vetera Christianorum" 15. Rome: Edizioni dell'Ateneo, 1980.

BÖTTRICH, Christfried. "Das slavische Henochbuch." In *Apokalypsen*. Jüdische Schriften aus hellenistisch-römischer Zeit 5/7. Gütersloh: Mohn, 1995.

———. "Konturen des 'Menschensohnes' in äthHen 37–71." In *Gottessohn und Menschensohn: Exegetische Studien zu zwei Paradigmen biblischer Intertextualität*, herausgegeben von Dieter Sänger, 53–90. Biblisch-theologische Studien 67. Neukirchen-Vluyn: Neukirchener, 2004.

BOULLUEC, Alain Le. "Die 'Schule' von Alexandrien." In *Die Zeit des Anfangs (bis 250)*, herausgegeben von Luce Pietri, 576–621. Die Geschichte des Christentums: Religion—Politik—Kultur 1. Freiburg: Herder, 2003.

———. *La notion d'hérésie dans la littérature grecque IIe–IIIe siècles.* Tome 2, *Clément d'Alexandrie et Origène.* Études Augustiniennes. Paris: Études Augustiniennes, 1985.

BOUSSET, Wilhelm. *Apophthegmata. Studien zur Geschichte des ältesten Mönchtums.* Tübingen: Mohr Siebeck, 1923.

————. *Jüdisch-christlicher Schulbetrieb in Alexandria und Rom: Literarische Untersuchungen zu Philo und Clemens von Alexandrien, Justin und Irenäus*. FRLANT 23. Göttingen: Vandenhoeck & Ruprecht, 1915.

BOUSTAN, Ra'Anan S. "The Study of Heikhalot Literature: Between Mystical Experience and Textual Artifact." *Currents in Biblical Research* 6 (2007): 130–160.

BOUYER, Louis. "Mysticism: An Essay on the History of the Word." In *Understanding Mysticism*, edited by Richard Woods, 42–55. London: Athlone Press, 1980.

BOVON, François. *Das Evangelium nach Lukas*. Tlbd. 1, *Lk 1,1–9,50*. EKKNT III/1. Zürich: Benziger / Neukirchen-Vluyn: Neukirchener, 1989.

————. *Das Evangelium nach Lukas*. Tlbd. 4, *Lk 19,28–24,53*. EKKNT III/4. Neukirchen-Vluyn: Neukirchener / Düsseldorf: Patmos Verlag, 2009.

BOWERSOCK, Glen W. *Martyrdom and Rome*. The Wiles Lectures given at the Queen's University of Belfast. Cambridge: Cambridge University Press, 1995.

BOYARIN, Daniel. *Border Lines: The Partition of Judaeo-Christianity*. Philadelphia: University of Pennsylvania Press, 2004.

————. *Dying for God: Martyrdom and the Making of Christianity and Judaism*. Stanford: Stanford University Press, 1999.

BRACHT, Katharina. "God and Methodius: Use of, and Background to, the Term ἀπροσδεής as a Description of God in the Works of Methodius of Olympus." In *God in Early Christian Thought: Essays in Memory of Lloyd G. Patterson*, edited by Andrew B. McGowan, Brian E. Daley, and Timothy J. Gaden, 105–122. SuppVC 94. Leiden: Brill, 2009.

BRADSHAW, Paul F. "Liturgy and 'Living Literature.'" In *Liturgy in Dialogue: Essays in Memory of Ronald Jasper*, edited by Paul Bradshaw and Bryan Spinks, 138–153. London: SPCK, 1994.

————. *The Search for the Origins of Christian Worship: Sources and Methods for the Study of Early Liturgy*. 2nd ed. London: SPCK; New York: Oxford University Press, 2002.

BRÄNDLE, Rudolf. *Johannes Chrysostomus: Bischof—Reformer—Märtyrer*. Stuttgart: Kohlhammer, 1999.

BRAKKE, David. *Athanasius and the Politics of Asceticism*. OECS. Oxford: Clarendon; New York: Oxford University Press, 1995.

————. *Demons and the Making of the Monk: Spiritual Combat in Early Christianity*. Cambridge, Mass./London: Harvard University Press, 2006.

BRANDT, Wilhelm. *Elchasai, ein Religionsstifter und sein Werk: Beiträge zur jüdischen, christlichen und allgemeinen Religionsgeschichte in späthellenistischer Zeit, mit Berücksichtigung der Sekten der syrischen Sampsäer und der arabaischen Mghtasila*. Leipzig: Hinrichs, 1912. (= Amsterdam: Philo Press, 1971.)

BRANKAER, Johanna. *Die Gnosis: Texte und Kommentar*. Wiesbaden: Marixverlag, 2010.

BRATKE, Eduard. *Das sogenannte Religionsgespräch am Hof der Sasaniden*. TU 19/3. Leipzig: Hinrichs, 1899.

BRAUN, René. *Deus Christianorum: Recherches sur le vocabulaire doctrinal de Tertullien*. 2e éd. revue et augmentée. Études Augustiniennes. Paris: Études Augustiniennes, 1977.

BRENK, Frederick E. "In the Light of the Moon: Demonology in the Early Imperial Period." In *ANRW* II, *Prinzipat*, 16.3, *Religion (Heidentum: Römische Religion, Allgemeines [Forts.])*, herausgegeben von Wolfgang Haase, 2068–2145. Berlin/New York: De Gruyter, 1986.

BRENNECKE, Hanns Ch. "Die Styliten als Römer." In *Leitbilder aus Kunst und Literatur*, herausgegeben von Jürgen Dummer und Meinolf Vielberg, 9–30. Altertumswissenschaftliches Kolloquium 5. Stuttgart: Steiner, 2002.

———. "Wie man einen Heiligen politisch instrumentalisiert: Der Heilige Simeon Stylites und die Synode von Chalkedon." In *Theologie und Kultur: Geschichten einer Wechselbeziehung; Festschrift zum einhundertfünfzigjährigen Bestehen des Lehrstuhls für Christliche Archäologie und Kirchliche Kunst an der Humboldt-Universität zu Berlin*, herausgegeben von Gerlinde Strohmaier-Wiederanders, 237–260. Halle: Gursky, 1999.

BREYTENBACH, Cilliers. *Paulus und Barnabas in der Provinz Galatien: Studien zu Apostelgeschichte 13f.; 16,6; 18,23 und den Adressaten des Galaterbriefes*. AGJU 38. Leiden: Brill, 1996.

BRINKER, Wolfram. "Seele." In *Platon-Lexikon: Begriffswörterbuch zu Platon und der platonischen Tradition*, herausgegeben von Christian Schäfer, 253–258. Darmstadt: Wissenschaftliche Buchgesellschaft, 2007.

BROCK, Sebastian. "Clothing Metaphors as a Means of Theological Expression in Syriac Tradition." In *Typus, Symbol, Allegorie bei den östlichen Vätern und ihre Parallelen im Mittelalter*, herausgegeben von Margot Schmidt in Zusammenarbeit mit Carl F. Geyer, 11–40. Eichstätter Beiträge 4. Regensburg: Pustet, 1982.

———. "Jewish Traditions in Syriac Sources." *JJS* 30 (1979): 212–232.

———. "A Report from a Supporter of Severos on Trouble in Alexandria." In *Synaxis katholike. Beiträge zu Gottesdienst und Geschichte der fünf altkirchlichen Patriarchate für Heinzgerd Brakmann zum 70. Geburtstag*, herausgegeben von Diliana Atanassova und Tinatin Chronz, 47–64. Orientalia—patristica—oecumenica 6/1. Wien/Berlin: Lit-Verlag, 2014.

BRODERSEN, Kai. *Die sieben Weltwunder: Legendäre Kunst- und Bauwerke der Antike*. C. H. Beck Wissen in der Beck'schen Reihe 2029. 7. Aufl. München: Beck, 2007.

BROEK, Roelof van den. "The Sarapis Oracle in Macrobius, Sat. I, 20, 16f." In *Hommages à Maarten J. Vermaseren: Recueil d'études offert par les auteurs de la Série Études préliminaires aux religions orientales dans l'Empire romain à Maarten J. Vermaseren à l'occasion de son soixantième anniversaire le 7 avril 1978*, tome 1, édité par Margreet B. de Boer et T. A. Edridge, 123–141. Études préliminaires aux religions orientales dans l'Empire romain 68. Leiden: Brill, 1978.

BROISE, Henri, et Yvon THÉBERT. "Élagabal et le complexe religieux de la Vigna Barberini: Heliogabalium in Palatino monte iuxta aedes imperatorias consecravit eique templum fecit (HA, Ant. Heliog., III, 4)." *Mélanges de l'École française de Rome: Antiquité* 111 (1999): 729–747.

BROISE, René de la. *Mamerti Claudiani Vita Ejusque Doctrina de Anima Hominis: Thesim Facultati Litterarum Parisiensi Proponebat.* Paris: Retaux-Bray, 1890.

BROWN, Peter. *The Body and Society.* Twentieth anniversary edition with a new introduction. Columbia Classics in Religion. New York: Columbia University Press, 2008.

———. *The Body and Society: Men, Women and Sexual Renunciation in Early Christianity.* Lectures on the History of Religions 13. New York: Columbia University Press, 1988.

———. *A Life of Learning.* Charles Homer Haskins Lecture for 2003. ACLS Occasional Paper 55. Available online at http://www.acls.org/Publications/OP/Haskins/2003_PeterBrown.pdf (last accessed 1 May 2019).

———. *The Ransom of the Soul: Afterlife and Wealth in Early Western Christianity.* Cambridge, Mass./London: Harvard University Press, 2015.

———. "Report." In *Symbolae Osloenses Debate: The World of Late Antiquity Revisited* (= Symbolae Osloenses 72) (1997): 5–30.

BROX, Norbert. "Der einfache Glaube und die Theologie: Zur altkirchlichen Geschichte eines Dauerproblems." *Kairos* 14 (1972): 161–187. (= idem, *Das Frühchristentum: Schriften zur Historischen Theologie*, herausgegeben von Franz Dünzl, Alfons Fürst und Ferdinand R. Prostmeier, 305–336. Freiburg: Herder, 2000.)

———. "'Doketismus'—eine Problemanzeige." *Zeitschrift für Kirchengeschichte* 95 (1984): 301–314.

BULHART, Vinzenz. "Buytaert, Eligius M.: L'héritage littéraire d'Eusèbe d'Émèse (book review)." *Gnomon* 30 (1958): 537–540.

BULTMANN, Rudolf. *Kerygma und Mythos.* Bd. 1, *Ein theologisches Gespräch*, herausgegeben von Hans-Werner Bartsch. Theologische Forschung 1. 5. erweiterte Aufl. Hamburg-Bergstedt: Reich, 1967.

———. *Kerygma und Mythos.* Bd. 2, *Diskussionen und Stimmen des In- und Auslandes,* herausgegeben von Hans-Werner Bartsch. Theologische Forschung 2. Hamburg-Bergstedt: Reich, 1965.

———. *Kerygma und Mythos.* Bd. 3, *Das Gespräch mit der Philosophie*, herausgegeben von Hans-Werner Bartsch. Theologische Forschung 5. Hamburg-Bergstedt: Reich, 1966.

———. *Kerygma und Mythos.* Bd. 4, *Das Gespräch mit der Philosophie*, herausgegeben von Hans-Werner Bartsch. Theologische Forschung 8. Hamburg-Bergstedt: Reich, 1966.

———. *Neues Testament und Mythologie: Das Problem der Entmythologisierung der neutestamentlichen Verkündigung.* Nachdruck der 1941 erschienenen Fassung, herausgegeben von Eberhard Jüngel. Beiträge zur Evangelischen Theologie 96. München: Kaiser, 1985.

———. "Welchen Sinn hat es, von Gott zu reden?" *Theologische Blätter* 4 (1925): 129–135. (= idem, *Glauben und Verstehen: Gesammelte Aufsätze.* Bd. 1, 26–37. Tübingen: Mohr Siebeck, 1933.)

———. "Zum Problem der Entmythologisierung." In *Kerygma und Mythos.* Bd. 2, *Diskussionen und Stimmen des In- und Auslandes*, herausgegeben von Hans-Werner Bartsch, 179–208. Theologische Forschung 2. Hamburg-Bergstedt: Reich, 1965.

BUMAZHNOV, Dmitrij. *Der Mensch als Gottes Bild im christlichen Ägypten: Studien zu Gen 1,26 in zwei koptischen Quellen des 4.–5. Jahrhunderts.* Studien und Texte zu Antike und Christentum 34. Tübingen: Mohr Siebeck, 2006.

————. "Einige Aspekte der Nachwirkung des Ankoratus und des Panarion des hl. Epiphanius von Salamis in der früheren monastischen Tradition." *Adamantius* 11 (2005): 158–178.

————. "Kann man Gott festhalten? Eine frühchristliche Diskussion und deren Hintergründe." In *Christianity in Egypt: Literary Production and Intellectual Trends; Studies in Honor of Tito Orlandi*, edited by Paola Buzi und Alberto Camplani, 165–176. Studia Ephemeridis Augustinianum 125. Rome: Institutum Patristicum Augustinianum, 2011.

————. *Visio mystica im Spannungsfeld frühchristlicher Überlieferungen: Die Lehre der sogenannten Antoniusbriefe von der Gottes- und Engelschau und das Problem unterschiedlicher spiritueller Traditionen im frühen ägyptischen Mönchtum.* Studien und Texte zu Antike und Christentum 52. Tübingen: Mohr Siebeck, 2009.

BUNGE, Gabriel. "Aktive und kontemplative Weise des Betens im Traktat *De oratione* des Evagrios Pontikos." *Studia Monastica* 41 (1999): 211–227. (= idem, *"Die Lehren der heiligen Väter" (RB 73, 2): Aufsätze zu Evagrios Pontikos aus drei Jahrzehnten*, herausgegeben von Jakobus Kaffanke, 23–40. Weisungen der Väter 11. Beuron: Beuroner Kunstverlag, 2011.)

————. *Das Geistgebet: Studien zum Traktat De oratione des Evagrios Pontikos.* Schriftenreihe des Zentrums patristischer Spiritualität Koinonia im Erzbistum Köln 25. Köln: Luthe, 1987.

————. "Hénade ou Monade? Au sujet de deux notions centrales de la terminologie évagrienne." *Le Muséon* 102 (1989): 69–91.

————. *"In Geist und Wahrheit": Studien zu den 153 Kapiteln "Über das Gebet" des Evagrios Pontikos.* Übersetzt von Hagia Witzenrath. Hereditas 27. Bonn: Borengässer, 2010.

————. "Mysterium Unitatis: Der Gedanke der Einheit von Schöpfer und Geschöpf in der evagrianischen Mystik." *Freiburger Zeitschrift für Philosophie und Theologie* 36 (1989): 449–469. (= idem, *"Die Lehren der heiligen Väter" (RB 73, 2): Aufsätze zu Evagrios Pontikos aus drei Jahrzehnten*, herausgegeben von Jakobus Kaffanke, 98–120. Weisungen der Väter 11. Beuron: Beuroner Kunstverlag, 2011.)

————. "Origenismus-Gnostizismus: Zum geistesgeschichtlichen Standort des Evagrios Pontikos." *VC* 40 (1986): 24–54. (= idem, *"Die Lehren der heiligen Väter" (RB 73, 2): Aufsätze zu Evagrios Pontikos aus drei Jahrzehnten*, herausgegeben von Jakobus Kaffanke, 121–154. Weisungen der Väter 11. Beuron: Beuroner Kunstverlag, 2011.)

BURGER, Christoph. *Aedificatio, fructus, utilitas: Johannes Gerson als Professor der Theologie und Kanzler der Universität Paris.* BHT 70. Tübingen: Mohr Siebeck, 1986.

BURGESS, Richard W., and Jitse H. F. DIJKSTRA. "The 'Alexandrian World Chronicle,' Its *Consularia* and the Date of the Destruction of the Serapeum (with an Appendix on the *Praefecti Augustales*)." *Millennium* 10 (2013): 39–113.

BURRUS, Virginia. "Carnal Excess: Flesh at the Limits of Imagination." *JECS* 17 (2009): 247–265.

BUTLER, Judith. *Bodies That Matter: On the Discursive Limits of "Sex."* New York/London: Routledge, 1993.

BUTTERWECK, Christel. *"Martyriumssehnsucht" in der Alten Kirche? Studien zur Darstellung und Deutung frühchristlicher Martyrien.* BHT 87. Tübingen: Mohr Siebeck, 1995.

BUYTAERT, Eligius M. "L'authenticité des dix-sept opuscules contenus dans le MS T. 523 sous le nom d'Eusèbe d'Emèse." *Revue d'histoire ecclésiastique* 43 (1948): 5–89.

———. *L'héritage littéraire d'Eusèbe d'Émèse: Étude critique et historique, textes.* Bibliothèque du Muséon 24. Louvain: Bureaux du Muséon, 1949.

BYNUM, Caroline Walker. "The Female Body and Religious Practice in the Later Middle Ages." In idem, *Fragmentation and Redemption: Essays on Gender and the Human Body in Medieval Religion*, 181–238. New York: Zone Books, 1992.

———. *The Resurrection of the Body in Western Christianity, 200–1336.* Lectures on the History of Religions. New Series 15. New York: Columbia University Press, 1995.

———. "Why All the Fuss about the Body? A Medievalist's Perspective." *Critical Inquiry* 22 (1995): 1–33.

CAMPENHAUSEN, Hans Freiherr von. *Bearbeitungen und Interpolationen des Polykarpmartyriums.* Sitzungsberichte der Heidelberger Akademie der Wissenschaften. Philosophisch-historische Klasse 3/1957. Heidelberg: Winter, 1957. (= idem, *Aus der Frühzeit des Christentums: Studien zur Kirchengeschichte des ersten und zweiten Jahrhunderts.* Tübingen: Mohr Siebeck, 1963.)

———. *Die Idee des Martyriums in der alten Kirche.* 2. durchgesehene und ergänzte Aufl. Göttingen: Vandenhoeck & Ruprecht, 1964.

CARNEY, James, Robin DUNBAR, Anna MACHIN, Tamás DÁVID-BARRETT, and Mauro SILVA JÚNIOR. "Social Psychology and the Comic-Book Superhero: A Darwinian Approach." *Philosophy and Literature* 38 (2014): A195–A215.

CASEY, Robert P. "Clement of Alexandria and the Beginnings of Christian Platonism." *HTR* 18 (1925): 39–101.

CASIDAY, Augustine. *Reconstructing the Theology of Evagrius Ponticus: Beyond Heresy.* Cambridge: Cambridge University Press, 2013.

CASPARI, Carl P. "Ein Glaubensbekenntniss des Bischofs Johannes von Jerusalem (386–417) in syrischer Übersetzung aus einer nitrischen Handschrift, sammt Allem, was uns sonst von Johannes übrig geblieben." In idem, *Ungedruckte, unbeachtete und wenig beachtete Quellen zur Geschichte des Taufsymbols und des Glaubenssymbols*, Tl. 1. Christiania: Malling, 1866. (= Brüssel: Culture et Civilisation, 1964.)

CAVALLERA, Ferdinand. *Le schisme d'Antioche (IVᵉ—Vᵉ siècle)*. Paris: Picard, 1905.

———. *Saint Jérôme, sa vie et son œuvre*. Spicilegium Sacrum Lovaniense 1 et 2. Louvain: Spicilegium Sacrum Lovaniense, 1922.

CERTEAU, Michel de. "'Mystique' au XVIIᵉ siecle: Le probleme du langage 'mystique.'" In *L'Homme devant Dieu: Mélanges Henri de Lubac*, 2: 267–291. Paris: Aubier, 1964.

CHADWICK, Henry. "The Latin Epitome of Melito's Homily on the Pascha." *JTS* 11 (1960): 76–82.

———. "Origen, Celsus, and the Resurrection of the Body." *HTR* 41 (1948): 83–102.

———. "Origen, Celsus, and the Stoa." *JTS* 48 (1947): 34–49.

———. *The Sentences of Sextus: A Contribution to the History of Early Christian Ethics*. Texts and Studies, n.s., 5. Cambridge: Cambridge University Press, 1959.

CHADWICK, Owen. *John Cassian: A Study in Primitive Monasticism*. Cambridge: Cambridge University Press, 1950. (= 2008.)

CHANIOTIS, Angelos. "Das Bankett des Damas und der Hymnos des Sosandros: Öffentlicher Diskurs über Rituale in den griechischen Städten der Kaiserzeit." In *Ritualdynamik: Kulturübergreifende Studien zur Theorie und Geschichte rituellen Handelns*, herausgegeben von Dietrich Harth und Gerrit J. Schenk, 291–304. Heidelberg: Synchron, 2004.

———. "Old Wine in a New Skin: Tradition and Innovation in the Cult Foundation of Alexander of Abonouteichos." *Electrum* 6 (2002): 67–85.

CHANTRAINE, Pierre. *Interférences de vocabulaire entre le grec et les langues européennes*. Studii clasice 2. Bucarest: Ed. academiei republicii populare romîne, 1960.

CHARLESWORTH, James H., and Carol A. NEWSOM, eds. *Angelic Liturgy: Songs of the Sabbath Sacrifice*. The Dead Sea Scrolls 4B. Tübingen: Mohr Siebeck, 1999.

CHATZIDAKIS, Manolis, and Gerry WALTERS. "An Encaustic Icon of Christ at Sinai." *Art Bulletin* 49 (1967): 197–208.

CHERBONNIER, Edmond La Beaume. "In Defense of Anthropomorphism." In *Reflections on Mormonism: Judaeo-Christian Parallels; Papers Delivered at the Religious Studies Center Symposium, Brigham Young University, March 10–11, 1978*, edited by Truman G. Madsen, 155–174. Religious Studies Series 4. Provo, Utah: Religious Studies Center, Brigham Young University and Bookcraft, 1978.

———. "The Logic of Biblical Anthropomorphism." *HTR* 55 (1962): 187–206.

CHESNUT, Glenn F. *The First Christian Histories: Eusebius, Socrates, Sozomen, Theodoret, and Evagrius*. 2nd ed., rev. and enlarged. Macon, Ga.: Mercer University Press; Leuven: Peeters, 1986.

CHESNUT, Roberta C. *Three Monophysite Christologies: Severus of Antioch, Philoxenus of Mabbug, and Jacob of Sarug*. Oxford Theological Monographs. Oxford: Oxford University Press, 1976.

CHICKERING, Roger. *Karl Lamprecht: A German Academic Life (1856–1915)*. Atlantic Highlands, N.J.: Humanities Press, 1993.

CHIESA, Bruno, and Wilfrid LOCKWOOD. *Ya'qūb al-Qirqisānī on Jewish Sects and Christianity: A Translation of 'Kitāb al-anwār,' Book I with Two Introductory Essays.* Judentum und Umwelt 10. Frankfurt am Main: Lang, 1984.

CHITTY, Derwas J. *The Desert a City: An Introduction to the Study of Egyptian and Palestinian Monasticism under the Christian Empire.* Crestwood, N.Y.: St Vladimir's Seminary Press, 1995. (= Oxford: Blackwell, 1966.)

CHRIST, Franz. *Menschlich von Gott reden: Das Problem des Anthropomorphismus bei Schleiermacher.* Ökumenische Theologie 10. Einsiedeln/Zürich/Köln: Benziger; Gütersloh: Gütersloher Verlagshaus Mohn, 1982.

CIRILLO, Luigi. *Elchasai e gli elchasaiti: Un contributo alla storia delle comunità giudeo-cristiane.* Cosenza: Marra, 1984.

CLARK, Elizabeth A. *The Origenist Controversy: The Cultural Construction of an Early Christian Debate.* Princeton, N.J.: Princeton University Press, 1992.

CLAUSS, Manfred. *Kaiser und Gott: Herrscherkult im römischen Reich.* Stuttgart/Leipzig: Teubner, 1999.

———. *Mithras: Kult und Mysterien.* München: Beck, 1990.

CLEMEN, Carl. "Tempel und Kult in Hierapolis." In *Pisciculi: Studien zur Religion und Kultur des Altertums; Franz Josef Dölger zum sechzigsten Geburtstage dargeboten von Freunden, Verehrern und Schülern*, herausgegeben von Theodor Klauser und Adolf Rücker, 66–69. Münster: Aschendorff, 1939.

CLEMEN, Otto. "Eine seltsame Christusreliquie." *Archiv für Kulturgeschichte* 7 (1909): 137–144. (= idem, *Kleine Schriften zur Reformationsgeschichte (1897–1944).* Bd. 3, *1907–1911*, herausgegeben von Ernst Koch, 193–200. Leipzig: Zentralantiquariat, 1983.)

COAKLEY, Sarah. "Introduction: Religion and the Body." In *Religion and the Body*, edited by Sarah Coakley, 1–12. Cambridge Studies in Religious Traditions 8. Cambridge/New York: Cambridge University Press, 1997.

COARELLI, Filippo. "Heliogabalus, templum; Heliogabalium." In *Lexicon Topographicum Urbis Romae*, a cura di Eva M. Steinby, 3: 10f. Rome: Edizioni Quasar, 1996.

COHEN, Martin S. *The Shi'ur Qomah: Liturgy and Theurgy in Pre-Kabbalistic Jewish Mysticism.* Lanham, Md./London: University Press of America, 1983.

———. *The Shi'ur Qomah: Texts and Recensions.* TSAJ 9. Tübingen: Mohr Siebeck, 1985.

COLISH, Marcia L. *The Stoic Tradition from Antiquity to the Early Middle Ages.* Vol. 2, *Stoicism in Christian Latin Thought through the Sixth Century.* Second impression with addenda et corrigenda. Leiden: Brill, 1990.

COLLINS, John J. *The Apocalyptic Imagination: An Introduction to Jewish Apocalyptic Literature.* 2nd ed. The Bible Resource Series. Grand Rapids/Cambridge: Eerdmans, 1998.

———. "The Son of Man in First-Century Judaism." *NTS* 38 (1992): 448–466.

COLLINS, Roger J. "Faustus von Reji." In *Theologische Realenzyklopädie,* 11: 63–67. Berlin/New York: De Gruyter, 1983.

COLPE, Carsten. *Einleitung in die Schriften aus Nag Hammadi*. Jerusalemer Theologisches Forum 16. Münster: Aschendorff, 2011.

———. "υἱὸς τοῦ ἀνθρώπου." In *Theologisches Wörterbuch zum Neuen Testament* 8: 407–481. Stuttgart: Kohlhammer, 1969.

CORBOUD, Pierre. "L'oratoire et les niches-oratoires: Les lieux de la prière." In *Le site monastique copte des Kellia: Sources historiques et explorations archéologiques*. Actes du Colloque de Genève 13 au 15 août 1984, édité par Philippe Bridel, 85–92. Carouge: Mission Suisse d'Archéologie Copte de l'Université de Genève, 1986.

COURCELLE, Pierre. "La première expérience augustinienne de l'extase." In *Augustinus Magister: Congrès International Augustinien, Paris, 21–24 Septembre 1954, Actes*. Tome 1, Communications, 53–57. Paris: Études Augustiniennes, 1954.

———. *Les lettres grecques en Occident: De Macrobe à Cassiodore*. Bibliothèque des écoles françaises 159. Paris: E. de Boccard, 1948.

———. *Recherches sur les Confessions de Saint Augustin*. Nouvelle édition augmentée et illustrée. Paris: De Boccard, 1968.

COURTH, Franz. *Trinität: In der Schrift und Patristik*. Handbuch der Dogmengeschichte. Bd. 2, *Der trinitarische Gott—die Schöpfung—die Sünde*. Fasc. 1a. Freiburg im Breisgau: Herder, 1988.

CROUZEL, Henri. "La doctrine origénienne du corps ressuscité." *Bulletin de littérature ecclésiastique* 81 (1980): 175–200, 241–266. (= idem, *Les fins dernières selon Origène*, nr. VI and VII. Collected Studies Series CS 320. Aldershot: Variorum, 1990.)

———. "Les critiques adressées par Méthode et ses contemporains à la doctrine origénienne du corps ressuscité." *Gregorianum* 53 (1972): 679–716.

———. *Origène et la philosophie*. Théologie 52. Paris: Aubier, 1962.

———. *Théologie de l'image de dieu chez Origène*. Théologie 34. Paris: Aubier, 1956.

CUMONT, Franz. *Die orientalischen Religionen im römischen Heidentum*. Bearbeitet von August Burckhardt-Brandenberg. 9. unveränderte Aufl., reprografischer Nachdruck der 3. dt. Aufl. Stuttgart: Teubner, 1989. (= 1931.)

CZAPLA, Bruno. *Gennadius als Litterarhistoriker: Eine quellenkritische Untersuchung der Schrift des Gennadius von Marseille "De viris illustribus."* Kirchengeschichtliche Studien 4/1. Münster: Schöningh, 1898.

DAFNI, Evangelia G. "ΣΑΡΞ ΜΟΥ ΕΞ ΑΥΤΩΝ (LXX-Hosea IX 2): Zur Theologie der Sprache in der Septuaginta." *VT* 51 (2001): 336–353.

DALGISH, Edward R. "Bethel (Deity)." In *The Anchor Bible Dictionary*, 1: 706–710. New York: Doubleday, 1992.

DAM, Raymond van. *Leadership and Community in Late Antique Gaul*. The Transformation of the Classical Heritage 8. Berkeley/Los Angeles/London: University of California Press, 1985.

DAN, Joseph. "Jewish Gnosticism?" In *Jewish Studies Quarterly* 2 (1995): 309–328.

D'ANNA, Alberto. *Pseudo-Giustino, Sulla Resurrezione: Discorso cristiano del II secolo*. Letteratura Cristiana Antica. Brescia: Morcelliana, 2001.

DANZ, Christian. "Der Atheismusstreit um Fichte." In *Philosophisch-theologische Streitsachen: Pantheismusstreit—Atheismusstreit—Theismusstreit*, herausgegeben von Georg Essen und Christian Danz, 135–213. Darmstadt: Wissenschaftliche Buchgesellschaft, 2012.

DAROCA, Javier Campos, et Juan L. LOPEZ CRUCES. "Maxime de Tyr." In *Dictionnaire des philosophes antiques*, publié sous la direction de Richard Goulet, 4: 324–348. Paris: Éditions du Centre national de la Recherche scientifique, 2005.

DASSMANN, Ernst. "Ambrosius." In *Augustinus-Lexikon*, 1: 270–285. Basel: Schwabe, 1986–1994.

DAWSON, David. "Transcendence as Embodiment: Augustine's Domestication of Gnosis." *Modern Theology* 10 (1994): 1–26.

DEAKLE, David W. "Harnack & Cerdo: A Reexamination of the Patristic Evidence for Marcion's Mentor." In *Marcion und seine kirchengeschichtliche Wirkung: Marcion and His Impact on Church History; Vorträge der Internationalen Fachkonferenz zu Marcion, gehalten vom 15.–18. August 2001 in Mainz*, herausgegeben von Gerhard May und Katharina Greschat in Gemeinschaft mit Martin Meiser, 177–191. TU 150. Berlin/New York: De Gruyter, 2002.

DECHOW, Jon F. *Dogma and Mysticism in Early Christianity: Epiphanius of Cyprus and the Legacy of Origen*. North American Patristic Society. Patristic Monograph Series 13. Macon, Ga.: Scholar's Press, 1988.

DECLERCK, José. "Théophile d'Alexandrie contre Origène: Nouveaux Fragments de l'Epistula Synodalis Prima (Clavis patrum Graecorum 2595)." *Byzantion* 54 (1984): 495–507.

DECRET, François. *L'Afrique Manichéenne (IVᵉ—Vᵉ siècles): Étude historique et doctrinale*. Tome 1. Paris: Études Augustiniennes, 1978.

DEGHAYE, Pierre. "Die Natur als Leib Gottes in Jacob Böhmes Theosophie." In *Gott, Natur und Mensch in der Sicht Jacob Böhmes und seiner Rezeption*, herausgegeben von Jan Garewicz und Alois M. Haas, 71–111. Wolfenbütteler Arbeiten zur Barockforschung 24. Wiesbaden: Harrassowitz, 1994.

DEHANDSCHUTTER, Boudewijn. "The New Testament and the Martyrdom of Polycarp." In *Trajectories through the New Testament and the Apostolic Fathers*, edited by Andrew F. Gregory and Christopher Tuckett, 395–406. Oxford: Oxford University Press, 2005.

DE LANGE, Nicholas R. *Origen and the Jews*. Studies in Jewish-Christian Relations in Third-Century Palestine. University of Cambridge Oriental Publications 25. Cambridge: Cambridge University Press, 1976.

DELBRÜCK, Richard. "Uranius of Emesa." *Numismatic Chronicle and Journal of the Royal Numismatic Society* 8 (1948): 11–29.

DELEEUW, Patricia. "A Peaceful Pluralism: The Durene Mithraeum, Synagogue, and Christian Building." In *Dura Europos: Crossroads of Antiquity*, edited by Lisa R. Brody and Gail L. Hoffman, 189–199. Chesnut Hill, Mass.: McMullen Museum of Art, Boston College, 2011.

DEUBNER, Ludwig. *Attische Feste*. Berlin: Heinrich Keller, 1932. (= Berlin: Akademie-Verlag, 1956.)

————. "Speichel." In *Handwörterbuch des deutschen Aberglaubens*, 149–155. Augsburg: Weltbild, 2000. (= Berlin: De Gruyter, 1937.)

DEUSE, Werner. *Untersuchungen zur mittelplatonischen und neuplatonischen Seelenlehre*. Akademie der Wissenschaften und der Literatur. Abhandlungen der Geistes- und Sozialwissenschaftlichen Klasse. Einzelveröffentlichung 3. Wiesbaden: Steiner, 1983.

DEVOS, Paul. "Silvie la sainte pèlerine." *Analecta Bollandiana* (1973): 105–121.

————. "Silvie la sainte pèlerine: II. En Occident." *Analecta Bollandiana* 92 (1974): 321–343.

DIEBNER, Bernd Jörg. *Zephanjas Apokalypse*. Jüdische Schriften aus hellenistisch-römischer Zeit V/9. Gütersloh: Gütersloher Verlagshaus Mohn, 2003.

DIELS, Hermann. *Doxographi Graeci collegit, recensuit prolegominis indicibusque instruxit*. 4th ed. Berlin: De Gruyter, 1965.

————. "Eine Quelle des Stobäus." *Rheinisches Museum für Philologie* 30 (1875): 172–181.

DIETRICH, Bernard C. "Divine epiphanies in Homer." *Numen* 30 (1983): 53–79.

DIETRICH, Manfried. "Das Kultbild in Mesopotamien." In *"Jahwe und seine Aschera": Anthropomorphes Kultbild in Mesopotamien, Ugarit und Israel; Das biblische Bilderverbot*, herausgegeben von Manfried Dietrich und Oswald Loretz, 7–38. Ugaritisch-Biblische Literatur 9. Münster: UGARIT-Verlag, 1992.

DIHLE, Albrecht. "Vom sonnenhaften Auge." In *Platonismus und Christentum: Festschrift für Heinrich Dörrie*, herausgegeben von Horst-Dieter Blume und Friedhelm Mann, 84–91. Jahrbuch für Antike und Christentum. Ergänzungsband 10. Münster: Aschendorff, 1983.

DILLON, John. "Iamblichus of Chalcis (c. 240–325 A.D.)." In *ANRW*, II, *Prinzipat*, 36.2, *Philosophie, Wissenschaften, Technik: Philosophie*, herausgegeben von Wolfgang Haase, 862–909. Berlin/New York: De Gruyter, 1987.

————. "The Nature of God in the *'Quod Deus.'"* In David WINSTON and John DILLON, *Two Treatises of Philo of Alexandria: A Commentary on De Gigantibus and Quod Deus Sit Immutabilis*, 217–227. Brown Judaic Studies 25. Chico, Calif.: Scholars Press, 1983.

DILLON, John, and Wilhelm H. WUELLNER, eds. *The Transcendence of God in Philo: Some Possible Sources*. The Center for Hermeneutical Studies in Hellenistic and Modern Culture, Protocol of the Sixteenth Colloquy, 20 April 1975. Series Colloquy 16. Berkeley: Graduate Theological Union and University of California, 1975.

DI MARCO, Michele. *La polemica sull'anima tra "Fausto di Riez" e Claudiano Mamerto*. Studia Ephemeridis Augustinianum 51. Roma: Institutum patristicum Augustinianum, 1995.

DINZELBACHER, Peter. "Barbara Feichtinger und Helmut Seng, Hg. *Die Christen und der Körper: Aspekte der Körperlichkeit in der christlichen Literatur der Spätantike* (Rezension)." *Plekos* 8 (2006): 73–76.

————. *Christliche Mystik im Abendland: Ihre Geschichte von den Anfängen bis zum Ende des Mittelalters*. Paderborn: Schöningh, 1994.

DITTENBERGER, Wilhelm. *Sylloge Inscriptionum Graecarum, Volumen alterum.* 3. Aufl. Leipzig: Hirzel, 1917. (= Hildesheim u.a.: Olms, 1982.)

DOBSCHÜTZ, Ernst von. *Christusbilder: Untersuchungen zur christlichen Legende.* Beilagen, TU 18/1–4. Leipzig: Hinrichs, 1899.

———. *Das Kerygma Petri kritisch untersucht.* TU 11/1. Leipzig: Hinrichs, 1893.

DODDS, Eric R., ed. and trans. *Proclus: The Elements of Theology; A Revised Text with Translation, Introduction, and Commentary.* Oxford: Oxford University Press, 1963.

DÖHLER, Marietheres. *Acta Petri: Text, Übersetzung und Kommentar zu den Actus Vercellenses.* Diss. theol. masch., Berlin, 2015.

DOHMEN, Christoph. *Das Bilderverbot: Seine Entstehung und seine Entwicklung im Alten Testament.* Bonner biblische Beiträge 62. 2. durchgesehene und um ein Nachwort erweiterte Aufl. Frankfurt am Main: Athenäum, 1987.

DÖLGER, Franz J. *Die Sonne der Gerechtigkeit und der Schwarze: Eine religionsgeschichtliche Studie zum Taufgelöbnis.* 2. um hinterlassene Nachträge des Verfassers verm. Aufl. Liturgiewissenschaftliche Quellen und Forschungen 14. Münster: Aschendorff, 1971.

———. *ΙΧΘΥΣ: Der heilige Fisch in den antiken Religionen und im Christentum.* Bd. 2. Rome: Spithöver / Münster: Aschendorff, 1922.

———. *Sol salutis: Gebet und Gesang im christlichen Altertum, mit besonderer Rücksicht auf die Ostung in Gebet und Liturgie.* 3. um Hinweise vermehrte Aufl. Liturgiewissenschaftliche Quellen und Forschungen 16/17. Münster: Aschendorff, 1971.

DONATI, Silvia. "Ägidius von Roms Kritik an Thomas von Aquins Lehre der hylomorphen Zusammensetzung der Himmelskörper." In *Thomas von Aquin: Werk und Wirkung im Licht neuer Forschungen*, herausgegeben von Albert Zimmermann, 377–396. Miscellanea mediaevalia 19. Berlin/New York: De Gruyter, 1988.

DONOHUE, Alice A. "The Greek Images of the Gods: Considerations on Terminology and Methodology." *Hephaistos* 15 (1997): 31–45.

DORANDI, Tiziano. "Démétrios Lacon." In *Dictionnaire des philosophes antiques*, publié sous la direction de Richard Goulet, 2: 637–641. Paris: Éditions du Centre national de la Recherche scientifique, 1994.

DÖRING, Klaus. *Die Megariker: Kommentierte Sammlung der Testimonien.* Studien zur antiken Philosophie 2. Amsterdam: Grüner, 1971.

DORIVAL, Gilles. "Justin et la resurrection des morts." In *La resurrection chez les Pères*, 101–118. Cahiers de Biblia Patristica 7. Strasbourg: Université Marc Bloch, 2003.

———. "Nouvelles remarques sur la forme du *Traité des Principes* d'Origène." *Recherches Augustiniennes* 22 (1987): 67–108.

———. "Origène d'Alexandrie." In *Dictionnaire des philosophes antiques*, publié sous la direction de Richard Goulet, 4: 807–842. Paris: Éditions du Centre national de la Recherche scientifique, 2005.

———. "Origène et la résurrection de la chair." In *Origeniana Quarta: Die Referate des 4. Internationalen Origeneskongresses (Innsbruck, 2.–6.*

September 1985), herausgegeben von Lothar Lies, 291–321. Innsbrucker Theologische Studien 19. Innsbruck/Wien: Tyrolia, 1987.

————. "Remarques sur la forme du Peri Archôn." In *Origeniana: Premier colloque international des études origéniennes (Montserrat, 18–21 septembre 1973)*, dirigé par Henri Crouzel, Gennaro Lomiento, et Josep Rius-Camps, 33–45. Quaderni di "Vetera Christianorum" 12. Bari: Istituto di letteratura cristiana antica, Università di Bari, 1975.

DORMEYER, Detlev. *Die Passion Jesu als Verhaltensmodell: Literarische und theologische Analyse der Traditions- und Redaktionsgeschichte der Markuspassion.* Neutestamentliche Abhandlungen Neue Folge 11. Münster: Aschendorff, 1974.

DORNSEIFF, Franz. *Das Alphabet in Mystik und Magie.* Stoicheia: Studien zur Geschichte des antiken Weltbildes und der griechischen Wissenschaft 7. 2. Aufl. Leipzig: Reprint-Verlag, 1994. (= Leipzig: Teubner, 1925.)

DÖRRIE, Heinrich. "Der Platoniker Eudoros von Alexandreia." *Hermes* 79 (1944): 25–38. (= idem, *Platonica minora.* Studia et testimonia antiqua 8. München: Fink, 1976.)

————. *Platonica Minora.* Studia et testimonia antiqua 8. München: Fink, 1976.

————. "Platons Begriff der Seele und dessen weitere Ausgestaltung im Neuplatonismus." In *Seele: Ihre Wirklichkeit, ihr Verhältnis zum Leib und zur menschlichen Person*, herausgegeben von Klaus Kremer, 18–45. Studien zur Problemgeschichte der antiken und mittelalterlichen Philosophie 10. Leiden/Köln: Brill, 1984.

————. *Porphyrios' "Symmikta zetemata": Ihre Stellung in System und Geschichte des Neuplatonismus nebst einem Kommentar zu den Fragmenten.* Zetemata 20. München: Beck, 1959.

————. "Porphyrius' Lehre von der Seele." In *Porphyre: Huit exposés suivis de discussions: Vandoeuvres-Genève, 30 août–5 sept. 1965*, édité par Heinrich Dörrie, 165–192. Entretiens sur l'antiquité classique 12. Genève: Fondation Hardt, 1966. (= idem, *Platonica Minora*, 441–453. Studia et testimonia antiqua 8. München: W. Fink, 1976.)

DÖRRIE, Heinrich, und Matthias BALTES. *Die philosophische Lehre des Platonismus: Einige grundlegende Axiome/Platonische Physik (im antiken Verständnis) I; Bausteine 101–124; Text, Übersetzung, Kommentar.* Der Platonismus in der Antike. Grundlagen—System—Entfaltung 4. Stuttgart-Bad Cannstatt: Frommann-Holzboog, 1996.

————. *Die philosophische Lehre des Platonismus: Von der "Seele" als der Ursache aller sinnvollen Abläufe, Bausteine 151–168; Text, Übersetzung, Kommentar.* Der Platonismus in der Antike: Grundlagen—System—Entwicklung. 6/1. Stuttgart-Bad Cannstatt: Frommann-Holzboog, 2002.

DOUGLAS, Mary. *Natural Symbols: Explorations in Cosmology.* New York: Pantheon Books, 1970.

————. *Purity and Danger: An Analysis of Concepts of Pollution and Taboo.* With a new preface by the author. New York/London: Routledge, 2002. (= New York: Praeger, 1966.)

DRAGUET, René. *Julien d'Halicarnasse et sa controverse avec Sévère d'Antioche sur l'incorruptibilité du corps du Christ: Étude d'histoire littéraire et doctrinale suivie des fragments dogmatiques de Julien (texte syriaces et traduction grecque).* Louvain: Smeesters, 1924.

DRAZIN, Israel. "Dating Targum Onkelos by Means of the Tannaitic Midrashim." *JJS* 50 (1999): 246–258.

DRECHSLER, Wolfgang, und Rainer KATTEL. "Mensch und Gott bei Xenophanes." In *Gott und Mensch im Dialog: Festschrift für Otto Kaiser zum 80. Geburtstag,* herausgegeben von Markus Witte, 1: 111–129. Beihefte zur Zeitschrift für die alttestamentliche Wissenschaft 345. Berlin/New York: De Gruyter, 2004.

DRECOLL, Volker H., und Mirjam KUDELLA. *Augustin und der Manichäismus.* Tübingen: Mohr Siebeck, 2011.

DRESS, Walter. *Die Theologie Gersons.* Gütersloh: Bertelsmann, 1931.

DRIOTON, Étienne. "La discussion d'un moine anthropomorphite Audien avec le patriarche Théophile d'Alexandrie en l'année 399." *Revue de l'orient chrétien* 20 [= 2. sér. 10] (1915–1917): 92–100, 113–128.

DROBNER, Hubertus R. "15 Jahre Forschung zu Melito von Sardes (1965–1980): Eine kritische Bibliographie." *VC* 36 (1982): 313–333.

DROZDEK, Adam. "Epicurean Gods." *Classica et Mediaevalia* 56 (2005): 155–166.

DUDEN, Barbara. *Geschichte unter der Haut: Ein Eisenacher Arzt und seine Patientinnen um 1730.* Stuttgart: Klett-Cotta, 1987.

DULAEY, Martine. "Les relations entre Lérins et Marseille: Eucher et Cassien." In *Lérins, une île sainte de l'antiquité au moyen âge,* édité par Yann Codou et Michel Lauwers, 63–82. Collection d'études médiévales de Nice 9. Turnhout: Brepols, 2009.

DUNN, Geoffrey D. "Mary's Virginity *in partu* and Tertullian's Anti-docetism in *De carne Christi* reconsidered." *JTS* 58 (2007): 467–484.

DUNN, James D. G. *The Parting of the Ways between Christianity and Judaism and Their Significance for the Character of Christianity.* London: SCM Press, 1991.

DURAND, Matthieu-Georges de. "Evagre le Pontique et le 'Dialogue sur la vie de saint Jean Chrysostome.'" *Bulletin de littérature ecclésiastique* 3 (1976): 191–206.

EASTERLING, Henry J. "Quinta natura." *Museum Helveticum* 21 (1964): 73–85.

EBELING, Gerhard. "Genie des Herzens unter dem Genius saeculi—J. C. Lavater als Theologe." In *Das Antlitz Gottes im Antlitz des Menschen: Zugänge zu Johann Kaspar Lavater,* herausgegeben von Karl Pestalozzi und Horst Weigelt, 23–60. Arbeiten zur Geschichte des Pietismus 31. Göttingen: Vandenhoeck & Ruprecht, 1994.

———. "Zum Verständnis von R. Bultmanns Aufsatz: 'Welchen Sinn hat es, von Gott zu reden?'" In idem, *Wort und Glaube.* Bd. 2, *Beiträge zur Fundamentaltheologie und zur Lehre von Gott,* 343–71. Tübingen: Mohr Siebeck, 1969.

EBIED, Rifaat Y., and Lionel R. WICKHAM. "Timothy Aelurus: Against the Definition of the Council of Chalcedon." In *After Chalcedon: Studies in*

Theology and Church History, Offered to Albert van Roey for His Seventieth Birthday, edited by Carl Laga, 115–166. Orientalia Lovaniensia Analecta 18. Leuven: Peeters, 1985.

EDWARDS, Mark J. "The *Clementina*: A Christian Response to the Pagan Novel." *Classical Quarterly* 42 (1992): 459–474.

———. "Further Reflections on the Platonism of Origen." *Adamantius* 18 (2012): 317–324.

———. "Ignatius and the Second Century: An Answer to R. Hübner." *Zeitschrift für Antikes Christentum* 2 (1998): 214–226.

———. "Middle Platonism on the Beautiful and the Good." *Mnemosyne* 44 (1991): 161–167.

———. *Origen against Plato*. Ashgate Studies in Philosophy & Theology in Late Antiquity. Aldershot: Ashgate, 2002.

———. "Origen no Gnostic; Or, on the Corporeality of Man." *JTS* 43 (1992): 23–37.

———. "Xenophanes Christianus?" *Greek, Roman and Byzantine Studies* 32 (1991): 219–228.

EGO, Beate. "Trauer und Erlösung: Zum Motiv der Hand Gottes in 3Hen §§ 68–70." In *La Main de Dieu. Die Hand Gottes*, édité par René Kieffer et Jan Bergman, 171–188. WUNT 94. Tübingen: Mohr Siebeck, 1997.

EHRHARD, Albert. *Überlieferung und Bestand der hagiographischen und homiletischen Literatur der griechischen Kirche von den Anfängen bis zum Ende des 16. Jahrhunderts*. TU 52/2. Berlin: Akademie-Verlag, 1952.

———. "Zur literarhistorischen und theologischen Würdigung der Texte." In Walter E. CRUM, *Der Papyruscodex saec. VI–VII der Philippsbibliothek in Cheltenham: Koptische theologische Schriften*, mit einem Beitrag von Albert Ehrhard, 129–171. Schriften der Wissenschaftlichen Gesellschaft in Straßburg 18. Straßburg: Trübner, 1915.

EIJK, Philip van der. "The Matter of Mind: Aristotle on the Biology of 'Psychic' Processes and the Bodily Aspects of Thinking." In *Aristotelische Biologie: Intentionen, Methoden, Ergebnisse*, herausgegeben von Wolfgang Kullmann und Sabine Föllinger, 221–258. Philosophie der Antike 6. Stuttgart: Steiner, 1997.

EILBERG-SCHWARTZ, Howard. *God's Phallus and Other Problems for Men and Monotheism*. Boston: Beacon Press, 1994.

EISSFELDT, Otto. "Der Gott Bethel." *Archiv für Religionswissenschaft* 28 (1930): 1–30. (= idem, *Kleine Schriften*, Bd. 1, herausgegeben von Rudolf Sellheim und Fritz Maas, 206–233. Tübingen: Mohr Siebeck, 1962.)

———. "Gott und das Meer in der Bibel." In *Studia Orientalia, Joanni Pedersen septuagenario A.D. VII id. nov. anno MCMLIII a collegis, discipulis, amicis dictata*, 76–84. Kopenhagen: Munksgaard, 1953. (= idem, *Kleine Schriften*, Bd. 3, 256–264. Tübingen: Mohr Siebeck, 1966.)

ELIAS, Norbert. *The Civilizing Process*. Translated by Edmund Jephcott. New York: Urizen Books, 1978.

———. *Über den Prozess der Zivilisation: Soziogenetische und psychogenetische Untersuchungen*. Bd. 1, *Wandlungen des Verhaltens in den weltlichen Oberschichten des Abendlandes*. Bd. 2, *Wandlungen der*

Gesellschaft: Entwurf zu einer Theorie der Zivilisation. Basel: Verlag Haus zum Falken, 1939.

ELIOR, Rachel. "The Foundations of Early Jewish Mysticism: The Lost Calendar and the Transformed Heavenly Chariot." In *Wege mystischer Gotteserfahrung: Judentum, Christentum und Islam. Mystical Approaches to God: Judaism, Christianity, and Islam,* herausgegeben von Peter Schäfer unter Mitarbeit von Elisabeth Müller-Luckner, 1–18. Schriften des Historischen Kollegs. Kolloquien 65. München: Oldenbourg Verlag, 2006.

———. "From Earthly Temple to Heavenly Shrines: Prayer and Sacred Song in the Hekhalot Literature and Its Relation to Temple Traditions." *Jewish Studies Quarterly* 4 (1997): 217–267.

———. *The Three Temples: On the Emergence of Jewish Mysticism.* The Littman Library of Jewish Civilization. Oxford/Portland, Ore.: Littman Library of Jewish Civilization, 2004.

ELM, Susanna. "The Dog That Did Not Bark: Doctrine and Patriarchical Authority in the Conflict between Theophilus of Alexandria and John Chrysostom of Constantinople." In *Christian Origins: Theology, Rhetoric and Community,* edited by Lewis Ayres and Gareth Jones, 68–93. London/New York: Routledge, 1998.

ELORDUY, Eleuterio. "El influjo estoíco en Orígenes." In *Origeniana: Premier colloque international des études origéniennes (Montserrat, 18–21 septembre 1973),* dirigé par Henri Crouzel, Gennaro Lomiento, et Josep Rius-Camps, 277–288. Quaderni di "Vetera Christianorum" 12. Bari: Istituto di letteratura cristiana antica, Università di Bari, 1975.

ENDSJØ, Dag Ø. "Immortal Bodies, before Christ: Bodily Continuity in Ancient Greece and 1 Corinthians." *Journal for the Study of the New Testament* 30 (2008): 417–436.

ENGEMANN, Josef. "Zu den Dreifaltigkeitsdarstellungen der frühchristlichen Kunst: Gab es im 4. Jahrhundert anthropomorphe Trinitätsbilder?" In *Jahrbuch für Antike und Christentum* 19 (1976): 157–172.

EPP, Eldon Jay. "The New Testament Papyri at Oxyrhynchus in Their Social and Intellectual Context." In *Sayings of Jesus: Canonical and Non-Canonical: Essays in Honour of Tjitze Baarda,* edited by William L. Petersen, Johan S. Vos, and Henk J. de Jonge, 47–68. Supplements to Novum Testamentum 89. Leiden: Brill, 1997. (= idem, *Perspectives on New Testament Textual Criticism: Collected Essays, 1962–2004,* 497–520. Supplements to Novum Testamentum 116. Leiden: Brill, 2005.)

ERBSE, Hartmut. *Untersuchungen zur Funktion der Götter im homerischen Epos.* Untersuchungen zur antiken Literatur und Geschichte 24. Berlin/New York: De Gruyter, 1986.

ERLER, Michael. "§ 18. Demetrios Lakon." In *Die hellenistische Philosophie,* herausgegeben von Hellmut Flashar: Grundriss der Philosophie, begründet von Friedrich Ueberweg; Bd. 4, *Die Philosophie der Antike,* 256–267. Völlig neu bearbeitete Ausgabe. Basel: Schwabe, 1994.

ESBROECK, Michel van. "Les Œuvres de Méliton de Sardes en Géorgien." *Bedi Kartlisa: Revue de kartvélologie* 31 (1973): 48–63.

————. "Nouveaux fragments de Méliton de Sardes dans une homélie grégorienne sur la croix." *Analecta Bollandiana* 90 (1972): 63–99.

ESSER, Gerhard. *Die Seelenlehre Tertullians*. Paderborn: Schöningh, 1893.

ESTIENNE, Sylvia. "*Simulacra Deorum* versus *Ornamenta Aedium*: The Status of Divine Images in the Temples of Rome." In *Divine Images and Human Imaginations in Ancient Greece and Rome*, edited by Joannis Mylonopoulos, 257–271. Religions in the Graeco-Roman World 170. Leiden: Brill, 2010.

EVELYN WHITE, Hugh G. *The Monasteries of the Wâdi 'n Natrûn*. Pt. 2, *The History of the Monasteries of Nitria and of Scetis*. Edited by Walter Hauser. Publications of the Metropolitan Museum of Art Egyptian Expedition. New York: Metropolitan Museum, 1932. (= New York: Arno Press, 1973.)

FALCON, Andrea. *Aristotelianism in the First Century BCE: Xenarchus of Seleucia*. Cambridge: Cambridge University Press, 2011.

FANTINO, Jacques. *L'homme, image de Dieu, chez saint Irénée de Lyon*. Paris: Les éditions du Cerf, 1985.

FATTI, Federico. "*Pontifex tantus*: Giovanni, Epifanio e le origini della prima controversia origenista." *Adamantius* 19 (2013): 30–49.

FAUTH, Wolfgang. *Helios Megistos: Zur synkretistischen Theologie der Spätantike*. Religions in the Graeco-Roman World 125. Leiden: Brill, 1995.

FAVALE, Agostino. *Teofilo d'Alessandria (345 c.—412): Scritti, vita e dottrina*. Biblioteca del Salesianum 41. Torino: Società Editrice Internazionale, 1958.

FAYE, Eugène de. *Origène: Sa vie, son oeuvre, sa pensée*. Tome 3, *La doctrine*. Paris: Ernest Leroux, 1928.

FEICHTINGER, Barbara. "Einleitung." In *Die Christen und der Körper: Aspekte der Körperlichkeit in der christlichen Literatur der Spätantike*, herausgegeben von Barbara Feichtinger und Helmut Seng, 9–26. Beiträge zur Altertumskunde 184. Leipzig/München: K. G. Saur, 2004.

FELDMANN, Erich. *Der Einfluss des Hortensius und des Manichäismus auf das Denken des jungen Augustinus*. Diss. theol., Münster, 1975.

————. *Die "Epistula Fundamenti" der nordafrikanischen Manichäer: Versuch einer Rekonstruktion*. Altenberge: CIS, 1987.

FELDMEIER, Reinhard. *Der erste Brief des Petrus*. Theologischer Handkommentar zum Neuen Testament 15/I. Leipzig: Evangelische Verlagsanstalt, 2005.

FELLMANN, Ferdinand. *Orientierung Philosophie: Was sie kann, was sie will*. Rowohlts Enzyklopädie 55601. Reinbek bei Hamburg: Rowohlts Taschenbuchverlag, 1998.

FERRARIS, Maurizio. *Manifesto of New Realism*. Translated by Sarah De Sanctis. Foreword by Graham Harman. New York: State University of New York Press, 2014.

FESTUGIERE, André-Jean. *La révélation d'Hermès Trismégiste*. Tome 2, *Le dieu cosmique*. Paris: Les Belles Lettres, 1986. (= Paris: Gabalda, 1949.)

————. *La révélation d'Hermès Trismégiste*. Tome 4, *Le dieu inconnu et la gnose*. Études Biblique. Paris: Gabalda, 1954.

————. *L'idéal religieux des Grecs et l'Évangile*. Études bibliques. 2ᵉ éd. Paris: Librairie Lecoffre / J. Gabalda, 1981.

FEUERBACH, Ludwig. *Das Wesen des Christentums*. Bearbeitet von Wolfgang Harich und Werner Schuffenhauer. Gesammelte Werke, Bd. 5. Berlin: Akademie Verlag, 1984.

FICHTE, Johann G. *J. G. Fichte's . . . Appellation an das Publicum über die durch ein Churf. Sächs: Confiscationsrescript ihm beigemessenen atheistischen Aeusserungen*, 191–333. Jena/Leipzig: Gabler; Tübingen: Cotta, 1799. (= FICHTE, Immanuel H., Hg. *Fichtes Werke*. Bd. 5, *Zur Religionsphilosophie*. Berlin: Veit, 1846. [= Berlin: De Gruyter, 1971].)

————. "Ueber den Grund unseres Glaubens an eine göttliche Weltregierung." *Philosophisches Journal* 8 (1798): 1–20. (= FICHTE, Immanuel H., Hg. *Fichtes Werke*. Bd. 5, *Zur Religionsphilosophie*, 175–189. Berlin: Veit, 1846. [= Berlin: De Gruyter, 1971].)

FILLION-LAHILLE, Janine. *Le De ira de Sénèque et la philosophie stoïcienne des passions*. Études et commentaires. Paris: Klincksieck, 1984.

FINAMORE, John F. *Iamblichus and the Theory of the Vehicle of the Soul*. American Classical Studies 14. Chico, Calif.: Scholars Press, 1985.

FINKEL, Joshua. *Maḳ'āla fi teḥiyat ha-metim: Maimonides' Treatise on Resurrection*. Proceedings of the American Academy for Jewish Research 9. New York: ha-Aḳademyah ha-ameriḳanit le-mada'e ha-yahadut, 1939.

FINKELBERG, Aryeh. "Studies in Xenophanes." *Harvard Studies in Classical Philology* 93 (1990): 103–167.

FINKELBERG, Margalit. "Two Kinds of Representations in Greek Religious Art." In *Representations in Religion: Studies in Honor of Moshe Barash*, edited by Jan Assmann and Albert I. Baumgarten, 27–41. Studies in the History of Religions 89. Leiden: Brill, 2001.

FISHER, Seymour. "Body Image." In *International Encyclopedia of the Social Sciences*, edited by David L. Sills, 2: 113–116. New York: Macmillan, 1968.

FLOROVSKY, Georges. "The Anthropomorphites in the Egyptian Desert: Part I." In *Akten des XI. Internationalen Byzantinistenkongresses München 1958*, herausgegeben von Franz Dölger und Hans-Georg Beck, 154–159. München: Beck, 1960. (= idem, *Collected Works*, vol. 4, *Aspects of Church History*, edited by Richard S. Haugh, 89–96. Belmont, Mass.: Nordland, 1975.)

————. "Theophilus of Alexandria and Apa Aphu of Pemdje: The Anthropomorphites in the Egyptian Desert: Part II." In *Harry Austryn Wolfson Jubilee Volume on the Occasion of His Seventy-Fifth Birthday. Sefer hayovel likhevod Tsevi Volfson*, 275–310, vol. 1, English Section. Jerusalem: American Academy for Jewish Research, 1965. (= idem, *Collected Works*, vol. 4, *Aspects of Church History*, edited by Richard S. Haugh, 97–129, 290–296. Belmont, Mass.: Nordland, 1975.)

FOLEY, Helene P., ed. and trans. *The Homeric "Hymn to Demeter": Translation, Commentary, and Interpretative Essays.* Princeton, N.J.: Princeton University Press, 1993.

FONTENROSE, Joseph. *Didyma: Apollo's Oracle, Cult, and Companions.* Berkeley/Los Angeles/London: University of California Press, 1988.

FORSCHNER, Maximilian. "Die pervertierte Vernunft: Zur stoischen Theorie der Affekte." *Philosophisches Jahrbuch* 87 (1983): 258–280.

FÖRSTER, Niclas. *Marcus Magus: Kult, Lehre und Gemeindeleben einer valentinianischen Gnostikergruppe; Sammlung der Quellen und Kommentar.* WUNT 114. Tübingen: Mohr Siebeck, 1999.

FORTIN, Ernest L. *Christianisme et culture philosophique au cinquième siècle: La querelle de l'âme humaine en Occident.* Études Augustiniennes. Paris: Études Augustiniennes, 1959.

———. "Saint Augustin et la doctrine néoplatonicienne de l'âme (Ep. 137,11)." In *Augustinus Magister: Congrès international Augustinien, Paris, 21–23 Septembre 1954, Actes*, 3: 371–380. Paris: Études Augustiniennes, 1954.

FOSSUM, Jarl. "Sects and Movements." In *The Samaritans*, edited by Alan D. Crown, 293–396. Tübingen: Mohr Siebeck, 1989.

FOSTER, Paul. "Polymorphic Christology: Its Origins and Development in Early Christianity." *JTS* 58 (2007): 66–99.

FOX, Robin L. *Pagans and Christians in the Mediterranean World from the Second Century AD to the Conversion of Constantine.* London: Penguin Books, 1986.

FRANK, Karl S. *ΑΓΓΕΛΙΚΟΣ ΒΙΟΣ. Begriffsanalytische und begriffsgeschichtliche Untersuchung zum "engelgleichen Leben" im frühen Mönchtum.* Beiträge zur Geschichte des alten Mönchtums und des Benediktinerordens 26. Münster: Aschendorff, 1964.

———. "Fiktive Mündlichkeit als Grundstruktur der monastischen Literatur." In *Biblica et apocrypha, orientalia, ascetica: Papers Presented at the Eleventh International Conference on Patristic Studies Held in Oxford 1991*, vol. 2, edited by Elizabeth A. Livingstone, 356–375. StPatr 25. Leuven: Peeters, 1993.

FRANKENBERG, Wilhelm. *Die syrischen Clementinen mit griechischem Paralleltext: Eine Vorarbeit zu dem literargeschichtlichen Problem der Sammlung.* TU 48/3. Leipzig: Hinrichs, 1937.

FRANZMANN, Majella. "Imitatio Christi: Copying the Death of the Founder and Gaining Paradise." In *A Wandering Galilean: Essays in Honour of Seán Freyne*, edited by Zuleika Rodgers, 367–383. Supplements to the Journal for the Study of Judaism 132. Leiden: Brill, 2009.

FRATEANTONIO, Christa. *Religion und Städtekonkurrenz: Zum politischen und kulturellen Kontext von Pausanias' Periegese.* Millennium-Studien 23. Berlin/New York: De Gruyter, 2009.

FREDRIKSEN, Paula. "Vile Bodies: Paul and Augustine on the Resurrection of the Flesh." In *Biblical Hermeneutics in Historical Perspective: Studies in Honor of Karlfried Froehlich on His Sixtieth Birthday*, edited by Mark S. Burrows and Paul Rorem, 75–87. Grand Rapids: Eeerdmans, 1991.

FREND, William H. C. *The Rise of the Monophysite Movement*. Cambridge: Cambridge University Press, 1972.

FRENSCHKOWSKI, Marco. *Offenbarung und Epiphanie*. Bd. 1, *Grundlagen des spätantiken und frühchristlichen Offenbarungsglaubens*. WUNT 2/79. Tübingen: Mohr Siebeck, 1995.

———. *Offenbarung und Epiphanie*. Bd. 2, *Die verborgene Epiphanie in Spätantike und frühem Christentum*. WUNT 2/80. Tübingen: Mohr Siebeck, 1997.

FREUD, Sigmund. *Das Unbehagen in der Kultur* (1930). Studienausgabe Bd. 9. Frankfurt am Main: S. Fischer, 1974.

FREY, Martin. *Untersuchungen zur Religion und Religionspolitik des Kaisers Elagabal*. Historia. Einzelschriften 62. Stuttgart: Steiner, 1989.

FRICKEL, Josef. *Das Dunkel um Hippolyt von Rom: Ein Lösungsversuch; Die Schriften Elenchos und Contra Noëtum*. Grazer Theologische Studien 13. Graz: Institut für ökumenische Theologie und Patrologie, 1988.

———. *Die "Apophasis Megale" in Hippolyt's Refutatio (VI 9–18): Eine Paraphrase zur Apophasis Simons*. Orientalia Christiana Analecta 182. Rome: Pontificium Institutum Orientalium Studiorum, 1968.

FRIEDLÄNDER, Julius. "Die unter Hadrian in Elis geprägte Münze mit der Darstellung der Bildsäule des olympischen Zeus von Phidias." *Berliner Blätter für Münz-, Siegel- und Wappenkunde* 3 (1866): 21–26.

FRIEDLÄNDER, Moritz. *Der vorchristliche jüdische Gnosticismus*. Göttingen: Vandenhoeck & Ruprecht, 1898.

FRITSCH, Charles T. *The Anti-anthropomorphisms of the Greek Pentateuch*. Princeton Oriental Texts 10. Princeton, N.J.: Princeton University Press, 1943.

FROHNHOFEN, Herbert. *ΑΠΑΘΕΙΑ ΤΟΥ ΘΕΟΥ: Über die Affektlosigkeit Gottes in der griechischen Antike und bei den griechischsprachigen Kirchenvätern bis zu Gregorios Thaumaturgos*. Europäische Hochschulschriften 23. Theologie 318. Frankfurt am Main: Lang, 1987.

FUCHS, Albert. "Die 'Seesturmperikope' Mk 4,35–41 parr. im Wandel der urkirchlichen Verkündigung." In *Weihbischof Dr. Alois Stöger: Exeget zwischen Bibelkommission und Offenbarungskonstitution*, herausgegeben von Ferdinand Staudinger und Heinrich Wurz, 101–133. Studien zum neuen Testament und seiner Umwelt 15. St. Pölten: Philosophisch-Theologische Hochschule der Diözese, 1990.

FÜHRER, Joseph. "Zur Geschichte des Elagabaliums und der Athena Parthenos des Pheidias." *Römische Mitteilungen* 7 (1892): 158–165.

FUHRER, Therese. "Augustins Modellierung des manichäischen Gottesbildes in den Confessiones." In *Monotheistische Denkfiguren in der Spätantike*, herausgegeben von Alfons Fürst, Luise Ahmend, Christian Gers-Uphaus und Stefan Klug, 179–195. Studien zu Antike und Christentum 81. Tübingen: Mohr Siebeck, 2013.

FUHRMANN, Manfred. "Die Mönchsgeschichten des Hieronymus: Formexperimente in erzählender Literatur." In *Christianisme et formes littéraires de l'antiquité tardive en Occident: Huit exposés suivis de discussions*, avec la participation de Helena Junod-Ammerbauer et François Paschoud, entretiens préparés et présidés par Manfred Fuhrmann, Vandoeuvres-Genève, 23–28 août 1976, 41–89. Entretiens sur l'antiquité classique 23. Genève: Fondation Hardt, 1977.

FUNKE, Hermann. "Götterbild." In *Reallexikon für Antike und Christentum* 11: 659–828. Stuttgart: Hiersemann, 1981.

FÜRST, Alfons. "Hieronymus gegen Origenes: Die Vision Jesajas im ersten Origenismusstreit." *Revue d'Études Augustiniennes* 53 (2007): 199–233. (= idem, *Von Origenes und Hieronymus zu Augustinus: Studien zur antiken Theologiegeschichte*, 239–274. Arbeiten zur Kirchengeschichte 115. Berlin/New York: De Gruyter, 2011.)

GALVAO-SOBRINHO, Carlos R. "Embodied Theologies: Christian Identity and Violence in Alexandria in the Early Arian Controversy." In *Violence in Late Antiquity: Perceptions and Practices,* edited by Harold Allen Drake, 321–331. Aldershot/Burlington, Vt.: Ashgate, 2006.

GASPARO, Giulia Sfameni. "Protologia ed encratismo: Esempi di esegesi encratita di Gen 1–3." *Augustinianum* 22 (1982): 75–89.

GASTER, Moses. "Das Schiur Komah." *Monatsschrift für Geschichte und Wissenschaft des Judentums* 37 (1893): 179–185, 213–230. (= idem, *Studies and Texts*, vol. 2, 1330–1353. New York: KTAV, 1971.)

GAUER, Heinz. *Texte zum byzantinischen Bilderstreit: Der Synodalbrief der drei Patriarchen des Ostens von 836 und seine Verwandlung in sieben Jahrhunderten.* Studien und Texte zur Byzantinistik 1. Frankfurt am Main: Lang, 1994.

GAUGER, Jörg-Dieter. "Eine missverstandene Strabonstelle (zum Judenbericht XVI 2,37)." *Historia* 28 (1979): 211–224.

GAUSE, Ute. *Paracelsus (1493–1541): Genese und Entfaltung seiner frühen Theologie.* Spätmittelalter und Reformation. Neue Reihe 4. Tübingen: Mohr Siebeck, 1993.

GEERLINGS, Wilhelm. "*Libri Platonicorum*: Die philosophische Bildung Augustins." In *Platon in der abendländischen Geistesgeschichte: Neue Forschungen zum Platonismus*, herausgegeben von Theo Kobusch und Burkhard Mojsisch, 60–70. Darmstadt: Wissenschaftliche Buchgesellschaft, 1997.

GEEST, Paul van. *The Incomprehensibility of God: Augustine as a Negative Theologian.* Late Antique History and Religion 4. (= The Mystagogy of the Church Fathers 1.) Leuven: Peeters, 2011.

GEHRKE, Hans-Joachim. *Geschichte des Hellenismus.* Oldenbourg Grundriss der Geschichte 1B. 4. Aufl. München: Oldenbourg Verlag, 2008.

GEMEINHARDT, Peter. *Antonius: Der erste Mönch; Leben—Lehre—Legende.* München: Beck, 2013.

―――. "Volksfrömmigkeit in der spätantiken Hagiographie: Potential und Grenzen eines umstrittenen Konzepts." *ZTK* 110 (2013): 410–438.

GERBER, Douglas E. "Pindar, Nemean Six: A Commentary." *Harvard Studies in Classical Philology* 99 (1999): 33–91.

GERHARDS, Albert, and Clemens LEONHARD, eds. *Jewish and Christian Liturgy and Worship: New Insights into Its History and Interaction.* Jewish and Christian Perspectives Series 15. Leiden/Boston: Brill, 2007.

GERHARDT, Volker. *Individualität. Das Element der Welt*. Beck'sche Reihe 1381. München: Beck, 2000.

GERLACH, Jens. "Die Figur des Scharlatans bei Lukian." In *Lukian, Der Tod des Peregrinos: Ein Scharlatan auf dem Scheiterhaufen*, herausgegeben, übersetzt und mit Beiträgen versehen von Peter Pilhofer, Manuel Baumbach, Jens Gerlach und Dirk U. Hansen, 150–152. SAPERE 9. Darmstadt: Wissenschaftliche Buchgesellschaft, 2005.

GESTRICH, Reinhold. *Schönheit Gottes: Anstösse zu einer neuen Wahrnehmung*. Ästhetik—Theologie—Liturgik 47. Berlin: LIT, 2007.

GEUDTNER, Otto. *Die Seelenlehre der chaldäischen Orakel*. Beiträge zur klassischen Philologie 35. Meisenheim am Glan: Anton Hain, 1971.

GILL, Mary L. "The Theory of the Elements in *De Caelo* 3 and 4." In *New Perspectives on Aristotle's "De Caelo,"* edited by Alan C. Bowen and Christian Wildberg, 139–162. Philosophia Antiqua 177. Leiden: Brill, 2009.

GLADIGOW, Burkhard. "Epiphanie, Statuette, Kultbild: Griechische Gottesvorstellungen im Wechsel von Kontext und Medium." *Visible Religion* 7 (1990): 98–121.

———. "Zur Ikonographie und Pragmatik römischer Kultbilder." In *Iconologia sacra: Mythos, Bildkunst und Dichtung in der Religions- und Sozialgeschichte Alteuropas; Festschrift Karl Hauck zum 75. Geburtstag*, herausgegeben von Hagen Keller und Nikolaus Staubach, 9–24. Arbeiten zur Frühmittelalterforschung 23. Berlin/New York: De Gruyter, 1994.

GLANCY, Jennifer A. *Corporal Knowledge: Early Christian Bodies*. New York/Oxford: Oxford University Press, 2010.

GLESSMER, Uwe. *Einleitung in die Targume zum Pentateuch*. TSAJ 48. Tübingen: Mohr Siebeck, 1995.

GMIRKIN, Russell E. *Berossus and Genesis, Manetho and Exodus: Hellenistic Histories and the Date of the Pentateuch*. Library of Hebrew Bible. Old Testament Studies 433. New York/London: T&T Clark, 2006.

GOETHE, Johann Wolfgang von. *Berliner Ausgabe: Poetische Werke; Gedichte und Singspiele*. Bd. 2, *Gedichte: Nachlese und Nachlaß*. Berlin: Aufbau-Verlag, 1979.

GÖGLER, Rolf. *Zur Theologie des biblischen Wortes bei Origenes*. Düsseldorf: Patmos, 1963.

GOLB, Norman. "Who Were the Maġārīya?" *Journal of the American Oriental Society* 80 (1960): 347–359.

GOLDSCHMIDT, Victor. "ὑπάρχειν et ὑφεστάναι dans la philosophie stoïcienne." *Revue des Études Grecques* 85 (1972): 331–444.

GOLDSTEIN, Jonathan. "The Central Composition of the West Wall of the Synagogue in Dura-Europos." *Journal of the Ancient Near Eastern Society* 16/17 (1984/1985): 99–142.

GOLITZIN, Alexander. "'The Demons Suggest an Illusion of God's Glory in a Form': Controversy over the Divine Body and Vision of Glory in Some Late Fourth, Early Fifth Monastic Literature." *Studia Monastica* 44 (2002): 13–43.

———. "The Form of God and Vision of the Glory: Some Thoughts on the Anthropomorphite Controversy of 399 AD." In *Mistagogia—experienţa lui Dumnezeu n Orthodoxie: Studii de théologie misticâ*, 184–267. Colecţia Mistica. Sibiu: Editura Deisis, 1998.

GOODENOUGH, Erwin R. *Symbolism in the Dura Synagogue*. Vol. 3, *Illustrations*. Jewish Symbols in the Greco-Roman Period 11 (= Bollingen Series 37/11). New York: Pantheon Books, 1964.

GOODRICH, Richard J. *Contextualizing Cassian: Aristocrats, Asceticism, and Reformation in Fifth-Century Gaul*. OECS. Oxford: Oxford University Press, 2007.

GÖRANSSON, Tryggve. *Albinus, Alcinous, Arius Didymus*. Studia Graeca et Latina Gothoburgensia 61. Göteborg: Acta Universitatis Gothoburgensis, 1995.

GORDON, Richard L. "The Real and the Imaginary: Production and the Religion in the Graeco-Roman World." *Art History* 2 (1979): 5–34.

GOTTSCHALK, Hans B. *Heraclides of Pontus*. Oxford: Clarendon, 1980.

GOTTSTEIN, Alon G. "The Body as Image of God in Rabbinic Literature." *HTR* 87 (1994): 171–195.

GOULD, Graham. "The Image of God and the Anthropomorphite Controversy in Fourth Century Monasticism." In *Origeniana Quinta: Historica— Text and Method—Biblica—Philosophica—Theologica—Origenism and Later Developments; Papers of the 5th International Origen Congress, Boston College, 14–18 August 1989*, edited by Robert J. Daly, 549–557. BETL 105. Leuven: University Press / Uitgeverij Peeters, 1992.

GOULD, Josiah B. *The Philosophy of Chrysippus*. Philosophia Antiqua 17. Leiden: Brill, 1970.

GOULDER, Michael D. "Ignatius' 'Docetists.'" *VC* 53 (1999): 16–30.

GOULET, Richard. "Augustin et le *De regressu animae* de Porphyre." In *Augustin philosophe et prédicateur: Hommage à Goulven Madec*, édité par Isabelle Bochet, 67–110. Collection des Études Augustiniennes. Série Antiquité 195. Paris: Institut des Études Augustiniennes, 2012.

GOURINAT, Jean-Baptiste. *Les stoïciens et l'âme*. Philosophies. Paris: Presses Universitaires de France, 1996.

GRABBE, Lester L. "Aristobulus of Alexandria (the Philosopher)." In *Encyclopedia of the Bible and Its Reception*, 2: 724–726. Berlin/New York: De Gruyter, 2009.

———. *A History of the Jews and Judaism in the Second Temple Period*. Vol. 2, *The Early Hellenistic Period (335–175 BCE)*. Library of Second Temple Studies 68. London/New York: T&T Clark, 2008.

GRAETZ, Heinrich. "Die mystische Literatur in der gaonäischen Epoche." *Monatsschrift für Geschichte und Wissenschaft des Judentums* 8 (1859): 67–78, 103–118, 140–153.

GRAF, Fritz. *Gottesnähe und Schadenzauber: Die Magie in der griechisch-römischen Antike*. München: Beck, 1996.

———. "An Oracle against Pestilence from a Western Anatolian Town." *Zeitschrift für Papyrologie und Epigraphik* 92 (1992): 267–279.

———. "Plutarch und die Götterbilder." In *Gott und die Götter bei Plutarch: Götterbilder—Gottesbilder—Weltbilder*, herausgegeben von Rainer

Hirsch-Luipold, 251–266. Religionsgeschichtliche Versuche und Vorarbeiten 54. Berlin/New York: De Gruyter, 2005.

GRANT, Edward. *Planets, Stars, and Orbs: The Medieval Cosmos, 1200–1687.* Cambridge: Cambridge University Press, 1994.

GRANT, Robert M. *The Early Christian Doctrine of God.* Charlottesville: University Press of Virginia, 1966.

GRAPPONE, Antonio. "Annotazioni sulla cronologia delle omelie di Origene." *Augustinianum* 41 (2001): 27–58.

GRAUBNER, Hans. "Zum Problem des Anthropomorphismus in der Theologie (Hume, Kant, Hamann)." In *Johann Georg Hamann und England: Hamann und die englischsprachige Aufklärung; Acta des siebten Internationalen Hamann-Kolloquiums zu Marburg/Lahn 1996*, herausgegeben von Bernhard Gajek, 381–395. Regensburger Beiträge zur deutschen Sprach- und Literaturwissenschaft, Reihe B, Untersuchungen 69. Frankfurt am Main/Berlin/Bern: Peter Lang, 1999.

GRAUMANN, Thomas. "Reading *De oratione*: Aspects of Religious Practice in the Condemnation of Origen." In *Origeniana Nona: Origen and the Religious Practice of His Time; Papers of the 9th International Origen Congress, Pécs, Hungary, 29 August–2 September 2005*, edited by György Heidl and Robert Somos, 159–177. BETL 228. Leuven: Peeters, 2009.

GREATREX, Geoffrey. Introduction to *The Chronicle of Pseudo-Zachariah Rhetor: Church and War in Late Antiquity*, edited by Geoffrey Greatrex, translated by Robert R. Phenix and Cornelia B. Horn, with contributions by Sebastian P. Brock and Witold Witakowski, 3–31. Translated Texts for Historians 55. Liverpool: Liverpool University Press, 2011.

GREENBERG, Moshe. *Ezekiel 1–20: A New Translation with Introduction and Commentary.* The Anchor Bible 22. Garden City, N.Y.: Doubleday, 1983.

GRESCHAT, Katharina. *Apelles und Hermogenes: Zwei theologische Lehrer des zweiten Jahrhunderts.* Supplements to Vigiliae Christiane 48. Leiden: Brill, 2000.

———. "Selbstentfaltung Gottes in der Geschichte bei Irenäus von Lyon? Zur Kritik an einer weitverbreiteten Auffassung." In *Gott in der Geschichte: Zum Ringen um das Verständnis von Heil und Unheil in der Geschichte des Christentums*, herausgegeben von Mariano Delgado und Volker Leppin, 71–84. Studien zur christlichen Religions- und Kulturgeschichte 18. Fribourg: Academic Press; Stuttgart: Kohlhammer, 2013.

GRIFFIN, Carl W., and David L. PAULSEN. "Augustine and the Corporeality of God." *HTR* 95 (2002): 97–118.

GRIFFIN, Jasper. *Homer on Life and Death.* Oxford: Oxford University Press, 1980.

GRILLMEIER, Alois Kardinal. "Das 'Gebet zu Jesus' und das 'Jesus-Gebet': Eine neue Quelle zum 'Jesus-Gebet' aus dem Weißen Kloster." In *After Chalcedon: Studies in Theology and Church History, Offered to Albert van Roey for his Seventieth Birthday*, edited by Carl Laga, 187–202. Orientalia Lovaniensia Analecta 18. Leuven: Peeters, 1985.

————. *Jesus der Christus im Glauben der Kirche*. Bd. 1, *Von der Apostolischen Zeit bis zum Konzil von Chalcedon (451)*. Unter Mitarbeit von Theresia Hainthaler. 3. verbesserte und ergänzte Aufl. Freiburg/Basel/Wien: Herder, 1990.

————. *Jesus der Christus im Glauben der Kirche*. Bd. 2/2, *Die Kirche von Konstantinopel im 6. Jahrhundert*. Unter Mitarbeit von Theresia Hainthaler. Freiburg/Basel/Wien: Herder, 1989.

————. *Jesus der Christus im Glauben der Kirche*. Bd. 2/3, *Die Kirchen von Jerusalem und Antiochien nach 451 und bis 600*. Mit Beiträgen von Alois Grillmeier, Theresia Hainthaler, Tanios Bou Mansour und Luise Abramowski. Herausgegeben von Theresia Hainthaler. Freiburg/Basel/Wien: Herder 2002.

————. *Jesus der Christus im Glauben der Kirche*. Bd. 2/4, *Die Kirche von Alexandrien mit Nubien und Äthiopien nach 451*. Unter Mitarbeit von Theresia Hainthaler. Freiburg/Basel/Wien: Herder, 1990.

GROSS, Walter. "Die Gottesebenbildlichkeit des Menschen nach Gen 1,26.27 in der Diskussion des letzten Jahrzehnts." *Biblische Notizen* 68 (1993): 35–48.

GROSSE KRACHT, Hermann-Josef. "Kult des Individuums oder Sakralität der Person: Ungeklärte Beziehungen und neue Verständigungschancen zwischen Theologie und Sozialtheorie." In *Der moderne Glaube an die Menschenwürde: Philosophie, Soziologie und Theologie im Gespräch mit Hans Joas*, herausgegeben von Hermann-Josef Grosse Kracht, 223–241. Bielefeld: transcript, 2014.

GRUBER, Margareta. "Zwischen Bilderverbot und 'Vera Icon' oder: Wie viel Bild ist von Christus erlaubt?" *Lebendiges Zeugnis* 60 (2005): 100–115.

GRUENWALD, Ithamar. *Apocalyptic and Merkavah Mysticism*. Arbeiten zur Geschichte des antiken Judentums 14. Leiden: Brill, 1980.

GRÜTZMACHER, Georg. "Hilarion." In *Realencyclopädie für protestantische Theologie und Kirche*, 8: 54–56. Leipzig: Hinrichs, 1900.

GRUND, Alexandra. "'Aus der Schönheit Vollendung strahlt Gott auf' (Ps 50,2): Bemerkungen zur Wahrnehmung des Schönen in den Psalmen." In *"Wie schön sind deine Zelte, Jakob!" Beiträge zur Ästhetik des Alten Testaments*, herausgegeben von Alexandra Grund u.a., 100–129. Biblisch-Theologische Studien 60. Neukirchen-Vluyn: Neukirchener, 2003.

GRUNDMANN, Walter. "καλός." In *Theologisches Wörterbuch zum Neuen Testament* 3: 539–553. Stuttgart: Kohlhammer, 1938.

GRYPEOU, Emmanouela. "Höllenreisen und engelgleiches Leben: Die Rezeption von apokalyptischen Traditionen in der koptisch-monastischen Literatur." In *Christliches Ägypten in der spätantiken Zeit: Akten der zweiten Tübinger Tagung zum Christlichen Orient (7.–8. Dezember 2007)*, herausgegeben von Dmitrij Bumazhnov, 43–54. Studien und Texte zu Antike und Christentum 79. Tübingen: Mohr Siebeck, 2013.

GUELICH, Robert A. *Mark 1–8:26*. World Biblical Commentary 34A. Dallas: Word Books, 1989.

GUILLAUMONT, Antoine. "Das Jesusgebet bei den Mönchen Ägyptens." In idem, *An den Wurzeln des christlichen Mönchtums: Aufsätze*, ins Deutsche übertragen von Hagia Witzenrath. Weisungen der Väter 4. Beuron: Beuroner Kunstverlag, 2007.

———. "Evagrius Ponticus." In *Theologische Realenzyklopädie*, 10: 565–570. Berlin: De Gruyter, 1977.

———. "Histoire des moines aux Kellia." *Orientalia Lovaniensia Periodica* 8 (1977): 187–203.

———. "La vision de l'intellect par lui-même dans la mystique Évagrienne." *Mélanges de l'Université Saint-Joseph* 50 (1984): 255–262. (= idem, *Études sur la spiritualité de l'Orient chrétien.* Spiritualité orientale. Série Monachisme primitif 66. Bégrolles en Mauges: Abbaye de Bellefontaine, 1996.)

———. *Les "Kephalaia Gnostica" d'Évagre le Pontique et l'histoire de l'Origénisme chez les Grecs et les Syriens.* Patristica Sorbonensia 5. Paris: Éditions du Seuil, 1962.

———. "Une inscription copte sur la 'prière de Jésus.'" *Orientalia Christiana Periodica* 34 (1968): 310–325. (= idem, *Aux origines du monachisme chrétien: Pour une phénoménologie du monachisme*, 168–183. Spiritualité orientale 30. Bégrolles en Mauges: Abbaye de Bellefontaine, 1979.)

———. *Un philosophe au désert: Évagre le Pontique.* Textes et Traditions 8. Paris: Vrin, 2004.

GUINOT, Jean-N. *L'exégèse de Théodoret de Cyr.* Théologie historique 100. Paris: Beauchesne, 1995.

GUMBRECHT, Hans U. "Incarnation, Now: Five Brief Thoughts and a Non-conclusive Ending." *Communication and Critical/Cultural Studies* 8 (2011): 207–213.

GUNDEL, Wilhelm. *Dekane und Dekansternbilder: Ein Beitrag zur Geschichte der Sternbilder der Kulturvölker.* Mit einer Untersuchung über die ägyptischen Sternbilder und Gottheiten der Dekanae von Siegfried Schott. Studien der Bibliothek Warburg 19. Glückstadt/Hamburg: Augustin, 1936.

———. "Teukros 5)." In *Paulys Realencyclopädie der classischen Altertumswissenschaft*, 5A/1: 1132–1134. München: Alfred Druckenmüller, 1934.

GUNDRY, Robert Horton. *Sōma in Biblical Theology: With Emphasis on Pauline Anthropology.* Society for New Testament Studies. Monograph Series 29. Cambridge/New York: Cambridge University Press, 1976.

HAAS, Christopher. *Alexandria in Late Antiquity: Topography and Social Conflict.* Baltimore: Johns Hopkins University Press, 1997.

HABER, Honi Fern, and Gail WEISS, eds. *Perspectives on Embodiment: The Intersections of Nature and Culture.* New York: Routledge, 1999.

HABERMEHL, Peter. *Perpetua und der Ägypter oder die Bilder des Bösen im frühen afrikanischen Christentum: Ein Versuch zur Passio sanctarum Perpetua[e] et Felicitatis.* TU 140. Berlin/New York: De Gruyter, 2004.

———. *Petronius, Satyrica 79–141: Ein philologisch-literarischer Kommentar.* Bd. 1, *Sat. 79–110.* Texte und Kommentare 27/1. Berlin/New York: De Gruyter, 2006.

HACHLILI, Rachel. "The Zodiac in Ancient Jewish Art." *Bulletin of the American Schools of Oriental Research* 228 (1977): 61–77.

HADOT, Ilsetraut. "Erziehung und Bildung bei Augustin." In *Internationales Symposion über den Stand der Augustinus-Forschung, vom 12. bis 16. April 1987 im Schloss Rauischholzhausen der Justus-Liebig-Universität Gießen*, herausgegeben von Cornelius Mayer und Karl Heinz Chelius, 127–130. Cassiciacum 39/1 (= Res et Signa 1). Würzburg: Augustinus-Verlag, 1989.

HADOT, Pierre. *Marius Victorinus: Recherches sur sa vie et ses œuvres*. Paris: Institut des Études Augustiniennes, 1971.

HAHN, Johannes. "The Conversion of the Cult Statues: The Destruction of the Serapeion 392 A.D. and the Transformation of Alexandria into the 'Christ-Loving City.'" In *From Temple to Church: Destruction and Renewal of Local Cultic Topography in Late Antiquity*, edited by Johnnes Hahn, Stephen Emmel, and Ulrich Gotter, 335–366. Religions in the Graeco-Roman World 163. Leiden: Brill, 2008.

———. *Gewalt und religiöser Konflikt: Studien zu den Auseinandersetzungen zwischen Christen, Heiden und Juden im Osten des Römischen Reiches (von Konstantin bis Theodosius II.)*. Klio. Beihefte. Neue Folge 8. Berlin: Akademie-Verlag, 2004.

———. "'*Vetustus error extinctus est*'—Wann wurde das Sarapeion von Alexandria zerstört?" *Historia* 55 (2006): 368–383.

HÄKKINEN, Sakari. "Ebionites." In *A Companion to Second-Century Christian "Heretics*," edited by Antti Marjanen and Petri Luomanen, 247–278. SuppVC 76. Leiden: Brill, 2005.

HÅLAND, Evy J. "Athena's Peplos: Weaving as a Core Female Activity in Ancient and Modern Greece." *Cosmos* 20 (2004): 155–182.

HALBFASS, Wilhelm. "Evidenz." In *Historisches Wörterbuch der Philosophie*, 2: 829–832. Basel: Schwabe, 1972.

HALFWASSEN, Jens. *Der Aufstieg zum Einen: Untersuchungen zu Platon und Plotin*. Beiträge zur Altertumskunde 9. Stuttgart: Teubner, 1992.

———. "Platonismus II. Religionsphilosophisch." In *Religion in Geschichte und Gegenwart: Handwörterbuch für Theologie und Religionswissenschaft*, 6: 1387–1389. 4. Aufl. Tübingen: Mohr Siebeck, 2003.

———. "Schönheit und Bild im Neuplatonismus." In *Neuplatonismus und Ästhetik: Zur Transformationsgeschichte des Schönen*, herausgegeben von Verena Olejniczak Lobsien und Claudia Olk, 43–57. Transformationen der Antike 2. Berlin/New York: De Gruyter, 2007.

HALL, Robert G. "Isaiah's Ascent to See the Beloved: An Ancient Jewish Source for the Ascension of Isaiah." *Journal of Biblical Literature* 113 (1994): 463–484.

HALLEUX, André de. "La définition christologique à Chalcédoine." *Revue théologique de Louvain* 7 (1976): 3–23, 155–170. (= idem, *Patrologie et Oecuménisme: Recueil d'Études*. BETL 93. Leuven: Peeters, 1990.)

HÄLLSTRÖM, Gunnar af. *Fides simpliciorum according to Origen of Alexandria*. Societas Scientiarum Fennica. Commentationes Humanarum Litterarum 76. Helsinki: Finnish Society of Science and Letters, 1984.

HALPERIN, David J. *The Faces of the Chariot: Early Jewish Responses to Ezekiel's Vision*. TSAJ 16. Tübingen: Mohr Siebeck, 1988.

————. *The Merkabah in Rabbinic Literature*. American Oriental Studies 62. New Haven, Conn.: American Oriental Society, 1980.

HAMACHER, Elisabeth. "Die Sabbatopferlieder im Streit um Ursprung und Anfänge der jüdischen Mystik." *Journal for the Study of Judaism* 27 (1996): 119–154.

HARDER, Günther. "φθείρω κτλ." In *Theologisches Wörterbuch zum Neuen Testament*, 94–106. Stuttgart: Kohlhammer, 1973.

HARKER, Andrew. *Loyalty and Dissidence in Roman Egypt: The Case of the Acta Alexandrinorum*. Cambridge: Cambridge University Press, 2008.

HARL, Marguerite. *Origène et la fonction révélatrice du verbe incarné*. Paris: Éditions du Seuil, 1958.

————. "Structure et cohérence du Peri Archôn." In *Origeniana: Premier colloque international des études origéniennes (Montserrat, 18–21 septembre 1973)*, dirigé par Henri Crouzel, Gennaro Lomiento, et Josep Rius-Camps, 11–45. Quaderni di "Vetera Christianorum" 12. Bari: Istituto di letteratura cristiana antica, Università di Bari, 1975.

HÅRLEMAN, Einar. *De Claudiano Mamerto Gallicae Latinitatis Scriptore Quaestiones*. Uppsala: A. B. Lundequistska Bokhandeln, 1938.

HARNACK, Adolf von. "Brandt, Wilhelm: Elchasai, ein Religionsstifter und sein Werk (Rezension)." *Theologische Literaturzeitung* 37 (1912): 683f.

————. *Das Wesen des Christentums*. Leipzig: Hinrichs, 1929. (= Herausgegeben und kommentiert von Trutz Rendtorff. Gütersloh: Kaiser, 1999. = Herausgegeben von Claus-Dieter Osthövener. 2. durchgesehene Aufl. Tübingen: Mohr Siebeck, 2007.)

————. *Der kirchengeschichtliche Ertrag der exegetischen Arbeiten des Origenes*. Teil 2, *Die beiden Testamente mit Ausschluss des Hexateuchs und des Richterbuchs*. TU 42/4. Leipzig: Hinrichs, 1919.

————. *Die Hypotyposen des Theognost*. TU 24/3. Leipzig: Hinrichs, 1903.

————. *Die Überlieferung der griechischen Apologeten des 2. Jahrhunderts in der alten Kirche und im Mittelalter*. TU 1/1–2. Leipzig: Hinrichs, 1882. (= Berlin: Akademie-Verlag, 1991.)

————. *Lehrbuch der Dogmengeschichte*. Bd. 1, *Die Entstehung des kirchlichen Dogmas*. 4. neu durchgearbeitete und vermehrte Aufl. Tübingen: Mohr Siebeck, 1909.

————. *Marcion: Das Evangelium vom fremden Gott; Eine Monographie zur Geschichte der Grundlegung der katholischen Kirche*. Neue Studien zu Marcion. TU 45 und 44/4. 2. verbesserte und vermehrte Aufl. Leipzig: Hinrichs, 1924. (= Darmstadt: Wissenschaftliche Buchgesellschaft, 1960.)

HARRÉ, Rom. "Mind-Body Dualism." In *International Encyclopedia of the Social & Behavioral Sciences*, edited by Neil J. Smelser and Paul B. Baltes, 14: 9885–9889. Amsterdam: Elsevier, 2001.

HARRIES, Jill. *Sidonius Apollinaris and the Fall of Rome AD 407–485*. Oxford: Oxford University Press, 1994.

HARRIS, Jonathan Gil. *Foreign Bodies and the Body Politic: Discourses of Social Pathology in Early Modern England*. Cambridge: Cambridge University Press 1998.

Hartenstein, Friedhelm. *Das Angesicht JHWHs: Studien zu seinem höfischen und kultischen Bedeutungshintergrund in den Psalmen und in Exodus 32–34*. FAT 55. Tübingen: Mohr Siebeck, 2008.

———. "JHWHs Wesen im Wandel: Vorüberlegungen zu einer Theologie des Alten Testaments." *Theologische Literaturzeitung* 137 (2012): 3–20.

———. "Vom Sehen und Schauen Gottes: Überlegungen zu einer theologischen Ästhetik aus der Sicht des Alten Testaments." In *Marburger Jahrbuch Theologie XXII* (= Marburger Theologische Studien 110). Leipzig: Evangelische Verlagsanstalt, 2010.

———. "Wolkendunkel und Himmelsfeste: Zur Genese und Kosmologie der Vorstellung des himmlischen Heiligtums JHWHs." In *Das biblische Weltbild und seine altorientalischen Kontexte*, herausgegeben von Bernd Janowski und Beate Ego, in Zusammenarbeit mit Annette Krüger, 125–179. FAT 32. Tübingen: Mohr Siebeck, 2001.

Hartmann, Andreas. "Judenhass und Martyrium: Zum kulturgeschichtlichen Kontext der *Acta Alexandrinorum*." In *Zwischen Antike und Moderne: Festschrift für Jürgen Malitz zum 65. Geburtsta*, dargebracht von Kollegen, Freunden, Schülern und Weggefährten, derausgegeben von Andreas Hartmann und Gregor Weber, 119–209. Speyer: Kartoffeldruck-Verlag Brodersen, 2012.

Harvey, Arnold D. *Body Politic: Political Metaphor and Political Violence.* Cambridge: Cambridge Scholars, 2007.

Harvey, Susan Ashbrook. "Locating the Sensing Body: Perception and Religious Identity in Late Antiquity." In *Religion and the Self in Antiquity*, edited by David Brakke, Michael L. Satlow, and Steven Weitzman, 140–162. Bloomington: Indiana University Press, 2005.

Hasselhoff, Görge K. *Dicit Rabbi Moyses: Studien zum Bild von Moses Maimonides im lateinischen Westen vom 13. bis 15. Jahrhundert*. 2. Aufl. mit ein Nachwort. Würzburg: Königshausen & Neumann, 2005.

Hausherr, Irénée. "Le *De oratione* d'Évagre le Pontique en Syriaque et en Arabe." *Orientalia Christiana Periodica* 5 (1939): 7–71.

———. "Les grands courants de la spiritualité orientale." *Orientalia Christiana Periodica* 1 (1935): 114–138.

———. "Le *Traité de l'oraison* d'Évagre le Pontique (Pseudo-Nil)." *Revue d'Ascétique et de Mystique* 15 (1934): 34–93, 113–70.

———. *Noms du Christ et voies d'oraison*. Orientalia Christiana Analecta 157. Rome: Pontificium Institutum orientalium studiorum, 1960.

Heck, Eberhard. "Perrin, Michel: Lactance, *La colère de dieu* (Rezension)." *Gnomon* 57 (1985): 145–148.

Heidrich, Peter. "Mystik, mystisch." In *Historisches Wörterbuch der Philosophie*, 6: 268–273. Darmstadt: Wissenschaftliche Buchgesellschaft, 1984.

Heil, John Paul. *The Transfiguration of Jesus: Narrative Meaning and Function of Mark 9:2–8, Matt 17:1–8 and Luke 9:28–36*. Analecta biblica 144. Rome: Edizione Pontificio Istituto Biblico, 2000.

Heimgartner, Martin. *Pseudojustin—Über die Auferstehung: Text und Studie*. Patristische Texte und Studien 54. Berlin/New York: De Gruyter, 2001.

HEINRICH, Elisabeth. "Religionskritik im Spannungsfeld von logischer und genealogischer Argumentation." In *Kritik der Religion: Zur Aktualität einer unerledigten philosophischen und theologischen Aufgabe*, herausgegeben von Ingolf U. Dalferth und Hans-Peter Großhans, 95–116. Religion in Philosophy and Theology 23. Tübingen: Mohr Siebeck, 2006.

HEINZE, Richard. *Tertullians Apologeticum.* Berichte über Verhandlungen der Königlich Sächsischen Gesellschaft der Wissenschaften. Philologisch-historische Klasse 62. Heft 10. Leipzig: Teubner, 1910.

HEINZELMANN, Martin. "Gallische Prosopographie 260–527." *Francia* 10 (1982): 531–718.

HEITSCH, Ernst. "Das Wissen des Xenokrates." *Rheinisches Museum* 109 (1966): 193–235.

———. "Hesiod." In idem, *Gesammelte Schriften*, Bd. 2, *Zur griechischen Philosophie*. Beiträge zur Altertumskunde 153. Berlin/New York: De Gruyter, 2002.

HELDERMAN, Jan. *Die Anapausis im Evangelium Veritatis: Eine vergleichende Untersuchung des valentinianisch-gnostischen Heilsgutes der Ruhe im Evangelium Veritatis und in anderen Schriften der Nag-Hammadi-Bibliothek.* Nag Hammadi Studies 18. Leiden: Brill, 1984.

HELSSIG, Rudolf. *Die lateinischen und deutschen Handschriften der Universitätsbibliothek Leipzig.* Bd. 1, *Die theologischen Handschriften*, Tl. 1 (Ms 1–500). Wiesbaden: Harrassowitz, 1995.

HEMER, Colin J. *The Book of Acts in the Settings of Hellenistic History.* Edited by Conrad H. Gempf. WUNT 49. Tübingen: Mohr Siebeck, 1989.

HENGEL, Martin. "Der Finger und die Herrschaft Gottes in Lk 11,20." In *La Main de Dieu. Die Hand Gottes*, édité par René Kieffer et Jan Bergman, 87–106. WUNT 94. Tübingen: Mohr Siebeck, 1997. (= idem, *Jesus und die Evangelien: Kleine Schriften V*, herausgegeben von Claus-Jürgen Thornton, 644–663. WUNT 211. Tübingen: Mohr Siebeck, 2007.)

———. *Juden, Griechen und Barbaren: Aspekte der Hellenisierung des Judentums in vorchristlicher Zeit.* Stuttgarter Bibelstudien 76. Stuttgart: Verlag Katholisches Bibelwerk, 1976.

———. *Judentum und Hellenismus: Studien zu ihrer Begegnung unter besonderer Berücksichtigung Palästinas bis zur Mitte des 2. Jahrhunderts vor Christus.* WUNT 10. 3. durchgesehene Aufl. Tübingen: Mohr Siebeck, 1988.

———. "Mors turpissima Crucis: Die Kreuzigung in der antiken Welt und die 'Torheit' des 'Wortes vom Kreuz.'" In *Rechtfertigung: FS Ernst Käsemann zum 70. Geburtstag*, herausgegeben von Johannes Friedrich, Wolfgang Pöhlmann und Peter Stuhlmacher, 123–184. Tübingen: Mohr Siebeck; Göttingen: Vandenhoeck & Ruprecht, 1976. (= idem, *Studien zum Urchristentum: Kleine Schriften VI*, herausgegeben von Claus-Jürgen Thornton, 594–652. WUNT 234. Tübingen: Mohr Siebeck, 2008.)

———. "'Setze dich zu meiner Rechten!' Die Inthronisation Christi zur Rechten Gottes und Psalm 110,1." In idem, *Studien zur Christologie: Kleine Schriften IV*, herausgegeben von Claus-Jürgen Thornton, 281–367.

Tübingen: Mohr Siebeck, 2006. (= Philonenko, Marc, ed., *Le trône de Dieu*, 108–194. WUNT 69. Tübingen: Mohr Siebeck, 1993.)

Hengel, Martin, in collaboration with Christoph Markschies. *The "Hellenization" of Judaea in the First Century after Christ*. London: SCM Press, 1989.

Hengel, Martin, und Anna M. Schwemer. *Geschichte des frühen Christentums*. Bd. 1, *Jesus und das Judentum*. Tübingen: Mohr Siebeck, 2007.

Hengelbrock, Jürgen. "Affekt." In *Historisches Wörterbuch der Philosophie*, 1: 89–93. Darmstadt: Wissenschaftliche Buchgesellschaft, 1971.

Hennessey, Lawrence R. "A Philosophical Issue in Origen's Eschatology: The Three Senses of Incorporeality." In *Origeniana Quinta: Historica—Text and Method—Biblica—Philosophica—Theologica—Origenism and Later Developments; Papers of the 5th International Origen Congress Boston College (14–18 August 1989)*, edited by Robert J. Daly, 373–380. BETL 105. Leuven: Peeters, 1992.

Henry, Paul. *La vision d'Ostie: Sa place dans la vie et l'œuvre de saint Augustin*. Paris: Vrin, 1938. (= "Die Vision zu Ostia." In *Zum Augustin-Gespräch der Gegenwart, herausgegeben von Carl Andresen*, 201–270. Wege der Forschung 5. Darmstadt: Wissenschaftliche Buchgesellschaft, 1962.)

———. *Plotin et l'Occident: Firmicus Maternus, Marius Victorinus, Saint Augustin et Macrobe*. Spicilegium Sacrum Lovaniense 15. Louvain: Spicilegium Sacrum Lovaniense, 1934.

Herrmann, Florian. *Strategien der Todesdarstellung in der Markuspassion: Ein literaturgeschichtlicher Vergleich*. Novum Testamentum et Orbis Antiquus. (= Studien zur Umwelt des Neuen Testaments 86). Göttingen: Vandenhoeck & Ruprecht, 2010.

Herrmann, Klaus. "Jüdische Gnosis? Dualismus und 'gnostische' Motive in der frühen jüdischen Mystik." In *Zugänge zur Gnosis: Akten zur Tagung der Patristischen Arbeitsgemeinschaft vom 02.–05.01.2011 in Berlin-Spandau*, herausgegeben von Christoph Markschies und Johannes van Oort, 43–90. Studien der Patristischen Arbeitsgemeinschaft 12. Leuven/Walpole, Mass.: Peeters, 2013.

———, Hg. *Massekhet Hekhalot: Traktat von den himmlischen Palästen; Edition, Übersetzung und Kommentar*. TSAJ 39. Tübingen: Mohr Siebeck, 1994.

———. "Text und Fiktionen: Zur Textüberlieferung des Shi'ur Qoma." *Frankfurter Judaistische Beiträge* 16 (1988): 89–142.

Herzog, Rudolf. *Die Wunderheilungen von Epidauros: Ein Beitrag zur Geschichte der Medizin und der Religion*. Philologus. Supplement 22/3. Leipzig: Dieterich, 1931.

Heussi, Karl. *Untersuchungen zu Nilus dem Asketen*. TU 42/2. Leipzig: Hinrichs, 1917.

Heyden, Katharina. *Die "Erzählung des Aphroditian": Thema und Variation einer Legende im Spannungsfeld von Christentum und Heidentum*. Studien und Texte zu Antike und Christentum 53. Tübingen: Mohr Siebeck, 2009.

HEZSER, Catherine. *Lohnmetaphorik und Arbeitswelt in Mt 20,1–16: Das Gleichnis von den Arbeitern im Weinberg im Rahmen rabbinischer Lohngleichnisse.* Novum Testamentum et Orbis Antiquus 15. Fribourg: Universitäts-Verlag; Göttingen: Vandenhoeck & Ruprecht, 1990.

HILGENFELD, Adolf. "Der gnostische und der kanonische Johannes über das Leben Jesu." *Zeitschrift für wissenschaftliche Theologie* 43 (1900): 1–61.

———. *Die clementinischen Recognitionen und Homilien, nach ihrem Ursprung und Inhalt.* Jena: Schreiber, 1848.

———. *Ketzergeschichte des Urchristenthums urkundlich dargestellt.* Leipzig: Fues, 1884. (= Darmstadt: Wissenschaftliche Buchgesellschaft, 1963.)

HILGERT, Earle. "Symbolismus und Heilsgeschichte in den Evangelien: Ein Beitrag zu den Seesturm- und Gerasenererzählungen." In *Oikonomia: Heilsgeschichte als Thema der Theologie; Oscar Cullmann zum 65. Geburtstag gewidmet*, herausgegeben von Felix Christ, 51–56. Hamburg-Bergstedt: Reich, 1967.

HIMMELFARB, Martha. *Ascent to Heaven in Jewish and Christian Apocalypses.* New York: Oxford University Press, 1993.

———. "Heavenly Ascent and the Relationship of the Apocalypses and the *Hekhalot* Literature." *Hebrew Union College Annual* 59 (1988): 73–100.

———. "Merkavah Mysticism since Scholem: Rachel Elior's *The Three Temples.*" In *Wege mystischer Gotteserfahrung: Judentum, Christentum und Islam. Mystical Approaches to God: Judaism, Christianity, and Islam*, herausgegeben von Peter Schäfer unter Mitarbeit von Elisabeth Müller-Luckner, 19–36. Schriften des Historischen Kollegs. Kolloquien 65. München: Oldenbourg Verlag, 2006.

HIRSCHBERG, Martin. *Studien zur Geschichte der "simplices" in der Alten Kirche: Ein Beitrag zum Problem der Schichtungen in der menschlichen Erkenntnis.* Berlin: maschinenschriftlich vervielfältigt, 1944.

HOEK, Annewies van den. "*Papyrus Berolinensis 20915* in the Context of other Early Christian Writings from Egypt." In *Origeniana Octava: Origen and the Alexandrian Tradition: Papers of the 8th International Origen Congress Pisa, 27–31 August 2001, Lorenzo Perrone*, edited in collaboration with Paolo Bernardini and Diego Marchini, 75–92. BETL 164. Leuven: Peeters, 2003.

HOFFMANN, Wolfgang. Ὁ θεὸς ἀπροσδεής: *Gottes Bedürfnislosigkeit in den Schriften der frühen Väterzeit.* Teildruck einer maschinenschriftlichen Dissertation an der Gregoriana Rom 1965. Bonn: n.n., 1966.

HOFIUS, Otfried. "'Der in des Vaters Schoß ist' Joh 1,18." In idem und Hans-Christian Kammler, *Johannesstudien: Untersuchungen zur Theologie des vierten Evangeliums*, 24–32. WUNT 88. Tübingen: Mohr Siebeck, 1996.

HOLL, Karl. "Die Zeitfolge des ersten origenistischen Streits." In idem, *Gesammelte Aufsätze zur Kirchengeschichte*, Bd. 2, *Der Osten*, 310–335. Tübingen: Mohr Siebeck, 1928.

HÖLSCHER, Fernande. *Die Macht der Gottheit im Bild: Archäologische Studien zur griechischen Götterstatue.* Heidelberg: Verlag Antike, 2017.

HOMMEL, Hildebrecht. *Symmetrie im Spiegel der Antike.* Sitzungsberichte der Heidelberger Akademie der Wissenschaften. Philosophisch-historische Klasse 5/1986. Heidelberg: Winter, 1987.

HOPKINS, Clark. "The Excavation of the Dura Synagogue Paintings." In *The Dura-Europos Synagogue: A Re-evaluation (1932–1972)*, edited by Joseph Gutmann, 15f. Chamberburg, Pa.: American Academy of Religion, 1973.

HOPPE, Heinrich. *Beiträge zur Sprache und Kritik Tertullians.* Publications of the New Society of Letters at Lund 14. Lund: Gleerup, 1932.

HORN, Hans Jürgen "Stoische Symmetrie und Theorie des Schönen in der Kaiserzeit." In *ANRW* II, *Prinzipat*, 36.3, *Philosophie, Wissenschaften, Technik: Philosophie (Stoizismus)*, herausgegeben von Wolfgang Haase, 1454–1472. Berlin/New York: De Gruyter, 1989.

HORST, Pieter van der. "'The Finger of God': Miscellaneous Notes on Luke 11:20 and Its *Umwelt.*" In *Sayings of Jesus: Canonical and Non-canonical: Essays in Honour of Tjitze Baarda*, edited by William L. Petersen, Johan S. Vos, and Henk J. de Jonge, 89–103. Novum Testamentum Supplements 89. Leiden: Brill, 1997.

———. "Moses' Throne Vision in Ezekiel the Dramatist." *JJS* 34 (1983): 21–29. (= idem, *Essays on the Jewish World of Early Christianity*, 63–71. Novum Testamentum et Orbis Antiquus 14. Göttingen: Vandenhoeck & Ruprecht/Fribourg: Universitäts-Verlag, 1986.)

———. "Some Notes on the 'Exagoge' of Ezekiel." *Mnemosyne* 37 (1984): 354–375. (= idem, *Essays on the Jewish World of Early Christianity*, 72–93. Novum Testamentum et Orbis Antiquus 14. Göttingen: Vandenhoeck & Ruprecht; Fribourg: Universitäts-Verlag, 1986.)

HORSTMANN, Axel. "Mythos, Mythologie VI: 20. Jahrhundert." In *Historisches Wörterbuch der Philosophie*, 6: 300–318. Darmstadt: Wissenschaftliche Buchgesellschaft, 1984.

HOSSFELD, Frank-Lothar. "Das Buch Ezechiel." In *Einleitung in das Alte Testament*, herausgegeben von Christian Frevel, 592–621. 8. vollständig überarbeitete Aufl. Kohlhammer Studienbücher Theologie 1/1. Stuttgart: Kohlhammer, 2012.

HOVORUN, Cyril. *Will, Action and Freedom: Christological Controversies in the Seventh Century.* The Medieval Mediterranean 77. Leiden: Brill, 2008.

HUBER, Irene. *Rituale der Seuchen- und Schadensabwehr im Vorderen Orient und Griechenland: Formen kollektiver Krisenbewältigung in der Antike.* Oriens et Occidens 10. Stuttgart: Steiner, 2005.

HÜBNER, Reinhard M. *Die Einheit des Leibes bei Gregor von Nyssa: Untersuchungen zum Ursprung der "physischen" Erlösungslehre.* Philosophia Patrum 2. Leiden: Brill, 1974.

———. *Die Wahrheit des Mythos.* München: Beck, 1985.

———. "Melito von Sardes und Noët von Smyrna." In *Oecumenica et Patristica: Festschrift für Wilhelm Schneemelcher zum 75. Geburtstag*, herausgegeben von Damaskinos Papandreou, Wolfgang A. Bienert und Knut Schäferdiek, 219–240. Stuttgart/Berlin/Köln: Kohlhammer, 1989.

(= idem, *Der paradox Eine: Antignostischer Monarchianismus im zweiten Jahrhundert*, mit einem Beitrag von Markus Vinzent. SuppVC 50. Leiden: Brill, 1999.)

―――. "Mythos: Philosophisch." In *Theologische Realenzyklopädie* 23: 597–608. Berlin/New York: De Gruyter, 1994.

―――. "Thesen zur Echtheit und Datierung der sieben Briefe des Ignatius von Antiochien." *Zeitschrift für Antikes Christentum* 1 (1997): 44–72.

HUFFMAN, Carl A. *Archytas of Tarentum: Pythagorean, Philosopher and Mathematician King*. Cambridge: Cambridge University Press, 2005.

HULTSCH, Friedrich. *Griechische und römische Metrologie*. 2. Aufl. Berlin: Weidmann, 1882.

HUME, David. *Dialogues concerning Natural Religion*. Pt. 4, *A Treatise of Human Nature Being an Attempt to Introduce the Experimental Method of Reasoning into Moral Subjects and Dialogues concerning Natural Religion*. Edited with preliminary dissertations and notes by Thomas Hill Green and Thomas Hodge Grose. Vol. 2. Aalen: Scientia Verlag, 1964. (= London, 1886.)

HUNT, Edward D. *Holy Land Pilgrimage in the Later Roman Empire AD 312– 460*. Oxford: Clarendon, 1998.

―――. "St. Silvia of Aquitaine: The Role of a Theodosian Pilgrim in the Society of East and West." *JTS* 23 (1972): 351–373.

HUNT, Hannah. *Clothed in the Body: Asceticism, the Body and the Spiritual in the Late Antique Era*. Ashgate Studies in Philosophy & Theology in Late Antiquity. Farnham, Surrey/Burlington, Vt.: Ashgate, 2012.

HUTTON, Jeremy M. "Southern, Northern and Transjordanian Perspectives." In *Religious Diversity in Israel and Juda*, edited by Francesca Stavrakopoulou and John Barton, 149–174. London/New York: T&T Clark, 2010.

HYATT, J. Philip. "The Deity Bethel and the Old Testament." *Journal of the American Oriental Society* 59 (1939): 81–89.

ICKS, Martijn. *The Crimes of Elagabalus: The Life and Legacy of Rome's Decadent Boy Emperor*. London: I. B. Tauris, 2011.

IRMSCHER, Johannes. "Das Buch des Elchasai." In *Neutestamentliche Apokryphen in deutscher Übersetzung*. Bd. 2, *Apostolisches, Apokalypsen und Verwandtes*, herausgegeben von Wilhelm Schneemelcher, 5. Aufl. der von Edgar Hennecke begründeten Sammlung, 619–623. Tübingen: Mohr Siebeck, 1989.

―――. "Die Anfänge der koptischen Papyrologie." In *Graeco-Coptica: Griechen und Kopten im byzantinischen Ägypten* [Referate der V. Koptologischen Arbeitskonferenz, 25.–27. Mai 1983], herausgegeben von Peter Nagel, 121–136. Wissenschaftliche Beiträge der Martin-Luther-Universität Halle-Wittenberg 48/1984. Halle, Saale: Universität Halle-Wittenberg, 1984.

ISRAEL, W. "Die Vita S. Hilarionis des Hieronymus als Quelle für die Anfänge des Mönchtums kritisch untersucht." *Zeitschrift für wissenschaftliche Theologie* 23 (1880): 129–165.

ISRAELI, Yael, and David MEVORAH, eds. *Cradle of Christianity*. Exhibition at the Israel Museum Jerusalem, Weisbord Exhibition Pavillon, Spring 2000–Winter 2001. Jerusalem: Israel Museum, 2000.

IVANKA, Endre von. "ΚΕΦΑΛΑΙΑ: Eine byzantinische Literaturform und ihre antiken Wurzeln." *Byzantinsche Zeitschrift* 47 (1954): 285–291.

JACOBS, Andrew S. *Christ Circumcised: A Study in Early Christian History and Difference*. Philadelphia: University of Pennsylvania Press, 2012.

JACOBSEN, Anders-Christian Lund. "The Constitution of Man according to Irenaeus and Origen." In *Körper und Seele: Aspekte spätantiker Anthropologie*, herausgegeben von Barbara Feichtinger, Stephen Lake und Helmut Seng, 67–94. Beiträge zur Altertumskunde 215. München/ Leipzig: K. G. Saur, 2006.

———. "The Importance of Genesis 1–3 in the Theology of Irenaeus." *Zeitschrift für Antikes Christentum* 8 (2005): 299–316.

JACOBSON, Howard. *The Exagoge of Ezekiel*. Cambridge: Cambridge University Press, 1983.

———. "A Philonic Rejection of Plato." *Mnemosyne* 57 (2004): 488f.

JACOBY, Felix. *Diagoras ὁ ἄθεος*. Abhandlungen der Deutschen Akademie der Wissenschaften zu Berlin. Klasse für Sprachen, Literatur und Kunst 3/1959. Berlin: Akademie, 1959.

———. "Hekataios 4) Hekataios aus Abdera." In *Paulys Realencyclopädie der classischen Altertumswissenschaft*, 7/2: 2750–2769. München: Alfred Druckenmüller, 1912.

JAEGER, Werner. *Die Theologie der frühen griechischen Denker*. Stuttgart: Kohlhammer, 2009. (= 1953.)

———. "Greeks and Jews: The First Greek Records of Jewish Religion and Civilization." *Journal of Religion* 18 (1938): 127–143.

———. *Paideia: Die Formung des griechischen Menschen*. Bd. 1. Berlin/ Leipzig: De Gruyter, 1934.

JAMMER, Max. *Concepts of Space: The History of Theories of Space in Physics*. Cambridge, Mass.: Havard University Press, 1954.

JANOWITZ, Naomi. "God's Body: Theological and Ritual Roles of *Shi'ur Komah*." In *People of the Body: Jews and Judaism from an Embodied Perspective*, edited by Howard Eilberg-Schwartz, 183–202. Albany: University of the State of New York Press, 1992.

JANOWSKI, Bernd. "Das biblische Weltbild: Eine methodologische Skizze." In *Das biblische Weltbild und seine altorientalischen Kontexte*, herausgegeben von Beate Ego und Bernd Janowski, 229–260. FAT 32. Tübingen: Mohr Siebeck, 2001.

———. "Keruben und Zion: Thesen zur Entstehung der Zionstradition." In idem, *Gottes Gegenwart in Israel*, 247–280. Beiträge zur Theologie des Alten Testaments 1. Neukirchen-Vluyn: Neukirchener, 1993.

JANTZEN, Grace. *God's World, God's Body*. Philadelphia: Westminster Press, 1984.

JASTROW, Marcus. *A Dictionary of the Targumim, the Talmud Babli and Yerushalmi, and the Midrashic Literature*. London: Luzac, 1903/1905. (= Peabody, Mass.: Hendrickson, 2005.)

JELLINEK, Adolf. *Beiträge zur Geschichte der Kabbala.* Bd. 2. Leipzig: Fritzsche, 1852.

————, Hg. *Beth ha-Midrasch: Sammlung kleiner Midraschim und vermischter Abhandlungen aus der ältern jüdischen Literatur.* Nach Handschriften und Druckwerken gesammelt und nebst Einleitungen herausgegeben. Tl. 6. Jerusalem: Bamberger & Wahrmann, 1938. (= Leipzig/Wien: Wahrmann, 1877.)

JEWETT, Robert. *Paul's Anthropological Terms: A Study of Their Use in Conflict Settings.* AGAJU 10. Leiden: Brill, 1971.

JOAS, Hans. *Die Sakralität der Person: Eine neue Genealogie der Menschenrechte.* Berlin: Suhrkamp, 2011.

JONES, Arnold H., John R. MARTINDALE, and John MORRIS. *The Prosopography of the Later Roman Empire.* Vol. 1, *A.D. 260–395.* Cambridge: Cambridge University Press, 1971.

JONES, Christopher P. "The Olympieion and the Hadrianeion at Ephesos." *Journal of Hellenic Studies* 113 (1993): 149–152.

JONES, F. Stanley. "The *Book of Elchasai* in Its Relevance for Manichean Instruction with a Supplement: *Book of Elchasai* Reconstructed and Translated." In idem, *Pseudoclementina*, 359–397.

————. "The Genre of the *Book of Elchasai*: A Primitive Church Order, Not an Apocalypse." In idem, *Pseudoclementina*, 398–416.

————. "Marcionism in the *Pseudo-Clementines*." In idem, *Pseudoclementina*, 152–171.

————. *Pseudoclementina Elchasaiticaque inter Judaeochristiana: Collected Studies.* Orientalia Lovaniensia Analecta 203. Leuven/Paris/Walpole, Mass.: Peeters, 2012.

————. "The Pseudo-Clementines: A History of Research." In idem, *Pseudoclementina*, 50–113.

JORDAN, Hermann. *Armenische Irenaeusfragmente.* Mit deutscher Übersetzung nach Dr. Willy Lüdtke, zum Teil erstmalig herausgegeben und untersucht. TU 36/3. Leipzig: Hinrichs, 1913.

JORI, Alberto. "Geschichte der Lehre vom ersten Körper (Äther)." In *Aristoteles: Über den Himmel*, übersetzt und erläutert von Alberto Jori, Aristoteles Werke in deutscher Übersetzung 12/3, 193–259. Berlin: Akademie-Verlag, 2009.

JOUSSARD, G. "Une citation et un ouvrage de saint Hippolyte sous le nom de saint Irénée?" *Revue des sciences religieuses* 17 (1937): 290–305.

JUGIE, Martin. "Gaïanité." In *Dictionnaire de théologie catholique*, 6: 1002–1022. Paris: Letouzey et Ané, 1920.

JÜLICHER, Adolf. "Bemerkungen zu der Abhandlung des Herrn Holl 'Die Zeitfolge des ersten origenistischen Streits.'" In Karl Holl, *Gesammelte Aufsätze zur Kirchengeschichte*, Bd. 2, *Der Osten*, 335–350. Tübingen: Mohr Siebeck, 1928.

————. "Eutyches 5." In *Paulys Realencyclopädie der classischen Altertumswissenschaft*, 6/1: 1527–1529. Stuttgart: Alfred Druckenmüller, 1907.

Jung, Franz, Hg. *Hilarius von Arles: Leben des heiligen Honoratus. Eine Textstudie zum Mönchtum und Bischofswesen im spätantiken Gallien.* Fohren-Linden: Carthusianus, 2013.

Jüngel, Eberhard. "Anthropomorphismus als Grundproblem neuzeitlicher Hermeneutik." In idem, *Wertlose Wahrheit: Zur Identität und Relevanz des christlichen Glaubens*, 110–131. Theologische Erörterungen 3. 2., um ein Register erweiterte Aufl. Tübingen: Mohr Siebeck, 2003.

———. "Die Wahrheit des Mythos und die Notwendigkeit der Entmythologisierung." In idem, *Indikative der Gnade—Imperative der Freiheit*, 40–57. Theologische Erörterungen 4. Tübingen: Mohr Siebeck, 2000.

———. *Gott als Geheimnis der Welt: Zur Begründung der Theologie des Gekreuzigten im Streit zwischen Theismus und Atheismus.* 8., erneut durchgesehene Aufl. Tübingen: Mohr Siebeck, 2010.

Junod, Éric. "Polymorphie du Dieu Saveur." In *Gnosticisme et Monde Hellénistique: Actes du Colloque de Louvain-la-Neuve (11–14 mars 1980)*, édité par Julien Ries, 38–46. Louvain-la-Neuve: Université catholique de Louvain, Institute orientaliste, 1982.

———. "Wodurch unterscheiden sich die Homilien des Origenes von seinen Kommentaren?" In *Predigt in der Alten Kirche*, herausgegeben von Ekkehard Mühlenberg und Johannes van Oort, 50–81. Studien der Patristischen Arbeitsgemeinschaft 3. Kampen: Kok Pharos, 1994.

Kaeser, Bert. "Die Körper der Götter und die Wahrheit der Bilder." In *Die Unsterblichen: Götter Griechenlands*, herausgegeben von den Staatlichen Antikensammlungen und Glyptothek München, 52–79. Lindenberg im Allgäu: Kunstverlag Josef Fink, 2012.

Kaiser, Otto. "Der eine Gott und die Götter der Welt." In idem, *Zwischen Athen und Jerusalem: Studien zur griechischen und biblischen Theologie, ihrer Eigenart und ihrem Verhältnis*, 135–152. Beihefte zur Zeitschrift für die alttestamentliche Wissenschaft 320. Berlin/New York: De Gruyter, 2003.

———. *Der Gott des Alten Testaments: Theologie des Alten Testaments. Tl. 2, Jahwe, der Gott Israels, Schöpfer der Welt und des Menschen.* Uni-Taschenbücher. Wissenschaft 2024. Göttingen: Vandenhoeck & Ruprecht, 1998.

Kaiser-Minn, Helga. *Die Erschaffung des Menschen auf den spätantiken Monumenten des 3. und 4. Jahrhunderts.* Jahrbuch für Antike und Christentum. Ergänzungsbände 6. Münster: Aschendorff, 1981.

Kannengiesser, Charles. "Das Vermächtnis des 'fleißigen Origenes' zur Theologie des Athanasius." In *Origeniana septima: Origenes in den Auseinandersetzungen des vierten Jahrhunderts* [7. Internationales Origeneskolloquium, vom 25. bis zum 29. August 1997, Hofgeismar], herausgegeben von Wolfgang A. Bienert, 173–186. BETL 137. Leuven: University Press/Peeters, 1999.

———. "Origen, Systematician in *De Principiis*." In *Origeniana Quinta: Historica–Text and Method—Biblica—Philosophica—Theologica—Origenism and Later Developments; Papers of the 5th International*

Origen Congress Boston College, 14–18 August 1989, edited by Robert J. Daly, 395–405. BETL 105. Leuven: Peeters, 1992.

Kant, Immanuel. *Kritik der reinen Vernunft.* Kants Gesammelte Schriften, herausgegeben von der Königlich Preußischen Akademie der Wissenschaften. Bd. 3. Berlin: De Gruyter, 1911.

———. *Prolegomena to Any Future Metaphysics That Will Be Able to Come Forward as Science: With Selections from the "Critique of Pure Reason."* Translated from the German by Gary Carl Hatfield. Rev. ed. Cambridge Texts in the History of Philosophy. Cambridge: Cambridge University Press, 2004. (= idem, *Prolegomena zu einer jeden künftigen Metaphysik, die als Wissenschaft wird auftreten können.* Kants Gesammelte Schriften. Herausgegeben von der Königlich Preußischen Akademie der Wissenschaften. Bd. 4, 253–383. Berlin: De Gruyter, 1903–1911.)

Kantorowicz, Ernst H. *The King's Two Bodies: A Study in Medieval Political Theology.* Princeton, N.J.: Princeton University Press, 1957.

Karpp, Heinrich. *Probleme altchristlicher Anthropologie: Biblische Anthropologie und philosophische Psychologie bei den Kirchenvätern des dritten Jahrhunderts.* Beiträge zur Förderung christlicher Theologie 44/3. Gütersloh: Bertelsmann, 1950.

Kasser, Rodolphe. "La 'prière de Jésus' Kelliote réexaminée en quelques points." *Orientalia Christiana Periodica* 62 (1996): 407–410.

———. "Le monachisme copte." In *Les Kellia, ermitages coptes en Basse-Egypte.* Musée d'art et d'histoire Genève, 12 octobre 1989–7 janvier 1990. Genève: Éditions du Tricorne, 1989.

———. "Sortir du monde: Réflexions sur la situation et le développement des établissements monastiques aux Kellia." *Revue de théologie et de philosophie* 109 (1976): 111–124.

Kattenbusch, Ferdinand. *Das apostolische Symbol: Seine Entstehung, sein geschichtlicher Sinn, seine ursprüngliche Stellung im Kultus und in der Theologie der Kirche.* Bd. 2, *Verbreitung und Bedeutung des Taufsymbols.* Leipzig: Hinrichs, 1900.

Kaulbach, Friedrich. "Leib, Körper: II. Neuzeit." In *Historisches Wörterbuch der Philosophie*, 5: 178–185. Darmstadt: Wissenschaftliche Buchgesellschaft, 1980.

Kearns, Emily. "The Gods in the Homeric Epics." In *The Cambridge Companion to Homer*, edited by Robert Fowler, 59–73. Cambridge: Cambridge University Press, 2004.

Keil, Bruno. "Ein neues Bruchstück des Diagoras von Melos." *Hermes* 55 (1920): 63–67.

Kelley, Nicole. *Knowledge and Religious Authority in the Pseudo-Clementines: Situating the Recognitions in Fourth Century Syria.* WUNT 2/213. Tübingen: Mohr Siebeck, 2006.

Kellner, Karl A. *Heortologie oder die geschichtliche Entwicklung des Kirchenjahres und der Heiligenfeste: Von den ältesten Zeiten bis zur Gegenwart.* 3. Aufl. Freiburg: Herder, 1911.

KELLY, Christopher J. *Cassian's Conferences: Scriptural Interpretation and the Monastic Ideal.* Ashgate New Critical Thinking in Religion, Theology and Biblical Studies Series. Farnham/Burlington, Vt: Ashgate, 2012.

KELLY, John N. *Early Christian Creeds.* 3rd ed. London: Longman, 1972.

———. *Golden Mouth: The Story of John Chrysostom—Ascetic, Preacher, Bishop.* London: Duckworth, 1995.

———. *Jerome: His Life, Writings, and Controversies.* London: Duckworth, 1975.

KERMANI, Navid. *God Is Beautiful: The Aesthetic Experience of the Quran.* Translated from the German by Tony Crawford. Cambridge: Polity Press, 2014.

KERN, Otto, Hg. *Die Inschriften von Magnesia am Maeander.* Berlin: W. Spemann, 1900.

KESSLER, Herbert L. "409 Two Copies of Minatures from the Cotton Genesis." In *Age of Spirituality: Late Antique and Christian Art, Third to Seventh Century: Catalogue of the Exhibition at the Metropolitan Museum of Art, November 19, 1977, through February 12, 1978*, edited by Kurt Weitzmann, 458. Princeton, N.J.: Princeton University Press, 1977.

KIHN, Heinrich. *Theodor von Mopsuestia und Junilius Africanus als Exegeten, nebst einer kritischen Textausgabe von des letzteren Instituta regularia divinae legis.* Freiburg: Herder, 1880.

KIM, Young R. "Epiphanius of Cyprus vs. John of Jerusalem: An Improper Ordination and the Escalation of the Origenist Controversy." In *Episcopal Elections in Late Antiquity*, edited by John Leemans, Peter van Nuffelen, Shawn W. J. Keough, and Carla Nicoloaye, 411–422. Arbeiten zur Kirchengeschichte 119. Berlin/Boston: De Gruyter, 2011.

KIPPENBERG, Hans G. *Garizim und Synagoge: Traditionsgeschichtliche Untersuchungen zur samaritanischen Religion der aramäischen Periode.* Religionsgeschichtliche Versuche und Vorarbeiten 30. Berlin: De Gruyter, 1971.

KISSLING, Robert C. "The OXHMA—ΠΝΕΥΜΑ of the Neo-Platonists and the *De insomniis* of Synesius of Cyrene." *American Journal of Philology* 43 (1922): 318–330.

KITZLER, Petr. *"Nihil enim anima si non corpus*: Tertullian und die Körperlichkeit der Seele." *Wiener Studien* 122 (2009): 145–169.

KLAUCK, Hans-Josef. *Allegorie und Allegorese in synoptischen Gleichnistexten.* Neutestamentliche Abhandlungen. Neue Folge 13. Münster: Aschendorff, 1978.

KLAUSER, Theodor. "Der Festkalender der Alten Kirche im Spannungsfeld jüdischer Traditionen, christlicher Glaubensvorstellungen und missionarischen Anpassungswillens." In *Kirchengeschichte als Missionsgeschichte*, Bd. 1, *Die alte Kirche*, herausgegeben von Heinzgünther Frohnes und Uwe W. Knorr, 377–388. München: Kaiser, 1974.

KLOCH-KORNITZ, Peter von. "Zum Anfang von Pindars Nemea VI." *Hermes* 89 (1961): 370f.

KLOOS, Kari. "Seeing the Invisible God: Augustine's Reconfiguration of Theophany Narrative Exegesis." *Augustinian Studies* 36 (2005): 397–420.

KOBUSCH, Theo. "Nichts, Nichtseiendes." In *Historisches Wörterbuch der Philosophie*, 6: 805–836. Darmstadt: Wissenschaftliche Buchgesellschaft, 1984.

KOCH, Anton F. "Topos (1)/Raum." In *Aristoteles-Lexikon*, herausgegeben von Otfried Höffe, 603–605. Kröners Taschenausgabe 459. Stuttgart: Kröner, 2005.

KOCH, Hal. *Pronoia und Paideusis: Studien über Origenes und sein Verhältnis zum Platonismus*. Arbeiten zur Kirchengeschichte 22. Berlin: De Gruyter, 1932.

KOCH, Klaus. *Daniel*. Tlbd. 1, *Daniel 1–4*. Biblischer Kommentar 22. Neukirchen-Vluyn: Neukirchener Verlag der Erziehungsvereins, 2005.

KÖCKERT, Charlotte. *Christliche Kosmologie und kaiserzeitliche Philosophie: Die Auslegung des Schöpfungsberichtes bei Origenes, Basilius und Gregor von Nyssa vor dem Hintergrund kaiserzeitlicher Timaeus-Interpretationen*. Studien und Texte zu Antike und Christentum 56. Tübingen: Mohr Siebeck, 2009.

KOENEN, Klaus. *Bethel: Geschichte, Kult und Theologie*. Orbis Biblicus et Orientalis. Fribourg, Schweiz/Göttingen: Universitätsverlag / Vandenhoeck & Ruprecht, 2003.

———. "'Süßes geht vom Starken aus' (Ri 14,14): Vergleiche zwischen Gott und Tier im Alten Testament." *Evangelische Theologie* 55 (1995): 174–197.

KOGAN-ZEHAVI, Elena. "The Tomb and Memorial of a Chain-Wearing Anachorite at Khirbet Tabaliya, Near Jerusalem." *Atiqot* 35 (1998): 135–148.

KOHLBACHER, Michael. "Unpublizierte Fragmente des Markianos von Bethlehem (nunc CPG 3898 a-d)." In *Horizonte der Christenheit: Festschrift für Friedrich Heyer zu seinem 85. Geburtstag*, herausgegeben von Michael Kohlbacher und Markus Lesinski, 137–167. Oikonomia 34. Erlangen: Lehrstuhl für Geschichte und Theologie des christlichen Ostens, 1994.

KOOTEN, George H. van. *Cosmic Christology in Paul and the Pauline School: Colossians and Ephesians in the Context of Graeco-Roman Cosmology, with a New Synopsis of the Greek Texts*. WUNT 2/ 171. Tübingen: Mohr Siebeck, 2003.

KÖPF, Ulrich. "Erfahrung III. Theologiegeschichtlich 1. Mittelalter und Reformation." In *Theologische Realenzyklopädie*, 10: 109–116. Berlin/New York: De Gruyter, 1982.

———. "Politische Theologie im Mittelalter." *Theologische Rundschau* 58 (1993): 437–444.

KÖRTING, Corinna. *Zion in den Psalmen*. FAT 48. Tübingen: Mohr Siebeck, 2006.

KÖSTERS, Oliver. *Die Trinitätslehre des Epiphanius von Salamis: Ein Kommentar zum "Ancoratus."* Forschungen zur Kirchen- und Dogmengeschichte 86. Göttingen: Vandenhoeck & Ruprecht, 2003.

KÖTTING, Bernhard. *Peregrinatio Religiosa: Wallfahrten in der Antike und das Pilgerwesen in der alten Kirche*. Forschungen zur Volkskunde 33–35. 2. Aufl. Münster: Stenderhoff, 1980. (= Münster: Regensberg, 1950.)

————. "Wohlgeruch der Heiligkeit." In *Jenseitsvorstellungen in Antike und Christentum, Gedenkschrift für Alfred Stuiber.* Jahrbuch für Antike und Christentum. Supplementband 9. Münster: Aschendorff, 1982.

KÖTZSCHE, Lieselotte. "Hand II (ikonographisch)." In *Reallexikon für Antike und Christentum*, 13: 402–482. Stuttgart: Hiersemann, 1986.

KOUTRAS, Dimitrios N. "The Beautiful according to Dionysius." In *Neoplatonism and Western Aesthetics*, edited by Aphrodite Alexandrakis and Nicholas J. Moutafakis, 31–40. Studies in Neoplatonism, Ancient and Modern 12. Albany: State University of New York Press, 2002.

KRAELING, Carl H. *The Synagogue.* Reprinted, with new foreword and indices. The Excavations at Dura-Europos conducted by Yale University and the French Academy of Inscriptions and Letters, Final Report 8/1. New York: KTAV, 1979. (= New Haven, Conn.: Yale University Press, 1956.)

KRAMER, Bärbel. "Didymus von Alexandrien (311–398)." In *Theologische Realenzyklopädie*, 8: 741–746. Berlin/New York: De Gruyter, 1981.

KRÄMER, Gudrun. "Ja, er kann. Islam als *empowerment.*" In *Was ist der Mensch?* herausgegeben von Detlev Ganten, Volker Gerhardt, Jan-Christoph Heilinger und Julian Nida-Rümelin, 159–161. Humanprojekt. Interdisziplinäre Anthropologie 3. Berlin/New York: De Gruyter, 2008.

KRÄMER, Hans. "Die ältere Akademie." In *Die Philosophie der Antike*, Bd. 3, *Ältere Akademie—Aristoteles—Peripatos*, herausgegeben von Hellmut Flashar, 1–174. Grundriss der Geschichte der Philosophie, begründet von Friedrich Ueberweg, völlig neu bearbeitete Ausgabe. Basel/Stuttgart: Schwabe, 1983.

KRAUSS, Samuel. *Griechische und lateinische Lehnwörter im Talmud, Midrasch und Targum.* Mit Bemerkungen von Immanuel Löw. Berlin: Calvary, 1899. (= Hildesheim: Olms, 1987.)

KREMER, Klaus. *Die neuplatonische Seinsphilosophie und ihre Wirkung auf Thomas von Aquin.* Studien zur Problemgeschichte der antiken und mittelalterlichen Philosophie 1. Leiden: Brill, 1966.

KRETSCHMAR, Georg. "Jüdische und christliche Kunst." In *Abraham unser Vater: Juden und Christen im Gespräch über die Bibel; Festschrift für Otto Michel zum 60. Geburtstag*, herausgegeben von Otto Betz, Martin Hengel und Peter Schmidt, 295–319. Arbeiten zur Geschichte des Spätjudentums und Urchristentums 5. Leiden/Köln: Brill, 1963.

————. *Studien zur frühchristlichen Trinitätstheologie.* BHT 21. Tübingen: Mohr Siebeck, 1956.

KREUZER, Johann. "Der Abgrund des Bewusstseins: Erinnerung und Selbsterkenntnis im zehnten Buch." In *Die Confessiones des Augustinus von Hippo: Einführung und Interpretation zu den dreizehn Büchern*, herausgegeben von Norbert Fischer und Cornelius Mayer, 445–487. Forschungen zur europäischen Geistesgeschichte 1. Freiburg: Herder, 1998.

KRÜGER, Gustav. "Doketen." In *Realencyklopädie für protestantische Theologie und Kirche*, 4: 764f. 3. Aufl. Leipzig: Hinrichs, 1898.

KRÜGER, Julian. *Oxyrhynchos in der Kaiserzeit: Studien zur Topographie und Literaturrezeption.* Europäische Hochschulschriften 3. Reihe Geschichte und ihre Hilfswissenschaften 441. Frankfurt am Main/New York: Lang, 1990.

KÜBEL, Paul. "Zum Aufbau von Origenes' DE PRINCIPIIS." *VC* 25 (1971): 31–39.

KUHN, Peter. *Offenbarungsstimmen im Antiken Judentum: Untersuchungen zur Bat Qol und verwandten Phänomenen.* TSAJ 20. Tübingen: Mohr Siebeck, 1989.

KULIK, Alexander. "The Gods of Nahor: A Note on the Pantheon of the Apocalypse of Abraham." *JJS* 54 (2003): 228–232.

KULLMANN, Wolfgang. *Aristoteles und die moderne Wissenschaft.* Philosophie der Antike 5. Stuttgart: Steiner, 1998.

———. "Gods and Men in the *Iliad* and *Odyssey*." In idem, *Homerische Motive: Beiträge zur Entstehung, Eigenart und Wirkung von "Ilias" und "Odyssee,"* herausgegeben von Roland J. Müller, 243–263. Stuttgart: Steiner, 1992. (= *Harvard Studies in Classical Philology* 89 [1985]: 1–23.)

KÜLZER, Andreas. "Die Festbriefe (ΕΠΙΣΤΟΛΑΙ ΕΟΡΤΑΣΤΙΚΑΙ): Eine wenig beachtete Untergattung der byzantinischen Briefliteratur." *Byzantinische Zeitschrift* 91 (1998): 379–390.

KURZ, Otto. "The Date of the Alexandrian World Chronicle." In *Kunsthistorische Forschungen, Otto Pächt zu seinem 70. Geburtstag,* herausgegeben von Artur Rosenauser, 17–22. Salzburg: Residenz, 1972.

LABROUSSE, Mireille. "Les origines du monastère (Vᵉ–VIIIᵉ siècle)." In *Histoire de l'abbaye de Lérins,* 23–124. Bégrolles-en-Mauges: Abbaye de Bellefontaine, 2005.

LACKNER, Wolfgang. "Zum Zusatz zu Epiphanios' von Salamis Panarion, Kap. 64." *VC* 27 (1973): 56–58.

LALLEMAN, Pieter J. "Polymorphy of Christ." In *The Apocryphal Acts of John,* edited by Jan N. Bremmer, 97–118. Studies on the Apocryphal Acts of the Apostles 1. Kampen: Kok Pharos, 1995.

LAMBERTON, Robert. "Homer in Antiquity." In *A New Companion to Homer,* edited by Ian Morris and Barry Powell, 33–54. Leiden: Brill, 1996.

LAMPE, Peter. "Paul's Concept of a Spiritual Body." In *Resurrection: Theological and Scientific Assessments,* edited by Ted Peters, Robert J. Russell, and Michael Welker, 103–114. Grand Rapids/Cambridge: Eerdmans 2002.

LAMPE, Peter, und Adolf M. RITTER. "Vinzent, Markus: Christ's Resurrection in Early Christianity and the Making of the New Testament (Rezension)." *Zeitschrift für Antikes Christentum* 17 (2013): 580–588.

LAMPRECHT, Karl. *Deutsche Geschichte: Ergänzungs-Band; Zur jüngsten deutschen Vergangenheit.* Bd. 2/2, *Innere Politik, äußere Politik.* 4. Aufl. Berlin: Gaertner, 1921.

LANGE, Christian. *Mia energeia: Untersuchungen zur Einigungspolitik des Kaisers Heraclius und des Patriarchen Sergius von Constantinopel.* Studien und Texte zu Antike und Christentum 66. Tübingen: Mohr Siebeck, 2012.

LANGKAMMER, Hugolin. "Jes 53 und 1 Petr 2, 21–25. Zur christologischen Interpretation der Leidenstheologie von Jes 53." *Bibel und Liturgie* 60 (1987): 90–98.

LANNE, Emmanuel. "La 'Prière de Jésus' dans la tradition égyptienne: Témoignage des psalies et des inscriptions." *Irénikon* 50 (1977): 163–203.

LAQUEUR, Thomas. *Making Sex: Body and Gender from the Greeks to Freud.* Cambridge, Mass./London: Harvard University Press, 1990.

LARDET, Pierre. *L'apologie de Jérôme contre Rufin: Un commentaire.* SuppVC 15. Leiden: Brill, 1993.

LAUSBERG, Marion. *Untersuchungen zu Senecas Fragmenten.* Untersuchungen zur antiken Literatur und Geschichte 7. Berlin: De Gruyter, 1970.

LECHNER, Thomas. *Ignatius adversus Valentinianos? Chronologische und theologiegeschichtliche Studien zu den Briefen des Ignatius von Antiochien.* SuppVC 47. Leiden: Brill, 1999.

LECLERCQ, Henri. "Chronique alexandrine." In *Dictionnaire d'archéologie chrétienne et de liturgie,* 3/1: 1546–1553. Paris: Letouzey et Ané, 1911.

———. "Dieu." In *Dictionnaire d'archéologie chrétienne et de liturgie,* 4/1: 821–824. Paris: Letouzey et Ané, 1920.

LEDEGANG, Fred. "Anthropomorphites and Origenists in Egypt at the End of the Fourth Century." In *Origeniana Septima: Origenes in den Auseinandersetzungen des 4. Jahrhunderts* [7. Internationales Origeneskolloquium, vom 25. bis zum 29. August 1997, Hofgeismar], herausgegeben von Wolfgang Bienert und Uwe Kühneweg, 375–781. BETL. Leuven: University Press / Uitgeverij Peeters, 1999.

LEHMANN, Henning J. *Per Piscatores: Orsardaukh; Studies in the Armenian Version of a Collection of Homilies by Eusebius of Emesa and Severian of Gabala.* Aarhus: Eget, 1975.

LEHMANN, Karl. "The Dome of Heaven." *Art Bulletin* 22 (1945): 1–17.

LEIBNIZ, Gottfried W. "Causa Dei Asserta per Justitiam Ejus cum Caeteris Ejus Perfectionibus Cunctis Actionibus Conciliatam." In idem, *Opera Philosophica Quae Exstant Latina Gallica Germanica Omnia,* instruxit Johann Eduard Erdmann, 653–665. Faksimiledruck der Ausgabe 1840 durch weitere Textstücke ergänzt und mit einem Vorwort versehen von Renate Vollbrecht. Aalen: Scientia Verlag, 1959. (= *Die philosophischen Schriften von Gottfried Wilhelm Leibniz,* Bd. 6, herausgegeben von Carl I. Gerhardt, 439–462. Hildesheim: Olms, 1961.)

LEIPOLDT, Johannes. *Schenute von Atripe und die Entstehung des national ägyptischen Christentums.* TU 25/1. Leipzig: Hinrichs, 1903.

LEJEUNE, Albert. *Euclide et Ptolémée: Deux stades de l'optique géométrique grecque.* Recueil de travaux d'histoire et de philologie 3/31. Louvain: Bibliothèque de l'Université, 1948.

———. *L'optique de Claude Ptolémée dans la version latine d'après l'arabe de l'émir Eugène de Sicile: Édition critique et exégétique.* Augmentée d'une traduction française et de compléments. Collection des travaux de l'Académie Internationale d'Histoire des Sciences 31. Leiden: Brill, 1989.

LEONHARD, Clemens. *The Jewish Pesach and the Origins of the Christian Easter: Open Questions in Current Research.* Studia Judaica 35. Berlin/New York: De Gruyter, 2006.

LEPPIN, Volker. *Die christliche Mystik.* C. H. Beck Wissen in der Beck'schen Reihe 2415. München: Beck, 2007.

LERAUX, Jean-Marie. "Jean Chrysostome et la querelle origéniste." In *Epektasis: Mélanges patristiques offerts au Cardinal Jean Danielou,* édité par Jacques Fontaine et Charles Kannengiesser, 335–341. Paris: Beauchesne, 1972.

LESHER, James H. *Xenophanes of Colophon: Fragments; A Text and Translation with a Commentary.* Phoenix. Supplementary vol. 30 (= Phoenix Pre-Socratics 4). Toronto/London: University of Toronto Press, 1992.

LEVINE, Lee I. "The Synagogue of Dura-Europos." In *Ancient Synagogues Revealed,* 172–177. Jerusalem: Israel Exploration Society, 1981.

———. *Visual Judaism in Late Antiquity: Historical Contexts of Jewish Art.* New Haven, Conn./London: Yale University Press, 2012.

LEWIS, Nicola Denzey, and Justine A. BLOUNT. "Rethinking the Origins of the Nag Hammadi Codices." *Journal of Biblical Literature* 133 (2014): 399–419.

LICHTENBERG, Georg C. *Briefwechsel.* Bd. 4, *1793–1799.* Im Auftrag der Akademie der Wissenschaften zu Göttingen herausgegeben von Ulrich Joost und Albrecht Schöne. München: Beck, 1992.

LIEGLE, Josef. *Der Zeus des Phidias.* Berlin: Weidmann, 1932.

LIES, Lothar. *Origenes' "Peri Archon": Eine undogmatische Dogmatik; Einführung und Erläuterung.* Werkinterpretationen. Darmstadt: Wissenschaftliche Buchgesellschaft, 1992.

LIETZMANN, Hans. *Apollinaris von Laodicea und seine Schule: Texte und Untersuchungen.* Hildesheim/New York: Olms, 1970. (= Tübingen: Mohr Siebeck, 1904.)

LIEU, Judith. "'The Parting of the Ways': Theological Construct or Historical Reality?" *Journal for the Study of the New Testament* 17 (1995): 101–119.

LIGHTFOOT, Jane L. *Lucian on the Syrian Goddess.* Edited with introduction, translation, and commentary. Oxford: Oxford University Press, 2003.

LINDEMANN, Andreas. "Antwort auf die 'Thesen zur Echtheit und Datierung der sieben Briefe des Ignatius von Antiochien.'" *Zeitschrift für Antikes Christentum* 1 (1997): 185–194.

LOBECK, Christian A. *Aglaophamus Sive de Theologiae Mysticae Graecorum Causis, Idemque Poetarum Orphicorum Dispersas Reliquias Collegit, Libri Tres Scripsit.* Bd. 1. Königsberg: Borntraeger, 1829. (= Darmstadt: Wissenschaftliche Buchgesellschaft, 1961.)

LOCK, Margaret. "Cultivating the Body: Anthropology and Epistemologies of Bodily Practise and Knowledge." *Annual Review of Anthropology* 22 (1993): 133–155.

LOEWE, Raphael. "The Divine Garment and Shi'ur Qomah." *HTR* 58 (1965): 153–160.

LOHMEYER, Ernst. *Vom göttlichen Wohlgeruch.* Sitzungsberichte der Heidelberger Akademie der Wissenschaften. Philosophisch-historische Klasse 9. Heidelberg: Winter, 1919.

LÖHR, Winrich A. "Christianity as Philosophy: Problems and Perspectives of an Ancient Intellectual Project." *VC* 64 (2010): 160–188.

––––––. "Deutungen der Passion bei Heiden und Christen im zweiten und dritten Jahrhundert." In *Deutungen des Todes Jesu im Neuen Testament*, herausgegeben von Jörg Frey und Jens Schröter, 545–574. 2. durchgesehene und mit einer neuen Einleitung versehene Aufl. Universitätstaschenbücher 2953. Tübingen: Mohr Siebeck, 2012.

––––––. "Did Marcion Distinguish between a Just God and a Good God?" In *Marcion und seine kirchengeschichtliche Wirkung: Marcion and His Impact on Church History; Vorträge der internationalen Fachkonferenz zu Marcion, gehalten vom 15.–18. August 2001 in Mainz*, herausgegeben von Gerhard May und Katharina Greschat in Gemeinschaft mit Martin Meiser, 131–146. Texte und Untersuchungen 150. Berlin/New York: De Gruyter, 2002.

––––––. "Doketismus." In *Religion in Geschichte und Gegenwart*, 2: 925–927. 4. Aufl. Tübingen: Mohr Siebeck, 2000.

––––––. "Theophilus von Alexandrien." In *Theologische Realenzyklopädie*, 33: 364–368. Berlin/New York: De Gruyter, 2002.

LOHSE, Eduard. *Die Briefe an die Kolosser und an Philemon.* Kritisch-exegetischer Kommentar IX/2. Göttingen: Vandenhoeck & Ruprecht, 1968.

LONA, Horacio E. *Über die Auferstehung des Fleisches: Studien zur frühchristlichen Eschatologie.* BZNW 66. Berlin/New York: De Gruyter, 1993.

LOOFS, Friedrich. "Die 'Ketzerei' Justinians." In *Harnack-Ehrung: Beiträge zur Kirchengeschichte, ihrem Lehrer Adolf von Harnack zu seinem siebzigsten Geburtstage (7. Mai 1921) dargebracht von einer Reihe seiner Schüler*, 232–248. Leipzig: Hinrichs, 1921. (= idem, *Patristica: Ausgewählte Aufsätze zur Alten Kirche*, herausgegeben von Hanns Christof Brennecke und Jörg Ulrich, 369–385. Arbeiten zur Kirchengeschichte 71. Berlin/New York: De Gruyter, 1999.

––––––. *Leontius von Byzanz und die gleichnamigen Schriftsteller der griechischen Kirche.* TU 3/1–2. Leipzig: Hinrichs, 1887.

LORENZ, Maren. *Leibhaftige Vergangenheit: Einführung in die Körpergeschichte.* Historische Einführungen 4. Tübingen: edition discord, 2000.

LORENZEN, Stefanie. *Das paulinische Eikon-Konzept.* WUNT 2/250. Tübingen: Mohr Siebeck, 2008.

LOURENÇO, Frederico. "A 'Cloud of Metaphysics' in Pindar: The Opening of Nemean 6." *Humanitas* 63 (2011): 61–73.

LOUTH, Andrew. "The Body in Western Catholic Christianity." In *Religion and the Body*, edited by Sarah Coakley, 111–130. Cambridge: Cambridge University Press, 1997.

LOYEN, André. "La mère de Fauste de Riez (Sidoine Apollinaire C. XVI v. 84)." *Bulletin de la littérature ecclésiastique* 73 (1972): 167–169.

LUBOMIERSKI, Nina. *Die Vita Sinuthii: Form- und Überlieferungsgeschichte der hagiographischen Texte über Schenute den Archimandriten.* Studien und Texte zu Antike und Christentum 45. Tübingen: Mohr Siebeck, 2007.

LUIJENDIJK, AnneMarie. *Greetings in the Lord: Early Christians and the Oxyrhynchus Papyri.* Harvard Theological Studies 60. Cambridge, Mass.: Harvard University Press, 2008.

LÜTCKE, Karl-Heinrich. "Animae quantitate (De-)." In *Augustinus-Lexikon*, 1: 350–356. Basel: Schwabe, 1986–1994.

———. *"Auctoritas" bei Augustin: Mit einer Einleitung zur römischen Vorgeschichte des Begriffs.* Tübinger Beiträge zur Altertumswissenschaft 44. Stuttgart: Kohlhammer, 1968.

LUTTIKHUIZEN, Gerard P. *The Revelation of Elchasai: Investigations into the Evidence for a Mesopotamian Jewish Apocalypse of the Second Century and Its Reception by Judeo-Christian Propagandists.* TSAJ 8. Tübingen: Mohr Siebeck, 1985.

LUZ, Ulrich. *Das Evangelium nach Matthäus.* Tlbd 1, *Mt 1–7.* 2. durchgesehene Aufl. EKKNT 1/1. Zürich/Neukirchen-Vluyn: Benziger/Neukirchener, 1989.

MAAS, Paul. "Die ikonoklastische Episode in dem Brief des Epiphanios an Johannes." *Byzantinische Zeitschrift* 30 (1929/1930): 279–286. (= idem, *Kleine Schriften*, herausgegeben von Wolfgang Buchwald, 437–445. München: Beck, 1973.)

MACH, Michael. "Philo von Alexandrien." In *Theologische Realenzyklopädie*, 26: 523–531. Berlin: De Gruyter, 1996.

MACMULLEN, Ramsay. *Christianizing the Roman Empire A.D. 100–400.* New Haven, Conn./London: Yale University Press, 1984.

MADEC, Goulven. "Christus." In *Augustinus-Lexikon*, 1: 845–908. Basel: Schwabe, 1986–1994.

———. *Saint Ambroise et la philosophie.* Paris: Études Augustiniennes, 1974.

MADOZ, José. "Un caso de materialismo en España en el siglo IV." *Revista española de teología* 8 (1948): 203–230.

MADYDA, Ladislaus. *De pulchritudine imaginum deorum quid auctores Graeci saec. 2 p. Chr. n. iudicaverint.* Polska Akademia umiejętności. Archiwum filologiczne 16. Warschau/Krakau: Gebethner et Wolff, 1939.

MAIER, Christl M. "Körperliche und emotionale Aspekte JHWHs aus der Genderperspektive." In *Göttliche Körper—Göttliche Gefühle: Was leisten anthropomorphe und anthropopathische Götterkonzepte im Alten Orient und im Alten Testament*, herausgegeben von Andreas Wagner, 171–189. Orbis Biblicus et Orientalis 270. Fribourg: Academic Press; Göttingen: Vandenhoeck & Ruprecht, 2014.

MAIER, Paul L. *Caspar Schwenckfeld on the Person and Work of Christ: A Study of Schwenckfeldian Theology at Its Core.* Van Gorcum's theologische bibliotheek 33. Assen: van Gorcum, 1959. (= Eugene, Ore.: Wipf and Stock, 2004.)

MALAMOUD, Charles, et Jean-Pierre VERNANT, éds. *Corps de Dieux.* Collection Folio: Histoire 120. Paris: Gallimard, 2003. (= Le temps de la reflexion 7. Paris: Gallimard, 1986.)

MALLWITZ, Alfred. *Olympia und seine Bauten*. München: Prestel-Verlag, 1972.
MANDOUZE, André. "'L'extase d'Ostie': Possibilités et limites de la méthode des parallèles textuels." In *Augustinus Magister: Congrès International Augustinien, Paris, 21–24 Septembre 1954, Actes*, tome 1, *Communications*, 67–84. Paris: Études Augustiniennes, 1954.
———. *Prosopographie de l'Afrique Chrétienne (303–533)*. D'après la documentation élaborée par Anne-Marie La Bonnardière. Prosopographie chrétienne du Bas-Empire 1. Paris: Éditions du Centre National de la Recherche Scientifique, 1982.
MANSFELD, Jaap. "Aspects of Epicurean Theology." *Mnemosyne* 46 (1993): 172–210.
———. "De Melisso Xenophane Gorgia: Pyrrhonizing Aristotelianism." *Rheinisches Museum für Philologie* 131 (1988): 239–276.
MARIEV, Sergei. "Proklos and Plethon on Beauty." In *Aesthetics and Theurgy in Byzantium*, edited by Sergei Mariev and Wiebke-Marie Stock, 57–74. Byzantinisches Archiv 25. Berlin/Boston: De Gruyter, 2013.
MARKSCHIES, Christoph. *Ambrosius von Mailand und die Trinitätstheologie: Kirchen- und theologiegeschichtliche Studien zu Antiarianismus und Neunizänismus bei Ambrosius und im lateinischen Westen (364–381)*. BHT 90. Tübingen: Mohr Siebeck, 1995.
———. *Christian Theology and Its Institutions in the Early Roman Empire: Prolegomena to a History of Early Christian Theology*. Translated from the German by Wayne Coppins. Baylor-Mohr Siebeck Studies in Early Christianity. Waco, Tex.: Baylor University Press; Tübingen: Mohr Siebeck, 2015.
———. *Das antike Christentum: Frömmigkeit, Lebensformen, Institutionen*. 2. durchgesehene und erweiterte Aufl. Beck'sche Reihe 1692. München: Beck, 2012.
———. "Der genaue Blick: Welche Moden haben uns wo die Qualität verdorben?" In *What the Hell Is Quality? Qualitätsstandards in den Geisteswissenschaften*, herausgegeben von Elisabeth Lack und Christoph Markschies, 134–144. Frankfurt am Main/New York: Campus-Verlag, 2008.
———. "Der religiöse Pluralismus und das antike Christentum—eine neue Deutung der Gnosis." In idem, *Gnosis und Christentum*, 53–82. Berlin: Berlin University Press, 2009.
———. "Die Seele als Bild der Welt—gestern, heute, morgen." *Berichte und Abhandlungen der Berlin-Brandenburgischen Akademie der Wissenschaften* 14 (2009): 9–24.
———. "Epiphanios von Salamis." In *Der Neue Pauly: Enzyklopädie der Antike*, 3: 1152f. Stuttgart/Weimar: Metzler, 1997.
———. "'. . . et tamen non tres Dii, sed unus Deus . . .' Zum Stand der Erforschung der altkirchlichen Trinitätstheologie." In idem, *Alta Trinità Beata: Gesammelte Studien zur altkirchlichen Trinitätstheologie*, 286–309. Tübingen: Mohr Siebeck, 2000.
———. "'. . . für die Gemeinde im Grossen und Ganzen nicht geeignet . . .'? Erwägungen zu Absicht und Wirkung der Predigten des Origenes." In

idem, *Origenes und sein Erbe: Gesammelte Studien*, 35–62. TU 160. Berlin/New York: De Gruyter, 2007.

———. *Gibt es eine "Theologie der gotischen Kathedrale"? Nochmals: Suger von Saint-Denis und Sankt Dionys vom Areopag.* Abhandlungen der Heidelberger Akademie der Wissenschaften. Philosophisch-historische Klasse 1/1995. Heidelberg: Winter, 1995.

———. "Gnostische und andere Bilderbücher in der Antike." *Zeitschrift für Antikes Christentum* 9 (2005): 100–121. (= idem, *Gnosis und Christentum*, 113–160. Berlin: Berlin University Press, 2009.)

———. *Hellenisierung des Christentums: Sinn und Unsinn einer historischen Deutungskategorie.* Forum Theologische Literaturzeitung 25. Leipzig: Evangelische Verlags-Anstalt, 2012.

———. "Hohe Theologie und schlichte Frömmigkeit? Einige Beobachtungen zum Verhältnis von Theologie und Frömmigkeit in der Antike." In *Volksglaube im antiken Christentum*, herausgegeben von Heike Grieser und Andreas Merkt, 456–471. Darmstadt: Wissenschaftliche Buchgesellschaft, 2009.

———. "Individuality in Some Gnostic Authors: With a Few Remarks on the Interpretation of Ptolemaeus, Epistula ad Floram." *Zeitschrift für Antikes Christentum* 15 (2011): 411–430.

———. "Innerer Mensch." In *Reallexikon für Antike und Christentum*, 18: 266–312. Stuttgart: Hiersemann, 1998.

———. *Kaiserzeitliche christliche Theologie und ihre Institutionen: Prolegomena zu einer Geschichte der antiken christlichen Theologie.* Tübingen: Mohr Siebeck, 2007.

———. "Kastration und Magenprobleme? Einige neue Blicke auf das asketische Leben des Origenes." In *Origeniana Nona: Origen and the Religious Practise of His Time: Papers of the 9th International Origen Congress, Pécs, Hungary, 29 August–2 September 2005*, edited by György Heidl and Róbert Somos in collaboration with Csaba Németh, 255–271. BETL 228. Leuven: Peeters, 2009. (= idem, *Origenes und sein Erbe: Gesammelte Studien.* TU 160. Berlin/New York: De Gruyter, 2007.)

———. "Körper und Körperlichkeit im antiken Mönchtum." In *Die Christen und der Körper: Aspekte der Körperlichkeit in der christlichen Literatur der Spätantike*, herausgegeben von Barbara Feichtinger und Helmut Seng, 189–212. Beiträge zur Altertumskunde 170. München: Saur, 2004.

———. "Kreuz." In *Erinnerungsorte des Christentums*, herausgegeben von Christoph Markschies und Hubert Wolf unter Mitarbeit von Barbara Schüler, 574–591. München: Beck, 2010.

———. "New Research on Ptolemaeus Gnosticus." *Zeitschrift für Antikes Christentum* 4 (2000): 225–254.

———. "Nochmals: Valentinus und die Gnostikoi; Beobachtungen zu Irenaeus, haer. I 30,15 und Tertullian, Val. 4,2." *VC* 51 (1997): 179–187.

———. "Odysseus und Orpheus—christlich gelesen." In *Griechische Mythologie und frühes Christentum*, herausgegeben von Raban von Haehling, 227–253. Darmstadt: Wissenschaftliche Buchgesellschaft, 2005.

————. "On Classifying Creeds the Classical German Way: 'Privat-Bekenntnisse' ('Private Creeds')." In *Biblica, Philosophica, Theologica, Ethica: Papers Presented at the Sixteenth International Conference on Patristic Studies Held in Oxford 2011*, vol. 11, edited by Markus Vinzent, 259–271. StPatr 63. Leuven/Paris/Walpole, Mass.: Peeters, 2013.

————. *Origenes und sein Erbe*. Gesammelte Studien, TU 160. Berlin/New York: De Gruyter, 2007.

————. "'Sessio ad dexteram': Bemerkungen zu einem altchristlichen Bekenntnismotiv in der christologischen Diskussion der altchristlichen Theologen." In idem, *Alta Trinità Beata: Gesammelte Studien zur alt-kirchlichen Trinitätstheologie*, 1–69. Tübingen: Mohr Siebeck, 2000. (= In *Le trône de Dieu*, édité par Marc Philonenko, 252–317. WUNT 69. Tübingen: Mohr Siebeck, 1993.)

————. "Theologische Diskussionen zur Zeit Konstantins: Arius, der 'aria-nische' Streit und das Konzil von Nicaea, die nachnizänischen Ausein-andersetzungen bis 337." In *Das Entstehen der einen Christenheit (250–430)*, herausgegeben von Charles (†) und Luce Piétri, 271–344. Die Geschichte des Christentums: Religion—Politik—Kultur 2. Freiburg: Herder, 1996. (= idem, *Alta Trinità Beata: Gesammelte Studien zur alt-kirchlichen Trinitätstheologie*, 99–195. Tübingen: Mohr Siebeck, 2000.)

————. "Valentinian Gnosticism: Toward the Anatomy of a School." In *The Nag Hammadi Library after Fifty Years: Proceedings of the 1995 Soci-ety of Biblical Literature Commemoration*, edited by John D. Turner and Anne M. McGuire, 401–438. Nag Hammadi Studies 44. Leiden: Brill, 1997.

————. "Valentinianische Gnosis in Alexandrien und Ägypten." In *Orige-niana Octava: Origen and the Alexandrian Tradition. Origene e la tra-dizione Alessandrina; Papers of the 8th International Origen Congress Pisa, 27–31 August 2001*, edited by Lorenzo Perrone, 331–346. BETL 164. Leuven: Peeters, 2004.

————. *Valentinus Gnosticus? Untersuchungen zur valentinianischen Gno-sis mit einem Kommentar zu den Fragmenten Valentins*. WUNT 65. Tübingen: Mohr Siebeck, 1992.

————. "Vergangenheit, Gegenwart und Zukunft der Ideengeschichte: Zum Werk Hans von Campenhausens." In *Hans Freiherr von Campenhausen: Weg, Werk und Wirkung*, herausgegeben von Christoph Markschies, 9–27. Schriften der Philosophisch-historischen Klasse der Heidelberger Akade-mie der Wissenschaften 43/2007. Heidelberg: Winter, 2008.

————. "Welche Funktion hat der Mythos in gnostischen Systemen? Oder: Ein gescheiterter Denkversuch zum Thema 'Heil und Geschichte.'" In *Heil und Geschichte: Die Geschichtsbezogenheit des Heils und das Problem der Heilsgeschichte in der biblischen Tradition und in der theologischen Deutung*, herausgegeben von Jörg Frey, Stefan Krauter und Hermann Lichtenberger, 513–534. WUNT 248. Tübingen: Mohr Siebeck, 2009. (= idem, *Gnosis und Christentum*, 83–112. Berlin: Berlin University Press, 2009.)

MARSILI, Salvatore. *Giovanni Cassiano ed Evagrio Pontico: Dottrina sulla carità e contemplazione.* Studia Anselmiana 5. Rome: Herder, 1936.

MARTIN, Annick. *Athanase d'Alexandrie et l'Église d'Égypte au IVe Siècle (328–373).* Collection de l'École Française de Rome 216. Rome: École Française, 1996.

MAUSS, Marcel. "Techniques of the Body." *Economy and Society* 2 (1973): 70–88. (= *Journal de psychologie normale et pathologique* 32 [1935]: 271–293.)

MAY, Gerhard. "Markions Genesisauslegung und die 'Antithesen.'" In idem, *Markion: Gesammelte Aufsätze*, herausgegeben von Katharina Greschat und Martin Meiser, 43–50. Veröffentlichungen des Instituts für Europäische Geschichte Mainz. Abteilung für abendländische Religionsgeschichte. Beiheft 68. Mainz: Philipp von Zabern, 2005.

———. "Markion und der Gnostiker Kerdon." In idem, *Markion: Gesammelte Aufsätze*, herausgegeben von Katharina Greschat und Martin Meiser, 63–73. Veröffentlichungen des Instituts für Europäische Geschichte Mainz. Abteilung für abendländische Religionsgeschichte. Beiheft 68. Mainz: Philipp von Zabern, 2005.

———. *Schöpfung aus dem Nichts: Die Entstehung der Lehre von der creatio ex nihilo.* Arbeiten zur Kirchengeschichte 48. Berlin/New York: De Gruyter, 1978.

MAYBAUM, Siegmund. *Die Anthropomorphien und Anthropopathien bei Onkelos und den späteren Targumin mit besonderer Berücksichtigung der Ausdrücke Memra, Jekara und Schechintha.* Breslau: Schletter'sche Buchhandlung, 1870.

MAYER, Wendy. "John Chrysostom as Bishop: The View from Antioch." *Journal of Ecclesiastical History* 55 (2004): 455–466.

McCABE, Donald F. *Inscriptions of Ionia.* Princeton, N.J.: Institute for Advanced Study, 1984.

McGINN, Bernard. *The Foundations of Mysticism.* Vol. 1, *The Presence of God: A History of Western Christian Mysticism.* London: SCM Press, 1991.

McGOWAN, Andrew B., Brian E. DALEY, and Timothy J. GADEN, eds. *God in Early Christian Thought: Essays in Memory of Lloyd G. Patterson.* SuppVC 94. Leiden: Brill, 2009.

McKENZIE, Judith S., Sheila GIBSON, and Andres T. REYES. "Reconstructing the Serapeum in Alexandria from the Archaeological Evidence." *Journal of Roman Studies* 94 (2004): 73–121.

MEIER, Mischa. *Anastasios I: Die Entstehung des Byzantinischen Reiches.* Stuttgart: Klett-Cotta, 2009.

MEIJERING, Eginhard P. *Die Hellenisierung des Christentums im Urteil Adolf von Harnacks.* Verhandelingen der Koninklijke Nederlandse Akademie van Wetenschappen, Afd. Letterkunde, Nieuwe Reeks, deel 128. Amsterdam: North-Holland, 1985.

———. "Some Reflections on Cyril of Alexandria's Rejection of Anthropomorphism." *Nieuw Theologisch Tijdschrift* 28 (1974): 295–301.

MELCHER, Robert. *Der 8. Brief des hl. Basilius, ein Werk des Evagrius Pontikus*. Münsterische Beiträge zur Theologie 1. Münster: Aschendorff, 1923.

MENN, Stephen "Aristotle and Plato on God as Nous and as the Good." *Review of Metaphysics* 45 (1992): 543–573.

———. *Plato on God as Nous*. Journal of the History of Philosophy Monograph Series. South Bend, Ind.: St. Augustine's Press, 2002. (= Carbondale: Southern Illinois University Press, 1995.)

MERKELBACH, Reinhold. "Der griechische Wortschatz und die Christen." *Zeitschrift für Papyrologie und Epigraphik* 18 (1995): 101–148.

———. "Gefesselte Götter." In idem, *Hestia und Erigone: Gesammelte Aufsätze*, herausgegeben von Wolfgang Blümel u.a., 17–30. Stuttgart/ Leipzig: Teubner, 1996.

———. *Isis Regina—Zeus Sarapis: Die griechisch-ägyptische Religion nach den Quellen dargestellt*. 2. Aufl. München/Leipzig: Teubner, 2001.

———. *Mithras*. Königstein/Taunus: Hain, 1984.

MERKELBACH, Reinhold, und Josef STAUBER, Hg. *Steinepigramme aus dem griechischen Osten*. Bd. 1, *Die Westküste Kleinasiens von Knidos bis Ilion*. Stuttgart/Leipzig: Teubner, 1998.

MERKI, Hubert. ὁμοίωσις θεῷ. *Von der platonischen Angleichung an Gott zur Gottähnlichkeit bei Gregor von Nyssa*. Paradosis 7. Freiburg, Schweiz: Paulusdruckerei, 1952.

MERKLEIN, Helmut. "Christus als Bild Gottes im Neuen Testament." *Jahrbuch für Biblische Theologie* 13 (1998): 53–75.

MESHEL, Ze'ev. *Kuntillet 'Ajrud (Horvat Teman): An Iron Age II Religious Site on the Judah-Sinai Border*. Jerusalem: Israel Exploration Society, 2012.

METTINGER, Tryggve N. D. *No Graven Image? Israelite Aniconism in Its Ancient Near Eastern Context*. Coniectanea biblica. Old Testament Series 42. Stockholm: Almqvist & Wiksell International, 1995.

MEULI, Karl. "Die gefesselten Götter." In idem, *Gesammelte Schriften*, mit Benutzung des Nachlasses herausgegeben von Thomas Gelzer, 2: 1035–1081. Basel: Schwabe, 1975.

MICHL, Johann. "Engel II (jüdisch)." In *Reallexikon für Antike und Christentum*, 5: 60–97. Stuttgart: Hiersemann, 1962.

MIDDELL, Matthias. *Weltgeschichtsschreibung im Zeitalter der Verfachlichung und Professionalisierung: Das Leipziger Institut für Kultur- und Universalgeschichte 1890–1990*. 3 Bde. Leipzig: Akademische Verlagsanstalt, 2004.

MILGROM, Jacob. "The Dura Synagogue and Visual Midrash." In *Scriptures for the Modern World*, edited by Paul R. Cheesman and C. Wilfred Griggs, 29–60. Provo, Utah: Religious Studies Center, Brigham Young University, 1984.

MILLER, Patricia Cox. *The Corporeal Imagination: Signifying the Holy in Late Ancient Christianity*. Philadelphia: University of Pennsylvania Press, 2009.

MIMOUNI, Simon C. *Early Judeo-Christianity: Historical Essays*. Translated by Robyn Fréchet. Interdisciplinary Studies in Ancient Culture and Religion 13. Leuven/Walpole, Mass.: Peeters, 2012.

MITCHELL, Margaret M. "Allegory: IV. Christianity; A. Greek Patristics and Orthodox Churches; B. Latin Patristics and Early Medieval Times." In *Encyclopedia of the Bible and Its Reception*, 1: 796–800. Berlin/New York: De Gruyter, 2009.

MOINGT, Joseph. *Théologie trinitaire de Tertullien*. Tome 1, *Histoire, Doctrine, Méthodes*. Théologie 68. Paris: Aubier, 1966.

———. *Théologie trinitaire de Tertullien*. Tome 2, *Substantialité et individualité*. Théologie 68. Paris: Aubier, 1966.

MÖLLENDORFF, Peter von. "Nesselrath, Heinz-Günther: Lukian und die antike Philosophie (Rezension)." *Plekos* 4 (2002): 1–10.

MONACI CASTAGNO, Adele. "Origene ed 'i molti': Due religiosità a contrasto." *Augustinianum* 21 (1981): 99–117.

MONTERO, Consuelo Ruiz. "Chariton von Aphrodisias: Ein Überblick." In *ANRW* II, *Prinzipat*, 34.2, *Sprache und Literatur (einzelne Autoren seit der hadrianischen Zeit und Allgemeines zur Literatur des 2. und 3. Jahrhunderts)*, herausgegeben von Wolfgang Haase, 1006–1054. Berlin/New York: De Gruyter, 1993.

MORAUX, Paul. "Quinta Essentia." In *Paulys Realencyclopädie der classischen Altertumswissenschaft*, 24: 1171–1263. Stuttgart: Metzler, 1963.

MOREAU, Joseph. "Épicure et la physique des dieux." *Revue des Études Anciennes* 70 (1968): 286–294.

MORESCHINI, Claudio. "Tertulliano tra Stoicismo e Platonismo." In *Kerygma und Logos: Beiträge zu den geistesgeschichtlichen Beziehungen zwischen Antike und Christentum; Festschrift für Carl Andresen zum 70. Geburtstag*, herausgegeben von Adolf Martin Ritter, 367–379. Göttingen: Vandenhoeck & Ruprecht, 1979.

MORIN, Germain. "Notes liturgiques." *Revue Bénédictine* 30 (1913): 226–234.

MORRAY-JONES, Christopher R. A. "The Body of the Glory: Approaching the New Testament from the Perspective of Shiur Koma Traditions." In *The Mystery of God: Early Jewish Mysticism and the New Testament*, edited by Christopher R. A. Morray-Jones and Christopher Rowland, 501–610. Leiden: Brill, 2009.

MOSCHOS, Dimitrios. *Eschatologie im ägyptischen Mönchtum: Die Rolle christlicher eschatologischer Denkvarianten in der Geschichte des frühen ägyptischen Mönchtums und seiner sozialen Funktion*. Studien zu Antike und Christentum 59. Tübingen: Mohr Siebeck, 2010.

MOSS, Candida R. "The Discourse of Voluntary Martyrdom: Ancient and Modern." *Church History* 81 (2012): 531–551.

———. "Heavenly Healing: Eschatological Cleansing and the Resurrection of the Dead in Early Church." *Journal of the American Academy of Religion* 79 (2011): 991–1017.

———. "Nailing Down and Tying Up: Lessons in Intertextual Impossibility from the Martyrdom of Polycarp." *VC* 67 (2013): 117–136.

———. "On the Dating of Polycarp: Rethinking the Place of the *Martyrdom of Polycarp* in the History of Christianity." *Early Christianity* 1 (2010): 539–574.

———. *The Other Christs: Imitating Jesus in Ancient Christian Ideologies of Martyrdom*. Oxford: Oxford University Press, 2010.

MOST, Glenn W. "From Logos to Mythos." In *From Myth to Reason? Studies in the Development of Greek Thought*, edited by Richard Buxton, 25–47. Oxford: Oxford University Press, 1999.

———. "Schöne (das)." In *Historisches Wörterbuch der Philosophie*, 8: 1343–1351. Darmstadt: Wissenschaftliche Buchgesellschaft, 1992.

MOURANT, John A. "Ostia Reexamined: A Study in the Concept of Mystical Experience." *Philosophy of Religion* 1 (1970): 34–45.

MUEHLBERGER, Ellen. *Angels in Late Ancient Christianity*. Oxford: Oxford University Press, 2013.

MUELLER, Gustav E. "Plato and the Gods." *Philosophical Review* 45 (1936): 457–472.

MÜHLENBERG, Ekkehard. "Bowersock, Glen W., *Martyrdom and Rome* (Book Review)." *JTS* 47 (1996): 275–279.

———. *Die Unendlichkeit Gottes bei Gregor von Nyssa: Gregors Kritik am Gottesbegriff der klassischen Metaphysik*. Forschungen zur Kirchen- und Dogmengeschichte 16. Göttingen 1966.

MUILENBURG, James. "The Son of Man in Daniel and the Ethiopic Apocalypse of Enoch." *Journal of Biblical Literature* 79 (1960): 197–209.

MÜLLER, Carl W. "Chariton von Aphrodisias und die Theorie des Romans in der Antike." In *Antike und Abendland* 22 (1976): 115–136. (= idem, *Legende—Novelle—Roman: Dreizehn Kapitel zur erzählenden Prosaliteratur der Antike*. Göttingen: Vandenhoeck & Ruprecht, 2006.)

MÜLLER, Nikolaus. "Christusbilder." In *Realenzyklopädie für protestantische Theologie und Kirche*, 4: 63–82. 3. Aufl. Leipzig: Hinrichs, 1898.

MUNOA, Phillip B. *Four Powers in Heaven: The Interpretation of Daniel 7 in the Testament of Abraham*. Journal for the Study of the Pseudepigrapha. Supplement 28. Sheffield: Sheffield Academic Press, 1998.

MUSIL, Robert. *Der Mann ohne Eigenschaften: Roman*. Herausgegeben von Adolf Frisé, neu durchgesehene und verbesserte Ausgabe. Rowohlt Jahrhundert 1 (= rororo 4001). Reinbek: Rowohlt, 1990.

MUYLDERMANS, Joseph. "Euagriana." *Le Muséon* 44 (1931): 37–68.

———. *Evagriana syriaca: Textes inédits du British Museum et de la Vaticane*. Édite et traduits. Bibliothèque du Muséon 31. Louvain: Publications universitaires, 1952.

MYLLYKOSKI, Matti. "Die Kraft des Herrn: Erwägungen zur Christologie des Petrusevangeliums." In *Das Evangelium des Petrus: Texte, Kontexte, Intertexte*, herausgegeben von Thomas J. Kraus und Tobias Nicklas, 301–326. TU 158. Berlin/New York: De Gruyter, 2007.

NAAB, Erich. *Augustinus: Über Schau und Gegenwart des unsichtbaren Gottes*. Texte mit Einführung und Übersetzung. Mystik in Geschichte und Gegenwart. TU 1/14. Stuttgart-Bad Cannstatt: Frommann-Holzboog, 1998.

NÄGELSBACH, Karl F. von. *Carl Friedrich von Nägelsbach's Homerische Theo-logie*. 2. Auflage. Nach dem Auftrag des verewigten Verfassers bearbeitet von Georg Autenrieth. Nürnberg: Geiger'sche Verlags-Buchhandlung, 1861.

———. *Die nachhomerische Theologie des griechischen Volksglaubens bis auf Alexander*. Nürnberg: Conrad Geiger, 1857. (= Hildesheim: Olms, 2004.)

NAUTIN, Pierre. "Études de chronologie hiéronymienne (393–397)." *Revue des Études Augustiniennes* 18 (1972): 209–218.

———. "La lettre de Théophile d'Alexandrie à l'Église de Jérusalem et la réponse de Jean de Jérusalem (Juin–Juillet 396)." *Revue d'Histoire Ecclé-siastique* 69 (1974): 365–394.

———. *Le dossier d'Hippolyte et de Méliton dans les florilèges dogmatiques et chez historiens modernes*. Patristica 1. Paris: Les éditions du Cerf, 1953.

———. "Ὁμοούσιος *unius esse* (Jérôme, ep. XCIII)." *VC* 15 (1961): 40–45.

———. *Origène: Sa vie et son œuvre*. Christianisme antique 1. Paris: Beau-chesne, 1977.

NEANDER, August. *Allgemeine Geschichte der christlichen Religion und Kirche*. Bd. 2. Gotha: Perthes, 1864.

NEGEL, Joachim. *Feuerbach weiterdenken: Studien zum religionskritischen Projektionsargument*. Religion—Geschichte—Gesellschaft 51. Berlin: LIT, 2014.

NEHRING, Przemyslaw. "Jerome's Vita Hilarionis: A Rhetorical Analysis of Its Structure." *Augustinianum* 43 (2003): 417–434.

NERI, Marino. *Dio, l'anima e l'uomo: L'epistolario di Fausto di Riez*. Rome: Aracne, 2011.

NESSELRATH, Heinz-Günther. "Lukian und die antike Philosophie." In *Lukian, ΦΙΛΟΨΕΥΔΕΙΣ Η ΑΠΙΣΤΩΝ: Die Lügenfreunde oder; Der Ungläubige*, eingeleitet, übersetzt und mit interpretierenden Essays versehen von Mar-tin Ebner, Holger Gzella, Heinz-Günther Nesselrath und Ernst Ribbat, 135–152. SAPERE 3. 2. Aufl. Darmstadt: Wissenschaftliche Buchge-sellschaft, 2002.

NESTLE, Wilhelm. *Vom Mythos zum Logos: Die Selbstentfaltung des griechi-schen Denkens von Homer bis auf die Sophistik und Sokrates*. 2. Aufl. Stuttgart: Kröner, 1975.

NEUSNER, Jacob. "Is the God of Judaism Incarnate?" *Religious Studies* 24 (1988): 213–238.

NEUWIRTH, Angelika. *Der Koran als Text der Spätantike: Ein europäischer Zugang*. Berlin: Verlag der Weltreligionen, 2010.

NEWIGER, Hans-Joachim. *Untersuchungen zu Gorgias' Schrift über das Nicht-seiende*. Berlin: De Gruyter, 1973.

NEWSOM, Carol A. *Songs of the Sabbath Sacrifice: A Critical Edition*. Harvard Semitic Studies 27. Atlanta: Scholar's Press, 1985.

NIEHR, Herbert. "Das Buch Daniel." In *Einleitung in das Alte Testament*, 8. vollständig überarbeitete Aufl., herausgegeben von Christian Frevel, 610–621. Kohlhammer Studienbücher Theologie 1/1. Stuttgart: Kohlhammer, 2012.

Nɪʟssoɴ, Martin P. *Griechische Feste von religiöser Bedeutung mit Ausschluss der attischen*. Leipzig: Teubner, 1906.

Noᴇᴛʜʟɪᴄʜs, Karl L. "Heidenverfolgung." In *Reallexikon für Antike und Christentum*, 13: 1149–1190. Stuttgart: Hiersemann, 1986.

———. "Kaisertum und Heidentum im 5. Jahrhundert." In *Heiden und Christen im 5. Jahrhundert*, herausgegeben von Johannes van Oort und Dietmar Wyrwa, 1–31. Studien der Patristischen Arbeitsgemeinschaft 5. Leuven: Peeters, 1998.

Noʟʟᴇ́, Johannes. "Die Münzen von Elis (Kat.–Nr. 1–50)." In *Olympia: Geld und Sport in der Antike*, herausgegeben von Manfred Gutgesell und Anne V. Siebert, 17–30. Museum Kestnerianum 7. Hannover: Kestner-Museum, 2004.

Noʀᴅᴇɴ, Eduard. *Agnostos Theos: Untersuchungen zur Formengeschichte religiöser Rede*. Leipzig: Teubner, 1912. (= Darmstadt: Wissenschaftliche Buchgesellschaft, 1956.)

———. "Jahve und Moses in hellenistischer Theologie." In *Festgabe von Fachgenossen und Freunden A. von Harnack zum siebzigsten Geburtstag dargebracht*, herausgegeben von Karl Holl, 292–301. Tübingen: Mohr Siebeck, 1921.

Noʀᴛᴍᴀɴɴ, Ulrich. "Schêma/Figur, Form." In *Aristoteles-Lexikon*, herausgegeben von Otfried Höffe, 520f. Kröners Taschenausgabe 459. Stuttgart: Kröner, 2005.

Noᴡᴀᴋ, Kurt. *Schleiermacher: Leben, Werk und Wirkung*. Göttingen: Vandenhoeck & Ruprecht, 2002.

Nᴜ̈ᴛzᴇʟ, Johannes M. *Die Verklärungserzählung im Markusevangelium: Eine redaktionsgeschichtliche Untersuchung*. Forschung zur Bibel 6. Würzburg: Echter, 1971.

Oʙʙɪɴᴋ, Dirk. "'All Gods Are True' in Epicurus." In *Traditions of Theology: Studies in Hellenistic Theology, Its Background and Aftermath*, edited by Dorothea Frede and André Laks, 183–222. Philosophia Antiqua 89. Leiden: Brill, 2002.

Oʙᴇʀᴅoʀғᴇʀ, Bernd. "The Dignity of Human Personhood and the Concept of the 'Image of God.'" In *The Depth of the Human Person: A Multidisciplinary Approach*, edited by Michael Welker, 257–273. Grand Rapids/ Cambridge: 2014.

O'Coɴɴᴇʟʟ, Robert J. "Augustine's Rejection of the Fall of the Soul." *Augustinian Studies* 4 (1973): 1–32.

———. "Ennead VI, 4 and 5 in the Works of Saint Augustine." *Revue des études augustiniennes* 9 (1963): 1–39.

O'Dᴀʟʏ, Gerard J. P. "Anima, animus." In *Augustinus-Lexikon*, 1: 315–340. Basel: Schwabe, 1986–1994.

Oᴅᴇʙᴇʀɢ, Hugo, ed. *3 Enoch, or the Hebrew Book of Enoch*. Translated for the first time with introduction, commentary, and critical notes by Hugo Odeberg. Cambridge: Cambridge University Press, 1928.

O'Doɴɴᴇʟʟ, James J. *Augustine Confessions*. Vol. 2, *Commentary on Books 1–7*. Oxford: Clarendon, 1992.

————. *Augustine Confessions*. Vol. 3, *Commentary on Books 8–13*. Indexes. Oxford: Clarendon, 1992.

————. "Memoria." In *Augustinus-Lexikon*, 3: 1249–1257. Basel: Schwabe, 2004–2010.

OETINGER, Friedrich C. "Leib, Soma." In idem, *Biblisches und emblematisches Wörterbuch*, herausgegeben von Gerhard Schäfer in Verbindung mit Otto Betz, Reinhard Breymayer, Eberhard Gutekunst, Ursula Hardmeier, Roland Pietsch und Guntram Spindler. 2 Bde. Bd. 1: *Text*, und Bd. 2: *Anmerkungen*. Texte zur Geschichte des Pietismus 7/3. Berlin/New York: De Gruyter, 1999.

————. "Offenbaren, Phaneroo." In idem, *Biblisches und emblematisches Wörterbuch*, herausgegeben von Gerhard Schäfer in Verbindung mit Otto Betz, Reinhard Breymayer, Eberhard Gutekunst, Ursula Hardmeier, Roland Pietsch und Guntram Spindler, 246,30–248,4. 2 Bde. Bd. 1: Text, und Bd. 2: Anmerkungen. Texte zur Geschichte des Pietismus 7/3. Berlin/New York: De Gruyter, 1999.

O'HAGAN, Angelo P. *Material Re-creation in the Apostolic Fathers*. TU 100. Berlin: Akademie-Verlag, 1968.

ÖHLER, Markus. "Die Verklärung (Mk 9,1–8): Die Ankunft der Herrschaft Gottes auf Erden." *Novum Testamentum* 38 (1996): 197–217.

————. *Elia im Neuen Testament: Untersuchungen zur Bedeutung des alttestamentlichen Propheten im frühen Christentum*. BZNW 88. Berlin/New York: De Gruyter, 1997.

OHST, Martin. *Schleiermacher und die Bekenntnisschriften: Eine Untersuchung zu seiner Reformations- und Protestantismusdeutung*. BHT 77. Tübingen: Mohr Siebeck, 1989.

OLIN, Margaret. "'Early Christian Synagogues' and 'Jewish Art Historians': The Discovery of the Synagogue of Dura-Europos." *Marburger Jahrbuch für Kunstwissenschaft* 27 (2000): 7–28.

OLOFSSON, Staffan. *God Is My Rock: A Study of Translation Technique and Theological Exegesis in the Septuagint*. Stockholm: Almqvist & Wiksell International, 1990.

O'LOUGHLIN, Thomas. "The 'Libri Platonicorum' and Augustine's Conversions." In *The Relationship between Neoplatonism and Christianity: Proceedings of the First Patristic Conference at Maynooth*, edited by Thomas Finan and Vincent Twomey, 101–125. Dublin: Four Courts Press, 1992.

O'MEARA, John J. *Porphyry's Philosophy from Oracles in Augustine*. Paris: Études Augustiniennes, 1959.

————. "Porphyry's Philosophy from Oracles in Eusebius' *Praeparatio Evangelica* and Augustine's Dialogues of Cassiciacum." *Recherches Augustiniennes* 6 (1969): 103–138.

OORT, Johannes van. "Elkesaiten." In *Religion in Geschichte und Gegenwart*, 2: 1227f. 4. Aufl. Tübingen: Mohr Siebeck, 2000.

————. "The Young Augustine's Knowledge of Manichaeism: An Analysis of the *Confessions* and Some Other Relevant Texts." *VC* 62 (2008): 441–466.

OPELT, Ilona. "Des Hieronymus' Heiligenbiographien." *Römische Quartalschrift* 74 (1979): 145–177.

———. *Hieronymus' Streitschriften.* Heidelberg: Winter, 1973.

OPITZ, Hans-Georg. "Theophilus von Alexandrien." In *Paulys Realencyclopädie der classischen Altertumswissenschaft,* 5A/2: 2149–2165. München: Alfred Druckenmüller, 1934.

OPPENHEIM, Philippus. *Das Mönchskleid im christlichen Altertum.* Römische Quartalschrift. 28. Supplementheft. Freiburg: Herder, 1931.

OPPERMANN, Hans. *Zeus Panamaros.* Religionsgeschichtliche Versuche und Vorarbeiten 19/3. Gießen: Alfred Töpelmann, 1924.

———. "Falco, Victorius de: Iamblichi Theologoumena arithmeticae (Rezension)." *Gnomon* 5 (1929): 545–558.

OPTENDRENK, Theo. *Die Religionspolitik des Kaisers Elagabal im Spiegel der Historia Augusta.* Habelts Dissertationsdrucke. Reihe Alte Geschichte. Heft 6. Bonn: Habelt, 1969.

ORBE, Antonio. *Antropología de San Ireneo.* Biblioteca de Autores Cristianos 286. Madrid: La Editorial Catolica, 1969.

ORLANDI, Tito. "Agathonicus of Tarsus." In *Coptic Encyclopedia,* 1: 69f. New York: Macmillan, 1991.

———. "Coptic Literature." In *The Roots of Egyptian Christianity,* edited by Birger A. Pearson and James E. Goehring, 51–81. Studies in Antiquity and Christianity. Philadelphia: Fortress Press, 1992. (= 1986.)

———. "Egyptian Monasticism and the Beginnings of the Coptic Literature." In *Carl-Schmidt-Kolloquium an der Martin-Luther-Universität 1988,* herausgegeben von Peter Nagel, 129–142. Martin-Luther-Universität Halle-Wittenberg. Wissenschaftliche Beiträge 23/1990 (K 9). Halle: Martin-Luther-Universität Halle-Wittenberg, 1990.

———. "Il *dossier* copto di Agatonico di Tarso: Studia letterario e storico." In *Studies presented to Hans Jacob Polotsky,* edited by Dwight W. Young, 269–299. East Gloucester, Mass.: Pirtle & Polson, 1981.

———. "La Cristologia nei testi catechetici Copti." In *Cristologia e catechesi patristica,* tome 1, *Convegno di studio e aggior-namento Pontificium Institutum Altioris Latinitatis (Facoltà di Lettere cristiane e classiche) Roma, 17–19 febbraio 1979,* a cura di Sergio Felici, 213–229. Biblioteca di scienze religiose 31. Rome: LAS, 1980.

———. "La tradizione di Melitone in Egitto e l'omelia *De anima et corpore.*" *Augustinianum* 37 (1997): 37–50.

———. "Theophilus of Alexandria in Coptic Literature." In *Monastica et ascetica, orientalia, e Saeculo Secundo, Origen, Athanasius, Cappadocian Fathers, Chrysostom, Augustine: Papers presented to the Seventh International Conference on Patristic Studies held in Oxford 1975,* edited by Elizabeth A. Livingstone, 100–104. StPatr 16/2. (= TU 129. Berlin: Akademie-Verlag, 1985.)

ORLOV, Andrei. *The Enoch-Metatron Tradition.* TSAJ 107. Tübingen: Mohr Siebeck, 2005.

———. "Ex 33 on God's Face: A Lesson from the Enochic Tradition." In *Seminar Papers 39: Society of Biblical Literature Annual Meeting 2000.*

Atlanta: Society of Biblical Literature, 2000. (= idem, *From Apocalypticism to Merkabah Mysticism*, 311–326. Leiden: Brill, 2006.)
———. "The Face as the Heavenly Counterpart of the Visionary in the Slavonic Ladder of Jacob." In *Of Scribes and Sages: Early Jewish Interpretation and Transmission of Scripture*, edited by Craig A. Evans, 2: 59–76. Studies in Scripture in Early Judaism and Christianity 9. London: T&T Clark, 2004. (= idem, *From Apocalypticism to Merkabah Mysticism*, 399–422. Leiden: Brill, 2006.)
———. "God's Face in the Enochic Tradition." In *Paradise Now: Essays on Early Jewish and Christian Mysticism*, edited by April D. DeConick, 179–193. Symposium Series 11. Atlanta: Society of Biblical Literature; Leiden: Brill, 2006.
———. "'The Gods of My Father Terah': Abraham the Iconoclast and the Polemics with the Divine Body Traditions in the *Apocalypse of Abraham*." *Journal for the Study of the Pseudepigrapha* 18 (2008): 33–53. (= idem, *Divine Manifestations in the Slavonic Pseudepigrapha*, 217–235. Orientalia Judaica Christiana 2. Piscataway, N.Y.: Gorgias, 2009.)
———. *Heavenly Priesthood in the Apocalypse of Abraham*. Cambridge: Cambridge University Press, 2013.
———. "In the Mirror of the Divine Face: The Enochic Features of the Exagoge of Ezekiel the Tragedian." In *The Significance of Sinai: Traditions about Sinai and Divine Revelation in Judaism and Christianity*, edited by George J. Brooke, Hindy Najman, and Loren Stuckenbruck, 183–199. Themes in Biblical Narrative 12. Leiden: Brill, 2008.
———. "'Without Measure and without Analogy': The Tradition of the Divine Body in *2 (Slavonic) Enoch*." In idem, *From Apocalypticism to Merkabah Mysticism: Studies in the Slavonic Pseudepigrapha*. Journal for the Study of Judaism Supplements 114. Leiden: Brill, 2007.
OSBORN, Eric. *Irenaeus of Lyon*. Cambridge: Cambridge University Press, 2001.
OSTHÖVENER, Claus-Dieter. "Literarische und religiöse Deutungskultur im Werk Robert Musils." In *Protestantismus zwischen Aufklärung und Moderne: Festschrift für Ulrich Barth*, herausgegeben von Roderich Barth, Claus-Dieter Osthövener und Arnulf von Scheliha, 286–300. Beiträge zur rationalen Theologie 16. Frankfurt am Main: Lang, 2005.
OTTEN, Willamien. "Christ's Birth of a Virgin Who Became a Wife: Flesh and Speech in Tertullian's *De carne Christi*." VC 51 (1997): 247–260.
OTTOSSON, Magnus. "היכל." In *Theologisches Wörterbuch zum Alten Testament*, 2: 408–415. Stuttgart: Kohlhammer, 1977.
OVERWIEN, Oliver. "Kampf um Gallien: Die Briefe des Sidonius Apollinaris zwischen Literatur und Politik." *Hermes* 137 (2009): 93–117.
PAFFENROTH, Kim. "Notes and Observations: Paulsen on Augustine; An Incorporeal or Nonanthropomorphic God." HTR 86 (1993): 233–235.
PÄLTZ, Eberhard H. "Böhme, Jacob (1575–1624)." In *Theologische Realenzyklopädie*, 6: 748–754. Berlin/New York: De Gruyter, 1980.
PANNENBERG, Wolfhart. *Systematische Theologie*. Bd. 1. Göttingen: Vandenhoeck & Ruprecht, 1988.

PARKE, Herbert W. *Festivals of the Athenians*. Aspects of Greek and Roman Life. London: Thames and Hudson, 1986.

PASQUALI, Giorgio. "Doxographica aus Basiliusscholien." *Nachrichten der Königlichen Gesellschaft der Wissenschaften zu Göttingen: Philosophisch-historische Klasse*, 194–228. Berlin: Weidmannsche Buchhandlung, 1910.

PASSONI, Anna Dell'Acqua. "Innovazioni lessicali e attributi divini: Una caratteristica del giudaismo alessandrino?" In *La parola di Dio cresceva (At 12,24): Scritti in onore di Carlo Maria Martini nel suo 70. Compleanno*, a cura di Rinaldo Favris, 87–108. Supplementi alla Rivista Biblica 33. Bologna: EDB, 1998.

PATMORE, Hector M. *Adam, Satan, and the King of Tyre: The Interpretation of Ezekiel 28:11–19 in Late Antiquity*. Jewish and Christian Perspectives 20. Leiden: Brill, 2012.

PATTERSON, Paul A. *Visions of Christ: The Anthropomorphite Controversy of 399 CE*. Studien zu Antike und Christentum 68. Tübingen: Mohr Siebeck, 2012.

PAULSEN, David L. "Early Christian Belief in a Corporeal Deity: Origen and Augustine as Reluctant Witnesses." *HTR* 83 (1990): 105–116.

———. "Reply to Kim Paffenroth's Comment." *HTR* 86 (1993): 235–239.

PAX, Elpidius. "Epiphanie." In *Reallexikon für Antike und Christentum*, 5: 832–909. Stuttgart: Hiersemann, 1962.

PEERS, Glenn. *Subtle Bodies: Representing Angels in Byzantium*. The Transformation of the Classical Heritage 32. Berkeley/Los Angeles/London: University of California Press, 2001.

PEÑA, Ignacio, Pascal CASTELLANA, et Romuald FERNÁNDEZ. *Les reclus syriens: Recherches sur les anciennes formes de vie solitaire en Syrie*. Publications of the Studium biblicum franciscanum. Collectio minor 23. Mailand: Centro Propaganda e Stampa, 1980.

PEPIN, Jean. *Idées grecques sur l'homme et sur Dieu*. Collection d'Études anciennes. Paris: Les Belles-Lettres, 1971.

———. "Remarques sur la théorie de l'exégèse allégorique chez Philon." In *Philon d'Alexandrie: Lyon, 11–15 Septembre 1966*. Colloques nationaux du Centre National de la Recherche Scientifique. Paris: Éditions du Centre National de la Recherche Scientifique, 1967.

———. *Théologie cosmique et théologie chrétienne (Ambroise, Exam. I 1, 1–4)*. Bibliothèque de philosophie contemporaine. Histoire de la philosophie et philosophie générale. Paris: Presses universitaires de France, 1964.

———. "Une nouvelle source de saint Augustin: Le ζητήματα de Porphyre. Sur l'union de l'âme et du corps." In *Revue des études anciennes* 66 (1964): 53–107.

PERLER, Othmar. "Méliton 'Peri Pascha' 56 et la traduction géorgienne." In *Forma futuri: Studi in onore del Cardinale Michele Pellegrino*, a cura di Terenzio Alimonti, Francesco Bolgiani, et al. 334–349. Turin: Bottega d'Erasmo, 1975. (= idem, *Sapientia et caritas: Gesammelte Aufsätze zum 90. Geburtstag*, herausgegeben von Dirk van Damme, Otto Wermelinger, et al., 349–364. Paradosis 29. Freiburg, Schweiz: Universitätsverlag, 1990.)

————. "Recherches sur le Peri Pascha de Méliton." *Recherches de science religieuse* 51 (1963): 407–421. (= idem, *Sapientia et caritas: Gesammelte Aufsätze zum 90. Geburtstag*, herausgegeben von Dirk van Damme and Otto Wermelinger, 315–329. Paradosis 29. Freiburg, Schweiz: Universitätsverlag, 1990.)

PERRIN, Michel. *L'homme antique et chrétien: L'anthropologie de Lactance 250–325*. Théologie historique 59. Paris: Beauchesne, 1981.

PERRONE, Lorenzo. "Il 'Dialogo contro gli aftartodoceti' di Leonzio di Bisanzio e Severo di Antiochia." *Cristianesimo nella storia* 1 (1980): 411–442.

————. *La preghiera secondo Origene: L'impossibilità donate*. Letteratura Cristiana antica 24. Brescia: Morcelliana, 2011.

PERRY, Ben E. *Secundus the Silent Philosopher*. American Philological Association Philological Monographs 22. Ithaca, N.Y.: American Philological Association, 1964.

PESCH, Rudolf. *Das Markusevangelium*. Tl. 1, *Einleitung und Kommentar zu Kap. 1,1–8,26*. Herders Theologischer Kommentar zum Neuen Testament II. 4. Aufl. Freiburg/Basel/Wien: Herder, 1984.

PETERSMANN, Hubert. "Religion, Superstition and Parody in Petronius' *Cena Trimalchionis*." In *Groningen Colloquia on the Novel*, Bd. 6., herausgegeben von Heinz Hofmann, 75–85. Groningen: Forsten, 1996.

PETERSON, Erik. "Einige Bemerkungen zum Hamburger Papyrusfragment der Acta Pauli." *VC* 3 (1949): 142–162. (= idem, *Frühkirche, Judentum und Gnosis: Studien und Untersuchungen*. Freiburg: Herder, 1959. [= Darmstadt: Wissenschaftliche Buchgesellschaft, 1982.])

————. "Theologie der Kleidung." *Wort und Wahrheit* 2 (1947): 193–199. (= idem, *Marginalien zur Theologie und andere Schriften*, 20–27. Mit einer Einführung von Barbara Nichtweiß und Erik Peterson. Ausgewählte Schriften 2. Würzburg: Echter, 1995.)

————. "Theologie des Kleides." *Benediktinische Monatsschrift* 16 (1934): 347–356. (= idem, *Marginalien zur Theologie und andere Schriften*, 10–19. Mit einer Einführung von Barbara Nichtweiß und Erik Peterson. Ausgewählte Schriften 2. Würzburg: Echter, 1995.)

PÉTREMENT, Simone. *A Separate God: The Christian Origins of Gnosticism*. Translated by Carol Harrison. London: Darton, Longman and Todd, 1991. (= idem, *Le Dieu séparé: Les origines du Gnosticisme*. Paris: Les éditions du Cerf, 1984.)

PETRY, Sven. *Die Entgrenzung JHWHs: Monolatrie, Bilderverbot und Monotheismus im Deuteronomium, in Deuterojesaja und im Ezechielbuch*. FAT 2/27. Tübingen: Mohr Siebeck, 2007.

PFEIFFER, Henrik. "Die Herkunft Jahwes und ihre Zeugen." *Berliner Theologische Zeitschrift* 30 (2013): (11–43) 36–40.

PFISTER, Friedrich. "Epiphanie." In *Paulys Realencyclopädie der classischen Altertumswissenschaft*, Supplementband 4: 277–323. München: Alfred Druckenmüller, 1924.

PHILIPP, Hanna. "Zu Polyklets Schrift 'Kanon.'" In *Polyklet: Der Bildhauer der griechischen Klassik; Ausstellung im Liebieghaus Museum alter*

Plastik Frankfurt am Main, herausgegeben von Herbert Beck, Peter C. Bol und Maraike Bückling, 135–155. Mainz: Zabern, 1990.

PHILIPPSON, Robert. "Die Quelle der Epikureischen Götterlehre in Ciceros erstem Buche De natura deorum." *Symbolae Osloenses* 19 (1939): 15–40.

———. "Zur epikureischen Götterlehre." *Hermes* 51 (1916): 568–608.

PIETRI, Charles, et Luce PIETRI. *Prosopographie de l'Italie chrétienne (313–604)*. Tome 1, *A–K*. Prosopographie chrétienne du Bas-Empire 2/1. Rome: École Française de Rome, 1999.

———. *Prosopographie de l'Italie chrétienne (313–604)*. Tome 2, *L–Z*. Prosopographie chrétienne du Bas-Empire 2/2. Rome: École Française de Rome, 2000.

PINES, Shlomo. "Points of Similarity between the Exposition of the Doctrine of the Sefirot in the Sefer Yezira and a Text of the Pseudo-Clementine Homilies: The Implications of this Resemblance." *Proceedings of the Israel Academy of Sciences and Humanities* 7 (1989): 63–141.

PLATT, Verity. *Facing the Gods: Epiphany and Representation in the Graeco-Roman Art, Literature and Religion*. Greek Culture in the Roman World. Cambridge: Cambridge University Press, 2011.

PLESCH, Julius. *Die Originalität und literarische Form der Mönchsbiographien des hl. Hieronymus*. Beilage zum Programm des Wittelsbacher-Gymnasiums München. München: Wolf, 1910.

PLÖGER, Otto. *Das Buch Daniel*. Kommentar zum Alten Testament 18. Gütersloh: Mohn, 1965.

PLOWDEN, Edmund. *The Commentaries, or Reports of Edmund Plowden: . . . Containing Divers Cases upon Matters of Law, Argued and Adjudged in the Several Reigns of King Edward VI., Queen Mary, King and Queen Philip and Mary, and Queen Elizabeth [1548–1579]. To Which Are Added, The Quæries of Mr. Plowden. In Two Parts*. London: Brooke, 1816.

POHLENZ, Max. *Die Stoa: Geschichte einer geistigen Bewegung*. 7. Aufl. Göttingen: Vandenhoeck & Ruprecht, 1992.

POULSEN, Richard C. *The Body as Text: In a Perpetual Age of Non-reason*. New York: Peter Lang, 1996.

PRAECHTER, Karl. "Syrianos." In *Realencyclopädie der classischen Altertumswissenschaften*, 4A/2: 1728–1775. Stuttgart: Alfred Druckenmüller, 1932.

PRESTIGE, George L. *God in Patristic Thought*. London: Heinemann, 1936. (= Eugene, Ore.: Wipf & Stock, 2008.)

PRIGENT, Pierre. *Justin et l'Ancien Testament: L'argumentation scripturaire du traité de Justin contre toutes les hérésies comme source principale du Dialogue avec Tryphon et de la Première Apologie*. Études bibliques. Paris: Gabalda, 1964.

———. "La main de Dieu dans l'iconographie du paléo-christianisme." In *La Main de Dieu. Die Hand Gottes*, édité par René Kieffer et Jan Bergman, 141–156. Tübingen: Mohr Siebeck, 1997.

———. *Le judaïsme et l'image*. TSAJ 24. Tübingen: Mohr Siebeck, 1990.

PRIMMER, Adolf. Ἀπάθεια und Ἔλεος *im Gottesbegriff des Origenes*. Wien: Diss. phil., masch., 1956.

PRINZ, Friedrich. *Frühes Mönchtum im Frankenreich: Kultur und Gesellschaft in Gallien, den Rheinlanden und Bayern am Beispiel der monastischen Entwicklung (4. bis 8. Jahrhundert)*. München: Oldenbourg, 1965.

PRINZIVALLI, Emanuela. "Aspetti esegetico-dottrinali del dibattito nel IV secolo sulle tesi origeniane in materia escatologica." *Annali di storia dell'esegesi* 11 (1994): 433–460.

PUJIULA, Martin. *Körper und christliche Lebensweise: Clemens von Alexandreia und sein Paidagogos*. Millennium-Studien zur Kultur und Geschichte des ersten Jahrtausends n. Chr. 9. Berlin/New York: De Gruyter, 2006.

QUISPEL, Gilles. "Ezekiel 1:26 in Jewish Mysticism and Gnosis." *VC* 34 (1980): 1–13.

———. *Makarius, das Thomasevangelium und das Lied von der Perle*. Supplements to Novum Testamentum 15. Leiden: Brill, 1967.

———. "Sein und Gestalt." In idem, *Gnostic Studies*, vol. 2. Uitgaven van het Nederlands Historisch-Archeologisch Instituut te Istanbul 34/2. İstanbul: Nederlands Historisch-Archaeologisch Institut in het Nabije Oosten, 1975.

RADKE, Gyburg. *Die Theorie der Zahl im Platonismus: Ein systematisches Lehrbuch*. Tübingen/Basel: Francke, 2003.

RAMELLI, Ilaria. "Allegory: II. Judaism." In *Encyclopedia of the Bible and Its Reception*, 1: 785–793. Berlin/New York: De Gruyter, 2009.

———. "Evagrius and Gregory: Nazianzen or Nyssen? Cappadocian (and Origenian) Influence on Evagrius." In *Greek, Roman, and Byzantine Studies* 53 (2013): 117–137.

RAMELLI, Ilaria, e Giulio LUCCHETTA. *Allegoria*. Vol. 1, *L'età classica*. Introduzione e cura di Roberto Radice. Temi metafisici e problemi del pensiero antico. Studi e testi 98. Mailand: Vita e Pensiero, 2004.

RAPP, Christof. "Pathos/Widerfahrnis, Affekt." In *Aristoteles-Lexikon*, herausgegeben von Otfried Höffe, 427–436. Kröners Taschenausgabe 459. Stuttgart: Kröner, 2005.

RAPP, Christof, und Tim WAGNER. "Eidos/Gestalt, Art, Form." In *Aristoteles-Lexikon*, herausgegeben von Otfried Höffe, 147–158. Kröners Taschenausgabe 459. Stuttgart: Kröner, 2005.

RAPP, Claudia. *Holy Bishops in Late Antiquity: The Nature of Christian Leadership in a Time of Transition*. The Transformation of the Classical Heritage 37. Berkeley: California University Press, 2005.

REBENICH, Stefan. *Hieronymus und sein Kreis: Prosopographische und sozialgeschichtliche Untersuchungen*. Historia. Einzelschriften 72. Stuttgart: Steiner, 1992.

REED, Annette Yoshiko. "Rethinking (Jewish-)Christian Evidence for Jewish Mysticism." In *Hekhalot Literature in Context: Between Byzantium and Babylonia*, edited by Ra'anan Boustan, Martha Himmelfarb, and Peter Schäfer, 349–377. TSAJ 153. Tübingen: Mohr Siebeck, 2013.

REED, Annette Yoshiko, and Adam H. BECKER. "Traditional Models and New Directions." In *The Ways That Never Parted: Jews and Christians in Late Antiquity and the Early Middle Ages*, edited by Adam H. Becker and Annette Y. Reed, 1–34. Texts and Studies in Ancient Judaism 95. Tübingen: Mohr Siebeck 2003.

REED, Annette Yoshiko, F. Stanley JONES, and Claude MIMOUNI. "Two Books on Jewish-Christianity." *Annali di Storia dell'Esegesi* 30 (2013): 93–101.

REHLING, Bernhard. *De Fausti Reiensis epistula tertia: Commentatio Historica*. Diss. phil. Münster 1898. Münster: Aschendorff, 1898.

REHM, Albert, und Richard HARDER, Hg. *Didyma*. Tl. 2, *Die Inschriften*. Mainz: von Zabern/Berlin: Mann, 1958.

REHM, Bernhard. "Zur Entstehung der pseudoclementinischen Schriften." *Zeitschrift für die neutestamentliche Wissenschaft* 37 (1938): 77–184.

REINBOLD, Wolfgang. *Der älteste Bericht über den Tod Jesu: Literarische Analyse und historische Kritik der Passionsdarstellungen der Evangelien*. BZNW 69. Berlin/New York: De Gruyter, 1994.

REINDL, Joseph. *Das Angesicht Gottes im Sprachgebrauch des Alten Testaments*. Erfurter Theologische Studien 25. Leipzig: St. Benno, 1970.

REINHARDT, Karl. *Poseidonios über Ursprung und Entartung: Interpretation zweier kulturgeschichtlicher Fragmente*. Orient und Antike 6. Heidelberg: Winter, 1928.

REININK, Gerrit J. "'Das Land Seiris' (Sir) und das Volk der Serer in jüdischen und christlichen Traditionen." *JSJ* 6 (1975): 72–85.

REITZENSTEIN, Richard. *Die hellenistischen Mysterienreligionen nach ihren Grundgedanken und Wirkungen*. 3. Aufl. Leipzig: Teubner, 1927.

———. *"Historia Monachorum" und "Historia Lausiaca": Eine Studie zur Geschichte des Mönchtums und der frühchristlichen Begriffe Gnostiker und Pneumatiker*. Forschungen zur Religion und Literatur des Alten und Neuen Testaments 24. Göttingen: Vandenhoeck & Ruprecht, 1916.

———. *Poimandres: Studien zur griechisch-ägyptischen und frühchristlichen Literatur*. Leipzig: Teubner, 1904.

RENGER, Almut-Barbara, und Alexandra STELLMACHER. "Der Asketen- als Wissenskörper: Zum verkörperlichten Wissen des Simeon Stylites in ausgewählten Texten der Spätantike." *Zeitschrift für Religions- und Geistesgeschichte* 62 (2010): 313–338.

RENTSCH, Thomas. "Theologie, negative." In *Historisches Wörterbuch der Philosophie*, 10: 1102–1105. Darmstadt: Wissenschaftliche Buchgesellschaft, 1998.

RESCH, Alfred. *Agrapha: Aussercanonische Schriftfragmente, gesammelt und untersucht*. In zweiter, völlig neu bearbeiteter, durch alttestamentliche Agrapha vermehrter Aufl. herausgegeben. TU 30/3–4. Leipzig: Hinrichs, 1906.

REYNDERS, Bruno. *Lexique comparé du texte Grec et des versions Latine, Arménienne et Syriaque de l'"Adversus Haereses" de Saint Irénée*. Tome 2, *Index des mots Latins*. Corpus scriptorum Christianorum orientalium 142. Subsidia 6. Louvain: Durbecq, 1954.

———. *Vocabulaire de la "Demonstration" et des fragments de Saint Irénée*. Louvain: Éditions de Chevetogne, 1958.

RICHARD, Marcel. "Léonce de Jérusalem et Léonce de Byzance." *Mélanges de Science Religieuse* 1 (1944): 35–88. (= idem, *Opera minora*. Tome 3, nr. 59. Turnhout: Brepols/Leuven: Peeters, 1977.)

———. "Nouveaux fragments de Théophile d'Alexandrie." *Nachrichten der Akademie der Wissenschaften zu Göttingen* 2 (1975): 57–65. (= idem, *Opera minora*. Tome 2, nr. 39. Turnhout/Leuven: Peeters, 1977.)

———. "Témoins Grecs des fragments XIII et XV de Méliton de Sardes." *Le Muséon* 85 (1972): 309–336. (= idem, *Opera minora*. Tome 1, nr. 7. Turnhout: Brepols/Leuven: Peeters, 1976.)

———. "Une homélie de Théophile d'Alexandrie sur l'institution de l'Eucharistie." *Revue d'histoire eccléstiastique* 33 (1937): 46–54. (= idem, *Opera minora*. Tome 2, nr. 37. Turnhout: Brepols/Leuven: Peeters, 1977.) (= idem, "Les écrits de Théophile d'Alexandrie." *Muséon* 52 [1939]: 33–50.)

RICHTER, Gerhard. *Oikonomia: Der Gebrauch des Wortes Oikonomia im Neuen Testament, bei den Kirchenvätern und in der theologischen Literatur bis ins 20. Jahrhundert*. Arbeiten zur Kirchengeschichte 90. Berlin/New York: De Gruyter, 2005.

RIEDMATTEN, Henri de. *Les actes du procès de Paul de Samosate: Étude sur la Christologie du III⁰ au IV⁰ siècle*. Paradosis 6. Fribourg: Éditions St-Paul, 1952.

RIEDWEG, Christoph. *Mysterienterminologie bei Platon, Philon und Klemens von Alexandrien*. Untersuchungen zur antiken Literatur und ihrer Geschichte 26. Berlin/New York: De Gruyter, 1987.

RINGGREN, Helmer. "יפה‎," and "תמונה‎." In *Theologisches Wörterbuch zum Alten Testament*, 3: 787–790. Stuttgart: Kohlhammer, 1982.

RITTER, Stefan. "Münzbilder im Kontext: Zeus und Olympia auf elischen Stateren des 4. Jahrhunderts v. Chr." In *Konstruktionen von Wirklichkeit: Bilder im Griechenland des 5. und 4. Jahrhunderts v. Chr.*, herausgegeben von Ralf von den Hoff und Stefan Schmidt, 89–105. Stuttgart: Steiner, 2001.

ROBERT, Louis. *Hellenica: Recueil d'épigraphie, de numismatique et antiquités grecques*. Tome 11. Limoges/Paris: Adrien-Maisonneuve, 1960.

ROBINSON, James M. *The Pachomian Monastic Library at the Chester Beatty Library and the Bibliothèque Bodmer*. Occasional Papers of the Institute for Antiquity and Christianity 19. Claremont: Institute for Antiquity and Christianity, 1990.

———. *The Story of the Bodmer Papyri: From the First Monastery's Library in Upper Egypt to Geneva and Dublin*. Eugene, Ore.: Cascade Books, 2011.

ROBINSON, Stephen E., et al. "God the Father." In *Encylopedia of Mormonism*, edited by Daniel H. Ludlow, 2: 548–552. New York: Macmillan, 1992.

ROHDE, Erwin. *Der griechische Roman und seine Vorläufer*. 3. durch einen zweiten Anhang vermehrte Aufl. Leipzig: Breitkopf & Härtel, 1914.

RÖHR, Werner, Hg. *Appellation an das Publikum . . . Dokumente zum Atheismusstreit um Fichte, Forberg, Niethammer: Jena 1798/99*. Reclams Universal-Bibliothek 1179. Leipzig: Reclam, 1987.

RÖLLI, Marc. "Philosophische Anthropologie im 19. Jahrhundert—Zwischen Leib und Körper." In *Leiblichkeit: Geschichte und Aktualität eines Konzepts*, herausgegeben von Emmanuel Alloa, Thomas Bedorf, Christian Grüny und Tobias N. Klass, 149–161. UTB, Mittlere Reihe 3633. Tübingen: Mohr Siebeck, 2012.

ROME, Giles of (= Aegidius Romanus). *Errores Philosophorum: Critical Text with Notes and Introduction.* Edited by Josef Koch. Translated by John O. Riedl. Milwaukee, Wis.: Marquette University Press, 1944.

ROMENY, Robert B. ter Haar. *A Syrian in Greek Dress: The Use of Greek, Hebrew and Syriac Biblical Texts in Eusebius of Emesa's Commentary on Genesis.* Traditio Exegetica Graeca 6. Leuven: Peeters, 1997.

ROSCHER, Wilhelm. "Helios." In *Ausführliches Lexikon der griechischen und römischen Mythologie,* 1/2: 1993–2026. Leipzig: Teubner, 1890.

ROSENAU, Hartmut. "Gott höchst persönlich: Zur Rehabilitierung der Rede von der Personalität Gottes im Durchgang durch den Pantheismus- und Atheismusstreit." In *Marburger Jahrbuch Theologie XIX: Personalität Gottes,* herausgegeben von Wilfried Härle und Reiner Preul, 47–76. Leipzig: Evangelische Verlagsanstalt, 2007.

———. *Mit Gott reden—von Gott reden: Das Personsein des dreieinigen Gottes; Votum des Theologischen Ausschusses der Union Evangelischer Kirchen (UEK) in der EKD.* Herausgegeben von Michael Beintker und Martin Heimbucher. Evangelische Impulse 3. Neukirchen-Vluyn: Neukirchener, 2011.

ROSTOVTZEFF, Michael. *Dura Europos and Its Art.* Oxford: Clarendon, 1938.

ROUSSEAU, Philip. *Ascetics, Authority, and the Church in the Age of Jerome and Cassian.* 2nd ed. Notre Dame, Ind.: University of Notre Dame Press, 2010.

ROUSSELLE, Aline. *Porneia: On Desire and the Body in Antiquity.* Oxford: Basil Blackwell, 1988. (= idem, *Porneia: De la maîtrise du corps à la privation sensorielle; IIe–IVe siècles de l'ère chrétienne.* Les chemins de l'histoire. Paris: Presses Universitaires de France, 1983.)

ROWLAND, Christopher. *The Open Heaven: A Study of Apocalyptic in Judaism and Early Christianity.* Eugene, Ore.: Wipf and Stock, 2002. (= London: SPCK, 1982.)

———. "Things to Which Angels Long to Look: Approaching Mysticism from the Perspective of the New Testament and the Jewish Apocalypses." In Christopher Rowland and Christopher R. Morray-Jones, *The Mystery of God: Early Jewish Mysticism and the New Testament,* 3–215. Compendia Rerum Iudaicarum ad Novum Testamentum 3/12. Leiden/Boston: Brill, 2009.

———. "The Visions of God in Apocalyptic Literature." *Journal for the Study of Judaism in the Persian, Hellenistic, and Roman Period* 10 (1979): 137–154.

RUBENSON, Samuel. "Evagrios Pontikos und die Theologie der Wüste." In *Logos: Festschrift für Luise Abramowski zum 8. Juli 1993,* herausgegeben von Hanns C. Brennecke, Ernst L. Grasmück und Christoph Markschies, 384–401. BZNW 67. Berlin/New York: De Gruyter, 1993.

———. "Origen in the Egyptian Monastic Tradition of the Fourth Century." In *Origeniana septima: Origenes in den Auseinandersetzungen des vierten Jahrhunderts* [7. Internationales Origeneskolloquium, vom 25. bis zum 29. August 1997, Hofgeismar], herausgegeben von Wolfgang A. Bienert, 319–337. BETL 137. Leuven: University Press / Uitgeverij Peeters, 1999.

RUBIN, Nissan, and Admiel KOSMAN. "The Clothing of the Primordial Adam as a Symbol of Apocalyptic Time in the Midrashic Sources." *HTR* 90 (1997): 155–174.

RUDOLPH, Kurt. *Antike Baptisten: Zu den Überlieferungen über frühjüdische und -christliche Taufsekten.* Sitzungsberichte der Sächsischen Akademie der Wissenschaften zu Leipzig, Philologisch-historische Klasse 4/121. Berlin: Akademie-Verlag, 1981. (= idem, *Gnosis und spätantike Religionsgeschichte: Gesammelte Aufsätze.* Nag Hammadi and Manichaean Studies 42. Leiden: Brill, 1996.)

RUH, Kurt. *Geschichte der abendländischen Mystik.* Bd. 1, *Die Grundlegung durch die Kirchenväter und die Mönchstheologie des 12. Jahrhunderts.* München: Beck, 1990.

———. "Vorbemerkungen zu einer neuen Geschichte der abendländischen Mystik im Mittelalter." In idem, *Kleine Schriften,* Bd. 2, *Scholastik und Mystik im Mittelalter,* herausgegeben von Volker Mertens, 337–363. Berlin/New York: De Gruyter, 1984.

RUNIA, David T. "The Beginning of the End: Philo of Alexandria and Hellenistic Theology." In *Traditions of Theology: Studies in Hellenistic Theology, Its Background and Aftermath,* edited by Dorothea Frede and André Laks, 281–316. Philosophia Antiqua 89. Leiden/Boston/Cologne: Brill, 2002.

———. *Philo of Alexandria and the Timaeus of Plato.* Philosophia Antiqua 44. Leiden: Brill, 1986.

RÜPKE, Jörg. *Aberglauben oder Individualität? Religiöse Abweichung im römischen Reich.* Tübingen: Mohr Siebeck, 2011.

RUSSELL, Norman. "Theophilus and Cyril of Alexandria on the Divine Image." In *Origeniana Octava: Origen and the Alexandrian Tradition; Papers of the 8th International Origen Congress Pisa, 27–31 August 2001,* edited by Lorenzo Perrone, in collaboration with Paolo Bernardini and Diego Marchini, 2: 939–946. BETL 164. Leuven: Peeters, 2003.

———. *Theophilus of Alexandria.* The Early Church Fathers. London/New York: Routledge, 2007.

RÜTHER, Theodor. *Die sittliche Forderung der Apatheia in den ersten beiden christlichen Jahrhunderten und bei Klemens von Alexandrien: Ein Beitrag zur Geschichte des christlichen Vollkommenheitsbegriffes.* Freiburger Theologische Studien 63. Freiburg: Herder, 1949.

RYNOR, Duncan H. "The Faith of the Simpliciores: A Patriarch's Dilemma." In *Cappadocian Fathers, Chrysostom and His Greek Contemporaries, Augustine, Donatism and Pelagianism,* edited by Elizabeth A. Livingstone, 165–169. StPatr 22. Leuven: Peeters, 1989.

ŞAHIN, Mehmet Ç. *Die Inschriften von Stratonikeia.* Tl. 1, *Panamara.* Inschriften griechischer Städte aus Kleinasien 21. Bonn: Habelt, 1981. (= *Steinepigramme aus dem griechischen Osten,* herausgegeben von Reinhold Merkelbach und Josef Stauber. Bd. 1, *Die Westküste Kleinasiens von Knidos bis Ilion.* Stuttgart/Leipzig: Teubner, 1998.)

———. *Die Inschriften von Stratonikeia.* Tl. 2/1, *Lagina, Stratonikeia und Umgebung.* Inschriften griechischer Städte aus Kleinasien 22/1. Bonn: Habelt, 1981.

SALLES, Ricardo. "'Εκπύρωσις and the Goodness of God in Cleanthes." *Phronesis* 50 (2005): 56–78.

SALOMONS, Robert P. *Einige Wiener Papyri.* Studia Amstelodamensia ad Epigraphicam, Ius Antiquum et Papyrologicam Pertinentia 4. Amsterdam: Hakkert, 1976.

SAMBURSKY, Shmuel. "On the Origin and Significance of the Term Gematria." *JJS* 29 (1978): 35–38.

SANDERS, Kirk R. "Cicero *De natura deorum* 1.48f.: Quasi Corpus?" *Mnemosyne* 4 (2004): 215–218.

SANDMEL, Samuel. "Parallelomania." *Journal of Biblical Literature* 81 (1962): 1–13. (= idem, "'Parallelomania': The Presidential Address Given before the Society of Biblical Literature, December 27, 1961." In *Presidential Voices: The Society of Biblical Literature in the Twentieth Century*, edited by Harold W. Attridge and James C. VanderKam, 107–118. Biblical Scholarship in North America 22. Leiden/Boston: Brill, 2006.)

SCHÄFER, Peter. "Bibelübersetzungen II. Targumim." In *Theologische Realenzyklopädie*, 6: 216–228. Berlin/New York: De Gruyter, 1980.

———. *Die Geburt des Judentums aus dem Geist des Christentums.* Tria Corda. Jenaer Vorlesungen zu Judentum, Antike und Christentum 6. Tübingen: Mohr Siebeck, 2010.

———. *Geniza-Fragmente zur Hekhalot-Literatur.* TSAJ 6. Tübingen: Mohr Siebeck, 1984.

———. *The Hidden and Manifest God: Some Major Themes in Early Jewish Mysticism.* Translated by Aubrey Pomerance. Albany: State University of New York Press, 1992. (= idem, *Der verborgene und der offenbare Gott: Hauptthemen der frühen jüdischen Mystik.* Tübingen: Mohr Siebeck, 1991.)

———. "Jewish Liturgy and Magic." In *Geschichte—Tradition—Reflexion: Festschrift für Martin Hengel zum 70. Geburtstag*, vol. 1, *Judentum*, herausgegeben von Peter Schäfer u.a., 541–555. Tübingen: Mohr Siebeck, 1996.

———. "New Testament and Hekhalot Literature: The Journey into Heaven in Paul and Merkavah Mysticism." In idem, *Hekhalot-Studien*, 234–249. TSAJ 19. Tübingen: Mohr Siebeck, 1988.

———. *The Origins of Jewish Mysticism.* Princeton, N.J.: Princeton University Press, 2009.

———. "*Shi'ur Qoma*: Rezensionen und Urtext." In idem, *Hekhalot-Studien*, 75–83. TSAJ 19. Tübingen: Mohr Siebeck, 1988.

SCHÄFER, Peter, and Joseph DAN, eds. *Gershom Scholem's Major Trends in Jewish Mysticism: 50 Years After; Proceedings of the Sixth International Conference on the History of Jewish Mysticism.* Tübingen: Mohr Siebeck, 1993.

SCHÄFER, Peter, Margarete SCHLÜTER, und Hans Georg VON MUTIUS, Hg. *Synopse zur Hekhalot-Literatur.* TSAJ 2. Tübingen Mohr Siebeck, 1981.

SCHART, Aaron. "Die 'Gestalt' YHWHs: Ein Beitrag zur Körpermetaphorik alttestamentlicher Rede von Gott." *Theologische Zeitschrift* 55 (1999): 26–43.

Schäublin, Christoph. *Untersuchungen zur Methode und Herkunft der antiochenischen Exegese.* Theophaneia 23. Köln/Bonn: Hanstein, 1974.

Scheer, Tanja S. *Die Gottheit und ihr Bild: Untersuchungen zur Funktion griechischer Kultbilder in Reli-gion und Politik.* Zetemata 105. München: Beck, 2000.

Schelhas, Johannes. "Der Leib als Schöpfung." *Neue Zeitschrift für Systematische Theologie und Religionsphilosophie* 55 (2013): 33–53.

Schenke, Hans-Martin. "The Phenomenon and Significance of Gnostic Sethianism." In *The Rediscovery of Gnosticism: Proceedings of the International Conference on Gnosticism at Yale, New Haven, Connecticut, March 28–31, 1978,* edited by Bentley Layton, 588–616, vol. 2, *Sethian Gnosticism.* Studies in the History of Religion 41/2. Leiden: Brill, 1981.

———. "Vorwort." In *Koptisch-Gnostische Schriften.* Bd. 1, *Die Pistis Sophia, die beiden Bücher des Jeû, unbekanntes altgnostisches Werk,* Herausgegeben von Carl Schmidt, 4. um das Vorwort erw. Aufl., Herausgegeben von Hans-Martin Schenke [mit den Nachträgen der 2. Aufl. von Walter C. Till, 1954], xvi–xxxiv. GCS. Berlin: Akademie-Verlag, 1984.

Scherer, Eckart. "Sinne, die." In *Historisches Wörterbuch der Philosophie,* 9: 824–869. Darmstadt: Wissenschaftliche Buchgesellschaft, 1995.

Schibli, Hermann S. "Hierocles of Alexandria and the Vehicle of the Soul." *Hermes* 121 (1993): 109–117.

Schiebe, Marianne Wifstrand. "Sind die epikureischen Götter 'thought-constructs'?" *Mnemosyne* 56 (2003): 703–727.

Schiering, Wolfgang. *Die Werkstatt des Pheidias in Olympia.* Tl. 2, *Werkstattfunde.* Olympische Forschungen 18. Berlin/New York: De Gruyter, 1991.

Schiffman, Laurence H. "Merkavah Speculation at Qumran: The 4Q Serekh Shirot Olat ha-Shabbat." In *Mystics, Philosophers, and Politicians: Essays in Jewish Intellectual History in Honor of Alexander Altmann,* edited by Jehuda Reinharz and Daniel Swetschinski with the collaboration of Kalman P. Bland, 15–47. Duke Monographs in Medieval and Renaissance Studies 5. Durham, N.C.: Duke University Press, 1982.

Schille, Gottfried. "Die Seesturmerzählung Markus 4:35–41 als Beispiel neutestamentlicher Aktualisierung." *Zeitschrift für die neutestamentliche Wissenschaft* 56 (1965): 30–40.

Schindler, Alfred. "Augustin, Augustinismus I." In *Theologische Realenzyklopädie,* 4: 646–698. Berlin/New York: De Gruyter, 1979.

Schiwietz, Stephan. *Das morgenländische Mönchtum.* Bd. 2, *Das Mönchtum auf Sinai und in Palästina im vierten Jahrhundert.* Mainz: Kirchheim, 1913.

———. *Das morgenländische Mönchtum.* Bd. 3, *Das Mönchtum in Syrien und Mesopotamien und das Aszetentum in Persien.* Mödling bei Wien: Missionsdruckerei St. Gabriel, 1938.

Schlapkohl, Corinna. *Persona Est Naturae Rationabilis Individua Substantia: Boethius und die Debatte über den Personbegriff.* Marburger Theologische Studien 56. Marburg an der Lahn: N. G. Elwert, 1999.

Schleiermacher, Friedrich D. *Der christliche Glaube nach den Grundsätzen der evangelischen Kirche im Zusammenhange dargestellt.* 2. Aufl. Berlin

1830/1831. Herausgegeben von Rolf Schäfer. Kritische Gesamtausgabe 1/13. Tlbd. 1. Berlin/New York: De Gruyter, 2003.

SCHMID, Wolfgang. "Claudianus Mamertus." In *Reallexikon für Antike und Christentum*, 3: 169–179. Stuttgart: Hiersemann, 1957.

SCHMIDT, Carl. *Studien zu den Pseudo-Clementinen, nebst einem Anhange: Die älteste römische Bischofsliste und die Pseudo-Clementinen*. TU 46/1. Leipzig: Hinrichs, 1929.

SCHMIDT, Francis. *Le testament grec d'Abraham: Introduction, édition critique des deux recensions grecques, traduit par Francis Schmidt*. Texts and Studies in Ancient Judaism 11. Tübingen: Mohr Siebeck, 1986.

SCHMIDT, Werner H. "Mythos III: Alttestamentlich." In *Theologische Realenzyklopädie*, 23: 625–644. Berlin/New York: De Gruyter, 1994.

SCHMIDTKE, Alfred. *Neue Fragmente und Untersuchungen zu den judenchristlichen Evangelien: Ein Beitrag zur Literatur und Geschichte der Judenchristen*. TU 37/1. Leipzig: Hinrichs, 1911.

SCHMITHALS, Walter. *Wunder und Glaube: Eine Auslegung von Markus 4,35–6,6a*. Biblische Studien 59. Neukirchen-Vluyn: Neukirchener, 1970.

SCHMITT, Arbogast. "Symmetrie und Schönheit. Plotins Kritik an hellenistischen Proportionslehren und ihre unterschiedliche Wirkungsgeschichte in Mittelalter und früher Neuzeit." In *Neuplatonismus und Ästhetik: Zur Transformationsgeschichte des Schönen*, herausgegeben von Verena O. Lobsien und Claudia Olk, 59–84. Transformationen der Antike 2. Berlin/New York: De Gruyter, 2007.

SCHMITT, Carl. *Politische Theologie: Vier Kapitel zur Lehre von der Souveränität*. 8. Aufl. Berlin: Duncker & Humblot, 2004. (= 1922.)

SCHMOLDT, Hans. "עתק." In *Theologisches Wörterbuch zum Alten Testament*, 6: 487–489. Stuttgart: Kohlhammer, 1989.

SCHNEEMELCHER, Wilhelm. "Der Sermo 'De anima et corpore': Ein Werk Alexander von Alexandriens?" In *Festschrift für Günther Dehn, zum 75. Geburtstag am 18. April 1957 dargebracht von der Evangelisch-Theologischen Fakultät der Rheinischen Friedrich-Wilhelms-Universität zu Bonn*, herausgegeben von Wilhelm Schneemelcher, 119–143. Neukirchen-Vluyn: Erziehungsverein, 1957.

———. "Die Kirchweihsynode von Antiochien 341." In *Bonner Festgabe Johannes Straub zum 65. Geburtstag am 18. Oktober 1977*, dargebracht von Kollegen und Schülern, herausgegeben von Adolf Lippold, 319–346. Bonner Jahrbücher, Beihefte 39. Bonn: Habelt, 1977. (= idem, *Reden und Aufsätze: Beiträge zur Kirchengeschichte und zum ökumenischen Gespräch*, 94–125. Tübingen: Mohr Siebeck, 1991.)

SCHNELLE, Udo. *Antidoketische Christologie im Johannesevangelium: Eine Untersuchung zur Stellung des 4. Evangeliums in der johanneischen Schule*. Forschungen zur Religion und Literatur des Alten und Neuen Testaments 144. Göttingen: Vandenhoeck & Ruprecht, 1987.

———. *Paulus: Leben und Denken*. De Gruyter Lehrbuch. Berlin/New York: De Gruyter, 2003.

SCHOEDEL, William R. *The Letters of Ignatius: A Commentary on the Seven Letters of Ignatius.* Hermeneia: A Critical & Historical Commentary on the Bible. Philadelphia: Fortress, 1985.

SCHOEPS, Hans J. *Vom himmlischen Fleisch Christi: Eine dogmengeschichtliche Untersuchung.* Sammlung gemeinverständlicher Vorträge und Schriften aus dem Gebiet der Theologie und Religionsgeschichte 195/196. Tübingen: Mohr Siebeck, 1951.

SCHOLEM, Gershom G. *Jewish Gnosticism, Merkabah Mysticism, and Talmudic Tradition: Based on the Israel Goldstein Lectures, Delivered at the Jewish Theological Seminary of America, New York.* New York: Jewish Theological Seminary of America, 1965.

———. *Major Trends in Jewish Mysticism.* 3rd ed. London: Thames and Hudson, 1955

———. *Major Trends in Jewish Mysticism: 50 Years After; Proceedings of the Sixth International Conference on the History of Jewish Mysticism.* Edited by Peter Schäfer and Joseph Dan. Tübingen: Mohr Siebeck, 1993. (= 3. Aufl. New York: Schocken Books, 1961.)

———. "Odeberg, Hugo: 3 Enoch or The Hebrew Book of Enoch (Rezension)." *Orientalische Literaturzeitung* 33 (1930): 193–197.

———. *Origins of the Kabbalah.* Edited by R. J. Zwi Werblowsky. Translated from the German by Allan Arkush. Princeton, N.J.: Princeton University Press, 1987.

SCHÖLLGEN, Georg. "Die Ignatianen als pseudepigraphisches Briefcorpus: Anmerkungen zu den Thesen von Reinhard M. Hübner." *Zeitschrift für Antikes Christentum* 2 (1998): 16–25.

SCHORN-SCHÜTTE, Luise. *Karl Lamprecht: Kulturgeschichtsschreibung zwischen Wissenschaft und Politik.* Schriftenreihe der Historischen Kommission bei der Bayerischen Akademie der Wissenschaften 22. Göttingen: Vandenhoeck & Ruprecht, 1984.

SCHREIBER, Johannes. *Die Markuspassion: Eine redaktionsgeschichtliche Untersuchung.* BZNW 68. 2. Aufl. Berlin/New York: De Gruyter, 1993.

SCHROEDER, Caroline T. *Monastic Bodies: Discipline and Salvation in Shenoute of Atripe.* Divinations: Rereading Late Ancient Religion. Philadelphia: University of Pennsylvania Press, 2007.

SCHROER, Silvia, und Thomas STAUBLI. *Die Körpersymbolik der Bibel.* Darmstadt: Wissenschaftliche Buchgesellschaft, 1998.

SCHUCHHARDT, Walter-Herwig. "Athena Parthenos." In *Antike Plastik: Forschungen zur griechischen und römischen Skulptur* 2 (1963): 31–53.

SCHULZ, Dietrich. "Zum Kanon Polyklets." *Hermes* 83 (1955): 200–220.

SCHULZE, Martin. *Die Schrift des Claudianus Mamertus: Presbyters zu Vienne, über das Wesen der Seele (De statu animae).* Diss. phil. Leipzig, 1883. Dresden: Rammingsche Buchdruckerei, 1883.

SCHÜTTE, Hans-Walter, und Rainer FABIAN. "Anthropomorphismus II." In *Historisches Wörterbuch der Philosophie*, 1: 377f. Basel/Stuttgart: Schwabe, 1971.

SCHWABL, Hans. "Zeus Tl. II." In *Paulys Realencyclopädie der classischen Altertumswissenschaft*, Supplementband, 15: 994–1411. München: Alfred Druckenmüller, 1978.

SCHWANZ, Peter. *Imago Dei als christologisch-anthropologisches Problem in der Geschichte der Alten Kirche von Paulus bis Clemens von Alexandrien*. Arbeiten zur Kirchengeschichte und Religionswissenschaft 2. Halle: Niemeyer, 1969.

SCHWARTZ, Daniel R. "Diodorus Siculus 40.3—Hecataeus or Pseudo Hecataeus?" In *Jews and Gentiles in the Holy Land in the Days of the Second Temple, the Mishnah, and the Talmud: A Collection of Articles*, edited by Menachem Mor, Aharon Oppenheimer, Jack Pastor, and Daniel R. Schwartz, 181–198. Jerusalem: Yad Ben-Zvi Press, 2003.

SCHWARTZ, Eduard. *Codex Vaticanus Gr. 1431: Eine antichalkedonische Sammlung aus der Zeit Kaiser Zenos*. Abhandlungen der Bayerischen Akademie der Wissenschaften. Philosophisch-historische Abteilung 32/6. München: Oldenbourg, 1927.

———. "Der Prozess des Eutyches." *Sitzungsberichte der Bayerischen Akademie der Wissenschaften: Philosophisch-historische Klasse* 5 (1929): 1–52.

———. *Eine fingierte Korrespondenz mit Paulus dem Samosatener*. Sitzungsberichte der Bayerischen Akademie der Wissenschaften, philosophisch-philologische und historische Klasse 3/1927. München: Bayerische Akademie der Wissenschaften, 1927.

———. "Unzeitgemäße Beobachtungen zu den Clementinen." *Zeitschrift für die neutestamentliche Wissenschaft* 31 (1932): 151–198.

———. "Von Konstantins Tod bis Sardika 342." In *Nachrichten von der Königlichen Gesellschaft der Wissenschaften zu Göttingen: Philosophisch-historische Klasse*, 469–522. Göttingen: Vandenhoeck & Ruprecht, 1911. (= idem, *Zur Geschichte des Athanasius*, 265–334. Gesammelte Schriften 3. Bd. Berlin: De Gruyter, 1959.)

SCHWARTZ, Howard. "Does God Have a Body? The Problem of Metaphor and Literal Language in Biblical Interpretation." In *Bodies, Embodiment, and Theology in the Hebrew Bible*, edited by S. Tamar Kamionkowski and Wonil Kim, 201–237. Library of Hebrew Bible 465. New York/London: T&T Clark, 2010.

SCHWEMER, Anna M. "Gott als König und seine Königsherrschaft in den Sabbatliedern aus Qumran." In *Königsherrschaft Gottes und himmlischer Kult im Judentum, Urchristentum und in der hellenistischen Welt*, herausgegeben von Martin Hengel und Anna M. Schwemer, 45–119. WUNT 55. Tübingen: Mohr Siebeck, 1991.

———. "Gottes Hand und die Propheten: Zum Wandel der Metapher 'Hand Gottes' in frühjüdischer Zeit." In *La main de Dieu. Die Hand Gottes*, édité par René Kieffer et Jan Bergman, 65–85. WUNT 94. Tübingen: Mohr Siebeck, 1997.

SCIBONA, Concetta Giuffrè. "The Doctrine of Soul in Manichaeism and Augustine." In *"In Search of Truth": Augustine, Manichaeism and Other Gnosticism; Studies for Johannes van Oort at Sixty*, edited by Jacob A. van den Berg, 377–418. Nag Hammadi and Manichaean Studies 74. Leiden: Brill, 2011.

SCOPELLO, Madeleine. "Haeresibus ad Quoduultdeum (De-)." In *Augustinus-Lexikon*, 3: 278–290. Basel: Schwabe, 2004.

SCOTT, Alan B. *Origen and the Life of the Stars: A History of an Idea*. OECS. Oxford: Clarendon; New York: Oxford University Press, 1991.

SCOTT, Walter. *Hermetica: The Ancient Greek and Latin Writings Which Contain Religious or Philosophic Teachings Ascribed to Hermes Trismegistus*. Vol. 3, *Commentary: Latin Asclepius and Stobaei Hermetica*. Oxford: Clarendon, 1936.

SEDLEY, David. "The Origins of Stoic God." In *Traditions of Theology: Studies in Hellenistic Theology, Its Background and Aftermath*, edited by Dorothea Frede and André Laks, 41–84. Philosophia Antiqua 89. Leiden: Brill, 2002.

SEGAL, Alan F. "Heavenly Ascent in Hellenistic Judaism, Early Christianity and Their Environment." In *ANRW* II, *Prinzipat*, 23.2, *Religion (Vorkonstantinisches Christentum: Verhältnis zu römischem Staat und heidnischer Religion)*, herausgegeben von Wolfgang Haase, 1333–1394. Berlin/New York: De Gruyter, 1980.

———. *Two Powers in Heaven: Early Rabbinic Reports about Christianity and Gnosticism*. Studies in Judaism in Late Antiquity 25. Leiden: Brill, 1977.

SEIDL, Horst. "Möglichkeit." In *Historisches Wörterbuch der Philosophie*, 6: 72–92. Darmstadt: Wissenschaftliche Buchgesellschaft, 1984.

SELLIN, Gerhard. "Gotteserkenntnis und Gotteserfahrung bei Philo von Alexandrien." In *Monotheismus und Christologie: Zur Gottesfrage im hellenistischen Judentum und im Urchristentum*, herausgegeben von Hans-Josef Klauck, 17–40. Quaestiones Disputatae 138. Freiburg/Basel/Wien: Herder, 1992.

SELTMAN, Charles T. *The Temple Coins of Olympia*. Reprinted from "Nomisma" VIII, IX, XI. With a foreword by William Ridgeway. Cambridge: Bowes & Bowes, 1921.

SENG, Helmut. "Seele und Kosmos bei Macrobius." In *Körper und Seele: Aspekte spätantiker Anthropologie*, herausgegeben von Barbara Feichtinger, Stephen Lake und Helmut Seng, 115–141. Beiträge zur Altertumskunde 215. München/Leipzig: K. G. Saur, 2006.

SHEPHERD, Massey H., Jr. "The Anthropomorphic Controversy in the Time of Theophilus of Alexandria." *Church History* 7 (1938): 263–273.

SHERIDAN, Mark. *Language for God in Patristic Tradition: Wrestling with Biblical Anthropomorphism*. Downers Grove, Ill.: IVP Academic, 2015.

SIMON, Gérard. *Der Blick, das Sein und die Erscheinung in der antiken Optik: Anhang; Die Wissenschaft vom Sehen und die Darstellung des Sichtbaren*. Aus dem Französischen von Heinz Jatho. München: Fink, 1992.

SIMONETTI, Manlio. "Fausto di Riez e i Macedoniani." *Augustinianum* 17 (1977): 333–354.

———. "Modelli culturali nella cristianità orientale del II–III secolo." In *De Tertullien aux Mozarabes: Mélanges offerts à Jacques Fontaine, membre de l'institut, à l'occasion de son 70ᵉ anniversaire, par ses élèves, amis et collègues*, Institut de Recherche et d'Histoire des Textes, comité, édité par Louis Holtz, 381–392. Tome 1, *Antiquité tardive et christianisme ancien (IIIᵉ–VIᵉ siècles)*. Collection des études augustiniennes 132. Paris: Institute d'Études Augustiniennes, 1992. (= idem, *Orthodossia ed eresia tra I e II secolo*, 315–331. Armarium 5. Soveria Manelli/Messina: Rubbettino, 1994.)

———. *Orthodossia ed eresia tra I e II secolo*. Armarium 5. Messina: Soveria Manelli, 1994.

———. "Osservazioni sulla struttura del *De principiis* di Origene." *Rivista di filologia e di istruzione classica* 90 (1962): 273–290, 372–393.

Sinn, Ulrich. "Olympia—Zeustempel und Wettkampfstätte." In *Erinnerungsorte der Antike: Die griechische Welt*, herausgegeben von Elke Stein-Hölkeskamp und Karl-Joachim Hölkeskamp, 79–97. München: Beck, 2010.

Sizgorich, Thomas. *Violence and Belief in Late Antiquity: Militant Devotion in Christianity and Islam*. Divinations: Rereading Late Ancient Religion. Philadelphia: University of Pennsylvania Press, 2009.

Skarsaune, Oskar. "Justin Märtyrer." In *Theologische Realenzyklopädie*, 17: 471–478. Berlin/New York: De Gruyter, 1988.

Skinner, Quentin. "Bedeutung und Verstehen in der Ideengeschichte." In *Die Cambridge School der politischen Ideengeschichte*, herausgegeben von Martin Mulsow und Andreas Mahler, 21–87. Suhrkamp taschenbuch wissenschaft 1925. Berlin: Suhrkamp, 2010.

Smith, Geoffrey. *Guilt by Association: Heresy Catalogues in Early Christianity*. OECS. Oxford: Oxford University Press, 2014.

Snell, Bruno. *Die Entdeckung des Geistes: Studien zur Entstehung des europäischen Denkens bei den Griechen*. 9. Aufl. Göttingen: Vandenhoeck & Ruprecht, 2009.

Sokolowski, Franciszek. *Lois sacrées de l'Asie Mineure*. École française d'Athenes. Trauvaux et mémoires 9. Paris: De Boccard, 1955.

Sokolowski, Kurt. "Emotion." In *Allgemeine Psychologie*, herausgegeben von Jochen Müsseler und Wolfgang Prinz, 337–384. Spektrum Lehrbuch. Heidelberg: Spektrum, 2002.

Solmsen, Friedrich. "The Background of Plato's Theology." *Transactions and Proceedings of the American Philological Association* 67 (1936): 208–218.

Sommer, Benjamin D. *The Bodies of God and the World of Ancient Israel*. Cambridge: Cambridge University Press, 2009.

Sorabji, Richard. *Matter, Space and Motion: Theories in Antiquity and Their Sequel*. Ithaca, N.Y.: Cornell University Press, 1988.

Sowaal, Alice. "Cartesian Bodies." *Canadian Journal of Philosophy* 34 (2004): 217–240.

Spanneut, Michel. "*Apatheia* ancienne, *Apatheia* chrétienne: 1ᵉʳᵉ partie; L'*apatheia* ancienne." In *ANRW*, II, *Prinzipat*, 36.7, *Philosophie, Wissenschaften, Technik: Systematische Themen; Indirekte Überlieferungen; Allgemeines; Nachträge*, herausgegeben von Wolfgang Haase, 4641–4717. Berlin/New York: De Gruyter, 1978.

————. "L' 'apatheia' chrétienne aux quatre premiers siècles." *Proche-Orient chrétien* 52 (2002): 165–302.

————. *Le Stoïcisme des pères de l'Église: De Clément de Rome à Clément d'Alexandrie*. Patristica Sorbonensia 1. Nouvelle éd., revue et augmentée. Paris: Éditions du Seuil, 1969.

SPECK, Paul. *Ich bin's nicht, Kaiser Konstantin ist es gewesen*. ΠΟΙΚΙΛΑ BYZANTINA 10. Bonn: Habelt, 1990.

SPEICH, Nikolaus. *Die Proportionslehre des menschlichen Körpers: Antike, Mittelalter, Renaissance*. Andelfingen: Akeret, 1957.

SPERBER-HARTMANN, Doris. *Das Gebet als Aufstieg zu Gott: Untersuchungen zur Schrift De oratione des Evagrius Ponticus*. Early Christianity in the Context of Antiquity 10. Frankfurt am Main: Lang, 2011.

SPEYER, Wolfgang. *Die literarische Fälschung im heidnischen und christlichen Altertum: Ein Versuch ihrer Deutung*. Handbuch der Altertumswissenschaft 1/2. München: Beck, 1971.

————. "Spuren der 'Genesis' in Ovids Metamorphosen." In *Kontinuität und Wandel: Lateinische Poesie von Naevius; Franco Munari zum 65. Geburtstag*, herausgegeben von Ulrich J. Stache, 90–99. Hildesheim: Weidmann, 1986.

SPICKERMANN, Wolfgang. "Lukian und die (Götter)bilder." In *Römische Götterbilder der mittleren und späten Kaiserzeit*, herausgegeben von Dietrich Boschung und Alfred Schäfer, 87–108. Morphomata 22. Paderborn: Wilhelm Fink, 2015.

SPINOZA, Baruch de. *Epistolae, Stelkonstige Reeckening van den Regenboog, Reeckening van Kanssen—(Nachbericht)*. Im Auftrag der Heidelberger Akademie der Wissenschaften herausgegeben von Carl Gebhardt. Spinoza Opera Bd. 4. Heidelberg: Winter, 1972. (= 1925.)

STADEN, Heinrich von. "Body, Soul, and Nerves: Epicurus, Herophilus, Erasistratus, the Stoics, and Galen." In *Psyche and Soma: Physicians and Metaphysicians on the Mind-Body Problem from Antiquity to Enlightenment*, edited by John P. Wright and Paul Potter, 79–116. Oxford: Clarendon, 2000.

STAEHELIN, Hans. *Die gnostischen Quellen Hippolyts in seiner Hauptschrift "Gegen die Häretiker."* TU 6/3. Leipzig: Hinrichs, 1890.

STÄHLI, Hans-Peter. *Antike Synagogenkunst*. Stuttgart: Calwer Verlag, 1988.

STARK, Isolde. "Religiöse Elemente im antiken Roman." In *Der antike Roman: Untersuchungen zur literarischen Kommunikation und Gattungsgeschichte*, von einem Autorenkollektiv unter Leitung von Heinrich Kuch, 135–149. Berlin: Akademie-Verlag, 1989.

STEAD, Christopher G. "Augustine, the *Meno* and the Subconscious Mind." In *Die Weltlichkeit des Glaubens in der Alten Kirche: Festschrift für Ulrich Wickert zum siebzigsten Geburtstag*, herausgegeben von Dietmar Wyrwa in Verbindung mit Barbara Aland und Christoph Schäublin, 339–345. BZNW 85. Berlin/New York: De Gruyter, 1997.

————. "Gott V. Alte Kirche." In *Theologische Realenzyklopädie*, 6: 652–657. Berlin/New York: De Gruyter, 1980.

STEIDLE, Basilius. "Neue Untersuchungen zu Origenes' Περὶ ἀρχῶν." *Zeitschrift für die neutestamentliche Wissenschaft und Kunde der älteren Kirche* 40 (1941): 236–243.

STEIMER, Bruno. *Vertex Traditionis: Die Gattung der altchristlichen Kirchenordnungen.* BZNW 63. Berlin/New York: De Gruyter, 1992.

STEIN, Edmund. *Die allegorische Exegese des Philo aus Alexandria.* Beihefte zur Zeitschrift für die alttestamentliche Wissenschaft 51. Gießen: Alfred Töpelmann, 1929.

STEIN, Markus. *Manichaica Latina.* Bd. 2, *Manichaei epistula fundamenti: Text, Übersetzung, Erläuterungen.* Abhandlungen der Nordrhein-Westfälischen Akademie der Wissenschaften. Sonderreihe Papyrologica Coloniensia 27/2. Paderborn/München/Wien/Zürich: Schöningh, 2002.

STEMBERGER, Günter. "Die Bedeutung des Tierkreises auf Mosaikfußböden spätantiker Synagogen." *Kairos* 17 (1975): 23–56.

STERN, Menahem, ed. *Greek and Latin Authors on Jews and Judaism.* Vol. 1, *From Herodotus to Plutarch.* Publications of the Israel Academy of Sciences and Humanities. Jerusalem: Academy of Sciences and Humanities, 1974.

STERN, Sacha. "Rachel Elior on Ancient Jewish Calendars: A Critique." *Aleph* 5 (2005): 287–292.

STEWART, Columba. *Cassian the Monk.* Oxford Studies in Historical Theology. New York/Oxford: Oxford University Press, 1998.

―――. "Imageless Prayer and the Theological Vision of Evagrius Ponticus." *JECS* 9 (2001): 173–204.

―――. "John Cassian's Schema of Eight Principal Faults and His Debt to Origen and Evagrius." In *Jean Cassien entre l'orient et l'occident: Actes du colloque international organisé par le New Europe College en collaboration avec la Ludwig Boltzmann Gesellschaft, Bucarest, 27–28 septembre 2001,* édité par Cristian Bădiliţă et Attila Jakab, 205–220. Paris: Beauchesne/Iaşi: Polirom, 2003.

[STRACK, Hermann L., und] Paul BILLERBECK. *Das Evangelium nach Markus, Lukas und Johannes und die Apostelgeschichte, erklärt aus Talmud und Midrasch.* Kommentar zum Neuen Testament aus Talmud und Midrasch 2. 9. Aufl. München: Beck, 1989.

―――. *Kommentar zum Neuen Testament aus Talmud und Midrasch.* Bd. 4, *Exkurse zu einzelnen Stellen des Neuen Testaments: Abhandlungen zur neutestamentlichen Theologie und Archäologie.* Tl. 1. München: Beck, 1928.

STRAUSS, Leo. "How to Begin to Study the *Guide of the Perplexed*." In *The Guide of the Perplexed by Moses Maimonides,* translated by Shlomo Pines, xi–lvii. Chicago: University of Chicago Press, 1963.

STRECKER, Georg. *Das Judenchristentum in den Pseudoklementinen.* TU 70. 2. bearbeitete und erweiterte Aufl. Berlin: Akademie-Verlag, 1981.

―――. "Elkesai." In *Reallexikon für Antike und Christentum,* 4: 1171–1186. Stuttgart: Hiersemann, 1959.

STROHEKER, Karl F. *Der senatorische Adel im spätantiken Gallien.* Darmstadt: Wissenschaftliche Buchgesellschaft; Tübingen: Alma Mater Verlag, 1948.

STROUMSA, Guy. "Form(s) of God: Some Notes on Metatron and Christ." *Harvard Thelogical Review* 76 (1983): 269–288.

———. "The Incorporeality of God: Context and Implications of Origen's Position." *Religion* 13 (1983): 345–358.

———. "Jewish and Gnostic Traditions among the Audians." In *Sharing the Sacred: Religious Contacts and Conflicts in the Holy Land, First– Fifteenth Centuries CE*, edited by Arieh Kofsky and Guy G. Stroumsa, 97–108. Jerusalem: Yad Izhak Ben-Zvi, 1998. (= idem, *Barbarian Philosophy: The Religious Revolution of Early Christianity*, 258–267. WUNT 112. Tübingen: Mohr Siebeck, 1999.)

———. "Le couple de l'Ange et de l'Esprit: Traditions juives et chrétiennes." *Révue Biblique* 88 (1981): 42–61.

———. "Polymorphie divine et transformations d'un mythologème: L' 'Apocryphon de Jean' et ses sources." *VC* 35 (1981): 412–434.

STROUMSA, Sarah. *Maimonides in His World: Portrait of a Mediterranean Thinker.* Princeton, N.J.: Princeton University Press, 2011.

———. "Twelfth Century Concepts of Soul and Body: The Maimonidean Controversy in Baghdad." In *Self, Soul, and Body in Religious Experience*, edited by Albert I. Baumgarten, Jan Assmann, and Guy G. Stroumsa, 313–334. Studies in the History of Religions 78. Leiden/Boston/Köln: Brill, 1998.

STRUKER, Arnold. *Die Gottebenbildlichkeit des Menschen in der christlichen Literatur der ersten zwei Jahrhunderte: Ein Beitrag zur Geschichte der Exegese von Genesis 1,26.* Münster: Aschendorff, 1913.

STRUTWOLF, Holger. *Gnosis als System: Zur Rezeption der valentinianischen Gnosis bei Origenes.* Forschungen zur Kirchen- und Dogmengeschichte 56. Göttingen: Vandenhoeck & Ruprecht, 1993.

STRZYGOWSKI, Josef. "Wilperts Kritik meiner alexandrinischen Weltchronik." *Römische Quartalsschrift* 24 (1910): 172–175.

STUDER, Basil. *Gratia Christi—Gratia Dei bei Augustinus von Hippo: Christozentrismus oder Theozentrismus?* Studia Ephemeridis "Augustinianum" 40. Rome: Institutum Patristicum "Augustinianum," 1993.

———. "Incarnazione." In *Origene: Dizionario; La cultura, il pensiero, le opere*, a cura di Adele Monaci Castagno, 225–229. Rome: Città Nuova Editrice, 2000.

———. "Kritische Fragen zu einer Geschichte des christologischen Dogmas." *Augustinianum* 34 (1994): 489–500.

———. "Zur Frage der dogmatischen Terminologie in der lateinischen Übersetzung von Origenes' *De Principiis*." In idem, *Dominus Salvator: Studien zur Christologie und Exegese der Kirchenväter*, 67–89. Studia Anselmiana 107. Rome: Pontificio Ateneo S. Anselmo, 1992.

———. *Zur Theophanie-Exegese Augustins: Untersuchung zu einem Ambrosius-Zitat in der Schrift "De videndo Deo" (ep. 147).* Studia Anselmiana 59. Rome: Herder/Rome: Editrice Anselmiana, 1971.

SULLIVAN, Kevin. "Sexuality and Gender of Angels." In *Paradise Now: Essays on Early Jewish and Christian Mysticism*, edited by April D. De Conick,

27–35. Society of Biblical Literature Symposium Series 11. Leiden: Brill, 2004.

SULLIVAN, Lawrence E. "Knowledge of the Body in the Study of Religion." *History of Religions* 30 (1990): 86–99.

SUMNEY, Jerry L. "Those Who 'Ignorantly Deny Him': The Opponents of Ignatius of Antioch." *JECS* 1 (1993): 345–365.

SUNDERMANN, Werner. *Mitteliranische manichäische Texte kirchenge-schichtlichen Inhalts.* Mit einem Appendix von Nicholas Sims-Williams. Schriften zur Geschichte und Kultur des Alten Orients. Berliner Turfan-texte 11. Berlin: Akademie-Verlag, 1981.

SYCHOWSKI, Stanislaus von. *Hieronymus als Litterarhistoriker: Eine quellen-kritische Untersuchung der Schrift des Heiligen Hieronymus "De viris illustribus."* Kirchengeschichtliche Studien 2/2. Münster: Schöningh, 1894.

SZLEZÁK, Thomas Alexander. *Pseudo-Archytas über die Kategorien: Texte zur griechischen Aristoteles-Exegese.* Peripatoi 4. Berlin/New York: De Gruyter, 1972.

TANNER, Jakob. "Body, History of." In *International Encyclopedia of the Social & Behavioral Sciences,* edited by Neil J. Smelser and Paul B. Baltes, 2: 1277–1282. Amsterdam: Elsevier, 2001.

TARDIEU, Michel. "Heraiskos." In *Der neue Pauly: Enzyklopädie der Antike,* 363. Stuttgart/Weimar: Metzler, 1998.

TEREZIS, Christos, and Kalomoira POLYCHRONOPOULOU. "The Sense of Beauty (κάλλος) in Proclus the Neoplatonist." In *Neoplatonism and Western Aesthetics,* edited by Aphrodite Alexandrakis and Nicholas J. Moutafakis, 53–60. Studies in Neoplatonism, Ancient and Modern 12. Albany: State University of New York Press, 2002.

TESELLE, Eugene. "Credere." In *Augustinus-Lexikon,* 1: 119–131. Basel: Schwabe, 1986–1994.

THEILER, Willy. "Courcelle, Pierre. Recherches sur les Confessions de Saint Augustin (Rezension)." *Gnomon* 25 (1953): 113–122.

———. *Die Vorbereitung des Neuplatonismus.* Berlin/Zürich: Weidmann, 1964. (= 1934.)

———. "Erinnerung." In *Reallexikon für Antike und Christentum,* 6: 43–54. Stuttgart: Hiersemann, 1966.

THEISSEN, Gerd. *Urchristliche Wundergeschichten: Ein Beitrag zur formge-schichtlichen Erforschung der synoptischen Tradition.* Studien zum Neuen Testament 8. 6. Aufl. Gütersloh: Gütersloher Verlagshaus Mohn, 1990.

THEISSEN, Gerd, und Annette MERZ. *Der historische Jesus: Ein Lehrbuch.* 2. durchgesehene Aufl. Göttingen: Vandenhoeck & Ruprecht, 1997.

THEOBALD, Michael. "Jesus, Sohn des Ananias, und Jesus, Sohn des Josef." *Welt und Umwelt der Bibel* 56 (2010): 36–39.

THEUNISSEN, Michael. *Pindar: Menschenlos und Wende der Zeit.* 2. durch-gesehene Aufl. München: Beck, 2002.

THOM, Johan C. *Cleanthes' Hymn to Zeus: Text, Translation, and Commentary*. Studien und Texte zu Antike und Christentum 33. Tübingen: Mohr Siebeck, 2005.

THOMA, Clemens. "Gott III. Judentum." In *Theologische Realenzyklopädie*, 6: 626–654. Berlin/New York: De Gruyter, 1980.

THOMASSEN, Einar. *The Spiritual Seed: The Church of the "Valentinians."* Nag Hammadi and Manichaean Studies 60. Leiden/Boston: Brill, 2006.

THOMÉ, Horst. "Weltbild." In *Historisches Wörterbuch der Philosophie*, 12: 460–463. Darmstadt: Wissenschaftliche Buchgesellschaft, 2004.

THYEN, Hartwig. *Das Johannesevangelium*. Handbuch zum Neuen Testament 6. Tübingen: Mohr Siebeck.

TÖLLE-KASTENBEIN, Renate. *Das Olympieion in Athen*. Arbeiten zur Archäologie. Köln/Weimar/Wien: Böhlau, 1994.

TORRANCE, Iain R. "Severus von Antiochien." In *Theologische Realenzyklopädie*, 31: 184–186. Berlin/New York: De Gruyter, 2000.

TRÖGER, Karl W. "Doketistische Christologie in Nag-Hammadi-Texten: Ein Beitrag zum Doketismus in frühchristlicher Zeit." *Kairos* 19 (1977): 45–52.

TURNER, Bryan S. *The Body and Society: Explorations in Social Theory*. 3rd ed. London/Los Angeles: SAGE, 2008.

———. "Recent Developments in the Theory of the Body." In *The Body: Social Process and Cultural Theory*, edited by Mike Featherstone, Mike Hepworth, and Bryan S. Turner, 1–35. London/Newbury Park, Calif.: SAGE, 1991.

TURNER, Cuthbert H. "The *Liber Ecclesiasticorum Dogmatum* attributed to Gennadius." *JTS* 7 (1906): 89–99.

TURNER, John D. *Sethian Gnosticism and the Platonic Tradition*. Bibliothèque Copte de Nag Hammadi. Section "Études" 6. Québec: Les Presses de l'Université Laval, 2001. (= Louvain/Paris: Peeters, 2001.)

TZAMALIKOS, Panagiōtēs. "Origen and the Stoic View of Time." *Journal of the History of Ideas* 52 (1991): 531–561.

———. *Origen: Philosophy of History & Eschatology*. SuppVC 85. Leiden/Boston: Brill, 2007.

UEBELE, Wolfram. *"Viele Verführer sind in die Welt hinausgegangen": Die Gegner in den Briefen des Ignatius von Antiochien und in den Johannesbriefen*. Beiträge zur Wissenschaft vom Alten und Neuen Testament 151. Stuttgart: Kohlhammer, 2001.

UTHEMANN, Karl-Heinz. "Kaiser Justinian als Kirchenpolitiker und Theologe." In idem, *Christus, Kosmos, Diatribe: Themen der frühen Kirche als Beiträge zu einer historischen Theologie*, 257–331. Arbeiten zur Kirchengeschichte 93. Berlin/New York: De Gruyter, 2005.

VAN RIEL, Gerd. *Plato's Gods*. Ashgate Studies in the History of Philosophical Theology. Surrey/Burlington, Vt.: Ashgate, 2013.

VANNIER, Marie-Anne. "Jean Cassien, historiographe du monachisme égyptien?" In *L'historiographie de l'église des premiers siècles*, édité par Bernard Pouderon et Yves-Marie Duval, 149–158. Théologie historique 114. Paris: Beauchesne, 2001.

VASILIEV, Alexander Alexandrovic. "The Life of Saint Theodore of Edessa." *Byzantion* 16 (1942/1943): 165–225.

VERNANT, Jean-Pierre. "Mortals and Immortals: The Body of the Divine." In idem, *Mortals and Immortals: Collected Essays*, edited by Froma I. Zeitlin, 27–49. Princeton, N.J.: Princeton University Press, 1992.

VERSNEL, Hendrik S. "What Did Ancient Man See When He *Saw* a God? Some Reflections on Greco-Roman Epiphany." In *Effigies Dei: Essays on the History of Religions*, edited by Dirk van der Plas, 42–55. Studies in the History of Religions 51. Leiden: Brill, 1987.

VICTOR, Ulrich. "Die Religionen und religiösen Vorstellungen im Römischen Reich im 1. und 2. Jahrhundert n.Chr." In *Antike Kultur und Neues Testament: Die wichtigsten Hintergründe und Hilfsmittel zum Verständnis der neutestamentlichen Schriften*, herausgegeben von Ulrich Victor, Carsten P. Thiede und Urs Stingelin, 87–170. Basel/Gießen: Brunnen Verlag, 2003.

———, Hg. *Lukian von Samosata: Alexandros oder der Lügenprophet*. Religions in the Graeco-Roman World 132. Leiden: Brill, 1997.

VIELBERG, Meinolf. *Klemens in den pseudoklementinischen Recognitionen: Studien zur literarischen Form des spätantiken Romans*. TU 145. Berlin: Akademie-Verlag, 2000.

VINZENT, Markus. *Christ's Resurrection in Early Christianity and the Making of the New Testament*. Farnham, Surrey: Ashgate, 2011.

———. "Das 'heidnische' Ägypten im 5. Jahrhundert." In *Heiden und Christen im 5. Jahrhundert*, herausgegeben von Johannes van Oort und Dietmar Wyrwa, 32–65. Studien der Patristischen Arbeitsgemeinschaft 5. Leuven: Peeters, 1998.

———. "'Ich bin kein körperloses Geistwesen': Zum Verhältnis von κήρυγμα Πέτρου, 'Doctrina Petri' und IgnSm 3." In Reinhard M. Hübner, *Der paradox Eine: Antignostischer Monarchianismus im zweiten Jahrhundert*, mit einem Beitrag von Markus Vinzent, 241–286. SuppVC 50. Leiden/ Boston/Köln: Brill, 1999.

VLIZOS, Stavros. "Das Vorbild des Zeus aus Olympia." In *Römische Götterbilder der mittleren und späten Kaiserzeit*, herausgegeben von Dietrich Boschung und Alfred Schäfer, 41–69. Morphomata 22. Paderborn: Wilhelm Fink, 2015.

———. *Der thronende Zeus: Eine Untersuchung zur statuarischen Ikonographie des Gottes in der spätklassischen und hellenischen Kunst*. Internationale Archäologie 62. Rahden, Westfalen: M. Leidorf, 1999.

VOGT, Ernst. "Tragiker Ezechiel." In *Poetische Schriften*, 124. Jüdische Schriften aus hellenistisch-römischer Zeit 4/3. Gütersloh: Mohn, 1983.

VOGT, Hermann J. "Bemerkungen zur Echtheit der Ignatiusbriefe." *Zeitschrift für Antikes Christentum* 3 (1999): 50–63.

VOGÜÉ, Adalbert de. *Histoire littéraire du mouvement monastique dans l'antiquité. Premier Partie: Le monachisme latin*. Tome 2, *De l'Itinéraire d'Égerie à l'éloge funèbre de Népotien (384–396)*. Patrimoines christianisme. Paris: Les éditions du Cerf, 1993.

————. *Histoire littéraire du mouvement monastique dans l'antiquité.* Tome 3, *Jérôme, Augustin et Rufin au tournant du siècle (391–405).* Paris: Les éditions du Cerf, 1996.

————. *Histoire littéraire du mouvement monastique dans l'antiquité.* Tome 6, *Les derniers ècrits de Jérôme et l'œuvre de Jean Cassien.* Patrimoines christianisme. Paris: Les éditions du Cerf, 2002.

————. "Pour comprendre Cassien: Un survol des Conférences." *Collectanea Cisterciensia* 39 (1979): 250–272. (= idem, *De Saint Pachôme à Jean Cassien: Études littéraires et doctrinales sur le monachisme égyptien à ses débuts*, 303–330. Studia Anselmiana 120. Rome: Pontificio ateneo S. Anselmo, 1996.

VÖLKER, Walter. "Basilius, Ep. 366 und Clemens Alexandrinus." *VC* 7 (1953): 23–26.

VOLLENWEIDER, Samuel. "Zwischen Monotheismus und Engelchristologie: Überlegungen zur Frühgeschichte des Christusglaubens." *ZTK* 99 (2002): 21–44.

VON WILAMOWITZ-MOELLENDORFF, Ulrich. "Der Zeus von Olympia." In idem, *Reden und Vorträge*, 3. vermehrte Auflage, 199–221. Berlin: Weidmann-sche Buchhandlung, 1913.

————. "Ein Stück aus dem Ancoratus des Epiphanios." In *Sitzungsberichte der preußischen Akademie der Wissenschaften, philologisch-historische Klasse*, 759–772. Berlin: Verlag der Königlichen Akademie der Wissenschaften, 1911.

————. *Euripides Herakles erklärt.* Bd. 1. Zweite Bearbeitung. Berlin: Weidmann, 1895.

————. "Kern, Otto: Die Inschriften von Magnesia am Maeander (Rezension)." In idem, *Kleine Schriften*, Bd. 5/1, *Geschichte, Epigraphik, Archäologie*, 343–368. Berlin: Akademie-Verlag, 1971.

WACHT, Manfred. *Aeneas von Gaza als Apologet: Seine Kosmologie im Verhältnis zum Platonismus.* Theophaneia 21. Bonn: Hanstein, 1969.

WÄCHTER, Ludwig. "Astrologie und Schicksalsglaube im rabbinischen Judentum." *Kairos* 11 (1969): 181–200.

WAGNER, Andreas. "Das synthetische Bedeutungsspektrum hebräischer Körperbezeichnungen." *Biblische Zeitschrift* 51 (2007): 257–265.

————. *Gottes Körper: Zur alttestamentlichen Vorstellung der Menschengestaltigkeit Gottes.* Gütersloh: Gütersloher Verlagshaus, 2010.

WAINWRIGHT, William J. "God's Body." *Journal of the American Academy of Religion* 42 (1974): 470–481.

WAITZ, Hans. "Das Buch des Elchasai, das heilige Buch der judenchristlichen Sekte der Sobiai." In *Harnack-Ehrung: Beiträge zur Kirchengeschichte, ihrem Lehrer Adolf von Harnack zu seinem siebzigsten Geburtstage (7. Mai 1921) dargebracht von einer Reihe seiner Schüler*, 87–104. Leipzig: Hinrichs, 1921.

————. "Die Lösung des pseudoclementinischen Problems." *Zeitschrift für Kirchengeschichte* 59 (1940): 304–341.

————. *Die Pseudoklementinen: Homilien und Rekognitionen:Eine quellenkritische Untersuchung.* TU 25/4. Leipzig: Hinrichs, 1904.

————. "Neues zur Text- und Literarkritik der Pseudoklementinen?" *Zeitschrift für Kirchengeschichte* 52 (1933): 305–318.

WALLRAFF, Martin. *Der Kirchenhistoriker Sokrates: Untersuchungen zu Geschichtsdarstellung, Methode und Person.* Forschungen zur Kirchen- und Dogmengeschichte 68. Göttingen: Vandenhocck & Ruprecht, 1997.

WALTER, Hans. *Das griechische Heiligtum, dargestellt am Heraion von Samos.* Stuttgart: Urachhaus, 1990.

WALTER, Jochen. *Pagane Texte und Wertvorstellungen bei Lactanz.* Hypomnemata 165. Göttingen: Vandenhoeck & Ruprecht, 2006.

WALTER, Nikolaus. *Der Thoraausleger Aristobulos: Untersuchungen zu seinen Fragmenten und zu pseudepigraphischen Resten der jüdisch-hellenistischen Literatur.* TU 86. Berlin: Akademie-Verlag, 1964.

————. "Fragmente jüdisch-hellenistischer Exegeten: Aristobulos, Demetrios, Aristeas." In *Jüdische Schriften aus hellenistisch-römischer Zeit*, Bd. 3, Lieferung 2, *Unterweisungen in lehrhafter Form.* Gütersloh: Gütersloher Verlagshaus Mohn, 1975.

WANKENNE, Jules. "Consentius." In *Augustinus-Lexikon*, 1: 1236–1239. Basel: Schwabe, 1986–1994.

WARE, Kallistos. "'My Helper and My Enemy': The Body in Greek Christianity." In *Religion and the Body*, edited by Sarah Coakley, 90–110. Cambridge: Cambridge University Press, 1997.

WASCHKE, Ernst-Joachim. "תמונה." In *Theologisches Wörterbuch zum Alten Testament*, 8: 677–680. Stuttgart: Kohlhammer, 1995.

WASZINK, Jan Hendrik. *Quinti Septimi Florentis Tertulliani De Anima.* SuppVC 100. Leiden/Boston: Brill, 2010.

WATTS, Edward J. *Riot in Alexandria: Tradition and Group Dynamics in Late Antique Pagan and Christian Communities.* Transformation of the Classical Heritage 46. Berkeley: University of California Press, 2010.

WEBB, Stephen H. *Jesus Christ, Eternal God: Heavenly Flesh and the Metaphysics of Matter.* Oxford: Oxford University Press, 2012.

WEBER, Dorothea. "Augustinus, *De Genesi contra Manichaeos*: Zu Augustins Darstellung und Widerlegung der manichäischen Kritik am biblischen Schöpfungsbericht." In *Augustine and Manichaeism in the Latin West: Proceedings of the Fribourg-Utrecht Symposium of the International Association of Manichaean Studies (IAMS)*, edited by Johannes van Oort, Otto Wermelinger, and Gregor Wurst, 298–306. Nag Hammadi and Manichaean Studies 49. Leiden/Boston/Köln: Brill, 2001.

————. "Textprobleme in Augustinus, De Genesi contra Manichaeos." *Wiener Studien* 111 (1998): 211–230.

WEED, Jennifer Hart. "Maimonides and Aquinas: A Medieval Misunderstanding?" *Revista Portuguesa de Filosofia* 64 (2008): 379–396.

WEHNERT, Jürgen. "Abriss der Entstehungsgeschichte des pseudoklementischen Romans." *Apocrypha* 3 (1992): 211–236.

————. "'Das Geheimnis der Siebenzahl': Spekulationen über die unendliche Gestalt Gottes in den pseudoklementinischen Homilien, Buch 16 und 17." In *Nouvelles intrigues pseudo-Clémentines. Plots in the Pseudo-Clementine Romance: Actes du deuxième colloque international sur la littérature apocryphe chrétienne, Lausanne—Genève, 30 août–2 septembre 2006*, édités par Frédéric Amsler, Albert Frey, Charlotte Touati, et Renée Girardet, 461–467. Publications de l'Institut Romand des Sciences Bibliques 6. Prahins: Éditions du Zèbre, 2008.

———. "Literarkritik und Sprachanalyse: Kritische Anmerkungen zum gegenwärtigen Stand der Pseudoklementinen-Forschung." *Zeitschrift für die neutestamentliche Wissenschaft* 74 (1983): 268–301.

———. "Petrus *versus* Paulus in den pseudoklementinischen Homilien 17." In *Christians as a Religious Minority in a Multicultural City: Modes of Interaction and Identity Formation in Early Imperial Rome; Studies on the Basis of a Seminar at the Second Conference of the European Association for Biblical Studies (EABS) from July 8–12, 2001, in Rome*, edited by Jürgen Zangenberg and Michael Labahn, 175–185. Journal for the Study of the New Testament. Supplement Series 243. London/New York: T&T Clark, 1980.

———. *Pseudoklementinische Homilien: Einführung und Übersetzung.* Kommentare zur apokryphen Literatur 1/1. Göttingen: Vandenhoeck & Ruprecht, 2010.

WEHR, Lothar. *Arznei der Unsterblichkeit: Die Eucharistie bei Ignatius von Antiochien und im Johannesevangelium.* Neutestamentliche Abhandlungen 18. Münster: Aschendorff, 1987.

WEIGANDT, Peter. *Der Doketismus im Urchristentum und in der theologischen Entwicklung des zweiten Jahrhunderts.* Diss. theol. masch., Heidelberg, 1961.

WEIGELT, Horst. "Kaspar Schwenckfeld." In *Theologische Realenzyklopädie*, 30: 712–719. Berlin/New York: De Gruyter, 1980.

WEIL, Eric. "Remarques sur le matérialisme des Stoïciens." In *Mélanges Alexandre Koyré*, publiés à l'occasion de son soixante-dixième anniversaire, tome 2, *L'aventure de l'esprit*, 556–572. Histoire de la pensée 13. Paris: Hermann, 1964.

WEINRICH, Harald. "Metapher." In *Historisches Wörterbuch der Philosophie*, 5: 1179–1186. Basel: Schwabe, 1971.

WEISS, Adolf. *Mose Ben Maimon, Führer der Unschlüssigen.* Übersetzung und Kommentar von Adolf Weiß, mit einer Einleitung von Johann Meier. Philosophische Bibliothek 184a-c. 2. Aufl. Hamburg: Meiner, 1995.

WEITZMANN, Kurt. *The Monastery of Saint Catherine at Mount Sinai: The Icons.* Vol. 1, *From the Sixth to the Tenth Century.* Princeton, N.J.: Princeton University Press, 1976.

WEITZMANN, Kurt, and Herbert L. KESSLER. *The Frescoes of the Dura Synagogue and Christian Art.* Dumbarton Oaks Studies 28. Washington, D.C.: Dumbarton Oaks Research Library and Collection, 1990.

WELTEN, Peter. "Lade—Tempel—Jerusalem: Zur Theologie der Chronikbücher." In *Textgemäß: Aufsätze und Beiträge zur Hermeneutik des Alten Testaments; Festschrift für Ernst Würthwein zum 70. Geburtstag*, herausgegeben von Antonius H. Gunneweg und Otto Kaiser, 169–183. Göttingen: Vandenhoeck & Ruprecht, 1979.

WENDLAND, Paul. "Eine doxographische Quelle Philo's." *Sitzungsberichte der königlich preussischen Akademie der Wissenschaften zu Berlin* 23 (1897): 1074–1079.

WENNING, Robert. "The Betyls of Petra." *Bulletin of the American School of Oriental Research* 234 (2001): 79–95.

WESSEL, Klaus. "Christusbild." In *Reallexikon zur byzantinischen Kunst*, 1: 966–1047. Stuttgart: Hiersemann, 1966.

———. "Hand Gottes." In *Reallexikon zur byzantinischen Kunst*, 2: 950–962. Stuttgart: Hiersemann, 1971.

WHITTAKER, John. "Ἐπέκεινα νοῦ καὶ οὐσίας." *VC* 23 (1969): 91–104. (= idem, *Studies in Platonism and Patristic Thought*, nr. XIII. Collected Studies Series CS 201. London: Variorum Reprints, 1984.)

———. "God and Time in Philo of Alexandria." In idem, *God—Time—Being: Two Studies in the Transcendental Tradition in Greek Philosophy*, 33–57. Symbolae Osloenses. Fascicle Supplement 23. Oslo: Universitetsforlaget, 1971.

WICKHAM, Lionel R. "Eucherius von Lyon." In *Theologische Realenzyklopädie*, 10: 522–525. Berlin/New York: De Gruyter, 1982.

WIKENHAUSER, Alfred. "Die Traumgesichte des Neuen Testaments in religionsgeschichtlicher Sicht." In *Pisciculi: Studien zur Religion und Kultur des Altertums; Franz Josef Dölger zum sechzigsten Geburtstage dargeboten von Freunden, Verehrern und Schülern*, herausgegeben von Theodor Klauser und Adolf Rücker, 320–333. Münster: Aschendorff, 1939.

WILDBERG, Christian. *John Philoponus' Criticism of Aristotle's Theory of Aether*. Peripatoi 16. Berlin/New York: De Gruyter, 1988.

WILLEITNER, Joachim. *Die ägyptischen Oasen: Städte, Tempel und Gräber in der libyschen Wüste*. Zaberns Bildbände zur Archäologie. Mainz: Zabern, 2003.

WILLIAMS, Rowan. "Origenes/Origenismus." In *Theologische Realenzyklopädie*, 25: 397–420. Berlin/New York: De Gruyter, 1995.

WILPERT, Joseph. "Beiträge zur christlichen Archäologie XIII: Das Bild des Patriarchen Theophilos in einer alexandrinischen Weltchronik." *Römische Quartalschrift* 24 (1910): 3–29.

WILSON, Robert R. McLachlan. "The Early History of the Exegesis of Gen. 1:26." In *Papers Presented to the Second International Conference on Patristic Studies Held at Christ Church Oxford*, edited by Kurt Aland and Frank L. Cross, 420–437. StPatr 1. (= TU 63.) Berlin: Akademie-Verlag, 1957.

WILSON, Walter T. *The Sentences of Sextus*. Society of Biblical Literature. Wisdom Literature from the Ancient World 1. Atlanta: Society of Biblical Literature, 2012.

WINGREN, Gustaf. *Man and the Incarnation: A Study in the Biblical Theology of Irenaeus*. Translated by Ross Mackenzie. Edinburgh/London: Oliver and Boyd, 1959.

WINKELMANN, Friedhelm. "Einige Bemerkungen zu den Aussagen des Rufinus von Aquileia und des Hieronymus über ihre Übersetzungstheorie und -methode." In *Kyriakon: Festschrift Johannes Quasten in Two Volumes*, vol. 2., edited by Patrick Granfield and Josef A. Jungmann, 532–547. Münster: Aschendorff, 1970.

WINKLER, Gabriele. "Die Licht-Erscheinung bei der Taufe Jesu und der Ursprung des Epiphaniefestes: Eine Untersuchung griechischer, syrischer, armenischer und lateinischer Quellen." *Oriens christianus* 78 (1994): 177–229.

WINLING, Raymond. "Nouvelle Théologie." In *Theologische Realenzyklopädie*, 24: 668–675. Berlin/New York: De Gruyter, 1994.

WINN, Robert E. *Eusebius of Emesa: Church and Theology in the Mid-Fourth Century.* Washington, D.C.: Catholic University of America Press, 2011.

———. "The Natural World in the Sermons of Eusebius of Emesa." *VC* 59 (2005): 31–53.

WINTER, Paul. *On the Trial of Jesus.* 2nd ed. Revised by Tom Alec Burkill and Geza Vermes. Studia Judaica 1. Berlin/New York: De Gruyter, 1974.

WINTERLING, Aloys. "Wie modern war die Antike? Was soll die Frage?" In *Geschichte denken: Perspektiven auf die Geschichtsschreibung heute*, herausgegeben von Michael Wildt, 12–34. Göttingen: Vandenhoeck & Ruprecht, 2014.

WIPPEL, John F. *The Metaphysical Thought of Thomas Aquinas: From Finite Being to Uncreated Being.* Monographs of the Society for Medieval and Renaissance Philosophy 1. Washington, D.C.: Catholic University of America Press, 2000.

———. "Quidditative Knowledge of God according to Thomas Aquinas." In *Graceful Reason: Essays in Ancient and Medieval Philosophy Presented to Joseph Owens on the Occasion of His Seventy-Fifth Birthday and the Fiftieth Anniversary of His Ordination*, edited by Lloyd P. Gerson, 273–299. Papers in Mediaeval Studies 4. Toronto: Pontifical Institute of Mediaeval Studies, 1983.

WISSE, Frederik. "Stalking Those Elusive Sethians." In *The Rediscovery of Gnosticism: Proceedings of the International Conference on Gnosticism at Yale, New Haven, Connecticut, March 28–31, 1978*, edited by Bentley Layton, 563–576, vol. 2, *Sethian Gnosticism*. Leiden: Brill, 1981.

WISSOWA, Georg. *Religion und Kultus der Römer.* 2. Aufl. Handbuch der Altertumswissenschaften 4/5. München: Beck, 1912. (= 1971.)

WLOSOK, Antonie. *Laktanz und die philosophische Gnosis: Untersuchungen zu Geschichte und Terminologie der gnostischen Erlösungsvorstellung.* Abhandlungen der Heidelberger Akademie der Wissenschaften. Philosophisch-historische Klasse 2/1960. Heidelberg: Winter, 1960.

———. "Römischer Religions- und *Gottesbegriff* in heidnischer und christlicher Zeit." *Antike und Abendland* 16 (1970): 39–53. (= *Res Humanae— Res Divinae: Kleine Schriften*, herausgegeben von Eberhard Heck und Ernst A. Schmidt, 15–34. Bibliothek der klassischen Altertumswissenschaften 2/84. Heidelberg: Winter, 1990.)

———. "Vater und Vatervorstellungen in der römischen Kultur." In *Das Vaterbild im Abendland*, Bd. 1, *Rom, frühes Christentum, Mittelalter, Neuzeit, Gegenwart*, herausgegeben von Hubertus Tellenbach, 18–54. Stuttgart: Kohlhammer, 1978. (= *Res Humanae—Res Divinae: Kleine*

Schriften, herausgegeben von Eberhard Heck und Ernst A. Schmidt, 35–83. Bibliothek der klassischen Altertumswissenschaften 2/84. Heidelberg: Winter, 1990.)

———. "§ 570. L. Caecilius Firmianus Lactantius." In *Restauration und Erneuerung: Die lateinische Literatur von 284 bis 374 n.Chr.*, herausgegeben von Reinhart Herzog, 383–385. Handbuch der lateinischen Literatur der Antike, Bd. 5 (= Handbuch der Altertumswissenschaft 8/5). München: Beck, 1989.

WOLFSON, Harry Austryn. "The Aristotelian Predicables and Maimonides' Division of Attributes." In idem, *Studies in the History of Philosophy and Religion*, edited by Isadore Twersky and George H. Williams, 2: 161–194. Cambridge, Mass.: Harvard University Press, 1977. (= *Essays and Studies in Memory of Linda R. Miller*, edited by Israel Davidson, 201–234. New York: Jewish Theological Seminary of America, 1938.)

———. *The Philosophy of the Kalam*. Structure and Growth of Philosophic Systems from Plato to Spinoza 4. Cambridge, Mass./London: Harvard University Press, 1976.

WOLTER, Michael. *Das Lukasevangelium*. Handbuch zum Neuen Testament 5. Tübingen: Mohr Siebeck, 2008.

WOODS David. "Ammianus Marcellinus and Bishop Eusebius of Emesa." *JTS* 54 (2003): 585–591.

WROTH, Warwick. *Catalogue of the Greek Coins of Galatia, Cappadocia and Syria*. A Catalogue of the Greek Coins in the British Museum 20. London: Printed by the Order of the Trustees of the British Museum, 1899.

WURST, Gregor. *Die Homilie "De anima et corpore," ein Werk des Meliton von Sardes? Einleitung, synoptische Edition, Übersetzung und Kommentar*. Bd. 2, *Einleitung, Kommentar (Habil. Masch.)*. Freiburg, Schweiz: Verlag, 2000.

WYRWA, Dietmar. *Die christliche Platonaneignung in den Stromateis des Clemens von Alexandrien*. Arbeiten zur Kirchengeschichte 53. Berlin/New York: De Gruyter, 1983.

———. "Kosmos und Heilsgeschichte bei Irenäus von Lyon." In *Die Weltlichkeit des Glaubens in der Alten Kirche: Festschrift für Ulrich Wickert zum siebzigsten Geburtstag*, in Verbindung mit Barbara Aland und Christoph Schäublin, herausgegeben von Dietmar Wyrwa, 443–480. BZNW 85. Berlin/New York: De Gruyter, 1997.

YARRY, Jacques. "Une semi hérésie syro-egyptienne: L'audianisme." *Bulletin de l'Institut Français d'Archéologie Orientale* 63 (1965): 169–195.

YOUNG, Frances M. "God's Image: The 'Elephant in the Room' in the Fourth Century?" In *Studia Patristica: Including Papers Presented at the National Conference on Patristic Studies Held at Cambridge in the Faculty of Divinity under Allen Brent, Thomas Graumann and Judith Lieu in 2009*, edited by Allen Brent and Markus Vinzent, 57–72. StPatr 50. Leuven/Paris/Walpole, Mass.: Peeters, 2011.

YUVAL, Israel J. "Christianity in the Talmud: Parallelomania or Parallelophobia?" In *Transforming Relations: Essays on Jews and Christians, throughout History in Honor of Michael A. Signer*, edited by Franklin T. Harkins, 50–74. Notre Dame, Ind.: University of Notre Dame Press, 2010.

———. "Passover in the Middle Ages." In *Passover and Easter: Origin and History to Modern Time*, edited by Paul F. Bradshaw and Lawrence A. Hoffman, 127–160. Two Liturgical Traditions 5. Notre Dame, Ind.: University of Notre Dame Press, 1999.

ZACHHUBER, Johannes. "Überseiend; überwesentlich." In *Historisches Wörterbuch der Philosophie*, 11: 58–63. Darmstadt: Wissenschaftliche Buchgesellschaft, 2001.

———. "Weltbild, Weltanschauung, Religion: Ein Paradigma intellektueller Diskurse im 19. Jahrhundert." In *Die Welt als Bild: Interdisziplinäre Beiträge zur Visualität von Weltbildern*, herausgegeben von Christoph Markschies und Johannes Zachhuber, 211–282. Arbeiten zur Kirchengeschichte 107. Berlin/New York: De Gruyter, 2008.

———. "Weltseele." In *Historisches Wörterbuch der Philosophie*, 12: 516–521. Darmstadt: Wissenschaftliche Buchgesellschaft, 2004.

ZEDLER, Johann H. "Leib, lat. *Corpus*, franz. *Corps*." In *Grosses vollständiges Universal-Lexicon*, 16: 1504f. Graz: Akademische Verlagsanstalt, 1961. (= Halle/Leipzig: Johann H. Zedler, 1737.)

ZEEGERS-VANDER, Nicole Vorst. *Les citations des poètes grecs chez les apologistes chrétiens du IIe siècle*. Université de Louvain. Recueil de travaux d'histoire et de philologie sér. 4, 47. Louvain: Bureau du Recueil, Bibliothèque de l'Université, 1972.

ZEKL, Hans G. "Raum I. Griechische Antike." In *Historisches Wörterbuch der Philosophie*, 8: 67–82. Darmstadt: Wissenschaftliche Buchgesellschaft, 1992.

ZELLER, Dieter. "Bedeutung und religionsgeschichtlicher Hintergrund der Verwandlung Jesu." In *Authenticating the Activities of Jesus*, edited by Bruce Chilton, 303–321. New Testament Tools and Studies 28/2. Leiden: Brill, 1999.

———. "Die Menschwerdung des Sohnes Gottes im Neuen Testament und die antike Religionsgeschichte." In *Menschwerdung Gottes—Vergöttlichung von Menschen*, herausgegeben von Dieter Zeller, 141–176. Novum Testamentum et Orbis Antiquus 7. Fribourg: Universitätsverlag/Göttingen: Vandenhoeck & Ruprecht, 1988.

———. "Gott bei Philo von Alexandrien." In *Der Gott Israels im Zeugnis des Neuen Testaments*, herausgegeben von Ulrich Busse, 32–57. Quaestiones Disputatae 201. Freiburg/Basel/Wien: Herder, 2003. (= idem, *Studien zu Philo und Paulus*, 13–36. Bonner Biblische Beiträge 165. Göttingen/Bonn: Vandenhoeck & Ruprecht Unipress / University Press, 2011.)

———. "La metamorphose de Jésus comme épiphanie (Mc 9,2–8)." In *L' Evangile exploré: Mélanges offerts à Simon Légasse à l'occasion de ses soixante-dix ans*, publié sous la direction de Alain Marchadour, 167–186. Lectio Divina 166. Paris: Les éditions du Cerf, 1996.

ZIAS, Joseph, and Eliezer SEKELES. "The Crucified Man from Giv'at ha-Mivtar: A Reappraisal." *Israel Exploration Journal* 35 (1985): 22–27.

ZIEBRITZKI, Henning. *Heiliger Geist und Weltseele: Das Problem der dritten Hypostase bei Origenes, Plotin und ihren Vorläufern*. BHT 84. Tübingen: Mohr Siebeck, 1994.

ZIEGLER, Konrat. "Plutarchos (2) von Chaironeia." In *Paulys Realencyclopädie der classischen Altertumswissenschaft*, 21/1: 636–962. München: Alfred Druckenmüller, 1951.

ZIMMERLI, Walther. *Ezechiel*. Tlbd. 1, *Ezechiel 1–24*. 2. verbesserte, durch ein neues Vorwort und einen Literaturnachtrag erweiterte Aufl. Biblischer Kommentar Altes Testament 13/1. Neukirchen-Vluyn: Neukirchener, 1979.

ZIMMERMANN, Franz. "Des Claudianus Mamertus Schrift: 'De statu animae libri tres.'" *Divus Thomas* 1 (1914): 238–256, 332–368, and 440–495.

ZINTZEN, Clemens. "Mystik und Magie in der neuplatonischen Philosophie." *Rheinisches Museum* 108 (1965): 71–100. (= idem, *Athen—Rom—Florenz: Ausgewählte Kleine Schriften*, herausgegeben von Dorothee Gall und Peter Riemer, 53–96. Hildesheim: Olms, 2000.)

ZÖCKLER, Theodor. "Hilarion von Gaza: Eine Rettung." *Neue Jahrbücher für deutsche Theologie* 3 (1894): 146–178.

ZÖLLNER, Frank. *Vitruvs Proportionsfigur: Quellenkritische Studien zur Kunstliteratur im 15. und 16. Jahrhundert*. Manuskripte für Kunstwissenschaft in der Wernerschen Verlagsgesellschaft. Worms: Werner, 1987.

ZUNTZ, Günther. "Baitylos und Bethel." *Classica et Mediaevalia* 8 (1946): 169–219.

INDEX OF PASSAGES

By Marie-Christin Barleben and Almut Bockisch

XVII 7.3 (I, 232.17–20): 309–310, 487n141
XVII 8.1 (I, 233.4–7): 203, 433n134
XVII 8.3–5 (I, 233.4–19): 203, 433n135
XVII 8.9 (I, 233.29–234.3): 204, 433n140
XVII 9.1–10.3 (I, 234L7–235.2): 204–
205, 434n142
XVII 10.1 (I, 235.5–9): 205, 434n145
XVII 10.2 (I, 234.21–235.2): 206,
434n151
XVII 10.5 (I, 235.5–9): 204–205, 434n142
XVII 10.5 (I, 235.7–9): 201, 432n118
XVII 11.2 (I, 235.11–14): 206, 435n153
XVII 16.2–6 (I, 238.9–16): 206–207,
435n156
XX 7.6f. (I, 272.21–26): 209, 437n176

Recognitiones Clementinae
III 30.5: 207, 435n158
VIII 15.4: 48, 358n181

Commodianus

Instructiones adversus gentium
I 18.5: 82, 374n45

Cosmas Indicopleustes

Topographia Christiana
X 17: 238, 450n331

Cyrillus Alexandrinus

Solutiones ad Tiberium
1 (137 Wickham): 268, 467n507

De dogmatum solutione
Quaestio 1 (549.3–8 Pusey): 268, 467n508
Responsio 1 (549.9–17 Pusey): 268,
467n509
Responsio 1 (550.1–6 Pusey): 268,
467n510
Responsio 1 (550.6–10 Pusey): 268,
467n511

Cyrillus Scythopolitanus

Vita S. Sabae
41: 253–254, 460n433

Ps.-Dionysius Areopagita

De divinis nominibus
4.7: 147, 406n116

De mystica theologia
1.1: 138, 402n67

Dionysius Cartusianus

*Sermo Septimus in Festo Johannis
Apostolae et Evangelistae*
31: 138, 402n64

Epiphanius Constantiensis

Ancoratus
54.1: 273, 469n535

De fide
13.5: 253, 460n432

Panarion haereses
19.1.1 together with 2.1: 168, 414n224
19.1.4: 165, 166, 413n207, 413n213
19.2.1: 166, 413n211
19.4.1–2: 168, 414n225
30.14.3: 296, 480n76
30.17.6f.: 169, 415n228
30.17.6: 297, 481n79
31.7.2: 172, 416n243
31.13.4: 173, 417n252
31.17.12: 176, 419n272
33.3.1–7,10: 172, 416n245
34.3.4: 172, 416n246, 417n247
34.4.7: 172–173, 417n251
34.4.11 and 5.1: 173, 417n254
34.5.5–7: 174, 418n258
34.6.4: 173, 417n256
42.3–5: 297, 481n81
53.1.9: 169, 415n229
64.4.1: 245, 454n378
70.2.4f.: 260, 464nn468–469
70.15.5: 260, 464n470

Epiphanius Monachus

Vita Mariae
*302**.5:* 179, 420n284
*302**.5–8:* 179, 420n287

Eusebius Caesariensis

Praeparatio Evangelica
III 9.9: 48, 102, 357n178, 384n14
VIII 9.38: 28, 346n57
VIII 10.1: 28, 346n58

III 8.2f.: 289, 476–477n36
III 9.1: 70–71, 289, 369n293, 477n38
III 10.2: 289, 477n39
IV 4.3: 199, 431n106

Adversus Praxean
7.8: 69–70, 368n286
27.4: 287, 475n24
27.6: 287, 475n23
27.7f.: 288, 475n25

Apologeticum
47.6: 48, 69, 358n180, 368n283
50.7f.: 254, 461n436

De anima
5.2: 109, 387n66
22.2: 109, 387n63

De carne Christi
2.1f.: 289–290, 477n42
11.3–4: 109, 388n67
11.4: 70, 288, 368n287, 476n29
15.2: 288, 297, 476n28, 481n83

De praescriptione haereticorum
30.1–2: 199, 431n106

Ps.-Tertullianus
Adversus omnes haereses
6.1: 289, 476n34
6.5: 297, 481n80

Theodoretus Cyrrhensis
Commentaria in Isaiam
XIX 63.2: 219, 442n234

Epistulae
82: 288, 476n31

Graecarum Affectionum Curatio
II 113: 48, 357n178
III 72: 33, 349n85

Historia monachorum
26.12: 281, 472n574
26.22: 281, 472n575
26.23: 281, 472n578

Theophilus Alexandrinus
Epistulae
fr. 7: 258, 463n457

fr. 8 (63.34f. Richard): 255, 461n441
fr. 8 (64.1–3 Richard): 255, 461n442

Tractatus contra Origenem de vision Esaie
2 (OWD 10, 338.1–11 Fürst/Hengstermann): 270–271, 468n525
2 (OWD 10, 342.15–23 Fürst/Hengstermann): 271–272, 468n531
2 (OWD 10, 338.21f. Fürst/Hengstermann): 271, 468n529
2 (OWD 10, 338.22–24 Fürst/Hengstermann): 271, 468n526

Zacharias Rhetor Mitylenaeus
Ammonius sive De mundi opificio disputatio
248–260: 275, 469n544
1233–1241: 275, 469n543

ALII AUCTORES
Aëtius
Placita philosophorum
I 3.18: 42, 354n146
I 6.1: 215, 440n212
I 7.33: 45, 357n167
I 14.6: 52, 360n205

Agathias
Historiae
II 21: 149, 407n129

Alcinous
Epitome doctrinae Platonicae sive Διδασκαλικός
7.4: 157, 410n170
10.7: 61, 102, 365nn246–247, 384n13
10.8: 61, 365n249
14.7: 102, 384n14
15.2: 102, 384n17
15.4: 102, 384n15

Alexander Aphrodisiensis
De mixtione
3: 46, 357n170

Herodotus

Historiae
II 6.3: 149, 167, 407n129, 414n219

Hesiodus

Opera et dies
251–253: 76, 371n12

Theogonia
33: 91, 379n101
105: 91, 379n101

Hesychius

Π 659: 149, 407n129

Hierocles

*In aureum Pythagoreorum carmen
commentarius*
26.1f.: 112, 389–390n94

Homerus

Ilias
I 194–198: 92, 380n111
III 396–398: 92, 380n112
V 339: 91, 380n103
V 339–342: 91, 380n108
V 341: 91, 380n105

Odyssea
XVII 485–487: 38, 285, 352n123, 474n10

Hymni Homerici in Cererem
275f.: 201–202, 432n122
275–281: 92, 380n109

Iamblichus

De anima
26: 112, 389n89

De mysteriis
I 19: 77, 371n19
V 19: 77, 371n18
V 23: 77, 371nn21–22
VII 5: 151, 407–408nn140–141

Fragmenta in Platonis Timaeum
81: 112, 389n91
84: 112, 389n90

Ps.-Iamblichus

Theologumena Arithmeticae
1: 165, 412n205
6: 204, 205, 433–434n141, 434n148
7: 205, 434n147

Iohannes Philoponus

In Aristotelem De anima
I prooemium (CAG XV, 9.4–9 Hayduck):
49, 358n186

Iohannes Lydus

De ostentis prooemium
8: 84, 376n65

Iohannes Stobaeus

Anthologium
I 1: 34, 350n92
I 1.12: 45, 356n166
I 3.9: 299, 482n89
I 8.42: 43–44, 355n156
I 10.16c: 52, 360n205
I 21.5: 52, 360n205
I 49.60: 111, 388n80
II 7.13: 93, 381n117

Flavius Iosephus

Bellum Iudaicum
VI 304f.: 312, 488n151

Lucianus

De Syria dea
10: 84, 100, 376n63, 383n4

Imagines
4: 86, 376n72

Lucretius

De rerum natura
VI 75–78: 41, 354n141

Macrobius

Somnium Scipionis
I 11.12: 112, 113, 389n92, 390n98
I 12.13f.: 112, 389n93

Apocryphon of John

(NHC II,1)
p. 3.22f.: 72, 369n299

Pistis Sophia
I 6: 175, 418n265
II 63: 175, 418n266

Second Logos of the Great Seth

(NHC VII,2)
p. 56.20–25: 71, 369n297

INSCRIPTIONS

Didyma
no. 496 A, p. 299: 87, 377n81

Corpus Inscriptionum Graecorum
II no. 2715: 83, 375n55

Die Inschriften von Magnesia am Maeander
no. 98, p. 82–84: 85, 376n69

MANDAICA ET MANICHAICA

Codex Manichaicus Coloniensis
p. 94.9f.: 165, 413n208

PAPYRI, OSTRACA

Papyri Graecae Magicae
XII 242–244: 40, 354n137
XIII 766–772: 40, 354n137
XXI 3–7: 40, 354n137

INDEX OF PEOPLE

By Marie-Christin Barleben and Almut Bockisch

ANCIENT PEOPLE

Acacius, Martyrer, 287
Aeneas of Gaza, 275
Agathonicus of Tarsus, 314–315
Albinus, Procurator, 311–312
Alcibiades, 167–168
Alcinous, 61, 67, 102
Alexander of Alexandria, 186
Alexander of Aphrodisias, 46
Alexander the Great, 28, 30
Alexandra, Priestess, 87
Ambrose of Milan, 35, 104, 118, 121, 223, 228, 229, 230
Ammonius Saccas, 59
Amun, Monk, 245
Anastasius of Sinai, 191
Anatolius of Laodicaea, 205
Anaxarchos, Philosopher, 254
Anthony, Monk, 252, 276
Apelles, 297
Aphou, Monk, 259–264, 268, 269, 273
Apollinaris of Laodicea, 198, 209–210
Apuleius of Madaurus, 86, 100, 101, 112, 117
Aqiba, Rabbi, 144, 145, 146, 148, 156, 160
Aratus, 29
Archytas of Tarento, 108, 117
Aristobul, 28–30, 127
Aristotle, 11, 32, 36, 48–52, 81, 101, 103, 108, 109, 112, 116, 200, 202, 212, 213, 215, 279

Arius, 208, 241, 245
Arnobius of Sicca, 163, 164
Arnobius the Younger, 110
Arsenius, Monk, 270
Athanasius of Alexandria, 186, 217, 244, 252
Athenagoras, 51, 61, 62, 197
Atticus, 50
Audius, 260
Augustine of Hippo, 38, 104, 112, 116, 117, 118, 119–122, 124, 126, 211, 222–231, 271, 301–302
Augustus, 94
Aurelius Prudentius Clemens, 76
Basil of Caesarea, 51, 104, 164, 245, 265, 295
Callixtus, 167
Celsus, 47, 67, 69
Cerdo, 289
Chariton, 88
Chrysipp of Soli, 21, 44–45, 46, 47–48, 52
Cicero, Marcus Tullius, 23, 41–43, 49, 52, 86, 104, 118, 120, 222, 228
Claudianus Mamertus, 103–105, 114–119, 122–126
Claudius, Emporer, 216
Claudius Ptolemaeus, 296
Cleanthes, 45
Clement of Alexandria, 31, 32–33, 48, 62–63, 134, 142, 176–177, 202, 212, 276, 292–293, 294–295

Commodian, 82
Consentius, 301
Constantine, 166, 217
Constantius, 217
Cosmas Indicopleustes, 238
Crispus, 118, 212
Cyril of Alexandria, 209, 238, 267–268, 269, 303

Damascius, 77, 113
Decius, Emporer, 287
Demetrius Lacon, 42
Democritus, 254
Dio Chrysostom, 78, 80–82, 101
Diagoras of Melos, 77
Didymus the Blind, 241, 246
Diocletian, 211
Diodor Siculus, 30
Diodor of Tarsus, 303
Diogenes of Babylon, 45, 46
Diogenes Laertius, 44, 87
Dionysus the Areopagite, 138

Elagabal, 26
Elchasai/Elxai, 165–171, 178, 296–297
Elisha Ben Abuyah, 145
Epictetus, 80
Epicurus, 21, 32, 41–42, 44, 48, 304
Epiphanius of Salamis, 166, 167, 168–169, 172, 174, 238, 239–243, 245, 254, 260, 262, 273, 296
Eratostrathenes, 112
Eucherius of Lyon, 104, 118
Euclid, 296
Eudorus of Alexandria, 164–165
Eunapius, Philosopher, 278
Euripides, 75
Eusebius of Caesarea, 28, 29, 33, 48, 57, 104, 166, 184, 185, 208, 318
Eusebius of Emesa, 211, 216–222
Eustathius of Antioch, 274
Eutyches, Monk, 306
Evagrius Ponticus, 245–251, 255, 265, 266
Evagrius the Scholiast, 306

Faustus of Riez, 103, 104, 105–109, 110, 111, 113–114, 115, 117, 123, 126
Flavius Rufinus, Prefect, 241
Flora, 172

Gaius Velleius, 41, 42
Galen, 112, 113, 154, 155, 203
Gennadius of Marseille, 105, 110, 258, 259
George of Laodicea, 216, 217
Gessius, Philosopher, 275

Gregor of Elvira, 292
Gregory of Nazianz, 104, 118, 245, 247, 265
Gregor of Nyssa, 265, 267

Hadrian, 76, 78
Hecataeus of Abdera, 21
Hecataeus of Miletus, 30
Heraclas of Alexandria, 272
Heraclides Ponticus, 49
Ps.-Heraclitus, 22
Heraclitus, 48
Heraiscus, 76, 77, 137
Herodotus, 149
Hermias of Alexandria, 112, 113
Hesiod, 76, 91, 92
Hilarion of Gaza, 276–278
Hilary of Poitiers, 110, 118
Hippolytus, 47–48, 167–169, 170, 295–296
Hippon of Metapontus, 117
Homer, 22, 38, 77, 79, 82, 90–92, 201, 285
Hosius of Cordoba, 274

Iamblichus, 77, 108, 112, 151
Ignatius of Antioch, 57, 290, 291, 316, 317–318, 319
Irenaeus of Lyon, 59, 172, 173, 174, 175, 182, 188, 193–198, 210, 293, 295
Isaac, Monk, 256, 257
Isidore, Philosopher, 77
Isidore, Presbyter, 239, 242, 243
Italica, 225, 226

Jacobus, Monk, 253
Jerome, xvi, 57, 104, 107, 115, 185, 211, 217, 235, 238, 239, 240, 241, 242, 243, 253, 270, 271, 276–277, 292
John of Caesarea, 198, 304
John Cassian, 107, 115, 126, 256, 257, 264–266
John Chrysostom, 243
John Damascene, 302
John of Jerusalem, 238, 239, 240, 241, 242, 243, 267, 268
John Lydus, 84
Josephus Flavius, 311
Julian the Apostate, 76
Julian of Halicarnassus, 305–306
Julius Cassianus, 292–293, 294, 295
Justin the Martyr, 61
Justinian, 235, 272, 306–307

Lactantius, 104, 211–216
Leontius of Byzantium, 304
Lucian of Samosata, 84, 100
Lucretius, 41, 42

MEDIEVAL AND MODERN PEOPLE